CUMULATIVE PROBABILITIES FOR THE STANDARD NORMAL DISTRIBUTION

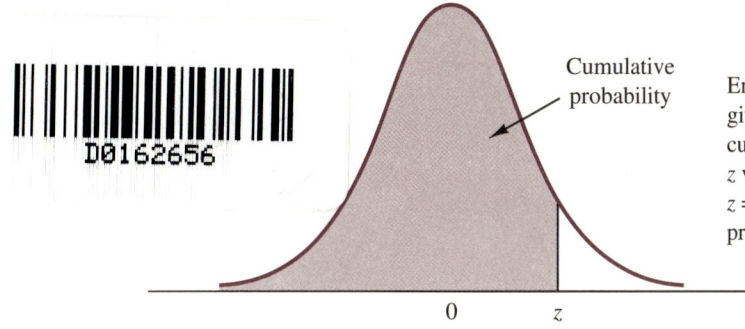

Cumulative probability

Entries in the table give the area under the curve to the left of the z value. For example, for z = 1.25, the cumulative probability is .8944.

z	.00	.01	.02	.03	.04	.05	.06	.07	.08	.09
.0	.5000	.5040	.5080	.5120	.5160	.5199	.5239	.5279	.5319	.5359
.1	.5398	.5438	.5478	.5517	.5557	.5596	.5636	.5675	.5714	.5753
.2	.5793	.5832	.5871	.5910	.5948	.5987	.6026	.6064	.6103	.6141
.3	.6179	.6217	.6255	.6293	.6331	.6368	.6406	.6443	.6480	.6517
.4	.6554	.6591	.6628	.6664	.6700	.6736	.6772	.6808	.6844	.6879
.5	.6915	.6950	.6985	.7019	.7054	.7088	.7123	.7157	.7190	.7224
.6	.7257	.7291	.7324	.7357	.7389	.7422	.7454	.7486	.7517	.7549
.7	.7580	.7611	.7642	.7673	.7704	.7734	.7764	.7794	.7823	.7852
.8	.7881	.7910	.7939	.7967	.7995	.8023	.8051	.8078	.8106	.8133
.9	.8159	.8186	.8212	.8238	.8264	.8289	.8315	.8340	.8365	.8389
1.0	.8413	.8438	.8461	.8485	.8508	.8531	.8554	.8577	.8599	.8621
1.1	.8643	.8665	.8686	.8708	.8729	.8749	.8770	.8790	.8810	.8830
1.2	.8849	.8869	.8888	.8907	.8925	.8944	.8962	.8980	.8997	.9015
1.3	.9032	.9049	.9066	.9082	.9099	.9115	.9131	.9147	.9162	.9177
1.4	.9192	.9207	.9222	.9236	.9251	.9265	.9279	.9292	.9306	.9319
1.5	.9332	.9345	.9357	.9370	.9382	.9394	.9406	.9418	.9429	.9441
1.6	.9452	.9463	.9474	.9484	.9495	.9505	.9515	.9525	.9535	.9545
1.7	.9554	.9564	.9573	.9582	.9591	.9599	.9608	.9616	.9625	.9633
1.8	.9641	.9649	.9656	.9664	.9671	.9678	.9686	.9693	.9699	.9706
1.9	.9713	.9719	.9726	.9732	.9738	.9744	.9750	.9756	.9761	.9767
2.0	.9772	.9778	.9783	.9788	.9793	.9798	.9803	.9808	.9812	.9817
2.1	.9821	.9826	.9830	.9834	.9838	.9842	.9846	.9850	.9854	.9857
2.2	.9861	.9864	.9868	.9871	.9875	.9878	.9881	.9884	.9887	.9890
2.3	.9893	.9896	.9898	.9901	.9904	.9906	.9909	.9911	.9913	.9913
2.4	.9918	.9920	.9922	.9925	.9927	.9929	.9931	.9932	.9934	.9936
2.5	.9938	.9940	.9941	.9943	.9945	.9946	.9948	.9949	.9951	.9952
2.6	.9953	.9955	.9956	.9957	.9959	.9960	.9961	.9962	.9963	.9964
2.7	.9965	.9966	.9967	.9968	.9969	.9970	.9971	.9972	.9973	.9974
2.8	.9974	.9975	.9976	.9977	.9977	.9978	.9979	.9979	.9980	.9981
2.9	.9981	.9982	.9982	.9983	.9984	.9984	.9985	.9985	.9986	.9986
3.0	.9986	.9987	.9987	.9988	.9988	.9989	.9989	.9989	.9990	.9990

Solutions designed for the way you teach today's students . . .

From the day you choose to adopt a Thomson South-Western text through the final exams, we are committed to providing the best materials available to support your teaching *and* your students' learning. That's why this text is supported by two **FREE** resources that provide great educational value while making your own course preparation easier than ever before.

Book Companion Website

Available 24 hours a day from any computer with Internet access, the *Book Companion Website* for this text provides invaluable resources that you and your students can access anytime, anywhere.

Students can access an unmatched array of interactive learning tools – for instance, self-testing, reinforcement activities, and links to the best and most relevant information on the Internet. For instructors, the site can feature course outlines and learning objectives, suggested activities and exercises, and much more.

* Specific resources can vary by title. For detailed information or a demonstration, contact your Thomson South-Western sales representative.

Resource Integration Guide

Your one-stop source for course organization and preparation!
Accessible from the *Book Companion Website*, the *Resource Integration Guide* is an indispensable tool that helps you get the most from your textbook and its supplementary package.

A detailed grid lists all of the resources you can use to enhance your course – such as lecture outlines, PowerPoint® presentations, online resources, testing options, and much more. You'll soon wonder how you ever did without this valuable course preparation tool!

THOMSON
SOUTH-WESTERN

Preview the companion site for this text and download your *Resource Integration Guide* at: **http://asw.swlearning.com**

ISBN 0-324-40068-3

MODERN BUSINESS STATISTICS

WITH MICROSOFT® EXCEL, 2e

David R. Anderson
University of Cincinnati

Dennis J. Sweeney
University of Cincinnati

Thomas A. Williams
Rochester Institute of Technology

THOMSON
™
SOUTH-WESTERN

Australia · Brazil · Canada · Mexico · Singapore · Spain · United Kingdom · United States

THOMSON
SOUTH-WESTERN

Modern Business Statistics with Microsoft® Excel, Second Edition

David R. Anderson, Dennis J. Sweeney, Thomas A. Williams

VP/Editorial Director:
Jack W. Calhoun

Editor-in-Chief:
Alex von Rosenberg

Sr. Acquisitions Editor:
Charles McCormick

Sr. Developmental Editor:
Alice Denny

Sr. Marketing Manager:
Larry Qualls

Sr. Production Editor:
Deanna Quinn

Manager of Technology, Editorial:
Vicky True

Technology Project Editor:
Kelly Reid

Web Coordinator:
Scott Cook

Manufacturing Coordinator:
Diane Lohman

Production House:
BookMasters, Inc.

Printer:
R.R. Donnelley
Willard, OH

Art Director:
Chris Miller

Cover Designer:
Fuson Design

Cover Images:
© Digital Vision

Photography Manager:
Deanna Ettinger

Photo Researcher:
Terri Miller

Library of Congress Control Number:
2005923750

For more information about our products, contact us at:

Thomson Learning Academic Resource Center

1-800-423-0563

Thomson Higher Education
5191 Natorp Boulevard
Mason, OH 45040

USA

Dedicated to
Krista, Justin, Mark, and Colleen
Mark, Linda, Brad, Tim, Scott, and Lisa
Cathy, David, and Kristin

Brief Contents

Preface xxi

About the Authors xxxi

Chapter 1 Data and Statistics 1

Chapter 2 Descriptive Statistics: Tabular and Graphical Presentations 28

Chapter 3 Descriptive Statistics: Numerical Measures 87

Chapter 4 Introduction to Probability 153

Chapter 5 Discrete Probability Distributions 198

Chapter 6 Continuous Probability Distributions 238

Chapter 7 Sampling and Sampling Distributions 269

Chapter 8 Interval Estimation 306

Chapter 9 Hypothesis Tests 345

Chapter 10 Statistical Inference About Means and Proportions with Two Populations 391

Chapter 11 Inferences About Population Variances 439

Chapter 12 Tests of Goodness of Fit and Independence 465

Chapter 13 Analysis of Variance and Experimental Design 497

Chapter 14 Simple Linear Regression 559

Chapter 15 Multiple Regression 648

Chapter 16 Regression Analysis: Model Building 702

Chapter 17 Nonparametric Methods 754

Chapter 18 Statistical Methods for Quality Control 795

Chapter 19 Decision Analysis 830

Chapter 20 Sample Survey   On CD

Appendix A References and Bibliography 868

Appendix B Tables 870

Appendix C Summation Notation 881

Appendix D Self-Test Solutions and Answers to Even-Numbered
Exercises 883

Appendix E Using Excel Functions 927

Index 933

Contents

Preface xxi

About the Authors xxxi

Chapter 1 Data and Statistics 1

Statistics in Practice: Businessweek 2

1.1 Applications in Business and Economics 3
    Accounting 3
    Finance 3
    Marketing 4
    Production 4
    Economics 4

1.2 Data 5
    Elements, Variables, and Observations 5
    Scales of Measurement 6
    Qualitative and Quantitative Data 7
    Cross-Sectional and Time Series Data 7

1.3 Data Sources 8
    Existing Sources 8
    Statistical Studies 9
    Data Acquisition Errors 12

1.4 Descriptive Statistics 12

1.5 Statistical Inference 14

1.6 Statistical Analysis Using Microsoft Excel 16
    Data Sets and Excel Worksheets 16
    Using Excel for Statistical Analysis 16

Summary 19

Glossary 20

Supplementary Exercises 20

Appendix 1.1 An Introduction to SWStat+ 26

Chapter 2 Descriptive Statistics: Tabular and Graphical Presentations 28

Statistics in Practice: Colgate-Palmolive Company 29

2.1 Summarizing Qualitative Data 30
    Frequency Distribution 30
    Using Excel's COUNTIF Function to Construct a Frequency
        Distribution 31
    Relative Frequency and Percent Frequency Distributions 32

Using Excel to Construct Relative Frequency and Percent Frequency
    Distributions 33
Bar Graphs and Pie Charts 34
Using Excel's Chart Wizard to Construct Bar Graphs and Pie Charts 34

2.2   Summarizing Quantitative Data 39
Frequency Distribution 39
Using Excel's FREQUENCY Function to Construct a Frequency Distribution 41
Relative Frequency and Percent Frequency Distributions 43
Histogram 43
Using Excel's Chart Wizard to Construct a Histogram 44
Cumulative Distributions 46
Using Excel's Histogram Tool to Construct a Frequency Distribution
    and Histogram 49

2.3   Exploratory Data Analysis: The Stem-and-Leaf Display 56

2.4   Crosstabulations and Scatter Diagrams 61
Crosstabulation 61
Using Excel's PivotTable Report to Construct a Crosstabulation 64
Simpson's Paradox 67
Scatter Diagram and Trendline 68
Using Excel's Chart Wizard to Construct a Scatter Diagram and a Trendline 70

Summary 76
Glossary 78
Key Formulas 78
Supplementary Exercises 79
Case Problem Pelican Stores 85

Chapter 3   Descriptive Statistics: Numerical Measures   87

Statistics in Practice: Small Fry Design 88
3.1   Measures of Location 89
Mean 89
Median 90
Mode 91
Using Excel to Compute the Mean, Median, and Mode 92
Percentiles 93
Quartiles 94
Using Excel's Rank and Percentile Tool to Compute Percentiles and
    Quartiles 95

3.2   Measures of Variability 101
Range 102
Interquartile Range 102
Variance 103
Standard Deviation 104
Using Excel to Compute the Sample Variance and Sample Standard
    Deviation 106
Coefficient of Variation 106
Using Excel's Descriptive Statistics Tool 106

3.3 Measures of Distribution Shape, Relative Location, and Detecting Outliers 111
Distribution Shape 111
z-Scores 113
Chebyshev's Theorem 114
Empirical Rule 114
Detecting Outliers 115

3.4 Exploratory Data Analysis 118
Five-Number Summary 118
Box Plot 119

3.5 Measures of Association Between Two Variables 123
Covariance 123
Interpretation of the Covariance 125
Correlation Coefficient 127
Interpretation of the Correlation Coefficient 128
Using Excel to Compute the Covariance and Correlation Coefficient 130

3.6 The Weighted Mean and Working with Grouped Data 133
Weighted Mean 133
Grouped Data 134

Summary 139
Glossary 139
Key Formulas 140
Supplementary Exercises 142
Case Problem 1 Pelican Stores 147
Case Problem 2 National Health Care Association 148
Case Problem 3 Business Schools of Asia-Pacific 149
Appendix 3.1 Constructing a Box Plot Using SWStat+ 149

Chapter 4 Introduction to Probability 153

Statistics in Practice: Morton International 154
4.1 Experiments, Counting Rules, and Assigning Probabilities 155
Counting Rules, Combinations, and Permutations 156
Assigning Probabilities 160
Probabilities for the KP&L Project 162

4.2 Events and Their Probabilities 165
4.3 Some Basic Relationships of Probability 169
Complement of an Event 169
Addition Law 170

4.4 Conditional Probability 175
Independent Events 179
Multiplication Law 179

4.5 Bayes' Theorem 183
Tabular Approach 186
Using Excel to Compute Posterior Probabilities 187

Summary 190
Glossary 190

Key Formulas 191
Supplemental Exercises 192
Case Problem Hamilton County Judges 196

Chapter 5   Discrete Probability Distributions   198

Statistics in Practice: Citibank 199
5.1 Random Variables 199
     Discrete Random Variables 200
     Continuous Random Variables 201
5.2 Discrete Probability Distributions 202
5.3 Expected Value and Variance 208
     Expected Value 208
     Variance 208
     Using Excel to Compute the Expected Value, Variance, and Standard
         Deviation 209
5.4 Binomial Probability Distribution 213
     A Binomial Experiment 214
     Martin Clothing Store Problem 215
     Using Excel to Compute Binomial Probabilities 219
     Expected Value and Variance for the Binomial Probability Distribution 221
5.5 Poisson Probability Distribution 224
     An Example Involving Time Intervals 224
     An Example Involving Length or Distance Invervals 225
     Using Excel to Compute Poisson Probabilities 226
5.6 Hypergeometric Probability Distribution 229
     Using Excel to Compute Hypergeometric Probabilities 231
Summary 233
Glossary 233
Key Formulas 234
Supplementary Exercises 235

Chapter 6   Continuous Probability Distributions   238

Statistics in Practice: Procter & Gamble 239
6.1 Uniform Probability Distribution 240
     Area as a Measure of Probability 241
6.2 Normal Probability Distribution 244
     Normal Curve 244
     Standard Normal Probability Distribution 246
     Computing Probabilities for Any Normal Probability Distribution 251
     Grear Tire Company Problem 252
     Using Excel to Compute Normal Probabilities 254
6.3 Exponential Probability Distribution 259
     Computing Probabilities for the Exponential Distribution 260
     Relationship Between the Poisson and Exponential Distributions 261
     Using Excel to Compute Exponential Probabilities 261

Summary 264
Glossary 264
Key Formulas 264
Supplementary Exercises 265
Case Problem Specialty Toys 267

Chapter 7   Sampling and Sampling Distributions   269

Statistics in Practice: Meadwestvaco Corporation 270
7.1   The Electronics Associates Sampling Problem 271
7.2   Simple Random Sampling 272
    Sampling from a Finite Population 272
    Sampling from an Infinite Population 276
7.3   Point Estimation 278
7.4   Introduction to Sampling Distributions 281
7.5   Sampling Distribution of $\bar{x}$ 284
    Expected Value of $\bar{x}$ 284
    Standard Deviation of $\bar{x}$ 285
    Form of the Sampling Distribution of $\bar{x}$ 286
    Sampling Distribution of $\bar{x}$ for the EAI Problem 288
    Practical Value of the Sampling Distribution of $\bar{x}$ 288
    Relationship Between Sample Size and the Sampling Distribution
       of $\bar{x}$ 290
7.6   Sampling Distribution of $\bar{p}$ 294
    Expected Value of $\bar{p}$ 294
    Standard Deviation of $\bar{p}$ 295
    Form of the Sampling Distribution of $\bar{p}$ 295
    Practical Value of the Sampling Distribution of $\bar{p}$ 296
7.7   Sampling Methods 299
    Stratified Random Sampling 299
    Cluster Sampling 299
    Systematic Sampling 300
    Convenience Sampling 301
    Judgment Sampling 301
Summary 302
Glossary 302
Key Formulas 303
Supplementary Exercises 303

Chapter 8   Interval Estimation   306

Statistics in Practice: Food Lion 307
8.1   Population Mean: σ Known 308
    Margin of Error and the Interval Estimate 308
    Using Excel 312
    Practical Advice 314

8.2   Population Mean: σ Unknown 316
    Margin of Error and the Interval Estimate 317
    Using Excel 320
    Practical Advice 321
    Using a Small Sample 321
    Summary of Interval Estimation Procedures 323
8.3   Determining the Sample Size 326
8.4   Population Proportion 329
    Using Excel 330
    Determining the Sample Size 332
Summary 336
Glossary 337
Key Formulas 337
Supplement Exercises 338
Case Problem 1 Bock Investment Services 341
Case Problem 2 Gulf Real Estate Properties 341
Case Problem 3 Metropolitan Research, Inc. 344

Chapter 9   Hypothesis Tests   345

Statistics in Practice: John Morrell & Company 346
9.1   Developing Null and Alternative Hypotheses 347
    Testing Research Hypotheses 347
    Testing the Validity of a Claim 347
    Testing in Decision-Making Situations 348
    Summary of Forms for Null and Alternative Hypotheses 348
9.2   Type I and Type II Errors 349
9.3   Population Mean: σ Known 352
    One-Tailed Test 352
    Two-Tailed Test 358
    Using Excel 361
    Summary and Practical Advice 362
    Relationship Between Interval Estimation and Hypothesis Testing 364
9.4   Population Mean: σ Unknown 368
    One-Tailed Test 369
    Two-Tailed Test 370
    Using Excel 372
    Summary and Practical Advice 374
9.5   Population Proportion 378
    Using Excel 380
    Summary 382
Summary 384
Glossary 385
Key Formulas 385
Supplementary Exercises 386
Case Problem 1 Quality Associates, Inc. 388
Case Problem 2 Unemployment Study 390

Chapter 10 Statistical Inference About Means and Proportions with Two Populations 391

Statistics in Practice: Fisons Corporation 392

10.1 Inferences About the Difference Between Two Population Means: σ_1 and σ_2 Known 393
Interval Estimation of $\mu_1 - \mu_2$ 393
Using Excel to Construct a Confidence Interval 395
Hypothesis Tests About $\mu_1 - \mu_2$ 397
Using Excel to Conduct a Hypothesis Test 399
Practical Advice 401

10.2 Inferences About the Difference Between Two Population Means: σ_1 and σ_2 Unknown 403
Interval Estimation of $\mu_1 - \mu_2$ 404
Using Excel to Construct a Confidence Interval 405
Hypothesis Tests About $\mu_1 - \mu_2$ 407
Using Excel to Conduct a Hypothesis Test 409
Practical Advice 411

10.3 Inferences About the Difference Between Two Population Means: Matched Samples 415
Using Excel to Conduct a Hypothesis Test 417

10.4 Inferences About the Difference Between Two Population Proportions 422
Interval Estimation of $p_1 - p_2$ 422
Using Excel to Construct a Confidence Interval 424
Hypothesis Tests About $p_1 - p_2$ 426
Using Excel to Conduct a Hypothesis Test 427

Summary 432

Glossary 432

Key Formulas 432

Supplementary Exercises 434

Case Problem Par, Inc. 437

Chapter 11 Inferences About Population Variances 439

Statistics in Practice: U.S. General Accounting Office 440

11.1 Inferences About a Population Variance 441
Interval Estimation 441
Using Excel to Construct a Confidence Interval 445
Hypothesis Testing 446
Using Excel to Conduct a Hypothesis Test 449

11.2 Inferences About Two Population Variances 453
Using Excel to Conduct a Hypothesis Test 458

Summary 461

Key Formulas 461

Supplementary Exercises 462

Case Problem Air Force Training Program 463

Chapter 12 Tests of Goodness of Fit and Independence   465

Statistics in Practice: United Way 466

12.1 Goodness of Fit Test: A Multinomial Population 467
Using Excel to Conduct a Goodness of Fit Test 470

12.2 Test of Independence 473
Using Excel to Conduct a Test of Independence 477

12.3 Goodness of Fit Test: Poisson and Normal Distributions 481
Poisson Distribution 481
Using Excel to Conduct a Goodness of Fit Test 485
Normal Distribution 485
Using Excel to Conduct a Goodness of Fit Test 489

Summary 491

Glossary 491

Key Formulas 492

Supplementary Exercises 492

Case Problem A Bipartisan Agenda for Change 496

Chapter 13 Analysis of Variance and Experimental Design   497

Statistics in Practice: Burke Marketing Services, Inc. 498

13.1 Introduction to Analysis of Variance 498
Assumptions for Analysis of Variance 500
A Conceptual Overview 500

13.2 Analysis of Variance: Testing for the Equality of k Population Means 502
Between-Treatments Estimate of Population Variance 503
Within-Treatments Estimate of Population Variance 504
Comparing the Variance Estimates: The F Test 505
ANOVA Table 507
Using Excel 507

13.3 Multiple Comparison Procedures 513
Fisher's LSD 513
Type I Error Rates 516

13.4 Introduction to Experimental Design 518
Data Collection 520

13.5 Completely Randomized Designs 521
Between-Treatments Estimate of Population Variance 521
Within-Treatments Estimate of Population Variance 521
Comparing the Variance Estimates: The F Test 522
ANOVA Table 522
Using Excel 522
Pairwise Comparisons 523

13.6 Randomized Block Design 528
Air Traffic Controller Stress Test 528
ANOVA Procedure 529
Computations and Conclusions 530
Using Excel 532

13.7 Factorial Experiments 535
ANOVA Procedure 537
Computations and Conclusions 538
Using Excel 539
Summary 545
Glossary 546
Key Formulas 546
Supplementary Exercises 549
Case Problem 1 Wentworth Medical Center 556
Case Problem 2 Compensation for ID Professionals 557

Chapter 14 Simple Linear Regression 559

Statistics in Practice: Alliance Data Systems 560
14.1 Simple Linear Regression Model 561
Regression Model and Regression Equation 561
Estimated Regression Equation 562
14.2 Least Squares Method 564
Using Excel to Develop a Scatter Diagram and Compute the Estimated
Regression Equation 568
14.3 Coefficient of Determination 576
Using Excel to Compute the Coefficient of Determination 580
Correlation Coefficient 580
14.4 Model Assumptions 585
14.5 Testing for Significance 586
Estimate of σ^2 587
t Test 587
Confidence Interval for β_1 589
F Test 590
Some Cautions About the Interpretation of Significance Tests 592
14.6 Excel's Regression Tool 596
Using Excel's Regression Tool for the Armand's Pizza Parlors Example 596
Interpretation of Estimated Regression Equation Output 598
Interpretation of ANOVA Output 598
Interpretation of Regression Statistics Output 599
**14.7 Using the Estimated Regression Equation for Estimation and
Prediction 602**
Point Estimation 602
Interval Estimation 602
Confidence Interval Estimate of the Mean Value of y 602
Prediction Interval Estimate of an Individual Value of y 604
Using Excel to Develop Confidence and Prediction Interval Estimates 606
14.8 Residual Analysis: Validating Model Assumptions 610
Residual Plot Against x 612
Residual Plot Against $\hat{y}$ 614
Using Excel's Regression Tool to Construct a Residual Plot 614
Standardized Residuals 615

Using Excel to Construct a Standardized Residual Plot 618
Normal Probability Plot 618

14.9 Outliers and Influential Observations 622
Detecting Outliers 622
Detecting Influential Observations 625

Summary 629

Glossary 629

Key Formulas 630

Supplementary Exercises 632

Case Problem 1 Spending and Student Achievement 638

Case Problem 2 U.S. Department of Transportation 639

Case Problem 3 Alumni Giving 640

Case Problem 4 Major League Baseball Teams Values 642

Appendix 14.1 Calculus-Based Derivation of Least Squares Formulas 642

Appendix 14.2 Test for Significance Using Correlation 644

Appendix 14.3 Regression Analysis with SWStat+ 645

Chapter 15 Multiple Regression 648

Statistics in Practice: International Paper 649

15.1 Multiple Regression Model 650
Regression Model and Regression Equation 650
Estimated Multiple Regression Equation 650

15.2 Least Squares Method 651
An Example: Butler Trucking Company 652
Using Excel's Regression Tool to Develop the Estimated Multiple Regression Equation 655
Note on Interpretation of Coefficients 656

15.3 Multiple Coefficient of Determination 661

15.4 Model Assumptions 664

15.5 Testing for Significance 666
F Test 666
t Test 669
Multicollinearity 670

15.6 Using the Estimated Regression Equation for Estimation and Prediction 673

15.7 Qualitative Independent Variables 675
An Example: Johnson Filtration, Inc. 676
Interpreting the Parameters 678
More Complex Qualitative Variables 680

15.8 Residual Analysis 684
Residual Plot Against $\hat{y}$ 684
Standardized Residual Plot Against $\hat{y}$ 684

Summary 688

Glossary 689

Key Formulas 689

Supplementary Exercises 690

Case Problem 1 Consumer Research, Inc. 696

Case Problem 2 Predicting Student Proficiency Test Scores 697

Case Problem 3 Alumni Giving 698

Appendix 15.1 Multiple Regression Analysis with SWStat+ 700

Chapter 16 Regression Analysis: Model Building 702

Statistics in Practice: Monsanto Company 703

16.1 General Linear Model 704

Modeling Curvilinear Relationships 704

Interaction 706

Transformations Involving the Dependent Variable 710

Nonlinear Models That Are Intrinsically Linear 713

16.2 Determining When to Add or Delete Variables 717

General Case 719

16.3 Analysis of a Larger Problem 724

16.4 Variable Selection Procedures 728

Stepwise Regression 728

Forward Selection 729

Backward Elimination 729

Using Excel to Perform the Backward Elimination Procedure 729

Best-Subsets Regression 731

16.5 Residual Analysis 734

Autocorrelation and the Durbin-Watson Test 735

16.6 Multiple Regression Approach to Analysis of Variance and Experimental Design 741

Summary 745

Glossary 746

Key Formulas 746

Supplementary Exercises 746

Case Problem 1 Unemployment Study 750

Case Problem 2 Fuel Economy for Cars 752

Chapter 17 Nonparametric Methods 754

Statistics in Practice: West Shell Realtors 755

17.1 Sign Test 757

Small-Sample Case 757

Using Excel 759

Large-Sample Case 760

Using Excel 761

Hypothesis Test About a Median 762

Using Excel 763

17.2 Wilcoxon Signed Rank Test 765

Using Excel 768

17.3   Mann-Whitney-Wilcoxon Rank Sum Test 771
Small-Sample Case 772
Large-Sample Case 775
Using Excel 777

17.4   Kruskal-Wallis Test 780
Using Excel 782

17.5   Rank Correlation 785
Test for Significant Rank Correlation 787
Using Excel 788

Summary 791

Glossary 791

Key Formulas 791

Supplementary Exercises 792

Chapter 18   Statistical Methods for Quality Control   795

Statistics in Practice: Dow Chemical 796

18.1   Philosophies and Frameworks 797
Malcolm Baldrige National Quality Award 797
ISO 9000 798
Six Sigma 798

18.2   Statistical Process Control 800
Control Charts 801
$\bar{x}$ Chart: Process Mean and Standard Deviation Known 802
$\bar{x}$ Chart: Process Mean and Standard Deviation Unknown 804
R Chart 807
Using Excel to Construct an R Chart and an $\bar{x}$ Chart 809
p Chart 812
np Chart 814
Interpretation of Control Charts 815

18.3   Acceptance Sampling 817
KALI, Inc.: An Example of Acceptance Sampling 819
Computing the Probability of Accepting a Lot 819
Selecting an Acceptance Sampling Plan 821
Multiple Sampling Plans 823

Summary 825

Glossary 826

Key Formulas 827

Supplementary Exercises 828

Chapter 19   Decision Analysis   830

Statistics in Practice: Ohio Edison Company 831

19.1   Problem Formulation 832
Payoff Tables 833
Decision Trees 833

19.2   Decision Making with Probabilities 834
      Expected Value Approach 834
      Expected Value of Perfect Information 836
19.3   Decision Analysis with Sample Information 842
      Decision Tree 843
      Decision Strategy 844
      Expected Value of Sample Information 847
19.4   Computing Branch Probabilities Using Bayes' Theorem 853
Summary 857
Glossary 858
Key Formulas 859
Case Problem Lawsuit Defense Strategy 859
Appendix 19.1 Solving the PDC Problem with TreePlan 860

Chapter 20 Sample Survey   On CD

Appendix A: References and Bibliography 868

Appendix B: Tables 870

Appendix C: Summation Notation 881

Appendix D: Self-Test Solutions and Answers to Even-Numbered Exercises 883

Appendix E: Using Excel Functions 927

Index 933

Preface

The purpose of *Modern Business Statistics with Microsoft® Excel* is to give students, primarily in the fields of business administration and economics, an introduction to the field of statistics and its many applications. The text is applications oriented and written with the needs of the nonmathematician in mind; the mathematical prerequisite is knowledge of algebra.

Applications of data analysis and statistical methodology are an integral part of the organization and presentation of the text material. The discussion and development of each technique is presented in an application setting, with the statistical results providing insights to decisions and solutions to problems.

Although the book is applications oriented, we have taken care to provide a sound methodological development and to use notation that is generally accepted for the topic being covered. Hence, students will find that this text provides good preparation for the study of more advanced material. A bibliography to guide further study is included in an appendix.

Use of Microsoft® Excel for Statistical Analysis

Modern Business Statistics with Microsoft® Excel is first and foremost a statistics textbook that emphasizes statistical concepts and applications. But, since most practical problems are too large to be solved using hand calculations, some type of statistical software package is required to solve these problems. There are several excellent statistical packages available today. However, because most students and potential employers value spreadsheet experience, many schools now use a spreadsheet package in their statistics courses. Microsoft Excel is the most widely used spreadsheet package in business as well as in colleges and universities. We have written *Modern Business Statistics with Microsoft® Excel* especially for statistics courses in which Excel is used as the software package.

Excel has been integrated within each of the chapters, and plays an integral part in providing an application orientation. We assume that readers using this text are familiar with Excel basics such as selecting cells, entering formulas, copying, and so on. We build on that familiarity by showing how to use the appropriate Excel statistical functions and data analysis tools.

The discussion of using Excel to perform a statistical procedure appears in a subsection immediately following the discussion of the statistical procedure. We believe that this style enables us to fully integrate the use of Excel throughout the text, but still maintain the primary emphasis on the statistical methodology being discussed. In each of these subsections, we use a standard format for setting up a worksheet for statistical analysis. There are three primary tasks: Enter Data, Enter Functions and Formulas, and Apply Tools. We believe a consistent framework for applying Excel helps users to focus on the statistical methodology without getting bogged down in the details of using Excel.

In presenting worksheet figures we often use a nested approach in which the worksheet shown in the background displays the formulas, and the worksheet shown in the foreground shows the values computed using the formulas.

Following is Figure 2.1 from the text, which is displayed to explain use of color in Excel figures. We use purple to highlight the data from the sample (soft drink purchases in this

FIGURE 2.1   FREQUENCY DISTRIBUTION FOR SOFT DRINK PURCHASES
CONSTRUCTED USING EXCEL'S COUNTIF FUNCTION

	A	B	C	D	E
1	**Brand Purchased**		**Soft Drink**	**Frequency**	
2	Coke Classic		Coke Classic	=COUNTIF($A$2:$A$51,C2)	
3	Diet Coke		Diet Coke	=COUNTIF($A$2:$A$51,C3)	
4	Pepsi-Cola		Dr. Pepper	=COUNTIF($A$2:$A$51,C4)	
5	Diet Coke		Pepsi-Cola	=COUNTIF($A$2:$A$51,C5)	
6	Coke Classic		Sprite	=COUNTIF($A$2:$A$51,C6)	
7	Coke Classic				
8	Dr. Pepper				
9	Diet Coke				
10	Pepsi-Cola				
45	Pepsi-Cola				
46	Pepsi-Cola				
47	Pepsi-Cola				
48	Coke Classic				
49	Dr. Pepper				
50	Pepsi-Cola				
51	Sprite				
52					

	A	B	C	D	E
1	**Brand Purchased**		**Soft Drink**	**Frequency**	
2	Coke Classic		Coke Classic	19	
3	Diet Coke		Diet Coke	8	
4	Pepsi-Cola		Dr. Pepper	5	
5	Diet Coke		Pepsi-Cola	13	
6	Coke Classic		Sprite	5	
7	Coke Classic				
8	Dr. Pepper				
9	Diet Coke				
10	Pepsi-Cola				
45	Pepsi-Cola				
46	Pepsi-Cola				
47	Pepsi-Cola				
48	Coke Classic				
49	Dr. Pepper				
50	Pepsi-Cola				
51	Sprite				
52					

*Note: Rows 11–44
are hidden.*

figure) and green to highlight the cells containing Excel functions and formulas. The green
cells show the functions and formulas in the background worksheet and they show the values
obtained using the formulas in the foreground worksheet. A third color (yellow) is used in
certain figures to highlight material that is printed by Excel as a result of using one of the
data analysis tools.

Changes in the Second Edition

We appreciate the acceptance and positive response to the first edition of *Modern Business
Statistics with Microsoft® Excel*. Accordingly, in making modifications for this new edition,
we have maintained the presentation style and readability of the first edition. The significant changes in the new edition are summarized here.

Content Revisions

- **Descriptive Statistics:** New sections have been added on the shape of distributions
  in Chapters 2 and 3. Skewness is introduced as an important measure of the shape
  of a distribution. In later chapters, we now mention the need for larger sample sizes
  in interval estimation and hypothesis testing applications involving a skewed popu-

lation. Crosstabulation material has been expanded to include more discussion of percentage distributions. Simpson's paradox is used to point out a source of potentially erroneous conclusions when working with crosstabulations.

- **Probability Distributions:** The cumulative standard normal probability table has been expanded to show cumulative probabilities from $z = -3.09$ to $z = 3.09$. This enables hand calculations to parallel the approach that Excel uses to compute probabilities using the NORMSDIST and NORMDIST functions, and it makes it easier to compute lower tail p-values. A discussion of the mean, variance, and standard deviation has been added for the Poisson and hypergeometric distributions in Chapter 5 and the exponential distribution in Chapter 6.

- **Interval Estimation:** In the first edition, we followed a large sample/small sample approach for interval estimation of a population mean in Chapter 8. In this second edition, we present interval estimation using the σ known and σ unknown paradigm. The standard normal distribution is used in all cases where the population standard deviation can be assumed known. The t distribution is used in all cases where the population standard deviation is estimated by the sample standard deviation. This approach simplifies the methodology for the student and is consistent with computer-based procedures provided by Excel. In the σ unknown case, the new approach provides slightly improved results over the previous large-sample approximation. A t distribution table with up to 100 degrees of freedom is included as Table 2 of Appendix B. This change carries into hypothesis tests about a population mean in Chapter 9 and statistical inferences about the means of two populations in Chapter 10.

- **Hypothesis Testing Using p-values:** Another change in the new edition is the emphasis on the use of p-values for hypothesis testing. With more and more use of statistical software packages for data analysis, p-values are clearly preferred to the traditional test statistic and rejection region approach. As a result, we now use p-values as the primary method for hypothesis testing applications in Chapters 9 to 16.

- **New Procedure for Two Sample Inferences:** We provide new methodology for inferences about the means of two populations when the population standard deviations are unknown. The methodology is based on the t distribution and is more general in that it can be applied whether or not the population variances are equal. The student no longer has to consider making the equal population variance assumption and making the pooled variance calculation.

- **New Chapter on Decision Analysis:** We have added a new Chapter 19 on decision analysis. Payoff tables, decision trees, and the development of optimal decision strategies are discussed. The Excel add-in TreePlan is available on the Student CD packaged with each new book.

Solutions Manual

In response to suggestions from users, we have revised the solutions manual extensively. In conjunction with hand solution of exercises, the use of Excel functions and formulas is shown where appropriate. In particular, results provided using Excel's probability distribution functions (e.g., BINOMDIST, NORMSDIST, and so on) and data analysis tools are shown.

New Examples and Exercises Based on Real Data

We have added approximately 150 new examples and exercises based on real data and recent reference sources of statistical information. Using articles from the *Wall Street Journal, USA Today, Fortune, Barron's,* and data from a variety of other sources, we draw from actual studies to develop explanations and to create exercises that demonstrate many uses of statistics in business and economics. We believe that the use of real data helps generate more student interest in the material and enables the student to learn about both the statistical methodology and it application. The second edition of the text contains approximately 300 examples and exercises based on real data.

New Case Problems

We have added several new case problems to this edition, bringing the total number of case problems in the text to twenty-seven. The new case problems appear in the chapters on descriptive statistics, probability distributions, regression analysis, and decision analysis. These case problems provide students with the opportunity to analyze somewhat larger data sets and prepare managerial reports based on the results of the analysis.

New Statistics in Practice

Each chapter begins with a Statistics in Practice article that describes an application of the statistical methodology to be covered in the chapter. Practitioners at companies such as Colgate-Palmolive, Citibank, Procter & Gamble, Monsanto, and others have provided Statistics in Practice. This edition includes three new Statistics in Practice: Food Lion (Chapter 8), John Morrell & Company (Chapter 9) and Alliance Data Systems (Chapter 14).

New Materials for Microsoft Excel

All Excel materials have been updated to be consistent with Microsoft Excel 2003, and two options have been added to enhance learning and extend the use of Excel.

- *EasyStat: Digital Tutor for Microsoft® Excel,* **Version 2.** This online tutorial makes it easier for students to learn how to use Excel to perform statistical analysis. In each digital video, one of the textbook authors demonstrates how Excel can be used to perform a particular statistical procedure. Students may purchase an online subscription for EasyStat Digital Tutor at *http//easystat.swlearning.com.*
- **Coverage of Excel Add-in** *SWStat+,* **Version 2.** For the second edition, the instructor now has the option of using *SWStat+*, a comprehensive Excel add-in. *SWStat+* is covered in the appendixes of selected chapters, and the software may be bundled with the text for student purchase.

Features and Pedagogy

Anderson, Sweeney, and Williams have continued many of the features that appeared in the first edition. Some of the important ones are noted here.

Methods Exercises and Applications Exercises

The end-of-section exercises are split into two parts: Methods and Applications. The Methods exercises require users to use the formulas and make computations. The Applications exercises require students to apply the chapter material in real-world situations. Thus, students focus on the computational "nuts and bolts" and then move on to the subtleties of statistical application and interpretation.

Self-Test Exercises

Some exercises are identified as self-test exercises. Completely worked-out solutions for these exercises are provided in an appendix at the end of the book. Students can attempt the self-text exercises and immediately check the solutions to evaluate their understanding of the concepts presented in the chapter.

Margin Annotations and Notes and Comments

Margin annotations that highlight key points and provide additional insights for the student are a key feature of this text. These annotations, which appear in the margins, are designed to provide emphasis and enhance understanding of the terms and concepts being presented in the text.

At the end of many sections, we provide Notes and Comments designed to give the student additional insights about the statistical methodology and its application. Notes and Comments include warnings about limitations of the methodology, recommendations for application, brief descriptions of technical considerations, and other matters.

Data Files Accompany the Text

More than 200 data files are available on the Student CD that is packaged with new copies of the text. Data set logos are used in the text to identify the data sets that are available on the CD. Data sets for all case problems, as well as data sets and worksheets for larger exercises, are included.

Ancillary Learning and Teaching Materials

For Students

Several print and online resources are available to help the student save time as well as learn how to use Excel.

- A **Student CD** is packaged free with each new text. It provides Excel worksheets for all text examples, exercises, and Case Problems; the TreePlan add-in and manual; and a PredInt add-in with directions. If necessary, the student CD may be purchased at the text's website, *http://asw.swlearning.com.*
- **EasyStat Digital Tutor for Microsoft® Excel, Version 2.** These online tutorials make it easier than ever for students to learn how to use Excel to perform statistical analysis. For more information, visit *http://easystat.swlearning.com.*
- The **Study Guide** (ISBN: 0-324-23326-4), prepared by John Loucks of St. Edward's University, provides the student with significant supplementary study materials. For each chapter, it contains key concepts, review materials, example problems worked out in full detail, exercises with answers, and self-test questions with answers. The Study Guide may be purchased online at *http://asw.swlearning.com.*

For Instructors

Instructor support materials are available to adopters from the Thomson Learning™ Academic Resource Center at 800-423-0563 or through http://*www.sw.learning.com.* All instructor ancillaries are provided on a single **Instructor's Resource CD-Rom** (ISBN: 0-324-23327-2). Included in this convenient format are:

- **Solutions Manual**—The *Solutions Manual* prepared by the authors, includes solutions for all problems in the text.
- **Solutions for Case Problems**—Also prepared by the authors, solutions to all case problems presented in the text are included here.
- **PowerPoint™ Presentation Slides**—Prepared by John Loucks of St. Edwards University, the presentation slides contain a teaching outline that incorporates graphics to help instructors create even more stimulating lectures. New for the second edition, the

slides include animation. The slides may be adapted using Microsoft® PowerPoint software to facilitate classroom or online use.

- **Test Bank** and **ExamView**™—Prepared also by John Loucks, the Test Bank includes multiple-choice questions and problems for each chapter. ExamView™ Pro computerized testing software enables instructors to create, edit, store and print exams.

Also, at the request of the instructor, a print version of the Solutions Manual can be packaged with the text for student purchase.

Two other online products provide course management tools to improve efficiency and record keeping.

- **Ilrn® Business Statistics Homework**
  This new tool enables instructors to assign and automatically grade the exercises from the text. The online gradebook will save time and enable instructors to assess class progress in real time and adjust lectures as necessary. For more information, visit *http://asw.swlearning.com.*

- **WebTutor Toolbox for Blackboard® or WebCT**™
  This online tool provides web-based learning resources for students as well as powerful communication and other course management tools for the instructor. Talk with your Thomson representative about how to package this interactive online resource with each new student text.

Acknowledgements

We would like to acknowledge the work of our reviewers who provided comments and suggestions of ways to continue to improve our text. Thanks to:

Darl Bien, University of Denver

Thomas W. Bolland, Ohio University

Terry Dielman, Texas Christian University

Mohammed A. El-Saidi, Ferris State University

Nicolas Farnum, California State University, Fullerton

Abe Feinberg, California State University, Northridge

V. Daniel Guide, Duquesne University

Alan Humphrey, University of Rhode Island

Kenneth Klassen, California State University, Northridge

June Lapidus, Roosevelt University

John Lawrence, California State University, Fullerton

Lynne Pastor, Carnegie Mellon University

Barry Pasternack, California State University, Fullerton

William Struning, Seton Hall University

We also express appreciation for the significant input we gained from instructors who participated in a large survey held in early 2004.

Michelle Boddy, Baker College

Alan Brokaw, Michigan Tech University

Nancy Brooks, University of Vermont

Yvonne Brown, Pima Community College

Robert Burgess, Georgia Tech

Von L. Burton, Athens State University

John R Carpenter, Cornerstone University

Alan S. Chesen, Wright State University

Michael Cicero, Highline Community College

Ping Deng, Maryville University

Sarvanan Devaraj, Notre Dame University

Cassandra DiRienzo, Elon University

Jianjun Du, University of Houston, Victoria

John N. Dyer, Georgia Southern University

Robert M. Escudero, Pepperdine University

Maggie Williams Flint, Northeast State Tech Community College

James Flynn, Cleveland State University

Alan F. Foltz, Drury University

Ronald L. Friesen, Bluffton College

Richard Gebhart, University of Tulsa

Paul Gentine, Bethany College

Deborah J. Gougeon, University of Scranton

Jeffrey Gropp, DePauw University

Rhonda Hensley, North Carolina A&T University

Wade Jackson, University of Memphis

Timmy James, Northwest Shoals Community College

Naser Kamleh, Wallace Community College

Mark P. Karscig, Central Missouri State University

Joseph Kosler, Indiana University of Pennsylvania

Howard Kittleson, Riverland Community College

Eileen Quinn Knight, St Xavier University, Chicago

Bharat Kolluri, University of Hartford

David A. Kravitz, George Mason University

Laura Kuhl, University of Phoenix, Cleveland Campus

John Lawrence, California State University, Fullerton

Tenpao Lee, Niagara University

Robert Lindsey, College of Charleston

Michael Machiorlatti, City College of San Francisco

Malik B. Malik, University of Maryland Eastern Shore

Lee McClain, Western Washington University

Timothy E. McDaniel, Buena Vista University

Kim I. Melton, North Georgia College & State University

Brian Metz, Cabrini College

John M. Miller, Sam Houston State University

Jack Muryn, University of Wisconsin, Washington County

Ceyhun Ozgur, Valparaiso University

Michael Parzen, Emory University

Barry Pasternack, California State University, Fullerton

Ranjna Patel, Bethune-Cookman College

Jennifer M. Platania, Elon University

Irene Powell, Grinnell College

Narseeyappa Rajanikanth, Mississippi Valley State University

Ronny Richardson, Southern Polytechnic State University

Leonard E Ross, California State University, Pomona

Probir Roy, University of Missouri, Kansas City

Randall K. Russell, Yavapai College

Alan Safer, California State University, Long Beach

David Satava, University of Houston, Victoria

Richard W. Schrader, Bellarmine University

Larry Seifert, Webster University

John Seydel, Arkansas State University

Robert Simoneau, Keene State College

Harvey A. Singer, George Mason University

Clifford Sowell, Berea College

William Stein, Texas A&M University

Timothy S. Sullivan, Southern Illinois University, Edwardsville

Lee Tangedahk, University of Montana

Alexander Thomson, Schoolcraft College

Suzanne Tilleman, Montana State University Northern

Daniel Tschopp, Daemen College (NY)

Jack Vaughn, University of Texas, El Paso

John Vogt, Newman University

Geoffrey L. Wallace, University of Wisconsin, Madison

Michael Wiemann, Metro Community Colleges

John Wiorkowski, University of Texas, Dallas

Guoqiang Peter Zhang, Georgia Southern University

Zhe George Zhang, Western Washington University

Deborah G. Ziegler, Hannibal-LaGrange College

We would like to recognize the following individuals who have helped us in the past and continue to influence our writing.

Glen Archibald, University of Mississippi

Mike Bourke, Houston Baptist University

Peter Bryant, University of Colorado,

Terri L. Byczkowski, University of Cincinnati

Ying Chien, University of Scranton

Robert Cochran, University of Wyoming

Murray Côté, University of Florida

David W. Cravens, Texas Christian University

Robert Carver, Stonehill College

Tom Dahlstrom, Eastern College

Ronald Ehresman, Baldwin-Wallace College

Michael Ford, Rochester Institute of Technology

Phil Fry, Boise State University

Paul Guy, California State University, Chico

Alan Humphrey, University of Rhode Island

Ann Hussein, Philadelphia College of Textiles and Science

Ben Isselhardt, Rochester Institute of Technology

Jeffery Jarrett, University of Rhode Island

Barry Kadets, Bryant College

David Krueger, St. Cloud State University

Martin S. Levy, University of Cincinnati

Don Marx, University of Alaska, Anchorage

Ka-sing Man, Georgetown University

Tom McCullough, University of California, Berkeley

Mario Miranda, The Ohio State University

Mitchell Muesham, Sam Houston State University

Richard O'Connell, Miami University of Ohio

Alan Olinsky, Bryant College

Tom Pray, Rochester Institute of Technology

Harold Rahmlow, St. Joseph's University

Derrick Reagle, Fordham University

Tom Ryan, Case Western Reserve University

Bill Seaver, University of Tennessee

Alan Smith, Robert Morris College

David Tufte, University of New Orleans

Jack Vaughn, University of Texas, El Paso

Ari Wijetunga, Morehead State University

J. E. Willis, Louisiana State University

Mustafa Yilmaz, Northeastern University

A special thanks is owed to our associates from business and industry that supplied the Statistics in Practice features. We recognize them individually by a credit line in each of the articles. Finally, we are also indebted to our senior acquisitions editor Charles McCormick, Jr., our senior developmental editor Alice Denny, our senior production editor Deanna Quinn, our senior marketing manager Larry Qualls, and others at Thomson Business and Economics for their editorial counsel and support during the preparation of this text.

David R. Anderson
Dennis J. Sweeney
Thomas A. Williams

David R. Anderson.   David R. Anderson is Professor of Quantitative Analysis in the College of Business Administration at the University of Cincinnati. Born in Grand Forks, North Dakota, he earned his B.S., M.S., and Ph.D. degrees from Purdue University. Professor Anderson has served as Head of the Department of Quantitative Analysis and Operations Management and as Associate Dean of the College of Business Administration. In addition, he was the coordinator of the College's first Executive Program.

At the University of Cincinnati, Professor Anderson has taught introductory statistics for business students as well as graduate-level courses in regression analysis, multivariate analysis, and management science. He has also taught statistical courses at the Department of Labor in Washington, D.C. He has been honored with nominations and awards for excellence in teaching and excellence in service to student organizations.

Professor Anderson has coauthored ten textbooks in the areas of statistics, management science, linear programming, and production and operations management. He is an active consultant in the field of sampling and statistical methods.

Dennis J. Sweeney.   Dennis J. Sweeney is Professor of Quantitative Analysis and Founder of the Center for Productivity Improvement at the University of Cincinnati. Born in Des Moines, Iowa, he earned a B.S.B.A. degree from Drake University and his M.B.A. and D.B.A. degrees from Indiana University where he was an NDEA Fellow. During 1978–79, Professor Sweeney worked in the management science group at Procter & Gamble; during 1981–82, he was a visiting professor at Duke University. Professor Sweeney served as Head of the Department of Quantitative Analysis and as Associate Dean of the College of Business Administration at the University of Cincinnati.

Professor Sweeney has published more than 30 articles and monographs in the area of management science and statistics. The National Science Foundation, IBM, Procter & Gamble, Federated Department Stores, Kroger, and Cincinnati Gas & Electric have funded his research, which has been published in *Management Science*, *Operations Research*, *Mathematical Programming*, *Decision Sciences*, and other journals.

Professor Sweeney has coauthored 10 textbooks in the areas of statistics, management science, linear programming, and production and operations management.

Thomas A. Williams.   Thomas A. Williams is Professor of Management Science in the College of Business at Rochester Institute of Technology. Born in Elmira, New York, he earned his B.S. degree at Clarkson University. He did his graduate work at Rensselaer Polytechnic Institute, where he received his M.S. and Ph.D. degrees.

Before joining the College of Business at RIT, Professor Williams served for seven years as a faculty member in the College of Business Administration at the University of Cincinnati, where he developed the undergraduate program in Information Systems and then served as its coordinator. At RIT he was the first chairman of the Decision Sciences Department. He teaches courses in management science and statistics, as well as graduate courses in regression and decision analysis.

Professor Williams is the coauthor of eleven textbooks in the areas of management science, statistics, production and operations management, and mathematics. He has been a consultant for numerous *Fortune* 500 companies and has worked on projects ranging from the use of data analysis to the development of large-scale regression models.

CHAPTER 1

Data and Statistics

CONTENTS

STATISTICS IN PRACTICE:
BUSINESSWEEK

1.1 APPLICATIONS IN BUSINESS
AND ECONOMICS
Accounting
Finance
Marketing
Production
Economics

1.2 DATA
Elements, Variables, and
Observations
Scales of Measurement

Qualitative and Quantitative Data
Cross-Sectional and Time
Series Data

1.3 DATA SOURCES
Existing Sources
Statistical Studies
Data Acquisition Errors

1.4 DESCRIPTIVE STATISTICS

1.5 STATISTICAL INFERENCE

1.6 STATISTICAL ANALYSIS
USING MICROSOFT EXCEL
Data Sets and Excel Worksheets
Using Excel for Statistical
Analysis

BUSINESSWEEK*
NEW YORK, NEW YORK

With a global circulation of more than 1 million, *BusinessWeek* is the most widely read business magazine in the world. More than 200 dedicated reporters and editors in 26 bureaus worldwide deliver a variety of articles of interest to the business and economic community. Along with feature articles on current topics, the magazine contains regular sections on International Business, Economic Analysis, Information Processing, and Science & Technology. Information in the feature articles and the regular sections helps readers stay abreast of current developments and assess the impact of those developments on business and economic conditions.

Most issues of *BusinessWeek* provide an in-depth report on a topic of current interest. Often, the in-depth reports contain statistical facts and summaries that help the reader understand the business and economic information. For example, the January 12, 2004, issue described the economic outlook by industry for 2004; the December 6, 2004 issue included a special report on the pricing of goods made in China; and the January 3, 2005, issue provided information about where to invest in 2005. In addition, the weekly *BusinessWeek Investor* provides statistics about the state of the economy, including production indexes, stock prices, mutual funds, and interest rates.

BusinessWeek also uses statistics and statistical information in managing its own business. For example, an annual survey of subscribers helps the company learn about subscriber demographics, reading habits, likely purchases, lifestyles, and so on. *BusinessWeek* managers use statistical summaries from the survey to provide better services to subscribers and advertisers. One recent North American subscriber survey indicated that 90% of

BusinessWeek uses statistical facts and summaries in many of its articles. © Terri Miller/E-Visual Communications, Inc.

BusinessWeek subscribers use a personal computer at home and that 64% of *BusinessWeek* subscribers are involved with computer purchases at work. Such statistics alert *BusinessWeek* managers to subscriber interest in articles about new developments in computers. The results of the survey are also made available to potential advertisers. The high percentage of subscribers using personal computers at home and the high percentage of subscribers involved with computer purchases at work would be an incentive for a computer manufacturer to consider advertising in *BusinessWeek*.

In this chapter, we discuss the types of data available for statistical analysis and describe how the data are obtained. We introduce descriptive statistics and statistical inference as ways of converting data into meaningful and easily interpreted statistical information.

*The authors are indebted to Charlene Trentham, Research Manager at *BusinessWeek*, for providing this Statistics in Practice.

Frequently, we see the following kinds of statements in newspaper and magazine articles:

- A Jupiter Media survey found that 31% of adult males spend 10 or more hours a week watching television. For adult women, it was 26% (*The Wall Street Journal,* January 26, 2004).
- General Motors, the leader in automotive cash rebates, provided an average cash incentive of $4300 per vehicle during 2003 (*USA Today,* January 23, 2004).
- More than 40% of Marriott International managers work their way up through the ranks (*Fortune,* January 20, 2003).

- Employees in management and finance had a median annual salary of $49,712 for 2003 (*The World Almanac,* 2004).
- Employers plan to hire 12.7% more college graduates in 2004 than they did in 2003 (Collegiate Employment Research Institute, Michigan State University, February 2004).
- The New York Yankees have the highest payroll in major league baseball. In 2003, team payroll was $152,749,814 with a median of $4,575,000 per player (*USA Today,* September 1, 2003).
- The Dow Jones Industrial Average closed at 10,759 on December 21, 2004 (*The Wall Street Journal,* December 22, 2004).

The numerical facts in the preceding statements (31%, 26%, $4300, 40%, $49,712, 12.7%, $152,749,814, $4,575,000, and 10,759) are called statistics. Thus, in everyday usage, the term *statistics* refers to numerical facts. However, the field, or subject, of statistics involves much more than numerical facts. In a broad sense, **statistics** is the art and science of collecting, analyzing, presenting, and interpreting data. Particularly in business and economics, the information provided by collecting, analyzing, presenting, and interpreting data gives managers and decision makers a better understanding of the business and economic environment and thus enables them to make more informed and better decisions. In this text, we emphasize the use of statistics for business and economic decision making.

Chapter 1 begins with some illustrations of the applications of statistics in business and economics. In Section 1.2 we define the term *data* and introduce the concept of a data set. This section also introduces key terms such as *variables* and *observations,* discusses the difference between quantitative and qualitative data, and illustrates the uses of cross-sectional and time series data. Section 1.3 discusses how data can be obtained from existing sources or through survey and experimental studies designed to obtain new data. The important role that the Internet now plays in obtaining data is also highlighted. The uses of data in developing descriptive statistics and in making statistical inferences are described in Sections 1.4 and 1.5.

1.1   Applications in Business and Economics

In today's global business and economic environment, anyone can access vast amounts of statistical information. The most successful managers and decision makers understand the information and know how to use it effectively. In this section, we provide examples that illustrate some of the uses of statistics in business and economics.

Accounting

Public accounting firms use statistical sampling procedures when conducting audits for their clients. For instance, suppose an accounting firm wants to determine whether the amount of accounts receivable shown on a client's balance sheet fairly represents the actual amount of accounts receivable. Usually the large number of individual accounts receivable makes reviewing and validating every account too time-consuming and expensive. As common practice in such situations, the audit staff selects a subset of the accounts called a sample. After reviewing the accuracy of the sampled accounts, the auditors draw a conclusion as to whether the accounts receivable amount shown on the client's balance sheet is acceptable.

Finance

Financial analysts use a variety of statistical information to guide their investment recommendations. In the case of stocks, the analysts review a variety of financial data including price/earnings ratios and dividend yields. By comparing the information for an individual stock with information about the stock market averages, a financial analyst can begin to draw a conclusion as to whether an individual stock is over- or underpriced. For example, *Barron's* (January 6, 2003) reported that the average price/earnings ratio for the 30 stocks in the Dow Jones Industrial Average was 22.36. General Electric showed a price/earnings ratio of 16. In this case, the statistical information on price/earnings ratios indicated a lower price in comparison to earnings for General Electric than the average for the Dow Jones stocks. Therefore, a financial analyst might conclude that General Electric was underpriced. This and other information about General Electric would help the analyst make a buy, sell, or hold recommendation for the stock.

Marketing

Electronic scanners at retail checkout counters collect data for a variety of marketing research applications. For example, data suppliers such as ACNielsen and Information Resources, Inc., purchase point-of-sale scanner data from grocery stores, process the data, and then sell statistical summaries of the data to manufacturers. Manufacturers spend hundreds of thousands of dollars per product category to obtain this type of scanner data. Manufacturers also purchase data and statistical summaries on promotional activities such as special pricing and the use of in-store displays. Brand managers can review the scanner statistics and the promotional activity statistics to gain a better understanding of the relationship between promotional activities and sales. Such analyses often prove helpful in establishing future marketing strategies for the various products.

Production

Today's emphasis on quality makes quality control an important application of statistics in production. A variety of statistical quality control charts are used to monitor the output of a production process. In particular, an x-bar chart can be used to monitor the average output. Suppose, for example, that a machine fills containers with 12 ounces of a soft drink. Periodically, a production worker selects a sample of containers and computes the average number of ounces in the sample. This average, or x-bar value, is plotted on an x-bar chart. A plotted value above the chart's upper control limit indicates overfilling, and a plotted value below the chart's lower control limit indicates underfilling. The process is termed "in control" and allowed to continue as long as the plotted x-bar values fall between the chart's upper and lower control limits. Properly interpreted, an x-bar chart can help determine when adjustments are necessary to correct a production process.

Economics

Economists frequently provide forecasts about the future of the economy or some aspect of it. They use a variety of statistical information in making such forecasts. For instance, in forecasting inflation rates, economists use statistical information on such indicators as the Producer Price Index, the unemployment rate, and manufacturing capacity utilization. Often these statistical indicators are entered into computerized forecasting models that predict inflation rates.

Applications of statistics such as those described in this section are an integral part of this text. Such examples provide an overview of the breadth of statistical applications. To supplement these examples, practitioners in the fields of business and economics provided chapter-opening Statistics in Practice articles that introduce the material covered in each chapter. The Statistics in Practice applications show the importance of statistics in a wide variety of business and economic situations.

1.2 Data

Data are the facts and figures collected, analyzed, and summarized for presentation and interpretation. All the data collected in a particular study are referred to as the **data set** for the study. Table 1.1 shows a data set containing information for 25 of the shadow stocks tracked by the American Association of Individual Investors. Shadow stocks are common stocks of smaller companies that are not closely followed by Wall Street analysts.

Elements, Variables, and Observations

Elements are the entities on which data are collected. For the data set in Table 1.1, each individual company's stock is an element; the element names appear in the first column. With 25 stocks, the data set contains 25 elements.

TABLE 1.1   DATA SET FOR 25 SHADOW STOCKS

CD file

Shadow02

Company	Exchange	Ticker Symbol	Market Cap ($ millions)	Price/ Earnings Ratio	Gross Profit Margin (%)
DeWolfe Companies	AMEX	DWL	36.4	8.4	36.7
North Coast Energy	OTC	NCEB	52.5	6.2	59.3
Hansen Natural Corp.	OTC	HANS	41.1	14.6	44.8
MarineMax, Inc.	NYSE	HZO	111.5	7.2	23.8
Nanometrics Incorporated	OTC	NANO	228.6	38.0	53.3
TeamStaff, Inc.	OTC	TSTF	92.1	33.5	4.1
Environmental Tectonics	AMEX	ETC	51.1	35.8	35.9
Measurement Specialties	AMEX	MSS	101.8	26.8	37.6
SEMCO Energy, Inc.	NYSE	SEN	193.4	18.7	23.6
Party City Corporation	OTC	PCTY	97.2	15.9	36.4
Embrex, Inc.	OTC	EMBX	136.5	18.9	59.5
Tech/Ops Sevcon, Inc.	AMEX	TO	23.2	20.7	35.7
ARCADIS NV	OTC	ARCAF	173.4	8.8	9.6
Qiao Xing Universal Tele.	OTC	XING	64.3	22.1	30.8
Energy West Incorporated	OTC	EWST	29.1	9.7	16.3
Barnwell Industries, Inc.	AMEX	BRN	27.3	7.4	73.4
Innodata Corporation	OTC	INOD	66.1	11.0	29.6
Medical Action Industries	OTC	MDCI	137.1	26.9	30.6
Instrumentarium Corp.	OTC	INMRY	240.9	3.6	52.1
Petroleum Development	OTC	PETD	95.9	6.1	19.4
Drexler Technology Corp.	OTC	DRXR	233.6	45.6	53.6
Gerber Childrenswear Inc.	NYSE	GCW	126.9	7.9	25.8
Gaiam, Inc.	OTC	GAIA	295.5	68.2	60.7
Artesian Resources Corp.	OTC	ARTNA	62.8	20.5	45.5
York Water Company	OTC	YORW	92.2	22.9	74.2

Source: American Association of Individual Investors, http://www.aaii.com (February 2002).

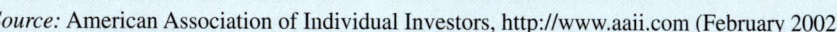

A **variable** is a characteristic of interest for the elements. The data set in Table 1.1 includes the following five variables:

- *Exchange:* Where the stock is traded—NYSE (New York Stock Exchange), AMEX (American Stock Exchange), and OTC (over-the-counter)
- *Ticker Symbol:* The abbreviation used to identify the stock on the exchange listing
- *Market Cap:* Total value of company (share price multiplied by number of shares outstanding)
- *Price/Earnings Ratio:* Market price per share divided by the most recent 12 months' earnings per share
- *Gross Profit Margin:* Gross profit as a percentage of sales

Measurements collected on each variable for every element in a study provide the data. The set of measurements obtained for a particular element is called an **observation**. Referring to Table 1.1, we see that the set of measurements for the first observation (DeWolfe Companies) is AMEX, DWL, 36.4, 8.4, and 36.7. The set of measurements for the second observation (North Coast Energy) is OTC, NCEB, 52.5, 6.2, and 59.3, and so on. A data set with 25 elements contains 25 observations.

Scales of Measurement

Data collection requires one of the following scales of measurement: nominal, ordinal, interval, or ratio. The scale of measurement determines the amount of information contained in the data and indicates the most appropriate data summarization and statistical analyses.

When the data for a variable consist of labels or names used to identify an attribute of the element, the scale of measurement is considered a **nominal scale**. For example, referring to the data in Table 1.1, we see that the scale of measurement for the exchange variable is nominal because NYSE, AMEX, and OTC are labels used to identify where the company's stock is traded. In cases where the scale of measurement is nominal, a numeric code as well as nonnumeric labels may be used. For example, to facilitate data collection and to prepare the data for entry into a computer database, we might use a numeric code by letting 1 denote the New York Stock Exchange, 2 denote the American Stock Exchange, and 3 denote over-the-counter. In this case the numeric values 1, 2, and 3 provide the labels used to identify where the stock is traded. The scale of measurement is nominal even though the data appear as numeric values.

The scale of measurement for a variable is called an **ordinal scale** if the data exhibit the properties of nominal data and the order or rank of the data is meaningful. For example, Eastside Automotive sends customers a questionnaire designed to obtain data on the quality of its automotive repair service. Each customer provides a repair service rating of excellent, good, or poor. Because the data obtained are the labels—excellent, good, or poor—the data have the properties of nominal data. In addition, the data can be ranked, or ordered, with respect to the service quality. Data recorded as excellent indicate the best service, followed by good and then poor. Thus, the scale of measurement is ordinal. Note that the ordinal data can also be recorded using a numeric code. For example, we could use 1 for excellent, 2 for good, and 3 for poor to maintain the properties of ordinal data. Thus, data for an ordinal scale may be either nonnumeric or numeric.

The scale of measurement for a variable becomes an **interval scale** if the data show the properties of ordinal data and the interval between values is expressed in terms of a fixed unit of measure. Interval data are always numeric. Scholastic Aptitude Test (SAT) scores are an example of interval-scaled data. For example, three students with SAT scores of 1120, 1050, and 970 can be ranked or ordered in terms of best performance to poorest performance. In addition, the differences between the scores are meaningful. For instance, student 1 scored $1120 - 1050 = 70$ points more than student 2, while student 2 scored $1050 - 970 = 80$ points more than student 3.

The scale of measurement for a variable is a **ratio scale** if the data have all the properties of interval data and the ratio of two values is meaningful. Variables such as distance, height, weight, and time use the ratio scale of measurement. This scale requires that a zero value be included to indicate that nothing exists for the variable at the zero point. For example, consider the cost of an automobile. A zero value for the cost would indicate that the automobile has no cost and is free. In addition, if we compare the cost of $30,000 for one automobile to the cost of $15,000 for a second automobile, the ratio property shows that the first automobile is $30,000/$15,000 = 2 times, or twice, the cost of the second automobile.

Qualitative and Quantitative Data

Qualitative data are often referred to as categorical data.

Data can also be classified as either qualitative or quantitative. **Qualitative data** include labels or names used to identify an attribute of each element. Qualitative data use either the nominal or ordinal scale of measurement and may be nonnumeric or numeric. **Quantitative data** require numeric values that indicate how much or how many. Quantitative data are obtained using either the interval or ratio scale of measurement.

The statistical method appropriate for summarizing data depends upon whether the data are qualitative or quantitative.

A **qualitative variable** is a variable with qualitative data, and a **quantitative variable** is a variable with quantitative data. The statistical analysis appropriate for a particular variable depends upon whether the variable is qualitative or quantitative. If the variable is qualitative, the statistical analysis is rather limited. We can summarize qualitative data by counting the number of observations in each qualitative category or by computing the proportion of the observations in each qualitative category. However, even when the qualitative data use a numeric code, arithmetic operations such as addition, subtraction, multiplication, and division do not provide meaningful results. Section 2.1 discusses ways for summarizing qualitative data.

On the other hand, arithmetic operations often provide meaningful results for a quantitative variable. For example, for a quantitative variable, the data may be added and then divided by the number of observations to compute the average value. This average is usually meaningful and easily interpreted. In general, more alternatives for statistical analysis are possible when the data are quantitative. Section 2.2 and Chapter 3 provide ways of summarizing quantitative data.

Cross-Sectional and Time Series Data

For purposes of statistical analysis, distinguishing between cross-sectional data and time series data is important. **Cross-sectional data** are data collected at the same or approximately the same point in time. The data in Table 1.1 are cross-sectional because they describe the five variables for the 25 shadow stocks at the same point in time. **Time series data** are data collected over several time periods. For example, Figure 1.1 provides a graph of the U.S. city average price per gallon for unleaded regular gasoline. The graph shows a sharp increase in the average price per gallon beginning in January 2004. From January 2004 to December 2004, the average price per gallon increased from $1.49 to $1.87. Most of the statistical methods presented in this text apply to cross-sectional rather than time series data.

FIGURE 1.1   U.S. CITY AVERAGE PRICE PER GALLON FOR UNLEADED REGULAR GASOLINE

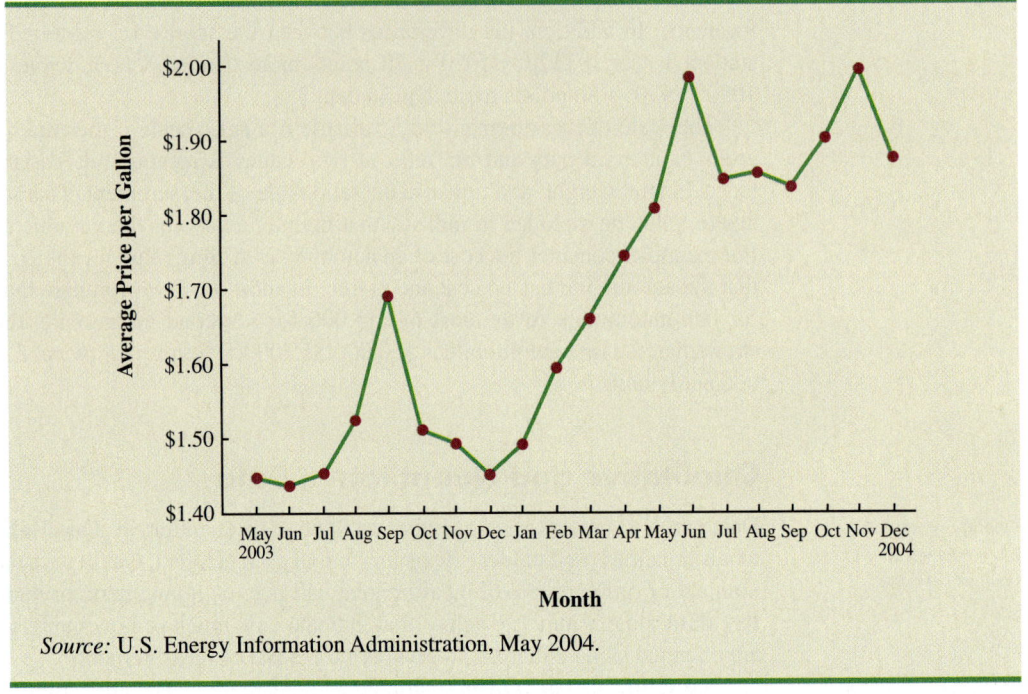

Source: U.S. Energy Information Administration, May 2004.

NOTES AND COMMENTS

1. An observation is the set of measurements obtained for each element in a data set. Hence, the number of observations is always the same as the number of elements. The number of measurements obtained for each element equals the number of variables. Hence, the total number of data items can be determined by multiplying the number of observations by the number of variables.

2. Quantitative data may be discrete or continuous. Quantitative data that measure how many (e.g., number of calls received in 5 minutes) are discrete. Quantitative data that measure how much (e.g., weight or time) are continuous because no separation occurs between the possible data values.

 # Data Sources

Data can be obtained from existing sources or from surveys and experimental studies designed to collect new data.

Existing Sources

In some cases, data needed for a particular application already exist. Companies maintain a variety of databases about their employees, customers, and business operations. Data on employee salaries, ages, and years of experience can usually be obtained from internal personnel records. Other internal records contain data on sales, advertising expenditures, distribution costs, inventory levels, and production quantities. Most companies also maintain detailed data about their customers. Table 1.2 shows some of the data commonly available from internal company records.

TABLE 1.2 EXAMPLES OF DATA AVAILABLE FROM INTERNAL COMPANY RECORDS

Source	Some of the Data Typically Available
Employee records	Name, address, social security number, salary, number of vacation days, number of sick days, and bonus
Production records	Part or product number, quantity produced, direct labor cost, and materials cost
Inventory records	Part or product number, number of units on hand, reorder level, economic order quantity, and discount schedule
Sales records	Product number, sales volume, sales volume by region, and sales volume by customer type
Credit records	Customer name, address, phone number, credit limit, and accounts receivable balance
Customer profile	Age, gender, income level, household size, address, and preferences

Organizations that specialize in collecting and maintaining data make available substantial amounts of business and economic data. Companies access these external data sources through leasing arrangements or by purchase. Dun & Bradstreet, Bloomberg, and Dow Jones & Company are three firms that provide extensive business database services to clients. ACNielsen and Information Resources, Inc., built successful businesses collecting and processing data that they sell to advertisers and product manufacturers.

Data are also available from a variety of industry associations and special interest organizations. The Travel Industry Association of America maintains travel-related information such as the number of tourists and travel expenditures by states. Such data would be of interest to firms and individuals in the travel industry. The Graduate Management Admission Council maintains data on test scores, student characteristics, and graduate management education programs. Most of the data from these types of sources are available to qualified users at a modest cost.

The Internet continues to grow as an important source of data and statistical information. Almost all companies maintain Web sites that provide general information about the company as well as data on sales, number of employees, number of products, product prices, and product specifications. In addition, a number of companies now specialize in making information available over the Internet. As a result, one can obtain access to stock quotes, meal prices at restaurants, salary data, and an almost infinite variety of information.

Government agencies are another important source of existing data. For instance, the U.S. Department of Labor maintains considerable data on employment rates, wage rates, size of the labor force, and union membership. Table 1.3 lists selected governmental agencies and some of the data they provide. Most government agencies that collect and process data also make the results available through a Web site. For instance, the U.S. Census Bureau has a wealth of data at its Web site, www.census.gov. Figure 1.2 shows the homepage for the U.S. Census Bureau.

Statistical Studies

The largest experimental statistical study ever conducted is believed to be the 1954 Public Health Service experiment for the Salk polio vaccine. Nearly 2 million children in grades 1, 2, and 3 were selected from throughout the United States.

Sometimes the data needed for a particular application are not available through existing sources. In such cases, the data can often be obtained by conducting a statistical study. Statistical studies can be classified as either *experimental* or *observational*.

In an experimental study, a variable of interest is first identified. Then one or more other variables are identified and controlled so that data can be obtained about how they influence the variable of interest. For example, a pharmaceutical firm might be interested in conducting

TABLE 1.3   EXAMPLES OF DATA AVAILABLE FROM SELECTED GOVERNMENT AGENCIES

Government Agency	Some of the Data Available
Census Bureau *http://www.census.gov*	Population data, number of households, and household income
Federal Reserve Board *http://www.federalreserve.gov*	Data on the money supply, installment credit, exchange rates, and discount rates
Office of Management and Budget *http://www.whitehouse.gov/omb*	Data on revenue, expenditures, and debt of the federal government
Department of Commerce *http://www.doc.gov*	Data on business activity, value of shipments by industry, level of profits by industry, and growing and declining industries
Bureau of Labor Statistics *http://www.bls.gov*	Consumer spending, hourly earnings, unemployment rate, safety records, and international statistics

FIGURE 1.2   U.S. CENSUS BUREAU HOMEPAGE

an experiment to learn about how a new drug affects blood pressure. Blood pressure is the variable of interest in the study. The dosage level of the new drug is another variable that is hoped to have a causal effect on blood pressure. To obtain data about the effect of the new drug, researchers select a sample of individuals. The dosage level of the new drug is controlled, as different groups of individuals are given different dosage levels. Before and after data on blood pressure are collected for each group. Statistical analysis of the experimental data can help determine how the new drug affects blood pressure.

Studies of smokers and nonsmokers are observational studies because researchers do not determine or control who will smoke and who will not smoke.

Nonexperimental, or observational, statistical studies make no attempt to control the variables of interest. A survey is perhaps the most common type of observational study. For instance, in a personal interview survey, research questions are first identified. Then a questionnaire is designed and administered to a sample of individuals. Some restaurants use observational studies to obtain data about their customers' opinions of the quality of food, service, atmosphere, and so on. A questionnaire used by the Lobster Pot Restaurant in Redington Shores, Florida, is shown in Figure 1.3. Note that the customers completing the questionnaire are asked to provide ratings for five variables: food quality, friendliness of service, promptness of service, cleanliness, and management. The response categories of excellent, good, satisfactory, and unsatisfactory provide ordinal data that enable Lobster Pot's managers to assess the quality of the restaurant's operation.

Managers wanting to use data and statistical analyses as aids to decision making must be aware of the time and cost required to obtain the data. The use of existing data sources

FIGURE 1.3 CUSTOMER OPINION QUESTIONNAIRE USED BY THE LOBSTER POT RESTAURANT, REDINGTON SHORES, FLORIDA

The
LOBSTER
Pot
RESTAURANT

*W*e are happy you stopped by the Lobster Pot Restaurant and want to make sure you will come back. So, if you have a little time, we will really appreciate it if you will fill out this card. Your comments and suggestions are extremely important to us. Thank you!

Server's Name _____

	Excellent	Good	Satisfactory	Unsatisfactory
Food Quality	❑	❑	❑	❑
Friendly Service	❑	❑	❑	❑
Prompt Service	❑	❑	❑	❑
Cleanliness	❑	❑	❑	❑
Management	❑	❑	❑	❑

Comments _____
_____
What prompted your visit to us? _____
_____

Please drop in suggestion box at entrance. Thank you.

is desirable when data must be obtained in a relatively short period of time. If important data are not readily available from an existing source, the additional time and cost involved in obtaining the data must be taken into account. In all cases, the decision maker should consider the contribution of the statistical analysis to the decision-making process. The cost of data acquisition and the subsequent statistical analysis should not exceed the savings generated by using the information to make a better decision.

Data Acquisition Errors

Managers should always be aware of the possibility of data errors in statistical studies. Using erroneous data can be worse than not using any data at all. An error in data acquisition occurs whenever the data value obtained is not equal to the true or actual value that would be obtained with a correct procedure. Such errors can occur in a number of ways. For example, an interviewer might make a recording error, such as a transposition in writing the age of a 24-year-old person as 42, or the person answering an interview question might misinterpret the question and provide an incorrect response.

Experienced data analysts take great care in collecting and recording data to ensure that errors are not made. Special procedures can be used to check for internal consistency of the data. For instance, such procedures would indicate that the analyst should review the accuracy of data for a respondent shown to be 22 years of age but reporting 20 years of work experience. Data analysts also review data with unusually large and small values, called outliers, which are candidates for possible data errors. In Chapter 3 we present some of the methods statisticians use to identify outliers.

Errors often occur during data acquisition. Blindly using any data that happen to be available or using data that were acquired with little care can result in misleading information and bad decisions. Thus, taking steps to acquire accurate data can help ensure reliable and valuable decision-making information.

 # 1.4   Descriptive Statistics

Most of the statistical information in newspapers, magazines, company reports, and other publications consists of data that are summarized and presented in a form that is easy for the reader to understand. Such summaries of data, which may be tabular, graphical, or numerical, are referred to as **descriptive statistics**.

Refer again to the data set in Table 1.1 showing data on 25 shadow stocks. Methods of descriptive statistics can be used to provide summaries of the information in this data set. For example, a tabular summary of the data for the qualitative variable Exchange is shown in Table 1.4. A graphical summary of the same data, called a bar graph, is shown in Figure 1.4. These types of tabular and graphical summaries generally make the data easier to interpret. Re-

TABLE 1.4   FREQUENCIES AND PERCENT FREQUENCIES FOR THE EXCHANGE VARIABLE

Exchange	Frequency	Percent Frequency
New York Stock Exchange (NYSE)	3	12
American Stock Exchange (AMEX)	5	20
Over-the-counter (OTC)	17	68
Totals	25	100

FIGURE 1.4   BAR GRAPH FOR THE EXCHANGE VARIABLE

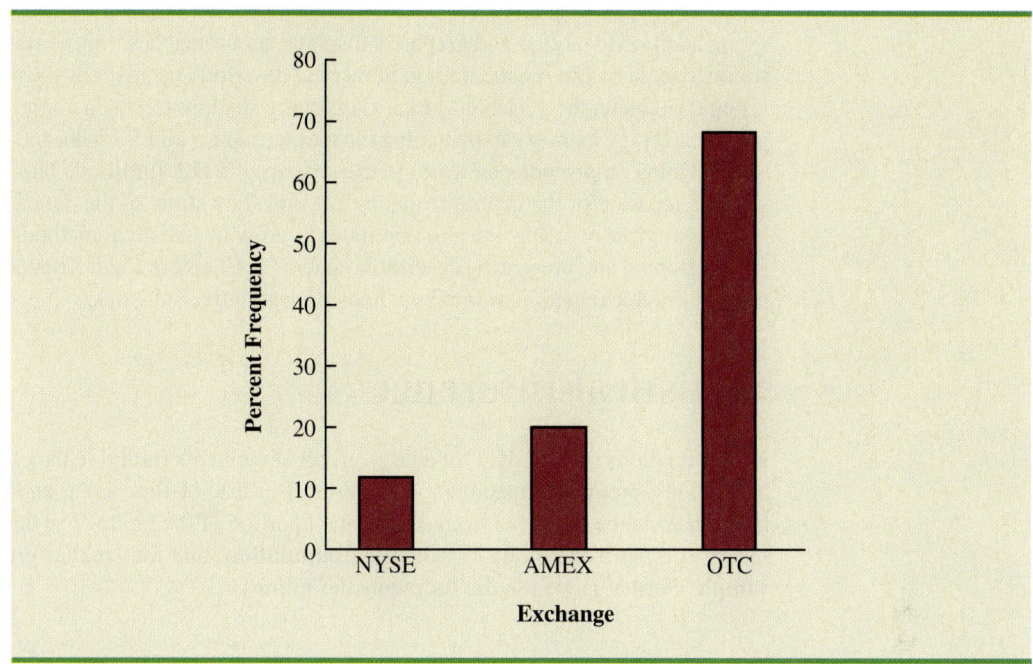

ferring to Table 1.4 and Figure 1.4, we can see easily that the majority of the stocks in the data set are traded over the counter. On a percentage basis, 68% are traded over the counter, 20% are traded on the American Stock Exchange, and 12% are traded on the New York Stock Exchange.

A graphical summary of the data for the quantitative variable Gross Profit Margin for the shadow stocks, called a histogram, is provided in Figure 1.5. The histogram makes it

FIGURE 1.5   HISTOGRAM OF GROSS PROFIT MARGIN (%) FOR 25 SHADOW STOCKS

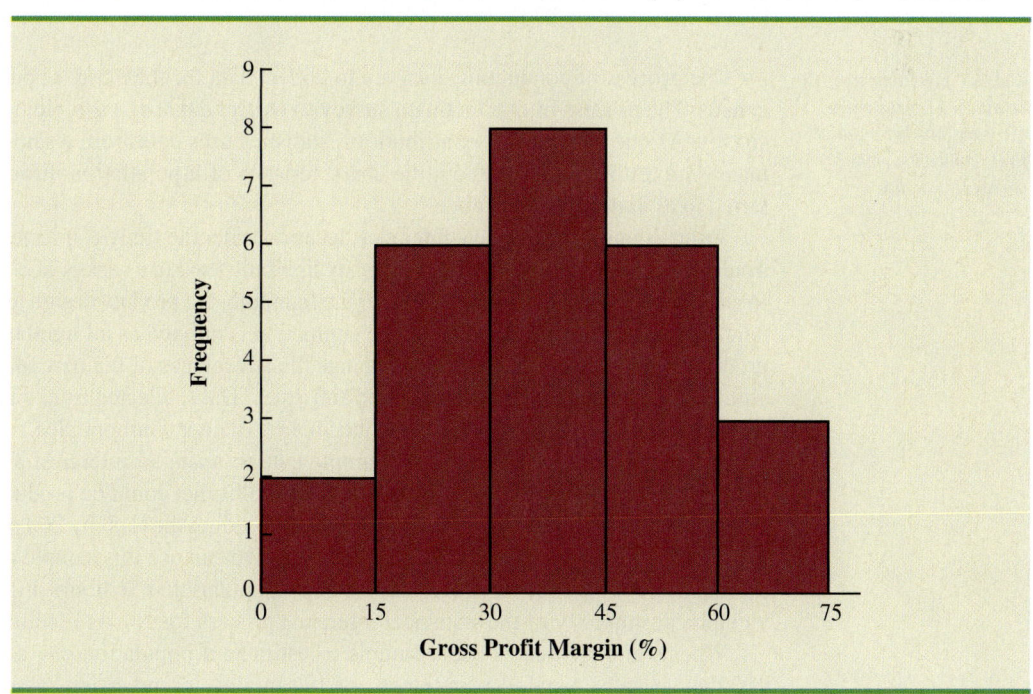

easy to see that the gross profit margins range from 0% to 75%, with the highest concentrations between 30% and 45%.

In addition to tabular and graphical displays, numerical descriptive statistics are used to summarize data. The most common numerical descriptive statistic is the average, or mean. Using the data on the variable Market Cap for the shadow stocks in Table 1.1, we can compute the average market cap by adding the market cap for all 25 stocks and dividing the sum by 25. Doing so provides an average market cap of $112.4 million. This average demonstrates a measure of the central tendency, or central location, of the data for that variable.

In a number of fields, interest continues to grow in statistical methods that can be used for developing and presenting descriptive statistics. Chapters 2 and 3 devote attention to the tabular, graphical, and numerical methods of descriptive statistics.

1.5 Statistical Inference

Many situations require data for a large group of elements (individuals, companies, voters, households, products, customers, and so on). Because of time, cost, and other considerations, data can be collected from only a small portion of the group. The larger group of elements in a particular study is called the **population**, and the smaller group is called the **sample**. Formally, we use the following definitions.

POPULATION

A population is the set of all elements of interest in a particular study.

SAMPLE

A sample is a subset of the population.

The U.S. government conducts a census every 10 years. Market research firms conduct sample surveys every day.

The process of conducting a survey to collect data for the entire population is called a **census**. The process of conducting a survey to collect data for a sample is called a **sample survey**. As one of its major contributions, statistics uses data from a sample to make estimates and test hypotheses about the characteristics of a population through a process referred to as **statistical inference**.

As an example of statistical inference, let us consider the study conducted by Norris Electronics. Norris manufactures a high-intensity lightbulb used in a variety of electrical products. In an attempt to increase the useful life of the lightbulb, the product design group developed a new lightbulb filament. In this case, the population is defined as all lightbulbs that could be produced with the new filament. To evaluate the advantages of the new filament, 200 bulbs with the new filament were manufactured and tested. Data collected from this sample showed the number of hours each lightbulb operated before filament burnout. See Table 1.5.

Suppose Norris wants to use the sample data to make an inference about the average hours of useful life for the population of all lightbulbs that could be produced with the new filament. Adding the 200 values in Table 1.5 and dividing the total by 200 provides the sample average lifetime for the lightbulbs: 76 hours. We can use this sample result to estimate that the average lifetime for the lightbulbs in the population is 76 hours. Figure 1.6 provides a graphical summary of the statistical inference process for Norris Electronics.

Whenever statisticians use a sample to estimate a population characteristic of interest, they usually provide a statement of the quality, or precision, associated with the

TABLE 1.5 HOURS UNTIL BURNOUT FOR A SAMPLE OF 200 LIGHTBULBS
FOR THE NORRIS ELECTRONICS EXAMPLE

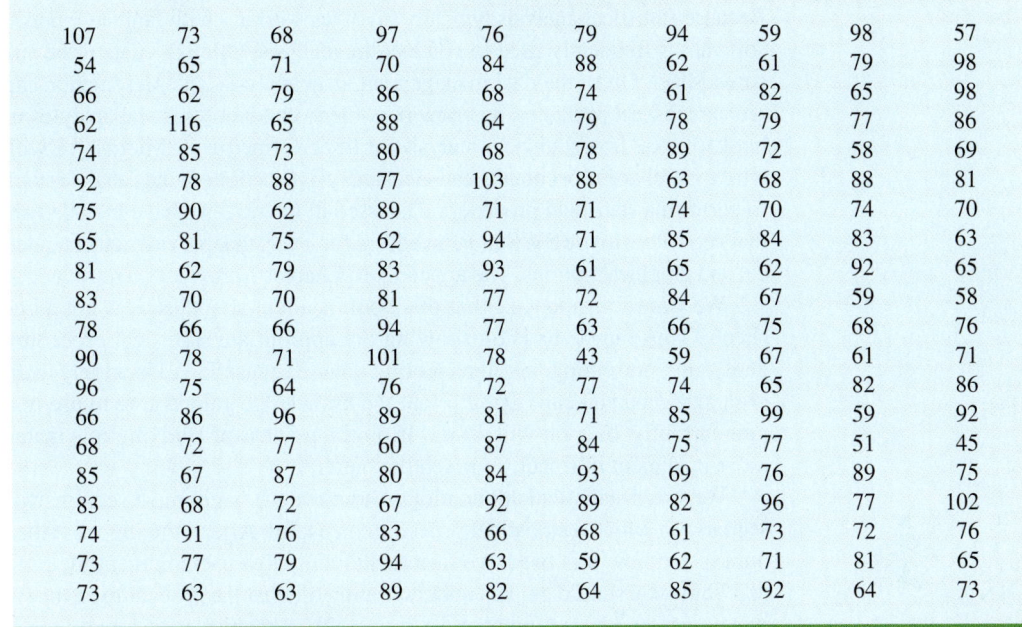

107	73	68	97	76	79	94	59	98	57
54	65	71	70	84	88	62	61	79	98
66	62	79	86	68	74	61	82	65	98
62	116	65	88	64	79	78	79	77	86
74	85	73	80	68	78	89	72	58	69
92	78	88	77	103	88	63	68	88	81
75	90	62	89	71	71	74	70	74	70
65	81	75	62	94	71	85	84	83	63
81	62	79	83	93	61	65	62	92	65
83	70	70	81	77	72	84	67	59	58
78	66	66	94	77	63	66	75	68	76
90	78	71	101	78	43	59	67	61	71
96	75	64	76	72	77	74	65	82	86
66	86	96	89	81	71	85	99	59	92
68	72	77	60	87	84	75	77	51	45
85	67	87	80	84	93	69	76	89	75
83	68	72	67	92	89	82	96	77	102
74	91	76	83	66	68	61	73	72	76
73	77	79	94	63	59	62	71	81	65
73	63	63	89	82	64	85	92	64	73

estimate. For the Norris example, the statistician might state that the point estimate of
the average lifetime for the population of new lightbulbs is 76 hours with a margin of
error of ± 4 hours. Thus, an interval estimate of the average lifetime for all lightbulbs
produced with the new filament is 72 hours to 80 hours. The statistician can also state
how confident he or she is that the interval from 72 hours to 80 hours contains the population average.

FIGURE 1.6 THE PROCESS OF STATISTICAL INFERENCE FOR THE NORRIS
ELECTRONICS EXAMPLE

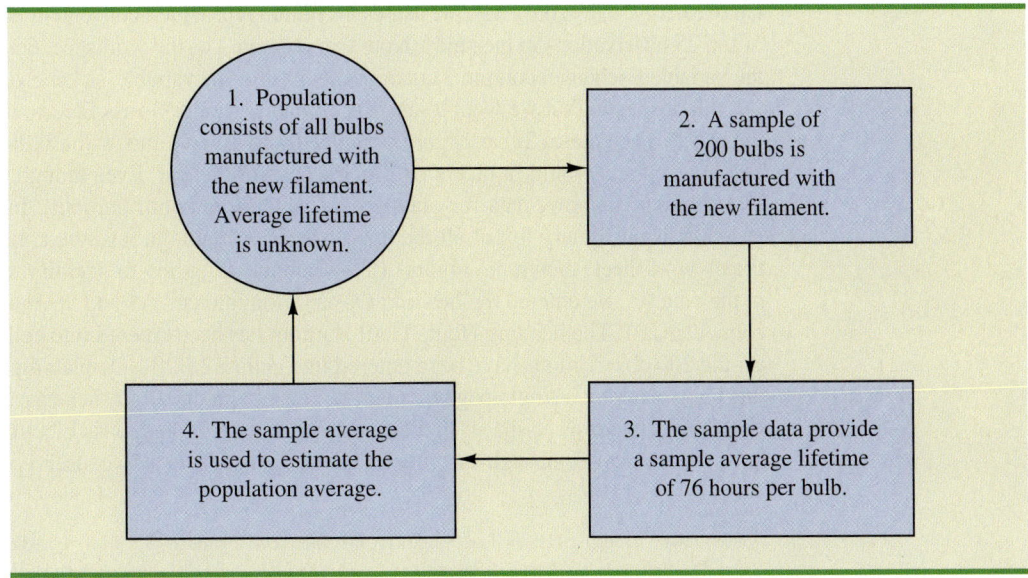

1.6 Statistical Analysis Using Microsoft Excel

Because statistical analysis typically involves working with large amounts of data, computer software is frequently used to conduct the analysis. Often the data to be analyzed reside in a spreadsheet. Given the data management, data analysis, and presentation capabilities of modern spreadsheet packages, it is now possible to conduct statistical analyses using them. In this book we show how statistical analysis can be performed using Microsoft Excel. In selected cases where Excel does not contain statistical analysis functions or data analysis tools that can be used to perform a statistical procedure discussed in the text, we have included chapter appendixes that show how to use SWStat+, an add-in for Excel that provides an extended range of statistical and graphical options. The appendix to Chapter 1 provides an introduction to SWStat+.

We want to emphasize that this book is about statistics; it is not a book about spreadsheets. Thus our focus is on showing the appropriate statistical procedures for collecting, analyzing, presenting, and interpreting data. Because Excel is widely available in business organizations, you can expect to put the knowledge gained here to use in the setting where you currently, or soon will, work. If, in the process of studying this material, you become more proficient in Excel, so much the better.

We stress statistical applications, therefore we begin most sections with an application scenario in which a statistical procedure is useful. After showing what the statistical procedure is and how it is used, we turn to showing how to implement the procedure using Excel. Thus, you should gain an understanding of what the procedure is, the situations in which it is useful, and how to implement it using the capabilities of Excel.

Data Sets and Excel Worksheets

Data sets are organized in Excel worksheets in much the same way as the data set for the 25 shadow stocks appears in Table 1.1. Figure 1.7 shows an Excel worksheet for that data set. Note that row 1 and column A contain labels. Cells B1:F1 contain the variable names and cells A2:A26 contain the observation names. Cells B2:F26 contain the data that were collected. A purple screen highlights the data. The data are the focus of the statistical analysis. Except for the headings in row 1, each row in the worksheet corresponds to an observation and each column corresponds to a variable. For instance, row 2 of the worksheet contains the data for the first observation, DeWolfe Companies, row 3 contains the data for the second observation, North Coast Energy, and so on. Thus, the names in column A provide a convenient way to refer to each of the 25 observations in the study. Note that column 2 of the worksheet contains the data for the variable Exchange, column 3 contains the data for the variable Ticker Symbol, and so on.

Suppose now that we want to use Excel to analyze the Norris Electronics data shown in Table 1.5. The data in Table 1.5 are organized into 10 columns with 20 data values in each column so that it would fit nicely on a single page of the text. Even though the table has several columns, it shows data for only one variable (hours until burnout). In statistical worksheets, it is customary to put all the data for each variable in a single column. Refer to the Excel worksheet shown in Figure 1.8. To make it easier to identify each observation in the data set, we entered the heading Observation into cell A1 and the numbers 1–200 into cells A2:A201. The heading Hours Until Burnout has been entered into cell B1, and the data for the 200 observations have been entered into cells B2:B201. Displaying a worksheet with this many rows on a single page of a textbook is not practical. In such cases we will hide selected rows to conserve space. In the Excel worksheet for the Norris Electronics problem we have hidden rows 7 through 195 (observations 6 through 194) to conserve space.*

---

*To hide rows 7 through 195 in the Excel worksheet, first select rows 7 through 195. Then, right-click and choose the Hide option. To redisplay rows 7 through 195, just select rows 6 and 196, right-click, and select the Unhide option.

FIGURE 1.7   EXCEL WORKSHEET FOR THE SHADOW STOCK DATA SET

	A	B	C	D	E	F	G
1	Company	Exchange	Ticker Symbol	Market Cap ($ millions)	Price/Earnings Ratio	Gross Profit Margin (%)	
2	DeWolfe Companies	AMEX	DWL	36.4	8.4	36.7	
3	North Coast Energy	OTC	NCEB	52.5	6.2	59.3	
4	Hansen Natural Corp.	OTC	HANS	41.1	14.6	44.8	
5	MarineMax, Inc.	NYSE	HZO	111.5	7.2	23.8	
6	Nanometrics Incorporated	OTC	NANO	228.6	38.0	53.3	
7	TeamStaff, Inc.	OTC	TSTF	92.1	33.5	4.1	
8	Environmental Tectonics	AMEX	ETC	51.1	35.8	35.9	
9	Measurement Specialties	AMEX	MSS	101.8	26.8	37.6	
10	SEMCO Energy, Inc.	NYSE	SEN	193.4	18.7	23.6	
11	Party City Corporation	OTC	PCTY	97.2	15.9	36.4	
12	Embrex, Inc.	OTC	EMBX	136.5	18.9	59.5	
13	Tech/Ops Sevcon, Inc.	AMEX	TO	23.2	20.7	35.7	
14	ARCADIS NV	OTC	ARCAF	173.4	8.8	9.6	
15	Qiao Xing Universal Tele.	OTC	XING	64.3	22.1	30.8	
16	Energy West Incorporated	OTC	EWST	29.1	9.7	16.3	
17	Barnwell Industries, Inc.	AMEX	BRN	27.3	7.4	73.4	
18	Innodata Corporation	OTC	INOD	66.1	11.0	29.6	
19	Medical Action Industries	OTC	MDCI	137.1	26.9	30.6	
20	Instrumentarium Corp.	OTC	INMRY	240.9	3.6	52.1	
21	Petroleum Development	OTC	PETD	95.9	6.1	19.4	
22	Drexler Technology Corp.	OTC	DRXR	233.6	45.6	53.6	
23	Gerber Childrenswear Inc.	NYSE	GCW	126.9	7.9	25.8	
24	Gaiam, Inc.	OTC	GAIA	295.5	68.2	60.7	
25	Artesian Resources Corp.	OTC	ARTNA	62.8	20.5	45.5	
26	York Water Company	OTC	YORW	92.2	22.9	74.2	
27							

FIGURE 1.8   EXCEL WORKSHEET FOR THE NORRIS ELECTRONICS DATA SET

Note: Rows 7–195 are hidden.

	A	B	C
1	Observation	Hours until Burnout	
2	1	107	
3	2	54	
4	3	66	
5	4	62	
6	5	74	
196	195	45	
197	196	75	
198	197	102	
199	198	76	
200	199	65	
201	200	73	
202			

Using Excel for Statistical Analysis

In this text, we are careful to separate the discussion of a statistical procedure from the discussion of using Excel to implement the procedure. The material that discusses the use of Excel will usually be set apart in sections with headings such as Using Excel's COUNTIF Function to Construct a Frequency Distribution, Using Excel's Chart Wizard to Construct Bar Graphs and Pie Charts, and so on. In using Excel for statistical analysis, three tasks may be needed: Enter Data; Enter Functions and Formulas; and Apply Tools.

Enter Data: Select cell locations for the data and enter the data along with appropriate descriptive labels.

Enter Functions and Formulas: Select cell locations, enter Excel functions and formulas, and provide descriptive material to identify the results.

Apply Tools: Use Excel's tools for data management, data analysis, and presentation.

Our approach will be to describe how these tasks are performed each time we use Excel to implement a statistical procedure. It will always be necessary to enter data. But, depending upon the complexity of the statistical analysis, only one of the last two tasks may be needed.

To illustrate how the discussion of using Excel will appear throughout the book, we will show how to use Excel's AVERAGE function to compute the average lifetime for the 200 burnout times in Table 1.5. Refer to Figure 1.9 as we describe the tasks involved. The worksheet shown in the foreground of Figure 1.9 displays the data for the problem and shows the results of the analysis. It is called a **value worksheet**. The worksheet shown in the background displays the Excel formula used to compute the average lifetime and is called the **formula worksheet.** A purple screen is used to highlight the data in both worksheets. In addition, a green screen is used to highlight functions and formulas in the formula worksheet and the corresponding results in the value worksheet.

FIGURE 1.9   COMPUTING THE AVERAGE LIFETIME OF LIGHTBULBS FOR NORRIS ELECTRONICS USING EXCEL'S AVERAGE FUNCTION

	A	B	C	D	E	F
1	Observation	Hours until Burnout				
2	1	107		Average Lifetime	=AVERAGE(B2:B201)	
3	2	54				
4	3	66				
5	4	62				
6	5	74				
196	195	45				
197	196	75				
198	197	102				
199	198	76				
200	199	65				
201	200	73				
202						

	A	B	C	D	E	F
1	Observation	Hours until Burnout				
2	1	107		Average Lifetime	76	
3	2	54				
4	3	66				
5	4	62				
6	5	74				
196	195	45				
197	196	75				
198	197	102				
199	198	76				
200	199	65				
201	200	73				
202						

Note: Rows 7–195 are hidden.

Enter Data: The labels Observation and Hours Until Burnout are entered into cells A1:B1. The numbers 1–200 are entered into cells A2:A201 to identify each of the observations, and the data showing the hours until burnout for each observation are entered into cells B2:B201 of the worksheet.

Enter Functions and Formulas: Excel's AVERAGE function can be used to compute the average lifetime for the 200 lightbulbs. We can compute the average lifetime by entering the following formula into cell E2:

$$=\text{AVERAGE}(\text{B2:B201})$$

To identify the result, the label Average Lifetime is entered into cell D2. Note that for this problem, the Apply Tools task was not required. The value worksheet shows that the value computed using the AVERAGE function is 76 hours.

Summary

Statistics is the art and science of collecting, analyzing, presenting, and interpreting data. Nearly every college student majoring in business or economics is required to take a course in statistics. We began the chapter by describing typical statistical applications for business and economics.

Data consist of the facts and figures that are collected and analyzed. Four scales of measurement used to obtain data on a particular variable include nominal, ordinal, interval, and ratio. The scale of measurement for a variable is nominal when the data are labels or names used to identify an attribute of an element. The scale is ordinal if the data demonstrate the properties of nominal data and the order or rank of the data is meaningful. The scale is interval if the data demonstrate the properties of ordinal data and the interval between values is expressed in terms of a fixed unit of measure. Finally, the scale of measurement is ratio if the data show all the properties of interval data and the ratio of two values is meaningful.

For purposes of statistical analysis, data can be classified as qualitative or quantitative. Qualitative data use labels or names to identify an attribute of each element. Qualitative data use either the nominal or ordinal scale of measurement and may be nonnumeric or numeric. Quantitative data are numeric values that indicate how much or how many. Quantitative data use either the interval or ratio scale of measurement. Ordinary arithmetic operations are meaningful only if the data are quantitative. Therefore, statistical computations used for quantitative data are not always appropriate for qualitative data.

In Sections 1.4 and 1.5 we introduced the topics of descriptive statistics and statistical inference. Descriptive statistics are the tabular, graphical, and numerical methods used to summarize data. The process of statistical inference uses data obtained from a sample to make estimates or test hypotheses about the characteristics of a population.

In the last section of the chapter we provided an introduction to the use of Excel for statistical analysis. We showed that data sets are organized in Excel worksheets in much the same way as the data set for the shadow stocks presented in Table 1.1. That is, the columns in the worksheet correspond to variables in the data set and the rows correspond to observations. We also introduced the approach that will be used throughout the text to describe the use of Excel for statistical analysis. Three tasks may be needed: Enter Data; Enter Functions and Formulas; and Apply Tools. As an illustration, we showed how Excel's AVERAGE function could be used to compute the average lifetime for the 200 observations in the Norris Electronics data set.

Glossary

Statistics The art and science of collecting, analyzing, presenting, and interpreting data.
Data The facts and figures collected, analyzed, and summarized for presentation and interpretation.
Data set All the data collected in a particular study.
Elements The entities on which data are collected.
Variable A characteristic of interest for the elements.
Observation The set of measurements obtained for a particular element.
Nominal scale The scale of measurement for a variable when the data use labels or names to identify an attribute of an element. Nominal data may be nonnumeric or numeric.
Ordinal scale The scale of measurement for a variable if the data exhibit the properties of nominal data and the order or rank of the data is meaningful. Ordinal data may be nonnumeric or numeric.
Interval scale The scale of measurement for a variable if the data demonstrate the properties of ordinal data and the interval between values is expressed in terms of a fixed unit of measure. Interval data are always numeric.
Ratio scale The scale of measurement for a variable if the data demonstrate all the properties of interval data and the ratio of two values is meaningful. Ratio data are always numeric.
Qualitative data Labels or names used to identify an attribute of each element. Qualitative data use either the nominal or ordinal scale of measurement and may be nonnumeric or numeric.
Quantitative data Numeric values that indicate how much or how many of something. Quantitative data are obtained using either the interval or ratio scale of measurement.
Qualitative variable A variable with qualitative data.
Quantitative variable A variable with quantitative data.
Cross-sectional data Data collected at the same or approximately the same point in time.
Time series data Data collected over several time periods.
Descriptive statistics Tabular, graphical, and numerical summaries of data.
Population The set of all elements of interest in a particular study.
Sample A subset of the population.
Census A survey to collect data on the entire population.
Sample survey A survey to collect data on a sample.
Statistical inference The process of using data obtained from a sample to make estimates or test hypotheses about the characteristics of a population.
Value worksheet A worksheet that displays the data for the problem and shows the results of the analysis.
Formula worksheet A worksheet that displays the Excel formulas used to create the results shown in the value worksheet.

Supplementary Exercises

1. Discuss the differences between statistics as numerical facts and statistics as a discipline or field of study.

2. *Condé Nast Traveler* magazine conducts an annual survey of subscribers in order to determine the best places to stay throughout the world. Table 1.6 shows a sample of nine European hotels (*Condé Nast Traveler*, January 2000). The price of a standard double room during the hotel's high season ranges from $ (lowest price) to $$$$ (highest price). The overall score includes subscribers' evaluations of each hotel's rooms, service, restaurants, location/atmosphere, and public areas; a higher overall score corresponds to a higher level of satisfaction.

TABLE 1.6   RATINGS FOR NINE PLACES TO STAY IN EUROPE

Hotel

Name of Property	Country	Room Rate	Number of Rooms	Overall Score
Graveteye Manor	England	$$	18	83.6
Villa d'Este	Italy	$$$$	166	86.3
Hotel Prem	Germany	$	54	77.8
Hotel d'Europe	France	$$	47	76.8
Palace Luzern	Switzerland	$$	326	80.9
Royal Crescent Hotel	England	$$$	45	73.7
Hotel Sacher	Austria	$$$	120	85.5
Duc de Bourgogne	Belgium	$	10	76.9
Villa Gallici	France	$$	22	90.6

Source: Condé Nast Traveler, January 2000.

    a.   How many elements are in this data set?
    b.   How many variables are in this data set?
    c.   Which variables are qualitative and which variables are quantitative?
    d.   What type of measurement scale is used for each of the variables?

3. Refer to Table 1.6.
    a.   What is the average number of rooms for the nine hotels?
    b.   Compute the average overall score.
    c.   What is the percentage of hotels located in England?
    d.   What is the percentage of hotels with a room rate of $$?

4. All-in-one sound systems, called minisystems, typically include an AM/FM tuner, a dual-cassette tape deck, and a CD changer in a book-sized box with two separate speakers. The data in Table 1.7 show the retail price, sound quality, CD capacity, FM tuning sensitivity and selectivity, and the number of tape decks for a sample of 10 minisystems (*Consumer Reports Buying Guide 2002*).
    a.   How many elements does this data set contain?
    b.   What is the population?
    c.   Compute the average price for the sample.
    d.   Using the results in part (c), estimate the average price for the population.

5. Consider the data set for the sample of 10 minisystems in Table 1.7.
    a.   How many variables are in the data set?
    b.   Which of the variables are quantitative and which are qualitative?

TABLE 1.7   A SAMPLE OF 10 MINISYSTEMS

Minisystems

Brand and Model	Price ($)	Sound Quality	CD Capacity	FM Tuning	Tape Decks
Aiwa NSX-AJ800	250	Good	3	Fair	2
JVC FS-SD1000	500	Good	1	Very Good	0
JVC MX-G50	200	Very Good	3	Excellent	2
Panasonic SC-PM11	170	Fair	5	Very Good	1
RCA RS 1283	170	Good	3	Poor	0
Sharp CD-BA2600	150	Good	3	Good	2
Sony CHC-CL1	300	Very Good	3	Very Good	1
Sony MHC-NX1	500	Good	5	Excellent	2
Yamaha GX-505	400	Very Good	3	Excellent	1
Yamaha MCR-E100	500	Very Good	1	Excellent	0

    c. What is the average CD capacity for the sample?

    d. What percentage of the minisystems provides an FM tuning rating of very good or excellent?

    e. What percentage of the minisystems includes two tape decks?

6. Columbia House provides CDs to its mail-order club members. A Columbia House Music Survey asked new club members to complete an 11-question survey. Some of the questions asked were:

    a. How many CDs have you bought in the last 12 months?

    b. Are you currently a member of a national mail-order book club? (Yes or No)

    c. What is your age?

    d. Including yourself, how many people (adults and children) are in your household?

    e. What kind of music are you interested in buying? (15 categories were listed, including hard rock, soft rock, adult contemporary, heavy metal, rap, and country.)

    Comment on whether each question provides qualitative or quantitative data.

7. A *Barron's* subscriber survey (September 15, 2000) asked subscribers to indicate their employment status. The data were recorded with 1 denoting employed full-time, 2 denoting employed part-time, 3 denoting retired, and 4 denoting unemployed (homemaker, student, etc.).

    a. The variable is employment status. Is it a qualitative or quantitative variable?

    b. What type of measurement scale is being used for this variable?

8. The Gallup organization conducted a telephone survey with a randomly selected national sample of 1005 adults, 18 years and older. The survey asked the respondents, "How would you describe your own physical health at this time?" (http://www.gallup.com, February 7, 2002). Response categories were Excellent, Good, Only Fair, Poor, and No Opinion.

    a. What was the sample size for this survey?

    b. Are the data qualitative or quantitative?

    c. Would it make more sense to use averages or percentages as a summary of the data for this question?

    d. Of the respondents, 29% said their personal health was excellent. How many individuals provided this response?

9. The Commerce Department reported receiving the following applications for the Malcolm Baldrige National Quality Award: 23 from large manufacturing firms, 18 from large service firms, and 30 from small businesses.

    a. Is type of business a qualitative or quantitative variable?

    b. What percentage of the applications came from small businesses?

10. *The Wall Street Journal* subscriber survey (October 13, 2003) asked 46 questions about subscriber characteristics and interests. State whether each of the following questions provided qualitative or quantitative data and indicate the measurement scale appropriate for each.

    a. What is your age?

    b. Are you male or female?

    c. When did you first start reading the *WSJ*? High school, college, early career, mid-career, late career, or retirement?

    d. How long have you been in your present job or position?

    e. What type of vehicle are you considering for your next purchase? Nine response categories include sedan, sports car, SUV, minivan, and so on.

11. State whether each of the following variables is qualitative or quantitative and indicate its measurement scale.

    a. Annual sales

    b. Soft-drink size (small, medium, large)

    c. Employee classification (GS1 through GS18)

    d. Earnings per share

    e. Method of payment (cash, check, credit card)

FIGURE 1.10 EARNINGS FOR VOLKSWAGEN

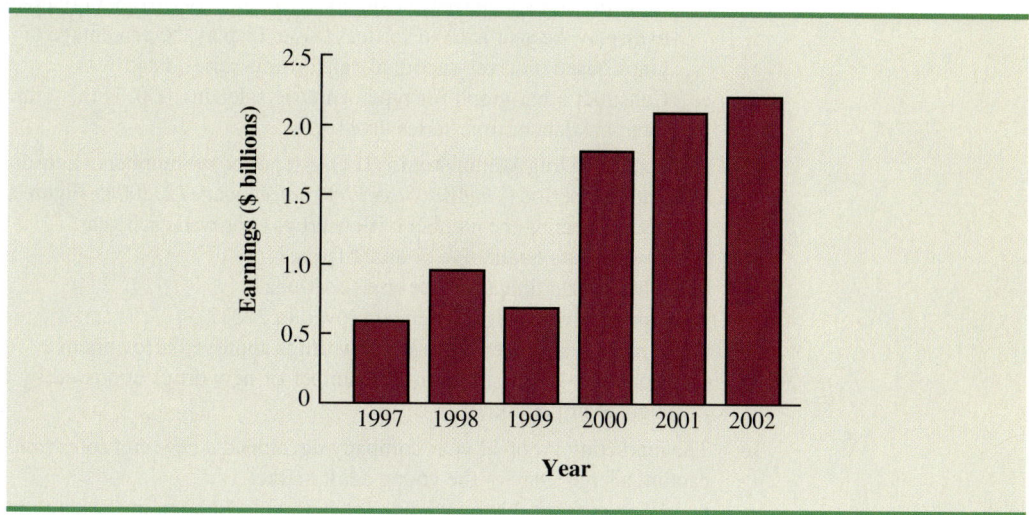

12. The Hawaii Visitors Bureau collects data on visitors to Hawaii. The following questions were among 16 asked in a questionnaire handed out to passengers during incoming airline flights in June 2003.
    - This trip to Hawaii is my: 1st, 2nd, 3rd, 4th, etc.
    - The primary reason for this trip is: (10 categories including vacation, convention, honeymoon)
    - Where I plan to stay: (11 categories including hotel, apartment, relatives, camping)
    - Total days in Hawaii
    a. What is the population being studied?
    b. Is the use of a questionnaire a good way to reach the population of passengers on incoming airline flights?
    c. Comment on each of the four questions in terms of whether it will provide qualitative or quantitative data.

SELF test

13. Figure 1.10 provides a bar graph summarizing the earnings and estimated earnings for Volkswagen for the years 1997 to 2002 (*BusinessWeek,* July 23, 2001).
    a. Are the data qualitative or quantitative?
    b. Are the data time series or cross-sectional?
    c. What is the variable of interest?
    d. Comment on the trend in Volkswagen's earnings over time. Would you expect to see an increase or decrease in 2003?

14. The Recording Industry of America keeps track of recorded music sales by type of music, format, and age group. The following data show the percentage of music sales by type (*The New York Times 2002 Almanac*).

CD file

Music

Type	1996	1997	1998	1999	2000
Rock	32.6	32.5	25.7	25.2	24.8
Country	12.1	11.2	12.8	10.8	10.7
R&B	12.1	11.2	12.8	10.5	9.7
Pop	9.3	9.4	10.0	10.3	11.0
Rap	8.9	10.1	9.7	10.8	12.9
Gospel	4.3	4.5	6.3	5.1	4.8
Classical	3.4	2.8	3.3	3.5	2.7
Jazz	3.3	2.8	1.9	3.0	2.9
Other	14.0	15.5	17.5	20.8	20.5

a. Is the type of music a qualitative or quantitative variable?
b. Construct a graph of rock music sales over the five-year period; use the horizontal axis to display the year and the vertical axis to display the percentage of music sales. Is this graph based on cross-sectional data or time series data?
c. Construct a bar graph for type of music sales in 2000. Is this graph based on cross-sectional data or time series data?

15. The Food and Drug Administration (FDA) reported the number of new drugs approved over an eight-year period (*The Wall Street Journal,* January 12, 2004). Figure 1.11 provides a bar graph summarizing the number of new drugs approved each year.
a. Are the data qualitative or quantitative?
b. Are the data time series or cross-sectional?
c. How many new drugs were approved in 2003?
d. In what year were the fewest new drugs approved? How many?
e. Comment on the trend in the number of new drugs approved by the FDA over the eight-year period.

16. The marketing group at your company developed a new diet soft drink that it claims will capture a large share of the young adult market.
a. What data would you want to see before deciding to invest substantial funds in introducing the new product into the marketplace?
b. How would you expect the data mentioned in part (a) to be obtained?

17. A manager of a large corporation recommends a $10,000 raise be given to keep a valued subordinate from moving to another company. What internal and external sources of data might be used to decide whether such a salary increase is appropriate?

18. A survey of 430 business travelers found 155 business travelers used a travel agent to make the travel arrangements (*USA Today,* November 20, 2003).
a. Develop a descriptive statistic that can be used to estimate the percentage of all business travelers who use a travel agent to make travel arrangements.
b. The survey reported that the most frequent way business travelers make travel arrangements is by using an online travel site. If 44% of business travelers surveyed made

FIGURE 1.11   NUMBER OF NEW DRUGS APPROVED BY THE FOOD AND DRUG ADMINISTRATION

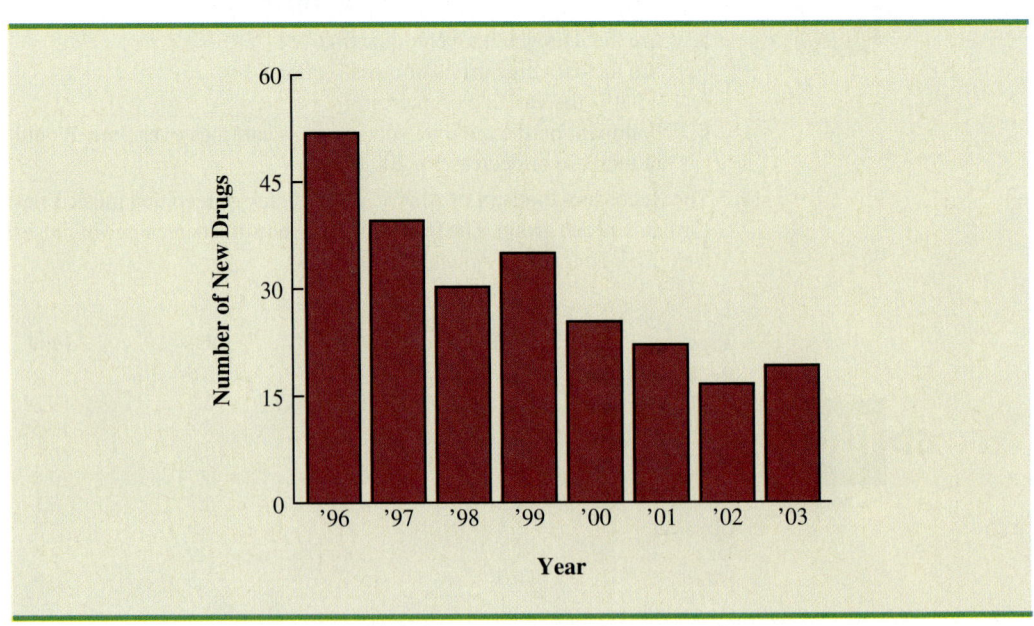

their arrangements this way, how many of the 430 business travelers used an online travel site?

c. Are the data on how travel arrangements are made qualitative or quantitative?

19. A *BusinessWeek* North American subscriber study collected data from a sample of 2861 subscribers. Fifty-nine percent of the respondents indicated an annual income of $75,000 or more, and 50% reported having an American Express credit card.

a. What is the population of interest in this study?

b. Is annual income a qualitative or quantitative variable?

c. Is ownership of an American Express card a qualitative or quantitative variable?

d. Does this study involve cross-sectional or time series data?

e. Describe any statistical inferences *BusinessWeek* might make on the basis of the survey.

20. A survey of 131 investment managers in *Barron's* Big Money poll revealed the following (*Barron's,* October 28, 2002):

- 43% of managers classified themselves as bullish or very bullish on the stock market.
- The average expected return over the next 12 months for equities was 11.2%.
- 21% selected health care as the sector most likely to lead the market in the next 12 months.
- When asked to estimate how long it would take for technology and telecom stocks to resume sustainable growth, the managers' average response was 2.5 years.

a. Cite two descriptive statistics.

b. Make an inference about the population of all investment managers concerning the average return expected on equities over the next 12 months.

c. Make an inference about the length of time it will take for technology and telecom stocks to resume sustainable growth.

21. A seven-year medical research study reported that women whose mothers took the drug DES during pregnancy were *twice* as likely to develop tissue abnormalities that might lead to cancer as were women whose mothers did not take the drug.

a. This study involved the comparison of two populations. What were the populations?

b. Do you suppose the data were obtained in a survey or an experiment?

c. For the population of women whose mothers took the drug DES during pregnancy, a sample of 3980 women showed 63 developed tissue abnormalities that might lead to cancer. Provide a descriptive statistic that could be used to estimate the number of women out of 1000 in this population who have tissue abnormalities.

d. For the population of women whose mothers did not take the drug DES during pregnancy, what is the estimate of the number of women out of 1000 who would be expected to have tissue abnormalities?

e. Medical studies often use a relatively large sample (in this case, 3980). Why?

22. In the fall of 2003, Arnold Schwarzenegger challenged Governor Gray Davis for the governorship of California. A Policy Institute of California survey of registered voters reported Arnold Schwarzenegger in the lead with an estimated 54% of the vote (*Newsweek,* September 8, 2003).

a. What was the population for this survey?

b. What was the sample for this survey?

c. Why was a sample used in this situation? Explain.

23. Nielsen Media Research conducts weekly surveys of television viewing throughout the United States, publishing both rating and market share data. The Nielsen rating is the percentage of households with televisions watching a program, while the Nielsen share is the percentage of households watching a program among those households with televisions in use. For example, Nielsen Media Research results for the 2003 Baseball World Series between the New York Yankees and the Florida Marlins showed a rating of 12.8% and a share of 22% (Associated Press, October 27, 2003). Thus, 12.8% of households with televisions were watching the World Series and 22% of households with televisions in use were watching the World Series. Based on the rating and share data for major television programs, Nielsen publishes a weekly ranking of television programs as well as a weekly ranking of the four major networks: ABC, CBS, NBC, and Fox.

    a.   What is Nielsen Media Research attempting to measure?

    b.   What is the population?

    c.   Why would a sample be used in this situation?

    d.   What kinds of decisions or actions are based on the Nielsen rankings?

24.   A sample of midterm grades for five students showed the following results: 72, 65, 82, 90, 76. Which of the following statements are correct, and which should be challenged as being too generalized?

    a.   The average midterm grade for the sample of five students is 77.

    b.   The average midterm grade for all students who took the exam is 77.

    c.   An estimate of the average midterm grade for all students who took the exam is 77.

    d.   More than half of the students who take this exam will score between 70 and 85.

    e.   If five other students are included in the sample, their grades will be between 65 and 90.

Appendix 1.1   An Introduction to SWStat+

Excel 2003 does not contain statistical functions or data analysis tools to perform all of the statistical procedures discussed in the text. SWStat+ is an Excel add-in that extends the range of statistical and graphical options. In some cases, we include a chapter appendix that shows the steps required to accomplish a statistical procedure using SWStat+. For those students who want to make more extensive use of the software, SWStat+ offers an excellent Help facility. The SWStat+ Help system includes detailed explanations of the statistical and graphical options available, as well as descriptions and definitions of the types of output provided.

    The purpose of this appendix is to explain how to install SWStat+ so that it can be accessed from an Excel worksheet, and to provide a brief introduction to its use.

Installing and Running SWStat+

The label on the SWStat+ CD provides instructions for installing the SWStat+ software on your computer. After installing the SWStat+ software, you must perform the following steps to use it as an Excel add-in.

When you perform the steps to make SWStat+ a permanent add-in, you will be asked whether you want to enable macros. You must enable macros to run SWStat+.

Step 1. Open Excel

Step 2. Select the **Tools** menu

Step 3. Choose **Add-Ins**

Step 4. Click the **Browse** button

Step 5. When the Browse dialog box appears:

           Locate the **SWStat2** folder and double-click

           Double-click the **SWStat2** icon

These steps will add SWStat2 (version 2) to the list of add-ins available in Excel, and SWStat+ will appear on the menu bar each time you run Excel. If you decide later that you do not want SWStat+ to be loaded each time you open Excel, choose **Tools**, then **Add-Ins**, and remove the check in the SWStat2 box.

Using SWStat+

More information can be found quickly using the Search/Index function of the SWStat+ Help system.

To use SWStat+ for a particular application you must first create a Data Area for the data set you will be working with. We will use the Excel worksheet for the shadow stock data set that appeared in Figure 1.7 to show how to create a data area that tells SWStat+ where the data to be analyzed reside. Then we will show how to do some simple statistical analysis with that data.

Creating a Data Area   The purpose of creating a data area is to tell SWStat+ where the data to be analyzed reside and whether row or column labels are present. The following steps will create a data area for the shadow stock data.

Step 1. Open the Shadow02 workbook on the CD accompanying the text
Step 2. Select any cell in the data set (say, C5)
Step 3. Select the **SWStat+** menu
Step 4. Choose **Data Area**
Step 5. Choose **Set New Data Area** from the list of Data Area options
Step 6. When the SWStat+ Data Area dialog box appears:
Select the **Set New** tab
Select **With column headers**
Select **With row headers**
Click **Set data area**

Note that the row and column labels are highlighted in yellow and the entire data area (including labels) is enclosed by a blue border. In addition, a Results worksheet has been added to the workbook. All the output generated using SWStat+ will be placed in this worksheet.

The SWStat+ toolbar in the right margin of your window contains shortcuts for many SWStat+ tasks. For instance, steps 3, 4, and 5 above can be replaced by clicking the second button from the top on the toolbar: Set Data Area with both Column and Row Headers.

Constructing a Bar Chart   Once the data area has been created, any of the options in the SWStat+ system can be used to analyze the data. For instance, the following steps will generate the bar graph for the qualitative variable, Exchange, shown in Figure 1.4.

Step 1. Select the **SWStat+** menu
Step 2. Choose **Charts and Graphs**
Step 3. When the SWStat+: Charts and Graphs dialog box appears:
Select the **One Variable** tab
Select **Column Chart**
Select **Exchange** in the Variables list
Select **2D Column %** in the Style list
Click **Show Chart**

A bar graph of the Exchange variable will appear in the Results worksheet. In step 3 we selected Column Chart to produce the bar graph. Had we selected the Bar Chart option instead, the graph obtained would have been displayed horizontally instead of vertically. In other words, the Column Chart option and the Bar Chart option provide two alternatives for displaying essentially the same graph.

Many more options for analyzing data can be accessed from the SWStat+ menu by selecting the Statistics option. Alternatively, all of the options available on the SWStat+ menu can also be accessed from the SWStat+ toolbar.

CHAPTER 2

Descriptive Statistics: Tabular and Graphical Presentations

CONTENTS

STATISTICS IN PRACTICE:
COLGATE-PALMOLIVE COMPANY

2.1 SUMMARIZING
QUALITATIVE DATA
Frequency Distribution
Using Excel's COUNTIF
   Function to Construct a
   Frequency Distribution
Relative Frequency and Percent
   Frequency Distributions
Using Excel to Construct
   Relative Frequency and
   Percent Frequency
   Distributions
Bar Graphs and Pie Charts
Using Excel's Chart Wizard to
   Construct Bar Graphs and Pie
   Charts

2.2 SUMMARIZING
QUANTITATIVE DATA
Frequency Distribution
Using Excel's FREQUENCY
   Function to Construct a
   Frequency Distribution

Relative Frequency and Percent
   Frequency Distributions
Histogram
Using Excel's Chart Wizard to
   Construct a Histogram
Cumulative Distributions
Using Excel's Histogram Tool to
   Construct a Frequency
   Distribution and Histogram

2.3 EXPLORATORY DATA
ANALYSIS: THE STEM-AND-
LEAF DISPLAY

2.4 CROSSTABULATIONS AND
SCATTER DIAGRAMS
Crosstabulation
Using Excel's PivotTable Report
   to Construct a Crosstabulation
Simpson's Paradox
Scatter Diagram and Trendline
Using Excel's Chart Wizard to
   Construct a Scatter Diagram
   and a Trendline

STATISTICS *in* PRACTICE

COLGATE-PALMOLIVE COMPANY*
NEW YORK, NEW YORK

The Colgate-Palmolive Company started as a small soap and candle shop in New York City in 1806. Today, Colgate-Palmolive employs more than 40,000 people working in more than 200 countries and territories around the world. Although best known for its brand names of Colgate, Palmolive, Ajax, and Fab, the company also markets Mennen, Hill's Science Diet, and Hill's Prescription Diet products.

The Colgate-Palmolive Company uses statistics in its quality assurance program for home laundry detergent products. One concern is customer satisfaction with the quantity of detergent in a carton. Every carton in each size category is filled with the same amount of detergent by weight, but the volume of detergent is affected by the density of the detergent powder. For instance, if the powder density is on the heavy side, a smaller volume of detergent is needed to reach the carton's specified weight. As a result, the carton may appear to be underfilled when opened by the consumer.

To control the problem of heavy detergent powder, limits are placed on the acceptable range of powder density. Statistical samples are taken periodically, and the density of each powder sample is measured. Data summaries are then provided for operating personnel so that corrective action can be taken if necessary to keep the density within the desired quality specifications.

A frequency distribution for the densities of 150 samples taken over a one-week period and a histogram are shown in the accompanying table and figure. Density levels above .40 are unacceptably high. The frequency distribution and histogram show that the operation is meeting its quality guidelines with all of the densities less than or equal to .40. Managers viewing these statistical summaries would be pleased with the quality of the detergent production process.

In this chapter, you will learn about tabular and graphical methods of descriptive statistics such as frequency distributions, bar graphs, histograms, stem-and-leaf displays, crosstabulations, and others. The goal of these methods is to summarize data so that the data can be easily understood and interpreted.

Statistical summaries help maintain the quality of these Colgate-Palmolive products. © Joe Higgins/South-Western.

Frequency Distribution of Density Data

Density	Frequency
.29–.30	30
.31–.32	75
.33–.34	32
.35–.36	9
.37–.38	3
.39–.40	1
Total	150

Histogram of Density Data

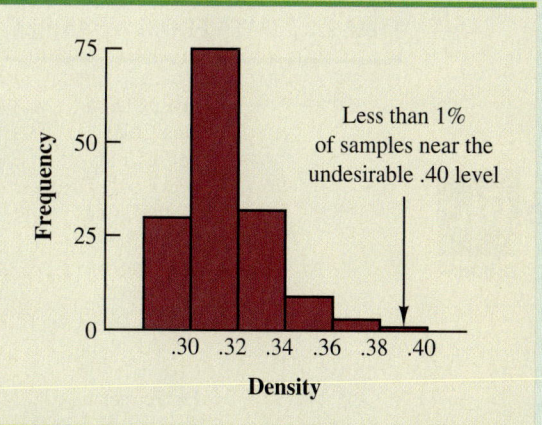

*The authors are indebted to William R. Fowle, Manager of Quality Assurance, Colgate-Palmolive Company, for providing this Statistics in Practice.

As indicated in Chapter 1, data can be classified as either qualitative or quantitative. **Qualitative data** use labels or names to identify categories of like items. **Quantitative data** are numerical values that indicate how much or how many.

This chapter introduces tabular and graphical methods commonly used to summarize both qualitative and quantitative data. Tabular and graphical summaries of data can be found in annual reports, newspaper articles, and research studies. Everyone is exposed to these types of presentations. Hence, it is important to understand how they are prepared and how they should be interpreted. We begin with tabular and graphical methods for summarizing data concerning a single variable. The last section introduces methods for summarizing data when the relationship between two variables is of interest.

Excel's wide variety of functions and tools for descriptive statistics is used extensively in this chapter. The Chart Wizard and PivotTable Report are two Excel tools that are extremely valuable in summarizing and presenting data. The Chart Wizard has extensive capabilities for developing graphical presentations and the PivotTable Report provides crosstabulations for data sets involving more than one variable.

2.1   Summarizing Qualitative Data

Frequency Distribution

We begin the discussion of how tabular and graphical methods can be used to summarize qualitative data with the definition of a **frequency distribution**.

> **FREQUENCY DISTRIBUTION**
>
> A frequency distribution is a tabular summary of data showing the number (frequency) of items in each of several nonoverlapping classes.

The following example demonstrates the construction and interpretation of a frequency distribution for qualitative data. Coke Classic, Diet Coke, Dr. Pepper, Pepsi-Cola, and Sprite are five popular soft drinks. Assume that the data in Table 2.1 show the soft drink selected in a sample of 50 soft drink purchases.

TABLE 2.1   DATA FROM A SAMPLE OF 50 SOFT DRINK PURCHASES

SoftDrink

Coke Classic	Sprite	Pepsi-Cola
Diet Coke	Coke Classic	Coke Classic
Pepsi-Cola	Diet Coke	Coke Classic
Diet Coke	Coke Classic	Coke Classic
Coke Classic	Diet Coke	Pepsi-Cola
Coke Classic	Coke Classic	Dr. Pepper
Dr. Pepper	Sprite	Coke Classic
Diet Coke	Pepsi-Cola	Diet Coke
Pepsi-Cola	Coke Classic	Pepsi-Cola
Pepsi-Cola	Coke Classic	Pepsi-Cola
Coke Classic	Coke Classic	Pepsi-Cola
Dr. Pepper	Pepsi-Cola	Pepsi-Cola
Sprite	Coke Classic	Coke Classic
Coke Classic	Sprite	Dr. Pepper
Diet Coke	Dr. Pepper	Pepsi-Cola
Coke Classic	Pepsi-Cola	Sprite
Coke Classic	Diet Coke	

TABLE 2.2

FREQUENCY
DISTRIBUTION OF
SOFT DRINK
PURCHASES

Soft Drink	Frequency
Coke Classic	19
Diet Coke	8
Dr. Pepper	5
Pepsi-Cola	13
Sprite	5
Total	50

To develop a frequency distribution for these data, we count the number of times each soft drink appears in Table 2.1. Coke Classic appears 19 times, Diet Coke appears 8 times, Dr. Pepper appears 5 times, Pepsi-Cola appears 13 times, and Sprite appears 5 times. These counts are summarized in the frequency distribution in Table 2.2.

This frequency distribution provides a summary of how the 50 soft drink purchases are distributed across the five soft drinks. It offers more insight than the original data shown in Table 2.1. Viewing the frequency distribution, we see that Coke Classic is the leader, Pepsi-Cola is second, Diet Coke is third, and Sprite and Dr. Pepper are tied for fourth. The frequency distribution summarizes information about the popularity of the five best-selling soft drinks.

Let us examine how Excel can be used to count the frequencies and construct a frequency distribution for the soft drink data in Table 2.1.

Using Excel's COUNTIF Function to Construct a Frequency Distribution

Two tasks are involved in using Excel's COUNTIF function to construct a frequency distribution: Enter Data and Enter Functions and Formulas. Refer to Figure 2.1 as we describe the tasks involved. The formula worksheet is in the background; the value worksheet is in the foreground.

FIGURE 2.1   FREQUENCY DISTRIBUTION FOR SOFT DRINK PURCHASES
CONSTRUCTED USING EXCEL'S COUNTIF FUNCTION

	A	B	C	D	E
1	Brand Purchased		Soft Drink	Frequency	
2	Coke Classic		Coke Classic	=COUNTIF($A$2:$A$51,C2)	
3	Diet Coke		Diet Coke	=COUNTIF($A$2:$A$51,C3)	
4	Pepsi-Cola		Dr. Pepper	=COUNTIF($A$2:$A$51,C4)	
5	Diet Coke		Pepsi-Cola	=COUNTIF($A$2:$A$51,C5)	
6	Coke Classic		Sprite	=COUNTIF($A$2:$A$51,C6)	
7	Coke Classic				
8	Dr. Pepper				
9	Diet Coke				
10	Pepsi-Cola				
45	Pepsi-Cola				
46	Pepsi-Cola				
47	Pepsi-Cola				
48	Coke Classic				
49	Dr. Pepper				
50	Pepsi-Cola				
51	Sprite				
52					

	A	B	C	D	E
1	Brand Purchased		Soft Drink	Frequency	
2	Coke Classic		Coke Classic	19	
3	Diet Coke		Diet Coke	8	
4	Pepsi-Cola		Dr. Pepper	5	
5	Diet Coke		Pepsi-Cola	13	
6	Coke Classic		Sprite	5	
7	Coke Classic				
8	Dr. Pepper				
9	Diet Coke				
10	Pepsi-Cola				
45	Pepsi-Cola				
46	Pepsi-Cola				
47	Pepsi-Cola				
48	Coke Classic				
49	Dr. Pepper				
50	Pepsi-Cola				
51	Sprite				
52					

*Note: Rows 11–44
are hidden.*

Enter Data: The label "Brand Purchased" and the data for the 50 soft drink purchases are entered into cells A1:A51.

Enter Functions and Formulas: Excel's COUNTIF function can be used to count the number of times each soft drink appears in cells A2:A51. We first entered a label and the soft drink names into cells C1:C6 and D1. Then, to count the number of times that Coke Classic appears, we entered the following formula into cell D2:

$$=COUNTIF(\$A\$2:\$A\$51,C2)$$

To count the number of times the other soft drinks appear, we copied the same formula into cells D3:D6.

The value worksheet, in the foreground of Figure 2.1, shows the values computed using these cell formulas; we see that the Excel worksheet shows the same frequency distribution that we developed in Table 2.2.

Relative Frequency and Percent Frequency Distributions

A frequency distribution shows the number (frequency) of items in each of several nonoverlapping classes. However, we are often interested in the proportion, or percentage, of items in each class. The *relative frequency* of a class equals the fraction or proportion of items belonging to a class. For a data set with n observations, the relative frequency of each class can be determined as follows:

RELATIVE FREQUENCY

$$\text{Relative frequency of a class} = \frac{\text{Frequency of the class}}{n} \qquad \textbf{(2.1)}$$

The *percent frequency* of a class is the relative frequency multiplied by 100.

A **relative frequency distribution** gives a tabular summary of data showing the relative frequency for each class. A **percent frequency distribution** summarizes the percent frequency of the data for each class. Table 2.3 shows a relative frequency distribution and a percent frequency distribution for the soft drink data. In Table 2.3 we see that the relative frequency for Coke Classic is 19/50 = .38, the relative frequency for Diet Coke is 8/50 = .16, and so on. From the percent frequency distribution, we see that 38% of the purchases were Coke Classic, 16% of the purchases were Diet Coke, and so on. We can also note that 38% + 26% + 16% = 80% of the purchases were the top three soft drinks.

TABLE 2.3   RELATIVE AND PERCENT FREQUENCY DISTRIBUTIONS
OF SOFT DRINK PURCHASES

Soft Drink	Relative Frequency	Percent Frequency
Coke Classic	.38	38
Diet Coke	.16	16
Dr. Pepper	.10	10
Pepsi-Cola	.26	26
Sprite	.10	10
Total	1.00	100

Using Excel to Construct Relative Frequency and Percent Frequency Distributions

Extending the worksheet shown in Figure 2.1, we can develop the relative frequency and percent frequency distributions shown in Table 2.3. Refer to Figure 2.2 as we describe the tasks involved. The formula worksheet is in the background; the value worksheet is in the foreground.

Enter Data: The label "Brand Purchased" and the data for the 50 soft drink purchases are entered into cells A1:A51.

Enter Functions and Formulas: The information in cells C1:D6 is the same as in Figure 2.1. Excel's SUM function is used in cell D7 to compute the sum of the frequencies in cells D2:D6. The resulting value of 50 is the number of observations in the data set. To compute the relative frequency for Coke Classic using equation (2.1), we entered the formula =D2/$D$7 into cell E2; the result, 0.38, is the relative frequency for Coke Classic. Copying cell E2 to cells E3:E6 computes the relative frequencies for each of the other soft drinks.

To compute the percent frequency for Coke Classic we entered the formula =E2*100 into cell F2. The result, 38, indicates that 38% of the soft drink purchases were Coke Classic. Copying cell F2 to cells F3:F6 computes the percent frequencies for each of the other soft drinks. Finally, copying cell D7 to cells E7:F7 computes the total of the relative frequencies (1.00) and the total of the percent frequencies (100).

FIGURE 2.2 RELATIVE FREQUENCY AND PERCENT FREQUENCY DISTRIBUTIONS OF SOFT DRINK PURCHASES CONSTRUCTED USING EXCEL

	A	B	C	D	E	F	G
1	Brand Purchased		Soft Drink	Frequency	Relative Frequency	Percent Frequency	
2	Coke Classic		Coke Classic	=COUNTIF($A$2:$A$51,C2)	=D2/$D$7	=E2*100	
3	Diet Coke		Diet Coke	=COUNTIF($A$2:$A$51,C3)	=D3/$D$7	=E3*100	
4	Pepsi-Cola		Dr. Pepper	=COUNTIF($A$2:$A$51,C4)	=D4/$D$7	=E4*100	
5	Diet Coke		Pepsi-Cola	=COUNTIF($A$2:$A$51,C5)	=D5/$D$7	=E5*100	
6	Coke Classic		Sprite	=COUNTIF($A$2:$A$51,C6)	=D6/$D$7	=E6*100	
7	Coke Classic		Total	=SUM(D2:D6)	=SUM(E2:E6)	=SUM(F2:F6)	
8	Dr. Pepper						
9	Diet Coke						
10	Pepsi-Cola						
45	Pepsi-Cola						
46	Pepsi-Cola						
47	Pepsi-Cola						
48	Coke Classic						
49	Dr. Pepper						
50	Pepsi-Cola						
51	Sprite						
52							

	A	B	C	D	E	F	G
1	Brand Purchased		Soft Drink	Frequency	Relative Frequency	Percent Frequency	
2	Coke Classic		Coke Classic	19	0.38	38	
3	Diet Coke		Diet Coke	8	0.16	16	
4	Pepsi-Cola		Dr. Pepper	5	0.1	10	
5	Diet Coke		Pepsi-Cola	13	0.26	26	
6	Coke Classic		Sprite	5	0.1	10	
7	Coke Classic		Total	50	1.00	100	
8	Dr. Pepper						
9	Diet Coke						
10	Pepsi-Cola						
45	Pepsi-Cola						
46	Pepsi-Cola						
47	Pepsi-Cola						
48	Coke Classic						
49	Dr. Pepper						
50	Pepsi-Cola						
51	Sprite						
52							

Note: Rows 11–44 are hidden.

Bar Graphs and Pie Charts

A **bar graph**, or bar chart, is a graphical device for depicting qualitative data summarized in a frequency, relative frequency, or percent frequency distribution. On one axis of the graph (usually the horizontal axis), we specify the labels that are used for the classes (categories). A frequency, relative frequency, or percent frequency scale can be used for the other axis of the graph (usually the vertical axis). Then, using a bar of fixed width drawn above each class label, we extend the length of the bar until we reach the frequency, relative frequency, or percent frequency of the class. For qualitative data, the bars should be separated to emphasize the fact that each class is separate. Figure 2.3 shows a bar graph of the frequency distribution for the 50 soft drink purchases. Note how the graphical presentation shows Coke Classic, Pepsi-Cola, and Diet Coke to be the most preferred brands.

In quality control applications, bar graphs are used to identify the most important causes of problems. When the bars are arranged in descending order of height from left to right with the most frequently occurring cause appearing first, the bar graph is called a pareto *diagram. This diagram is named for its founder, Vilfredo Pareto, an Italian economist.*

The **pie chart** provides another graphical device for presenting relative frequency and percent frequency distributions for qualitative data. To construct a pie chart, we first draw a circle to represent all of the data. Then we use the relative frequencies to subdivide the circle into sectors, or parts, that correspond to the relative frequency for each class. For example, because a circle contains 360 degrees and Coke Classic shows a relative frequency of .38, the sector of the pie chart labeled Coke Classic consists of .38(360) = 136.8 degrees. The sector of the pie chart labeled Diet Coke consists of .16(360) = 57.6 degrees. Similar calculations for the other classes yield the pie chart in Figure 2.4. The numerical values shown for each sector can be frequencies, relative frequencies, or percent frequencies.

Using Excel's Chart Wizard to Construct Bar Graphs and Pie Charts

Excel's Chart Wizard provides a general tool for constructing a variety of graphical displays, including bar graphs and pie charts. We illustrate its use by showing how to construct the bar graph for soft drink purchases. The Chart Wizard tool allows us to go beyond what can be done with functions and formulas alone. When such tools are used, a third task is needed for worksheet construction: Apply Tools.

The same data and functions and formulas that were used in Figure 2.1 are used here. Thus, the chart we are going to develop is an extension of that worksheet. Refer to Fig-

FIGURE 2.3   BAR GRAPH OF SOFT DRINK PURCHASES

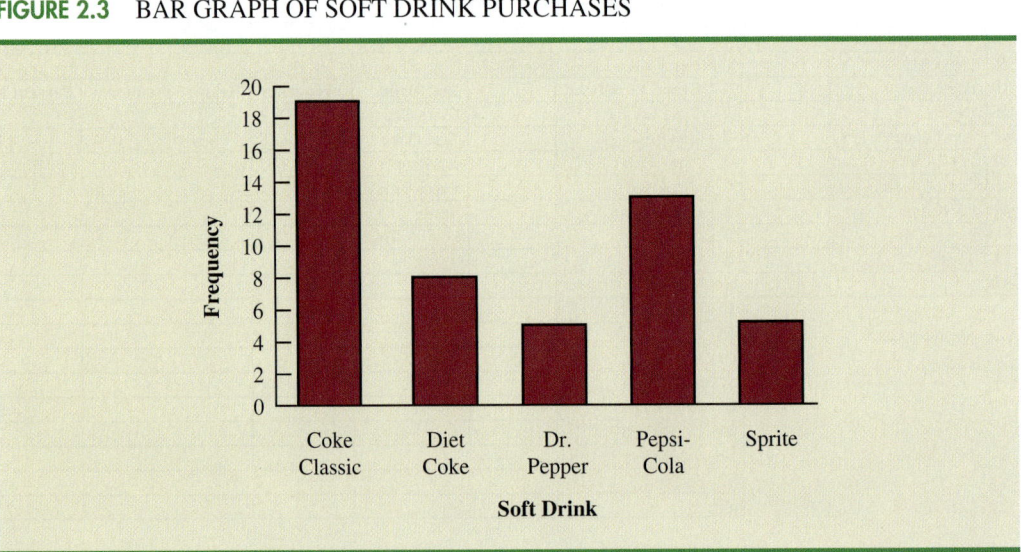

FIGURE 2.4   PIE CHART OF SOFT DRINK PURCHASES

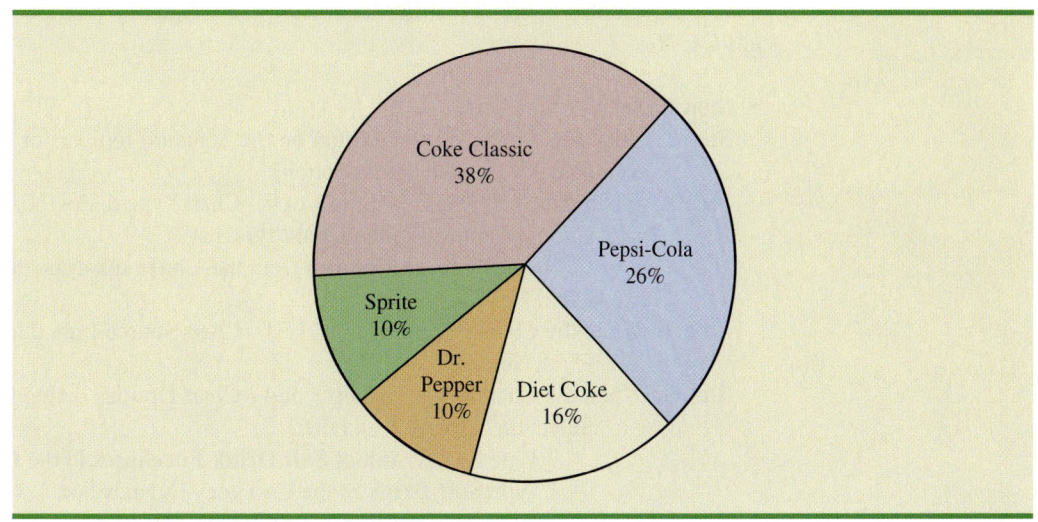

ure 2.5 as we describe the Apply Tools task. The value worksheet is in the background; the chart developed using the Excel Chart Wizard is in the foreground.

Enter Data: Same as in Figure 2.1.

Enter Functions and Formulas: Same as in Figure 2.1.

FIGURE 2.5   BAR GRAPH OF SOFT DRINK PURCHASES CONSTRUCTED USING EXCEL'S CHART WIZARD

	A	B	C	D	E	F	G	H	I	J
1	**Brand Purchased**		**Soft Drink**	**Frequency**						
2	Coke Classic		Coke Classic	19						
3	Diet Coke		Diet Coke	8						
4	Pepsi-Cola		Dr. Pepper	5						
5	Diet Coke		Pepsi-Cola	13						
6	Coke Classic		Sprite	5						
7	Coke Classic									
8	Dr. Pepper									
9	Diet Coke									
10	Pepsi-Cola									
45	Pepsi-Cola									
46	Pepsi-Cola									
47	Pepsi-Cola									
48	Coke Classic									
49	Dr. Pepper									
50	Pepsi-Cola									
51	Sprite									
52										
53										
54										
55										
56										
57										

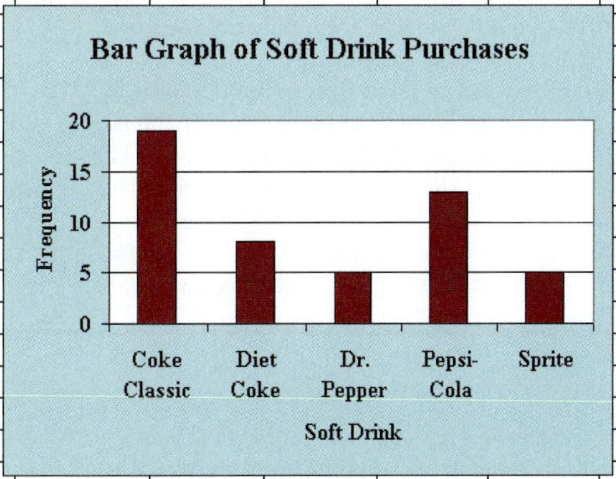

Apply Tools: The following steps describe how to use Excel's Chart Wizard to construct a bar graph for the soft drink data using the frequency distribution appearing in cells C1:D6.

Step 1. Select cells C1:D6

Step 2. Click the **Chart Wizard** button on the Standard toolbar (or select the **Insert** menu and choose the **Chart** option)

Step 3. When the Chart Wizard - Step 1 of 4 - Chart Type dialog box appears:
Choose **Column** in the **Chart type** list
Choose **Clustered Column** from the **Chart sub-type** display
Click **Next >**

Step 4. When the Chart Wizard - Step 2 of 4 - Chart Source Data dialog box appears:
Click **Next >**

Step 5. When the Chart Wizard - Step 3 of 4 - Chart Options dialog box appears:
Select the **Titles** tab and then
Type **Bar Graph of Soft Drink Purchases** in the **Chart title** box
Type **Soft Drink** in the **Category (X)** axis box
Type **Frequency** in the **Value (Y)** axis box
Select the **Legend** tab and then
Remove the check in the **Show legend** box
Click **Next >**

Step 6. When the Chart Wizard - Step 4 of 4 - Chart Location dialog box appears:
Specify a location for the new chart (we used the default setting of the current worksheet)
Click **Finish**

The resulting bar graph (chart) is shown in Figure 2.5.*

Excel's Chart Wizard can produce a pie chart for the soft drink data in a similar fashion. The major difference is that in step 3 we would choose **Pie** in the Chart type list.

NOTES AND COMMENTS

1. Often the number of classes in a frequency distribution is the same as the number of categories found in the data, as is the case for the soft drink purchase data in this section. The data involve only five soft drinks, and a separate frequency distribution class was defined for each one. Data that included all soft drinks would require many categories, most of which would have a small number of purchases. Most statisticians recommend that classes with smaller frequencies be grouped into an aggregate class called "other." Categories with frequencies of 5% or less would most often be treated in this fashion.

2. The sum of the frequencies in any frequency distribution always equals the number of observations. The sum of the relative frequencies in any relative frequency distribution always equals 1.00, and the sum of the percentages in a percent frequency distribution always equals 100.

---

*The bar graph in Figure 2.5 is slightly larger than what was provided by Excel after selecting **Finish**. Resizing an Excel chart is not difficult. First, select the chart. Small black squares, called sizing handles, will appear on the chart border. Click on the sizing handles and drag them to resize the figure to your preference.

Exercises

Methods

1. The response to a question has three alternatives: A, B, and C. A sample of 120 responses provides 60 A, 24 B, and 36 C. Show the frequency and relative frequency distributions.

2. A partial relative frequency distribution is given.

Class	Relative Frequency
A	.22
B	.18
C	.40
D	

   a. What is the relative frequency of class D?
   b. The total sample size is 200. What is the frequency of class D?
   c. Show the frequency distribution.
   d. Show the percent frequency distribution.

3. A questionnaire provides 58 Yes, 42 No, and 20 No Opinion answers.
   a. In the construction of a pie chart, how many degrees would be in the section of the pie showing the Yes answers?
   b. How many degrees would be in the section of the pie showing the No answers?
   c. Construct a pie chart.
   d. Construct a bar graph.

Applications

TVMedia

4. The top four primetime television shows were *CSI, ER, Everybody Loves Raymond,* and *Friends* (Nielsen Media Research, January 11, 2004). Data indicating the preferred shows for a sample of 50 viewers follow.

CSI	Friends	CSI	CSI	CSI
CSI	CSI	Raymond	ER	ER
Friends	CSI	ER	Friends	CSI
ER	ER	Friends	CSI	Raymond
CSI	Friends	CSI	CSI	Friends
ER	ER	ER	Friends	Raymond
CSI	Friends	Friends	CSI	Raymond
Friends	Friends	Raymond	Friends	CSI
Raymond	Friends	ER	Friends	CSI
CSI	ER	CSI	Friends	ER

   a. Are these data qualitative or quantitative?
   b. Provide frequency and percent frequency distributions.
   c. Construct a bar graph and a pie chart.
   d. On the basis of the sample, which television show has the largest viewing audience? Which one is second?

Names

TABLE 2.4

**THE EIGHT
BEST-SELLING
PAPERBACK
BUSINESS BOOKS**

- *The 7 Habits of Highly Effective People*
- *Investing For Dummies*
- *The Ernst & Young Tax Guide 2000*
- *The Millionaire Next Door*
- *The Motley Fool Investment Guide*
- *Rich Dad, Poor Dad*
- *The Wall Street Journal Guide to Understanding Money and Investing*
- *What Color Is Your Parachute? 2000*

BWBooks

SELF test

5. In alphabetical order, the six most common last names in the United States are Brown, Davis, Johnson, Jones, Smith, and Williams (*Time Almanac 2001*). Assume that a sample of 50 individuals with one of these last names provided the following data.

Brown	Williams	Williams	Williams	Brown
Smith	Jones	Smith	Johnson	Smith
Davis	Smith	Brown	Williams	Johnson
Johnson	Smith	Smith	Johnson	Brown
Williams	Davis	Johnson	Williams	Johnson
Williams	Johnson	Jones	Smith	Brown
Johnson	Smith	Smith	Brown	Jones
Jones	Jones	Smith	Smith	Davis
Davis	Jones	Williams	Davis	Smith
Jones	Johnson	Brown	Johnson	Davis

Summarize the data by constructing the following:

a. Relative and percent frequency distributions
b. A bar graph
c. A pie chart
d. Based on these data, what are the three most common last names?

6. The eight best-selling paperback business books are listed in Table 2.4 (*BusinessWeek*, April 3, 2000). Suppose a sample of book purchases provided the following data:

7 Habits	Dad	7 Habits	Millionaire	Millionaire	WSJ Guide
Motley	Millionaire	Tax Guide	7 Habits	Dad	Dummies
Millionaire	Motley	Dad	Dad	Parachute	Dad
Dad	7 Habits	WSJ Guide	WSJ Guide	WSJ Guide	7 Habits
Motley	WSJ Guide	Millionaire	7 Habits	Millionaire	Millionaire
Millionaire	7 Habits	Millionaire	7 Habits	Motley	Motley
Motley	7 Habits	Dad	Dad	Dad	Dad
7 Habits	WSJ Guide	Tax Guide	Millionaire	Motley	Tax Guide
Motley	Motley	Millionaire	Millionaire	Dad	Dummies
Millionaire	Millionaire	Millionaire	Dad	Millionaire	Dad

a. Construct frequency and percent frequency distributions for the data. Group any books with a frequency of 5% or less in an "other" category.
b. Rank the best-selling books.
c. What percentage of the sales are represented by *The Millionaire Next Door* and *Rich Dad, Poor Dad*?

7. Leverock's Waterfront Steakhouse in Maderia Beach, Florida, uses a questionnaire to ask customers how they rate the server, food quality, cocktails, prices, and atmosphere at the restaurant. Each characteristic is rated on a scale of outstanding (O), very good (V), good (G), average (A), and poor (P). Use descriptive statistics to summarize the following data collected on food quality. What is your feeling about the food quality ratings at the restaurant?

G	O	V	G	A	O	V	O	V	G	O	V	A
V	O	P	V	O	G	A	O	O	O	G	O	V
V	A	G	O	V	P	V	O	O	G	O	O	V
O	G	A	O	V	O	O	G	V	A	G		

8. Data for a sample of 55 members of the Baseball Hall of Fame in Cooperstown, New York, are shown here. Each observation indicates the primary position played by the Hall of Famers: pitcher (P), catcher (H), 1st base (1), 2nd base (2), 3rd base (3), shortstop (S), left field (L), center field (C), and right field (R).

L	P	C	H	2	P	R	1	S	S	1	L	P	R	P
P	P	P	R	C	S	L	R	P	C	C	P	P	R	P
2	3	P	H	L	P	1	C	P	P	P	S	1	L	R
R	1	2	H	S	3	H	2	L	P					

a. Use frequency and relative frequency distributions to summarize the data.
b. What position provides the most Hall of Famers?
c. What position provides the fewest Hall of Famers?
d. What outfield position (L, C, or R) provides the most Hall of Famers?
e. Compare infielders (1, 2, 3, and S) to outfielders (L, C, and R).

9. About 60% of small and medium-sized businesses are family-owned. A TEC International Inc. survey asked the chief executive officers (CEOs) of family-owned businesses how they became the CEO (*The Wall Street Journal,* December 16, 2003). Responses were that the CEO inherited the business, the CEO built the business, or the CEO was hired by the family-owned firm. A sample of 26 CEOs of family-owned businesses provided the following data on how each became the CEO.

CEOs

Built	Built	Built	Inherited
Inherited	Built	Inherited	Built
Inherited	Built	Built	Built
Built	Hired	Hired	Hired
Inherited	Inherited	Inherited	Built
Built	Built	Built	Hired
Built	Inherited		

a. Provide a frequency distribution.
b. Provide a percent frequency distribution.
c. Construct a bar graph.
d. What percentage of CEOs of family-owned businesses became the CEO because they inherited the business? What is the primary reason a person becomes the CEO of a family-owned business?

10. A 2001 Merrill Lynch Client Satisfaction Survey asked clients to indicate how satisfied they were with their financial consultant. Client responses were coded 1 to 7, with 1 indicating "not at all satisfied" and 7 indicating "extremely satisfied." Assume that the following data are from a sample of 60 responses for a particular financial consultant.

Client

5	7	6	6	7	5	5	7	3	6
7	7	6	6	6	5	5	6	7	7
6	6	4	4	7	6	7	6	7	6
5	7	5	7	6	4	7	5	7	6
6	5	3	7	7	6	6	6	6	5
5	6	6	7	7	5	6	4	6	6

a. Comment on why these data are qualitative.
b. Provide a frequency distribution and a relative frequency distribution for the data.
c. Provide a bar graph.
d. On the basis of your summaries, comment on the clients' overall evaluation of the financial consultant.

2.2   Summarizing Quantitative Data

Frequency Distribution

TABLE 2.5

YEAR-END AUDIT TIMES (IN DAYS)

12	14	19	18
15	15	18	17
20	27	22	23
22	21	33	28
14	18	16	13

As defined in Section 2.1, a frequency distribution is a tabular summary of data showing the number (frequency) of items in each of several nonoverlapping classes. This definition holds for quantitative as well as qualitative data. However, with quantitative data we must be more careful in defining the nonoverlapping classes to be used in the frequency distribution.

For example, consider the quantitative data in Table 2.5. These data show the time in days required to complete year-end audits for a sample of 20 clients of Sanderson and Clifford, a small public accounting firm. The three steps necessary to define the classes for a frequency distribution with quantitative data are:

1. Determine the number of nonoverlapping classes.
2. Determine the width of each class.
3. Determine the class limits.

Let us demonstrate these steps by developing a frequency distribution for the audit time data in Table 2.5.

CD file

Audit

Number of Classes   Classes are formed by specifying ranges that will be used to group the data. As a general guideline, we recommend using between 5 and 20 classes. For a small number of data items, as few as five or six classes may be used to summarize the data. For a larger number of data items, a larger number of classes is usually required. The goal is to use enough classes to show the variation in the data, but not so many classes that some contain only a few data items. Because the number of data items in Table 2.5 is relatively small ($n = 20$), we chose to develop a frequency distribution with five classes.

Making the classes the same width reduces the chance of inappropriate interpretations by the user.

Width of the Classes   The second step in constructing a frequency distribution for quantitative data is to choose a width for the classes. As a general guideline, we recommend that the width be the same for each class. Thus the choices of the number of classes and the width of classes are not independent decisions. A larger number of classes means a smaller class width, and vice versa. To determine an approximate class width, we begin by identifying the largest and smallest data values. Then, with the desired number of classes specified, we can use the following expression to determine the approximate class width.

$$\text{Approximate class width} = \frac{\text{Largest data value} - \text{Smallest data value}}{\text{Number of classes}} \qquad \textbf{(2.2)}$$

The approximate class width given by equation (2.2) can be rounded to a more convenient value based on the preference of the person developing the frequency distribution. For example, an approximate class width of 9.28 might be rounded to 10 simply because 10 is a more convenient class width to use in presenting a frequency distribution.

For the data involving the year-end audit times, the largest data value is 33 and the smallest data value is 12. Because we decided to summarize the data with five classes, using equation (2.2) provides an approximate class width of $(33 - 12)/5 = 4.2$. We therefore decided to round up and use a class width of five days in the frequency distribution.

No single frequency distribution is best for a data set. Different people may construct different, but equally acceptable, frequency distributions. The goal is to reveal the natural grouping and variation in the data.

In practice, the number of classes and the appropriate class width are determined by trial and error. Once a possible number of classes is chosen, equation (2.2) is used to find the approximate class width. The process can be repeated for a different number of classes. Ultimately, the analyst uses judgment to determine the combination of the number of classes and class width that provides the best frequency distribution for summarizing the data.

For the audit time data in Table 2.5, after deciding to use five classes, each with a width of five days, the next task is to specify the class limits for each of the classes.

Class Limits   Class limits must be chosen so that each data item belongs to one and only one class. The *lower class limit* identifies the smallest possible data value assigned to the class. The *upper class limit* identifies the largest possible data value assigned to the class. In developing frequency distributions for qualitative data, we did not need to specify class limits because each data item naturally fell into a separate class. But with quantitative data, such as the audit times in Table 2.5, class limits are necessary to determine where each data value belongs.

Using the audit time data in Table 2.5, we selected 10 days as the lower class limit and 14 days as the upper class limit for the first class. This class is denoted 10–14 in Table 2.6. The smallest data value, 12, is included in the 10–14 class. We then selected 15 days as the

TABLE 2.6 FREQUENCY DISTRIBUTION FOR THE AUDIT TIME DATA

Audit Time (days)	Frequency
10–14	4
15–19	8
20–24	5
25–29	2
30–34	1
Total	20

lower class limit and 19 days as the upper class limit of the next class. We continued defining the lower and upper class limits to obtain a total of five classes: 10–14, 15–19, 20–24, 25–29, and 30–34. The largest data value, 33, is included in the 30–34 class. The difference between the lower class limits of adjacent classes is the class width. Using the first two lower class limits of 10 and 15, we see that the class width is $15 - 10 = 5$.

With the number of classes, class width, and class limits determined, a frequency distribution can be obtained by counting the number of data values belonging to each class. For example, the data in Table 2.5 show that four values—12, 14, 14, and 13—belong to the 10–14 class. Thus, the frequency for the 10–14 class is 4. Continuing this counting process for the 15–19, 20–24, 25–29, and 30–34 classes provides the frequency distribution in Table 2.6. Using this frequency distribution, we can observe the following:

1. The most frequently occurring audit times are in the class of 15–19 days. Eight of the 20 audit times belong to this class.
2. Only one audit required 30 or more days.

Other conclusions are possible, depending on the interests of the person viewing the frequency distribution. The value of a frequency distribution is that it provides insights about the data that are not easily obtained by viewing the data in their original unorganized form.

Class Midpoint In some applications, we want to know the midpoints of the classes in a frequency distribution for quantitative data. The **class midpoint** is the value halfway between the lower and upper class limits. For the audit time data, the five class midpoints are 12, 17, 22, 27, and 32.

Using Excel's FREQUENCY Function to Construct a Frequency Distribution

Constructing a frequency distribution for quantitative data using Excel's COUNTIF function is cumbersome. Here we show how to use Excel's FREQUENCY function to construct a frequency distribution for quantitative data. The FREQUENCY function has two inputs: the range for the data, and the upper limits for the classes used. Unlike most Excel functions, it provides multiple values (in this case the class frequencies) as output. Because of the multiple output values, we must enter the FREQUENCY function in a special way as an array formula.

Refer to Figure 2.6 as we describe the tasks involved in using the FREQUENCY function to create a frequency distribution for the audit time data. The formula worksheet is in the background; the value worksheet is in the foreground.

Enter Data: The label Audit Time and the 20 audit times have been entered into cells A1:A21. Descriptive headings have been entered into cells C1:E1, and labels to identify the chosen classes have been entered using text format into cells C2:C6. The class upper limits used by Excel's FREQUENCY function have been entered into cells D2:D6.

FIGURE 2.6 FREQUENCY DISTRIBUTION FOR AUDIT TIME DATA CONSTRUCTED USING EXCEL'S FREQUENCY FUNCTION

	A	B	C	D	E	F
1	Audit Time		Audit Time	Upper Limit	Frequency	
2	12		10-14	14	=FREQUENCY(A2:A21,D2:D6)	
3	15		15-19	19	=FREQUENCY(A2:A21,D2:D6)	
4	20		20-24	24	=FREQUENCY(A2:A21,D2:D6)	
5	22		25-29	29	=FREQUENCY(A2:A21,D2:D6)	
6	14		30-34	34	=FREQUENCY(A2:A21,D2:D6)	
7	14					
8	15					
9	27					
10	21					
11	18					
12	19					
13	18					
14	22					
15	33					
16	16					
17	18					
18	17					
19	23					
20	28					
21	13					
22						

	A	B	C	D	E	F
1	Audit Time		Audit Time	Upper Limit	Frequency	
2	12		10-14	14	4	
3	15		15-19	19	8	
4	20		20-24	24	5	
5	22		25-29	29	2	
6	14		30-34	34	1	
7	14					
8	15					
9	27					
10	21					
11	18					
12	19					
13	18					
14	22					
15	33					
16	16					
17	18					
18	17					
19	23					
20	28					
21	13					
22						

Enter Functions and Formulas: Excel's FREQUENCY function is used in cells E2:E6 to compute the class frequencies. The following steps describe how to create and enter an array formula that uses the FREQUENCY function to develop a frequency distribution for the audit time data.

Step 1. Select cells E2:E6, the cells where we want the frequencies to appear

Step 2. Type, but do not enter, the following formula:
=FREQUENCY(A2:A21,D2:D6)

You must hold down the Ctrl and Shift keys while pressing the Enter key to enter an array formula.

Step 3. Press CTRL+SHIFT+ENTER and the array formula will be entered into each of the cells E2:E6

The results are shown in Figure 2.6. Because we entered an array formula into cells E2:E6, the formula that Excel displays in each of these cells is the same, but the values calculated are not. They are the frequencies for each class. The range of cells for the upper class limits (D2:D6) used as the second input for the FREQUENCY function tells Excel which frequency to put into each cell of the output range (E2:E6). The frequency for the class with an upper limit of 14 is placed in the first cell (E2), the frequency for the class with an upper limit of 19 is placed in the second cell (E3), and so on.

TABLE 2.7 RELATIVE AND PERCENT FREQUENCY DISTRIBUTIONS FOR THE AUDIT TIME DATA

Audit Time (days)	Relative Frequency	Percent Frequency
10–14	.20	20
15–19	.40	40
20–24	.25	25
25–29	.10	10
30–34	.05	5
Total	1.00	100

Relative Frequency and Percent Frequency Distributions

We define the relative frequency and percent frequency distributions for quantitative data in the same manner as for qualitative data. First, recall that the relative frequency is the proportion of the observations belonging to a class. With n observations,

$$\text{Relative frequency of class} = \frac{\text{Frequency of the class}}{n}$$

The percent frequency of a class is the relative frequency multiplied by 100.

Based on the class frequencies in Table 2.6 and with $n = 20$, Table 2.7 shows the relative frequency distribution and percent frequency distribution for the audit time data. Note that .40 of the audits, or 40%, required from 15 to 19 days. Only .05 of the audits, or 5%, required 30 or more days. Again, additional interpretations and insights can be obtained by using Table 2.7.

Histogram

A common graphical presentation of quantitative data is a **histogram**. This graphical summary can be prepared for data previously summarized in either a frequency, relative frequency, or percent frequency distribution. A histogram is constructed by placing the variable of interest on the horizontal axis and the frequency, relative frequency, or percent frequency on the vertical axis. The frequency, relative frequency, or percent frequency of each class is shown by drawing a rectangle whose base is determined by the class limits on the horizontal axis and whose height is the corresponding frequency, relative frequency, or percent frequency.

Figure 2.7 is a histogram for the audit time data.* Note that the class with the greatest frequency is shown by the rectangle appearing above the class of 15–19 days. The height of the rectangle shows that the frequency of this class is 8. A histogram for the relative or percent frequency distribution of these data would look the same as the histogram in Figure 2.7 with the exception that the vertical axis would be labeled with relative or percent frequency values.

As Figure 2.7 shows, the adjacent rectangles of a histogram touch one another. Unlike a bar graph, a histogram contains no natural separation between the rectangles of adjacent classes. This format is the usual convention for histograms. Because the classes for the audit time data are stated as 10–14, 15–19, 20–24, 25–29, and 30–34, one-unit spaces of 14 to 15, 19 to 20, 24 to 25, and 29 to 30 would seem to be needed between the classes. These spaces are eliminated when constructing a histogram. Eliminating the spaces

---

* In Figure 2.7 the labels used to identify each rectangle are the same as the labels we used to identify each class in the frequency distribution. Another commonly used convention is to label the horizontal axis using the class midpoints. In this case, the first rectangle would be labelled at 12, the midpoint of the first class; the second rectangle would be labelled at 17, the midpoint of the second class; and so on.

FIGURE 2.7   HISTOGRAM FOR THE AUDIT TIME DATA

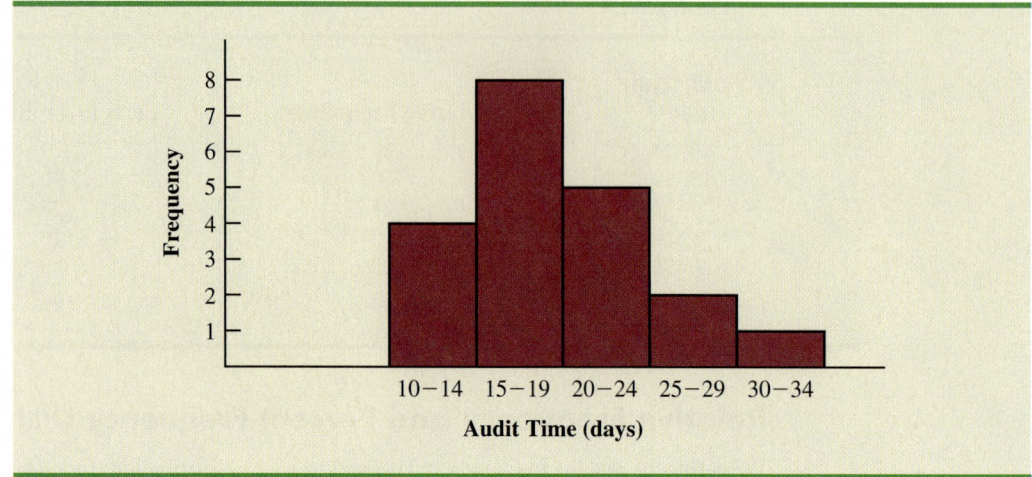

between classes in a histogram for the audit time data helps show that all values between the lower limit of the first class and the upper limit of the last class are possible.

One of the most important uses of a histogram is to provide information about the shape, or form, of a distribution. Figure 2.8 contains four histograms constructed from relative frequency distributions. Panel A shows the histogram for a set of data moderately skewed to the left. A histogram is said to be skewed to the left if its tail extends farther to the left. This histogram is typical for exam scores, with no scores above 100%, most of the scores above 70%, and only a few really low scores. Panel B shows the histogram for a set of data moderately skewed to the right. A histogram is said to be skewed to the right if its tail extends farther to the right. An example of this type of histogram would be for data such as housing prices; a few very expensive houses create the skewness in the right tail.

Panel C shows a symmetric histogram. In a symmetric histogram, the left tail mirrors the shape of the right tail. Histograms for data found in applications are never perfectly symmetric, but the histogram for many applications may be roughly symmetric. Data for SAT scores, heights and weights of people, and so on lead to histograms that are roughly symmetric. Panel D shows a histogram highly skewed to the right. This histogram was constructed from data on the amount of customer purchases over one day at a women's apparel store. Data from applications in business and economics often lead to histograms that are skewed to the right. For instance, data on housing prices, salaries, purchase amounts, and so on often result in histograms skewed to the right.

Using Excel's Chart Wizard to Construct a Histogram

We can use Excel's Chart Wizard to construct a histogram for the audit time data. Refer to Figures 2.9, 2.10, and 2.11 as we describe the tasks involved.

Enter Data: Same as in Figure 2.6.

Enter Functions and Formulas: Same as in Figure 2.6.

Apply Tools: The following steps describe how to use Excel's Chart Wizard to produce a histogram for the audit time data using the class frequencies appearing in cells E2:E6 of the worksheet shown in Figure 2.9.

    Step 1. Select cells E2:E6
    Step 2. Click the **Chart Wizard** button on the Standard toolbar (or select the **Insert** menu and choose the **Chart** option)

FIGURE 2.8   HISTOGRAMS SHOWING DIFFERING LEVELS OF SKEWNESS

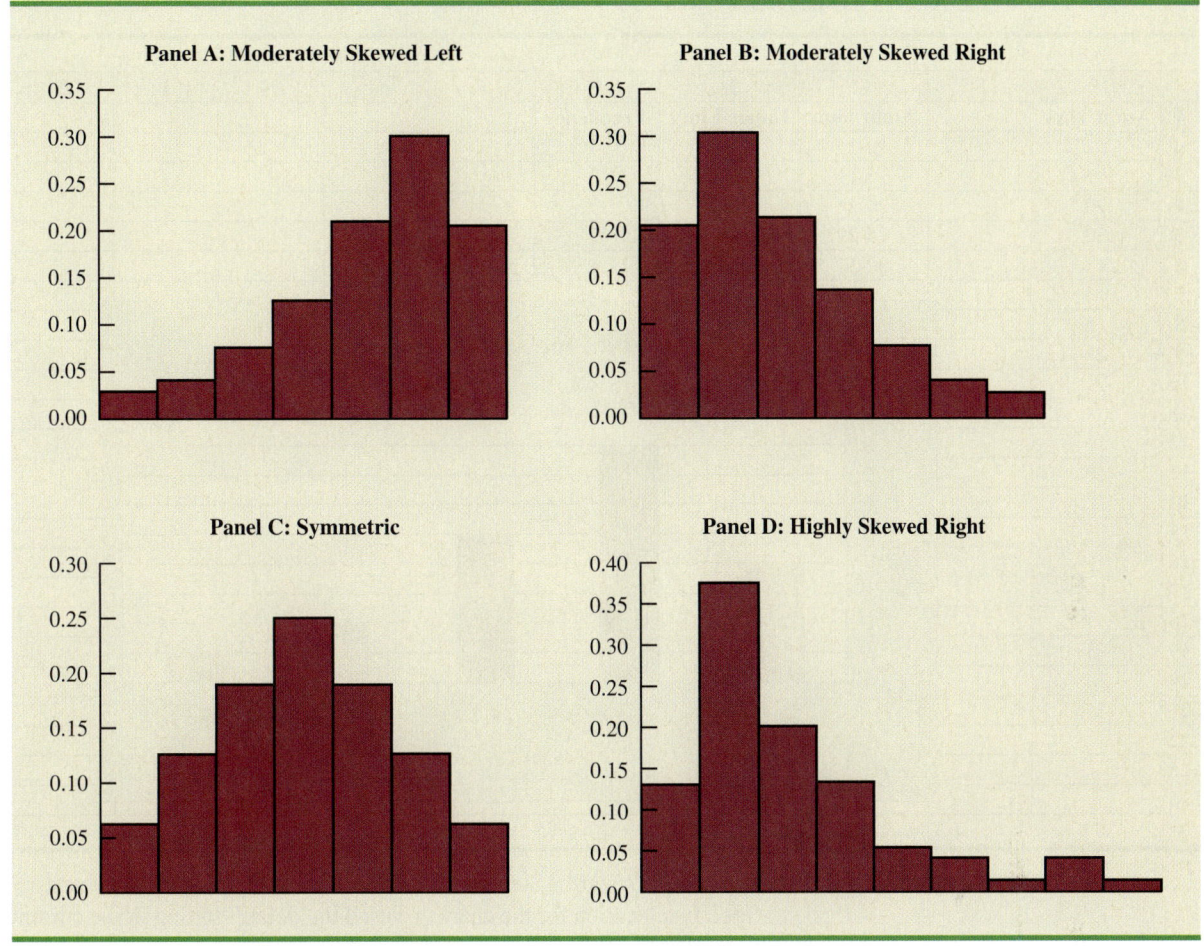

Step 3. When the Chart Wizard - Step 1 of 4 - Chart Type dialog box appears:
   Choose **Column** in the **Chart type** list
   Choose **Clustered Column** from the **Chart sub-type** display
   Click **Next >**

Step 4. When the Chart Wizard - Step 2 of 4 - Chart Source Data dialog box appears:
   Select the **Series** tab and then
   Enter C2:C6 in the **Category (X) axis labels** box
   Click **Next >**

Step 5. When the Chart Wizard - Step 3 of 4 - Chart Options dialog box appears:
   Select the **Titles** tab and then
      Type **Histogram for Audit Time Data** in the **Chart title** box
      Type **Audit Time in Days** in the **Category (X)** axis box
      Type **Frequency** in the **Value (Y)** axis box
   Select the **Legend** tab and then
      Remove the check in the **Show legend** box
   Click **Next >**

FIGURE 2.9   INITIAL HISTOGRAM CONSTRUCTED USING EXCEL'S CHART WIZARD
FOR THE AUDIT TIME DATA

	A	B	C	D	E	F	G	H	I	J
1	Audit Time		Audit Time	Upper Limit	Frequency					
2	12		10-14	14	4					
3	15		15-19	19	8					
4	20		20-24	24	5					
5	22		25-29	29	2					
6	14		30-34	34	1					
7	14									
8	15									
9	27									
10	21									
11	18									
12	19									
13	18									
14	22									
15	33									
16	16									
17	18									
18	17									
19	23									
20	28									
21	13									
22										
23										
24										

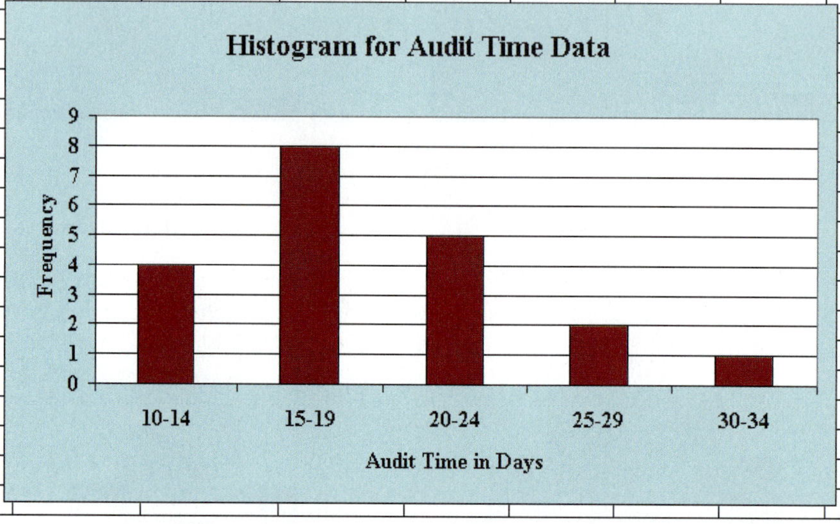

Histogram for Audit Time Data

Step 6. When the Chart Wizard - Step 4 of 4 - Chart Location dialog box appears:
Specify a location for the chart (we used the default setting of the current
worksheet)
Click **Finish**

The worksheet displayed in Figure 2.9 shows the column chart produced by Excel. Note
the gaps between the rectangles. Because the adjacent rectangles in a histogram must touch,
we need to edit the chart in order to eliminate the gap between each of the rectangles. The
following steps describe this process. Refer to Figure 2.10 as we describe the steps.

Step 1. Right-click on any rectangle in the column chart to produce a list of options
Step 2. Select the **Format Data Series** option
Step 3. When the Format Data Series dialog box appears:
Select the **Options** tab and then
Enter **0** in the **Gap width** box
Click **OK**

Figure 2.11 displays the histogram produced by Excel. It is the same histogram that we developed earlier in Figure 2.7. The size of the chart can now be adjusted to suit user preference.

Cumulative Distributions

A variation of the frequency distribution that provides another tabular summary of quantitative data is the **cumulative frequency distribution**. The cumulative frequency distribution uses the number of classes, class widths, and class limits developed for the frequency
distribution. However, rather than showing the frequency of each class, the cumulative fre-

FIGURE 2.10 REMOVING THE GAPS BETWEEN CLASSES TO DISPLAY A HISTOGRAM FOR THE AUDIT TIME DATA

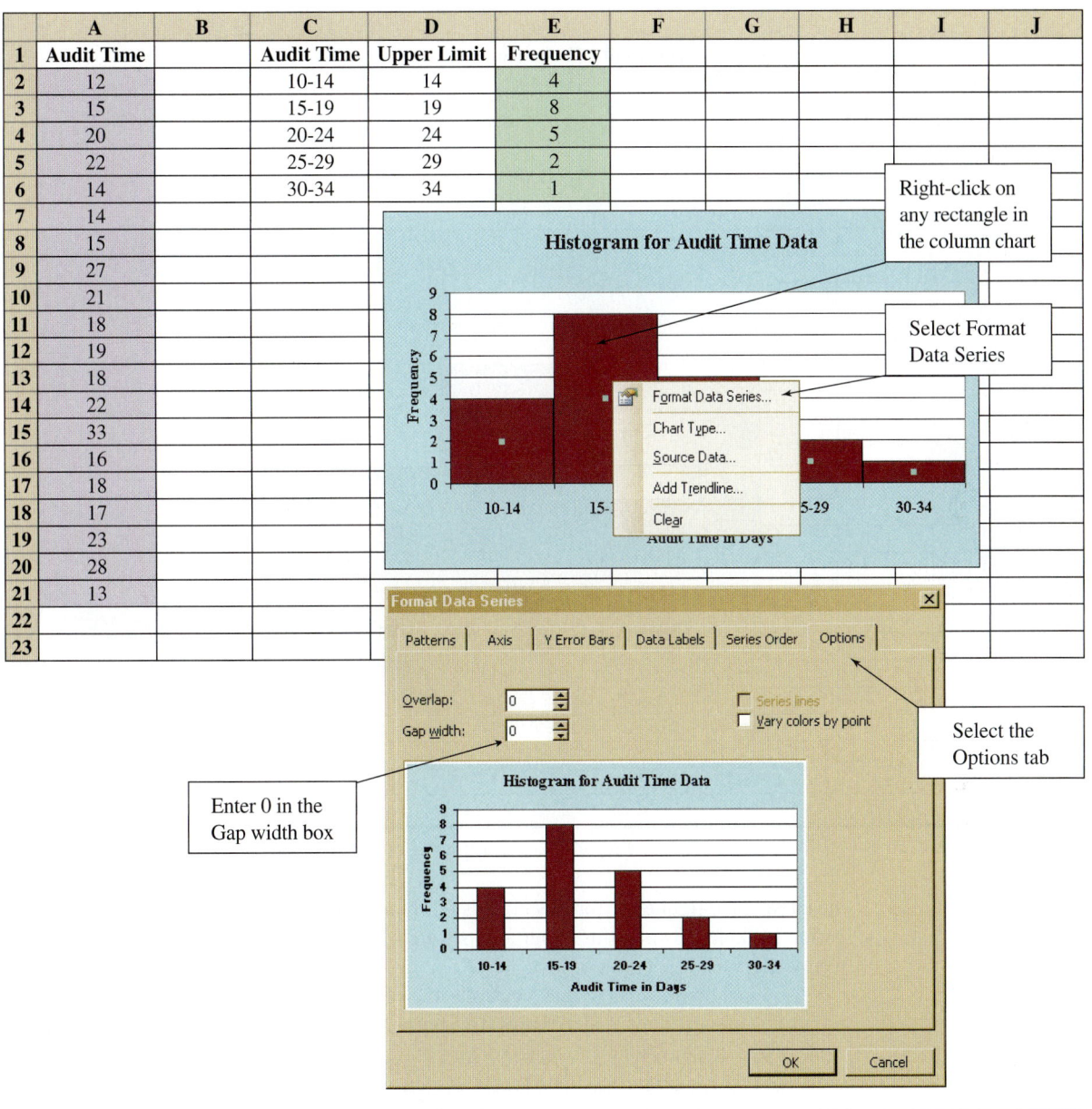

quency distribution shows the number of data items with values *less than or equal to the upper class limit* of each class. The first two columns of Table 2.8 provide the cumulative frequency distribution for the audit time data.

To understand how the cumulative frequencies are determined, consider the class with the description "less than or equal to 24." The cumulative frequency for this class is simply the sum of the frequencies for all classes with data values less than or equal to 24. For the frequency distribution in Table 2.6, the sum of the frequencies for classes 10–14, 15–19, and 20–24 indicates that $4 + 8 + 5 = 17$ data values are less than or equal to 24. Hence,

FIGURE 2.11   FINAL HISTOGRAM CONSTRUCTED USING EXCEL'S CHART WIZARD FOR THE AUDIT
TIME DATA

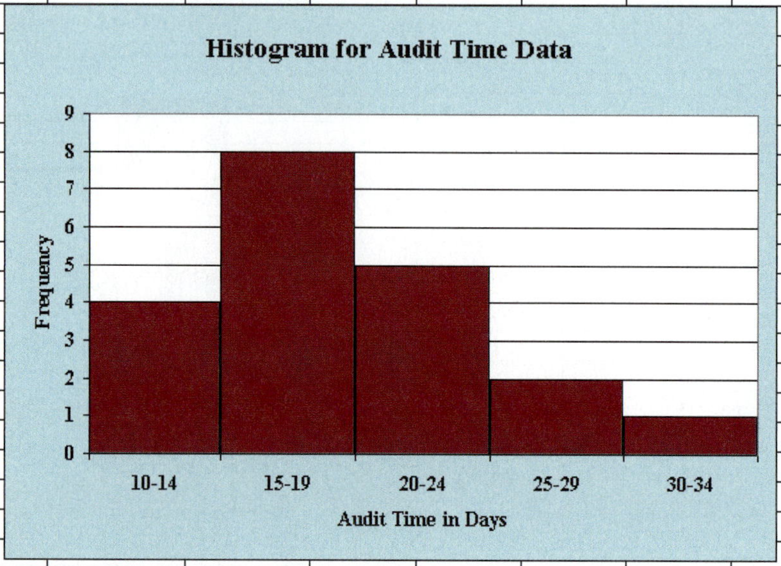

	A	B	C	D	E	F	G	H	I	J
1	Audit Time		Audit Time	Upper Limit	Frequency					
2	12		10-14	14	4					
3	15		15-19	19	8					
4	20		20-24	24	5					
5	22		25-29	29	2					
6	14		30-34	34	1					
7	14									
8	15									
9	27									
10	21									
11	18									
12	19									
13	18									
14	22									
15	33									
16	16									
17	18									
18	17									
19	23									
20	28									
21	13									
22										
23										
24										
25										
26										
27										
28										

the cumulative frequency for this class is 17. In addition, the cumulative frequency distribution in Table 2.8 shows that four audits were completed in 14 days or less and 19 audits were completed in 29 days or less.

As a final point, we note that a **cumulative relative frequency distribution** shows the proportion of data items, and a **cumulative percent frequency distribution** shows the percentage of data items with values less than or equal to the upper limit of each class. The cumulative relative frequency distribution can be computed either by summing the relative frequencies in the relative frequency distribution or by dividing the cumulative frequencies by the total number of items. Using the latter approach, we found the cumulative relative frequencies in column 3 of Table 2.8 by dividing the cumulative frequencies in column 2 by the total number of items ($n = 20$). The cumulative percent frequencies were again computed by multiplying the relative frequencies by 100. The cumulative relative and percent frequency distributions show that .85 of the audits, or 85%, were completed in 24 days or less; .95 of the audits, or 95%, were completed in 29 days or less; and so on.

A graph of a cumulative distribution, called an **ogive**, shows data values on the horizontal axis and either the cumulative frequencies, the cumulative relative frequencies, or the cumulative percent frequencies on the vertical axis. Figure 2.12 illustrates an ogive for the cumulative frequencies of the audit time data in Table 2.8.

TABLE 2.8 CUMULATIVE FREQUENCY, CUMULATIVE RELATIVE FREQUENCY, AND CUMULATIVE PERCENT FREQUENCY DISTRIBUTIONS FOR THE AUDIT TIME DATA

Audit Time (days)	Cumulative Frequency	Cumulative Relative Frequency	Cumulative Percent Frequency
Less than or equal to 14	4	.20	20
Less than or equal to 19	12	.60	60
Less than or equal to 24	17	.85	85
Less than or equal to 29	19	.95	95
Less than or equal to 34	20	1.00	100

The ogive is constructed by plotting a point corresponding to the cumulative frequency of each class. Because the classes for the audit time data are 10–14, 15–19, 20–24, and so on, one-unit gaps appear from 14 to 15, 19 to 20, and so on. These gaps are eliminated by plotting points halfway between the class limits. Thus, 14.5 is used for the 10–14 class, 19.5 is used for the 15–19 class, and so on. The "less than or equal to 14" class with a cumulative frequency of 4 is shown on the ogive in Figure 2.12 by the point located at 14.5 on the horizontal axis and 4 on the vertical axis. The "less than or equal to 19" class with a cumulative frequency of 12 is shown by the point located at 19.5 on the horizontal axis and 12 on the vertical axis. Note that one additional point is plotted at the left end of the ogive. This point starts the ogive by showing that no data values fall below the 10–14 class. It is plotted at 9.5 on the horizontal axis and 0 on the vertical axis. The plotted points are connected by straight lines to complete the ogive.

Using Excel's Histogram Tool to Construct a Frequency Distribution and Histogram

In illustrating how to use Excel to summarize quantitative data, we used the FREQUENCY function to construct a frequency distribution and the Chart Wizard to construct a histogram. Microsoft Excel also provides a set of data analysis tools that can be accessed through

FIGURE 2.12 OGIVE FOR THE AUDIT TIME DATA

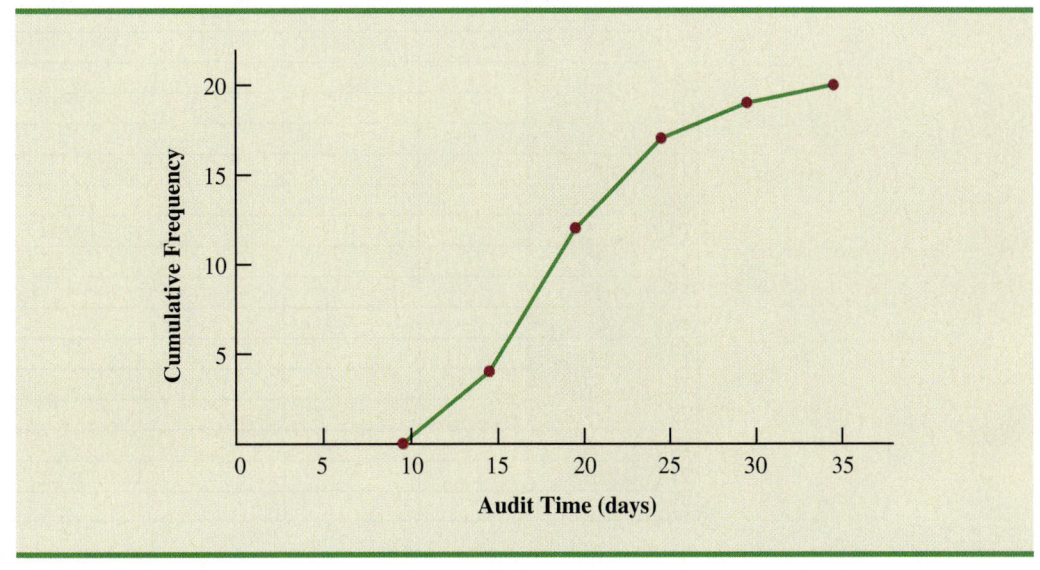

the Tools menu. The data analysis tool for constructing frequency distributions and histograms is the Histogram tool. It can save steps when both a frequency distribution and a histogram are desired. Here we show how it is used by constructing a frequency distribution and a histogram for the audit time data in Table 2.5.

Enter Data: The label Audit Time and the data for the 20 audit times have been entered into cells A1:A21 of the worksheet shown in Figure 2.13.

Enter Functions and Formulas: No functions and formulas are needed.

Apply Tools: Excel's Histogram tool requires the identification of what are called *bins* for each class in the frequency distribution using the class upper limits. Hence, five bins with upper limits of 14, 19, 24, 29, and 34 are needed for the audit time data. The bin upper limits must be entered in ascending order in a column or row of the worksheet. Descriptive labels have been entered into cells C1:D1, the class limits 10–14, 15–19, and so on, have been entered using text format into cells C2:C6, and the bin upper limits have been entered into cells D2:D6 of the worksheet in Figure 2.13.

The following steps describe how to use the Histogram tool to produce a frequency distribution and a histogram consisting of five classes, or bins, for the audit time data.

*Note: If the **Data Analysis** option does not appear when you select the **Tools** menu, choose **Add-Ins**, and check **Analysis ToolPak** to install it.*

Step 1. Select the **Tools** menu
Step 2. Choose the **Data Analysis** option
Step 3. Choose **Histogram** from the list of Analysis Tools
Step 4. When the Histogram dialog box appears (see Figure 2.14):
       Enter A1:A21 in the **Input Range** box
       Enter D1:D6 in the **Bin Range** box

FIGURE 2.13   WORKSHEET FOR AUDIT TIME DATA AFTER CREATING BINS USING UPPER CLASS LIMITS

	A	B	C	D	E
1	**Audit Time**		**Audit Time**	**Upper Limit**	
2	12		10-14	14	
3	15		15-19	19	
4	20		20-24	24	
5	22		25-29	29	
6	14		30-34	34	
7	14				
8	15				
9	27				
10	21				
11	18				
12	19				
13	18				
14	22				
15	33				
16	16				
17	18				
18	17				
19	23				
20	28				
21	13				
22					

FIGURE 2.14   DIALOG BOX FOR HISTOGRAM TOOL

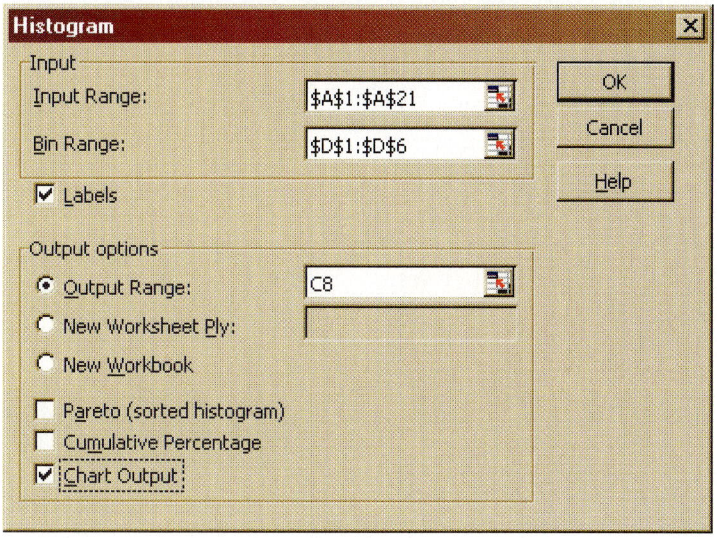

Select **Labels**
Select **Output Range**
Enter C8 in the **Output Range** box (it tells Excel where to display the frequency distribution)
Select **Chart Output** (to request a histogram)
Click **OK**

The worksheet shown in Figure 2.15 displays the frequency distribution and the histogram created using these steps. The frequency distribution is displayed in cells C8:D14. Note that Excel added a row to the frequency distribution with a label of "More" in order to provide for the possibility that we might have entered too few bin values.

To present the frequency distribution in the format of Table 2.6, some editing is required. Paste the contents of cells C1:C6 into cells C8:C13 and clear the contents of cells C14:D14. To present the histogram in the form of Figure 2.7 some editing of it is also required.

Step 1. Right-click on the legend title (Frequency) and select **Clear**
Step 2. Left-click on the horizontal axis title (Upper Limit), type **Audit Time**, and press **Enter**
Step 3. Remove the gaps between bars the same way as when using the Chart Wizard (see Figure 2.9)

The worksheet now appears as shown in Figure 2.16.

As we have just seen, the Histogram tool can be used to construct both a frequency distribution and histogram in one series of steps. Previously, we showed how to use the FREQUENCY function and the Chart Wizard to accomplish the same thing. The advantage of using the FREQUENCY function and Chart Wizard is that the results remain linked to the data. Thus, a change in the data will prompt an automatic update of the frequency distribution and histogram. With the Histogram tool, the results are not linked to the data so a change in the data requires that we reconstruct the frequency distribution and histogram.

FIGURE 2.15 INITIAL FREQUENCY DISTRIBUTION AND HISTOGRAM CONSTRUCTED USING HISTOGRAM TOOL

	A	B	C	D	E	F	G	H	I	J	K	L
1	**Audit Time**		**Audit Time**	**Upper Limit**								
2	12		10-14	14								
3	15		15-19	19								
4	20		20-24	24								
5	22		25-29	29								
6	14		30-34	34								
7	14											
8	15		*Upper Limit*	*Frequency*								
9	27		14	4								
10	21		19	8								
11	18		24	5								
12	19		29	2								
13	18		34	1								
14	22		More	0								
15	33											
16	16											
17	18											
18	17											
19	23											
20	28											
21	13											
22												

FIGURE 2.16 FINAL FREQUENCY DISTRIBUTION AND HISTOGRAM CONSTRUCTED USING HISTOGRAM TOOL

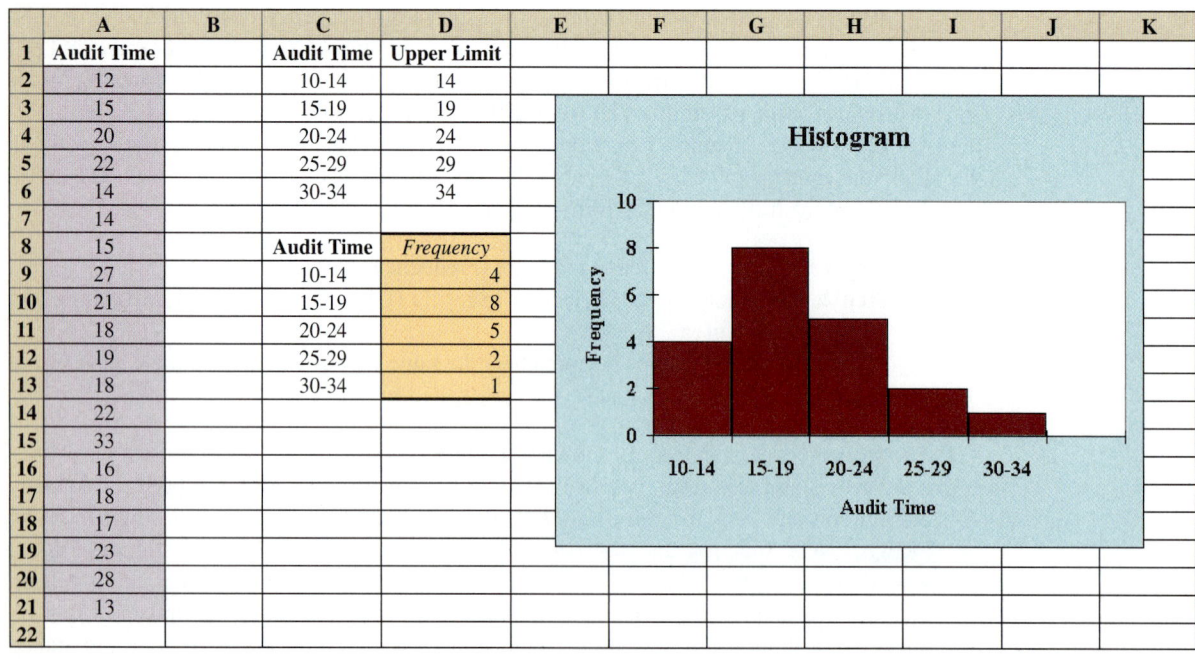

	A	B	C	D	E	F	G	H	I	J	K
1	**Audit Time**		**Audit Time**	**Upper Limit**							
2	12		10-14	14							
3	15		15-19	19							
4	20		20-24	24							
5	22		25-29	29							
6	14		30-34	34							
7	14										
8	15		**Audit Time**	*Frequency*							
9	27		10-14	4							
10	21		15-19	8							
11	18		20-24	5							
12	19		25-29	2							
13	18		30-34	1							
14	22										
15	33										
16	16										
17	18										
18	17										
19	23										
20	28										
21	13										
22											

NOTES AND COMMENTS

1. A bar graph and a histogram are essentially the same thing; both are graphical presentations of the data in a frequency distribution. A histogram is just a bar graph with no separation between bars. For some discrete quantitative data, a separation between bars is also appropriate. Consider, for example, the number of classes in which a college student is enrolled. The data may only assume integer values. Intermediate values such as 1.5, 2.73, and so on are not possible. With continuous quantitative data, however, such as the audit times in Table 2.5, a separation between bars is not appropriate.

2. The appropriate values for the class limits with quantitative data depend on the level of accuracy of the data. For instance, with the audit time data of Table 2.5 the limits used were integer values. If the data were rounded to the nearest tenth of a day (e.g., 12.3, 14.4, and so on), then the limits would be stated in tenths of days. For instance, the first class would be 10.0–14.9. If the data were recorded to the nearest hundredth of a day (e.g., 12.34, 14.45, and so on), the limits would be stated in hundredths of days. For instance, the first class would be 10.00–14.99.

3. An *open-end* class requires only a lower class limit or an upper class limit. For example, in the audit time data of Table 2.5, suppose two of the audits had taken 58 and 65 days. Rather than continue with the classes of width 5 with classes 35–39, 40–44, 45–49, and so on, we could simplify the frequency distribution to show an open-end class of "35 or more." This class would have a frequency of 2. Most often the open-end class appears at the upper end of the distribution. Sometimes an open-end class appears at the lower end of the distribution, and occasionally such classes appear at both ends.

4. The last entry in a cumulative frequency distribution always equals the total number of observations. The last entry in a cumulative relative frequency distribution always equals 1.00 and the last entry in a cumulative percent frequency distribution always equals 100.

Exercises

Methods

11.   Consider the following data.

Frequency

14	21	23	21	16
19	22	25	16	16
24	24	25	19	16
19	18	19	21	12
16	17	18	23	25
20	23	16	20	19
24	26	15	22	24
20	22	24	22	20

   a.   Develop a frequency distribution using classes of 12–14, 15–17, 18–20, 21–23, and 24–26.
   b.   Develop a relative frequency distribution and a percent frequency distribution using the classes in part (a).

12.   Consider the following frequency distribution.

Class	Frequency
10–19	10
20–29	14
30–39	17
40–49	7
50–59	2

Construct a cumulative frequency distribution and a cumulative relative frequency distribution.

13. Construct a histogram and an ogive for the data in exercise 12.

14. Consider the following data.

8.9	10.2	11.5	7.8	10.0	12.2	13.5	14.1	10.0	12.2
6.8	9.5	11.5	11.2	14.9	7.5	10.0	6.0	15.8	11.5

a. Construct a frequency distribution.
b. Construct a percent frequency distribution.

Applications

15. A doctor's office staff studied the waiting times for patients who arrive at the office with a request for emergency service. The following data with waiting times in minutes were collected over a one-month period.

2   5   10   12   4   4   5   17   11   8   9   8   12   21   6   8   7   13   18   3

Use classes of 0–4, 5–9, and so on in the following:
a. Show the frequency distribution.
b. Show the relative frequency distribution.
c. Show the cumulative frequency distribution.
d. Show the cumulative relative frequency distribution.
e. What proportion of patients needing emergency service wait 9 minutes or less?

16. Consider the following two frequency distributions. The first frequency distribution shows the annual adjusted gross income in the United States for individuals earning less than $200,000 (Internal Revenue Service, March 2003). The second frequency distribution shows exam scores for students in a college statistics course.

Income ($1000s)	Frequency (millions)	Exam Score	Frequency
0–24	60	Below 30	2
25–49	33	30–39	5
50–74	20	40–49	6
75–99	6	50–59	13
100–124	4	60–69	32
125–149	2	70–79	78
150–174	1	80–89	43
175–199	1	90–99	21
Total	**127**	**Total**	**200**

a. Develop a histogram for the annual income data. What evidence of skewness does it show? Does this skewness make sense? Explain.
b. Develop a histogram for the exam score data. What evidence of skewness does it show? Explain.
c. Develop a histogram for the data in exercise 11. What evidence of skewness does it show? What is the general shape of the distribution?

17. Mendelsohn Media Research provided survey data on the annual amount of household purchases by families with an annual income of $75,000 or more (*Money*, 2001). Assume that the following data from a sample of 25 households show the dollars spent in the past year on books and magazines.

Spending

280	496	382	202	287
266	119	10	385	135
475	255	379	267	24
42	25	283	110	423
160	123	16	243	363

a. Construct a frequency distribution and relative frequency distribution for the data.
b. Provide a histogram. Comment on the shape of the distribution.
c. Comment on the annual spending on books and magazines for families in the sample.

18. Wageweb conducts surveys of salary data and presents summaries on its Web site. Wageweb reported annual salaries of marketing vice presidents ranged from $85,090 to $190,054 (http://www.Wageweb.com, April 12, 2000). Assume the following data come from a sample of the annual salaries for 50 marketing vice presidents. Data are in thousands of dollars.

CD file

Wageweb

145	95	148	112	132
140	162	118	170	144
145	127	148	165	138
173	113	104	141	142
116	178	123	141	138
127	143	134	136	137
155	93	102	154	142
134	165	123	124	124
138	160	157	138	131
114	135	151	138	157

a. What are the lowest and highest salaries?
b. Use a class width of $15,000 and prepare tabular summaries of the annual salary data.
c. What proportion of the annual salaries are $135,000 or less?
d. What percentage of the annual salaries are more than $150,000?
e. Prepare a histogram. Comment on the shape of the distribution.

19. Sorting through unsolicited e-mail and spam affects the productivity of office workers. An InsightExpress survey monitored office workers to determine the unproductive time per day devoted to unsolicited e-mail and spam (*USA Today,* November 13, 2003). The following data show a sample of time in minutes devoted to this task.

2	4	8	4
8	1	2	32
12	1	5	7
5	5	3	4
24	19	4	14

Summarize the data by constructing the following:
a. A frequency distribution (classes 1–5, 6–10, 11–15, 16–20, and so on)
b. A relative frequency distribution
c. A cumulative frequency distribution
d. A cumulative relative frequency distribution
e. An ogive
f. What percentage of office workers spend 5 minutes or less on unsolicited e-mail and spam? What percentage of office workers spend more than 10 minutes a day on this task?

20. The top 20 concert tours and their average ticket price for shows in North America are shown here. The list is based on data provided to the trade publication *Pollstar* by concert promoters and venue managers (Associated Press, November 21, 2003).

CD file

Concerts

Concert Tour	Ticket Price	Concert Tour	Ticket Price
Bruce Springsteen	$72.40	Toby Keith	$37.76
Dave Matthews Band	44.11	James Taylor	44.93
Aerosmith/KISS	69.52	Alabama	40.83
Shania Twain	61.80	Harper/Johnson	33.70
Fleetwood Mac	78.34	50 Cent	38.89
Radiohead	39.50	Steely Dan	36.38
Cher	64.47	Red Hot Chili Peppers	56.82
Counting Crows	36.48	R.E.M.	46.16
Timberlake/Aguilera	74.43	American Idols Live	39.11
Mana	46.48	Mariah Carey	56.08

Summarize the data by constructing the following:
a. A frequency distribution and a percent frequency distribution
b. A histogram
c. What concert had the most expensive average ticket price? What concert had the least expensive average ticket price?
d. Comment on what the data indicate about the average ticket prices of the top concert tours.

21. The *Nielsen Home Technology Report* provided information about home technology and its usage by persons age 12 and older. The following data are the hours of personal computer usage during one week for a sample of 50 persons.

CD file

Computer

4.1	1.5	10.4	5.9	3.4	5.7	1.6	6.1	3.0	3.7
3.1	4.8	2.0	14.8	5.4	4.2	3.9	4.1	11.1	3.5
4.1	4.1	8.8	5.6	4.3	3.3	7.1	10.3	6.2	7.6
10.8	2.8	9.5	12.9	12.1	0.7	4.0	9.2	4.4	5.7
7.2	6.1	5.7	5.9	4.7	3.9	3.7	3.1	6.1	3.1

Summarize the data by constructing the following:
a. A frequency distribution (use a class width of 3 hours)
b. A relative frequency distribution
c. A histogram
d. An ogive
e. Comment on what the data indicate about personal computer usage at home.

2.3 Exploratory Data Analysis: The Stem-and-Leaf Display

The techniques of **exploratory data analysis** consist of simple arithmetic and easy-to-draw graphs that can be used to summarize data quickly. One technique—referred to as a **stem-and-leaf display**—can be used to show both the rank order and shape of a data set simultaneously.

To illustrate the use of a stem-and-leaf display, consider the data in Table 2.9. These data result from a 150-question aptitude test given to 50 individuals recently interviewed for a position at Haskens Manufacturing. The data indicate the number of questions answered correctly.

To develop a stem-and-leaf display, we first arrange the leading digits of each data value to the left of a vertical line. To the right of the vertical line, we record the last digit for each

TABLE 2.9 NUMBER OF QUESTIONS ANSWERED CORRECTLY ON AN APTITUDE TEST

CD file

ApTest

112	72	69	97	107
73	92	76	86	73
126	128	118	127	124
82	104	132	134	83
92	108	96	100	92
115	76	91	102	81
95	141	81	80	106
84	119	113	98	75
68	98	115	106	95
100	85	94	106	119

data value. Based on the top row of data in Table 2.9 (112, 72, 69, 97, and 107), the first five entries in constructing a stem-and-leaf display would be as follows:

```
 6 | 9
 7 | 2
 8 |
 9 | 7
10 | 7
11 | 2
12 |
13 |
14 |
```

For example, the data value 112 shows the leading digits 11 to the left of the line and the last digit 2 to the right of the line. Similarly, the data value 72 shows the leading digit 7 to the left of the line and last digit 2 to the right of the line. Continuing to place the last digit of each data value on the line corresponding to its leading digit(s) provides the following:

```
 6 | 9 8
 7 | 2 3 6 3 6 5
 8 | 6 2 3 1 1 0 4 5
 9 | 7 2 2 6 2 1 5 8 8 5 4
10 | 7 4 8 0 2 6 6 0 6
11 | 2 8 5 9 3 5 9
12 | 6 8 7 4
13 | 2 4
14 | 1
```

With this organization of the data, sorting the digits on each line into rank order is simple. Doing so provides the stem-and-leaf display shown here.

```
 6 | 8 9
 7 | 2 3 3 5 6 6
 8 | 0 1 1 2 3 4 5 6
 9 | 1 2 2 2 4 5 5 6 7 8 8
10 | 0 0 2 4 6 6 6 7 8
11 | 2 3 5 5 8 9 9
12 | 4 6 7 8
13 | 2 4
14 | 1
```

The numbers to the left of the vertical line (6, 7, 8, 9, 10, 11, 12, 13, and 14) form the *stem*, and each digit to the right of the vertical line is a *leaf*. For example, consider the first row with a stem value of 6 and leaves of 8 and 9.

```
6 | 8   9
```

This row indicates that two data values have a first digit of six. The leaves show that the data values are 68 and 69. Similarly, the second row

$$7 \mid 2 \quad 3 \quad 3 \quad 5 \quad 6 \quad 6$$

indicates that six data values have a first digit of seven. The leaves show that the data values are 72, 73, 73, 75, 76, and 76.

To focus on the shape indicated by the stem-and-leaf display, let us use a rectangle to contain the leaves of each stem. Doing so, we obtain the following.

```
 6 | 8  9
 7 | 2  3  3  5  6  6
 8 | 0  1  1  2  3  4  5  6
 9 | 1  2  2  2  4  5  5  6  7  8  8
10 | 0  0  2  4  6  6  6  7  8
11 | 2  3  5  5  8  9  9
12 | 4  6  7  8
13 | 2  4
14 | 1
```

Rotating this page counterclockwise onto its side provides a picture of the data that is similar to a histogram with classes of 60–69, 70–79, 80–89, and so on.

Although the stem-and-leaf display may appear to offer the same information as a histogram, it has two primary advantages.

1. The stem-and-leaf display is easier to construct by hand.
2. Within a class interval, the stem-and-leaf display provides more information than the histogram because the stem-and-leaf shows the actual data.

In a stretched stem-and-leaf display, whenever a stem value is stated twice, the first value corresponds to leaf values of 0–4, and the second value corresponds to leaf values of 5–9.

Just as a frequency distribution or histogram has no absolute number of classes, neither does a stem-and-leaf display have an absolute number of rows or stems. If we believe that our original stem-and-leaf display condensed the data too much, we can easily stretch the display by using two or more stems for each leading digit. For example, to use two stems for each leading digit, we would place all data values ending in 0, 1, 2, 3, and 4 in one row and all values ending in 5, 6, 7, 8, and 9 in a second row. The following stretched stem-and-leaf display illustrates this approach.

```
 6 | 8  9
 7 | 2  3  3
 7 | 5  6  6
 8 | 0  1  1  2  3  4
 8 | 5  6
 9 | 1  2  2  2  4
 9 | 5  5  6  7  8  8
10 | 0  0  2  4
10 | 6  6  6  7  8
11 | 2  3
11 | 5  5  8  9  9
12 | 4
12 | 6  7  8
13 | 2  4
13 |
14 | 1
```

Note that values 72, 73, and 73 have leaves in the 0–4 range and are shown with the first stem value of 7. The values 75, 76, and 76 have leaves in the 5–9 range and are shown with the second stem value of 7. This stretched stem-and-leaf display is similar to a frequency distribution with intervals of 65–69, 70–74, 75–79, and so on.

The preceding example showed a stem-and-leaf display for data with as many as three digits. Stem-and-leaf displays for data with more than three digits are possible. For example, consider the following data on the number of hamburgers sold by a fast-food restaurant for each of 15 weeks.

1565	1852	1644	1766	1888	1912	2044	1812
1790	1679	2008	1852	1967	1954	1733	

A stem-and-leaf display of these data follows.

Leaf unit = 10

15	6			
16	4	7		
17	3	6	9	
18	1	5	5	8
19	1	5	6	
20	0	4		

A single digit is used to define each leaf in a stem-and-leaf display. The leaf unit indicates how to multiply the stem-and-leaf numbers in order to approximate the original data. Leaf units may be 100, 10, 1, 0.1, and so on.

Note that a single digit is used to define each leaf and that only the first three digits of each data value have been used to construct the display. At the top of the display we have specified Leaf unit = 10. To illustrate how to interpret the values in the display, consider the first stem, 15, and its associated leaf, 6. Combining these numbers, we obtain 156. To reconstruct an approximation of the original data value, we must multiply this number by 10, the value of the *leaf unit*. Thus, 156 × 10 = 1560 is an approximation of the original data value used to construct the stem-and-leaf display. Although it is not possible to reconstruct the exact data value from this stem-and-leaf display, the convention of using a single digit for each leaf enables stem-and-leaf displays to be constructed for data having a large number of digits. For stem-and-leaf displays where the leaf unit is not shown, the leaf unit is assumed to equal 1.

Exercises

Methods

22. Construct a stem-and-leaf display for the following data.

70	72	75	64	58	83	80	82
76	75	68	65	57	78	85	72

23. Construct a stem-and-leaf display for the following data.

11.3	9.6	10.4	7.5	8.3	10.5	10.0
9.3	8.1	7.7	7.5	8.4	6.3	8.8

24. Construct a stem-and-leaf display for the following data. Use a leaf unit of 10.

1161	1206	1478	1300	1604	1725	1361	1422
1221	1378	1623	1426	1557	1730	1706	1689

Applications

25. A psychologist developed a new test of adult intelligence. The test was administered to 20 individuals, and the following data were obtained.

| 114 | 99 | 131 | 124 | 117 | 102 | 106 | 127 | 119 | 115 |
| 98 | 104 | 144 | 151 | 132 | 106 | 125 | 122 | 118 | 118 |

Construct a stem-and-leaf display for the data.

26. The American Association of Individual Investors conducts an annual survey of discount brokers. The following prices charged are from a sample of 24 discount brokers (*AAII Journal*, January 2003). The two types of trades are a broker-assisted trade of 100 shares at $50 per share and an online trade of 500 shares at $50 per share.

Broker

Broker	Broker-Assisted 100 Shares at $50/Share	Online 500 Shares at $50/Share	Broker	Broker-Assisted 100 Shares at $50/Share	Online 500 Shares at $50/Share
Accutrade	30.00	29.95	Merrill Lynch Direct	50.00	29.95
Ameritrade	24.99	10.99	Muriel Siebert	45.00	14.95
Banc of America	54.00	24.95	NetVest	24.00	14.00
Brown & Co.	17.00	5.00	Recom Securities	35.00	12.95
Charles Schwab	55.00	29.95	Scottrade	17.00	7.00
CyberTrader	12.95	9.95	Sloan Securities	39.95	19.95
E*TRADE Securities	49.95	14.95	Strong Investments	55.00	24.95
First Discount	35.00	19.75	TD Waterhouse	45.00	17.95
Freedom Investments	25.00	15.00	T. Rowe Price	50.00	19.95
Harrisdirect	40.00	20.00	Vanguard	48.00	20.00
Investors National	39.00	62.50	Wall Street Discount	29.95	19.95
MB Trading	9.95	10.55	York Securities	40.00	36.00

a. Round the trading prices to the nearest dollar and develop a stem-and-leaf display for 100 shares at $50 per share. Comment on what you learned about broker-assisted trading prices.

b. Round the trading prices to the nearest dollar and develop a stretched stem-and-leaf display for 500 shares online at $50 per share. Comment on what you learned about online trading prices.

27. The prices per share for the 30 companies making up the Dow Jones Industrial Average are shown here (*The Wall Street Journal*, April 9, 2004).

StockPrices

Company	$/Share	Company	$/Share
Alcoa	$34	Honeywell	$35
Altria Group	55	IBM	93
American Express	52	Intel	27
American International	76	Johnson & Johnson	51
Boeing	41	J.P. Morgan Chase	41
Caterpillar	82	McDonald's	29
Citigroup	52	Merck	45
Coca-Cola	51	Microsoft	25
Disney	26	Pfizer	36
DuPont	43	Procter & Gamble	106
ExxonMobil	42	SBE Communications	24
General Electric	31	3M	82
General Motors	47	United Technologies	90
Hewlett-Packard	23	Verizon	37
Home Depot	36	Wal-Mart Stores	57

a. Develop a stem-and-leaf display.
b. Use the stem-and-leaf display to answer the following questions:
    •   What does the grouping of the data in the stem-and-leaf display tell you about the prices per share for the 30 Dow Jones companies?
    •   What is the price-per-share range for the majority of the companies?
    •   How many companies have a price per share of $36?
    •   What is the most frequently appearing price per share?
    •   What should be considered a relatively high price per share? What percentage of the companies have a price per share in this range? Which companies have a price per share in this range, and what is the price per share for each?
c. Use *The Wall Street Journal* or another business publication to find the current price per share for each of the 30 Dow Jones Industrial Average companies. Construct a stem-and-leaf display for these data and use the display to comment on any changes in the prices per share since April 2004.

28. The 2004 Naples, Florida, mini marathon (13.1 miles) had 1228 registrants (*The Naples Daily News,* January 17, 2004). Competition was held in six age groups. The following data show the ages for a sample of 40 individuals who participated in the marathon.

Marathon

49	33	40	37	56
44	46	57	55	32
50	52	43	64	40
46	24	30	37	43
31	43	50	36	61
27	44	35	31	43
52	43	66	31	50
72	26	59	21	47

a. Show a stretched stem-and-leaf display.
b. What age group had the largest number of runners?
c. What age occurred most frequently?
d. A *Naples Daily News* feature article emphasized the number of runners who were "20-something." What percentage of the runners were in the 20-something age group? What do you suppose was the focus of the article?

2.4   Crosstabulations and Scatter Diagrams

Crosstabulations and scatter diagrams are used to summarize data in a way that reveals the relationship between two variables.

Thus far in this chapter, we focused on tabular and graphical methods used to summarize the data for *one variable at a time.* Often a manager or decision maker requires tabular and graphical methods that will assist in the understanding of the *relationship between two variables.* Crosstabulation and scatter diagrams are two such methods.

Crosstabulation

A **crosstabulation** is a tabular summary of data for two variables. Let us illustrate the use of a crosstabulation by considering the following application based on data from Zagat's Restaurant Survey. The quality rating and the meal price data were collected for a sample of 300 restaurants located in the Los Angeles area. Table 2.10 shows the data for the first 10 restaurants. Data on a restaurant's quality rating and typical meal price are reported. Quality rating is a qualitative variable with rating categories of good, very good, and excellent. Meal price is a quantitative variable that ranges from $10 to $49.

A crosstabulation of the data for this application is shown in Table 2.11. The left and top margin labels define the classes for the two variables. In the left margin, the row labels (good, very good, and excellent) correspond to the three classes of the quality rating variable. In the top margin, the column labels ($10–19, $20–29, $30–39, and $40–49) correspond to the four classes of the meal price variable. Each restaurant in the sample provides a quality

TABLE 2.10   QUALITY RATING AND MEAL PRICE FOR 300 LOS ANGELES RESTAURANTS

CD file

Restaurant

Restaurant	Quality Rating	Meal Price ($)
1	Good	18
2	Very Good	22
3	Good	28
4	Excellent	38
5	Very Good	33
6	Good	28
7	Very Good	19
8	Very Good	11
9	Very Good	23
10	Good	13
.	.	.
.	.	.
.	.	.

rating and a meal price. Thus, each restaurant in the sample is associated with a cell appearing in one of the rows and one of the columns of the crosstabulation. For example, restaurant 5 is identified as having a very good quality rating and a meal price of $33. This restaurant belongs to the cell in row 2 and column 3 of Table 2.11. In constructing a crosstabulation, we simply count the number of restaurants that belong to each of the cells in the crosstabulation table.

In reviewing Table 2.11, we see that the greatest number of restaurants in the sample (64) have a very good rating and a meal price in the $20–29 range. Only two restaurants have an excellent rating and a meal price in the $10–19 range. Similar interpretations of the other frequencies can be made. In addition, note that the right and bottom margins of the cross-tabulation provide the frequency distributions for quality rating and meal price separately. From the frequency distribution in the right margin, we see that data on quality ratings show that 84 of the restaurants were rated good, 150 were rated very good, and 66 were rated excellent. Similarly, the bottom margin shows the frequency distribution for the meal price variable.

Dividing the totals in the right margin of the crosstabulation by the total for that column provides a relative and percent frequency distribution for the quality rating variable.

Quality Rating	Relative Frequency	Percent Frequency
Good	.28	28
Very Good	.50	50
Excellent	.22	22
Total	1.00	100

TABLE 2.11   CROSSTABULATION OF QUALITY RATING AND MEAL PRICE
FOR 300 LOS ANGELES RESTAURANTS

	Meal Price				
Quality Rating	**$10–19**	**$20–29**	**$30–39**	**$40–49**	**Total**
Good	42	40	2	0	84
Very Good	34	64	46	6	150
Excellent	2	14	28	22	66
Total	78	118	76	28	300

From the percent frequency distribution we see that 28% of the restaurants were rated good, 50% were rated very good, and 22% were rated excellent.

Dividing the totals in the bottom row of the crosstabulation by the total for that row provides a relative and percent frequency distribution for the meal price variable.

Meal Price	Relative Frequency	Percent Frequency
$10–19	.26	26
$20–29	.39	39
$30–39	.25	25
$40–49	.09	9
Total	1.00	100

Note that the sum of the values in each column does not add up exactly to the column total, because the values being summed are rounded. From the percent frequency distribution we see that 26% of the meal prices are in the lowest price class ($10–19), 39% are in the next higher class, and so on.

The frequency and relative frequency distributions constructed from the margins of a crosstabulation provide information about each of the variables individually, but they do not shed any light on the relationship between the variables. The primary value of a crosstabulation lies in the insight it offers about the relationship between the variables. A review of the crosstabulation in Table 2.11 reveals that higher meal prices are associated with the higher quality restaurants, and the lower meal prices are associated with the lower quality restaurants.

Converting the entries in a crosstabulation into row percentages or column percentages can provide more insight into the relationship between the two variables. For row percentages, the results of dividing each frequency in Table 2.11 by its corresponding row total are shown in Table 2.12. Each row of Table 2.12 is a percent frequency distribution of meal price for one of the quality rating categories. Of the restaurants with the lowest quality rating (good), we see that the greatest percentages are for the less expensive restaurants (50% have $10–19 meal prices and 47.6% have $20–29 meal prices). Of the restaurants with the highest quality rating (excellent), we see that the greatest percentages are for the more expensive restaurants (42.4% have $30–39 meal prices and 33.4% have $40–49 meal prices). Thus, we continue to see that the more expensive meals are associated with the higher quality restaurants.

Crosstabulation is widely used for examining the relationship between two variables. In practice, the final reports for many statistical studies include a large number of crosstabulation tables. In the Los Angeles restaurant survey, the crosstabulation is based on one qualitative variable (quality rating) and one quantitative variable (meal price). Crosstabulations can also be developed when both variables are qualitative and when both variables are quantitative. When quantitative variables are used, however, we must first create classes for the values of the variable. For instance, in the restaurant example we grouped the meal prices into four classes ($10–19, $20–29, $30–39, and $40–49).

TABLE 2.12   ROW PERCENTAGES FOR EACH QUALITY RATING CATEGORY

Quality Rating	Meal Price $10–19	$20–29	$30–39	$40–49	Total
Good	50.0	47.6	2.4	0.0	100
Very Good	22.7	42.7	30.6	4.0	100
Excellent	3.0	21.2	42.4	33.4	100

Using Excel's PivotTable Report to Construct a Crosstabulation

Excel's PivotTable Report provides a general tool for summarizing the data for two or more variables simultaneously. We will illustrate the use of Excel's PivotTable Report by showing how to develop a crosstabulation of quality ratings and meal prices for the sample of 300 restaurants located in the Los Angeles area.

Enter Data: The labels "Restaurant," "Quality Rating," and "Meal Price ($)" have been entered into cells A1:C1 of the worksheet shown in Figure 2.17. The data for each of the 300 restaurants in the sample have been entered into cells B2:C301.

Enter Functions and Formulas: No functions and formulas are needed.

Apply Tools: Starting with the worksheet in Figure 2.17, the following steps will produce a crosstabulation.

> **Step 1.** Select the **Data** menu
> **Step 2.** Choose **PivotTable and PivotChart Report**
> **Step 3.** When the PivotTable and PivotChart Wizard - Step 1 of 3 dialog box appears:
> > Choose **Microsoft Office Excel list or database**
> > Choose **PivotTable**
> > Click **Next**
> **Step 4.** When the PivotTable and PivotChart Wizard - Step 2 of 3 dialog box appears:
> > Enter A1:C301 in the **Range:** box
> > Click **Next**

FIGURE 2.17   EXCEL WORKSHEET CONTAINING RESTAURANT DATA

CD file

Restaurant

Note: Rows 12–291 are hidden.

	A	B	C	D
1	Restaurant	Quality Rating	Meal Price ($)	
2	1	Good	18	
3	2	Very Good	22	
4	3	Good	28	
5	4	Excellent	38	
6	5	Very Good	33	
7	6	Good	28	
8	7	Very Good	19	
9	8	Very Good	11	
10	9	Very Good	23	
11	10	Good	13	
292	291	Very Good	23	
293	292	Very Good	24	
294	293	Excellent	45	
295	294	Good	14	
296	295	Good	18	
297	296	Good	17	
298	297	Good	16	
299	298	Good	15	
300	299	Very Good	38	
301	300	Very Good	31	
302				

Step 5. When the PivotTable and PivotChart Wizard - Step 3 of 3 dialog box appears:
     Select **New Worksheet**
     Click **Layout**
Step 6. When the PivotTable and PivotChart Wizard - Layout diagram appears
     (see Figure 2.18):
          Drag the **Quality Rating** field button to the **ROW** section of the diagram
          Drag the **Meal Price ($)** field button to the **COLUMN** section of the
          diagram
          Drag the **Restaurant** field button to the **Data** section of the diagram
          Double-click the **Sum of Restaurant** field button in the DATA section
          When the PivotTable Field dialog box appears:
               Choose **Count** under **Summarize by**
               Click **OK** (Figure 2.19 shows the completed layout diagram)
          Click **OK**
Step 7. When the PivotTable and PivotChart Wizard - Step 3 of 3 dialog box reappears:
     Click **Finish**

A portion of the output generated by Excel is shown in Figure 2.20. Note that the output that appears in columns D through AK is hidden so the results can be shown on one page. The row labels (Excellent, Good, and Very Good) and row totals (66, 84, 150, and 300) that appear in Figure 2.20 are the same as the row labels and row totals shown in Table 2.11. But they are in a different order. To put them in the order Good, Very Good, Excellent, follow these steps.

Step 1. Right-click on Excellent in cell A5
Step 2. Choose **Order**
Step 3. Select **Move to End**

In Figure 2.20, one column is designated for each possible value of meal price. For example, column B contains a count of restaurants with a $10 meal price, column C contains a count of restaurants with an $11 meal price, and so on. To view the PivotTable Report in

FIGURE 2.18   PIVOTTABLE AND PIVOTCHART WIZARD - LAYOUT DIAGRAM

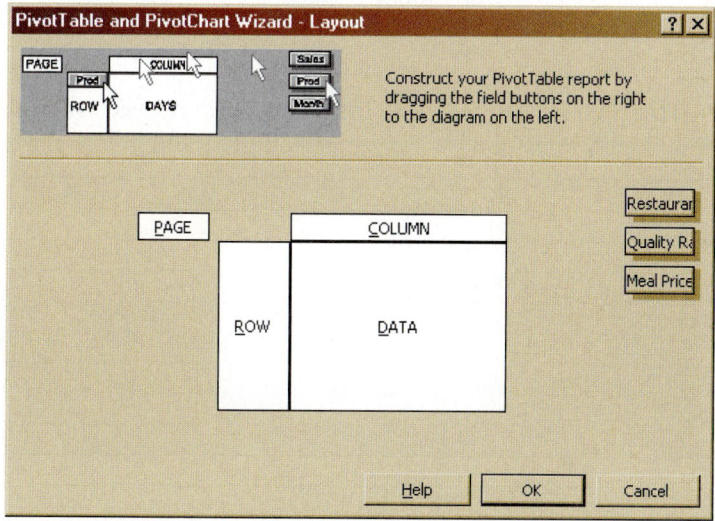

FIGURE 2.19   COMPLETED LAYOUT DIAGRAM

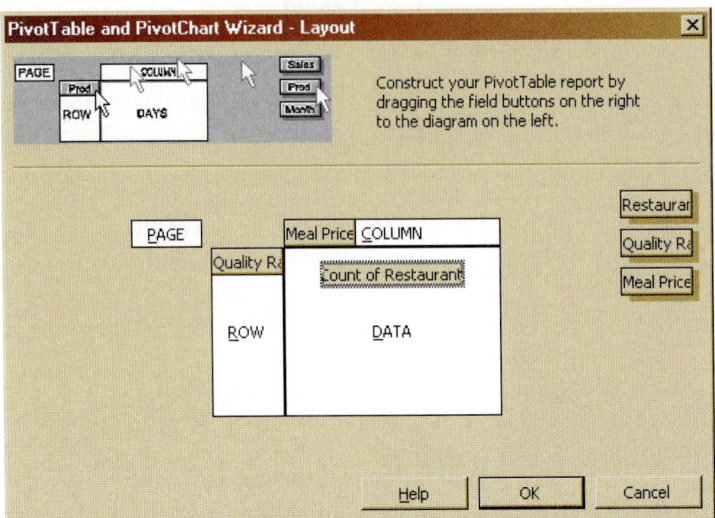

a form similar to that shown in Table 2.11, we must group the columns into four price categories: $10–19, $20–29, $30–39, and $40–49. The steps necessary to group the columns for the worksheet shown in Figure 2.20 follow.

Step 1. Right-click on Meal Price ($) in cell B3 of the PivotTable
Step 2. Choose **Group and Show Detail**
        Choose **Group**
Step 3. When the Grouping dialog box appears:
        Enter 10 in the **Starting at** box
        Enter 49 in the **Ending at** box
        Enter 10 in the **By** box
        Click **OK**

By grouping the columns we create a frequency distribution for the quantitative variable, meal price.

The revised PivotTable output is shown in Figure 2.21. It is the final PivotTable. Note that it provides the same information as the crosstabulation shown in Table 2.11.

FIGURE 2.20   INITIAL PIVOTTABLE REPORT (COLUMNS D:AK ARE HIDDEN.)

	A	B	C	AL	AM	AN	AO
1							
2							
3	Count of Restaurant	Meal Price ($)					
4	Quality Rating	10	11	47	48	Grand Total	
5	Excellent			2	2	66	
6	Good	6	4			84	
7	Very Good	1	4		1	150	
8	Grand Total	7	8	2	3	300	
9							
10							

FIGURE 2.21   FINAL PIVOTTABLE REPORT FOR RESTAURANT DATA

	A	B	C	D	E	F	G
1							
2							
3	**Count of Restaurant**	**Meal Price ($)**					
4	**Quality Rating**	10-19	20-29	30-39	40-49	**Grand Total**	
5	Good	42	40	2		84	
6	Very Good	34	64	46	6	150	
7	Excellent	2	14	28	22	66	
8	Grand Total	78	118	76	28	300	
9							
10							

Simpson's Paradox

The data in two or more crosstabulations are often combined or aggregated to produce a summary crosstabulation showing how two variables are related. In such cases, we must be careful in drawing conclusions about the relationship between the two variables in the aggregated crosstabulation. In some cases the conclusions based upon the aggregated crosstabulation can be completely reversed if we look at the unaggregated data, an occurrence known as **Simpson's paradox**. To provide an illustration of Simpson's paradox we consider an example involving the analysis of verdicts for two judges in two types of courts.

Judges Ron Luckett and Dennis Kendall presided over cases in Common Pleas Court and Municipal Court during the past three years. Some of the verdicts they rendered were appealed. In most of these cases the appeals court upheld the original verdicts, but in some cases those verdicts were reversed. For each judge, a crosstabulation was developed based upon two variables: Verdict (upheld or reversed) and Type of Court (Common Pleas and Municipal). Suppose that the two crosstabulations were then combined by aggregating the type of court data. The resulting aggregated crosstabulation contains two variables: Verdict (upheld or reversed) and Judge (Luckett or Kendall). This crosstabulation shows the number of appeals in which the verdict was upheld and the number in which the verdict was reversed for both judges. The following crosstabulation shows these results along with the column percentages in parentheses next to each value.

	Judge		
Verdict	**Luckett**	**Kendall**	**Total**
Upheld	129 (86%)	110 (88%)	239
Reversed	21 (14%)	15 (12%)	36
Total (%)	150 (100%)	125 (100%)	275

A review of the column percentages shows that 14% of the verdicts were reversed for Judge Luckett, but only 12% of the verdicts were reversed for Judge Kendall. Thus, we might conclude that Judge Kendall is doing a better job because a higher percentage of his verdicts are being upheld. A problem arises with this conclusion, however.

The following crosstabulations show the cases tried by Luckett and Kendall in the two courts; column percentages are also shown in parentheses next to each value.

	Judge Luckett					**Judge Kendall**		
Verdict	**Common Pleas**	**Municipal Court**	**Total**		**Verdict**	**Common Pleas**	**Municipal Court**	**Total**
Upheld	29 (91%)	100 (85%)	129		**Upheld**	90 (90%)	20 (80%)	110
Reversed	3 (9%)	18 (15%)	21		**Reversed**	10 (10%)	5 (20%)	15
Total (%)	32 (100%)	118 (100%)	150		**Total (%)**	100 (100%)	25 (100%)	125

From the crosstabulation and column percentages for Luckett, we see that his verdicts were upheld in 91% of the Common Pleas Court cases and in 85% of the Municipal Court cases. From the crosstabulation and column percentages for Kendall, we see that his verdicts were upheld in 90% of the Common Pleas Court cases and in 80% of the Municipal Court cases. Comparing the column percentages for the two judges, we see that Judge Luckett demonstrates a better record than Judge Kendall in both courts. This result contradicts the conclusion we reached when we aggregated the data across both courts for the original crosstabulation. It appeared then that Judge Kendall had the better record. This example illustrates Simpson's paradox.

The original crosstabulation was obtained by aggregating the data in the separate crosstabulations for the two courts. Note that for both judges the percentage of appeals that resulted in reversals was much higher in Municipal Court than in Common Pleas Court. Because Judge Luckett tried a much higher percentage of his cases in Municipal Court, the aggregated data favored Judge Kendall. When we look at the crosstabulations for the two courts separately, however, Judge Luckett clearly shows the better record. Thus, for the original crosstabulation, we see that the *type of court* is a hidden variable that cannot be ignored when evaluating the records of the two judges.

Because of Simpson's paradox, we need to be especially careful when drawing conclusions using aggregated data. Before drawing any conclusions about the relationship between two variables shown for a crosstabulation involving aggregated data, you should investigate whether any hidden variables could affect the results.

Scatter Diagram and Trendline

A **scatter diagram** is a graphical presentation of the relationship between two quantitative variables, and a **trendline** is a line that provides an approximation of the relationship. As an illustration, consider the advertising/sales relationship for a stereo and sound equipment store in San Francisco. On 10 occasions during the past three months, the store used weekend television commercials to promote sales at its stores. The managers want to investigate whether a relationship exists between the number of commercials shown and sales at the store during the following week. Sample data for the 10 weeks with sales in hundreds of dollars are shown in Table 2.13.

Figure 2.22 shows the scatter diagram and the trendline* for the data in Table 2.13. The number of commercials (x) is shown on the horizontal axis and the sales (y) are shown on the vertical axis. For week 1, $x = 2$ and $y = 50$. A point with those coordinates is plotted on

---

*The equation of the trendline is $y = 4.95x + 36.15$. The slope of the trendline is 4.95 and the y-intercept (the point where the line intersects the y axis) is 36.15. We will discuss in detail the interpretation of the slope and y-intercept for a linear trendline in Chapter 14 when we study simple linear regression.

TABLE 2.13 SAMPLE DATA FOR THE STEREO AND SOUND EQUIPMENT STORE

CD file

Stereo

Week	Number of Commercials x	Sales ($100s) y
1	2	50
2	5	57
3	1	41
4	3	54
5	4	54
6	1	38
7	5	63
8	3	48
9	4	59
10	2	46

the scatter diagram. Similar points are plotted for the other nine weeks. Note that during two of the weeks one commercial was shown, during two of the weeks two commercials were shown, and so on.

The scatter diagram in Figure 2.22 indicates a positive relationship between the number of commercials and sales. Higher sales are associated with a higher number of commercials. The relationship is not perfect in that all points are not on a straight line. However, the general pattern of the points and the trendline suggest that the overall relationship is positive.

Some general scatter diagram patterns and the types of relationships they suggest are shown in Figure 2.23. The top left panel depicts a positive relationship similar to the one for the number of commercials and sales example. In the top right panel, the scatter diagram shows no apparent relationship between the variables. The bottom panel depicts a negative relationship where y tends to decrease as x increases.

FIGURE 2.22 SCATTER DIAGRAM AND TRENDLINE FOR THE STEREO AND SOUND EQUIPMENT STORE

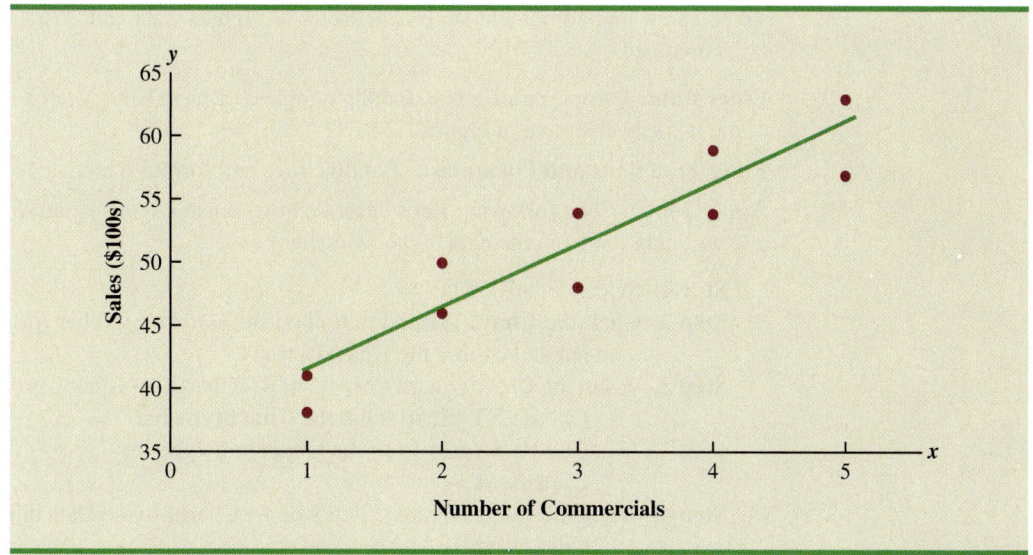

FIGURE 2.23   TYPES OF RELATIONSHIPS DEPICTED BY SCATTER DIAGRAMS

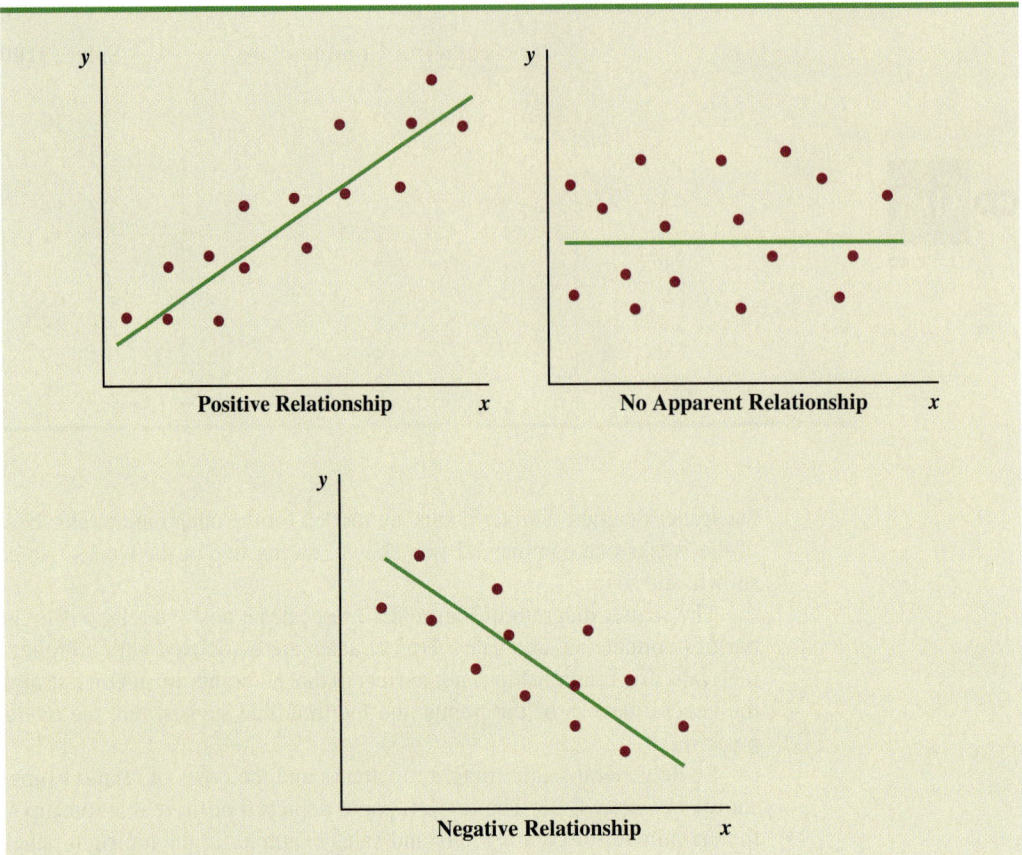

Using Excel's Chart Wizard to Construct a Scatter Diagram and a Trendline

We can use Excel's Chart Wizard to construct a scatter diagram and a trendline for the stereo and sound equipment store data. Refer to Figures 2.24 and 2.25 as we describe the tasks involved.

Enter Data: Appropriate labels and the sample data have been entered into cells A1:C11 of the worksheet shown in Figure 2.24.

Enter Functions and Formulas: No functions and formulas are needed.

Apply Tools: The following steps describe how to use Excel's Chart Wizard to produce a scatter diagram from the data in the worksheet.

> **Step 1.** Select cells B1:C11
> **Step 2.** Click the **Chart Wizard** button on the standard toolbar (or select the **Insert** menu and choose the **Chart** option)
> **Step 3.** When the Chart Wizard - Step 1 of 4 - Chart Type dialog box appears:
>> Choose **XY (Scatter)** in the **Chart type** list
>> Choose **Scatter** from the **Chart sub-type** display
>> Click **Next >**
> **Step 4.** When the Chart Wizard - Step 2 of 4 - Chart Source Data dialog box appears:
>> Click **Next >**

FIGURE 2.24 SCATTER DIAGRAM FOR STEREO AND SOUND EQUIPMENT STORE USING EXCEL'S CHART WIZARD

	A	B	C	D	E	F	H	H	I
1	Week	No. of Commercials	Sales Volume						
2	1	2	50						
3	2	5	57						
4	3	1	41						
5	4	3	54						
6	5	4	54						
7	6	1	38						
8	7	5	63						
9	8	3	48						
10	9	4	59						
11	10	2	46						
12									
13									
14									
15									
16									
17									
18									
19									
20									

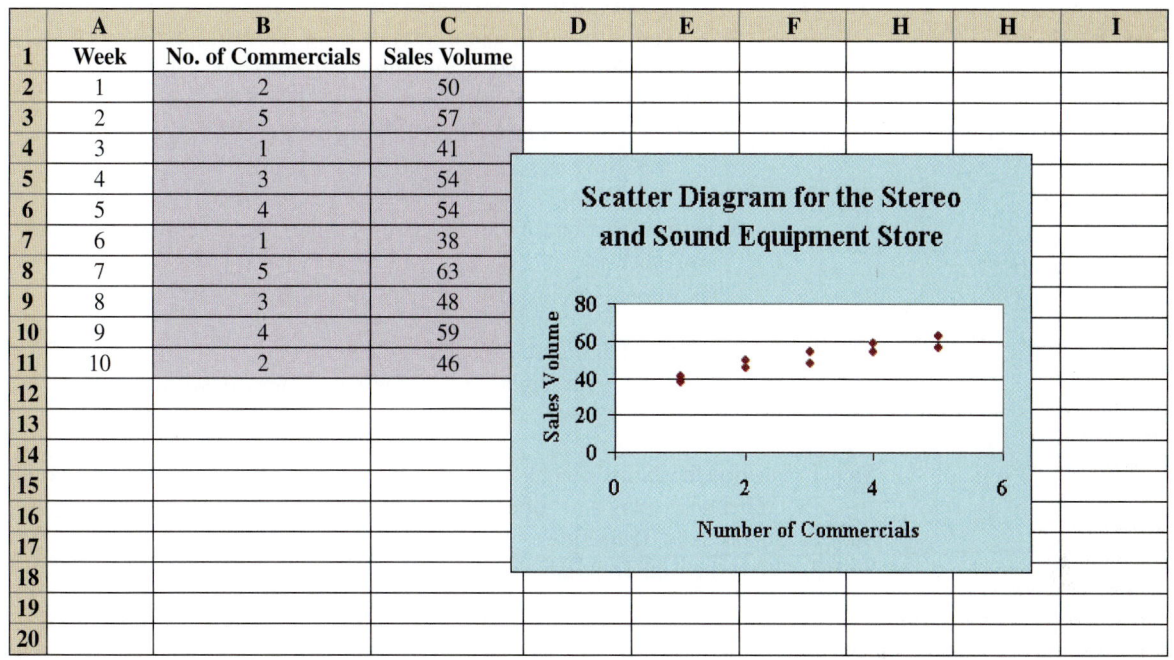

FIGURE 2.25 SCATTER DIAGRAM AND TRENDLINE FOR STEREO AND SOUND EQUIPMENT STORE USING EXCEL'S CHART WIZARD

	A	B	C	D	E	F	H	H	I
1	Week	No. of Commercials	Sales Volume						
2	1	2	50						
3	2	5	57						
4	3	1	41						
5	4	3	54						
6	5	4	54						
7	6	1	38						
8	7	5	63						
9	8	3	48						
10	9	4	59						
11	10	2	46						
12									
13									
14									
15									
16									
17									
18									
19									
20									

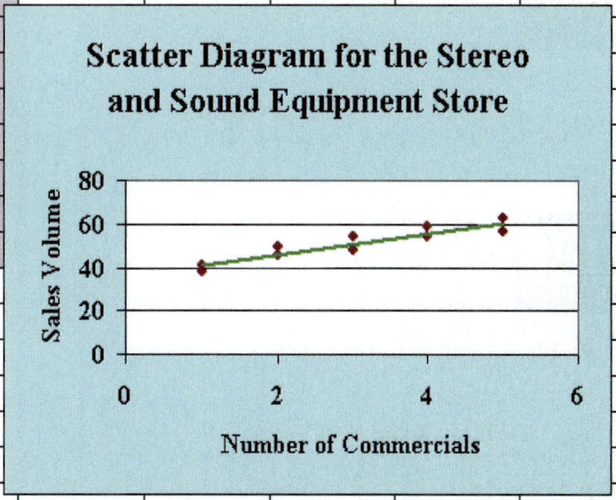

Step 5. When the Chart Wizard - Step 3 of 4 - Chart Options dialog box appears:
Select the **Titles** tab and then
Type **Scatter Diagram for the Stereo and Sound Equipment Store** in the **Chart title:** box
Type **Number of Commercials** in the **Value (X) axis:** box
Type **Sales Volume** in the **Value (Y) axis:** box
Select the **Legend** tab and then
Remove the check in the **Show legend** box
Click **Next >**

Step 6. When the Chart Wizard - Step 4 of 4 - Chart Location dialog box appears:
Specify a location for the chart (we used the default setting of the current worksheet)
Click **Finish**

The worksheet displayed in Figure 2.24 shows the scatter diagram produced by Excel. (We enlarged the scatter diagram slightly.) The following steps describe how to add a trendline.

Step 1. Position the mouse pointer over any data point in the scatter diagram and right-click to display a list of options

Step 2. Choose **Add Trendline**

Step 3. When the Add Trendline dialog box appears:
Select the **Type** tab and then
Choose **Linear** from the **Trend/Regression type** display
Click **OK**

The worksheet displayed in Figure 2.25 shows the scatter diagram with the trendline added.

Exercises

Methods

29. The following data are for 30 observations involving two qualitative variables, x and y. The categories for x are A, B, and C; the categories for y are 1 and 2.

Observation	x	y	Observation	x	y
1	A	1	16	B	2
2	B	1	17	C	1
3	B	1	18	B	1
4	C	2	19	C	1
5	B	1	20	B	1
6	C	2	21	C	2
7	B	1	22	B	1
8	C	2	23	C	2
9	A	1	24	A	1
10	B	1	25	B	1
11	A	1	26	C	2
12	B	1	27	C	2
13	C	2	28	A	1
14	C	2	29	B	1
15	C	2	30	B	2

a.   Develop a crosstabulation for the data, with x as the row variable and y as the column variable.
b.   Compute the row percentages.
c.   Compute the column percentages.
d.   What is the relationship, if any, between x and y?

30.   The following 20 observations are for two quantitative variables, x and y.

Scatter

Observation	x	y	Observation	x	y
1	−22	22	11	−37	48
2	−33	49	12	34	−29
3	2	8	13	9	−18
4	29	−16	14	−33	31
5	−13	10	15	20	−16
6	21	−28	16	−3	14
7	−13	27	17	−15	18
8	−23	35	18	12	17
9	14	−5	19	−20	−11
10	3	−3	20	−7	−22

a.   Develop a scatter diagram for the relationship between x and y.
b.   What is the relationship, if any, between x and y?

Applications

31.   The following crosstabulation shows household income by educational level of the head of household (*Statistical Abstract of the United States: 2002*).

Educational Level	Household Income ($1000s)					Total
	Under 25	25.0–49.9	50.0–74.9	75.0–99.9	100 or more	
Not H.S. graduate	9285	4093	1589	541	354	15862
H.S. graduate	10150	9821	6050	2737	2028	30786
Some college	6011	8221	5813	3215	3120	26380
Bachelor's degree	2138	3985	3952	2698	4748	17521
Beyond bach. deg.	813	1497	1815	1589	3765	9479
Total	28397	27617	19219	10780	14015	100028

a.   Compute the row percentages and identify the percent frequency distributions of income for households in which the head of household is a high school graduate and in which the head of household holds a bachelor's degree.
b.   What percentage of households headed by high school graduates earn $75,000 or more? What percentage of households headed by bachelor's degree recipients earn $75,000 or more?
c.   Construct percent frequency histograms of income for households headed by persons with a high school degree and for those headed by persons with a bachelor's degree. Is any relationship evident between household income and educational level?

32.   Refer again to the crosstabulation of household income by educational level shown in exercise 31.
a.   Compute column percentages and identify the percent frequency distributions displayed. What percentage of the heads of households did not graduate from high school?
b.   What percentage of the households earning $100,000 or more were headed by a person having schooling beyond a bachelor's degree? What percentage of the households

headed by a person with schooling beyond a bachelor's degree earned over $100,000? Why are these two percentages different?

c. Compare the percent frequency distributions for those households earning "Under 25," "100 or more," and for "Total." Comment on the relationship between household income and educational level of the head of household.

33. Recently, management at Oak Tree Golf Course received a few complaints about the condition of the greens. Several players complained that the greens are too fast. Rather than react to the comments of just a few players, the Golf Association conducted a survey of 100 male and 100 female golfers. The survey results are summarized here.

Male Golfers				**Female Golfers**		
	Greens Condition				**Greens Condition**	
Handicap	**Too Fast**	**Fine**		**Handicap**	**Too Fast**	**Fine**
Under 15	10	40		Under 15	1	9
15 or more	25	25		15 or more	39	51

a. Combine these two crosstabulations into one with Male, Female as the row labels and the column labels Too Fast and Fine. Which group shows the highest percentage saying that the greens are too fast?

b. Refer to the initial crosstabulations. For those players with handicaps under 15 (better players), which group (male or female) shows the highest percentage saying the greens are too fast?

c. Refer to the initial crosstabulations. For those players with handicaps 15 or more, which group (male or female) shows the highest percentage saying the greens are too fast?

d. What conclusions can you draw about the preferences of men and women concerning the speed of the greens? Are the conclusions you draw from part (a) as compared with parts (b) and (c) consistent? Explain any apparent inconsistencies.

34. Table 2.14 provides financial data for a sample of 36 companies whose stock trades on the New York Stock Exchange (*Investor's Business Daily,* April 7, 2000). The data on Sales/Margins/ROE are a composite rating based on a company's sales growth rate, its profit margins, and its return on equity (ROE). EPS Rating is a measure of growth in earnings per share for the company.

a. Prepare a crosstabulation of the data on Sales/Margins/ROE (rows) and EPS Rating (columns). Use classes of 0–19, 20–39, 40–59, 60–79, and 80–99 for EPS Rating.

b. Compute row percentages and comment on any relationship between the variables.

35. Refer to the data in Table 2.14.

a. Prepare a crosstabulation of the data on Sales/Margins/ROE and Industry Group Relative Strength.

b. Prepare a frequency distribution for the data on Sales/Margins/ROE.

c. Prepare a frequency distribution for the data on Industry Group Relative Strength.

d. How has the crosstabulation helped in preparing the frequency distributions in parts (b) and (c)?

36. Refer to the data in Table 2.14.

a. Prepare a scatter diagram of the data on EPS Rating and Relative Price Strength.

b. Comment on the relationship, if any, between the variables. (The meaning of the EPS Rating is described in exercise 34. Relative Price Strength is a measure of the change in the stock's price over the past 12 months. Higher values indicate greater strength.)

TABLE 2.14   FINANCIAL DATA FOR A SAMPLE OF 36 COMPANIES

IBD

Company	EPS Rating	Relative Price Strength	Industry Group Relative Strength	Sales/Margins/ ROE
Advo	81	74	B	A
Alaska Air Group	58	17	C	B
Alliant Tech	84	22	B	B
Atmos Energy	21	9	C	E
Bank of Am.	87	38	C	A
Bowater PLC	14	46	C	D
Callaway Golf	46	62	B	E
Central Parking	76	18	B	C
Dean Foods	84	7	B	C
Dole Food	70	54	E	C
Elec. Data Sys.	72	69	A	B
Fed. Dept. Store	79	21	D	B
Gateway	82	68	A	A
Goodyear	21	9	E	D
Hanson PLC	57	32	B	B
ICN Pharm.	76	56	A	D
Jefferson PLC	80	38	D	C
Kroger	84	24	D	A
Mattel	18	20	E	D
McDermott	6	6	A	C
Monaco	97	21	D	A
Murphy Oil	80	62	B	B
Nordstrom	58	57	B	C
NYMAGIC	17	45	D	D
Office Depot	58	40	B	B
Payless Shoes	76	59	B	B
Praxair	62	32	C	B
Reebok	31	72	C	E
Safeway	91	61	D	A
Teco Energy	49	48	D	B
Texaco	80	31	D	C
US West	60	65	B	A
United Rental	98	12	C	A
Wachovia	69	36	E	B
Winnebago	83	49	D	A
York International	28	14	D	B

Source: Investor's Business Daily, April 7, 2000.

37. The National Football League rates prospects by position on a scale that ranges from 5 to 9. The ratings are interpreted as follows: 8–9 should start the first year; 7.0–7.9 should start; 6.0–6.9 will make the team as a backup; and 5.0–5.9 can make the club and contribute. Table 2.15 shows the position, weight, speed (seconds for 40 yards), and ratings for 40 NFL prospects (*USA Today*, April 14, 2000).

a. Prepare a crosstabulation of the data on Position (rows) and Speed (columns). Use classes of 4.00–4.49, 4.50–4.99, 5.00–5.49, and 5.50–5.99 for speed.

b. Comment on the relationship between Position and Speed based upon the crosstabulation developed in part (a).

c. Develop a scatter diagram of the data on Speed and Rating. Use the vertical axis for Rating.

d. Comment on the relationship, if any, between Speed and Rating.

TABLE 2.15   NATIONAL FOOTBALL LEAGUE RATINGS FOR 40 DRAFT PROSPECTS

NFL

Observation	Name	Position	Weight	Speed	Rating
1	Peter Warrick	Wide receiver	194	4.53	9
2	Plaxico Burress	Wide receiver	231	4.52	8.8
3	Sylvester Morris	Wide receiver	216	4.59	8.3
4	Travis Taylor	Wide receiver	199	4.36	8.1
5	Laveranues Coles	Wide receiver	192	4.29	8
6	Dez White	Wide receiver	218	4.49	7.9
7	Jerry Porter	Wide receiver	221	4.55	7.4
8	Ron Dugans	Wide receiver	206	4.47	7.1
9	Todd Pinkston	Wide receiver	169	4.37	7
10	Dennis Northcutt	Wide receiver	175	4.43	7
11	Anthony Lucas	Wide receiver	194	4.51	6.9
12	Darrell Jackson	Wide receiver	197	4.56	6.6
13	Danny Farmer	Wide receiver	217	4.6	6.5
14	Sherrod Gideon	Wide receiver	173	4.57	6.4
15	Trevor Gaylor	Wide receiver	199	4.57	6.2
16	Cosey Coleman	Guard	322	5.38	7.4
17	Travis Claridge	Guard	303	5.18	7
18	Kaulana Noa	Guard	317	5.34	6.8
19	Leander Jordan	Guard	330	5.46	6.7
20	Chad Clifton	Guard	334	5.18	6.3
21	Manula Savea	Guard	308	5.32	6.1
22	Ryan Johanningmeir	Guard	310	5.28	6
23	Mark Tauscher	Guard	318	5.37	6
24	Blaine Saipaia	Guard	321	5.25	6
25	Richard Mercier	Guard	295	5.34	5.8
26	Damion McIntosh	Guard	328	5.31	5.3
27	Jeno James	Guard	320	5.64	5
28	Al Jackson	Guard	304	5.2	5
29	Chris Samuels	Offensive tackle	325	4.95	8.5
30	Stockar McDougle	Offensive tackle	361	5.5	8
31	Chris McIngosh	Offensive tackle	315	5.39	7.8
32	Adrian Klemm	Offensive tackle	307	4.98	7.6
33	Todd Wade	Offensive tackle	326	5.2	7.3
34	Marvel Smith	Offensive tackle	320	5.36	7.1
35	Michael Thompson	Offensive tackle	287	5.05	6.8
36	Bobby Williams	Offensive tackle	332	5.26	6.8
37	Darnell Alford	Offensive tackle	334	5.55	6.4
38	Terrance Beadles	Offensive tackle	312	5.15	6.3
39	Tutan Reyes	Offensive tackle	299	5.35	6.1
40	Greg Robinson-Ran	Offensive tackle	333	5.59	6

Summary

A set of data, even if modest in size, is often difficult to interpret directly in the form in which it is gathered. Tabular and graphical methods provide procedures for organizing and summarizing data so that patterns are revealed and the data are more easily interpreted. Frequency distributions, relative frequency distributions, percent frequency distributions, bar graphs, and pie charts were presented as tabular and graphical procedures for summarizing qualitative data. Frequency distributions, relative frequency distributions, percent frequency distributions, histograms, cumulative frequency distributions, cumulative relative frequency distributions, cumulative percent frequency distributions, and ogives were presented as ways of summarizing quantitative data. A stem-and-leaf display provides an exploratory data analysis technique that can be used to summarize quantitative data. Cross-tabulation was presented as a tabular method for summarizing data for two variables. The scatter diagram was introduced as a graphical method for showing the relationship between two quantitative variables. Figure 2.26 shows the tabular and graphical methods presented in this chapter.

For most of the statistical methods introduced, we showed how they can be implemented using Excel. The COUNTIF and FREQUENCY functions can be used to construct frequency distributions for a single variable, and the PivotTable Report can be used to prepare a crosstabulation for a two-variable data set. The Chart Wizard provides extensive graphical presentations. We showed how it can be used to construct bar graphs, pie charts, histograms, and scatter diagrams. We also showed how to use the Histogram tool to construct a frequency distribution and a histogram for quantitative data.

If you have trouble recalling which Excel function to use in a particular situation, or have difficulty using a function, Excel's Insert Function dialog box has been designed to provide help. We describe how to use it in Appendix E: Using Excel Functions.

FIGURE 2.26   TABULAR AND GRAPHICAL METHODS FOR SUMMARIZING DATA

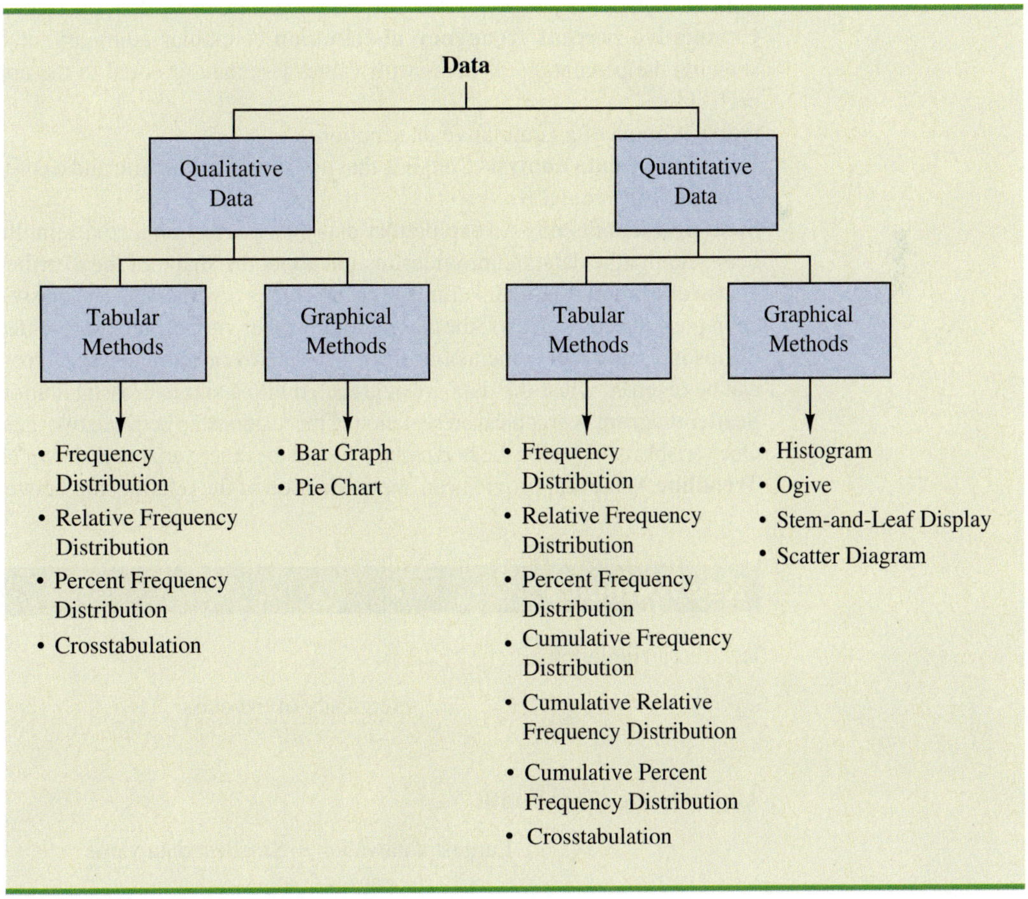

Glossary

Qualitative data Labels or names used to identify categories of like items.

Quantitative data Numerical values that indicate how much or how many.

Frequency distribution A tabular summary of data showing the number (frequency) of items in each of several nonoverlapping classes.

Relative frequency distribution A tabular summary of data showing the fraction or proportion of items in each of several nonoverlapping classes.

Percent frequency distribution A tabular summary of data showing the percentage of items in each of several nonoverlapping classes.

Bar graph A graphical device for depicting qualitative data that have been summarized in a frequency, relative frequency, or percent frequency distribution.

Pie chart A graphical device for presenting data summaries based on subdivision of a circle into sectors that correspond to the relative frequency for each class.

Class midpoint The value halfway between the lower and upper class limits.

Histogram A graphical presentation of a frequency distribution, relative frequency distribution, or percent frequency distribution of quantitative data constructed by placing the class intervals on the horizontal axis and the frequencies, relative frequencies, or percent frequencies on the vertical axis.

Cumulative frequency distribution A tabular summary of quantitative data showing the number of items with values less than or equal to the upper class limit of each class.

Cumulative relative frequency distribution A tabular summary of quantitative data showing the fraction or proportion of items with values less than or equal to the upper class limit of each class.

Cumulative percent frequency distribution A tabular summary of quantitative data showing the percentage of items with values less than or equal to the upper class limit of each class.

Ogive A graph of a cumulative distribution.

Exploratory data analysis Methods that use simple arithmetic and easy-to-draw graphs to summarize data quickly.

Stem-and-leaf display An exploratory data analysis technique that simultaneously rank orders quantitative data and provides insight about the shape of the distribution.

Crosstabulation A tabular summary of data for two variables. The classes for one variable are represented by the rows; the classes for the other variable are represented by the columns.

Simpson's paradox Conclusions drawn from two or more separate crosstabulations that can be reversed when the data are aggregated into a single crosstabulation.

Scatter diagram A graphical presentation of the relationship between two quantitative variables. One variable is shown on the horizontal axis and the other variable is shown on the vertical axis.

Trendline A line that provides an approximation of the relationship between two variables.

Key Formulas

Relative Frequency

$$\frac{\text{Frequency of the class}}{n} \tag{2.1}$$

Approximate Class Width

$$\frac{\text{Largest data value} - \text{Smallest data value}}{\text{Number of classes}} \tag{2.2}$$

Supplementary Exercises

38. The five top-selling vehicles during 2003 were the Chevrolet Silverado/C/K pickup, Dodge Ram pickup, Ford F-Series pickup, Honda Accord, and Toyota Camry (*Motor Trend,* 2003). Data from a sample of 50 vehicle purchases are presented in Table 2.16.

TABLE 2.16   DATA FOR 50 VEHICLE PURCHASES

CD file

AutoData

Silverado	Ram	Accord	Camry	Camry
Silverado	Silverado	Camry	Ram	F-Series
Ram	F-Series	Accord	Ram	Ram
Silverado	F-Series	F-Series	Silverado	Ram
Ram	Ram	Accord	Silverado	Camry
F-Series	Ram	Silverado	Accord	Silverado
Camry	F-Series	F-Series	F-Series	Silverado
F-Series	Silverado	F-Series	F-Series	Ram
Silverado	Silverado	Camry	Camry	F-Series
Silverado	F-Series	F-Series	Accord	Accord

a. Develop a frequency and percent frequency distribution.
b. What is the best-selling pickup truck, and what is the best-selling passenger car?
c. Show a pie chart.

39. Each of the *Fortune* 1000 companies belongs to one of several industry classifications (*Fortune,* April 17, 2000). A sample of 20 companies with their corresponding industry classification follows.

Company	Industry Classification
IBP	Food
Intel	Electronics
Coca-Cola	Beverage
Union Carbide	Chemicals
General Electric	Electronics
Motorola	Electronics
Kellogg	Food
Dow Chemical	Chemicals
Campbell Soup	Food
Ralston Purina	Food
Borden	Food
McDonnell Douglas	Aerospace
Morton International	Chemicals
Quaker Oats	Food
PepsiCo	Beverage
Maytag	Electronics
Textron	Aerospace
Sara Lee	Food
Harris	Electronics
Eaton	Electronics

a. Provide a frequency distribution showing the number of companies in each industry.
b. Provide a percent frequency distribution.
c. Provide a bar graph for the data.

40. *Golf Magazine*'s Top 100 Teachers were asked the question, "What is the most critical area that prevents golfers from reaching their potential?" The possible responses were lack of accuracy, poor approach shots, poor mental approach, lack of power, limited practice, poor putting, poor short game, and poor strategic decisions. The data obtained follow (*Golf Magazine*, February 2002):

Golf

Mental approach	Mental approach	Short game	Short game	Short game
Practice	Accuracy	Mental approach	Accuracy	Putting
Power	Approach shots	Accuracy	Short game	Putting
Accuracy	Mental approach	Mental approach	Accuracy	Power
Accuracy	Accuracy	Short game	Power	Short game
Accuracy	Putting	Mental approach	Strategic decisions	Accuracy
Short game	Power	Mental approach	Approach shots	Short game
Practice	Practice	Mental approach	Power	Power
Mental approach	Short game	Mental approach	Short game	Strategic decisions
Accuracy	Short game	Accuracy	Mental approach	Short game
Mental approach	Putting	Mental approach	Mental approach	Putting
Practice	Putting	Practice	Short game	Putting
Power	Mental approach	Short game	Practice	Strategic decisions
Accuracy	Short game	Accuracy	Practice	Putting
Accuracy	Short game	Accuracy	Short game	Putting
Accuracy	Approach shots	Short game	Mental approach	Practice
Short game	Short game	Strategic decisions	Short game	Short game
Practice	Practice	Short game	Practice	Strategic decisions
Mental approach	Strategic decisions	Strategic decisions	Power	Short game
Accuracy	Practice	Practice	Practice	Accuracy

a. Develop a frequency and percent frequency distribution.
b. Which four critical areas most often prevent golfers from reaching their potential?

41. The data in Table 2.17 show the book value per share for the 30 stocks that compose the Dow Jones Industrial Average (*Barron's,* March 10, 2003).
   a. Construct a frequency distribution to summarize the data. Use a class width of 6.00.
   b. Develop a relative frequency distribution.

TABLE 2.17   BOOK VALUE PER SHARE FOR DOW JONES INDUSTRIAL AVERAGE STOCKS

Dow

Company	Book Value per Share	Company	Book Value per Share
AT&T	14.59	Home Depot	7.71
Alcoa	12.30	Honeywell	11.25
Altria Group	8.96	IBM	13.37
American Express	9.04	Intel	5.39
Boeing	12.92	International Paper	21.37
Caterpillar	16.18	Johnson & Johnson	7.79
Citigroup	15.09	J.P. Morgan Chase	20.31
Coca-Cola	4.57	McDonald's	7.30
Disney	11.28	Merck	6.89
DuPont	14.17	Microsoft	8.49
Eastman Kodak	9.93	Procter & Gamble	8.80
ExxonMobil	10.62	SBE Communications	9.69
General Electric	5.43	3M	14.93
General Motors	35.15	United Technologies	17.36
Hewlett-Packard	7.33	Wal-Mart Stores	7.85

   c. Construct a cumulative frequency distribution.

   d. Construct a cumulative relative frequency distribution.

   e. Construct a histogram as a graphical representation of the data. Comment on the shape of the distribution.

42. The closing prices of 40 common stocks follow (*Barron's,* January 3, 2005).

Comstock

29.63	34.00	43.25	8.75	37.88	8.63	7.63	30.38	35.25	19.38
9.25	16.50	38.00	53.38	16.63	1.25	48.38	18.00	9.38	9.25
10.00	25.02	18.00	8.00	28.50	24.25	21.63	18.50	33.63	31.13
32.25	29.63	79.38	11.38	38.88	11.50	52.00	14.00	9.00	33.50

   a. Construct frequency and relative frequency distributions.

   b. Construct cumulative frequency and cumulative relative frequency distributions.

   c. Construct a histogram.

   d. Using your summaries, make comments and observations about the price of common stock.

43. Ninety-four shadow stocks were reported by the American Association of Individual Investors. The term *shadow* indicates stocks for small to medium-sized firms not followed closely by the major brokerage houses. Information on where the stock was traded—New York Stock Exchange (NYSE), American Stock Exchange (AMEX), and over-the-counter (OTC)—the earnings per share, and the price/earnings ratio were provided for the following sample of 20 shadow stocks.

Shadow

Stock	Exchange	Earnings per Share ($)	Price/Earnings Ratio
Chemi-Trol	OTC	.39	27.30
Candie's	OTC	.07	36.20
TST/Impreso	OTC	.65	12.70
Unimed Pharm.	OTC	.12	59.30
Skyline Chili	AMEX	.34	19.30
Cyanotech	OTC	.22	29.30
Catalina Light.	NYSE	.15	33.20
DDL Elect.	NYSE	.10	10.20
Euphonix	OTC	.09	49.70
Mesa Labs	OTC	.37	14.40
RCM Tech.	OTC	.47	18.60
Anuhco	AMEX	.70	11.40
Hello Direct	OTC	.23	21.10
Hilite Industries	OTC	.61	7.80
Alpha Tech.	OTC	.11	34.60
Wegener Group	OTC	.16	24.50
U.S. Home & Garden	OTC	.24	8.70
Chalone Wine	OTC	.27	44.40
Eng. Support Sys.	OTC	.89	16.70
Int. Remote Imaging	AMEX	.86	4.70

   a. Provide frequency and relative frequency distributions for the exchange data. Where are most shadow stocks listed?

   b. Provide frequency and relative frequency distributions for the earnings per share and price/earnings ratio data. Use classes of 0.00–0.19, 0.20–0.39, and so on, for the earnings per share data and classes of 0.0–9.9, 10.0–19.9, and so on for the price/earnings ratio data. What observations and comments can you make about the shadow stocks?

44. A state-by-state listing of per capita personal income follows (Bureau of Economic Analysis, *Current Population Survey,* March 2000).

Income

Ala.	21,500	Ky.	21,551	N.D.	21,708
Alaska	25,771	La.	21,385	Ohio	25,239
Ariz.	23,152	Maine	23,002	Okla.	21,056
Ark.	20,393	Md.	30,023	Ore.	24,775
Calif.	27,579	Mass.	32,902	Penn.	26,889
Colo.	28,821	Mich.	25,979	R.I.	26,924
Conn.	37,700	Minn.	27,667	S.C.	21,387
Del.	29,932	Miss.	18,998	S.D.	22,201
D.C.	37,325	Mo.	24,447	Tenn.	23,615
Fla.	25,922	Mont.	20,427	Texas	25,028
Ga.	25,106	Neb.	24,786	Utah	21,096
Hawaii	26,210	Nev.	27,360	Vt.	24,217
Idaho	21,080	N.H.	29,219	Va.	27,489
Ill.	28,976	N.J.	33,953	Wash.	28,066
Ind.	24,302	N.M.	20,008	W. Va.	19,373
Iowa	24,007	N.Y.	31,679	Wis.	25,184
Kan.	25,049	N.C.	24,122	Wyo.	23,225

Develop a frequency distribution, a relative frequency distribution, and a histogram.

45. *Drug Store News* (September 2002) provided data on annual pharmacy sales for the leading pharmacy retailers in the United States. The following data are annual sales in millions.

Retailer	Sales	Retailer	Sales
Ahold USA	$ 1700	Medicine Shoppe	$ 1757
CVS	12700	Rite-Aid	8637
Eckerd	7739	Safeway	2150
Kmart	1863	Walgreens	11660
Kroger	3400	Wal-Mart	7250

a. Show a stem-and-leaf display.
b. Identify the annual sales levels for the smallest, median, and largest drug retailers.
c. What are the two largest drug retailers?

46. The daily high and low temperatures for 20 cities follow (*USA Today,* May 9, 2000).

HighLow

City	High	Low	City	High	Low
Athens	75	54	Melbourne	66	50
Bangkok	92	74	Montreal	64	52
Cairo	84	57	Paris	77	55
Copenhagen	64	39	Rio de Janeiro	80	61
Dublin	64	46	Rome	81	54
Havana	86	68	Seoul	64	50
Hong Kong	81	72	Singapore	90	75
Johannesburg	61	50	Sydney	68	55
London	73	48	Tokyo	79	59
Manila	93	75	Vancouver	57	43

a. Prepare a stem-and-leaf display for the high temperatures.
b. Prepare a stem-and-leaf display for the low temperatures.

c. Compare the stem-and-leaf displays from parts (a) and (b), and make some comments about the differences between daily high and low temperatures.

d. Use the stem-and-leaf display from part (a) to determine the number of cities having a high temperature of 80 degrees or above.

e. Provide frequency distributions for both high and low temperature data.

47. Refer to the data set in exercise 46.

a. Develop a scatter diagram to show the relationship between the two variables, high temperature and low temperature.

b. Comment on the relationship between high and low temperatures.

48. A study of job satisfaction was conducted for four occupations. Job satisfaction was measured using an 18-item questionnaire with each question receiving a response score of 1 to 5 with higher scores indicating greater satisfaction. The sum of the 18 scores provides the job satisfaction score for each individual in the sample. The data are as follow.

CD file

OccupSat

Occupation	Satisfaction Score	Occupation	Satisfaction Score	Occupation	Satisfaction Score
Lawyer	42	Physical Therapist	78	Systems Analyst	60
Physical Therapist	86	Systems Analyst	44	Physical Therapist	59
Lawyer	42	Systems Analyst	71	Cabinetmaker	78
Systems Analyst	55	Lawyer	50	Physical Therapist	60
Lawyer	38	Lawyer	48	Physical Therapist	50
Cabinetmaker	79	Cabinetmaker	69	Cabinetmaker	79
Lawyer	44	Physical Therapist	80	Systems Analyst	62
Systems Analyst	41	Systems Analyst	64	Lawyer	45
Physical Therapist	55	Physical Therapist	55	Cabinetmaker	84
Systems Analyst	66	Cabinetmaker	64	Physical Therapist	62
Lawyer	53	Cabinetmaker	59	Systems Analyst	73
Cabinetmaker	65	Cabinetmaker	54	Cabinetmaker	60
Lawyer	74	Systems Analyst	76	Lawyer	64
Physical Therapist	52				

a. Provide a crosstabulation of occupation and job satisfaction score.

b. Compute the row percentages for your crosstabulation in part (a).

c. What observations can you make concerning the level of job satisfaction for these occupations?

49. Do larger companies generate more revenue? The following data show the number of employees and annual revenue for a sample of 20 *Fortune* 1000 companies (*Fortune,* April 17, 2000).

CD file

RevEmps

Company	Employees	Revenue ($ millions)	Company	Employees	Revenue ($ millions)
Sprint	77,600	19,930	American Financial	9,400	3,334
Chase Manhattan	74,801	33,710	Fluor	53,561	12,417
Computer Sciences	50,000	7,660	Phillips Petroleum	15,900	13,852
Wells Fargo	89,355	21,795	Cardinal Health	36,000	25,034
Sunbeam	12,200	2,398	Borders Group	23,500	2,999
CBS	29,000	7,510	MCI Worldcom	77,000	37,120
Time Warner	69,722	27,333	Consolidated Edison	14,269	7,491
Steelcase	16,200	2,743	IBP	45,000	14,075
Georgia-Pacific	57,000	17,796	Super Value	50,000	17,421
Toro	1,275	4,673	H&R Block	4,200	1,669

a. Prepare a scatter diagram to show the relationship between the variables Revenue and Employees.
b. Comment on any relationship between the variables.

50. A survey of commercial buildings served by the Cincinnati Gas & Electric Company asked what main heating fuel was used and what year the building was constructed. A partial crosstabulation of the findings follows.

Year Constructed	Fuel Type				
	Electricity	Natural Gas	Oil	Propane	Other
1973 or before	40	183	12	5	7
1974–1979	24	26	2	2	0
1980–1986	37	38	1	0	6
1987–1991	48	70	2	0	1

a. Complete the crosstabulation by showing the row totals and column totals.
b. Show the frequency distributions for year constructed and for fuel type.
c. Prepare a crosstabulation showing column percentages.
d. Prepare a crosstabulation showing row percentages.
e. Comment on the relationship between year constructed and fuel type.

51. Table 2.18 contains a portion of the data on the file named Fortune on the CD that accompanies the text. It provides data on stockholders' equity, market value, and profits for a sample of 50 *Fortune* 500 companies.
a. Prepare a crosstabulation for the variables Stockholders' Equity and Profit. Use classes of 0–200, 200–400, . . . , 1000–1200 for Profit, and classes of 0–1200, 1200–2400, . . . , 4800–6000 for Stockholders' Equity.
b. Compute the row percentages for your crosstabulation in part (a).
c. What relationship, if any, do you notice between Profit and Stockholders' Equity?

52. Refer to the data set in Table 2.18.
a. Prepare a crosstabulation for the variables Market Value and Profit.
b. Compute the row percentages for your crosstabulation in part (a).
c. Comment on any relationship between the variables.

TABLE 2.18   DATA FOR A SAMPLE OF 50 *FORTUNE* 500 COMPANIES

Fortune

Company	Stockholders' Equity ($1000s)	Market Value ($1000s)	Profit ($1000s)
AGCO	982.1	372.1	60.6
AMP	2698.0	12017.6	2.0
Apple Computer	1642.0	4605.0	309.0
Baxter International	2839.0	21743.0	315.0
Bergen Brunswick	629.1	2787.5	3.1
Best Buy	557.7	10376.5	94.5
Charles Schwab	1429.0	35340.6	348.5
.	.	.	.
.	.	.	.
.	.	.	.
Walgreen	2849.0	30324.7	511.0
Westvaco	2246.4	2225.6	132.0
Whirlpool	2001.0	3729.4	325.0
Xerox	5544.0	35603.7	395.0

53. Refer to the data set in Table 2.18.
    a. Prepare a scatter diagram to show the relationship between the variables Profit and Stockholders' Equity.
    b. Comment on any relationship between the variables.

54. Refer to the data set in Table 2.18.
    a. Prepare a scatter diagram to show the relationship between the variables Market Value and Stockholders' Equity.
    b. Comment on any relationship between the variables.

Case Problem   Pelican Stores

Pelican Stores, a division of National Clothing, is a chain of women's apparel stores operating throughout the country. The chain recently ran a promotion in which discount coupons were sent to customers of other National Clothing stores. Data collected for a sample of 100 in-store credit card transactions at Pelican Stores during one day while the promotion was running are contained in the file named PelicanStores. Table 2.19 shows a portion of the data set. The Proprietary Card method of payment refers to charges made using a National Clothing charge card. Customers who made a purchase using a discount coupon are referred to as promotional customers and customers who made a purchase but did not use a discount coupon are referred to as regular customers. Because the promotional coupons were not sent to regular Pelican Stores customers, management considers the sales made to people presenting the promotional coupons as sales it would not otherwise make. Of course, Pelican also hopes that the promotional customers will continue to shop at its stores.

Most of the variables shown in Table 2.19 are self-explanatory, but two of the variables require some clarification.

Items   The total number of items purchased
Net Sales   The total amount ($) charged to the credit card

Pelican's management would like to use this sample data to learn about its customer base and to evaluate the promotion involving discount coupons.

TABLE 2.19   DATA FOR A SAMPLE OF 100 CREDIT CARD PURCHASES AT PELICAN STORES

PelicanStores

Customer	Type of Customer	Items	Net Sales	Method of Payment	Gender	Marital Status	Age
1	Regular	1	39.50	Discover	Male	Married	32
2	Promotional	1	102.40	Proprietary Card	Female	Married	36
3	Regular	1	22.50	Proprietary Card	Female	Married	32
4	Promotional	5	100.40	Proprietary Card	Female	Married	28
5	Regular	2	54.00	MasterCard	Female	Married	34
.	.	.	.	.	.	.	.
.	.	.	.	.	.	.	.
.	.	.	.	.	.	.	.
96	Regular	1	39.50	MasterCard	Female	Married	44
97	Promotional	9	253.00	Proprietary Card	Female	Married	30
98	Promotional	10	287.59	Proprietary Card	Female	Married	52
99	Promotional	2	47.60	Proprietary Card	Female	Married	30
100	Promotional	1	28.44	Proprietary Card	Female	Married	44

Managerial Report

Use the tabular and graphical methods of descriptive statistics to help management develop a customer profile and to evaluate the promotional campaign. At a minimum, your report should include the following:

1. Percent frequency distribution for key variables.
2. A bar graph or pie chart showing the number of customer purchases attributable to the method of payment.
3. A crosstabulation of type of customer (regular or promotional) versus net sales. Comment on any similarities or differences present.
4. A scatter diagram to explore the relationship between net sales and customer age.

CHAPTER 3

Descriptive Statistics: Numerical Measures

CONTENTS

STATISTICS IN PRACTICE:
SMALL FRY DESIGN

3.1 MEASURES OF LOCATION
Mean
Median
Mode
Using Excel to Compute the
    Mean, Median, and Mode
Percentiles
Quartiles
Using Excel's Rank and
    Percentile Tool to Compute
    Percentiles and Quartiles

3.2 MEASURES OF VARIABILITY
Range
Interquartile Range
Variance
Standard Deviation
Using Excel to Compute the
    Sample Variance and Sample
    Standard Deviation
Coefficient of Variation
Using Excel's Descriptive
    Statistics Tool

3.3 MEASURES OF
DISTRIBUTION SHAPE,
RELATIVE LOCATION, AND
DETECTING OUTLIERS
Distribution Shape

z-Scores
Chebyshev's Theorem
Empirical Rule
Detecting Outliers

3.4 EXPLORATORY DATA
ANALYSIS
Five-Number Summary
Box Plot

3.5 MEASURES OF
ASSOCIATION BETWEEN
TWO VARIABLES
Covariance
Interpretation of the Covariance
Correlation Coefficient
Interpretation of the Correlation
    Coefficient
Using Excel to Compute the
    Covariance and Correlation
    Coefficient

3.6 THE WEIGHTED MEAN AND
WORKING WITH GROUPED
DATA
Weighted Mean
Grouped Data

SMALL FRY DESIGN*
SANTA ANA, CALIFORNIA

Founded in 1997, Small Fry Design is a toy and accessory company that designs and imports products for infants. The company's product line includes teddy bears, mobiles, musical toys, rattles, and security blankets and features high-quality soft toy designs with an emphasis on color, texture, and sound. The products are designed in the United States and manufactured in China.

Small Fry Design uses independent representatives to sell the products to infant furnishing retailers, children's accessory and apparel stores, gift shops, upscale department stores, and major catalog companies. Currently, Small Fry Design products are distributed in more than 1000 retail outlets throughout the United States.

Cash flow management is one of the most critical activities in the day-to-day operation of this company. Ensuring sufficient incoming cash to meet both current and ongoing debt obligations can mean the difference between business success and failure. A critical factor in cash flow management is the analysis and control of accounts receivable. By measuring the average age and dollar value of outstanding invoices, management can predict cash availability and monitor changes in the status of accounts receivable. The company set the following goals: the average age for outstanding invoices should not exceed 45 days, and the dollar value of invoices more than 60 days old should not exceed 5% of the dollar value of all accounts receivable.

In a recent summary of accounts receivable status, the following descriptive statistics were provided for the age of outstanding invoices:

Mean	40 days
Median	35 days
Mode	31 days

A new Small Fry Design mobile. © Photo courtesy of Small Fry Design, Inc.

Interpretation of these statistics shows that the mean or average age of an invoice is 40 days. The median shows that half of the invoices remain outstanding 35 days or more. The mode of 31 days, the most frequent invoice age, indicates that the most common length of time an invoice is outstanding is 31 days. The statistical summary also showed that only 3% of the dollar value of all accounts receivable was more than 60 days old. Based on the statistical information, management was satisfied that accounts receivable and incoming cash flow were under control.

In this chapter, you will learn how to compute and interpret some of the statistical measures used by Small Fry Design. In addition to the mean, median, and mode, you will learn about other descriptive statistics such as the range, variance, standard deviation, percentiles, and correlation. These numerical measures will assist in the understanding and interpretation of data.

*The authors are indebted to John A. McCarthy, President of Small Fry Design, for providing this Statistics in Practice.

In Chapter 2 we discussed tabular and graphical presentations used to summarize data. In this chapter, we present several numerical measures that provide additional alternatives for summarizing data.

We start by developing numerical summary measures for data sets consisting of a single variable. When a data set contains more than one variable, the same numerical measures can be computed separately for each variable. However, in the two-variable case, we will also develop measures of the relationship between the variables.

Numerical measures of location, dispersion, shape, and association are introduced. If the measures are computed for data from a sample, they are called **sample statistics**. If the measures are computed for data from a population, they are called **population parameters**. In statistical inference, a sample statistic is referred to as the **point estimator** of the corresponding population parameter. In Chapter 7 we will discuss in more detail the process of point estimation.

Several more of Excel's statistical functions are introduced in this chapter. In most cases we introduce them with little digression from the flow of the statistical material. But, at the end of Section 3.2, we pause to show how Excel's Descriptive Statistics tool can be used to perform the work of several functions by providing a summary of the most commonly used descriptive statistics. If you experience trouble using any of the statistical functions, recall that Excel's Insert Function dialog box is designed to provide help (see Appendix E: Using Excel Functions).

3.1 Measures of Location

Mean

Perhaps the most important measure of location is the **mean**, or average value, for a variable. The mean provides a measure of central location for the data. If the data are from a sample, the mean is denoted by $\bar{x}$; if the data are from a population, the mean is denoted by the Greek letter μ (mu).

In statistical formulas, it is customary to denote the value of variable x for the first observation by x_1, the value of variable x for the second observation by x_2, and so on. In general, the value of variable x for the ith observation is denoted by x_i. For a sample with n observations, the formula for the sample mean is as follows.

The sample mean $\bar{x}$ is a sample statistic.

SAMPLE MEAN

$$\bar{x} = \frac{\Sigma x_i}{n}$$

(3.1)

In the preceding formula, the numerator is the sum of the values of the n observations. That is,

$$\Sigma x_i = x_1 + x_2 + \cdots + x_n$$

The Greek letter Σ is the summation sign.

To illustrate the computation of a sample mean, let us consider the following class size data for a sample of five college classes.

$$46 \quad 54 \quad 42 \quad 46 \quad 32$$

We use the notation x_1, x_2, x_3, x_4, x_5 to represent the number of students in each of the five classes.

$$x_1 = 46 \qquad x_2 = 54 \qquad x_3 = 42 \qquad x_4 = 46 \qquad x_5 = 32$$

Hence, to compute the sample mean, we can write

$$\bar{x} = \frac{\Sigma x_i}{n} = \frac{x_1 + x_2 + x_3 + x_4 + x_5}{5} = \frac{46 + 54 + 42 + 46 + 32}{5} = 44$$

The sample mean class size is 44 students.

Another illustration of the computation of a sample mean is given in the following situation. Suppose that a college placement office sent a questionnaire to a sample of business

TABLE 3.1   MONTHLY STARTING SALARIES FOR A SAMPLE OF 12 BUSINESS SCHOOL
GRADUATES

Salary

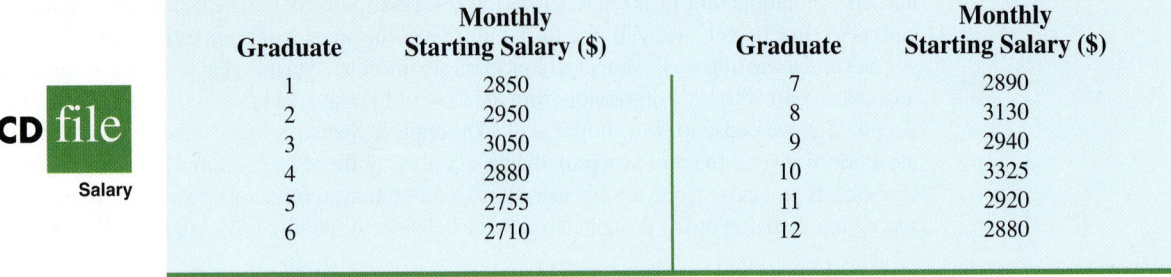

Graduate	Monthly Starting Salary ($)	Graduate	Monthly Starting Salary ($)
1	2850	7	2890
2	2950	8	3130
3	3050	9	2940
4	2880	10	3325
5	2755	11	2920
6	2710	12	2880

school graduates requesting information on monthly starting salaries. Table 3.1 shows the
collected data. The mean monthly starting salary for the sample of 12 business college
graduates is computed as

$$\bar{x} = \frac{\Sigma x_i}{n} = \frac{x_1 + x_2 + \cdots + x_{12}}{12}$$

$$= \frac{2850 + 2950 + \cdots + 2880}{12}$$

$$= \frac{35{,}280}{12} = 2940$$

Equation (3.1) shows how the mean is computed for a sample with n observations. The
formula for computing the mean of a population remains the same, but we use different notation to indicate that we are working with the entire population. The number of observations in a population is denoted by N and the symbol for a population mean is μ.

The sample mean $\bar{x}$ is a point estimator of the population mean μ.

POPULATION MEAN

$$\mu = \frac{\Sigma x_i}{N} \tag{3.2}$$

Median

The **median** is another measure of central location for a variable. The median is the value
in the middle when the data are arranged in ascending order (smallest value to largest
value). With an odd number of observations, the median is the middle value. An even number of observations has no single middle value. In this case, we follow convention and define the median as the average of the values for the middle two observations. For
convenience the definition of the median is restated as follows.

MEDIAN

Arrange the data in ascending order (smallest value to largest value).

(a) For an odd number of observations, the median is the middle value.
(b) For an even number of observations, the median is the average of the two middle values.

Let us apply this definition to compute the median class size for the sample of five college classes. Arranging the data in ascending order provides the following list.

$$32 \quad 42 \quad 46 \quad 46 \quad 54$$

Because $n = 5$ is odd, the median is the middle value. Thus the median class size is 46 students. Even though this data set contains two observations with values of 46, each observation is treated separately when we arrange the data in ascending order.

Suppose we also compute the median starting salary for the 12 business college graduates in Table 3.1. We first arrange the data in ascending order.

$$2710 \quad 2755 \quad 2850 \quad 2880 \quad 2880 \quad \underbrace{2890 \quad 2920}_{\text{Middle Two Values}} \quad 2940 \quad 2950 \quad 3050 \quad 3130 \quad 3325$$

Because $n = 12$ is even, we identify the middle two values: 2890 and 2920. The median is the average of these values.

$$\text{Median} = \frac{2890 + 2920}{2} = 2905$$

The median is the measure of location most often reported for annual income and property value data because a few extremely large incomes or property values can inflate the mean. In such cases, the median is the preferred measure of central location.

Although the mean is the more commonly used measure of central location, in some situations the median is preferred. The mean is influenced by extremely small and large data values. For instance, suppose that one of the graduates (see Table 3.1) had a starting salary of $10,000 per month (maybe the individual's family owns the company). If we change the highest monthly starting salary in Table 3.1 from $3325 to $10,000 and recompute the mean, the sample mean changes from $2940 to $3496. The median of $2905, however, is unchanged, because $2890 and $2920 are still the middle two values. With the extremely high starting salary included, the median provides a better measure of central location than the mean. We can generalize to say that whenever a data set contains extreme values, the median is often the preferred measure of central location.

Mode

A third measure of location is the **mode**. The mode is defined as follows.

MODE

The mode is the value that occurs with greatest frequency.

To illustrate the identification of the mode, consider the sample of five class sizes. The only value that occurs more than once is 46. Because this value, occurring with a frequency of 2, has the greatest frequency, it is the mode. As another illustration, consider the sample of starting salaries for the business school graduates. The only monthly starting salary that occurs more than once is $2880. Because this value has the greatest frequency, it is the mode.

Situations can arise for which the greatest frequency occurs at two or more different values. In these instances more than one mode exists. If the data contain exactly two modes, we say that the data are *bimodal*. If data contain more than two modes, we say that the data are *multimodal*. In multimodal cases the mode is almost never reported because listing three or more modes would not be particularly helpful in describing a location for the data.

The mode is an important measure of location for qualitative data. For example, the qualitative data set in Table 2.2 resulted in the following frequency distribution for soft drink purchases.

Soft Drink	Frequency
Coke Classic	19
Diet Coke	8
Dr. Pepper	5
Pepsi-Cola	13
Sprite	5
Total	50

The mode, or most frequently purchased soft drink, is Coke Classic. For this type of data it obviously makes no sense to speak of the mean or median. The mode provides the information of interest, the most frequently purchased soft drink.

Using Excel to Compute the Mean, Median, and Mode

Excel provides functions for computing the mean, median, and mode. We illustrate the use of these Excel functions by computing the mean, median, and mode for the starting salary data in Table 3.1. Refer to Figure 3.1 as we describe the tasks involved. The formula worksheet is in the background; the value worksheet is in the foreground.

FIGURE 3.1   EXCEL WORKSHEET USED TO COMPUTE THE MEAN, MEDIAN, AND MODE
FOR STARTING SALARIES

	A	B	C	D	E	F
1	Graduate	Starting Salary		Mean	=AVERAGE(B2:B13)	
2	1	2850		Median	=MEDIAN(B2:B13)	
3	2	2950		Mode	=MODE(B2:B13)	
4	3	3050				
5	4	2880				
6	5	2755				
7	6	2710				
8	7	2890				
9	8	3130				
10	9	2940				
11	10	3325				
12	11	2920				
13	12	2880				
14						

	A	B	C	D	E	F
1	Graduate	Starting Salary		Mean	2940	
2	1	2850		Median	2905	
3	2	2950		Mode	2880	
4	3	3050				
5	4	2880				
6	5	2755				
7	6	2710				
8	7	2890				
9	8	3130				
10	9	2940				
11	10	3325				
12	11	2920				
13	12	2880				
14						

Enter Data: Labels and the starting salary data are entered into cells A1:B13 of the worksheet.

Enter Functions and Formulas: Excel's AVERAGE function can be used to compute the mean by entering the following formula into cell E1:

$$=\text{AVERAGE(B2:B13)}$$

If the data are bimodal or multimodal, Excel's MODE function will incorrectly identify a single mode.

Similarly, the formulas =MEDIAN(B2:B13) and =MODE(B2:B13) are entered into cells E2 and E3, respectively, to compute the median and the mode. The labels Mean, Median, and Mode are entered into cells D1:D3 to identify the output.

The formulas in cells E1:E3 are displayed in the formula worksheet in the background of Figure 3.1. The worksheet in the foreground shows the values computed using the Excel functions. Note that the mean (2940), median (2905), and mode (2880) are the same as we computed earlier.

Percentiles

A **percentile** provides information about how the data are spread over the interval from the smallest value to the largest value. For data that do not contain numerous repeated values, the pth percentile divides the data into two parts. Approximately p percent of the observations have values less than the pth percentile; approximately $(100 - p)$ percent of the observations have values greater than the pth percentile. The pth percentile is formally defined as follows.

> **PERCENTILE**
>
> The pth percentile is a value such that *at least* p percent of the observations are less than or equal to this value and *at least* $(100 - p)$ percent of the observations are greater than or equal to this value.

Colleges and universities frequently report admission test scores in terms of percentiles. For instance, suppose an applicant obtains a raw score of 54 on the verbal portion of an admission test. How this student performed in relation to other students taking the same test may not be readily apparent. However, if the raw score of 54 corresponds to the 70th percentile, we know that approximately 70% of the students scored lower than this individual and approximately 30% of the students scored higher than this individual.

The following procedure can be used to compute the pth percentile.

> **CALCULATING THE pTH PERCENTILE**
>
> *Following these steps makes it easy to calculate percentiles.*
>
> **Step 1.** Arrange the data in ascending order (smallest value to largest value).
> **Step 2.** Compute an index i
>
> $$i = \left(\frac{p}{100}\right)n$$
>
> where p is the percentile of interest and n is the number of observations.

> **Step 3.** (a) If i *is not an integer, round up.* The next integer *greater* than i denotes the position of the pth percentile.
> (b) If i *is an integer,* the pth percentile is the average of the values in positions i and $i + 1$.

As an illustration of this procedure, let us determine the 85th percentile for the starting salary data in Table 3.1.

Step 1. Arrange the data in ascending order.

2710　2755　2850　2880　2880　2890　2920　2940　2950　3050　3130　3325

Step 2.

$$i = \left(\frac{p}{100}\right)n = \left(\frac{85}{100}\right)12 = 10.2$$

Step 3. Because i is not an integer, *round up*. The position of the 85th percentile is the next integer greater than 10.2, the 11th position.

Returning to the data, we see that the 85th percentile is the data value in the 11th position, or 3130.

As another illustration of this procedure, let us consider the calculation of the 50th percentile for the starting salary data. Applying step 2, we obtain

$$i = \left(\frac{50}{100}\right)12 = 6$$

Because i is an integer, step 3(b) states that the 50th percentile is the average of the sixth and seventh data values; thus, the 50th percentile is $(2890 + 2920)/2 = 2905$. Note that the *50th percentile is also the median.*

Quartiles

Quartiles are just specific percentiles; thus, the steps for computing percentiles can be applied directly in the computation of quartiles.

It is often desirable to divide data into four parts, with each part containing approximately one-fourth, or 25%, of the observations. Figure 3.2 shows a data distribution divided into four parts. The division points are referred to as the **quartiles** and are defined as

Q_1 = first quartile, or 25th percentile

Q_2 = second quartile, or 50th percentile (also the median)

Q_3 = third quartile, or 75th percentile

The starting salary data are again arranged in ascending order. We already identified Q_2, the second quartile (median), as 2905.

2710　2755　2850　2880　2880　2890　2920　2940　2950　3050　3130　3325

The computations of quartiles Q_1 and Q_3 require the use of the rule for finding the 25th and 75th percentiles. These calculations follow.

For Q_1,

$$i = \left(\frac{p}{100}\right)n = \left(\frac{25}{100}\right)12 = 3$$

FIGURE 3.2 LOCATION OF THE QUARTILES

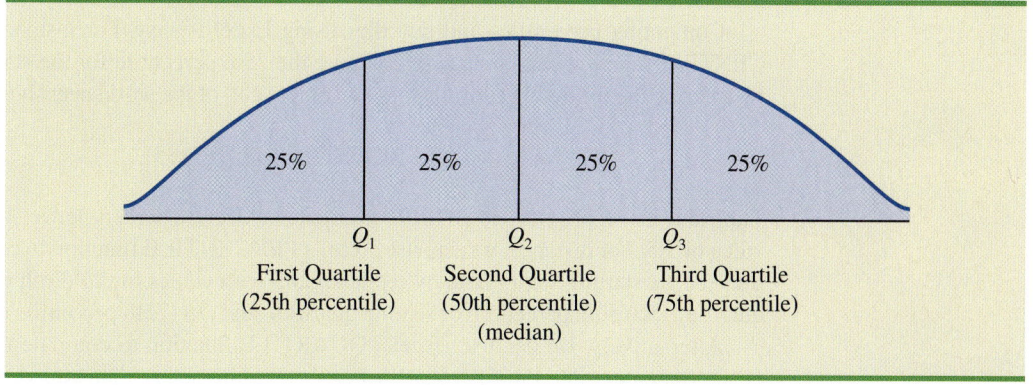

Because i is an integer, step 3(b) indicates that the first quartile, or 25th percentile, is the average of the third and fourth data values; thus, $Q_1 = (2850 + 2880)/2 = 2865$.

For Q_3,

$$i = \left(\frac{p}{100}\right)n = \left(\frac{75}{100}\right)12 = 9$$

Again, because i is an integer, step 3(b) indicates that the third quartile, or 75th percentile, is the average of the ninth and tenth data values; thus, $Q_3 = (2950 + 3050)/2 = 3000$.

The quartiles divide the starting salary data into four parts, with each part containing 25% of the observations.

$$2710 \quad 2755 \quad 2850 \mid 2880 \quad 2880 \quad 2890 \mid 2920 \quad 2940 \quad 2950 \mid 3050 \quad 3130 \quad 3325$$

$$Q_1 = 2865 \qquad\qquad Q_2 = 2905 \qquad\qquad Q_3 = 3000$$
$$\text{(Median)}$$

We defined the quartiles as the 25th, 50th, and 75th percentiles. Thus, we computed the quartiles in the same way as percentiles. However, other conventions are sometimes used to compute quartiles, and the actual values reported for quartiles may vary slightly depending on the convention used. Nevertheless, the objective of all procedures for computing quartiles is to divide the data into four equal parts.

Using Excel's Rank and Percentile Tool to Compute Percentiles and Quartiles

Computer software packages do not all use the same method to compute percentiles and quartiles. The formula Excel uses to compute the location (L_p) of the pth percentile is

$$L_p = \left(\frac{p}{100}\right)n + \left(1 - \frac{p}{100}\right)$$

For instance, Excel would compute the location of the 85th percentile for the starting salary data as follows:

$$L_{85} = (.85)12 + (1 - .85) = 10.20 + .15 = 10.35$$

The value of $L_{85} = 10.35$ indicates that the 85th percentile is between the 10th and the 11th observations in rank order from the bottom up. It is the value of observation 10 (3050) plus

.35 of the difference between observation 10 and observation 11 (3130). Therefore, the 85th percentile is $3050 + .35(3130 - 3050) = 3050 + .35(80) = 3078.$*

Computing percentiles and quartiles using Excel is easy. For instance, Excel's PERCENTILE function can be used to compute the 85th percentile for the starting salary data by entering the following formula into any empty cell of the worksheet shown in Figure 3.1:

$$=\text{PERCENTILE(B2:B13,.85)}$$

The value Excel provides is 3078. To compute a different percentile we simply change the value of .85. For instance, we can use Excel's PERCENTILE function to compute the quartiles for the starting salary data by replacing .85 with values of .25 (25th percentile or first quartile), .50 (50th percentile or second quartile), and .75 (75th percentile or third quartile).

Alternatively, we can use Excel's QUARTILE function to compute the quartiles. For example, to compute the first quartile for the starting salary data we would enter the following formula into an empty cell of the worksheet in Figure 3.1.

If the value of 1 in the QUARTILE function is changed to 0, Excel computes the minimum value in the data set. If the value of 1 is changed to 4, Excel computes the maximum value.

$$=\text{QUARTILE(B2:B3,1)}$$

The value Excel provides is 2872.5. We can compute the second quartile or median by replacing the value of 1 with 2, and the third quartile by replacing the value of 1 with 3.

Computing percentiles and quartiles is useful for a data analyst who is interested in getting a feel for how the values in a data set are distributed. However, if you are a student who wants to know how the starting salary you received ranks compared to all the other starting salaries, then what you would like to do is to take your salary and compute its rank and percentile. Or perhaps you know your raw score on an exam and would like to know its rank and percentile. Excel's Rank and Percentile tool can be used to provide this information for an entire data set.

We illustrate the use of Excel's Rank and Percentile tool by computing the ranks and percentiles for the starting salaries in Table 3.1. Refer to Figure 3.3 as we present the steps involved.

Enter Data: Labels and the starting salary data are entered into cells A1:B13.

Enter Functions and Formulas: No functions and formulas are needed.

Apply Tools: The following steps will compute the rank and percentile for each observation.

Note: If the Data Analysis option does not appear when you select the Tools menu, choose Add-Ins, and check Analysis ToolPak to install it.

Step 1. Select the **Tools** menu
Step 2. Choose **Data Analysis**
Step 3. Choose **Rank and Percentile** from the list of Analysis Tools
Step 4. When the Rank and Percentile dialog box appears:
> Enter B1:B13 in the **Input Range** box
> Select **Grouped by Columns**
> Select **Labels in First Row**
> Select **Output Range**
> Enter D1 in the **Output Range** box
>> (Any cell where the upper left corner of the output is desired may be entered here.)
> Click **OK**

---

* The value Excel computed for the 85th percentile does not strictly satisfy the definition of the 85th percentile because only 83% of the values are less than or equal to 3078. Our procedure would round up in this case to obtain 3130 as the value satisfying the definition of the 85th percentile. For larger data sets, the difference between the approximate value provided by Excel and the value computed using our three-step procedure is not of practical significance.

FIGURE 3.3   USING EXCEL'S RANK AND PERCENTILE TOOL FOR STARTING SALARIES

	A	B	C	D	E	F	G	H
1	Graduate	Starting Salary		Point	Starting Salary	Rank	Percent	
2	1	2850		10	3325	1	100.00%	
3	2	2950		8	3130	2	90.90%	
4	3	3050		3	3050	3	81.80%	
5	4	2880		2	2950	4	72.70%	
6	5	2755		9	2940	5	63.60%	
7	6	2710		11	2920	6	54.50%	
8	7	2890		7	2890	7	45.40%	
9	8	3130		4	2880	8	27.20%	
10	9	2940		12	2880	8	27.20%	
11	10	3325		1	2850	10	18.10%	
12	11	2920		5	2755	11	9.00%	
13	12	2880		6	2710	12	0.00%	
14								

Excel interpolates over the interval from 0 to n when computing percentiles for a data set.

The output from using the Rank and Percentile tool appears in cells D1:G13. Cells F2:F13 contain the rank of each observation. The highest salary is given a rank of 1 and the lowest salary is given a rank of 12. Cells G2:G13 show the percentile each salary represents. For instance, the percentile for 2850 is 18.1% because 2 of the other 11 salaries are smaller than 2850. The lowest salary is the 0th percentile and the highest salary is the 100th percentile. The percentiles increase by (1/11)100% as we move up from the lowest salary to the highest, except for ties. In the case of a tie, Excel gives the tied values the same rank and percentile. Note that the two observations with the same value (2880) both received a rank of 8 and a percentile of 27.20%.

NOTES AND COMMENTS

It is better to use the median than the mean as a measure of central location when a data set contains extreme values. Another measure, sometimes used when extreme values are present, is the *trimmed mean*. It is obtained by deleting a percentage of the smallest and largest values from a data set and then computing the mean of the remaining values. For example, the 5% trimmed mean is obtained by removing the smallest 5% and the largest 5% of the data values and then computing the mean of the remaining values. Using the sample with $n = 12$ starting salaries, $0.05(12) = 0.6$. Rounding this value to 1 indicates that the 5% trimmed mean would remove the 1 smallest data value and the 1 largest data value. The 5% trimmed mean using the 10 remaining observations is 2924.50.

Exercises

Methods

1. Consider a sample with data values of 10, 20, 12, 17, and 16. Compute the mean and median.

2. Consider a sample with data values of 10, 20, 21, 17, 16, and 12. Compute the mean and median.

3. Consider a sample with data values of 27, 25, 20, 15, 30, 34, 28, and 25. Compute the 20th, 25th, 65th, and 75th percentiles.

4. Consider a sample with data values of 53, 55, 70, 58, 64, 57, 53, 69, 57, 68, and 53. Compute the mean, median, and mode.

Applications

5. The Dow Jones Travel Index reported what business travelers pay for hotel rooms per night in major U.S. cities (*The Wall Street Journal,* January 16, 2004). The hotel room rates for 20 cities are as follows:

Hotels

Atlanta	$163	Minneapolis	$125
Boston	177	New Orleans	167
Chicago	166	New York	245
Cleveland	126	Orlando	146
Dallas	123	Phoenix	139
Denver	120	Pittsburgh	134
Detroit	144	San Francisco	167
Houston	173	Seattle	162
Los Angeles	160	St. Louis	145
Miami	192	Washington, D.C.	207

a. What is the mean hotel room rate?
b. What is the median hotel room rate?
c. What is the mode?
d. What is the first quartile?
e. What is the third quartile?

6. J. D. Powers and Associates surveyed cell phone users in order to learn about the minutes of cell phone usage per month (Associated Press, June 2002). Minutes per month for a sample of 15 cell phone users are shown here.

615	135	395
430	830	1180
690	250	420
265	245	210
180	380	105

a. What is the mean number of minutes of usage per month?
b. What is the median number of minutes of usage per month?
c. What is the 85th percentile?
d. J. D. Powers and Associates reported that the average wireless subscriber plan allows up to 750 minutes of usage per month. What do the data suggest about cell phone subscribers' utilization of their monthly plan?

7. The American Association of Individual Investors conducted an annual survey of discount brokers (*AAII Journal,* January 2003). The commissions charged by 24 discount brokers for two types of trades, a broker-assisted trade of 100 shares at $50 per share and an online trade of 500 shares at $50 per share, are shown in Table 3.2.
a. Compute the mean, median, and mode for the commission charged on a broker-assisted trade of 100 shares at $50 per share.
b. Compute the mean, median, and mode for the commission charged on an online trade of 500 shares at $50 per share.
c. Which costs more, a broker-assisted trade of 100 shares at $50 per share or an online trade of 500 shares at $50 per share?
d. Is the cost of a transaction related to the amount of the transaction?

TABLE 3.2 COMMISSIONS CHARGED BY DISCOUNT BROKERS

Broker

Broker	Broker-Assisted 100 Shares at $50/Share	Online 500 Shares at $50/Share	Broker	Broker-Assisted 100 Shares at $50/Share	Online 500 Shares at $50/Share
Accutrade	30.00	29.95	Merrill Lynch Direct	50.00	29.95
Ameritrade	24.99	10.99	Muriel Siebert	45.00	14.95
Banc of America	54.00	24.95	NetVest	24.00	14.00
Brown & Co.	17.00	5.00	Recom Securities	35.00	12.95
Charles Schwab	55.00	29.95	Scottrade	17.00	7.00
CyberTrader	12.95	9.95	Sloan Securities	39.95	19.95
E*TRADE Securities	49.95	14.95	Strong Investments	55.00	24.95
First Discount	35.00	19.75	TD Waterhouse	45.00	17.95
Freedom Investments	25.00	15.00	T. Rowe Price	50.00	19.95
Harrisdirect	40.00	20.00	Vanguard	48.00	20.00
Investors National	39.00	62.50	Wall Street Discount	29.95	19.95
MB Trading	9.95	10.55	York Securities	40.00	36.00

Source: AAII Journal, January 2003.

8. Millions of Americans get up each morning and telecommute to work from offices in their home. Following is a sample of age data for individuals working at home.

18	54	20	46	25	48	53	27	26	37
40	36	42	25	27	33	28	40	45	25

a. Compute the mean and mode.
b. The median age of the population of all adults is 35.5 years (*The World Almanac,* 2004). Use the median age of the preceding data to comment on whether the at-home workers tend to be younger or older than the population of all adults.
c. Compute the first and third quartiles.
d. Compute and interpret the 32nd percentile.

9. Media Matrix collected data showing the most popular Web sites when browsing at home and at work (*Business 2.0,* January 2000). The following data show the number of unique visitors (thousands) for the top 25 Web sites when browsing at home.

Websites

Web Site	Unique Visitors (1000s)
about.com	5538
altavista.com	7391
amazon.com	7986
angelfire.com	8917
aol.com	23863
bluemountainarts.com	6786
ebay.com	8296
excite.com	10479
geocities.com	15321
go.com	14330
hotbot.com	5760
hotmail.com	11791
icq.com	5052

(*continued*)

Web Site	Unique Visitors (1000s)
looksmart.com	5984
lycos.com	9950
microsoft.com	15593
msn.com	23505
netscape.com	14470
passport.com	11299
real.com	6785
snap.com	5730
tripod.com	7970
xoom.com	5652
yahoo.com	26796
zdnet.com	5133

   a. Compute the mean and median.

   b. Do you think it would be better to use the mean or the median as the measure of central location for these data? Explain.

   c. Compute the first and third quartiles.

   d. Compute and interpret the 85th percentile.

10. An American Hospital Association survey found that most hospital emergency rooms are operating at full capacity (Associated Press, April 9, 2002). The survey collected data on the emergency room waiting times for hospitals where the emergency room is operating at full capacity and for hospitals where the emergency room is in balance and rarely operates at capacity. Sample data showing waiting times in minutes are as follows.

ER Waiting Times for Hospitals at Full Capacity		ER Waiting Times for Hospitals in Balance	
87	59	60	39
80	110	54	32
47	83	18	56
73	79	29	26
50	50	45	37
93	66	34	38
72	115		

   a. Compute the mean and median emergency room waiting times for hospitals operating at full capacity.

   b. Compute the mean and median emergency room waiting times for hospitals operating in balance.

   c. What observations can you make about emergency room waiting times based on these results? Would the American Hospital Association express concern with the statistical results shown here?

11. In automobile mileage and gasoline-consumption testing, 13 automobiles were road tested for 300 miles in both city and highway driving conditions. The following data were recorded for miles-per-gallon performance.

City: 16.2 16.7 15.9 14.4 13.2 15.3 16.8 16.0 16.1 15.3 15.2 15.3 16.2
Highway: 19.4 20.6 18.3 18.6 19.2 17.4 17.2 18.6 19.0 21.1 19.4 18.5 18.7

Use the mean, median, and mode to make a statement about the difference in performance for city and highway driving.

12. The following data show the price, picture capacity, and battery life (minutes) for 20 digital cameras (*PC World,* January 2000).

Cameras

Camera	Price ($)	Picture Capacity	Battery Life (minutes)
Agfa Ephoto CL30	349	36	25
Canon PowerShot A50	499	106	75
Canon PowerShot Pro70	999	96	118
Epson PhotoPC 800	699	120	99
Fujifilm DX-10	299	30	229
Fujifilm MX-2700	699	141	124
Fujifilm MX-2900 Zoom	899	141	88
HP PhotoSmart C200	299	80	68
Kodak DC215 Zoom	399	54	159
Kodak DC265 Zoom	899	180	186
Kodak DC280 Zoom	799	245	143
Minolta Dimage EX Zoom 1500	549	105	38
Nikon Coolpix 950	999	32	88
Olympus D-340R	299	122	161
Olympus D-450 Zoom	499	122	62
Ricoh RDC-500	699	99	56
Sony Cybershot DSC-F55	699	63	69
Sony Mavica MVC-FD73	599	40	186
Sony Mavica MVC-FD88	999	40	88
Toshiba PDR-M4	599	124	142

   a. Compute the mean price.
   b. Compute the mean picture capacity.
   c. Compute the mean battery life.
   d. If you had to select one camera from this list, which camera would you choose? Explain.

Measures of Variability

In addition to measures of location, it is often desirable to consider measures of variability, or dispersion. For example, suppose that you are a purchasing agent for a large manufacturing firm and that you regularly place orders with two different suppliers. After several months of operation, you find that the mean number of days required to fill orders is 10 days for both of the suppliers. The histograms summarizing the number of working days required to fill orders from the suppliers are shown in Figure 3.4. Although the mean number of days is 10 for both suppliers, do the two suppliers demonstrate the same degree of reliability in terms of making deliveries on schedule? Note the dispersion, or variability, in delivery times indicated by the histograms. Which supplier would you prefer?

For most firms, receiving materials and supplies on schedule is important. The seven- or eight-day deliveries shown for J.C. Clark Distributors might be viewed favorably; however, a few of the slow 13- to 15-day deliveries could be disastrous in terms of keeping a workforce busy and production on schedule. This example illustrates a situation in which the variability in the delivery times may be an overriding consideration in selecting a supplier. For most purchasing agents, the lower variability shown for Dawson Supply, Inc., would make Dawson the preferred supplier.

We turn now to a discussion of some commonly used measures of variability.

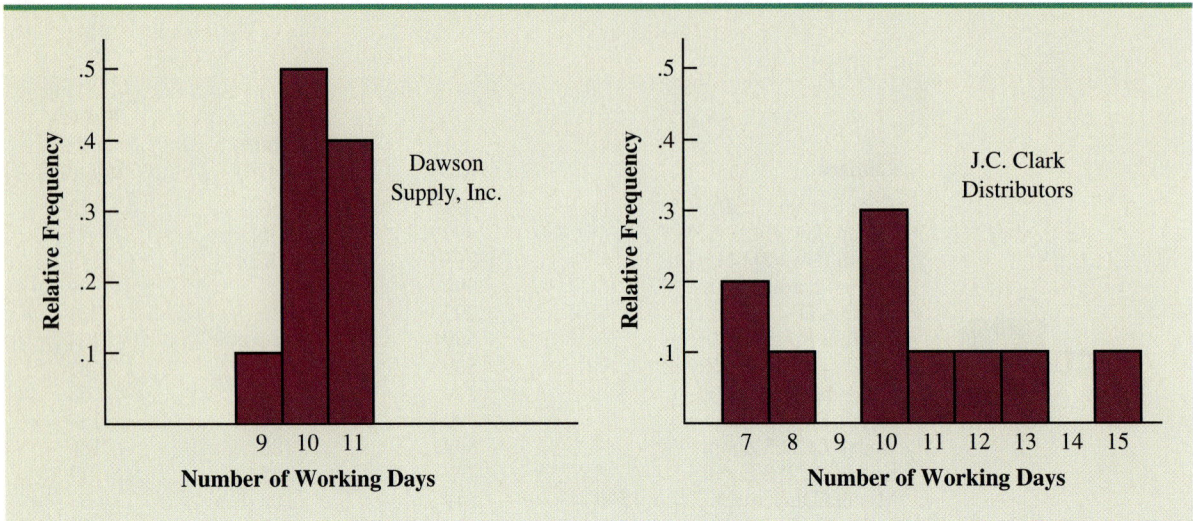

Range

The simplest measure of variability is the **range**.

> RANGE
>
> $$\text{Range} = \text{Largest value} - \text{Smallest value}$$

Let us refer to the data on starting salaries for business school graduates in Table 3.1. The largest starting salary is 3325 and the smallest is 2710. The range is $3325 - 2710 = 615$.

Although the range is the easiest of the measures of variability to compute, it is seldom used as the only measure. The reason is that the range is based on only two of the observations and thus is highly influenced by extreme values. Suppose one of the graduates received a starting salary of $10,000 per month. In this case, the range would be $10,000 - 2710 = 7290$ rather than 615. This large value for the range would not be especially descriptive of the variability in the data because 11 of the 12 starting salaries are closely grouped between 2710 and 3130.

Interquartile Range

A measure of variability that overcomes the dependency on extreme values is the **interquartile range (IQR)**. This measure of variability is the difference between the third quartile, Q_3, and the first quartile, Q_1. In other words, the interquartile range is the range for the middle 50% of the data.

> INTERQUARTILE RANGE
>
> $$IQR = Q_3 - Q_1 \tag{3.3}$$

For the data on monthly starting salaries, the quartiles are $Q_3 = 3000$ and $Q_1 = 2865$. Thus, the interquartile range is $3000 - 2865 = 135$.

Variance

The **variance** is a measure of variability that utilizes all the data. The variance is based on the difference between the value of each observation (x_i) and the mean. The difference between each x_i and the mean ($\bar{x}$ for a sample, μ for a population) is called a *deviation about the mean*. For a sample, a deviation about the mean is written ($x_i - \bar{x}$); for a population, it is written ($x_i - \mu$). In the computation of the variance, the deviations about the mean are *squared*.

If the data are for a population, the average of the squared deviations is called the *population variance*. The population variance is denoted by the Greek symbol σ^2 (sigma squared). For a population of N observations and with μ denoting the population mean, the definition of the population variance is as follows.

POPULATION VARIANCE

$$\sigma^2 = \frac{\Sigma(x_i - \mu)^2}{N} \tag{3.4}$$

In most statistical applications, the data being analyzed are for a sample. When we compute a sample variance, we are often interested in using it to estimate the population variance σ^2. Although a detailed explanation is beyond the scope of this text, it can be shown that if the sum of the squared deviations about the sample mean is divided by $n - 1$, and not n, the resulting sample variance provides an unbiased estimate of the population variance. For this reason, the *sample variance,* denoted by s^2, is defined as follows.

The sample variance s^2 is the estimator of the population variance σ^2.

SAMPLE VARIANCE

$$s^2 = \frac{\Sigma(x_i - \bar{x})^2}{n - 1} \tag{3.5}$$

To illustrate the computation of the sample variance, we will use the data on class size for the sample of five college classes as presented in Section 3.1. A summary of the data, including the computation of the deviations about the mean and the squared deviations about the mean, is shown in Table 3.3. The sum of squared deviations about the mean is $\Sigma(x_i - \bar{x})^2 = 256$. Hence, with $n - 1 = 4$, the sample variance is

$$s^2 = \frac{\Sigma(x_i - \bar{x})^2}{n - 1} = \frac{256}{4} = 64$$

Before moving on, let us note that the units associated with the sample variance often cause confusion. Because the values being summed in the variance calculation $(x_i - \bar{x})^2$ are squared, the units associated with the sample variance are also *squared*. For instance, the sample variance for the class size data is $s^2 = 64$ (students)^2. The squared units associated with variance make it difficult to obtain an intuitive understanding and interpretation of the numerical value of the variance. We recommend that you think of the variance as a measure useful in comparing the amount of variability for two or more variables. In a comparison of the variables, the one with the largest variance shows the most variability. Further interpretation of the value of the variance may not be necessary.

The variance is useful in comparing the variability of two or more variables.

As another illustration of computing a sample variance, consider the starting salaries listed in Table 3.1 for the 12 business school graduates. In Section 3.1, we showed that the

TABLE 3.3 COMPUTATION OF DEVIATIONS AND SQUARED DEVIATIONS ABOUT THE MEAN FOR THE CLASS SIZE DATA

Number of Students in Class (x_i)	Mean Class Size ($\bar{x}$)	Deviation About the Mean ($x_i - \bar{x}$)	Squared Deviation About the Mean ($x_i - \bar{x})^2$
46	44	2	4
54	44	10	100
42	44	−2	4
46	44	2	4
32	44	−12	144
		0	256
		$\Sigma(x_i - \bar{x})$	$\Sigma(x_i - \bar{x})^2$

sample mean starting salary was 2940. A summary of the data, including the computation of the deviations about the mean and the squared deviations about the mean, is shown in Figure 3.5. The worksheet in the background shows the Excel formulas used to compute the results shown in the value worksheet in the foreground. The sum of the squared deviations about the mean is $\Sigma(x_i - \bar{x})^2 = 301{,}850$ (see cell E14). Hence, with $n - 1 = 11$, the sample variance is

$$s^2 = \frac{\Sigma(x_i - \bar{x})^2}{n - 1} = \frac{301{,}850}{11} = 27{,}440.91$$

Using the definition to compute the sample variance helps us to realize that the variance measures variability as a function of the squared deviations about the mean.

The method we used for computing the sample variance for starting salaries is the same method that we used to compute the sample variance for the class size data (see Table 3.3). We used the definition as given by equation (3.5). The only difference is that this time we use an Excel worksheet to ease the computational burden. Later we will see that Excel provides a function for obtaining the sample variance directly without entering all the formulas needed to compute the sum of the squared deviations about the mean.

Note that in Table 3.3 and Figure 3.5 we show both the sum of the deviations about the mean and the sum of the squared deviations about the mean. For any data set, the sum of the deviations about the mean will *always equal zero*. Note that in Table 3.3 and Figure 3.5, $\Sigma(x_i - \bar{x}) = 0$. The positive deviations and negative deviations cancel each other, causing the sum of the deviations about the mean to equal zero.

Standard Deviation

The **standard deviation** is defined to be the positive square root of the variance. Following the notation we adopted for a sample variance and a population variance, we use s to denote the sample standard deviation and σ to denote the population standard deviation. The standard deviation is derived from the variance in the following way.

The sample standard deviation s is the estimator of the population standard deviation σ.

STANDARD DEVIATION

$$\text{Sample standard deviation} = s = \sqrt{s^2} \tag{3.6}$$

$$\text{Population standard deviation} = \sigma = \sqrt{\sigma^2} \tag{3.7}$$

FIGURE 3.5 EXCEL WORKSHEET USED TO COMPUTE THE DEVIATIONS AND SQUARED DEVIATIONS ABOUT THE MEAN FOR THE STARTING SALARIES

	A	B	C	D	E	F
1	**Graduate**	**Starting Salary**	**Sample Mean**	**Deviation about the Mean**	**Squared Deviation about the Mean**	
2	1	2850	=AVERAGE($B$2:$B$13)	=B2-C2	=D2^2	
3	2	2950	=AVERAGE($B$2:$B$13)	=B3-C3	=D3^2	
4	3	3050	=AVERAGE($B$2:$B$13)	=B4-C4	=D4^2	
5	4	2880	=AVERAGE($B$2:$B$13)	=B5-C5	=D5^2	
6	5	2755	=AVERAGE($B$2:$B$13)	=B6-C6	=D6^2	
7	6	2710	=AVERAGE($B$2:$B$13)	=B7-C7	=D7^2	
8	7	2890	=AVERAGE($B$2:$B$13)	=B8-C8	=D8^2	
9	8	3130	=AVERAGE($B$2:$B$13)	=B9-C9	=D9^2	
10	9	2940	=AVERAGE($B$2:$B$13)	=B10-C10	=D10^2	
11	10	3325	=AVERAGE($B$2:$B$13)	=B11-C11	=D11^2	
12	11	2920	=AVERAGE($B$2:$B$13)	=B12-C12	=D12^2	
13	12	2880	=AVERAGE($B$2:$B$13)	=B13-C13	=D13^2	
14				=SUM(D2:D13)	=SUM(E2:E13)	
15						

	A	B	C	D	E	F
1	**Graduate**	**Starting Salary**	**Sample Mean**	**Deviation about the Mean**	**Squared Deviation about the Mean**	
2	1	2850	2940	-90	8100	
3	2	2950	2940	10	100	
4	3	3050	2940	110	12100	
5	4	2880	2940	-60	3600	
6	5	2755	2940	-185	34225	
7	6	2710	2940	-230	52900	
8	7	2890	2940	-50	2500	
9	8	3130	2940	190	36100	
10	9	2940	2940	0	0	
11	10	3325	2940	385	148225	
12	11	2920	2940	-20	400	
13	12	2880	2940	-60	3600	
14				0	301850	
15						

Recall that the sample variance for the sample of class sizes in five college classes is $s^2 = 64$. Thus, the sample standard deviation is $s = \sqrt{64} = 8$. For the data on starting salaries, the sample standard deviation is $s = \sqrt{27,440.91} = 165.65$.

The standard deviation is easier to interpret than the variance because the standard deviation is measured in the same units as the data.

What is gained by converting the variance to its corresponding standard deviation? Recall that the units associated with the variance are squared. For example, the sample variance for the starting salary data of business school graduates is $s^2 = 27,440.91$ (dollars)^2. Because the standard deviation is the square root of the variance, the units of the variance, dollars squared, are converted to dollars in the standard deviation. Thus, the standard deviation of the starting salary data is $165.65. In other words, the standard deviation is measured in the same units as the original data. For this reason the standard deviation is more easily compared to the mean and other statistics that are measured in the same units as the original data.

Using Excel to Compute the Sample Variance and Sample Standard Deviation

Excel provides functions for computing the sample variance and sample standard deviation, which we will illustrate using the starting salary data. Refer to Figure 3.6 as we describe the steps involved. Figure 3.6 is an extension of Figure 3.1 where we showed how to use Excel functions to compute the mean, median, and mode. The formula worksheet is in the background; the value worksheet is in the foreground.

Enter Data: Labels and the starting salary data are entered into cells A1:B13 of the worksheet.

Enter Functions and Formulas: The Excel AVERAGE, MEDIAN, and MODE functions are entered into cells E1:E3 as described earlier. Excel's VAR function can be used to compute the sample variance by entering the following formula into cell E4:

$$=VAR(B2:B13)$$

Similarly, the formula =STDEV(B2:B13) is entered into cell E5 to compute the sample standard deviation. Appropriate labels are entered into cells D1:D5 to identify the output.

The value worksheet, in the foreground, shows the values computed using the Excel functions. Note that the sample variance and sample standard deviation are the same as we computed earlier using the definitions.

Coefficient of Variation

The coefficient of variation is a relative measure of variability; it measures the standard deviation relative to the mean.

In some situations we may be interested in a descriptive statistic that indicates how large the standard deviation is relative to the mean. This measure is called the **coefficient of variation** and is usually expressed as a percentage.

COEFFICIENT OF VARIATION

$$\left(\frac{\text{Standard deviation}}{\text{Mean}} \times 100 \right)\% \qquad \text{(3.8)}$$

For the class size data, we found a sample mean of 44 and a sample standard deviation of 8. The coefficient of variation is $[(8/44) \times 100]\% = 18.2\%$. In words, the coefficient of variation tells us that the sample standard deviation is 18.2% of the value of the sample mean. For the starting salary data with a sample mean of 2940 and a sample standard deviation of 165.65, the coefficient of variation, $[(165.65/2940) \times 100]\% = 5.6\%$, tells us the sample standard deviation is only 5.6% of the value of the sample mean. In general, the coefficient of variation is a useful statistic for comparing the variability of variables that have different standard deviations and different means.

Using Excel's Descriptive Statistics Tool

As we have seen, Excel provides statistical functions to compute descriptive statistics for a data set. These functions can be used to compute one statistic at a time (e.g., mean, variance, etc.). Excel also provides a variety of data analysis tools. One of these, called Descriptive Statistics, allows the user to compute a variety of descriptive statistics at once. We show here how it can be used to compute descriptive statistics for the starting salary data in Table 3.1. Refer to Figures 3.7 and 3.8 as we describe the steps involved.

FIGURE 3.6 EXCEL WORKSHEET USED TO COMPUTE THE SAMPLE VARIANCE AND THE SAMPLE STANDARD DEVIATION FOR STARTING SALARIES

	A	B	C	D	E	F
1	Graduate	Starting Salary		Mean	=AVERAGE(B2:B13)	
2	1	2850		Median	=MEDIAN(B2:B13)	
3	2	2950		Mode	=MODE(B2:B13)	
4	3	3050		Variance	=VAR(B2:B13)	
5	4	2880		Standard Deviation	=STDEV(B2:B13)	
6	5	2755				
7	6	2710				

	A	B	C	D	E	F
1	Graduate	Starting Salary		Mean	2940	
2	1	2850		Median	2905	
3	2	2950		Mode	2880	
4	3	3050		Variance	27440.91	
5	4	2880		Standard Deviation	165.65	
6	5	2755				
7	6	2710				
8	7	2890				
9	8	3130				
10	9	2940				
11	10	3325				
12	11	2920				
13	12	2880				
14						

(Figure 3.6 left worksheet data, rows 8–14)

	A	B
8	7	2890
9	8	3130
10	9	2940
11	10	3325
12	11	2920
13	12	2880
14		

FIGURE 3.7 DESCRIPTIVE STATISTICS DIALOG BOX FOR THE STARTING SALARY DATA

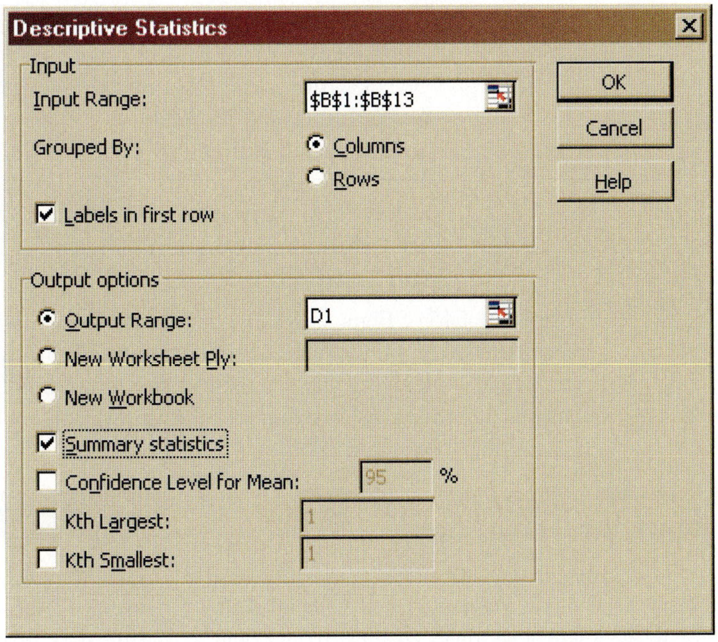

Descriptive Statistics dialog box:

Input
Input Range: $B$1:$B$13
Grouped By: ● Columns ○ Rows
☑ Labels in first row

Output options
● Output Range: D1
○ New Worksheet Ply:
○ New Workbook
☑ Summary statistics
☐ Confidence Level for Mean: 95 %
☐ Kth Largest: 1
☐ Kth Smallest: 1

OK Cancel Help

FIGURE 3.8 USING EXCEL TO COMPUTE DESCRIPTIVE STATISTICS FOR STARTING SALARIES

	A	B	C	D	E	F
1	Graduate	Starting Salary		*Starting Salary*		
2	1	2850				
3	2	2950		Mean	2940	
4	3	3050		Standard Error	47.8199	
5	4	2880		Median	2905	
6	5	2755		Mode	2880	
7	6	2710		Standard Deviation	165.653	
8	7	2890		Sample Variance	27440.91	
9	8	3130		Kurtosis	1.7189	
10	9	2940		Skewness	1.0911	
11	10	3325		Range	615	
12	11	2920		Minimum	2710	
13	12	2880		Maximum	3325	
14				Sum	35280	
15				Count	12	
16						

Enter Data: Labels and the starting salary data are entered into cells A1:B13 of the worksheet.

Enter Functions and Formulas: No functions and formulas are needed.

Apply Analysis Tools: The following steps describe how to use Excel's Descriptive Statistics tool for these data:

Step 1. Select the **Tools** menu
Step 2. Choose the **Data Analysis** option
Step 3. Choose **Descriptive Statistics** from the list of **Analysis Tools**
Step 4. When the Descriptive Statistics dialog box appears (see Figure 3.7):
   Enter B1:B13 in the **Input Range** box
   Select **Grouped By Columns**
   Select **Labels in First Row**
   Select **Output Range**
   Enter D1 in the **Output Range** box (to identify the upper left corner of the section of the worksheet where the descriptive statistics will appear)
   Select **Summary Statistics**
   Click **OK**

Cells D1:E15 of Figure 3.8 show the descriptive statistics provided by Excel. A yellow screen is used to highlight the results. The boldfaced entries are the descriptive statistics we have covered. The descriptive statistics that are not boldfaced are either covered subsequently in the text or discussed in more advanced texts.

NOTES AND COMMENTS

1. The standard deviation is a commonly used measure of the risk associated with investing in stock and stock funds (*BusinessWeek*, January 17, 2000). It provides a measure of how

monthly returns fluctuate around the long-run average return.

2. Rounding the value of the sample mean $\bar{x}$ and the values of the squared deviations $(x_i - \bar{x})^2$

may introduce errors when a calculator is used in the computation of the variance and standard deviation. To reduce rounding errors, we recommend carrying at least six significant digits during intermediate calculations. The resulting variance or standard deviation can then be rounded to fewer digits.

3. An alternative formula for the computation of the sample variance is

$$s^2 = \frac{\Sigma x_i^2 - n\bar{x}^2}{n - 1}$$

where $\Sigma x_i^2 = x_1^2 + x_2^2 + \cdots + x_n^2$.

Exercises

Methods

13. Consider a sample with data values of 10, 20, 12, 17, and 16. Compute the range and interquartile range.

14. Consider a sample with data values of 10, 20, 12, 17, and 16. Compute the variance and standard deviation.

15. Consider a sample with data values of 27, 25, 20, 15, 30, 34, 28, and 25. Compute the range, interquartile range, variance, and standard deviation.

Applications

16. A bowler's scores for six games were 182, 168, 184, 190, 170, and 174. Using these data as a sample, compute the following descriptive statistics.
    a. Range   c. Standard deviation
    b. Variance   d. Coefficient of variation

17. A home theater in a box is the easiest and cheapest way to provide surround sound for a home entertainment center. A sample of prices is shown here (*Consumer Reports Buying Guide,* 2004). The prices are for models with a DVD player and for models without a DVD player.

Models with DVD Player	Price ($)	Models without DVD Player	Price ($)
Sony HT-1800DP	450	Pioneer HTP-230	300
Pioneer HTD-330DV	300	Sony HT-DDW750	300
Sony HT-C800DP	400	Kenwood HTB-306	360
Panasonic SC-HT900	500	RCA RT-2600	290
Panasonic SC-MTI	400	Kenwood HTB-206	300

   a. Compute the mean price for models with a DVD player and the mean price for models without a DVD player. What is the additional price paid to have a DVD player included in a home theater unit?
   b. Compute the range, variance, and standard deviation for the two samples. What does this information tell you about the prices for models with and without a DVD player?

18. Car rental rates per day for a sample of seven Eastern U.S. cities are as follows (*The Wall Street Journal,* January 16, 2004).

City	Daily Rate ($)
Boston	43
Atlanta	35
Miami	34

(*continued*)

City	Daily Rate ($)
New York	58
Orlando	30
Pittsburgh	30
Washington, D.C.	36

a. Compute the mean, variance, and standard deviation for the car rental rates.
b. A similar sample of seven Western U.S. cities showed a sample mean car rental rate of $38 per day. The variance and standard deviation were 12.3 and 3.5, respectively. Discuss any difference between the car rental rates in Eastern and Western U.S. cities.

19. The *Los Angeles Times* regularly reports the air quality index for various areas of Southern California. A sample of air quality index values for Pomona provided the following data: 28, 42, 58, 48, 45, 55, 60, 49, and 50.
   a. Compute the range and interquartile range.
   b. Compute the sample variance and sample standard deviation.
   c. A sample of air quality index readings for Anaheim provided a sample mean of 48.5, a sample variance of 136, and a sample standard deviation of 11.66. What comparisons can you make between the air quality in Pomona and that in Anaheim on the basis of these descriptive statistics?

20. The following data were used to construct the histograms of the number of days required to fill orders for Dawson Supply, Inc., and J.C. Clark Distributors (see Figure 3.2).

Dawson Supply Days for Delivery: 11   10   9   10   11   11   10   11   10   10
Clark Distributors Days for Delivery: 8   10   13   7   10   11   10   7   15   12

Use the range and standard deviation to support the previous observation that Dawson Supply provides the more consistent and reliable delivery times.

21. How do grocery costs compare across the country? Using a market basket of 10 items including meat, milk, bread, eggs, coffee, potatoes, cereal, and orange juice, *Where to Retire* magazine calculated the cost of the market basket in six cities and in six retirement areas across the country (*Where to Retire,* November/December 2003). The data with market basket cost to the nearest dollar are as follows:

City	Cost ($)	Retirement Area	Cost ($)
Buffalo, NY	33	Biloxi-Gulfport, MS	29
Des Moines, IA	27	Asheville, NC	32
Hartford, CT	32	Flagstaff, AZ	32
Los Angeles, CA	38	Hilton Head, SC	34
Miami, FL	36	Fort Myers, FL	34
Pittsburgh, PA	32	Santa Fe, NM	31

a. Compute the mean, variance, and standard deviation for the sample of cities and the sample of retirement areas.
b. What observations can be made based on the two samples?

Broker

22. The American Association of Individual Investors conducted an annual survey of discount brokers (*AAII Journal,* January 2003). The commissions charged by 24 discount brokers for two types of trades, a broker-assisted trade of 100 shares at $50 per share and an on-line trade of 500 shares at $50 per share, are shown in Table 3.2.
   a. Compute the range and interquartile range for each type of trade.
   b. Compute the variance and standard deviation for each type of trade.

c. Compute the coefficient of variation for each type of trade.

d. Compare the variability of cost for the two types of trades.

23. *PC World* provided ratings for 15 notebook PCs (*PC World*, February 2000). A 100-point scale was used to provide an overall rating for each notebook. A score in the 90s is exceptional, while one in the 70s is good. The overall ratings for the 15 notebooks are shown here.

CD file

Notebook

Notebook	Overall Rating
AMS Tech Roadster 15CTA380	67
Compaq Armada M700	78
Compaq Prosignia Notebook 150	79
Dell Inspiron 3700 C466GT	80
Dell Inspiron 7500 R500VT	84
Dell Latitude Cpi A366XT	76
Enpower ENP-313 Pro	77
Gateway Solo 9300LS	92
HP Pavilion Notebook PC	83
IBM ThinkPad I Series 1480	78
Micro Express NP7400	77
Micron TransPort NX PII-400	78
NEC Versa SX	78
Sceptre Soundx 5200	73
Sony VAIO PCG-F340	77

Compute the range, interquartile range, variance, and standard deviation for this sample of notebook PCs.

24. The following times were recorded by the quarter-mile and mile runners of a university track team (times are in minutes).

Quarter-Mile Times:	.92	.98	1.04	.90	.99
Mile Times:	4.52	4.35	4.60	4.70	4.50

After viewing this sample of running times, one of the coaches commented that the quarter-milers turned in the more consistent times. Use the standard deviation and the coefficient of variation to summarize the variability in the data. Does the use of the coefficient of variation indicate that the coach's statement should be qualified?

3.3 Measures of Distribution Shape, Relative Location, and Detecting Outliers

We have described several measures of location and variability for data. In addition, it is often important to have a measure of the shape of a distribution. In Chapter 2 we noted that a histogram provides a graphical display showing the shape of a distribution. An important numerical measure of the shape of a distribution is called **skewness**.

Distribution Shape

Shown in Figure 3.9 are four histograms constructed from relative frequency distributions. The histograms in Panels A and B are moderately skewed. The one in Panel A is skewed to the left; its skewness is −.85. The histogram in Panel B is skewed to the right; its skewness is +.85. The histogram in Panel C is symmetric; its skewness is zero. The histogram in Panel D is highly skewed to the right; its skewness is 1.62. For data skewed to the left, the skewness is negative; for data skewed to the right, the skewness is positive. If the data are symmetric, the skewness is zero.

FIGURE 3.9 HISTOGRAMS SHOWING THE SKEWNESS FOR FOUR DISTRIBUTIONS

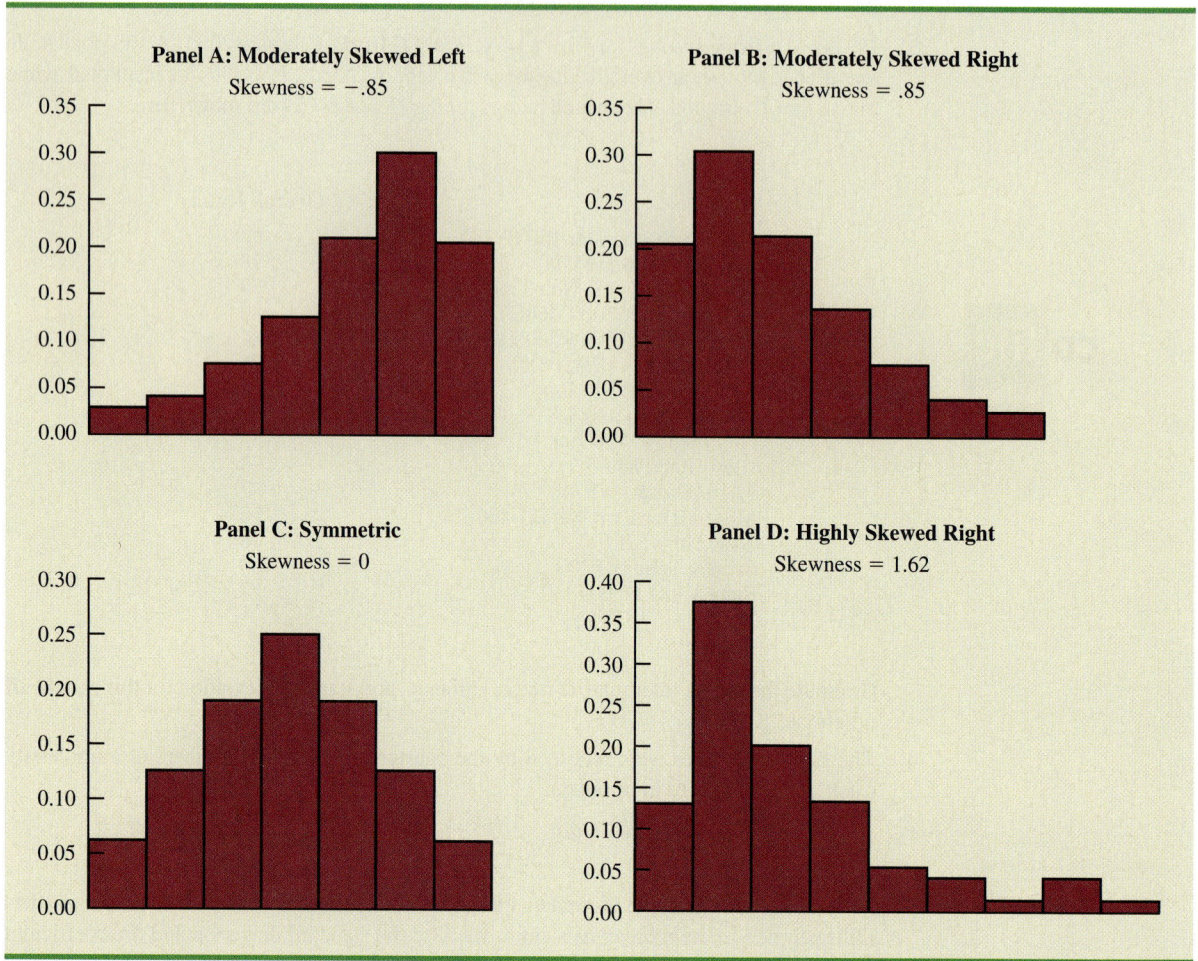

The formula used to compute skewness is somewhat complex.* However, the skewness can be easily computed using Excel. In Section 3.2 we showed how Excel's Descriptive Statistics tool can be used to compute descriptive statistics for the starting salary data in Table 3.1; the results were shown in the worksheet in Figure 3.8. The label Skewness in cell D10 and the corresponding value of 1.0911 in cell E10 indicates that the starting salary data are moderately to highly skewed to the right.

For a symmetric distribution, the mean and the median are equal. When the data are positively skewed, the mean will usually be greater than the median; when the data are negatively skewed, the mean will usually be less than the median. The data used to construct the histogram in Panel D are customer purchases at a women's apparel store. The mean purchase amount is $77.60 and the median purchase amount is $59.70. The relatively few large purchase amounts tend to increase the mean, while the median remains unaffected by the large purchase amounts. The median provides the preferred measure of location when the data are highly skewed.

Excel's SKEW function can also be used to compute the skewness by entering the following formula into any empty cell of the worksheet in Figure 3.8: =SKEW(B2:B13).

---

*The formula for the skewness of sample data:

$$\text{Skewness} = \frac{n}{(n-1)(n-2)} \sum \left(\frac{x_i - \bar{x}}{s} \right)^3$$

z-Scores

In addition to measures of location, variability, and shape, we are also interested in the relative location of values within a data set. Measures of relative location help us determine how far a particular value is from the mean.

By using both the mean and standard deviation, we can determine the relative location of any observation. Suppose we have a sample of n observations, with the values denoted by $x_1, x_2, \ldots, x_n$. In addition, assume that the sample mean, $\bar{x}$, and the sample standard deviation, s, are already computed. Associated with each value, x_i, is another value called its **z-score**. Equation (3.9) shows how the z-score is computed for each x_i.

Excel's STANDARDIZE function can be used to compute the z-score. But it is just as easy to enter a cell formula to compute z_i.

z-SCORE

$$z_i = \frac{x_i - \bar{x}}{s} \qquad\qquad \textbf{(3.9)}$$

where

$z_i =$ the z-score for x_i
$\bar{x} =$ the sample mean
$s =$ the sample standard deviation

The z-score is often called the *standardized value*. The z-score, z_i, can be interpreted as the *number of standard deviations x_i is from the mean $\bar{x}$*. For example, $z_1 = 1.2$ would indicate that x_1 is 1.2 standard deviations greater than the sample mean. Similarly, $z_2 = -.5$ would indicate that x_2 is .5, or 1/2, standard deviation less than the sample mean. A z-score greater than zero occurs for observations with a value greater than the mean, and a z-score less than zero occurs for observations with a value less than the mean. A z-score of zero indicates that the value of the observation is equal to the mean.

The z-score for any observation can be interpreted as a measure of the relative location of the observation in a data set. Thus, observations in two different data sets with the same z-score can be said to have the same relative location in terms of being the same number of standard deviations from the mean.

The z-scores for the class size data are computed in Table 3.4. Recall the previously computed sample mean, $\bar{x} = 44$, and sample standard deviation, $s = 8$. The z-score of -1.50 for the fifth observation shows it is farthest from the mean; it is 1.50 standard deviations below the mean.

TABLE 3.4 z-SCORES FOR THE CLASS SIZE DATA

Number of Students in Class (x_i)	Deviation About the Mean ($x_i - \bar{x}$)	z-Score $\left(\dfrac{x_i - \bar{x}}{s}\right)$
46	2	$2/8 =$ .25
54	10	$10/8 =$ 1.25
42	-2	$-2/8 =$ $-.25$
46	2	$2/8 =$ .25
32	-12	$-12/8 =$ -1.50

Chebyshev's Theorem

Chebyshev's theorem enables us to make statements about the proportion of data values that must be within a specified number of standard deviations of the mean.

> CHEBYSHEV'S THEOREM
>
> At least $(1 - 1/z^2)$ of the data values must be within z standard deviations of the mean, where z is any value greater than 1.

Some of the implications of this theorem, with $z = 2, 3,$ and 4 standard deviations, follow.

- At least .75, or 75%, of the data values must be within $z = 2$ standard deviations of the mean.
- At least .89, or 89%, of the data values must be within $z = 3$ standard deviations of the mean.
- At least .94, or 94%, of the data values must be within $z = 4$ standard deviations of the mean.

For an example using Chebyshev's theorem, suppose that the midterm test scores for 100 students in a college business statistics course had a mean of 70 and a standard deviation of 5. How many students had test scores between 60 and 80? How many students had test scores between 58 and 82?

For the test scores between 60 and 80, we note that 60 is two standard deviations below the mean and 80 is two standard deviations above the mean. Using Chebyshev's theorem, we see that at least .75, or at least 75%, of the observations must have values within two standard deviations of the mean. Thus, at least 75% of the students must have scored between 60 and 80.

Chebyshev's theorem requires $z > 1$; but z need not be an integer.

For the test scores between 58 and 82, we see that $(58 - 70)/5 = -2.4$ indicates 58 is 2.4 standard deviations below the mean and that $(82 - 70)/5 = +2.4$ indicates 82 is 2.4 standard deviations above the mean. Applying Chebyshev's theorem with $z = 2.4$, we have

$$\left(1 - \frac{1}{z^2}\right) = \left(1 - \frac{1}{(2.4)^2}\right) = .826$$

At least 82.6% of the students must have test scores between 58 and 82.

Empirical Rule

The empirical rule is based on the normal probability distribution, which will be discussed in Chapter 6. The normal distribution is used extensively throughout the text.

One of the advantages of Chebyshev's theorem is that it applies to any data set regardless of the shape of the distribution of the data. Indeed, it could be used with any of the distributions in Figure 3.9. In many practical applications, however, data exhibit a symmetric mound-shaped or bell-shaped distribution like the one shown in Figure 3.10. When the data are believed to approximate this distribution, the **empirical rule** can be used to determine the percentage of data values that must be within a specified number of standard deviations of the mean.

> EMPIRICAL RULE
>
> For data having a bell-shaped distribution:
>
> - Approximately 68% of the data values will be within one standard deviation of the mean.
> - Approximately 95% of the data values will be within two standard deviations of the mean.
> - Almost all of the data values will be within three standard deviations of the mean.

FIGURE 3.10   A SYMMETRIC MOUND-SHAPED OR BELL-SHAPED DISTRIBUTION

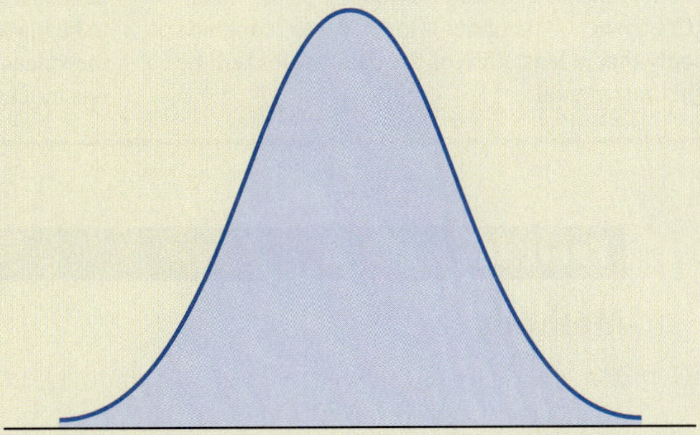

For example, liquid detergent cartons are filled automatically on a production line. Filling weights frequently have a bell-shaped distribution. If the mean filling weight is 16 ounces and the standard deviation is .25 ounces, we can use the empirical rule to draw the following conclusions.

- Approximately 68% of the filled cartons will have weights between 15.75 and 16.25 ounces (within one standard deviation of the mean).
- Approximately 95% of the filled cartons will have weights between 15.50 and 16.50 ounces (within two standard deviations of the mean).
- Almost all filled cartons will have weights between 15.25 and 16.75 ounces (within three standard deviations of the mean).

Detecting Outliers

Sometimes a data set will have one or more observations with unusually large or unusually small values. These extreme values are called **outliers**. Experienced statisticians take steps to identify outliers and then review each one carefully. An outlier may be a data value that has been incorrectly recorded. If so, it can be corrected before further analysis. An outlier may also be from an observation that was incorrectly included in the data set; if so, it can be removed. Finally, an outlier may be an unusual data value that has been recorded correctly and belongs in the data set.

It is a good idea to check for outliers before making decisions based on data analysis. Errors are often made in recording data and entering data into the computer. Outliers should not necessarily be deleted, but their accuracy and appropriateness should be verified.

Standardized values (z-scores) can be used to identify outliers. Recall that the empirical rule allows us to conclude that for data with a bell-shaped distribution, almost all the data values will be within three standard deviations of the mean. Hence, in using z-scores to identify outliers, we recommend treating any data value with a z-score less than -3 or greater than $+3$ as an outlier. Such data values can then be reviewed for accuracy and to determine whether they belong in the data set.

Refer to the z-scores for the class size data in Table 3.4. The z-score of -1.50 shows the fifth class size is farthest from the mean. However, this standardized value is well within the -3 to $+3$ guideline for outliers. Thus, the z-scores do not indicate that outliers are present in the class size data.

NOTES AND COMMENTS

1. Chebyshev's theorem is applicable for any data set and can be used to state the minimum number of data values that will be within a certain number of standard deviations of the mean. If the data are known to be approximately bell-shaped, more can be said. For instance, the empirical rule allows us to say that *approximately* 95% of the data values will be within two standard deviations of the mean; Chebyshev's theorem allows us to conclude only that at least 75% of the data values will be in that interval.

2. Before analyzing a data set, statisticians usually make a variety of checks to ensure the validity of data. In a large study it is not uncommon for errors to be made in recording data values or in entering the values into a computer. Identifying outliers is one tool used to check the validity of the data.

Exercises

Methods

25. Consider a sample with data values of 10, 20, 12, 17, and 16. Compute the z-score for each of the five observations.

26. Consider a sample with a mean of 500 and a standard deviation of 100. What are the z-scores for the following data values: 520, 650, 500, 450, and 280?

27. Consider a sample with a mean of 30 and a standard deviation of 5. Use Chebyshev's theorem to determine the percentage of the data within each of the following ranges.
    a.   20 to 40
    b.   15 to 45
    c.   22 to 38
    d.   18 to 42
    e.   12 to 48

28. Suppose the data have a bell-shaped distribution with a mean of 30 and a standard deviation of 5. Use the empirical rule to determine the percentage of data within each of the following ranges.
    a.   20 to 40
    b.   15 to 45
    c.   25 to 35

Applications

29. The results of a national survey showed that on average, adults sleep 6.9 hours per night (2000 Omnibus Sleep in America Poll). Suppose that the standard deviation is 1.2 hours.
    a.   Use Chebyshev's theorem to calculate the percentage of individuals who sleep between 4.5 and 9.3 hours.
    b.   Use Chebyshev's theorem to calculate the percentage of individuals who sleep between 3.9 and 9.9 hours.
    c.   Assume that the number of hours of sleep follows a bell-shaped distribution. Use the empirical rule to calculate the percentage of individuals who sleep between 4.5 and 9.3 hours per day. How does this result compare to the value that you obtained using Chebyshev's theorem in part (a)?

30. The Energy Information Administration reported that the mean retail price per gallon of regular grade gasoline was $1.47 (*The Wall Street Journal,* January 30, 2003). Suppose that the standard deviation was $.08 and that the retail price per gallon has a bell-shaped distribution.
    a.   What percentage of regular grade gasoline sold between $1.39 and $1.55 per gallon?
    b.   What percentage of regular grade gasoline sold between $1.39 and $1.63 per gallon?
    c.   What percentage of regular grade gasoline sold for more than $1.63 per gallon?

31. The national average for the verbal portion of the College Board's Scholastic Aptitude Test (SAT) is 507 (*The World Almanac,* 2004). The College Board periodically rescales the test scores such that the standard deviation is approximately 100. Answer the following questions using a bell-shaped distribution and the empirical rule for the verbal test scores.

    a.   What percentage of students have an SAT verbal score greater than 607?

    b.   What percentage of students have an SAT verbal score greater than 707?

    c.   What percentage of students have an SAT verbal score between 407 and 507?

    d.   What percentage of students have an SAT verbal score between 307 and 607?

32.   The high costs in the California real estate market have caused families who cannot afford to buy bigger homes to consider backyard sheds as an alternative form of housing expansion. Many are using the backyard structures for home offices, art studios, and hobby areas as well as for additional storage. The mean price of a customized wooden, shingled backyard structure is $3100 (*Newsweek,* September 29, 2003). Assume that the standard deviation is $1200.

    a.   What is the z-score for a backyard structure costing $2300?

    b.   What is the z-score for a backyard structure costing $4900?

    c.   Interpret the z-scores in parts (a) and (b). Comment on whether either should be considered an outlier.

    d.   The *Newsweek* article described a backyard shed-office combination built in Albany, California, for $13,000. Should this structure be considered an outlier? Explain.

33.   Wageweb conducts surveys of salary data and presents summaries on its Web site. Salaries reported for benefits managers ranged from $50,935 to $79,577 (http://www.Wageweb.com, April 12, 2000). Assume the following data are a sample of the annual salaries for 30 benefits managers. Data are in thousands of dollars.

CD file

WageWeb

57.7	64.4	62.1	59.1	71.1
63.0	64.7	61.2	66.8	61.8
64.2	63.3	62.2	61.2	59.4
63.0	66.7	60.3	74.0	62.8
68.7	63.8	59.2	60.3	56.6
59.3	69.5	61.7	58.9	63.1

    a.   Compute the mean and standard deviation for the sample data.

    b.   Using the mean and standard deviation computed in part (a) as estimates of the mean and standard deviation of salary for the population of benefits managers, use Chebyshev's theorem to determine the percentage of benefits managers with an annual salary between $55,000 and $71,000.

    c.   Develop a histogram for the sample data. Computer software provides .97 as the measure of skewness. Does it appear reasonable to assume that the distribution of annual salary can be approximated by a bell-shaped distribution?

    d.   Assume that the distribution of annual salary is bell-shaped. Using the mean and standard deviation computed in part (a) as estimates of the mean and standard deviation of salary for the population of benefits managers, use the empirical rule to determine the percentage of benefits managers with an annual salary between $55,000 and $71,000. Compare your answer with the value computed in part (b).

    e.   Do the sample data contain any outliers?

34.   A sample of 10 NCAA college basketball game scores provided the following data (*USA Today,* January 26, 2004).

CD file

NCAA

Winning Team	Points	Losing Team	Points	Winning Margin
Arizona	90	Oregon	66	24
Duke	85	Georgetown	66	19
Florida State	75	Wake Forest	70	5
Kansas	78	Colorado	57	21
Kentucky	71	Notre Dame	63	8
Louisville	65	Tennessee	62	3

(*continued*)

Winning Team	Points	Losing Team	Points	Winning Margin
Oklahoma State	72	Texas	66	6
Purdue	76	Michigan State	70	6
Stanford	77	Southern Cal	67	10
Wisconsin	76	Illinois	56	20

   a.   Compute the mean and standard deviation for the points scored by the winning team.

   b.   Assume that the points scored by the winning teams for all NCAA games follow a bell-shaped distribution. Using the mean and standard deviation found in part (a), estimate the percentage of all NCAA games in which the winning team scores 84 or more points. Estimate the percentage of NCAA games in which the winning team scores more than 90 points.

   c.   Compute the mean and standard deviation for the winning margin. Do the data contain outliers? Explain.

35.   *Consumer Review* posts reviews and ratings of a variety of products on the Internet. The following is a sample of 20 speaker systems and their ratings (http://www.audioreview.com). The ratings are on a scale of 1 to 5, with 5 being best.

Speakers

Speaker	Rating	Speaker	Rating
Infinity Kappa 6.1	4.00	ACI Sapphire III	4.67
Allison One	4.12	Bose 501 Series	2.14
Cambridge Ensemble II	3.82	DCM KX-212	4.09
Dynaudio Contour 1.3	4.00	Eosone RSF1000	4.17
Hsu Rsch. HRSW12V	4.56	Joseph Audio RM7si	4.88
Legacy Audio Focus	4.32	Martin Logan Aerius	4.26
Mission 73li	4.33	Omni Audio SA 12.3	2.32
PSB 400i	4.50	Polk Audio RT12	4.50
Snell Acoustics D IV	4.64	Sunfire True Subwoofer	4.17
Thiel CS1.5	4.20	Yamaha NS-A636	2.17

   a.   Compute the mean and the median.

   b.   Compute the first and third quartiles.

   c.   Compute the standard deviation.

   d.   The skewness of this data is -1.67. Comment on the shape of the distribution.

   e.   What are the z-scores associated with Allison One and Omni Audio?

   f.   Do the data contain any outliers? Explain.

3.4 Exploratory Data Analysis

In Chapter 2 we introduced the stem-and-leaf display as a technique of exploratory data analysis. Recall that exploratory data analysis enables us to use simple arithmetic and easy-to-draw pictures to summarize data. In this section we continue exploratory data analysis by considering five-number summaries and box plots.

Five-Number Summary

In a **five-number summary**, the following five numbers are used to summarize the data.

   1. Smallest value

   2. First quartile (Q_1)

   3. Median (Q_2)

4. Third quartile (Q_3)
5. Largest value

The easiest way to develop a five-number summary is to first place the data in ascending order. Then it is easy to identify the smallest value, the three quartiles, and the largest value. The monthly starting salaries shown in Table 3.1 for a sample of 12 business school graduates are repeated here in ascending order.

$$2710 \quad 2755 \quad 2850 \quad \bigg| \quad 2880 \quad 2880 \quad 2890 \quad \bigg| \quad 2920 \quad 2940 \quad 2950 \quad \bigg| \quad 3050 \quad 3130 \quad 3325$$

$$Q_1 = 2865 \qquad\qquad Q_2 = 2905 \qquad\qquad Q_3 = 3000$$
$$\text{(Median)}$$

The median of 2905 and the quartiles $Q_1 = 2865$ and $Q_3 = 3000$ were computed in Section 3.1. Reviewing the data shows a smallest value of 2710 and a largest value of 3325. Thus, the five-number summary for the salary data is 2710, 2865, 2905, 3000, 3325. Approximately one-fourth, or 25%, of the observations are between adjacent numbers in a five-number summary.

Box Plot

A **box plot** is a graphical summary of data that is based on a five-number summary. A key to the development of a box plot is the computation of the median and the quartiles, Q_1 and Q_3. The interquartile range, IQR $= Q_3 - Q_1$, is also used. Figure 3.11 is the box plot for the monthly starting salary data. The steps used to construct the box plot follow.

Box plots provide another way to identify outliers. But they do not necessarily identify the same values as those with a z-score less than -3 or greater than $+3$. Either or both procedures may be used.

1. A box is drawn with the ends of the box located at the first and third quartiles. For the salary data, $Q_1 = 2865$ and $Q_3 = 3000$. This box contains the middle 50% of the data.
2. A vertical line is drawn in the box at the location of the median (2905 for the salary data).
3. By using the interquartile range, IQR $= Q_3 - Q_1$, *limits* are located. The limits for the box plot are 1.5(IQR) below Q_1 and 1.5(IQR) above Q_3. For the salary data, IQR $= Q_3 - Q_1 = 3000 - 2865 = 135$. Thus, the limits are $2865 - 1.5(135) = 2662.5$ and $3000 + 1.5(135) = 3202.5$. Data outside these limits are considered *outliers*.
4. The dashed lines in Figure 3.11 are called *whiskers*. The whiskers are drawn from the ends of the box to the smallest and largest values *inside the limits* computed in step 3. Thus, the whiskers end at salary values of 2710 and 3130.
5. Finally, the location of each outlier is shown with the symbol *. In Figure 3.11 we see one outlier, 3325.

FIGURE 3.11 BOX PLOT OF THE STARTING SALARY DATA WITH LINES SHOWING THE LOWER AND UPPER LIMITS

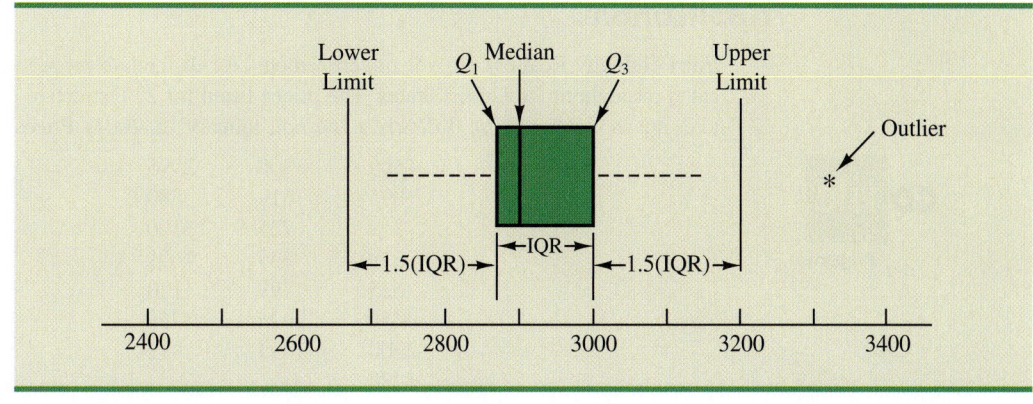

FIGURE 3.12   BOX PLOT OF THE STARTING SALARY DATA

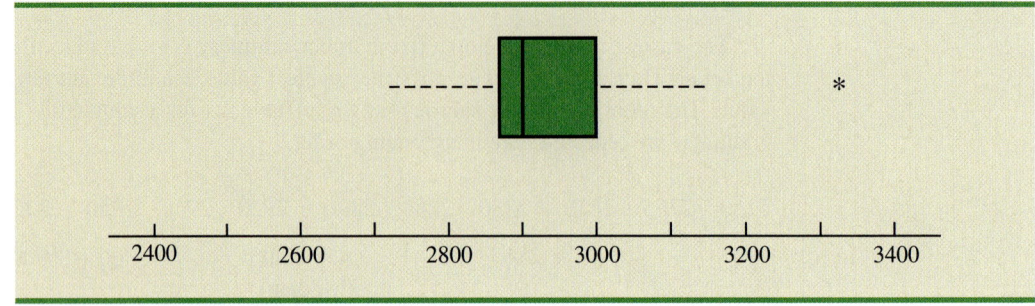

In Figure 3.11 we included lines showing the location of the upper and lower limits. These lines were drawn to show how the limits are computed and where they are located for the salary data. Although the limits are always computed, generally they are not drawn on the box plots. Figure 3.12 shows the usual appearance of a box plot for the salary data.

NOTES AND COMMENTS

1. An advantage of the exploratory data analysis procedures is that they are easy to use; few numerical calculations are necessary. We simply sort the data values into ascending order and identify the five-number summary. The box plot can then be constructed. It is not necessary to compute the mean and the standard deviation for the data.

2. Excel 2003 does not contain a procedure for constructing box plots. In Appendix 3.1, we show how to construct a box plot for the starting salary data using SWStat+, an Excel add-in.

Exercises

Methods

36. Consider a sample with data values of 27, 25, 20, 15, 30, 34, 28, and 25. Provide the five-number summary for the data.

37. Show the box plot for the data in exercise 36.

38. Show the five-number summary and the box plot for the following data: 5, 15, 18, 10, 8, 12, 16, 10, 6.

39. A data set has a first quartile of 42 and a third quartile of 50. Compute the lower and upper limits for the corresponding box plot. Should a data value of 65 be considered an outlier?

Applications

40. Ebby Halliday Realtors provide advertisements for distinctive properties and estates located throughout the United States. The prices listed for 22 distinctive properties and estates are shown here (*The Wall Street Journal,* January 16, 2004). Prices are in thousands.

Property

1500	700	2995
895	619	880
719	725	3100
619	739	1699
625	799	1120
4450	2495	1250
2200	1395	912
1280		

a. Provide a five-number summary.
b. Compute the lower and upper limits.
c. The highest priced property, $4,450,000, is listed as an estate overlooking White Rock Lake in Dallas, Texas. Should this property be considered an outlier? Explain.
d. Should the second highest priced property listed for $3,100,000 be considered an outlier? Explain.
e. Show a box plot.

41. Annual sales, in millions of dollars, for 21 pharmaceutical companies follow.

8408	1374	1872	8879	2459	11413
608	14138	6452	1850	2818	1356
10498	7478	4019	4341	739	2127
3653	5794	8305			

a. Provide a five-number summary.
b. Compute the lower and upper limits.
c. Do the data contain any outliers?
d. Johnson & Johnson's sales are the largest on the list at $14,138 million. Suppose a data entry error (a transposition) had been made and the sales had been entered as $41,138 million. Would the method of detecting outliers in part (c) identify this problem and allow for correction of the data entry error?
e. Show a box plot.

42. Major League Baseball payrolls continue to escalate. Team payrolls in millions are as follows (*The Miami Herald,* May 22, 2002).

Payroll

Team	Payroll ($)	Team	Payroll ($)
Anaheim	62	Milwaukee	50
Arizona	103	Minnesota	40
Atlanta	93	Montreal	39
Baltimore	60	NY Mets	95
Boston	108	NY Yankees	126
Chi Cubs	76	Oakland	40
Chi White Sox	57	Philadelphia	58
Cincinnati	45	Pittsburgh	42
Cleveland	79	San Diego	41
Colorado	57	San Francisco	78
Detroit	55	Seattle	90
Florida	42	St. Louis	74
Houston	63	Tampa Bay	34
Kansas City	47	Texas	105
Los Angeles	95	Toronto	77

a. What is the median team payroll?
b. Provide a five-number summary.
c. Is the $126 million payroll for the New York Yankees an outlier? Explain.
d. Show a box plot.

43. New York Stock Exchange (NYSE) Chairman Richard Grasso and NYSE Board of Directors came under fire for the large compensation package being paid to Grasso. When it comes to salary plus bonus, Grasso's $8.5 million out-earned the top executives of all major financial services companies. The data that follow show total annual salary plus bonus paid

to the top executives of 14 financial services companies (*The Wall Street Journal*, September 17, 2003). Data are in millions.

Company	Salary and Bonus ($)	Company	Salary and Bonus ($)
Aetna	3.5	Fannie Mae	4.3
AIG	6.0	Federal Home Loan	0.8
Allstate	4.1	Fleet Boston	1.0
American Express	3.8	Freddie Mac	1.2
Chubb	2.1	Mellon Financial	2.0
Cigna	1.0	Merrill Lynch	7.7
Citigroup	1.0	Wells Fargo	8.0

a. What is the median annual salary plus bonus paid to the top executive of the 14 financial service companies?
b. Provide a five-number summary.
c. Should Grasso's $8.5 million annual salary plus bonus be considered an outlier for this group of top executives? Explain.
d. Show a box plot.

44. A listing of 46 mutual funds and their 12-month total return percentage is shown in Table 3.5 (*Smart Money*, February 2004).

Mutual

a. What are the mean and median return percentages for these mutual funds?
b. What are the first and third quartiles?
c. Provide a five-number summary.
d. Do the data contain any outliers? Show a box plot.

TABLE 3.5   TWELVE-MONTH RETURN FOR MUTUAL FUNDS

Mutual Fund	Return (%)	Mutual Fund	Return (%)
Alger Capital Appreciation	23.5	Nations Small Company	21.4
Alger LargeCap Growth	22.8	Nations SmallCap Index	24.5
Alger MidCap Growth	38.3	Nations Strategic Growth	10.4
Alger SmallCap	41.3	Nations Value Inv	10.8
AllianceBernstein Technology	40.6	One Group Diversified Equity	10.0
Federated American Leaders	15.6	One Group Diversified Int'l	10.9
Federated Capital Appreciation	12.4	One Group Diversified Mid Cap	15.1
Federated Equity-Income	11.5	One Group Equity Income	6.6
Federated Kaufmann	33.3	One Group Int'l Equity Index	13.2
Federated Max-Cap Index	16.0	One Group LargeCap Growth	13.6
Federated Stock	16.9	One Group LargeCap Value	12.8
Janus Adviser Int'l Growth	10.3	One Group MidCap Growth	18.7
Janus Adviser Worldwide	3.4	One Group MidCap Value	11.4
Janus Enterprise	24.2	One Group SmallCap Growth	23.6
Janus High-Yield	12.1	PBHG Growth	27.3
Janus Mercury	20.6	Putnam Europe Equity	20.4
Janus Overseas	11.9	Putnam Int'l Capital Opportunity	36.6
Janus Worldwide	4.1	Putnam International Equity	21.5
Nations Convertible Securities	13.6	Putnam Int'l New Opportunity	26.3
Nations Int'l Equity	10.7	Strong Advisor MidCap Growth	23.7
Nations LargeCap Enhd. Core	13.2	Strong Growth 20	11.7
Nations LargeCap Index	13.5	Strong Growth Inv	23.2
Nation MidCap Index	19.5	Strong LargeCap Growth	14.5

3.5 Measures of Association Between Two Variables

Thus far we examined numerical methods used to summarize the data for *one variable at a time*. Often a manager or decision maker is interested in the *relationship between two variables*. In this section we present covariance and correlation as measures of the relationship between two variables.

We begin by reconsidering the application concerning a stereo and sound equipment store in San Francisco as presented in Section 2.4. The store's manager wants to determine the relationship between the number of weekend television commercials shown and the sales at the store during the following week. Sample data with sales expressed in hundreds of dollars are provided in Table 3.6. It shows 10 observations ($n = 10$), one for each week. The scatter diagram and trendline in Figure 3.13 shows a positive relationship, with higher sales (y) associated with a greater number of commercials (x). In fact, the trendline suggests that a straight line could be used as an approximation of the relationship. In the following discussion, we introduce **covariance** as a measure of the linear association between two variables.

Covariance

For a sample of size n with the observations (x_1, y_1), (x_2, y_2), and so on, the sample covariance is defined as follows:

SAMPLE COVARIANCE

$$s_{xy} = \frac{\Sigma(x_i - \bar{x})(y_i - \bar{y})}{n - 1}$$ **(3.10)**

This formula pairs each x_i with a y_i. We then sum the products obtained by multiplying the deviation of each x_i from its sample mean $\bar{x}$ by the deviation of the corresponding y_i from its sample mean $\bar{y}$; this sum is then divided by $n - 1$.

TABLE 3.6 SAMPLE DATA FOR THE STEREO AND SOUND EQUIPMENT STORE

CD file

Stereo

Week	Number of Commercials x	Sales Volume ($100s) y
1	2	50
2	5	57
3	1	41
4	3	54
5	4	54
6	1	38
7	5	63
8	3	48
9	4	59
10	2	46

FIGURE 3.13   SCATTER DIAGRAM AND TRENDLINE FOR THE STEREO AND SOUND
EQUIPMENT STORE

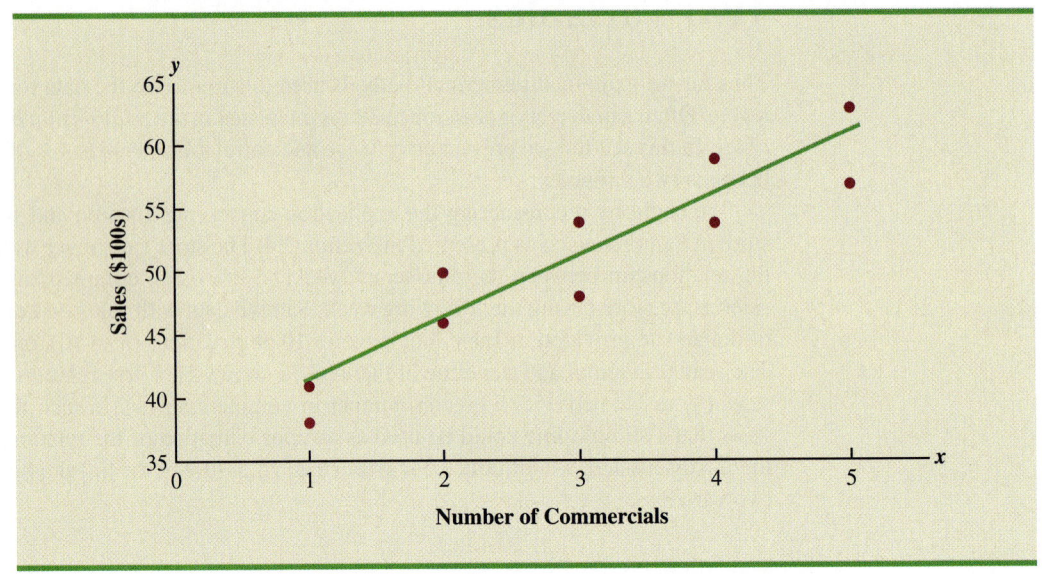

To measure the strength of the linear relationship between the number of commercials
x and the sales volume y in the stereo and sound equipment store problem, we use equation (3.10) to compute the sample covariance. The calculations in Table 3.7 show the
computation of $\Sigma(x_i - \bar{x})(y_i - \bar{y})$. Note that $\bar{x} = 30/10 = 3$ and $\bar{y} = 510/10 = 51$. Using
equation (3.10), we obtain a sample covariance of

$$s_{xy} = \frac{\Sigma(x_i - \bar{x})(y_i - \bar{y})}{n - 1} = \frac{99}{9} = 11$$

TABLE 3.7   CALCULATIONS FOR THE SAMPLE COVARIANCE

	x_i	y_i	$x_i - \bar{x}$	$y_i - \bar{y}$	$(x_i - \bar{x})(y_i - \bar{y})$
	2	50	−1	−1	1
	5	57	2	6	12
	1	41	−2	−10	20
	3	54	0	3	0
	4	54	1	3	3
	1	38	−2	−13	26
	5	63	2	12	24
	3	48	0	−3	0
	4	59	1	8	8
	2	46	−1	−5	5
Totals	30	510	0	0	99

$$s_{xy} = \frac{\Sigma(x_i - \bar{x})(y_i - \bar{y})}{n - 1} = \frac{99}{10 - 1} = 11$$

The formula for computing the covariance of a population of size N is similar to equation (3.10), but we use different notation to indicate that we are working with the entire population.

POPULATION COVARIANCE

$$\sigma_{xy} = \frac{\Sigma(x_i - \mu_x)(y_i - \mu_y)}{N}$$

(3.11)

In equation (3.11) we use the notation μ_x for the population mean of the variable x and μ_y for the population mean of the variable y. The population covariance σ_{xy} is defined for a population of size N.

Interpretation of the Covariance

To aid in the interpretation of the sample covariance, consider Figure 3.14. It is the same as the scatter diagram of Figure 3.13 with a vertical dashed line at $\bar{x} = 3$ and a horizontal dashed line at $\bar{y} = 51$. The lines divide the graph into four quadrants. Points in quadrant I correspond to x_i greater than $\bar{x}$ and y_i greater than $\bar{y}$, points in quadrant II correspond to x_i less than $\bar{x}$ and y_i greater than $\bar{y}$, and so on. Thus, the value of $(x_i - \bar{x})(y_i - \bar{y})$ must be positive for points in quadrant I, negative for points in quadrant II, positive for points in quadrant III, and negative for points in quadrant IV.

The covariance is a measure of the linear association between two variables.

If the value of s_{xy} is positive, the points with the greatest influence on s_{xy} must be in quadrants I and III. Hence, a positive value for s_{xy} indicates a positive linear association between x and y; that is, as the value of x increases, the value of y increases. If the value of s_{xy} is negative, however, the points with the greatest influence on s_{xy} are in quadrants II and IV. Hence, a negative value for s_{xy} indicates a negative linear association between x and y; that is, as the value of x increases, the value of y decreases. Finally, if the points are evenly distributed across all four quadrants, the value of s_{xy} will be close to zero, indicating no linear association between x and y. Figure 3.15 shows the values of s_{xy} that can be expected with three different types of scatter diagrams.

FIGURE 3.14 PARTITIONED SCATTER DIAGRAM FOR THE STEREO AND SOUND EQUIPMENT STORE

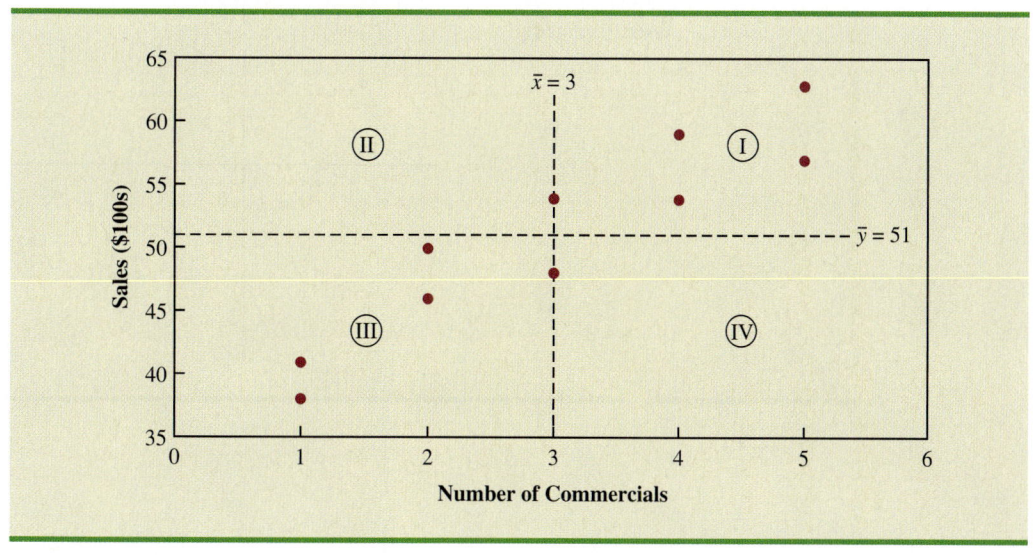

FIGURE 3.15   INTERPRETATION OF SAMPLE COVARIANCE

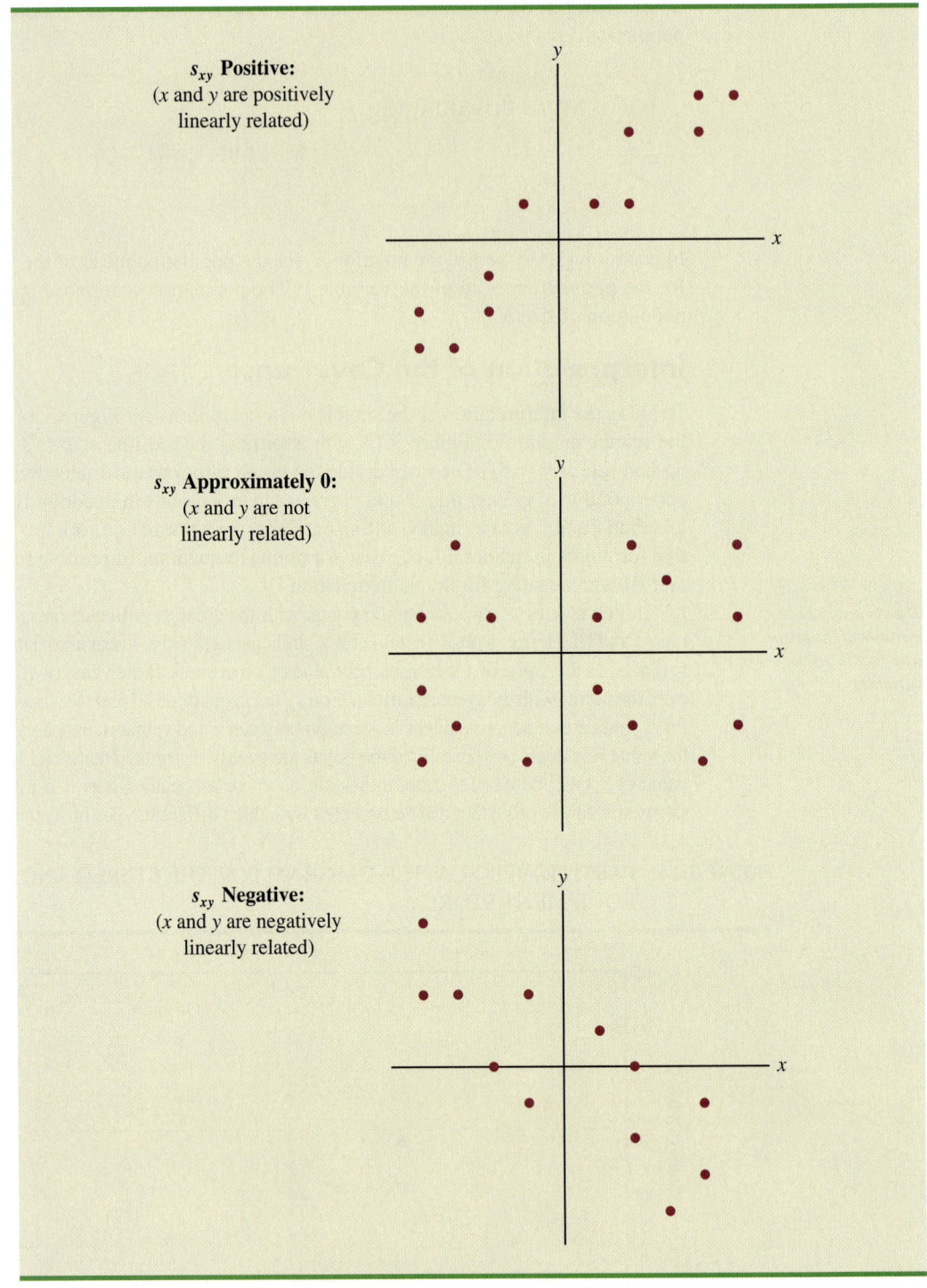

Referring again to Figure 3.14, we see that the scatter diagram for the stereo and sound equipment store follows the pattern in the top panel of Figure 3.15. As we should expect, the value of the sample covariance indicates a positive linear relationship with $s_{xy} = 11$.

From the preceding discussion, it might appear that a large positive value for the covariance indicates a strong positive linear relationship and that a large negative value indicates a strong negative linear relationship. However, one problem with using covariance as a measure of the strength of the linear relationship is that the value of the covariance depends on the units of measurement for x and y. For example, suppose we are interested in the relationship between height x and weight y for individuals. Clearly the strength of the relationship should be the same whether we measure height in feet or inches. Measuring the height in inches, however, gives us much larger numerical values for $(x_i - \bar{x})$ than when we measure height in feet. Thus, with height measured in inches, we would obtain a larger value for the numerator $\Sigma(x_i - \bar{x})(y_i - \bar{y})$ in equation (3.10)—and hence a larger covariance—when in fact the relationship does not change. A measure of the relationship between two variables that is not affected by the units of measurement for x and y is the **correlation coefficient**.

Correlation Coefficient

For sample data, the Pearson product moment correlation coefficient is defined as follows.

PEARSON PRODUCT MOMENT CORRELATION COEFFICIENT: SAMPLE DATA

$$r_{xy} = \frac{s_{xy}}{s_x s_y} \tag{3.12}$$

where

r_{xy} = sample correlation coefficient
s_{xy} = sample covariance
s_x = sample standard deviation of x
s_y = sample standard deviation of y

Equation (3.12) shows that the Pearson product moment correlation coefficient for sample data (commonly referred to more simply as the *sample correlation coefficient*) is computed by dividing the sample covariance by the product of the sample standard deviation of x and the sample standard deviation of y.

Let us now compute the sample correlation coefficient for the stereo and sound equipment store. Using the data in Table 3.7, we can compute the sample standard deviations for the two variables.

$$s_x = \sqrt{\frac{\Sigma(x_i - \bar{x})^2}{n-1}} = \sqrt{\frac{20}{9}} = 1.49$$

$$s_y = \sqrt{\frac{\Sigma(y_i - \bar{y})^2}{n-1}} = \sqrt{\frac{566}{9}} = 7.93$$

Now, because $s_{xy} = 11$, the sample correlation coefficient equals

$$r_{xy} = \frac{s_{xy}}{s_x s_y} = \frac{11}{(1.49)(7.93)} = +.93$$

The formula for computing the correlation coefficient for a population, denoted by the Greek letter ρ_{xy} (rho, pronounced "row"), follows.

PEARSON PRODUCT MOMENT CORRELATION COEFFICIENT:
POPULATION DATA

The sample correlation coefficient r_{xy} is the estimator of the population correlation coefficient ρ_{xy}.

$$\rho_{xy} = \frac{\sigma_{xy}}{\sigma_x \sigma_y}$$ (3.13)

where

ρ_{xy} = population correlation coefficient
σ_{xy} = population covariance
σ_x = population standard deviation for x
σ_y = population standard deviation for y

The sample correlation coefficient r_{xy} provides an estimate of the population correlation coefficient ρ_{xy}.

Interpretation of the Correlation Coefficient

First let us consider a simple example that illustrates the concept of a perfect positive linear relationship. The scatter diagram in Figure 3.16 depicts the relationship between x and y based on the following sample data.

x_i	y_i
5	10
10	30
15	50

FIGURE 3.16   SCATTER DIAGRAM DEPICTING A PERFECT POSITIVE
LINEAR RELATIONSHIP

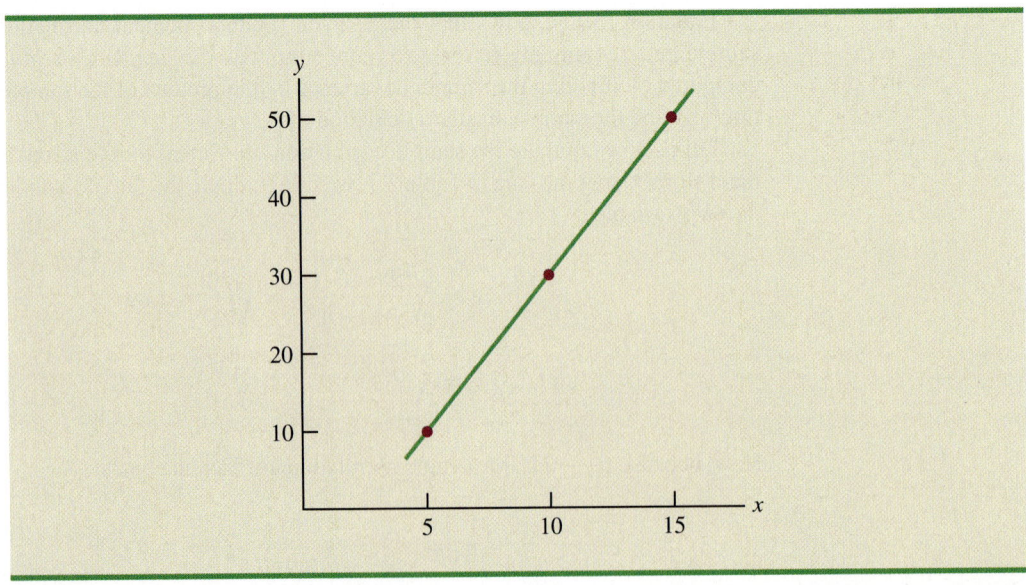

The straight line drawn through each of the three points shows a perfect linear relationship between x and y. In order to apply equation (3.12) to compute the sample correlation we must first compute s_{xy}, s_x, and s_y. Some of the computations are shown in Table 3.8. Using the results in Table 3.8, we find

$$s_{xy} = \frac{\Sigma(x_i - \bar{x})(y_i - \bar{y})}{n - 1} = \frac{200}{2} = 100$$

$$s_x = \sqrt{\frac{\Sigma(x_i - \bar{x})^2}{n - 1}} = \sqrt{\frac{50}{2}} = 5$$

$$s_y = \sqrt{\frac{\Sigma(y_i - \bar{y})^2}{n - 1}} = \sqrt{\frac{800}{2}} = 20$$

$$r_{xy} = \frac{s_{xy}}{s_x s_y} = \frac{100}{5(20)} = 1$$

The correlation coefficient ranges from −1 to +1. Values close to −1 or +1 indicate a strong linear relationship. The closer the correlation is to zero, the weaker the relationship.

Thus, we see that the value of the sample correlation coefficient is 1.

In general, it can be shown that if all the points in a data set fall on a positively sloped straight line, the value of the sample correlation coefficient is +1; that is, a sample correlation coefficient of +1 corresponds to a perfect positive linear relationship between x and y. Moreover, if the points in the data set fall on a straight line having negative slope, the value of the sample correlation coefficient is −1; that is, a sample correlation coefficient of −1 corresponds to a perfect negative linear relationship between x and y.

Let us now suppose that a certain data set indicates a positive linear relationship between x and y but that the relationship is not perfect. The value of r_{xy} will be less than 1, indicating that the points in the scatter diagram are not all on a straight line. As the points deviate more and more from a perfect positive linear relationship, the value of r_{xy} becomes smaller and smaller. A value of r_{xy} equal to zero indicates no linear relationship between x and y, and values of r_{xy} near zero indicate a weak linear relationship.

For the data involving the stereo and sound equipment store, recall that $r_{xy} = +.93$. Therefore, we conclude that a strong positive linear relationship exists between the number of commercials and sales. More specifically, an increase in the number of commercials is associated with an increase in sales.

In closing, we note that correlation provides a measure of linear association and not necessarily causation. A high correlation between two variables does not mean that changes in one variable will cause changes in the other variable. For example, we may find that the quality rating and the typical meal price of restaurants are positively correlated. However, simply increasing the meal price at a restaurant will not cause the quality rating to increase.

TABLE 3.8   COMPUTATIONS USED IN CALCULATING THE SAMPLE CORRELATION COEFFICIENT

	x_i	y_i	$x_i - \bar{x}$	$(x_i - \bar{x})^2$	$y_i - \bar{y}$	$(y_i - \bar{y})^2$	$(x_i - \bar{x})(y_i - \bar{y})$
	5	10	−5	25	−20	400	100
	10	30	0	0	0	0	0
	15	50	5	25	20	400	100
Totals	30	90	0	50	0	800	200

$\bar{x} = 10$ $\bar{y} = 30$

Using Excel to Compute the Covariance and Correlation Coefficient

Excel's COVAR function is designed for a population and Excel's CORREL function is designed for a sample.

Excel provides functions that can be used to compute the covariance and correlation coefficient. But you must be careful when using these functions because the covariance function treats the data as a population and the correlation function treats the data as a sample. Thus, the result obtained using Excel's covariance function must be adjusted to provide the sample covariance. We show here how these functions can be used to compute the sample covariance and the sample correlation coefficient for the stereo and sound equipment store data. Refer to Figure 3.17 as we present the steps involved. The formula worksheet is in the background; the value worksheet is in the foreground.

Enter Data: Labels and data on commercials and sales are entered into cells A1:C11 of the worksheet.

Enter Functions and Formulas: Excel's covariance function, COVAR, can be used to compute the population covariance by entering the following formula into cell F1:

$$=COVAR(B2:B11,C2:C11)$$

Similarly, the formula =CORREL(B2:B11,C2:C11) is entered into cell F2 to compute the sample correlation coefficient. The labels Population Covariance and Sample Correlation are entered into cells E1 and E2 to identify the output.

The formulas in cells F1:F2 are displayed in the worksheet in the background of Figure 3.17. The worksheet in the foreground shows the values computed using the Excel functions. Note that, except for rounding, the value of the sample correlation coefficient (.9305) is the same as we computed earlier using equation (3.12). However, the result provided by the COVAR function, 9.9, was obtained by treating the data as a population. Thus, we must adjust the Excel result of 9.9 to obtain the sample covariance. The adjustment is rather simple. First, note that the formula for the population covariance, equation (3.11), re-

FIGURE 3.17   EXCEL WORKSHEET USED TO COMPUTE THE COVARIANCE AND CORRELATION COEFFICIENT

	A	B	C	D	E	F	G
1	Week	Commercials	Sales		Population Covariance	=COVAR(B2:B11,C2:C11)	
2	1	2	50		Sample Correlation	=CORREL(B2:B11,C2:C11)	
3	2	5	57				
4	3	1	41				
5	4	3	54				
6	5	4	54				
7	6	1	38				
8	7	5	63				
9	8	3	48				
10	9	4	59				
11	10	2	46				
12							

	A	B	C	D	E	F	G
1	Week	Commercials	Sales		Population Covariance	9.9	
2	1	2	50		Sample Correlation	0.9305	
3	2	5	57				
4	3	1	41				
5	4	3	54				
6	5	4	54				
7	6	1	38				
8	7	5	63				
9	8	3	48				
10	9	4	59				
11	10	2	46				
12							

quires dividing by the total number of observations in the data set. But the formula for the sample covariance, equation (3.10), requires dividing by the total number of observations minus 1. So to use the Excel result of 9.9 to compute the sample covariance, we simply multiply 9.9 by $n/(n-1)$. With $n = 10$, we obtain

$$s_{xy} = \left(\frac{10}{9}\right)9.9 = 11$$

Thus, the sample covariance for the stereo and sound equipment data is 11.

Exercises

Methods

45. Five observations taken for two variables follow.

x_i	4	6	11	3	16
y_i	50	50	40	60	30

 a. Develop a scatter diagram with x on the horizontal axis.
 b. What does the scatter diagram developed in part (a) indicate about the relationship between the two variables?
 c. Compute and interpret the sample covariance.
 d. Compute and interpret the sample correlation coefficient.

46. Five observations taken for two variables follow.

x_i	6	11	15	21	27
y_i	6	9	6	17	12

 a. Develop a scatter diagram for these data.
 b. What does the scatter diagram indicate about a relationship between x and y?
 c. Compute and interpret the sample covariance.
 d. Compute and interpret the sample correlation coefficient.

Applications

47. Nielsen Media Research provides two measures of the television viewing audience: a television program *rating,* which is the percentage of households with televisions watching a program, and a television program *share,* which is the percentage of households watching a program among those with televisions in use. The following data show the Nielsen television ratings and share data for the Major League Baseball World Series over a nine-year period (Associated Press, October 27, 2003).

Rating	19	17	17	14	16	12	15	12	13
Share	32	28	29	24	26	20	24	20	22

 a. Develop a scatter diagram with rating on the horizontal axis.
 b. What is the relationship between rating and share? Explain.
 c. Compute and interpret the sample covariance.
 d. Compute the sample correlation coefficient. What does this value tell us about the relationship between rating and share?

48. A department of transportation's study on driving speed and mileage for midsize automobiles resulted in the following data.

Driving Speed	30	50	40	55	30	25	60	25	50	55
Mileage	28	25	25	23	30	32	21	35	26	25

Compute and interpret the sample correlation coefficient.

49. *PC World* provided ratings for 15 notebook PCs (*PC World*, February 2000). The performance score is a measure of how fast a PC can run a mix of common business applications as compared to a baseline machine. For example, a PC with a performance score of 200 is twice as fast as the baseline machine. A 100-point scale was used to provide an overall rating for each notebook tested in the study. A score in the 90s is exceptional, while one in the 70s is good. Table 3.9 shows the performance scores and the overall ratings for the 15 notebooks.
   a. Compute the sample correlation coefficient.
   b. What does the sample correlation coefficient tell about the relationship between the performance score and the overall rating?

50. The Dow Jones Industrial Average (DJIA) and the Standard & Poor's (S&P) 500 Index are both used as measures of overall movement in the stock market. The DJIA is based on the price movements of 30 large companies; the S&P 500 is an index composed of 500 stocks. Some say the S&P 500 is a better measure of stock market performance because it is broader based. The closing price for the DJIA and the S&P 500 for 10 weeks, beginning with February 11, 2000, are shown (*Barron's*, April 17, 2000).

CD file
DowS&P

Date	Dow Jones	S&P 500	Date	Dow Jones	S&P 500
February 11	10425	1387	March 17	10595	1464
February 18	10220	1346	March 24	11113	1527
February 25	9862	1333	March 31	10922	1499
March 3	10367	1409	April 7	11111	1516
March 10	9929	1395	April 14	10306	1357

   a. Compute the sample correlation coefficient for these data.
   b. Discuss the association between the DJIA and the S&P 500 Index.

TABLE 3.9   PERFORMANCE SCORES AND OVERALL RATINGS FOR 15 NOTEBOOK PCs

CD file
PCs

Notebook	Performance Score	Overall Rating
AMS Tech Roadster 15CTA380	115	67
Compaq Armada M700	191	78
Compaq Prosignia Notebook 150	153	79
Dell Inspiron 3700 C466GT	194	80
Dell Inspiron 7500 R500VT	236	84
Dell Latitude Cpi A366XT	184	76
Enpower ENP-313 Pro	184	77
Gateway Solo 9300LS	216	92
HP Pavilion Notebook PC	185	83
IBM ThinkPad I Series 1480	183	78
Micro Express NP7400	189	77
Micron TransPort NX PII-400	202	78
NEC Versa SX	192	78
Sceptre Soundx 5200	141	73
Sony VAIO PCG-F340	187	77

51.   The daily high and low temperatures for 12 U.S. cities are as follows (Weather Channel, January 25, 2004).

Temperature

City	High	Low	City	High	Low
Albany	9	−8	Los Angeles	62	47
Boise	32	26	New Orleans	71	55
Cleveland	21	19	Portland	43	36
Denver	37	10	Providence	18	8
Des Moines	24	16	Raleigh	28	24
Detroit	20	17	Tulsa	55	38

a.   What is the sample mean daily high temperature?
b.   What is the sample mean daily low temperature?
c.   What is the correlation between the high and low temperatures?

3.6   The Weighted Mean and Working with Grouped Data

In Section 3.1, we presented the mean as one of the most important measures of central location. The formula for the mean of a sample with n observations is restated as follows.

$$\bar{x} = \frac{\Sigma x_i}{n} = \frac{x_1 + x_2 + \cdots + x_n}{n} \qquad \textbf{(3.14)}$$

In this formula, each x_i is given equal importance or weight. Although this practice is most common, in some instances, the mean is computed by giving each observation a weight that reflects its importance. A mean computed in this manner is referred to as a **weighted mean**.

Weighted Mean

The weighted mean is computed as follows:

WEIGHTED MEAN

$$\bar{x} = \frac{\Sigma w_i x_i}{\Sigma w_i} \qquad \textbf{(3.15)}$$

where

$$x_i = \text{value of observation } i$$
$$w_i = \text{weight for observation } i$$

When the data are from a sample, equation (3.15) provides the weighted sample mean. When the data are from a population, μ replaces $\bar{x}$ and equation (3.15) provides the weighted population mean.

As an example of the need for a weighted mean, consider the following sample of five purchases of a raw material over the past three months.

Purchase	Cost per Pound ($)	Number of Pounds
1	3.00	1200
2	3.40	500
3	2.80	2750
4	2.90	1000
5	3.25	800

Note that the cost per pound varies from $2.80 to $3.40, and the quantity purchased varies from 500 to 2750 pounds. Suppose that a manager asked for information about the mean cost per pound of the raw material. Because the quantities ordered vary, we must use the formula for a weighted mean. The five cost-per-pound data values are $x_1 = 3.00$, $x_2 = 3.40$, $x_3 = 2.80$, $x_4 = 2.90$, and $x_5 = 3.25$. The weighted mean cost per pound is found by weighting each cost by its corresponding quantity. For this example, the weights are $w_1 = 1200$, $w_2 = 500$, $w_3 = 2750$, $w_4 = 1000$, and $w_5 = 800$. Using equation (3.15), the weighted mean is calculated as follows:

$$\bar{x} = \frac{1200(3.00) + 500(3.40) + 2750(2.80) + 1000(2.90) + 800(3.25)}{1200 + 500 + 2750 + 1000 + 800}$$

$$= \frac{18,500}{6250} = 2.96$$

Thus, the weighted mean computation shows that the mean cost per pound for the raw material is $2.96. Note that using equation (3.14) rather than the weighted mean formula would have provided misleading results. In this case, the mean of the five cost-per-pound values is $(3.00 + 3.40 + 2.80 + 2.90 + 3.25)/5 = 15.35/5 = \$3.07$, which overstates the actual mean cost per pound purchased.

The choice of weights for a particular weighted mean computation depends upon the application. An example that is well known to college students is the computation of a grade point average (GPA). In this computation, the data values generally used are 4 for an A grade, 3 for a B grade, 2 for a C grade, 1 for a D grade, and 0 for an F grade. The weights are the number of credits hours earned for each grade. Exercise 54 at the end of this section provides an example of this weighted mean computation. In other weighted mean computations, quantities such as pounds, dollars, or volume are frequently used as weights. In any case, when observations vary in importance, the analyst must choose the weight that best reflects the importance of each observation in the determination of the mean.

Computing a grade point average is a good example of the use of a weighted mean.

Grouped Data

In most cases, measures of location and variability are computed by using the individual data values. Sometimes, however, data are available only in a grouped or frequency distribution form. In the following discussion, we show how the weighted mean formula can be used to obtain approximations of the mean, variance, and standard deviation for **grouped data**.

In Section 2.2 we provided a frequency distribution of the time in days required to complete year-end audits for the public accounting firm of Sanderson and Clifford. The frequency distribution of audit times based on a sample of 20 clients is shown again in Table 3.10. Based on this frequency distribution, what is the sample mean audit time?

TABLE 3.10   FREQUENCY DISTRIBUTION OF AUDIT TIMES

Audit Time (days)	Frequency
10–14	4
15–19	8
20–24	5
25–29	2
30–34	1
Total	20

To compute the mean using only the grouped data, we treat the midpoint of each class as being representative of the items in the class. Let M_i denote the midpoint for class i and let f_i denote the frequency of class i. The weighted mean formula (3.15) is then used with the data values denoted as M_i and the weights given by the frequencies f_i. In this case, the denominator of equation (3.15) is the sum of the frequencies, which is the sample size n. That is, $\Sigma f_i = n$. Thus, the equation for the sample mean for grouped data is as follows.

SAMPLE MEAN FOR GROUPED DATA

$$\bar{x} = \frac{\Sigma f_i M_i}{n} \tag{3.16}$$

where

$$M_i = \text{the midpoint for class } i$$
$$f_i = \text{the frequency for class } i$$
$$n = \text{the sample size}$$

With the class midpoints, M_i, halfway between the class limits, the first class of 10–14 in Table 3.10 has a midpoint at $(10 + 14)/2 = 12$. The five class midpoints and the weighted mean computation for the audit time data are summarized in Table 3.11. As can be seen, the sample mean audit time is 19 days.

TABLE 3.11   COMPUTATION OF THE SAMPLE MEAN AUDIT TIME FOR GROUPED DATA

Audit Time (days)	Class Midpoint (M_i)	Frequency (f_i)	$f_i M_i$
10–14	12	4	48
15–19	17	8	136
20–24	22	5	110
25–29	27	2	54
30–34	32	1	32
		20	380

$$\text{Sample mean } \bar{x} = \frac{\Sigma f_i M_i}{n} = \frac{380}{20} = 19 \text{ days}$$

To compute the variance for grouped data, we use a slightly altered version of the formula for the variance provided in equation (3.5). In equation (3.5), the squared deviations of the data about the sample mean $\bar{x}$ were written $(x_i - \bar{x})^2$. However, with grouped data, the values are not known. In this case, we treat the class midpoint, M_i, as being representative of the x_i values in the corresponding class. Thus, the squared deviations about the sample mean, $(x_i - \bar{x})^2$, are replaced by $(M_i - \bar{x})^2$. Then, just as we did with the sample mean calculations for grouped data, we weight each value by the frequency of the class, f_i. The sum of the squared deviations about the mean for all the data is approximated by $\Sigma f_i(M_i - \bar{x})^2$. The term $n - 1$ rather than n appears in the denominator in order to make the sample variance the estimate of the population variance. Thus, the following formula is used to obtain the sample variance for grouped data.

SAMPLE VARIANCE FOR GROUPED DATA

$$s^2 = \frac{\Sigma f_i(M_i - \bar{x})^2}{n - 1} \qquad \textbf{(3.17)}$$

The calculation of the sample variance for audit times based on the grouped data from Table 3.10 is shown in Table 3.12. As can be seen, the sample variance is 30.

The standard deviation for grouped data is simply the square root of the variance for grouped data. For the audit time data, the sample standard deviation is $s = \sqrt{30} = 5.48$.

Before closing this section on computing measures of location and dispersion for grouped data, we note that formulas (3.16) and (3.17) are for a sample. Population summary measures are computed similarly. The grouped data formulas for a population mean and variance follow.

POPULATION MEAN FOR GROUPED DATA

$$\mu = \frac{\Sigma f_i M_i}{N} \qquad \textbf{(3.18)}$$

TABLE 3.12   COMPUTATION OF THE SAMPLE VARIANCE OF AUDIT TIMES FOR GROUPED DATA (SAMPLE MEAN $\bar{x} = 19$)

Audit Time (days)	Class Midpoint (M_i)	Frequency (f_i)	Deviation ($M_i - \bar{x}$)	Squared Deviation ($M_i - \bar{x})^2$	$f_i(M_i - \bar{x})^2$
10–14	12	4	−7	49	196
15–19	17	8	−2	4	32
20–24	22	5	3	9	45
25–29	27	2	8	64	128
30–34	32	1	13	169	169
		20			570
					$\Sigma f_i(M_i - \bar{x})^2$

Sample variance $s^2 = \dfrac{\Sigma f_i(M_i - \bar{x})^2}{n - 1} = \dfrac{570}{19} = 30$

POPULATION VARIANCE FOR GROUPED DATA

$$\sigma^2 = \frac{\Sigma f_i (M_i - \mu)^2}{N}$$

(3.19)

NOTES AND COMMENTS

In computing descriptive statistics for grouped data, the class midpoints are used to approximate the data values in each class. As a result, the descriptive statistics for grouped data approximate the descriptive statistics that would result from using the original data directly. We therefore recommend computing descriptive statistics from the original data rather than from grouped data whenever possible.

Exercises

Methods

52. Consider the following data and corresponding weights.

x_i	Weight (w_i)
3.2	6
2.0	3
2.5	2
5.0	8

a. Compute the weighted mean.
b. Compute the sample mean of the four data values without weighting. Note the difference in the results provided by the two computations.

53. Consider the sample data in the following frequency distribution.

Class	Midpoint	Frequency
3–7	5	4
8–12	10	7
13–17	15	9
18–22	20	5

a. Compute the sample mean.
b. Compute the sample variance and sample standard deviation.

Applications

54. The grade point average for college students is based on a weighted mean computation. For most colleges, the grades are given the following data values: A (4), B (3), C (2), D (1), and F (0). After 60 credit hours of course work, a student at State University earned 9 credit hours of A, 15 credit hours of B, 33 credit hours of C, and 3 credit hours of D.
a. Compute the student's grade point average.
b. Students at State University must maintain a 2.5 grade point average for their first 60 credit hours of course work in order to be admitted to the business college. Will this student be admitted?

55. *Bloomberg Personal Finance* (July/August 2001) included the following companies in its recommended investment portfolio. For a portfolio value of $25,000, the recommended dollar amounts allocated to each stock are shown.

Company	Portfolio ($)	Estimated Growth Rate (%)	Dividend Yield (%)
Citigroup	3000	15	1.21
General Electric	5500	14	1.48
Kimberly-Clark	4200	12	1.72
Oracle	3000	25	0.00
Pharmacia	3000	20	0.96
SBC Communications	3800	12	2.48
WorldCom	2500	35	0.00

   a. Using the portfolio dollar amounts as the weights, what is the weighted average estimated growth rate for the portfolio?
   b. What is the weighted average dividend yield for the portfolio?

56. A service station recorded the following frequency distribution for the number of gallons of gasoline sold per car in a sample of 680 cars.

Gasoline (gallons)	Frequency
0–4	74
5–9	192
10–14	280
15–19	105
20–24	23
25–29	6
Total	680

   Compute the mean, variance, and standard deviation for these grouped data. If the service station expects to service about 120 cars on a given day, estimate the total number of gallons of gasoline that will be sold.

57. A survey of subscribers to *Fortune* magazine asked the following question: "How many of the last four issues have you read?" Suppose that the following frequency distribution summarizes 500 responses.

Number Read	Frequency
0	15
1	10
2	40
3	85
4	350
Total	500

   a. What is the mean number of issues read by a *Fortune* subscriber?
   b. What is the standard deviation of the number of issues read?

Summary

In this chapter we introduced several descriptive statistics that can be used to summarize the location, variability, and shape of a data distribution. Unlike the tabular and graphical procedures introduced in Chapter 2, the measures introduced in this chapter summarize the data in terms of numerical values. When the numerical values obtained are for a sample, they are called sample statistics. When the numerical values obtained are for a population, they are called population parameters. Some of the sample statistics and population parameters discussed follow.

In statistical inference, the sample statistic is referred to as the point estimator of the population parameter.

	Sample Statistic	Population Parameter
Mean	$\bar{x}$	μ
Variance	s^2	σ^2
Standard deviation	s	σ
Covariance	s_{xy}	σ_{xy}
Correlation	r_{xy}	ρ_{xy}

As measures of central location, we defined the mean, median, and mode. Then the concept of percentiles was used to describe other locations in the data set. Next, we presented the range, interquartile range, variance, standard deviation, and coefficient of variation as measures of variability or dispersion. Our primary measure of the shape of a data distribution was the skewness. Negative values indicate a data distribution skewed to the left. Positive values indicate a data distribution skewed to the right. We then described how the mean and standard deviation could be used, applying Chebyshev's theorem and the empirical rule, to provide more information about the distribution of data and to identify outliers.

In Section 3.4 we showed how to develop a five-number summary and a box plot to provide simultaneous information about the location, variability, and shape of the distribution. In Section 3.5 we introduced covariance and the correlation coefficient as measures of association between two variables. In the final section, we showed how to compute a weighted mean and how to calculate a mean, variance, and standard deviation for grouped data.

Most of the descriptive statistics discussed in this chapter can be computed using the functions and tools available in Excel. We showed how to use many of these functions as well as the Descriptive Statistics tool.

Glossary

Sample statistic A numerical value used as a summary measure for a sample (e.g., the sample mean, $\bar{x}$, the sample variance, s^2, and the sample standard deviation, s).

Population parameter A numerical value used as a summary measure for a population (e.g., the population mean, μ, the population variance, σ^2, and the population standard deviation, σ).

Point estimator The sample statistic, such as $\bar{x}$, s^2, and s, used to estimate the corresponding population parameter.

Mean A measure of central location computed by summing the data values and dividing by the number of observations.

Median A measure of central location provided by the value in the middle when the data are arranged in ascending order.

Mode A measure of location, defined as the value that occurs with greatest frequency.

Percentile A value such that at least p percent of the observations are less than or equal to this value and at least $(100 - p)$ percent of the observations are greater than or equal to this value. The 50th percentile is the median.

Quartiles The 25th, 50th, and 75th percentiles, referred to as the first quartile, the second quartile (median), and third quartile, respectively. The quartiles can be used to divide a data set into four parts, with each part containing approximately 25% of the data.

Range A measure of variability, defined to be the largest value minus the smallest value.

Interquartile range (IQR) A measure of variability, defined to be the difference between the third and first quartiles.

Variance A measure of variability based on the squared deviations of the data values about the mean.

Standard deviation A measure of variability computed by taking the positive square root of the variance.

Coefficient of variation A measure of relative variability computed by dividing the standard deviation by the mean and multiplying by 100.

Skewness A measure of the shape of a data distribution. Data skewed to the left result in negative skewness; a symmetric data distribution results in zero skewness; and data skewed to the right result in positive skewness.

z-score A value computed by dividing the deviation about the mean $(x_i - \bar{x})$ by the standard deviation s. A z-score is referred to as a standardized value and denotes the number of standard deviations x_i is from the mean.

Chebyshev's theorem A theorem that can be used to make statements about the proportion of data values that must be within a specified number of standard deviations of the mean.

Empirical rule A rule that can be used to compute the percentage of data values that must be within one, two, and three standard deviations of the mean for data that exhibit a bell-shaped distribution.

Outlier An unusually small or unusually large data value.

Five-number summary An exploratory data analysis technique that uses five numbers to summarize the data: smallest value, first quartile, median, third quartile, and largest value.

Box plot A graphical summary of data based on a five-number summary.

Covariance A measure of linear association between two variables. Positive values indicate a positive relationship; negative values indicate a negative relationship.

Correlation coefficient A measure of linear association between two variables that takes on values between -1 and $+1$. Values near $+1$ indicate a strong positive linear relationship; values near -1 indicate a strong negative linear relationship; and values near zero indicate the lack of a linear relationship.

Weighted mean The mean obtained by assigning each observation a weight that reflects its importance.

Grouped data Data in a grouped or a frequency distribution form.

Key Formulas

Sample Mean

$$\bar{x} = \frac{\Sigma x_i}{n} \tag{3.1}$$

Population Mean

$$\mu = \frac{\Sigma x_i}{N} \tag{3.2}$$

Interquartile Range

$$\text{IQR} = Q_3 - Q_1 \tag{3.3}$$

Population Variance

$$\sigma^2 = \frac{\Sigma(x_i - \mu)^2}{N} \tag{3.4}$$

Sample Variance

$$s^2 = \frac{\Sigma(x_i - \bar{x})^2}{n - 1} \tag{3.5}$$

Standard Deviation

$$\text{Sample standard deviation} = s = \sqrt{s^2} \tag{3.6}$$
$$\text{Population standard deviation} = \sigma = \sqrt{\sigma^2} \tag{3.7}$$

Coefficient of Variation

$$\left(\frac{\text{Standard deviation}}{\text{Mean}} \times 100\right)\% \tag{3.8}$$

z-Score

$$z_i = \frac{x_i - \bar{x}}{s} \tag{3.9}$$

Sample Covariance

$$s_{xy} = \frac{\Sigma(x_i - \bar{x})(y_i - \bar{y})}{n - 1} \tag{3.10}$$

Population Covariance

$$\sigma_{xy} = \frac{\Sigma(x_i - \mu_x)(y_i - \mu_y)}{N} \tag{3.11}$$

Pearson Product Moment Correlation Coefficient: Sample Data

$$r_{xy} = \frac{s_{xy}}{s_x s_y} \tag{3.12}$$

Pearson Product Moment Correlation Coefficient: Population Data

$$\rho_{xy} = \frac{\sigma_{xy}}{\sigma_x \sigma_y} \tag{3.13}$$

Weighted Mean

$$\bar{x} = \frac{\Sigma w_i x_i}{\Sigma w_i} \tag{3.15}$$

Sample Mean for Grouped Data

$$\bar{x} = \frac{\Sigma f_i M_i}{n} \tag{3.16}$$

Sample Variance for Grouped Data

$$s^2 = \frac{\Sigma f_i (M_i - \bar{x})^2}{n - 1} \qquad \textbf{(3.17)}$$

Population Mean for Grouped Data

$$\mu = \frac{\Sigma f_i M_i}{N} \qquad \textbf{(3.18)}$$

Population Variance for Grouped Data

$$\sigma^2 = \frac{\Sigma f_i (M_i - \mu)^2}{N} \qquad \textbf{(3.19)}$$

Supplementary Exercises

58. According to the 2003 Annual Consumer Spending Survey, the average monthly Bank of America Visa credit card charge was $1838 (*U.S. Airways Attaché Magazine,* December 2003). A sample of monthly credit card charges provides the following data.

Visa

236	1710	1351	825	7450
316	4135	1333	1584	387
991	3396	170	1428	1688

   a. Compute the mean and median.
   b. Compute the first and third quartiles.
   c. Compute the range and interquartile range.
   d. Compute the variance and standard deviation.
   e. The skewness measure for these data is 2.12. Comment on the shape of this distribution. Is it the shape you would expect? Why or why not?
   f. Do the data contain outliers?

59. The total annual compensation for a board member at one of the nation's 100 biggest public companies is based in part on the cash retainer, an annual payment for serving on the board. In addition to the cash retainer, a board member may receive a stock retainer, a stock grant, a stock option, and a fee for attending board meetings. The total compensation can easily exceed $100,000 even with an annual retainer as low as $15,000. The following data show the cash retainer (in $1000s) for a sample of 20 of the nation's biggest public companies (*USA Today,* April 17, 2000).

Retainer

Company	Cash Retainer
American Express	64
Bank of America	36
Boeing	26
Chevron	35
Dell Computer	40
DuPont	35
ExxonMobil	40
Ford Motor	30
General Motors	60
International Paper	36
Kroger	28
Lucent Technologies	50

Company	Cash Retainer
Motorola	20
Procter & Gamble	55
Raytheon	40
Sears Roebuck	30
Texaco	15
United Parcel Service	55
Wal-Mart Stores	25
Xerox	40

Compute the following descriptive statistics.
a. Mean, median, and mode
b. The first and third quartiles
c. The range and interquartile range
d. The variance and the standard deviation
e. Coefficient of variation

60. Dividend yield is the annual dividend per share a company pays divided by the current market price per share expressed as a percentage. A sample of 10 large companies provided the following dividend yield data (*The Wall Street Journal,* January 16, 2004).

Company	Yield %	Company	Yield %
Altria Group	5.0	General Motors	3.7
American Express	0.8	JPMorgan Chase	3.5
Caterpillar	1.8	McDonald's	1.6
Eastman Kodak	1.9	United Technology	1.5
ExxonMobil	2.5	Wal-Mart Stores	0.7

a. What are the mean and median dividend yields?
b. What are the variance and standard deviation?
c. Which company provides the highest dividend yield?
d. What is the z-score for McDonald's? Interpret this z-score.
e. What is the z-score for General Motors? Interpret this z-score.
f. Based on z-scores, do the data contain any outliers?

61. According to Forrester Research, Inc., approximately 19% of Internet users play games online. The following data show the number of unique users (in thousands) for the month of March for 10 game sites (*The Wall Street Journal,* April 17, 2000).

Site	Unique Users
aolgames.com	9416
extremelotto.com	3955
freelotto.com	12901
gamesville.com	4844
iwin.com	7410
prizecentral.com	4899
shockwave.com	5582
speedyclick.com	6628
uproar.com	8821
webstakes.com	7499

Using these data, compute the mean, median, variance, and standard deviation.

62. The typical household income for a sample of 20 cities follows (*Places Rated Almanac*, 2000). Data are in thousands of dollars.

Income

City	Income	City	Income
Akron, OH	74.1	Hartford, CT	89.1
Atlanta, GA	82.4	Lancaster, PA	75.2
Birmingham, AL	71.2	Madison, WI	78.8
Bismark, ND	62.8	Naples, FL	100.0
Cleveland, OH	79.2	Nashville, TN	77.3
Columbia, SC	66.8	Philadelphia, PA	87.0
Danbury, CT	132.3	Savannah, GA	67.8
Denver, CO	82.6	Toledo, OH	71.2
Detroit, MI	85.3	Trenton, NJ	106.4
Fort Lauderdale, FL	75.8	Washington, DC	97.4

a. Compute the mean and standard deviation for the sample data.
b. Using the mean and standard deviation computed in part (a) as estimates of the mean and standard deviation of household income for the population of all cities, use Chebyshev's theorem to determine the range within which 75% of the household incomes for the population of all cities must fall.
c. Assume that the distribution of household income is bell-shaped. Using the mean and standard deviation computed in part (a) as estimates of the mean and standard deviation of household income for the population of all cities, use the empirical rule to determine the range within which 95% of the household incomes for the population of all cities must fall. Compare your answer with the value in part (b).
d. Do the sample data contain any outliers?

63. Public transportation and the automobile are two methods an employee can use to get to work each day. Samples of times recorded for each method are shown. Times are in minutes.

Public Transportation:	28	29	32	37	33	25	29	32	41	34
Automobile:	29	31	33	32	34	30	31	32	35	33

a. Compute the sample mean time to get to work for each method.
b. Compute the sample standard deviation for each method.
c. On the basis of your results from parts (a) and (b), which method of transportation should be preferred? Explain.
d. Develop a box plot for each method. Does a comparison of the box plots support your conclusion in part (c)?

64. The typical household income and typical home price for a sample of 20 cities follow (*Places Rated Almanac*, 2000). Data are in thousands of dollars.

Cities

City	Income	Home Price
Bismark, ND	62.8	92.8
Columbia, SC	66.8	116.7
Savannah, GA	67.8	108.1
Birmingham, AL	71.2	130.9
Toledo, OH	71.2	101.1
Akron, OH	74.1	114.9
Lancaster, PA	75.2	125.9
Fort Lauderdale, FL	75.8	145.3
Nashville, TN	77.3	125.9
Madison, WI	78.8	145.2

City	Income	Home Price
Cleveland, OH	79.2	135.8
Atlanta, GA	82.4	126.9
Denver, CO	82.6	161.9
Detroit, MI	85.3	145.0
Philadelphia, PA	87.0	151.5
Hartford, CT	89.1	162.1
Washington, DC	97.4	191.9
Naples, FL	100.0	173.6
Trenton, NJ	106.4	168.1
Danbury, CT	132.3	234.1

a. What is the value of the sample covariance? Does it indicate a positive or a negative linear relationship between income and home price?

b. What is the sample correlation coefficient?

65. The following data show the media expenditures ($ millions) and shipments in millions of barrels (bbls.) for 10 major brands of beer.

Beer

Brand	Media Expenditures ($ millions)	Shipments in bbls. (millions)
Budweiser	120.0	36.3
Bud Light	68.7	20.7
Miller Lite	100.1	15.9
Coors Light	76.6	13.2
Busch	8.7	8.1
Natural Light	0.1	7.1
Miller Genuine Draft	21.5	5.6
Miller High Life	1.4	4.4
Busch Lite	5.3	4.3
Milwaukee's Best	1.7	4.3

a. What is the sample covariance? Does it indicate a positive or negative relationship between media expenditures and shipments?

b. What is the sample correlation coefficient?

66. *Road & Track* provided the following sample of the tire ratings and load-carrying capacity of automobiles tires.

Tire Rating	Load-Carrying Capacity
75	853
82	1047
85	1135
87	1201
88	1235
91	1356
92	1389
93	1433
105	2039

a. Develop a scatter diagram for the data with tire rating on the x-axis.

b. What is the sample correlation coefficient, and what does it tell you about the relationship between tire rating and load-carrying capacity?

67. The following data show the trailing 52-weeks primary share earnings and book values as reported by 10 companies (*The Wall Street Journal*, March 13, 2000).

Company	Book Value	Earnings	Company	Book Value	Earnings
Am Elec	25.21	2.69	Enron Cp.	7.44	1.27
Columbia En	23.20	3.01	Peco	13.61	3.15
Con Ed	25.19	3.13	Pub Sv Ent	21.86	3.29
Duke Energy	20.17	2.25	Southn Co.	8.77	1.86
Edison Int'l	13.55	1.79	Unicom	23.22	2.74

   a. Develop a scatter diagram for the data with book value on the *x*-axis.
   b. What is the sample correlation coefficient, and what does it tell you about the relationship between the earnings per share and the book value?

68. A forecasting technique referred to as moving averages uses the average or mean of the most recent *n* periods to forecast the next value for time series data. With a three-period moving average, the most recent three periods of data are used in the forecast computation. Consider a product with the following demand for the first three months of the current year: January (800 units), February (750 units), and March (900 units).
   a. What is the three-month moving average forecast for April?
   b. A variation of this forecasting technique is called weighted moving averages. The weighting allows the more recent time series data to receive more weight or more importance in the computation of the forecast. For example, a weighted three-month moving average might give a weight of 3 to data one month old, a weight of 2 to data two months old, and a weight of 1 to data three months old. Use the data given to provide a three-month weighted moving average forecast for April.

69. The days to maturity for a sample of five money market funds are shown here. The dollar amounts invested in the funds are provided. Use the weighted mean to determine the mean number of days to maturity for dollars invested in these five money market funds.

Days to Maturity	Dollar Value ($ millions)
20	20
12	30
7	10
5	15
6	10

70. Automobiles traveling on a road with a posted speed limit of 55 miles per hour are checked for speed by a state police radar system. Following is a frequency distribution of speeds.

Speed (miles per hour)	Frequency
45–49	10
50–54	40
55–59	150
60–64	175
65–69	75
70–74	15
75–79	10
Total	475

a. What is the mean speed of the automobiles traveling on this road?
b. Compute the variance and the standard deviation.

Case Problem 1   Pelican Stores

Pelican Stores, a division of National Clothing, is a chain of women's apparel stores operating throughout the country. The chain recently ran a promotion in which discount coupons were sent to customers of other National Clothing stores. Data collected for a sample of 100 in-store credit card transactions at Pelican Stores during one day while the promotion was running are contained in the file named PelicanStores. Table 3.13 shows a portion of the data set. The Proprietary Card method of payment refers to charges made using a National Clothing charge card. Customers who made a purchase using a discount coupon are referred to as promotional customers and customers who made a purchase but did not use a discount coupon are referred to as regular customers. Because the promotional coupons were not sent to regular Pelican Stores customers, management considers the sales made to people presenting the promotional coupons as sales it would not otherwise make. Of course, Pelican also hopes that the promotional customers will continue to shop at its stores.

Most of the variables shown in Table 3.13 are self-explanatory, but two of the variables require some clarification.

Items   The total number of items purchased
Net Sales   The total amount ($) charged to the credit card

Pelican's management would like to use this sample data to learn about its customer base and to evaluate the promotion involving discount coupons.

TABLE 3.13   DATA FOR A SAMPLE OF 100 CREDIT CARD PURCHASES AT PELICAN STORES

PelicanStores

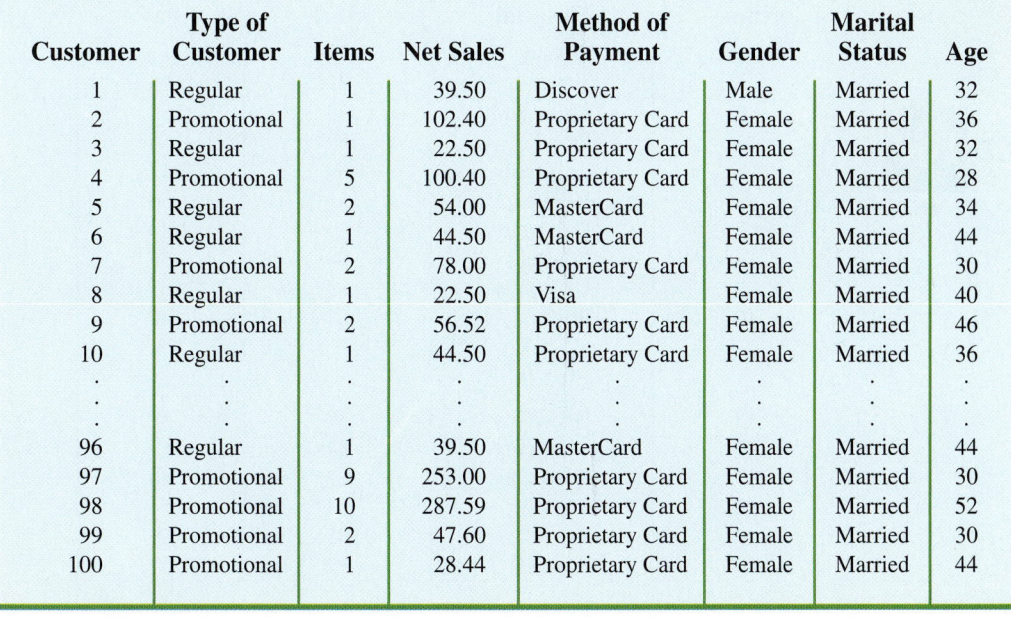

Customer	Type of Customer	Items	Net Sales	Method of Payment	Gender	Marital Status	Age
1	Regular	1	39.50	Discover	Male	Married	32
2	Promotional	1	102.40	Proprietary Card	Female	Married	36
3	Regular	1	22.50	Proprietary Card	Female	Married	32
4	Promotional	5	100.40	Proprietary Card	Female	Married	28
5	Regular	2	54.00	MasterCard	Female	Married	34
6	Regular	1	44.50	MasterCard	Female	Married	44
7	Promotional	2	78.00	Proprietary Card	Female	Married	30
8	Regular	1	22.50	Visa	Female	Married	40
9	Promotional	2	56.52	Proprietary Card	Female	Married	46
10	Regular	1	44.50	Proprietary Card	Female	Married	36
⋮	⋮	⋮	⋮	⋮	⋮	⋮	⋮
96	Regular	1	39.50	MasterCard	Female	Married	44
97	Promotional	9	253.00	Proprietary Card	Female	Married	30
98	Promotional	10	287.59	Proprietary Card	Female	Married	52
99	Promotional	2	47.60	Proprietary Card	Female	Married	30
100	Promotional	1	28.44	Proprietary Card	Female	Married	44

Managerial Report

Use the methods of descriptive statistics presented in this chapter to summarize the data and comment on your findings. At a minimum, your report should include the following:

1. Descriptive statistics on net sales and descriptive statistics on net sales by various classifications of customers.
2. Descriptive statistics concerning the relationship between age and net sales.

Case Problem 2   # National Health Care Association

The National Health Care Association is concerned about the shortage of nurses the health care profession is projecting for the future. To learn the current degree of job satisfaction among nurses, the association sponsored a study of hospital nurses throughout the country. As part of this study, 50 nurses in a sample indicated their degree of satisfaction with their work, their pay, and their opportunities for promotion. Each of the three aspects of satisfaction was measured on a scale from 0 to 100, with larger values indicating higher degrees of satisfaction. The data collected also showed the type of hospital employing the nurses. The types of hospitals were Private, Veterans Administration (VA), and University. A portion of the data is shown in Table 3.14. The complete data set can be found on the CD accompanying the text in the file named Health.

Managerial Report

Use methods of descriptive statistics to summarize the data. Present the summaries that will be beneficial in communicating the results to others. Discuss your findings. Specifically, comment on the following questions.

1. On the basis of the entire data set and the three job satisfaction variables, what aspect of the job is most satisfying for the nurses? What appears to be the least satisfying? In what area(s), if any, do you feel improvements should be made? Discuss.

TABLE 3.14   SATISFACTION SCORE DATA FOR A SAMPLE OF 50 NURSES

CD file

Health

Nurse	Hospital	Work	Pay	Promotion
1	Private	74	47	63
2	VA	72	76	37
3	University	75	53	92
4	Private	89	66	62
5	University	69	47	16
6	Private	85	56	64
7	University	89	80	64
8	Private	88	36	47
9	University	88	55	52
10	Private	84	42	66
.	.	.	.	.
.	.	.	.	.
.	.	.	.	.
45	University	79	59	41
46	University	84	53	63
47	University	87	66	49
48	VA	84	74	37
49	VA	95	66	52
50	Private	72	57	40

2. On the basis of descriptive measures of variability, what measure of job satisfaction appears to generate the greatest difference of opinion among the nurses? Explain.

3. What can be learned about the types of hospitals? Does any particular type of hospital seem to have better levels of job satisfaction than the other types? Do your results suggest any recommendations for learning about and improving job satisfaction? Discuss.

4. What additional descriptive statistics and insights can you use to learn about and possibly improve job satisfaction?

Case Problem 3   Business Schools of Asia-Pacific

Asian

The pursuit of a higher education degree in business is now international. A survey shows that more and more Asians choose the Master of Business Administration degree route to corporate success (*Asia, Inc.,* September 1997). The number of applicants for MBA courses at Asia-Pacific schools continues to increase about 30% a year. In 1997, the 74 business schools in the Asia-Pacific region reported a record 170,000 applications for the 11,000 full-time MBA degrees to be awarded in 1999. A main reason for the surge in demand is that an MBA can greatly enhance earning power.

Across the region, thousands of Asians show an increasing willingness to temporarily shelve their careers and spend two years in pursuit of a theoretical business qualification. Courses in these schools are notoriously tough and include economics, banking, marketing, behavioral sciences, labor relations, decision making, strategic thinking, business law, and more. *Asia, Inc.* provided the data set in Table 3.15, which shows some of the characteristics of the leading Asia-Pacific business schools.

Managerial Report

Use the methods of descriptive statistics to summarize the data in Table 3.15. Discuss your findings.

1. Include a summary for each variable in the data set. Make comments and interpretations based on maximums and minimums, as well as the appropriate means and proportions. What new insights do these descriptive statistics provide concerning Asia-Pacific business schools?

2. Summarize the data to compare the following:
   a. Any difference between local and foreign tuition costs.
   b. Any difference between mean starting salaries for schools requiring and not requiring work experience.
   c. Any difference between starting salaries for schools requiring and not requiring English tests.

3. Do starting salaries appear to be related to tuition?

4. Present any additional graphical and numerical summaries that will be beneficial in communicating the data in Table 3.15 to others.

Appendix 3.1   Constructing a Box Plot Using SWStat+

We discussed the box plot in Section 3.4. A box plot is a graphical display of data based on a five-number summary: smallest value, first quartile, median, third quartile, and largest value. Excel 2003 does not have a procedure for constructing a box plot. In this appendix we describe the steps required to construct a box plot for the starting salary data using SWStat+. First, we must create the data area.

TABLE 3.15   DATA FOR 25 ASIA-PACIFIC BUSINESS SCHOOLS

Business School	Full-Time Enrollment	Students per Faculty	Local Tuition ($)	Foreign Tuition ($)	Age	%Foreign	GMAT	English Test	Work Experience	Starting Salary ($)
Melbourne Business School	200	5	24,420	29,600	28	47	Yes	No	Yes	71,400
University of New South Wales (Sydney)	228	4	19,993	32,582	29	28	Yes	No	Yes	65,200
Indian Institute of Management (Ahmedabad)	392	5	4,300	4,300	22	0	No	No	No	7,100
Chinese University of Hong Kong	90	5	11,140	11,140	29	10	Yes	No	No	31,000
International University of Japan (Niigata)	126	4	33,060	33,060	28	60	Yes	Yes	No	87,000
Asian Institute of Management (Manila)	389	5	7,562	9,000	25	50	Yes	No	Yes	22,800
Indian Institute of Management (Bangalore)	380	5	3,935	16,000	23	1	Yes	No	No	7,500
National University of Singapore	147	6	6,146	7,170	29	51	Yes	Yes	Yes	43,300
Indian Institute of Management (Calcutta)	463	8	2,880	16,000	23	0	No	No	No	7,400
Australian National University (Canberra)	42	2	20,300	20,300	30	80	Yes	Yes	Yes	46,600
Nanyang Technological University (Singapore)	50	5	8,500	8,500	32	20	Yes	No	Yes	49,300
University of Queensland (Brisbane)	138	17	16,000	22,800	32	26	No	No	Yes	49,600
Hong Kong University of Science and Technology	60	2	11,513	11,513	26	37	Yes	No	Yes	34,000
Macquarie Graduate School of Management (Sydney)	12	8	17,172	19,778	34	27	No	No	Yes	60,100
Chulalongkorn University (Bangkok)	200	7	17,355	17,355	25	6	Yes	No	Yes	17,600
Monash Mt. Eliza Business School (Melbourne)	350	13	16,200	22,500	30	30	Yes	Yes	Yes	52,500
Asian Institute of Management (Bangkok)	300	10	18,200	18,200	29	90	No	Yes	Yes	25,000
University of Adelaide	20	19	16,426	23,100	30	10	No	Yes	Yes	66,000
Massey University (Palmerston North, New Zealand)	30	15	13,106	21,625	37	35	No	Yes	Yes	41,400
Royal Melbourne Institute of Technology Business Graduate School	30	7	13,880	17,765	32	30	No	Yes	Yes	48,900
Jamnalal Bajaj Institute of Management Studies (Bombay)	240	9	1,000	1,000	24	0	No	No	Yes	7,000
Curtin Institute of Technology (Perth)	98	15	9,475	19,097	29	43	Yes	No	Yes	55,000
Lahore University of Management Sciences	70	14	11,250	26,300	23	2.5	No	No	No	7,500
Universiti Sains Malaysia (Penang)	30	5	2,260	2,260	32	15	No	Yes	Yes	16,000
De La Salle University (Manila)	44	17	3,300	3,600	28	3.5	Yes	No	Yes	13,100

Creating the Data Area

Step 1. Select any cell in the starting salary data set
Step 2. Select the **SWStat+** menu
Step 3. Choose **Data Area**
Step 4. Choose **Set New Data Area** from the list of Data Area options
Step 5. When the SWStat+ Data Area dialog box appears:

    Select the **Set New** tab
    Select **With column headers**
    Select **With row headers**
    Click **Set data area**

After creating the data area, the row and column labels are highlighted in yellow and the entire data set (including labels) is surrounded by a blue border.

The worksheet in Figure 3.18 shows the starting salary data set with the SWStat+ data area highlighted. A Results worksheet has also been added to the workbook. (View the Worksheet tabs to see where the Results worksheet is located.)

Constructing a Box Plot

We are now ready to use SWStat+ to create a box plot for the starting salary data. The necessary steps are as follows:

Step 1. Select the **SWStat+** menu
Step 2. Choose **Charts and Graphs**
Step 3. When the SWStat+: Charts and Graphs dialog box appears:

    Select the **One Variable** tab
    Select **Box Plot**
    Select **Starting Salary** in the Variables list
    Select **Modified** in the Style list
    Click **Show Chart**

FIGURE 3.18   STARTING SALARY DATA AFTER SETTING THE DATA AREA USING SWStat+

	A	B	C	D
1	**Graduate**	**Starting Salary**		
2	1	2850		
3	2	2950		
4	3	3050		
5	4	2880		
6	5	2755		
7	6	2710		
8	7	2890		
9	8	3130		
10	9	2940		
11	10	3325		
12	11	2920		
13	12	2880		
14				
15				
16				

A box plot is now displayed in the Results worksheet. We can resize it as desired using the following steps.

Step 1. Position the mouse pointer over the horizontal axis and right-click
Step 2. Select **Format Axis**
Step 3. When the Format Axis dialog box appears:
Select the **Scale** tab
Enter 2400 in the **Minimum** box
Enter 3400 in the **Maximum** box
Click **OK**

The resulting box plot is shown in Figure 3.19. It is similar to the one shown in Figure 3.12.

FIGURE 3.19   SWStat+ RESULTS WORKSHEET SHOWING BOX PLOT

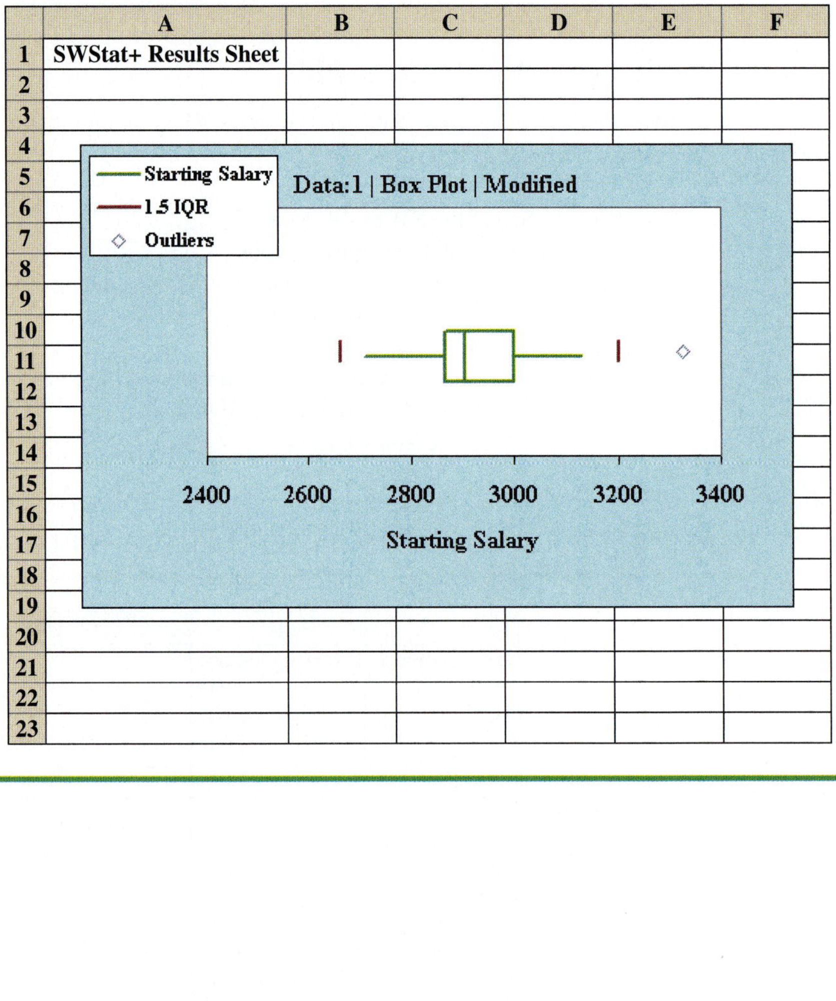

CHAPTER 4

Introduction to Probability

CONTENTS

STATISTICS IN PRACTICE:
MORTON INTERNATIONAL

4.1 EXPERIMENTS, COUNTING
RULES, AND ASSIGNING
PROBABILITIES
Counting Rules, Combinations,
and Permutations
Assigning Probabilities
Probabilities for the KP&L
Project

4.2 EVENTS AND THEIR
PROBABILITIES

4.3 SOME BASIC
RELATIONSHIPS OF
PROBABILITY
Complement of an Event
Addition Law

4.4 CONDITIONAL
PROBABILITY
Independent Events
Multiplication Law

4.5 BAYES' THEOREM
Tabular Approach
Using Excel to Compute
Posterior Probabilities

STATISTICS *in* PRACTICE

MORTON INTERNATIONAL*
CHICAGO, ILLINOIS

Morton International is a company with businesses in salt, household products, rocket motors, and specialty chemicals. Carstab Corporation, a subsidiary of Morton International, produces specialty chemicals and offers a variety of chemicals designed to meet the unique specifications of its customers. For one particular customer, Carstab produced an expensive catalyst used in chemical processing. Some, but not all, of the lots produced by Carstab met the customer's specifications for the product.

Carstab's customer agreed to test each lot after receiving it and determine whether the catalyst would perform the desired function. Lots that did not pass the customer's test would be returned to Carstab. Over time, Carstab found that the customer was accepting 60% of the lots and returning 40%. In probability terms, each Carstab shipment to the customer had a .60 probability of being accepted and a .40 probability of being returned.

Neither Carstab nor its customer was pleased with these results. In an effort to improve service, Carstab explored the possibility of duplicating the customer's test prior to shipment. However, the high cost of the special testing equipment made that alternative infeasible. Carstab's chemists then proposed a new, relatively low-cost test designed to indicate whether a lot would pass the customer's test. The probability question of interest was: What is the probability that a lot will pass the customer's test if it has passed the new Carstab test?

Morton Salt: "When It Rains It Pours." © Joe Higgins/South-Western.

A sample of lots was produced and subjected to the new Carstab test. Only lots that passed the new test were sent to the customer. Probability analysis of the data indicated that if a lot passed the Carstab test, it had a .909 probability of passing the customer's test and being accepted. Alternatively, if a lot passed the Carstab test, it had only a .091 probability of being returned. The probability analysis provided key supporting evidence for the adoption and implementation of the new testing procedure at Carstab. The new test resulted in an immediate improvement in customer service and a substantial reduction in shipping and handling costs for returned lots.

The probability of a lot being accepted by the customer after passing the new Carstab test is called a conditional probability. In this chapter, you will learn how to compute this and other probabilities that are helpful in decision making.

*The authors are indebted to Michael Haskell of Morton International for providing this Statistics in Practice.

Managers often base their decisions on an analysis of uncertainties such as the following:

1. What are the chances that sales will decrease if we increase prices?
2. What is the likelihood a new assembly method will increase productivity?
3. How likely is it that the project will be finished on time?
4. What is the chance that a new investment will be profitable?

Some of the earliest work on probability originated in a series of letters between Pierre de Fermat and Blaise Pascal in the 1650s.

Probability is a numerical measure of the likelihood that an event will occur. Thus, probabilities can be used as measures of the degree of uncertainty associated with the four events previously listed. If probabilities are available, we can determine the likelihood of each event occurring.

Probability values are always assigned on a scale from 0 to 1. A probability near zero indicates an event is unlikely to occur; a probability near 1 indicates an event is almost cer-

FIGURE 4.1 PROBABILITY AS A NUMERICAL MEASURE OF THE LIKELIHOOD OF AN EVENT OCCURRING

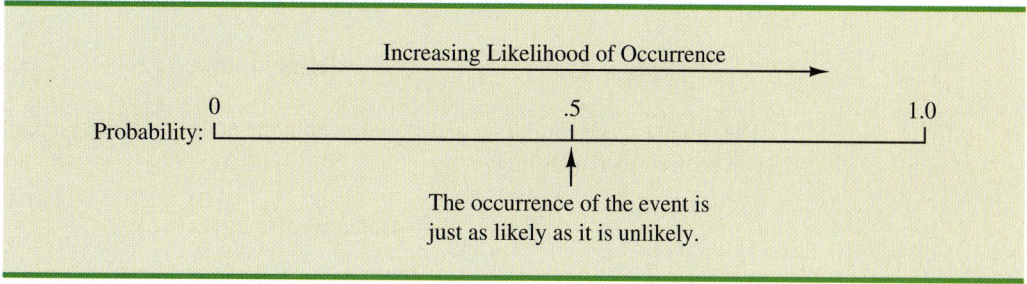

tain to occur. Other probabilities between 0 and 1 represent degrees of likelihood that an event will occur. For example, if we consider the event "rain tomorrow," we understand that when the weather report indicates "a near-zero probability of rain," it means almost no chance of rain. However, if a .90 probability of rain is reported, we know that rain is likely to occur. A .50 probability indicates that rain is just as likely to occur as not. Figure 4.1 depicts the view of probability as a numerical measure of the likelihood of an event occurring.

4.1 Experiments, Counting Rules, and Assigning Probabilities

In discussing probability, we define an **experiment** as a process that generates well-defined outcomes. On any single repetition of an experiment, one and only one of the possible experimental outcomes will occur. Several examples of experiments and their associated outcomes follow.

Experiment	**Experimental Outcomes**
Toss a coin	Head, tail
Select a part for inspection	Defective, nondefective
Conduct a sales call	Purchase, no purchase
Roll a die	1, 2, 3, 4, 5, 6
Play a football game	Win, lose, tie

By specifying all possible experimental outcomes, we identify the **sample space** for an experiment.

SAMPLE SPACE

The sample space for an experiment is the set of all experimental outcomes.

Experimental outcomes are also called sample points.

An experimental outcome is also called a **sample point** to identify it as an element of the sample space.

Consider the first experiment in the preceding table—tossing a coin. The upward face of the coin—a head or a tail—determines the experimental outcomes (sample points). If we let S denote the sample space, we can use the following notation to describe the sample space.

$$S = \{\text{Head, Tail}\}$$

The sample space for the second experiment in the table—selecting a part for inspection—can be described as follows:

$$S = \{\text{Defective, Nondefective}\}$$

Both of the experiments just described have two experimental outcomes (sample points). However, suppose we consider the fourth experiment listed in the table—rolling a die. The possible experimental outcomes, defined as the number of dots appearing on the upward face of the die, are the six points in the sample space for this experiment.

$$S = \{1, 2, 3, 4, 5, 6\}$$

Counting Rules, Combinations, and Permutations

Being able to identify and count the experimental outcomes is a necessary step in assigning probabilities. We now discuss three useful counting rules.

Multiple-Step Experiments The first counting rule applies to multiple-step experiments. Consider the experiment of tossing two coins. Let the experimental outcomes be defined in terms of the pattern of heads and tails appearing on the upward faces of the two coins. How many experimental outcomes are possible for this experiment? The experiment of tossing two coins can be thought of as a two-step experiment in which step 1 is the tossing of the first coin and step 2 is the tossing of the second coin. If we use H to denote a head and T to denote a tail, (H, H) indicates the experimental outcome with a head on the first coin and a head on the second coin. Continuing this notation, we can describe the sample space (S) for this coin-tossing experiment as follows:

$$S = \{(H, H), (H, T), (T, H), (T, T)\}$$

Thus, we see that four experimental outcomes are possible. In this case, we can easily list all of the experimental outcomes.

The counting rule for multiple-step experiments makes it possible to determine the number of experimental outcomes without listing them.

COUNTING RULE FOR MULTIPLE-STEP EXPERIMENTS

If an experiment can be described as a sequence of k steps with n_1 possible outcomes on the first step, n_2 possible outcomes on the second step, and so on, then the total number of experimental outcomes is given by $(n_1) (n_2) \ldots (n_k)$.

Viewing the experiment of tossing two coins as a sequence of first tossing one coin ($n_1 = 2$) and then tossing the other coin ($n_2 = 2$), we can see from the counting rule that there are $(2)(2) = 4$ distinct experimental outcomes. As shown, they are $S = \{(H, H), (H, T), (T, H), (T, T)\}$. The number of experimental outcomes in an experiment involving tossing six coins is $(2)(2)(2)(2)(2)(2) = 64$.

Without the tree diagram, one might think only three experimental outcomes are possible for two tosses of a coin: 0 heads, 1 head, and 2 heads.

A **tree diagram** is a graph that helps in visualizing a multiple-step experiment. Figure 4.2 shows a tree diagram for the experiment of tossing two coins. The sequence of steps moves from left to right through the tree. Step 1 corresponds to tossing the first coin, and step 2 corresponds to tossing the second coin. For each step, the two possible outcomes are head or tail. Note that for each possible outcome at step 1 two branches correspond to the two possible outcomes at step 2. Each of the points on the right end of the tree corresponds to an experimental outcome. Each path through the tree from the leftmost node to one of the nodes at the right side of the tree corresponds to a unique sequence of outcomes.

Let us now see how the counting rule for multiple-step experiments can be used in the analysis of a capacity expansion project for the Kentucky Power & Light Company (KP&L). KP&L is starting a project designed to increase the generating capacity of one of its plants in northern Kentucky. The project is divided into two sequential stages or steps: stage 1 (design) and stage 2 (construction). Even though each stage will be scheduled and controlled as closely as possible, management cannot predict beforehand the exact time required to complete each stage of the project. An analysis of similar construction projects revealed possible completion times for the design stage of 2, 3, or 4 months and possible completion times for the construction stage of 6, 7, or 8 months. In addition, because of the critical need for additional electrical power, management set a goal of 10 months for the completion of the entire project.

Because this project has three possible completion times for the design stage (step 1) and three possible completion times for the construction stage (step 2), the counting rule for multiple-step experiments can be used to show that there are $(3)(3) = 9$ experimental outcomes. To describe the experimental outcomes, we use a two-number notation; for instance, (2, 6) indicates that the design stage is completed in 2 months and the construction stage is completed in 6 months. This experimental outcome results in a total of $2 + 6 = 8$ months to complete the entire project. Table 4.1 summarizes the nine experimental outcomes for the KP&L problem. The tree diagram in Figure 4.3 shows how the nine outcomes (sample points) occur.

The counting rule and tree diagram help the project manager identify the experimental outcomes and determine the possible project completion times. From the information in

FIGURE 4.2 TREE DIAGRAM FOR THE EXPERIMENT OF TOSSING TWO COINS

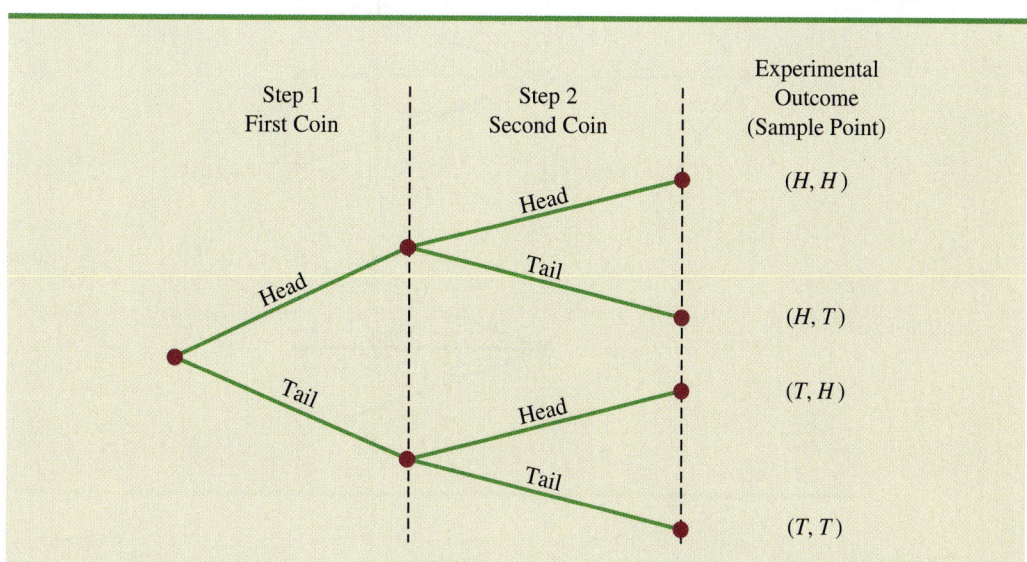

TABLE 4.1   EXPERIMENTAL OUTCOMES (SAMPLE POINTS) FOR THE KP&L PROJECT

Completion Time (months)		Notation for Experimental Outcome	Total Project Completion Time (months)
Stage 1 Design	**Stage 2 Construction**		
2	6	(2, 6)	8
2	7	(2, 7)	9
2	8	(2, 8)	10
3	6	(3, 6)	9
3	7	(3, 7)	10
3	8	(3, 8)	11
4	6	(4, 6)	10
4	7	(4, 7)	11
4	8	(4, 8)	12

FIGURE 4.3   TREE DIAGRAM FOR THE KP&L PROJECT

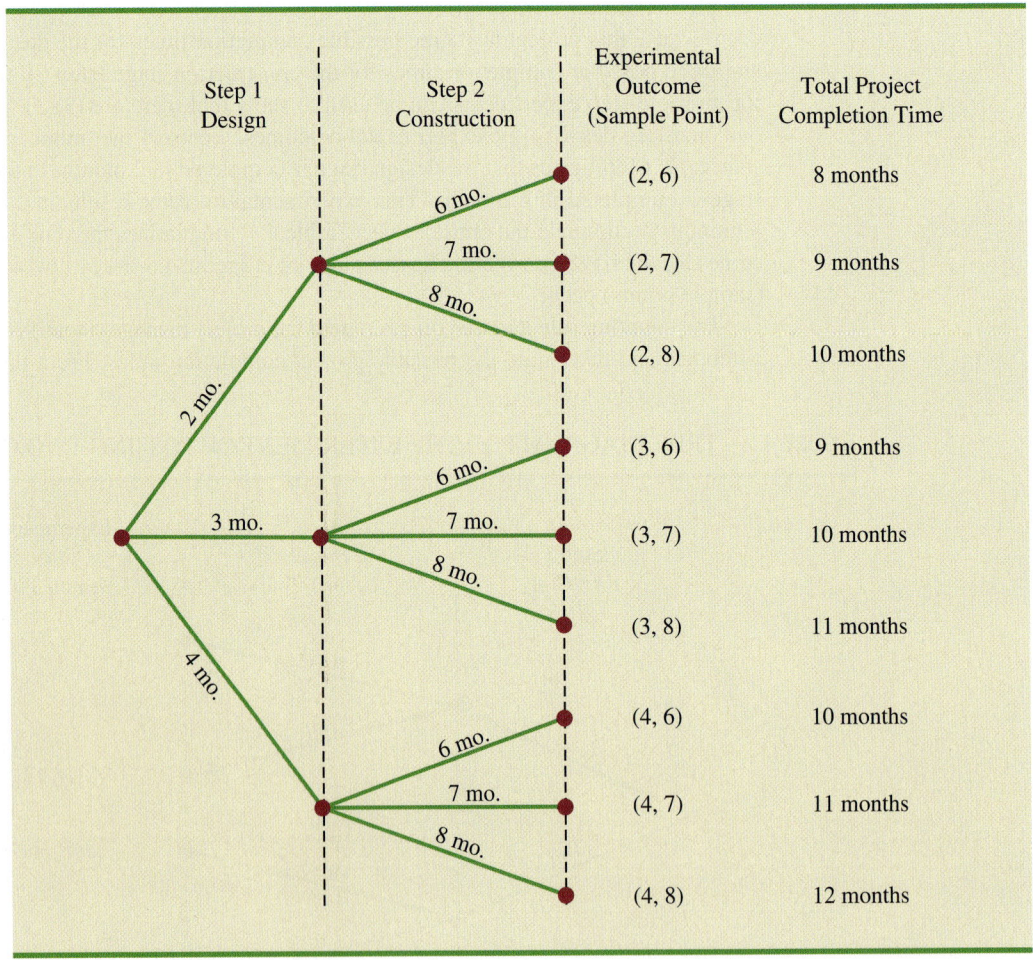

Figure 4.3, we see that the project will be completed in 8 to 12 months, with six of the nine experimental outcomes providing the desired completion time of 10 months or less. Even though identifying the experimental outcomes may be helpful, we need to consider how probability values can be assigned to the experimental outcomes before making an assessment of the probability that the project will be completed within the desired 10 months.

Combinations A second useful counting rule allows one to count the number of experimental outcomes when the experiment involves selecting n objects from a (usually larger) set of N objects. It is called the counting rule for combinations.

COUNTING RULE FOR COMBINATIONS

The number of combinations of N objects taken n at a time is

$$C_n^N = \binom{N}{n} = \frac{N!}{n!(N-n)!} \tag{4.1}$$

where
$$N! = N(N-1)(N-2)\cdots(2)(1)$$
$$n! = n(n-1)(n-2)\cdots(2)(1)$$

and, by definition, $0! = 1$

The notation ! means *factorial;* for example, 5 factorial is $5! = (5)(4)(3)(2)(1) = 120$.

In sampling from a finite population of size N, the counting rule for combinations is used to find the number of different samples of size n that can be selected.

As an illustration of the counting rule for combinations, consider a quality control procedure in which an inspector randomly selects two of five parts to test for defects. In a group of five parts, how many combinations of two parts can be selected? The counting rule in equation (4.1) shows that with $N = 5$ and $n = 2$, we have

$$C_2^5 = \binom{5}{2} = \frac{5!}{2!(5-2)!} = \frac{(5)(4)(3)(2)(1)}{(2)(1)(3)(2)(1)} = \frac{120}{12} = 10$$

Thus, 10 outcomes are possible for the experiment of randomly selecting two parts from a group of five. If we label the five parts as A, B, C, D, and E, the 10 combinations or experimental outcomes can be identified as AB, AC, AD, AE, BC, BD, BE, CD, CE, and DE.

As another example, consider that the Ohio lottery system uses the random selection of six integers from a group of 47 to determine the weekly lottery winner. The counting rule for combinations, equation (4.1), can be used to determine the number of ways six different integers can be selected from a group of 47.

$$\binom{47}{6} = \frac{47!}{6!(47-6)!} = \frac{47!}{6!41!} = \frac{(47)(46)(45)(44)(43)(42)}{(6)(5)(4)(3)(2)(1)} = 10,737,573$$

The counting rule for combinations shows that the chance of winning the lottery is very unlikely.

The counting rule for combinations tells us that more than 10 million experimental outcomes are possible in the lottery drawing. An individual who buys a lottery ticket has 1 chance in 10,737,573 of winning.

Permutations A third counting rule that is sometimes useful is the counting rule for permutations. It allows one to compute the number of experimental outcomes when n objects are to be selected from a set of N objects where the order of selection is important. The same n objects selected in a different order is considered a different experimental outcome.

COUNTING RULE FOR PERMUTATIONS

The number of permutations of N objects taken n at a time is given by

$$P_n^N = n!\binom{N}{n} = \frac{N!}{(N-n)!} \qquad (4.2)$$

The counting rule for permutations closely relates to the one for combinations; however, an experiment results in more permutations than combinations for the same number of objects because every selection of n objects can be ordered in $n!$ different ways.

As an example, consider again the quality control process in which an inspector selects two of five parts to inspect for defects. How many permutations may be selected? The counting rule in equation (4.2) shows that with $N = 5$ and $n = 2$, we have

$$P_2^5 = \frac{5!}{(5-2)!} = \frac{5!}{3!} = \frac{(5)(4)(3)(2)(1)}{(3)(2)(1)} = \frac{120}{6} = 20$$

Thus, 20 outcomes are possible for the experiment of randomly selecting two parts from a group of five when the order of selection must be taken into account. If we label the parts A, B, C, D, and E, the 20 permutations are AB, BA, AC, CA, AD, DA, AE, EA, BC, CB, BD, DB, BE, EB, CD, DC, CE, EC, DE, and ED.

Assigning Probabilities

Now let us see how probabilities can be assigned to experimental outcomes. The three approaches most frequently used are the classical, relative frequency, and subjective methods. Regardless of the method used, two **basic requirements for assigning probabilities** must be met.

BASIC REQUIREMENTS FOR ASSIGNING PROBABILITIES

1. The probability assigned to each experimental outcome must be between 0 and 1, inclusively. If we let E_i denote the ith experimental outcome and $P(E_i)$ its probability, then this requirement can be written as

$$0 \le P(E_i) \le 1 \text{ for all } i \qquad (4.3)$$

2. The sum of the probabilities for all the experimental outcomes must equal 1. For n experimental outcomes, this requirement can be written as

$$P(E_1) + P(E_2) + \cdots + P(E_n) = 1 \qquad (4.4)$$

The **classical method** of assigning probabilities is appropriate when all the experimental outcomes are equally likely. If n experimental outcomes are possible, a probability of $1/n$ is assigned to each experimental outcome. When using this approach, the two basic requirements for assigning probabilities are automatically satisfied.

For an example, consider the experiment of tossing a fair coin; the two experimental outcomes—head and tail—are equally likely. Because one of the two equally likely outcomes is a head, the probability of observing a head is 1/2, or .50. Similarly, the probability of observing a tail is also 1/2, or .50.

As another example, consider the experiment of rolling a die. It would seem reasonable to conclude that the six possible outcomes are equally likely, and hence each outcome is assigned a probability of 1/6. If $P(1)$ denotes the probability that one dot appears on the upward face of the die, then $P(1) = 1/6$. Similarly, $P(2) = 1/6$, $P(3) = 1/6$, $P(4) = 1/6$, $P(5) = 1/6$, and $P(6) = 1/6$. Note that these probabilities satisfy the two basic requirements of equations (4.3) and (4.4) because each of the probabilities is greater than or equal to zero and they sum to 1.0.

The **relative frequency method** of assigning probabilities is appropriate when data are available to estimate the proportion of the time the experimental outcome will occur if the experiment is repeated a large number of times. As an example consider a study of waiting times in the X-ray department for a local hospital. A clerk recorded the number of patients waiting for service at 9:00 A.M. on 20 successive days and obtained the following results.

Number Waiting	Number of Days Outcome Occurred
0	2
1	5
2	6
3	4
4	3
Total	20

These data show that on 2 of the 20 days, zero patients were waiting for service; on 5 of the days, one patient was waiting for service; and so on. Using the relative frequency method, we would assign a probability of 2/20 = .10 to the experimental outcome of zero patients waiting for service, 5/20 = .25 to the experimental outcome of one patient waiting, 6/20 = .30 to two patients waiting, 4/20 = .20 to three patients waiting, and 3/20 = .15 to four patients waiting. As with the classical method, using the relative frequency method automatically satisfies the two basic requirements of equations (4.3) and (4.4).

The **subjective method** of assigning probabilities is most appropriate when one cannot realistically assume that the experimental outcomes are equally likely and when little relevant data are available. When the subjective method is used to assign probabilities to the experimental outcomes, we may use any information available, such as our experience or intuition. After considering all available information, a probability value that expresses our *degree of belief* (on a scale from 0 to 1) that the experimental outcome will occur is specified. Because subjective probability expresses a person's degree of belief, it is personal. Using the subjective method, different people can be expected to assign different probabilities to the same experimental outcome.

The subjective method requires extra care to ensure that the two basic requirements of equations (4.3) and (4.4) are satisfied. Regardless of a person's degree of belief, the probability value assigned to each experimental outcome must be between 0 and 1, inclusive, and the sum of all the probabilities for the experimental outcomes must equal 1.

Consider the case in which Tom and Judy Elsbernd make an offer to purchase a house. Two outcomes are possible:

$$E_1 = \text{their offer is accepted}$$
$$E_2 = \text{their offer is rejected}$$

Judy believes that the probability their offer will be accepted is .8; thus, Judy would set $P(E_1) = .8$ and $P(E_2) = .2$. Tom, however, believes that the probability that their offer will be accepted is .6; hence, Tom would set $P(E_1) = .6$ and $P(E_2) = .4$. Note that Tom's probability estimate for E_1 reflects a greater pessimism that their offer will be accepted.

Bayes' theorem (see Section 4.5) provides a means for combining subjectively determined prior probabilities with probabilities obtained by other means to obtain revised, or posterior, probabilities.

Both Judy and Tom assigned probabilities that satisfy the two basic requirements. The fact that their probability estimates are different emphasizes the personal nature of the subjective method.

Even in business situations where either the classical or the relative frequency approach can be applied, managers may want to provide subjective probability estimates. In such cases, the best probability estimates often are obtained by combining the estimates from the classical or relative frequency approach with subjective probability estimates.

Probabilities for the KP&L Project

To perform further analysis on the KP&L project, we must develop probabilities for each of the nine experimental outcomes listed in Table 4.1. On the basis of experience and judgment, management concluded that the experimental outcomes were not equally likely. Hence, the classical method of assigning probabilities could not be used. Management then decided to conduct a study of the completion times for similar projects undertaken by KP&L over the past three years. The results of a study of 40 similar projects are summarized in Table 4.2.

After reviewing the results of the study, management decided to employ the relative frequency method of assigning probabilities. Management could have provided subjective probability estimates, but felt that the current project was quite similar to the 40 previous projects. Thus, the relative frequency method was judged best.

In using the data in Table 4.2 to compute probabilities, we note that outcome (2, 6)— stage 1 completed in 2 months and stage 2 completed in 6 months—occurred six times in the 40 projects. We can use the relative frequency method to assign a probability of $6/40 = .15$ to this outcome. Similarly, outcome (2, 7) also occurred in six of the 40 projects, providing a $6/40 = .15$ probability. Continuing in this manner, we obtain the probability assignments for the sample points of the KP&L project shown in Table 4.3. Note that $P(2, 6)$ represents the probability of the sample point (2, 6), $P(2, 7)$ represents the probability of the sample point (2, 7), and so on.

TABLE 4.2   COMPLETION RESULTS FOR 40 KP&L PROJECTS

Completion Time (months)		Sample Point	Number of Past Projects Having These Completion Times
Stage 1 Design	Stage 2 Construction		
2	6	(2, 6)	6
2	7	(2, 7)	6
2	8	(2, 8)	2
3	6	(3, 6)	4
3	7	(3, 7)	8
3	8	(3, 8)	2
4	6	(4, 6)	2
4	7	(4, 7)	4
4	8	(4, 8)	6
		Total	40

TABLE 4.3   PROBABILITY ASSIGNMENTS FOR THE KP&L PROJECT BASED
ON THE RELATIVE FREQUENCY METHOD

Sample Point	Project Completion Time	Probability of Sample Point
(2, 6)	8 months	$P(2, 6) = 6/40 = $ .15
(2, 7)	9 months	$P(2, 7) = 6/40 = $ .15
(2, 8)	10 months	$P(2, 8) = 2/40 = $ .05
(3, 6)	9 months	$P(3, 6) = 4/40 = $ .10
(3, 7)	10 months	$P(3, 7) = 8/40 = $ .20
(3, 8)	11 months	$P(3, 8) = 2/40 = $ .05
(4, 6)	10 months	$P(4, 6) = 2/40 = $ .05
(4, 7)	11 months	$P(4, 7) = 4/40 = $ .10
(4, 8)	12 months	$P(4, 8) = 6/40 = $ .15
		Total 1.00

NOTES AND COMMENTS

1. In statistics, the notion of an experiment differs somewhat from the notion of an experiment in the physical sciences. In the physical sciences, researchers usually conduct an experiment in a laboratory or a controlled environment in order to learn about cause and effect. In statistical experiments, probability determines outcomes. Even though the experiment is repeated in ex-actly the same way, an entirely different outcome may occur. Because of this influence of proba-bility on the outcome, the experiments of statis-tics are sometimes called *random experiments*.

2. When drawing a sample without replacement from a population of size N, the counting rule for combinations is used to find the number of different samples of size n that can be selected.

Exercises

Methods

1. An experiment has three steps with three outcomes possible for the first step, two outcomes possible for the second step, and four outcomes possible for the third step. How many ex-perimental outcomes exist for the entire experiment?

2. How many ways can three items be selected from a group of six items? Use the letters A, B, C, D, E, and F to identify the items, and list each of the different combinations of three items.

3. How many permutations of three items can be selected from a group of six? Use the letters A, B, C, D, E, and F to identify the items, and list each of the permutations of items B, D, and F.

4. Consider the experiment of tossing a coin three times.
   a.   Develop a tree diagram for the experiment.
   b.   List the experimental outcomes.
   c.   What is the probability for each experimental outcome?

5. Suppose an experiment has five equally likely outcomes: E_1, E_2, E_3, E_4, E_5. Assign proba-bilities to each outcome and show that the requirements in equations (4.3) and (4.4) are satisfied. What method did you use?

6. An experiment with three outcomes has been repeated 50 times, and it was learned that E_1 occurred 20 times, E_2 occurred 13 times, and E_3 occurred 17 times. Assign probabilities to the outcomes. What method did you use?

7. A decision maker subjectively assigned the following probabilities to the four outcomes of an experiment: $P(E_1) = .10$, $P(E_2) = .15$, $P(E_3) = .40$, and $P(E_4) = .20$. Are these probability assignments valid? Explain.

Applications

8. In the city of Milford, applications for zoning changes go through a two-step process: a review by the planning commission and a final decision by the city council. At step 1 the planning commission reviews the zoning change request and makes a positive or negative recommendation concerning the change. At step 2 the city council reviews the planning commission's recommendation and then votes to approve or to disapprove the zoning change. Suppose the developer of an apartment complex submits an application for a zoning change. Consider the application process as an experiment.
   a. How many sample points are there for this experiment? List the sample points.
   b. Construct a tree diagram for the experiment.

9. Simple random sampling uses a sample of size n from a population of size N to obtain data that can be used to make inferences about the characteristics of a population. Suppose that, from a population of 50 bank accounts, we want to take a random sample of four accounts in order to learn about the population. How many different random samples of four accounts are possible?

10. Venture capital can provide a big boost in funds available to companies. According to Venture Economics (*Investor's Business Daily*, April 28, 2000), of 2374 venture capital disbursements, 1434 were to companies in California, 390 were to companies in Massachusetts, 217 were to companies in New York, and 112 were to companies in Colorado. Twenty-two percent of the companies receiving funds were in the early stages of development and 55% of the companies were in an expansion stage. Suppose you want to randomly choose one of these companies to learn about how venture capital funds are used.
   a. What is the probability the company chosen will be from California?
   b. What is the probability the company chosen will not be from one of the four states mentioned?
   c. What is the probability the company will not be in the early stages of development?
   d. Assuming the companies in the early stages of development were evenly distributed across the country, how many Massachusetts companies receiving venture capital funds were in their early stages of development?
   e. The total amount of funds invested was $32.4 billion. Estimate the amount that went to Colorado.

11. The National Highway Traffic Safety Administration (NHTSA) conducted a survey to learn about how drivers throughout the United States are using seat belts (Associated Press, August 25, 2003). Sample data consistent with the NHTSA survey are as follows.

	Driver Using Seat Belt?	
Region	**Yes**	**No**
Northeast	148	52
Midwest	162	54
South	296	74
West	252	48
Total	858	228

   a. For the United States, what is the probability that a driver is using a seat belt?
   b. The seat belt usage probability for a U.S. driver a year earlier was .75. NHTSA chief Dr. Jeffrey Runge had hoped for a .78 probability in 2003. Would he have been pleased with the 2003 survey results?

   c. What is the probability of seat belt usage by region of the country? What region has the highest seat belt usage?

   d. What proportion of the drivers in the sample came from each region of the country? What region had the most drivers selected? What region had the second most drivers selected?

   e. Assuming the total number of drivers in each region is the same, do you see any reason why the probability estimate in part (a) might be too high? Explain.

12.   The Powerball lottery is played twice each week in 23 states, the Virgin Islands, and the District of Columbia. To play Powerball a participant must purchase a ticket for $1 and then select five numbers from the digits 1 through 53 and a Powerball number from the digits 1 through 42. To determine the winning numbers for each game, lottery officials draw five white balls out of a drum with 53 white balls, and one red ball out of a drum with 42 red balls. To win the jackpot, a participant's numbers must match the numbers on the five white balls in any order and the number on the red Powerball. In August 2001, four winners shared a jackpot of $295 million by matching the numbers 8-17-22-42-47 plus Powerball number 21. In addition to the jackpot, a variety of other prizes is awarded each time the game is played. For instance, a prize of $100,000 is paid if the participant's five numbers match the numbers on the five white balls (http://www.powerball.com, March 25, 2003).

   a. Compute the number of ways the first five numbers can be selected.

   b. What is the probability of winning a prize of $100,000 by matching the numbers on the five white balls?

   c. What is the probability of winning the Powerball jackpot?

13.   A company that manufactures toothpaste is studying five different package designs. Assuming that one design is just as likely to be selected by a consumer as any other design, what selection probability would you assign to each of the package designs? In an actual experiment, 100 consumers were asked to pick the design they preferred. The following data were obtained. Do the data confirm the belief that one design is just as likely to be selected as another? Explain.

Design	Number of Times Preferred
1	5
2	15
3	30
4	40
5	10

Events and Their Probabilities

In the introduction to this chapter we used the term *event* much as it would be used in everyday language. Then, in Section 4.1 we introduced the concept of an experiment and its associated experimental outcomes or sample points. Sample points and events provide the foundation for the study of probability. As a result, we must now introduce the formal definition of an **event** as it relates to sample points. Doing so will provide the basis for determining the probability of an event.

EVENT

An event is a collection of sample points.

For an example, let us return to the KP&L project and assume that the project manager is interested in the event that the entire project can be completed in 10 months or less. Referring to Table 4.3, we see that six sample points—(2, 6), (2, 7), (2, 8), (3, 6), (3, 7), and (4, 6)—provide a project completion time of 10 months or less. Let C denote the event that the project is completed in 10 months or less; we write

$$C = \{(2, 6), (2, 7), (2, 8), (3, 6), (3, 7), (4, 6)\}$$

Event C is said to occur if *any one* of these six sample points appears as the experimental outcome.

Other events that might be of interest to KP&L management include the following.

$L = $ The event that the project is completed in *less* than 10 months

$M = $ The event that the project is completed in *more* than 10 months

Using the information in Table 4.3, we see that these events consist of the following sample points.

$$L = \{(2, 6), (2, 7), (3, 6)\}$$
$$M = \{(3, 8), (4, 7), (4, 8)\}$$

A variety of additional events can be defined for the KP&L project, but in each case the event must be identified as a collection of sample points for the experiment.

Given the probabilities of the sample points shown in Table 4.3, we can use the following definition to compute the probability of any event that KP&L management might want to consider.

PROBABILITY OF AN EVENT

The probability of any event is equal to the sum of the probabilities of the sample points in the event.

Using this definition, we calculate the probability of a particular event by adding the probabilities of the sample points (experimental outcomes) that make up the event. We can now compute the probability that the project will take 10 months or less to complete. Because this event is given by $C = \{(2, 6), (2, 7), (2, 8), (3, 6), (3, 7), (4, 6)\}$, the probability of event C, denoted $P(C)$, is given by

$$P(C) = P(2, 6) + P(2, 7) + P(2, 8) + P(3, 6) + P(3, 7) + P(4, 6)$$

Refer to the sample point probabilities in Table 4.3; we have

$$P(C) = .15 + .15 + .05 + .10 + .20 + .05 = .70$$

Similarly, because the event that the project is completed in less than 10 months is given by $L = \{(2, 6), (2, 7), (3, 6)\}$, the probability of this event is given by

$$P(L) = P(2, 6) + P(2, 7) + P(3, 6)$$
$$= .15 + .15 + .10 = .40$$

Finally, for the event that the project is completed in more than 10 months, we have $M = \{(3, 8), (4, 7), (4, 8)\}$ and thus

$$P(M) = P(3, 8) + P(4, 7) + P(4, 8)$$
$$= .05 + .10 + .15 = .30$$

Using these probability results, we can now tell KP&L management that there is a .70 probability that the project will be completed in 10 months or less, a .40 probability that the project will be completed in less than 10 months, and a .30 probability that the project will be completed in more than 10 months. This procedure of computing event probabilities can be repeated for any event of interest to the KP&L management.

Any time that we can identify all the sample points of an experiment and assign probabilities to each, we can compute the probability of an event using the definition. However, in many experiments the large number of sample points makes the identification of the sample points, as well as the determination of their associated probabilities, extremely cumbersome, if not impossible. In the remaining sections of this chapter, we present some basic probability relationships that can be used to compute the probability of an event without knowledge of all the sample point probabilities.

NOTES AND COMMENTS

1. The sample space, S, is an event. Because it contains all the experimental outcomes, it has a probability of 1; that is, $P(S) = 1$.
2. When the classical method is used to assign probabilities, the assumption is that the experimental outcomes are equally likely. In such cases, the probability of an event can be computed by counting the number of experimental outcomes in the event and dividing the result by the total number of experimental outcomes.

Exercises

Methods

14. An experiment has four equally likely outcomes: E_1, E_2, E_3, and E_4.
    a. What is the probability that E_2 occurs?
    b. What is the probability that any two of the outcomes occur (e.g., E_1 or E_3)?
    c. What is the probability that any three of the outcomes occur (e.g., E_1 or E_2 or E_4)?

15. Consider the experiment of selecting a playing card from a deck of 52 playing cards. Each card corresponds to a sample point with a 1/52 probability.
    a. List the sample points in the event an ace is selected.
    b. List the sample points in the event a club is selected.
    c. List the sample points in the event a face card (jack, queen, or king) is selected.
    d. Find the probabilities associated with each of the events in parts (a), (b), and (c).

16. Consider the experiment of rolling a pair of dice. Suppose that we are interested in the sum of the face values showing on the dice.
    a. How many sample points are possible? (*Hint:* Use the counting rule for multiple-step experiments.)
    b. List the sample points.
    c. What is the probability of obtaining a value of 7?
    d. What is the probability of obtaining a value of 9 or greater?
    e. Because each roll has six possible even values (2, 4, 6, 8, 10, and 12) and only five possible odd values (3, 5, 7, 9, and 11), the dice should show even values more often than odd values. Do you agree with this statement? Explain.
    f. What method did you use to assign the probabilities requested?

Applications

17. Refer to the KP&L sample points and sample point probabilities in Tables 4.2 and 4.3.
    a. The design stage (stage 1) will run over budget if it takes 4 months to complete. List the sample points in the event the design stage is over budget.
    b. What is the probability that the design stage is over budget?
    c. The construction stage (stage 2) will run over budget if it takes 8 months to complete. List the sample points in the event the construction stage is over budget.
    d. What is the probability that the construction stage is over budget?
    e. What is the probability that both stages are over budget?

18. Suppose that a manager of a large apartment complex provides the following subjective probability estimates about the number of vacancies that will exist next month.

Vacancies	Probability
0	.05
1	.15
2	.35
3	.25
4	.10
5	.10

Provide the probability of each of the following events.
   a. No vacancies
   b. At least four vacancies
   c. Two or fewer vacancies

19. The National Sporting Goods Association conducted a survey of persons 7 years of age or older about participation in sports activities (*Statistical Abstract of the United States: 2002*). The total population in this age group was reported at 248.5 million, with 120.9 million male and 127.6 million female. The number of participants for the top five sports activities appears here.

Activity	Participants (millions)	
	Male	Female
Bicycle riding	22.2	21.0
Camping	25.6	24.3
Exercise walking	28.7	57.7
Exercising with equipment	20.4	24.4
Swimming	26.4	34.4

   a. For a randomly selected female, estimate the probability of participation in each of the sports activities.
   b. For a randomly selected male, estimate the probability of participation in each of the sports activities.
   c. For a randomly selected person, what is the probability the person participates in exercise walking?
   d. Someone tells you they saw an exercise walker. What is the probability the walker is a woman? What is the probability the walker is a man?

20. *Fortune* magazine publishes an annual issue containing information on *Fortune* 500 companies. The following data show the six states with the largest number of *Fortune* 500 companies as well as the number of companies headquartered in those states (*Fortune*, April 17, 2000).

State	Number of Companies
New York	56
California	53
Texas	43
Illinois	37
Ohio	28
Pennsylvania	28

Suppose a *Fortune* 500 company is chosen for a follow-up questionnaire. What are the probabilities of the following events?
a.   Let N be the event the company is headquartered in New York. Find $P(N)$.
b.   Let T be the event the company is headquartered in Texas. Find $P(T)$.
c.   Let B be the event the company is headquartered in one of these six states. Find $P(B)$.

21. The U.S. population by age is as follows (*The World Almanac 2004*). The data are in millions of people.

Age	Number
19 and under	80.5
20 to 24	19.0
25 to 34	39.9
35 to 44	45.2
45 to 54	37.7
55 to 64	24.3
65 and over	35.0

Assume that a person will be randomly chosen from this population.
a.   What is the probability the person is 20 to 24 years old?
b.   What is the probability the person is 20 to 34 years old?
c.   What is the probability the person is 45 years or older?

Some Basic Relationships of Probability

Complement of an Event

Given an event A, the **complement of** A is defined to be the event consisting of all sample points that are *not* in A. The complement of A is denoted by A^c. Figure 4.4 is a diagram, known as a **Venn diagram**, which illustrates the concept of a complement. The rectangular area represents the sample space for the experiment and as such contains all possible sample points. The circle represents event A and contains only the sample points that belong to A. The shaded region of the rectangle contains all sample points not in event A and is by definition the complement of A.

In any probability application, either event A or its complement A^c must occur. Therefore, we have

$$P(A) + P(A^c) = 1$$

FIGURE 4.4   COMPLEMENT OF EVENT *A* IS SHADED

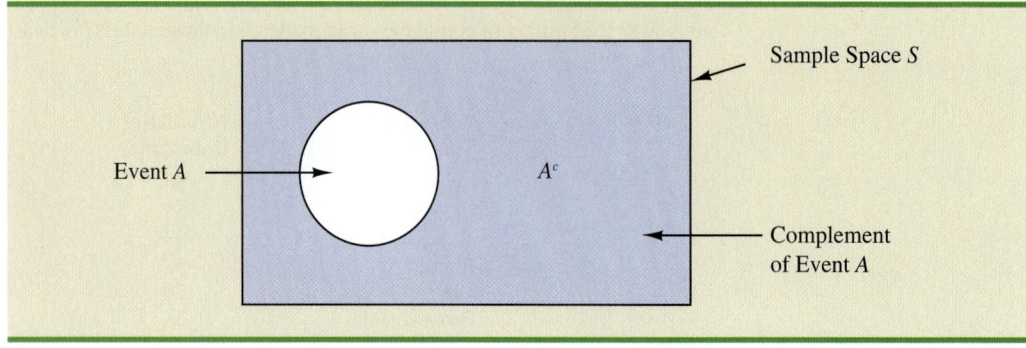

Solving for *P(A)*, we obtain the following result.

COMPUTING PROBABILITY USING THE COMPLEMENT

$$P(A) = 1 - P(A^c)$$

$$(4.5)$$

Equation (4.5) shows that the probability of an event *A* can be computed easily if the probability of its complement, $P(A^c)$, is known.

As an example, consider the case of a sales manager who, after reviewing sales reports, states that 80% of new customer contacts result in no sale. By allowing *A* to denote the event of a sale and A^c to denote the event of no sale, the manager is stating that $P(A^c) = .80$. Using equation (4.5), we see that

$$P(A) = 1 - P(A^c) = 1 - .80 = .20$$

We can conclude that a new customer contact has a .20 probability of resulting in a sale.

In another example, a purchasing agent states a .90 probability that a supplier will send a shipment that is free of defective parts. Using the complement, we can conclude that there is a $1 - .90 = .10$ probability that the shipment will contain defective parts.

Addition Law

The addition law is used to compute the probability that at least one of two events occurs. That is, with events *A* and *B* we are interested in knowing the probability that event *A* or event *B* or both occur.

Before we present the addition law, we need to discuss two concepts related to the combination of events: the *union* of events and the *intersection* of events. Given two events *A* and *B*, the **union of *A* and *B*** is defined as follows.

UNION OF TWO EVENTS

The *union* of *A* and *B* is the event containing *all* sample points belonging to *A or B or both*. The union is denoted by $A \cup B$.

The Venn diagram in Figure 4.5 depicts the union of events *A* and *B*. Note that the two circles contain all the sample points in event *A* as well as all the sample points in event *B*.

FIGURE 4.5   UNION OF EVENTS A AND B IS SHADED

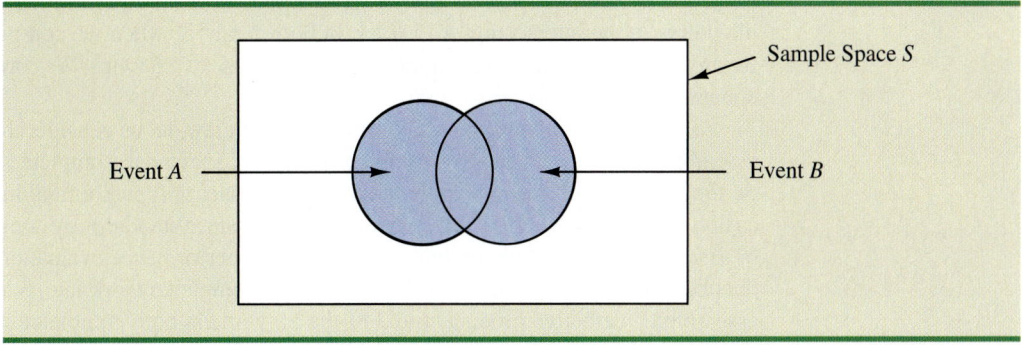

The fact that the circles overlap indicates that some sample points are contained in both A and B.

The definition of the **intersection of A and B** follows.

> **INTERSECTION OF TWO EVENTS**
>
> Given two events A and B, the *intersection* of A and B is the event containing the sample points belonging to *both A and B*. The intersection is denoted by $A \cap B$.

The Venn diagram depicting the intersection of events A and B is shown in Figure 4.6. The area where the two circles overlap is the intersection; it contains the sample points that are in both A and B.

Let us now continue with a discussion of the addition law. The **addition law** provides a way to compute the probability that event A or event B or both occur. In other words, the addition law is used to compute the probability of the union of two events. The addition law is written as follows.

> **ADDITION LAW**
>
> $$P(A \cup B) = P(A) + P(B) - P(A \cap B) \qquad \textbf{(4.6)}$$

FIGURE 4.6   INTERSECTION OF EVENTS A AND B IS SHADED

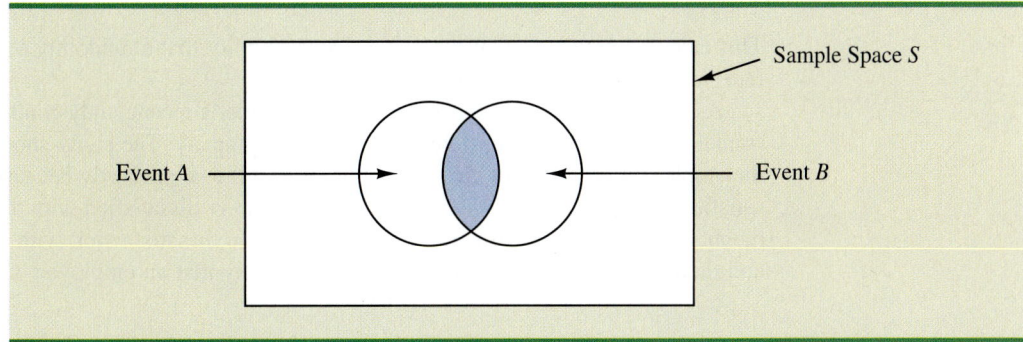

To understand the addition law intuitively, note that the first two terms in the addition law, $P(A) + P(B)$, account for all the sample points in $A \cup B$. However, because the sample points in the intersection $A \cap B$ are in both A and B, when we compute $P(A) + P(B)$, we are in effect counting each of the sample points in $A \cap B$ twice. We correct for this overcounting by subtracting $P(A \cap B)$.

As an example of an application of the addition law, let us consider the case of a small assembly plant with 50 employees. Each worker is expected to complete work assignments on time and in such a way that the assembled product will pass a final inspection. On occasion, some of the workers fail to meet the performance standards by completing work late or assembling a defective product. At the end of a performance evaluation period, the production manager found that 5 of the 50 workers completed work late, 6 of the 50 workers assembled a defective product, and 2 of the 50 workers both completed work late *and* assembled a defective product.

Let

$$L = \text{the event that the work is completed late}$$
$$D = \text{the event that the assembled product is defective}$$

The relative frequency information leads to the following probabilities.

$$P(L) = \frac{5}{50} = .10$$

$$P(D) = \frac{6}{50} = .12$$

$$P(L \cap D) = \frac{2}{50} = .04$$

After reviewing the performance data, the production manager decided to assign a poor performance rating to any employee whose work was either late or defective; thus the event of interest is $L \cup D$. What is the probability that the production manager assigned an employee a poor performance rating?

Note that the probability question is about the union of two events. Specifically, we want to know $P(L \cup D)$. Using equation (4.6), we have

$$P(L \cup D) = P(L) + P(D) - P(L \cap D)$$

Knowing values for the three probabilities on the right side of this expression, we can write

$$P(L \cup D) = .10 + .12 - .04 = .18$$

This calculation tells us that there is a .18 probability that a randomly selected employee received a poor performance rating.

As another example of the addition law, consider a recent study conducted by the personnel manager of a major computer software company. The study showed that 30% of the employees who left the firm within two years did so primarily because they were dissatisfied with their salary, 20% left because they were dissatisfied with their work assignments, and 12% of the former employees indicated dissatisfaction with *both* their salary and their work assignments. What is the probability that an employee who leaves within two years does so because of dissatisfaction with salary, dissatisfaction with the work assignment, or both?

Let

S = the event that the employee leaves because of dissatisfaction with salary

W = the event that the employee leaves because of dissatisfaction with the work assignment

We have $P(S) = .30$, $P(W) = .20$, and $P(S \cap W) = .12$. Using equation (4.6), the addition law, we have

$$P(S \cup W) = P(S) + P(W) - P(S \cap W) = .30 + .20 - .12 = .38$$

We find a .38 probability that an employee leaves for salary or work assignment reasons.

Before we conclude our discussion of the addition law, let us consider a special case that arises for **mutually exclusive events**.

> MUTUALLY EXCLUSIVE EVENTS
>
> Two events are said to be mutually exclusive if the events have no sample points in common.

Events A and B are mutually exclusive if, when one event occurs, the other cannot occur. Thus, a requirement for A and B to be mutually exclusive is that their intersection must contain no sample points. The Venn diagram depicting two mutually exclusive events A and B is shown in Figure 4.7. In this case $P(A \cap B) = 0$ and the addition law can be written as follows.

> ADDITION LAW FOR MUTUALLY EXCLUSIVE EVENTS
> $$P(A \cup B) = P(A) + P(B)$$

FIGURE 4.7   MUTUALLY EXCLUSIVE EVENTS

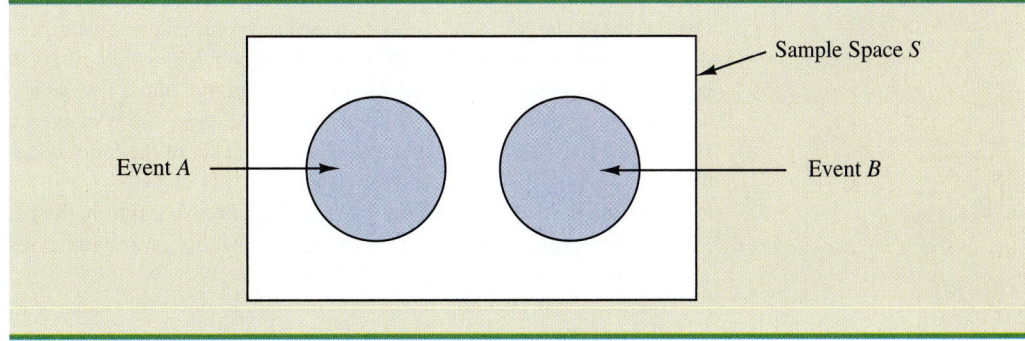

Exercises

Methods

22. Suppose that we have a sample space with five equally likely experimental outcomes: E_1, E_2, E_3, E_4, E_5. Let

$$A = \{E_1, E_2\}$$
$$B = \{E_3, E_4\}$$
$$C = \{E_2, E_3, E_5\}$$

   a. Find $P(A)$, $P(B)$, and $P(C)$.
   b. Find $P(A \cup B)$. Are A and B mutually exclusive?
   c. Find A^c, C^c, $P(A^c)$, and $P(C^c)$.
   d. Find $A \cup B^c$ and $P(A \cup B^c)$.
   e. Find $P(B \cup C)$.

23. Suppose that we have a sample space $S = \{E_1, E_2, E_3, E_4, E_5, E_6, E_7\}$, where $E_1, E_2, \ldots,$ E_7 denote the sample points. The following probability assignments apply: $P(E_1) = .05$, $P(E_2) = .20$, $P(E_3) = .20$, $P(E_4) = .25$, $P(E_5) = .15$, $P(E_6) = .10$, and $P(E_7) = .05$. Let

$$A = \{E_1, E_4, E_6\}$$
$$B = \{E_2, E_4, E_7\}$$
$$C = \{E_2, E_3, E_5, E_7\}$$

   a. Find $P(A)$, $P(B)$, and $P(C)$.
   b. Find $A \cup B$ and $P(A \cup B)$.
   c. Find $A \cap B$ and $P(A \cap B)$.
   d. Are events A and C mutually exclusive?
   e. Find B^c and $P(B^c)$.

Applications

24. Clarkson University surveyed alumni to learn more about what they think of Clarkson. One part of the survey asked respondents to indicate whether their overall experience at Clarkson fell short of expectations, met expectations, or surpassed expectations. The results showed that 4% of the respondents did not provide a response, 26% said that their experience fell short of expectations, and 65% of the respondents said that their experience met expectations (*Clarkson Magazine,* Summer 2001).
   a. If we chose an alumnus at random, what is the probability that the alumnus would say the Clarkson experience surpassed expectations?
   b. If we chose an alumnus at random, what is the probability that the alumnus would say the Clarkson experience met or surpassed expectations?

25. Data on the 30 largest bond funds provided one-year and five-year percentage returns for the period ending March 31, 2000 (*The Wall Street Journal,* April 10, 2000). Suppose we consider a one-year return in excess of 2% to be high and a five-year return in excess of 44% to be high. One-half of the funds had a one-year return in excess of 2%, 12 of the funds had a five-year return in excess of 44%, and six of the funds had both a one-year return in excess of 2% and a five-year return in excess of 44%.
   a. Find the probability of a fund having a high one-year return, the probability of a fund having a high five-year return, and the probability of a fund having both a high one-year return and a high five-year return.
   b. What is the probability that a fund had a high one-year return or a high five-year return or both?
   c. What is the probability that a fund had neither a high one-year return nor a high five-year return?

26. Data on the 30 largest stock and balanced funds provided one-year and five-year percentage returns for the period ending March 31, 2000 (*The Wall Street Journal,* April 10, 2000). Suppose we consider a one-year return in excess of 50% to be high and a five-year return in excess of 300% to be high. Nine of the funds had one-year returns in excess of 50%, seven of the funds had five-year returns in excess of 300%, and five of the funds had both one-year returns in excess of 50% and five-year returns in excess of 300%.
    a. What is the probability of a high one-year return, and what is the probability of a high five-year return?
    b. What is the probability of both a high one-year return and a high five-year return?
    c. What is the probability of neither a high one-year return nor a high five-year return?

27. A 2001 preseason NCAA football poll asked respondents to answer the question, "Will the Big Ten or the Pac-10 have a team in this year's national championship game, the Rose Bowl?" Of the 13,429 respondents, 2961 said the Big Ten would, 4494 said the Pac-10 would, and 6823 said neither the Big Ten nor the Pac-10 would have a team in the Rose Bowl (http://www.yahoo.com, August 30, 2001).
    a. What is the probability that a respondent said neither the Big Ten nor the Pac-10 will have a team in the Rose Bowl?
    b. What is the probability that a respondent said either the Big Ten or the Pac-10 will have a team in the Rose Bowl?
    c. Find the probability that a respondent said both the Big Ten and the Pac-10 would have a team in the Rose Bowl.

28. A survey of magazine subscribers showed that 45.8% rented a car during the past 12 months for business reasons, 54% rented a car during the past 12 months for personal reasons, and 30% rented a car during the past 12 months for both business and personal reasons.
    a. What is the probability that a subscriber rented a car during the past 12 months for business or personal reasons?
    b. What is the probability that a subscriber did not rent a car during the past 12 months for either business or personal reasons?

29. High school seniors with strong academic records apply to the nation's most selective colleges in greater numbers each year. Because the number of slots remains relatively stable, some colleges reject more early applicants. The University of Pennsylvania received 2851 applications for early admission. Of this group, it admitted 1033 students, rejected 854 outright, and deferred 964 to the regular admissions pool. Penn admitted about 18% of the applicants in the regular admissions pool for a total class size (number of early admissions plus number of regular admissions) of 2375 students (*USA Today,* January 24, 2001). Let E, R, and D represent the events that a student who applies for early admission is admitted, rejected outright, or deferred to the regular admissions pool; and let A represent the event that a student in the regular admissions pool is admitted.
    a. Use the data to estimate $P(E)$, $P(R)$, and $P(D)$.
    b. Are events E and D mutually exclusive? Find $P(E \cap D)$.
    c. For the 2375 students admitted to Penn, what is the probability that a randomly selected student was accepted for early admission?
    d. Suppose a student applies to Penn for early admission. What is the probability the student will be admitted for early admission or be accepted for admission in the regular admissions pool?

4.4 Conditional Probability

Often, the probability of an event is influenced by whether a related event already occurred. Suppose we have an event A with probability $P(A)$. If we obtain new information and learn that a related event, denoted by B, already occurred, we will want to take advantage of this information by calculating a new probability for event A. This new probability of event A is called a **conditional probability** and is written $P(A \mid B)$. We use the notation | to indicate that we are considering the probability of event A *given* the condition that event B has occurred. Hence, the notation $P(A \mid B)$ reads "the probability of A given B."

As an illustration of the application of conditional probability, consider the situation of the promotion status of male and female officers of a major metropolitan police force in the eastern United States. The police force consists of 1200 officers, 960 men and 240 women. Over the past two years, 324 officers on the police force received promotions. The specific breakdown of promotions for male and female officers is shown in Table 4.4.

After reviewing the promotion record, a committee of female officers raised a discrimination case on the basis that 288 male officers had received promotions but only 36 female officers had received promotions. The police administration argued that the relatively low number of promotions for female officers was due not to discrimination, but to the fact that relatively few females are members of the police force. Let us show how conditional probability could be used to analyze the discrimination charge.

Let

$$M = \text{event an officer is a man}$$
$$W = \text{event an officer is a woman}$$
$$A = \text{event an officer is promoted}$$
$$A^c = \text{event an officer is not promoted}$$

Dividing the data values in Table 4.4 by the total of 1200 officers enables us to summarize the available information with the following probability values.

$$P(M \cap A) = 288/1200 = .24 = \text{probability that a randomly selected officer is a man } and \text{ is promoted}$$

$$P(M \cap A^c) = 672/1200 = .56 = \text{probability that a randomly selected officer is a man } and \text{ is not promoted}$$

$$P(W \cap A) = 36/1200 = .03 = \text{probability that a randomly selected officer is a woman } and \text{ is promoted}$$

$$P(W \cap A^c) = 204/1200 = .17 = \text{probability that a randomly selected officer is a woman } and \text{ is not promoted}$$

Because each of these values gives the probability of the intersection of two events, the probabilities are called **joint probabilities**. Table 4.5, which provides a summary of the probability information for the police officer promotion situation, is referred to as a *joint probability table*.

The values in the margins of the joint probability table provide the probabilities of each event separately. That is, $P(M) = .80$, $P(W) = .20$, $P(A) = .27$, and $P(A^c) = .73$. These

TABLE 4.4   PROMOTION STATUS OF POLICE OFFICERS OVER THE PAST TWO YEARS

	Men	Women	Total
Promoted	288	36	324
Not Promoted	672	204	876
Total	960	240	1200

TABLE 4.5   JOINT PROBABILITY TABLE FOR PROMOTION STATUS OF POLICE OFFICERS

Joint probabilities appear in the body of the table.	Men (*M*)	Women (*W*)	Total
Promoted (*A*)	.24	.03	.27
Not Promoted (*A^c*)	.56	.17	.73
Total	.80	.20	1.00

Marginal probabilities appear in the margins of the table.

probabilities are referred to as **marginal probabilities** because of their location in the margins of the joint probability table. We note that the marginal probabilities are found by summing the joint probabilities in the corresponding row or column of the joint probability table. For instance, the marginal probability of being promoted is $P(A) = P(M \cap A) + P(W \cap A) = .24 + .03 = .27$. From the marginal probabilities, we see that 80% of the force is male, 20% of the force is female, 27% of all officers received promotions, and 73% were not promoted.

Let us begin the conditional probability analysis by computing the probability that an officer is promoted given that the officer is a man. In conditional probability notation, we are attempting to determine $P(A \mid M)$. To calculate $P(A \mid M)$, we first realize that this notation simply means that we are considering the probability of the event A (promotion) given that the condition designated as event M (the officer is a man) is known to exist. Thus $P(A \mid M)$ tells us that we are now concerned only with the promotion status of the 960 male officers. Because 288 of the 960 male officers received promotions, the probability of being promoted given that the officer is a man is 288/960 = .30. In other words, given that an officer is a man, that officer had a 30% chance of receiving a promotion over the past two years.

This procedure was easy to apply because the values in Table 4.4 show the number of officers in each category. We now want to demonstrate how conditional probabilities such as $P(A \mid M)$ can be computed directly from related event probabilities rather than the frequency data of Table 4.4.

We have shown that $P(A \mid M) = 288/960 = .30$. Let us now divide both the numerator and denominator of this fraction by 1200, the total number of officers in the study.

$$P(A \mid M) = \frac{288}{960} = \frac{288/1200}{960/1200} = \frac{.24}{.80} = .30$$

We now see that the conditional probability $P(A \mid M)$ can be computed as .24/.80. Refer to the joint probability table (Table 4.5). Note in particular that .24 is the joint probability of events A and M; that is, $P(A \cap M) = .24$. Also note that .80 is the marginal probability that a randomly selected officer is a man; that is, $P(M) = .80$. Thus, the conditional probability $P(A \mid M)$ can be computed as the ratio of the joint probability $P(A \cap M)$ to the marginal probability $P(M)$.

$$P(A \mid M) = \frac{P(A \cap M)}{P(M)} = \frac{.24}{.80} = .30$$

The fact that conditional probabilities can be computed as the ratio of a joint probability to a marginal probability provides the following general formula for conditional probability calculations for two events A and B.

CONDITIONAL PROBABILITY

$$P(A \mid B) = \frac{P(A \cap B)}{P(B)} \tag{4.7}$$

or

$$P(B \mid A) = \frac{P(A \cap B)}{P(A)} \tag{4.8}$$

The Venn diagram in Figure 4.8 is helpful in obtaining an intuitive understanding of conditional probability. The circle on the right shows that event B has occurred; the portion of the circle that overlaps with event A denotes the event $(A \cap B)$. We know that once event B has occurred, the only way that we can also observe event A is for the event $(A \cap B)$ to occur. Thus, the ratio $P(A \cap B)/P(B)$ provides the conditional probability that we will observe event A given that event B has already occurred.

Let us return to the issue of discrimination against the female officers. The marginal probability in row 1 of Table 4.5 shows that the probability of promotion of an officer is $P(A) = .27$ (regardless of whether that officer is male or female). However, the critical issue in the discrimination case involves the two conditional probabilities $P(A \mid M)$ and $P(A \mid W)$. That is, what is the probability of a promotion *given* that the officer is a man, and what is the probability of a promotion *given* that the officer is a woman? If these two probabilities are equal, a discrimination argument has no basis because the chances of a promotion are the same for male and female officers. However, a difference in the two conditional probabilities will support the position that male and female officers are treated differently in promotion decisions.

We already determined that $P(A \mid M) = .30$. Let us now use the probability values in Table 4.5 and the basic relationship of conditional probability in equation (4.7) to compute

FIGURE 4.8   CONDITIONAL PROBABILITY $P(A \mid B) = P(A \cap B)/P(B)$

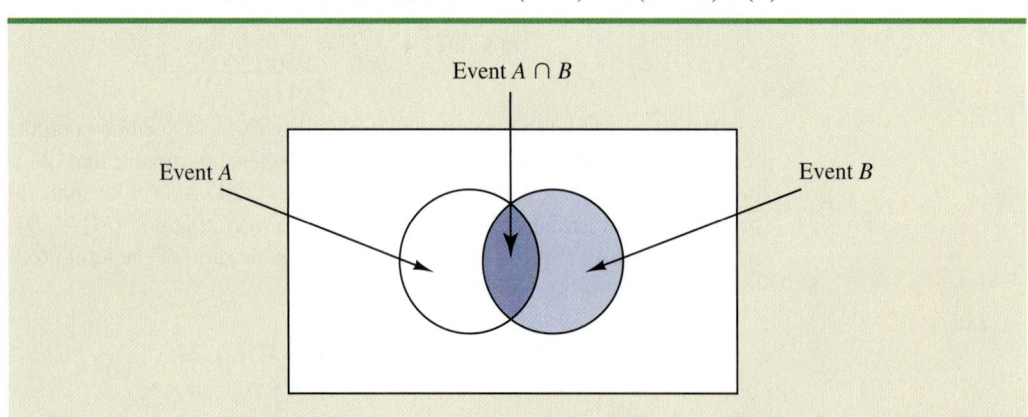

the probability that an officer is promoted given that the officer is a woman; that is, $P(A \mid W)$. Using equation (4.7), with W replacing B, we obtain

$$P(A \mid W) = \frac{P(A \cap W)}{P(W)} = \frac{.03}{.20} = .15$$

What conclusion do you draw? The probability of a promotion given that the officer is a man is .30, twice the .15 probability of a promotion given that the officer is a woman. Although the use of conditional probability does not in itself prove that discrimination exists in this case, the conditional probability values support the argument presented by the female officers.

Independent Events

In the preceding illustration, $P(A) = .27$, $P(A \mid M) = .30$, and $P(A \mid W) = .15$. We see that the probability of a promotion (event A) is affected or influenced by whether the officer is a man or a woman. Particularly, because $P(A \mid M) \neq P(A)$, we would say that events A and M are dependent events. That is, the probability of event A (promotion) is altered or affected by knowing that event M (the officer is a man) exists. Similarly, with $P(A \mid W) \neq P(A)$, we would say that events A and W are *dependent events*. However, if the probability of event A is not changed by the existence of event M—that is, $P(A \mid M) = P(A)$—we would say that events A and M are **independent events**. This situation leads to the following definition of the independence of two events.

INDEPENDENT EVENTS

Two events A and B are independent if

$$P(A \mid B) = P(A) \qquad\qquad \textbf{(4.9)}$$

or

$$P(B \mid A) = P(B) \qquad\qquad \textbf{(4.10)}$$

Otherwise, the events are dependent.

Multiplication Law

Whereas the addition law of probability is used to compute the probability of a union of two events, the multiplication law is used to compute the probability of the intersection of two events. The multiplication law is based on the definition of conditional probability. Using equations (4.7) and (4.8) and solving for $P(A \cap B)$, we obtain the **multiplication law**.

MULTIPLICATION LAW

$$P(A \cap B) = P(B)P(A \mid B) \qquad\qquad \textbf{(4.11)}$$

or

$$P(A \cap B) = P(A)P(B \mid A) \qquad\qquad \textbf{(4.12)}$$

To illustrate the use of the multiplication law, consider a newspaper circulation department where it is known that 84% of the households in a particular neighborhood subscribe to the daily edition of the paper. If we let D denote the event that a household subscribes to the daily edition, $P(D) = .84$. In addition, it is known that the probability that a household that already holds a daily subscription also subscribes to the Sunday edition (event S) is .75; that is, $P(S \mid D) = .75$.

What is the probability that a household subscribes to both the Sunday and daily editions of the newspaper? Using the multiplication law, we compute the desired $P(S \cap D)$ as

$$P(S \cap D) = P(D)P(S \mid D) = .84(.75) = .63$$

We now know that 63% of the households subscribe to both the Sunday and daily editions.

Before concluding this section, let us consider the special case of the multiplication law when the events involved are independent. Recall that events A and B are independent if $P(A \mid B) = P(A)$ or $P(B \mid A) = P(B)$. Hence, using equations (4.11) and (4.12) for the special case of independent events, we obtain the following multiplication law.

MULTIPLICATION LAW FOR INDEPENDENT EVENTS

$$P(A \cap B) = P(A)P(B) \qquad\qquad \textbf{(4.13)}$$

To compute the probability of the intersection of two independent events, we simply multiply the corresponding probabilities. Note that the multiplication law for independent events provides another way to determine whether A and B are independent. That is, if $P(A \cap B) = P(A)P(B)$, then A and B are independent; if $P(A \cap B) \neq P(A)P(B)$, then A and B are dependent.

As an application of the multiplication law for independent events, consider the situation of a service station manager who knows from past experience that 80% of the customers use a credit card when they purchase gasoline. What is the probability that the next two customers purchasing gasoline will each use a credit card? If we let

$$A = \text{the event that the first customer uses a credit card}$$
$$B = \text{the event that the second customer uses a credit card}$$

then the event of interest is $A \cap B$. Given no other information, we can reasonably assume that A and B are independent events. Thus,

$$P(A \cap B) = P(A)P(B) = (.80)(.80) = .64$$

To summarize this section, we note that our interest in conditional probability is motivated by the fact that events are often related. In such cases, we say the events are dependent and the conditional probability formulas in equations (4.7) and (4.8) must be used to compute the event probabilities. If two events are not related, they are independent; in this case neither event's probability is affected by whether the other event occurred.

NOTES AND COMMENTS

Do not confuse the notion of mutually exclusive events with that of independent events. Two events with nonzero probabilities cannot be both mutually exclusive and independent. If one mutually exclusive event is known to occur, the other cannot occur; thus, the probability of the other event occurring is reduced to zero. They are therefore dependent.

Exercises

Methods

30. Suppose that we have two events, A and B, with $P(A) = .50$, $P(B) = .60$, and $P(A \cap B) = .40$.
    a. Find $P(A \mid B)$.
    b. Find $P(B \mid A)$.
    c. Are A and B independent? Explain.

31.   Assume that we have two events, A and B, that are mutually exclusive. Assume further that
      we know P(A) = .30 and P(B) = .40.
      a.   What is P(A ∩ B)?
      b.   What is P(A | B)?
      c.   A student in statistics argues that the concepts of mutually exclusive events and inde-
           pendent events are really the same, and that if events are mutually exclusive they must
           be independent. Do you agree with this statement? Use the probability information in
           this problem to justify your answer.
      d.   What general conclusion would you make about mutually exclusive and independent
           events given the results of this problem?

Applications

32.   Due to rising health insurance costs, 43 million people in the United States go without
      health insurance (*Time,* December 1, 2003). Sample data representative of the national
      health insurance coverage for individuals 18 years of age and older are shown here.

		Health Insurance	
		Yes	**No**
Age	**18 to 34**	750	170
	35 and over	950	130

      a.   Develop a joint probability table for these data and use the table to answer the re-
           maining questions.
      b.   What do the marginal probabilities tell you about the age of the U.S. population?
      c.   What is the probability that a randomly selected individual does not have health in-
           surance coverage?
      d.   If the individual is between the ages of 18 and 34, what is the probability that the in-
           dividual does not have health insurance coverage?
      e.   If the individual is age 35 or over, what is the probability that the individual does not
           have health insurance coverage?
      f.   If the individual does not have health insurance, what is the probability that the indi-
           vidual is in the 18 to 34 age group?
      g.   What does the probability information tell you about health insurance coverage in the
           United States?

33.   In a survey of MBA students, the following data were obtained on students' first reason for
      application to the school in which they matriculated.

		Reason for Application			
		School Quality	**School Cost or Convenience**	**Other**	**Total**
Enrollment Status	**Full Time**	421	393	76	890
	Part Time	400	593	46	1039
	Total	821	986	122	1929

      a.   Develop a joint probability table for these data.
      b.   Use the marginal probabilities of school quality, school cost or convenience, and other
           to comment on the most important reason for choosing a school.

c.   If a student goes full time, what is the probability that school quality is the first reason for choosing a school?

d.   If a student goes part time, what is the probability that school quality is the first reason for choosing a school?

e.   Let *A* denote the event that a student is full time and let *B* denote the event that the student lists school quality as the first reason for applying. Are events *A* and *B* independent? Justify your answer.

34. The following table shows the probabilities of blood types in the general population (Hoxworth Blood Center, Cincinnati, Ohio, March 2003).

	A	B	AB	O
Rh+	.34	.09	.04	.38
Rh−	.06	.02	.01	.06

a.   What is the probability a person will have type O blood?

b.   What is the probability a person will be Rh−?

c.   What is the probability a person will be Rh− given he or she has type O blood?

d.   What is the probability a person will have type B blood given he or she is Rh+?

e.   What is the probability a married couple will both be Rh−?

f.   What is the probability a married couple will both have type AB blood?

35. The U.S. Bureau of Labor Statistics collected data on the occupations of workers 25 to 64 years old. The following table shows the number of male and female workers (in millions) in each occupation category (*Statistical Abstract of the United States: 2002*).

Occupation	Male	Female
Managerial/Professional	19079	19021
Tech./Sales/Administrative	11079	19315
Service	4977	7947
Precision Production	11682	1138
Operators/Fabricators/Labor	10576	3482
Farming/Forestry/Fishing	1838	514

a.   Develop a joint probability table.

b.   What is the probability of a female worker being a manager or professional?

c.   What is the probability of a male worker being in precision production?

d.   Is occupation independent of gender? Justify your answer with a probability calculation.

36. Reggie Miller of the Indiana Pacers is the National Basketball Association's best career free throw shooter, making 89% of his shots (*USA Today*, January 22, 2004). Assume that late in a basketball game, Reggie Miller is fouled and is awarded two shots.

a.   What is the probability that he will make both shots?

b.   What is the probability that he will make at least one shot?

c.   What is the probability that he will miss both shots?

d.   Late in a basketball game, a team often intentionally fouls an opposing player in order to stop the game clock. The usual strategy is to intentionally foul the other team's worst free throw shooter. Assume that the Indiana Pacers' center makes 58% of his free throw shots. Calculate the probabilities for the center as shown in parts (a), (b), and (c), and show that intentionally fouling the Indiana Pacers' center is a better strategy than intentionally fouling Reggie Miller.

37. A purchasing agent placed rush orders for a particular raw material with two different suppliers, *A* and *B*. If neither order arrives in four days, the production process must be shut down until at least one of the orders arrives. The probability that supplier *A* can deliver the material in four days is .55. The probability that supplier *B* can deliver the material in four days is .35.
    a. What is the probability that both suppliers will deliver the material in four days? Because two separate suppliers are involved, we are willing to assume independence.
    b. What is the probability that at least one supplier will deliver the material in four days?
    c. What is the probability that the production process will be shut down in four days because of a shortage of raw material (i.e., both orders are late)?

38. The Minneapolis Heart Institute Foundation conducted a study to determine the benefit of follow-up care for patients discharged from a hospital after treatment for a heart attack (*The Wall Street Journal,* November 11, 2002). Out of 2060 patients, 1070 did not return for follow-up treatment and 990 did. Within 24 months, 14 of the patients receiving follow-up treatment died, and 29 of the patients not receiving follow-up treatment died. Within 54 months, 20 of the patients receiving follow-up treatment died, and 49 of the patients not receiving follow-up treatment died.
    a. What is the probability of a patient dying within 24 months of being discharged after treatment for a heart attack?
    b. Using the data for 24 months after discharge, compute the conditional probabilities of dying for patients receiving and not receiving follow-up treatment.
    c. Is the probability of dying within 24 months of discharge independent of whether the person receives follow-up treatment? Explain.
    d. Using the data for 54 months after discharge, compute the conditional probabilities of dying for patients receiving and not receiving follow-up treatment.
    e. Would you recommend enrolling in a follow-up treatment program to a friend?

4.5 Bayes' Theorem

In the discussion of conditional probability, we indicated that revising probabilities when new information is obtained is an important phase of probability analysis. Often, we begin the analysis with initial or **prior probability** estimates for specific events of interest. Then, from sources such as a sample, a special report, or a product test, we obtain additional information about the events. Given this new information, we update the prior probability values by calculating revised probabilities, referred to as **posterior probabilities**. **Bayes' theorem** provides a means for making these probability calculations. The steps in this probability revision process are shown in Figure 4.9.

As an application of Bayes' theorem, consider a manufacturing firm that receives shipments of parts from two different suppliers. Let A_1 denote the event that a part is from supplier 1 and A_2 denote the event that a part is from supplier 2. Currently, 65% of the parts purchased by the company are from supplier 1 and the remaining 35% are from supplier 2. Hence, if a part is selected at random, we would assign the prior probabilities $P(A_1) = .65$ and $P(A_2) = .35$.

The quality of the purchased parts varies with the source of supply. Historical data suggest that the quality ratings of the two suppliers are as shown in Table 4.6. If we let *G*

FIGURE 4.9 PROBABILITY REVISION USING BAYES' THEOREM

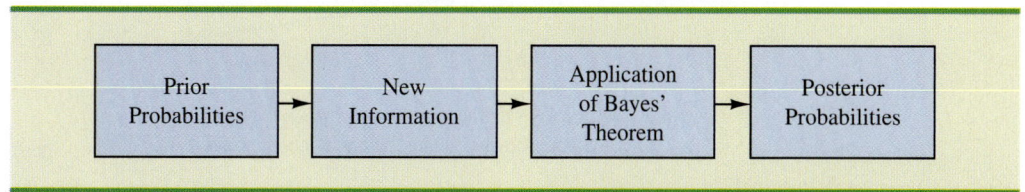

TABLE 4.6   HISTORICAL QUALITY LEVELS OF TWO SUPPLIERS

	Percentage Good Parts	Percentage Bad Parts
Supplier 1	98	2
Supplier 2	95	5

denote the event that a part is good and B denote the event that a part is bad, the information in Table 4.6 provides the following conditional probability values.

$$P(G \mid A_1) = .98 \quad P(B \mid A_1) = .02$$
$$P(G \mid A_2) = .95 \quad P(B \mid A_2) = .05$$

The tree diagram in Figure 4.10 depicts the process of the firm receiving a part from one of the two suppliers and then discovering that the part is good or bad as a two-step experiment. We see that four experimental outcomes are possible; two correspond to the part being good and two correspond to the part being bad.

Each of the experimental outcomes is the intersection of two events, so we can use the multiplication rule to compute the probabilities. For instance,

$$P(A_1, G) = P(A_1 \cap G) = P(A_1)P(G \mid A_1)$$

The process of computing these joint probabilities can be depicted in what is called a probability tree (see Figure 4.11). From left to right through the tree, the probabilities for each branch at step 1 are prior probabilities and the probabilities for each branch at step 2 are conditional probabilities. To find the probabilities of each experimental outcome, we simply multiply the probabilities on the branches leading to the outcome. Each of these joint probabilities is shown in Figure 4.11 along with the known probabilities for each branch.

Suppose now that the parts from the two suppliers are used in the firm's manufacturing process and that a machine breaks down because it attempts to process a bad part. Given

FIGURE 4.10   TREE DIAGRAM FOR TWO-SUPPLIER EXAMPLE

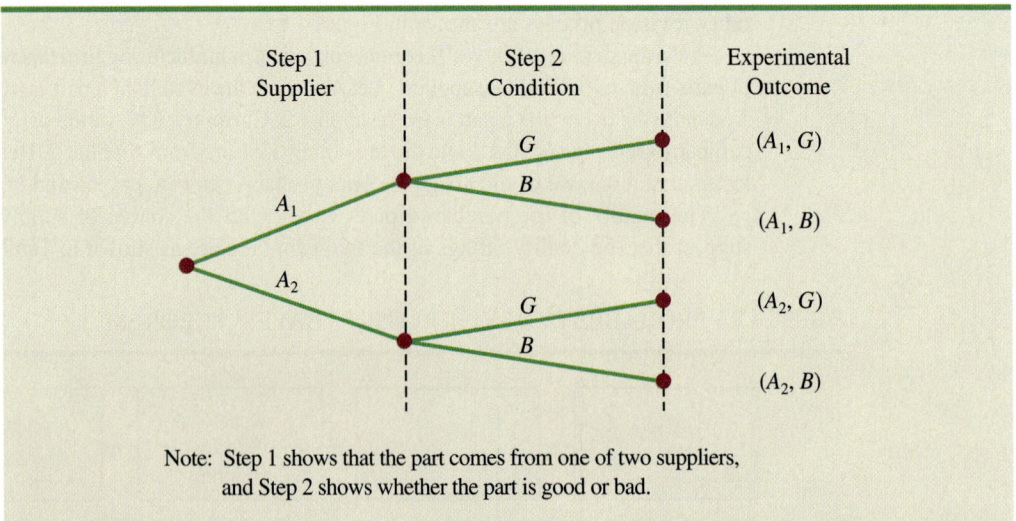

Note: Step 1 shows that the part comes from one of two suppliers, and Step 2 shows whether the part is good or bad.

FIGURE 4.11 PROBABILITY TREE FOR TWO-SUPPLIER EXAMPLE

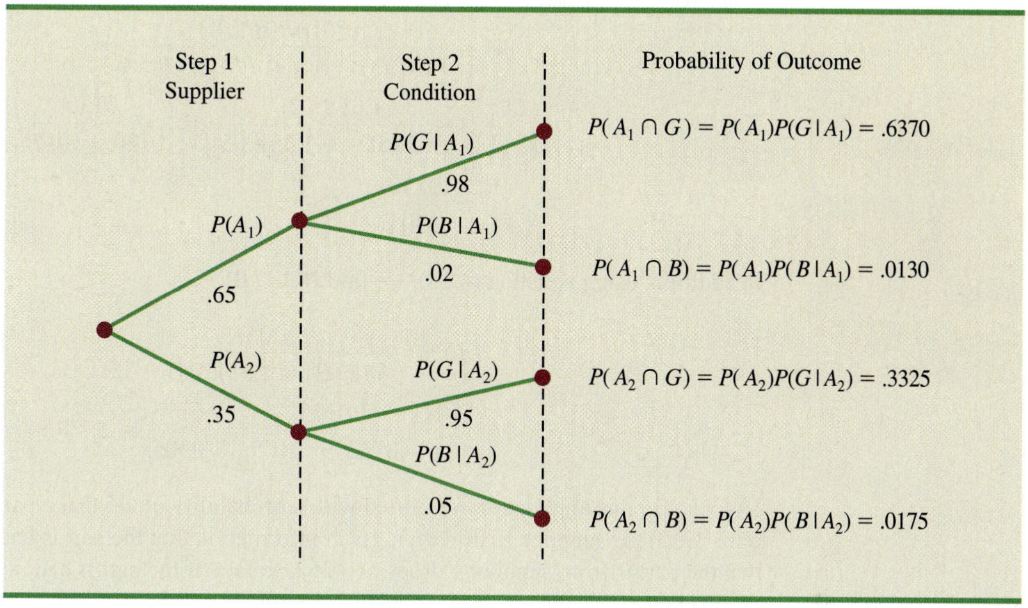

the information that the part is bad, what is the probability that it came from supplier 1 and what is the probability that it came from supplier 2? With the information in the probability tree (Figure 4.11), Bayes' theorem can be used to answer these questions.

Letting B denote the event that the part is bad, we are looking for the posterior probabilities $P(A_1 \mid B)$ and $P(A_2 \mid B)$. From the law of conditional probability, we know that

$$P(A_1 \mid B) = \frac{P(A_1 \cap B)}{P(B)} \qquad (4.14)$$

Referring to the probability tree, we see that

$$P(A_1 \cap B) = P(A_1)P(B \mid A_1) \qquad (4.15)$$

To find $P(B)$, we note that event B can occur in only two ways: $(A_1 \cap B)$ and $(A_2 \cap B)$. Therefore, we have

$$\begin{aligned} P(B) &= P(A_1 \cap B) + P(A_2 \cap B) \\ &= P(A_1)P(B \mid A_1) + P(A_2)P(B \mid A_2) \end{aligned} \qquad (4.16)$$

Substituting from equations (4.15) and (4.16) into equation (4.14) and writing a similar result for $P(A_2 \mid B)$, we obtain Bayes' theorem for the case of two events.

The Reverend Thomas Bayes (1702–1761), a Presbyterian minister, is credited with the original work leading to the version of Bayes' theorem in use today.

BAYES' THEOREM (TWO-EVENT CASE)

$$P(A_1 \mid B) = \frac{P(A_1)P(B \mid A_1)}{P(A_1)P(B \mid A_1) + P(A_2)P(B \mid A_2)} \qquad (4.17)$$

$$P(A_2 \mid B) = \frac{P(A_2)P(B \mid A_2)}{P(A_1)P(B \mid A_1) + P(A_2)P(B \mid A_2)} \qquad (4.18)$$

Using equation (4.17) and the probability values provided in the example, we have

$$P(A_1 \mid B) = \frac{P(A_1)P(B \mid A_1)}{P(A_1)P(B \mid A_1) + P(A_2)P(B \mid A_2)}$$

$$= \frac{(.65)(.02)}{(.65)(.02) + (.35)(.05)} = \frac{.0130}{.0130 + .0175}$$

$$= \frac{.0130}{.0305} = .4262$$

In addition, using equation (4.18), we find $P(A_2 \mid B)$.

$$P(A_2 \mid B) = \frac{(.35)(.05)}{(.65)(.02) + (.35)(.05)}$$

$$= \frac{.0175}{.0130 + .0175} = \frac{.0175}{.0305} = .5738$$

Note that in this application we started with a probability of .65 that a part selected at random was from supplier 1. However, given information that the part is bad, the probability that the part is from supplier 1 drops to .4262. In fact, if the part is bad, it has better than a 50-50 chance that it came from supplier 2; that is, $P(A_2 \mid B) = .5738$.

Bayes' theorem is applicable when the events for which we want to compute posterior probabilities are mutually exclusive and their union is the entire sample space.* For the case of n mutually exclusive events $A_1, A_2, \ldots, A_n$, whose union is the entire sample space, Bayes' theorem can be used to compute any posterior probability $P(A_i \mid B)$ as shown here.

BAYES' THEOREM

$$P(A_i \mid B) = \frac{P(A_i)P(B \mid A_i)}{P(A_1)P(B \mid A_1) + P(A_2)P(B \mid A_2) + \cdots + P(A_n)P(B \mid A_n)} \quad \textbf{(4.19)}$$

With prior probabilities $P(A_1), P(A_2), \ldots, P(A_n)$ and the appropriate conditional probabilities $P(B \mid A_1), P(B \mid A_2), \ldots, P(B \mid A_n)$, equation (4.19) can be used to compute the posterior probability of the events $A_1, A_2, \ldots, A_n$.

Tabular Approach

A tabular approach is helpful in conducting the Bayes' theorem calculations. Such an approach is shown in Table 4.7 for the two supplier example. The computations shown there are done in the following steps.

Step 1. Prepare the following three columns:
Column 1—The mutually exclusive events A_i for which posterior probabilities are desired
Column 2—The prior probabilities $P(A_i)$ for the events
Column 3—The conditional probabilities $P(B \mid A_i)$ of the new information B given each event

Step 2. In column 4, compute the joint probabilities $P(A_i \cap B)$ for each event and the new information B by using the multiplication law. These joint probabilities are

---

*If the union of events is the entire sample space, the events are said to be *collectively exhaustive*.

TABLE 4.7 TABULAR APPROACH TO BAYES' THEOREM CALCULATIONS FOR THE TWO-SUPPLIER EXAMPLE

(1) Events A_i	(2) Prior Probabilities $P(A_i)$	(3) Conditional Probabilities $P(B \mid A_i)$	(4) Joint Probabilities $P(A_i \cap B)$	(5) Posterior Probabilities $P(A_i \mid B)$
A_1	.65	.02	.0130	.0130/.0305 = .4262
A_2	.35	.05	.0175	.0175/.0305 = .5738
	1.00		$P(B) = .0305$	1.0000

found by multiplying the prior probabilities in column 2 by the corresponding conditional probabilities in column 3; that is, $P(A_i \cap B) = P(A_i)P(B \mid A_i)$.

Step 3. Sum the joint probabilities in column 4. The sum is the probability of the new information, $P(B)$. Thus we see in Table 4.7 that there is a .0130 probability that the part came from supplier 1 and is bad and a .0175 probability that the part came from supplier 2 and is bad. Because these are the only two ways in which a bad part can be obtained, the sum .0130 + .0175 shows an overall probability of .0305 of finding a bad part from the combined shipments of the two suppliers.

Step 4. In column 5, compute the posterior probabilities using the basic relationship of conditional probability.

$$P(A_i \mid B) = \frac{P(A_i \cap B)}{P(B)}$$

Note that the joint probabilities $P(A_i \cap B)$ are in column 4 and the probability $P(B)$ is the sum of column 4.

Using Excel to Compute Posterior Probabilities

The tabular approach to Bayes' theorem can be easily implemented within an Excel worksheet. In this subsection we show how the Bayes' theorem calculations shown in Table 4.7 can be made. Refer to Figure 4.12 as we describe the tasks involved. The formula worksheet is in the background; the value worksheet is in the foreground.

Enter Data: Labels are placed in rows 1 and 2 and the two mutually exclusive events are identified in cells A3:A4. The prior probabilities were entered into cells B3:B4 and the conditional probabilities were entered into cells C3:C4.

FIGURE 4.12 EXCEL WORKSHEET FOR COMPUTING POSTERIOR PROBABILITIES

	A	B	C	D	E	F
1		Prior	Conditional	Joint	Posterior	
2	Events	Probabilities	Probabilities	Probabilities	Probabilities	
3	A1	0.65	0.02	=B3*C3	=D3/$D$5	
4	A2	0.35	0.05	=B4*C4	=D4/$D$5	
5		=SUM(B3:B4)		=SUM(D3:D4)	=SUM(E3:E4)	
6						

	A	B	C	D	E	F
1		Prior	Conditional	Joint	Posterior	
2	Events	Probabilities	Probabilities	Probabilities	Probabilities	
3	A1	0.65	0.02	0.0130	0.4262	
4	A2	0.35	0.05	0.0175	0.5738	
5		1		0.0305	1.0000	
6						

Enter Functions and Formulas: The formulas in cells D3:D4 show that the joint probabilities are the product of the prior probabilities in column B and the conditional probabilities in column C. The results, shown in cells D3:D4 of the value worksheet, are the same as those shown in Table 4.7. The sum in cell D5 shows that the probability of finding a bad part is .0305. This probability is the denominator in Bayes' theorem. The formulas in cells E3:E4 provide the posterior probabilities. From the value worksheet we see that they are the same as the posterior probabilities in Table 4.7.

Note that the same worksheet could be used to find the posterior probabilities of the two suppliers given a good part is found. The prior probabilities in cells B3:B4 would not change. But we would replace the conditional probabilities in cells C3:C4 with the values .98 and .95, respectively. Doing so would provide $P(A_1 \mid G) = .6570$ and $P(A_2 \mid G) = .3430$ in cells E3:E4.

This worksheet can also be modified to handle Bayes' theorem calculations for more than two events. Just add a row for each additional event and move the sum row down.

NOTES AND COMMENTS

1. Bayes' theorem is used extensively in decision analysis. The prior probabilities are often subjective estimates provided by a decision maker. Sample information is obtained and posterior probabilities are computed for use in choosing the best decision.

2. An event and its complement are mutually exclusive, and their union is the entire sample space. Thus, Bayes' theorem is always applicable for computing posterior probabilities of an event and its complement.

Exercises

Methods

39. The prior probabilities for events A_1 and A_2 are $P(A_1) = .40$ and $P(A_2) = .60$. It is also known that $P(A_1 \cap A_2) = 0$. Suppose $P(B \mid A_1) = .20$ and $P(B \mid A_2) = .05$.
    a. Are A_1 and A_2 mutually exclusive? Explain.
    b. Compute $P(A_1 \cap B)$ and $P(A_2 \cap B)$.
    c. Compute $P(B)$.
    d. Use Bayes' theorem to compute $P(A_1 \mid B)$ and $P(A_2 \mid B)$.

40. The prior probabilities for events A_1, A_2, and A_3 are $P(A_1) = .20$, $P(A_2) = .50$, and $P(A_3) = .30$. The conditional probabilities of event B given A_1, A_2, and A_3 are $P(B \mid A_1) = .50$, $P(B \mid A_2) = .40$, and $P(B \mid A_3) = .30$.
    a. Compute $P(B \cap A_1)$, $P(B \cap A_2)$, and $P(B \cap A_3)$.
    b. Use Bayes' theorem, equation (4.19), to compute the posterior probability $P(A_2 \mid B)$.
    c. Use the tabular approach to applying Bayes' theorem to compute $P(A_1 \mid B)$, $P(A_2 \mid B)$, and $P(A_3 \mid B)$.

Applications

41. A consulting firm submitted a bid for a large research project. The firm's management initially felt they had a 50-50 chance of getting the project. However, the agency to which the bid was submitted subsequently requested additional information on the bid. Past experience indicates that for 75% of the successful bids and 40% of the unsuccessful bids the agency requested additional information.
    a. What is the prior probability of the bid being successful (i.e., prior to the request for additional information)?

    b.   What is the conditional probability of a request for additional information given that the bid will ultimately be successful?

    c.   Compute the posterior probability that the bid will be successful given a request for additional information.

42.   A local bank reviewed its credit card policy with the intention of recalling some of its credit cards. In the past approximately 5% of cardholders defaulted, leaving the bank unable to collect the outstanding balance. Hence, management established a prior probability of .05 that any particular cardholder will default. The bank also found that the probability of missing a monthly payment is .20 for customers who do not default. Of course, the probability of missing a monthly payment for those who default is 1.

    a.   Given that a customer missed one or more monthly payments, compute the posterior probability that the customer will default.

    b.   The bank would like to recall its card if the probability that a customer will default is greater than .20. Should the bank recall its card if the customer misses a monthly payment? Why or why not?

43.   Small cars get better gas mileage, but they are not as safe as bigger cars. Small cars accounted for 18% of the vehicles on the road, but accidents involving small cars led to 11,898 fatalities during a recent year (*Reader's Digest,* May 2000). Assume the probability a small car is involved in an accident is .18. The probability of an accident involving a small car leading to a fatality is .128 and the probability of an accident not involving a small car leading to a fatality is .05. Suppose you learn of an accident involving a fatality. What is the probability a small car was involved? Assume that the likelihood of getting into an accident is independent of car size.

44.   The American Council of Education reported that 47% of college freshmen earn a degree and graduate within five years (Associated Press, May 6, 2002). Assume that graduation records show women make up 50% of the students who graduated within five years, but only 45% of the students who did not graduate within five years. The students who had not graduated within five years either dropped out or were still working on their degrees.

    a.   Let A_1 = the student graduated within five years

           A_2 = the student did not graduate within five years

            W = the student is a female student

       Using the given information, what are the values for $P(A_1)$, $P(A_2)$, $P(W \mid A_1)$, and $P(W \mid A_2)$?

    b.   What is the probability that a female student will graduate within five years?

    c.   What is the probability that a male student will graduate within five years?

    d.   Given the preceding results, what are the percentage of women and the percentage of men in the entering freshman class?

45.   In an article about investment growth, *Money* magazine reported that drug stocks show powerful long-term trends and offer investors unparalleled potential for strong and steady gains. The federal Health Care Financing Administration supports this conclusion through its forecast that annual prescription drug expenditures will reach $366 billion by 2010, up from $117 billion in 2000. Many individuals age 65 and older rely heavily on prescription drugs. For this group, 82% take prescription drugs regularly, 55% take three or more prescriptions regularly, and 40% currently use five or more prescriptions. In contrast, 49% of people under age 65 take prescriptions regularly, with 37% taking three or more prescriptions regularly and 28% using five or more prescriptions (*Money,* September 2001). The U.S. Census Bureau reports that of the 281,421,906 people in the United States, 34,991,753 are age 65 years and older (U.S. Census Bureau, *Census 2000*).

    a.   Compute the probability that a person in the United States is age 65 or older.

    b.   Compute the probability that a person takes prescription drugs regularly.

    c.   Compute the probability that a person is age 65 or older and takes five or more prescriptions.

    d.   Given a person uses five or more prescriptions, compute the probability that the person is age 65 or older.

Summary

In this chapter we introduced basic probability concepts and illustrated how probability analysis can be used to provide helpful information for decision making. We described how probability can be interpreted as a numerical measure of the likelihood that an event will occur. In addition, we saw that the probability of an event can be computed either by summing the probabilities of the experimental outcomes (sample points) comprising the event or by using the relationships established by the addition, conditional probability, and multiplication laws of probability. For cases in which additional information is available, we showed how Bayes' theorem can be used to obtain revised or posterior probabilities.

Glossary

Probability A numerical measure of the likelihood that an event will occur.

Experiment A process that generates well-defined outcomes.

Sample space The set of all experimental outcomes.

Sample point An element of the sample space. A sample point represents an experimental outcome.

Tree diagram A graphical representation that helps in visualizing a multiple-step experiment.

Basic requirements for assigning probabilities Two requirements that restrict the manner in which probability assignments can be made: (1) for each experimental outcome E_i we must have $0 \leq P(E_i) \leq 1$; (2) considering all experimental outcomes, we must have $P(E_1) + P(E_2) + \cdots + P(E_n) = 1$.

Classical method A method of assigning probabilities that is appropriate when all the experimental outcomes are equally likely.

Relative frequency method A method of assigning probabilities that is appropriate when data are available to estimate the proportion of the time the experimental outcome will occur if the experiment is repeated a large number of times.

Subjective method A method of assigning probabilities on the basis of judgment.

Event A collection of sample points.

Complement of A The event consisting of all sample points that are not in A.

Venn diagram A graphical representation for showing symbolically the sample space and operations involving events in which the sample space is represented by a rectangle and events are represented as circles within the sample space.

Union of A and B The event containing all sample points belonging to A or B or both. The union is denoted $A \cup B$.

Intersection of A and B The event containing the sample points belonging to both A and B. The intersection is denoted $A \cap B$.

Addition law A probability law used to compute the probability of the union of two events. It is $P(A \cup B) = P(A) + P(B) - P(A \cap B)$. For mutually exclusive events, $P(A \cap B) = 0$; in this case the addition law reduces to $P(A \cup B) = P(A) + P(B)$.

Mutually exclusive events Events that have no sample points in common; that is, $A \cap B$ is empty and $P(A \cap B) = 0$.

Conditional probability The probability of an event given that another event already occurred. The conditional probability of A given B is $P(A \mid B) = P(A \cap B)/P(B)$.

Joint probability The probability of two events both occurring; that is, the probability of the intersection of two events.

Marginal probability The values in the margins of a joint probability table that provide the probabilities of each event separately.

Independent events Two events A and B where $P(A \mid B) = P(A)$ or $P(B \mid A) = P(B)$; that is, the events have no influence on each other.

Multiplication law A probability law used to compute the probability of the intersection of two events. It is $P(A \cap B) = P(B)P(A \mid B)$ or $P(A \cap B) = P(A)P(B \mid A)$. For independent events it reduces to $P(A \cap B) = P(A)P(B)$.

Prior probabilities Initial estimates of the probabilities of events.

Posterior probabilities Revised probabilities of events based on additional information.

Bayes' theorem A method used to compute posterior probabilities.

Key Formulas

Counting Rule for Combinations

$$C_n^N = \binom{N}{n} = \frac{N!}{n!(N-n)!} \tag{4.1}$$

Counting Rule for Permutations

$$P_n^N = n!\binom{N}{n} = \frac{N!}{(N-n)!} \tag{4.2}$$

Computing Probability Using the Complement

$$P(A) = 1 - P(A^c) \tag{4.5}$$

Addition Law

$$P(A \cup B) = P(A) + P(B) - P(A \cap B) \tag{4.6}$$

Conditional Probability

$$P(A \mid B) = \frac{P(A \cap B)}{P(B)} \tag{4.7}$$

$$P(B \mid A) = \frac{P(A \cap B)}{P(A)} \tag{4.8}$$

Multiplication Law

$$P(A \cap B) = P(B)P(A \mid B) \tag{4.11}$$

$$P(A \cap B) = P(A)P(B \mid A) \tag{4.12}$$

Multiplication Law for Independent Events

$$P(A \cap B) = P(A)P(B) \tag{4.13}$$

Bayes' Theorem

$$P(A_i \mid B) = \frac{P(A_i)P(B \mid A_i)}{P(A_1)P(B \mid A_1) + P(A_2)P(B \mid A_2) + \cdots + P(A_n)P(B \mid A_n)} \tag{4.19}$$

Supplementary Exercises

46. In a *Business Week*/Harris Poll, 1035 adults were asked about their attitudes toward business (*Business Week,* September 11, 2000). One question asked: "How would you rate large U.S. companies on making good products and competing in a global environment?" The responses were: excellent—18%, pretty good—50%, only fair—26%, poor—5%, and don't know/no answer—1%.
     a. What is the probability that a respondent rated U.S. companies pretty good or excellent?
     b. How many respondents rated U.S. companies poor?
     c. How many respondents did not know or did not answer?

47. A financial manager made two new investments—one in the oil industry and one in municipal bonds. After a one-year period, each of the investments will be classified as either successful or unsuccessful. Consider the making of the two investments as an experiment.
     a. How many sample points exist for this experiment?
     b. Show a tree diagram and list the sample points.
     c. Let O = the event that the oil industry investment is successful and M = the event that the municipal bond investment is successful. List the sample points in O and in M.
     d. List the sample points in the union of the events $(O \cup M)$.
     e. List the sample points in the intersection of the events $(O \cap M)$.
     f. Are events O and M mutually exclusive? Explain.

48. In early 2003, President Bush proposed eliminating the taxation of dividends to shareholders on the grounds that it was double taxation. Corporations pay taxes on the earnings that are later paid out in dividends. In a poll of 671 Americans, TechnoMetrica Market Intelligence found that 47% favored the proposal, 44% opposed it, and 9% were not sure (*Investor's Business Daily,* January 13, 2003). In looking at the responses across party lines the poll showed that 29% of Democrats were in favor, 64% of Republicans were in favor, and 48% of Independents were in favor.
     a. How many of those polled favored elimination of the tax on dividends?
     b. What is the conditional probability in favor of the proposal given the person polled is a Democrat?
     c. Is party affiliation independent of whether one is in favor of the proposal?
     d. If we assume people's responses were consistent with their own self-interest, which group do you believe will benefit most from passage of the proposal?

49. A study of 31,000 hospital admissions in New York State found that 4% of the admissions led to treatment-caused injuries. One-seventh of these treatment-caused injuries resulted in death, and one-fourth were caused by negligence. Malpractice claims were filed in one out of 7.5 cases involving negligence, and payments were made in one out of every two claims.
     a. What is the probability a person admitted to the hospital will suffer a treatment-caused injury due to negligence?
     b. What is the probability a person admitted to the hospital will die from a treatment-caused injury?
     c. In the case of a negligent treatment-caused injury, what is the probability a malpractice claim will be paid?

50. A telephone survey to determine viewer response to a new television show obtained the following data.

Rating	Frequency
Poor	4
Below average	8
Average	11
Above average	14
Excellent	13

a. What is the probability that a randomly selected viewer will rate the new show as average or better?

b. What is the probability that a randomly selected viewer will rate the new show below average or worse?

51. The following crosstabulation shows household income by educational level of the head of household (*Statistical Abstract of the United States: 2002*).

Education Level	Household Income ($1000s)					
	Under 25	25.0– 49.9	50.0– 74.9	75.0– 99.9	100 or more	Total
Not H.S. Graduate	9,285	4,093	1,589	541	354	15,862
H.S. Graduate	10,150	9,821	6,050	2,737	2,028	30,786
Some College	6,011	8,221	5,813	3,215	3,120	26,380
Bachelor's Degree	2,138	3,985	3,952	2,698	4,748	17,521
Beyond Bach. Deg.	813	1,497	1,815	1,589	3,765	9,479
Total	28,397	27,617	19,219	10,780	14,015	100,028

a. Develop a joint probability table.

b. What is the probability of a head of household not being a high school graduate?

c. What is the probability of a head of household having a bachelor's degree or more education?

d. What is the probability of a household headed by someone with a bachelor's degree earning $100,000 or more?

e. What is the probability of a household having income below $25,000?

f. What is the probability of a household headed by someone with a bachelor's degree earning less than $25,000?

g. Is household income independent of educational level?

52. A GMAC MBA new-matriculants survey provided the following data for 2018 students.

Age Group	Applied to More Than One School	
	Yes	No
23 and under	207	201
24–26	299	379
27–30	185	268
31–35	66	193
36 and over	51	169

a. For a randomly selected MBA student, prepare a joint probability table for the experiment consisting of observing the student's age and whether the student applied to one or more schools.

b. What is the probability that a randomly selected applicant is 23 or under?

c. What is the probability that a randomly selected applicant is older than 26?

d. What is the probability that a randomly selected applicant applied to more than one school?

53. Refer again to the data from the GMAC new-matriculants survey in exercise 52.

a. Given that a person applied to more than one school, what is the probability that the person is 24–26 years old?

b. Given that a person is in the 36-and-over age group, what is the probability that the person applied to more than one school?

c. What is the probability that a person is 24–26 years old or applied to more than one school?

d.   Suppose a person is known to have applied to only one school. What is the probability that the person is 31 or more years old?
e.   Is the number of schools applied to independent of age? Explain.

54.   An IBD/TIPP poll conducted to learn about attitudes toward investment and retirement (*Investor's Business Daily,* May 5, 2000) asked male and female respondents how important they felt level of risk was in choosing a retirement investment. The following joint probability table was constructed from the data provided. "Important" means the respondent said level of risk was either important or very important.

	Male	Female	Total
Important	.22	.27	.49
Not Important	.28	.23	.51
Total	.50	.50	1.00

a.   What is the probability a survey respondent will say level of risk is important?
b.   What is the probability a male respondent will say level of risk is important?
c.   What is the probability a female respondent will say level of risk is important?
d.   Is the level of risk independent of the gender of the respondent? Why or why not?
e.   Do male and female attitudes toward risk differ?

55.   A large consumer goods company ran a television advertisement for one of its soap products. On the basis of a survey that was conducted, probabilities were assigned to the following events.

B = individual purchased the product
S = individual recalls seeing the advertisement
$B \cap S$ = individual purchased the product and recalls seeing the advertisement

The probabilities assigned were $P(B) = .20$, $P(S) = .40$, and $P(B \cap S) = .12$.
a.   What is the probability of an individual's purchasing the product given that the individual recalls seeing the advertisement? Does seeing the advertisement increase the probability that the individual will purchase the product? As a decision maker, would you recommend continuing the advertisement (assuming that the cost is reasonable)?
b.   Assume that individuals who do not purchase the company's soap product buy from its competitors. What would be your estimate of the company's market share? Would you expect that continuing the advertisement will increase the company's market share? Why or why not?
c.   The company also tested another advertisement and assigned it values of $P(S) = .30$ and $P(B \cap S) = .10$. What is $P(B \mid S)$ for this other advertisement? Which advertisement seems to have had the bigger effect on customer purchases?

56.   Cooper Realty is a small real estate company located in Albany, New York, specializing primarily in residential listings. They recently became interested in determining the likelihood of one of their listings being sold within a certain number of days. An analysis of company sales of 800 homes in previous years produced the following data.

		Days Listed Until Sold			
		Under 30	31–90	Over 90	Total
	Under $150,000	50	40	10	100
	$150,000–$199,999	20	150	80	250
Initial Asking Price	$200,000–$250,000	20	280	100	400
	Over $250,000	10	30	10	50
	Total	100	500	200	800

a. If A is defined as the event that a home is listed for more than 90 days before being sold, estimate the probability of A.

b. If B is defined as the event that the initial asking price is under $150,000, estimate the probability of B.

c. What is the probability of $A \cap B$?

d. Assuming that a contract was just signed to list a home with an initial asking price of less than $150,000, what is the probability that the home will take Cooper Realty more than 90 days to sell?

e. Are events A and B independent?

57. A company studied the number of lost-time accidents occurring at its Brownsville, Texas, plant. Historical records show that 6% of the employees suffered lost-time accidents last year. Management believes that a special safety program will reduce such accidents to 5% during the current year. In addition, it estimates that 15% of employees who had lost-time accidents last year will experience a lost-time accident during the current year.

a. What percentage of the employees will experience lost-time accidents in both years?

b. What percentage of the employees will suffer at least one lost-time accident over the two-year period?

58. The Dallas IRS auditing staff, concerned with identifying potentially fraudulent tax returns, believes that the probability of finding a fraudulent return given that the return contains deductions for contributions exceeding the IRS standard is .20. Given that the deductions for contributions do not exceed the IRS standard, the probability of a fraudulent return decreases to .02. If 8% of all returns exceed the IRS standard for deductions due to contributions, what is the best estimate of the percentage of fraudulent returns?

59. An oil company purchased an option on land in Alaska. Preliminary geologic studies assigned the following prior probabilities.

$$P(\text{high-quality oil}) = .50$$
$$P(\text{medium-quality oil}) = .20$$
$$P(\text{no oil}) = .30$$

a. What is the probability of finding oil?

b. After 200 feet of drilling on the first well, a soil test is taken. The probabilities of finding the particular type of soil identified by the test follow.

$$P(\text{soil} \mid \text{high-quality oil}) = .20$$
$$P(\text{soil} \mid \text{medium-quality oil}) = .80$$
$$P(\text{soil} \mid \text{no oil}) = .20$$

How should the firm interpret the soil test? What are the revised probabilities, and what is the new probability of finding oil?

60. Companies that do business over the Internet can often obtain probability information about Web site visitors from previous Web sites visited. The article "Internet Marketing" (*Interfaces,* March/April 2001) described how clickstream data on Web sites visited could be used in conjunction with a Bayesian updating scheme to determine the gender of a Web site visitor. Par Fore created a Web site to market golf equipment and apparel. Management would like a certain offer to appear for female visitors and a different offer to appear for male visitors. From a sample of past Web site visits, management learned that 60% of the visitors to ParFore.com are male and 40% are female.

a. What is the prior probability that the next visitor to the Web site will be female?

b. Suppose you know that the current visitor to ParFore.com previously visited the Dillard's Web site, and that women are three times as likely to visit the Dillard's Web site as men. What is the revised probability that the current visitor to ParFore.com is female? Should you display the offer that appeals more to female visitors or the one that appeals more to male visitors?

Case Problem   # Hamilton County Judges

Hamilton County judges try thousands of cases each year. In an overwhelming majority of the cases disposed, the verdict stands as rendered. However, some cases are appealed, and of those appealed, some of the cases are reversed. Kristen DelGuzzi of *The Cincinnati Enquirer* conducted a study of cases handled by Hamilton County judges over a three-year period. Shown in Table 4.8 are the results for 182,908 cases handled (disposed) by 38 judges in Common Pleas Court, Domestic Relations Court, and Municipal Court. Two of the judges (Dinkelacker and Hogan) did not serve in the same court for the entire three-year period.

The purpose of the newspaper's study was to evaluate the performance of the judges. Appeals are often the result of mistakes made by judges, and the newspaper wanted to know which judges were doing a good job and which were making too many mistakes. You are called in to assist in the data analysis. Use your knowledge of probability and conditional probability to help with the ranking of the judges. You also may be able to analyze the likelihood of appeal and reversal for cases handled by different courts.

Managerial Report

Prepare a report with your rankings of the judges. Also, include an analysis of the likelihood of appeal and case reversal in the three courts. At a minimum, your report should include the following:

1. The probability of cases being appealed and reversed in the three different courts.
2. The probability of a case being appealed for each judge.
3. The probability of a case being reversed for each judge.
4. The probability of reversal given an appeal for each judge.
5. Rank the judges within each court. State the criteria you used and provide a rationale for your choice.

TABLE 4.8   TOTAL CASES DISPOSED, APPEALED, AND REVERSED IN HAMILTON COUNTY COURTS

CD file

Judge

Common Pleas Court		
Judge	**Total Cases Disposed**	**Appealed Cases**	**Reversed Cases**
Fred Cartolano	3,037	137	12
Thomas Crush	3,372	119	10
Patrick Dinkelacker	1,258	44	8
Timothy Hogan	1,954	60	7
Robert Kraft	3,138	127	7
William Mathews	2,264	91	18
William Morrissey	3,032	121	22
Norbert Nadel	2,959	131	20
Arthur Ney, Jr.	3,219	125	14
Richard Niehaus	3,353	137	16
Thomas Nurre	3,000	121	6
John O'Connor	2,969	129	12
Robert Ruehlman	3,205	145	18
J. Howard Sundermann	955	60	10
Ann Marie Tracey	3,141	127	13
Ralph Winkler	3,089	88	6
Total	**43,945**	**1762**	**199**

Domestic Relations Court		
Judge	**Total Cases Disposed**	**Appealed Cases**	**Reversed Cases**
Penelope Cunningham	2,729	7	1
Patrick Dinkelacker	6,001	19	4
Deborah Gaines	8,799	48	9
Ronald Panioto	12,970	32	3
Total	**30,499**	**106**	**17**

Municipal Court		
Judge	**Total Cases Disposed**	**Appealed Cases**	**Reversed Cases**
Mike Allen	6,149	43	4
Nadine Allen	7,812	34	6
Timothy Black	7,954	41	6
David Davis	7,736	43	5
Leslie Isaiah Gaines	5,282	35	13
Karla Grady	5,253	6	0
Deidra Hair	2,532	5	0
Dennis Helmick	7,900	29	5
Timothy Hogan	2,308	13	2
James Patrick Kenney	2,798	6	1
Joseph Luebbers	4,698	25	8
William Mallory	8,277	38	9
Melba Marsh	8,219	34	7
Beth Mattingly	2,971	13	1
Albert Mestemaker	4,975	28	9
Mark Painter	2,239	7	3
Jack Rosen	7,790	41	13
Mark Schweikert	5,403	33	6
David Stockdale	5,371	22	4
John A. West	2,797	4	2
Total	**108,464**	**500**	**104**

CHAPTER 5

Discrete Probability Distributions

CONTENTS

STATISTICS IN PRACTICE:
CITIBANK

5.1 RANDOM VARIABLES
   Discrete Random Variables
   Continuous Random Variables

5.2 DISCRETE PROBABILITY
   DISTRIBUTIONS

5.3 EXPECTED VALUE AND
   VARIANCE
   Expected Value
   Variance
   Using Excel to Compute the
      Expected Value, Variance, and
      Standard Deviation

5.4 BINOMIAL PROBABILITY
   DISTRIBUTION
   A Binomial Experiment
   Martin Clothing Store Problem

   Using Excel to Compute
      Binomial Probabilities
   Expected Value and Variance for
      the Binomial Probability
      Distribution

5.5 POISSON PROBABILITY
   DISTRIBUTION
   An Example Involving Time
      Intervals
   An Example Involving Length or
      Distance Intervals
   Using Excel to Compute Poisson
      Probabilities

5.6 HYPERGEOMETRIC
   PROBABILITY DISTRIBUTION
   Using Excel to Compute
      Hypergeometric Probabilities

CITIBANK*
LONG ISLAND CITY, NEW YORK

Citibank, a division of Citigroup, makes available a wide range of financial services, including checking and savings accounts, loans and mortgages, insurance, and investment services, within the framework of a unique strategy for delivering those services called Citibanking. Citibanking entails a consistent brand identity all over the world, consistent product offerings, and high-level customer service. Citibanking lets you manage your money anytime, anywhere, anyway you choose. Whether you need to save for the future or borrow for today, you can do it all at Citibank.

Citibanking's state-of-the-art automatic teller machines (ATMs) located in Citicard Banking Centers (CBCs) let customers do all their banking in one place with the touch of a finger, 24 hours a day, 7 days a week. More than 150 different banking functions from deposits to managing investments can be performed with ease. Citibanking ATMs are so much more than just cash machines that customers today use them for 80% of their transactions.

Each Citibank CBC operates as a waiting line system with randomly arriving customers seeking service at one of the ATMs. If all ATMs are busy, the arriving customers wait in line. Periodic CBC capacity studies are used to analyze customer waiting times and to determine whether additional ATMs are needed.

Data collected by Citibank showed that the random customer arrivals followed a probability distribution known as the Poisson distribution. Using the Poisson distribution, Citibank can compute probabilities for the number of customers arriving at a CBC during any time period and make decisions concern-

A Citibank ATM in Manhattan. © PhotoDisc/Getty Images.

ing the number of ATMs needed. For example, let x = the number of customers arriving during a one-minute period. Assuming that a particular CBC has a mean arrival rate of two customers per minute, the following table shows the probabilities for the number of customers arriving during a one-minute period.

x	Probability
0	.1353
1	.2707
2	.2707
3	.1804
4	.0902
5 or more	.0527

Discrete probability distributions, such as the one used by Citibank, are the topic of this chapter. In addition to the Poisson distribution, you will learn about the binomial and hypergeometric distributions and how they can be used to provide helpful probability information.

*The authors are indebted to Ms. Stacey Karter, Citibank, for providing this Statistics in Practice.

In this chapter we continue the study of probability by introducing the concepts of random variables and probability distributions. The focus of this chapter is discrete probability distributions. Three special discrete probability distributions—the binomial, Poisson, and hypergeometric—are covered.

5.1 Random Variables

In Chapter 4 we defined the concept of an experiment and its associated experimental outcomes. A random variable provides a means for describing experimental outcomes using numerical values. Random variables must assume numerical values.

Random variables must assume numerical values.

> RANDOM VARIABLE
>
> A **random variable** is a numerical description of the outcome of an experiment.

In effect, a random variable associates a numerical value with each possible experimental outcome. The particular numerical value of the random variable depends on the outcome of the experiment. A random variable can be classified as being either *discrete* or *continuous* depending on the numerical values it assumes.

Discrete Random Variables

A random variable that may assume either a finite number of values or an infinite sequence of values such as 0, 1, 2, . . . is referred to as a **discrete random variable**. For example, consider the experiment of an accountant taking the certified public accountant (CPA) examination. The examination has four parts. We can define a random variable as x = the number of parts of the CPA examination passed. It is a discrete random variable because it may assume the finite number of values 0, 1, 2, 3, or 4.

As another example of a discrete random variable, consider the experiment of cars arriving at a tollbooth. The random variable of interest is x = the number of cars arriving during a one-day period. The possible values for x come from the sequence of integers 0, 1, 2, and so on. Hence, x is a discrete random variable assuming one of the values in this infinite sequence.

Although the outcomes of many experiments can naturally be described by numerical values, others cannot. For example, a survey question might ask an individual to recall the message in a recent television commercial. This experiment would have two possible outcomes: the individual cannot recall the message and the individual can recall the message. We can still describe these experimental outcomes numerically by defining the discrete random variable x as follows: let x = 0 if the individual cannot recall the message and x = 1 if the individual can recall the message. The numerical values for this random variable are arbitrary (we could use 5 and 10), but they are acceptable in terms of the definition of a random variable—namely, x is a random variable because it provides a numerical description of the outcome of the experiment.

Table 5.1 provides some additional examples of discrete random variables. Note that in each example the discrete random variable assumes a finite number of values or an infinite sequence of values such as 0, 1, 2, ... These types of discrete random variables are discussed in detail in this chapter.

TABLE 5.1   EXAMPLES OF DISCRETE RANDOM VARIABLES

Experiment	Random Variable (x)	Possible Values for the Random Variable
Contact five customers	Number of customers who place an order	0, 1, 2, 3, 4, 5
Inspect a shipment of 50 radios	Number of defective radios	0, 1, 2, $\cdots$, 49, 50
Operate a restaurant for one day	Number of customers	0, 1, 2, 3, $\cdots$
Sell an automobile	Gender of the customer	0 if male; 1 if female

Continuous Random Variables

A random variable that may assume any numerical value in an interval or collection of intervals is called a **continuous random variable**. Experimental outcomes based on measurement scales such as time, weight, distance, and temperature can be described by continuous random variables. For example, consider an experiment of monitoring incoming telephone calls to the claims office of a major insurance company. Suppose the random variable of interest is $x = $ the time between consecutive incoming calls in minutes. This random variable may assume any value in the interval $x \geq 0$. Actually, an infinite number of values are possible for x, including values such as 1.26 minutes, 2.751 minutes, 4.3333 minutes, and so on. As another example, consider a 90-mile section of interstate highway I-75 north of Atlanta, Georgia. For an emergency ambulance service located in Atlanta, we might define the random variable as $x = $ number of miles to the location of the next traffic accident along this section of I-75. In this case, x would be a continuous random variable assuming any value in the interval $0 \leq x \leq 90$. Additional examples of continuous random variables are listed in Table 5.2. Note that each example describes a random variable that may assume any value in an interval of values. Continuous random variables and their probability distributions will be the topic of Chapter 6.

TABLE 5.2   EXAMPLES OF CONTINUOUS RANDOM VARIABLES

Experiment	Random Variable (x)	Possible Values for the Random Variable
Operate a bank	Time between customer arrivals in minutes	$x \geq 0$
Fill a soft drink can (max = 12.1 ounces)	Number of ounces	$0 \leq x \leq 12.1$
Construct a new library	Percentage of project complete after six months	$0 \leq x \leq 100$
Test a new chemical process	Temperature when the desired reaction takes place (min 150° F; max 212° F)	$150 \leq x \leq 212$

NOTES AND COMMENTS

One way to determine whether a random variable is discrete or continuous is to think of the values of the random variable as points on a line segment. Choose two points representing values of the random variable. If the entire line segment between the two points also represents possible values for the random variable, then the random variable is continuous.

Exercises

Methods

1. Consider the experiment of tossing a coin twice.
   a. List the experimental outcomes.
   b. Define a random variable that represents the number of heads occurring on the two tosses.
   c. Show what value the random variable would assume for each of the experimental outcomes.
   d. Is this random variable discrete or continuous?

2. Consider the experiment of a worker assembling a product.
    a. Define a random variable that represents the time in minutes required to assemble the product.
    b. What values may the random variable assume?
    c. Is the random variable discrete or continuous?

Applications

3. Three students scheduled interviews for summer employment at the Brookwood Institute. In each case the interview results in either an offer for a position or no offer. Experimental outcomes are defined in terms of the results of the three interviews.
    a. List the experimental outcomes.
    b. Define a random variable that represents the number of offers made. Is the random variable continuous?
    c. Show the value of the random variable for each of the experimental outcomes.

4. Suppose we know home mortgage rates for 12 Florida lending institutions. Assume that the random variable of interest is the number of lending institutions in this group that offers a 30-year fixed rate of 8.5% or less. What values may this random variable assume?

5. To perform a certain type of blood analysis, lab technicians must perform two procedures. The first procedure requires either one or two separate steps, and the second procedure requires either one, two, or three steps.
    a. List the experimental outcomes associated with performing the blood analysis.
    b. If the random variable of interest is the total number of steps required to do the complete analysis (both procedures), show what value the random variable will assume for each of the experimental outcomes.

6. Listed is a series of experiments and associated random variables. In each case, identify the values that the random variable can assume and state whether the random variable is discrete or continuous.

Experiment	Random Variable (x)
a. Take a 20-question examination	Number of questions answered correctly
b. Observe cars arriving at a tollbooth for 1 hour	Number of cars arriving at tollbooth
c. Audit 50 tax returns	Number of returns containing errors
d. Observe an employee's work	Number of nonproductive hours in an eight-hour workday
e. Weigh a shipment of goods	Number of pounds

5.2   Discrete Probability Distributions

The **probability distribution** for a random variable describes how probabilities are distributed over the values of the random variable. For a discrete random variable x, the probability distribution is defined by a **probability function**, denoted by $f(x)$. The probability function provides the probability for each value of the random variable.

As an illustration of a discrete random variable and its probability distribution, consider the sales of automobiles at DiCarlo Motors in Saratoga, New York. Over the past 300 days of operation, sales data show 54 days with no automobiles sold, 117 days with 1 automobile sold, 72 days with 2 automobiles sold, 42 days with 3 automobiles sold, 12 days with 4 automobiles sold, and 3 days with 5 automobiles sold. Suppose we consider the experiment of selecting a day of operation at DiCarlo Motors and define the random variable of interest as $x =$ the number of automobiles sold during a day. From historical data, we know

x is a discrete random variable that can assume the values 0, 1, 2, 3, 4, or 5. In probability function notation, $f(0)$ is the probability of 0 automobiles sold, $f(1)$ is the probability of 1 automobile sold, and so on. Because historical data show 54 of 300 days with 0 automobiles sold, we assign the value $54/300 = .18$ to $f(0)$, indicating that the probability of 0 automobiles being sold during a day is .18. Similarly, because 117 of 300 days had 1 automobile sold, we assign the value $117/300 = .39$ to $f(1)$, indicating that the probability of exactly 1 automobile being sold during a day is .39. Continuing in this way for the other values of the random variable, we compute the values for $f(2), f(3), f(4),$ and $f(5)$ as shown in Table 5.3, the probability distribution for the number of automobiles sold during a day at DiCarlo Motors.

A primary advantage of defining a random variable and its probability distribution is that once the probability distribution is known, it is relatively easy to determine the probability of a variety of events that may be of interest to a decision maker. For example, using the probability distribution for DiCarlo Motors as shown in Table 5.3, we see that the most probable number of automobiles sold during a day is 1 with a probability of $f(1) = .39$. In addition, there is an $f(3) + f(4) + f(5) = .14 + .04 + .01 = .19$ probability of selling three or more automobiles during a day. These probabilities, plus others the decision maker may ask about, provide information that can help the decision maker understand the process of selling automobiles at DiCarlo Motors.

In the development of a probability function for any discrete random variable, the following two conditions must be satisfied.

These conditions are the analogs to the two basic requirements for assigning probabilities to experimental outcomes presented in Chapter 4.

REQUIRED CONDITIONS FOR A DISCRETE PROBABILITY FUNCTION

$$f(x) \geq 0 \qquad \textbf{(5.1)}$$
$$\Sigma f(x) = 1 \qquad \textbf{(5.2)}$$

Table 5.3 shows that the probabilities for the random variable x satisfy equation (5.1); $f(x)$ is greater than or equal to 0 for all values of x. In addition, because the probabilities sum to 1, equation (5.2) is satisfied. Thus, the DiCarlo Motors probability function is a valid discrete probability function.

We can also present probability distributions graphically. In Figure 5.1 the values of the random variable x for DiCarlo Motors are shown on the horizontal axis and the probability associated with these values is shown on the vertical axis.

In addition to tables and graphs, a formula that gives the probability function, $f(x)$, for every value of x is often used to describe probability distributions. The simplest example of

TABLE 5.3 PROBABILITY DISTRIBUTION FOR THE NUMBER OF AUTOMOBILES SOLD DURING A DAY AT DICARLO MOTORS

x	$f(x)$
0	.18
1	.39
2	.24
3	.14
4	.04
5	.01
Total	1.00

FIGURE 5.1   GRAPHICAL REPRESENTATION OF THE PROBABILITY DISTRIBUTION
FOR THE NUMBER OF AUTOMOBILES SOLD DURING A DAY AT
DICARLO MOTORS

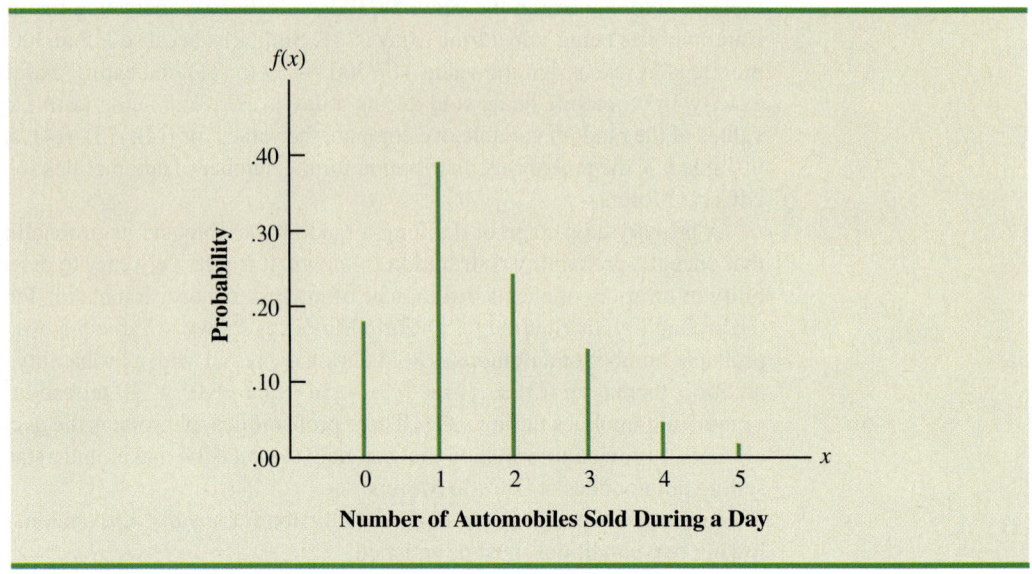

a discrete probability distribution given by a formula is the **discrete uniform probability distribution**. Its probability function is defined by equation (5.3).

DISCRETE UNIFORM PROBABILITY FUNCTION

$$f(x) = 1/n \qquad\qquad (5.3)$$

where

n = the number of values the random variable may assume

For example, suppose that for the experiment of rolling a die we define the random variable x to be the number of dots on the upward face. For this experiment, $n = 6$ values are possible for the random variable; $x = 1, 2, 3, 4, 5, 6$. Thus, the probability function for this discrete uniform random variable is

$$f(x) = 1/6 \qquad x = 1, 2, 3, 4, 5, 6$$

The possible values of the random variable and the associated probabilities are shown.

x	$f(x)$
1	1/6
2	1/6
3	1/6
4	1/6
5	1/6
6	1/6

As another example, consider the random variable x with the following discrete probability distribution.

x	$f(x)$
1	1/10
2	2/10
3	3/10
4	4/10

This probability distribution can be defined by the formula

$$f(x) = \frac{x}{10} \qquad \text{for } x = 1, 2, 3, \text{ or } 4$$

Evaluating $f(x)$ for a given value of the random variable will provide the associated probability. For example, using the preceding probability function, we see that $f(2) = 2/10$ provides the probability that the random variable assumes a value of 2.

The more widely used discrete probability distributions generally are specified by formulas. Three important cases are the binomial, Poisson, and hypergeometric distributions; these distributions are discussed later in the chapter.

Exercises

Methods

7.   The probability distribution for the random variable x follows.

x	$f(x)$
20	.20
25	.15
30	.25
35	.40

    a.   Is this probability distribution valid? Explain.
    b.   What is the probability that $x = 30$?
    c.   What is the probability that x is less than or equal to 25?
    d.   What is the probability that x is greater than 30?

Applications

8.   The following data were collected by counting the number of operating rooms in use at Tampa General Hospital over a 20-day period: On 3 of the days only one operating room was used, on 5 of the days two were used, on 8 of the days three were used, and on 4 days all four of the hospital's operating rooms were used.
    a.   Use the relative frequency approach to construct a probability distribution for the number of operating rooms in use on any given day.
    b.   Draw a graph of the probability distribution.
    c.   Show that your probability distribution satisfies the required conditions for a valid discrete probability distribution.

9. Nationally, 38% of fourth-graders cannot read an age-appropriate book. The following data show the number of children, by age, identified as learning disabled under special education. Most of these children have reading problems that should be identified and corrected before third grade. Current federal law prohibits most children from receiving extra help from special education programs until they fall behind by approximately two years' worth of learning, and that typically means third grade or later (*USA Today,* September 6, 2001).

Age	Number of Children
6	37,369
7	87,436
8	160,840
9	239,719
10	286,719
11	306,533
12	310,787
13	302,604
14	289,168

Suppose that we want to select a sample of children identified as learning disabled under special education for a program designed to improve reading ability. Let x be a random variable indicating the age of one randomly selected child.
   a. Use the data to develop a probability distribution for x. Specify the values for the random variable and the corresponding values for the probability function $f(x)$.
   b. Draw a graph of the probability distribution.
   c. Show that the probability distribution satisfies equations (5.1) and (5.2).

10. Table 5.4 shows the percent frequency distributions of job satisfaction scores for a sample of information systems (IS) senior executives and IS middle managers. The scores range from a low of 1 (very dissatisfied) to a high of 5 (very satisfied).

TABLE 5.4 PERCENT FREQUENCY DISTRIBUTION OF JOB SATISFACTION SCORES FOR INFORMATION SYSTEMS EXECUTIVES AND MIDDLE MANAGERS

Job Satisfaction Score	IS Senior Executives (%)	IS Middle Managers (%)
1	5	4
2	9	10
3	3	12
4	42	46
5	41	28

   a. Develop a probability distribution for the job satisfaction score of a senior executive.
   b. Develop a probability distribution for the job satisfaction score of a middle manager.
   c. What is the probability a senior executive will report a job satisfaction score of 4 or 5?
   d. What is the probability a middle manager is very satisfied?
   e. Compare the overall job satisfaction of senior executives and middle managers.

11. A technician services mailing machines at companies in the Phoenix area. Depending on the type of malfunction, the service call can take 1, 2, 3, or 4 hours. The different types of malfunctions occur at about the same frequency.

a. Develop a probability distribution for the duration of a service call.
b. Draw a graph of the probability distribution.
c. Show that your probability distribution satisfies the conditions required for a discrete probability function.
d. What is the probability a service call will take 3 hours?
e. A service call has just come in, but the type of malfunction is unknown. It is 3:00 P.M. and service technicians usually get off at 5:00 P.M. What is the probability the service technician will have to work overtime to fix the machine today?

12. The director of admissions at Lakeville Community College subjectively assessed a probability distribution for x, the number of entering students, as follows.

x	$f(x)$
1000	.15
1100	.20
1200	.30
1300	.25
1400	.10

a. Is this probability distribution valid? Explain.
b. What is the probability of 1200 or fewer entering students?

13. A psychologist determined that the number of sessions required to obtain the trust of a new patient is either 1, 2, or 3. Let x be a random variable indicating the number of sessions required to gain the patient's trust. The following probability function has been proposed.

$$f(x) = \frac{x}{6} \quad \text{for } x = 1, 2, \text{ or } 3$$

a. Is this probability function valid? Explain.
b. What is the probability that it takes exactly 2 sessions to gain the patient's trust?
c. What is the probability that it takes at least 2 sessions to gain the patient's trust?

14. The following table is a partial probability distribution for the MRA Company's projected profits (x = profit in $1000s) for the first year of operation (the negative value denotes a loss).

x	$f(x)$
-100	.10
0	.20
50	.30
100	.25
150	.10
200	

a. What is the proper value for $f(200)$? What is your interpretation of this value?
b. What is the probability that MRA will be profitable?
c. What is the probability that MRA will make at least $100,000?

5.3   Expected Value and Variance

Expected Value

The **expected value**, or mean, of a random variable is a measure of the central location for the random variable. The formula for the expected value of a discrete random variable x follows.

The expected value is a weighted average of the values the random variable may assume. The weights are the probabilities.

> **EXPECTED VALUE OF A DISCRETE RANDOM VARIABLE**
>
> $$E(x) = \mu = \Sigma x f(x) \qquad \text{(5.4)}$$

Both the notations $E(x)$ and μ are used to denote the expected value of a random variable.

The expected value does not have to be a value the random variable can assume.

Equation (5.4) shows that to compute the expected value of a discrete random variable, we must multiply each value of the random variable by the corresponding probability $f(x)$ and then add the resulting products. Using the DiCarlo Motors automobile sales example from Section 5.2, we show the calculation of the expected value for the number of automobiles sold during a day in Table 5.5. The sum of the entries in the $xf(x)$ column shows that the expected value of x is 1.50 automobiles per day. We therefore know that although sales of 0, 1, 2, 3, 4, or 5 automobiles are possible on any one day, over time DiCarlo can anticipate selling an average of 1.50 automobiles per day. Assuming 30 days of operation during a month, we can use the expected value of 1.50 to forecast average monthly sales of 30(1.50) = 45 automobiles.

Variance

Even though the expected value provides the mean value for the random variable, we often need a measure of variability, or dispersion. Just as we used the variance in Chapter 3 to summarize the variability in data, we now use **variance** to summarize the variability in the values of a random variable. The formula for the variance of a discrete random variable follows.

The variance is a weighted average of the squared deviations of a random variable from its mean. The weights are the probabilities.

> **VARIANCE OF A DISCRETE RANDOM VARIABLE**
>
> $$\text{Var}(x) = \sigma^2 = \Sigma(x - \mu)^2 f(x) \qquad \text{(5.5)}$$

TABLE 5.5   CALCULATION OF THE EXPECTED VALUE FOR THE NUMBER OF AUTOMOBILES SOLD DURING A DAY AT DICARLO MOTORS

x	$f(x)$	$xf(x)$
0	.18	0(.18) = .00
1	.39	1(.39) = .39
2	.24	2(.24) = .48
3	.14	3(.14) = .42
4	.04	4(.04) = .16
5	.01	5(.01) = .05
		1.50

$$E(x) = \mu = \Sigma x f(x)$$

TABLE 5.6   CALCULATION OF THE VARIANCE FOR THE NUMBER OF AUTOMOBILES
SOLD DURING A DAY AT DICARLO MOTORS

x	$x - \mu$	$(x - \mu)^2$	$f(x)$	$(x - \mu)^2 f(x)$
0	$0 - 1.50 = -1.50$	2.25	.18	$2.25(.18) = $ .4050
1	$1 - 1.50 = -.50$	.25	.39	$.25(.39) = $ .0975
2	$2 - 1.50 = .50$	.25	.24	$.25(.24) = $ .0600
3	$3 - 1.50 = 1.50$	2.25	.14	$2.25(.14) = $ .3150
4	$4 - 1.50 = 2.50$	6.25	.04	$6.25(.04) = $ .2500
5	$5 - 1.50 = 3.50$	12.25	.01	$12.25(.01) = $ .1225
				1.2500

$$\sigma^2 = \Sigma(x - \mu)^2 f(x)$$

As equation (5.5) shows, an essential part of the variance formula is the deviation, $x - \mu$, which measures how far a particular value of the random variable is from the expected value, or mean, μ. In computing the variance of a random variable, the deviations are squared and then weighted by the corresponding value of the probability function. The sum of these weighted squared deviations for all values of the random variable is referred to as the *variance*. The notations Var(x) and σ^2 are both used to denote the variance of a random variable.

The calculation of the variance for the probability distribution of the number of automobiles sold during a day at DiCarlo Motors is summarized in Table 5.6. We see that the variance is 1.25. The **standard deviation**, σ, is defined as the positive square root of the variance. Thus, the standard deviation for the number of automobiles sold during a day is

$$\sigma = \sqrt{1.25} = 1.118$$

The standard deviation is measured in the same units as the random variable ($\sigma = 1.118$ automobiles) and therefore is often preferred in describing the variability of a random variable. The variance σ^2 is measured in squared units and is thus more difficult to interpret.

Using Excel to Compute the Expected Value, Variance, and Standard Deviation

The calculations involved in computing the expected value and variance for a discrete random variable can easily be made in an Excel worksheet. One approach is to enter the formulas necessary to make the calculations in Tables 5.5 and 5.6. An easier way, however, is to make use of Excel's SUMPRODUCT function. In this subsection we show how to use the SUMPRODUCT function to compute the expected value and variance for daily automobile sales at DiCarlo Motors. Refer to Figure 5.2 as we describe the tasks involved. The formula worksheet is in the background; the value worksheet is in the foreground.

Enter Data: The data needed are the values for the random variable and the corresponding probabilities. Labels, values for the random variable, and the corresponding probabilities are entered in cells A1:B7.

Enter Functions and Formulas: The SUMPRODUCT function multiplies each value in one range by the corresponding value in another range and sums the products. To use the

FIGURE 5.2   EXCEL WORKSHEET FOR EXPECTED VALUE, VARIANCE, AND STANDARD DEVIATION

	A	B	C	D
1	Sales	Probability	Sq Dev from Mean	
2	0	0.18	=(A2-$B$9)^2	
3	1	0.39	=(A3-$B$9)^2	
4	2	0.24	=(A4-$B$9)^2	
5	3	0.14	=(A5-$B$9)^2	
6	4	0.04	=(A6-$B$9)^2	
7	5	0.01	=(A7-$B$9)^2	
8				
9	Mean	=SUMPRODUCT(A2:A7,B2:B7)		
10				
11	Variance	=SUMPRODUCT(C2:C7,B2:B7)		
12				
13	Std Deviation	=SQRT(B11)		
14				

	A	B	C	D
1	Sales	Probability	Sq Dev from Mean	
2	0	0.18	2.25	
3	1	0.39	0.25	
4	2	0.24	0.25	
5	3	0.14	2.25	
6	4	0.04	6.25	
7	5	0.01	12.25	
8				
9	Mean	1.5		
10				
11	Variance	1.25		
12				
13	Std Deviation	1.118034		
14				

SUMPRODUCT function to compute the expected value of daily automobile sales at Di-Carlo Motors, we entered the following formula into cell B9:

$$=SUMPRODUCT(A2:A7,B2:B7)$$

Note that the first range, A2:A7, contains the values for the random variable, daily automobile sales. The second range, B2:B7, contains the corresponding probabilities. Thus, the SUMPRODUCT function in cell B9 is computing A2*B2 + A3*B3 + A4*B4 + A5*B5 + A6*B6 + A7*B7; hence, it is applying the formula in equation (5.4) to compute the expected value. The result, shown in cell B9 of the value worksheet, is 1.5.

The formulas in cells C2:C7 are used to compute the squared deviations from the expected value or mean of 1.5 (the mean is in cell B9). The results, shown in the value worksheet, are the same as the results shown in Table 5.6. The formula necessary to compute the variance for daily automobile sales was entered into cell B11. It uses the SUMPRODUCT function to multiply each value in the range C2:C7 by each corresponding value in the range B2:B7 and sums the products. The result, shown in the value worksheet, is 1.25. Because the standard deviation is the square root of the variance, we entered the formula =SQRT(B11) into cell B13 to compute the standard deviation for daily automobile sales. The result, shown in the value worksheet, is 1.118034.

Exercises

Methods

15. The following table provides a probability distribution for the random variable x.

x	$f(x)$
3	.25
6	.50
9	.25

a.   Compute $E(x)$, the expected value of x.
b.   Compute σ^2, the variance of x.
c.   Compute σ, the standard deviation of x.

16.   The following table provides a probability distribution for the random variable y.

y	$f(y)$
2	.20
4	.30
7	.40
8	.10

a.   Compute $E(y)$.
b.   Compute Var(y) and σ.

Applications

17.   A volunteer ambulance service handles 0 to 5 service calls on any given day. The probability distribution for the number of service calls is as follows.

Number of Service Calls	Probability	Number of Service Calls	Probability
0	.10	3	.20
1	.15	4	.15
2	.30	5	.10

a.   What is the expected number of service calls?
b.   What is the variance in the number of service calls? What is the standard deviation?

18.   The American Housing Survey reported the following data on the number of bedrooms in owner-occupied and renter-occupied houses in central cities (http://www.census.gov, March 31, 2003).

	Number of Houses (1000s)	
Bedrooms	**Renter-Occupied**	**Owner-Occupied**
0	547	23
1	5012	541
2	6100	3832
3	2644	8690
4 or more	557	3783

a.   Define a random variable x = number of bedrooms in renter-occupied houses and develop a probability distribution for the random variable. (Let $x = 4$ represent 4 or more bedrooms.)
b.   Compute the expected value and variance for the number of bedrooms in renter-occupied houses.
c.   Define a random variable y = number of bedrooms in owner-occupied houses and develop a probability distribution for the random variable. (Let $y = 4$ represent 4 or more bedrooms.)
d.   Compute the expected value and variance for the number of bedrooms in owner-occupied houses.
e.   What observations can you make from a comparison of the number of bedrooms in renter-occupied versus owner-occupied homes?

19. The National Basketball Association (NBA) records a variety of statistics for each team. Two of these statistics are the percentage of field goals made by the team and the percentage of three-point shots made by the team. For a portion of the 2004 season, the shooting records of the 29 teams in the NBA showed the probability of scoring two points by making a field goal was .44, and the probability of scoring three points by making a three-point shot was .34 (http://www.nba.com, January 3, 2004).

   a. What is the expected value of a two-point shot for these teams?
   b. What is the expected value of a three-point shot for these teams?
   c. If the probability of making a two-point shot is greater than the probability of making a three-point shot, why do coaches allow some players to shoot the three-point shot if they have the opportunity? Use expected value to explain your answer.

20. The probability distribution for damage claims paid by the Newton Automobile Insurance Company on collision insurance follows.

Payment ($)	Probability	Payment ($)	Probability
0	.90	2000	.01
400	.04	4000	.01
1000	.03	6000	.01

   a. Use the expected collision payment to determine the collision insurance premium that would enable the company to break even.
   b. The insurance company charges an annual rate of $260 for the collision coverage. What is the expected value of the collision policy for a policyholder? (*Hint:* It is the expected payments from the company minus the cost of coverage.) Why does the policyholder purchase a collision policy with this expected value?

21. The following probability distributions of job satisfaction scores for a sample of information systems (IS) senior executives and IS middle managers range from a low of 1 (very dissatisfied) to a high of 5 (very satisfied).

	Probability	
Job Satisfaction Score	IS Senior Executives	IS Middle Managers
1	.05	.04
2	.09	.10
3	.03	.12
4	.42	.46
5	.41	.28

   a. What is the expected value of the job satisfaction score for senior executives?
   b. What is the expected value of the job satisfaction score for middle managers?
   c. Compute the variance of job satisfaction scores for executives and middle managers.
   d. Compute the standard deviation of job satisfaction scores for both probability distributions.
   e. Compare the overall job satisfaction of senior executives and middle managers.

22. The demand for a product of Carolina Industries varies greatly from month to month. The probability distribution in the following table, based on the past two years of data, shows the company's monthly demand.

Unit Demand	Probability	Unit Demand	Probability
300	.20	500	.35
400	.30	600	.15

a. If the company bases monthly orders on the expected value of the monthly demand, what should Carolina's monthly order quantity be for this product?

b. Assume that each unit demanded generates $70 in revenue and that each unit ordered costs $50. How much will the company gain or lose in a month if it places an order based on your answer to part (a) and the actual demand for the item is 300 units?

23. The 2002 New York City Housing and Vacancy Survey showed a total of 59,324 rent-controlled housing units and 236,263 rent-stabilized units built in 1947 or later. For these rental units, the probability distributions for the number of persons living in the unit are given (http://www.census.gov, January 12, 2004).

Number of Persons	Rent-Controlled	Rent-Stabilized
1	.61	.41
2	.27	.30
3	.07	.14
4	.04	.11
5	.01	.03
6	.00	.01

a. What is the expected value of the number of persons living in each type of unit?

b. What is the variance of the number of persons living in each type of unit?

c. Make some comparisons between the number of persons living in rent-controlled units and the number of persons living in rent-stabilized units.

24. The J. R. Ryland Computer Company is considering a plant expansion to enable the company to begin production of a new computer product. The company's president must determine whether to make the expansion a medium- or large-scale project. Demand for the new product is uncertain, which for planning purposes may be low demand, medium demand, or high demand. The probability estimates for demand are .20, .50, and .30, respectively. Letting x and y indicate the annual profit in thousands of dollars, the firm's planners developed the following profit forecasts for the medium- and large-scale expansion projects.

		Medium-Scale Expansion Profit		Large-Scale Expansion Profit	
		x	$f(x)$	y	$f(y)$
	Low	50	.20	0	.20
Demand	Medium	150	.50	100	.50
	High	200	.30	300	.30

a. Compute the expected value for the profit associated with the two expansion alternatives. Which decision is preferred for the objective of maximizing the expected profit?

b. Compute the variance for the profit associated with the two expansion alternatives. Which decision is preferred for the objective of minimizing the risk or uncertainty?

5.4 Binomial Probability Distribution

The binomial probability distribution is a discrete probability distribution that has many applications. It is associated with a multiple-step experiment that we call the binomial experiment.

A Binomial Experiment

A **binomial experiment** exhibits the following four properties.

PROPERTIES OF A BINOMIAL EXPERIMENT

1. The experiment consists of a sequence of n identical trials.
2. Two outcomes are possible on each trial. We refer to one outcome as a *success* and the other outcome as a *failure*.
3. The probability of a success, denoted by p, does not change from trial to trial. Consequently, the probability of a failure, denoted by $1 - p$, does not change from trial to trial.
4. The trials are independent.

Jakob Bernoulli (1654–1705), the first of the Bernoulli family of Swiss mathematicians, published a treatise on probability that contained the theory of permutations and combinations, as well as the binomial theorem.

If properties 2, 3, and 4 are present, we say the trials are generated by a Bernoulli process. If, in addition, property 1 is present, we say we have a binomial experiment. Figure 5.3 depicts one possible sequence of successes and failures for a binomial experiment involving eight trials.

In a binomial experiment, our interest is in the *number of successes occurring in the n trials*. If we let x denote the number of successes occurring in the n trials, we see that x can assume the values of 0, 1, 2, 3, . . . , n. Because the number of values of x is finite, x is a *discrete* random variable. The probability distribution associated with this random variable is called the **binomial probability distribution**. For example, consider the experiment of tossing a coin five times and on each toss observing whether the coin lands with a head or a tail on its upward face. Suppose we want to count the number of heads appearing over the five tosses. Does this experiment satisfy the properties of a binomial experiment? What is the random variable of interest? Note that:

1. The experiment consists of five identical trials; each trial involves the tossing of one coin.
2. Two outcomes are possible for each trial: a head or a tail. We can designate head a success and tail a failure.
3. The probability of a head and the probability of a tail are the same for each trial, with $p = .5$ and $1 - p = .5$.
4. The trials or tosses are independent because the outcome on any one trial is not affected by what happens on other trials or tosses.

FIGURE 5.3   ONE POSSIBLE SEQUENCE OF SUCCESSES AND FAILURES FOR AN EIGHT-TRIAL BINOMIAL EXPERIMENT

Property 1:   The experiment consists of $n = 8$ identical trials.

Property 2:   Each trial results in either success (S) or failure (F).

Trials ⟶	1	2	3	4	5	6	7	8
Outcomes ⟶	S	F	F	S	S	F	S	S

Enter Data: We entered the number of trials (10) into cell D1, the probability of success (.3) into cell D2, and the values for the random variable into cells B5:B15.

Enter Functions and Formulas: The binomial probabilities for each value of the random variable are computed in column C and the cumulative probabilities are computed in column D. We entered the formula =BINOMDIST(B5,$D$1,$D$2,FALSE) into cell C5 to compute the probability of 0 successes in 10 trials. Note that we used FALSE as the fourth input in the BINOMDIST function. The probability (.0282) is shown in cell C5 of the value worksheet. The formula in cell C5 is simply copied to cells C6:C15 to compute the remaining probabilities.

To compute the cumulative probabilities we start by entering the formula =BINOMDIST (B5,$D$1,$D$2,TRUE) into cell D5. Note that we used TRUE as the fourth input in the BINOMDIST function. The formula in cell D5 is then copied to cells D6:D15 to compute the remaining cumulative probabilities. In cell D5 of the value worksheet we see that the cumulative probability for $x = 0$ is the same as the probability for $x = 0$. Each of the remaining cumulative probabilities is the sum of the previous cumulative probability and the individual probability in column C. For instance, the cumulative probability for $x = 4$ is given by $.6496 + .2001 = .8497$. Note also that the cumulative probability for $x = 10$ is 1. The cumulative probability of $x = 9$ is also 1 because the probability of $x = 10$ is zero (to four decimal places of accuracy).

Expected Value and Variance for the Binomial Probability Distribution

In Section 5.3 we provided formulas for computing the expected value and variance of a discrete random variable. In the special case where the random variable has a binomial probability distribution with a known number of trials n and a known probability of success p, the general formulas for the expected value and variance can be simplified. The results follow.

EXPECTED VALUE AND VARIANCE FOR THE BINOMIAL PROBABILITY DISTRIBUTION

$$E(x) = \mu = np \tag{5.9}$$

$$\text{Var}(x) = \sigma^2 = np(1 - p) \tag{5.10}$$

For the Martin Clothing Store problem with three customers, we can use equation (5.9) to compute the expected number of customers who will make a purchase.

$$E(x) = np = 3(.30) = .9$$

Suppose that for the next month the Martin Clothing Store forecasts 1000 customers will enter the store. What is the expected number of customers who will make a purchase? The answer is $\mu = np = (1000)(.3) = 300$. Thus, to increase the expected number of purchases, Martin's must induce more customers to enter the store and/or somehow increase the probability that any individual customer will make a purchase after entering.

The np chart and lot acceptance sampling are quality control procedures that are excellent examples of the use of the binomial distribution. These procedures are discussed in Chapter 18, Statistical Methods for Quality Control.

For the Martin Clothing Store problem with three customers, we see that the variance and standard deviation for the number of customers who will make a purchase are

$$\sigma^2 = np(1 - p) = 3(.3)(.7) = .63$$
$$\sigma = \sqrt{.63} = .79$$

For the next 1000 customers entering the store, the variance and standard deviation for the number of customers who will make a purchase are

$$\sigma^2 = np(1 - p) = 1000(.3)(.7) = 210$$
$$\sigma = \sqrt{210} = 14.49$$

NOTES AND COMMENTS

Statisticians have developed tables that give probabilities and cumulative probabilities for a binomial random variable. These tables can be found in some statistics textbooks. With modern calculators and the capability of the BINOMDIST function in Microsoft Excel, such tables are unnecessary.

Exercises

Methods

25. Consider a binomial experiment with two trials and $p = .4$.
    a. Draw a tree diagram for this experiment (see Figure 5.4).
    b. Compute the probability of one success, $f(1)$.
    c. Compute $f(0)$.
    d. Compute $f(2)$.
    e. Compute the probability of at least one success.
    f. Compute the expected value, variance, and standard deviation.

26. Consider a binomial experiment with $n = 10$ and $p = .10$.
    a. Compute $f(0)$.
    b. Compute $f(2)$.
    c. Compute $P(x \leq 2)$.
    d. Compute $P(x \geq 1)$.
    e. Compute $E(x)$.
    f. Compute Var(x) and σ.

27. Consider a binomial experiment with $n = 20$ and $p = .70$.
    a. Compute $f(12)$.
    b. Compute $f(16)$.
    c. Compute $P(x \geq 16)$.
    d. Compute $P(x \leq 15)$.
    e. Compute $E(x)$.
    f. Compute Var(x) and σ.

Applications

28. A Harris Interactive survey for InterContinental Hotels & Resorts asked respondents, "When traveling internationally, do you generally venture out on your own to experience culture, or stick with your tour group and itineraries?" The survey found that 23% of the respondents stick with their tour group (*USA Today*, January 21, 2004).
    a. In a sample of six international travelers, what is the probability that two will stick with their tour group?
    b. In a sample of six international travelers, what is the probability that at least two will stick with their tour group?
    c. In a sample of 10 international travelers, what is the probability that none will stick with the tour group?

29. According to a *BusinessWeek*/Harris poll of 1035 adults, 40% of those surveyed agreed strongly with the proposition that business has too much power over American life (*Business-Week,* September 11, 2000). Assume this percentage is representative of the American population. In a sample of 20 individuals taken from a cross-section of the American population, what is the probability that at least five of these individuals will feel that business has too much power over American life?

30. When a new machine is functioning properly, only 3% of the items produced are defective. Assume that we will randomly select two parts produced on the machine and that we are interested in the number of defective parts found.
    a. Describe the conditions under which this situation would be a binomial experiment.
    b. Draw a tree diagram similar to Figure 5.4 showing this problem as a two-trial experiment.
    c. How many experimental outcomes result in exactly one defect being found?
    d. Compute the probabilities associated with finding no defects, exactly one defect, and two defects.

31. Nine percent of undergraduate students carry credit card balances greater than $7000 (*Reader's Digest,* July 2002). Suppose 10 undergraduate students are selected randomly to be interviewed about credit card usage.
    a. Is the selection of 10 students a binomial experiment? Explain.
    b. What is the probability that two of the students will have a credit card balance greater than $7000?
    c. What is the probability that none will have a credit card balance greater than $7000?
    d. What is the probability that at least three will have a credit card balance greater than $7000?

32. Military radar and missile detection systems are designed to warn a country of an enemy attack. A reliability question is whether a detection system will be able to identify an attack and issue a warning. Assume that a particular detection system has a .90 probability of detecting a missile attack. Use the binomial probability distribution to answer the following questions.
    a. What is the probability that a single detection system will detect an attack?
    b. If two detection systems are installed in the same area and operate independently, what is the probability that at least one of the systems will detect the attack?
    c. If three systems are installed, what is the probability that at least one of the systems will detect the attack?
    d. Would you recommend that multiple detection systems be used? Explain.

33. Fifty percent of Americans believed the country was in a recession, even though technically the economy had not shown two straight quarters of negative growth (*BusinessWeek,* July 30, 2001). For a sample of 20 Americans, make the following calculations.
    a. Compute the probability that exactly 12 people believed the country was in a recession.
    b. Compute the probability that no more than five people believed the country was in a recession.
    c. How many people would you expect to say the country was in a recession?
    d. Compute the variance and standard deviation of the number of people who believed the country was in a recession.

34. Forty percent of business travelers carry either a cell phone or a laptop (*USA Today,* September 12, 2000). For a sample of 15 business travelers, make the following calculations.
    a. Compute the probability that three of the travelers carry a cell phone or laptop.
    b. Compute the probability that 12 of the travelers carry neither a cell phone nor a laptop.
    c. Compute the probability that at least three of the travelers carry a cell phone or a laptop.

35. A university found that 20% of its students withdraw without completing the introductory statistics course. Assume that 20 students registered for the course this semester.
    a. Compute the probability that two or fewer will withdraw.
    b. Compute the probability that exactly four will withdraw.
    c. Compute the probability that more than three will withdraw.
    d. Compute the expected number of withdrawals.

36. For the special case of a binomial random variable, we stated that the variance could be computed using the formula $\sigma^2 = np(1 - p)$. For the Martin Clothing Store problem with $n = 3$ and $p = .3$ we found $\sigma^2 = np(1 - p) = 3(.3)(.7) = .63$. Use the general definition of variance for a discrete random variable, equation (5.5), and the probabilities in Table 5.7 to verify that the variance is in fact .63.

37. Seventy-two percent of Americans have online access (*CNBC,* December 3, 2001). In a random sample of 30 people, what is the expected number of persons with online access? What are the variance and standard deviation?

5.5   Poisson Probability Distribution

The Poisson probability distribution is often used to model random arrivals in waiting line situations.

In this section we consider a discrete random variable that is often useful in estimating the number of occurrences over a specified interval of time or space. For example, the random variable of interest might be the number of arrivals at a car wash in one hour, the number of repairs needed in 10 miles of highway, or the number of leaks in 100 miles of pipeline. If the following two properties are satisfied, the number of occurrences is a random variable described by the **Poisson probability distribution**.

> **PROPERTIES OF A POISSON EXPERIMENT**
>
> 1. The probability of an occurrence is the same for any two intervals of equal length.
> 2. The occurrence or nonoccurrence in any interval is independent of the occurrence or nonoccurrence in any other interval.

The **Poisson probability function** is defined by equation (5.11).

Siméon Poisson taught mathematics at the Ecole Polytechnique in Paris from 1802 to 1808. In 1837, he published a work entitled, "Researches on the Probability of Criminal and Civil Verdicts," which includes a discussion of what later became known as the Poisson distribution.

> **POISSON PROBABILITY FUNCTION**
>
> $$f(x) = \frac{\mu^x e^{-\mu}}{x!} \qquad (5.11)$$
>
> where
>
> $f(x)$ = the probability of x occurrences in an interval
> μ = expected value or mean number of occurrences in an interval
> e = 2.71828

Before we consider a specific example to see how the Poisson distribution can be applied, note that the number of occurrences, x, has no upper limit. It is a discrete random variable that may assume an infinite sequence of values ($x = 0, 1, 2, \ldots$).

An Example Involving Time Intervals

Bell Labs uses the Poisson distribution to model the arrival of phone calls.

Suppose that we are interested in the number of arrivals at the drive-up teller window of a bank during a 15-minute period on weekday mornings. If we can assume that the probability of a car arriving is the same for any two time periods of equal length and that the arrival or nonarrival of a car in any time period is independent of the arrival or nonarrival in any other time period, the Poisson probability function is applicable. Suppose these assumptions are satisfied and an analysis of historical data shows that the average number of cars arriving in a 15-minute period of time is 10; in this case, the following probability function applies.

$$f(x) = \frac{10^x e^{-10}}{x!}$$

The random variable here is x = number of cars arriving in any 15-minute period.

If management wanted to know the probability of exactly five arrivals in 15 minutes, we would set $x = 5$ and thus obtain

$$\begin{array}{c}\text{Probability of exactly}\\\text{5 arrivals in 15 minutes}\end{array} = f(5) = \frac{10^5 e^{-10}}{5!} = .0378$$

This probability was obtained by using a calculator to evaluate the probability function. Microsoft Excel also provides a function, called POISSON, for computing Poisson probabilities and cumulative probabilities. This function is easier to use when numerous probabilities and cumulative probabilities are desired. We show how to compute these probabilities with Excel at the end of this section.

A property of the Poisson distribution is that the mean and variance are equal.

In the preceding example, the mean of the Poisson distribution is $\mu = 10$ arrivals per 15-minute period. A property of the Poisson distribution is that the mean of the distribution and the variance of the distribution are *equal*. Thus, the variance for the number of arrivals during 15-minute periods is $\sigma^2 = 10$. The standard deviation is $\sigma = \sqrt{10} = 3.16$.

Our illustration involves a 15-minute period, but other time periods can be used. Suppose we want to compute the probability of one arrival in a three-minute period. Because 10 is the expected number of arrivals in a 15-minute period, we see that 10/15 = 2/3 is the expected number of arrivals in a one-minute period and that (2/3)(3 minutes) = 2 is the expected number of arrivals in a three-minute period. Thus, the probability of x arrivals in a three-minute time period with $\mu = 2$ is given by the following Poisson probability function.

$$f(x) = \frac{2^x e^{-2}}{x!}$$

The probability of one arrival in a three-minute period is calculated as follows:

$$\begin{array}{c}\text{Probability of exactly}\\\text{1 arrival in 3 minutes}\end{array} = f(1) = \frac{2^1 e^{-2}}{1!} = .2707$$

Earlier we computed the probability of five arrivals in a 15-minute period; it was .0378. Note that the probability of one arrival in a 3-minute period (.2707) is not the same. When computing a Poisson probability for a different time interval, we must first convert the mean arrival rate to the time period of interest and then compute the probability.

An Example Involving Length or Distance Intervals

Let us illustrate an application not involving time intervals in which the Poisson distribution is useful. Suppose we are concerned with the occurrence of major defects in a highway one month after resurfacing. We will assume that the probability of a defect is the same for any two highway intervals of equal length and that the occurrence or nonoccurrence of a defect in any one interval is independent of the occurrence or nonoccurrence of a defect in any other interval. Hence, the Poisson distribution can be applied.

Suppose we learn that major defects one month after resurfacing occur at the average rate of two per mile. Let us find the probability of no major defects in a particular three-mile section of the highway. Because we are interested in an interval with a length of three miles, μ = (2 defects/mile)(3 miles) = 6 represents the expected number of major defects over the three-mile section of highway. Using equation (5.11), the probability of no major defects is $f(0) = 6^0 e^{-6}/0! = .0025$. Thus, it is unlikely that no major defects will occur in the three-mile section. In fact, this example indicates a $1 - .0025 = .9975$ probability of at least one major defect in the three-mile highway section.

Using Excel to Compute Poisson Probabilities

The Excel function for computing Poisson probabilities and cumulative probabilities is called POISSON. It works in much the same way as the Excel function for computing binomial probabilities. Here we show how to use it to compute Poisson probabilities and cumulative probabilities. To illustrate, we use the example introduced earlier in this section; cars arrive at a bank drive-up teller window at the mean rate of 10 per 15-minute time interval. Refer to Figure 5.8 as we describe the tasks involved.

Enter Data: In order to compute a Poisson probability we must know the mean number of occurrences (μ) per time period and the number of occurrences for which we want to compute the probability (x). For the drive-up teller window example, the occurrences of interest are the arrivals of cars. The mean arrival rate is 10, which has been entered in cell D1. Earlier in this section, we computed the probability of 5 arrivals. But suppose we now want to compute the probability of zero up through 20 arrivals. To do so, we enter the values 0, 1, 2, . . . , 20 into cells A4:A24.

Enter Functions and Formulas: The POISSON function has three inputs: the first is the value of x, the second is the value of μ, and the third is FALSE or TRUE. We choose FALSE

FIGURE 5.8   EXCEL WORKSHEET FOR COMPUTING POISSON PROBABILITIES

	A	B	C	D	E
1			Mean No. of Occurrences	10	
2					
3	No. of Arrivals (x)	Probability f(x)			
4	0	=POISSON(A4,$D$1,FALSE)			
5	1	=POISSON(A5,$D$1,FALSE)			
6	2	=POISSON(A6,$D$1,FALSE)			
7	3	=POISSON(A7,$D$1,FALSE)			
8	4	=POISSON(A8,$D$1,FALSE)			
9	5	=POISSON(A9,$D$1,FALSE)			
10	6	=POISSON(A10,$D$1,FALSE)			
11	7	=POISSON(A11,$D$1,FALSE)			
12	8	=POISSON(A12,$D$1,FALSE)			
13	9	=POISSON(A13,$D$1,FALSE)			
14	10	=POISSON(A14,$D$1,FALSE)			
15	11	=POISSON(A15,$D$1,FALSE)			
16	12	=POISSON(A16,$D$1,FALSE)			
17	13	=POISSON(A17,$D$1,FALSE)			
18	14	=POISSON(A18,$D$1,FALSE)			
19	15	=POISSON(A19,$D$1,FALSE)			
20	16	=POISSON(A20,$D$1,FALSE)			
21	17	=POISSON(A21,$D$1,FALSE)			
22	18	=POISSON(A22,$D$1,FALSE)			
23	19	=POISSON(A23,$D$1,FALSE)			
24	20	=POISSON(A24,$D$1,FALSE)			
25					

	A	B	C	D	E	F	G	H	I
1		Mean No. of Occurrences		10					
2									
3	No. of Arrivals (x)	Probability f(x)							
4	0	0.0000							
5	1	0.0005							
6	2	0.0023							
7	3	0.0076							
8	4	0.0189							
9	5	0.0378							
10	6	0.0631							
11	7	0.0901							
12	8	0.1126							
13	9	0.1251							
14	10	0.1251							
15	11	0.1137							
16	12	0.0948							
17	13	0.0729							
18	14	0.0521							
19	15	0.0347							
20	16	0.0217							
21	17	0.0128							
22	18	0.0071							
23	19	0.0037							
24	20	0.0019							
25									

for the third argument if a probability is desired. The formula =POISSON(A4, \$D\$1,FALSE) has been entered into cell B4 to compute the probability of 0 arrivals in a 15-minute period. The value worksheet in the foreground shows that the probability of 0 arrivals is 0.0000. The formula in cell B4 is copied to cells B5:B24 to compute the probabilities for 1 through 20 arrivals. Note, in cell B9 of the value worksheet, that the probability of 5 arrivals is .0378. This result is the same as we calculated earlier in the text.

Notice how easy it was to compute all the probabilities for 0 through 20 arrivals using the POISSON function. These calculations would take quite a bit of work using a calculator. We have also used Excel's Chart Wizard to develop a graph of the Poisson probability distribution of arrivals. See the value worksheet in Figure 5.8. This chart gives a nice graphical presentation of the probabilities for the various number of arrival possibilities in a 15-minute interval. We can quickly see that the most likely number of arrivals is 9 or 10 and that the probabilities fall off rather smoothly for smaller and larger values.

Let us now see how cumulative probabilities are generated using Excel's POISSON function. It is really a simple extension of what we have already done. We again use the example of arrivals at a drive-up teller window. Refer to Figure 5.9 as we describe the tasks involved.

FIGURE 5.9   EXCEL WORKSHEET FOR COMPUTING CUMULATIVE POISSON PROBABILITIES

	A	B	C	D	E
1			Mean No. of Occurrences	10	
2					
3	No. of Arrivals (x)	Probability f(x)			
4	0	=POISSON(A4,\$D\$1,TRUE)			
5	1	=POISSON(A5,\$D\$1,TRUE)			
6	2	=POISSON(A6,\$D\$1,TRUE)			
7	3	=POISSON(A7,\$D\$1,TRUE)			
8	4	=POISSON(A8,\$D\$1,TRUE)			
9	5	=POISSON(A9,\$D\$1,TRUE)			
10	6	=POISSON(A10,\$D\$1,TRUE)			
11	7	=POISSON(A11,\$D\$1,TRUE)			
12	8	=POISSON(A12,\$D\$1,TRUE)			
13	9	=POISSON(A13,\$D\$1,TRUE)			
14	10	=POISSON(A14,\$D\$1,TRUE)			
15	11	=POISSON(A15,\$D\$1,TRUE)			
16	12	=POISSON(A16,\$D\$1,TRUE)			
17	13	=POISSON(A17,\$D\$1,TRUE)			
18	14	=POISSON(A18,\$D\$1,TRUE)			
19	15	=POISSON(A19,\$D\$1,TRUE)			
20	16	=POISSON(A20,\$D\$1,TRUE)			
21	17	=POISSON(A21,\$D\$1,TRUE)			
22	18	=POISSON(A22,\$D\$1,TRUE)			
23	19	=POISSON(A23,\$D\$1,TRUE)			
24	20	=POISSON(A24,\$D\$1,TRUE)			
25					

	A	B	C	D	E
1		Mean No. of Occurrences		10	
2					
3	No. of Arrivals (x)	Probability f(x)			
4	0	0.0000			
5	1	0.0005			
6	2	0.0028			
7	3	0.0103			
8	4	0.0293			
9	5	0.0671			
10	6	0.1301			
11	7	0.2202			
12	8	0.3328			
13	9	0.4579			
14	10	0.5830			
15	11	0.6968			
16	12	0.7916			
17	13	0.8645			
18	14	0.9165			
19	15	0.9513			
20	16	0.9730			
21	17	0.9857			
22	18	0.9928			
23	19	0.9965			
24	20	0.9984			
25					

Enter Data: To compute cumulative Poisson probabilities we must provide the mean number of occurrences (μ) per time period and the values of x that we are interested in. The mean arrival rate (10) has been entered into cell D1. Suppose we want to compute the cumulative probabilities for a number of arrivals ranging from zero up through 20. To do so, we enter the values 0, 1, 2, . . . , 20 into cells A4:A24.

Enter Functions and Formulas: Refer to the formula worksheet in the background of Figure 5.8. The formulas we enter into cells B4:B24 of Figure 5.9 are the same as in Figure 5.8 with one exception. Instead of FALSE for the third argument we enter the word TRUE to obtain cumulative probabilities. After entering these formulas into cells B4:B24 of the worksheet in Figure 5.9 the cumulative probabilities shown were obtained.

Note, in Figure 5.9, that the probability of 5 or fewer arrivals is .0671 and that the probability of 4 or fewer arrivals is .0293. Thus, the probability of exactly 5 arrivals is the difference in these two numbers: $f(5) = .0671 - .0293 = .0378$. We computed this probability earlier in this section and in Figure 5.8. Using these cumulative probabilities it is easy to compute the probability that a random variable lies within a certain interval. For instance, suppose we wanted to know the probability of more than 5 and fewer than 16 arrivals. We would just find the cumulative probability of 15 arrivals and subtract from that the cumulative probability for 5 arrivals. Referring to Figure 5.9 to obtain the appropriate probabilities, we obtain $.9513 - .0671 = .8842$. With such a high probability, we could conclude that 6 to 15 cars will arrive in most 15-minute intervals. Using the cumulative probability for 20 arrivals, we can also conclude that the probability of more than 20 arrivals in a 15-minute period is $1 - .9984 = .0016$; thus, there is almost no chance of more than 20 cars arriving.

Exercises

Methods

38.   Consider a Poisson distribution with $\mu = 3$.
    a.   Write the appropriate Poisson probability function.
    b.   Compute $f(2)$.
    c.   Compute $f(1)$.
    d.   Compute $P(x \geq 2)$.

39.   Consider a Poisson distribution with a mean of two occurrences per time period.
    a.   Write the appropriate Poisson probability function.
    b.   What is the expected number of occurrences in three time periods?
    c.   Write the appropriate Poisson probability function to determine the probability of x occurrences in three time periods.
    d.   Compute the probability of two occurrences in one time period.
    e.   Compute the probability of six occurrences in three time periods.
    f.   Compute the probability of five occurrences in two time periods.

Applications

40.   Phone calls arrive at the rate of 48 per hour at the reservation desk for Regional Airways.
    a.   Compute the probability of receiving three calls in a five-minute interval of time.
    b.   Compute the probability of receiving exactly 10 calls in 15 minutes.

c. Suppose no calls are currently on hold. If the agent takes five minutes to complete the current call, how many callers do you expect to be waiting by that time? What is the probability that none will be waiting?

d. If no calls are currently being processed, what is the probability that the agent can take three minutes for personal time without being interrupted by a call?

41. During the period of time that a local university takes phone-in registrations, calls come in at the rate of one every two minutes.
a. What is the expected number of calls in one hour?
b. What is the probability of three calls in five minutes?
c. What is the probability of no calls in a five-minute period?

42. More than 50 million guests stayed at bed and breakfasts (B&Bs) last year. The Web site for the Bed and Breakfast Inns of North America (http://www.cimarron.net), which averages approximately seven visitors per minute, enables many B&Bs to attract guests without waiting years to be mentioned in guidebooks (*Time,* September 2001).
a. Compute the probability of no Web site visitors in a one-minute period.
b. Compute the probability of two or more Web site visitors in a one-minute period.
c. Compute the probability of one or more Web site visitors in a 30-second period.
d. Compute the probability of five or more Web site visitors in a one-minute period.

43. Airline passengers arrive randomly and independently at the passenger-screening facility at a major international airport. The mean arrival rate is 10 passengers per minute.
a. Compute the probability of no arrivals in a one-minute period.
b. Compute the probability that three or fewer passengers arrive in a one-minute period.
c. Compute the probability of no arrivals in a 15-second period.
d. Compute the probability of at least one arrival in a 15-second period.

44. From 1990 through 1999, an average of approximately 26 aircraft accidents per year involved one or more passenger fatalities. Since 2000, the average decreased to 15 accidents per year (*The World Almanac and Book of Facts,* 2004). Assume that aircraft accidents continue to occur at the rate of 15 per year.
a. Compute the mean number of aircraft accidents per month.
b. Compute the probability of no accidents during a month.
c. Compute the probability of exactly one accident during a month.
d. Compute the probability of more than one accident during a month.

45. The National Safety Council reported that air bag–related fatalities dropped to 18 in the year 2000 (http://www.nsc.org).
a. Compute the expected number of air bag–related fatalities per month.
b. Compute the probability of no air bag–related fatalities in a month.
c. Compute the probability of two or more air bag–related fatalities in a month.

5.6 Hypergeometric Probability Distribution

The **hypergeometric probability distribution** is closely related to the binomial distribution. The two probability distributions differ in two key ways. With the hypergeometric distribution, the trials are not independent; and the probability of success changes from trial to trial.

In the usual notation for the hypergeometric distribution, r denotes the number of elements in the population of size N labeled success, and $N - r$ denotes the number of elements in the population labeled failure. The **hypergeometric probability function** is used to compute the probability that in a random selection of n elements, selected without replacement, we obtain x elements labeled success and $n - x$ elements labeled failure. For this outcome to occur, we must obtain x successes from the r successes in the population and $n - x$ failures from the $N - r$ failures. The hypergeometric probability function provides $f(x)$, the probability of obtaining x successes in a sample of size n.

HYPERGEOMETRIC PROBABILITY FUNCTION

$$f(x) = \frac{\binom{r}{x}\binom{N - r}{n - x}}{\binom{N}{n}} \qquad \text{for } 0 \le x \le r \qquad (5.12)$$

where

$$f(x) = \text{probability of } x \text{ successes in } n \text{ trials}$$
$$n = \text{number of trials}$$
$$N = \text{number of elements in the population}$$
$$r = \text{number of elements in the population labeled success}$$

Note that $\binom{N}{n}$ represents the number of ways a sample of size n can be selected from a population of size N; $\binom{r}{x}$ represents the number of ways that x successes can be selected from a total of r successes in the population; and $\binom{N - r}{n - x}$ represents the number of ways that $n - x$ failures can be selected from a total of $N - r$ failures in the population.

To illustrate the computations involved in using equation (5.12), let us consider the following quality control application. Electric fuses produced by Ontario Electric are packaged in boxes of 12 units each. Suppose an inspector randomly selects 3 of the 12 fuses in a box for testing. If the box contains exactly 5 defective fuses, what is the probability that the inspector will find exactly 1 of the 3 fuses defective? In this application, $n = 3$ and $N = 12$. With $r = 5$ defective fuses in the box the probability of finding $x = 1$ defective fuse is

$$f(1) = \frac{\binom{5}{1}\binom{7}{2}}{\binom{12}{3}} = \frac{\left(\frac{5!}{1!4!}\right)\left(\frac{7!}{2!5!}\right)}{\left(\frac{12!}{3!9!}\right)} = \frac{(5)(21)}{220} = .4773$$

Now suppose that we wanted to know the probability of finding *at least* 1 defective fuse. The easiest way to answer this question is to first compute the probability that the inspector does not find any defective fuses. The probability of $x = 0$ is

$$f(0) = \frac{\binom{5}{0}\binom{7}{3}}{\binom{12}{3}} = \frac{\left(\frac{5!}{0!5!}\right)\left(\frac{7!}{3!4!}\right)}{\left(\frac{12!}{3!9!}\right)} = \frac{(1)(35)}{220} = .1591$$

Because the probability of zero defective fuses is $f(0) = .1591$, we conclude that the probability of finding at least 1 defective fuse is $1 - .1591 = .8409$. Thus, there is a reasonably high probability that the inspector will find at least 1 defective fuse.

The expected value and variance of a hypergeometric distribution are as follows.

$$E(x) = \mu = n\left(\frac{r}{N}\right) \tag{5.13}$$

$$\text{Var}(x) = \sigma^2 = n\left(\frac{r}{N}\right)\left(1 - \frac{r}{N}\right)\left(\frac{N-n}{N-1}\right) \tag{5.14}$$

In the preceding example $n = 3$, $r = 5$, and $N = 12$. Thus, the mean and variance for the number of defective fuses is

$$\mu = n\left(\frac{r}{N}\right) = 3\left(\frac{5}{12}\right) = 1.25$$

$$\sigma^2 = n\left(\frac{r}{N}\right)\left(1 - \frac{r}{N}\right)\left(\frac{N-n}{N-1}\right) = 3\left(\frac{5}{12}\right)\left(1 - \frac{5}{12}\right)\left(\frac{12-3}{12-1}\right) = .60$$

The standard deviation is $\sigma = \sqrt{.60} = .77$.

Using Excel to Compute Hypergeometric Probabilities

The Excel function for computing hypergeometric probabilities is called HYPGEOMDIST. It only computes probabilities, not cumulative probabilities. The HYPGEOMDIST function has four inputs: x, n, r, N. Its usage is similar to that of BINOMDIST for the binomial distribution and POISSON for the Poisson distribution, so we dispense with showing a worksheet figure and just show the usage of the formula. Let us reconsider the example of selecting 3 fuses for inspection from a fuse box containing 12 fuses, 5 of which are defective. We want to compute the probability that 1 of the 3 fuses selected is defective. In this case $x = 1$, $n = 3$, $r = 5$, and $N = 12$. So the appropriate formula to place in a cell of an Excel worksheet would be =HYPGEOMDIST(1,3,5,12). Placing this formula in a cell of an Excel worksheet provides a hypergeometric probability of .4773.

If we want to know the probability that none of the 3 fuses selected is defective, we have $x = 0$, $n = 3$, $r = 5$, and $N = 12$. So using the HYPGEOMDIST function to compute the probability of randomly selecting 3 fuses without any being defective we would enter the following formula into an Excel worksheet: =HYPGEOMDIST(0,3,5,12). The probability computed is .1591.

NOTES AND COMMENTS

Consider a hypergeometric distribution with n trials. Let $p = (r/N)$ denote the probability of a success on the first trial. If the population size is large, the term $(N - n)/(N - 1)$ in equation (5.14) approaches 1. As a result, the expected value and variance can be written $E(x) = np$ and $\text{Var}(x) = np(1 - p)$. Note that these expressions are the same as the expressions used to compute the expected value and variance of a binomial distribution, as in equations (5.9) and (5.10). When the population size is large, a hypergeometric distribution can be approximated by a binomial distribution with n trials and a probability of success $p = (r/N)$.

Exercises

Methods

46. Suppose $N = 10$ and $r = 3$. Compute the hypergeometric probabilities for the following values of n and x.
   a. $n = 4, x = 1$.
   b. $n = 2, x = 2$.
   c. $n = 2, x = 0$.
   d. $n = 4, x = 2$.

47. Suppose $N = 15$ and $r = 4$. What is the probability of $x = 3$ for $n = 10$?

Applications

48. In a survey conducted by the Gallup Organization, respondents were asked, "What is your favorite sport to watch?" Football and basketball ranked number one and two in terms of preference (http://www.gallup.com, January 3, 2004). Assume that in a group of 10 individuals, seven preferred football and three preferred basketball. A random sample of three of these individuals is selected.
   a.   What is the probability that exactly two preferred football?
   b.   What is the probability that the majority (either two or three) preferred football?

49. Blackjack, or twenty-one as it is frequently called, is a popular gambling game played in Las Vegas casinos. A player is dealt two cards. Face cards (jacks, queens, and kings) and tens have a point value of 10. Aces have a point value of 1 or 11. A 52-card deck contains 16 cards with a point value of 10 (jacks, queens, kings, and tens) and four aces.
   a.   What is the probability that both cards dealt are aces or 10-point cards?
   b.   What is the probability that both of the cards are aces?
   c.   What is the probability that both of the cards have a point value of 10?
   d.   A blackjack is a 10-point card and an ace for a value of 21. Use your answers to parts (a), (b), and (c) to determine the probability that a player is dealt blackjack. (*Hint:* Part (d) is not a hypergeometric problem. Develop your own logical relationship as to how the hypergeometric probabilities from parts (a), (b), and (c) can be combined to answer this question.)

50. Axline Computers manufactures personal computers at two plants, one in Texas and the other in Hawaii. The Texas plant has 40 employees; the Hawaii plant has 20. A random sample of 10 employees is to be asked to fill out a benefits questionnaire.
   a.   What is the probability that none of the employees in the sample work at the plant in Hawaii?
   b.   What is the probability that one of the employees in the sample works at the plant in Hawaii?
   c.   What is the probability that two or more of the employees in the sample work at the plant in Hawaii?
   d.   What is the probability that nine of the employees in the sample work at the plant in Texas?

51. The 2003 Zagat Restaurant Survey provides food, decor, and service ratings for some of the top restaurants across the United States. For 15 top-ranking restaurants located in Boston, the average price of a dinner, including one drink and tip, was $48.60. You are leaving for a business trip to Boston and will eat dinner at three of these restaurants. Your company will reimburse you for a maximum of $50 per dinner. Business associates familiar with these restaurants have told you that the meal cost at one-third of these restaurants will exceed $50. Suppose that you randomly select three of these restaurants for dinner.
   a.   What is the probability that none of the meals will exceed the cost covered by your company?
   b.   What is the probability that one of the meals will exceed the cost covered by your company?

c. What is the probability that two of the meals will exceed the cost covered by your company?
d. What is the probability that all three of the meals will exceed the cost covered by your company?

52. A shipment of 10 items has two defective and eight nondefective items. In the inspection of the shipment, a sample of items will be selected and tested. If a defective item is found, the shipment of 10 items will be rejected.
    a. If a sample of three items is selected, what is the probability that the shipment will be rejected?
    b. If a sample of four items is selected, what is the probability that the shipment will be rejected?
    c. If a sample of five items is selected, what is the probability that the shipment will be rejected?
    d. If management would like a .90 probability of rejecting a shipment with two defective and eight nondefective items, how large a sample would you recommend?

Summary

A random variable provides a numerical description of the outcome of an experiment. The probability distribution for a random variable describes how the probabilities are distributed over the values the random variable can assume. For any discrete random variable x, the probability distribution is defined by a probability function, denoted by $f(x)$, which provides the probability associated with each value of the random variable. Once the probability function is defined, we can compute the expected value, variance, and standard deviation for the random variable.

The binomial distribution can be used to determine the probability of x successes in n trials whenever the experiment has the following properties:

1. The experiment consists of a sequence of n identical trials.
2. Two outcomes are possible on each trial, one called success and the other failure.
3. The probability of a success p does not change from trial to trial. Consequently, the probability of failure, $1 - p$, does not change from trial to trial.
4. The trials are independent.

When the four properties hold, the binomial probability function can be used to determine the probability of obtaining x successes in n trials. Formulas were also presented for the mean and variance of the binomial distribution.

The Poisson distribution is used when it is desirable to determine the probability of obtaining x occurrences over an interval of time or space. The following assumptions are necessary for the Poisson distribution to be applicable.

1. The probability of an occurrence of the event is the same for any two intervals of equal length.
2. The occurrence or nonoccurrence of the event in any interval is independent of the occurrence or nonoccurrence of the event in any other interval.

A third discrete probability distribution, the hypergeometric, was introduced in Section 5.6. Like the binomial, it is used to compute the probability of x successes in n trials. But, in contrast to the binomial, the probability of success changes from trial to trial.

Glossary

Random variable A numerical description of the outcome of an experiment.
Discrete random variable A random variable that may assume either a finite number of values or an infinite sequence of values.

Continuous random variable A random variable that may assume any numerical value in an interval or collection of intervals.

Probability distribution A description of how the probabilities are distributed over the values of the random variable.

Probability function A function, denoted by $f(x)$, that provides the probability that x assumes a particular value for a discrete random variable.

Discrete uniform probability distribution A probability distribution for which each possible value of the random variable has the same probability.

Expected value A measure of the central location of a random variable.

Variance A measure of the variability, or dispersion, of a random variable.

Standard deviation The positive square root of the variance.

Binomial experiment An experiment having the four properties stated at the beginning of Section 5.4.

Binomial probability distribution A probability distribution showing the probability of x successes in n trials of a binomial experiment.

Binomial probability function The function used to compute binomial probabilities.

Poisson probability distribution A probability distribution showing the probability of x occurrences of an event over a specified interval of time or space.

Poisson probability function The function used to compute Poisson probabilities.

Hypergeometric probability distribution A probability distribution showing the probability of x successes in n trials from a population with r successes and $N - r$ failures.

Hypergeometric probability function The function used to compute hypergeometric probabilities.

Key Formulas

Discrete Uniform Probability Function

$$f(x) = 1/n \tag{5.3}$$

where

$$n = \text{the number of values the random variable may assume}$$

Expected Value of a Discrete Random Variable

$$E(x) = \mu = \Sigma x f(x) \tag{5.4}$$

Variance of a Discrete Random Variable

$$\text{Var}(x) = \sigma^2 = \Sigma(x - \mu)^2 f(x) \tag{5.5}$$

Number of Experimental Outcomes Providing Exactly x Successes in n Trials

$$\binom{n}{x} = \frac{n!}{x!(n - x)!} \tag{5.6}$$

Binomial Probability Function

$$f(x) = \binom{n}{x} p^x (1 - p)^{(n-x)} \tag{5.8}$$

Expected Value for the Binomial Distribution

$$E(x) = \mu = np \tag{5.9}$$

Variance for the Binomial Distribution

$$\text{Var}(x) = \sigma^2 = np(1 - p) \tag{5.10}$$

Poisson Probability Function

$$f(x) = \frac{\mu^x e^{-\mu}}{x!} \tag{5.11}$$

Hypergeometric Probability Function

$$f(x) = \frac{\binom{r}{x}\binom{N - r}{n - x}}{\binom{N}{n}} \quad \text{for } 0 \leq x \leq r \tag{5.12}$$

Expected Value for the Hypergeometric Distribution

$$E(x) = \mu = n\left(\frac{r}{N}\right) \tag{5.13}$$

Variance for the Hypergeometric Distribution

$$\text{Var}(x) = \sigma^2 = n\left(\frac{r}{N}\right)\left(1 - \frac{r}{N}\right)\left(\frac{N - n}{N - 1}\right) \tag{5.14}$$

Supplementary Exercises

53. The *Barron's* Big Money Poll asked 131 investment managers across the United States about their short-term investment outlook (*Barron's,* October 28, 2002). Their responses showed 4% were very bullish, 39% were bullish, 29% were neutral, 21% were bearish, and 7% were very bearish. Let x be the random variable reflecting the level of optimism about the market. Set $x = 5$ for very bullish down through $x = 1$ for very bearish.
   a. Develop a probability distribution for the level of optimism of investment managers.
   b. Compute the expected value for the level of optimism.
   c. Compute the variance and standard deviation for the level of optimism.
   d. Comment on what your results imply about the level of optimism and its variability.

54. The American Association of Individual Investors publishes an annual guide to the top mutual funds (*The Individual Investor's Guide to the Top Mutual Funds,* 22e, American Association of Individual Investors, 2003). Table 5.8 contains their ratings of the total risk for 29 categories of mutual funds.

TABLE 5.8   RISK RATING FOR 29 CATEGORIES OF MUTUAL FUNDS

Total Risk	Number of Fund Categories
Low	7
Below Average	6
Average	3
Above Average	6
High	7

a.   Let $x = 1$ for low risk up through $x = 5$ for high risk, and develop a probability distribution for level of risk.

b.   What are the expected value and variance for total risk?

c.   It turns out that 11 of the fund categories were bond funds. For the bond funds, 7 categories were rated low and 4 were rated below average. Compare the total risk of the bond funds with the 18 categories of stock funds.

55.   The budgeting process for a midwestern college resulted in expense forecasts for the coming year (in $ millions) of $9, $10, $11, $12, and $13. Because the actual expenses are unknown, the following respective probabilities are assigned: .3, .2, .25, .05, and .2.

a.   Show the probability distribution for the expense forecast.

b.   What is the expected value of the expense forecast for the coming year?

c.   What is the variance of the expense forecast for the coming year?

d.   If income projections for the year are estimated at $12 million, comment on the financial position of the college.

56.   A survey conducted by the Bureau of Transportation Statistics (BTS) showed that the average commuter spends about 26 minutes on a one-way door-to-door trip from home to work. In addition, 5% of commuters reported a one-way commute of more than one hour (http://www.bts.gov, January 12, 2004).

a.   If 20 commuters are surveyed on a particular day, what is the probability that 3 will report a one-way commute of more than one hour?

b.   If 20 commuters are surveyed on a particular day, what is the probability that none will report a one-way commute of more than one hour?

c.   If a company has 2000 employees, what is the expected number of employees that have a one-way commute of more than one hour?

d.   If a company has 2000 employees, what is the variance and standard deviation of the number of employees that have a one-way commute of more than one hour?

57.   A company is planning to interview Internet users to learn how its proposed Web site will be received by different age groups. According to the Census Bureau, 40% of individuals ages 18 to 54 and 12% of individuals age 55 and over use the Internet (*Statistical Abstract of the United States: 2000*).

a.   How many people from the 18–54 age group must be contacted to find an expected number of at least 10 Internet users?

b.   How many people from the age group 55 and over must be contacted to find an expected number of at least 10 Internet users?

c.   If you contact the number of 18- to 54-year-old people suggested in part (a), what is the standard deviation of the number who will be Internet users?

d.   If you contact the number of people age 55 and older suggested in part (b), what is the standard deviation of the number who will be Internet users?

58.   Many companies use a quality control technique called acceptance sampling to monitor incoming shipments of parts, raw materials, and so on. In the electronics industry, component parts are commonly shipped from suppliers in large lots. Inspection of a sample of n components can be viewed as the n trials of a binomial experiment. The outcome for each component tested (trial) will be that the component is classified as good or defective. Reynolds Electronics accepts a lot from a particular supplier if the defective components in the lot do not exceed 1%. Suppose a random sample of five items from a recent shipment is tested.

a.   Assume that 1% of the shipment is defective. Compute the probability that no items in the sample are defective.

b.   Assume that 1% of the shipment is defective. Compute the probability that exactly one item in the sample is defective.

c.   What is the probability of observing one or more defective items in the sample if 1% of the shipment is defective?

d.   Would you feel comfortable accepting the shipment if one item was found to be defective? Why or why not?

59. The unemployment rate is 4.1% (*Barron's,* September 4, 2000). Assume that 100 employable people are selected randomly.
    a. What is the expected number of people who are unemployed?
    b. What are the variance and standard deviation of the number of people who are unemployed?

60. A poll conducted by Zogby International showed that of those Americans who said music plays a "very important" role in their lives, 30% said their local radio stations "always" play the kind of music they like (http://www.zogby.com, January 12, 2004). Suppose a sample of 800 people who say music plays an important role in their lives is taken.
    a. How many would you expect to say that their local radio stations always play the kind of music they like?
    b. What is the standard deviation of the number of respondents who think their local radio stations always play the kind of music they like?
    c. What is the standard deviation of the number of respondents who do not think their local radio stations always play the kind of music they like?

61. Cars arrive at a car wash randomly and independently; the probability of an arrival is the same for any two time intervals of equal length. The mean arrival rate is 15 cars per hour. What is the probability that 20 or more cars will arrive during any given hour of operation?

62. A new automated production process averages 1.5 breakdowns per day. Because of the cost associated with a breakdown, management is concerned about the possibility of having three or more breakdowns during a day. Assume that breakdowns occur randomly, that the probability of a breakdown is the same for any two time intervals of equal length, and that breakdowns in one period are independent of breakdowns in other periods. What is the probability of having three or more breakdowns during a day?

63. A regional director responsible for business development in the state of Pennsylvania is concerned about the number of small business failures. If the mean number of small business failures per month is 10, what is the probability that exactly four small businesses will fail during a given month? Assume that the probability of a failure is the same for any two months and that the occurrence or nonoccurrence of a failure in any month is independent of failures in any other month.

64. Customer arrivals at a bank are random and independent; the probability of an arrival in any one-minute period is the same as the probability of an arrival in any other one-minute period. Answer the following questions, assuming a mean arrival rate of three customers per minute.
    a. What is the probability of exactly three arrivals in a one-minute period?
    b. What is the probability of at least three arrivals in a one-minute period?

65. A deck of playing cards contains 52 cards, four of which are aces. What is the probability that the deal of a five-card hand provides:
    a. A pair of aces?
    b. Exactly one ace?
    c. No aces?
    d. At least one ace?

66. Through the week ending September 16, 2001, Tiger Woods was the leading money winner on the PGA Tour, with total earnings of $5,517,777. Of the top 10 money winners, seven players used a Titleist brand golf ball (http://www.pgatour.com). Suppose that we randomly select two of the top 10 money winners.
    a. What is the probability that exactly one uses a Titleist golf ball?
    b. What is the probability that both use Titleist golf balls?
    c. What is the probability that neither uses a Titleist golf ball?

CHAPTER 6

Continuous Probability Distributions

CONTENTS

STATISTICS IN PRACTICE:
PROCTER & GAMBLE

6.1 UNIFORM PROBABILITY
DISTRIBUTION
Area as a Measure of Probability

6.2 NORMAL PROBABILITY
DISTRIBUTION
Normal Curve
Standard Normal Probability
Distribution
Computing Probabilities for Any
Normal Probability
Distribution

Grear Tire Company Problem
Using Excel to Compute Normal
Probabilities

6.3 EXPONENTIAL
PROBABILITY
DISTRIBUTION
Computing Probabilities for the
Exponential Distribution
Relationship Between the
Poisson and Exponential
Distributions
Using Excel to Compute
Exponential Probabilities

STATISTICS *in* PRACTICE

PROCTER & GAMBLE*
CINCINNATI, OHIO

Procter & Gamble (P&G) produces and markets such products as detergents, disposable diapers, over-the-counter pharmaceuticals, dentifrices, bar soaps, mouthwashes, and paper towels. Worldwide, it has the leading brand in more categories than any other consumer products company.

As a leader in the application of statistical methods in decision making, P&G employs people with diverse academic backgrounds: engineering, statistics, operations research, and business. The major quantitative technologies for which these people provide support are probabilistic decision and risk analysis, advanced simulation, quality improvement, and quantitative methods (e.g., linear programming, regression analysis, probability analysis).

The Industrial Chemicals Division of P&G is a major supplier of fatty alcohols derived from natural substances such as coconut oil and from petroleum-based derivatives. The division wanted to know the economic risks and opportunities of expanding its fatty-alcohol production facilities, so it called in P&G's experts in probabilistic decision and risk analysis to help. After structuring and modeling the problem, they determined that the key to profitability was the cost difference between the petroleum- and coconut-based raw materials. Future costs were unknown, but the analysts were able to approximate them with the following continuous random variables.

x = the coconut oil price per pound of fatty alcohol

and

y = the petroleum raw material price per pound
    of fatty alcohol

Because the key to profitability was the difference between these two random variables, a third random variable, $d = x - y$, was used in the analysis. Experts were interviewed to determine

Some of Procter & Gamble's many well-known products. © Joe Higgins/South-Western.

the probability distributions for x and y. In turn, this information was used to develop a probability distribution for the difference in prices d. This continuous probability distribution showed a .90 probability that the price difference would be $.0655 or less and a .50 probability that the price difference would be $.035 or less. In addition, there was only a .10 probability that the price difference would be $.0045 or less.[†]

The Industrial Chemicals Division thought that being able to quantify the impact of raw material price differences was key to reaching a consensus. The probabilities obtained were used in a sensitivity analysis of the raw material price difference. The analysis yielded sufficient insight to form the basis for a recommendation to management.

The use of continuous random variables and their probability distributions was helpful to P&G in analyzing the economic risks associated with its fatty-alcohol production. In this chapter, you will gain an understanding of continuous random variables and their probability distributions including one of the most important probability distributions in statistics, the normal distribution.

---

*The authors are indebted to Joel Kahn of Procter & Gamble for providing this Statistics in Practice.

[†]The price differences stated here have been modified to protect proprietary data.

In the preceding chapter we discussed discrete random variables and their probability distributions. In this chapter we turn to the study of continuous random variables. Specifically, we discuss three continuous probability distributions: the uniform, the normal, and the exponential.

A fundamental difference separates discrete and continuous random variables in terms of how probabilities are computed. For a discrete random variable, the probability function $f(x)$ provides the probability that the random variable assumes a particular value. With continuous random variables, the counterpart of the probability function is the **probability density function**, also denoted by $f(x)$. The difference is that the probability density function does not directly provide probabilities. However, the area under the graph of $f(x)$ corresponding to a given interval does provide the probability that the continuous random variable x assumes a value in that interval. So when we compute probabilities for continuous random variables we are computing the probability that the random variable assumes any value in an interval.

Because the area under the graph of $f(x)$ at any particular point is zero, one of the implications of the definition of probability for continuous random variables is that the probability of any particular value of the random variable is zero. In Section 6.1 we demonstrate these concepts for a continuous random variable that has a uniform distribution.

Much of the chapter is devoted to describing and showing applications of the normal distribution. The normal distribution is of major importance because of its wide applicability and its extensive use in statistical inference. The chapter closes with a discussion of the exponential distribution. The exponential distribution is useful in applications involving waiting times, service times, etc.

6.1 Uniform Probability Distribution

Consider the random variable x representing the flight time of an airplane traveling from Chicago to New York. Suppose the flight time can be any value in the interval from 120 minutes to 140 minutes. Because the random variable x can assume any value in that interval, x is a continuous rather than a discrete random variable. Let us assume that sufficient actual flight data are available to conclude that the probability of a flight time within any 1-minute interval is the same as the probability of a flight time within any other 1-minute interval contained in the larger interval from 120 to 140 minutes. With every 1-minute interval being equally likely, the random variable x is said to have a **uniform probability distribution**. The probability density function, which defines the uniform distribution for the flight-time random variable, is

Whenever the probability is proportional to the length of the interval, the random variable is uniformly distributed.

$$f(x) = \begin{cases} 1/20 & \text{for } 120 \leq x \leq 140 \\ 0 & \text{elsewhere} \end{cases}$$

Figure 6.1 is a graph of this probability density function. In general, the uniform probability density function for a random variable x is defined by the following formula.

UNIFORM PROBABILITY DENSITY FUNCTION

$$f(x) = \begin{cases} \dfrac{1}{b - a} & \text{for } a \leq x \leq b \\ 0 & \text{elsewhere} \end{cases} \tag{6.1}$$

For the flight-time random variable, $a = 120$ and $b = 140$.

FIGURE 6.1   UNIFORM PROBABILITY DISTRIBUTION FOR FLIGHT TIME

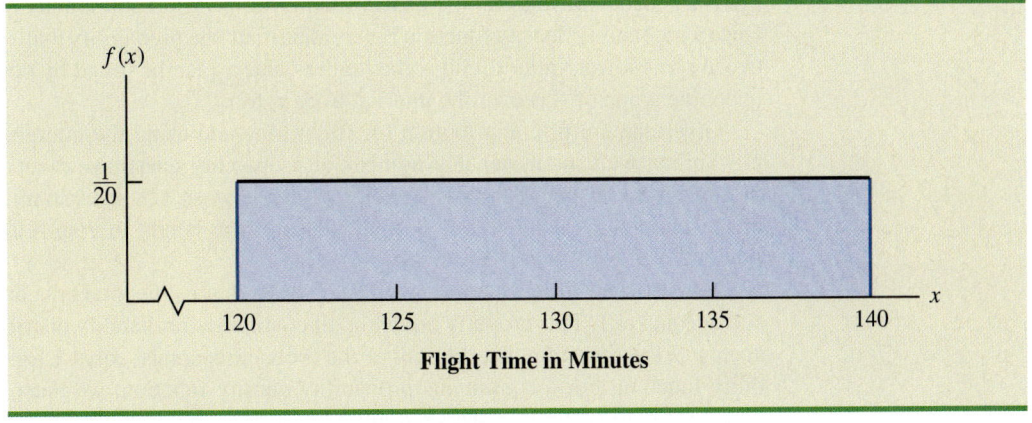

As noted in the introduction, for a continuous random variable, we consider probability only in terms of the likelihood that a random variable assumes a value within a specified interval. In the flight time example, an acceptable probability question is: What is the probability that the flight time is between 120 and 130 minutes? That is, what is $P(120 \leq x \leq 130)$? Because the flight time must be between 120 and 140 minutes and because the probability is described as being uniform over this interval, we feel comfortable saying $P(120 \leq x \leq 130) = .50$. In the following subsection we show that this probability can be computed as the area under the graph of $f(x)$ from 120 to 130 (see Figure 6.2).

Area as a Measure of Probability

Let us make an observation about the graph in Figure 6.2. Consider the area under the graph of $f(x)$ in the interval from 120 to 130. The area is rectangular, and the area of a rectangle is simply the width multiplied by the height. With the width of the interval equal to $130 - 120 = 10$ and the height equal to the value of the probability density function $f(x) = 1/20$, we have area $=$ width $\times$ height $= 10(1/20) = 10/20 = .50$.

FIGURE 6.2   AREA PROVIDES PROBABILITY OF A FLIGHT TIME BETWEEN 120
            AND 130 MINUTES

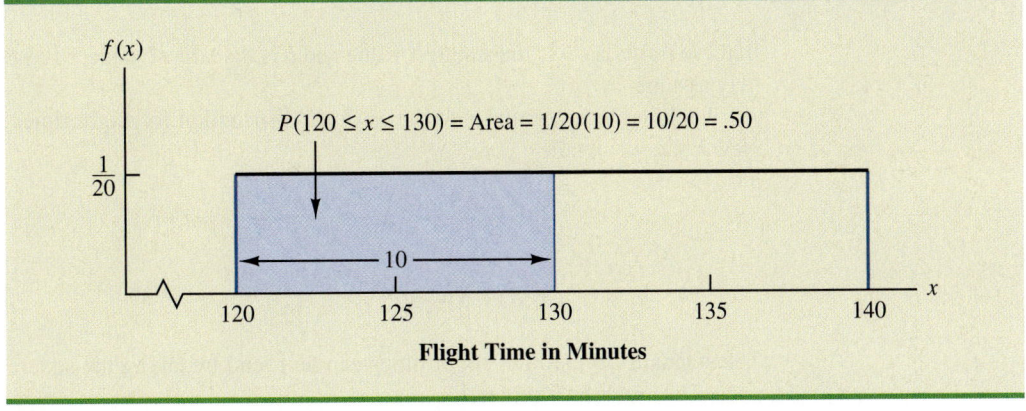

What observation can you make about the area under the graph of $f(x)$ and probability? They are identical! Indeed, this observation is valid for all continuous random variables. Once a probability density function $f(x)$ is identified, the probability that x takes a value between some lower value x_1 and some higher value x_2 can be found by computing the area under the graph of $f(x)$ over the interval from x_1 to x_2.

Given the uniform distribution for flight time and using the interpretation of area as probability, we can answer any number of probability questions about flight times. For example, what is the probability of a flight time between 128 and 136 minutes? The width of the interval is $136 - 128 = 8$. With the uniform height of $f(x) = 1/20$, we see that $P(128 \leq x \leq 136) = 8(1/20) = .40$.

Note that $P(120 \leq x \leq 140) = 20(1/20) = 1$; that is, the total area under the graph of $f(x)$ is equal to 1. This property holds for all continuous probability distributions and is the analog of the condition that the sum of the probabilities must equal 1 for a discrete probability function. For a continuous probability density function, we must also require that $f(x) \geq 0$ for all values of x. This requirement is the analog of the requirement that $f(x) \geq 0$ for discrete probability functions.

Two major differences stand out between the treatment of continuous random variables and the treatment of their discrete counterparts.

To see that the probability of any single point is 0, refer to Figure 6.2 and compute the probability of a single point, say, $x = 125$. $P(x = 125) = P(125 \leq x \leq 125) = 0(1/20) = 0$.

1. We no longer talk about the probability of the random variable assuming a particular value. Instead, we talk about the probability of the random variable assuming a value within some given interval.

2. The probability of a continuous random variable assuming a value within some given interval from x_1 to x_2 is defined to be the area under the graph of the probability density function between x_1 and x_2. Because a single point is an interval of zero width, this implies that the probability of a continuous random variable assuming any particular value exactly is zero. It also means that the probability of a continuous random variable assuming a value in any interval is the same whether or not the endpoints are included.

The calculation of the expected value and variance for a continuous random variable is analogous to that for a discrete random variable. However, because the computational procedure involves integral calculus, we leave the derivation of the appropriate formulas to more advanced texts.

For the uniform continuous probability distribution introduced in this section, the formulas for the expected value and variance are

$$E(x) = \frac{a + b}{2}$$

$$\text{Var}(x) = \frac{(b - a)^2}{12}$$

In these formulas, a is the smallest value and b is the largest value that the random variable may assume.

Applying these formulas to the uniform distribution for flight times from Chicago to New York, we obtain

$$E(x) = \frac{(120 + 140)}{2} = 130$$

$$\text{Var}(x) = \frac{(140 - 120)^2}{12} = 33.33$$

The standard deviation of flight times can be found by taking the square root of the variance. Thus, $\sigma = 5.77$ minutes.

NOTES AND COMMENTS

To see more clearly why the height of a probability density function is not a probability, think about a random variable with the following uniform probability distribution.

$$f(x) = \begin{cases} 2 & \text{for } 0 \leq x \leq .5 \\ 0 & \text{elsewhere} \end{cases}$$

The height of the probability density function, $f(x)$, is 2 for values of x between 0 and .5. However, we know probabilities can never be greater than 1. Thus, we see that $f(x)$ cannot be interpreted as the probability of x.

Exercises

Methods

1. The random variable x is known to be uniformly distributed between 1.0 and 1.5.
   a. Show the graph of the probability density function.
   b. Compute $P(x = 1.25)$.
   c. Compute $P(1.0 \leq x \leq 1.25)$.
   d. Compute $P(1.20 < x < 1.5)$.

2. The random variable x is known to be uniformly distributed between 10 and 20.
   a. Show the graph of the probability density function.
   b. Compute $P(x < 15)$.
   c. Compute $P(12 \leq x \leq 18)$.
   d. Compute $E(x)$.
   e. Compute Var(x).

Applications

3. Delta Airlines quotes a flight time of 2 hours, 5 minutes for its flights from Cincinnati to Tampa. Suppose we believe that actual flight times are uniformly distributed between 2 hours and 2 hours, 20 minutes.
   a. Show the graph of the probability density function for flight time.
   b. What is the probability that the flight will be no more than 5 minutes late?
   c. What is the probability that the flight will be more than 10 minutes late?
   d. What is the expected flight time?

4. Most computer languages include a function that can be used to generate random numbers. In Excel, the RAND function can be used to generate random numbers between 0 and 1. If we let x denote a random number generated using RAND, then x is a continuous random variable with the following probability density function.

$$f(x) = \begin{cases} 1 & \text{for } 0 \leq x \leq 1 \\ 0 & \text{elsewhere} \end{cases}$$

   a. Graph the probability density function.
   b. What is the probability of generating a random number between .25 and .75?
   c. What is the probability of generating a random number with a value less than or equal to .30?
   d. What is the probability of generating a random number with a value greater than .60?
   e. Generate 50 random numbers by entering =RAND() into 50 cells of an Excel worksheet.
   f. Compute the mean and standard deviation for the random numbers in part (e).

5. The driving distance for the top 100 golfers on the PGA tour is between 284.7 and 310.6 yards (*Golfweek*, March 29, 2003). Assume that the driving distance for these golfers is uniformly distributed over this interval.
   a. Give a mathematical expression for the probability density function of driving distance.
   b. What is the probability the driving distance for one of these golfers is less than 290 yards?
   c. What is the probability the driving distance for one of these golfers is at least 300 yards?
   d. What is the probability the driving distance for one of these golfers is between 290 and 305 yards?
   e. How many of these golfers drive the ball at least 290 yards?

6. The label on a bottle of liquid detergent shows the contents to be 12 ounces per bottle. The production operation fills the bottle uniformly according to the following probability density function.

$$f(x) = \begin{cases} 8 & \text{for } 11.975 \le x \le 12.100 \\ 0 & \text{elsewhere} \end{cases}$$

   a. What is the probability that a bottle will be filled with between 12 and 12.05 ounces?
   b. What is the probability that a bottle will be filled with 12.02 or more ounces?
   c. Quality control accepts a bottle that is filled to within .02 ounces of the number of ounces shown on the container label. What is the probability that a bottle of this liquid detergent will fail to meet the quality control standard?

7. Suppose we are interested in bidding on a piece of land and we know one other bidder is interested.* The seller announced that the highest bid in excess of $10,000 will be accepted. Assume that the competitor's bid x is a random variable that is uniformly distributed between $10,000 and $15,000.
   a. Suppose you bid $12,000. What is the probability that your bid will be accepted?
   b. Suppose you bid $14,000. What is the probability that your bid will be accepted?
   c. What amount should you bid to maximize the probability that you get the property?
   d. Suppose you know someone who is willing to pay you $16,000 for the property. Would you consider bidding less than the amount in part (c)? Why or why not?

 6.2 # Normal Probability Distribution

Abraham de Moivre, a French mathematician, published The Doctrine of Chances *in 1733. He derived the normal distribution.*

The most important probability distribution for describing a continuous random variable is the **normal probability distribution**. The normal distribution has been used in a wide variety of practical applications in which the random variables are heights and weights of people, test scores, scientific measurements, amounts of rainfall, and other similar values. It is also widely used in statistical inference, which is the major topic of the remainder of this book. In such applications, the normal distribution provides a description of the likely results obtained through sampling.

Normal Curve

The form, or shape, of the normal distribution is illustrated by the bell-shaped normal curve in Figure 6.3. The probability density function that defines the bell-shaped curve of the normal distribution follows.

---

*This exercise is based on a problem suggested to us by Professor Roger Myerson of Northwestern University.

FIGURE 6.3   BELL-SHAPED CURVE FOR THE NORMAL DISTRIBUTION

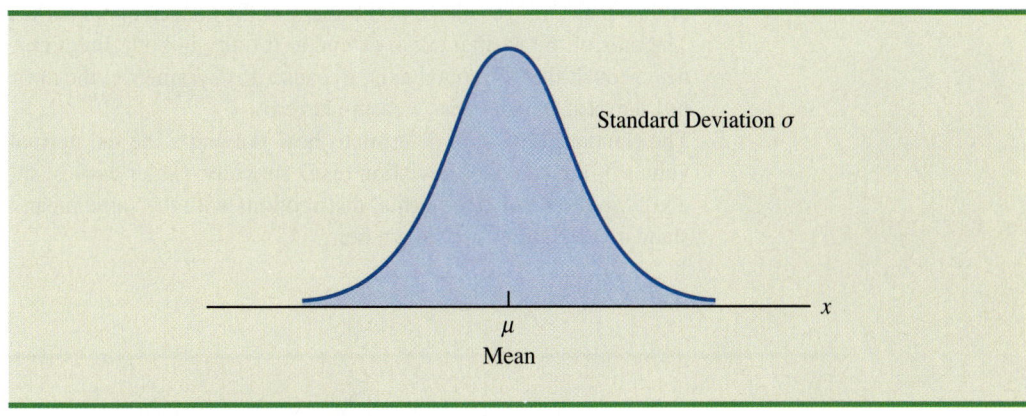

NORMAL PROBABILITY DENSITY FUNCTION

$$f(x) = \frac{1}{\sigma\sqrt{2\pi}} e^{-(x-\mu)^2/2\sigma^2}$$ **(6.2)**

where

μ = mean
σ = standard deviation
π = 3.14159
e = 2.71828

We make several observations about the characteristics of the normal distribution.

The normal curve has two parameters, μ and σ. They determine the location and shape of the normal distribution.

1. The entire family of normal distributions is differentiated by two parameters: the mean μ and the standard deviation σ.
2. The highest point on the normal curve is at the mean, which is also the median and mode of the distribution.
3. The mean of the distribution can be any numerical value: negative, zero, or positive. Three normal distributions with the same standard deviation but three different means (-10, 0, and 20) are shown here.

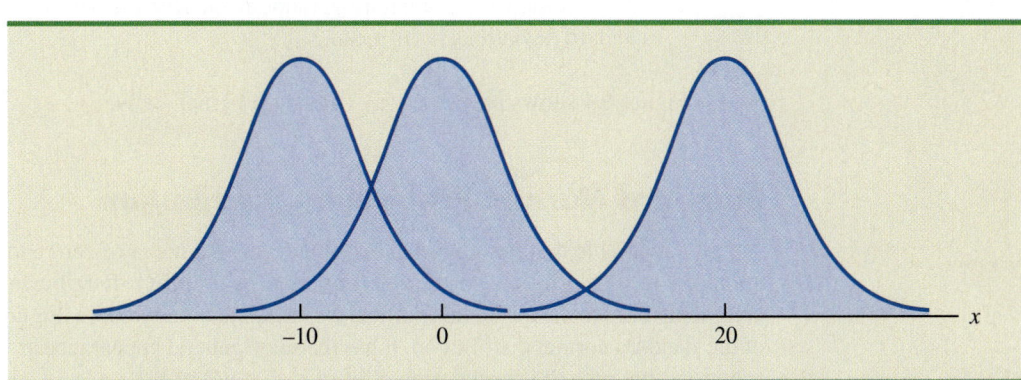

4. The normal distribution is symmetric, with the shape of the normal curve to the left of the mean a mirror image of the shape of the normal curve to the right of the mean. The tails of the normal curve extend to infinity in both directions and theoretically never touch the horizontal axis. Because it is symmetric, the normal distribution is not skewed; its skewness measure is zero.

5. The standard deviation determines how flat and wide the normal curve is. Larger values of the standard deviation result in wider, flatter curves, showing more variability in the data. Two normal distributions with the same mean but with different standard deviations are shown here.

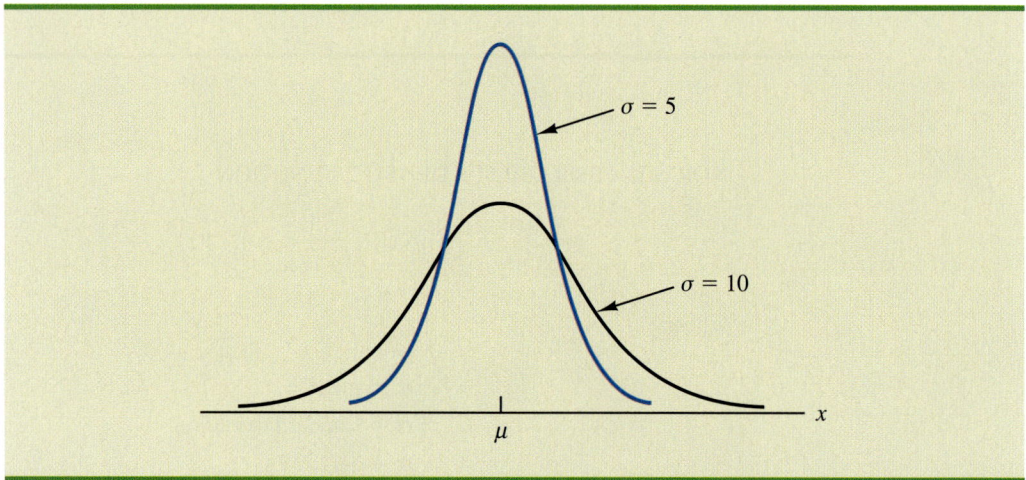

6. Probabilities for the normal random variable are given by areas under the normal curve. The total area under the curve for the normal distribution is 1. Because the distribution is symmetric, the area under the curve to the left of the mean is .50 and the area under the curve to the right of the mean is .50.

7. The percentage of values in some commonly used intervals are:
   a. 68.3% of the values of a normal random variable are within plus or minus one standard deviation of its mean.
   b. 95.4% of the values of a normal random variable are within plus or minus two standard deviations of its mean.
   c. 99.7% of the values of a normal random variable are within plus or minus three standard deviations of its mean.

These percentages are the basis for the empirical rule introduced in Section 3.3.

Figure 6.4 shows properties (a), (b), and (c) graphically.

Standard Normal Probability Distribution

A random variable that has a normal distribution with a mean of zero and a standard deviation of one is said to have a **standard normal probability distribution**. The letter z is commonly used to designate this particular normal random variable. Figure 6.5 is the graph of the standard normal distribution. It has the same general appearance as other normal distributions, but with the special properties of $\mu = 0$ and $\sigma = 1$.

FIGURE 6.4 AREAS UNDER THE CURVE FOR ANY NORMAL DISTRIBUTION

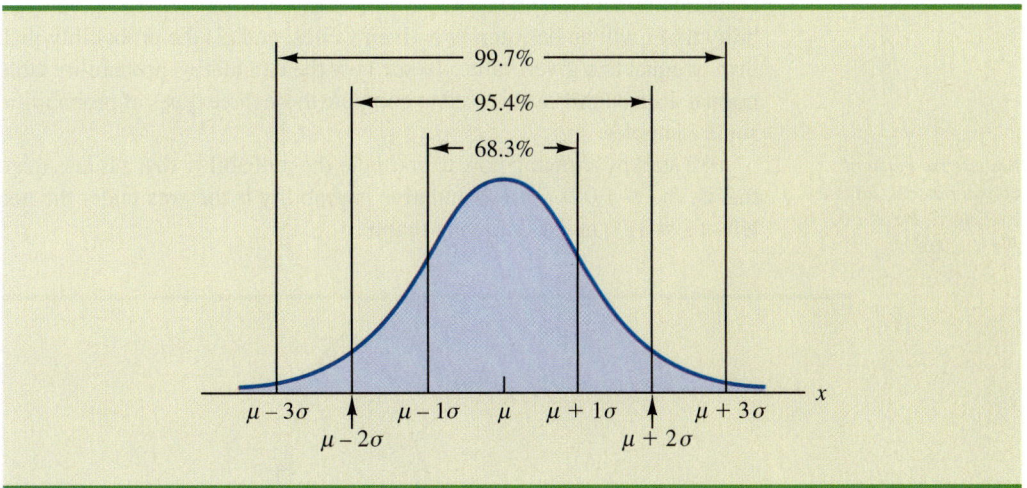

FIGURE 6.5 THE STANDARD NORMAL DISTRIBUTION

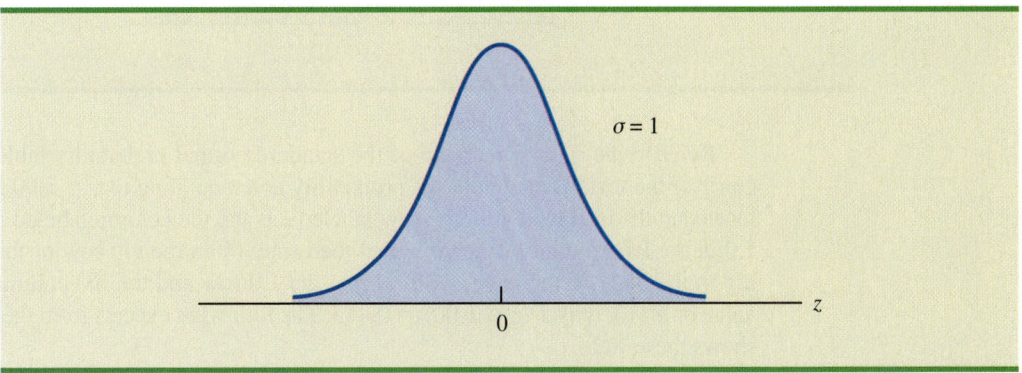

Because $\mu = 0$ and $\sigma = 1$, the formula for the standard normal probability density function is a simpler version of equation (6.2).

STANDARD NORMAL DENSITY FUNCTION

$$f(z) = \frac{1}{\sqrt{2\pi}} e^{-z^2/2}$$

As with other continuous random variables, probability calculations with any normal distribution are made by computing areas under the graph of the probability density function. Thus, to find the probability that a normal random variable is within any specific interval, we must compute the area under the normal curve over that interval.

For the standard normal distribution, areas under the normal curve have been computed and are available in tables that can be used to compute probabilities. Such a table appears on the two pages inside the front cover of the text. The table on the left-hand page contains areas, or cumulative probabilities, for z values less than or equal to the mean of zero. The table on the right-hand page contains areas, or cumulative probabilities, for z values greater than or equal to the mean of zero.

For the normal probability density function, the height of the normal curve varies and more advanced mathematics is required to compute the areas that represent probability.

The three types of probabilities we need to compute include (1) the probability that the standard normal random variable z will be less than or equal to a given value; (2) the probability that z will be between two given values; and (3) the probability that z will be greater than or equal to a given value. To see how the cumulative probability table for the standard normal distribution can be used to compute these three types of probabilities, let us consider some examples.

Because the standard normal random variable is continuous, $P(z \leq 1.00) = P(z < 1.00)$.

We start by showing how to compute the probability that z is less than or equal to 1.00; that is, $P(z \leq 1.00)$. This cumulative probability is the area under the normal curve to the left of $z = 1.00$ in the following graph.

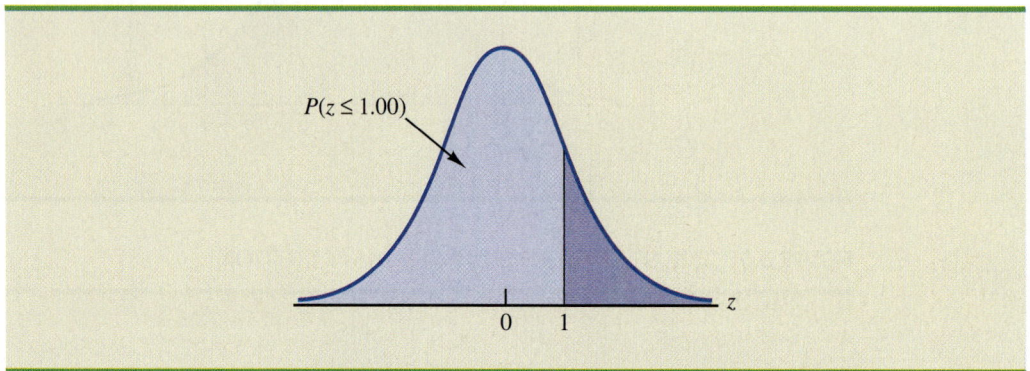

Refer to the right-hand page of the standard normal probability table inside the front cover of the text. The cumulative probability corresponding to $z = 1.00$ is the table value located at the intersection of the row labeled 1.0 and the column labeled .00. First we find 1.0 in the left column of the table and then find .00 in the top row of the table. By looking in the body of the table, we find that the 1.0 row and the .00 column intersect at the value of .8413; thus, $P(z \leq 1.00) = .8413$. The following excerpt from the probability table shows these steps.

z	.00	.01	.02
.			
.			
.			
.9	.8159	.8186	.8212
1.0	.8413	.8438	.8461
1.1	.8643	.8665	.8686
1.2	.8849	.8869	.8888
.			
.			
.			

$P(z \leq 1.00)$

To illustrate the second type of probability calculation we show how to compute the probability that z is in the interval between $-.50$ and 1.25; that is, $P(-.50 \leq z \leq 1.25)$. The following graph shows this area, or probability.

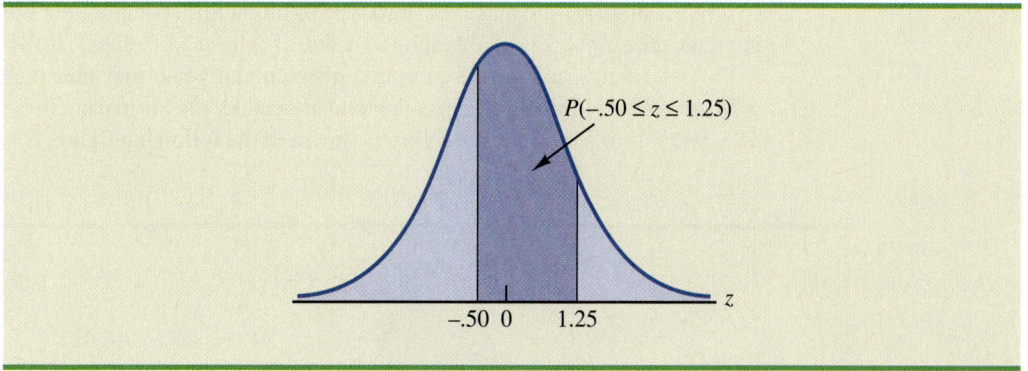

Three steps are required to compute this probability. First, we find the area under the normal curve to the left of $z = 1.25$. Second, we find the area under the normal curve to the left of $z = -.50$. Finally, we subtract the area to the left of $z = -.50$ from the area to the left of $z = 1.25$ to find $P(-.50 \leq z \leq 1.25)$.

To find the area under the normal curve to the left of $z = 1.25$, we first locate the 1.2 row in the standard normal probability table and then move across to the .05 column. Because the table value in the 1.2 row and the .05 column is .8944, $P(z \leq 1.25) = .8944$. Similarly, to find the area under the curve to the left of $z = -.50$ we use the left-hand page of the table to locate the table value in the $-.5$ row and the .00 column; with a table value of .3085, $P(z \leq -.50) = .3085$. Thus, $P(-.50 \leq z \leq 1.25) = P(z \leq 1.25) - P(z \leq -.50) = .8944 - .3085 = .5859$.

Let us consider another example of computing the probability that z is in the interval between two given values. Often it is of interest to compute the probability that a normal random variable assumes a value within a certain number of standard deviations of the mean. Suppose we want to compute the probability that the standard normal random variable is within one standard deviation of the mean; that is, $P(-1.00 \leq z \leq 1.00)$. To compute this probability we must find the area under the curve between -1.00 and 1.00. Earlier we found that $P(z \leq 1.00) = .8413$. Referring again to the table inside the front cover of the book, we find that the area under the curve to the left of $z = -1.00$ is .1587, so $P(z \leq -1.00) = .1587$. Therefore, $P(-1.00 \leq z \leq 1.00) = P(z \leq 1.00) - P(z \leq -1.00) = .8413 - .1587 = .6826$. This probability is shown graphically in the following figure.

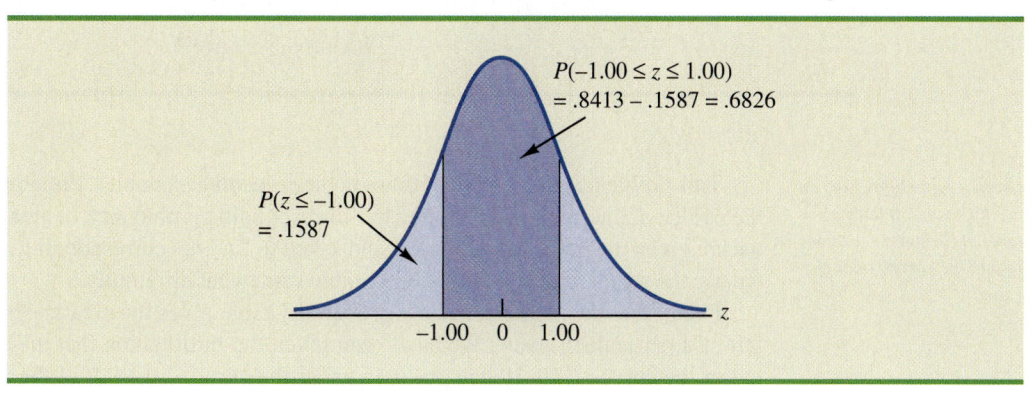

To illustrate how to make the third type of probability computation, suppose we want to compute the probability of obtaining a z value of at least 1.58; that is, $P(z \geq 1.58)$. The value in the $z = 1.5$ row and the .08 column of the cumulative normal table is .9429; thus, $P(z \leq 1.58) = .9429$. However, because the total area under the normal curve is 1, $P(z \geq 1.58) = 1 - .9429 = .0571$. This probability is shown in the following figure.

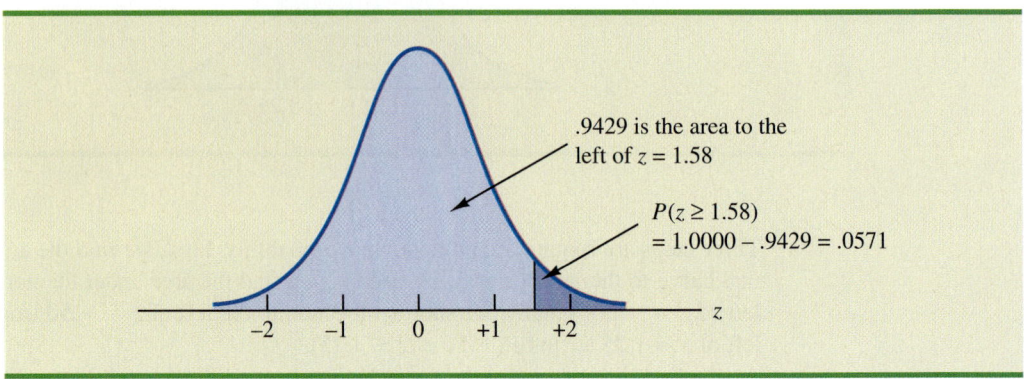

In the preceding illustrations, we showed how to compute probabilities given specified z values. In some situations, we are given a probability and are interested in working backward to find the corresponding z value. Suppose we want to find a z value such that the probability of obtaining a larger z value is .10. The following figure shows this situation graphically.

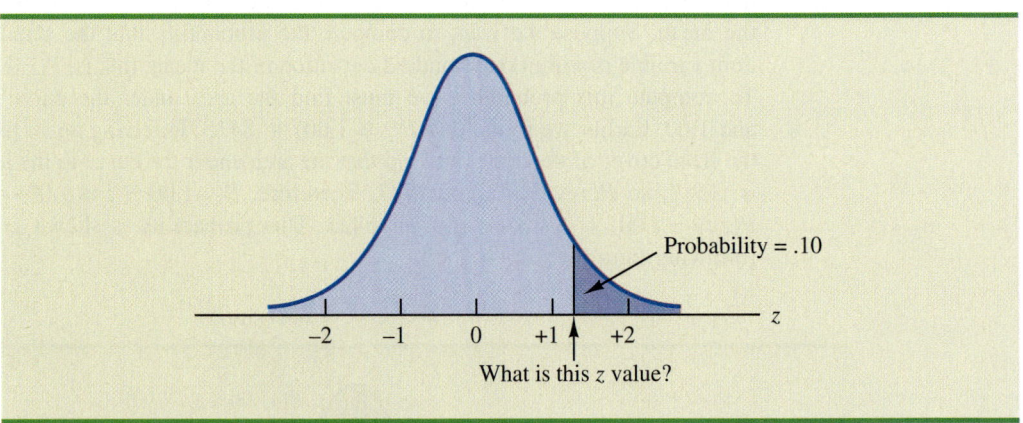

Given a probability, we can use the standard normal table in an inverse fashion to find the corresponding z value.

This problem is the inverse of those in the preceding examples. Previously, we specified the z value of interest and then found the corresponding probability, or area. In this example, we are given the probability, or area, and asked to find the corresponding z value. To do so, we use the standard normal probability table somewhat differently.

Recall that the standard normal probability table gives the area under the curve to the left of a particular z value. We have been given the information that the area in the upper tail of the curve is .10. Hence, the area under the curve to the left of the unknown z value must equal .9000. Scanning the body of the table, we find .8997 is the cumulative probability value closest to .9000. The section of the table providing this result follows.

z	.06	.07	.08	.09
.				
.				
.				
1.0	.8554	.8577	.8599	.8621
1.1	.8770	.8790	.8810	.8830
1.2	.8962	.8980	.8997	.9015
1.3	.9131	.9147	.9162	.9177
1.4	.9279	.9292	.9306	.9319
.				
.				
.				

Cumulative probability value
closest to .9000

Reading the *z* value from the left-most column and the top row of the table, we find that the corresponding *z* value is 1.28. Thus, an area of approximately .9000 (actually .8997) will be to the left of $z = 1.28$.* In terms of the question originally asked, there is an approximately .10 probability of a *z* value larger than 1.28.

Later we will show how Excel can be used to obtain these probabilities.

The examples illustrate that the table of cumulative probabilities for the standard normal probability distribution can be used to find probabilities associated with values of the standard normal random variable *z*. Two types of questions can be asked. The first type of question specifies a value, or values, for *z* and asks us to use the table to determine the corresponding areas or probabilities. The second type of question provides an area, or probability, and asks us to use the table to determine the corresponding *z* value. Thus, we need to be flexible in using the standard normal probability table to answer the desired probability question. In most cases, sketching a graph of the standard normal probability distribution and shading the appropriate area will help to visualize the situation and aid in determining the correct answer.

Computing Probabilities for Any Normal Probability Distribution

The reason for discussing the standard normal distribution so extensively is that probabilities for all normal distributions are computed by using the standard normal distribution. That is, when we have a normal distribution with any mean μ and any standard deviation σ, we answer probability questions about the distribution by first converting to the standard normal distribution. Then we can use the standard normal probability table and the appropriate *z* values to find the desired probabilities. The formula used to convert any normal random variable *x* with mean μ and standard deviation σ to the standard normal random variable *z* follows.

The formula for the standard normal random variable is similar to the formula we introduced in Chapter 3 for computing z-scores for a data set.

CONVERTING TO THE STANDARD NORMAL RANDOM VARIABLE

$$z = \frac{x - \mu}{\sigma}$$

(6.3)

*We could use interpolation in the body of the table to get a better approximation of the *z* value that corresponds to an area of .9000. Doing so to provide one more decimal place of accuracy would yield a *z* value of 1.282. However, in most practical situations, sufficient accuracy is obtained by simply using the table value closest to the desired probability.

A value of x equal to its mean μ results in $z = (\mu - \mu)/\sigma = 0$. Thus, we see that a value of x equal to its mean μ corresponds to $z = 0$. Now suppose that x is one standard deviation above its mean; that is, $x = \mu + \sigma$. Applying equation (6.3), we see that the corresponding z value is $z = [(\mu + \sigma) - \mu]/\sigma = \sigma/\sigma = 1$. Thus, an x value that is one standard deviation above its mean corresponds to $z = 1$. In other words, *we can interpret z as the number of standard deviations that the normal random variable x is from its mean μ.*

To see how this conversion enables us to compute probabilities for any normal distribution, suppose we have a normal distribution with $\mu = 10$ and $\sigma = 2$. What is the probability that the random variable x is between 10 and 14? Using equation (6.3), we see that at $x = 10$, $z = (x - \mu)/\sigma = (10 - 10)/2 = 0$ and that at $x = 14$, $z = (14 - 10)/2 = 4/2 = 2$. Thus, the answer to our question about the probability of x being between 10 and 14 is given by the equivalent probability that z is between 0 and 2 for the standard normal distribution. In other words, the probability that we are seeking is the probability that the random variable x is between its mean and two standard deviations above the mean. Using $z = 2.00$ and the standard normal probability table inside the front cover of the text, we see that $P(z \leq 2) = .9772$. Because $P(z \leq 0) = .5000$, we can compute $P(.00 \leq z \leq 2.00) = P(z \leq 2) - P(z \leq 0) = .9772 - .5000 = .4772$. Hence the probability that x is between 10 and 14 is .4772.

Grear Tire Company Problem

We turn now to an application of the normal probability distribution. Suppose the Grear Tire Company developed a new steel-belted radial tire to be sold through a national chain of discount stores. Because the tire is a new product, Grear's managers believe that the mileage guarantee offered with the tire will be an important factor in the acceptance of the product. Before finalizing the tire mileage guarantee policy, Grear's managers want probability information about $x =$ number of miles the tires will last.

From actual road tests with the tires, Grear's engineering group estimated that the mean tire mileage is $\mu = 36{,}500$ miles and that the standard deviation is $\sigma = 5000$. In addition, the data collected indicate that a normal distribution is a reasonable assumption. What percentage of the tires can be expected to last more than 40,000 miles? In other words, what is the probability that the tire mileage, x, will exceed 40,000? This question can be answered by finding the area of the darkly shaded region in Figure 6.6.

FIGURE 6.6   GREAR TIRE COMPANY MILEAGE DISTRIBUTION

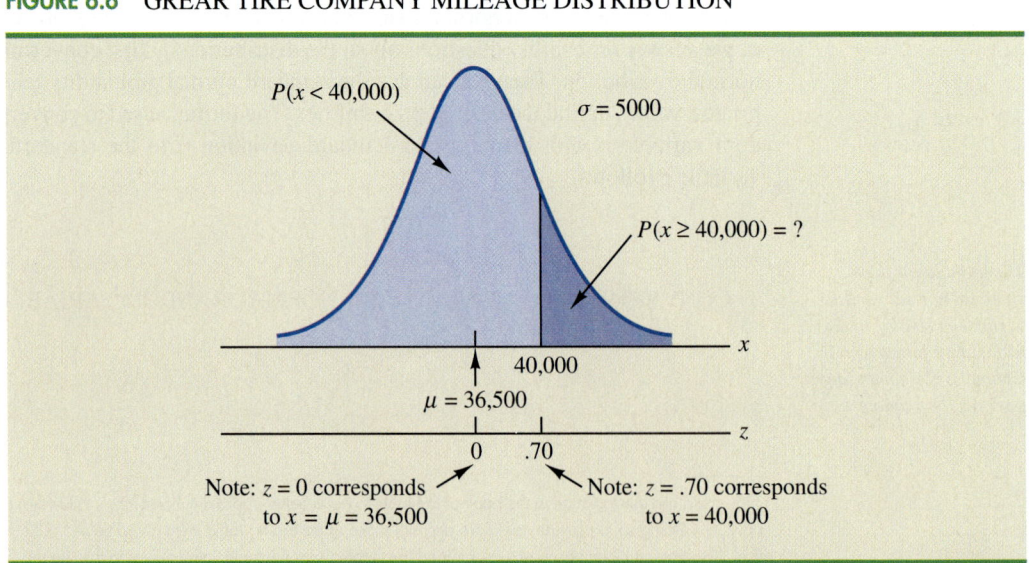

At $x = 40{,}000$, we have

$$z = \frac{x - \mu}{\sigma} = \frac{40{,}000 - 36{,}500}{5000} = \frac{3500}{5000} = .70$$

Refer now to the bottom of Figure 6.6. We see that a value of $x = 40{,}000$ on the Grear Tire normal distribution corresponds to a value of $z = .70$ on the standard normal distribution. Using the standard normal probability table, we see that the area under the standard normal curve to the left of $z = .70$ is .7580. Thus, $1.000 - .7580 = .2420$ is the probability that z will exceed .70 and hence x will exceed 40,000. We can conclude that about 24.2% of the tires will exceed 40,000 in mileage.

Let us now assume that Grear is considering a guarantee that will provide a discount on replacement tires if the original tires do not provide the guaranteed mileage. What should the guarantee mileage be if Grear wants no more than 10% of the tires to be eligible for the discount guarantee? This question is interpreted graphically in Figure 6.7.

According to Figure 6.7, the area under the curve to the left of the unknown guarantee mileage must be .10. So, we must first find the z-value that cuts off an area of .10 in the left tail of a standard normal distribution. Using the standard normal probability table, we see that $z = -1.28$ cuts off an area of .10 in the lower tail. Hence, $z = -1.28$ is the value of the standard normal random variable corresponding to the desired mileage guarantee on the Grear Tire normal distribution. To find the value of x corresponding to $z = -1.28$, we have

The guarantee mileage we need to find is 1.28 standard deviations below the mean. Thus, $x = \mu - 1.28\sigma$.

$$z = \frac{x - \mu}{\sigma} = -1.28$$
$$x - \mu = -1.28\sigma$$
$$x = \mu - 1.28\sigma$$

With $\mu = 36{,}500$ and $\sigma = 5000$,

$$x = 36{,}500 - 1.28(5000) = 30{,}100$$

With the guarantee set at 30,000 miles, the actual percentage eligible for the guarantee will be 9.68%.

Thus, a guarantee of 30,100 miles will meet the requirement that approximately 10% of the tires will be eligible for the guarantee. Perhaps, with this information, the firm will set its tire mileage guarantee at 30,000 miles.

FIGURE 6.7   GREAR'S DISCOUNT GUARANTEE

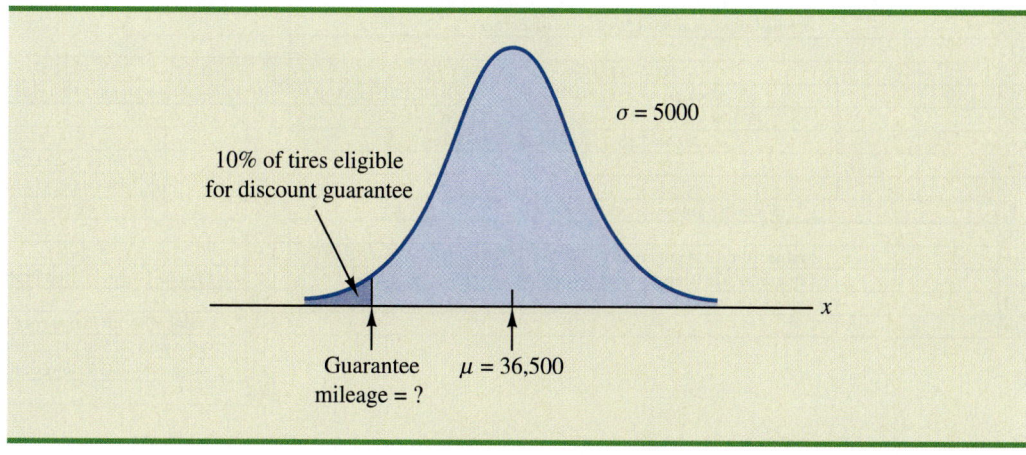

Again, we see the important role that probability distributions play in providing decision-making information. Namely, once a probability distribution is established for a particular application, it can be used to obtain probability information about the problem. Probability does not make a decision recommendation directly, but it provides information that helps the decision maker better understand the risks and uncertainties associated with the problem. Ultimately, this information may assist the decision maker in reaching a good decision.

Using Excel to Compute Normal Probabilities

Excel provides two functions for computing probabilities and z values for a standard normal probability distribution: NORMSDIST and NORMSINV. The NORMSDIST function computes the cumulative probability given a z value, and the NORMSINV function computes the z value given a cumulative probability. Two similar functions, NORMDIST and NORMINV, are available for computing the cumulative probability and the x value for any normal distribution. We begin by showing how to use the NORMSDIST and NORMSINV functions.

The letter S that appears in the name of the NORMSDIST and NORMSINV functions reminds us that these functions relate to the standard normal probability distribution.

The NORMSDIST function provides the area under the standard normal curve to the left of a given z value; thus, it provides the same cumulative probability we would obtain if we used the standard normal probability table inside the front cover of the text. Using the NORMSDIST function is just like having Excel look up cumulative normal probabilities for you. The NORMSINV function is the inverse of the NORMSDIST function; it takes a cumulative probability as input and provides the z value corresponding to that cumulative probability.

Let's see how both of these functions work by computing the probabilities and z values obtained earlier in this section using the standard normal probability table. Refer to Figure 6.8 as we describe the tasks involved. The formula worksheet is in the background; the value worksheet is in the foreground.

Enter Data: No data are entered in the worksheet. We will simply enter the appropriate z values and probabilities directly into the formulas as needed.

Enter Functions and Formulas: The NORMSDIST function has one input: the z value for which we want to obtain the cumulative probability. To illustrate the use of the NORMSDIST function we compute the four probabilities shown in cells D3:D6 of Figure 6.8.

FIGURE 6.8 EXCEL WORKSHEET FOR COMPUTING PROBABILITIES AND z VALUES FOR THE STANDARD NORMAL DISTRIBUTION

	A	B	C	D	E
1			**Probabilities: Standard Normal Distribution**		
2					
3			$P(z \leq 1)$	=NORMSDIST(1)	
4			$P(-.50 \leq z \leq 1.25)$	=NORMSDIST(1.25)-NORMSDIST(-0.5)	
5			$P(-1.00 \leq z \leq 1.00)$	=NORMSDIST(1)-NORMSDIST(-1)	
6			$P(z \geq 1.58)$	=1-NORMSDIST(1.58)	
7					
8					
9			**Finding z-values Given Probabilities**		
10					
11			z value with .10 in upper tail	=NORMSINV(0.9)	
12			z value with .025 in upper tail	=NORMSINV(0.975)	
13			z value with .025 in lower tail	=NORMSINV(0.025)	
14					

	A	B	C	D	E
1		**Probabilities: Standard Normal Distribution**			
2					
3			$P(z \leq 1)$	0.8413	
4			$P(-.50 \leq z \leq 1.25)$	0.5858	
5			$P(-1.00 \leq z \leq 1.00)$	0.6827	
6			$P(z \geq 1.58)$	0.0571	
7					
8					
9		**Finding z-values Given Probabilities**			
10					
11			z value with .10 in upper tail	1.28	
12			z value with .025 in upper tail	1.96	
13			z value with .025 in lower tail	-1.96	
14					

To compute the cumulative probability to the left of a given z value (area in lower tail), we simply evaluate NORMSDIST at the z value. For instance, to compute $P(z \leq 1)$ we entered the formula =NORMSDIST(1) into cell D3. The result, .8413, is the same as obtained using the standard normal probability table.

To compute the probability of z being in an interval we compute the value of NORMS-DIST at the upper endpoint of the interval and subtract the value of NORMSDIST at the lower endpoint of the interval. For instance, to find $P(-.50 \leq z \leq 1.25)$, we enter the formula =NORMSDIST(1.25)−NORMSDIST(−.50) into cell D4. The interval probability in cell D5 is computed in a similar fashion.

The probability in cell D4, 0.5858, differs from what we computed earlier (.5859) due to rounding.

To compute the probability to the right of a given z value (upper tail area), we must subtract the cumulative probability represented by the area under the curve below the z value (lower tail area) from 1. For example, to compute $P(z \geq 1.58)$ we entered the formula =1-NORMSDIST(1.58) into cell D6.

To compute the z value for a given cumulative probability (lower tail area), we use the NORMSINV function. To find the z value corresponding to an upper tail probability of .10, we note that the corresponding lower tail area is .90 and enter the formula =NORMSINV(0.9) into cell D11. Actually, NORMSINV(0.9) gives us the z value providing a cumulative probability (lower tail area) of .9. But it is also the z value associated with an upper tail area of .10.

Two other z values are computed in Figure 6.8. These z values will be used extensively in succeeding chapters. To compute the z value corresponding to an upper tail probability of .025, we entered the formula =NORMSINV(0.975) into cell D12. To compute the z value corresponding to a lower tail probability of .025, we entered the formula =NORMSINV(0.025) into cell D13. We see that $z = 1.96$ corresponds to an upper tail probability of .025, and $z = -1.96$ corresponds to a lower tail probability of .025.

Let us now turn to the Excel functions for computing cumulative probabilities and x values for any normal distribution. The NORMDIST function provides the area under the normal curve to the left of a given value of the random variable x; thus it provides cumulative probabilities. The NORMINV function is the inverse of the NORMDIST function; it takes a cumulative probability as input and provides the value of x corresponding to that cumulative probability. The NORMDIST and NORMINV functions do the same thing for any normal distribution that the NORMSDIST and NORMSINV functions do for the standard normal distribution.

Let's see how both of these functions work by computing probabilities and x values for the Grear Tire Company example introduced earlier in this section. Recall that the lifetime of a Grear tire has a mean of 36,500 miles and a standard deviation of 5000 miles. Refer to Figure 6.9 as we describe the tasks involved. The formula worksheet is in the background; the value worksheet is in the foreground.

Enter Data: No data are entered in the worksheet. We simply enter the appropriate x values and probabilities directly into the formulas as needed.

Enter Functions and Formulas: The NORMDIST function has four inputs: (1) the x value we want to compute the cumulative probability for, (2) the mean, (3) the standard deviation, and (4) a value of TRUE or FALSE. For the fourth input, we enter TRUE if a cumulative probability is desired, and we enter FALSE if the height of the curve is desired. Because we will always be using NORMDIST to compute cumulative probabilities, we will always choose TRUE for the fourth input.

To compute the cumulative probability to the left of a given x value (lower tail area), we simply evaluate NORMDIST at the x value. For instance, to compute the probability that a Grear tire will last 20,000 miles or less, we entered the formula =NORMDIST(20000,36500,5000, TRUE) into cell D3. The value worksheet shows that this cumulative probability is .0005. So, we can conclude that almost all Grear tires will last at least 20,000 miles.

To compute the probability of x being in an interval we compute the value of NORMDIST at the upper endpoint of the interval and subtract the value of NORMDIST at

FIGURE 6.9 EXCEL WORKSHEET FOR COMPUTING PROBABILITIES AND *x* VALUES FOR THE NORMAL DISTRIBUTION

	A	B	C	D	E	F
1			Probabilities: Normal Distribution			
2						
3			P(x <= 20000)	=NORMDIST(20000,36500,5000,TRUE)		
4			P(20000 <= x <= 40000)	=NORMDIST(40000,36500,5000,TRUE)-NORMDIST(20000,36500,5000,TRUE)		
5			P(x >= 40000)	=1-NORMDIST(40000,36500,5000,TRUE)		
6						
7			Finding x values Given Probabilities			
8						
9			x value with .10 in lower tail	=NORMINV(0.1,36500,5000)		
10			x value with .025 in upper tail	=NORMINV(0.975,36500,5000)		
11						

	A	B	C	D	E	F
1		Probabilities: Normal Distribution				
2						
3			P(x <= 20000)	0.0005		
4			P(20000 <= x <= 40000)	0.7576		
5			P(x >= 40000)	0.2420		
6						
7		Finding x values Given Probabilities				
8						
9		x value with .10 in lower tail		30092.24		
10		x value with .025 in upper tail		46299.82		
11						

the lower endpoint of the interval. The formula in cell D4 provides the probability that a tire's lifetime is between 20,000 and 40,000 miles, $P(20{,}000 \le x \le 40{,}000)$. In the value worksheet, we see that this probability is .7576.

To compute the probability to the right of a given *x* value (upper tail area), we must subtract the cumulative probability represented by the area under the curve below the *x* value (lower tail area) from 1. The formula in cell D5 computes the probability that a Grear tire will last for at least 40,000 miles. We see that this probability is .2420.

To compute the *x* value for a given cumulative probability, we use the NORMINV function. The NORMINV function has only three inputs. The first input is the cumulative probability; the second and third inputs are the mean and standard deviation. For instance, to compute the tire mileage corresponding to a lower tail area of .1 for Grear Tire, we enter the formula =NORMINV(0.1,36500,5000) into cell D9. From the value worksheet, we see that 10% of the Grear tires will last for 30,092.24 miles or less.

To compute the minimum tire mileage for the top 2.5% of Grear tires, we want to find the value of *x* corresponding to an area of .025 in the upper tail. This calculation is the same as finding the *x* value that provides a cumulative probability of .975. Thus we entered the formula =NORMINV(0.975,36500,5000) into cell D10 to compute this tire mileage. From the value worksheet, we see that 2.5% of the Grear tires will last at least 46,299.82 miles.

EXERCISES

Methods

8. Using Figure 6.4 as a guide, sketch a normal curve for a random variable *x* that has a mean of $\mu = 100$ and a standard deviation of $\sigma = 10$. Label the horizontal axis with values of 70, 80, 90, 100, 110, 120, and 130.

9. A random variable is normally distributed with a mean of $\mu = 50$ and a standard deviation of $\sigma = 5$.
   a. Sketch a normal curve for the probability density function. Label the horizontal axis with values of 35, 40, 45, 50, 55, 60, and 65. Figure 6.4 shows that the normal curve almost touches the horizontal axis at three standard deviations below and at three standard deviations above the mean (in this case at 35 and 65).
   b. What is the probability the random variable will assume a value between 45 and 55?
   c. What is the probability the random variable will assume a value between 40 and 60?

10. Draw a graph for the standard normal distribution. Label the horizontal axis at values of $-3, -2, -1, 0, 1, 2,$ and 3. Then use the table of probabilities for the standard normal distribution inside the front cover of the text to compute the following probabilities.
    a. $P(z \le 1.5)$
    b. $P(z \le 1)$
    c. $P(1 \le z \le 1.5)$
    d. $P(0 < z < 2.5)$

11. Given that z is a standard normal random variable, compute the following probabilities.
    a. $P(z \le -1.0)$
    b. $P(z \ge -1)$
    c. $P(z \ge -1.5)$
    d. $P(-2.5 \le z)$
    e. $P(-3 < z \le 0)$

12. Given that z is a standard normal random variable, compute the following probabilities.
    a. $P(0 \le z \le .83)$
    b. $P(-1.57 \le z \le 0)$
    c. $P(z > .44)$
    d. $P(z \ge -.23)$
    e. $P(z < 1.20)$
    f. $P(z \le -.71)$

13. Given that z is a standard normal random variable, compute the following probabilities.
    a. $P(-1.98 \le z \le .49)$
    b. $P(.52 \le z \le 1.22)$
    c. $P(-1.75 \le z \le -1.04)$

14. Given that z is a standard normal random variable, find z for each situation.
    a. The area to the left of z is .9750.
    b. The area between 0 and z is .4750.
    c. The area to the left of z is .7291.
    d. The area to the right of z is .1314.
    e. The area to the left of z is .6700.
    f. The area to the right of z is .3300.

15. Given that z is a standard normal random variable, find z for each situation.
    a. The area to the left of z is .2119.
    b. The area between $-z$ and z is .9030.
    c. The area between $-z$ and z is .2052.
    d. The area to the left of z is .9948.
    e. The area to the right of z is .6915.

16. Given that z is a standard normal random variable, find z for each situation.
    a. The area to the right of z is .01.
    b. The area to the right of z is .025.
    c. The area to the right of z is .05.
    d. The area to the right of z is .10.

Applications

17. The average amount parents and children spent per child on back-to-school clothes in Autumn 2001 was $527 (CNBC, September 5, 2001). Assume the standard deviation is $160 and that the amount spent is normally distributed.
    a. What is the probability that the amount spent on a randomly selected child is more than $700?
    b. What is the probability that the amount spent on a randomly selected child is less than $100?
    c. What is the probability that the amount spent on a randomly selected child is between $450 and $700?
    d. What is the probability that the amount spent on a randomly selected child is no more than $300?

18. The average stock price for companies making up the S&P 500 is $30, and the standard deviation is $8.20 (*BusinessWeek,* Special Annual Issue, Spring 2003). Assume the stock prices are normally distributed.
    a. What is the probability a company will have a stock price of at least $40?
    b. What is the probability a company will have a stock price no higher than $20?
    c. How high does a stock price have to be to put a company in the top 10%?

19. The average amount of precipitation in Dallas, Texas, during the month of April is 3.5 inches (*The World Almanac,* 2000). Assume that a normal distribution applies and that the standard deviation is .8 inches.
    a. What percentage of the time does the amount of rainfall in April exceed 5 inches?
    b. What percentage of the time is the amount of rainfall in April less than 3 inches?
    c. A month is classified as extremely wet if the amount of rainfall is in the upper 10% for that month. How much precipitation must fall in April for it to be classified as extremely wet?

20. In January 2003, the American worker spent an average of 77 hours logged on to the Internet while at work (CNBC, March 15, 2003). Assume the population mean is 77 hours, the times are normally distributed, and that the standard deviation is 20 hours.
    a. What is the probability that in January 2003 a randomly selected worker spent fewer than 50 hours logged on to the Internet?
    b. What percentage of workers spent more than 100 hours in January 2003 logged on to the Internet?
    c. A person is classified as a heavy user if he or she is in the upper 20% of usage. In January 2003, how many hours did a worker have to be logged on to the Internet to be considered a heavy user?

21. A person must score in the upper 2% of the population on an IQ test to qualify for membership in Mensa, the international high-IQ society (*US Airways Attache,* September 2000). If IQ scores are normally distributed with a mean of 100 and a standard deviation of 15, what score must a person have to qualify for Mensa?

22. According to the Bureau of Labor Statistics, the average weekly pay for a U.S. production worker was $441.84 (*The World Almanac,* 2000). Assume that available data indicate that production worker wages were normally distributed with a standard deviation of $90.
    a. What is the probability that a worker earned between $400 and $500 per week?
    b. How much did a production worker have to earn per week to be in the top 20% of wage earners?
    c. For a randomly selected production worker, what is the probability the worker earned less than $250 per week?

23. The time needed to complete a final examination in a particular college course is normally distributed with a mean of 80 minutes and a standard deviation of 10 minutes. Answer the following questions.

a. What is the probability of completing the exam in one hour or less?
b. What is the probability that a student will complete the exam in more than 60 minutes but less than 75 minutes?
c. Assume that the class has 60 students and that the examination period is 90 minutes in length. How many students do you expect will be unable to complete the exam in the allotted time?

24. The daily trading volumes (millions of shares) for stocks traded on the New York Stock Exchange for 12 days in August and September are shown here (*Barron's*, August 7, 2000, September 4, 2000, and September 11, 2000).

917	983	1046
944	723	783
813	1057	766
836	992	973

The probability distribution of trading volume is approximately normal.
a. Compute the mean and standard deviation for the daily trading volume to use as estimates of the population mean and standard deviation.
b. What is the probability that on a particular day the trading volume will be less than 800 million shares?
c. What is the probability that trading volume will exceed 1 billion shares?
d. If the exchange wants to issue a press release on the top 5% of trading days, what volume will trigger a release?

25. The average ticket price for a Washington Redskins football game was $81.89 for the 2001 season (*USA Today*, September 6, 2001). With the additional costs of parking, food, drinks, and souvenirs, the average cost for a family of four to attend a game totaled $442.54. Assume the normal distribution applies and that the standard deviation is $65.
a. What is the probability that a family of four will spend more than $400?
b. What is the probability that a family of four will spend $300 or less?
c. What is the probability that a family of four will spend between $400 and $500?

Exponential Probability Distribution

The **exponential probability distribution** may be used for random variables such as the time between arrivals at a car wash, the time required to load a truck, the distance between major defects in a highway, and so on. The exponential probability density function follows.

EXPONENTIAL PROBABILITY DENSITY FUNCTION

$$f(x) = \frac{1}{\mu} e^{-x/\mu} \qquad \text{for } x \geq 0, \mu > 0 \tag{6.4}$$

where μ = expected value or mean

As an example of the exponential distribution, suppose that x represents the loading time for a truck at the Schips loading dock and follows such a distribution. If the mean, or average, loading time is 15 minutes ($\mu = 15$), the appropriate probability density function for x is

$$f(x) = \frac{1}{15} e^{-x/15}$$

Figure 6.10 is the graph of this probability density function.

FIGURE 6.10   EXPONENTIAL DISTRIBUTION FOR THE SCHIPS LOADING
DOCK EXAMPLE

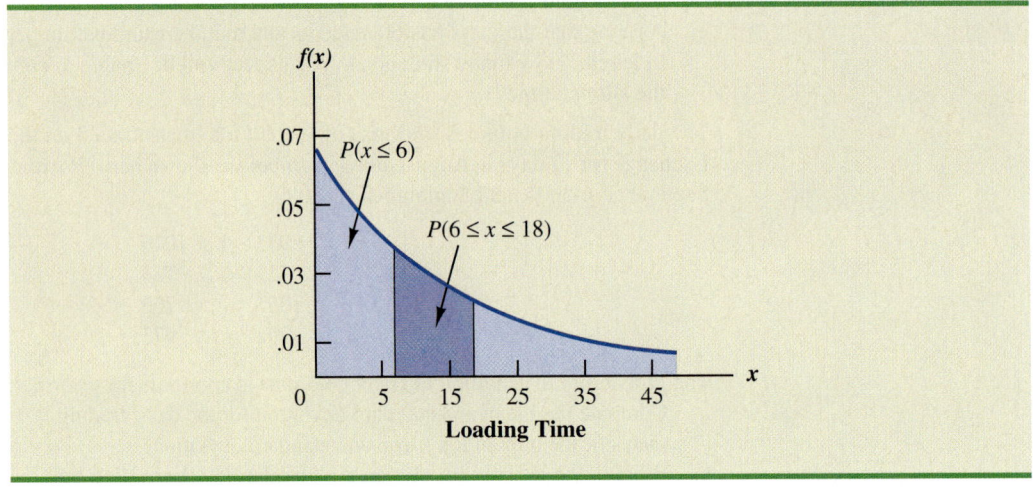

Computing Probabilities for the Exponential Distribution

In waiting line applications, the exponential distribution is often used for service time.

As with any continuous probability distribution, the area under the curve corresponding to an interval provides the probability that the random variable assumes a value in that interval. In the Schips loading dock example, the probability that loading a truck will take 6 minutes or less $P(x \le 6)$ is defined to be the area under the curve in Figure 6.10 from $x = 0$ to $x = 6$. Similarly, the probability that the loading time will be 18 minutes or less $P(x \le 18)$ is the area under the curve from $x = 0$ to $x = 18$. Note also that the probability that the loading time will be between 6 minutes and 18 minutes $P(6 \le x \le 18)$ is given by the area under the curve from $x = 6$ to $x = 18$.

To compute exponential probabilities such as those just described, we use the following formula. It provides the cumulative probability of obtaining a value for the exponential random variable of less than or equal to some specific value denoted by x_0.

EXPONENTIAL DISTRIBUTION: CUMULATIVE PROBABILITIES

$$P(x \le x_0) = 1 - e^{-x_0/\mu} \tag{6.5}$$

For the Schips loading dock example, $x = $ loading time in minutes and $\mu = 15$ minutes. Using equation (6.5)

$$P(x \le x_0) = 1 - e^{-x_0/15}$$

Hence, the probability that loading a truck will take 6 minutes or less is

$$P(x \le 6) = 1 - e^{-6/15} = .3297$$

Using equation (6.5), we calculate the probability of loading a truck in 18 minutes or less.

$$P(x \le 18) = 1 - e^{-18/15} = .6988$$

Thus, the probability that loading a truck will take between 6 minutes and 18 minutes is equal to .6988 − .3297 = .3691. Probabilities for any other interval can be computed similarly.

A property of the exponential distribution is that the mean and standard deviation are equal.

   In the preceding example, the mean time it takes to load a truck is $\mu = 15$ minutes. A property of the exponential distribution is that the mean of the distribution and the standard deviation of the distribution are *equal.* Thus, the standard deviation for the time it takes to load a truck is $\sigma = 15$ minutes. The variance is $\sigma^2 = (15)^2 = 225$.

Relationship Between the Poisson and Exponential Distributions

In Section 5.5 we introduced the Poisson distribution as a discrete probability distribution that is often useful in examining the number of occurrences of an event over a specified interval of time or space. Recall that the Poisson probability function is

$$f(x) = \frac{\mu^x e^{-\mu}}{x!}$$

where

$$\mu = \text{expected value or mean number of}$$
$$\text{occurrences over a specified interval}$$

If arrivals follow a Poisson distribution, the time between arrivals must follow an exponential distribution.

The continuous exponential probability distribution is related to the discrete Poisson distribution. If the Poisson distribution provides an appropriate description of the number of occurrences per interval, the exponential distribution provides a description of the length of the interval between occurrences.

   To illustrate this relationship, suppose the number of cars that arrive at a car wash during one hour is described by a Poisson probability distribution with a mean of 10 cars per hour. The Poisson probability function that gives the probability of x arrivals per hour is

$$f(x) = \frac{10^x e^{-10}}{x!}$$

Because the average number of arrivals is 10 cars per hour, the average time between cars arriving is

$$\frac{1 \text{ hour}}{10 \text{ cars}} = .1 \text{ hour/car}$$

Thus, the corresponding exponential distribution that describes the time between the arrivals has a mean of $\mu = .1$ hour per car; as a result, the appropriate exponential probability density function is

$$f(x) = \frac{1}{.1} e^{-x/.1} = 10e^{-10x}$$

Using Excel to Compute Exponential Probabilities

Excel's EXPONDIST function can be used to compute exponential probabilities. We will illustrate by computing probabilities associated with the time it takes to load a truck at the Schips loading dock. This example was introduced at the beginning of the section. Refer to Figure 6.11 as we describe the tasks involved. The formula worksheet is in the background; the value worksheet is in the foreground.

FIGURE 6.11 EXCEL WORKSHEET FOR COMPUTING PROBABILITIES FOR THE EXPONENTIAL PROBABILITY DISTRIBUTION

	A	B	C	D	E	F	G
1			Probabilities: Exponential Distribution				
2							
3			$P(x \le 18)$	=EXPONDIST(18,1/15,TRUE)			
4			$P(6 \le x \le 18)$	=EXPONDIST(18,1/15,TRUE)-EXPONDIST(6,1/15,TRUE)			
5			$P(x \ge 8)$	=1-EXPONDIST(8,1/15,TRUE)			
6							

	A	B	C	D	E
1	Probabilities: Exponential Distribution				
2					
3			$P(x \le 18)$	0.6988	
4			$P(6 \le x \le 18)$	0.3691	
5			$P(x \ge 8)$	0.5866	
6					

Enter Data: No data are entered in the worksheet. We simply enter the appropriate values for the exponential random variable into the formulas as needed. The random variable is x = loading time.

Enter Functions and Formulas: The EXPONDIST function has three inputs: the first is the value of x, the second is $1/\mu$, and the third is TRUE or FALSE. We choose TRUE for the third input if a cumulative probability is desired and FALSE if the height of the probability density function is desired. We will always use TRUE because we will be computing cumulative probabilities.

The first probability we compute is the probability that the loading time is 18 minutes or less. For the Schips problem, $1/\mu$ = 1/15, so we enter the formula =EXPONDIST (18,1/15,TRUE) into cell D3 to compute the desired cumulative probability. From the value worksheet, we see that the probability of loading a truck in 18 minutes or less is .6988.

The second probability we compute is the probability that the loading time is between 6 and 18 minutes. To find this probability we first compute the cumulative probability for the upper endpoint of the time interval and subtract the cumulative probability for the lower endpoint of the interval. The formula we have entered into cell D4 calculates this probability. The value worksheet shows that this probability is .3691.

The last probability we calculate is the probability that the loading time is at least 8 minutes. Because the EXPONDIST function only computes cumulative (lower tail) probabilities, we compute this probability by entering the formula =1-EXPONDIST(8,1/15,TRUE) into cell D5. The value worksheet shows that the probability of a loading time of 8 minutes or more is .5866.

NOTES AND COMMENTS

As we can see in Figure 6.10, the exponential distribution is skewed to the right. Indeed, the skewness measure for exponential distributions is 2. The exponential distribution gives us a good idea what a skewed distribution looks like.

Exercises

Methods

26. Consider the following exponential probability density function.

$$f(x) = \frac{1}{8} e^{-x/8} \qquad \text{for } x \ge 0$$

a.   Find $P(x \leq 6)$.
b.   Find $P(x \leq 4)$.
c.   Find $P(x \geq 6)$.
d.   Find $P(4 \leq x \leq 6)$.

27. Consider the following exponential probability density function.

$$f(x) = \frac{1}{3} e^{-x/3} \qquad \text{for } x \geq 0$$

a.   Write the formula for $P(x \leq x_0)$.
b.   Find $P(x \leq 2)$.
c.   Find $P(x \geq 3)$.
d.   Find $P(x \leq 5)$.
e.   Find $P(2 \leq x \leq 5)$.

Applications

28. *Internet Magazine* monitors Internet service providers (ISPs) and provides statistics on their performance. The average time to download a Web page for free ISPs is approximately 20 seconds for European Web pages (*Internet Magazine,* January 2000). Assume the time to download a Web page follows an exponential distribution.
a.   What is the probability it will take less than 10 seconds to download a Web page?
b.   What is the probability it will take more than 30 seconds to download a Web page?
c.   What is the probability it will take between 10 and 30 seconds to download a Web page?

29. The time between arrivals of vehicles at a particular intersection follows an exponential probability distribution with a mean of 12 seconds.
a.   Sketch this exponential probability distribution.
b.   What is the probability that the arrival time between vehicles is 12 seconds or less?
c.   What is the probability that the arrival time between vehicles is 6 seconds or less?
d.   What is the probability of 30 or more seconds between vehicle arrivals?

30. The lifetime (hours) of an electronic device is a random variable with the following exponential probability density function.

$$f(x) = \frac{1}{50} e^{-x/50} \qquad \text{for } x \geq 0$$

a.   What is the mean lifetime of the device?
b.   What is the probability that the device will fail in the first 25 hours of operation?
c.   What is the probability that the device will operate 100 or more hours before failure?

31. Sparagowski & Associates conducted a study of service times at the drive-up window of fast-food restaurants. The average service time at McDonald's restaurants was 2.78 minutes (*The Cincinnati Enquirer,* July 9, 2000). Service times such as these frequently follow an exponential distribution.
a.   What is the probability that a customer's service time is less than 2 minutes?
b.   What is the probability that a customer's service time is more than 5 minutes?
c.   What is the probability that a customer's service time is more than 2.78 minutes?

32. According to a *Barron's* Primary Reader Survey, the average annual number of investment transactions for a subscriber is 30 (http://www.barronsmag.com, July 28, 2000). Suppose the number of transactions in a year follows the Poisson probability distribution.
a.   Show the probability distribution for the time between investment transactions.
b.   What is the probability of no transactions during the month of January for a particular subscriber?
c.   What is the probability that the next transaction will occur within the next half month for a particular subscriber?

Summary

This chapter extended the discussion of probability distributions to the case of continuous random variables. The major conceptual difference between discrete and continuous probability distributions involves the method of computing probabilities. With discrete distributions, the probability function $f(x)$ provides the probability that the random variable x assumes various values. With continuous distributions, the probability density function $f(x)$ does not provide probability values directly. Instead, probabilities are given by areas under the curve or graph of the probability density function $f(x)$. Because the area under the curve above a single point is zero, we observe that the probability of any particular value is zero for a continuous random variable.

Three continuous probability distributions—the uniform, normal, and exponential distributions—were treated in detail. The normal distribution is used widely in statistical inference and will be used extensively throughout the remainder of the text.

Glossary

Probability density function A function used to compute probabilities for a continuous random variable. The area under the graph of a probability density function over an interval represents probability.

Uniform probability distribution A continuous probability distribution for which the probability that the random variable will assume a value in any interval is the same for each interval of equal length.

Normal probability distribution A continuous probability distribution. Its probability density function is bell-shaped and determined by its mean μ and standard deviation σ.

Standard normal probability distribution A normal distribution with a mean of zero and a standard deviation of one.

Exponential probability distribution A continuous probability distribution that is useful in computing probabilities for the time it takes to complete a task.

Key Formulas

Uniform Probability Density Function

$$f(x) = \begin{cases} \dfrac{1}{b-a} & \text{for } a \leq x \leq b \\ 0 & \text{elsewhere} \end{cases} \tag{6.1}$$

Normal Probability Density Function

$$f(x) = \frac{1}{\sigma\sqrt{2\pi}} e^{-(x-\mu)^2/2\sigma^2} \tag{6.2}$$

Converting to the Standard Normal Random Variable

$$z = \frac{x-\mu}{\sigma} \tag{6.3}$$

Exponential Probability Density Function

$$f(x) = \frac{1}{\mu} e^{-x/\mu} \qquad \text{for } x \geq 0, \mu > 0 \qquad\qquad \textbf{(6.4)}$$

Exponential Distribution: Cumulative Probabilities

$$P(x \leq x_0) = 1 - e^{-x_0/\mu} \qquad\qquad \textbf{(6.5)}$$

Supplementary Exercises

33. A business executive, transferred from Chicago to Atlanta, needs to sell her house in Chicago quickly. The executive's employer has offered to buy the house for $210,000, but the offer expires at the end of the week. The executive does not currently have a better offer, but can afford to leave the house on the market for another month. From conversations with her realtor, the executive believes the price she will get by leaving the house on the market for another month is uniformly distributed between $200,000 and $225,000.
    a. If she leaves the house on the market for another month, what is the mathematical expression for the probability density function of the sales price?
    b. If she leaves it on the market for another month, what is the probability she will get at least $215,000 for the house?
    c. If she leaves it on the market for another month, what is the probability she will get less than $210,000?
    d. Should the executive leave the house on the market for another month? Why or why not?

34. The U.S. Bureau of Labor Statistics reports that the average annual expenditure on food and drink for all families is $5700 (*Money,* December 2003). Assume that annual expenditure on food and drink is normally distributed and that the standard deviation is $1500.
    a. What is the range of expenditures of the 10% of families with the lowest annual spending on food and drink?
    b. What percentage of families spend more than $7000 annually on food and drink?
    c. What is the range of expenditures for the 5% of families with the highest annual spending on food and drink?

35. Motorola used the normal distribution to determine the probability of defects and the number of defects expected in a production process. Assume a production process produces items with a mean weight of 10 ounces. Calculate the probability of a defect and the expected number of defects for a 1000-unit production run in the following situations.
    a. The process standard deviation is .15, and the process control is set at plus or minus one standard deviation. Units with weights less than 9.85 or greater than 10.15 ounces will be classified as defects.
    b. Through process design improvements, the process standard deviation can be reduced to .05. Assume the process control remains the same, with weights less than 9.85 or greater than 10.15 ounces being classified as defects.
    c. What is the advantage of reducing process variation, thereby causing process control limits to be at a greater number of standard deviations from the mean?

36. The average annual amount American households spend for daily transportation is $6312 (*Money,* August 2001). Assume that the amount spent is normally distributed.
    a. Suppose you learn that 5% of American households spend less than $1000 for daily transportation. What is the standard deviation of the amount spent?
    b. What is the probability that a household spends between $4000 and $6000?
    c. What is the range of spending for the 3% of households with the highest daily transportation cost?

37. *Condé Nast Traveler* publishes a Gold List of the top hotels all over the world. The Broadmoor Hotel in Colorado Springs contains 700 rooms and is on the 2004 Gold List (*Condé Nast Traveler,* January 2004). Suppose Broadmoor's marketing group forecasts a mean demand of 670 rooms for the coming weekend. Assume that demand for the upcoming weekend is normally distributed with a standard deviation of 30.
    a. What is the probability all the hotel's room will be rented?
    b. What is the probability 50 or more rooms will not be rented?
    c. Would you recommend the hotel consider offering a promotion to increase demand? What considerations would be important?

38. Ward Doering Auto Sales is considering offering a special service contract that will cover the total cost of any service work required on leased vehicles. From experience, the company manager estimates that yearly service costs are approximately normally distributed, with a mean of $150 and a standard deviation of $25.
    a. If the company offers the service contract to customers for a yearly charge of $200, what is the probability that any one customer's service costs will exceed the contract price of $200?
    b. What is Ward's expected profit per service contract?

39. Is lack of sleep causing traffic fatalities? A study conducted under the auspices of the National Highway Traffic Safety Administration found that the average number of fatal crashes caused by drowsy drivers each year was 1550 (*Business Week,* January 26, 2004). Assume the annual number of fatal crashes per year is normally distributed with a standard deviation of 300.
    a. What is the probability of fewer than 1000 fatal crashes in a year?
    b. What is the probability the number of fatal crashes will be between 1000 and 2000 for a year?
    c. For a year to be in the upper 5% with respect to the number of fatal crashes, how many fatal crashes would have to occur?

40. Assume that the test scores from a college admissions test are normally distributed, with a mean of 450 and a standard deviation of 100.
    a. What percentage of the people taking the test score between 400 and 500?
    b. Suppose someone receives a score of 630. What percentage of the people taking the test score better? What percentage score worse?
    c. If a particular university will not admit anyone scoring below 480, what percentage of the persons taking the test would be acceptable to the university?

41. According to *Advertising Age,* the average base salary for women working as copywriters in advertising firms is higher than the average base salary for men. The average base salary for women is $67,000 and the average base salary for men is $65,500 (*Working Woman,* July/August 2000). Assume salaries are normally distributed and that the standard deviation is $7000 for both men and women.
    a. What is the probability of a woman receiving a salary in excess of $75,000?
    b. What is the probability of a man receiving a salary in excess of $75,000?
    c. What is the probability of a woman receiving a salary below $50,000?
    d. How much would a woman have to make to have a higher salary than 99% of her male counterparts?

42. A machine fills containers with a particular product. The standard deviation of filling weights is known from past data to be .6 ounce. If only 2% of the containers hold less than 18 ounces, what is the mean filling weight for the machine? That is, what must μ equal? Assume the filling weights have a normal distribution.

43. The time in minutes for which a student uses a computer terminal at the computer center of a major university follows an exponential probability distribution with a mean of 36 minutes. Assume a student arrives at the terminal just as another student is beginning to work on the terminal.

a.   What is the probability that the wait for the second student will be 15 minutes or less?
b.   What is the probability that the wait for the second student will be between 15 and 45 minutes?
c.   What is the probability that the second student will have to wait an hour or more?

44.   The Web site for the Bed and Breakfast Inns of North America (http://www.cimarron.net) gets approximately seven visitors per minute (*Time,* September 2001). Suppose the number of Web site visitors per minute follows a Poisson probability distribution.
a.   What is the mean time between visits to the Web site?
b.   Show the exponential probability density function for the time between Web site visits.
c.   What is the probability no one will access the Web site in a 1-minute period?
d.   What is the probability no one will access the Web site in a 12-second period?

45.   The average travel time to work for New York City residents is 36.5 minutes (*Time Almanac,* 2001).
a.   Assume the exponential probability distribution is applicable and show the probability density function for the travel time to work for a typical New Yorker.
b.   What is the probability it will take a typical New Yorker between 20 and 40 minutes to travel to work?
c.   What is the probability it will take a typical New Yorker more than 40 minutes to travel to work?

46.   The time (in minutes) between telephone calls at an insurance claims office has the following exponential probability distribution.

$$f(x) = .50e^{-.50x} \qquad \text{for } x \geq 0$$

a.   What is the mean time between telephone calls?
b.   What is the probability of having 30 seconds or less between telephone calls?
c.   What is the probability of having 1 minute or less between telephone calls?
d.   What is the probability of having 5 or more minutes without a telephone call?

Case Problem   # Specialty Toys

Specialty Toys, Inc., sells a variety of new and innovative children's toys. Management learned that the preholiday season is the best time to introduce a new toy, because many families use this time to look for new ideas for December holiday gifts. When Specialty discovers a new toy with good market potential, it chooses an October market entry date.

In order to get toys in its stores by October, Specialty places one-time orders with its manufacturers in June or July of each year. Demand for children's toys can be highly volatile. If a new toy catches on, a sense of shortage in the marketplace often increases the demand to high levels and large profits can be realized. However, new toys can also flop, leaving Specialty stuck with high levels of inventory that must be sold at reduced prices. The most important question the company faces is deciding how many units of a new toy should be purchased to meet anticipated sales demand. If too few are purchased, sales will be lost; if too many are purchased, profits will be reduced because of low prices realized in clearance sales.

For the coming season, Specialty plans to introduce a new product called Weather Teddy. This variation of a talking teddy bear is made by a company in Taiwan. When a child presses Teddy's hand, the bear begins to talk. A built-in barometer selects one of five responses that predict the weather conditions. The responses range from "It looks to be a very nice day! Have fun" to "I think it may rain today. Don't forget your umbrella." Tests with the product show that, even though it is not a perfect weather predictor, its predictions are surprisingly good. Several of Specialty's managers claimed Teddy gave predictions of the weather that were as good as many local television weather forecasters.

As with other products, Specialty faces the decision of how many Weather Teddy units to order for the coming holiday season. Members of the management team suggested order quantities of 15,000, 18,000, 24,000, or 28,000 units. The wide range of order quantities suggested indicates considerable disagreement concerning the market potential. The product management team asks you for an analysis of the stock-out probabilities for various order quantities, an estimate of the profit potential, and to help make an order quantity recommendation. Specialty expects to sell Weather Teddy for $24 based on a cost of $16 per unit. If inventory remains after the holiday season, Specialty will sell all surplus inventory for $5 per unit. After reviewing the sales history of similar products, Specialty's senior sales forecaster predicted an expected demand of 20,000 units with a 0.90 probability that demand would be between 10,000 units and 30,000 units.

Managerial Report

Prepare a managerial report that addresses the following issues and recommends an order quantity for the Weather Teddy product.

1. Use the sales forecaster's prediction to describe a normal probability distribution that can be used to approximate the demand distribution. Sketch the distribution and show its mean and standard deviation.
2. Compute the probability of a stock-out for the order quantities suggested by members of the management team.
3. Compute the projected profit for the order quantities suggested by the management team under three scenarios: worst case in which sales = 10,000 units, most likely case in which sales = 20,000 units, and best case in which sales = 30,000 units.
4. One of Specialty's managers felt that the profit potential was so great that the order quantity should have a 70% chance of meeting demand and only a 30% chance of any stock-outs. What quantity would be ordered under this policy, and what is the projected profit under the three sales scenarios?
5. Provide your own recommendation for an order quantity and note the associated profit projections. Provide a rationale for your recommendation.

CHAPTER 7

Sampling and Sampling Distributions

CONTENTS

STATISTICS IN PRACTICE:
MEADWESTVACO CORPORATION

7.1 THE ELECTRONICS
ASSOCIATES SAMPLING
PROBLEM

7.2 SIMPLE RANDOM SAMPLING
Sampling from a Finite
Population
Sampling from an Infinite
Population

7.3 POINT ESTIMATION

7.4 INTRODUCTION TO
SAMPLING DISTRIBUTIONS

7.5 SAMPLING DISTRIBUTION
OF $\bar{x}$
Expected Value of $\bar{x}$
Standard Deviation of $\bar{x}$
Form of the Sampling
Distribution of $\bar{x}$

Sampling Distribution of $\bar{x}$ for
the EAI Problem
Practical Value of the Sampling
Distribution of $\bar{x}$
Relationship Between Sample
Size and the Sampling
Distribution of $\bar{x}$

7.6 SAMPLING DISTRIBUTION
OF $\bar{p}$
Expected Value of $\bar{p}$
Standard Deviation of $\bar{p}$
Form of the Sampling
Distribution of $\bar{p}$
Practical Value of the Sampling
Distribution of $\bar{p}$

7.7 SAMPLING METHODS
Stratified Random Sampling
Cluster Sampling
Systematic Sampling
Convenience Sampling
Judgment Sampling

STATISTICS *in* PRACTICE

MEADWESTVACO CORPORATION*
STAMFORD, CONNECTICUT

MeadWestvaco Corporation, a leading producer of packaging, coated and specialty papers, consumer and office products, and specialty chemicals, employs more than 30,000 people. It operates worldwide in 33 countries and serves customers located in approximately 100 countries. MeadWestvaco holds a leading position in paper production, with an annual capacity of 1.8 million tons. The company's products include textbook paper, glossy magazine paper, beverage packaging systems, and office products. MeadWestvaco's internal consulting group uses sampling to provide a variety of information that enables the company to obtain significant productivity benefits and remain competitive.

For example, MeadWestvaco maintains large woodland holdings, which supply the trees, or raw material, for many of the company's products. Managers need reliable and accurate information about the timberlands and forests to evaluate the company's ability to meet its future raw material needs. What is the present volume in the forests? What is the past growth of the forests? What is the projected future growth of the forests? With answers to these important questions MeadWestvaco's managers can develop plans for the future, including long-term planting and harvesting schedules for the trees.

How does MeadWestvaco obtain the information it needs about its vast forest holdings? Data collected from sample plots throughout the forests are the basis for learning about the population of trees owned by the company. To identify the sample plots, the timberland holdings are first divided into three sections based on location and types of tree. Using maps and random numbers, MeadWestvaco analysts identify random samples of ⅕- to ⅐-acre plots in each section of the

Random sampling of its forest holdings enables MeadWestvaco Corporation to meet future raw material needs. © Walter Hodges/Corbis.

forest. MeadWestvaco foresters collect data from these sample plots to learn about the forest population.

Foresters throughout the organization participate in the field data collection process. Periodically, two-person teams gather information on each tree in every sample plot. The sample data are entered into the company's continuous forest inventory (CFI) computer system. Reports from the CFI system include a number of frequency distribution summaries containing statistics on types of trees, present forest volume, past forest growth rates, and projected future forest growth and volume. Sampling and the associated statistical summaries of the sample data provide the reports essential for the effective management of MeadWestvaco's forests and timberlands.

In this chapter you will learn about simple random sampling and the sample selection process. In addition, you will learn how statistics such as the sample mean and sample proportion are used to estimate the population mean and population proportion. The important concept of a sampling distribution is also introduced.

The authors are indebted to Dr. Edward P. Winkofsky for providing this Statistics in Practice.

In Chapter 1, we defined a *population* and a *sample*. The definitions are restated here.

1. A *population* is the set of all the elements of interest in a study.
2. A *sample* is a subset of the population.

Numerical characteristics of a population, such as the mean and standard deviation, are called **parameters**. A primary purpose of statistical inference is to develop estimates and test hypotheses about population parameters using information contained in a sample.

Let us begin by citing two situations in which samples provide estimates of population parameters.

1. A tire manufacturer developed a new tire designed to provide an increase in mileage over the firm's current line of tires. To estimate the mean number of miles provided by the new tires, the manufacturer selected a sample of 120 new tires for testing. The test results provided a sample mean of 36,500 miles. Hence, an estimate of the mean tire mileage for the population of new tires is 36,500 miles.

2. Members of a political party were considering supporting a particular candidate for election to the U.S. Senate, and party leaders wanted an estimate of the proportion of registered voters favoring the candidate. The time and cost associated with contacting every individual in the population of registered voters were prohibitive. Hence, a sample of 400 registered voters was selected and 160 of the 400 voters indicated a preference for the candidate. An estimate of the proportion of the population of registered voters favoring the candidate is 160/400 = .40.

These two examples illustrate some of the reasons why samples are used. Note that in the tire mileage example, collecting the data on tire life involves wearing out each tire tested. Clearly it is not feasible to test every tire in the population; a sample is the only realistic way to obtain the desired tire mileage data. In the example involving the election, contacting every registered voter in the population is theoretically possible, but the time and cost in doing so are prohibitive; thus, a sample of registered voters is preferred.

A sample mean provides an estimate of a population mean, and a sample proportion provides an estimate of a population proportion. With estimates such as these, some estimation error can be expected. This chapter provides the basis for determining how large that error might be.

It is important to realize that sample results provide only *estimates* of the values of the population characteristics. We do not expect the sample mean of 36,500 miles to exactly equal the mean mileage for all tires in the population, nor do we expect exactly .40, or 40%, of the population of registered voters to favor the candidate. The reason is simply that the sample contains only a portion of the population. With proper sampling methods, the sample results will provide "good" estimates of the population parameters. But how good can we expect the sample results to be? Fortunately, statistical procedures are available for answering this question.

In this chapter we show how simple random sampling can be used to select a sample from a population. We then show how data obtained from a simple random sample can be used to compute estimates of a population mean, a population standard deviation, and a population proportion. In addition, we introduce the important concept of a sampling distribution. As we show, knowledge of the appropriate sampling distribution is what enables us to make statements about how close the sample estimates are to the corresponding population parameters. The last section discusses some alternatives to simple random sampling that are often employed in practice.

7.1   The Electronics Associates Sampling Problem

The director of personnel for Electronics Associates, Inc. (EAI), has been assigned the task of developing a profile of the company's 2500 managers. The characteristics to be identified include the mean annual salary for the managers and the proportion of managers having completed the company's management training program.

CD file

EAI

Using the 2500 managers as the population for this study, we can find the annual salary and the training program status for each individual by referring to the firm's personnel records. The data file containing this information for all 2500 managers in the population is on the CD that accompanies the text.

Using the EAI data set and the formulas presented in Chapter 3, we compute the population mean and the population standard deviation for the annual salary data.

$$\text{Population mean:}\quad \mu = \$51{,}800$$
$$\text{Population standard deviation:}\quad \sigma = \$4000$$

The data for the training program status show that 1500 of the 2500 managers completed the training program. Letting p denote the proportion of the population that completed the training program, we see that $p = 1500/2500 = .60$. The population mean annual salary ($\mu = \$51,800$), the population standard deviation of annual salary ($\sigma = \$4000$), and the population proportion that completed the training program ($p = .60$) are parameters of the population of EAI managers.

Often the cost of collecting information from a sample is substantially less than from a population, especially when personal interviews must be conducted to collect the information.

Now, suppose that the necessary information on all the EAI managers was not readily available in the company's database. The question we now consider is how the firm's director of personnel can obtain estimates of the population parameters by using a sample of managers rather than all 2500 managers in the population. Suppose that a sample of 30 managers will be used. Clearly, the time and the cost of developing a profile would be substantially less for 30 managers than for the entire population. If the personnel director could be assured that a sample of 30 managers would provide adequate information about the population of 2500 managers, working with a sample would be preferable to working with the entire population. Let us explore the possibility of using a sample for the EAI study by first showing how to select a sample of 30 managers.

7.2   Simple Random Sampling

Several methods can be used to select a sample from a population; one of the most common is **simple random sampling**. The definition of a simple random sample and the process of selecting a simple random sample depend on whether the population is *finite* or *infinite*. Because the EAI sampling problem involves a finite population of 2500 managers, we first consider sampling from a finite population.

Sampling from a Finite Population

A simple random sample of size n from a finite population of size N is defined as follows.

> **SIMPLE RANDOM SAMPLE (FINITE POPULATION)**
>
> A simple random sample of size n from a finite population of size N is a sample selected such that each possible sample of size n has the same probability of being selected.

The random numbers generated using Excel's RAND function follow a uniform probability distribution between 0 and 1.

The procedures used to select a simple random sample from a finite population are based upon the use of random numbers. We can use Excel's RAND function to generate a random number between 0 and 1 by entering the formula =RAND() into any cell in a worksheet. The number generated is called a random number because the mathematical procedure used by the RAND function guarantees that every number between 0 and 1 has the same probability of being selected. Let us see how these random numbers can be used to select a simple random sample.

Our procedure for selecting a simple random sample of size n from a population of size N involves two steps.

Step 1. Assign a random number to each element of the population.
Step 2. Select the n elements corresponding to the n smallest random numbers.

Because each set of n elements in the population has the same probability of being assigned the n smallest random numbers, each set of n elements has the same probability of being selected for the sample. If we select the sample using this two-step procedure, every sample of size n has the same probability of being selected; thus, the sample selected satisfies the definition of a simple random sample.

TABLE 7.1   NATIONAL BASEBALL LEAGUE TEAMS

Arizona	Milwaukee
Atlanta	Montreal
Chicago	New York
Cincinnati	Philadelphia
Colorado	Pittsburgh
Florida	San Diego
Houston	San Francisco
Los Angeles	St. Louis

Let us consider an example involving selecting a simple random sample of size $n = 5$ from a population of size $N = 16$. Table 7.1 contains a list of the 16 teams in the National Baseball League. Suppose we want to select a simple random sample of 5 teams to conduct in-depth interviews about how they manage their minor league franchises.

Step 1 of our simple random sampling procedure requires that we assign a random number to each of the 16 teams in the population. Figure 7.1 shows a worksheet used to generate a random number corresponding to each of the 16 teams in the population. The names of the baseball teams are in column A, and the random numbers generated are in column B. From the formula worksheet in the background we see that the formula =RAND( ) has been entered into cells B2:B17 to generate the random numbers between 0 and 1. From the value worksheet in the foreground we see that Arizona is assigned the random number .850862, Atlanta has been assigned the random number .706245, and so on.

FIGURE 7.1   WORKSHEET USED TO GENERATE A RANDOM NUMBER
CORRESPONDING TO EACH TEAM

CD file

National League

	A	B	C
1	Team	Random Numbers	
2	Arizona	=RAND()	
3	Atlanta	=RAND()	
4	Chicago	=RAND()	
5	Cincinnati	=RAND()	
6	Colorado	=RAND()	
7	Florida	=RAND()	
8	Houston	=RAND()	
9	Los Angeles	=RAND()	
10	Milwaukee	=RAND()	
11	Montreal	=RAND()	
12	New York	=RAND()	
13	Philadelphia	=RAND()	
14	Pittsburgh	=RAND()	
15	San Diego	=RAND()	
16	San Francisco	=RAND()	
17	St. Louis	=RAND()	
18			

	A	B	C
1	Team	Random Numbers	
2	Arizona	0.850862	
3	Atlanta	0.706245	
4	Chicago	0.724789	
5	Cincinnati	0.614784	
6	Colorado	0.553815	
7	Florida	0.857324	
8	Houston	0.179123	
9	Los Angeles	0.525636	
10	Milwaukee	0.471490	
11	Montreal	0.158452	
12	New York	0.523103	
13	Philadelphia	0.851552	
14	Pittsburgh	0.806185	
15	San Diego	0.327713	
16	San Francisco	0.374168	
17	St. Louis	0.066942	
18			

The second step is to select the five teams corresponding to the five smallest random numbers as our sample. Looking through the random numbers in Figure 7.1, we see that the team corresponding to the smallest random number (.066942) is St. Louis, and that the four teams corresponding to the next four smallest random numbers are Montreal, Houston, San Diego, and San Francisco. Thus, these five teams make up the simple random sample.

Searching through the list of random numbers in Figure 7.1 to find the five smallest random numbers is tedious, and it is easy to make mistakes. Excel's SORT procedure simplifies this step. We illustrate by sorting the list of baseball teams in Figure 7.1 to find the five teams corresponding to the five smallest random numbers. Refer to the foreground worksheet in Figure 7.1 as we describe the steps involved.

Step 1. Select cells A2:B17
Step 2. Select the **Data** menu
Step 3. Choose the **Sort** option
Step 4. When the Sort dialog box appears:
    Choose **Random Numbers** in the **Sort by** text box
    Choose **Ascending**
    Click **OK**

After completing these steps we obtain the worksheet shown in Figure 7.2.* The teams listed in rows 2–6 are the ones corresponding to the smallest five random numbers; they are our simple random sample. Note that the random numbers shown in Figure 7.2 are in ascending order, and that the teams are not in their original order. For instance, St. Louis is the

FIGURE 7.2 USING EXCEL'S SORT PROCEDURE TO SELECT THE SIMPLE RANDOM SAMPLE OF FIVE TEAMS

	A	B	C
1	Team	**Random Numbers**	
2	St. Louis	0.066942	
3	Montreal	0.158452	
4	Houston	0.179123	
5	San Diego	0.327713	
6	San Francisco	0.374168	
7	Milwaukee	0.471490	
8	New York	0.523103	
9	Los Angeles	0.525636	
10	Colorado	0.553815	
11	Cincinnati	0.614784	
12	Atlanta	0.706245	
13	Chicago	0.724789	
14	Pittsburgh	0.806185	
15	Arizona	0.850862	
16	Philadelphia	0.851552	
17	Florida	0.857324	
18			

* In order to show the random numbers from Figure 7.1 in ascending order in this worksheet, we turned off the automatic recalculation option prior to sorting for illustrative purposes. If the recalculation option were not turned off, a new set of random numbers would have been generated when the sort was completed. But the same five teams would be selected.

The Excel sort procedure for identifying the managers associated with the 30 smallest random numbers is especially valuable with such a large population.

last team listed in Figure 7.1, but it is the first team selected in the simple random sample. Montreal, the second team in our sample, is the tenth team in the original list, and so on.

We now use this simple random sampling procedure to select a simple random sample of 30 EAI managers from the population of 2500 EAI managers. We begin by generating 2500 random numbers, one for each manager in the population. Then we select 30 managers corresponding to the 30 smallest random numbers as our sample. Refer to Figure 7.3 as we describe the steps involved.

FIGURE 7.3   USING EXCEL TO SELECT A SIMPLE RANDOM SAMPLE WITHOUT REPLACEMENT

	A	B	C	D
1	**Manager**	**Annual Salary**	**Training Program**	**Random Numbers**
2	1	55769.50	No	0.613872
3	2	50823.00	Yes	0.473204
4	3	48408.20	No	0.549011
5	4	49787.50	No	0.047482
6	5	52801.60	Yes	0.531085
7	6	51767.70	No	0.994296
8	7	58346.60	Yes	0.189065
9	8	46670.20	No	0.020714
10	9	50246.80	Yes	0.647318
11	10	51255.00	No	0.524341
12	11	52546.60	No	0.764998
13	12	49512.50	Yes	0.255244
14	13	51753.00	Yes	0.010923
15	14	53547.10	No	0.238003
16	15	48052.20	No	0.635675
17	16	44652.50	Yes	0.177294
18	17	51764.90	Yes	0.415097
19	18	45187.80	Yes	0.883440
20	19	49867.50	Yes	0.476824
21	20	53706.30	Yes	0.101065
22	21	52039.50	Yes	0.775323
23	22	52973.60	No	0.011729
24	23	53372.50	No	0.762026
25	24	54592.00	Yes	0.066344
26	25	55738.10	Yes	0.776766
27	26	52975.10	Yes	0.828493
28	27	52386.20	Yes	0.841532
29	28	51051.60	Yes	0.899427
30	29	52095.60	Yes	0.486284
31	30	44956.50	No	0.264628

The formula in cells D2:D2501 is =RAND().

Note: Rows 32–2501 are not shown.

	A	B	C	D	E
1	**Manager**	**Annual Salary**	**Training Program**	**Random Numbers**	
2	812	49094.30	Yes	0.000193	
3	1411	53263.90	Yes	0.000484	
4	1795	49643.50	Yes	0.002641	
5	2095	49894.90	Yes	0.002763	
6	1235	47621.60	No	0.002940	
7	744	55924.00	Yes	0.002977	
8	470	49092.30	Yes	0.003182	
9	1606	51404.40	Yes	0.003448	
10	1744	50957.70	Yes	0.004203	
11	179	55109.70	Yes	0.005293	
12	1387	45922.60	Yes	0.005709	
13	1782	57268.40	No	0.005729	
14	1006	55688.80	Yes	0.005796	
15	278	51564.70	No	0.005966	
16	1850	56188.20	No	0.006250	
17	844	51766.00	Yes	0.006708	
18	2028	52541.30	No	0.007767	
19	1654	44980.00	Yes	0.008095	
20	444	51932.60	Yes	0.009686	
21	556	52973.00	Yes	0.009711	
22	2449	45120.90	Yes	0.010595	
23	13	51753.00	Yes	0.010923	
24	2187	54391.80	No	0.011364	
25	1633	50164.20	No	0.011603	
26	22	52973.60	No	0.011729	
27	1530	50241.30	No	0.013570	
28	820	52793.90	No	0.013669	
29	1258	50979.40	Yes	0.014042	
30	2349	55860.90	Yes	0.014532	
31	1698	57309.10	No	0.014539	

Enter Data: The first three columns of the worksheet in the background show the annual salary data and training program status for the first 30 managers in the population of 2500 EAI managers. (The complete worksheet contains all 2500 managers.)

Enter Functions and Formulas: In the background worksheet, the label **Random Numbers** has been entered into cell D1 and the formula =RAND() has been entered into cells D2:D2501 to generate a random number between 0 and 1 for each of the 2500 EAI managers. The random number generated for the first manager is 0.613872, the random number generated for the second manager is 0.473204, and so on.

Apply Tools: All that remains is to find the managers associated with the 30 smallest random numbers. To do so we sort the data in columns A through D into ascending order by the random numbers in column D.

Step 1. Select cells A2:D2501
Step 2. Select the **Data** menu
Step 3. Choose the **Sort** option
Step 4. When the Sort dialog box appears
Choose **Random Numbers** in the **Sort by** text box
Choose **Ascending**
Click **OK**

After completing these steps we obtain the worksheet shown in the foreground of Figure 7.3. The managers listed in rows 2–31 are the ones corresponding to the smallest 30 random numbers that were generated. Hence, this group of 30 managers is a simple random sample. Note that the random numbers shown in the foreground of Figure 7.3 are in ascending order, and that the managers are not in their original order. For instance, manager 812 in the population is associated with the smallest random number and is the first element in the sample, and manager 13 in the population (see row 14 of the background worksheet) has been included as the 22nd observation in the sample (row 23 of the foreground worksheet).

Sampling from an Infinite Population

In practice, a population being studied is usually considered infinite if it involves an ongoing process that makes listing or counting every element in the population impossible.

In some situations, the population is either infinite or so large that for practical purposes it must be treated as infinite. For example, suppose that a fast-food restaurant would like to obtain a profile of its customers by selecting a simple random sample of customers and asking each customer to complete a short questionnaire. In such situations, the ongoing process of customer visits to the restaurant can be viewed as coming from an infinite population. The definition of a simple random sample from an infinite population follows.

SIMPLE RANDOM SAMPLE (INFINITE POPULATION)

A simple random sample from an infinite population is a sample selected such that the following conditions are satisfied.

1. Each element selected comes from the population.
2. Each element is selected independently.

For infinite populations, a sample selection procedure must be specially devised to select the items independently and thus avoid a selection bias that gives higher selection probabilities to certain types of elements.

For the example of selecting a simple random sample of customers at a fast-food restaurant, the first requirement is satisfied by any customer who comes into the restaurant. The second requirement is satisfied by selecting customers independently. The purpose of the second requirement is to prevent selection bias. Selection bias would occur if, for instance, five consecutive customers selected were all friends who arrived together. We might expect these customers to exhibit similar profiles. Selection bias can be avoided by ensuring that the selection of a particular customer does not influence the selection of any other customer. In other words, the customers must be selected independently.

McDonald's, the fast-food restaurant leader, implemented a simple random sampling procedure for just such a situation. The sampling procedure was based on the fact that some customers presented discount coupons. Whenever a customer presented a discount coupon, the next customer served was asked to complete a customer profile questionnaire. Because arriving customers presented discount coupons randomly, and independently, this sampling plan ensured that customers were selected independently. Thus, the two requirements for a simple random sample from an infinite population were satisfied.

Infinite populations are often associated with an ongoing process that operates continuously over time. For example, parts being manufactured on a production line, transactions occurring at a bank, telephone calls arriving at a technical support center, and customers entering stores may all be viewed as coming from an infinite population. In such cases, a creative sampling procedure ensures that no selection bias occurs and that the sample elements are selected independently.

NOTES AND COMMENTS

The number of different simple random samples of size n that can be selected from a finite population of size N is

$$\frac{N!}{n!(N-n)!}$$

In this formula, $N!$ and $n!$ are the factorial computations discussed in Chapter 4. For the EAI problem with $N = 2500$ and $n = 30$, this expression can be used to show that approximately 2.75×10^{69} different simple random samples of 30 EAI managers are possible.

Exercises

Methods

1. Consider a finite population with five elements labeled A, B, C, D, and E. Ten possible simple random samples of size 2 can be selected.
    a. List the 10 samples beginning with AB, AC, and so on.
    b. Using simple random sampling, what is the probability that each sample of size 2 is selected?
    c. Suppose we use Excel's RAND function to assign random numbers to the five elements: A (.7266), B (.0476), C (.2459), D (.0957), E (.9408). List the simple random sample of size 2 that will be selected by using these random numbers.

2. Assume a finite population has 10 elements. Number the elements from 1 to 10 and use the following 10 random numbers to select a sample of size 4.

    .7545   .0936   .0341   .3242   .1449   .9060   .2420   .9773   .5428   .0729

3. The American League consists of 14 baseball teams. Suppose a sample of 5 teams is to be selected to conduct player interviews. The following table lists the 14 teams and the random numbers assigned by Excel's RAND function. Use these random numbers to select a sample of size 5.

American
League

Team	Random Number	Team	Random Number
New York	0.178624	Boston	0.290197
Baltimore	0.578370	Tampa Bay	0.867778
Toronto	0.965807	Minnesota	0.811810
Chicago	0.562178	Cleveland	0.960271
Detroit	0.253574	Kansas City	0.326836
Oakland	0.288287	Anaheim	0.895267
Texas	0.500879	Seattle	0.839071

4. The 10 most active issues on the New York Stock Exchange on September 17, 2004, are listed here (*The Sun News,* September 18, 2004).

| Nortel | General Electric | Lucent | Pfizer | Texas Instruments |
| Exxon/Mobil | Citigroup | Wal-Mart | EMC | Motorola |

Exchange authorities decided to sample three of these companies to investigate trading practices. Select a simple random sample of three companies for this investigation.

EAI

5. In this section we used a two-step procedure to select a simple random sample of 30 EAI managers. Use this procedure to select a simple random sample of 50 EAI managers.

6. Indicate whether the following populations should be considered finite or infinite.
   a. All registered voters in the state of California
   b. All television sets that could be produced by the Allentown, Pennsylvania, plant of the TV-M Company
   c. All orders that could be processed by a mail-order firm
   d. All emergency telephone calls that could come into a local police station
   e. All components that Fibercon, Inc., produced on the second shift on May 17

7.3　Point Estimation

Now that we described how to select a simple random sample, let us return to the sample selected for the EAI problem. The simple random sample of 30 managers selected using Excel and the corresponding data on annual salary and management training program participation are as shown in Table 7.2. The notation x_1, x_2, and so on is used to denote the annual salary of the first manager in the sample, the annual salary of the second manager in the sample, and so on. Participation in the management training program is indicated by Yes in the management training program column.

To estimate the value of a population parameter, we compute a corresponding characteristic of the sample, referred to as a **sample statistic**. For example, to estimate the population mean μ and the population standard deviation σ for the annual salary of EAI managers, we use the data in Table 7.2 to calculate the corresponding sample statistics: the sample mean $\bar{x}$ and the sample standard deviation s. Using the formulas for a sample mean and a sample standard deviation presented in Chapter 3, the sample mean is

$$\bar{x} = \frac{\Sigma x_i}{n} = \frac{1{,}554{,}420}{30} = \$51{,}814$$

TABLE 7.2 ANNUAL SALARY AND TRAINING PROGRAM STATUS FOR A SIMPLE
RANDOM SAMPLE OF 30 EAI MANAGERS

Annual Salary ($)	Management Training Program	Annual Salary ($)	Management Training Program
$x_1 = 49,094.30$	Yes	$x_{16} = 51,766.00$	Yes
$x_2 = 53,263.90$	Yes	$x_{17} = 52,541.30$	No
$x_3 = 49,643.50$	Yes	$x_{18} = 44,980.00$	Yes
$x_4 = 49,894.90$	Yes	$x_{19} = 51,932.60$	Yes
$x_5 = 47,621.60$	No	$x_{20} = 52,973.00$	Yes
$x_6 = 55,924.00$	Yes	$x_{21} = 45,120.90$	Yes
$x_7 = 49,092.30$	Yes	$x_{22} = 51,753.00$	Yes
$x_8 = 51,404.40$	Yes	$x_{23} = 54,391.80$	No
$x_9 = 50,957.70$	Yes	$x_{24} = 50,164.20$	No
$x_{10} = 55,109.70$	Yes	$x_{25} = 52,973.60$	No
$x_{11} = 45,922.60$	Yes	$x_{26} = 50,241.30$	No
$x_{12} = 57,268.40$	No	$x_{27} = 52,793.90$	No
$x_{13} = 55,688.80$	Yes	$x_{28} = 50,979.40$	Yes
$x_{14} = 51,564.70$	No	$x_{29} = 55,860.90$	Yes
$x_{15} = 56,188.20$	No	$x_{30} = 57,309.10$	No

and the sample standard deviation is

$$s = \sqrt{\frac{\Sigma(x_i - \bar{x})^2}{n - 1}} = \sqrt{\frac{325,009,260}{29}} = \$3348$$

To estimate p, the proportion of managers in the population who completed the management training program, we use the corresponding sample proportion $\bar{p}$. Let x denote the number of managers in the sample who completed the management training program. The data in Table 7.2 show that $x = 19$. Thus, with a sample size of $n = 30$, the sample proportion is

$$\bar{p} = \frac{x}{n} = \frac{19}{30} = .63$$

By making the preceding computations, we perform the statistical procedure called *point estimation.* We refer to the sample mean $\bar{x}$ as the **point estimator** of the population mean μ, the sample standard deviation s as the point estimator of the population standard deviation σ, and the sample proportion $\bar{p}$ as the point estimator of the population proportion p. The numerical value obtained for $\bar{x}$, s, or $\bar{p}$ is called the **point estimate**. Thus, for the simple random sample of 30 EAI managers shown in Table 7.2, $51,814 is the point estimate of μ, $3348 is the point estimate of σ, and .63 is the point estimate of p. Table 7.3 summarizes the sample results and compares the point estimates to the actual values of the population parameters.

As evident from Table 7.3, the point estimates differ somewhat from the corresponding population parameters. This difference is to be expected because a sample, and not the entire population, is being used to develop the point estimates. In the next chapter, we will show how to construct an interval estimate in order to provide information about how close the point estimate is to the population parameter.

TABLE 7.3   SUMMARY OF POINT ESTIMATES OBTAINED FROM A SIMPLE RANDOM
SAMPLE OF 30 EAI MANAGERS

Population Parameter	Parameter Value	Point Estimator	Point Estimate
μ = Population mean annual salary	$51,800	$\bar{x}$ = Sample mean annual salary	$51,814
σ = Population standard deviation for annual salary	$4000	s = Sample standard deviation for annual salary	$3348
p = Population proportion having completed the management training program	.60	$\bar{p}$ = Sample proportion having completed the management training program	.63

NOTES AND COMMENTS

In our discussion of point estimators, we use $\bar{x}$ to denote a sample mean and $\bar{p}$ to denote a sample proportion. Our use of $\bar{p}$ is based on the fact that the sample proportion is also a *sample mean*. Suppose that in a sample of size n with data values $x_1, x_2, \ldots,$ x_n, we let $x_i = 1$ when a characteristic of interest is present for the ith observation and $x_i = 0$ when the characteristic is not present. Then the sample pro-portion is computed by $\Sigma x_i/n$, which is the formula for a sample mean. We also like the consistency of using the bar over the letter to remind the reader that the sample proportion $\bar{p}$ estimates the population proportion just as the sample mean $\bar{x}$ estimates the population mean. Some texts use $\hat{p}$ instead of $\bar{p}$ to denote the sample proportion.

Exercises

Methods

7. The following data are from a simple random sample.

    5   8   10   7   10   14

    a.   What is the point estimate of the population mean?
    b.   What is the point estimate of the population standard deviation?

8. A survey question for a sample of 150 individuals yielded 75 Yes responses, 55 No responses, and 20 No Opinions.
    a.   What is the point estimate of the proportion in the population who respond Yes?
    b.   What is the point estimate of the proportion in the population who respond No?

Applications

9. A simple random sample of five months of sales data provided the following information:

Month	1	2	3	4	5
Units Sold	94	100	85	94	92

    a.   Develop a point estimate of the population mean number of units sold per month.
    b.   Develop a point estimate of the population standard deviation.

MutualFund

10. *BusinessWeek* published information on 283 equity mutual funds (*BusinessWeek*, January 26, 2004). A sample of 40 of those funds is contained in the data set MutualFund. Use the data set to answer the following questions.
    a.   Develop a point estimate of the proportion of the *BusinessWeek* equity funds that are load funds.

b.   Develop a point estimate of the proportion of funds that are classified as high risk.
c.   Develop a point estimate of the proportion of funds that have a below-average risk rating.

11.   *Appliance Magazine* provided estimates of the life expectancy of household appliances (*USA Today,* September 5, 2000). A simple random sample of 10 VCRs shows the following useful life in years.

$$6.5 \quad 8.0 \quad 6.2 \quad 7.4 \quad 7.0 \quad 8.4 \quad 9.5 \quad 4.6 \quad 5.0 \quad 7.4$$

a.   Develop a point estimate of the population mean life expectancy for VCRs.
b.   Develop a point estimate of the population standard deviation for life expectancy of VCRs.

12.   A sample of 50 *Fortune* 500 companies (*Fortune,* April 14, 2003) showed 5 were based in New York, 6 in California, 2 in Minnesota, and 1 in Wisconsin.
a.   Develop an estimate of the proportion of *Fortune* 500 companies based in New York.
b.   Develop an estimate of the number of *Fortune* 500 companies based in Minnesota.
c.   Develop an estimate of the proportion of *Fortune* 500 companies that are not based in these four states.

13.   A Louis Harris poll used a survey of 1008 adults to learn about how people feel about the economy (*BusinessWeek,* August 7, 2000). Responses were as follows:

595 adults   The economy is growing.
332 adults   The economy is staying about the same.
 81 adults   The economy is shrinking.

Develop a point estimate of the following population parameters.
a.   The proportion of all adults who feel the economy is growing
b.   The proportion of all adults who feel the economy is staying about the same
c.   The proportion of all adults who feel the economy is shrinking

14.   In this section we showed how a simple random sample of 30 EAI managers can be used to develop point estimates of the population mean annual salary, the population standard deviation for annual salary, and the population proportion having completed the management training program.

CD file

EAI

a.   Use Excel to select a simple random sample of 50 EAI managers.
b.   Develop a point estimate of the mean annual salary.
c.   Develop a point estimate of the population standard deviation for annual salary.
d.   Develop a point estimate of the population proportion having completed the management training program.

7.4   Introduction to Sampling Distributions

In the preceding section we said that the sample mean $\bar{x}$ is the point estimator of the population mean μ, and the sample proportion $\bar{p}$ is the point estimator of the population proportion p. For the simple random sample of 30 EAI managers shown in Table 7.2, the point estimate of μ is $\bar{x} = \$51,814$ and the point estimate of p is $\bar{p} = .63$. Suppose we select another simple random sample of 30 EAI managers and obtain the following point estimates:

Sample mean: $\bar{x} = \$52,670$
Sample proportion: $\bar{p} = .70$

Note that different values of $\bar{x}$ and $\bar{p}$ were obtained. Indeed, a second simple random sample of 30 EAI managers cannot be expected to provide the same point estimates as the first sample.

Now, suppose we repeat the process of selecting a simple random sample of 30 EAI managers over and over again, each time computing the values of $\bar{x}$ and $\bar{p}$. Table 7.4 contains a portion of the results obtained for 500 simple random samples, and Table 7.5 shows

TABLE 7.4   VALUES OF $\bar{x}$ AND $\bar{p}$ FROM 500 SIMPLE RANDOM SAMPLES OF 30 EAI MANAGERS

Sample Number	Sample Mean ($\bar{x}$)	Sample Proportion ($\bar{p}$)
1	51,814	.63
2	52,670	.70
3	51,780	.67
4	51,588	.53
.	.	.
.	.	.
.	.	.
500	51,752	.50

the frequency and relative frequency distributions for the 500 $\bar{x}$ values. Figure 7.4 shows the relative frequency histogram for the $\bar{x}$ values.

In Chapter 5 we defined a random variable as a numerical description of the outcome of an experiment. If we consider the process of selecting a simple random sample as an experiment, the sample mean $\bar{x}$ is a numerical description of the outcome of the experiment. Thus, the sample mean $\bar{x}$ is a random variable. As a result, just like other random variables, $\bar{x}$ has a mean or expected value, a standard deviation, and a probability distribution. Because the various possible values of $\bar{x}$ are the result of different simple random samples, the probability distribution of $\bar{x}$ is called the **sampling distribution** of $\bar{x}$. Knowledge of this sampling distribution and its properties will enable us to make probability statements about how close the sample mean $\bar{x}$ is to the population mean μ.

Let us return to Figure 7.4. We would need to enumerate every possible sample of 30 managers and compute each sample mean to completely determine the sampling distribution of $\bar{x}$. However, the histogram of 500 $\bar{x}$ values gives an approximation of this sampling distribution. From the approximation we observe the bell-shaped appearance of the distribution. We note that the largest concentration of the $\bar{x}$ values and the mean of the 500 $\bar{x}$ values are near the population mean $\mu = \$51,800$. We will describe the properties of the sampling distribution of $\bar{x}$ more fully in the next section.

The 500 values of the sample proportion $\bar{p}$ are summarized by the relative frequency histogram in Figure 7.5. As in the case of $\bar{x}$, $\bar{p}$ is a random variable. If every possible sample

TABLE 7.5   FREQUENCY DISTRIBUTION OF $\bar{x}$ FROM 500 SIMPLE RANDOM SAMPLES OF 30 EAI MANAGERS

Mean Annual Salary ($)	Frequency	Relative Frequency
49,500.00–49,999.99	2	.004
50,000.00–50,499.99	16	.032
50,500.00–50,999.99	52	.104
51,000.00–51,499.99	101	.202
51,500.00–51,999.99	133	.266
52,000.00–52,499.99	110	.220
52,500.00–52,999.99	54	.108
53,000.00–53,499.99	26	.052
53,500.00–53,999.99	6	.012
Totals	500	1.000

FIGURE 7.4 RELATIVE FREQUENCY HISTOGRAM OF $\bar{x}$ VALUES FROM 500 SIMPLE RANDOM SAMPLES OF 30 EAI MANAGERS

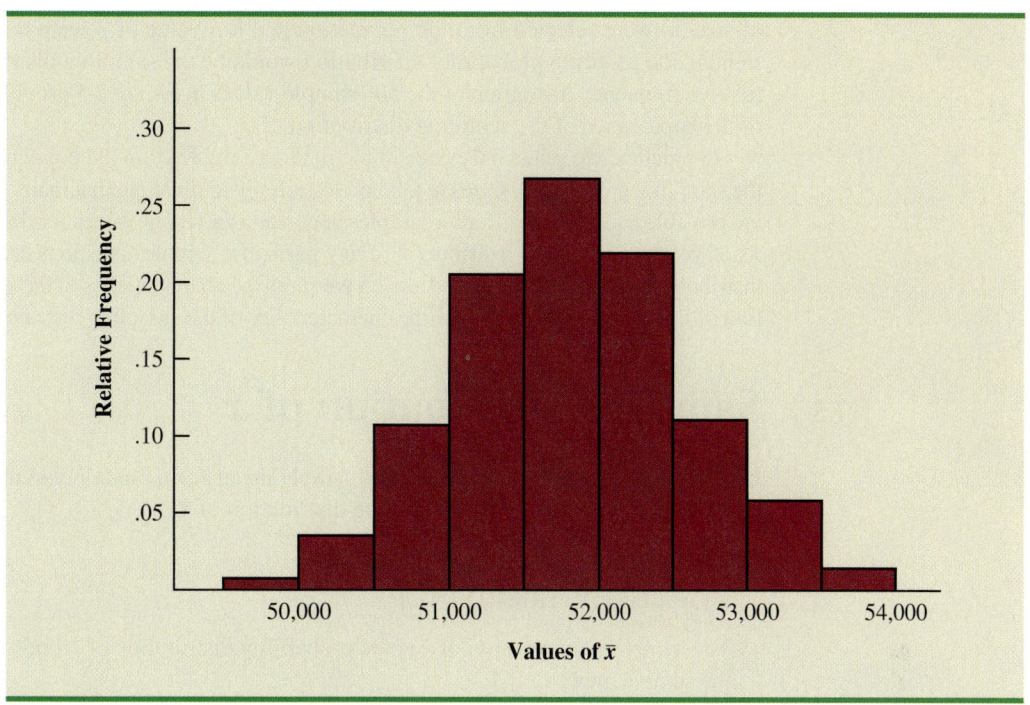

FIGURE 7.5 RELATIVE FREQUENCY HISTOGRAM OF $\bar{p}$ VALUES FROM 500 SIMPLE RANDOM SAMPLES OF 30 EAI MANAGERS

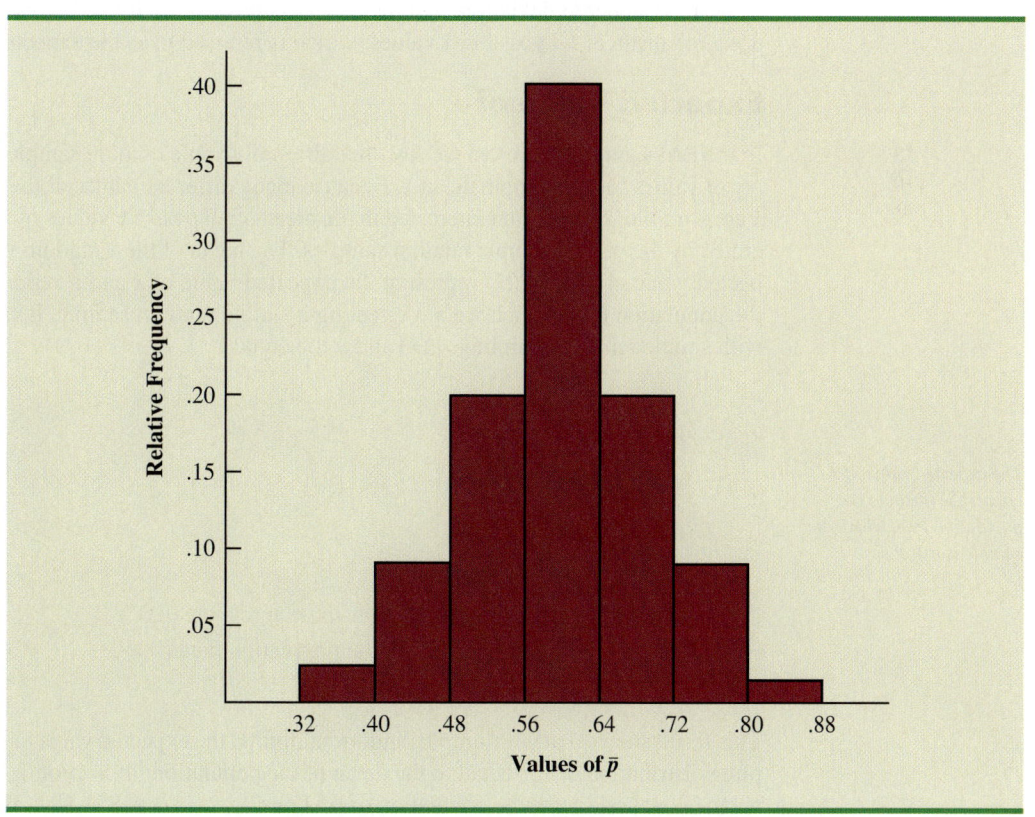

of size 30 were selected from the population and if a value of $\bar{p}$ were computed for each sample, the resulting probability distribution would be the sampling distribution of $\bar{p}$. The relative frequency histogram of the 500 sample values in Figure 7.5 provides a general idea of the appearance of the sampling distribution of $\bar{p}$.

In practice, we select only one simple random sample from the population. We repeated the sampling process 500 times in this section simply to illustrate that many different samples are possible and that the different samples generate a variety of values for the sample statistics $\bar{x}$ and $\bar{p}$. The probability distribution of any particular sample statistic is called the sampling distribution of the statistic. In Section 7.5 we show the characteristics of the sampling distribution of $\bar{x}$. In Section 7.6 we show the characteristics of the sampling distribution of $\bar{p}$.

7.5   Sampling Distribution of $\bar{x}$

In the previous section we said that the sample mean $\bar{x}$ is a random variable and its probability distribution is called the sampling distribution of $\bar{x}$.

> **SAMPLING DISTRIBUTION OF $\bar{x}$**
>
> The sampling distribution of $\bar{x}$ is the probability distribution of all possible values of the sample mean $\bar{x}$.

This section describes the properties of the sampling distribution of $\bar{x}$. Just as with other probability distributions we studied, the sampling distribution of $\bar{x}$ has an expected value or mean, a standard deviation, and a characteristic shape or form. Let us begin by considering the mean of all possible $\bar{x}$ values, which is referred to as the expected value of $\bar{x}$.

Expected Value of $\bar{x}$

In the EAI sampling problem we saw that different simple random samples result in a variety of values for the sample mean $\bar{x}$. Because many different values of the random variable $\bar{x}$ are possible, we are often interested in the mean of all possible values of $\bar{x}$ that can be generated by the various simple random samples. The mean of the $\bar{x}$ random variable is the expected value of $\bar{x}$. Let $E(\bar{x})$ represent the expected value of $\bar{x}$ and μ represent the mean of the population from which we are selecting a simple random sample. It can be shown that with simple random sampling, $E(\bar{x})$ and μ are equal.

> **EXPECTED VALUE OF $\bar{x}$**
>
> *The expected value of $\bar{x}$ equals the mean of the population from which the sample is selected.*
>
> $$E(\bar{x}) = \mu \tag{7.1}$$
>
> where
>
> $$E(\bar{x}) = \text{the expected value of } \bar{x}$$
> $$\mu = \text{the population mean}$$

This result shows that with simple random sampling, the expected value or mean of the sampling distribution of $\bar{x}$ is equal to the mean of the population. In Section 7.1 we saw that the mean annual salary for the population of EAI managers is $\mu = \$51,800$. Thus, according to equation (7.1), the mean of all possible sample means for the EAI study is also $\$51,800$.

When the expected value of a point estimator equals the population parameter, we say the point estimator is **unbiased**. Thus, equation (7.1) shows that $\bar{x}$ is an unbiased estimator of the population mean μ.

Standard Deviation of $\bar{x}$

Let us define the standard deviation of the sampling distribution of $\bar{x}$. We will use the following notation.

$$\sigma_{\bar{x}} = \text{the standard deviation of } \bar{x}$$
$$\sigma = \text{the standard deviation of the population}$$
$$n = \text{the sample size}$$
$$N = \text{the population size}$$

It can be shown that with simple random sampling, the standard deviation of $\bar{x}$ depends on whether the population is finite or infinite. The two formulas for the standard deviation of $\bar{x}$ follow.

STANDARD DEVIATION OF $\bar{x}$

Finite Population	*Infinite Population*	
$\sigma_{\bar{x}} = \sqrt{\dfrac{N-n}{N-1}}\left(\dfrac{\sigma}{\sqrt{n}}\right)$	$\sigma_{\bar{x}} = \dfrac{\sigma}{\sqrt{n}}$	**(7.2)**

In comparing the two formulas shown above, we see that the factor $\sqrt{(N-n)/(N-1)}$ is required for the finite population case but not for the infinite population case. This factor is commonly referred to as the **finite population correction factor**. In many practical sampling situations, we find that the population involved, although finite, is "large," whereas the sample size is relatively "small." In such cases the finite population correction factor $\sqrt{(N-n)/(N-1)}$ is close to 1. As a result, the difference between the values of the standard deviation of $\bar{x}$ for the finite and infinite population cases becomes negligible. Then, $\sigma_{\bar{x}} = \sigma/\sqrt{n}$ becomes a good approximation to the standard deviation of $\bar{x}$ even though the population is finite. This observation leads to the following general guideline, or rule of thumb, for computing the standard deviation of $\bar{x}$.

USE THE FOLLOWING EXPRESSION TO COMPUTE THE STANDARD DEVIATION OF $\bar{x}$

$$\sigma_{\bar{x}} = \frac{\sigma}{\sqrt{n}} \qquad \textbf{(7.3)}$$

whenever

1. The population is infinite; or
2. The population is finite *and* the sample size is less than or equal to 5% of the population size; that is, $n/N \le .05$.

Problem 17 shows that when $n/N \le .05$, the finite population correction factor has little effect on the value of $\sigma_{\bar{x}}$.

In cases where $n/N > .05$, the finite population version of formula (7.2) should be used in the computation of $\sigma_{\bar{x}}$. Unless otherwise noted, throughout the text we will assume that the population size is "large," $n/N \le .05$, and expression (7.3) can be used to compute $\sigma_{\bar{x}}$.

The term standard error *is used to refer to the standard deviation of a point estimator.*

Equation (7.3) shows that we need to know σ, the standard deviation of the population to compute $\sigma_{\bar{x}}$. To emphasize the difference between $\sigma_{\bar{x}}$ and σ, we refer to the standard deviation of $\bar{x}$, $\sigma_{\bar{x}}$, as the **standard error** of the mean. In general, the term *standard error* refers to the standard deviation of a point estimator. Later we will see that the value of the standard error of the mean is helpful in determining how far the sample mean may be from the population mean. Let us now return to the EAI example and compute the standard error of the mean associated with simple random samples of 30 EAI managers.

In Section 7.1 we saw that the standard deviation of annual salary for the population of 2500 EAI managers is $\sigma = 4000$. In this case, the population is finite, with $N = 2500$. However, with a sample size of 30, we have $n/N = 30/2500 = .012$. Because the sample size is less than 5% of the population size, we can ignore the finite population correction factor and use equation (7.3) to compute the standard error.

$$\sigma_{\bar{x}} = \frac{\sigma}{\sqrt{n}} = \frac{4000}{\sqrt{30}} = 730.3$$

Form of the Sampling Distribution of $\bar{x}$

The preceding results concerning the expected value and standard deviation for the sampling distribution of $\bar{x}$ are applicable for any population. The final step in identifying the characteristics of the sampling distribution of $\bar{x}$ is to determine the form or shape of the sampling distribution. We will consider two cases: (1) the population has a normal distribution; and (2) the population does not have a normal distribution.

Population Has a Normal Distribution In many situations it is reasonable to assume that the population from which we are selecting a simple random sample has a normal, or nearly normal, distribution. When the population has a normal distribution, the sampling distribution of $\bar{x}$ is normally distributed for any sample size.

Population Does Not Have a Normal Distribution When the population from which we are selecting a simple random sample does not have a normal distribution, the **central limit theorem** is helpful in identifying the shape of the sampling distribution of $\bar{x}$. A statement of the central limit theorem as it applies to the sampling distribution of $\bar{x}$ follows.

CENTRAL LIMIT THEOREM

In selecting simple random samples of size n from a population, the sampling distribution of the sample mean $\bar{x}$ can be approximated by a *normal distribution* as the sample size becomes large.

Figure 7.6 shows how the central limit theorem works for three different populations; each column refers to one of the populations. The top panel of the figure shows that none of the populations are normally distributed. Population I follows a uniform distribution. Population II is often called the rabbit-eared distribution. It is symmetric, but the more likely values fall in the tails of the distribution. Population III is shaped like the exponential distribution; it is skewed to the right.

The bottom three panels of Figure 7.6 show the shape of the sampling distribution for samples of size $n = 2$, $n = 5$, and $n = 30$. When the sample size is 2, we see that the shape of each sampling distribution is different from the shape of the corresponding population distribution. For samples of size 5, we see that the shape of the sampling distributions for Populations I and II already look similar to the shape of a normal distribution. Even though

FIGURE 7.6   ILLUSTRATION OF THE CENTRAL LIMIT THEOREM
FOR THREE POPULATIONS

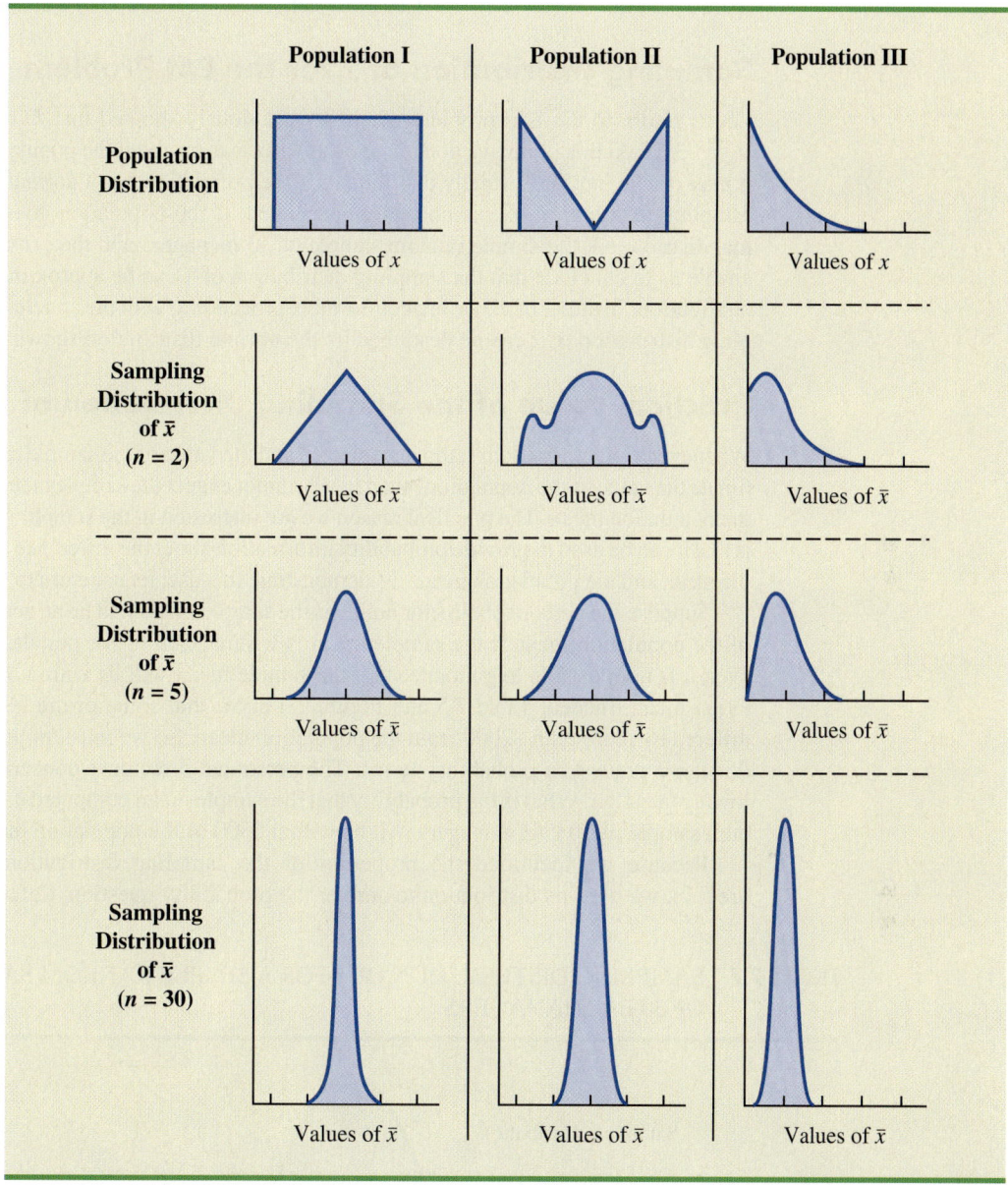

the shape of the sampling distribution for Population III begins to look similar to the shape of a normal distribution, some skewness to the right is still present. Finally, for samples of size 30, the shapes of each of the three sampling distributions are approximately normal.

From a practitioner standpoint, we often want to know how large the sample size needs to be before the central limit theorem applies and we can assume that the shape of the sampling distribution is approximately normal. Statistical researchers have investigated this question by studying the sampling distribution of $\bar{x}$ for a variety of populations and a variety of sample sizes. General statistical practice is to assume that, for most applications, the sampling distribution of $\bar{x}$ can be approximated by a normal distribution whenever the sample is size 30 or more. In cases where the population is highly skewed or outliers are present, samples of size 50 may be needed. Finally, if the population is discrete, the sample size needed for a normal approximation often depends on the population proportion. We say more about this issue when we discuss the sampling distribution of $\bar{p}$ in Section 7.6.

Sampling Distribution of $\bar{x}$ for the EAI Problem

Let us return to the EAI problem where we previously showed that $E(\bar{x}) = \$51,800$ and $\sigma_{\bar{x}} = 730.3$. At this point, we do not have any information about the population distribution; it may or may not be normally distributed. If the population has a normal distribution, the sampling distribution of $\bar{x}$ is normally distributed. If the population does not have a normal distribution, the simple random sample of 30 managers and the central limit theorem enable us to conclude that the sampling distribution of $\bar{x}$ can be approximated by a normal distribution. In either case, we are comfortable proceeding with the conclusion that the sampling distribution of $\bar{x}$ can be described by the normal distribution shown in Figure 7.7.

Practical Value of the Sampling Distribution of $\bar{x}$

Whenever a simple random sample is selected and the value of the sample mean is used to estimate the value of the population mean μ, we cannot expect the sample mean to exactly equal the population mean. The practical reason we are interested in the sampling distribution of $\bar{x}$ is that it can be used to provide probability information about the difference between the sample mean and the population mean. To demonstrate this use, let us return to the EAI problem.

Suppose the personnel director believes the sample mean will be an acceptable estimate of the population mean if the sample mean is within \$500 of the population mean. However, it is not possible to guarantee that the sample mean will be within \$500 of the population mean. Indeed, Table 7.5 and Figure 7.4 show that some of the 500 sample means differed by more than \$2000 from the population mean. So we must think of the personnel director's request in probability terms: The personnel director is concerned with the following question: What is the probability that the sample mean computed using a simple random sample of 30 EAI managers will be within \$500 of the population mean?

Because we identified the properties of the sampling distribution of $\bar{x}$ (see Figure 7.7), we use this distribution to answer the probability question. Refer to the sampling

FIGURE 7.7   SAMPLING DISTRIBUTION OF $\bar{x}$ FOR A SIMPLE RANDOM SAMPLE OF 30 EAI MANAGERS

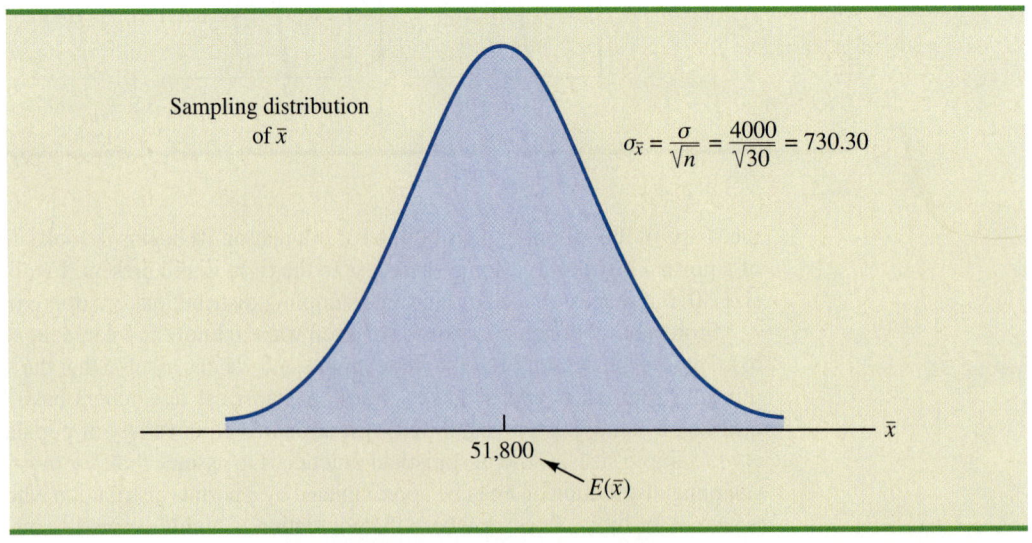

FIGURE 7.8 PROBABILITY OF A SAMPLE MEAN BEING WITHIN $500 OF THE POPULATION MEAN FOR A SIMPLE RANDOM SAMPLE OF 30 EAI MANAGERS

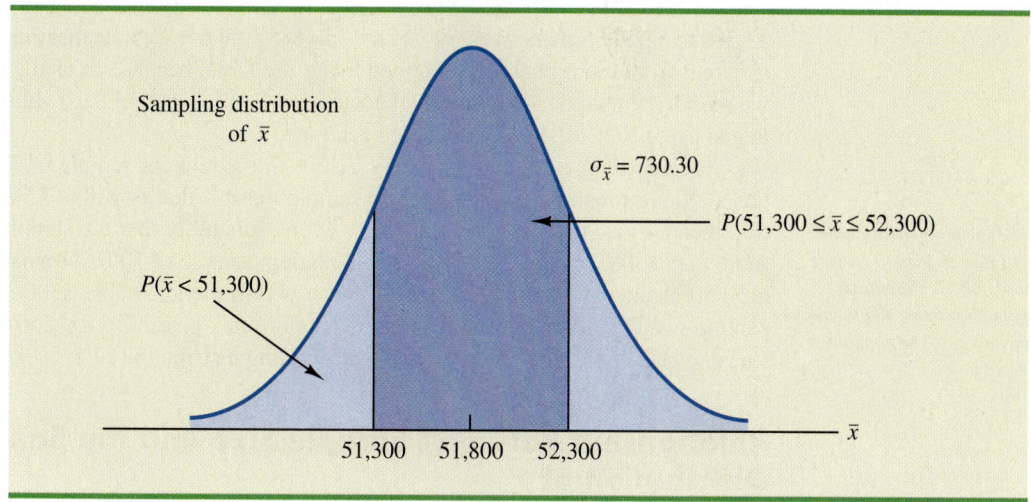

distribution of $\bar{x}$ shown again in Figure 7.8. With a population mean of $51,800, the personnel director wants to know the probability that $\bar{x}$ is between $51,300 and $52,300. This probability is given by the darkly shaded area of the sampling distribution shown in Figure 7.8. Because the sampling distribution is normally distributed, with mean 51,800 and standard error of the mean 730.3, we can use the standard normal probability table to find the area or probability.

We first calculate the z value at the upper endpoint of the interval (52,300) and use the table to find the area under the curve to the left of that point (left tail area). Then we compute the z value at the lower endpoint of the interval (51,300) and use the table to find the area under the curve to the left of that point (another left tail area). Subtracting the second tail area from the first gives us the desired probability.

At $\bar{x} = 52,300$, we have

$$z = \frac{52,300 - 51,800}{730.30} = .68$$

Referring to the standard normal probability table, we find a cumulative probability (area to the left of $z = .68$) of .7517.

At $\bar{x} = 51,300$, we have

$$z = \frac{51,300 - 51,800}{730.30} = -.68$$

The area under the curve to the left of $z = -.68$ is .2483. Therefore, $P(51,300 \leq \bar{x} \leq 52,300) = P(z \leq .68) - P(z < -.68) = .7517 - .2483 = .5034$.

The desired probability can also be computed using Excel's NORMDIST function. The advantage of using the NORMDIST function is that we do not have to make a separate computation of the z value. Evaluating the NORMDIST function at the upper endpoint of the interval provides the area under the curve to the left of 52,300. Entering the formula =NORMDIST(52300,51800,730.30,TRUE) into a cell of an Excel worksheet provides

Using Excel's NORMDIST function is easier and provides more accurate results than the tables.

.7532 for this cumulative probability. Evaluating the NORMDIST function at the lower endpoint of the interval provides the area under the curve to the left of 51,300. Entering the formula =NORMDIST(51300,51800,730.30,TRUE) into a cell of an Excel worksheet provides .2468 for this cumulative probability. The probability of $\bar{x}$ being in the interval from 51,300 to 52,300 is then given by .7532 − .2468 = .5064. We note that this result is slightly different from the probability obtained using the table, because in using the normal table we rounded to two decimal places of accuracy when computing the z value. The result obtained using NORMDIST is thus more accurate.

The preceding computations show that a simple random sample of 30 EAI managers has a .5064 probability of providing a sample mean $\bar{x}$ that is within $500 of the population mean. Thus, there is a 1 − .5064 = .4936 probability that the sampling error will be more than $500. In other words, a simple random sample of 30 EAI managers has roughly a 50-50 chance of providing a sample mean within the allowable $500. Perhaps a larger sample size should be considered. Let us explore this possibility by considering the relationship between the sample size and the sampling distribution of $\bar{x}$.

The sampling distribution of $\bar{x}$ can be used to provide probability information about how close the sample mean $\bar{x}$ is to the population mean μ.

Relationship Between Sample Size and the Sampling Distribution of $\bar{x}$

Suppose that in the EAI sampling problem we select a simple random sample of 100 EAI managers instead of the 30 originally considered. Intuitively, it would seem that with more data provided by the larger sample size, the sample mean based on $n = 100$ should provide a better estimate of the population mean than the sample mean based on $n = 30$. To see how much better, let us consider the relationship between the sample size and the sampling distribution of $\bar{x}$.

First note that $E(\bar{x}) = \mu$ regardless of the sample size. Thus, the mean of all possible values of $\bar{x}$ is equal to the population mean μ regardless of the sample size n. However, note that the standard error of the mean, $\sigma_{\bar{x}} = \sigma/\sqrt{n}$, is related to the square root of the sample size. Whenever the sample size is increased, the standard error of the mean $\sigma_{\bar{x}}$ is decreased. With $n = 30$, the standard error of the mean for the EAI problem is 730.30. However, with the increase in the sample size to $n = 100$, the standard error of the mean is decreased to

$$\sigma_{\bar{x}} = \frac{\sigma}{\sqrt{n}} = \frac{4000}{\sqrt{100}} = 400$$

The sampling distributions of $\bar{x}$ with $n = 30$ and $n = 100$ are shown in Figure 7.9. Because the sampling distribution with $n = 100$ provides a smaller standard error, the values of $\bar{x}$ vary less and tend to be grouped closer around the population mean than the values of $\bar{x}$ with $n = 30$.

We can use the sampling distribution of $\bar{x}$ for the case with $n = 100$ to compute the probability that a simple random sample of 100 EAI managers will provide a sample mean that is within $500 of the population mean. In this case the sampling distribution is normal with a mean of 51,800 and a standard deviation of 400 (see Figure 7.10). Again, we could compute the appropriate z values and use the standard normal probability distribution table to make this probability calculation. However, Excel's NORMDIST function is easier to use and provides more accurate results. Entering the formula =NORMDIST(52300,51800,400,TRUE) into a cell of an Excel worksheet provides the cumulative probability corresponding to $\bar{x} = 52,300$. The value provided by Excel is .8944. Entering the formula =NORMDIST (51300,51800,400,TRUE) into a cell of an Excel worksheet provides the cumulative proba-

FIGURE 7.9   COMPARISON OF THE SAMPLING DISTRIBUTIONS OF $\bar{x}$ FOR SIMPLE
RANDOM SAMPLES OF $n = 30$ AND $n = 100$ EAI MANAGERS

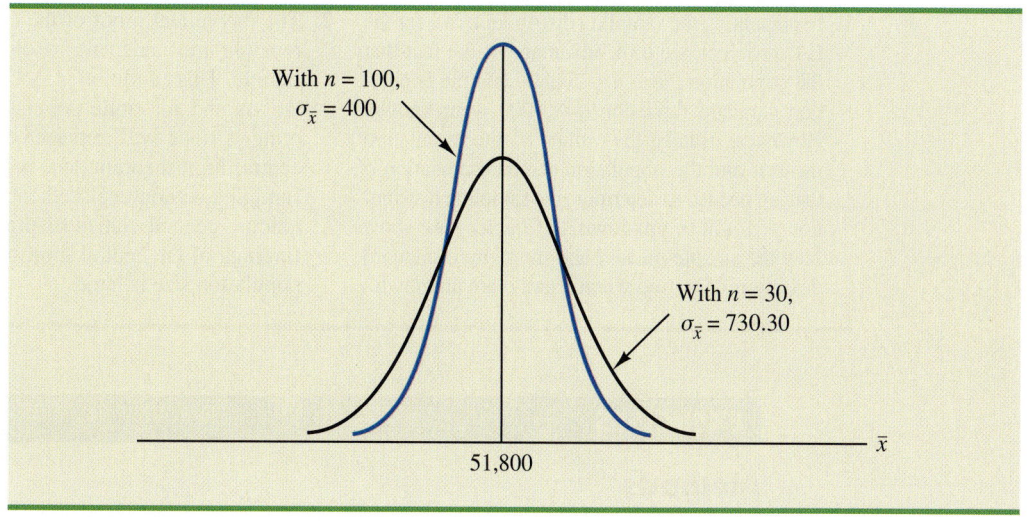

bility corresponding to $\bar{x} = 51,300$. The value provided by Excel is .1056. Thus, the probability of $\bar{x}$ being in the interval from 51,300 to 52,300 is given by .8944 − .1056 = .7888.
By increasing the sample size from 30 to 100 EAI managers, we increase the probability that
the sampling error will be $500 or less; that is, the probability of obtaining a sample mean
within $500 of the population mean increases from .5064 to .7888.

   The important point in this discussion is that as the sample size increases, the standard
error of the mean decreases. As a result, a larger sample size will provide a higher probability that the sample mean falls within a specified distance of the population mean.

FIGURE 7.10   PROBABILITY OF A SAMPLE MEAN BEING WITHIN $500
OF THE POPULATION MEAN FOR A SIMPLE RANDOM SAMPLE
OF 100 EAI MANAGERS

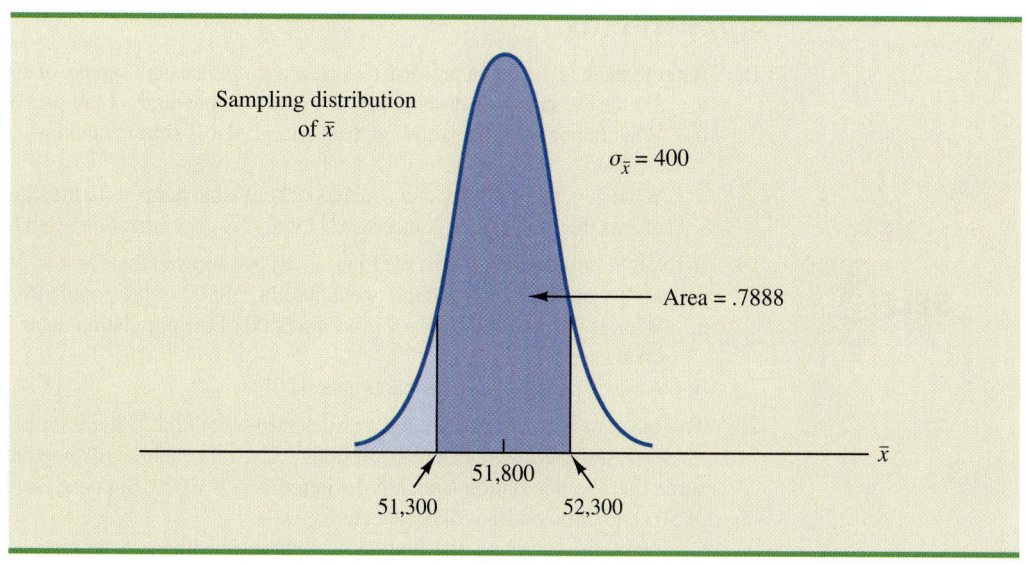

NOTES AND COMMENTS

1. In presenting the sampling distribution of $\bar{x}$ for the EAI problem, we took advantage of the fact that the population mean $\mu = 51,800$ and the population standard deviation $\sigma = 4000$ were known. However, usually the values of the population mean μ and the population standard deviation σ that are needed to determine the sampling distribution of $\bar{x}$ will be unknown. In Chapter 8 we show how the sample mean $\bar{x}$ and the sample standard deviation s are used when μ and σ are unknown.

2. The theoretical proof of the central limit theorem requires independent observations in the sample. This condition is met for infinite populations and for finite populations where sampling is done with replacement. Although the central limit theorem does not directly address sampling without replacement from finite populations, general statistical practice applies the findings of the central limit theorem when the population size is large.

EXERCISES

Methods

15. In a population with a mean of 200 and a standard deviation of 50, suppose a simple random sample of size 100 is selected and $\bar{x}$ is used to estimate μ.
    a. What is the probability that the sample mean will be within ± 5 of the population mean?
    b. What is the probability that the sample mean will be within ± 10 of the population mean?

16. Assume the population standard deviation is $\sigma = 25$. Compute the standard error of the mean, $\sigma_{\bar{x}}$, for sample sizes of 50, 100, 150, and 200. What can you say about the size of the standard error of the mean as the sample size is increased?

17. Suppose a simple random sample of size 50 is selected from a population with $\sigma = 10$. Find the value of the standard error of the mean in each of the following cases (use the finite population correction factor if appropriate).
    a. The population size is infinite.
    b. The population size is $N = 50,000$.
    c. The population size is $N = 5000$.
    d. The population size is $N = 500$.

Applications

18. Refer to the EAI sampling problem. Suppose a simple random sample of 60 managers is used.
    a. Sketch the sampling distribution of $\bar{x}$ when simple random samples of size 60 are used.
    b. What happens to the sampling distribution of $\bar{x}$ if simple random samples of size 120 are used?
    c. What general statement can you make about what happens to the sampling distribution of $\bar{x}$ as the sample size is increased? Does this generalization seem logical? Explain.

19. In the EAI sampling problem (see Figure 7.8), we showed that for $n = 30$, there was .5034 probability of obtaining a sample mean within $\pm\$500$ of the population mean.
    a. What is the probability that $\bar{x}$ is within $\$500$ of the population mean if a sample of size 60 is used?
    b. Answer part (a) for a sample of size 120.

20. The mean tuition cost at state universities throughout the United States is $\$4260$ per year (*St. Petersburg Times,* December 11, 2002). Use this value as the population mean and assume that the population standard deviation is $\sigma = \$900$. Suppose that a random sample of 50 state universities will be selected.
    a. Show the sampling distribution of $\bar{x}$ where $\bar{x}$ is the sample mean tuition cost for the 50 state universities.

    b.   What is the probability that the simple random sample will provide a sample mean within $250 of the population mean?

    c.   What is the probability that the simple random sample will provide a sample mean within $100 of the population mean?

21.   The College Board American College Testing Program reported a population mean SAT score of $\mu = 1020$ (*The World Almanac 2003*). Assume that the population standard deviation is $\sigma = 100$.

    a.   What is the probability that a random sample of 75 students will provide a sample mean SAT score within 10 of the population mean?

    b.   What is the probability a random sample of 75 students will provide a sample mean SAT score within 20 of the population mean?

22.   The mean annual starting salary for marketing majors is $34,000 (*Time,* May 8, 2000). Assume that for the population of graduates with a marketing major, the mean annual starting salary is $\mu = 34,000$, and the standard deviation is $\sigma = 2000$.

    a.   What is the probability that a simple random sample of marketing majors will have a sample mean within $\pm$250 of the population mean for each of the following sample sizes: 30, 50, 100, 200, and 400?

    b.   What is the advantage of a larger sample size when attempting to estimate the population mean?

23.   *BusinessWeek* conducted a survey of graduates from 30 top MBA programs (*BusinessWeek,* September 22, 2003). On the basis of the survey, assume that the mean annual salary for male and female graduates 10 years after graduation is $168,000 and $117,000, respectively. Assume the standard deviation for the male graduates is $40,000, and for the female graduates it is $25,000.

    a.   What is the probability that a simple random sample of 40 male graduates will provide a sample mean within $10,000 of the population mean, $168,000?

    b.   What is the probability that a simple random sample of 40 female graduates will provide a sample mean within $10,000 of the population mean, $117,000?

    c.   In which of the preceding two cases, part (a) or part (b), do we have a higher probability of obtaining a sample estimate within $10,000 of the population mean? Why?

    d.   What is the probability that a simple random sample of 100 male graduates will provide a sample mean more than $4000 below the population mean?

24.   The average annual cost of automobile insurance is $687 (*National Association of Insurance Commissioners,* January 2003). Use this value as the population mean and assume that the population standard deviation is $\sigma = \$230$. Consider a sample of 45 automobile insurance policies.

    a.   Show the sampling distribution of $\bar{x}$ where $\bar{x}$ is the sample mean annual cost of automobile insurance.

    b.   What is the probability that the sample mean is within $100 of the population mean?

    c.   What is the probability that the sample mean is within $25 of the population mean?

    d.   What sample size would you recommend if an insurance agency wanted the sample mean to estimate the population mean within $\pm$25?

25.   *Money* magazine reported that the average price of a gallon of gasoline in the United States during the first quarter of 2001 was $1.46 (*Money,* August 2001). Assume the price reported by *Money* is the population mean, and the population standard deviation is $\sigma = \$.15$.

    a.   What is the probability that the mean price for a sample of 30 gas stations is within $.03 of the population mean?

    b.   What is the probability that the mean price for a sample of 50 gas stations is within $.03 of the population mean?

    c.   What is the probability that the mean price for a sample of 100 gas stations is within $.03 of the population mean?

    d.   Would you recommend a sample size of 30, 50, or 100 to have at least a .95 probability that the sample mean is within $.03 of the population mean?

26. To estimate the mean age for a population of 4000 employees, a simple random sample of 40 employees is selected.
    a. Would you use the finite population correction factor in calculating the standard error of the mean? Explain.
    b. If the population standard deviation is $\sigma = 8.2$ years, compute the standard error both with and without the finite population correction factor. What is the rationale for ignoring the finite population correction factor whenever $n/N \leq .05$?
    c. What is the probability that the sample mean age of the employees will be within ± 2 years of the population mean age?

Sampling Distribution of $\bar{p}$

The sample proportion $\bar{p}$ is the point estimator of the population proportion p. The formula for computing the sample proportion is

$$\bar{p} = \frac{x}{n}$$

where

> x = the number of elements in the sample that possess the characteristic of interest
> n = sample size

As noted in Section 7.4, the sample proportion $\bar{p}$ is a random variable and its probability distribution is called the sampling distribution of $\bar{p}$.

> **SAMPLING DISTRIBUTION OF $\bar{p}$**
>
> The sampling distribution of $\bar{p}$ is the probability distribution of all possible values of the sample proportion $\bar{p}$.

To determine how close the sample proportion $\bar{p}$ is to the population proportion p, we need to understand the properties of the sampling distribution of $\bar{p}$: the expected value of $\bar{p}$, the standard deviation of $\bar{p}$, and the shape or form of the sampling distribution of $\bar{p}$.

Expected Value of $\bar{p}$

The expected value of $\bar{p}$, the mean of all possible values of $\bar{p}$, is equal to the population proportion p.

> **EXPECTED VALUE OF $\bar{p}$**
>
> $$E(\bar{p}) = p \tag{7.4}$$
>
> where
>
> > $E(\bar{p})$ = the expected value of $\bar{p}$
> > p = the population proportion

Because $E(\bar{p}) = p$, $\bar{p}$ is an unbiased estimator of p. Recall from Section 7.1 we noted that $p = .60$ for the EAI population, where p is the proportion of the population of managers who participated in the company's management training program. Thus, the expected value of $\bar{p}$ for the EAI sampling problem is .60.

Standard Deviation of $\bar{p}$

Just as we found for the standard deviation of $\bar{x}$, the standard deviation of $\bar{p}$ depends on whether the population is finite or infinite. The two formulas for computing the standard deviation of $\bar{p}$ follow.

STANDARD DEVIATION OF $\bar{p}$

Finite Population   *Infinite Population*

$$\sigma_{\bar{p}} = \sqrt{\frac{N-n}{N-1}} \sqrt{\frac{p(1-p)}{n}} \qquad \sigma_{\bar{p}} = \sqrt{\frac{p(1-p)}{n}} \qquad (7.5)$$

Comparing the two formulas in (7.5), we see that the only difference is the use of the finite population correction factor $\sqrt{(N-n)/(N-1)}$.

As was the case with the sample mean $\bar{x}$, the difference between the expressions for the finite population and the infinite population becomes negligible if the size of the finite population is large in comparison to the sample size. We follow the same rule of thumb that we recommended for the sample mean. That is, if the population is finite with $n/N \le .05$, we will use $\sigma_{\bar{p}} = \sqrt{p(1-p)/n}$. However, if the population is finite with $n/N > .05$, the finite population correction factor should be used. Again, unless specifically noted, throughout the text we will assume that the population size is large in relation to the sample size and thus the finite population correction factor is unnecessary.

In Section 7.5 we used standard error of the mean to refer to the standard deviation of $\bar{x}$. We stated that in general the term *standard error* refers to the standard deviation of a point estimator. Thus, for proportions we use *standard error of the proportion* to refer to the standard deviation of $\bar{p}$. Let us now return to the EAI example and compute the standard error of the proportion associated with simple random samples of 30 EAI managers.

For the EAI study we know that the population proportion of managers who participated in the management training program is $p = .60$. With $n/N = 30/2500 = .012$, we can ignore the finite population correction factor when we compute the standard error of the proportion. For the simple random sample of 30 managers, $\sigma_{\bar{p}}$ is

$$\sigma_{\bar{p}} = \sqrt{\frac{p(1-p)}{n}} = \sqrt{\frac{.60(1-.60)}{30}} = .0894$$

Form of the Sampling Distribution of $\bar{p}$

Now that we know the mean and standard deviation of $\bar{p}$, we want to consider the form of the sampling distribution of $\bar{p}$. Applying the central limit theorem as it relates to $\bar{p}$ produces the following result.

The sampling distribution of $\bar{p}$ can be approximated by a normal probability distribution whenever the sample size is large.

With $\bar{p}$, the sample size can be considered large whenever the following two conditions are satisfied.

$$np \geq 5$$
$$n(1 - p) \geq 5$$

In practical applications, when an estimate of a population proportion is desired, we find that sample sizes are almost always large enough to permit the use of a normal approximation for the sampling distribution of $\bar{p}$.

Recall that for the EAI sampling problem we know that the population proportion of managers who participated in the training program is $p = .60$. With a simple random sample of size 30, we have $np = 30(.60) = 18$ and $n(1 - p) = 30(.40) = 12$. Thus, the sampling distribution of $\bar{p}$ can be approximated by the normal distribution shown in Figure 7.11.

Practical Value of the Sampling Distribution of $\bar{p}$

The practical value of the sampling distribution of $\bar{p}$ is that it can be used to provide probability information about the difference between the sample proportion and the population proportion. For instance, suppose that in the EAI problem the personnel director wants to know the probability of obtaining a value of $\bar{p}$ that is within .05 of the population proportion of EAI managers who participated in the training program. That is, what is the probability of obtaining a sample with a sample proportion $\bar{p}$ between .55 and .65? The darkly shaded area in Figure 7.12 shows this probability. Using the fact that the sampling distribution of $\bar{p}$ can be approximated by a normal probability distribution with a mean of .60 and a standard error of $\sigma_{\bar{p}} = .0894$, we can use Excel's NORMDIST function to make this calculation. Entering the formula =NORMDIST(.65,.60,.0894,TRUE) into a cell of an Excel worksheet provides the cumulative probability corresponding to $\bar{p} = .65$. The value calculated by Excel is .7120. Entering the formula =NORMDIST(.55,.60,.0894,TRUE) into a cell of an Excel worksheet provides the cumulative probability corresponding to $\bar{p} = .55$. The value calculated by Excel is .2880. Thus, the probability of $\bar{p}$ being in the interval from .55 to .65 is given by .7120 − .2880 = .4240.

FIGURE 7.11   SAMPLING DISTRIBUTION OF $\bar{p}$ FOR THE PROPORTION OF EAI MANAGERS WHO PARTICIPATED IN THE MANAGEMENT TRAINING PROGRAM

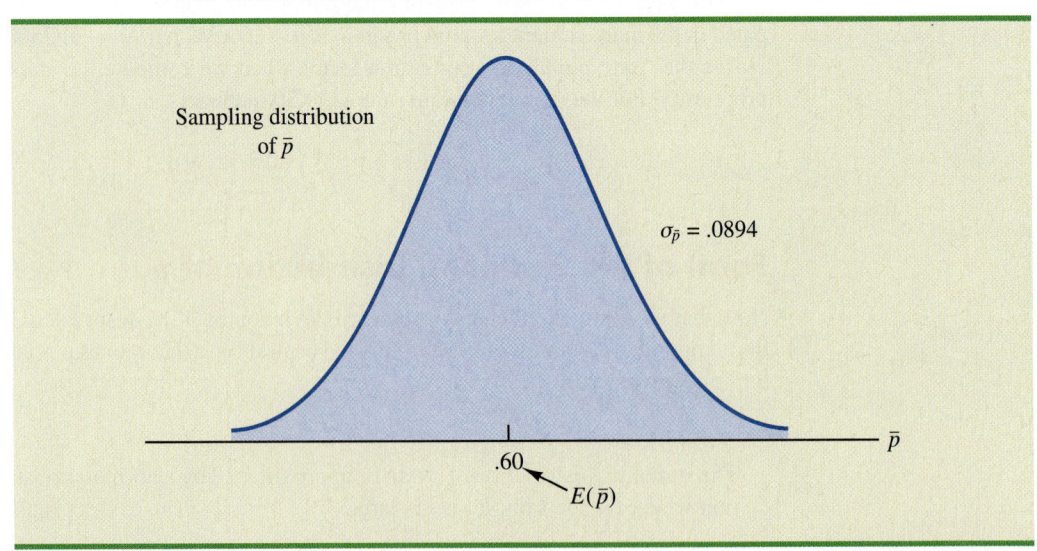

FIGURE 7.12   PROBABILITY OF OBTAINING $\bar{p}$ BETWEEN .55 AND .65

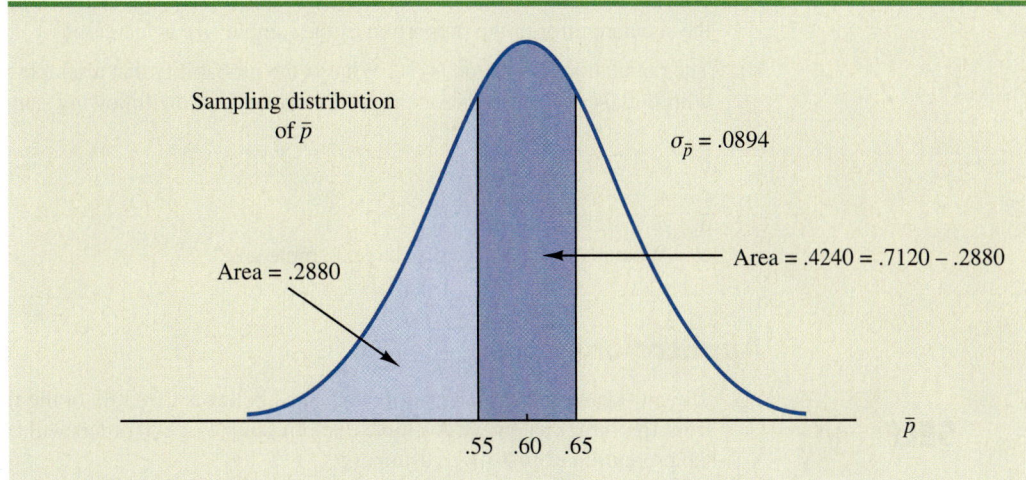

If we consider increasing the sample size to $n = 100$, the standard error of the proportion becomes

$$\sigma_{\bar{p}} = \sqrt{\frac{.60(1 - .60)}{100}} = .0490$$

With a sample size of 100 EAI managers, the probability of the sample proportion having a value within .05 of the population proportion can now be computed. Because the sampling distribution is approximately normal, with mean .60 and standard deviation .0490, we can use Excel's NORMDIST function to make this calculation. Entering the formula =NORMDIST(.65,.60,.0490,TRUE) into a cell of an Excel worksheet provides the cumulative probability corresponding to $\bar{p} = .65$. The value calculated by Excel is .8462. Entering the formula =NORMDIST(.55,.60,.0490,TRUE) into a cell of an Excel worksheet provides the cumulative probability corresponding to $\bar{p} = .55$. The value calculated by Excel is .1538. Thus, the probability of $\bar{p}$ being in the interval from .55 to .65 is given by $.8462 - .1538 = .6924$. Increasing the sample size increases the probability that the sampling error will be less than or equal to .05 by .2684 (from .4240 to .6924).

Exercises

Methods

27. A simple random sample of size 100 is selected from a population with $p = .40$.
    a. What is the expected value of $\bar{p}$?
    b. What is the standard error of $\bar{p}$?
    c. Show the sampling distribution of $\bar{p}$.
    d. What does the sampling distribution of $\bar{p}$ show?

28. A population proportion is .40. A simple random sample of size 200 will be taken and the sample proportion $\bar{p}$ will be used to estimate the population proportion.
    a. What is the probability that the sample proportion will be within $\pm.03$ of the population proportion?
    b. What is the probability that the sample proportion will be within $\pm.05$ of the population proportion?

29. Assume that the population proportion is .55. Compute the standard error of the proportion, $\sigma_{\bar{p}}$, for sample sizes of 100, 200, 500, and 1000. What can you say about the size of the standard error of the proportion as the sample size is increased?

30. The population proportion is .30. What is the probability that a sample proportion will be within $\pm.04$ of the population proportion for each of the following sample sizes?
    a. $n = 100$
    b. $n = 200$
    c. $n = 500$
    d. $n = 1000$
    e. What is the advantage of a larger sample size?

Applications

31. The president of Doerman Distributors, Inc., believes that 30% of the firm's orders come from first-time customers. A simple random sample of 100 orders will be used to estimate the proportion of first-time customers.
    a. Assume that the president is correct and $p = .30$. What is the sampling distribution of $\bar{p}$ for this study?
    b. What is the probability that the sample proportion $\bar{p}$ will be between .20 and .40?
    c. What is the probability that the sample proportion will be between .25 and .35?

32. *BusinessWeek* reported that 56% of the households in the United States have Internet access (*BusinessWeek*, May 21, 2001). Use a population proportion $p = .56$ and assume that a sample of 300 households will be selected.
    a. Show the sampling distribution of $\bar{p}$ where $\bar{p}$ is the sample proportion of households that have Internet access.
    b. What is the probability that the sample proportion will be within $\pm.03$ of the population proportion?
    c. Answer part (b) for sample sizes of 600 and 1000.

33. *Time*/CNN voter polls monitored public opinion for the presidential candidates during the 2000 presidential election campaign. One *Time*/CNN poll conducted by Yankelovich Partners, Inc., used a sample of 589 likely voters (*Time*, June 26, 2000). Assume the population proportion for a presidential candidate is $p = .50$. Let $\bar{p}$ be the sample proportion of likely voters favoring the presidential candidate.
    a. Show the sampling distribution of $\bar{p}$.
    b. What is the probability the *Time*/CNN poll will provide a sample proportion within $\pm.04$ of the population proportion?
    c. What is the probability the *Time*/CNN poll will provide a sample proportion within $\pm.03$ of the population proportion?
    d. What is the probability the *Time*/CNN poll will provide a sample proportion within $\pm.02$ of the population proportion?

34. Roper ASW conducted a survey to learn about American adults' attitudes toward money and happiness (*Money*, October 2003). Fifty-six percent of the respondents said they balance their checkbook at least once a month.
    a. Suppose a sample of 400 American adults were taken. Show the sampling distribution of the proportion of adults who balance their checkbook at least once a month.
    b. What is the probability that the sample proportion will be within $\pm.02$ of the population proportion?
    c. What is the probability that the sample proportion will be within $\pm.04$ of the population proportion?

35. The *Democrat and Chronicle* reported that 25% of the flights arriving at the San Diego airport during the first five months of 2001 were late (*Democrat and Chronicle*, July 23, 2001). Assume the population proportion is $p = .25$.

a.   Show the sampling distribution of $\bar{p}$, the proportion of late flights in a sample of 1000 flights.

b.   What is the probability that the sample proportion will be within $\pm.03$ of the population proportion if a sample of size 1000 is selected?

c.   Answer part (b) for a sample of 500 flights.

36.   The Grocery Manufacturers of America reported that 76% of consumers read the ingredients listed on a product's label. Assume the population proportion is $p = .76$ and a sample of 400 consumers is selected from the population.

a.   Show the sampling distribution of the sample proportion $\bar{p}$ where $\bar{p}$ is the proportion of the sampled consumers who read the ingredients listed on a product's label.

b.   What is the probability that the sample proportion will be within $\pm.03$ of the population proportion?

c.   Answer part (b) for a sample of 750 consumers.

37.   The Food Marketing Institute shows that 17% of households spend more than $100 per week on groceries. Assume the population proportion is $p = .17$ and a simple random sample of 800 households will be selected from the population.

a.   Show the sampling distribution of $\bar{p}$, the sample proportion of households spending more than $100 per week on groceries.

b.   What is the probability that the sample proportion will be within $\pm.02$ of the population proportion?

c.   Answer part (b) for a sample of 1600 households.

7.7 Sampling Methods

This section provides a brief introduction to sampling methods other than simple random sampling.

We described the simple random sampling procedure and discussed the properties of the sampling distributions of $\bar{x}$ and $\bar{p}$ when simple random sampling is used. However, simple random sampling is not the only sampling method available. Such methods as stratified random sampling, cluster sampling, and systematic sampling provide advantages over simple random sampling in some situations. In this section we briefly introduce these alternative sampling methods.

Stratified Random Sampling

In **stratified random sampling**, the elements in the population are first divided into groups called *strata,* such that each element in the population belongs to one and only one stratum. The basis for forming the strata, such as department, location, age, industry type, and so on, is at the discretion of the designer of the sample. However, the best results are obtained when the elements within each stratum are as much alike as possible. Figure 7.13 is a diagram of a population divided into *H* strata.

Stratified random sampling works best when the variance among elements in each stratum is relatively small.

After the strata are formed, a simple random sample is taken from each stratum. Formulas are available for combining the results for the individual stratum samples into one estimate of the population parameter of interest. The value of stratified random sampling depends on how homogeneous the elements are within the strata. If elements within strata are alike, the strata will have low variances. Thus relatively small sample sizes can be used to obtain good estimates of the strata characteristics. If strata are homogeneous, the stratified random sampling procedure provides results just as precise as those of simple random sampling by using a smaller total sample size.

Cluster Sampling

Cluster sampling works best when each cluster provides a small-scale representation of the population.

In **cluster sampling**, the elements in the population are first divided into separate groups called *clusters*. Each element of the population belongs to one and only one cluster (see Figure 7.14). A simple random sample of the clusters is then taken. All elements within each sampled cluster

FIGURE 7.13   DIAGRAM FOR STRATIFIED RANDOM SAMPLING

```
                          Population

        Stratum 1      Stratum 2     . . .    Stratum H
```

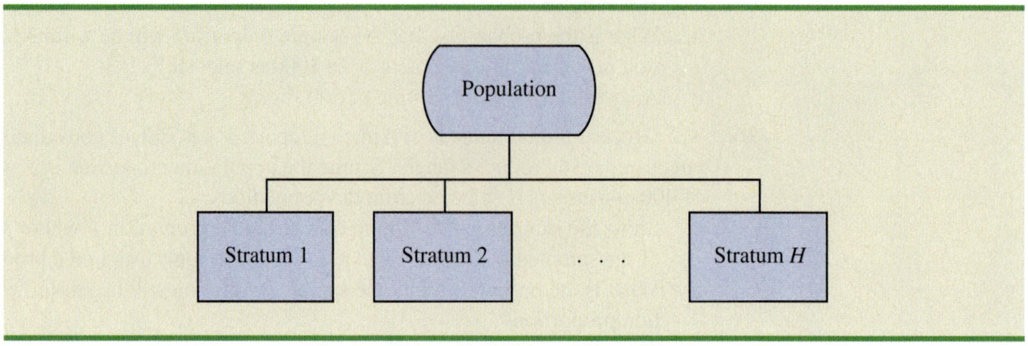

form the sample. Cluster sampling tends to provide the best results when the elements within the clusters are not alike. In the ideal case, each cluster is a representative small-scale version of the entire population. The value of cluster sampling depends on how representative each cluster is of the entire population. If all clusters are alike in this regard, sampling a small number of clusters will provide good estimates of the population parameters.

One of the primary applications of cluster sampling is area sampling, where clusters are city blocks or other well-defined areas. Cluster sampling generally requires a larger total sample size than either simple random sampling or stratified random sampling. However, it can result in cost savings because of the fact that when an interviewer is sent to a sampled cluster (e.g., a city-block location), many sample observations can be obtained in a relatively short time. Hence, a larger sample size may be obtainable with a significantly lower total cost.

Systematic Sampling

In some sampling situations, especially those with large populations, it is time-consuming to select a simple random sample by first finding a random number and then counting or searching through the list of the population until the corresponding element is found. An alternative to simple random sampling is **systematic sampling**. For example, if a sample size of 50 is desired from a population containing 5000 elements, we will sample one element for every $5000/50 = 100$ elements in the population. A systematic sample for this case involves selecting randomly one of the first 100 elements from the population list. Other sample elements are identified by starting with the first sampled element and then selecting every 100th element that follows in the population list. In effect, the sample of 50 is identified by moving systematically through the population and identifying every 100th element after the first randomly selected element. The sample of 50 usually will be easier to

FIGURE 7.14   DIAGRAM FOR CLUSTER SAMPLING

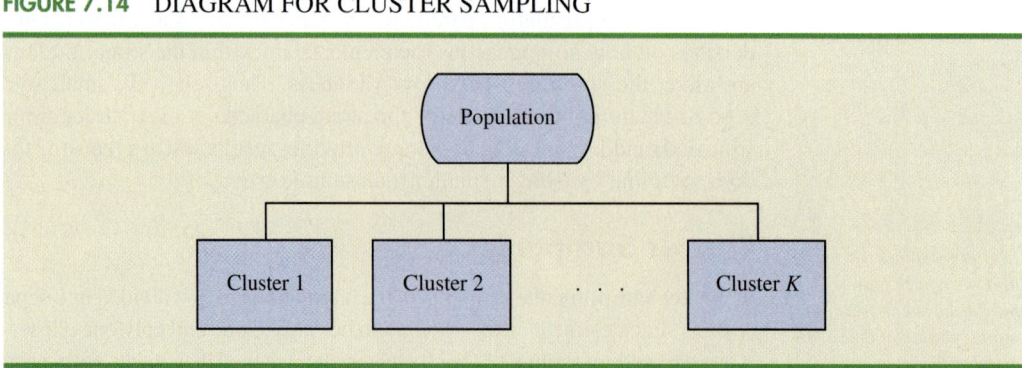

identify in this way than it would be if simple random sampling were used. Because the first element selected is a random choice, a systematic sample is usually assumed to have the properties of a simple random sample. This assumption is especially applicable when the list of elements in the population is a random ordering of the elements.

Convenience Sampling

The sampling methods discussed thus far are referred to as *probability sampling* techniques. Elements selected from the population have a known probability of being included in the sample. The advantage of probability sampling is that the sampling distribution of the appropriate sample statistic generally can be identified. Formulas such as the ones for simple random sampling presented in this chapter can be used to determine the properties of the sampling distribution. Then the sampling distribution can be used to make probability statements about the error associated with the sample results.

Convenience sampling is a *nonprobability sampling* technique. As the name implies, the sample is identified primarily by convenience. Elements are included in the sample without prespecified or known probabilities of being selected. For example, a professor conducting research at a university may use student volunteers to constitute a sample simply because they are readily available and will participate as subjects for little or no cost. Similarly, an inspector may sample a shipment of oranges by selecting oranges haphazardly from among several crates. Labeling each orange and using a probability method of sampling would be impractical. Samples such as wildlife captures and volunteer panels for consumer research are also convenience samples.

Convenience samples have the advantage of relatively easy sample selection and data collection; however, it is impossible to evaluate the "goodness" of the sample in terms of its representativeness of the population. A convenience sample may provide good results or it may not; no statistically justified procedure allows a probability analysis and inference about the quality of the sample results. Sometimes researchers apply statistical methods designed for probability samples to a convenience sample, arguing that the convenience sample can be treated as though it were a probability sample. However, this argument cannot be supported, and we should be cautious in interpreting the results of convenience samples that are used to make inferences about populations.

Judgment Sampling

One additional nonprobability sampling technique is **judgment sampling**. In this approach, the person most knowledgeable on the subject of the study selects elements of the population that he or she feels are most representative of the population. Often this method is a relatively easy way of selecting a sample. For example, a reporter may sample two or three senators, judging that those senators reflect the general opinion of all senators. However, the quality of the sample results depends on the judgment of the person selecting the sample. Again, great caution is warranted in drawing conclusions based on judgment samples used to make inferences about populations.

NOTES AND COMMENTS

We recommend using probability sampling methods: simple random sampling, stratified random sampling, cluster sampling, or systematic sampling. For these methods, formulas are available for evaluating the "goodness" of the sample results in terms of the closeness of the results to the population parameters being estimated. An evaluation of the goodness cannot be made with convenience or judgment sampling. Thus, great care should be used in interpreting the results based on nonprobability sampling methods.

Summary

In this chapter we presented the concepts of simple random sampling and sampling distributions. We demonstrated how a simple random sample can be selected and how the data collected for the sample can be used to develop point estimates of population parameters. Because different simple random samples provide different values for the point estimators, point estimators such as $\bar{x}$ and $\bar{p}$ are random variables. The probability distribution of such a random variable is called a sampling distribution. In particular, we described the sampling distributions of the sample mean $\bar{x}$ and the sample proportion $\bar{p}$.

In considering the characteristics of the sampling distributions of $\bar{x}$ and $\bar{p}$, we stated that $E(\bar{x}) = \mu$ and $E(\bar{p}) = p$. The expected values of $\bar{x}$ and $\bar{p}$ provide unbiased estimators of μ and p. After developing the standard deviation or standard error formulas for these estimators, we described the conditions necessary for the sampling distributions of $\bar{x}$ and $\bar{p}$ to follow a normal distribution. Other sampling methods, including stratified random sampling, cluster sampling, systematic sampling, convenience sampling, and judgment sampling, were discussed.

Glossary

Parameter A numerical characteristic of a population, such as a population mean μ, a population standard deviation σ, a population proportion p, and so on.

Simple random sample Finite population: a sample selected such that each possible sample of size n has the same probability of being selected. Infinite population: a sample selected such that each element comes from the same population and the elements are selected independently.

Sample statistic A sample characteristic, such as a sample mean $\bar{x}$, a sample standard deviation s, a sample proportion $\bar{p}$, and so on. The value of the sample statistic is used to estimate the value of the corresponding population parameter.

Point estimator The sample statistic, such as $\bar{x}$, s, or $\bar{p}$, that provides the point estimate of the population parameter.

Point estimate The value of a point estimator used in a particular instance as an estimate of a population parameter.

Sampling distribution A probability distribution consisting of all possible values of a sample statistic.

Unbiased A property of a point estimator that is present when the expected value of the point estimator is equal to the population parameter it estimates.

Finite population correction factor The term $\sqrt{(N - n)/(N - 1)}$ that is used in the formulas for $\sigma_{\bar{x}}$ and $\sigma_{\bar{p}}$ whenever a finite population, rather than an infinite population, is being sampled. The generally accepted rule of thumb is to ignore the finite population correction factor whenever $n/N \leq .05$.

Standard error The standard deviation of a point estimator.

Central limit theorem A theorem that enables one to use the normal probability distribution to approximate the sampling distribution of $\bar{x}$ whenever the sample size is large.

Stratified random sampling A probability sampling method in which the population is first divided into strata and a simple random sample is then taken from each stratum.

Cluster sampling A probability sampling method in which the population is first divided into clusters and then a simple random sample of the clusters is taken.

Systematic sampling A probability sampling method in which we randomly select one of the first k elements and then select every kth element thereafter.

Convenience sampling A nonprobability method of sampling whereby elements are selected for the sample on the basis of convenience.

Judgment sampling A nonprobability method of sampling whereby elements are selected for the sample based on the judgment of the person doing the study.

Key Formulas

Expected Value of $\bar{x}$

$$E(\bar{x}) = \mu \tag{7.1}$$

Standard Deviation of $\bar{x}$ (Standard Error)

Finite Population   *Infinite Population*

$$\sigma_{\bar{x}} = \sqrt{\frac{N-n}{N-1}}\left(\frac{\sigma}{\sqrt{n}}\right) \qquad \sigma_{\bar{x}} = \frac{\sigma}{\sqrt{n}} \tag{7.2}$$

Expected Value of $\bar{p}$

$$E(\bar{p}) = p \tag{7.4}$$

Standard Deviation of $\bar{p}$ (Standard Error)

Finite Population   *Infinite Population*

$$\sigma_{\bar{p}} = \sqrt{\frac{N-n}{N-1}}\sqrt{\frac{p(1-p)}{n}} \qquad \sigma_{\bar{p}} = \sqrt{\frac{p(1-p)}{n}} \tag{7.5}$$

Supplementary Exercises

Dining

38. Bob Miller, a food critic, wants to prepare an article on the quality of food at locally owned restaurants in Myrtle Beach, South Carolina. A list of 44 locally owned restaurants is contained in the data file named Dining that is on the CD accompanying the text (*Coastal Carolina Dining,* Fall 2004). Bob only has time to sample the food at five of these restaurants.
    a. In the data file the restaurants are listed in column A of an Excel worksheet. In column B we generated a random number for each of the restaurants in column A. Use these random numbers to select a simple random sample of five restaurants for Bob.
    b. Generate a new set of random numbers and use them to select a new simple random sample. Did you select the same restaurants?

39. Americans have become increasingly concerned about the rising cost of Medicare. In 1990, the average annual Medicare spending per enrollee was $3267; in 2003, the average annual Medicare spending per enrollee was $6883 (*Money,* Fall 2003). Suppose you hired a consulting firm to take a sample of fifty 2003 Medicare enrollees to further investigate the nature of expenditures. Assume the population standard deviation for 2003 was $2000.
    a. Show the sampling distribution of the mean amount of Medicare spending for a sample of fifty 2003 enrollees.
    b. What is the probability the sample mean will be within ±$300 of the population mean?
    c. What is the probability the sample mean will be greater than $7500? If the consulting firm tells you the sample mean for the Medicare enrollees they interviewed was $7500, would you question whether they followed correct simple random sampling procedures? Why or why not?

40. *BusinessWeek* surveyed MBA alumni 10 years after graduation (*BusinessWeek,* September 22, 2003). One finding was that alumni spend an average of $115.50 per week eating out socially. You have been asked to conduct a follow-up study by taking a sample of 40 of these MBA alumni. Assume the population standard deviation is $35.
    a. Show the sampling distribution of $\bar{x}$, the sample mean weekly expenditure for the 40 MBA alumni.
    b. What is the probability the sample mean will be within $10 of the population mean?
    c. Suppose you find a sample mean of $100. What is the probability of finding a sample mean of $100 or less? Would you consider this sample to be an unusually low spending group of alumni? Why or why not?

41. The mean television viewing time for Americans is 15 hours per week (*Money,* November 2003). Suppose a sample of 60 Americans is taken to further investigate viewing habits. Assume the population standard deviation for weekly viewing time is $\sigma = 4$ hours.
    a. What is the probability the sample mean will be within 1 hour of the population mean?
    b. What is the probability the sample mean will be within 45 minutes of the population mean?

42. The average annual salary for federal government employees in Indiana is $41,979 (*The World Almanac 2001*). Use this figure as the population mean and assume the population standard deviation is $\sigma = \$5000$. Suppose that a random sample of 50 federal government employees will be selected from the population.
    a. What is the value of the standard error of the mean?
    b. What is the probability that the sample mean will be more than $41,979?
    c. What is the probability the sample mean will be within $1000 of the population mean?
    d. How would the probability in part (c) change if the sample size were increased to 100?

43. Three firms carry inventories that differ in size. Firm A's inventory contains 2000 items, firm B's inventory contains 5000 items, and firm C's inventory contains 10,000 items. The population standard deviation for the cost of the items in each firm's inventory is $\sigma = 144$. A statistical consultant recommends that each firm take a sample of 50 items from its inventory to provide statistically valid estimates of the average cost per item. Managers of the small firm state that because it has the smallest population, it should be able to make the estimate from a much smaller sample than that required by the larger firms. However, the consultant states that to obtain the same standard error and thus the same precision in the sample results, all firms should use the same sample size regardless of population size.
    a. Using the finite population correction factor, compute the standard error for each of the three firms given a sample of size 50.
    b. What is the probability that for each firm the sample mean $\bar{x}$ will be within ± 25 of the population mean μ?

44. A researcher reports survey results by stating that the standard error of the mean is 20. The population standard deviation is 500.
    a. How large was the sample used in this survey?
    b. What is the probability that the point estimate was within ± 25 of the population mean?

45. A production process is checked periodically by a quality control inspector. The inspector selects simple random samples of 30 finished products and computes the sample mean product weights $\bar{x}$. If test results over a long period of time show that 5% of the $\bar{x}$ values are over 2.1 pounds and 5% are under 1.9 pounds, what are the mean and the standard deviation for the population of products produced with this process?

46. As of June 13, 2001, 30.5% of individual investors were bullish on the stock market short term (*AAII Journal,* July 2001). Answer the following questions assuming a sample of 200 individual investors is used.
    a. Show the sampling distribution of $\bar{p}$, the sample proportion of individual investors who are bullish on the market short term.

    b.   What is the probability that the sample proportion will be within $\pm.04$ of the population proportion?

    c.   What is the probability that the sample proportion will be within $\pm.02$ of the population proportion?

47.   A market research firm conducts telephone surveys with a 40% historical response rate. What is the probability that in a new sample of 400 telephone numbers, at least 150 individuals will cooperate and respond to the questions? In other words, what is the probability that the sample proportion will be at least 150/400 = .375?

48.   According to ORC International, 71% of Internet users connect their computers to the Internet by normal telephone lines (*USA Today,* January 18, 2000). Assume a population proportion $p = .71$.

    a.   What is the probability that a sample proportion from a simple random sample of 350 Internet users will be within $\pm.05$ of the population proportion?

    b.   What is the probability that a sample proportion from a simple random sample of 350 Internet users will be .75 or greater?

49.   The proportion of individuals insured by the All-Driver Automobile Insurance Company who received at least one traffic ticket during a five-year period is .15.

    a.   Show the sampling distribution of $\bar{p}$ if a random sample of 150 insured individuals is used to estimate the proportion having received at least one ticket.

    b.   What is the probability that the sample proportion will be within $\pm.03$ of the population proportion?

50.   Lori Jeffrey is a successful sales representative for a major publisher of college textbooks. Historically, Lori obtains a book adoption on 25% of her sales calls. Viewing her sales calls for one month as a sample of all possible sales calls, assume that a statistical analysis of the data yields a standard error of the proportion of .0625.

    a.   How large was the sample used in this analysis? That is, how many sales calls did Lori make during the month?

    b.   Let $\bar{p}$ indicate the sample proportion of book adoptions obtained during the month. Show the sampling distribution $\bar{p}$.

    c.   Using the sampling distribution of $\bar{p}$, compute the probability that Lori will obtain book adoptions on 30% or more of her sales calls during a one-month period.

CHAPTER 8

Interval Estimation

CONTENTS

STATISTICS IN PRACTICE:
FOOD LION

8.1 POPULATION MEAN:
σ KNOWN
Margin of Error and the Interval
Estimate
Using Excel
Practical Advice

8.2 POPULATION MEAN:
σ UNKNOWN
Margin of Error and the Interval
Estimate

Using Excel
Practical Advice
Using a Small Sample
Summary of Interval
Estimation Procedures

8.3 DETERMINING THE
SAMPLE SIZE

8.4 POPULATION PROPORTION
Using Excel
Determining the Sample Size

STATISTICS *in* PRACTICE

FOOD LION*
SALISBURY, NORTH CAROLINA

Founded in 1957 as Food Town, Food Lion is one of the largest supermarket chains in the United States with 1200 stores in 11 Southeastern and Mid-Atlantic states. The company sells more than 24,000 different products and offers nationally and regionally advertised brand-name merchandise, as well as a growing number of high-quality private label products manufactured especially for Food Lion. The company maintains its low price leadership and quality assurance through operating efficiencies such as standard store formats, innovative warehouse design, energy-efficient facilities, and data synchronization with suppliers. Food Lion looks to a future of continued innovation, growth, price leadership, and service to its customers.

Being in an inventory-intense business, Food Lion made the decision to adopt the LIFO (last-in, first-out) method of inventory valuation. This method matches current costs against current revenues, which minimizes the effect of radical price changes on profit and loss results. In addition, the LIFO method reduces net income thereby reducing income taxes during periods of inflation.

Food Lion establishes a LIFO index for each of seven inventory pools: Grocery, Paper/Household, Pet Supplies, Health & Beauty Aids, Dairy, Cigarette/Tobacco, and Beer/Wine. For example, a LIFO index of 1.008 for the Grocery pool would indicate that the company's grocery inventory value at current costs reflects a 0.8% increase due to inflation over the most recent one-year period.

A LIFO index for each inventory pool requires that the year-end inventory count for each product be valued at the current year-end cost and at the preceding year-end cost. To avoid ex-

The Food Lion store in the Cambridge Shopping Center, Charlotte, North Carolina. © Courtesy of Food Lion.

cessive time and expense associated with counting the inventory in all 1200 store locations, Food Lion selects a random sample of 50 stores. Year-end physical inventories are taken in each of the sample stores. The current-year and preceding-year costs for each item are then used to construct the required LIFO indexes for each inventory pool.

For a recent year, the sample estimate of the LIFO index for the Health & Beauty Aids inventory pool was 1.015. Using a 95% confidence level, Food Lion computed a margin of error of .006 for the sample estimate. Thus, the interval from 1.009 to 1.021 provided a 95% confidence interval estimate of the population LIFO index. This level of precision was judged to be very good.

In this chapter you will learn how to compute the margin of error associated with sample estimates. You will also learn how to use this information to construct and interpret interval estimates of a population mean and a population proportion.

---

*The authors are indebted to Keith Cunningham, Tax Director, and Bobby Harkey, Staff Tax Accountant, at Food Lion for providing this Statistics in Practice.

In Chapter 7, we stated that a point estimator is a sample statistic used to estimate a population parameter. For instance, the sample mean $\bar{x}$ is a point estimator of the population mean μ and the sample proportion $\bar{p}$ is a point estimator of the population proportion p. Because a point estimator cannot be expected to provide the exact value of the population parameter, an **interval estimate** is often computed by adding and subtracting a value, called the **margin of error**, to the point estimate. The general form of an interval estimate is as follows:

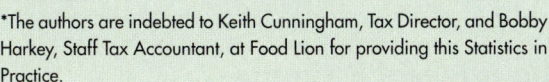

$$\text{Point estimate} \pm \text{Margin of error}$$

The purpose of an interval estimate is to provide information about how close the point estimate, provided by the sample, is to the value of the population parameter.

In this chapter we show how to compute interval estimates of a population mean μ and a population proportion p. The general form of an interval estimate of a population mean is

$$\bar{x} \pm \text{Margin of error}$$

Similarly, the general form of an interval estimate of a population proportion is

$$\bar{p} \pm \text{Margin of error}$$

The sampling distributions of $\bar{x}$ and $\bar{p}$ play key roles in computing these interval estimates.

8.1   Population Mean: σ Known

In order to develop an interval estimate of a population mean, either the population standard deviation σ or the sample standard deviation s must be used to compute the margin of error. In most applications σ is not known, and s is used to compute the margin of error. In some applications, however, large amounts of relevant historical data are available and can be used to estimate the population standard deviation prior to sampling. Also, in quality control applications where a process is assumed to be operating correctly, or "in control," it is appropriate to treat the population standard deviation as known. We refer to such cases as the **σ known** case. In this section we introduce an example in which it is reasonable to treat σ as known and show how to construct an interval estimate for this case.

Each week Lloyd's Department Store selects a simple random sample of 100 customers in order to learn about the amount spent per shopping trip. With x representing the amount spent per shopping trip, the sample mean $\bar{x}$ provides a point estimate of μ, the mean amount spent per shopping trip for the population of all Lloyd's customers. Lloyd's has been using the weekly survey for several years. Based on the historical data, Lloyd's now assumes a known value of $\sigma = \$20$ for the population standard deviation. The historical data also indicate that the population follows a normal distribution.

Lloyd's

During the most recent week, Lloyd's surveyed 100 customers ($n = 100$) and obtained a sample mean of $\bar{x} = \$82$. The sample mean amount spent provides a point estimate of the population mean amount spent per shopping trip, μ. In the discussion that follows, we show how to compute the margin of error for this estimate and develop an interval estimate of the population mean.

Margin of Error and the Interval Estimate

In Chapter 7 we showed that the sampling distribution of $\bar{x}$ can be used to compute the probability that $\bar{x}$ will be within a given distance of μ. In the Lloyd's example, the historical data show that the population of amounts spent is normally distributed with a standard deviation of $\sigma = 20$. So, using what we learned in Chapter 7, we can conclude that the sampling distribution of $\bar{x}$ follows a normal distribution with an unknown mean μ, and a known standard error of $\sigma_{\bar{x}} = \sigma/\sqrt{n} = 20/\sqrt{100} = 2$. This sampling distribution is shown in Figure 8.1.*

---

*We use the fact that the population of amounts spent has a normal distribution to conclude that the sampling distribution of $\bar{x}$ has a normal distribution. If the population did not have a normal distribution, we could rely on the central limit theorem and the large sample size of $n = 100$ to conclude that the sampling distribution of $\bar{x}$ is approximately normal. In either case, the sampling distribution of $\bar{x}$ would appear as shown in Figure 8.1.

FIGURE 8.1   SAMPLING DISTRIBUTION OF THE SAMPLE MEAN AMOUNT
SPENT FROM SIMPLE RANDOM SAMPLES OF 100 CUSTOMERS

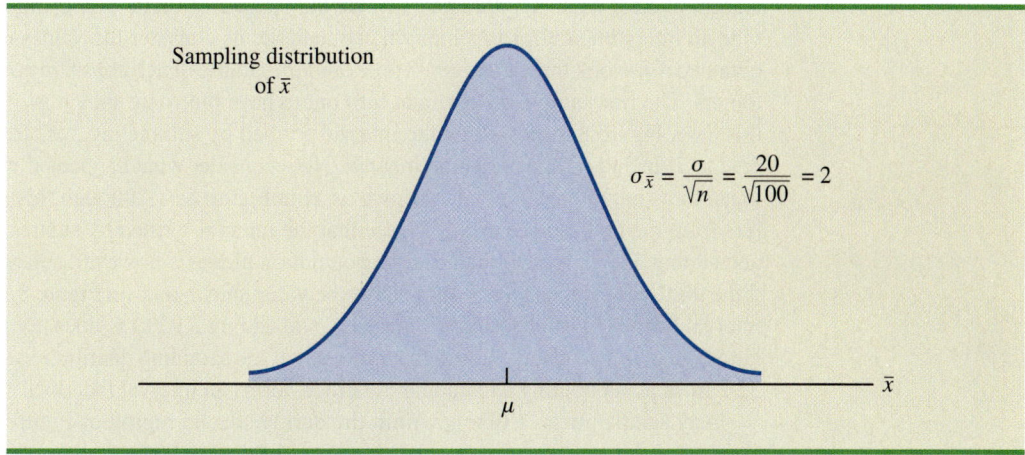

Because the sampling distribution shows how values of $\bar{x}$ are distributed around the population mean μ, the sampling distribution of $\bar{x}$ provides information about the possible differences between $\bar{x}$ and μ.

Using the standard normal probability table, we find that 95% of the values of any normally distributed random variable are within ± 1.96 standard deviations of the mean. Thus, when the sampling distribution of $\bar{x}$ is normally distributed, 95% of the $\bar{x}$ values must be within $\pm 1.96\sigma_{\bar{x}}$ of the mean μ. In the Lloyd's example we know that the sampling distribution of $\bar{x}$ is normally distributed with a standard error of $\sigma_{\bar{x}} = 2$. Because $\pm 1.96\sigma_{\bar{x}} = 1.96(2) = 3.92$, we can conclude that 95% of all $\bar{x}$ values obtained using a sample size of $n = 100$ will be within ± 3.92 of the population mean μ. See Figure 8.2.

FIGURE 8.2   SAMPLING DISTRIBUTION OF $\bar{x}$ SHOWING THE LOCATION OF SAMPLE
MEANS THAT ARE WITHIN 3.92 OF μ

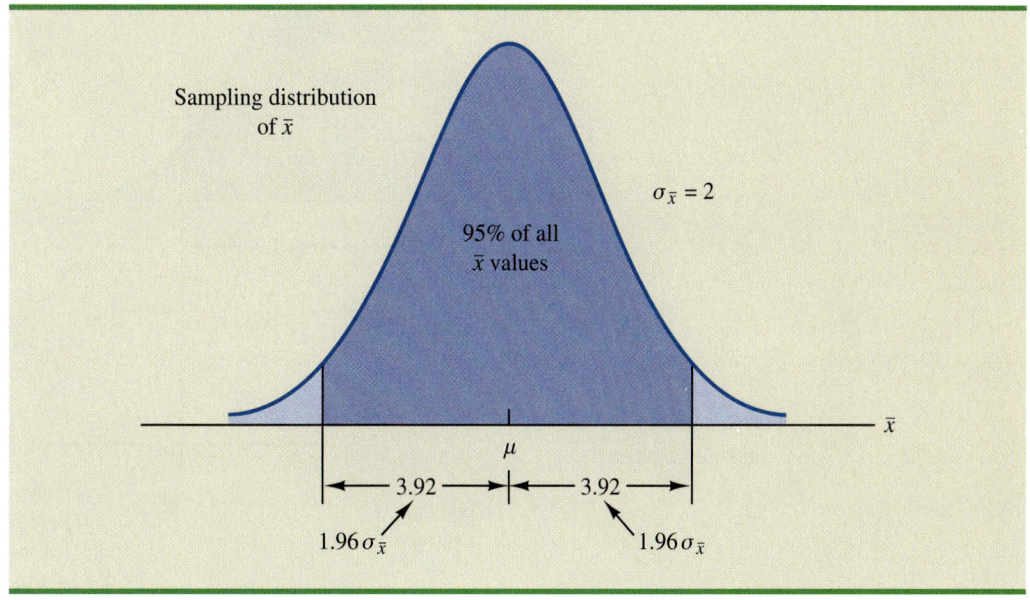

In the introduction to this chapter we said that the general form of an interval estimate of the population mean μ is $\bar{x} \pm$ margin of error. For the Lloyd's example, suppose we set the margin of error equal to 3.92 and compute the interval estimate of μ using $\bar{x} \pm 3.92$. To provide an interpretation for this interval estimate, let us consider the values of $\bar{x}$ that could be obtained if we took three *different* simple random samples, each consisting of 100 Lloyd's customers. The first sample mean might turn out to have the value shown as $\bar{x}_1$ in Figure 8.3. In this case, Figure 8.3 shows that the interval formed by subtracting 3.92 from $\bar{x}_1$ and adding 3.92 to $\bar{x}_1$ includes the population mean μ. Now consider what happens if the second sample mean turns out to have the value shown as $\bar{x}_2$ in Figure 8.3. Although this sample mean differs from the first sample mean, we see that the interval formed by subtracting 3.92 from $\bar{x}_2$ and adding 3.92 to $\bar{x}_2$ also includes the population mean μ. However, consider what happens if the third sample mean turns out to have the value shown as $\bar{x}_3$ in Figure 8.3. In this case, the interval formed by subtracting 3.92 from $\bar{x}_3$ and adding 3.92 to $\bar{x}_3$ does not include the population mean μ. Because $\bar{x}_3$ falls in the upper tail of the sampling distribution and is farther than 3.92 from μ, subtracting and adding 3.92 to $\bar{x}_3$ forms an interval that does not include μ.

Any sample mean $\bar{x}$ that is within the darkly shaded region of Figure 8.3 will provide an interval that contains the population mean μ. Because 95% of all possible sample means are in the darkly shaded region, 95% of all intervals formed by subtracting 3.92 from $\bar{x}$ and adding 3.92 to $\bar{x}$ will include the population mean μ.

Recall that during the most recent week, the quality assurance team at Lloyd's surveyed 100 customers and obtained a sample mean amount spent of $\bar{x} = 82$. Using $\bar{x} \pm 3.92$ to construct the interval estimate, we obtain 82 ± 3.92. Thus, the specific interval estimate of

FIGURE 8.3   INTERVALS FORMED FROM SELECTED SAMPLE MEANS AT LOCATIONS $\bar{x}_1$, $\bar{x}_2$, AND $\bar{x}_3$

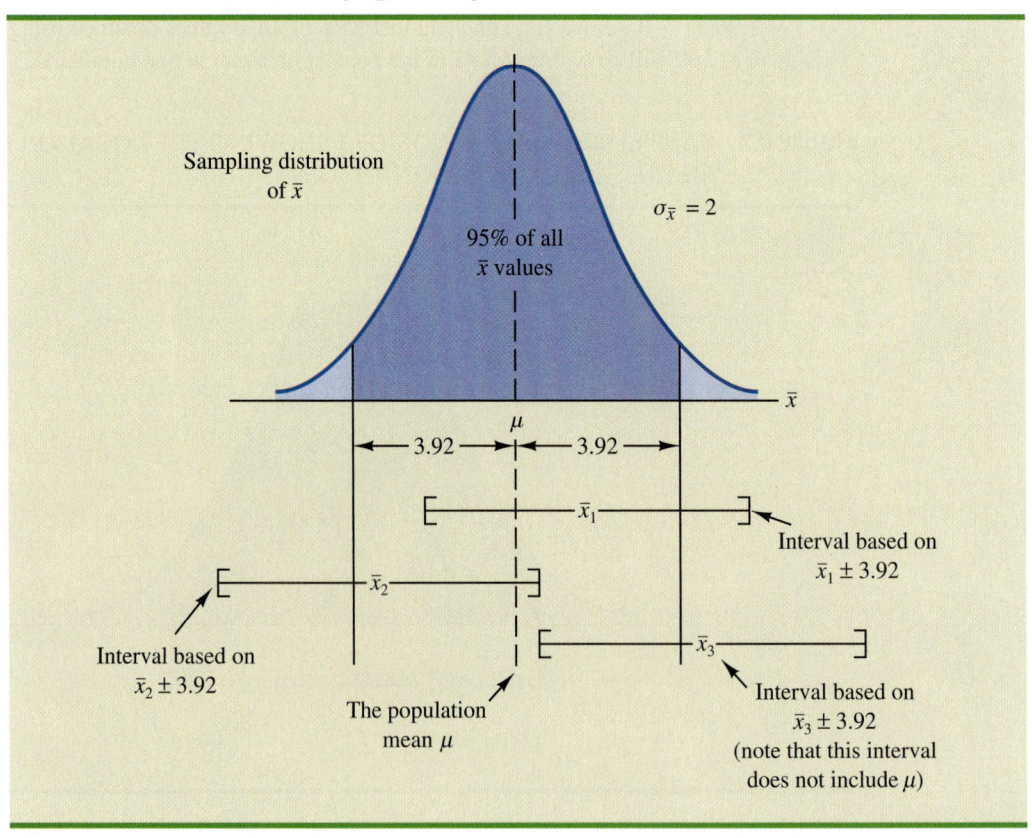

This discussion provides insight as to why the interval is called a 95% confidence interval.

μ based on the data from the most recent week is $82 - 3.92 = 78.08$ to $82 + 3.92 = 85.92$. Because 95% of all the intervals constructed using $\bar{x} \pm 3.92$ will contain the population mean, we say that we are 95% confident that the interval 78.08 to 85.92 includes the population mean μ. We say that this interval has been established at the 95% **confidence level**. The value .95 is referred to as the **confidence coefficient**, and the interval 78.08 to 85.92 is called the 95% **confidence interval**.

Another term sometimes associated with an interval estimate is the **level of significance**. The level of significance associated with an interval estimate is denoted by the Greek letter α. The level of significance and the confidence coefficient are related as follows:

$$\alpha = \text{Level of Significance} = 1 - \text{Confidence Coefficient}$$

The level of significance is also referred to as the significance level.

The level of significance is the probability that the interval estimation procedure will generate an interval that does not contain μ. For example, the level of significance corresponding to a .95 confidence coefficient is $\alpha = 1 - .95 = .05$. In Lloyd's case, the level of significance ($\alpha = .05$) is the probability of drawing a sample, computing the sample mean, and finding that $\bar{x}$ lies in one of the tails of the sampling distribution (see $\bar{x}_3$ in Figure 8.3). When the sample mean happens to fall in the tail of the sampling distribution (and it will 5% of the time), the confidence interval generated will not contain μ.

With the margin of error given by $z_{\alpha/2}(\sigma/\sqrt{n})$, the general form of an interval estimate of a population mean for the σ known case follows.

INTERVAL ESTIMATE OF A POPULATION MEAN: σ KNOWN

$$\bar{x} \pm z_{\alpha/2}\frac{\sigma}{\sqrt{n}} \qquad\qquad \textbf{(8.1)}$$

where $(1 - \alpha)$ is the confidence coefficient and $z_{\alpha/2}$ is the z value providing an area of $\alpha/2$ in the upper tail of the standard normal probability distribution.

Let us use expression (8.1) to construct a 95% confidence interval for the Lloyd's example. For a 95% confidence interval, the confidence coefficient is $(1 - \alpha) = .95$ and thus, $\alpha = .05$. Using the tables of areas for the standard normal distribution, an area of $\alpha/2 = .05/2 = .025$ in the upper tail provides $z_{.025} = 1.96$. With the Lloyd's sample mean $\bar{x} = 82$, $\sigma = 20$, and a sample size $n = 100$, we obtain

$$82 \pm 1.96\frac{20}{\sqrt{100}}$$

$$82 \pm 3.92$$

Thus, using expression (8.1), the margin of error is 3.92 and the 95% confidence interval is $82 - 3.92 = 78.08$ to $82 + 3.92 = 85.92$.

Although a 95% confidence level is frequently used, other confidence levels such as 90% and 99% may be considered. Values of $z_{\alpha/2}$ for the most commonly used confidence levels are shown in Table 8.1. Using these values and expression (8.1), the 90% confidence interval for the Lloyd's example is

$$82 \pm 1.645\frac{20}{\sqrt{100}}$$

$$82 \pm 3.29$$

TABLE 8.1   VALUES OF $z_{\alpha/2}$ FOR THE MOST COMMONLY USED CONFIDENCE LEVELS

Confidence Level	α	$\alpha/2$	$z_{\alpha/2}$
90%	.10	.05	1.645
95%	.05	.025	1.960
99%	.01	.005	2.576

Thus, at 90% confidence, the margin of error is 3.29 and the confidence interval is $82 - 3.29 = 78.71$ to $82 + 3.29 = 85.29$. Similarly, the 99% confidence interval is

$$82 \pm 2.576 \frac{20}{\sqrt{100}}$$

$$82 \pm 5.15$$

Thus, at 99% confidence, the margin of error is 5.15 and the confidence interval is $82 - 5.15 = 76.85$ to $82 + 5.15 = 87.15$.

Comparing the results for the 90%, 95%, and 99% confidence levels, we see that in order to have a higher degree of confidence, the margin of error and thus the width of the confidence interval must be larger.

Using Excel

We will use the Lloyd's Department Store data to illustrate how Excel can be used to construct an interval estimate of the population mean for the σ known case. Refer to Figure 8.4 as we describe the tasks involved. The formula worksheeet is in the background; the value worksheet appears in the foreground.

Enter Data: A label and the sales data are entered into cells A1:A101.

Enter Functions and Formulas: The sample size and sample mean are computed in cells D4:D5 using Excel's COUNT and AVERAGE functions, respectively. The value worksheet shows that the sample size is 100 and the sample mean is 82. The value of the known population standard deviation (20) is entered into cell D7 and the desired confidence coefficient (.95) is entered into cell D8. The level of significance is computed in cell D9 by entering the formula $=1-D8$; the value worksheet shows that the level of significance associated with a confidence coefficient of .95 is .05. The margin of error is computed in cell D11 using Excel's CONFIDENCE function. The CONFIDENCE function has three inputs: the level of significance (cell D9); the population standard deviation (cell D7); and the sample size (cell D4). Thus, to compute the margin of error associated with a 95% confidence interval, the following formula is entered into cell D11:

=CONFIDENCE(D9,D7,D4)

The resulting value of 3.92 is the margin of error associated with the interval estimate of the population mean amount spent per week.

Cells D13:D15 provide the point estimate and the lower and upper limits for the confidence interval. Because the point estimate is just the sample mean, the formula $=D5$ is entered into cell D13. To compute the lower limit of the 95% confidence interval, $\bar{x} -$ (margin of error), we enter the formula $=D13-D11$ into cell D14. To compute the upper limit of the 95% confidence interval, $\bar{x} +$ (margin of error), we enter the formula $=D13+D11$ into cell D15. The value worksheet shows a lower limit of 78.08 and an upper limit of 85.92. In other words, the 95% confidence interval for the population mean is from 78.08 to 85.92.

FIGURE 8.4 EXCEL WORKSHEET: CONSTRUCTING A 95% CONFIDENCE INTERVAL FOR LLOYD'S DEPARTMENT STORE

	A	B	C	D	E
1	Amount		Interval Estimate of a Population Mean:		
2	72		σ Known Case		
3	91				
4	74		Sample Size	=COUNT(A1:A101)	
5	115		Sample Mean	=AVERAGE(A1:A101)	
6	71				
7	120		Population Standard Deviation	20	
8	37		Confidence Coefficient	0.95	
9	96		Level of Significance	=1-D8	
10	91				
11	105		Margin of Error	=CONFIDENCE(D9,D7,D4)	
12	104				
13	89		Point Estimate	=D5	
14	70		Lower Limit	=D13-D11	
15	125		Upper Limit	=D13+D11	
16	43				
17	61				
100	71				
101	84				
102					

	A	B	C	D	E
1	Amount		Interval Estimate of a Population Mean:		
2	72		σ Known Case		
3	91				
4	74		Sample Size	100	
5	115		Sample Mean	82	
6	71				
7	120		Population Standard Deviation	20	
8	37		Confidence Coefficient	0.95	
9	96		Level of Significance	0.05	
10	91				
11	105		Margin of Error	3.92	
12	104				
13	89		Point Estimate	82	
14	70		Lower Limit	78.08	
15	125		Upper Limit	85.92	
16	43				
17	61				
100	71				
101	84				
102					

Note: Rows 18–99 are hidden.

A Template for Other Problems. To use this worksheet as a template for another problem of this type, we must first enter the new problem data in column A. Then, the cell formulas in cells D4 and D5 must be updated with the new data range and the known population standard deviation must be entered into cell D7. After doing so, the point estimate and a 95% confidence interval will be displayed into cells D13:D15. If a confidence interval with a different confidence coefficient is desired, we simply change the value in cell D8.

We can further simplify the use of Figure 8.4 as a template for other problems by eliminating the need to enter new data ranges in cells D4 and D5. To do so we rewrite the cell formulas as follows:

Cell D4: =COUNT(A:A)

Cell D5: =AVERAGE(A:A)

With the A:A method of specifying data ranges, Excel's COUNT function will count the number of numeric values in column A and Excel's AVERAGE function will compute the

The Lloyd's data set includes a worksheet titled Template that uses the A:A method for entering the data ranges.

average of the numeric values in column A. Thus, to solve a new problem it is only necessary to enter the new data into column A and enter the value of the known population standard deviation in cell D7.

This worksheet can also be used as a template for text exercises in which the sample size, sample mean, and the population standard deviation are given. In this type of situation we simply replace the values in cells D4, D5, and D7 with the given values of the sample size, sample mean, and the population standard deviation.

Practical Advice

If the population follows a normal distribution, the confidence interval provided by expression (8.1) is exact. In other words, if expression (8.1) were used repeatedly to generate 95% confidence intervals, exactly 95% of the intervals generated would contain the population mean. If the population does not follow a normal distribution, the confidence interval provided by expression (8.1) will be approximate. In this case, the quality of the approximation depends on both the distribution of the population and the sample size.

In most applications, a sample size of $n \geq 30$ is adequate when using expression (8.1) to develop an interval estimate of a population mean. If the population is not normally distributed, but is roughly symmetric, sample sizes as small as 15 can be expected to provide good approximate confidence intervals. With smaller sample sizes, expression (8.1) should only be used if the analyst believes, or is willing to assume, that the population distribution is at least approximately normal.

NOTES AND COMMENTS

1. The interval estimation procedure discussed in this section is based on the assumption that the population standard deviation σ is known. By σ known we mean that historical data or other information are available that permit us to obtain a good estimate of the population standard deviation prior to taking the sample that will be used to develop an estimate of the population mean. So technically we don't mean that σ is actually known with certainty. We just mean that we obtained a good estimate of the standard deviation prior to sampling and thus we won't be using the same sample to estimate both the population mean and the population standard deviation.

2. The sample size n appears in the denominator of the interval estimation expression (8.1). Thus, if a particular sample size provides too wide an interval to be of any practical use, we may want to consider increasing the sample size. With n in the denominator, a larger sample size will provide a smaller margin of error, a narrower interval, and greater precision. The procedure for determining the size of a simple random sample necessary to obtain a desired precision is discussed in Section 8.3.

Exercises

Methods

1. A simple random sample of 40 items resulted in a sample mean of 25. The population standard deviation is $\sigma = 5$.
    a. What is the standard error of the mean, $\sigma_{\bar{x}}$?
    b. At 95% confidence, what is the margin of error?

2. A simple random sample of 50 items from a population with $\sigma = 6$ resulted in a sample mean of 32.
    a. Provide a 90% confidence interval for the population mean.
    b. Provide a 95% confidence interval for the population mean.
    c. Provide a 99% confidence interval for the population mean.

3. A simple random sample of 60 items resulted in a sample mean of 80. The population standard deviation is $\sigma = 15$.
   a. Compute the 95% confidence interval for the population mean.
   b. Assume that the same sample mean was obtained from a sample of 120 items. Provide a 95% confidence interval for the population mean.
   c. What is the effect of a larger sample size on the interval estimate?

4. A 95% confidence interval for a population mean was reported to be 152 to 160. If $\sigma = 15$, what sample size was used in this study?

Applications

Restaurant

5. In an effort to estimate the mean amount spent per customer for dinner at an Atlanta restaurant, data were collected for a sample of 49 customers. The data collected are shown in the CD file named Restaurant. Based upon past studies the population standard deviation is assumed known with $\sigma = \$5$.
   a. At 95% confidence, what is the margin of error?
   b. Develop a 95% confidence interval estimate of the mean amount spent for dinner.

Nielsen

6. Nielsen Media Research conducted a study of household television viewing times during the 8 P.M. to 11 P.M. time period. The data contained in the CD file named Nielsen are consistent with the findings reported (*The World Almanac*, 2003). Based upon past studies the population standard deviation is assumed known with $\sigma = 3.5$ hours. Develop a 95% confidence interval estimate of the mean television viewing time per week during the 8 P.M. to 11 P.M. time period.

7. A survey of small businesses with Web sites found that the average amount spent on a site was $11,500 per year (*Fortune,* March 5, 2001). Given a sample of 60 small businesses and a population standard deviation of $\sigma = \$4000$, what is the margin of error? Use 95% confidence. What would you recommend if the study required a margin of error of $500?

8. The National Quality Research Center at the University of Michigan provides a quarterly measure of consumer opinions about products and services (*The Wall Street Journal,* February 18, 2003). A survey of 10 restaurants in the Fast Food/Pizza group showed a sample mean customer satisfaction index of 71. Past data indicate that the population standard deviation of the index has been relatively stable with $\sigma = 5$.
   a. What assumption should the researcher be willing to make if a margin of error is desired?
   b. Using 95% confidence, what is the margin of error?
   c. What is the margin of error if 99% confidence is desired?

GPA

9. A study was conducted of students admitted to the top graduate business schools. The data contained in the CD file named GPA show the undergraduate grade point average for students and is consistent with the findings reported ("Best Graduate Schools," *U.S. News and World Report,* 2001). Using past years' data, the population standard deviation can be assumed known with $\sigma = .28$. What is the 95% confidence interval estimate of the mean undergraduate grade point average for students admitted to the top graduate business schools?

10. *Playbill* magazine reported that the mean annual household income of its readers is $119,155 (*Playbill,* December 2003). Assume this estimate of the mean annual household income is based on a sample of 80 households and, based on past studies, the population standard deviation is known to be $\sigma = \$30,000$.
   a. Develop a 90% confidence interval estimate of the population mean.
   b. Develop a 95% confidence interval estimate of the population mean.
   c. Develop a 99% confidence interval estimate of the population mean.
   d. Discuss what happens to the width of the confidence interval as the confidence level is increased. Does this result seem reasonable? Explain.

8.2 Population Mean: σ Unknown

When developing an interval estimate of a population mean we usually do not have a good estimate of the population standard deviation either. In these cases, we must use the same sample to estimate μ and σ. This situation represents the **σ unknown** case. When s is used to estimate σ, the margin of error and the interval estimate for the population mean are based on a probability distribution known as the **t distribution**. Although the mathematical development of the t distribution is based on the assumption of a normal distribution for the population we are sampling from, research shows that the t distribution can be successfully applied in many situations where the population deviates significantly from normal. Later in this section we provide guidelines for using the t distribution if the population is not normally distributed.

William Sealy Gosset, writing under the name "Student," is the founder of the t distribution. Gosset, an Oxford graduate in mathematics, worked for the Guinness Brewery in Dublin, Ireland. He developed the t distribution while working on small-scale materials and temperature experiments.

The t distribution is a family of similar probability distributions, with a specific t distribution depending on a parameter known as the **degrees of freedom**. The t distribution with one degree of freedom is unique, as is the t distribution with two degrees of freedom, with three degrees of freedom, and so on. As the number of degrees of freedom increases, the difference between the t distribution and the standard normal distribution becomes smaller and smaller. Figure 8.5 shows t distributions with 10 and 20 degrees of freedom and their relationship to the standard normal probability distribution. Note that a t distribution with more degrees of freedom exhibits less variability and more closely resembles the standard normal distribution. Note also that the mean of the t distribution is zero.

We place a subscript on t to indicate an area in the upper tail of the t distribution. For example, just as we used $z_{.025}$ to indicate the z value providing a .025 area in the upper tail of a standard normal distribution, we will use $t_{.025}$ to indicate the t value providing a .025 area in the upper tail of a t distribution. In general, we will use the notation $t_{\alpha/2}$ to represent a t value with an area of $\alpha/2$ in the upper tail of the t distribution. See Figure 8.6.

FIGURE 8.5   COMPARISON OF THE STANDARD NORMAL DISTRIBUTION WITH t DISTRIBUTIONS HAVING 10 AND 20 DEGREES OF FREEDOM

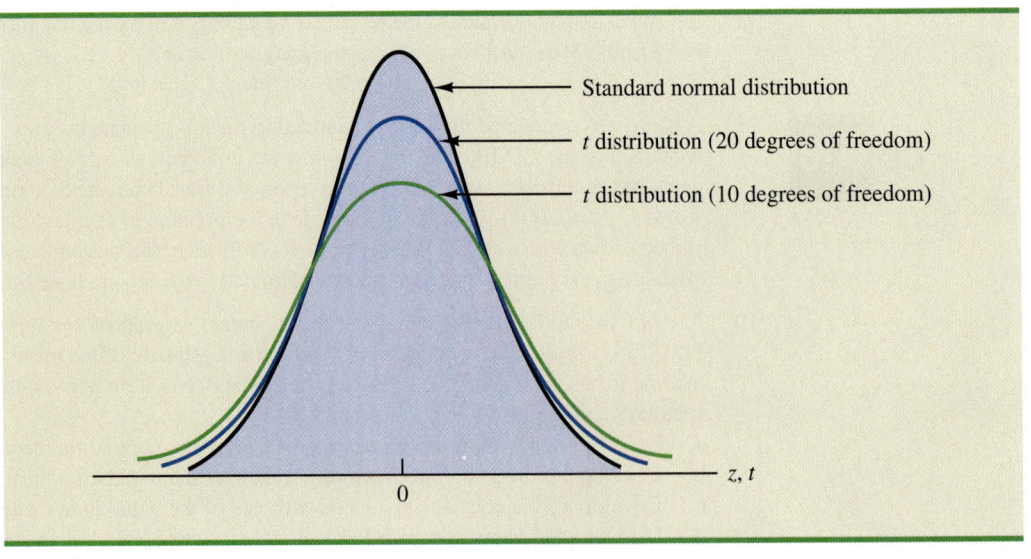

FIGURE 8.6 t DISTRIBUTION WITH $\alpha/2$ AREA OR PROBABILITY IN THE UPPER TAIL

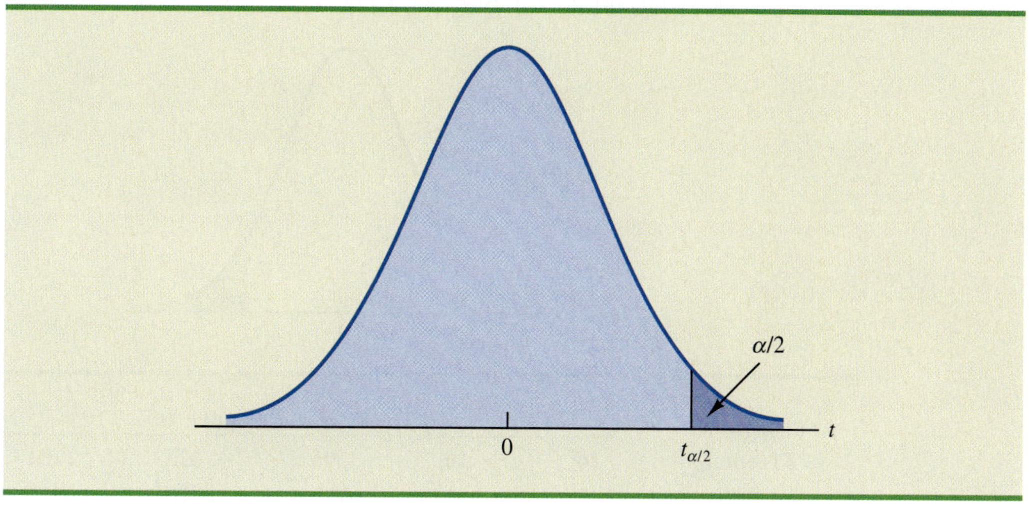

Table 8.2 provides the t value for upper tail areas of .20, .10, .05, .025, .01, and .005. Each row in the table corresponds to a separate t distribution with the degrees of freedom shown. For example, for a t distribution with 10 degrees of freedom, $t_{.025} = 2.228$. Similarly, for a t distribution with 20 degrees of freedom, $t_{.025} = 2.086$. As the degrees of freedom continue to increase, $t_{.025}$ approaches $z_{.025} = 1.96$. In fact, the standard normal distribution z values can be found in the infinite degrees of freedom row (labeled ∞) of the t distribution table. If the degrees of freedom exceed 100, the infinite degrees of freedom row can be used to approximate the actual t value; in other words, for more than 100 degrees of freedom, the standard normal z value provides a good approximation to the t value. Table 2 in Appendix B provides a more extensive t distribution table, with all the degrees of freedom from 1 to 100 included.

As the degrees of freedom increase, the t distribution approaches the standard normal distribution.

Margin of Error and the Interval Estimate

In Section 8.1 we showed that an interval estimate of a population mean for the σ known case is

$$\bar{x} \pm z_{\alpha/2}\frac{\sigma}{\sqrt{n}}$$

To compute an interval estimate of μ for the σ unknown case, the sample standard deviation s is used to estimate σ, and $z_{\alpha/2}$ is replaced by the t distribution value $t_{\alpha/2}$. The margin of error is then given by $t_{\alpha/2}s/\sqrt{n}$. With this margin of error, the general expression for an interval estimate of a population mean when σ is unknown follows.

INTERVAL ESTIMATE OF A POPULATION MEAN: σ UNKNOWN

$$\bar{x} \pm t_{\alpha/2}\frac{s}{\sqrt{n}} \tag{8.2}$$

where s is the sample standard deviation, $(1 - \alpha)$ is the confidence coefficient, and $t_{\alpha/2}$ is the t value providing an area of $\alpha/2$ in the upper tail of the t distribution with $n - 1$ degrees of freedom.

TABLE 8.2 *t* DISTRIBUTION TABLE FOR AN AREA OF $\alpha/2$ IN THE UPPER TAIL. EXAMPLE: WITH 10 DEGREES OF FREEDOM, THE *t* VALUE PROVIDING AN AREA OF .025 IN THE UPPER TAIL IS $t_{.025} = 2.228$

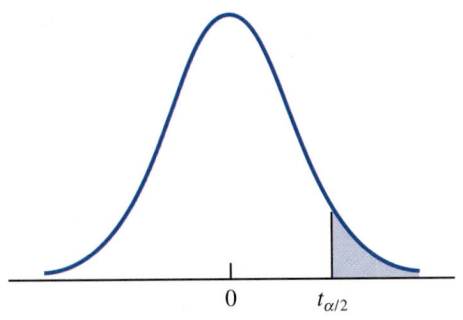

Degrees of Freedom	Area in Upper Tail					
	.20	**.10**	**.05**	**.025**	**.01**	**.005**
1	1.376	3.078	6.314	12.706	31.821	63.656
2	1.061	1.886	2.920	4.303	6.965	9.925
3	.978	1.638	2.353	3.182	4.541	5.841
4	.941	1.533	2.132	2.776	3.747	4.604
5	.920	1.476	2.015	2.571	3.365	4.032
6	.906	1.440	1.943	2.447	3.143	3.707
7	.896	1.415	1.895	2.365	2.998	3.499
8	.889	1.397	1.860	2.306	2.896	3.355
9	.883	1.383	1.833	2.262	2.821	3.250
10	.879	1.372	1.812	2.228	2.764	3.169
11	.876	1.363	1.796	2.201	2.718	3.106
12	.873	1.356	1.782	2.179	2.681	3.055
13	.870	1.350	1.771	2.160	2.650	3.012
14	.868	1.345	1.761	2.145	2.624	2.977
15	.866	1.341	1.753	2.131	2.602	2.947
16	.865	1.337	1.746	2.120	2.583	2.921
17	.863	1.333	1.740	2.110	2.567	2.898
18	.862	1.330	1.734	2.101	2.552	2.878
19	.861	1.328	1.729	2.093	2.539	2.861
20	.860	1.325	1.725	2.086	2.528	2.845
21	.859	1.323	1.721	2.080	2.518	2.831
22	.858	1.321	1.717	2.074	2.508	2.819
23	.858	1.319	1.714	2.069	2.500	2.807
24	.857	1.318	1.711	2.064	2.492	2.797
25	.856	1.316	1.708	2.060	2.485	2.787
26	.856	1.315	1.706	2.056	2.479	2.779
27	.855	1.314	1.703	2.052	2.473	2.771
28	.855	1.313	1.701	2.048	2.467	2.763
29	.854	1.311	1.699	2.045	2.462	2.756
30	.854	1.310	1.697	2.042	2.457	2.750
40	.851	1.303	1.684	2.021	2.423	2.704
50	.849	1.299	1.676	2.009	2.403	2.678
60	.848	1.296	1.671	2.000	2.390	2.660
80	.846	1.292	1.664	1.990	2.374	2.639
100	.845	1.290	1.660	1.984	2.364	2.626
∞	.842	1.282	1.645	1.960	2.326	2.576

Note: A more extensive table is provided as Table 2 of Appendix B.

The reason the number of degrees of freedom associated with the t value in expression (8.2) is $n - 1$ concerns the use of s as an estimate of the population standard deviation σ. The expression for the sample standard deviation is

$$s = \sqrt{\frac{\Sigma(x_i - \bar{x})^2}{n - 1}}$$

Degrees of freedom refer to the number of independent pieces of information that go into the computation of $\Sigma(x_i - \bar{x})^2$. The n pieces of information involved in computing $\Sigma(x_i - \bar{x})^2$ are as follows: $x_1 - \bar{x}, x_2 - \bar{x}, \ldots, x_n - \bar{x}$. In Section 3.2 we indicated that $\Sigma(x_i - \bar{x}) = 0$ for any data set. Thus, only $n - 1$ of the $x_i - \bar{x}$ values are independent; that is, if we know $n - 1$ of the values, the remaining value can be determined exactly by using the condition that the sum of the $x_i - \bar{x}$ values must be 0. Thus, $n - 1$ is the number of degrees of freedom associated with $\Sigma(x_i - \bar{x})^2$ and hence the number of degrees of freedom for the t distribution in expression (8.2).

To illustrate the interval estimation procedure for the σ unknown case, we will consider a study designed to estimate the mean credit card debt for the population of U.S. households. A sample of $n = 85$ households provided the credit card balances shown in Table 8.3. For this situation, no previous estimate of the population standard deviation σ is available. Thus, the sample data must be used to estimate both the population mean and the population standard deviation. Using the data in Table 8.3, we compute the sample mean $\bar{x} = \$5900$ and the sample standard deviation $s = \$3058$. With 95% confidence and $n - 1 = 84$ degrees of freedom, Table 2 in Appendix B provides $t_{.025} = 1.989$. We can now use expression (8.2) to compute an interval estimate of the population mean.

$$5900 \pm 1.989 \frac{3058}{\sqrt{85}}$$

$$5900 \pm 660$$

The point estimate of the population mean is $5900, the margin of error is $660, and the 95% confidence interval is $5900 - 660 = \$5240$ to $5900 + 660 = \$6560$. Thus, we are 95% confident that the population mean credit card balance for all households is between $5240 and $6560.

TABLE 8.3   CREDIT CARD BALANCES FOR A SAMPLE OF 85 HOUSEHOLDS

Balance

9619	5994	3344	7888	7581	9980
5364	4652	13627	3091	12545	8718
8348	5376	968	943	7959	8452
7348	5998	4714	8762	2563	4935
381	7530	4334	1407	6787	5938
2998	3678	4911	6644	5071	5266
1686	3581	1920	7644	9536	10658
1962	5625	3780	11169	4459	3910
4920	5619	3478	7979	8047	7503
5047	9032	6185	3258	8083	1582
6921	13236	1141	8660	2153	
5759	4447	7577	7511	8003	
8047	609	4667	14442	6795	
3924	414	5219	4447	5915	
3470	7636	6416	6550	7164	

Using Excel

We will use the credit card balances in Table 8.3 to illustrate how Excel can be used to construct an interval estimate of the population mean for the σ unknown case. We start by summarizing the date using Excel's Descriptive Statistics tool described in Chapter 3. Refer to Figure 8.7 as we describe the tasks involved. The formula worksheet is in the background; the value worksheet is in the foreground.

Enter Data: A label and the credit card balances are entered into cells A1:A86.

Apply Analysis Tools: The following steps describe how to use Excel's Descriptive Statistics tool for these data:

Step 1. Select the **Tools** menu
Step 2. Choose the **Data Analysis** option
Step 3. Choose **Descriptive Statistics** from the list of Analysis Tools
Step 4. When the Descriptive Statistics dialog box appears:
Enter A1:A86 in the **Input Range** box
Select **Grouped By Columns**
Select **Labels in First Row**
Select **Output Range**
Enter C4 in the **Output Range** box
Select **Summary Statistics**
Select **Confidence Level for Mean**
Enter 95 in the **Confidence Level for Mean** box
Click **OK**

FIGURE 8.7 EXCEL WORKSHEET: 95% CONFIDENCE INTERVAL FOR CREDIT CARD BALANCES

	A	B	C	D	E
1	Balance		*Balance*		
2	9619				
3	5364		Mean	5900	
4	8348		Standard Error	331.6867	
5	7348		Median	5759	
6	381		Mode	8047	
7	2998		Standard Deviation	3058	
8	1686		Sample Variance	9351364	
9	1962		Kurtosis	0.2327	
10	4920		Skewness	0.4076	
11	5047		Range	14061	
12	6921		Minimum	381	
13	5759		Maximum	14442	
14	8047		Sum	501500	
15	3924		Count	85	
16	3470		Confidence Level(95.0%)	660	
17	5994				
18	4652		Point Estimate	=D3	
19	5376		Lower Limit	=D18-D16	
20	5998		Upper Limit	=D18+D16	
85	7503				
86	1582				
87					

Note: Rows 21–84 are hidden.

	A	B	C	D	E	F
1	Balance		*Balance*			
2	9619				Point Estimate	
3	5364		Mean	5900		
4	8348		Standard Error	331.6867		
5	7348		Median	5759		
6	381		Mode	8047		
7	2998		Standard Deviation	3058		
8	1686		Sample Variance	9351364		
9	1962		Kurtosis	0.2327		
10	4920		Skewness	0.4076		
11	5047		Range	14061		
12	6921		Minimum	381		
13	5759		Maximum	14442		
14	8047		Sum	501500		
15	3924		Count	85	Margin of Error	
16	3470		Confidence Level(95.0%)	660		
17	5994					
18	4652		Point Estimate	5900		
19	5376		Lower Limit	5240		
20	5998		Upper Limit	6560		
85	7503					
86	1582					
87						

The sample mean ($\bar{x}$) is in cell D3. The margin of error, labeled "Confidence Level(95%)," appears in cell D16. The value worksheet shows $\bar{x} = 5900$ and a margin of error equal to 660.

Enter Functions and Formulas: Cells D18:D20 provide the point estimate and the lower and upper limits for the confidence interval. Because the point estimate is just the sample mean, the formula =D3 is entered into cell D18. To compute the lower limit of the 95% confidence interval, $\bar{x} -$ (margin of error), we enter the formula =D18-D16 into cell D19. To compute the upper limit of the 95% confidence interval, $\bar{x} +$ (margin of error), we enter the formula =D18+D16 into cell D20. The value worksheet shows a lower limit of 5240 and an upper limit of 6560. In other words, the 95% confidence interval for the population mean is from 5240 to 6560.

Practical Advice

If the population follows a normal distribution, the confidence interval provided by expression (8.2) is exact and can be used for any sample size. If the population does not follow a normal distribution, the confidence interval provided by expression (8.2) will be approximate. In this case, the quality of the approximation depends on both the distribution of the population and the sample size.

Larger sample sizes are needed if the distribution of the population is highly skewed or includes outliers.

In most applications, a sample size of $n \geq 30$ is adequate when using expression (8.2) to develop an interval estimate of a population mean. However, if the population distribution is highly skewed or contains outliers, most statisticians would recommend increasing the sample size to 50 or more. If the population is not normally distributed but is roughly symmetric, sample sizes as small as 15 can be expected to provide good approximate confidence intervals. With smaller sample sizes, expression (8.2) should only be used if the analyst believes, or is willing to assume, that the population distribution is at least approximately normal.

Using a Small Sample

In the following example we develop an interval estimate for a population mean when the sample size is small. As we already noted, an understanding of the distribution of the population becomes a factor in deciding whether the interval estimation procedure provides acceptable results.

Scheer Industries is considering a new computer-assisted program to train maintenance employees to do machine repairs. In order to fully evaluate the program, the director of manufacturing requested an estimate of the population mean time required for maintenance employees to complete the computer-assisted training.

A sample of 20 employees is selected, with each employee in the sample completing the training program. Data on the training time in days for the 20 employees are shown in Table 8.4. A histogram of the sample data appears in Figure 8.8. What can we say about the distribution of the population based on this histogram? First, the sample data do not support

TABLE 8.4   TRAINING TIME IN DAYS FOR A SAMPLE OF 20 SCHEER
INDUSTRIES EMPLOYEES

52	59	54	42
44	50	42	48
55	54	60	55
44	62	62	57
45	46	43	56

FIGURE 8.8   HISTOGRAM OF TRAINING TIMES FOR THE SCHEER INDUSTRIES SAMPLE

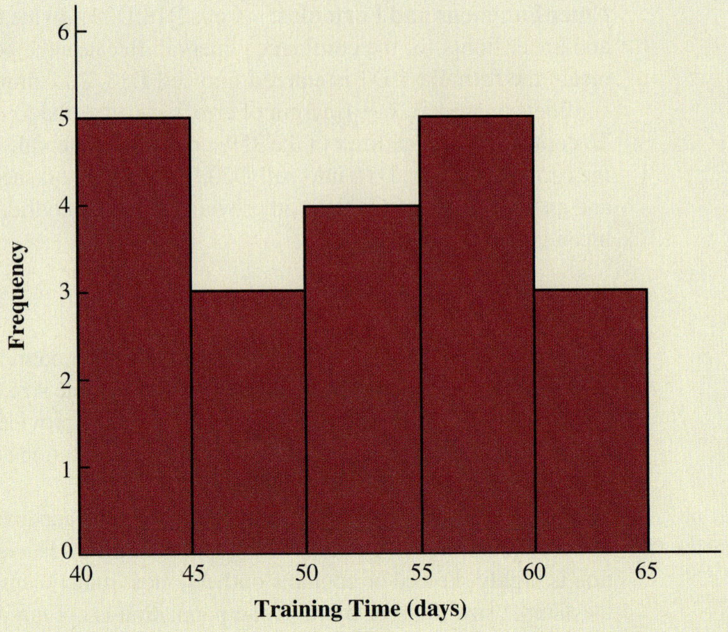

the conclusion that the distribution of the population is normal, yet we do not see any evidence of skewness or outliers. Therefore, using the guidelines in the previous subsection, we conclude that an interval estimate based on the t distribution appears acceptable for the sample of 20 employees.

We continue by computing the sample mean and sample standard deviation as follows.

$$\bar{x} = \frac{\Sigma x_i}{n} = \frac{1030}{20} = 51.5 \text{ days}$$

$$s = \sqrt{\frac{\Sigma(x_i - \bar{x})^2}{n-1}} = \sqrt{\frac{889}{20-1}} = 6.84 \text{ days}$$

For a 95% confidence interval, we use Table 8.2 and $n - 1 = 19$ degrees of freedom to obtain $t_{.025} = 2.093$. Expression (8.2) provides the interval estimate of the population mean.

$$51.5 \pm 2.093\left(\frac{6.84}{\sqrt{20}}\right)$$

$$51.5 \pm 3.2$$

The point estimate of the population mean is 51.5 days. The margin of error is 3.2 days and the 95% confidence interval is $51.5 - 3.2 = 48.3$ days to $51.5 + 3.2 = 54.7$ days.

Using a histogram of the sample data to learn about the distribution of a population is not always conclusive, but in many cases it provides the only information available. The histogram, along with judgment on the part of the analyst, can often be used to decide whether expression (8.2) can be used to develop the interval estimate.

FIGURE 8.9 SUMMARY OF INTERVAL ESTIMATION PROCEDURES FOR A POPULATION MEAN

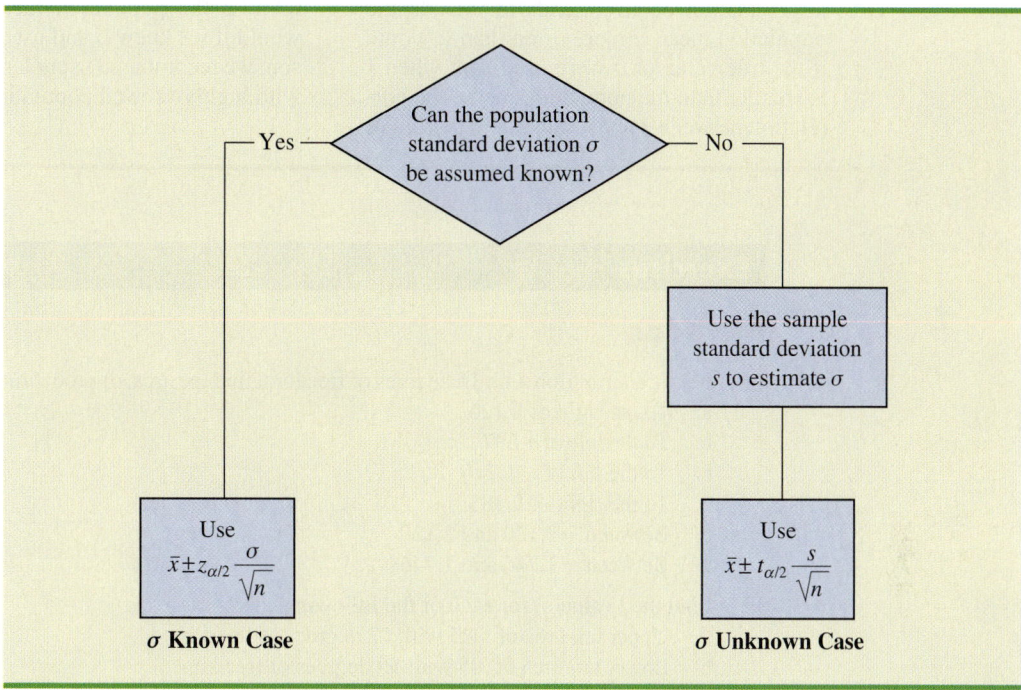

Summary of Interval Estimation Procedures

We provided two approaches to developing an interval estimate of a population mean. For the σ known case, σ and the standard normal distribution are used in expression (8.1) to compute the margin of error and to develop the interval estimate. For the σ unknown case, the sample standard deviation s and the t distribution are used in expression (8.2) to compute the margin of error and to develop the interval estimate.

A summary of the interval estimation procedures for the two cases is shown in Figure 8.9. In most applications, a sample size of $n \geq 30$ is adequate. If the population has a normal or approximately normal distribution, however, smaller sample sizes may be used. For the σ unknown case a sample size of $n \geq 50$ is recommended if the population distribution is believed to be highly skewed or has outliers.

NOTES AND COMMENTS

1. When σ is known, the margin of error, $z_{\alpha/2}(\sigma/\sqrt{n})$, is fixed and is the same for all samples of size n. When σ is unknown, the margin of error, $t_{\alpha/2}(s/\sqrt{n})$, varies from sample to sample. This variation occurs because the sample standard deviation s varies depending upon the sample selected. A large value for s provides a larger margin of error, while a small value for s provides a smaller margin of error.

2. What happens to confidence interval estimates when the population is skewed? Con-

sider a population that is skewed to the right with large data values stretching the distribution to the right. When such skewness exists, the sample mean $\bar{x}$ and the sample standard deviation s are positively correlated. Larger values of s tend to be associated with larger values of $\bar{x}$. Thus, when $\bar{x}$ is larger than the population mean, s tends to be larger than σ. This skewness causes the margin of error,

(continued)

$t_{\alpha/2}(s/\sqrt{n})$, to be larger than it would be with σ known. The confidence interval with the larger margin of error tends to include the population mean μ more often than it would if the true value of σ were used. But when $\bar{x}$ is smaller than the population mean, the correlation between $\bar{x}$ and s causes the margin of error to be small. In this case, the confidence interval with the smaller margin of error tends to miss the population mean more than it would if we knew σ and used it. For this reason, we recommend using larger sample sizes with highly skewed population distributions.

Exercises

Methods

11. For a t distribution with 16 degrees of freedom, find the area, or probability, in each region.
    a. To the right of 2.120
    b. To the left of 1.337
    c. To the left of -1.746
    d. To the right of 2.583
    e. Between -2.120 and 2.120
    f. Between -1.746 and 1.746

12. Find the t value(s) for each of the following cases.
    a. Upper tail area of .025 with 12 degrees of freedom
    b. Lower tail area of .05 with 50 degrees of freedom
    c. Upper tail area of .01 with 30 degrees of freedom
    d. Where 90% of the area falls between these two t values with 25 degrees of freedom
    e. Where 95% of the area falls between these two t values with 45 degrees of freedom
        (See Table 2 of Appendix B for a more extensive t table.)

13. The following sample data are from a normal population: 10, 8, 12, 15, 13, 11, 6, 5.
    a. What is the point estimate of the population mean?
    b. What is the point estimate of the population standard deviation?
    c. With 95% confidence, what is the margin of error for the estimation of the population mean?
    d. What is the 95% confidence interval for the population mean?

14. A simple random sample with $n = 54$ provided a sample mean of 22.5 and a sample standard deviation of 4.4. (See Table 2 of Appendix B for a more extensive t table.)
    a. Develop a 90% confidence interval for the population mean.
    b. Develop a 95% confidence interval for the population mean.
    c. Develop a 99% confidence interval for the population mean.
    d. What happens to the margin of error and the confidence interval as the confidence level is increased?

Applications

15. Sales personnel for Skillings Distributors submit weekly reports listing the customer contacts made during the week. A sample of 65 weekly reports showed a sample mean of 19.5 customer contacts per week. The sample standard deviation was 5.2. Provide 90% and 95% confidence intervals for the population mean number of weekly customer contacts for the sales personnel.

16. The mean number of hours of flying time for pilots at Continental Airlines is 49 hours per month (*The Wall Street Journal,* February 25, 2003). Assume that this mean was based on actual flying times for a sample of 100 Continental pilots and that the sample standard deviation was 8.5 hours.

a. At 95% confidence, what is the margin of error?

b. What is the 95% confidence interval estimate of the population mean flying time for the pilots?

c. The mean number of hours of flying time for pilots at United Airlines is 36 hours per month. Use your results from part (b) to discuss differences between the flying times for the pilots at the two airlines. *The Wall Street Journal* reported United Airlines as having the highest labor cost among all airlines. Does the information in this exercise provide insight as to why United Airlines might expect higher labor costs?

17. The International Air Transport Association surveys business travelers to develop quality ratings for transatlantic gateway airports. The maximum possible rating is 10. Suppose a simple random sample of 50 business travelers is selected and each traveler is asked to provide a rating for the Miami International Airport. The ratings obtained from the sample of 50 business travelers follow.

Miami

6	4	6	8	7	7	6	3	3	8	10	4	8
7	8	7	5	9	5	8	4	3	8	5	5	4
4	4	8	4	5	6	2	5	9	9	8	4	8
9	9	5	9	7	8	3	10	8	9	6		

Develop a 95% confidence interval estimate of the population mean rating for Miami.

18. Thirty fast-food restaurants including Wendy's, McDonald's, and Burger King were visited during the summer of 2000 (*The Cincinnati Enquirer,* July 9, 2000). During each visit, the customer went to the drive-through and ordered a basic meal such as a "combo" meal or a sandwich, fries, and shake. The time between pulling up to the menu board and receiving the filled order was recorded. The times in minutes for the 30 visits are as follows:

FastFood

0.9	1.0	1.2	2.2	1.9	3.6	2.8	5.2	1.8	2.1
6.8	1.3	3.0	4.5	2.8	2.3	2.7	5.7	4.8	3.5
2.6	3.3	5.0	4.0	7.2	9.1	2.8	3.6	7.3	9.0

a. Provide a point estimate of the population mean drive-through time at fast-food restaurants.

b. At 95% confidence, what is the margin of error?

c. What is the 95% confidence interval estimate of the population mean?

d. Discuss skewness that may be present in this population. What suggestion would you make for a repeat of this study?

19. A National Retail Foundation survey found households intended to spend an average of $649 during the December holiday season (*The Wall Street Journal,* December 2, 2002). Assume that the survey included 600 households and that the sample standard deviation was $175.

a. With 95% confidence, what is the margin of error?

b. What is the 95% confidence interval estimate of the population mean?

c. The prior year, the population mean expenditure per household was $632. Discuss the change in holiday season expenditures over the one-year period.

20. The American Association of Advertising Agencies records data on nonprogram minutes on half-hour, prime-time television shows. Representative data in minutes for a sample of 20 prime-time shows on major networks at 8:30 P.M. follow.

TVtime

6.0	6.6	5.8
7.0	6.3	6.2
7.2	5.7	6.4
7.0	6.5	6.2
6.0	6.5	7.2
7.3	7.6	6.8
6.0	6.2	

Assume a normal population and provide a point estimate and a 95% confidence interval for the mean number of nonprogram minutes on half-hour, prime-time television shows at 8:30 P.M.

21. Complaints about rising prescription drug prices caused the U.S. Congress to consider laws that would force pharmaceutical companies to offer prescription discounts to senior citizens without drug benefits. The House Government Reform Committee provided data on the prescription cost for some of the most widely used drugs (*Newsweek*, May 8, 2000). Assume the following data show a sample of the prescription cost in dollars for Zocor, a drug used to lower cholesterol.

| 110 | 112 | 115 | 99 | 100 | 98 | 104 | 126 |

Given a normal population, what is the 95% confidence interval estimate of the population mean cost for a prescription of Zocor?

22. The first few weeks of 2004 were good for the stock market. A sample of 25 large open-end funds showed the following year-to-date returns through January 16, 2004 (*Barron's*, January 19, 2004).

CD file

OpenEndFunds

7.0	3.2	1.4	5.4	8.5
2.5	2.5	1.9	5.4	1.6
1.0	2.1	8.5	4.3	6.2
1.5	1.2	2.7	3.8	2.0
1.2	2.6	4.0	2.6	0.6

a. What is the point estimate of the population mean year-to-date return for large open-end funds?

b. Given that the population has a normal distribution, develop a 95% confidence interval for the population mean year-to-date return for open-end funds.

8.3   Determining the Sample Size

In providing practical advice in the two preceding sections, we commented on the role of the sample size in providing approximate confidence intervals when the population is not normally distributed. In this section, we focus on another aspect of the sample size issue. We describe how to choose a sample size large enough to provide a desired margin of error. To see how this is done, we return to the σ known case presented in Section 8.1. Using expression (8.1), the interval estimate is

If a desired margin of error is selected prior to sampling, the procedures in this section can be used to determine the sample size necessary to satisfy the margin of error requirement.

$$\bar{x} \pm z_{\alpha/2} \frac{\sigma}{\sqrt{n}}$$

The quantity $z_{\alpha/2}(\sigma/\sqrt{n})$ is the margin of error. Thus, we see that $z_{\alpha/2}$, the population standard deviation σ, and the sample size n combine to determine the margin of error. Once we select a confidence coefficient $1 - \alpha$, $z_{\alpha/2}$ can be determined. Then, if we have a value for σ, we can determine the sample size n needed to provide any desired margin of error. Development of the formula used to compute the required sample size n follows.

Let E = the desired margin of error:

$$E = z_{\alpha/2} \frac{\sigma}{\sqrt{n}}$$

Solving for $\sqrt{n}$, we have

$$\sqrt{n} = \frac{z_{\alpha/2}\sigma}{E}$$

Squaring both sides of this equation, we obtain the following expression for the sample size.

Equation (8.3) can be used to provide a sample size recommendation. However, judgment on the part of the analyst should be used to determine whether the final sample size should be adjusted upward.

SAMPLE SIZE FOR AN INTERVAL ESTIMATE OF A POPULATION MEAN

$$n = \frac{(z_{\alpha/2})^2 \sigma^2}{E^2}$$

(8.3)

This sample size provides the desired margin of error at the chosen confidence level.

In equation (8.3) E is the margin of error that the user is willing to accept, and the value of $z_{\alpha/2}$ follows directly from the confidence level to be used in developing the interval estimate. Although user preference must be considered, 95% confidence is the most frequently chosen value ($z_{.025} = 1.96$).

Finally, use of equation (8.3) requires a value for the population standard deviation σ. However, even if σ is unknown, we can use equation (8.3) provided we have a preliminary or *planning value* for σ. In practice, one of the following procedures can be chosen.

A planning value for the population standard deviation σ must be specified before the sample size can be determined. Three methods of obtaining a planning value for σ are discussed here.

1. Use the estimate of the population standard deviation computed from data of previous studies as the planning value for σ.
2. Use a pilot study to select a preliminary sample. The sample standard deviation from the preliminary sample can be used as the planning value for σ.
3. Use judgment or a "best guess" for the value of σ. For example, we might begin by estimating the largest and smallest data values in the population. The difference between the largest and smallest values provides an estimate of the range for the data. Finally, the range divided by 4 is often suggested as a rough approximation of the standard deviation and thus an acceptable planning value for σ.

Let us demonstrate the use of equation (8.3) to determine the sample size by considering the following example. A previous study that investigated the cost of renting automobiles in the United States found a mean cost of approximately $55 per day for renting a midsize automobile. Suppose that the organization that conducted this study would like to conduct a new study in order to estimate the population mean daily rental cost for a midsize automobile in the United States. In designing the new study, the project director specifies that the population mean daily rental cost be estimated with a margin of error of $2 and a 95% level of confidence.

The project director specified a desired margin of error of $E = 2$, and the 95% level of confidence indicates $z_{.025} = 1.96$. Thus, we only need a planning value for the population standard deviation σ in order to compute the required sample size. At this point, an analyst reviewed the sample data from the previous study and found that the sample standard deviation for the daily rental cost was $9.65. Using 9.65 as the planning value for σ, we obtain

Equation (8.3) provides the minimum sample size needed to satisfy the desired margin of error requirement. If the computed sample size is not an integer, rounding up to the next integer value will provide a margin of error slightly smaller than required.

$$n = \frac{(z_{\alpha/2})^2 \sigma^2}{E^2} = \frac{(1.96)^2(9.65)^2}{2^2} = 89.43$$

Thus, the sample size for the new study needs to be at least 89.43 midsize automobile rentals in order to satisfy the project director's $2 margin-of-error requirement. In cases where the computed n is not an integer, we round up to the next integer value; hence, the recommended sample size is 90 midsize automobile rentals.

Exercises

Methods

23. How large a sample should be selected to provide a 95% confidence interval with a margin of error of 10? Assume that the population standard deviation is 40.

24. The range for a set of data is estimated to be 36.
    a. What is the planning value for the population standard deviation?
    b. At 95% confidence, how large a sample would provide a margin of error of 3?
    c. At 95% confidence, how large a sample would provide a margin of error of 2?

Applications

25. Refer to the Scheer Industries example in Section 8.2. Use 6.84 days as a planning value for the population standard deviation.
    a. Assuming 95% confidence, what sample size would be required to obtain a margin of error of 1.5 days?
    b. If the precision statement was made with 90% confidence, what sample size would be required to obtain a margin of error of 2 days?

26. *Bride's* magazine reported that the mean cost of a wedding is $19,000 (*USA Today*, April 17, 2000). Assume that the population standard deviation is $9400. *Bride's* plans to use an annual survey to monitor the cost of a wedding. Use 95% confidence.
    a. What is the recommended sample size if the desired margin of error is $1000?
    b. What is the recommended sample size if the desired margin of error is $500?
    c. What is the recommended sample size if the desired margin of error is $200?

27. Annual starting salaries for college graduates with degrees in business administration are generally expected to be between $30,000 and $45,000. Assume that a 95% confidence interval estimate of the population mean annual starting salary is desired. What is the planning value for the population standard deviation? How large a sample should be taken if the desired margin of error is
    a. $500?
    b. $200?
    c. $100?
    d. Would you recommend trying to obtain the $100 margin of error? Explain.

28. Smith Travel Research provides information on the one-night cost of hotel rooms throughout the United States (*USA Today*, July 8, 2002). Use $2 as the desired margin of error and $22.50 as the planning value for the population standard deviation to find the sample size recommended in (a), (b), and (c).
    a. A 90% confidence interval estimate of the population mean cost of hotel rooms
    b. A 95% confidence interval estimate of the population mean cost of hotel rooms
    c. A 99% confidence interval estimate of the population mean cost of hotel rooms
    d. When the desired margin of error is fixed, what happens to the sample size as the confidence level is increased? Would you recommend a 99% confidence level be used by Smith Travel Research? Discuss.

29. The travel-to-work time for residents of the 15 largest cities in the United States is reported in the *2003 Information Please Almanac*. Suppose that a preliminary simple random sample of residents of San Francisco is used to develop a planning value of 6.25 minutes for the population standard deviation.
    a. If we want to estimate the population mean travel-to-work time for San Francisco residents with a margin of error of 2 minutes, what sample size should be used? Assume 95% confidence.
    b. If we want to estimate the population mean travel-to-work time for San Francisco residents with a margin of error of 1 minute, what sample size should be used? Assume 95% confidence.

30. During the first quarter of 2003, the price/earnings (P/E) ratio for stocks listed on the New York Stock Exchange generally ranged from 5 to 60 (*The Wall Street Journal,* March 7, 2003). Assume that we want to estimate the population mean P/E ratio for all stocks listed on the exchange. How many stocks should be included in the sample if we want a margin of error of 3? Use 95% confidence.

8.4 Population Proportion

In the introduction to this chapter we said that the general form of an interval estimate of a population proportion p is

$$\bar{p} \pm \text{Margin of error}$$

The sampling distribution of $\bar{p}$ plays a key role in computing the margin of error for this interval estimate.

In Chapter 7 we said that the sampling distribution of $\bar{p}$ can be approximated by a normal distribution whenever $np \geq 5$ and $n(1 - p) \geq 5$. Figure 8.10 shows the normal approximation of the sampling distribution of $\bar{p}$. The mean of the sampling distribution of $\bar{p}$ is the population proportion p, and the standard error of $\bar{p}$ is

$$\sigma_{\bar{p}} = \sqrt{\frac{p(1 - p)}{n}} \tag{8.4}$$

Because the sampling distribution of $\bar{p}$ is normally distributed, if we choose $z_{\alpha/2}\sigma_{\bar{p}}$ as the margin of error in an interval estimate of a population proportion, we know that $100(1 - \alpha)\%$ of the intervals generated will contain the true population proportion. Unfortunately, $\sigma_{\bar{p}}$ cannot be used directly in the computation of the margin of error because p will not be known; p is what we are trying to estimate. So, $\bar{p}$ is substituted for p and the margin of error for an interval estimate of a population proportion is given by

$$\text{Margin of error} = z_{\alpha/2}\sqrt{\frac{\bar{p}(1 - \bar{p})}{n}} \tag{8.5}$$

FIGURE 8.10   NORMAL APPROXIMATION OF THE SAMPLING DISTRIBUTION OF $\bar{p}$

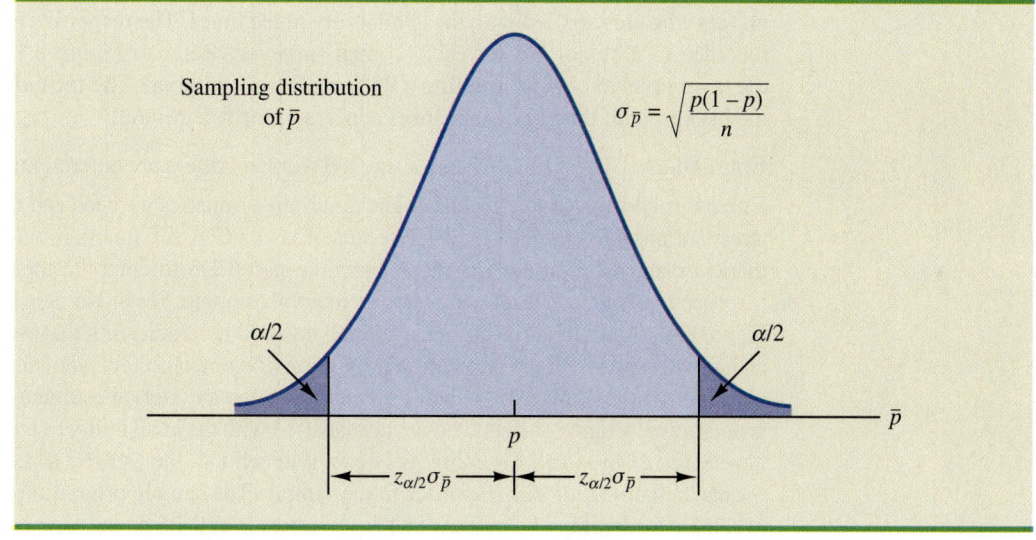

With this margin of error, the general expression for an interval estimate of a population proportion is as follows.

INTERVAL ESTIMATE OF A POPULATION PROPORTION

$$\bar{p} \pm z_{\alpha/2} \sqrt{\frac{\bar{p}(1 - \bar{p})}{n}} \qquad (8.6)$$

where $1 - \alpha$ is the confidence coefficient and $z_{\alpha/2}$ is the z value providing an area of $\alpha/2$ in the upper tail of the standard normal distribution.

When developing confidence intervals for proportions, the quantity $z_{\alpha/2}\sqrt{\bar{p}(1 - \bar{p})/n}$ provides the margin of error.

TeeTimes

The following example illustrates the computation of the margin of error and interval estimate for a population proportion. A national survey of 900 women golfers was conducted to learn how women golfers view their treatment at golf courses in the United States. The survey found that 396 of the women golfers were satisfied with the availability of tee times. Thus, the point estimate of the proportion of the population of women golfers who are satisfied with the availability of tee times is 396/900 = .44. Using expression (8.6) and a 95% confidence level,

$$\bar{p} \pm z_{\alpha/2} \sqrt{\frac{\bar{p}(1 - \bar{p})}{n}}$$

$$.44 \pm 1.96 \sqrt{\frac{.44(1 - .44)}{900}}$$

$$.44 \pm .0324$$

Thus, the margin of error is .0324 and the 95% confidence interval estimate of the population proportion is .4076 to .4724. Using percentages, the survey results enable us to state with 95% confidence that between 40.76% and 47.24% of all women golfers are satisfied with the availability of tee times.

Using Excel

Excel can be used to construct an interval estimate of the population proportion of women golfers who are satisfied with the availability of tee times. The responses in the survey were recorded as a Yes or No for each woman surveyed. Refer to Figure 8.11 as we describe the tasks involved in constructing a 95% confidence interval. The formula worksheet is in the background; the value worksheet appears in the foreground.

Enter Data: The Yes-No data for the 900 women golfers are entered into cells A2:A901.

Enter Functions and Formulas: The descriptive statistics we need and the response of interest are provided in cells D3:D6. Because Excel's COUNT function only works with numerical data, we used the COUNTA function in cell D3 to compute the sample size. The response for which we want to develop an interval estimate, Yes or No, is entered into cell D4. Figure 8.11 shows that Yes has been entered into cell D4, indicating that we want to develop an interval estimate of the population proportion of women golfers who are satisfied with the availability of tee times. If we had wanted to develop an interval estimate of the population proportion of women golfers who are not satisfied with the availability of tee times, we would have entered No in cell D4. With Yes entered in cell D4, the COUNTIF function in cell D5 counts the number of Yes responses in the sample. The sample proportion is then computed in cell D6 by dividing the number of Yes responses in cell D5 by the sample size in cell D3.

FIGURE 8.11   EXCEL WORKSHEET: 95% CONFIDENCE INTERVAL FOR SURVEY OF WOMEN GOLFERS

	A	B	C	D	E
1	Response		Interval Estimate of a Population Proportion		
2	Yes				
3	No		Sample Size	=COUNTA(A2:A901)	
4	Yes		Response of Interest	Yes	
5	Yes		Count for Response	=COUNTIF(A2:A901,D4)	
6	No		Sample Proportion	=D5/D3	
7	No				
8	No		Confidence Coefficient	0.95	
9	Yes		Level of Significance (alpha)	=1-D8	
10	Yes		z Value	=NORMSINV(1-D9/2)	
11	Yes				
12	No		Standard Error	=SQRT(D6*(1-D6)/D3)	
13	No		Margin of Error	=D10*D12	
14	Yes				
15	No		Point Estimate	=D6	
16	No		Lower Limit	=D15-D13	
17	Yes		Upper Limit	=D15+D13	
18	No				
900	Yes				
901	Yes				
902					

CD file

TeeTimes

Note: Rows 19 to 899 are hidden.

	A	B	C	D	E	F	G
1	Response		Interval Estimate of a Population Proportion				
2	Yes						
3	No		Sample Size	900			
4	Yes		Response of Interest	Yes	Enter Yes as the Response of Interest		
5	Yes		Count for Response	396			
6	No		Sample Proportion	0.44			
7	No						
8	No		Confidence Coefficient	0.95			
9	Yes		Level of Significance	0.05			
10	Yes		z Value	1.96			
11	Yes						
12	No		Standard Error	0.0165			
13	No		Margin of Error	0.0324			
14	Yes						
15	No		Point Estimate	0.44			
16	No		Lower Limit	0.4076			
17	Yes		Upper Limit	0.4724			
18	No						
900	Yes						
901	Yes						
902							

Cells D8:D10 are used to compute the appropriate z value. The confidence coefficient (0.95) is entered into cell D8 and the level of significance (α) is computed in cell D9 by entering the formula =1-D8. The z value corresponding to an upper tail area of $\alpha/2$ is computed by entering the formula =NORMSINV(1-D9/2) into cell D10. The value worksheet shows that $z_{.025} = 1.960$.

Cells D12:D13 provide the estimate of the standard error and the margin of error. In cell D12, we entered the formula =SQRT(D6*(1-D6)/D3) to compute the standard error using the sample proportion and the sample size as inputs. The formula =D10*D12 is entered into cell D13 to compute the margin of error.

Cells D15:D17 provide the point estimate and the lower and upper limits for a confidence interval. The point estimate in cell D15 is the sample proportion. The lower and upper limits in cells D16 and D17 are obtained by subtracting and adding the margin of error to the point estimate. We note that the 95% confidence interval for the proportion of women golfers who are satisfied with the availability of tee times is .4076 to .4724.

A Template for Other Problems. The worksheet in Figure 8.11 can be used as a template for developing confidence intervals about a population proportion p. To use this worksheet for another problem of this type, we must first enter the new problem data in column A. The response of interest would then be typed in cell D4 and the ranges for the formulas in cells D3 and D5 would be revised to correspond to the new data. After doing so, the point estimate and a 95% confidence interval will be displayed in cells D15:D17. If a confidence interval with a different confidence coefficient is desired, we simply change the value in cell D8.

Determining the Sample Size

Let us consider the question of how large the sample size should be to obtain an estimate of a population proportion at a specified level of precision. The rationale for the sample size determination in developing interval estimates of p is similar to the rationale used in Section 8.3 to determine the sample size for estimating a population mean.

Previously in this section we said that the margin of error associated with an interval estimate of a population proportion is $z_{\alpha/2}\sqrt{\bar{p}(1 - \bar{p})/n}$. The margin of error is based on the value of $z_{\alpha/2}$, the sample proportion $\bar{p}$, and the sample size n. Larger sample sizes provide a smaller margin of error and better precision.

Let E denote the desired margin of error.

$$E = z_{\alpha/2}\sqrt{\frac{\bar{p}(1 - \bar{p})}{n}}$$

Solving this equation for n provides a formula for the sample size that will provide a margin of error of size E.

$$n = \frac{(z_{\alpha/2})^2\bar{p}(1 - \bar{p})}{E^2}$$

Note, however, that we cannot use this formula to compute the sample size that will provide the desired margin of error because $\bar{p}$ will not be known until after we select the sample. What we need, then, is a planning value for $\bar{p}$ that can be used to make the computation. Using p^* to denote the planning value for $\bar{p}$, the following formula can be used to compute the sample size that will provide a margin of error of size E.

SAMPLE SIZE FOR AN INTERVAL ESTIMATE OF A POPULATION PROPORTION

$$n = \frac{(z_{\alpha/2})^2 p^*(1 - p^*)}{E^2} \qquad \textbf{(8.7)}$$

In practice, the planning value p^* can be chosen by one of the following procedures.

1. Use the sample proportion from a previous sample of the same or similar units.
2. Use a pilot study to select a preliminary sample. The sample proportion from this sample can be used as the planning value, p^*.
3. Use judgment or a "best guess" for the value of p^*.
4. If none of the preceding alternatives apply, use a planning value of $p^* = .50$.

Let us return to the survey of women golfers and assume that the company is interested in conducting a new survey to estimate the current proportion of the population of women golfers who are satisfied with the availability of tee times. How large should the sample be if the survey director wants to estimate the population proportion with a margin of error of .025 at 95% confidence? With $E = .025$ and $z_{\alpha/2} = 1.96$, we need a planning value p^* to answer the sample size question. Using the previous survey result of $\bar{p} = .44$ as the planning value p^*, equation (8.7) shows that

$$n = \frac{(z_{\alpha/2})^2 p^*(1 - p^*)}{E^2} = \frac{(1.96)^2(.44)(1 - .44)}{(.025)^2} = 1514.5$$

Thus, the sample size must be at least 1514.5 women golfers to satisfy the margin of error requirement. Rounding up to the next integer value indicates that a sample of 1515 women golfers is recommended to satisfy the margin of error requirement.

The fourth alternative suggested for selecting a planning value p^* is to use $p^* = .50$. This value of p^* is frequently used when no other information is available. To understand why, note that the numerator of equation (8.7) shows that the sample size is proportional to the quantity $p^*(1 - p^*)$. A larger value for the quantity $p^*(1 - p^*)$ will result in a larger sample size. Table 8.5 gives some possible values of $p^*(1 - p^*)$. Note that the largest value of $p^*(1 - p^*)$ occurs when $p^* = .50$. Thus, in case of any uncertainty about an appropriate planning value, we know that $p^* = .50$ will provide the largest sample size recommendation. In effect, we play it safe by recommending the largest possible sample size. If the sample proportion turns out to be different from the .50 planning value, the margin of error will be smaller than anticipated. Thus, in using $p^* = .50$, we guarantee that the sample size will be sufficient to obtain the desired margin of error.

In the survey of women golfers example, a planning value of $p^* = .50$ would have provided the sample size

$$n = \frac{(z_{\alpha/2})^2 p^*(1 - p^*)}{E^2} = \frac{(1.96)^2(.50)(1 - .50)}{(.025)^2} = 1536.6$$

Thus, a slightly larger sample size of 1537 women golfers would be recommended.

TABLE 8.5   SOME POSSIBLE VALUES FOR $p^*(1 - p^*)$

p^*	$p^*(1 - p^*)$	
.10	$(.10)(.90) = .09$	
.30	$(.30)(.70) = .21$	
.40	$(.40)(.60) = .24$	
.50	$(.50)(.50) = .25$	← Largest value for $p^*(1 - p^*)$
.60	$(.60)(.40) = .24$	
.70	$(.70)(.30) = .21$	
.90	$(.90)(.10) = .09$	

NOTES AND COMMENTS

The desired margin of error for estimating a population proportion is almost always .10 or less. In national public opinion polls conducted by organizations such as Gallup and Harris, a .03 or .04 margin of error is common. With such margins of error, equation (8.7) will almost always provide a sample size that is large enough to satisfy the requirements of $np \geq 5$ and $n(1 - p) \geq 5$ for using a normal distribution as an approximation for the sampling distribution of $\bar{p}$.

Exercises

Methods

31. A simple random sample of 400 individuals provides 100 Yes responses.
    a. What is the point estimate of the proportion of the population that would provide Yes responses?
    b. What is your estimate of the standard error of $\bar{p}$, $\sigma_{\bar{p}}$?
    c. Compute the 95% confidence interval for the population proportion.

32. A simple random sample of 800 elements generates a sample proportion $\bar{p} = .70$.
    a. Provide a 90% confidence interval for the population proportion.
    b. Provide a 95% confidence interval for the population proportion.

33. In a survey, the planning value for the population proportion is $p^* = .35$. How large a sample should be taken to provide a 95% confidence interval with a margin of error of .05?

34. At 95% confidence, how large a sample should be taken to obtain a margin of error of .03 for the estimation of a population proportion? Assume that past data are not available for developing a planning value for p^*.

Applications

35. A survey of 611 office workers investigated telephone answering practices, including how often each office worker was able to answer incoming telephone calls and how often incoming telephone calls went directly to voice mail (*USA Today,* April 21, 2002). A total of 281 office workers indicated that they never need voice mail and are able to take every telephone call.
    a. What is the point estimate of the proportion of the population of office workers who are able to take every telephone call?
    b. At 90% confidence, what is the margin of error?
    c. What is the 90% confidence interval for the proportion of the population of office workers who are able to take every telephone call?

36. A survey by the Society for Human Resource Management asked 346 job seekers why employees change jobs so frequently (*The Wall Street Journal,* March 28, 2000). The answer selected most (152 times) was "higher compensation elsewhere."
    a. What is the point estimate of the proportion of job seekers who would select "higher compensation elsewhere" as the reason for changing jobs?
    b. What is the 95% confidence interval estimate of the population proportion?

Job Satisfaction

37. Towers Perrin, a New York human resources consulting firm, conducted a survey of 1100 employees at medium-sized and large companies to determine how dissatisfied employees were with their jobs (*The Wall Street Journal,* January 29, 2003). The data are shown in the file named Job Satisfaction. A response of Yes indicates that the employee strongly dislikes the current work experience.
    a. What is the point estimate of the proportion of the population of employees who strongly dislike the current work experience?
    b. At 95% confidence, what is the margin of error?

    c.   What is the 95% confidence interval for the proportion of the population of employees who strongly dislike the current work experience?

    d.   Towers Perrin estimates that it costs employers one-third of an hourly employee's annual salary to find a successor and as much as 1.5 times the annual salary to find a successor for a highly compensated employee. What message did this survey send to employers?

38.   Audience profile data collected at the ESPN SportsZone Web site showed that 26% of the users were women (*USA Today,* January 21, 1998). Assume that this percentage was based on a sample of 400 users.

    a.   At 95% confidence, what is the margin of error associated with the estimated proportion of users who are women?

    b.   What is the 95% confidence interval for the population proportion of ESPN SportsZone Web site users who are women?

    c.   How large a sample should be taken if the desired margin of error is .03?

39.   An Employee Benefit Research Institute survey explored the reasons small business employers offer a retirement plan to their employees (*USA Today,* April 4, 2000). The reason "competitive advantage in recruitment/retention" was anticipated 33% of the time.

    a.   What sample size is recommended if a survey goal is to estimate the proportion of small business employers who offer a retirement plan primarily for "competitive advantage in recruitment/retention" with a margin of error of .03? Use 95% confidence.

    b.   Repeat part (a) using 99% confidence.

40.   The professional baseball home run record of 61 home runs in a season was held for 37 years by Roger Maris of the New York Yankees. However, between 1998 and 2001, three players—Mark McGwire, Sammy Sosa, and Barry Bonds—broke the standard set by Maris with Bonds holding the current record of 73 home runs in a single season. With the long-standing home run record being broken and with many other new offensive records being set, suspicion arose that baseball players might be using illegal muscle-building drugs called steroids. A *USA Today*/CNN/Gallup poll found that 86% of baseball fans think professional baseball players should be tested for steroids (*USA Today,* July 8, 2002). If 650 baseball fans were included in the sample, compute the margin of error and the 95% confidence interval for the population proportion of baseball fans who think professional baseball players should be tested for steroids.

41.   An American Express retail survey found that 16% of U.S. consumers used the Internet to buy gifts during the holiday season (*USA Today,* January 18, 2000). If 1285 customers participated in the survey, what is the margin of error and what is the interval estimate of the population proportion of customers using the Internet to buy gifts? Use 95% confidence.

42.   A poll for the presidential campaign sampled 491 potential voters in June. A primary purpose of the poll was to obtain an estimate of the proportion of potential voters who favor each candidate. Assume a planning value of $p^* = .50$ and a 95% confidence level.

    a.   For $p^* = .50$, what was the planned margin of error for the June poll?

    b.   Closer to the November election, better precision and smaller margins of error are desired. Assume the following margins of error are requested for surveys to be conducted during the presidential campaign. Compute the recommended sample size for each survey.

Survey	Margin of Error
September	.04
October	.03
Early November	.02
Pre-Election Day	.01

43. A Phoenix Wealth Management/Harris Interactive survey of 1500 individuals with net worth of $1 million or more provided a variety of statistics on wealthy people (*Business-Week,* September 22, 2003). The previous three-year period had been bad for the stock market, which motivated some of the questions asked.

    a. The survey reported that 53% of the respondents lost 25% or more of their portfolio value over the past three years. Develop a 95% confidence interval for the proportion of wealthy people who lost 25% or more of their portfolio value over the past three years.

    b. The survey reported that 31% of the respondents feel they have to save more for retirement to make up for what they lost. Develop a 95% confidence interval for the population proportion.

    c. Five percent of the respondents gave $25,000 or more to charity over the previous year. Develop a 95% confidence interval for the proportion who gave $25,000 or more to charity.

    d. Compare the margin of error for the interval estimates in parts (a), (b), and (c). How is the margin of error related to $\bar{p}$? When the same sample is being used to estimate a variety of proportions, which of the proportions should be used to choose the planning value p^*? Why do you think $p^* = .50$ is often used in these cases?

Summary

In this chapter we presented methods for developing interval estimates of a population mean and a population proportion. A point estimator may or may not provide a good estimate of a population parameter. The use of an interval estimate provides a measure of the precision of an estimate. Both the interval estimate of the population mean and the population proportion are of the form: point estimate ± margin of error.

We presented interval estimates for a population mean for two cases. In the σ known case, historical data or other information is used to develop an estimate of σ prior to taking a sample. Analysis of new sample data then proceeds based on the assumption that σ is known. In the σ unknown case, the sample data are used to estimate both the population mean and the population standard deviation. The final choice of which interval estimation procedure to use depends upon the analyst's understanding of which method provides the best estimate of σ.

In the σ known case, the interval estimation procedure is based on the assumed value of σ and the use of the standard normal distribution. In the σ unknown case, the interval estimation procedure uses the sample standard deviation s and the t distribution. In both cases the quality of the interval estimates obtained depends on the distribution of the population and the sample size. If the population is normally distributed the interval estimates will be exact in both cases, even for small sample sizes. If the population is not normally distributed, the interval estimates obtained will be approximate. Larger sample sizes will provide better approximations, but the more highly skewed the population is, the larger the sample size needs to be to obtain a good approximation. Practical advice about the sample size necessary to obtain good approximations was included in Sections 8.1 and 8.2. In most cases a sample of size 30 or more will provide good approximate confidence intervals.

The general form of the interval estimate for a population proportion is $\bar{p}$ ± margin of error. In practice the sample sizes used for interval estimates of a population proportion are generally large. Thus, the interval estimation procedure is based on the standard normal distribution.

Often a desired margin of error is specified prior to developing a sampling plan. We showed how to choose a sample size large enough to provide the desired precision.

Glossary

Interval estimate An estimate of a population parameter that provides an interval believed to contain the value of the parameter. For the interval estimates in this chapter, it has the form: point estimate $\pm$ margin of error.

Margin of error The $\pm$ value added to and subtracted from a point estimate in order to develop an interval estimate of a population parameter.

σ known The case when historical data or other information provides a good value for the population standard deviation prior to taking a sample. The interval estimation procedure uses this known value of σ in computing the margin of error.

Confidence level The confidence associated with an interval estimate. For example, if an interval estimation procedure provides intervals such that 95% of the intervals formed using the procedure will include the population parameter, the interval estimate is said to be constructed at the 95% confidence level.

Confidence coefficient The confidence level expressed as a decimal value. For example, .95 is the confidence coefficient for a 95% confidence level.

Confidence interval Another name for an interval estimate.

Level of significance The probability that the interval estimation procedure will generate an interval that does not contain μ.

σ unknown The more common case when no good basis exists for estimating the population standard deviation prior to taking the sample. The interval estimation procedure uses the sample standard deviation s in computing the margin of error.

t distribution A family of probability distributions that can be used to develop an interval estimate of a population mean whenever the population standard deviation σ is unknown and is estimated by the sample standard deviation s.

Degrees of freedom A parameter of the t distribution. When the t distribution is used in the computation of an interval estimate of a population mean, the appropriate t distribution has $n - 1$ degrees of freedom, where n is the size of the simple random sample.

Key Formulas

Interval Estimate of a Population Mean: σ Known

$$\bar{x} \pm z_{\alpha/2} \frac{\sigma}{\sqrt{n}} \tag{8.1}$$

Interval Estimate of a Population Mean: σ Unknown

$$\bar{x} \pm t_{\alpha/2} \frac{s}{\sqrt{n}} \tag{8.2}$$

Sample Size for an Interval Estimate of a Population Mean

$$n = \frac{(z_{\alpha/2})^2 \sigma^2}{E^2} \tag{8.3}$$

Interval Estimate of a Population Proportion

$$\bar{p} \pm z_{\alpha/2} \sqrt{\frac{\bar{p}(1 - \bar{p})}{n}} \tag{8.6}$$

Sample Size for an Interval Estimate of a Population Proportion

$$n = \frac{(z_{\alpha/2})^2 p^*(1 - p^*)}{E^2} \tag{8.7}$$

Supplementary Exercises

44. A survey of first-time home buyers found that the mean of annual household income was $50,000 (http://CNBC.com, July 11, 2000). Assume the survey used a sample of 400 first-time home buyers and assume that the population standard deviation is $20,500.
    a. At 95% confidence, what is the margin of error for this study?
    b. What is the 95% confidence interval for the population mean annual household income for first-time home buyers?

45. A survey conducted by the American Automobile Association showed that a family of four spends an average of $215.60 per day while on vacation. Suppose a sample of 64 families of four vacationing at Niagara Falls resulted in a sample mean of $252.45 per day and a sample standard deviation of $74.50.
    a. Develop a 95% confidence interval estimate of the mean amount spent per day by a family of four visiting Niagara Falls.
    b. Based on the confidence interval from part (a), does it appear that the population mean amount spent per day by families visiting Niagara Falls differs from the mean reported by the American Automobile Association? Explain.

46. The motion picture *Harry Potter and the Sorcerer's Stone* shattered the box office debut record previously held by *The Lost World: Jurassic Park* (*The Wall Street Journal,* November 19, 2001). A sample of 100 movie theaters showed that the mean three-day weekend gross was $25,467 per theater. The sample standard deviation was $4980.
    a. What is the margin of error for this study? Use 95% confidence.
    b. What is the 95% confidence interval estimate for the population mean weekend gross per theater?
    c. *The Lost World* took in $72.1 million in its first three-day weekend. *Harry Potter and the Sorcerer's Stone* was shown in 3672 theaters. What is an estimate of the total *Harry Potter and the Sorcerer's Stone* took in during its first three-day weekend?
    d. An Associated Press article claimed *Harry Potter* "shattered" the box office debut record held by *The Lost World*. Do your results agree with this claim?

47. Many stock market observers say that when the P/E ratio for stocks gets over 20 the market is overvalued. The P/E ratio is the stock price divided by the most recent 12 months of earnings. Suppose you are interested in seeing whether the current market is overvalued and would also like to know the proportion of companies that pay dividends. A random sample of 30 companies listed on the New York Stock Exchange (NYSE) is provided (*Barron's,* January 19, 2004).

NYSEStocks

Company	Dividend	P/E Ratio	Company	Dividend	P/E Ratio
Albertsons	Yes	14	NY Times A	Yes	25
BRE Prop	Yes	18	Omnicare	Yes	25
CityNtl	Yes	16	PallCp	Yes	23
DelMonte	No	21	PubSvcEnt	Yes	11
EnrgzHldg	No	20	SensientTch	Yes	11
Ford Motor	Yes	22	SmtProp	Yes	12
Gildan A	No	12	TJX Cos	Yes	21
HudsnUtdBcp	Yes	13	Thomson	Yes	30
IBM	Yes	22	USB Hldg	Yes	12
JeffPilot	Yes	16	US Restr	Yes	26
KingswayFin	No	6	Varian Med	No	41
Libbey	Yes	13	Visx	No	72
MasoniteIntl	No	15	Waste Mgt	No	23
Motorola	Yes	68	Wiley A	Yes	21
Ntl City	Yes	10	Yum Brands	No	18

a. What is a point estimate of the P/E ratio for the population of stocks listed on the New York Stock Exchange? Develop a 95% confidence interval.

b. Based on your answer to part (a), do you believe that the market is overvalued?

c. What is a point estimate of the proportion of companies on the NYSE that pay dividends? Is the sample size large enough to justify using the normal distribution to construct a confidence interval for this proportion? Why or why not?

Flights

48. US Airways conducted a number of studies that indicated a substantial savings could be obtained by encouraging Dividend Miles frequent flyer customers to redeem miles and schedule award flights online (*US Airways Attaché,* February 2003). One study collected data on the amount of time required to redeem miles and schedule an award flight over the telephone. A sample showing the time in minutes required for each of 150 award flights scheduled by telephone is contained in the data set Flights. Use Excel to help answer the following questions.

a. What is the sample mean number of minutes required to schedule an award flight by telephone?

b. What is the 95% confidence interval for the population mean time to schedule an award flight by telephone?

c. Assume a telephone ticket agent works 7.5 hours per day. How many award flights can one ticket agent be expected to handle a day?

d. Discuss why this information supported US Airways' plans to use an online system to reduce costs.

ActTemps

49. A survey by Accountemps asked a sample of 200 executives to provide data on the number of minutes per day office workers waste trying to locate mislabeled, misfiled, or misplaced items. Data consistent with this survey are contained in the data set ActTemps.

a. Use ActTemps to develop a point estimate of the number of minutes per day office workers waste trying to locate mislabeled, misfiled, or misplaced items.

b. What is the sample standard deviation?

c. What is the 95% confidence interval for the mean number of minutes wasted per day?

50. Mileage tests are conducted for a particular model of automobile. If a 98% confidence interval with a margin of error of 1 mile per gallon is desired, how many automobiles should be used in the test? Assume that preliminary mileage tests indicate the standard deviation is 2.6 miles per gallon.

51. In developing patient appointment schedules, a medical center wants to estimate the mean time that a staff member spends with each patient. How large a sample should be taken if the desired margin of error is two minutes at a 95% level of confidence? How large a sample should be taken for a 99% level of confidence? Use a planning value for the population standard deviation of eight minutes.

52. Annual salary plus bonus data for chief executive officers are presented in the *BusinessWeek* Annual Pay Survey. A preliminary sample showed that the standard deviation is $675 with data provided in thousands of dollars. How many chief executive officers should be in a sample if we want to estimate the population mean annual salary plus bonus with a margin of error of $100,000? (*Note:* The desired margin of error would be $E = 100$ if the data are in thousands of dollars.) Use 95% confidence.

53. The National Center for Education Statistics reported that 47% of college students work to pay for tuition and living expenses. Assume that a sample of 450 college students was used in the study.

a. Provide a 95% confidence interval for the population proportion of college students who work to pay for tuition and living expenses.

b. Provide a 99% confidence interval for the population proportion of college students who work to pay for tuition and living expenses.

c. What happens to the margin of error as the confidence is increased from 95% to 99%?

54. A *USA Today*/CNN/Gallup survey of 369 working parents found 200 who said they spend too little time with their children because of work commitments.
    a. What is the point estimate of the proportion of the population of working parents who feel they spend too little time with their children because of work commitments?
    b. At 95% confidence, what is the margin of error?
    c. What is the 95% confidence interval estimate of the population proportion of working parents who feel they spend too little time with their children because of work commitments?

55. Which would be hardest for you to give up: Your computer or your television? In a recent survey of 1677 U.S. Internet users, 74% of the young tech elite (average age of 22) say their computer would be very hard to give up (*PC Magazine*, February 3, 2004). Only 48% say their television would be very hard to give up.
    a. Develop a 95% confidence interval for the proportion of the young tech elite that would find it very hard to give up their computer.
    b. Develop a 99% confidence interval for the proportion of the young tech elite that would find it very hard to give up their television.
    c. In which case, part (a) or part (b), is the margin of error larger? Explain why.

56. A Roper Starch survey asked employees ages 18 to 29 whether they would prefer better health insurance or a raise in salary (*USA Today*, September 5, 2000). Answer the following questions assuming 340 of 500 employees said they would prefer better health insurance over a raise.
    a. What is the point estimate of the proportion of employees ages 18 to 29 who would prefer better health insurance?
    b. What is the 95% confidence interval estimate of the population proportion?

57. The *2003 Statistical Abstract of the United States* reported the percentage of people 18 years of age and older who smoke. Suppose that a study designed to collect new data on smokers and nonsmokers uses a preliminary estimate of the proportion who smoke of .30.
    a. How large a sample should be taken to estimate the proportion of smokers in the population with a margin of error of .02? Use 95% confidence.
    b. Assume that the study uses your sample size recommendation in part (a) and finds 520 smokers. What is the point estimate of the proportion of smokers in the population?
    c. What is the 95% confidence interval for the proportion of smokers in the population?

58. A well-known bank credit card firm wishes to estimate the proportion of credit card holders who carry a nonzero balance at the end of the month and incur an interest charge. Assume that the desired margin of error is .03 at 98% confidence.
    a. How large a sample should be selected if it is anticipated that roughly 70% of the firm's card holders carry a nonzero balance at the end of the month?
    b. How large a sample should be selected if no planning value for the proportion could be specified?

59. In a survey, 200 people were asked to identify their major source of news information; 110 stated that their major source was television news.
    a. Construct a 95% confidence interval for the proportion of people in the population who consider television their major source of news information.
    b. How large a sample would be necessary to estimate the population proportion with a margin of error of .05 at 95% confidence?

60. Although airline schedules and cost are important factors for business travelers when choosing an airline carrier, a *USA Today* survey found that business travelers list an airline's frequent flyer program as the most important factor. From a sample of $n = 1993$ business travelers who responded to the survey, 618 listed a frequent flyer program as the most important factor.
    a. What is the point estimate of the proportion of the population of business travelers who believe a frequent flyer program is the most important factor when choosing an airline carrier?

b. Develop a 95% confidence interval estimate of the population proportion.
c. How large a sample would be required to report the margin of error of .01 at 95% confidence? Would you recommend that *USA Today* attempt to provide this degree of precision? Why or why not?

Case Problem 1   Bock Investment Services

The goal of Bock Investment Services (BIS) is to be the leading money market advisory service in South Carolina. To provide better service for its present clients and to attract new clients, BIS developed a weekly newsletter. BIS is considering adding a new feature to the newsletter that will report the results of a weekly telephone survey of fund managers. To investigate the feasibility of offering this service, and to determine what type of information to include in the newsletter, BIS selected a simple random sample of 45 money market funds. A portion of the data obtained is shown in Table 8.6, which reports fund assets and yields for the past 7 and 30 days. Before calling the money market fund managers to obtain additional data, BIS decided to do some preliminary analysis of the data already collected.

Managerial Report

1. Use appropriate descriptive statistics to summarize the data on assets and yields for the money market funds.
2. Develop a 95% confidence interval estimate of the mean assets, mean 7-day yield, and mean 30-day yield for the population of money market funds. Provide a managerial interpretation of each interval estimate.
3. Discuss the implication of your findings in terms of how BIS could use this type of information in preparing its weekly newsletter.
4. What other information would you recommend that BIS gather to provide the most useful information to its clients?

Case Problem 2   Gulf Real Estate Properties

Gulf Real Estate Properties, Inc., is a real estate firm located in southwestern Florida. The company, which advertises itself as "expert in the real estate market," monitors condominium sales by collecting data on location, list price, sale price, and number of days it takes to sell each unit. Each condominium is classified as *Gulf View* if it is located directly on the Gulf of Mexico or *No Gulf View* if it is located on the bay or a golf course, near but not on the Gulf. Sample data from the Multiple Listing Service in Naples, Florida, provided recent sales data for 40 Gulf View condominiums and 18 No Gulf View condominiums.* Prices are in thousands of dollars. The data are shown in Table 8.7.

Managerial Report

1. Use appropriate descriptive statistics to summarize each of the three variables for the 40 Gulf View condominiums.
2. Use appropriate descriptive statistics to summarize each of the three variables for the 18 No Gulf View condominiums.
3. Compare your summary results. Discuss any specific statistical results that would help a real estate agent understand the condominium market.

---

*Data based on condominium sales reported in the Naples MLS (Coldwell Banker, June 2000).

TABLE 8.6   DATA FOR BOCK INVESTMENT SERVICES

Bock

Money Market Fund	Assets ($ millions)	7-Day Yield (%)	30-Day Yield (%)
Amcore	103.9	4.10	4.08
Alger	156.7	4.79	4.73
Arch MM/Trust	496.5	4.17	4.13
BT Instit Treas	197.8	4.37	4.32
Benchmark Div	2755.4	4.54	4.47
Bradford	707.6	3.88	3.83
Capital Cash	1.7	4.29	4.22
Cash Mgt Trust	2707.8	4.14	4.04
Composite	122.8	4.03	3.91
Cowen Standby	694.7	4.25	4.19
Cortland	217.3	3.57	3.51
Declaration	38.4	2.67	2.61
Dreyfus	4832.8	4.01	3.89
Elfun	81.7	4.51	4.41
FFB Cash	506.2	4.17	4.11
Federated Master	738.7	4.41	4.34
Fidelity Cash	13272.8	4.51	4.42
Flex-fund	172.8	4.60	4.48
Fortis	105.6	3.87	3.85
Franklin Money	996.8	3.97	3.92
Freedom Cash	1079.0	4.07	4.01
Galaxy Money	801.4	4.11	3.96
Government Cash	409.4	3.83	3.82
Hanover Cash	794.3	4.32	4.23
Heritage Cash	1008.3	4.08	4.00
Infinity/Alpha	53.6	3.99	3.91
John Hancock	226.4	3.93	3.87
Landmark Funds	481.3	4.28	4.26
Liquid Cash	388.9	4.61	4.64
MarketWatch	10.6	4.13	4.05
Merrill Lynch Money	27005.6	4.24	4.18
NCC Funds	113.4	4.22	4.20
Nationwide	517.3	4.22	4.14
Overland	291.5	4.26	4.17
Pierpont Money	1991.7	4.50	4.40
Portico Money	161.6	4.28	4.20
Prudential MoneyMart	6835.1	4.20	4.16
Reserve Primary	1408.8	3.91	3.86
Schwab Money	10531.0	4.16	4.07
Smith Barney Cash	2947.6	4.16	4.12
Stagecoach	1502.2	4.18	4.13
Strong Money	470.2	4.37	4.29
Transamerica Cash	175.5	4.20	4.19
United Cash	323.7	3.96	3.89
Woodward Money	1330.0	4.24	4.21

Source: Barron's, October 3, 1994.

TABLE 8.7   SALES DATA FOR GULF REAL ESTATE PROPERTIES

Gulf View Condominiums			No Gulf View Condominiums		
List Price	Sale Price	Days to Sell	List Price	Sale Price	Days to Sell
495.0	475.0	130	217.0	217.0	182
379.0	350.0	71	148.0	135.5	338
529.0	519.0	85	186.5	179.0	122
552.5	534.5	95	239.0	230.0	150
334.9	334.9	119	279.0	267.5	169
550.0	505.0	92	215.0	214.0	58
169.9	165.0	197	279.0	259.0	110
210.0	210.0	56	179.9	176.5	130
975.0	945.0	73	149.9	144.9	149
314.0	314.0	126	235.0	230.0	114
315.0	305.0	88	199.8	192.0	120
885.0	800.0	282	210.0	195.0	61
975.0	975.0	100	226.0	212.0	146
469.0	445.0	56	149.9	146.5	137
329.0	305.0	49	160.0	160.0	281
365.0	330.0	48	322.0	292.5	63
332.0	312.0	88	187.5	179.0	48
520.0	495.0	161	247.0	227.0	52
425.0	405.0	149			
675.0	669.0	142			
409.0	400.0	28			
649.0	649.0	29			
319.0	305.0	140			
425.0	410.0	85			
359.0	340.0	107			
469.0	449.0	72			
895.0	875.0	129			
439.0	430.0	160			
435.0	400.0	206			
235.0	227.0	91			
638.0	618.0	100			
629.0	600.0	97			
329.0	309.0	114			
595.0	555.0	45			
339.0	315.0	150			
215.0	200.0	48			
395.0	375.0	135			
449.0	425.0	53			
499.0	465.0	86			
439.0	428.5	158			

CD file

GulfProp

4. Develop a 95% confidence interval estimate of the population mean sales price and population mean number of days to sell for Gulf View condominiums. Interpret your results.

5. Develop a 95% confidence interval estimate of the population mean sales price and population mean number of days to sell for No Gulf View condominiums. Interpret your results.

6. Assume the branch manager requested estimates of the mean selling price of Gulf View condominiums with a margin of error of $40,000 and the mean selling price of No Gulf View condominiums with a margin of error of $15,000. Using 95% confidence, how large should the sample sizes be?

7. Gulf Real Estate Properties just signed contracts for two new listings: a Gulf View condominium with a list price of $589,000 and a No Gulf View condominium with a list price of $285,000. What is your estimate of the final selling price and number of days required to sell each of these units?

Case Problem 3   Metropolitan Research, Inc.

Metropolitan Research, Inc., a consumer research organization, conducts surveys designed to evaluate a wide variety of products and services available to consumers. In one particular study, Metropolitan looked at consumer satisfaction with the performance of automobiles produced by a major Detroit manufacturer. A questionnaire sent to owners of one of the manufacturer's full-sized cars revealed several complaints about early transmission problems. To learn more about the transmission failures, Metropolitan used a sample of actual transmission repairs provided by a transmission repair firm in the Detroit area. The following data show the actual number of miles driven for 50 vehicles at the time of transmission failure.

85,092	32,609	59,465	77,437	32,534	64,090	32,464	59,902
39,323	89,641	94,219	116,803	92,857	63,436	65,605	85,861
64,342	61,978	67,998	59,817	101,769	95,774	121,352	69,568
74,276	66,998	40,001	72,069	25,066	77,098	69,922	35,662
74,425	67,202	118,444	53,500	79,294	64,544	86,813	116,269
37,831	89,341	73,341	85,288	138,114	53,402	85,586	82,256
77,539	88,798						

Managerial Report

1. Use appropriate descriptive statistics to summarize the transmission failure data.

2. Develop a 95% confidence interval for the mean number of miles driven until transmission failure for the population of automobiles with transmission failure. Provide a managerial interpretation of the interval estimate.

3. Discuss the implication of your statistical finding in terms of the belief that some owners of the automobiles experienced early transmission failures.

4. How many repair records should be sampled if the research firm wants the population mean number of miles driven until transmission failure to be estimated with a margin of error of 5000 miles? Use 95% confidence.

5. What other information would you like to gather to evaluate the transmission failure problem more fully?

CHAPTER 9

Hypothesis Tests

CONTENTS

STATISTICS IN PRACTICE:
JOHN MORRELL & COMPANY

9.1 DEVELOPING NULL AND
ALTERNATIVE HYPOTHESES
Testing Research Hypotheses
Testing the Validity of a Claim
Testing in Decision-Making
  Situations
Summary of Forms for Null and
  Alternative Hypotheses

9.2 TYPE I AND TYPE II ERRORS

9.3 POPULATION MEAN:
σ KNOWN
One-Tailed Test
Two-Tailed Test

Using Excel
Summary and Practical Advice
Relationship Between Interval
  Estimation and Hypothesis
  Testing

9.4 POPULATION MEAN:
σ UNKNOWN
One-Tailed Test
Two-Tailed Test
Using Excel
Summary and Practical Advice

9.5 POPULATION PROPORTION
Using Excel
Summary

JOHN MORRELL & COMPANY*
CINCINNATI, OHIO

John Morrell & Company, which began in England in 1827, is considered the oldest continuously operating meat manufacturer in the United States. It is a wholly owned and independently managed subsidiary of Smithfield Foods, Smithfield, Virginia. John Morrell & Company offers an extensive product line of processed meats and fresh pork to consumers under 13 regional brands including John Morrell, E-Z-Cut, Tobin's First Prize, Dinner Bell, Hunter, Kretschmar, Rath, Rodeo, Shenson, Farmers Hickory Brand, Iowa Quality, and Peyton's. Each regional brand enjoys high brand recognition and loyalty among consumers.

Market research at Morrell provides management with up-to-date information on the company's various products and how the products compare with competing brands of similar products. A recent study investigated consumer preference for Morrell's Convenient Cuisine Beef Pot Roast compared to similar beef products from two major competitors. In the three-product comparison test, a sample of consumers was used to indicate how the products rated in terms of taste, appearance, aroma, and overall preference.

One research question concerned whether Morrell's Convenient Cuisine Beef Pot Roast was the preferred choice of more than 50% of the consumer population. Letting p indicate the population proportion preferring Morrell's product, the hypothesis test for the research question is as follows:

$$H_0: p \leq .50$$
$$H_a: p > .50$$

The null hypothesis H_0 indicates the preference for Morrell's product is less than or equal to 50%. If the sample data sup-

Convenient Cuisine fully cooked entrees allow consumers to heat and serve in the same microwaveable tray. © Courtesy of John Morrell's Convenient Cuisine products.

port rejecting H_0 in favor of the alternate hypothesis H_a, Morrell will draw the research conclusion that in a three-product comparison, their product is preferred by more than 50% of the consumer population.

In an independent taste test study using a sample of 224 consumers in Cincinnati, Milwaukee, and Los Angeles, 150 consumers selected the Morrell Convenient Cuisine Beef Pot Roast as the preferred product. Using statistical hypothesis testing procedures, the null hypothesis H_0 was rejected. The study provided statistical evidence supporting H_a and the conclusion that the Morrell product is preferred by more than 50% of the consumer population.

The point estimate of the population proportion was $\bar{p} = 150/224 = .67$. Thus, the sample data provided support for a food magazine advertisement showing that in a three-product taste comparison, Morrell's Convenient Cuisine Beef Pot Roast was "preferred 2 to 1 over the competition."

In this chapter we will discuss how to formulate hypotheses and how to conduct tests like the one used by Morrell. Through the analysis of sample data, we will be able to determine whether a hypothesis should or should not be rejected.

---

*The authors are indebted to Marty Butler, Vice President of Marketing, John Morrell, for providing this Statistics in Practice.

In Chapters 7 and 8 we showed how a sample could be used to develop point and interval estimates of population parameters. In this chapter we continue the discussion of statistical inference by showing how hypothesis testing can be used to determine whether a statement about the value of a population parameter should or should not be rejected.

In hypothesis testing we begin by making a tentative assumption about a population parameter. This tentative assumption is called the **null hypothesis** and is denoted by H_0. We then define another hypothesis, called the **alternative hypothesis**, which is the opposite of what is stated in the null hypothesis. The alternative hypothesis is denoted by H_a.

The hypothesis testing procedure uses data from a sample to test the two competing statements indicated by H_0 and H_a.

This chapter shows how hypothesis tests can be conducted about a population mean and a population proportion. We begin by providing examples that illustrate approaches to developing null and alternative hypotheses.

9.1   Developing Null and Alternative Hypotheses

Learning to formulate hypotheses correctly will take practice. Expect some initial confusion over the proper choice for H_0 and H_a. The examples in this section show a variety of forms for H_0 and H_a depending upon the application.

In some applications it may not be obvious how the null and alternative hypotheses should be formulated. Care must be taken to structure the hypotheses appropriately so that the hypothesis testing conclusion provides the information the researcher or decision maker wants. Guidelines for establishing the null and alternative hypotheses are given for three types of situations in which hypothesis testing procedures are commonly employed.

Testing Research Hypotheses

Consider a particular automobile model that currently attains an average fuel efficiency of 24 miles per gallon. A product research group developed a new fuel injection system specifically designed to increase the miles-per-gallon rating. To evaluate the new system, several will be manufactured, installed in automobiles, and subjected to research-controlled driving tests. Here the product research group is looking for evidence to conclude that the new system *increases* the mean miles-per-gallon rating. In this case, the research hypothesis is that the new fuel injection system will provide a mean miles-per-gallon rating exceeding 24; that is, $\mu > 24$. As a general guideline, a research hypothesis should be stated as the *alternative hypothesis*. Hence, the appropriate null and alternative hypotheses for the study are

$$H_0: \mu \leq 24$$
$$H_a: \mu > 24$$

The conclusion that the research hypothesis is true is made if the sample data contradict the null hypothesis.

If the sample results indicate that H_0 cannot be rejected, researchers cannot conclude that the new fuel injection system is better. Perhaps more research and subsequent testing should be conducted. However, if the sample results indicate that H_0 can be rejected, researchers can make the inference that $H_a: \mu > 24$ is true. With this conclusion, the researchers gain the statistical support necessary to state that the new system increases the mean number of miles per gallon. Production with the new system should be considered.

In research studies such as these, the null and alternative hypotheses should be formulated so that the rejection of H_0 supports the research conclusion. The research hypothesis therefore should be expressed as the alternative hypothesis.

Testing the Validity of a Claim

As an illustration of testing the validity of a claim, consider the situation of a manufacturer of soft drinks who states that two-liter containers of its products contain an average of at least 67.6 fluid ounces. A sample of two-liter containers will be selected, and the contents will be measured to test the manufacturer's claim. In this type of hypothesis testing situation, we generally assume that the manufacturer's claim is true unless the sample evidence is contradictory. Using this approach for the soft drink example, we would state the null and alternative hypotheses as follows.

$$H_0: \mu \geq 67.6$$
$$H_a: \mu < 67.6$$

A manufacturer's claim is usually given the benefit of the doubt and stated as the null hypothesis. The conclusion that the claim is false can be made if the null hypothesis is rejected.

If the sample results indicate H_0 cannot be rejected, the manufacturer's claim will not be challenged. However, if the sample results indicate H_0 can be rejected, the inference will be made that $H_a: \mu < 67.6$ is true. With this conclusion, statistical evidence indicates that the manufacturer's claim is incorrect and that the soft drink containers are being filled with a mean less than the claimed 67.6 ounces. Appropriate action against the manufacturer may be considered.

In situations involving testing the validity of a claim, the null hypothesis is generally based on the assumption that the claim is true. The alternative hypothesis is then formulated so that rejection of H_0 will provide statistical evidence that the stated assumption is incorrect. Action to correct the claim should be considered whenever H_0 is rejected.

Testing in Decision-Making Situations

In testing research hypotheses or testing the validity of a claim, action is taken if H_0 is rejected. In some instances, however, action must be taken both when H_0 cannot be rejected and when H_0 can be rejected. In general, this type of situation occurs when a decision maker must choose between two courses of action, one associated with the null hypothesis and another associated with the alternative hypothesis. For example, on the basis of a sample of parts from a shipment just received, a quality control inspector must decide whether to accept the shipment or to return the shipment to the supplier because it does not meet specifications. Assume that specifications for a particular part require a mean length of 2 inches per part. If the mean length is greater or less than the 2-inch standard, the parts will cause quality problems in the assembly operation. In this case, the null and alternative hypotheses would be formulated as follows.

$$H_0: \mu = 2$$
$$H_a: \mu \neq 2$$

If the sample results indicate H_0 cannot be rejected, the quality control inspector will have no reason to doubt that the shipment meets specifications, and the shipment will be accepted. However, if the sample results indicate H_0 should be rejected, the conclusion will be that the parts do not meet specifications. In this case, the quality control inspector will have sufficient evidence to return the shipment to the supplier. Thus, we see that for these types of situations, action is taken both when H_0 cannot be rejected and when H_0 can be rejected.

Summary of Forms for Null and Alternative Hypotheses

The hypothesis tests in this chapter involve two population parameters: the population mean and the population proportion. Depending on the situation, hypothesis tests about a population parameter may take one of three forms: two use inequalities in the null hypothesis; the third uses an equality in the null hypothesis. For hypothesis tests involving a population mean, we let μ_0 denote the hypothesized value and we must choose one of the following three forms for the hypothesis test.

The three possible forms for hypothesis tests about a population mean are shown here. Note that the equality always appears in the null hypothesis H_0.

$$
\begin{array}{lll}
H_0: \mu \geq \mu_0 & H_0: \mu \leq \mu_0 & H_0: \mu = \mu_0 \\
H_a: \mu < \mu_0 & H_a: \mu > \mu_0 & H_a: \mu \neq \mu_0
\end{array}
$$

For reasons that will be clear later, the first two forms are called one-tailed tests. The third form is called a two-tailed test.

In many situations, the choice of H_0 and H_a is not obvious and judgment is necessary to select the proper form. However, as the preceding forms show, the equality part of the expression (either $\geq$, $\leq$, or $=$) *always* appears in the null hypothesis. In selecting the proper form of H_0 and H_a, keep in mind that the alternative hypothesis is often what the test is attempting to establish. Hence, asking whether the user is looking for evidence to support $\mu < \mu_0$, $\mu > \mu_0$, or $\mu \neq \mu_0$ will help determine H_a. The following exercises are designed to provide practice in choosing the proper form for a hypothesis test involving a population mean.

Exercises

1. The manager of the Danvers-Hilton Resort Hotel stated that the mean guest bill for a weekend is $600 or less. A member of the hotel's accounting staff noticed that the total charges for guest bills have been increasing in recent months. The accountant will use a sample of weekend guest bills to test the manager's claim.
    a.   Which form of the hypotheses should be used to test the manager's claim? Explain.

    $$H_0: \mu \geq 600 \qquad H_0: \mu \leq 600 \qquad H_0: \mu = 600$$
    $$H_a: \mu < 600 \qquad H_a: \mu > 600 \qquad H_a: \mu \neq 600$$

    b.   What conclusion is appropriate when H_0 cannot be rejected?
    c.   What conclusion is appropriate when H_0 can be rejected?

2. The manager of an automobile dealership is considering a new bonus plan designed to increase sales volume. Currently, the mean sales volume is 14 automobiles per month. The manager wants to conduct a research study to see whether the new bonus plan increases sales volume. To collect data on the plan, a sample of sales personnel will be allowed to sell under the new bonus plan for a one-month period.
    a.   Develop the null and alternative hypotheses most appropriate for this research situation.
    b.   Comment on the conclusion when H_0 cannot be rejected.
    c.   Comment on the conclusion when H_0 can be rejected.

3. A production line operation is designed to fill cartons with laundry detergent to a mean weight of 32 ounces. A sample of cartons is periodically selected and weighed to determine whether underfilling or overfilling is occurring. If the sample data lead to a conclusion of underfilling or overfilling, the production line will be shut down and adjusted to obtain proper filling.
    a.   Formulate the null and alternative hypotheses that will help in deciding whether to shut down and adjust the production line.
    b.   Comment on the conclusion and the decision when H_0 cannot be rejected.
    c.   Comment on the conclusion and the decision when H_0 can be rejected.

4. Because of high production-changeover time and costs, a director of manufacturing must convince management that a proposed manufacturing method reduces costs before the new method can be implemented. The current production method operates with a mean cost of $220 per hour. A research study will measure the cost of the new method over a sample production period.
    a.   Develop the null and alternative hypotheses most appropriate for this study.
    b.   Comment on the conclusion when H_0 cannot be rejected.
    c.   Comment on the conclusion when H_0 can be rejected.

9.2   Type I and Type II Errors

The null and alternative hypotheses are competing statements about the population. Either the null hypothesis H_0 is true or the alternative hypothesis H_a is true, but not both. Ideally the hypothesis testing procedure should lead to the acceptance of H_0 when H_0 is true and the

TABLE 9.1 ERRORS AND CORRECT CONCLUSIONS IN HYPOTHESIS TESTING

		Population Condition	
		H_0 True	H_a True
Conclusion	Accept H_0	Correct Conclusion	Type II Error
	Reject H_0	Type I Error	Correct Conclusion

rejection of H_0 when H_a is true. Unfortunately, the correct conclusions are not always possible. Because hypothesis tests are based on sample information, we must allow for the possibility of errors. Table 9.1 illustrates the two kinds of errors that can be made in hypothesis testing.

The first row of Table 9.1 shows what can happen if the conclusion is to accept H_0. If H_0 is true, this conclusion is correct. However, if H_a is true, we make a **Type II error**; that is, we accept H_0 when it is false. The second row of Table 9.1 shows what can happen if the conclusion is to reject H_0. If H_0 is true, we make a **Type I error**; that is, we reject H_0 when it is true. However, if H_a is true, rejecting H_0 is correct.

Recall the hypothesis testing illustration discussed in Section 9.1 in which an automobile product research group developed a new fuel injection system designed to increase the miles-per-gallon rating of a particular automobile. With the current model obtaining an average of 24 miles per gallon, the hypothesis test was formulated as follows.

$$H_0: \mu \leq 24$$
$$H_a: \mu > 24$$

The alternative hypothesis, $H_a: \mu > 24$, indicates that the researchers are looking for sample evidence to support the conclusion that the population mean miles per gallon with the new fuel injection system is greater than 24.

In this application, the Type I error of rejecting H_0 when it is true corresponds to the researchers claiming that the new system improves the miles-per-gallon rating ($\mu > 24$) when in fact the new system is not any better than the current system. In contrast, the Type II error of accepting H_0 when it is false corresponds to the researchers concluding that the new system is not any better than the current system ($\mu \leq 24$) when in fact the new system improves miles-per-gallon performance.

For the miles-per-gallon rating hypothesis test, the null hypothesis is $H_0: \mu \leq 24$. Suppose the null hypothesis is true as an equality; that is, $\mu = 24$. The probability of making a Type I error when the null hypothesis is true as an equality is called the **level of significance**. Thus, for the miles-per-gallon rating hypothesis test, the level of significance is the probability of rejecting $H_0: \mu \leq 24$ when $\mu = 24$. Because of the importance of this concept, we now restate the definition of level of significance.

LEVEL OF SIGNIFICANCE

The level of significance is the probability of making a Type I error when the null hypothesis is true as an equality.

The Greek symbol α (alpha) is used to denote the level of significance, and common choices for α are .05 and .01.

In practice, the person conducting the hypothesis test specifies the level of significance. By selecting α, that person is controlling the probability of making a Type I error. If the cost of making a Type I error is high, small values of α are preferred. If the cost of making a Type I error is not too high, larger values of α are typically used. Applications of hypothesis testing that only control for the Type I error are often called *significance tests*. Most applications of hypothesis testing are of this type.

If the sample data are consistent with the null hypothesis H_0, we will follow the practice of concluding "do not reject H_0." This conclusion is preferred over "accept H_0," because the conclusion to accept H_0 puts us at risk of making a Type II error.

Although most applications of hypothesis testing control for the probability of making a Type I error, they do not always control for the probability of making a Type II error.* Hence, if we decide to accept H_0, we cannot determine how confident we can be with that decision. Because of the uncertainty associated with making a Type II error when conducting significance tests, statisticians often recommend that we use the statement "do not reject H_0" instead of "accept H_0." Using the statement "do not reject H_0" carries the recommendation to withhold both judgment and action. In effect, by not directly accepting H_0, the statistician avoids the risk of making a Type II error. Whenever the probability of making a Type II error has not been determined and controlled, we will not make the statement "accept H_0." In such cases, only two conclusions are possible: *do not reject H_0 or reject H_0.*

Exercises

5. Nielsen reported that young men in the United States watch 56.2 minutes of prime-time TV daily (*The Wall Street Journal Europe,* November 18, 2003). A researcher believes that young men in Germany spend more time watching prime-time TV. A sample of German young men will be selected by the researcher and the time they spend watching TV in one day will be recorded. The sample results will be used to test the following null and alternative hypotheses.

$$H_0: \mu \leq 56.2$$
$$H_a: \mu > 56.2$$

   a. What is the Type I error in this situation? What are the consequences of making this error?
   b. What is the Type II error in this situation? What are the consequences of making this error?

6. The label on a 3-quart container of orange juice claims that the orange juice contains an average of 1 gram of fat or less. Answer the following questions for a hypothesis test that could be used to test the claim on the label.
   a. Develop the appropriate null and alternative hypotheses.
   b. What is the Type I error in this situation? What are the consequences of making this error?
   c. What is the Type II error in this situation? What are the consequences of making this error?

7. Carpetland salespersons average $8000 per week in sales. Steve Contois, the firm's vice president, proposes a compensation plan with new selling incentives. Steve hopes that the results of a trial selling period will enable him to conclude that the compensation plan increases the average sales per salesperson.
   a. Develop the appropriate null and alternative hypotheses.
   b. What is the Type I error in this situation? What are the consequences of making this error?
   c. What is the Type II error in this situation? What are the consequences of making this error?

---

*More advanced texts describe procedures for determining and controlling the probability of making a Type II error. See, for example, Anderson, D. R., D. J. Sweeney, and T. A. Williams, *Statistics for Business and Economics,* 9th ed. (Cincinnati: South-Western, 2005).

8. Suppose a new production method will be implemented if a hypothesis test supports the conclusion that the new method reduces the mean operating cost per hour.
   a. State the appropriate null and alternative hypotheses if the mean cost for the current production method is $220 per hour.
   b. What is the Type I error in this situation? What are the consequences of making this error?
   c. What is the Type II error in this situation? What are the consequences of making this error?

Population Mean: σ Known

In Chapter 8 we said that the σ known case corresponds to applications in which historical data or other information is available that enables us to obtain a good estimate of the population standard deviation prior to sampling. In such cases the population standard deviation can, for all practical purposes, be considered known. In this section we show how to conduct a hypothesis test about a population mean for the σ known case.

The methods presented in this section are exact if the sample is selected from a population that is normally distributed. In cases where it is not reasonable to assume the population is normally distributed, these methods are still applicable if the sample size is large enough. We provide some practical advice concerning the population distribution and the sample size at the end of the section.

One-Tailed Test

One-tailed tests about a population mean take one of the following two forms.

Lower Tail Test	Upper Tail Test
$H_0: \mu \geq \mu_0$	$H_0: \mu \leq \mu_0$
$H_a: \mu < \mu_0$	$H_a: \mu > \mu_0$

Let us consider an example involving a lower tail test.

The Federal Trade Commission (FTC) periodically conducts statistical studies designed to test the claims that manufacturers make about their products. For example, the label on a large can of Hilltop Coffee states that the can contains 3 pounds of coffee. The FTC knows that Hilltop's production process cannot place exactly 3 pounds of coffee in each can, even if the mean filling weight for the population of all cans filled is 3 pounds per can. However, as long as the population mean filling weight is at least 3 pounds per can, the rights of consumers will be protected. Thus, the FTC interprets the label information on a large can of coffee as a claim by Hilltop that the population mean filling weight is at least 3 pounds per can. We will show how the FTC can check Hilltop's claim by conducting a lower tail hypothesis test.

The first step is to develop the null and alternative hypotheses for the test. If the population mean filling weight is at least 3 pounds per can, Hilltop's claim is correct. This result establishes the null hypothesis for the test. However, if the population mean filling weight is less than 3 pounds per can, Hilltop's claim is incorrect. This result establishes the alternative hypothesis. With μ denoting the population mean filling weight, the null and alternative hypotheses are as follows:

$$H_0: \mu \geq 3$$
$$H_a: \mu < 3$$

Note that the hypothesized value of the population mean is $\mu_0 = 3$.

If the sample data indicate that H_0 cannot be rejected, the statistical evidence does not support the conclusion that a label violation has occurred. Hence, no action should be taken against Hilltop. However, if the sample data indicate H_0 can be rejected, we will conclude that the alternative hypothesis, H_a: $\mu < 3$, is true. In this case a conclusion of underfilling and a charge of a label violation against Hilltop would be justified.

Suppose a sample of 36 cans of coffee is selected and the sample mean $\bar{x}$ is computed as an estimate of the population mean μ. If the value of the sample mean $\bar{x}$ is less than 3 pounds, the sample results will cast doubt on the null hypothesis. What we want to know is how much less than 3 pounds must $\bar{x}$ be before we would be willing to declare the difference significant and risk making a Type I error by falsely accusing Hilltop of a label violation. A key factor in addressing this issue is the value the decision maker selects for the level of significance.

As noted in the preceding section, the level of significance, denoted by α, is the probability of making a Type I error by rejecting H_0 when the null hypothesis is true as an equality. The decision maker must specify the level of significance. If the cost of making a Type I error is high, a small value should be chosen for the level of significance. If the cost is not high, a larger value is more appropriate. In the Hilltop Coffee study, the director of the FTC's testing program made the following statement: "If the company is meeting its weight specifications at $\mu = 3$, I do not want to take action against them. But, I am willing to risk a 1% chance of making such an error." From the director's statement, we set the level of significance for the hypothesis test at $\alpha = .01$. Thus, we must design the hypothesis test so that the probability of making a Type I error when $\mu = 3$ is .01.

For the Hilltop Coffee study, by developing the null and alternative hypotheses and specifying the level of significance for the test, we carry out the first two steps required in conducting every hypothesis test. We are now ready to perform the third step of hypothesis testing: collect the sample data and compute the value of what is called a test statistic.

Test Statistic. For the Hilltop Coffee study, previous FTC tests show that the population standard deviation can be assumed known with a value of $\sigma = .18$. In addition, these tests also show that the population of filling weights can be assumed to have a normal distribution. From the study of sampling distributions in Chapter 7 we know that if the population from which we are sampling is normally distributed, the sampling distribution of $\bar{x}$ will also be normally distributed. Thus, for the Hilltop Coffee study, the sampling distribution of $\bar{x}$ is normally distributed. With a known value of $\sigma = .18$ and a sample size of $n = 36$, Figure 9.1 shows the sampling distribution of $\bar{x}$ when the null hypothesis is true as an equality; that is, when $\mu = \mu_0 = 3$.* Note that the standard error of $\bar{x}$ is given by

The standard error of $\bar{x}$ is the standard deviation of the sampling distribution of $\bar{x}$.

$$\sigma_{\bar{x}} = \sigma/\sqrt{n} = .18/\sqrt{36} = .03.$$

FIGURE 9.1 SAMPLING DISTRIBUTION OF $\bar{x}$ FOR THE HILLTOP COFFEE STUDY WHEN THE NULL HYPOTHESIS IS TRUE AS AN EQUALITY ($\mu = 3$)

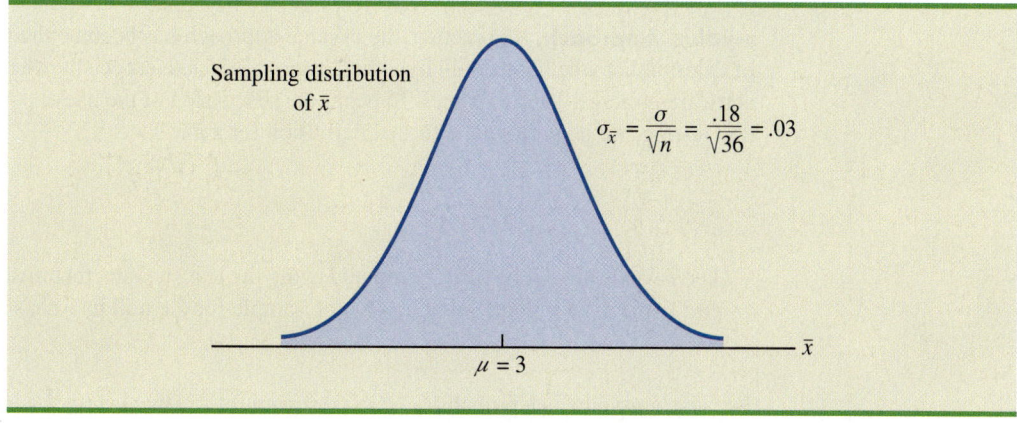

Sampling distribution of $\bar{x}$

$$\sigma_{\bar{x}} = \frac{\sigma}{\sqrt{n}} = \frac{.18}{\sqrt{36}} = .03$$

$\mu = 3$

*In constructing sampling distributions for hypothesis tests, it is assumed that H_0 is satisfied as an equality.

Because the sampling distribution of $\bar{x}$ is normally distributed, the sampling distribution of

$$z = \frac{\bar{x} - \mu_0}{\sigma_{\bar{x}}} = \frac{\bar{x} - 3}{.03}$$

is a standard normal distribution. A value of $z = -1$ means that the value of $\bar{x}$ is one standard error below the hypothesized value of the mean, a value of $z = -2$ means that the value of $\bar{x}$ is two standard errors below the hypothesized value of the mean, and so on. We can use the standard normal probability table to find the lower tail probability corresponding to any z value. For instance, the lower tail area at $z = -3.00$ is .0013. Hence, the probability of obtaining a value of z that is three or more standard errors below the mean is .0013. As a result, the probability of obtaining a value of $\bar{x}$ that is 3 or more standard errors below the hypothesized population mean $\mu_0 = 3$ is also .0013. Such a result is unlikely if the null hypothesis is true.

For hypothesis tests about a population mean in the σ known case, we use the standard normal random variable z as a **test statistic** to determine whether $\bar{x}$ deviates from the hypothesized value of μ enough to justify rejecting the null hypothesis. With $\sigma_{\bar{x}} = \sigma/\sqrt{n}$, the test statistic used in the σ known case is as follows.

> **TEST STATISTIC FOR HYPOTHESIS TESTS ABOUT A POPULATION MEAN: σ KNOWN**
>
> $$z = \frac{\bar{x} - \mu_0}{\sigma/\sqrt{n}} \tag{9.1}$$

The key question for a lower tail test is: How small must the test statistic z be before we choose to reject the null hypothesis? Two approaches can be used to answer this question.

The first approach uses the value of the test statistic z to compute a probability called a **p-value**. The p-value measures the support (or lack of support) provided by the sample for the null hypothesis and is the basis for determining whether the null hypothesis should be rejected given the level of significance. The second approach requires that we first determine a value for the test statistic called the **critical value**. For a lower tail test, the critical value serves as a benchmark for determining whether the value of the test statistic is small enough to reject the null hypothesis. We begin with the p-value approach.

p-value Approach. In practice, the p-value approach has become the preferred method of determining whether the null hypothesis can be rejected, especially when using computer software packages such as Excel. To begin our discussion of the use of p-values in hypothesis testing, we now provide a formal definition for a p-value.

> **p-VALUE**
>
> The p-value is a probability, computed using the test statistic, that measures the support (or lack of support) provided by the sample for the null hypothesis.

Because a p-value is a probability, it ranges from 0 to 1. In general, the larger the p-value, the more support the test statistic provides for the null hypothesis. On the other hand, a small p-value indicates a sample test statistic that is unusual given the assumption that H_0 is true.

Small p-values lead to rejection of H_0, whereas large p-values indicate the null hypothesis should not be rejected.

Two steps are required to use the p-value approach. First, we must use the value of the test statistic to compute the p-value. The method used to compute a p-value depends on whether the test is a lower tail, an upper tail, or a two-tailed test. For a lower tail test, the p-value is the probability of obtaining a value for the test statistic as small as or smaller than that provided by the sample. Thus, to compute the p-value for the lower tail test in the σ known case, we must find the area under the standard normal curve to the left of the test statistic. After computing the p-value, we must then decide whether it is small enough to reject the null hypothesis; as we will show, this decision involves comparing the p-value to the level of significance.

Coffee

Let us now illustrate the p-value approach by computing the p-value for the Hilltop Coffee lower tail test. Suppose the sample of 36 Hilltop coffee cans provides a sample mean of $\bar{x} = 2.92$ pounds. Is $\bar{x} = 2.92$ small enough to cause us to reject H_0? Because this is a lower tail test, the p-value is the area under the standard normal curve to the left of the test statistic. Using $\bar{x} = 2.92$, $\sigma = .18$, and $n = 36$, we compute the value of the test statistic z.

$$z = \frac{\bar{x} - \mu_0}{\sigma/\sqrt{n}} = \frac{2.92 - 3}{.18/\sqrt{36}} = -2.67$$

Thus, the p-value is the probability that the test statistic z is less than or equal to -2.67 (the area under the standard normal curve to the left of the test statistic).

Using the standard normal probability table, we find that the lower tail area at $z = -2.67$ is .0038. Figure 9.2 shows that $\bar{x} = 2.92$ corresponds to $z = -2.67$ and a p-value $= .0038$. This p-value indicates a small probability of obtaining a sample mean of $\bar{x} = 2.92$ (and a test statistic of -2.67) or smaller when sampling from a population with $\mu = 3$. This p-value does not provide much support for the null hypothesis, but is it small enough to cause us to reject H_0? The answer depends upon the level of significance for the test.

As noted previously, the director of the FTC's testing program selected a value of .01 for the level of significance. The selection of $\alpha = .01$ means that the director is willing to accept a probability of .01 of rejecting the null hypothesis when it is true as an equality ($\mu_0 = 3$). The sample of 36 coffee cans in the Hilltop Coffee study resulted in a p-value $= .0038$, which means that the probability of obtaining a value of $\bar{x} = 2.92$ or less when the null hypothesis is true as an equality is .0038. Because .0038 is less than or equal to $\alpha = .01$, we reject H_0. Therefore, we find sufficient statistical evidence to reject the null hypothesis at the .01 level of significance.

We can now state the general rule for determining whether the null hypothesis can be rejected when using the p-value approach. For a level of significance α, the rejection rule using the p-value approach is as follows:

REJECTION RULE USING p-VALUE

Reject H_0 if p-value $\leq \alpha$

In the Hilltop Coffee test, the p-value of .0038 resulted in the rejection of the null hypothesis. Although the basis for making the rejection decision involves a comparison of the p-value to the level of significance specified by the FTC director, the observed p-value of .0038 means that we would reject H_0 for any value of $\alpha \geq .0038$. For this reason, the p-value is also called the *observed level of significance*.

Excel's NORMDIST function makes it easy to compute p-values.

Excel's NORMSDIST function can also be used to compute the p-value for the Hilltop Coffee study. Entering the function $=$NORMSDIST(-2.67) into a cell of an Excel worksheet provides the cumulative probability (lower tail area) corresponding to $z = -2.67$. The result

FIGURE 9.2   *p*-VALUE FOR THE HILLTOP COFFEE STUDY WHEN $\bar{x} = 2.92$ AND $z = -2.67$

obtained is .0038, which is the same *p*-value we obtained using the standard normal probability table.

   Different decision makers may express different opinions concerning the cost of making a Type I error and may choose a different level of significance. By providing the *p*-value
as part of the hypothesis testing results, another decision maker can compare the reported
p-value to his or her own level of significance and possibly make a different decision with
respect to rejecting H_0.

Critical Value Approach.   For a lower tail test, the critical value is the value of the test
statistic that corresponds to an area of α (the level of significance) in the lower tail of the
sampling distribution of the test statistic. In other words, the critical value is the largest
value of the test statistic that will result in the rejection of the null hypothesis. Let us return
to the Hilltop Coffee example and see how this approach works.

   In the σ known case, the sampling distribution for the test statistic z is a standard normal distribution. Therefore, the critical value is the value of the test statistic that corresponds to an area of $\alpha = .01$ in the lower tail of a standard normal distribution. Using the
standard normal probability table, we find that $z = -2.33$ provides an area of .01 in the
lower tail (see Figure 9.3). Thus, if the sample results in a value of the test statistic that is
less than or equal to -2.33, the corresponding *p*-value will be less than or equal to .01; in
this case, we should reject the null hypothesis. Hence, for the Hilltop Coffee study the critical value rejection rule for a level of significance of .01 is

$$\text{Reject } H_0 \text{ if } z \leq -2.33$$

FIGURE 9.3 CRITICAL VALUE = -2.33 FOR THE HILLTOP COFFEE HYPOTHESIS TEST

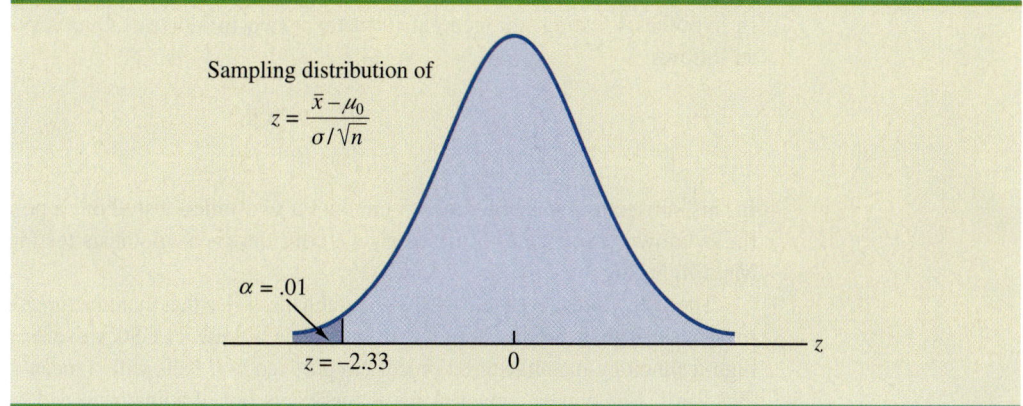

In the Hilltop Coffee example, $\bar{x} = 2.92$ and the test statistic is $z = -2.67$. Because $z = -2.67 < -2.33$, we can reject H_0 and conclude that Hilltop Coffee is underfilling cans.

We can generalize the rejection rule for the critical value approach to handle any level of significance. The rejection rule for a lower tail test follows.

REJECTION RULE FOR A LOWER TAIL TEST: CRITICAL VALUE APPROACH

$$\text{Reject } H_0 \text{ if } z \leq -z_\alpha$$

where $-z_\alpha$ is the critical value; that is, the z value that provides an area of α in the lower tail of the standard normal distribution.

The p-value approach to hypothesis testing and the critical value approach will always lead to the same rejection decision; that is, whenever the p-value is less than or equal to α, the value of the test statistic will be less than or equal to the critical value. The advantage of the p-value approach is that the p-value tells us *how* significant the results are (the observed level of significance). If we use the critical value approach, we only know that the results are significant at the stated level of significance.

At the beginning of this section, we said that one-tailed tests about a population mean take one of the following two forms:

Lower Tail Test	**Upper Tail Test**
$H_0: \mu \geq \mu_0$	$H_0: \mu \leq \mu_0$
$H_a: \mu < \mu_0$	$H_a: \mu > \mu_0$

We used the Hilltop Coffee study to illustrate how to conduct a lower tail test. We can use the same general approach to conduct an upper tail test. The test statistic z is still computed using equation (9.1). But, for an upper tail test, the p-value is the probability of obtaining a value for the test statistic as large as or larger than that provided by the sample. Thus, to compute the p-value for the upper tail test in the σ known case, we must find the area under the standard normal curve to the right of the test statistic. Using the critical value approach causes us to reject the null hypothesis if the value of the test statistic is greater than or equal to the critical value z_α; in other words, we reject H_0 if $z \geq z_\alpha$.

Two-Tailed Test

In hypothesis testing, the general form for a **two-tailed test** about a population mean is as follows:

$$H_0: \mu = \mu_0$$
$$H_a: \mu \neq \mu_0$$

In this subsection we show how to conduct a two-tailed test about a population mean for the σ known case. As an illustration, we consider the hypothesis testing situation facing MaxFlight, Inc.

The U.S. Golf Association (USGA) establishes rules that manufacturers of golf equipment must meet if their products are to be acceptable for use in USGA events. MaxFlight uses a high-technology manufacturing process to produce golf balls with a mean driving distance of 295 yards. Sometimes, however, the process gets out of adjustment and produces golf balls with a mean driving distance different from 295 yards. When the mean distance falls below 295 yards, the company worries about losing sales because the golf balls do not provide as much distance as advertised. When the mean distance passes 295 yards, MaxFlight's golf balls may be rejected by the USGA for exceeding the overall distance standard concerning carry and roll.

MaxFlight's quality control program involves taking periodic samples of 50 golf balls to monitor the manufacturing process. For each sample, a hypothesis test is conducted to determine whether the process has fallen out of adjustment. Let us develop the null and alternative hypotheses. We begin by assuming that the process is functioning correctly; that is, the golf balls being produced have a mean distance of 295 yards. This assumption establishes the null hypothesis. The alternative hypothesis is that the mean distance is not equal to 295 yards. With a hypothesized value of $\mu_0 = 295$, the null and alternative hypotheses for the MaxFlight hypothesis test are as follows:

$$H_0: \mu = 295$$
$$H_a: \mu \neq 295$$

If the sample mean $\bar{x}$ is significantly less than 295 yards or significantly greater than 295 yards, we will reject H_0. In this case, corrective action will be taken to adjust the manufacturing process. On the other hand, if $\bar{x}$ does not deviate from the hypothesized mean $\mu_0 = 295$ by a significant amount, H_0 will not be rejected and no action will be taken to adjust the manufacturing process.

The quality control team selected $\alpha = .05$ as the level of significance for the test. Data from previous tests conducted when the process was known to be in adjustment show that the population standard deviation can be assumed known with a value of $\sigma = 12$. Thus, with a sample size of $n = 50$, the standard error of $\bar{x}$ is

$$\sigma_{\bar{x}} = \frac{\sigma}{\sqrt{n}} = \frac{12}{\sqrt{50}} = 1.7$$

Because the sample size is large, the central limit theorem (see Chapter 7) allows us to conclude that the sampling distribution of $\bar{x}$ can be approximated by a normal distribution. Figure 9.4 shows the sampling distribution of $\bar{x}$ for the MaxFlight hypothesis test with a hypothesized population mean of $\mu_0 = 295$.

Suppose that a sample of 50 golf balls is selected and that the sample mean is $\bar{x} = 297.6$ yards. This sample mean provides support for the conclusion that the population mean is larger than 295 yards. Is this value of $\bar{x}$ enough larger than 295 to cause us to reject H_0 at the .05 level of significance? In the previous section we described two approaches that can be used to answer this question: the p-value approach and the critical value approach.

FIGURE 9.4 SAMPLING DISTRIBUTION OF $\bar{x}$ FOR THE MAXFLIGHT HYPOTHESIS TEST

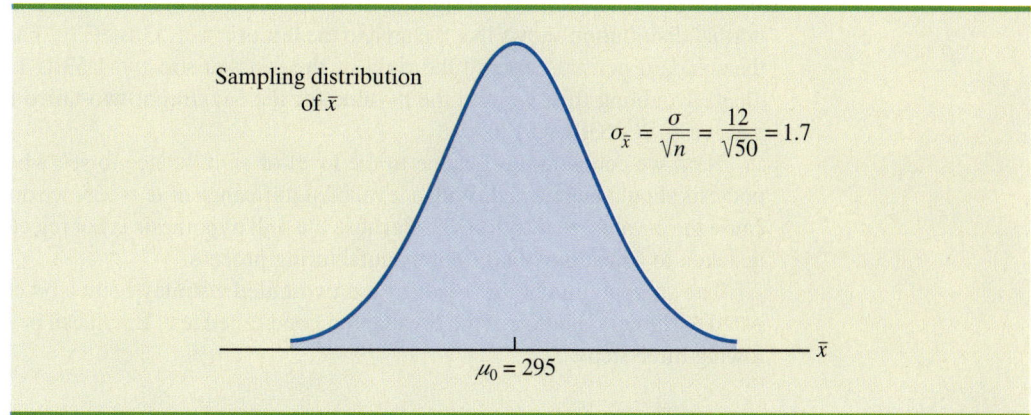

p-value Approach. Recall that the *p*-value is a probability, computed using the test statistic, that measures the support (or lack of support) provided by the sample for the null hypothesis. For a two-tailed test, values of the test statistic in *either* tail show a lack of support for the null hypothesis. For a two-tailed test, the *p*-value is the probability of obtaining a value for the test statistic *as unlikely as or more unlikely than* that provided by the sample. Let us see how the *p*-value is computed for the MaxFlight hypothesis test.

First we compute the value of the test statistic. For the σ known case, the test statistic *z* is a standard normal random variable. Using equation (9.1) with $\bar{x} = 297.6$, the value of the test statistic is

$$z = \frac{\bar{x} - \mu_0}{\sigma/\sqrt{n}} = \frac{297.6 - 295}{12/\sqrt{50}} = 1.53$$

Now to compute the *p*-value we must find the probability of obtaining a value for the test statistic *at least as unlikely as* $z = 1.53$. Clearly values of $z \geq 1.53$ are *at least as unlikely*. But, because this is a two-tailed test, values of $z \leq -1.53$ are also *at least as unlikely as* the value of the test statistic provided by the sample. Referring to Figure 9.5, we see that the two-tailed *p*-value in this case is given by $P(z \leq -1.53) + P(z \geq 1.53)$. Because the

FIGURE 9.5 *p*-VALUE FOR THE MAXFLIGHT HYPOTHESIS TEST

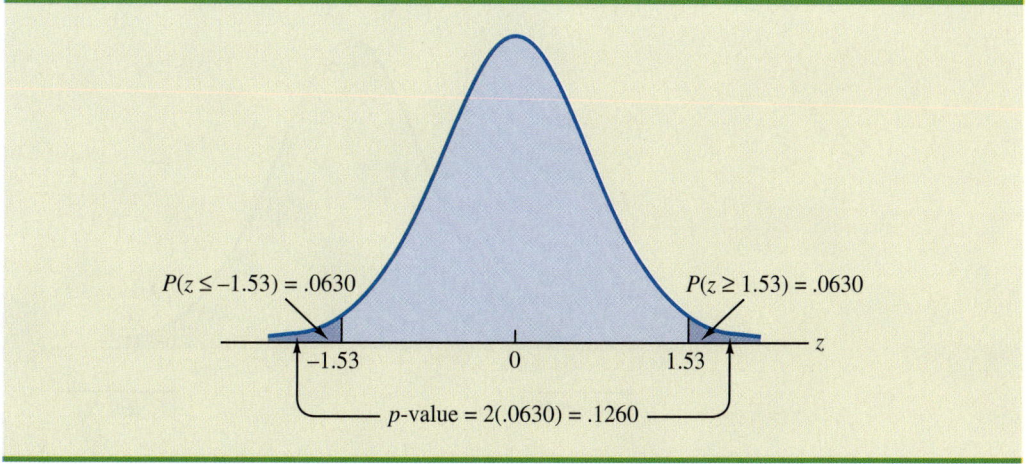

normal curve is symmetric, we can compute this probability by finding the area under the standard normal curve to the right of $z = 1.53$ and doubling it. The table for the standard normal distribution shows that the area to the left of $z = 1.53$ is .9370. Thus, the area under the standard normal curve to the right of the test statistic $z = 1.53$ is $1.0000 - .9370 = .0630$. Doubling this, we find the p-value for the MaxFlight two-tailed hypothesis test is p-value $= 2(.0630) = .1260$.

Next we compare the p-value to the level of significance to see whether the null hypothesis should be rejected. With a level of significance of $\alpha = .05$, we do not reject H_0 because the p-value $= .1260 > .05$. Because the null hypothesis is not rejected, no action will be taken to adjust the MaxFlight manufacturing process.

The computation of the p-value for a two-tailed test may seem a bit confusing as compared to the computation of the p-value for a one-tailed test. But, it can be simplified by following three steps.

COMPUTATION OF p-VALUE FOR A TWO-TAILED TEST

   1. Compute the value of the test statistic z.
   2. If the value of the test statistic is in the upper tail ($z > 0$), find the area under the standard normal curve to the right of z. If the value of the test statistic is in the lower tail ($z < 0$), find the area under the standard normal curve to the left of z.
   3. Double the tail area, or probability, obtained in step 2 to obtain the p-value.

Critical Value Approach.   Before leaving this section, let us see how the test statistic z can be compared to a critical value to make the hypothesis testing decision for a two-tailed test. Figure 9.6 shows that the critical values for the test will occur in both the lower and upper tails of the standard normal distribution. With a level of significance of $\alpha = .05$, the area in each tail beyond the critical values is $\alpha/2 = .05/2 = .025$. Using the standard normal probability table, we find the critical values for the test statistic are $-z_{.025} = -1.96$ and $z_{.025} = 1.96$. Thus, using the critical value approach, the two-tailed rejection rule is

$$\text{Reject } H_0 \text{ if } z \leq -1.96 \text{ or if } z \geq 1.96$$

Because the value of the test statistic for the MaxFlight study is $z = 1.53$, the statistical evidence will not permit us to reject the null hypothesis at the .05 level of significance.

FIGURE 9.6   CRITICAL VALUES FOR THE MAXFLIGHT HYPOTHESIS TEST

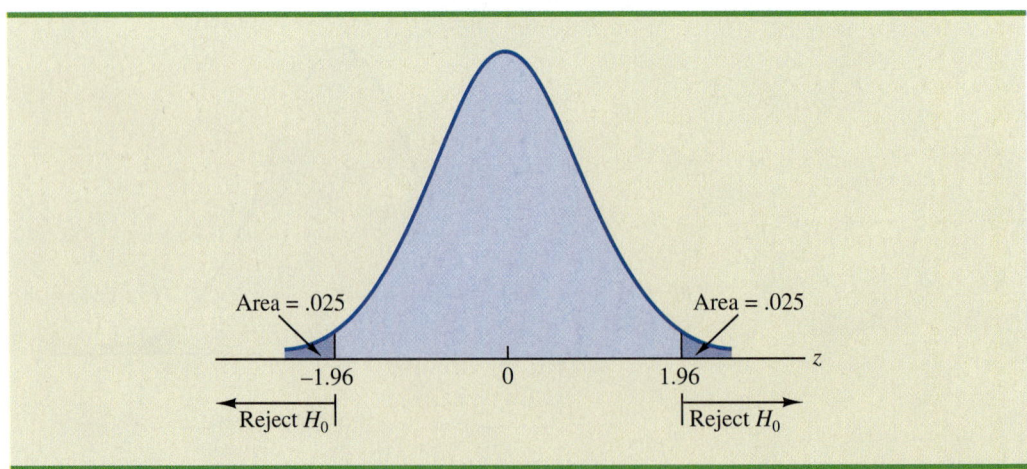

Using Excel

Excel can be used to conduct one-tailed and two-tailed hypothesis tests about a population mean for the σ known case using the *p*-value approach. Recall that the method used to compute a *p*-value depends upon whether the test is lower tail, upper tail, or two-tailed. Therefore, in the Excel procedure we describe we will use the sample results to compute three *p*-values: *p*-value (Lower Tail); *p*-value (Upper Tail); and *p*-value (Two Tail). The user can then choose α and draw a conclusion using whichever *p*-value is appropriate for the type of hypothesis test being conducted. We will illustrate using the MaxFlight two-tailed hypothesis test. Refer to Figure 9.7 as we describe the tasks involved. The formula worksheet is in the background; the value worksheet is in the foreground.

FIGURE 9.7   EXCEL WORKSHEET: HYPOTHESIS TEST FOR THE σ KNOWN CASE

	A	B	C	D	E
1	Yards		Hypothesis Test about a Population Mean:		
2	303		σ Known Case		
3	282				
4	289		Sample Size	=COUNT(A2:A51)	
5	298		Sample Mean	=AVERAGE(A2:A51)	
6	283				
7	317		Population Standard Deviation	12	
8	297		Hypothesized Value	295	
9	308				
10	317		Standard Error	=D7/SQRT(D4)	
11	293		Test Statistic z	=(D5-D8)/D10	
12	284				
13	290		*p*-value (Lower Tail)	=NORMSDIST(D11)	
14	304		*p*-value (Upper Tail)	=1-D13	
15	290		*p*-value (Two Tail)	=2*(MIN(D13,D14))	
16	311				
50	301				
51	292				
52					

	A	B	C	D	E
1	Yards		Hypothesis Test about a Population Mean:		
2	303		σ Known Case		
3	282				
4	289		Sample Size	50	
5	298		Sample Mean	297.6	
6	283				
7	317		Population Standard Deviation	12	
8	297		Hypothesized Value	295	
9	308				
10	317		Standard Error	1.6971	
11	293		Test Statistic z	1.5321	
12	284				
13	290		*p*-value (Lower Tail)	0.9372	
14	304		*p*-value (Upper Tail)	0.0628	
15	290		*p*-value (Two Tail)	0.1255	
16	311				
50	301				
51	292				
52					

CD file

GolfTest

Note: Rows 17–49 are hidden.

Enter Data: A label and the distance data for the sample of 50 golf balls are entered into cells A1:A51.

Enter Functions and Formulas: The descriptive statistics needed are provided in cells D4 and D5. Excel's COUNT and AVERAGE functions compute the sample size and the sample mean, respectively. The value of the known population standard deviation (12) is entered into cell D7, and the hypothesized value of the population mean (295) is entered into cell D8.

The standard error is obtained in cell D10 by entering the formula D7/SQRT(D4). The formula =(D5-D8)/D10 entered into cell D11 computes the test statistic $z(1.5321)$. To compute the p-value for a lower tail test, we enter the formula =NORMSDIST(D11) into cell D13. The p-value for an upper tail test is then computed in cell D14 as 1 minus the p-value for the lower tail test. Finally, the p-value for a two-tailed test is computed in cell D15 as 2 times the minimum of the 2 one-tailed p-values. The value worksheet shows that p-value (Lower Tail) = 0.9372, p-value (Upper Tail) = 0.0628, and p-value (Two Tail) = 0.1255.

The development of the worksheet is now complete. For the two-tailed MaxFlight problem we cannot reject $H_0 : \mu = 295$ using $\alpha = .05$ because the p-value (Two Tail) = 0.1255 is greater than α. Thus, the quality control manager has no reason to doubt that the manufacturing process is producing golf balls with a population mean distance of 295 yards.

A Template for Other Problems.   The worksheet in Figure 9.7 can be used as a template for conducting any one-tailed and two-tailed hypothesis tests for the σ known case. Just enter the appropriate data in column A, adjust the ranges for the formulas in cells D4 and D5, enter the population standard deviation in cell D7, and enter the hypothesized value in cell D8. The standard error, the test statistic, and the three p-values will then appear. Depending on the form of the hypothesis test (lower tail, upper tail, or two-tailed), we can then choose the appropriate p-value to make the rejection decision.

We can further simplify the use of Figure 9.7 as a template for other problems by eliminating the need to enter new data ranges in cells D4 and D5. To do so we rewrite the cell formulas as follows:

$$\text{Cell D4:} \quad =\text{COUNT(A:A)}$$
$$\text{Cell D5:} \quad =\text{AVERAGE(A:A)}$$

The GolfTest data set includes a worksheet titled Template that uses the A:A method for entering the data ranges.

With the A:A method of specifying data ranges, Excel's COUNT function will count the number of numeric values in column A and Excel's AVERAGE function will compute the average of the numeric values in column A. Thus, to solve a new problem it is only necessary to enter the new data in column A, enter the value of the known population standard deviation in cell D7, and enter the hypothesized value of the population mean in cell D8.

The worksheet can also be used as a template for text exercises in which n, $\bar{x}$, and σ are given. Just ignore the data in column A and enter the values for n, $\bar{x}$, and σ into cells D4, D5, and D7, respectively. Then enter the appropriate hypothesized value for the population mean into cell D8. The p-values corresponding to lower tail, upper tail, and two-tailed hypothesis tests will then appear in cells D13:D15.

Summary and Practical Advice

We presented examples of a lower tail test and a two-tailed test about a population mean. Based upon these examples, we can now summarize the hypothesis testing procedures about a population mean for the σ known case as shown in Table 9.2. Note that μ_0 is the hypothesized value of the population mean.

TABLE 9.2   SUMMARY OF HYPOTHESIS TESTS ABOUT A POPULATION MEAN: σ KNOWN CASE

	Lower Tail Test	**Upper Tail Test**	**Two-Tailed Test**
Hypotheses	$H_0: \mu \geq \mu_0$ $H_a: \mu < \mu_0$	$H_0: \mu \leq \mu_0$ $H_a: \mu > \mu_0$	$H_0: \mu = \mu_0$ $H_a: \mu \neq \mu_0$
Test Statistic	$z = \dfrac{\bar{x} - \mu_0}{\sigma/\sqrt{n}}$	$z = \dfrac{\bar{x} - \mu_0}{\sigma/\sqrt{n}}$	$z = \dfrac{\bar{x} - \mu_0}{\sigma/\sqrt{n}}$
Rejection Rule: ***p*-Value Approach**	Reject H_0 if p-value $\leq \alpha$	Reject H_0 if p-value $\leq \alpha$	Reject H_0 if p-value $\leq \alpha$
Rejection Rule: **Critical Value** **Approach**	Reject H_0 if $z \leq -z_\alpha$	Reject H_0 if $z \geq z_\alpha$	Reject H_0 if $z \leq -z_{\alpha/2}$ or if $z \geq z_{\alpha/2}$

The hypothesis testing steps followed in the two examples presented in this section are common to every hypothesis test.

STEPS OF HYPOTHESIS TESTING

Step 1. Develop the null and alternative hypotheses.
Step 2. Specify the level of significance.
Step 3. Collect the sample data and compute the value of the test statistic.

p-Value Approach

Step 4. Use the value of the test statistic to compute the *p*-value.
Step 5. Reject H_0 if the *p*-value $\leq \alpha$.

Critical Value Approach

Step 4. Use the level of significance to determine the critical value and the rejection rule.
Step 5. Use the value of the test statistic and the rejection rule to determine whether to reject H_0.

Practical advice about the sample size for hypothesis tests is similar to the advice we provided about the sample size for interval estimation in Chapter 8. In most applications, a sample size of $n \geq 30$ is adequate when using the hypothesis testing procedure described in this section. In cases where the sample size is less than 30, the distribution of the population from which we are sampling becomes an important consideration. If the population is normally distributed, the hypothesis testing procedure that we described is exact and can be used for any sample size. If the population is not normally distributed but is at least roughly symmetric, sample sizes as small as 15 can be expected to provide acceptable results. With smaller sample sizes, the hypothesis testing procedure presented in this section should only be used if the analyst believes, or is willing to assume, that the population is at least approximately normally distributed.

Relationship Between Interval Estimation and Hypothesis Testing

We close this section by discussing the relationship between interval estimation and hypothesis testing. In Chapter 8 we showed how to develop a confidence interval estimate of a population mean. For the σ known case, the confidence interval estimate of a population mean corresponding to a $1 - \alpha$ confidence coefficient is given by

$$\bar{x} \pm z_{\alpha/2} \frac{\sigma}{\sqrt{n}} \qquad (9.2)$$

Conducting a hypothesis test requires us first to develop the hypotheses about the value of a population parameter. In the case of the population mean, the two-tailed test takes the form

$$H_0: \mu = \mu_0$$
$$H_a: \mu \neq \mu_0$$

where μ_0 is the hypothesized value for the population mean. Using the two-tailed critical value approach, we do not reject H_0 for values of the sample mean $\bar{x}$ that are within $-z_{\alpha/2}$ and $+z_{\alpha/2}$ standard errors of μ_0. Thus, the do-not-reject region for the sample mean $\bar{x}$ in a two-tailed hypothesis test with a level of significance of α is given by

$$\mu_0 \pm z_{\alpha/2} \frac{\sigma}{\sqrt{n}} \qquad (9.3)$$

A close look at expressions (9.2) and (9.3) provides insight about the relationship between the estimation and hypothesis testing approaches to statistical inference. Note in particular that both procedures require the computation of the values $z_{\alpha/2}$ and $\sigma/\sqrt{n}$. Focusing on α, we see that a confidence coefficient of $(1 - \alpha)$ for interval estimation corresponds to a level of significance of α in hypothesis testing. For example, a 95% confidence interval corresponds to a .05 level of significance for hypothesis testing. Furthermore, expressions (9.2) and (9.3) show that, because $z_{\alpha/2}(\sigma/\sqrt{n})$ is the plus or minus value for both expressions, if $\bar{x}$ is in the do-not-reject region defined by expression (9.3), the hypothesized value μ_0 will be in the confidence interval defined by expression (9.2). Conversely, if the hypothesized value μ_0 is in the confidence interval defined by expression (9.2), the sample mean $\bar{x}$ will be in the do-not-reject region for the hypothesis $H_0: \mu = \mu_0$ as defined by expression (9.3). These observations lead to the following procedure for using a confidence interval to conduct a two-tailed hypothesis test.

A CONFIDENCE INTERVAL APPROACH TO TESTING A HYPOTHESIS OF THE FORM

$$H_0: \mu = \mu_0$$
$$H_a: \mu \neq \mu_0$$

1. Select a simple random sample from the population and use the value of the sample mean $\bar{x}$ to develop the confidence interval for the population mean μ.

$$\bar{x} \pm z_{\alpha/2} \frac{\sigma}{\sqrt{n}}$$

For a two-tailed hypothesis test, the null hypothesis can be rejected if the confidence interval does not include μ_0.

2. If the confidence interval contains the hypothesized value μ_0, do not reject H_0. Otherwise, reject H_0.

Let us return to the MaxFlight hypothesis test, which resulted in the following two-tailed test.

$$H_0: \mu = 295$$
$$H_a: \mu \neq 295$$

To test this hypothesis with a level of significance of $\alpha = .05$, we sampled 50 golf balls and found a sample mean distance of $\bar{x} = 297.6$ yards. Recall that the population standard deviation is $\sigma = 12$. Using these results with $z_{.025} = 1.96$, we find that the 95% confidence interval estimate of the population mean is

$$\bar{x} \pm z_{.025} \frac{\sigma}{\sqrt{n}}$$

$$297.6 \pm 1.96 \frac{12}{\sqrt{50}}$$

$$297.6 \pm 3.3$$

or

$$294.3 \text{ to } 300.9$$

This finding enables the quality control manager to conclude with 95% confidence that the mean distance for the population of golf balls is between 294.3 and 300.9 yards. Because the hypothesized value for the population mean, $\mu_0 = 295$, is in this interval, the hypothesis testing conclusion is that the null hypothesis, $H_0: \mu = 295$, cannot be rejected.

Note that this discussion and example pertain to two-tailed hypothesis tests about a population mean. However, the same confidence interval and two-tailed hypothesis testing relationship exist for other population parameters. The relationship can also be extended to one-tailed tests about population parameters. Doing so, however, requires the development of one-sided confidence intervals, which are rarely used in practice.

NOTES AND COMMENTS

We have shown how to compute p-values using Excel. The smaller the p-value the greater the evidence against H_0 and the more the evidence in favor of H_a. Here are some guidelines statisticians suggest for interpreting small p-values.

- Less than .01—Overwhelming evidence to conclude H_a is true.

- Between .01 and .05—Strong evidence to conclude H_a is true.
- Between .05 and .10—Weak evidence to conclude H_a is true.
- Greater than .10—Insufficient evidence to conclude H_a is true.

Exercises

Note to Student: Some of the exercises that follow ask you to use the p-value approach and others ask you to use the critical value approach. Both methods will provide the same hypothesis testing conclusion. We provide exercises with both methods to give you practice using both. In later sections and in following chapters, we will generally emphasize the p-value approach as the preferred method, but you may select either based on personal preference.

Methods

9. Consider the following hypothesis test:

$$H_0: \mu \geq 20$$
$$H_a: \mu < 20$$

A sample of 50 provided a sample mean of 19.4. The population standard deviation is 2.
   a. Compute the value of the test statistic.
   b. What is the p-value?
   c. Using $\alpha = .05$, what is your conclusion?
   d. What is the rejection rule using the critical value? What is your conclusion?

10. Consider the following hypothesis test:

$$H_0: \mu \leq 25$$
$$H_a: \mu > 25$$

A sample of 40 provided a sample mean of 26.4. The population standard deviation is 6.
   a. Compute the value of the test statistic.
   b. What is the p-value?
   c. At $\alpha = .01$, what is your conclusion?
   d. What is the rejection rule using the critical value? What is your conclusion?

11. Consider the following hypothesis test:

$$H_0: \mu = 15$$
$$H_a: \mu \neq 15$$

A sample of 50 provided a sample mean of 14.15. The population standard deviation is 3.
   a. Compute the value of the test statistic.
   b. What is the p-value?
   c. At $\alpha = .05$, what is your conclusion?
   d. What is the rejection rule using the critical value? What is your conclusion?

12. Consider the following hypothesis test:

$$H_0: \mu \geq 80$$
$$H_a: \mu < 80$$

A sample of 100 is used and the population standard deviation is 12. Compute the p-value and state your conclusion for each of the following sample results. Use $\alpha = .01$.
   a. $\bar{x} = 78.5$
   b. $\bar{x} = 77$
   c. $\bar{x} = 75.5$
   d. $\bar{x} = 81$

13. Consider the following hypothesis test:

$$H_0: \mu \leq 50$$
$$H_a: \mu > 50$$

A sample of 60 is used and the population standard deviation is 8. Use the critical value approach to state your conclusion for each of the following sample results. Use $\alpha = .05$.
   a. $\bar{x} = 52.5$
   b. $\bar{x} = 51$
   c. $\bar{x} = 51.8$

14.   Consider the following hypothesis test:

$$H_0: \mu = 22$$
$$H_a: \mu \neq 22$$

A sample of 75 is used and the population standard deviation is 10. Compute the p-value and state your conclusion for each of the following sample results. Use $\alpha = .01$.
a. $\bar{x} = 23$
b. $\bar{x} = 25.1$
c. $\bar{x} = 20$

Applications

15.   Individuals filing federal income tax returns prior to March 31 received an average refund of $1056. Consider the population of "last-minute" filers who mail their tax return during the last five days of the income tax period (typically April 10 to April 15).
a.   A researcher suggests that a reason individuals wait until the last five days is that on average these individuals receive lower refunds than do early filers. Develop appropriate hypotheses such that rejection of H_0 will support the researcher's contention.
b.   For a sample of 400 individuals who filed a tax return between April 10 and 15, the sample mean refund was $910. Based on prior experience a population standard deviation of $\sigma = \$1600$ may be assumed. What is the p-value?
c.   At $\alpha = .05$, what is your conclusion?
d.   Repeat the preceding hypothesis test using the critical value approach.

RentalRates

16.   Reis, Inc., a New York real estate research firm, tracks the cost of apartment rentals in the United States. In mid-2002, the nationwide mean apartment rental rate was $895 per month (*The Wall Street Journal,* July 8, 2002). Assume that, based on the historical quarterly surveys, a population standard deviation of $\sigma = \$225$ is reasonable. In a current study of apartment rental rates, a sample of 180 apartments nationwide provided the apartment rental rates shown in the CD file named RentalRates. Do the sample data enable Reis to conclude that the population mean apartment rental rate now exceeds the level reported in 2002?
a.   State the null and alternative hypotheses.
b.   What is the p-value?
c.   At $\alpha = .01$, what is your conclusion?
d.   What would you recommend Reis consider doing at this time?

17.   The mean length of a work week for the population of workers was reported to be 39.2 hours (*Investor's Business Daily,* September 11, 2000). Suppose that we would like to take a current sample of workers to see whether the mean length of a work week has changed from the previously reported 39.2 hours.
a.   State the hypotheses that will help us determine whether a change occurred in the mean length of a work week.
b.   Suppose a current sample of 112 workers provided a sample mean of 38.5 hours. Use a population standard deviation $\sigma = 4.8$ hours. What is the p-value?
c.   At $\alpha = .05$, can the null hypothesis be rejected? What is your conclusion?
d.   Repeat the preceding hypothesis test using the critical value approach.

18.   The average annual total return for U.S. Diversified Equity mutual funds from 1999 to 2003 was 4.1% (*Business Week,* January 26, 2004). A researcher would like to conduct a hypothesis test to see whether the returns for mid-cap growth funds over the same period are significantly different from the average for U.S. Diversified Equity funds.
a.   Formulate the hypotheses that can be used to determine whether the mean annual return for mid-cap growth funds differ from the mean for U.S. Diversified Equity funds.
b.   A sample of 40 mid-cap growth funds provides a mean return of $\bar{x} = 3.4\%$. Assume the population standard deviation for mid-cap growth funds is known from previous

studies to be $\sigma = 2\%$. Use the sample results to compute the test statistic and p-value for the hypothesis test.

c. At $\alpha = .05$, what is your conclusion?

19. In 2001, the U.S. Department of Labor reported the average hourly earnings for U.S. production workers to be $14.32 per hour (*The World Almanac 2003*). A sample of 75 production workers during 2003 showed a sample mean of $14.68 per hour. Assuming the population standard deviation $\sigma = \$1.45$, can we conclude that an increase occurred in the mean hourly earnings since 2001? Use $\alpha = .05$.

20. The national mean sales price for new one-family homes is $181,900 (*The New York Times Almanac 2000*). A sample of 40 one-family home sales in the South showed a sample mean of $166,400. Use a population standard deviation of $33,500.

a. Formulate the null and alternative hypotheses that can be used to determine whether the sample data support the conclusion that the population mean sales price for new one-family homes in the South is less than the national mean of $181,900.

b. What is the value of the test statistic?

c. What is the p-value?

d. At $\alpha = .01$, what is your conclusion?

Fowle

21. Fowle Marketing Research, Inc., bases charges to a client on the assumption that telephone surveys can be completed in a mean time of 15 minutes or less. If a longer mean survey time is necessary, a premium rate is charged. A sample of 35 surveys provided the survey times shown in the CD file named Fowle. Based upon past studies, the population standard deviation is assumed known with $\sigma = 4$ minutes. Is the premium rate justified?

a. Formulate the null and alternative hypotheses for this application.

b. Compute the value of the test statistic.

c. What is the p-value?

d. At $\alpha = .01$, what is your conclusion?

22. CCN and ActMedia provided a television channel targeted to individuals waiting in supermarket checkout lines. The channel showed news, short features, and advertisements. The length of the program was based on the assumption that the population mean time a shopper stands in a supermarket checkout line is 8 minutes. A sample of actual waiting times will be used to test this assumption and determine whether actual mean waiting time differs from this standard.

a. Formulate the hypotheses for this application.

b. A sample of 120 shoppers showed a sample mean waiting time of 8.5 minutes. Assume a population standard deviation $\sigma = 3.2$ minutes. What is the p-value?

c. At $\alpha = .05$, what is your conclusion?

d. Compute a 95% confidence interval for the population mean. Does it support your conclusion?

9.4 Population Mean: σ Unknown

In this section we describe how to conduct hypothesis tests about a population mean for the σ unknown case. Because the σ unknown case corresponds to situations in which an estimate of the population standard deviation cannot be developed prior to sampling, the sample must be used to develop an estimate of both μ and σ. Thus, to conduct a hypothesis test about a population mean for the σ unknown case, the sample mean $\bar{x}$ is used as an estimate of μ and the sample standard deviation s is used as an estimate of σ.

The steps of the hypothesis testing procedure for the σ unknown case are the same as those for the σ known case described in Section 9.3. But, with σ unknown, the computation of the test statistic and p-value is a bit different. Recall that for the σ known case, the sampling distribution of the test statistic has a standard normal distribution. For the σ unknown case, however, the sampling distribution of the test statistic follows the *t* distribution; it has slightly more variability because the sample is used to develop estimates of both μ and σ.

In Section 8.2 we showed that an interval estimate of a population mean for the σ unknown case is based on a probability distribution known as the *t* distribution. Hypothesis tests about a population mean for the σ unknown case are also based on the *t* distribution. For the σ unknown case, the test statistic has a *t* distribution with $n - 1$ degrees of freedom.

TEST STATISTIC FOR HYPOTHESIS TESTS ABOUT A POPULATION MEAN: σ UNKNOWN

$$t = \frac{\bar{x} - \mu_0}{s/\sqrt{n}} \qquad (9.4)$$

In Chapter 8 we said that the *t* distribution is based on an assumption that the population from which we are sampling has a normal distribution. However, research shows that this assumption can be relaxed considerably when the sample size is large enough. We provide some practical advice concerning the population distribution and sample size at the end of the section.

One-Tailed Test

AirRating

Let us consider an example of a one-tailed test about a population mean for the σ unknown case. A business travel magazine wants to classify transatlantic gateway airports according to the mean rating for the population of business travelers. A rating scale with a low score of 0 and a high score of 10 will be used, and airports with a population mean rating greater than 7 will be designated as superior service airports. The magazine staff surveyed a sample of 60 business travelers at each airport to obtain the ratings data. The sample for London's Heathrow Airport provided a sample mean rating of $\bar{x} = 7.25$ and a sample standard deviation of $s = 1.052$. Do the data indicate that Heathrow should be designated as a superior service airport?

We want to develop a hypothesis test for which the decision to reject H_0 will lead to the conclusion that the population mean rating for the Heathrow Airport is *greater* than 7. Thus, an upper tail test with H_a: $\mu > 7$ is required. The null and alternative hypotheses for this upper tail test are as follows:

$$H_0\text{: } \mu \leq 7$$
$$H_a\text{: } \mu > 7$$

We will use $\alpha = .05$ as the level of significance for the test.

Using equation (9.4) with $\bar{x} = 7.25$, $\mu_0 = 7$, $s = 1.052$, and $n = 60$, the value of the test statistic is

$$t = \frac{\bar{x} - \mu_0}{s/\sqrt{n}} = \frac{7.25 - 7}{1.052/\sqrt{60}} = 1.84$$

The sampling distribution of *t* has $n - 1 = 60 - 1 = 59$ degrees of freedom. Because the test is an upper tail test, the *p*-value is the area under the curve of the *t* distribution to the right of $t = 1.84$.

The *t* distribution table provided in most textbooks will not contain sufficient detail to determine the exact *p*-value, such as the *p*-value corresponding to $t = 1.84$. For instance, using Table 2 in Appendix B, the t distribution with 59 degrees of freedom provides the following information.

Area in Upper Tail	.20	.10	.05	.025	.01	.005
t Value (59 df)	.848	1.296	1.671	2.001	2.391	2.662

$$t = 1.84$$

We see that $t = 1.84$ is between 1.671 and 2.001. Although the table does not provide the exact p-value, the values in the "Area in Upper Tail" row show that the p-value must be less than .05 and greater than .025. With a level of significance of $\alpha = .05$, this placement is all we need to know to make the decision to reject the null hypothesis and conclude that Heathrow should be classified as a superior service airport.

In the upcoming "Using Excel" section, we illustrate how to use the TDIST function to compute the area in the lower tail of the t distribution when the value of the test statistic is negative.

Excel's TDIST function can be used to determine the exact p-value associated with the test statistic $t = 1.84$. The general form of the TDIST function is as follows:

$$\text{TDIST(test statistic,degrees of freedom,tails)}$$

Only nonnegative values are allowed for *test statistic*. If the value of *tails* is 1, the function returns the area in the upper tail of the t distribution corresponding to the value of the test statistic. In the Heathrow Airport study we found a value for the test statistic of $t = 1.84$. If we enter the function =TDIST(1.84,59,1) into an Excel worksheet, the value obtained is .0354. A p-value $= .0354 < .05$ leads to the rejection of the null hypothesis and to the conclusion that Heathrow should be classified as a superior service airport.

The critical value approach can also be used to make the rejection decision. With $\alpha = .05$ and the t distribution with 59 degrees of freedom, $t_{.05} = 1.671$ is the critical value for the test. The rejection rule is thus

$$\text{Reject } H_0 \text{ if } t \geq 1.671$$

With the test statistic $t = 1.84 \geq 1.671$, H_0 is rejected and we can conclude that Heathrow can be classified as a superior service airport.

Two-Tailed Test

To illustrate how to conduct a two-tailed test about a population mean for the σ unknown case, let us consider the hypothesis testing situation facing Holiday Toys. The company manufactures and distributes its products through more than 1000 retail outlets. In planning production levels for the coming winter season, Holiday must decide how many units of each product to produce prior to knowing the actual demand at the retail level. For this year's most important new toy, Holiday's marketing director is expecting demand to average 40 units per retail outlet. Prior to making the final production decision based upon this estimate, Holiday decided to survey a sample of 25 retailers in order to develop more information about the demand for the new product. Each retailer was provided with information about the features of the new toy along with the cost and the suggested selling price. Then each retailer was asked to specify an anticipated order quantity.

With μ denoting the population mean order quantity per retail outlet, the sample data will be used to conduct the following two-tailed hypothesis test:

$$H_0: \mu = 40$$
$$H_a: \mu \neq 40$$

If H_0 cannot be rejected, Holiday will continue its production planning based on the marketing director's estimate that the population mean order quantity per retail outlet will be $\mu = 40$ units. However, if H_0 is rejected. Holiday will immediately reevaluate its production plan for the product. A two-tailed hypothesis test is used because Holiday wants to reevaluate the production plan if the population mean quantity per retail outlet is less than anticipated or greater than anticipated. Because no historical data are available (it's a new product), the population mean μ and the population standard deviation must both be estimated using $\bar{x}$ and s from the sample data.

Orders

The sample of 25 retailers provided a mean of $\bar{x} = 37.4$ and a standard deviation of $s = 11.79$ units. Before going ahead with the use of the t distribution, the analyst constructed a histogram of the sample data in order to check on the form of the population distribution. The histogram of the sample data showed no evidence of skewness or any extreme outliers, so the analyst concluded that the use of the t distribution with $n - 1 = 24$ degrees of freedom was appropriate. Using equation (9.4) with $\bar{x} = 37.4$, $\mu_0 = 40$, $s = 11.79$, and $n = 25$, the value of the test statistic is

$$t = \frac{\bar{x} - \mu_0}{s/\sqrt{n}} = \frac{37.4 - 40}{11.79/\sqrt{25}} = -1.10$$

Because we have a two-tailed test, the p-value is two times the area under the curve for the t distribution to the left of $t = -1.10$. Using Table 2 in Appendix B, the t distribution table for 24 degrees of freedom provides the following information.

Area in Upper Tail	.20	.10	.05	.025	.01	.005
t Value (24 df)	.857	1.318	1.711	2.064	2.492	2.797

$t = 1.10$

The t distribution table only contains positive t values. Because the t distribution is symmetric, however, we can find the area under the curve to the right of $t = 1.10$ and double it to find the p-value. We see that $t = 1.10$ is between 0.857 and 1.318. From the "Area in Upper Tail" row, we see that the area in the tail to the right of $t = 1.10$ is between .20 and .10. Doubling these amounts, we see that the p-value must be between .40 and .20. With a level of significance of $\alpha = .05$, we now know that the p-value is greater than α. Therefore, H_0 cannot be rejected. Sufficient evidence is not available to conclude that Holiday should change its production plan for the coming season.

Excel's TDIST function can be used to determine the p-value for a two-tailed hypothesis test. Recall that the general form of the TDIST function is as follows:

TDIST(test statistic,degrees of freedom,tails)

Excel's TDIST function makes it easy to compute p-values.

Only nonnegative values are allowed for the test statistic and the value of tails is 1 or 2, depending upon whether the test is one- or two-tailed. For the two-tailed Holiday Toys hypothesis test, the value of the test statistic is -1.10, with 24 degrees of freedom. With 2 for the value of tails, entering the function =TDIST(1.10,24,2) into a cell of an Excel worksheet provides the area under the curve of the t distribution to the right of the value of 1.10 plus the area under the curve of the t distribution to the left of -1.10; it provides the p-value for the two-tailed Holiday Toys hypothesis test. The value obtained is .2822. With a level of significance of $\alpha = .05$, we cannot reject H_0 because the p-value is greater than α.

The test statistic can also be compared to the critical value to make the two-tailed hypothesis testing decision. With $\alpha = .05$ and the t distribution with 24 degrees of freedom,

$-t_{.025} = -2.064$ and $t_{.025} = 2.064$ are the critical values for the two-tailed test. The rejection rule using the test statistic is

$$\text{Reject } H_0 \text{ if } t \leq -2.064 \text{ or if } t \geq 2.064$$

Based on the test statistic $t = -1.10$, H_0 cannot be rejected. This result indicates that Holiday should continue its production planning for the coming season based on the expectation that $\mu = 40$.

Using Excel

Excel can be used to conduct one-tailed and two-tailed hypothesis tests about a population mean for the σ unknown case. The approach is similar to the procedure used in the σ known case. The sample data and the test statistic (t) are used to compute three p-values: p-value (Lower Tail), p-value (Upper Tail), and p-value (Two Tail). The user can then choose α and draw a conclusion using whichever p-value is appropriate for the type of hypothesis test being conducted.

Let's start by showing how to use Excel's TDIST function to compute a lower tail p-value. Previously, we showed that the general form of the TDIST function is as follows:

$$\text{TDIST(test statistic, degrees of freedom, tails)}$$

Recall that only nonnegative values are allowed for the test statistic and a tails value of 1 provides the area under the curve of the t distribution to the right of the value of the test statistic. For a lower tail hypothesis test the value of the test statistic is usually negative and the p-value is the area under the curve for the t distribution to the left of the test statistic. Because the t distribution is symmetric, the area under the curve to the left of the test statistic (the lower tail p-value) is the same as the area under the curve to the right of the negative of the test statistic. Thus, when the test statistic is *negative*, the TDIST function is used to compute the lower tail p-value in the following manner:

$$\text{TDIST(}-\text{test statistic, degrees of freedom, 1)}$$

To compute the p-value (Lower Tail) when the test statistic in *nonnegative*, we subtract the upper tail area provided by the TDIST function from 1 as follows:

$$\text{1-TDIST(test statistic, degrees of freedom, 1)}$$

We can use Excel's IF function to determine whether the value of the test statistic is negative or nonnegative and to specify how the TDIST function is used to compute the lower tail p-value.

$$\text{IF(test statistic} <0, \text{negative } t, \text{nonnegative } t)$$

where

$$\text{Negative } t: \text{ TDIST(-test statistic, degrees of freedom, 1)}$$
$$\text{Nonnegative } t: \text{ 1-TDIST(test statistic, degrees of freedom, 1)}$$

Thus, if the value of the test statistic is negative, the first form of the TDIST function is used to compute the lower tail p-value; if the value of the test statistic is nonnegative, the second form is used.

Once the lower tail p-value has been computed, it is easy to compute the upper tail and the two-tailed p-values. The upper tail p-value is just 1 minus the lower tail p-value.

And the two-tailed *p*-value is given by two times the smaller of the lower and upper tail *p*-values.

Let us now construct an Excel worksheet to conduct the two-tailed hypothesis test for the Holiday Toys study. Refer to Figure 9.8 as we describe the tasks involved. The formula worksheet is in the background; the value worksheet is in the foreground.

Enter Data: A label and the order quantity data for the sample of 25 retailers are entered into cells A1:A26.

Enter Functions and Formulas: The descriptive statistics needed are provided in cells D4:D6. Excel's COUNT, AVERAGE, and STDEV functions compute the sample size, the sample mean, and the sample standard deviation, respectively. The hypothesized value of the population mean (40) is entered into cell D8.

FIGURE 9.8   EXCEL WORKSHEET: HYPOTHESIS TEST FOR THE σ UNKNOWN CASE

	A	B	C	D	E
1	Units		Hypothesis Test about a Population Mean:		
2	26		σ Unknown Case		
3	23				
4	32		Sample Size	=COUNT(A2:A26)	
5	47		Sample Mean	=AVERAGE(A2:A26)	
6	45		Sample Standard Deviation	=STDEV(A2:A26)	
7	31				
8	47		Hypothesized Value	40	
9	59				
10	21		Standard Error	=D6/SQRT(D4)	
11	52		Test Statistic *t*	=(D5-D8)/D10	
12	45		Degrees of Freedom	=D4-1	
13	53				
14	34		*p*-value (Lower Tail)	=IF(D11<0,TDIST(-D11,D12,1),1-TDIST(D11,D12,1))	
15	45		*p*-value (Upper Tail)	=1-D14	
16	39		*p*-value (Two Tail)	=2*MIN(D14,D15)	
17	52				
25	30				
26	28				
27					

CD file

Orders

Note: Rows 18–24 are hidden.

	A	B	C	D	E	F
1	Units		Hypothesis Test about a Population Mean:			
2	26		σ Unknown Case			
3	23					
4	32		Sample Size	25		
5	47		Sample Mean	37.4		
6	45		Sample Standard Deviation	11.79		
7	31					
8	47		Hypothesized Value	40		
9	59					
10	21		Standard Error	2.3580		
11	52		Test Statistic *t*	-1.1026		
12	45		Degrees of Freedom	24		
13	53					
14	34		*p*-value (Lower Tail)	0.1406		
15	45		*p*-value (Upper Tail)	0.8594		
16	39		*p*-value (Two Tail)	0.2811		
17	52					
25	30					
26	28					
27						

Using the sample standard deviation as an estimate of the population standard deviation, an estimate of the standard error is obtained in cell D10 by dividing the sample standard deviation in cell D6 by the square root of the sample size in cell D4. The formula =(D5-D8)/D10 entered into cell D11 computes the test statistic $t(-1.1026)$. The degrees of freedom are computed in cell D12 as the sample size in cell D4 minus 1.

To compute the p-value for a lower tail test, we enter the following formula into cell D14:

$$=IF(D11<0,TDIST(-D11,D12,1),1-TDIST(D11,D12,1))$$

The p-value for an upper tail test is then computed in cell D15 as 1 minus the p-value for the lower tail test. Finally, the p-value for a two-tailed test is computed in cell D16 as 2 times the minimum of the 2 one-tailed p-values. The value worksheet shows that the three p-values are p-value (Lower Tail) = 0.1406, p-value (Upper Tail) = 0.8594, and p-value (Two Tail) = 0.2811.

The development of the worksheet is now complete. For the two-tailed Holiday Toys problem we cannot reject $H_0 : \mu = 40$ using $\alpha = .05$ because the p-value (Two Tail) = 0.2811 is greater than α. This result indicates that Holiday should continue its production planning for the coming season based on the expectation that $\mu = 40$. The worksheet in Figure 9.8 can also be used for any one-tailed hypothesis test involving the t distribution. If a lower tail test is required, compare the p-value (Lower Tail) with α to make the rejection decision. If an upper tail test is required, compare the p-value (Upper Tail) with α to make the rejection decision.

A Template for Other Problems. The worksheet in Figure 9.8 can be used as a template for any hypothesis tests about a population mean for the σ unknown case. Just enter the appropriate data in column A, adjust the ranges for the formulas in cells D4:D6, and enter the hypothesized value in cell D8. The standard error, the test statistic, and the three p-values will then appear. Depending on the form of the hypothesis test (lower tail, upper tail, or two-tailed), we can then choose the appropriate p-value to make the rejection decision.

We can further simplify the use of Figure 9.8 as a template for other problems by eliminating the need to enter new data ranges in cells D4:D6. To do so we rewrite the cell formulas as follows:

Cell D4: =COUNT(A:A)
Cell D5: =AVERAGE(A:A)
Cell D6: =STDEV(A:A)

The Orders data set includes a worksheet titled Template that uses the A:A method for entering the data ranges.

With the A:A method of specifying data ranges, Excel's COUNT function will count the number of numeric values in column A, Excel's AVERAGE function will compute the average of the numeric values in column A, and Excel's STDEV function will compute the standard deviation of the numeric values in Column A. Thus, to solve a new problem it is only necessary to enter the new data in column A and enter the hypothesized value of the population mean in cell D8.

Summary and Practical Advice

Table 9.3 provides a summary of the hypothesis testing procedures about a population mean for the σ unknown case. The key difference between these procedures and the ones for the σ known case is that s is used, instead of σ, in the computation of the test statistic. For this reason, the test statistic follows the t distribution.

The applicability of the hypothesis testing procedures of this section is dependent on the distribution of the population being sampled from and the sample size. When the popu-

TABLE 9.3 SUMMARY OF HYPOTHESIS TESTS ABOUT A POPULATION MEAN: σ UNKNOWN CASE

	Lower Tail Test	Upper Tail Test	Two-Tailed Test
Hypotheses	$H_0: \mu \geq \mu_0$ $H_a: \mu < \mu_0$	$H_0: \mu \leq \mu_0$ $H_a: \mu > \mu_0$	$H_0: \mu = \mu_0$ $H_a: \mu \neq \mu_0$
Test Statistic	$t = \dfrac{\bar{x} - \mu_0}{s/\sqrt{n}}$	$t = \dfrac{\bar{x} - \mu_0}{s/\sqrt{n}}$	$t = \dfrac{\bar{x} - \mu_0}{s/\sqrt{n}}$
Rejection Rule: **p-Value Approach**	Reject H_0 if p-value $\leq \alpha$	Reject H_0 if p-value $\leq \alpha$	Reject H_0 if p-value $\leq \alpha$
Rejection Rule: **Critical Value Approach**	Reject H_0 if $t \leq -t_\alpha$	Reject H_0 if $t \geq t_\alpha$	Reject H_0 if $t \leq -t_{\alpha/2}$ or if $t \geq t_{\alpha/2}$

lation is normally distributed, the hypothesis tests described in this section provide exact results for any sample size. When the population is not normally distributed, the procedures are approximations. Nonetheless, we find that sample sizes greater than 50 will provide good results in almost all cases. If the population is approximately normal, small sample sizes (e.g., $n < 15$) can provide acceptable results. In situations where the population cannot be approximated by a normal distribution, sample sizes of $n \geq 15$ will provide acceptable results as long as the population is not highly skewed and does not contain outliers. If the population is highly skewed or contains outliers, samples sizes approaching 50 are recommended.

Exercises

Methods

23. Consider the following hypothesis test:

$$H_0: \mu \leq 12$$
$$H_a: \mu > 12$$

A sample of 25 provided a sample mean $\bar{x} = 14$ and a sample standard deviation $s = 4.32$.
a. Compute the value of the test statistic.
b. What does the t distribution table (Table 2 in Appendix B) tell you about the p-value?
c. At $\alpha = .05$, what is your conclusion?
d. What is the rejection rule using the critical value? What is your conclusion?

 **SELF** test

24. Consider the following hypothesis test:

$$H_0: \mu = 18$$
$$H_a: \mu \neq 18$$

A sample of 48 provided a sample mean $\bar{x} = 17$ and a sample standard deviation $s = 4.5$.
a. Compute the value of the test statistic.
b. What does the t distribution table (Table 2 in Appendix B) tell you about the p-value?
c. At $\alpha = .05$, what is your conclusion?
d. What is the rejection rule using the critical value? What is your conclusion?

25. Consider the following hypothesis test:

$$H_0: \mu \geq 45$$
$$H_a: \mu < 45$$

A sample of 36 is used. Identify the *p*-value and state your conclusion for each of the following sample results. Use $\alpha = .01$.

a. $\bar{x} = 44$ and $s = 5.2$
b. $\bar{x} = 43$ and $s = 4.6$
c. $\bar{x} = 46$ and $s = 5.0$

26. Consider the following hypothesis test:

$$H_0: \mu = 100$$
$$H_a: \mu \neq 100$$

A sample of 65 is used. Identify the *p*-value and state your conclusion for each of the following sample results. Use $\alpha = .05$.

a. $\bar{x} = 103$ and $s = 11.5$
b. $\bar{x} = 96.5$ and $s = 11.0$
c. $\bar{x} = 102$ and $s = 10.5$

Applications

27. The Employment and Training Administration reported the U.S. mean unemployment insurance benefit of $238 per week (*The World Almanac 2003*). A researcher in the state of Virginia anticipated that sample data would show evidence that the mean weekly unemployment insurance benefit in Virginia was below the national level.

a. Develop appropriate hypotheses such that rejection of H_0 will support the researcher's contention.
b. For a sample of 100 individuals, the sample mean weekly unemployment insurance benefit was $231 with a sample standard deviation of $80. What is the *p*-value?
c. At $\alpha = .05$, what is your conclusion?
d. Repeat the preceding hypothesis test using the critical value approach.

28. The National Association of Professional Baseball Leagues, Inc., reported that attendance for 176 minor league baseball teams reached an all-time high during the 2001 season (*New York Times,* July 28, 2002). On a per-game basis, the mean attendance for minor league baseball was 3530 people per game. Midway through the 2002 season, the president of the association asked for an attendance report that would hopefully show that the mean attendance for 2002 was exceeding the 2001 level.

a. Formulate hypotheses that could be used determine whether the mean attendance per game in 2002 was greater than the previous year's level.
b. Assume that a sample of 92 minor league baseball games played during the first half of the 2002 season showed a mean attendance of 3740 people per game with a sample standard deviation of 810. What is the *p*-value?
c. At $\alpha = .01$, what is your conclusion?

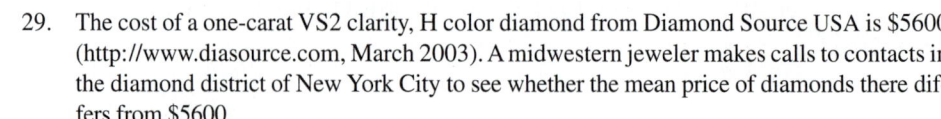

29. The cost of a one-carat VS2 clarity, H color diamond from Diamond Source USA is $5600 (http://www.diasource.com, March 2003). A midwestern jeweler makes calls to contacts in the diamond district of New York City to see whether the mean price of diamonds there differs from $5600.

a. Formulate hypotheses that can be used to determine whether the mean price in New York City differs from $5600.
b. A sample of 25 New York City contacts provided the prices shown in the CD file named Diamonds. What is the *p*-value?

c.   At $\alpha = .05$, can the null hypothesis be rejected? What is your conclusion?
d.   Repeat the preceding hypothesis test using the critical value approach.

30.   AOL Time Warner Inc.'s CNN has been the longtime ratings leader of cable television news. Nielsen Media Research indicated that the mean CNN viewing audience was 600,000 viewers per day during 2002 (*The Wall Street Journal,* March 10, 2003). Assume that for a sample of 40 days during the first half of 2003, the daily audience was 612,000 viewers with a sample standard deviation of 65,000 viewers.
a.   What are the hypotheses if CNN management would like information on any change in the CNN viewing audience?
b.   What is the *p*-value?
c.   Select your own level of significance. What is your conclusion?
d.   What recommendation would you make to CNN management in this application?

31.   Raftelis Financial Consulting reported that the mean quarterly water bill in the United States is $47.50 (*U.S. News & World Report,* August 12, 2002). Some water systems are operated by public utilities, whereas other water systems are operated by private companies. An economist pointed out that privatization does not equal competition and that monopoly powers provided to public utilities are now being transferred to private companies. The concern is that consumers end up paying higher-than-average rates for water provided by private companies. The water system for Atlanta, Georgia, is provided by a private company. A sample of 64 Atlanta consumers showed a mean quarterly water bill of $51 with a sample standard deviation of $12. At $\alpha = .05$, does the Atlanta sample support the conclusion that above-average rates exist for this private water system? What is your conclusion?

32.   According to the National Automobile Dealers Association, the mean price for used cars is $10,192. A manager of a Kansas City used car dealership reviewed a sample of 50 recent used car sales at the dealership in an attempt to determine whether the population mean price for used cars at this particular dealership differed from the national mean. The prices for the sample of 50 cars are shown in the CD file named Used Cars.
a.   Formulate the hypotheses that can be used to determine whether a difference exists in the mean price for used cars at the dealership.
b.   What is the *p*-value?
c.   At $\alpha = .05$, what is your conclusion?

33.   Callaway Golf Company's new forged titanium ERC driver has been described as "illegal" because it promises driving distances that exceed the USGA's standard. *Golf Digest* compared actual driving distances with the ERC driver and a USGA-approved driver with a population mean driving distance of 280 yards. Based on nine test drives, the mean driving distance by the ERC driver was 286.9 yards (*Golf Digest,* May 12, 2000). Answer the following questions assuming a sample standard deviation driving distance of 10 yards.
a.   Formulate the null and alternative hypotheses that can be used to determine whether the new ERC driver has a population mean driving distance greater than 280 yards.
b.   On average, how many yards farther did the golf ball travel with the ERC driver?
c.   At $\alpha = .05$, what is your conclusion?

34.   Joan's Nursery specializes in custom-designed landscaping for residential areas. The estimated labor cost associated with a particular landscaping proposal is based on the number of plantings of trees, shrubs, and so on to be used for the project. For cost-estimating purposes, managers use two hours of labor time for the planting of a medium-sized tree. Actual times from a sample of 10 plantings during the past month follow (times in hours).

1.7   1.5   2.6   2.2   2.4   2.3   2.6   3.0   1.4   2.3

With a .05 level of significance, test to see whether the mean tree-planting time differs from two hours.

a. State the null and alternative hypotheses.
b. Compute the sample mean.
c. Compute the sample standard deviation.
d. What is the p-value?
e. What is your conclusion?

 ## 9.5   Population Proportion

In this section we show how to conduct a hypothesis test about a population proportion p. Using p_0 to denote the hypothesized value for the population proportion, the three forms for a hypothesis test about a population proportion are as follows.

$$
\begin{array}{ccc}
H_0\colon p \geq p_0 & H_0\colon p \leq p_0 & H_0\colon p = p_0 \\
H_a\colon p < p_0 & H_a\colon p > p_0 & H_a\colon p \neq p_0
\end{array}
$$

The first form is called a lower tail test, the second form is called an upper tail test, and the third form is called a two-tailed test.

Hypothesis tests about a population proportion are based on the difference between the sample proportion $\bar{p}$ and the hypothesized population proportion p_0. The methods used to conduct the hypothesis test are similar to those used for hypothesis tests about a population mean. The only difference is that we use the sample proportion and its standard error to compute the test statistic. The p-value approach or the critical value approach is then used to determine whether the null hypothesis should be rejected.

Let us consider an example involving a situation faced by Pine Creek golf course. Over the past year, 20% of the players at Pine Creek were women. In an effort to increase the proportion of women players, Pine Creek implemented a special promotion designed to attract women golfers. One month after the promotion was implemented, the course manager requested a statistical study to determine whether the proportion of women players at Pine Creek had increased. Because the objective of the study is to determine whether the proportion of women golfers increased, an upper tail test with $H_a\colon p > .20$ is appropriate. The null and alternative hypotheses for the Pine Creek hypothesis test are as follows:

$$
\begin{array}{c}
H_0\colon p \leq .20 \\
H_a\colon p > .20
\end{array}
$$

If H_0 can be rejected, the test results will give statistical support for the conclusion that the proportion of women golfers increased and the promotion was beneficial. The course manager specified that a level of significance of $\alpha = .05$ be used in carrying out this hypothesis test.

The next step of the hypothesis testing procedure is to select a sample and compute the value of an appropriate test statistic. To show how this step is done for the Pine Creek upper tail test, we begin with a general discussion of how to compute the value of the test statistic for any form of a hypothesis test about a population proportion. The sampling distribution of $\bar{p}$, the point estimator of the population parameter p, is the basis for developing the test statistic.

When the null hypothesis is true as an equality, the expected value of $\bar{p}$ equals the hypothesized value p_0; that is, $E(\bar{p}) = p_0$. The standard error of $\bar{p}$ is given by

$$
\sigma_{\bar{p}} = \sqrt{\frac{p_0(1 - p_0)}{n}}
$$

In Chapter 7 we said that if $np \geq 5$ and $n(1 - p) \geq 5$, the sampling distribution of $\bar{p}$ can be approximated by a normal distribution.* Under these conditions, which usually apply in practice, the quantity

$$z = \frac{\bar{p} - p_0}{\sigma_{\bar{p}}} \qquad (9.5)$$

has a standard normal probability distribution. With $\sigma_{\bar{p}} = \sqrt{p_0(1 - p_0)/n}$, the standard normal random variable z is the test statistic used to conduct hypothesis tests about a population proportion.

TEST STATISTIC FOR HYPOTHESIS TESTS ABOUT A POPULATION PROPORTION

$$z = \frac{\bar{p} - p_0}{\sqrt{\dfrac{p_0(1 - p_0)}{n}}} \qquad (9.6)$$

CD file

WomenGolf

We can now compute the test statistic for the Pine Creek hypothesis test. Suppose a random sample of 400 players was selected, and that 100 of the players were women. The proportion of women golfers in the sample is

$$\bar{p} = \frac{100}{400} = .25$$

Using equation (9.6), the value of the test statistic is

$$z = \frac{\bar{p} - p_0}{\sqrt{\dfrac{p_0(1 - p_0)}{n}}} = \frac{.25 - .20}{\sqrt{\dfrac{.20(1 - .20)}{400}}} = \frac{.05}{.02} = 2.50$$

Because the Pine Creek hypothesis test is an upper tail test, the *p*-value is the probability that z is greater than or equal to $z = 2.50$; that is, it is the area under the standard normal curve to the right of $z = 2.50$. Using the standard normal probability table, we find that the area to the left of $z = 2.50$ is .9938. Thus, the *p*-value for the Pine Creek test is $1.0000 - .9938 = .0062$. Figure 9.9 shows this *p*-value calculation.

Recall that the course manager specified a level of significance of $\alpha = .05$. A *p*-value $= .0062 < .05$ gives sufficient statistical evidence to reject H_0 at the .05 level of significance. Thus, the test provides statistical support for the conclusion that the special promotion increased the proportion of women players at the Pine Creek golf course.

The decision whether to reject the null hypothesis can also be made using the critical value approach. The critical value corresponding to an area of .05 in the upper tail of a normal probability distribution is $z_{.05} = 1.645$. Thus, the rejection rule using the critical value approach is to reject H_0 if $z \geq 1.645$. Because $z = 2.50 > 1.645$, H_0 is rejected.

Again, we see that the *p*-value approach and the critical value approach lead to the same hypothesis testing conclusion, but the *p*-value approach provides more information. With a

---

*In most applications involving hypothesis tests of a population proportion, sample sizes are large enough to use the normal approximation. The exact sampling distribution of $\bar{p}$ is discrete with the probability for each value of $\bar{p}$ given by the binomial distribution. So hypothesis testing is a bit more complicated for small samples when the normal approximation cannot be used.

FIGURE 9.9   CALCULATION OF THE *p*-VALUE FOR THE PINE CREEK HYPOTHESIS TEST

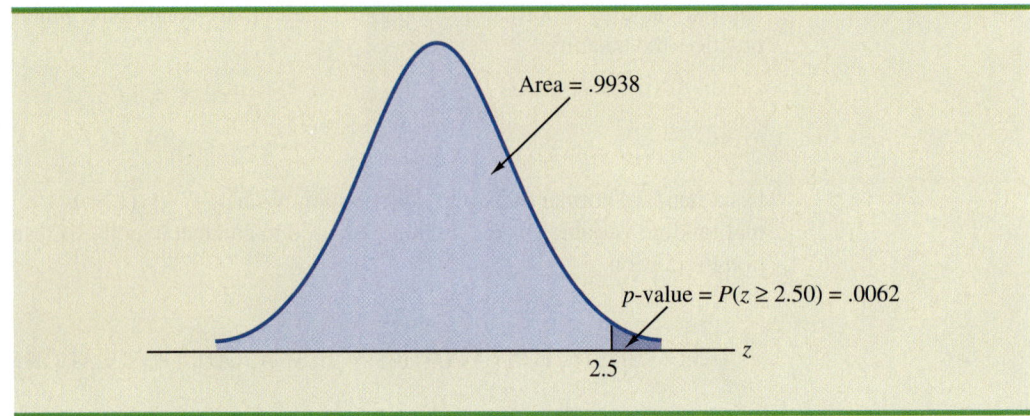

Area = .9938

p-value = $P(z \geq 2.50)$ = .0062

2.5

z

p-value = .0062, the null hypothesis would be rejected for any level of significance greater than or equal to .0062.

Using Excel

Excel can be used to conduct one-tailed and two-tailed hypothesis tests about a population proportion using the *p*-value approach. The procedure is similar to the approach used with Excel in conducting hypothesis tests about a population mean. The primary difference is that the test statistic is based on the sampling distribution of $\bar{x}$ for hypothesis tests about a population mean and on the sampling distribution of $\bar{p}$ for hypothesis tests about a population proportion. Thus, although different formulas are used to compute the test statistic needed to make the hypothesis testing decision, the computations of the critical value and the *p*-value for the tests are identical.

We will illustrate the procedure by showing how Excel can be used to conduct the upper tail hypothesis test for the Pine Creek golf course study. Refer to Figure 9.10 as we describe the tasks involved. The formula worksheet is in the background; the value worksheet is in the foreground.

Enter Data: A label and the gender of each golfer in the study are entered into cells A1:A401.

Enter Functions and Formulas: The descriptive statistics needed are provided in cells D3, D5, and D6. Because the data are not numeric, Excel's COUNTA function, not the COUNT function, is used in cell D3 to determine the sample size. We entered Female in cell D4 to identify the response for which we wish to compute a proportion. The COUNTIF function is then used in cell D5 to determine the number of responses of the type identified in cell D4. The sample proportion is then computed in cell D6 by dividing the response count by the sample size.

The hypothesized value of the population proportion (.20) is entered into cell D8. The standard error is obtained in cell D10 by entering the formula =SQRT(D8*(1-D8)/D3). The formula =(D6-D8)/D10 entered into cell D11 computes the test statistic *z* (2.50). To compute the *p*-value for a lower tail test, we enter the formula =NORMSDIST(D11) into cell D13. The *p*-value for an upper tail test is then computed in cell D14 as 1 minus the *p*-value for the lower tail test. Finally, the *p*-value for a two-tailed test is computed in cell D15 as 2 times the minimum of the 2 one-tailed *p*-values. The value worksheet shows that the three *p*-values are as follows: *p*-value (Lower Tail) = 0.9938; *p*-value (Upper Tail) = 0.0062; and *p*-value (Two Tail) = 0.0124.

The development of the worksheet is now complete. For the Pine Creek upper tail hypothesis test we reject the null hypothesis that the population proportion is .20 or less be-

FIGURE 9.10 EXCEL WORKSHEET: HYPOTHESIS TEST FOR PINE CREEK GOLF COURSE

	A	B	C	D	E
1	Golfer		**Hypothesis Test about a Population Proportion**		
2	Female				
3	Male		**Sample Size**	=COUNTA(A2:A401)	
4	Female		**Response of Interest**	Female	
5	Male		**Count for Response**	=COUNTIF(A2:A903,D4)	
6	Male		**Sample Proportion**	=D5/D3	
7	Female				
8	Male		**Hypothesized Value**	0.2	
9	Male				
10	Female		**Standard Error**	=SQRT(D8*(1-D8)/D3)	
11	Male		**Test Statistic** z	=(D6-D8)/D10	
12	Male				
13	Male		***p*-value (Lower Tail)**	=NORMSDIST(D11)	
14	Male		***p*-value (Upper Tail)**	=1-D13	
15	Male		***p*-value (Two Tail)**	=2*MIN(D13,D14)	
16	Female				
400	Male				
401	Male				
402					

	A	B	C	D	E	F
1	Golfer		**Hypothesis Test about a Population Proportion**			
2	Female					
3	Male		**Sample Size**	400		
4	Female		**Response of Interest**	Female		
5	Male		**Count for Response**	100		
6	Male		**Sample Proportion**	0.25		
7	Female					
8	Male		**Hypothesized Value**	0.20		
9	Male					
10	Female		**Standard Error**	0.02		
11	Male		**Test Statistic** z	2.5000		
12	Male					
13	Male		***p*-value (Lower Tail)**	0.9938		
14	Male		***p*-value (Upper Tail)**	0.0062		
15	Male		***p*-value (Two Tail)**	0.0124		
16	Female					
400	Male					
401	Male					
402						

Note: Rows 17 to 399 are hidden.

cause the *p*-value (Upper Tail) = 0.0062 is less than α = .05. Indeed, with this *p*-value we would reject the hull hypothesis for any level of significance of .0062 or greater.

A Template for Other Problems. The worksheet in Figure 9.10 can be used as a template for hypothesis tests about a population proportion whenever $np \geq 5$ and $n(1 - p) \geq 5$. Just enter the appropriate data in column A, adjust the ranges for the formulas in cells D3 and D5, enter the appropriate response in cell D4, and enter the hypothesized value in cell D8. The standard error, the test statistic, and the three *p*-values will then appear. Depending on the form of the hypothesis test (lower tail, upper tail, or two-tailed), we can then choose the appropriate *p*-value to make the rejection decision.

TABLE 9.4   SUMMARY OF HYPOTHESIS TESTS ABOUT A POPULATION PROPORTION

	Lower Tail Test	**Upper Tail Test**	**Two-Tailed Test**
Hypotheses	$H_0: p \geq p_0$ $H_a: p < p_0$	$H_0: p \leq p_0$ $H_a: p > p_0$	$H_0: p = p_0$ $H_a: p \neq p_0$
Test Statistic	$z = \dfrac{\bar{p} - p_0}{\sqrt{\dfrac{p_0(1 - p_0)}{n}}}$	$z = \dfrac{\bar{p} - p_0}{\sqrt{\dfrac{p_0(1 - p_0)}{n}}}$	$z = \dfrac{\bar{p} - p_0}{\sqrt{\dfrac{p_0(1 - p_0)}{n}}}$
Rejection Rule: **p-Value Approach**	Reject H_0 if p-value $\leq \alpha$	Reject H_0 if p-value $\leq \alpha$	Reject H_0 if p-value $\leq \alpha$
Rejection Rule: **Critical Value** **Approach**	Reject H_0 if $z \leq -z_\alpha$	Reject H_0 if $z \geq z_\alpha$	Reject H_0 if $z \leq -z_{\alpha/2}$ or if $z \geq z_{\alpha/2}$

Summary

The procedure used to conduct a hypothesis test about a population proportion is similar to the procedure used to conduct a hypothesis test about a population mean. Although we only illustrated how to conduct a hypothesis test about a population proportion for an upper tail test, similar procedures can be used for lower tail and two-tailed tests. Table 9.4 provides a summary of the hypothesis tests about a population proportion. We assume that $np \geq 5$ and $n(1 - p) \geq 5$; thus the normal probability distribution can be used to approximate the sampling distribution of $\bar{p}$.

Exercises

Methods

35. Consider the following hypothesis test:

$$H_0: p = .20$$
$$H_a: p \neq .20$$

A sample of 400 provided a sample proportion $\bar{p} = .175$.
a.   Compute the value of the test statistic.
b.   What is the p-value?
c.   At $\alpha = .05$, what is your conclusion?
d.   What is the rejection rule using the critical value? What is your conclusion?

36. Consider the following hypothesis test:

$$H_0: p \geq .75$$
$$H_a: p < .75$$

A sample of 300 items was selected. Compute the p-value and state your conclusion for each of the following sample results. Use $\alpha = .05$.
a. $\bar{p} = .68$ c. $\bar{p} = .70$
b. $\bar{p} = .72$ d. $\bar{p} = .77$

Applications

37. The Heldrich Center for Workforce Development found that 40% of Internet users received more than 10 e-mail messages per day (*USA Today,* May 7, 2000). A similar study on the use of e-mail was repeated in 2002.
    a. Formulate the hypotheses that can be used to determine whether the proportion of Internet users receiving more than 10 e-mail messages per day increased.
    b. If a sample of 425 Internet users found 189 receiving more than 10 e-mail messages per day, what is the *p*-value?
    c. At $\alpha = .05$, what is your conclusion?

38. A study by *Consumer Reports* showed that 64% of supermarket shoppers believe supermarket brands to be as good as national name brands. To investigate whether this result applies to its own product, the manufacturer of a national name-brand ketchup asked a sample of shoppers whether they believed that supermarket ketchup was as good as the national brand ketchup.
    a. Formulate the hypotheses that could be used to determine whether the percentage of supermarket shoppers who believe that the supermarket ketchup was as good as the national brand ketchup differed from 64%.
    b. If a sample of 100 shoppers showed 52 stating that the supermarket brand was as good as the national brand, what is the *p*-value?
    c. At $\alpha = .05$, what is your conclusion?
    d. Should the national brand ketchup manufacturer be pleased with this conclusion? Explain.

39. The National Center for Health Statistics released a report that stated 70% of adults do not exercise regularly (Associated Press, April 7, 2002). A researcher decided to conduct a study to see whether the claim made by the National Center for Health Statistics differed on a state-by-state basis.
    a. State the null and alternative hypotheses assuming the intent of the researcher is to identify states that differ from the 70% reported by the National Center for Health Statistics.
    b. At $\alpha = .05$, what is the research conclusion for the following states:

    >   Wisconsin: 252 of 350 adults did not exercise regularly
    >   California: 189 of 300 adults did not exercise regularly

40. Before the 2003 Super Bowl, ABC predicted that 22% of the Super Bowl audience would express an interest in seeing one of its forthcoming new television shows, including *8 Simple Rules, Are You Hot?,* and *Dragnet.* ABC ran commercials for these television shows during the Super Bowl. The day after the Super Bowl, Intermediate Advertising Group of New York sampled 1532 viewers who saw the commercials and found that 414 said that they would watch one of the ABC advertised television shows (*The Wall Street Journal,* January 30, 2003).
    a. What is the point estimate of the proportion of the audience that said they would watch the television shows after seeing the television commercials?
    b. At $\alpha = .05$, determine whether the intent to watch the ABC television shows significantly increased after seeing the television commercials. Formulate the appropriate hypotheses, compute the *p*-value, and state your conclusion.
    c. Why are such studies valuable to companies and advertising firms?

41. Microsoft Outlook is the most widely used e-mail manager. A Microsoft executive claims that Microsoft Outlook is used by at least 75% of Internet users. A sample of Internet users will be used to test this claim.
    a. Formulate the hypotheses that can be used to test the claim.
    b. A Merrill Lynch study reported that Microsoft Outlook is used by 72% of Internet users (CNBC, June 2000). Assume that the report was based on a sample size of 300 Internet users. What is the *p*-value?
    c. At $\alpha = .05$, should the executive's claim of at least 75% be rejected?

42. According to the Census Bureau's American Housing Survey, the primary reason people who move choose their new neighborhood is because the location is convenient to work (*USA Today*, December 24, 2002). Based on 1990 Census Bureau data, we know that 24% of the population of people who moved selected "location convenient to work" as the reason for selecting their new neighborhood. Assume a sample of 300 people who moved during 2003 found 93 did so to be closer to work. Do the sample data support the research conclusion that in 2003 more people are choosing where to live based on how close they will be to their work? What is the point estimate of the proportion of people who moved during 2003 that chose their new neighborhood because the location is convenient to work? What is your research conclusion? Use $\alpha = .05$.

43. An article about driving practices in Strathcona County, Alberta, Canada, claimed that 48% of drivers did not stop at stop sign intersections on county roads (*Edmonton Journal*, July 19, 2000). Two months later, a follow-up study collected data in order to see whether this percentage had changed.
    a. Formulate the hypotheses to determine whether the proportion of drivers who did not stop at stop sign intersections had changed.
    b. Assume the study found 360 of 800 drivers did not stop at stop sign intersections. What is the sample proportion? What is the *p*-value?
    c. At $\alpha = .05$, what is your conclusion?

44. In a cover story, *BusinessWeek* published information about sleep habits of Americans (*BusinessWeek*, January 26, 2004). The article noted that sleep deprivation causes a number of problems. The article noted that lack of sleep causes highway deaths. Fifty-one percent of adult drivers admit to driving while drowsy. A researcher hypothesized that this issue was an even bigger problem for night shift workers.
    a. Formulate the hypotheses that can be used to help determine whether more than 51% of the population of night shift workers admit to driving while drowsy.
    b. A sample of 500 night shift workers found that 232 admitted to driving while drowsy. What is the sample proportion? What is the *p*-value?
    c. At $\alpha = .01$, what is your conclusion?

45. Drugstore.com was the first e-commerce company to offer Internet drugstore retailing. Drugstore.com customers were provided the opportunity to buy health, beauty, personal care, wellness, and pharmaceutical replenishment products over the Internet. At the end of 10 months of operation, the company reported that 44% of orders were from repeat customers (*Drugstore.com Annual Report*, January 2, 2000). Assume that Drugstore.com will use a sample of customer orders each quarter to determine whether the proportion of orders from repeat customers changed from the initial $p = .44$.
    a. Formulate the null and alternative hypotheses.
    b. During the first quarter a sample of 500 orders showed 205 repeat customers. What is the *p*-value? Use $\alpha = .05$. What is your conclusion?
    c. During the second quarter a sample of 500 orders showed 245 repeat customers. What is the *p*-value? Use $\alpha = .05$. What is your conclusion?

Summary

Hypothesis testing is a statistical procedure that uses sample data to determine whether a statement about the value of a population parameter should or should not be rejected. The hypotheses are two competing statements about a population parameter. One statement is called the null hypothesis (H_0), and the other statement is called the alternative hypothesis (H_a). In Section 9.1 we provided guidelines for developing hypotheses for three situations frequently encountered in practice.

Whenever historical data or other information provides a basis for assuming that the population standard deviation is known, the hypothesis testing procedure is based on the standard normal distribution. Whenever σ is unknown, the sample standard deviation s is used to estimate σ and the hypothesis testing procedure is based on the t distribution. In both cases, the quality of results depends on both the form of the population distribution and the sample size. If the population has a normal distribution, both hypothesis testing procedures are applicable, even with small sample sizes. If the population is not normally distributed, larger sample sizes are needed. General guidelines about the sample size were provided in Sections 9.3 and 9.4. In the case of hypothesis tests about a population proportion, the hypothesis testing procedure uses a test statistic based on the standard normal distribution.

In all cases, the value of the test statistic is used to compute a p-value for the test. A p-value is a probability, computed using the test statistic, that measures the support (or lack of support) provided by the sample for the null hypothesis. If the p-value is less than or equal to the level of significance α, the null hypothesis can be rejected.

Hypothesis testing conclusions can also be made by comparing the value of the test statistic to a critical value. For lower tail tests, the null hypothesis is rejected if the value of the test statistic is less than or equal to the critical value. For upper tail tests, the null hypothesis is rejected if the value of the test statistic is greater than or equal to the critical value. Two-tailed tests consist of two critical values: one in the lower tail of the sampling distribution and one in the upper tail. In this case, the null hypothesis is rejected if the value of the test statistic is less than or equal to the critical value in the lower tail or greater than or equal to the critical value in the upper tail.

Glossary

Null hypothesis The hypothesis tentatively assumed true in the hypothesis testing procedure.
Alternative hypothesis The hypothesis concluded to be true if the null hypothesis is rejected.
Type II error The error of accepting H_0 when it is false.
Type I error The error of rejecting H_0 when it is true.
Level of significance The probability of making a Type I error when the null hypothesis is true as an equality.
One-tailed test A hypothesis test in which rejection of the null hypothesis occurs for values of the test statistic in one tail of its sampling distribution.
Test statistic A statistic whose value helps determine whether a null hypothesis can be rejected.
p-value A probability, computed using the test statistic, that measures the support (or lack of support) provided by the sample for the null hypothesis. For a lower tail test, the p-value is the probability of obtaining a value for the test statistic as small as or smaller than that provided by the sample. For an upper tail test, the p-value is the probability of obtaining a value for the test statistic as large as or larger than that provided by the sample. For a two-tailed test, the p-value is the probability of obtaining a value for the test statistic as unlikely as or more unlikely than that provided by the sample.
Critical value A value that is compared with the test statistic to determine whether H_0 should be rejected.
Two-tailed test A hypothesis test in which rejection of the null hypothesis occurs for values of the test statistic in either tail of its sampling distribution.

Key Formulas

Test Statistic for Hypothesis Tests About a Population Mean: σ Known

$$z = \frac{\bar{x} - \mu_0}{\sigma/\sqrt{n}}$$

(9.1)

Test Statistic for Hypothesis Tests About a Population Mean: σ Unknown

$$t = \frac{\bar{x} - \mu_0}{s/\sqrt{n}} \qquad \text{(9.4)}$$

Test Statistic for Hypothesis Tests About a Population Proportion

$$z = \frac{\bar{p} - p_0}{\sqrt{\dfrac{p_0(1 - p_0)}{n}}} \qquad \text{(9.6)}$$

Supplementary Exercises

46. A production line operates with a mean filling weight of 16 ounces per container. Over-filling or underfilling presents a serious problem and when detected requires the operator to shut down the production line to readjust the filling mechanism. From past data, a population standard deviation $\sigma = .8$ ounces is assumed. A quality control inspector selects a sample of 30 items every hour and at that time makes the decision of whether to shut down the line for readjustment. The level of significance is $\alpha = .05$.
    a. State the hypothesis test for this quality control application.
    b. If a sample mean of $\bar{x} = 16.32$ ounces was found, what is the p-value? What action would you recommend?
    c. If a sample mean of $\bar{x} = 15.82$ ounces was found, what is the p-value? What action would you recommend?
    d. Use the critical value approach. What is the rejection rule for the preceding hypothesis testing procedure? Repeat parts (b) and (c). Do you reach the same conclusion?

47. At Western University the historical mean of scholarship examination scores for freshman applications is 900. A historical population standard deviation $\sigma = 180$ is assumed known. Each year, the assistant dean uses a sample of applications to determine whether the mean examination score for the new freshman applications has changed.
    a. State the hypotheses.
    b. What is the 95% confidence interval estimate of the population mean examination score if a sample of 200 applications provided a sample mean $\bar{x} = 935$?
    c. Use the confidence interval to conduct a hypothesis test. Use $\alpha = .05$. What is your conclusion?
    d. What is the p-value?

48. The population mean annual salary for public school teachers in the state of New York is $45,250. A sample mean annual salary of public school teachers in New York City is $47,000 (*Time*, April 3, 2000). Assume the New York City results are based on a sample of 95 teachers. Assume the population standard deviation is $\sigma = \$6300$.
    a. Formulate the null and alternative hypotheses that can be used to determine whether the sample data support the conclusion that public school teachers in New York City have a higher mean salary than the public school teachers in the state of New York.
    b. What is the p-value?
    c. Use $\alpha = .01$. What is your conclusion?

49. According to the National Association of Colleges and Employers, the 2000 mean annual salary of business degree graduates in accounting was $37,000 (*Time*, May 8, 2000). In a follow-up study in June 2001, a sample of 48 graduating accounting majors provided a sample mean of $38,100 and a sample standard deviation of $5200.
    a. Formulate the null and alternative hypotheses that can be used to determine whether the sample data support the conclusion that June 2001 graduates in accounting have a mean salary greater than the 2000 mean annual salary of $37,000.

b. What is the p-value?

c. Use $\alpha = .05$. What is your conclusion?

50. The College Board reported that the average number of freshman class applications to public colleges and universities is 6000 (*USA Today,* December 26, 2002). During a recent application/enrollment period, a sample of 32 colleges and universities showed that the sample mean number of freshman class applications was 5812 with a sample standard deviation of 1140. Do the data indicate a change in the mean number of applications? Use $\alpha = .05$.

51. An extensive study of the cost of health care in the United States presented data showing that the mean spending per Medicare enrollee in 2003 was $6883 (*Money,* Fall 2003). To investigate differences across the country, a researcher took a sample of 40 Medicare enrollees in Indianapolis. For the Indianapolis sample, the mean 2003 Medicare spending was $5980 and the standard deviation was $2518.

a. State the hypotheses that should be used if we would like to determine whether the mean annual Medicare spending in Indianapolis is lower than the national mean.

b. Use the preceding sample results to compute the test statistic and the p-value.

c. Use $\alpha = .05$. What is your conclusion?

d. Repeat the hypothesis test using the critical value approach.

52. The Chamber of Commerce of a Florida Gulf Coast community advertises that area residential property is available at a mean cost of $125,000 or less per lot. Suppose a sample of 32 properties provided a sample mean of $130,000 per lot and a sample standard deviation of $12,500. Using a .05 level of significance, test the validity of the advertising claim.

53. The population mean earnings per share for financial services corporations including American Express, E*TRADE Group, Goldman Sachs, and Merrill Lynch was $3 (*BusinessWeek,* August 14, 2000). In 2001, a sample of 10 financial services corporations provided the following earnings per share data:

1.92	2.16	3.63	3.16	4.02	3.14	2.20	2.34	3.05	2.38

a. Formulate the null and alternative hypotheses that can be used to determine whether the population mean earnings per share in 2001 differ from the $3 reported in 2000.

b. Compute the sample mean.

c. Compute the sample standard deviation.

d. What is the p-value?

e. Use $\alpha = .05$. What is your conclusion?

54. A study by the Centers for Disease Control (CDC) found that 23.3% of adults are smokers and that roughly 70% of those who do smoke indicate that they want to quit (Associated Press, July 26, 2002). CDC reported that, of people who smoked at some point in their lives, 50% have been able to kick the habit. Part of the study suggested that the success rate for quitting rose by education level. Assume that a sample of 100 college graduates who smoked at some point in their lives showed that 64 had been able to successfully stop smoking.

a. State the hypotheses that can be used to determine whether the population of college graduates has a success rate higher than the overall population when it comes to breaking the smoking habit.

b. Given the sample data, what is the proportion of college graduates who, having smoked at some point in their lives, were able to stop smoking?

c. What is the p-value? At $\alpha = .01$, what is your hypothesis testing conclusion?

55. An airline promotion to business travelers is based on the assumption that two-thirds of business travelers use a laptop computer on overnight business trips.

a. State the hypotheses that can be used to test the assumption.

b. What is the sample proportion from an American Express–sponsored survey that found 355 of 546 business travelers use a laptop computer on overnight business trips?

c. What is the p-value?

d. Use $\alpha = .05$. What is your conclusion?

56. Shell Oil office workers were asked which work schedule appealed most: working five 8-hour days a week or working four 10-hour days a week (*USA Today,* September 11, 2000). Let $p =$ the proportion of the office worker population preferring the four-10-hour-days work week.
    a. State the hypotheses if Shell management is interested in statistical support that shows more than 50% of office workers prefer the four-10-hour-days work week.
    b. What is the sample proportion if a sample of 105 office workers showed 67 preferred the four-10-hour-days schedule?
    c. What is the p-value? Use $\alpha = .01$. What is your conclusion?

57. During the 2004 election year, new polling results were reported daily. In an IBD/TIPP poll of 910 adults, 503 respondents reported that they were optimistic about the national outlook, and President Bush's leadership index jumped 4.7 points to 55.3 (*Investor's Business Daily,* January 14, 2004).
    a. What is the sample proportion of respondents who are optimistic about the national outlook?
    b. A campaign manager wants to claim that this poll indicates that the majority of adults are optimistic about the national outlook. Construct a hypothesis test so that rejection of the null hypothesis will permit the conclusion that the proportion optimistic is greater than 50%.
    c. Use the polling data to compute the p-value for the hypothesis test in part (b). Explain to the manager what this p-value means about the level of significance of the results.

58. A radio station in Myrtle Beach announced that at least 90% of the hotels and motels would be full for the Memorial Day weekend. The station advised listeners to make reservations in advance if they planned to be in the resort over the weekend. On Saturday night a sample of 58 hotels and motels showed 49 with a no-vacancy sign and 9 with vacancies. What is your reaction to the radio station's claim after seeing the sample evidence? Use $\alpha = .05$ in making the statistical test. What is the p-value?

59. Environmental health indicators include air quality, water quality, and food quality. Twenty-five years ago, 47% of U.S. food samples contained pesticide residues (*U.S. News & World Report,* April 17, 2000). In a recent study, 44 of 125 food samples contained pesticide residues.
    a. State the hypotheses that can be used to show that the population proportion declined.
    b. What is the sample proportion?
    c. What is the p-value?
    d. Use $\alpha = .01$. What is your conclusion?

Case Problem 1   Quality Associates, Inc.

Quality Associates, Inc., a consulting firm, advises its clients about sampling and statistical procedures that can be used to control their manufacturing processes. In one particular application, a client gave Quality Associates a sample of 800 observations taken during a time in which that client's process was operating satisfactorily. The sample standard deviation for these data was .21; hence, with so much data, the population standard deviation was assumed to be .21. Quality Associates then suggested that random samples of size 30 be taken periodically to monitor the process on an ongoing basis. By analyzing the new samples, the client could quickly learn whether the process was operating satisfactorily. When the process was not operating satisfactorily, corrective action could be taken to eliminate the problem. The design specification indicated the mean for the process should be 12. The hypothesis test suggested by Quality Associates follows.

$$H_0: \mu = 12$$
$$H_a: \mu \neq 12$$

Corrective action will be taken any time H_0 is rejected.

The following samples were collected at hourly intervals during the first day of operation of the new statistical process control procedure. These data are available in the data set Quality.

Quality

Sample 1	Sample 2	Sample 3	Sample 4
11.55	11.62	11.91	12.02
11.62	11.69	11.36	12.02
11.52	11.59	11.75	12.05
11.75	11.82	11.95	12.18
11.90	11.97	12.14	12.11
11.64	11.71	11.72	12.07
11.80	11.87	11.61	12.05
12.03	12.10	11.85	11.64
11.94	12.01	12.16	12.39
11.92	11.99	11.91	11.65
12.13	12.20	12.12	12.11
12.09	12.16	11.61	11.90
11.93	12.00	12.21	12.22
12.21	12.28	11.56	11.88
12.32	12.39	11.95	12.03
11.93	12.00	12.01	12.35
11.85	11.92	12.06	12.09
11.76	11.83	11.76	11.77
12.16	12.23	11.82	12.20
11.77	11.84	12.12	11.79
12.00	12.07	11.60	12.30
12.04	12.11	11.95	12.27
11.98	12.05	11.96	12.29
12.30	12.37	12.22	12.47
12.18	12.25	11.75	12.03
11.97	12.04	11.96	12.17
12.17	12.24	11.95	11.94
11.85	11.92	11.89	11.97
12.30	12.37	11.88	12.23
12.15	12.22	11.93	12.25

Managerial Report

1. Conduct a hypothesis test for each sample at the .01 level of significance and determine what action, if any, should be taken. Provide the test statistic and p-value for each test.
2. Compute the standard deviation for each of the four samples. Does the assumption of .21 for the population standard deviation appear reasonable?
3. Compute limits for the sample mean $\bar{x}$ around $\mu = 12$ such that, as long as a new sample mean is within those limits, the process will be considered to be operating satisfactorily. If $\bar{x}$ exceeds the upper limit or if $\bar{x}$ is below the lower limit, corrective action will be taken. These limits are referred to as upper and lower control limits for quality control purposes.
4. Discuss the implications of changing the level of significance to a larger value. What mistake or error could increase if the level of significance is increased?

Case Problem 2   Unemployment Study

Each month the U.S. Bureau of Labor Statistics publishes a variety of unemployment statistics, including the number of individuals who are unemployed and the mean length of time the individuals have been unemployed. For November 1998, the Bureau of Labor Statistics reported that the national mean length of time of unemployment was 14.6 weeks.

The mayor of Philadelphia requested a study on the status of unemployment in the Philadelphia area. A sample of 50 unemployed residents of Philadelphia included data on their age and the number of weeks without a job. A portion of the data collected in November 1998 follows. The complete data set is available in the data file BLS.

BLS

Age	Weeks	Age	Weeks	Age	Weeks
56	22	22	11	25	12
35	19	48	6	25	1
22	7	48	22	59	33
57	37	25	5	49	26
40	18	40	20	33	13

Managerial Report

1. Use descriptive statistics to summarize the data.
2. Develop a 95% confidence interval estimate of the mean age of unemployed individuals in Philadelphia.
3. Conduct a hypothesis test to determine whether the mean duration of unemployment in Philadelphia is greater than the national mean duration of 14.6 weeks. Use a .01 level of significance. What is your conclusion?
4. Is there a relationship between the age of an unemployed individual and the number of weeks of unemployment? Explain.

CHAPTER 10

Statistical Inference About Means and Proportions with Two Populations

CONTENTS

STATISTICS IN PRACTICE: FISONS CORPORATION

10.1 INFERENCES ABOUT THE DIFFERENCE BETWEEN TWO POPULATION MEANS: σ_1 AND σ_2 KNOWN
Interval Estimation of $\mu_1 - \mu_2$
Using Excel to Construct a Confidence Interval
Hypothesis Tests About $\mu_1 - \mu_2$
Using Excel to Conduct a Hypothesis Test
Practical Advice

10.2 INFERENCES ABOUT THE DIFFERENCE BETWEEN TWO POPULATION MEANS: σ_1 AND σ_2 UNKNOWN
Interval Estimation of $\mu_1 - \mu_2$
Using Excel to Construct a Confidence Interval

Hypothesis Tests About $\mu_1 - \mu_2$
Using Excel to Conduct a Hypothesis Test
Practical Advice

10.3 INFERENCES ABOUT THE DIFFERENCE BETWEEN TWO POPULATION MEANS: MATCHED SAMPLES
Using Excel to Conduct a Hypothesis Test

10.4 INFERENCES ABOUT THE DIFFERENCE BETWEEN TWO POPULATION PROPORTIONS
Interval Estimation of $p_1 - p_2$
Using Excel to Construct a Confidence Interval
Hypothesis Tests About $p_1 - p_2$
Using Excel to Conduct a Hypothesis Test

FISONS CORPORATION
ROCHESTER, NEW YORK

Fisons Corporation, Rochester, New York, is a unit of Fisons Plc., UK. Fisons opened its U.S. operations in 1966.

Fisons Pharmaceutical Division uses extensive statistical procedures to test and develop new drugs. The testing process in the pharmaceutical industry usually consists of three stages: (1) preclinical testing, (2) testing for long-term usage and safety, and (3) clinical efficacy testing. At each successive stage, the chance that a drug will pass the rigorous tests decreases; however, the cost of further testing increases dramatically. Industry surveys indicate that on average the research and development for one new drug costs $250 million and takes 12 years. Hence, it is important to eliminate unsuccessful new drugs in the early stages of the testing process, as well as identify promising ones for further testing.

Statistics plays a major role in pharmaceutical research, where government regulations are stringent and rigorously enforced. In preclinical testing, a two- or three-population statistical study typically is used to determine whether a new drug should continue to be studied in the long-term usage and safety program. The populations may consist of the new drug, a control, and a standard drug. The preclinical testing process begins when a new drug is sent to the pharmacology group for evaluation of efficacy—the capacity of the drug to produce the desired effects. As part of the process, a statistician is asked to design an experiment that can be used to test the new drug. The design must specify the sample size and the statistical methods of analysis. In a two-population study, one sample is used to obtain data on the efficacy of the new drug (population 1) and a second sample is used to obtain data on the efficacy of a standard drug (population 2). Depending on the intended use, the new and standard drugs are tested in such disciplines as neurology, cardiology, and immunology. In most studies, the statistical method involves hypothesis testing for the difference between the means of the new drug population and the standard drug population. If a new drug

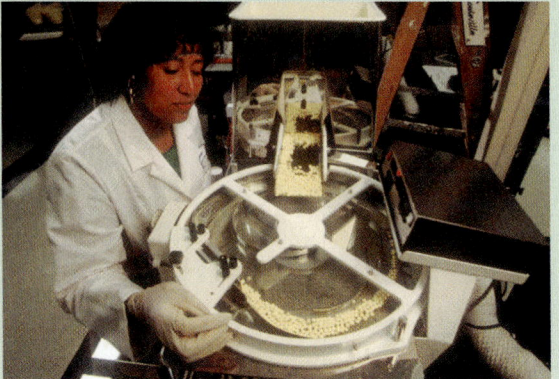

Statistical methods are used to test and develop new drugs. © Mark Richards/PhotoEdit.

lacks efficacy or produces undesirable effects in comparison with the standard drug, the new drug is rejected and withdrawn from further testing. Only new drugs that show promising comparisons with the standard drugs are forwarded to the long-term usage and safety testing program.

Further data collection and multipopulation studies are conducted in the long-term usage and safety testing program and in the clinical testing programs. The Food and Drug Administration (FDA) requires that statistical methods be defined prior to such testing to avoid data-related biases. In addition, to avoid human biases, some of the clinical trials are double or triple blind. That is, neither the subject nor the investigator knows what drug is administered to whom. If the new drug meets all requirements in relation to the standard drug, a new drug application (NDA) is filed with the FDA. The application is rigorously scrutinized by statisticians and scientists at the agency.

In this chapter you will learn how to construct interval estimates and conduct hypothesis tests about means and proportions with two populations. Techniques will be presented for analyzing independent random samples as well as matched samples.

In Chapters 8 and 9 we showed how to develop interval estimates and conduct hypothesis tests for situations involving a single population mean and a single population proportion. In this chapter we continue our discussion of statistical inference by showing how interval estimates and hypothesis tests can be developed for situations involving two populations, when the difference between the two population means or the two population proportions is of prime importance. For example, we may want to develop an interval estimate of the difference between the mean starting salary for a population of men and the mean starting salary for a population of women or conduct a hypothesis test to determine whether any difference is present between the proportion of defective parts in a population of parts produced by supplier A and the proportion of defective parts in a population of parts produced by supplier B. We begin our discussion of statistical inference about two populations by showing how to develop interval estimates and conduct hypothesis tests about the difference between the means of two populations when the standard deviations of the two populations are assumed known.

10.1 Inferences About the Difference Between Two Population Means: σ_1 and σ_2 Known

Letting μ_1 denote the mean of population 1 and μ_2 denote the mean of population 2, we will focus on inferences about the difference between the means: $\mu_1 - \mu_2$. To make an inference about this difference, we select a simple random sample of n_1 units from population 1 and a second simple random sample of n_2 units from population 2. The two samples, taken separately and independently, are referred to as independent simple random samples. In this section, we assume that information is available such that the two population standard deviations, σ_1 and σ_2, can be assumed known prior to collecting the samples. We refer to this situation as the σ_1 and σ_2 known case. In the following example we show how to compute a margin of error and develop an interval estimate of the difference between the two population means when σ_1 and σ_2 are known.

Interval Estimation of $\mu_1 - \mu_2$

HomeStyle sells furniture at two stores: one is located in the inner city and the other is located in a suburban shopping center. The regional manager noticed that products that sell well in one store do not always sell well in the other. The manager believes this situation may be attributable to differences in customer demographics at the two locations. Customers may differ in age, education, income, and so on. Suppose the manager asks us to investigate the difference between the mean ages of the customers who shop at the two stores.

Let us define population 1 as all customers who shop at the inner-city store and population 2 as all customers who shop at the suburban store.

μ_1 = mean of population 1 (i.e., the mean age of all customers who shop at the inner-city store)

μ_2 = mean of population 2 (i.e., the mean age of all customers who shop at the suburban store)

The difference between the two population means is $\mu_1 - \mu_2$.

To estimate $\mu_1 - \mu_2$, we will select a simple random sample of n_1 customers from population 1 and a simple random sample of n_2 customers from population 2. We then compute the two sample means.

$\bar{x}_1$ = sample mean age for the simple random sample of n_1 inner-city customers

$\bar{x}_2$ = sample mean age for the simple random sample of n_2 suburban customers

The point estimator of the difference between the two population means is the difference between the two sample means.

POINT ESTIMATOR OF THE DIFFERENCE BETWEEN TWO POPULATION MEANS

$$\bar{x}_1 - \bar{x}_2 \tag{10.1}$$

FIGURE 10.1   ESTIMATING THE DIFFERENCE BETWEEN TWO POPULATION MEANS

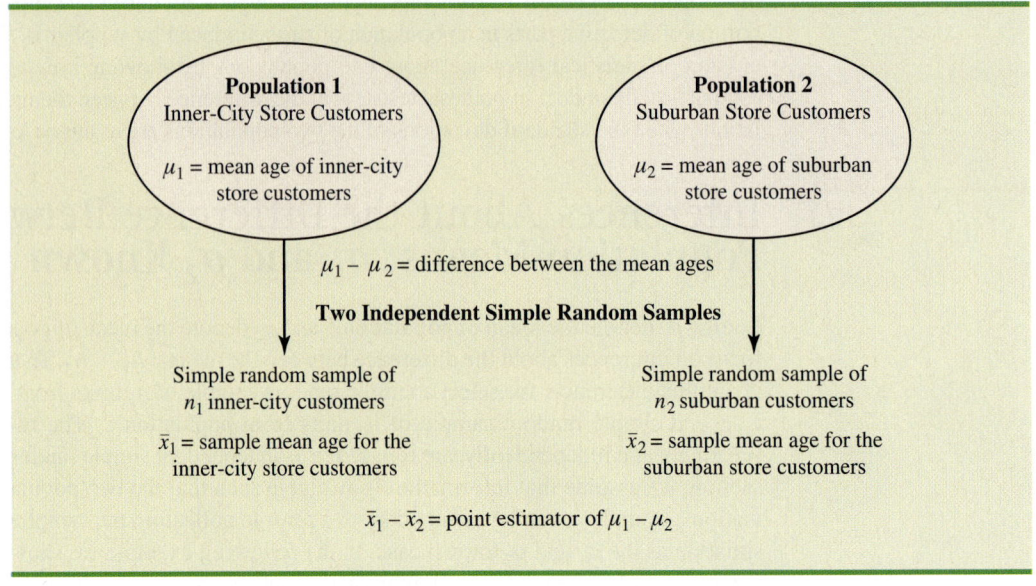

Figure 10.1 provides an overview of the process used to estimate the difference between two population means based on two independent simple random samples.

The standard error of $\bar{x}_1 - \bar{x}_2$ is the standard deviation of the sampling distribution of $\bar{x}_1 - \bar{x}_2$.

As with other point estimators, the point estimator $\bar{x}_1 - \bar{x}_2$ has a standard error that describes the variation in the sampling distribution of the estimator. With two independent simple random samples, the standard error of $\bar{x}_1 - \bar{x}_2$ is as follows:

STANDARD ERROR OF $\bar{x}_1 - \bar{x}_2$

$$\sigma_{\bar{x}_1 - \bar{x}_2} = \sqrt{\frac{\sigma_1^2}{n_1} + \frac{\sigma_2^2}{n_2}} \qquad (10.2)$$

If both populations have a normal distribution, or if the sample sizes are large enough that the central limit theorem enables us to conclude that the sampling distributions of $\bar{x}_1$ and $\bar{x}_2$ can be approximated by a normal distribution, the sampling distribution of $\bar{x}_1 - \bar{x}_2$ will have a normal distribution with mean given by $\mu_1 - \mu_2$.

As we showed in Chapter 8, an interval estimate is given by a point estimate $\pm$ a margin of error. When estimating the difference between two population means, the interval estimate takes the following form:

$$\bar{x}_1 - \bar{x}_2 \pm \text{Margin of error}$$

With the sampling distribution of $\bar{x}_1 - \bar{x}_2$ having a normal distribution, we can write the margin of error as follows:

The margin of error is given by multiplying the standard error by $z_{\alpha/2}$.

$$\text{Margin of error} = z_{\alpha/2}\sigma_{\bar{x}_1 - \bar{x}_2} = z_{\alpha/2}\sqrt{\frac{\sigma_1^2}{n_1} + \frac{\sigma_2^2}{n_2}} \qquad (10.3)$$

Thus the interval estimate of the difference between two population means is as follows:

INTERVAL ESTIMATE OF THE DIFFERENCE BETWEEN TWO POPULATION MEANS: σ_1 AND σ_2 KNOWN

$$\bar{x}_1 - \bar{x}_2 \pm z_{\alpha/2}\sqrt{\frac{\sigma_1^2}{n_1} + \frac{\sigma_2^2}{n_2}} \qquad \text{(10.4)}$$

where $1 - \alpha$ is the confidence coefficient.

Let us return to the HomeStyle example. Based on data from previous customer demographic studies, the two population standard deviations are assumed known with $\sigma_1 = 9$ years and $\sigma_2 = 10$ years. The data collected from the two independent simple random samples of HomeStyle customers provided the following results.

CD file

HomeStyle

	Inner-City Store	**Suburban Store**
Sample Size	$n_1 = 36$	$n_2 = 49$
Sample Mean	$\bar{x}_1 = 40$ years	$\bar{x}_2 = 35$ years

Using expression (10.1), we find that the point estimate of the difference between the mean ages of the two populations is $\bar{x}_1 - \bar{x}_2 = 40 - 35 = 5$ years. Thus, we estimate that the customers at the inner-city store have a mean age 5 years greater than the mean age of the suburban store customers. We can now use expression (10.4) to compute the margin of error and provide the interval estimate of $\mu_1 - \mu_2$. Using 95% confidence and $z_{\alpha/2} = z_{.025} = 1.96$, we have

$$\bar{x}_1 - \bar{x}_2 \pm z_{\alpha/2}\sqrt{\frac{\sigma_1^2}{n_1} + \frac{\sigma_2^2}{n_2}}$$

$$40 - 35 \pm 1.96\sqrt{\frac{9^2}{36} + \frac{10^2}{49}}$$

$$5 \pm 4.06$$

Thus, the margin of error is 4.06 years and the 95% confidence interval estimate of the difference between the two population means is $5 - 4.06 = .94$ years to $5 + 4.06 = 9.06$ years.

Using Excel to Construct a Confidence Interval

Excel's data analysis tools do not provide a procedure for developing interval estimates involving two population means. However, we can develop an Excel worksheet that can be used as a template to construct interval estimates. We will illustrate by constructing an interval estimate of the difference between the population means in the HomeStyle Furniture Stores study. Refer to Figure 10.2 as we describe the tasks involved. The formula worksheet is in the background; the value worksheet is in the foreground.

Enter Data: Column A contains the age data for the simple random sample of 36 inner-city customers, and column B contains the age data for the simple random sample of 49 suburban customers.

FIGURE 10.2   EXCEL WORKSHEET: CONSTRUCTING A 95% CONFIDENCE INTERVAL FOR HOMESTYLE FURNITURE STORES

	A	B	C	D	E	F	G
1	Inner City	Suburban		Interval Estimate of Difference in Population Means:			
2	38	29		σ_1 and σ_2 Known Case			
3	46	35					
4	32	39			Inner City	Suburban	
5	23	10		Sample Size	=COUNT(A2:A37)	=COUNT(B2:B50)	
6	39	37		Sample Mean	=AVERAGE(A2:A37)	=AVERAGE(B2:B50)	
7	40	52					
8	35	40		Population Standard Deviation	9	10	
9	35	37		Standard Error	=SQRT(E8^2/E5+F8^2/F5		
10	36	43					
11	41	38		Confidence Coefficient	0.95		
12	32	28		Level of Significance	=1-E11		
13	38	37		z Value	=NORMSINV(1-E12/2)		
14	44	51		Margin of Error	=E13*E9		
15	50	23					
16	47	25		Point Estimate of Difference	=E6-F6		
17	59	37		Lower Limit	=E16-E14		
18	38	38		Upper Limit	=E16+E14		
36	44	19					
37	62	40					
49		22					
50		47					
51							

	A	B	C	D	E	F	G
1	Inner City	Suburban		Interval Estimate of Difference in Population Means:			
2	38	29		σ_1 and σ_2 Known Case			
3	46	35					
4	32	39			Inner City	Suburban	
5	23	10		Sample Size	36	49	
6	39	37		Sample Mean	40	35	
7	40	52					
8	35	40		Population Standard Deviation	9	10	
9	35	37		Standard Error	2.07		
10	36	43					
11	41	38		Confidence Coefficient	0.95		
12	32	28		Level of Significance	0.05		
13	38	37		z Value	1.960		
14	44	51		Margin of Error	4.06		
15	50	23					
16	47	25		Point Estimate of Difference	5		
17	59	37		Lower Limit	0.94		
18	38	38		Upper Limit	9.06		
36	44	19					
37	62	40					
49		22					
50		47					
51							

Note: Rows 19–35 and 38–48 are hidden.

Enter Functions and Formulas: The descriptive statistics needed are provided in cells E5:F6. The known population standard deviations are entered into cells E8 and F8. Using the two population standard deviations and the sample sizes, the standard error of the point estimator, $\bar{x}_1 - \bar{x}_2$, is computed using equation (10.2) by entering the following formula into cell E9:

$$=SQRT(E8^2/E5+F8^2/F5)$$

Cells E11:E14 are used to compute the appropriate *z* value and the margin of error. The confidence coefficient is entered into cell E11 (.95) and the corresponding level of significance ($\alpha = 1 -$ confidence coefficient) is computed in cell E12. In cell E13, we used the NORMSINV function to compute the z value needed for the interval estimate. The margin of error is computed in cell E14 by multiplying the z value by the standard error.

In cell E16 the difference in the sample means is used to compute the point estimate of the difference in the two population means. The lower limit of the confidence interval is computed in cell E17 (.94) and the upper limit is computed in cell E18 (9.06); thus, the 95% confidence interval estimate of the difference in the two population means is .94 to 9.06.

A Template for Other Problems. This worksheet can be used as a template for developing interval estimates of the difference in population means when the population standard deviations are assumed known. For another problem of this type, we must first enter the new problem data in columns A and B. The data ranges in cells E5:F6 must be modified in order to compute the sample means and sample sizes for the new data. Also, the assumed known population standard deviations must be entered into cells E8 and F8. After doing so, the point estimate and a 95% confidence interval will be displayed in cells E16:E18. If a confidence interval with a different confidence coefficient is desired, we simply change the value in cell E11.

We can further simplify the use of Figure 10.2 as a template for other problems by eliminating the need to enter new data ranges in cells E5:F6. We rewrite the cell formulas as follows:

Cell E5:   =COUNT(A:A)
Cell F5:   =COUNT(B:B)
Cell E6:   =AVERAGE(A:A)
Cell F6:   =AVERAGE(B:B)

The HomeStyle data set includes a worksheet titled Template that uses the A:A and B:B methods for entering the data ranges.

Using the A:A method of specifying data ranges in cells E5 and E6, Excel's COUNT function will count the number of numeric values in column A and Excel's AVERAGE function will compute the average of the numeric values in column A. Similarly, using the B:B method of specifying data ranges in cells F5 and F6, Excel's COUNT function will count the number of numeric values in column B and Excel's AVERAGE function will compute the average of the numeric values in column B. Thus, to solve a new problem it is only necessary to enter the new data into columns A and B and enter the known population standard deviations in cells E8 and F8.

This worksheet can also be used as a template for text exercises in which the sample sizes, sample means, and population standard deviations are given. In this type of situation, no change in the data is necessary. We simply replace the values in cells E5:F6 and E8:F8 with the given values of the sample sizes, sample means, and population standard deviations. If something other than a 95% confidence interval is desired, the confidence coefficient in cell E11 must also be changed.

Hypothesis Tests About $\mu_1 - \mu_2$

Let us consider hypothesis tests about the difference between two population means. Using D_0 to denote the hypothesized difference between μ_1 and μ_2, the three forms for a hypothesis test are as follows:

$$H_0: \mu_1 - \mu_2 \geq D_0 \qquad H_0: \mu_1 - \mu_2 \leq D_0 \qquad H_0: \mu_1 - \mu_2 = D_0$$
$$H_a: \mu_1 - \mu_2 < D_0 \qquad H_a: \mu_1 - \mu_2 > D_0 \qquad H_a: \mu_1 - \mu_2 \neq D_0$$

In most applications, $D_0 = 0$. Using the two-tailed test as an example, when $D_0 = 0$ the null hypothesis is $H_0: \mu_1 - \mu_2 = 0$. In this case, the null hypothesis is that μ_1 and μ_2 are equal. Rejection of H_0 leads to the conclusion that $H_a: \mu_1 - \mu_2 \neq 0$ is true; that is, μ_1 and μ_2 are not equal.

The steps for conducting hypothesis tests presented in Chapter 9 are applicable here. We must choose a level of significance, compute the value of the test statistic, and find the

p-value to determine whether the null hypothesis should be rejected. With two independent simple random samples, we showed that the point estimator $\bar{x}_1 - \bar{x}_2$ has a standard error $\sigma_{\bar{x}_1 - \bar{x}_2}$ given by expression (10.2) and the sampling distribution of $\bar{x}_1 - \bar{x}_2$ can be described by a normal distribution. In this case, the test statistic for the difference between two population means when σ_1 and σ_2 are known is as follows.

TEST STATISTIC FOR HYPOTHESIS TESTS ABOUT $\mu_1 - \mu_2$: σ_1 AND σ_2 KNOWN

$$z = \frac{(\bar{x}_1 - \bar{x}_2) - D_0}{\sqrt{\dfrac{\sigma_1^2}{n_1} + \dfrac{\sigma_2^2}{n_2}}} \qquad (10.5)$$

Let us demonstrate the use of this test statistic in the following hypothesis testing example.

As part of a study to evaluate differences in education quality between two training centers, a standardized examination is given to individuals who are trained at the centers. The difference between the mean examination scores is used to assess quality differences between the centers. The population means for the two centers are as follows.

μ_1 = the mean examination score for the population
    of individuals trained at center A

μ_2 = the mean examination score for the population
    of individuals trained at center B

We begin with the tentative assumption that no difference exists between the training quality provided at the two centers. Hence, in terms of the mean examination scores, the null hypothesis is that $\mu_1 - \mu_2 = 0$. If sample evidence leads to the rejection of this hypothesis, we will conclude that the mean examination scores differ for the two populations. This conclusion indicates a quality differential between the two centers and suggests that a follow-up study investigating the reason for the differential may be warranted. The null and alternative hypotheses for this two-tailed test are written as follows.

$$H_0: \mu_1 - \mu_2 = 0$$
$$H_a: \mu_1 - \mu_2 \neq 0$$

The standardized examination given previously in a variety of settings always resulted in an examination score standard deviation near 10 points. Thus, we will use this information to assume that the population standard deviations are known with $\sigma_1 = 10$ and $\sigma_2 = 10$. An $\alpha = .05$ level of significance is specified for the study.

Independent simple random samples of $n_1 = 30$ individuals from training center A and $n_2 = 40$ individuals from training center B are taken. The respective sample means are $\bar{x}_1 = 82$ and $\bar{x}_2 = 78$. Do these data suggest a significant difference between the population means at the two training centers? To help answer this question, we compute the test statistic using equation (10.5).

$$z = \frac{(\bar{x}_1 - \bar{x}_2) - D_0}{\sqrt{\dfrac{\sigma_1^2}{n_1} + \dfrac{\sigma_2^2}{n_2}}} = \frac{(82 - 78) - 0}{\sqrt{\dfrac{10^2}{30} + \dfrac{10^2}{40}}} = 1.66$$

Next let us compute the p-value for this two-tailed test. Because the test statistic z is in the upper tail, we first compute the area under the curve to the right of $z = 1.66$. Using the standard normal distribution table, the area to the left of $z = 1.66$ is .9515. Thus, the area in the upper tail of the distribution is $1.0000 - .9515 = .0485$. Because this test is a two-tailed test, we must double the tail area: p-value $= 2(.0485) = .0970$. Following the usual rule to reject H_0 if p-value $\leq \alpha$, we see that the p-value of .0970 does not allow us to reject H_0 at the .05 level of significance. The sample results do not provide sufficient evidence to conclude that the training centers differ in quality.

In this chapter we will use the p-value approach to hypothesis testing as described in Chapter 9. However, if you prefer, the test statistic and the critical value rejection rule may be used. With $\alpha = .05$ and $z_{\alpha/2} = z_{.025} = 1.96$, the rejection rule employing the critical value approach would be reject H_0 if $z \leq -1.96$ or if $z \geq 1.96$. With $z = 1.66$, we reach the same do not reject H_0 conclusion.

In the preceding example, we demonstrated a two-tailed hypothesis test about the difference between two population means. Lower tail and upper tail tests can also be considered. These tests use the same test statistic as given in equation (10.5). The procedure for computing the p-value and the rejection rules for these one-tailed tests are the same as those presented in Chapter 9.

Using Excel to Conduct a Hypothesis Test

The Excel procedure used to conduct the hypothesis test to determine whether there is a significant difference in population means when σ_1 and σ_2 are assumed known is called *z-test: Two Sample for Means*. We illustrate using the sample data for exam scores at center A and at center B. With an assumed known standard deviation of 10 points at each center, the known variance of exam scores for each of the two populations is equal to $10^2 = 100$. Refer to the Excel worksheet shown in Figure 10.3 and the dialog box in Figure 10.4 as we describe the tasks involved.

Enter Data: Column A contains the examination score data for the simple random sample of 30 individuals trained at center A, and column B contains the examination score data for the simple random sample of 40 individuals trained at center B.

Apply Tools: The following steps will provide the information needed to conduct the hypothesis test to see whether there is a significant difference in test scores at the two centers.

> **Step 1.** Select the **Tools** menu
> **Step 2.** Choose **Data Analysis**
> **Step 3.** Choose *z*-**Test: Two Sample for Means** from the list of Analysis Tools
> **Step 4.** When the *z*-Test: Two Sample for Means dialog box appears (Figure 10.4):
> > Enter A1:A31 in the **Variable 1 Range** box
> > Enter B1:B41 in the **Variable 2 Range** box
> > Enter 0 in the **Hypothesized Mean Difference** box
> > Enter 100 in the **Variable 1 Variance (known)** box
> > Enter 100 in the **Variable 2 Variance (known)** box
> > Select **Labels**
> > Enter .05 in the **Alpha** box
> > Select **Output Range** and enter D4 in the box
> > Click **OK**

The value of the test statistic shown here (1.6562) and the p-value (.0977) differ slightly from those shown previously, because we rounded the test statistic to two places (1.66) in the text.

Descriptive statistics for the two samples are shown in cells E7:F9. The value of the test statistic, 1.6562, is shown in cell E11. The p-value for the test, labeled P(Z<=z) two-tail, is shown in cell E14. Because the p-value, 0.0977, is greater than the level of significance, $\alpha = .05$, we cannot conclude that the means for the two populations are different.

The z-test: Two Sample for Means can also be used to conduct one-tailed hypothesis tests. The only change required to make the hypothesis testing decision is that we need to use the p-value for a one-tailed test, labeled P(Z<=z) one-tail (see cell E12).

	A	B	C	D	E	F	G
1	**Center A**	**Center B**					
2	97	64					
3	95	85					
4	89	72		z-Test: Two Sample for Means			
5	79	64					
6	78	74			*Center A*	*Center B*	
7	87	93		**Mean**	82	78	
8	83	70		**Known Variance**	100	100	
9	94	79		**Observations**	30	40	
10	76	79		**Hypothesized Mean Difference**	0		
11	79	75		**z**	1.6562		
12	83	66		**P(Z<=z) one-tail**	0.0488		
13	84	83		**z Critical one-tail**	1.6449		
14	76	74		**P(Z<=z) two-tail**	0.0977		
15	82	70		**z Critical two-tail**	1.9600		
16	85	82					
17	85	82					
29	88	65					
30	60	78					
31	73	66					
32		84					
40		80					
41		76					
42							

Note: Rows 18–28 and 33–39 are hidden.

FIGURE 10.4   DIALOG BOX FOR EXCEL'S z-TEST: TWO SAMPLE FOR MEANS

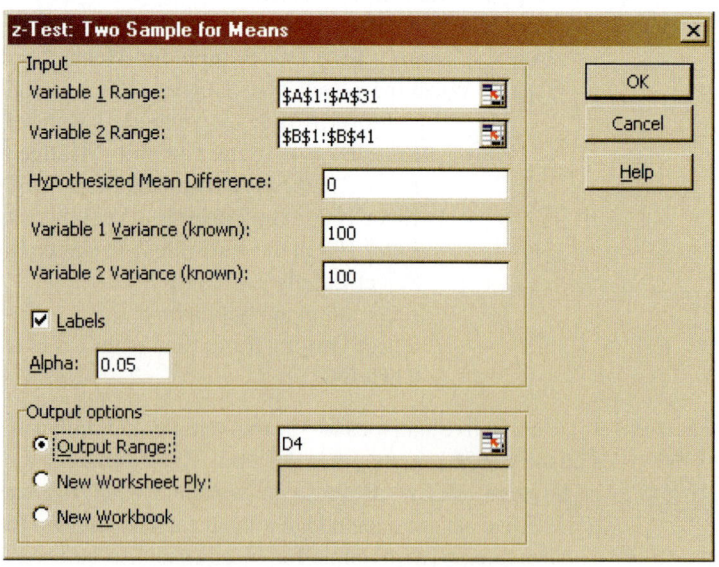

Practical Advice

In most applications of the interval estimation and hypothesis testing procedures presented in this section, random samples with $n_1 \geq 30$ and $n_2 \geq 30$ are adequate. In cases where either or both sample sizes are less than 30, the distributions of the populations become important considerations. In general, with smaller sample sizes, it is more important for the analyst to be satisfied that it is reasonable to assume that the distributions of the two populations are at least approximately normal.

Exercises

Methods

1. The following results are for two independent random samples taken from two populations.

Sample 1	Sample 2
$n_1 = 50$	$n_2 = 35$
$\bar{x}_1 = 13.6$	$\bar{x}_2 = 11.6$
$\sigma_1 = 2.2$	$\sigma_2 = 3.0$

   a. What is the point estimate of the difference between the two population means?
   b. Provide a 90% confidence interval for the difference between the two population means.
   c. Provide a 95% confidence interval for the difference between the two population means.

2. Consider the following hypothesis test.

$$H_0: \mu_1 - \mu_2 \leq 0$$
$$H_a: \mu_1 - \mu_2 > 0$$

The following results are for two independent samples taken from the two populations.

Sample 1	Sample 2
$n_1 = 40$	$n_2 = 50$
$\bar{x}_1 = 25.2$	$\bar{x}_2 = 22.8$
$\sigma_1 = 5.2$	$\sigma_2 = 6.0$

   a. What is the value of the test statistic?
   b. What is the p-value?
   c. With $\alpha = .05$, what is your hypothesis testing conclusion?

3. Consider the following hypothesis test.

$$H_0: \mu_1 - \mu_2 = 0$$
$$H_a: \mu_1 - \mu_2 \neq 0$$

The following results are for two independent samples taken from the two populations.

Sample 1	Sample 2
$n_1 = 80$	$n_2 = 70$
$\bar{x}_1 = 104$	$\bar{x}_2 = 106$
$\sigma_1 = 8.4$	$\sigma_2 = 7.6$

a.   What is the value of the test statistic?
b.   What is the p-value?
c.   With $\alpha = .05$, what is your hypothesis testing conclusion?

Applications

4.   Gasoline prices reached record high levels in 16 states during 2003 (*The Wall Street Journal,* March 7, 2003). Two of the affected states were California and Florida. The American Automobile Association reported a sample mean price of $2.04 per gallon in California and a sample mean price of $1.72 per gallon in Florida. Use a sample size of 40 for the California data and a sample size of 35 for the Florida data. Assume that prior studies indicating a population standard deviation of .10 in California and .08 in Florida are reasonable.
   a.   What is a point estimate of the difference between the population mean prices per gallon in California and Florida?
   b.   At 95% confidence, what is the margin of error?
   c.   What is the 95% confidence interval estimate of the difference between the population mean prices per gallon in the two states?

5.   A Cornell University study of wage differentials between men and women reported that one of the reasons wages for men are higher than wages for women is that men tend to have more years of work experience than women (*BusinessWeek,* August 28, 2000). Assume the following results were obtained for each group.

Men	Women
$n_1 = 100$	$n_2 = 85$
$\bar{x}_1 = 14.9$ years	$\bar{x}_2 = 10.3$ years
$\sigma_1 = 5.2$ years	$\sigma_2 = 3.8$ years

   a.   What is the point estimate of the difference between the two population means?
   b.   At 95% confidence, what is the margin of error?
   c.   What is the 95% confidence interval estimate of the difference between the two population means?

Mortgage

6.   The nation's 40,000 mortgage brokers are some of the most profitable small businesses in the United States. These low-profile companies find loans for companies in exchange for commissions. Mortgage Bankers Association of America provides data on the average size of loans handled by mortgage brokers (*The Wall Street Journal,* February 24, 2003). The CD file named Mortgage contains data from a sample of 250 loans made in 2001 and a sample of 270 loans made in 2002 that are consistent with these data. Based on historical loan data, the population standard deviations for loan amounts can be assumed known at $50,000 in 2001 and $55,000 in 2002. Do the sample data indicate an increase in the mean loan amount between 2001 and 2002? Use $\alpha = .05$.

7.   During the 2003 season, Major League Baseball took steps to speed up the play of baseball games in order to maintain fan interest (*CNN Headline News,* September 30, 2003). The following results come from a sample of 60 games played during the summer of 2002

and a sample of 50 games played during the summer of 2003. The sample mean shows the mean duration of the games included in each sample.

2002 Season	2003 Season
$n_1 = 60$	$n_2 = 50$
$\bar{x}_1 = 2$ hours, 52 minutes	$\bar{x}_2 = 2$ hours, 46 minutes

a. A research hypothesis was that the steps taken during the 2003 season would reduce the population mean duration of baseball games. Formulate the null and alternative hypotheses.

b. What is the point estimate of the reduction in the mean duration of games during the 2003 season?

c. Historical data indicate a population standard deviation of 12 minutes is a reasonable assumption for both years. Conduct the hypothesis test and report the *p*-value. At a .05 level of significance, what is your conclusion?

d. Provide a 95% confidence interval estimate of the reduction in the mean duration of games during the 2003 season.

e. What was the percentage reduction in the mean time of baseball games during the 2003 season? Should management be pleased with the results of the statistical analysis? Discuss. Should the length of baseball games continue to be an issue in future years? Explain.

8. Arnold Palmer and Tiger Woods are two of the best golfers to ever play the game. To show how these two golfers would compare if both were playing at the top of their game, the following sample data provide the results of 18-hole scores during a PGA tournament competition. Palmer's scores are from his 1960 season, while Woods' scores are from his 1999 season (*Golf Magazine,* February 2000).

Arnold Palmer	Tiger Woods
$n_1 = 112$	$n_2 = 84$
$\bar{x}_1 = 69.95$	$\bar{x}_2 = 69.56$

Use the sample results to test the hypothesis of no difference between the population mean 18-hole scores for the two golfers.

a. Assume a population standard deviation of 2.5 for both golfers. What is the value of the test statistic?

b. What is the *p*-value?

c. At $\alpha = .01$, what is your conclusion?

Inferences About the Difference Between Two Population Means: σ_1 and σ_2 Unknown

In this section we extend the discussion of inferences about the difference between two population means to the case when the two population standard deviations, σ_1 and σ_2, are unknown. In this case, we will use the sample standard deviations, s_1 and s_2, to estimate the unknown population standard deviations. When we use the sample standard deviations, the interval estimation and hypothesis testing procedures will be based on the *t* distribution rather than the standard normal distribution.

Interval Estimation of $\mu_1 - \mu_2$

In the following example we show how to compute a margin of error and develop an interval estimate of the difference between two population means when σ_1 and σ_2 are unknown. Clearwater National Bank is conducting a study designed to identify differences between checking account practices by customers at two of its branch banks. A simple random sample of 28 checking accounts is selected from the Cherry Grove Branch and an independent simple random sample of 22 checking accounts is selected from the Beechmont Branch. The current checking account balance is recorded for each of the checking accounts. A summary of the account balances follows:

CheckAcct

	Cherry Grove	**Beechmont**
Sample Size	$n_1 = 28$	$n_2 = 22$
Sample Mean	$\bar{x}_1 = \$1025$	$\bar{x}_2 = \$910$
Sample Standard Deviation	$s_1 = \$150$	$s_2 = \$125$

Clearwater National Bank would like to estimate the difference between the mean checking account balance maintained by the population of Cherry Grove customers and the population of Beechmont customers. Let us develop the margin of error and an interval estimate of the difference between these two population means.

In Section 10.1, we provided the following interval estimate for the case when the population standard deviations, σ_1 and σ_2, are known.

$$\bar{x}_1 - \bar{x}_2 \pm z_{\alpha/2}\sqrt{\frac{\sigma_1^2}{n_1} + \frac{\sigma_2^2}{n_2}}$$

When σ_1 and σ_2 are estimated by s_1 and s_2, the t distribution is used to make inferences about the difference between two population means.

With σ_1 and σ_2 unknown, we will use the sample standard deviations s_1 and s_2 to estimate σ_1 and σ_2 and replace $z_{\alpha/2}$ with $t_{\alpha/2}$. As a result, the interval estimate of the difference between two population means is given by the following expression:

> **INTERVAL ESTIMATE OF THE DIFFERENCE BETWEEN TWO POPULATION MEANS: σ_1 AND σ_2 UNKNOWN**
>
> $$\bar{x}_1 - \bar{x}_2 \pm t_{\alpha/2}\sqrt{\frac{s_1^2}{n_1} + \frac{s_2^2}{n_2}} \qquad (10.6)$$
>
> where $1 - \alpha$ is the confidence coefficient.

In this expression, the use of the t distribution is an approximation, but it provides excellent results and is relatively easy to use. The only difficulty that we encounter in using expression (10.6) is determining the appropriate degrees of freedom for $t_{\alpha/2}$. The formula used is as follows:

> **DEGREES OF FREEDOM: t DISTRIBUTION WITH TWO INDEPENDENT RANDOM SAMPLES**
>
> $$df = \frac{\left(\dfrac{s_1^2}{n_1} + \dfrac{s_2^2}{n_2}\right)^2}{\dfrac{1}{n_1 - 1}\left(\dfrac{s_1^2}{n_1}\right)^2 + \dfrac{1}{n_2 - 1}\left(\dfrac{s_2^2}{n_2}\right)^2} \qquad (10.7)$$

The Excel worksheet in Figure 10.5 makes this computation easy.

Let us return to the Clearwater National Bank example and show how to use expression (10.6) to provide a 95% confidence interval estimate of the difference between the population mean checking account balances at the two branch banks. The sample data show $n_1 = 28$, $\bar{x}_1 = \$1025$, and $s_1 = \$150$ for the Cherry Grove Branch, and $n_2 = 22$, $\bar{x}_2 = \$910$, and $s_2 = \$125$ for the Beechmont Branch. The calculation for degrees of freedom for $t_{\alpha/2}$ is as follows:

$$df = \frac{\left(\dfrac{s_1^2}{n_1} + \dfrac{s_2^2}{n_2}\right)^2}{\dfrac{1}{n_1 - 1}\left(\dfrac{s_1^2}{n_1}\right)^2 + \dfrac{1}{n_2 - 1}\left(\dfrac{s_2^2}{n_2}\right)^2} = \frac{\left(\dfrac{150^2}{28} + \dfrac{125^2}{22}\right)^2}{\dfrac{1}{28 - 1}\left(\dfrac{150^2}{28}\right)^2 + \dfrac{1}{22 - 1}\left(\dfrac{125^2}{22}\right)^2} = 47.8$$

We round the noninteger degrees of freedom *down* to 47 to provide a larger *t* value and a more conservative (wider) interval estimate. Using the *t* distribution table with 47 degrees of freedom, we find $t_{.025} = 2.012$. Using expression (10.6), we develop the 95% confidence interval estimate of the difference between the two population means as follows.

$$\bar{x}_1 - \bar{x}_2 \pm t_{.025}\sqrt{\frac{s_1^2}{n_1} + \frac{s_2^2}{n_2}}$$

$$1025 - 910 \pm 2.012\sqrt{\frac{150^2}{28} + \frac{125^2}{22}}$$

$$115 \pm 78$$

The point estimate of the difference between the population mean checking account balances at the two branches is $115 and the margin of error is $78. Thus the 95% confidence interval estimate of the difference between the two population means is $115 - 78 = \$37$ to $115 + 78 = \$193$.

This suggestion should help if you are using equation (10.7) to calculate the degrees of freedom by hand.

The computation of the degrees of freedom in equation (10.7) is cumbersome if you are doing the calculation by hand. However, note that the expressions s_1^2/n_1 and s_2^2/n_2 appear in both expression (10.6) and equation (10.7). These values only need to be computed once in order to evaluate both (10.6) and (10.7).

Using Excel to Construct a Confidence Interval

Excel's data analysis tools do not provide a procedure for developing interval estimates involving two population means. However, we can develop an Excel worksheet that can be used for a template to construct interval estimates. We will illustrate by constructing an interval estimate of the difference between the population means in the Clearwater National Bank study. Refer to Figure 10.5 as we describe the tasks involved. The formula worksheet is in the background; the value worksheet is in the foreground.

Enter Data: Column A contains the account balances for the simple random sample of 28 customers at the Cherry Grove Branch, and column B contains the account balances for the simple random sample of 22 customers at the Beechmont Branch.

Enter Functions and Formulas: The descriptive statistics needed are provided in cells E5:F7. Using the two sample standard deviations and the sample sizes, an estimate of the variance of the point estimator $\bar{x}_1 - \bar{x}_2$ is computed by entering the following formula into cell E9:

$$=E7\wedge2/E5 + F7\wedge2/F5$$

An estimate of the standard error is then computed in cell E10 by taking the square root of the variance.

FIGURE 10.5   EXCEL WORKSHEET: CONSTRUCTING A 95% CONFIDENCE INTERVAL FOR CLEARWATER NATIONAL BANK

	A	B	C	D	E	F	G
1	Cherry Grove	Beechmont		Interval Estimate of Difference in Population Means:			
2	1263	996.7			σ_1 and σ_2 Unknown Case		
3	897	897					
4	849	912			Cherry Grove	Beechmont	
5	891	894.9		Sample Size	=COUNT(A2:A29)	=COUNT(B2:B23)	
6	964	785		Sample Mean	=AVERAGE(A2:A29)	=AVERAGE(B2:B23)	
7	810	750.7		Sample Standard Deviation	=STDEV(A2:A29)	=STDEV(B2:B23)	
8	877	882.2					
9	899	1110		Estimate of Variance	=E7^2/E5+F7^2/F5		
10	847	907.2		Standard Error	=SQRT(E9)		
11	1070	1226.1					
12	1252	762.1		Confidence Coefficient	0.95		
13	920	835.5		Level of Significance	=1-E12		
14	1256	1048		Degrees of Freedom	=E9^2/((1/(E5-1))*(E7^2/E5)^2+(1/(F5-1)*(F7^2/F5)^2))		
15	1196	773.8		t Value	=TINV(E13,E14)		
16	1150	807		Margin of Error	=E15*E10		
17	1024	972					
18	1016	980		Point Estimate of Difference	=E6-F6		
19	1126	876.6		Lower Limit	=E18-E16		
20	1289	943		Upper Limit	=E18+E16		
21	1220	992.7					
22	912	704.3					
23	1026	962.9					
24	786						
25	989						
26	1133						
27	990						
28	999						
29	1049						
30							

	A	B	C	D	E	F	G
1	Cherry Grove	Beechmont		Interval Estimate of Difference in Population Means:			
2	1263	997			σ_1 and σ_2 Unknown Case		
3	897	897					
4	849	912			Cherry Grove	Beechmont	
5	891	895		Sample Size	28	22	
6	964	785		Sample Mean	1025	910	
7	810	751		Sample Standard Deviation	150	125	
8	877	882					
9	899	1110		Estimate of Variance	1513.8550		
10	847	907		Standard Error	38.9083		
11	1070	1226					
12	1252	762		Confidence Coefficient	0.95		
13	920	836		Level of Significance	0.05		
14	1256	1048		Degrees of Freedom	47.8		
15	1196	774		t Value	2.012		
16	1150	807		Margin of Error	78		
17	1024	972					
18	1016	980		Point Estimate of Difference	115		
19	1126	877		Lower Limit	37		
20	1289	943		Upper Limit	193		
21	1220	993					
22	912	704					
23	1026	963					
24	786						
25	989						
26	1133						
27	990						
28	999						
29	1049						
30							

Cells E12:E16 are used to compute the appropriate t value and the margin of error. The confidence coefficient is entered into cell E12 (.95) and the corresponding level of significance is computed in cell E13 ($\alpha = .05$). In cell E14, we used formula (10.7) to compute the degrees of freedom (47.8). In cell E15, we used the TINV function to compute the t value needed for the interval estimate. The margin of error is computed in cell E16 by multiplying the t value by the standard error.

In cell E18 the difference in the sample means is used to compute the point estimate of the difference in the two population means (115). The lower limit of the confidence interval is computed in cell E19 (37) and the upper limit is computed in cell E20 (193);

thus, the 95% confidence interval estimate of the difference in the two population means is 37 to 193.

A Template for Other Problems. This worksheet can be used as a template for developing interval estimates of the difference in population means when the population standard deviations are unknown. For another problem of this type, we must first enter the new problem data in columns A and B. The data ranges in cells E5:F7 must be modified in order to compute the sample means, sample sizes, and sample standard deviations for the new data. After doing so the point estimate and a 95% confidence interval will be displayed in cells E18:E20. If a confidence interval with a different confidence coefficient is desired, we simply change the value in cell E12.

We can further simplify the use of Figure 10.5 as a template for other problems by eliminating the need to enter new data ranges in cells E5:F7. We rewrite the cell formulas as follows:

Cell E5: =COUNT(A:A)
Cell F5: =COUNT(B:B)
Cell E6: =AVERAGE(A:A)
Cell F6: =AVERAGE(B:B)
Cell E7: =STDEV(A:A)
Cell F7: =STDEV(B:B)

The CheckAcct data set includes a worksheet titled Template that uses the A:A and B:B methods for entering the data ranges.

Using the A:A method of specifying data ranges in cells E5:F7, Excel's COUNT function will count the number of numeric values in column A, Excel's AVERAGE function will compute the average of the numeric values in column A, and Excel's STDEV function will compute the standard deviation of the numeric values in column A. Similarly, using the B:B method of specifying data ranges in cells F5:F7, Excel's COUNT function will count the number of numeric values in column B, Excel's AVERAGE function will compute the average of the numeric values in column B, and Excel's STDEV function will compute the standard deviation of the numeric values in column B. Thus, to solve a new problem it is only necessary to enter the new data into columns A and B.

This worksheet can also be used as a template for text exercises in which the sample sizes, sample means, and sample standard deviations are given. In this type of situation, no change in the data is necessary. We simply replace the values in cells E5:F7 with the given values of the sample sizes, sample means, and sample standard deviations. If something other than a 95% confidence interval is desired, the confidence coefficient in cell E12 must also be changed.

Hypothesis Tests About $\mu_1 - \mu_2$

Let us now consider hypothesis tests about the difference between the means of two populations when the population standard deviations σ_1 and σ_2 are unknown. Letting D_0 denote the hypothesized difference between μ_1 and μ_2, Section 10.1 showed that the test statistic used for the case where σ_1 and σ_2 are known is as follows.

$$z = \frac{(\bar{x}_1 - \bar{x}_2) - D_0}{\sqrt{\dfrac{\sigma_1^2}{n_1} + \dfrac{\sigma_2^2}{n_2}}}$$

The test statistic, z, follows the standard normal distribution.

When σ_1 and σ_2 are unknown, we use s_1 as an estimator of σ_1 and s_2 as an estimator of σ_2. Substituting these sample standard deviations for σ_1 and σ_2 provides the following test statistic when σ_1 and σ_2 are unknown.

TEST STATISTIC FOR HYPOTHESIS TESTS ABOUT $\mu_1 - \mu_2$: σ_1 AND σ_2 UNKNOWN

$$t = \frac{(\bar{x}_1 - \bar{x}_2) - D_0}{\sqrt{\dfrac{s_1^2}{n_1} + \dfrac{s_2^2}{n_2}}} \qquad \textbf{(10.8)}$$

The degrees of freedom for t are given by equation (10.7).

Let us demonstrate the use of this test statistic in the following hypothesis testing example.

Consider a new computer software package developed to help systems analysts reduce the time required to design, develop, and implement an information system. To evaluate the benefits of the new software package, a random sample of 24 systems analysts is selected. Each analyst is given specifications for a hypothetical information system. Then 12 of the analysts are instructed to produce the information system by using current technology. The other 12 analysts are trained in the use of the new software package and then instructed to use it to produce the information system.

This study involves two populations: a population of systems analysts using the current technology and a population of systems analysts using the new software package. In terms of the time required to complete the information system design project, the population means are as follow.

$\mu_1 = $ the mean project completion time for systems analysts using the current technology

$\mu_2 = $ the mean project completion time for systems analysts using the new software package

The researcher in charge of the new software evaluation project hopes to show that the new software package will provide a shorter mean project completion time. Thus, the researcher is looking for evidence to conclude that μ_2 is less than μ_1; in this case, the difference between the two population means, $\mu_1 - \mu_2$, will be greater than zero. The research hypothesis $\mu_1 - \mu_2 > 0$ is stated as the alternative hypothesis. Thus, the hypothesis test becomes

$$H_0: \mu_1 - \mu_2 \leq 0$$
$$H_a: \mu_1 - \mu_2 > 0$$

We will use $\alpha = .05$ as the level of significance.

Suppose that the 24 analysts complete the study with the results shown in Table 10.1. Using the test statistic in equation (10.8), we have

$$t = \frac{(\bar{x}_1 - \bar{x}_2) - D_0}{\sqrt{\dfrac{s_1^2}{n_1} + \dfrac{s_2^2}{n_2}}} = \frac{(325 - 286) - 0}{\sqrt{\dfrac{40^2}{12} + \dfrac{44^2}{12}}} = 2.27$$

TABLE 10.1   COMPLETION TIME DATA AND SUMMARY STATISTICS
FOR THE SOFTWARE TESTING STUDY

	Current Technology	New Software
	300	274
	280	220
	344	308
	385	336
	372	198
	360	300
	288	315
	321	258
	376	318
	290	310
	301	332
	283	263
Summary Statistics		
Sample size	$n_1 = 12$	$n_2 = 12$
Sample mean	$\bar{x}_1 = 325$ hours	$\bar{x}_2 = 286$ hours
Sample standard deviation	$s_1 = 40$	$s_2 = 44$

CD file

SoftwareTest

Computing the degrees of freedom using equation (10.7), we have

$$ df = \frac{\left(\dfrac{s_1^2}{n_1} + \dfrac{s_2^2}{n_2}\right)^2}{\dfrac{1}{n_1 - 1}\left(\dfrac{s_1^2}{n_1}\right)^2 + \dfrac{1}{n_2 - 1}\left(\dfrac{s_2^2}{n_2}\right)^2} = \frac{\left(\dfrac{40^2}{12} + \dfrac{44^2}{12}\right)^2}{\dfrac{1}{12 - 1}\left(\dfrac{40^2}{12}\right)^2 + \dfrac{1}{12 - 1}\left(\dfrac{44^2}{12}\right)^2} = 21.8 $$

Rounding down, we will use a t distribution with 21 degrees of freedom. This row of the t distribution table is as follows:

Area in Upper Tail	.20	.10	.05	.025	.01	.005
t Value (21 df)	.859	1.323	1.721	2.080	2.518	2.831

$t = 2.27$

Using the t distribution table, we can only determine a range for the p-value. Use of Excel shows the p-value = .0166.

With an upper tail test, the p-value is the area in the upper tail to the right of $t = 2.27$. From the preceding results, we see that the p-value is between .025 and .01. Thus, the p-value is less than $\alpha = .05$ and H_0 is rejected. The sample results enable the researcher to conclude that $\mu_1 - \mu_2 > 0$, or $\mu_2 < \mu_1$. Thus, the research study supports the conclusion that the new software package provides a smaller population mean completion time.

Using Excel to Conduct a Hypothesis Test

The Excel procedure used to conduct a hypothesis test to determine whether there is a significant difference in population means when the population standard deviations are unknown is called *t-test: Two-Sample Assuming Unequal Variances*. We illustrate using the sample data for the software evaluation study. Twelve systems analysts developed an information system using current technology, and 12 systems analysts developed an information system using a new software package. A one-tailed hypothesis test is to be conducted to see whether the mean completion time is shorter using the new software package. Refer to the

Excel worksheet shown in Figure 10.6 and the dialog box in Figure 10.7 as we describe the tasks involved.

Enter Data: Column A contains the completion time data for the simple random sample of 12 individuals using the current technology, and column B contains the completion time data for the simple random sample of 12 individuals using the new software.

Apply Tools: The following steps will provide the information needed to conduct the hypothesis test to see whether there is a significant difference in favor of the new software.

> **Step 1.** Select the **Tools** menu
> **Step 2.** Choose **Data Analysis**
> **Step 3.** Choose *t*-**Test: Two-Sample Assuming Unequal Variances** from the list of Analysis Tools
> **Step 4.** When the *t*-Test: Two-Sample Assuming Unequal Variances dialog box appears:
>> Enter A1:A13 in the **Variable 1 Range** box
>> Enter B1:B13 in the **Variable 2 Range** box
>> Enter 0 in the **Hypothesized Means Difference** box
>> Select **Labels**
>> Enter .05 in the **Alpha** box
>> Select **Output Range** and enter D1 in the box
>> Click **OK**

Descriptive statistics for the two samples are shown in cells E4:F6. The value of the test statistic, 2.2721, is shown in cell E9. The *p*-value for the test, labeled P(T <=t) one-tail, is shown in cell E10. Because the *p*-value, 0.0166, is less than the level of significance $\alpha = .05$, we can conclude that the mean completion time for the population using the new software package is smaller.

The *t*-test: Two-Sample Assuming Unequal Variances can also be used to conduct two-tailed hypothesis tests. The only change required to make the hypothesis testing decision is that we need to use the *p*-value for a two-tailed test, labeled P(T <=t) two-tail (see cell E12).

FIGURE 10.6   USING EXCEL TO CONDUCT A HYPOTHESIS TEST ABOUT EQUALITY OF MEAN PROJECT COMPLETION TIMES

	A	B	C	D	E	F	G
1	Current	New		t-Test: Two-Sample Assuming Unequal Variances			
2	300	274					
3	280	220			*Current*	*New*	
4	344	308		Mean	325	286	
5	385	336		Variance	1599.6364	1935.8182	
6	372	198		Observations	12	12	
7	360	300		Hypothesized Mean Difference	0		
8	288	315		df	22		
9	321	258		t Stat	2.2721		
10	376	318		P(T<=t) one-tail	0.0166		
11	290	310		t Critical one-tail	1.7171		
12	301	332		P(T<=t) two-tail	0.0332		
13	283	263		t Critical two-tail	2.0739		
14							

FIGURE 10.7   DIALOG BOX FOR EXCEL'S t-TEST: TWO-SAMPLE ASSUMING UNEQUAL VARIANCES

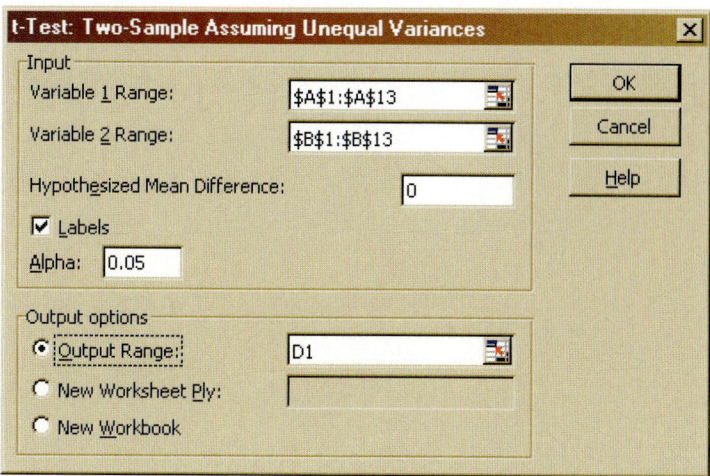

Practical Advice

The interval estimation and hypothesis testing procedures presented in this section are robust and can be used with relatively small sample sizes. In most applications, sample sizes that are equal or nearly equal and result in a total sample size of $n_1 + n_2 \geq 20$ will provide very good results even if the populations are not normal. However, larger sample sizes are recommended if the distributions of the populations are highly skewed or contain outliers. Smaller sample sizes should only be used if the analyst is satisfied that the distributions of the populations are at least approximately normal.

NOTES AND COMMENTS

Another approach used to make inferences about the difference between two population means when σ_1 and σ_2 are unknown is based on the assumption that the two population standard deviations are *equal* ($\sigma_1 = \sigma_2 = \sigma$). Under this assumption, the two sample standard deviations are combined to provide the following *pooled sample variance*:

$$s_p^2 = \frac{(n_1 - 1)s_1^2 + (n_2 - 1)s_2^2}{n_1 + n_2 - 2}$$

The t test statistic becomes

$$t = \frac{(\bar{x}_1 - \bar{x}_2) - D_0}{s_p\sqrt{\dfrac{1}{n_1} + \dfrac{1}{n_2}}}$$

and has $n_1 + n_2 - 2$ degrees of freedom. At this point, the computation of the p-value and the interpretation of the sample results are identical to the procedures discussed earlier in this section.

A difficulty with this procedure is that the assumption that the two population standard deviations are equal is usually difficult to verify. Unequal population standard deviations are frequently encountered. Using the pooled procedure may not provide satisfactory results especially if the sample sizes n_1 and n_2 are quite different.

The t procedure that we presented in this section does not require the assumption of equal population standard deviations and can be applied whether the population standard deviations are equal or not. It is a more general procedure and is recommended for most applications.

Exercises

Methods

9. The following results are for independent random samples taken from two populations.

Sample 1	Sample 2
$n_1 = 20$	$n_2 = 30$
$\bar{x}_1 = 22.5$	$\bar{x}_2 = 20.1$
$s_1 = 2.5$	$s_2 = 4.8$

    a. What is the point estimate of the difference between the two population means?
    b. What is the degrees of freedom for the t distribution?
    c. At 95% confidence, what is the margin of error?
    d. What is the 95% confidence interval for the difference between the two population means?

10. Consider the following hypothesis test.

$$H_0: \mu_1 - \mu_2 = 0$$
$$H_a: \mu_1 - \mu_2 \neq 0$$

The following results are from independent samples taken from two populations.

Sample 1	Sample 2
$n_1 = 35$	$n_2 = 40$
$\bar{x}_1 = 13.6$	$\bar{x}_2 = 10.1$
$s_1 = 5.2$	$s_2 = 8.5$

    a. What is the value of the test statistic?
    b. What is the value of the degrees of freedom for the t distribution?
    c. What is the p-value?
    d. At $\alpha = .05$, what is your conclusion?

11. Consider the following data for two independent random samples taken from two normal populations.

Sample 1	10	7	13	7	9	8
Sample 2	8	7	8	4	6	9

    a. Compute the two sample means.
    b. Compute the two sample standard deviations.
    c. What is the point estimate of the difference between the two population means?
    d. What is the 90% confidence interval estimate of the difference between the two population means?

Applications

12. The U.S. Department of Transportation provides the number of miles that residents of the 75 largest metropolitan areas travel per day in a car. Suppose that for a simple random sample of 50 Buffalo residents the mean is 22.5 miles a day and the standard deviation is 8.4 miles a day, and for an independent simple random sample of 40 Boston residents the mean is 18.6 miles a day and the standard deviation is 7.4 miles a day.

a. What is the point estimate of the difference between the mean number of miles that Buffalo residents travel per day and the mean number of miles that Boston residents travel per day?

b. What is the 95% confidence interval for the difference between the two population means?

CD file

Cargo

13. FedEx and United Parcel Service (UPS) are the world's two leading cargo carriers by volume and revenue (*The Wall Street Journal*, January 27, 2004). According to the Airports Council International, the Memphis International Airport (FedEx) and the Louisville International Airport (UPS) are two of the ten largest cargo airports in the world. The following random samples show the tons of cargo per day handled by these airports. Data are in thousands of tons.

Memphis					
9.1	15.1	8.8	10.0	7.5	10.5
8.3	9.1	6.0	5.8	12.1	9.3

Louisville					
4.7	5.0	4.2	3.3	5.5
2.2	4.1	2.6	3.4	7.0

a. Compute the sample mean and sample standard deviation for each airport.

b. What is the point estimate of the difference between the two population means? Interpret this value in terms of the higher-volume airport and a comparison of the volume difference between the two airports.

c. Develop a 95% confidence interval of the difference between the daily population means for the two airports.

14. Coastal areas of the United States including Cape Cod, the Outer Banks, the Carolinas, and the Gulf Coast had relatively high population growth rates during the 1990s. Data were collected on residents living in the coastal communities as well as on residents living in noncoastal areas throughout the United States (*USA Today*, July 21, 2000). Assume that the following sample results were obtained on the ages of individuals in the two populations:

Coastal Areas	Noncoastal Areas
$n_1 = 150$	$n_2 = 175$
$\bar{x}_1 = 39.3$ years	$\bar{x}_2 = 35.4$ years
$s_1 = 16.8$ years	$s_2 = 15.2$ years

Test the hypothesis of no difference between the two population means. Use $\alpha = .05$.

a. Formulate the null and alternative hypotheses.

b. What is the value of the test statistic?

c. What is the *p*-value?

d. What is your conclusion?

15. Injuries to Major League Baseball players have been increasing in recent years. For the period 1992 to 2001, league expansion caused Major League Baseball rosters to increase 15%. However, the number of players being put on the disabled list due to injury increased 32% over the same period (*USA Today*, July 8, 2002). A research question addressed whether Major League Baseball players being put on the disabled list are on the list longer in 2001 than players put on the disabled list a decade earlier.

a. Using the population mean number of days a player is on the disabled list, formulate null and alternative hypotheses that can be used to test the research question.
b. Assume that the following data apply:

	2001 Season	**1992 Season**
Sample size	$n_1 = 45$	$n_2 = 38$
Sample mean	$\bar{x}_1 = 60$ days	$\bar{x}_2 = 51$ days
Sample standard deviation	$s_1 = 18$ days	$s_2 = 15$ days

What is the point estimate of the difference between population mean number of days on the disabled list for 2001 compared to 1992? What is the percentage increase in the number of days on the disabled list?

c. Use $\alpha = .01$. What is your conclusion about the number of days on the disabled list? What is the p-value?
d. Do these data suggest that Major League Baseball should be concerned about the situation?

SATVerbal

16. The College Board provided comparisons of Scholastic Aptitude Test (SAT) scores based on the highest level of education attained by the test taker's parents. A research hypothesis was that students whose parents had attained a higher level of education would on average score higher on the SAT. During 2003, the overall mean SAT verbal score was 507 (*The World Almanac 2004*). SAT verbal scores for independent samples of students follow. The first sample shows the SAT verbal test scores for students whose parents are college graduates with a bachelor's degree. The second sample shows the SAT verbal test scores for students whose parents are high school graduates but do not have a college degree.

Student's Parents			
College Grads		**High School Grads**	
485	487	442	492
534	533	580	478
650	526	479	425
554	410	486	485
550	515	528	390
572	578	524	535
497	448		
592	469		

a. Formulate the hypotheses that can be used to determine whether the sample data support the hypothesis that students show a higher population mean verbal score on the SAT if their parents attained a higher level of education.
b. What is the point estimate of the difference between the means for the two populations?
c. Compute the p-value for the hypothesis test.
d. At $\alpha = .05$, what is your conclusion?

17. Periodically, Merrill Lynch customers are asked to evaluate Merrill Lynch financial consultants and services (2000 Merrill Lynch Client Satisfaction Survey). Higher ratings on the client satisfaction survey indicate better service with 7 the maximum service rating. Independent samples of service ratings for two financial consultants are summarized here. Consultant A has 10 years of experience, whereas consultant B has 1 year of experience. Use $\alpha = .05$ and test to see whether the consultant with more experience has the higher population mean service rating.

Consultant A	Consultant B
$n_1 = 16$	$n_2 = 10$
$\bar{x}_1 = 6.82$	$\bar{x}_2 = 6.25$
$s_1 = .64$	$s_2 = .75$

a. State the null and alternative hypotheses.
b. Compute the value of the test statistic.
c. What is the *p*-value?
d. What is your conclusion?

SAT

18. Educational testing companies provide tutoring, classroom learning, and practice tests in an effort to help students perform better on tests such as the Scholastic Aptitude Test (SAT). The test preparation companies claim that their courses will improve SAT score performances by an average of 120 points (*The Wall Street Journal*, January 23, 2003). A researcher is uncertain of this claim and believes that 120 points may be an overstatement in an effort to encourage students to take the test preparation course. In an evaluation study of one test preparation service, the researcher collects SAT score data for 35 students who took the test preparation course and 48 students who did not take the course. The CD file named SAT contains the scores for this study.
a. Formulate the hypotheses that can be used to test the researcher's belief that the improvement in SAT scores may be less than the stated average of 120 points.
b. Using $\alpha = .05$, what is your conclusion?
c. What is the point estimate of the improvement in the average SAT scores provided by the test preparation course? Provide a 95% confidence interval estimate of the improvement.
d. What advice would you have for the researcher after seeing the confidence interval?

10.3 Inferences About the Difference Between Two Population Means: Matched Samples

Suppose employees at a manufacturing company can use two different methods to perform a production task. To maximize production output, the company wants to identify the method with the shorter population mean completion time. Let μ_1 denote the population mean completion time for production method 1 and μ_2 denote the population mean completion time for production method 2. With no preliminary indication of the preferred production method, we begin by tentatively assuming that the two production methods have the same population mean completion time. Thus, the null hypothesis is $H_0: \mu_1 - \mu_2 = 0$. If this hypothesis is rejected, we can conclude that the population mean completion times differ. In this case, the method providing the shorter mean completion time would be recommended. The null and alternative hypotheses are written as follows.

$$H_0: \mu_1 - \mu_2 = 0$$
$$H_a: \mu_1 - \mu_2 \neq 0$$

In choosing the sampling procedure that will be used to collect production time data and test the hypotheses, we consider two alternative designs. One is based on **independent samples** and the other is based on **matched samples**.

1. *Independent sample design:* A simple random sample of workers is selected and each worker in the sample uses method 1. A second independent simple random sample of workers is selected and each worker in this sample uses method 2. The test of the difference between population means is based on the procedures in Section 10.2.

2. *Matched sample design:* One simple random sample of workers is selected. Each worker first uses one method and then uses the other method. The order of the two methods is assigned randomly to the workers, with some workers performing method 1 first and others performing method 2 first. Each worker provides a pair of data values, one value for method 1 and another value for method 2.

In the matched sample design the two production methods are tested under similar conditions (i.e., with the same workers); hence this design often leads to a smaller sampling error than the independent sample design. The primary reason is that in a matched sample design, variation between workers is eliminated because the same workers are used for both production methods.

Let us demonstrate the analysis of a matched sample design by assuming it is the method used to test the difference between population means for the two production methods. A random sample of six workers is used. The data on completion times for the six workers are given in Table 10.2. Note that each worker provides a pair of data values, one for each production method. Also note that the last column contains the difference in completion times d_i for each worker in the sample.

The key to the analysis of the matched sample design is to realize that we consider only the column of differences. Therefore, we have six data values (.6, −.2, .5, .3, .0, and .6) that will be used to analyze the difference between population means of the two production methods.

Let μ_d = the mean of the *difference* values for the population of workers. With this notation, the null and alternative hypotheses are rewritten as follows.

$$H_0: \mu_d = 0$$
$$H_a: \mu_d \neq 0$$

If H_0 is rejected, we can conclude that the population mean completion times differ.

The d notation is a reminder that the matched sample provides *difference* data. The sample mean and sample standard deviation for the six difference values in Table 10.2 follow.

Other than the use of the d notation, the formulas for the sample mean and sample standard deviation are the same ones used previously in the text.

$$\bar{d} = \frac{\Sigma d_i}{n} = \frac{1.8}{6} = .30$$

$$s_d = \sqrt{\frac{s\Sigma(d_i - \bar{d})^2}{n - 1}} = \sqrt{\frac{.56}{5}} = .3347$$

With the small sample of $n = 6$ workers, we need to make the assumption that the population of differences has a normal distribution. This assumption is necessary so that we may

TABLE 10.2   TASK COMPLETION TIMES FOR A MATCHED SAMPLE DESIGN

Worker	Completion Time for Method 1 (minutes)	Completion Time for Method 2 (minutes)	Difference in Completion Times (d_i)
1	6.0	5.4	.6
2	5.0	5.2	−.2
3	7.0	6.5	.5
4	6.2	5.9	.3
5	6.0	6.0	.0
6	6.4	5.8	.6

It is not necessary to make the assumption that the population has a normal distribution if the sample size is large. Sample size guidelines for using the t distribution were presented in Chapters 8 and 9.

use the t distribution for hypothesis testing and interval estimation procedures. Based on this assumption, the following test statistic has a t distribution with $n - 1$ degrees of freedom.

> **TEST STATISTIC FOR HYPOTHESIS TESTS INVOLVING MATCHED SAMPLES**
>
> $$t = \frac{\bar{d} - \mu_d}{s_d/\sqrt{n}}$$ **(10.9)**

Once the difference data are computed, the t distribution procedure for matched samples is the same as the one-population estimation and hypothesis testing procedures described in Chapters 8 and 9.

Let us use equation (10.9) to test the hypotheses $H_0: \mu_d = 0$ and $H_a: \mu_d \neq 0$, using $\alpha = .05$. Substituting the sample results $\bar{d} = .30$, $s_d = .3347$, and $n = 6$ into equation (10.9), we compute the value of the test statistic.

$$t = \frac{\bar{d} - \mu_d}{s_d/\sqrt{n}} = \frac{.30 - 0}{.3347/\sqrt{6}} = 2.20$$

Now let us compute the p-value for this two-tailed test. Because $t = 2.20 > 0$, the test statistic is in the upper tail of the t distribution. With $t = 2.20$, the area in the upper tail to the right of the test statistic can be found by using the t distribution table with degrees of freedom $= n - 1 = 6 - 1 = 5$. Information from the 5 degrees of freedom row of the t distribution table is as follows:

Area in Upper Tail	.20	.10	.05	.025	.01	.005
t Value (5 df)	0.920	1.476	2.015	2.571	3.365	4.032

$t = 2.20$

Thus, we see that the area in the upper tail is between .05 and .025. Because this test is a two-tailed test, we double these values to conclude that the p-value is between .10 and .05. This p-value is greater than $\alpha = .05$. Thus, the null hypothesis $H_0: \mu_d = 0$ is not rejected. Using Excel and the data in Table 10.2, we find the p-value $= .0795$.

We can also obtain an interval estimate of the difference between the two population means by using the single population methodology of Chapter 8. At 95% confidence, the calculation follows.

$$\bar{d} \pm t_{.025} \frac{s_d}{\sqrt{n}}$$

$$.3 \pm 2.571 \left(\frac{.3347}{\sqrt{6}} \right)$$

$$.3 \pm .35$$

Thus, the margin of error is .35 and the 95% confidence interval for the difference between the population means of the two production methods is $-.05$ minutes to .65 minutes.

Using Excel to Conduct a Hypothesis Test

Excel's t-Test: Paired Two Sample for Means tool can be used to conduct a hypothesis test about the difference between the population means when a matched sample design is used. We illustrate by conducting the hypothesis test involving the two production methods. Refer to the Excel worksheet shown in Figure 10.8 and the dialog box in Figure 10.9 as we describe the tasks involved.

FIGURE 10.8 USING EXCEL FOR A HYPOTHESIS TEST IN THE MATCHED SAMPLES STUDY

	A	B	C	D	E	F	G	H
1	Worker	Method 1	Method 2		t-Test: Paired Two Sample for Means			
2	1	6	5.4					
3	2	5	5.2			*Method 1*	*Method 2*	
4	3	7	6.5		**Mean**	6.1	5.8	
5	4	6.2	5.9		**Variance**	0.428	0.212	
6	5	6	6		**Observations**	6	6	
7	6	6.4	5.8		**Pearson Correlation**	0.8764		
8					**Hypothesized Mean Difference**	0		
9					df	5		
10					t Stat	2.196		
11					P(T<=t) one-tail	0.0398		
12					t Critical one-tail	2.015		
13					P(T<=t) two-tail	0.0795		
14					t Critical two-tail	2.571		
15								

Enter Data: Column A is used to identify each of the six workers who participated in the study. Column B contains the completion time data for each worker using method 1, and column C contains the completion time data for each worker using method 2.

Apply Tools: The following steps describe how to use Excel's t-Test: Paired Two Sample for Means tool to conduct the hypothesis test about the difference between the means of the two production methods

Step 1. Select the **Tools** menu
Step 2. Choose the **Data Analysis** option
Step 3. Choose **t-Test: Paired Two Sample for Means** from the list of Analysis Tools

FIGURE 10.9 DIALOG BOX FOR EXCEL'S t-TEST: PAIRED TWO SAMPLE FOR MEANS

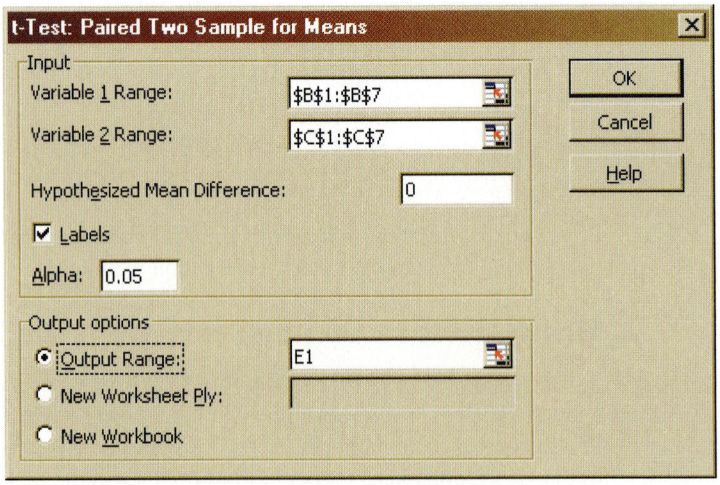

Step 4. When the t-Test: Paired Two Sample for Means dialog box appears (see Figure 10.9):

> Enter B1:B7 in the **Variable 1 Range** box
> Enter C1:C7 in the **Variable 2 Range** box
> Enter 0 in the **Hypothesized Mean Difference** box
> Select **Labels**
> Enter .05 in the **Alpha** box
> Select **Output Range**
> Enter E1 in the **Output Range** box (to identify the upper left corner of the section of the worksheet where the output will appear)
> Click **OK**

The results are shown in cells E1:G14 of the worksheet shown in Figure 10.8. The *p*-value for the test, labeled P(T $<=$ t) two-tail, is shown in cell F13. Because the *p*-value, 0.0795, is greater than the level of significance $\alpha = .05$, we cannot reject the null hypothesis that the mean completion times are equal.

The same procedure can also be used to conduct one-tailed hypothesis tests. The only change required to make the hypothesis testing decision is that we need to use the *p*-value for a one-tailed test, labeled P(T $<=$ t) one-tail (see cell F11).

NOTES AND COMMENTS

1. In the example presented in this section, workers performed the production task with first one method and then the other method. This example illustrates a matched sample design in which each sampled element (worker) provides a pair of data values. It is also possible to use different but "similar" elements to provide the pair of data values. For example, a worker at one location could be matched with a similar worker at another location (similarity based on age, education, gender, experience, etc.). The pairs of workers would provide the difference data that could be used in the matched sample analysis.

2. A matched sample procedure for inferences about two population means generally provides better precision than the independent sample approach; therefore, it is the recommended design. However, in some applications the matching cannot be achieved, or perhaps the time and cost associated with matching are excessive. In such cases, the independent sample design should be used.

Exercises

Methods

19. Consider the following hypothesis test.

$$H_0: \mu_d \leq 0$$
$$H_a: \mu_d > 0$$

The following data are from matched samples taken from two populations.

	Population	
Element	**1**	**2**
1	21	20
2	28	26
3	18	18
4	20	20
5	26	24

a. Compute the difference value for each element.
b. Compute $\bar{d}$.
c. Compute the standard deviation s_d.
d. Conduct a hypothesis test using $\alpha = .05$. What is your conclusion?

20. The following data are from matched samples taken from two populations.

		Population	
Element		**1**	**2**
1		11	8
2		7	8
3		9	6
4		12	7
5		13	10
6		15	15
7		15	14

a. Compute the difference value for each element.
b. Compute $\bar{d}$.
c. Compute the standard deviation s_d.
d. What is the point estimate of the difference between the two population means?
e. Provide a 95% confidence interval for the difference between the two population means.

Applications

21. A market research firm used a sample of individuals to rate the purchase potential of a particular product before and after the individuals saw a new television commercial about the product. The purchase potential ratings were based on a 0 to 10 scale, with higher values indicating a higher purchase potential. The null hypothesis stated that the mean rating "after" would be less than or equal to the mean rating "before." Rejection of this hypothesis would show that the commercial improved the mean purchase potential rating. Use $\alpha = .05$ and the following data to test the hypothesis and comment on the value of the commercial.

	Purchase Rating			**Purchase Rating**	
Individual	**After**	**Before**	**Individual**	**After**	**Before**
1	6	5	5	3	5
2	6	4	6	9	8
3	7	7	7	7	5
4	4	3	8	6	6

22. A sample of 10 international telephone calls provided Sprint and WorldCom calling rates per minute for calls from the United States (*World Traveler,* July 2000).

Country	Sprint	WorldCom	Country	Sprint	WorldCom
Australia	.46	.26	France	.46	.26
Belgium	.69	.40	Germany	.46	.26
Brazil	.92	.53	Hong Kong	.92	.40
Colombia	.55	.53	Japan	.69	.40
Denmark	.50	.26	United Kingdom	.46	.26

Provide a 95% confidence interval estimate of the difference between the two population means.

23. Bank of America's Consumer Spending Survey collected data on annual credit card charges in seven different categories of expenditures: transportation, groceries, dining out, household expenses, home furnishings, apparel, and entertainment (*U.S. Airways Attaché*, December 2003). Using data from a sample of 42 credit card accounts, assume that each account was used to identify the annual credit card charges for groceries (population 1) and the annual credit card charges for dining out (population 2). Using the difference data, the sample mean difference was $\bar{d} = \$850$, and the sample standard deviation was $s_d = \$1123$.

    a. Formulate the null and alternative hypotheses to test for no difference between the population mean credit card charges for groceries and the population mean credit card charges for dining out.

    b. Use a .05 level of significance. Can you conclude that the population means differ? What is the *p*-value?

    c. Which category, groceries or dining out, has a higher population mean annual credit card charge? What is the point estimate of the difference between the population means? What is the 95% confidence interval estimate of the difference between the population means?

24. Rental car gasoline prices per gallon were sampled at eight major airports. Data for Hertz and National car rental companies follow (*USA Today*, April 4, 2000).

Airport	Hertz	National	Airport	Hertz	National
Boston Logan	1.55	1.56	New York (JFK)	1.72	1.51
Chicago O'Hare	1.62	1.59	New York (LaGuardia)	1.67	1.50
Los Angeles	1.72	1.78	Orange County, CA	1.68	1.77
Miami	1.65	1.49	Washington (Dulles)	1.52	1.41

    Use $\alpha = .05$ to test the hypothesis of no difference between the population mean prices per gallon for the two companies.

25. In recent years, a growing array of entertainment options competes for consumer time. By 2004, cable television and radio surpassed broadcast television, recorded music, and the daily newspaper to become the two entertainment media with the greatest usage (*The Wall Street Journal*, January 26, 2004). Researchers used a sample of 15 individuals and collected data on the hours per week spent watching cable television and hours per week spent listening to the radio.

TVRadio

Individual	Television	Radio	Individual	Television	Radio
1	22	25	9	21	21
2	8	10	10	23	23
3	25	29	11	14	15
4	22	19	12	14	18
5	12	13	13	14	17
6	26	28	14	16	15
7	22	23	15	24	23
8	19	21			

    a. Use a .05 level of significance and test for a difference between the population mean usage for cable television and radio. What is the *p*-value?

    b. What is the sample mean number of hours per week spent watching cable television? What is the sample mean number of hours per week spent listening to radio? Which medium has the greater usage?

26. StreetInsider.com reported 2002 earnings per share data for a sample of major companies (February 12, 2003). Prior to 2002, financial analysts predicted the 2002 earnings per share for these same companies (*Barron's,* September 10, 2001). Use the following data to comment on differences between actual and estimated earnings per share.

Earnings

Company	Actual	Predicted
AT&T	1.29	0.38
American Express	2.01	2.31
Citigroup	2.59	3.43
Coca-Cola	1.60	1.78
DuPont	1.84	2.18
Exxon-Mobil	2.72	2.19
General Electric	1.51	1.71
Johnson & Johnson	2.28	2.18
McDonald's	0.77	1.55
Wal-Mart	1.81	1.74

a. Use $\alpha = .05$ and test for any difference between the population mean actual and population mean predicted earnings per share. What is the p-value? What is your conclusion?
b. What is the point estimate of the difference between the two means? Did the analysts tend to underestimate or overestimate the earnings?
c. At 95% confidence, what is the margin of error for the estimate in part (b)? What would you recommend based on this information?

10.4 Inferences About the Difference Between Two Population Proportions

Letting p_1 denote the proportion for population 1 and p_2 denote the proportion for population 2, we next consider inferences about the difference between the two population proportions: $p_1 - p_2$. To make an inference about this difference, we will select two independent random samples consisting of n_1 units from population 1 and n_2 units from population 2.

Interval Estimation of $p_1 - p_2$

In the following example, we show how to compute a margin of error and develop an interval estimate of the difference between two population proportions.

A tax preparation firm is interested in comparing the quality of work at two of its regional offices. By randomly selecting samples of tax returns prepared at each office and verifying the sample returns' accuracy, the firm will be able to estimate the proportion of erroneous returns prepared at each office. Of particular interest is the difference between these proportions.

p_1 = proportion of erroneous returns for population 1 (office 1)
p_2 = proportion of erroneous returns for population 2 (office 2)
$\bar{p}_1$ = sample proportion for a simple random sample from population 1
$\bar{p}_2$ = sample proportion for a simple random sample from population 2

The difference between the two population proportions is given by $p_1 - p_2$. The point estimator of $p_1 - p_2$ is as follows.

POINT ESTIMATOR OF THE DIFFERENCE BETWEEN TWO POPULATION PROPORTIONS

$$\bar{p}_1 - \bar{p}_2 \qquad \textbf{(10.10)}$$

Thus, the point estimator of the difference between two population proportions is the difference between the sample proportions of two independent simple random samples.

As with other point estimators, the point estimator $\bar{p}_1 - \bar{p}_2$ has a sampling distribution that reflects the possible values of $\bar{p}_1 - \bar{p}_2$ if we repeatedly took two independent random samples. The mean of this sampling distribution is $p_1 - p_2$ and the standard error is as follows:

$$\sigma_{\bar{p}_1 - \bar{p}_2} = \sqrt{\frac{p_1(1 - p_1)}{n_1} + \frac{p_2(1 - p_2)}{n_2}} \qquad \textbf{(10.11)}$$

Sample sizes involving proportions are usually large enough to use this approximation.

If the sample sizes are large enough that $n_1 p_1$, $n_1(1 - p_1)$, $n_2 p_2$, and $n_2(1 - p_2)$ are all greater than or equal to 5, the sampling distribution of $\bar{p}_1 - \bar{p}_2$ can be approximated by a normal distribution.

In the estimation of the difference between two population proportions, an interval estimate will take the following form:

$$\bar{p}_1 - \bar{p}_2 \pm \text{Margin of error}$$

With the sampling distribution of $\bar{p}_1 - \bar{p}_2$ approximated by a normal distribution, we would like to use $z_{\alpha/2}\sigma_{\bar{p}_1 - \bar{p}_2}$ as the margin of error. However, $\sigma_{\bar{p}_1 - \bar{p}_2}$ given by equation (10.11) involves the two unknown population proportions, p_1 and p_2. Thus, we use the sample proportion $\bar{p}_1$ to estimate p_1 and the sample proportion $\bar{p}_2$ to estimate p_2. The margin of error is thus.

$$\text{Margin of error} = z_{\alpha/2}\sqrt{\frac{\bar{p}_1(1 - \bar{p}_1)}{n_1} + \frac{\bar{p}_2(1 - \bar{p}_2)}{n_2}} \qquad \textbf{(10.12)}$$

The general form of an interval estimate of the difference between two population proportions is as follows.

INTERVAL ESTIMATE OF THE DIFFERENCE BETWEEN TWO POPULATION PROPORTIONS

$$\bar{p}_1 - \bar{p}_2 \pm z_{\alpha/2}\sqrt{\frac{\bar{p}_1(1 - \bar{p}_1)}{n_1} + \frac{\bar{p}_2(1 - \bar{p}_2)}{n_2}} \qquad \textbf{(10.13)}$$

where $1 - \alpha$ is the confidence coefficient.

Returning to the tax preparation example, we find that independent simple random samples from the two offices provide the following information.

Office 1	Office 2
$n_1 = 250$	$n_2 = 300$
Number of returns with errors = 35	Number of returns with errors = 27

TaxPrep

The sample proportions for the two offices follow.

$$\bar{p}_1 = \frac{35}{250} = .14$$

$$\bar{p}_2 = \frac{27}{300} = .09$$

The point estimate of the difference between the proportions of erroneous tax returns for the two populations is $\bar{p}_1 - \bar{p}_2 = .14 - .09 = .05$. Thus, we estimate that office 1 has a .05, or 5%, greater error rate than office 2.

Expression (10.13) can now be used to provide a margin of error and interval estimate of the difference between the two population proportions. Using a 90% confidence interval with $z_{\alpha/2} = z_{.05} = 1.645$, we have

$$\bar{p}_1 - \bar{p}_2 \pm z_{\alpha/2} \sqrt{\frac{\bar{p}_1(1 - \bar{p}_1)}{n_1} + \frac{\bar{p}_2(1 - \bar{p}_2)}{n_2}}$$

$$.14 - .09 \pm 1.645 \sqrt{\frac{.14(1 - .14)}{250} + \frac{.09(1 - .09)}{300}}$$

$$.05 \pm .045$$

Thus, the margin of error is .045, and the 90% confidence interval is .005 to .095.

Using Excel to Construct a Confidence Interval

We can create a worksheet for developing an interval estimate of the difference between population proportions. Let us illustrate by developing an interval estimate of the difference between the proportions of erroneous tax returns at the two offices of the tax preparation firm. Refer to Figure 10.10 as we describe the tasks involved. The formula worksheet is in the background; the value worksheet appears in the foreground.

Enter Data: Columns A and B contain Yes or No labels that indicate which of the tax returns from each office contain an error.

Enter Functions and Formulas: The descriptive statistics needed are provided in cells E5:F5 and E7:F8. Note that Excel's COUNTA function is used in cells E5 and F5 to count the number of observations for each of the samples. The value worksheet indicates 250 returns in the sample from office 1 and 300 returns in the sample from office 2. In cells E6 and F6, we type Yes to indicate the response of interest (an erroneous return). Excel's COUNTIF function is used in cells E7 and F7 to count the number of Yes responses from each office. Formulas entered into cells E8 and F8 compute the sample proportions. The confidence coefficient entered into cell E10 (.9) is used to compute the corresponding level of significance ($\alpha = .10$) in cell E11. In cell E12 we use the NORMSINV function to compute the z value needed to compute the margin of error for the interval estimate.

FIGURE 10.10   CONSTRUCTING A 90% CONFIDENCE INTERVAL FOR THE DIFFERENCE IN THE PROPORTION OF ERRONEOUS TAX RETURNS PREPARED BY TWO OFFICES

	A	B	C	D	E	F	G
1	Office 1	Office 2			Interval Estimate of Difference		
2	No	No			in Population Proportions		
3	No	No					
4	No	No			Office 1	Office 2	
5	No	No		Sample Size	=COUNTA(A2:A251)	=COUNTA(B2:B301)	
6	No	No		Response of Interest	Yes	Yes	
7	Yes	No		Count for Response	=COUNTIF(A2:A251,E6)	=COUNTIF(B2:B301,F6)	
8	No	No		Sample Proportion	=E7/E5	=F7/F5	
9	No	No					
10	No	No		Confidence Coefficient	0.9		
11	No	No		Level of Significance	=1-E10		
12	No	No		z Value	=NORMSINV(1-E11/2)		
13	No	No					
14	No	No		Standard Error	=SQRT(E8*(1-E8)/E5+F8*(1-F8)/F5)		
15	No	No		Margin of Error	=E12*E14		
16	No	No					
17	No	Yes		Point Estimate of Difference	=E8-F8		
18	Yes	No		Lower Limit	=E17-E15		
19	No	No		Upper Limit	=E17+E15		
250	Yes	No					
251	No	No					
300		No					
301		No					
302							

	A	B	C	D	E	F	G
1	Office 1	Office 2			Interval Estimate of Difference		
2	No	No			in Population Proportions		
3	No	No					
4	No	No			Office 1	Office 2	
5	No	No		Sample Size	250	300	
6	No	No		Response of Interest	Yes	Yes	
7	Yes	No		Count for Response	35	27	
8	No	No		Sample Proportion	0.14	0.09	
9	No	No					
10	No	No		Confidence Coefficient	0.9		
11	No	No		Level of Significance	0.1		
12	No	No		z Value	1.645		
13	No	No					
14	No	No		Standard Error	0.0275		
15	No	No		Margin of Error	0.0452		
16	No	No					
17	No	Yes		Point Estimate of Difference	0.05		
18	Yes	No		Lower Limit	0.0048		
19	No	No		Upper Limit	0.0952		
250	Yes	No					
251	No	No					
300		No					
301		No					
302							

Note: Rows 20–249 and 252–299 are hidden.

In cell E14, a point estimate of $\sigma_{\bar{p}_1-\bar{p}_2}$, the standard error of the point estimator $\bar{p}_1 - \bar{p}_2$, is computed based on the two sample proportions (E8 and F8) and sample sizes (E5 and F5). The margin of error is then computed in cell E15 by multiplying the z value by the estimate of the standard error.

The point estimate of the difference in the two population proportions is computed in cell E17 as the difference in the sample proportions; the result, shown in the value worksheet, is .05. The lower limit of the confidence interval is computed in cell E18 by subtracting the margin of error from the point estimate. The upper limit is computed in cell E19 by adding the margin of error to the point estimate. The value worksheet shows that the

90% confidence interval estimate of the difference in the two population proportions is .0048 to .0952.

A Template for Other Problems. This worksheet can be used as a template for other problems requiring an interval estimate of the difference in population proportions. The new data must be entered in columns A and B. The data ranges in the cells used to compute the sample size (E5:F5) and the cells used to compute a count of the response of interest (E7:F7) must be changed to correctly indicate the location of the new data. The response of interest must be typed into cells E6:F6. The 90% confidence interval for the new data will then appear in cells E17:E19. If an interval estimate with a different confidence coefficient is desired, simply change the entry in cell E10.

This worksheet can also be used as a template for solving text exercises in which the sample data have already been summarized. No change in the data section is necessary. Simply type the values for the given sample sizes in cells E5:F5 and type the given values for the sample proportions in cells E8:F8. The 90% confidence interval will then appear in cells E17:E19. If an interval estimate with a different confidence coefficient is desired, simply change the entry in cell E10.

Hypothesis Tests About $p_1 - p_2$

Let us now consider hypothesis tests about the difference between the proportions of two populations. We focus on tests involving no difference between the two population proportions. In this case, the three forms for a hypothesis test are as follows:

All hypotheses considered use 0 as the difference of interest.

$$H_0: p_1 - p_2 \geq 0 \qquad H_0: p_1 - p_2 \leq 0 \qquad H_0: p_1 - p_2 = 0$$
$$H_a: p_1 - p_2 < 0 \qquad H_a: p_1 - p_2 > 0 \qquad H_a: p_1 - p_2 \neq 0$$

When we assume H_0 is true as an equality, we have $p_1 - p_2 = 0$, which is the same as saying that the population proportions are equal, $p_1 = p_2$.

We will base the test statistic on the sampling distribution of the point estimator $\bar{p}_1 - \bar{p}_2$. In equation (10.11), we showed that the standard error of $\bar{p}_1 - \bar{p}_2$ is given by

$$\sigma_{\bar{p}_1 - \bar{p}_2} = \sqrt{\frac{p_1(1 - p_1)}{n_1} + \frac{p_2(1 - p_2)}{n_2}}$$

Under the assumption H_0 is true as an equality, the population proportions are equal and $p_1 = p_2 = p$. In this case, $\sigma_{\bar{p}_1 - \bar{p}_2}$ becomes

$$\sigma_{\bar{p}_1 - \bar{p}_2} = \sqrt{\frac{p(1 - p)}{n_1} + \frac{p(1 - p)}{n_2}} = \sqrt{p(1 - p)\left(\frac{1}{n_1} + \frac{1}{n_2}\right)} \qquad \textbf{(10.14)}$$

With p unknown, we pool, or combine, the point estimators from the two samples ($\bar{p}_1$ and $\bar{p}_2$) to obtain a single point estimator of p as follows:

$$\bar{p} = \frac{n_1 \bar{p}_1 + n_2 \bar{p}_2}{n_1 + n_2} \qquad \textbf{(10.15)}$$

This **pooled estimator of p** is a weighted average of $\bar{p}_1$ and $\bar{p}_2$.

Substituting $\bar{p}$ for p in equation (10.14), we obtain an estimate of the standard error of $\bar{p}_1 - \bar{p}_2$. This estimate of the standard error is used in the test statistic. The general form of the test statistic for hypothesis tests about the difference between two population proportions is the point estimator divided by the estimate of $\sigma_{\bar{p}_1 - \bar{p}_2}$.

> **TEST STATISTIC FOR HYPOTHESIS TESTS ABOUT $p_1 - p_2$**
>
> $$z = \frac{(\bar{p}_1 - \bar{p}_2)}{\sqrt{\bar{p}(1 - \bar{p})\left(\dfrac{1}{n_1} + \dfrac{1}{n_2}\right)}}$$
>
> **(10.16)**

This test statistic applies to large sample situations where $n_1 p_1$, $n_1(1 - p_1)$, $n_2 p_2$, and $n_2(1 - p_2)$ are all greater than or equal to 5.

Let us return to the tax preparation firm example and assume that the firm wants to use a hypothesis test to determine whether the error proportions differ between the two offices. A two-tailed test is required. The null and alternative hypotheses are as follows:

$$H_0: p_1 - p_2 = 0$$
$$H_a: p_1 - p_2 \neq 0$$

If H_0 is rejected, the firm can conclude that the error rates at the two offices differ. We will use $\alpha = .10$ as the level of significance.

The sample data previously collected showed $\bar{p}_1 = .14$ for the $n_1 = 250$ returns sampled at office 1 and $\bar{p}_2 = .09$ for the $n_2 = 300$ returns sampled at office 2. We continue by computing the pooled estimate of p.

$$\bar{p} = \frac{n_1 \bar{p}_1 + n_2 \bar{p}_2}{n_1 + n_2} = \frac{250(.14) + 300(.09)}{250 + 300} = .1127$$

Using this pooled estimate and the difference between the sample proportions, the value of the test statistic is as follows.

$$z = \frac{(\bar{p}_1 - \bar{p}_2)}{\sqrt{\bar{p}(1 - \bar{p})\left(\dfrac{1}{n_1} + \dfrac{1}{n_2}\right)}} = \frac{(.14 - .09)}{\sqrt{.1127(1 - .1127)\left(\dfrac{1}{250} + \dfrac{1}{300}\right)}} = 1.85$$

In computing the p-value for this two-tailed test, we first note that $z = 1.85$ is in the upper tail of the standard normal distribution. Using $z = 1.85$ and the standard normal distribution table, we find the area in the upper tail is $1.0000 - .9678 = .0322$. Doubling this area for a two-tailed test, we find the p-value $= 2(.0322) = .0644$. With the p-value less than $\alpha = .10$, H_0 is rejected at the .10 level of significance. The firm can conclude that the error rates differ between the two offices. This hypothesis testing conclusion is consistent with the earlier 90% confidence interval results that showed the interval estimate of the difference between the population error rates at the two offices to be .005 to .095, with office 1 having the higher error rate.

Using Excel to Conduct a Hypothesis Test

We can create a worksheet for conducting a hypothesis test about the difference between population proportions. Let us illustrate by testing to see whether there is a significant difference between the proportions of erroneous tax returns at the two offices of the tax preparation firm. Refer to Figure 10.11 as we describe the tasks involved. The formula worksheet is in the background; the value worksheet is in the foreground.

FIGURE 10.11   HYPOTHESIS TEST CONCERNING DIFFERENCE IN PROPORTION OF ERRONEOUS TAX RETURNS PREPARED BY TWO OFFICES

	A	B	C	D	E	F	G
1	Office 1	Office 2		Hypothesis Test Concerning Difference			
2	No	No		Between Population Proportions			
3	No	No					
4	No	No			Office 1	Office 2	
5	No	No		Sample Size	=COUNTA(A2:A251)	=COUNTA(B2:B301)	
6	No	No		Response of Interest	Yes	Yes	
7	Yes	No		Count for Response	=COUNTIF(A2:A251,E6)	=COUNTIF(B2:B301,F6)	
8	No	No		Sample Proportion	=E7/E5	=F7/F5	
9	No	No					
10	No	No		Hypothesized Value	0		
11	No	No		Point Estimate of Difference	=E8-F8		
12	No	No					
13	No	No		Pooled Estimate of p	=(E5*E8+F5*F8)/(E5+F5)		
14	No	No		Standard Error	=SQRT(E13*(1-E13)*(1/E5+1/F5))		
15	No	No		Test Statistic	=(E11-E10)/E14		
16	No	No					
17	No	Yes		p-value (Lower Tail)	=NORMSDIST(E15)		
18	Yes	No		p-value (Upper Tail)	=1-NORMSDIST(E15)		
19	No	No		p-value (Two Tail)	=2*MIN(E17,E18)		
250	Yes	No					
251	No	No					
300		No					
301		No					
302							

	A	B	C	D	E	F	G
1	Office 1	Office 2		Hypothesis Test Concerning Difference			
2	No	No		Between Population Proportions			
3	No	No					
4	No	No			Office 1	Office 2	
5	No	No		Sample Size	250	300	
6	No	No		Response of Interest	Yes	Yes	
7	Yes	No		Count for Response	35	27	
8	No	No		Sample Proportion	0.14	0.09	
9	No	No					
10	No	No		Hypothesized Value	0		
11	No	No		Point Estimate of Difference	0.05		
12	No	No					
13	No	No		Pooled Estimate of p	0.1127		
14	No	No		Standard Error	0.0271		
15	No	No		Test Statistic	1.8462		
16	No	No					
17	No	Yes		p-value (Lower Tail)	0.9676		
18	Yes	No		p-value (Upper Tail)	0.0324		
19	No	No		p-value (Two Tail)	0.0649		
250	Yes	No					
251	No	No					
300		No					
301		No					
302							

Note: Rows 20–249 and 252–299 are hidden.

Enter Data: Columns A and B contain Yes or No labels that indicate which of the tax returns from each office contain an error.

Enter Functions and Formulas: The descriptive statistics needed to perform the hypothesis test are provided in cells E5:F6 and E7:F8. They are the same as the ones used for an interval estimate (see Figure 10.10). The hypothesized value of the difference between the two populations is zero; it is entered into cell E10. In cell E11, the difference in the sample proportions is used to compute a point estimate of the difference in the two population proportions. Using the two sample proportions and sample sizes, a pooled estimate of the population proportion p is computed in cell E13; its value is .1127. Then, in cell E14, an estimate of $\sigma_{\bar{p}_1 - \bar{p}_2}$ is computed using equation (10.14), with the pooled estimate of p and the sample sizes.

The formula =(E11−E10)/E14 entered into cell E15 computes the test statistic z (1.8462). The NORMSDIST function is then used to compute the p-value (Lower Tail) and the p-value (Upper Tail) in cells E17 and E18. The p-value (Two Tail) is computed in cell E19 as twice the minimum of the 2 one-tailed p-values. The value worksheet shows that p-value (Two Tail) = .0649. Because the p-value = .0649 is less than the level of significance, $\alpha = .10$, we have sufficient evidence to reject the null hypothesis and conclude that the population proportions are not equal.

The p-value here (.0649) differs from the one we found using the cumulative normal probability tables (.0644) due to rounding.

This worksheet can be used as a template for hypothesis testing problems involving differences between population proportions. The new data can be entered into columns A and B. The ranges for the new data and the response of interest need to be revised in cells E5:F7. The remainder of the worksheet will then be updated as needed to conduct the hypothesis test. If a hypothesized difference other than 0 is to be used, the new value must be entered in cell E10.

To use this worksheet for exercises in which the sample statistics are given, just type in the given values for cells E5:F5 and E7:F8. The remainder of the worksheet will then be updated to conduct the hypothesis test. If a hypothesized difference other than 0 is to be used, the new value must be entered in cell E10.

Exercises

Methods

27. Consider the following results for independent samples taken from two populations.

Sample 1	Sample 2
$n_1 = 400$	$n_2 = 300$
$\bar{p}_1 = .48$	$\bar{p}_2 = .36$

a. What is the point estimate of the difference between the two population proportions?
b. Develop a 90% confidence interval for the difference between the two population proportions.
c. Develop a 95% confidence interval for the difference between the two population proportions.

28. Consider the hypothesis test

$$H_0: p_1 - p_2 \leq 0$$
$$H_a: p_1 - p_2 > 0$$

The following results are for independent samples taken from the two populations.

Sample 1	Sample 2
$n_1 = 200$	$n_2 = 300$
$\bar{p}_1 = .22$	$\bar{p}_2 = .16$

a. What is the p-value?
b. With $\alpha = .05$, what is your hypothesis testing conclusion?

Applications

29. A *BusinessWeek/*Harris survey asked senior executives at large corporations their opinions about the economic outlook for the future. One question was "Do you think that there will be an increase in the number of full-time employees at your company over the next 12 months?" In the current survey, 220 of 400 executives answered yes, while in a previous year's survey, 192 of 400 executives had answered yes. Provide a 95% confidence interval estimate for the difference between the proportions at the two points in time. What is your interpretation of the interval estimate?

30. In recent years, the number of people who use the Internet to obtain political news has grown. Often the political Web sites ask Internet users to register their opinions by participating in online surveys. Pew Research Center conducted a survey of its own to learn about the participation of Republicans and Democrats in online surveys (Associated Press, January 6, 2003). The following sample data apply.

Political Party	Sample Size	Participate in Online Surveys
Republican	250	115
Democrat	350	98

a. Compute the point estimate of the proportion of Republicans who indicate they would participate in online surveys. Compute the point estimate for the Democrats.
b. What is the point estimate of the difference between the two population proportions?
c. At 95% confidence, what is the margin of error?
d. Representatives of the scientific polling industry claim that the profusion of online surveys can confuse people about actual public opinion. Do you agree with this statement? Use the 95% confidence interval estimate of the difference between the Republican and Democrat population proportions to help justify your answer.

31. Slot machines are the favorite game at casinos throughout the United States (*Harrah's Survey 2002: Profile of the American Gamble*). The following sample data show the number of women and number of men who selected slot machines as their favorite game.

	Women	Men
Sample Size	320	250
Favorite Game–Slots	256	165

a. What is the point estimate of the proportion of women who say slots is their favorite game?
b. What is the point estimate of the proportion of men who say slots is their favorite game?
c. Provide a 95% confidence interval estimate of the difference between the proportion of women and proportion of men who say slots is their favorite game.

32. The Bureau of Transportation tracks the flight arrival performances of the 10 biggest airlines in the United States (*The Wall Street Journal,* March 4, 2003). Flights that arrive within 15 minutes of schedule are considered on time. Using sample data consistent with Bureau of Transportation statistics reported in January 2001 and January 2002, consider the following:

January 2001 A sample of 924 flights showed 742 on time.
January 2002 A sample of 841 flights showed 714 on time.

    a.   What is the point estimate of on-time flights in January 2001?

    b.   What is the point estimate of on-time flights in January 2002?

    c.   Let p_1 denote the population proportion of on-time flights in January 2001 and p_2 denote the population proportion of on-time flights in January 2002. State the hypotheses that could be tested to determine whether the major airlines improved on-time flight performance during the one-year period.

    d.   What is the p-value? At $\alpha = .05$, what is your conclusion?

33.   In a test of the quality of two television commercials, each commercial was shown in a separate test area six times over a one-week period. The following week a telephone survey was conducted to identify individuals who had seen the commercials. Those individuals were asked to state the primary message in the commercials. The following results were recorded.

	Commercial A	Commercial B
Number Who Saw Commercial	150	200
Number Who Recalled Message	63	60

    a.   Use $\alpha = .05$ and test the hypothesis that there is no difference in the recall proportions for the two commercials.

    b.   Compute a 95% confidence interval for the difference between the recall proportions for the two populations.

34.   During the 2003 Super Bowl, Miller Lite Beer's commercial referred to as "The Miller Lite Girls" ranked among the top three most effective advertisements aired during the Super Bowl (*USA Today*, December 29, 2003). The survey of advertising effectiveness, conducted by *USA Today*'s Ad Track poll, reported separate samples by respondent age group to learn about how the Super Bowl advertisement appealed to different age groups. The following sample data apply to the "The Miller Lite Girls" commercial.

Age Group	Sample Size	Liked the Ad a Lot
Under 30	100	49
30 to 49	150	54

    a.   Formulate a hypothesis test that can be used to determine whether there is a difference between the population proportions for the two age groups.

    b.   What is the point estimate of the difference between the two population proportions?

    c.   Conduct the hypothesis test and report the p-value. At $\alpha = .05$, what is your conclusion?

    d.   Discuss the appeal of the advertisements to the younger and the older age groups. Would the Miller Lite organization find the results of the *USA Today* Ad Track poll encouraging? Explain.

35.   A 2003 *New York Times*/CBS News poll sampled 523 adults who were planning a vacation during the next six months and found that 141 were expecting to travel by airplane (*New York Times News Service*, March 2, 2003). A similar survey question in a May 1993 *New York Times*/CBS News poll found that of 477 adults who were planning a vacation in the next six months, 81 were expecting to travel by airplane.

    a.   State the hypotheses that can be used to determine whether a significant change occurred in the population proportion planning to travel by airplane over the 10-year period.

    b.   What is the sample proportion expecting to travel by airplane in 2003? In 1993?

    c.   Use $\alpha = .01$ and test for a significant difference. What is your conclusion?

    d.   Discuss reasons that might provide an explanation for this conclusion.

36. *Yahoo! Internet Life* sponsored surveys in several metropolitan areas to estimate the proportion of adults using the Internet at work (*USA Today,* May 7, 2000). Results showed 40% of Washington, D.C., adults use the Internet at work, while 32% of San Francisco adults use the Internet at work. If the sample sizes are 240 and 250, respectively, do the sample results indicate that the population proportion of adults using the Internet at work in Washington, D.C., is greater than the population proportion in San Francisco? What is the *p*-value? Using $\alpha = .05$, what is the conclusion?

Summary

In this chapter we discussed procedures for developing interval estimates and conducting hypothesis tests involving two populations. First, we showed how to make inferences about the difference between two population means when independent simple random samples are selected. We first considered the case where the population standard deviations σ_1 and σ_2 could be assumed known. The standard normal distribution z was used to develop the interval estimate and served as the test statistic for hypothesis tests. We then considered the case where the population standard deviations were unknown and estimated by the sample standard deviations s_1 and s_2. In this case, the t distribution was used to develop the interval estimate and the t value served as the test statistic for hypothesis tests.

Inferences about the difference between two population means were then discussed for the matched sample design. In the matched sample design each element provides a pair of data values, one from each population. The difference between the paired data values is then used in the statistical analysis. The matched sample design is generally preferred to the independent sample design because the matched-sample procedure often improves the precision of the estimate.

Finally, interval estimation and hypothesis testing about the difference between two population proportions were discussed. Statistical procedures for analyzing the difference between two population proportions are similar to the procedures for analyzing the difference between two population means.

We showed how Excel can be used to develop the interval estimates and conduct the hypothesis tests discussed in the chapter. Many of the worksheets can be used as templates to solve problems encountered in practice as well as the exercises and case problems found in the text.

Glossary

Independent samples Samples selected from two populations in such a way that the elements making up one sample are chosen independently of the elements making up the other sample.

Matched samples Samples in which each data value of one sample is matched with a corresponding data value of the other sample.

Pooled estimator of *p* An estimator of a population proportion obtained by computing a weighted average of the point estimators obtained from two independent samples.

Key Formulas

Point Estimator of the Difference Between Two Population Means

$$\bar{x}_1 - \bar{x}_2 \qquad\qquad (10.1)$$

Standard Error of $\bar{x}_1 - \bar{x}_2$

$$\sigma_{\bar{x}_1-\bar{x}_2} = \sqrt{\frac{\sigma_1^2}{n_1} + \frac{\sigma_2^2}{n_2}} \tag{10.2}$$

Interval Estimate of the Difference Between Two Population Means: σ_1 and σ_2 Known

$$\bar{x}_1 - \bar{x}_2 \pm z_{\alpha/2}\sqrt{\frac{\sigma_1^2}{n_1} + \frac{\sigma_2^2}{n_2}} \tag{10.4}$$

Test Statistic for Hypothesis Tests About $\mu_1 - \mu_2$: σ_1 and σ_2 Known

$$z = \frac{(\bar{x}_1 - \bar{x}_2) - D_0}{\sqrt{\dfrac{\sigma_1^2}{n_1} + \dfrac{\sigma_2^2}{n_2}}} \tag{10.5}$$

Interval Estimate of the Difference Between Two Population Means: σ_1 and σ_2 Unknown

$$\bar{x}_1 - \bar{x}_2 \pm t_{\alpha/2}\sqrt{\frac{s_1^2}{n_1} + \frac{s_2^2}{n_2}} \tag{10.6}$$

Degrees of Freedom: t Distribution with Two Independent Random Samples

$$df = \frac{\left(\dfrac{s_1^2}{n_1} + \dfrac{s_2^2}{n_2}\right)^2}{\dfrac{1}{n_1-1}\left(\dfrac{s_1^2}{n_1}\right)^2 + \dfrac{1}{n_2-1}\left(\dfrac{s_2^2}{n_2}\right)^2} \tag{10.7}$$

Test Statistic for Hypothesis Tests About $\mu_1 - \mu_2$: σ_1 and σ_2 Unknown

$$t = \frac{(\bar{x}_1 - \bar{x}_2) - D_0}{\sqrt{\dfrac{s_1^2}{n_1} + \dfrac{s_2^2}{n_2}}} \tag{10.8}$$

Test Statistic for Hypothesis Tests Involving Matched Samples

$$t = \frac{\bar{d} - \mu_d}{s_d/\sqrt{n}} \tag{10.9}$$

Point Estimate of the Difference Between Two Population Proportions

$$\bar{p}_1 - \bar{p}_2 \tag{10.10}$$

Standard Error of $\bar{p}_1 - \bar{p}_2$

$$\sigma_{\bar{p}_1-\bar{p}_2} = \sqrt{\frac{p_1(1-p_1)}{n_1} + \frac{p_2(1-p_2)}{n_2}} \tag{10.11}$$

Interval Estimate of the Difference Between Two Population Proportions

$$\bar{p}_1 - \bar{p}_2 \pm z_{\alpha/2}\sqrt{\frac{\bar{p}_1(1-\bar{p}_1)}{n_1} + \frac{\bar{p}_2(1-\bar{p}_2)}{n_2}} \tag{10.13}$$

Standard Error of $\bar{p}_1 - \bar{p}_2$ **When** $p_1 = p_2 = p$

$$\sigma_{\bar{p}_1 - \bar{p}_2} = \sqrt{p(1-p)\left(\frac{1}{n_1} + \frac{1}{n_2}\right)} \tag{10.14}$$

Pooled Estimator of p **When** $p_1 = p_2 = p$

$$\bar{p} = \frac{n_1\bar{p}_1 + n_2\bar{p}_2}{n_1 + n_2} \tag{10.15}$$

Test Statistic for Hypothesis Tests About $p_1 - p_2$

$$z = \frac{(\bar{p}_1 - \bar{p}_2)}{\sqrt{\bar{p}(1-\bar{p})\left(\frac{1}{n_1} + \frac{1}{n_2}\right)}} \tag{10.16}$$

Supplementary Exercises

37. Safegate Foods, Inc., is redesigning the checkout lanes in its supermarkets throughout the country and is considering two designs. Tests on customer checkout times conducted at two stores where the two new systems have been installed result in the following summary of the data.

System A	System B
$n_1 = 120$	$n_2 = 100$
$\bar{x}_1 = 4.1$ minutes	$\bar{x}_2 = 3.4$ minutes
$\sigma_1 = 2.2$ minutes	$\sigma_2 = 1.5$ minutes

Test at the .05 level of significance to determine whether the population mean checkout times of the two systems differ. Which system is preferred?

38. Starting annual salaries for individuals with master's and bachelor's degrees in business were collected in two independent random samples. Use the following data to develop a 90% confidence interval estimate of the increase in starting salary that can be expected upon completion of a master's program.

Master's Degree	Bachelor's Degree
$n_1 = 60$	$n_2 = 80$
$\bar{x}_1 = \$45,000$	$\bar{x}_2 = \$35,000$
$\sigma_1 = \$4000$	$\sigma_2 = \$3500$

39. Three-megapixel digital cameras are typically the lightest, most compact, and easiest to use. However, if you plan to enlarge or crop images, you will probably want to spend more for a higher-resolution model. The following shows sample prices of five-megapixel and three-megapixel digital cameras (*Consumer Reports Buying Guide*, 2004).

Digital

Five-Megapixel		Three-Megapixel	
Model	**Price**	**Model**	**Price**
Nikon 5700	890	Kodak DX4330	280
Olympus C-5050	620	Canon A70	290
Sony DCS-F717	730	Sony DSC P8	370
Olympus C-5050	480	Minolta XI	400
Minolta 7Hi	1060	Sony DSC P72	310
HP 935	450	Nikon 3100	340
Pentax 550	540	Panasonic DMC-LC33	270
Canon S50	500	Pentax S	380
Kyocera TVS	890		
Minolta F300	440		

a. Provide a point estimate of the difference between population mean prices for the two types of digital cameras. What observation can you make about the price of the higher-quality five-megapixel model?

b. Develop a 95% confidence interval estimate of the difference between the two population mean prices.

40. Mutual funds are classified as *load* or *no-load* funds. Load funds require an investor to pay an initial fee based on a percentage of the amount invested in the fund. The no-load funds do not require this initial fee. Some financial advisors argue that the load mutual funds may be worth the extra fee because these funds provide a higher mean rate of return than the no-load mutual funds. A sample of 30 load mutual funds and a sample of 30 no-load mutual funds were selected. Data were collected on the annual return for the funds over a five-year period. The data are contained in the data set Mutual. The data for the first five load and first five no-load mutual funds are as follows.

Mutual

Mutual Funds—Load	Return	Mutual Funds—No Load	Return
American National Growth	15.51	Amana Income Fund	13.24
Arch Small Cap Equity	14.57	Berger One Hundred	12.13
Bartlett Cap Basic	17.73	Columbia International Stock	12.17
Calvert World International	10.31	Dodge & Cox Balanced	16.06
Colonial Fund A	16.23	Evergreen Fund	17.61

a. Formulate H_0 and H_a such that rejection of H_0 leads to the conclusion that the load mutual funds have a higher mean annual return over the five-year period.

b. Use the 60 mutual funds in the data set Mutual to conduct the hypothesis test. What is the *p*-value? At $\alpha = .05$, what is your conclusion?

41. The National Association of Home Builders provided data on the cost of the most popular home remodeling projects. Sample data on cost in thousands of dollars for two types of remodeling projects are as follows.

Kitchen	Master Bedroom	Kitchen	Master Bedroom
25.2	18.0	23.0	17.8
17.4	22.9	19.7	24.6
22.8	26.4	16.9	21.0
21.9	24.8	21.8	
19.7	26.9	23.6	

a.   Develop a point estimate of the difference between the population mean remodeling costs for the two types of projects.

b.   Develop a 90% confidence interval for the difference between the two population means.

42.   Typical prices of single-family homes in the state of Florida are shown for a sample of 15 metropolitan areas (*Naples Daily News,* February 23, 2003). Data are in thousands of dollars.

Florida

Metropolitan Area	January 2003	January 2002
Daytona Beach	117	96
Fort Lauderdale	207	169
Fort Myers	143	129
Fort Walton Beach	139	134
Gainesville	131	119
Jacksonville	128	119
Lakeland	91	85
Miami	193	165
Naples	263	233
Ocala	86	90
Orlando	134	121
Pensacola	111	105
Sarasota-Bradenton	168	141
Tallahassee	140	130
Tampa-St. Petersburg	139	129

a.   Use a matched-sample analysis to develop a point estimate of the population mean one-year increase in the price of single-family homes in Florida.

b.   Develop a 90% confidence interval estimate of the population mean one-year increase in the price of single-family homes in Florida.

c.   What was the percentage increase over the one-year period?

43.   Jupiter Media used a survey to determine how people use their free time. Watching television was the most popular activity selected by both men and women (*The Wall Street Journal,* January 26, 2004). The proportion of men and the proportion of women who selected watching television as their most popular leisure time activity can be estimated from the following sample data.

Gender	Sample Size	Watching Television
Men	800	248
Women	600	156

a.   State the hypotheses that can be used to test for a difference between the proportion for the population of men and the proportion for the population of women who selected watching television as their most popular leisure time activity.

b.   What is the sample proportion of men who selected watching television as their most popular leisure time activity? What is the sample proportion of women?

c.   Conduct the hypothesis test and compute the *p*-value. At a .05 level of significance, what is your conclusion?

d.   What is the margin of error and 95% confidence interval estimate of the difference between the population proportions?

44.   A large automobile insurance company selected samples of single and married male policy-holders and recorded the number who made an insurance claim over the preceding three-year period.

Single Policyholders	Married Policyholders
$n_1 = 400$	$n_2 = 900$
Number making claims $= 76$	Number making claims $= 90$

a. Use $\alpha = .05$. Test to determine whether the claim rates differ between single and married male policyholders.

b. Provide a 95% confidence interval for the difference between the proportions for the two populations.

45. Medical tests were conducted to learn about drug-resistant tuberculosis. Of 142 cases tested in New Jersey, 9 were found to be drug-resistant. Of 268 cases tested in Texas, 5 were found to be drug-resistant. Do these data suggest a statistically significant difference between the proportions of drug-resistant cases in the two states? Use a .02 level of significance. What is the p-value, and what is your conclusion?

46. In July 2001, the Harris Ad Track Research Service conducted a survey to evaluate the effectiveness of a major advertising campaign for Kodak cameras (*USA Today*, August 27, 2001). In a sample of 430 respondents, 38% thought the ads were very effective. In another sample of 285 respondents to other ad campaigns, 23% thought the ads were very effective.

a. Estimate the number of respondents who thought the Kodak ads were very effective and the number of respondents who felt the other ads were very effective.

b. Provide a 95% confidence interval for the difference in proportions.

c. On the basis of your results in part (b), do you believe the Kodak advertising campaign is more effective than most advertising campaigns?

47. In June 2001, 38% of fund managers surveyed believed that the core inflation rate would be higher in one year. One month later a similar survey revealed that 22% of fund managers expected the core inflation rate to be higher in one year (*Global Research Highlights*, Merrill Lynch, July 20, 2001). Assume that the sample size was 200 in both the June and July surveys.

a. Develop a point estimate of the difference between the June and July proportions of fund managers who felt the core inflation rate would be higher in one year.

b. Develop hypotheses such that rejection of the null hypothesis allows us to conclude that inflation expectations diminished between June and July.

c. Conduct a test of the hypotheses in part (b) using $\alpha = .01$. What is your conclusion?

Case Problem   Par, Inc.

Par, Inc., is a major manufacturer of golf equipment. Management believes that Par's market share could be increased with the introduction of a cut-resistant, longer-lasting golf ball. Therefore, the research group at Par has been investigating a new golf ball coating designed to resist cuts and provide a more durable ball. The tests with the coating have been promising.

One of the researchers voiced concern about the effect of the new coating on driving distances. Par would like the new cut-resistant ball to offer driving distances comparable to those of the current-model golf ball. To compare the driving distances for the two balls, 40 balls of both the new and current models were subjected to distance tests. The testing was performed with a mechanical hitting machine so that any difference between the mean distances for the two models could be attributed to a difference in the two models. The results of the tests, with distances measured to the nearest yard, follow. These data are available on the CD that accompanies the text.

Model		Model		Model		Model	
Current	**New**	**Current**	**New**	**Current**	**New**	**Current**	**New**
264	277	270	272	263	274	281	283
261	269	287	259	264	266	274	250
267	263	289	264	284	262	273	253
272	266	280	280	263	271	263	260
258	262	272	274	260	260	275	270
283	251	275	281	283	281	267	263
258	262	265	276	255	250	279	261
266	289	260	269	272	263	274	255
259	286	278	268	266	278	276	263
270	264	275	262	268	264	262	279

Golf

Managerial Report

1. Formulate and present the rationale for a hypothesis test that Par could use to compare the driving distances of the current and new golf balls.
2. Analyze the data to provide the hypothesis testing conclusion. What is the *p*-value for your test? What is your recommendation for Par, Inc.?
3. Provide descriptive statistical summaries of the data for each model.
4. What is the 95% confidence interval for the population mean of each model, and what is the 95% confidence interval for the difference between the means of the two populations?
5. Do you see a need for larger sample sizes and more testing with the golf balls? Discuss.

CHAPTER 11

Inferences About Population Variances

CONTENTS

STATISTICS IN PRACTICE:
U.S. GENERAL ACCOUNTING
OFFICE

11.1 INFERENCES ABOUT A
POPULATION VARIANCE
Interval Estimation
Using Excel to Construct a
Confidence Interval

Hypothesis Testing
Using Excel to Conduct a
Hypothesis Test

11.2 INFERENCES ABOUT TWO
POPULATION VARIANCES
Using Excel to Conduct a
Hypothesis Test

STATISTICS *in* PRACTICE

U.S. GENERAL ACCOUNTING OFFICE*
WASHINGTON, D.C.

The U.S. General Accounting Office (GAO) is an independent, nonpolitical audit organization in the legislative branch of the federal government. GAO evaluators determine the effectiveness of current and proposed federal programs. To carry out their duties, evaluators must be proficient in records review, legislative research, and statistical analysis techniques.

In one case, GAO evaluators studied a Department of Interior program established to help clean up the nation's rivers and lakes. As part of this program, federal grants were made to small cities throughout the United States. Congress asked the GAO to determine how effectively the program was operating. To do so, the GAO examined records and visited the sites of several waste treatment plants.

One objective of the GAO audit was to ensure that the effluent (treated sewage) at the plants met certain standards. Among other things the audits reviewed sample data on the oxygen content, the pH level, and the amount of suspended solids in the effluent. A requirement of the program was that a variety of tests be taken daily at each plant and that the collected data be sent periodically to the state engineering department. The GAO's investigation of the data showed whether various characteristics of the effluent were within acceptable limits.

For example, the mean or average pH level of the effluent was examined carefully. In addition, the variance in the reported pH levels was reviewed. The following hypothesis test was conducted about the variance in pH level for the population of effluent.

$$H_0: \sigma^2 = \sigma_0^2$$
$$H_a: \sigma^2 \neq \sigma_0^2$$

In this test, σ_0^2 is the population variance in pH level expected at a properly functioning plant. In one particular plant, the

Effluent at this facility must fall within a statistically determined pH range. © John Boyner/Corbis.

null hypothesis was rejected. Further analysis showed that this plant had a variance in pH level that was significantly less than normal.

The auditors visited the plant to examine the measuring equipment and to discuss their statistical findings with the plant manager. The auditors found that the measuring equipment was not being used because the operator did not know how to work it. Instead, the operator had been told by an engineer what level of pH was acceptable and had simply recorded similar values without actually conducting the test. The unusually low variance in this plant's data resulted in rejection of H_0. The GAO suspected that other plants might have similar problems and recommended an operator training program to improve the data collection aspect of the pollution control program.

In this chapter you will learn how to conduct statistical inferences about the variances of one and two populations. Two new probability distributions, the chi-square distribution and the F distribution, will be introduced and used to make interval estimates and hypothesis tests about population variances.

---

*The authors thank Art Foreman and Dale Ledman of the U.S. General Accounting Office for providing this Statistics in Practice.

In the preceding four chapters we examined methods of statistical inference involving population means and population proportions. In this chapter we expand the discussion to situations involving inferences about population variances. As an example of a case in which a variance can provide important decision-making information, consider the production process of filling containers with a liquid detergent product. The filling mechanism for the process is adjusted so that the mean filling weight is 16 ounces per container. Although a mean of 16 ounces is desired, the variance of the filling weights is also critical.

That is, even with the filling mechanism properly adjusted for the mean of 16 ounces, we cannot expect every container to have exactly 16 ounces. By selecting a sample of containers, we can compute a sample variance for the number of ounces placed in a container. This value will serve as an estimate of the variance for the population of containers being filled by the production process. If the sample variance is small, the production process will be continued. However, if the sample variance is excessive, overfilling and underfilling may be occurring even though the mean is correct at 16 ounces. In this case, the filling mechanism will be readjusted in an attempt to reduce the filling variance for the containers.

In many manufacturing applications, controlling the process variance is extremely important in maintaining quality.

In the first section we consider inferences about the variance of a single population. Subsequently, we will discuss procedures that can be used to make inferences about the variances of two populations.

11.1 Inferences About a Population Variance

The sample variance

$$s^2 = \frac{\Sigma(x_i - \bar{x})^2}{n - 1}$$

(11.1)

is the point estimator of the population variance σ^2. In using the sample variance as a basis for making inferences about a population variance, the sampling distribution of the quantity $(n - 1)s^2/\sigma^2$ is helpful. This sampling distribution is described as follows.

SAMPLING DISTRIBUTION OF $(n - 1)s^2/\sigma^2$

The chi-square distribution is based on sampling from a normal population.

Whenever a simple random sample of size n is selected from a normal population, the sampling distribution of

$$\frac{(n - 1)s^2}{\sigma^2}$$

(11.2)

has a chi-square distribution with $n - 1$ degrees of freedom.

Figure 11.1 shows some possible forms of the sampling distribution of $(n - 1)s^2/\sigma^2$.

Excel's CHIDIST function can be used to compute probabilities for the chi-square distribution.

Tables of areas or probabilities are readily available for the chi-square distribution. Since the sampling distribution of $(n - 1)s^2/\sigma^2$ is known to have a chi-square distribution whenever a simple random sample of size n is selected from a normal population, we can use the chi-square distribution to develop interval estimates and conduct hypothesis tests about a population variance.

Interval Estimation

To show how the chi-square distribution can be used to develop a confidence interval estimate of a population variance σ^2, suppose that we are interested in estimating the population variance for the container filling process mentioned in the chapter introduction. A sample of 20 containers is taken, and the sample variance for the filling weights is found to be $s^2 = .0025$. We know we cannot expect the variance of a sample of 20 containers to provide the exact value of the variance for the population of containers filled by the production process. Hence, our interest will be in developing an interval estimate for the population variance.

Detergent

FIGURE 11.1   EXAMPLES OF THE SAMPLING DISTRIBUTION OF $(n-1)s^2/\sigma^2$ (A CHI-SQUARE DISTRIBUTION)

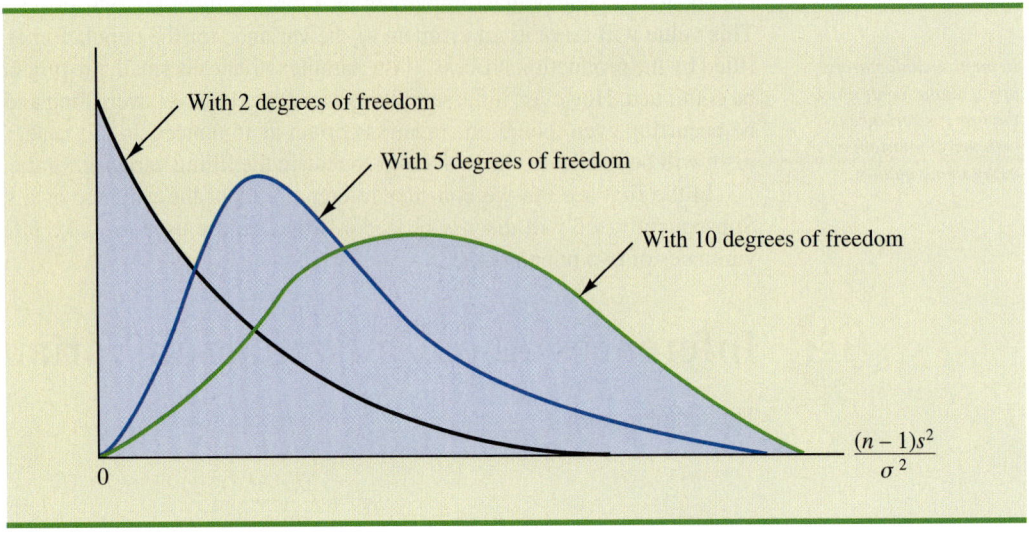

We will use the notation χ_α^2 to denote the value for the chi-square distribution that provides an area or probability of α to the *right* of the χ_α^2 value. For example, in Figure 11.2 the chi-square distribution with 19 degrees of freedom is shown with $\chi_{.025}^2 = 32.852$ indicating that 2.5% of the chi-square values are to the right of 32.852, and $\chi_{.975}^2 = 8.907$ indicating that 97.5% of the chi-square values are to the right of 8.907. Refer to Table 11.1 and verify that these chi-square values with 19 degrees of freedom (19th row of the table) are correct. Table 3 of Appendix B provides a more extensive table of chi-square values.

From the graph in Figure 11.2 we see that .95, or 95%, of the chi-square values are between $\chi_{.975}^2$ and $\chi_{.025}^2$. That is, there is a .95 probability of obtaining a χ^2 value such that

$$\chi_{.975}^2 \leq \chi^2 \leq \chi_{.025}^2$$

FIGURE 11.2   A CHI-SQUARE DISTRIBUTION WITH 19 DEGREES OF FREEDOM

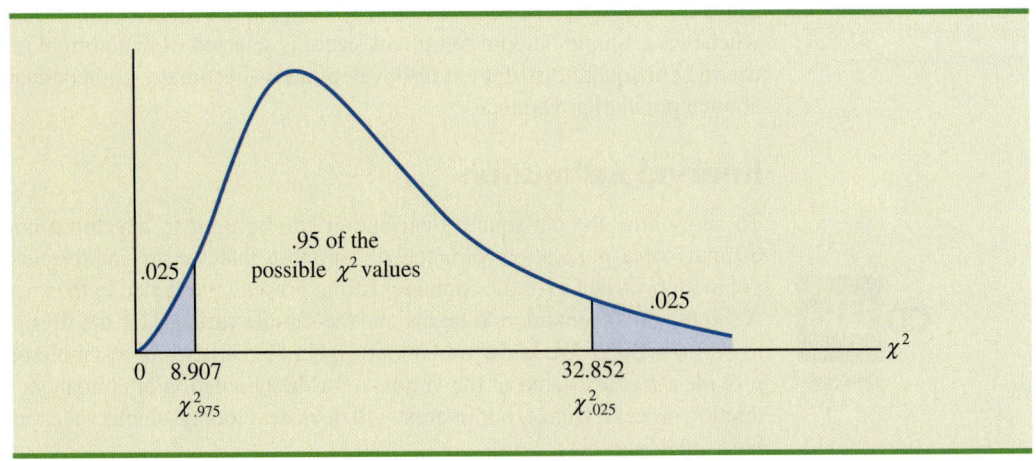

TABLE 11.1 SELECTED VALUES FROM THE CHI-SQUARE DISTRIBUTION TABLE*

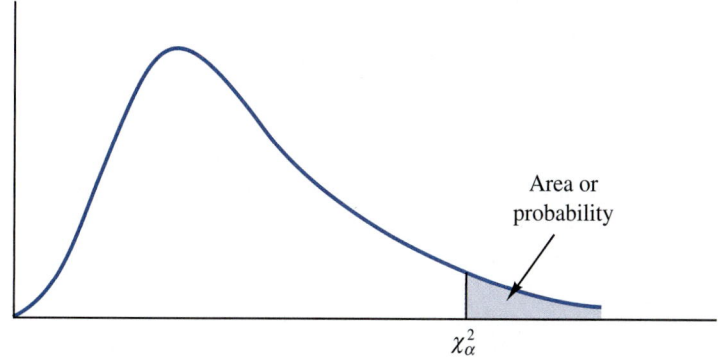

Degrees of Freedom	Area in Upper Tail							
	.99	**.975**	**.95**	**.90**	**.10**	**.05**	**.025**	**.01**
1	.000	.001	.004	.016	2.706	3.841	5.024	6.635
2	.020	.051	.103	.211	4.605	5.991	7.378	9.210
3	.115	.216	.352	.584	6.251	7.815	9.348	11.345
4	.297	.484	.711	1.064	7.779	9.488	11.143	13.277
5	.554	.831	1.145	1.610	9.236	11.070	12.832	15.086
6	.872	1.237	1.635	2.204	10.645	12.592	14.449	16.812
7	1.239	1.690	2.167	2.833	12.017	14.067	16.013	18.475
8	1.647	2.180	2.733	3.490	13.362	15.507	17.535	20.090
9	2.088	2.700	3.325	4.168	14.684	16.919	19.023	21.666
10	2.558	3.247	3.940	4.865	15.987	18.307	20.483	23.209
11	3.053	3.816	4.575	5.578	17.275	19.675	21.920	24.725
12	3.571	4.404	5.226	6.304	18.549	21.026	23.337	26.217
13	4.107	5.009	5.892	7.041	19.812	22.362	24.736	27.688
14	4.660	5.629	6.571	7.790	21.064	23.685	26.119	29.141
15	5.229	6.262	7.261	8.547	22.307	24.996	27.488	30.578
16	5.812	6.908	7.962	9.312	23.542	26.296	28.845	32.000
17	6.408	7.564	8.672	10.085	24.769	27.587	30.191	33.409
18	7.015	8.231	9.390	10.865	25.989	28.869	31.526	34.805
19	7.633	8.907	10.117	11.651	27.204	30.144	32.852	36.191
20	8.260	9.591	10.851	12.443	28.412	31.410	34.170	37.566
21	8.897	10.283	11.591	13.240	29.615	32.671	35.479	38.932
22	9.542	10.982	12.338	14.041	30.813	33.924	36.781	40.289
23	10.196	11.689	13.091	14.848	32.007	35.172	38.076	41.638
24	10.856	12.401	13.848	15.659	33.196	36.415	39.364	42.980
25	11.524	13.120	14.611	16.473	34.382	37.652	40.646	44.314
26	12.198	13.844	15.379	17.292	35.563	38.885	41.923	45.642
27	12.878	14.573	16.151	18.114	36.741	40.113	43.195	46.963
28	13.565	15.308	16.928	18.939	37.916	41.337	44.461	48.278
29	14.256	16.047	17.708	19.768	39.087	42.557	45.722	49.588
30	14.953	16.791	18.493	20.599	40.256	43.773	46.979	50.892
40	22.164	24.433	26.509	29.051	51.805	55.758	59.342	63.691
60	37.485	40.482	43.188	46.459	74.397	79.082	83.298	88.379
80	53.540	57.153	60.391	64.278	96.578	101.879	106.629	112.329
100	70.065	74.222	77.929	82.358	118.498	124.342	129.561	135.807

Note: A more extensive table is provided as Table 3 of Appendix B.

We stated in expression (11.2) that $(n - 1)s^2/\sigma^2$ follows a chi-square distribution, therefore we can substitute $(n - 1)s^2/\sigma^2$ for χ^2 and write

$$\chi^2_{.975} \leq \frac{(n - 1)s^2}{\sigma^2} \leq \chi^2_{.025} \qquad (11.3)$$

In effect, expression (11.3) provides an interval estimate in that .95, or 95%, of all possible values for $(n - 1)s^2/\sigma^2$ will be in the interval $\chi^2_{.975}$ to $\chi^2_{.025}$. We now need to do some algebraic manipulations with expression (11.3) to develop an interval estimate for the population variance σ^2. Working with the leftmost inequality in expression (11.3), we have

$$\chi^2_{.975} \leq \frac{(n - 1)s^2}{\sigma^2}$$

Thus

$$\sigma^2 \chi^2_{.975} \leq (n - 1)s^2$$

or

$$\sigma^2 \leq \frac{(n - 1)s^2}{\chi^2_{.975}} \qquad (11.4)$$

Performing similar algebraic manipulations with the rightmost inequality in expression (11.3) gives

$$\frac{(n - 1)s^2}{\chi^2_{.025}} \leq \sigma^2 \qquad (11.5)$$

The results of expressions (11.4) and (11.5) can be combined to provide

$$\frac{(n - 1)s^2}{\chi^2_{.025}} \leq \sigma^2 \leq \frac{(n - 1)s^2}{\chi^2_{.975}} \qquad (11.6)$$

Because expression (11.3) is true for 95% of the $(n - 1)s^2/\sigma^2$ values, expression (11.6) provides a 95% confidence interval estimate for the population variance σ^2.

Let us return to the problem of providing an interval estimate for the population variance of filling weights. Recall that the sample of 20 containers provided a sample variance of $s^2 = .0025$. With a sample size of 20, we have 19 degrees of freedom. As shown in Figure 11.2, we have already determined that $\chi^2_{.975} = 8.907$ and $\chi^2_{.025} = 32.852$. Using these values in expression (11.6) provides the following interval estimate for the population variance.

$$\frac{(19)(.0025)}{32.852} \leq \sigma^2 \leq \frac{(19)(.0025)}{8.907}$$

or

A confidence interval for a population standard deviation can be found by computing the square roots of the lower limit and upper limit of the confidence interval for the population variance.

$$.001446 \leq \sigma^2 \leq .005333$$

Taking the square root of these values provides the following 95% confidence interval for the population standard deviation.

$$.0380 \leq \sigma \leq .0730$$

Thus, we illustrated the process of using the chi-square distribution to establish interval estimates of a population variance and a population standard deviation. Note specifically that because $\chi^2_{.975}$ and $\chi^2_{.025}$ were used, the interval estimate has a .95 confidence coefficient. Extending expression (11.6) to the general case of any confidence coefficient, we have the following interval estimate of a population variance.

INTERVAL ESTIMATE OF A POPULATION VARIANCE

$$\frac{(n-1)s^2}{\chi^2_{\alpha/2}} \leq \sigma^2 \leq \frac{(n-1)s^2}{\chi^2_{(1-\alpha/2)}} \qquad \textbf{(11.7)}$$

where the χ^2 values are based on a chi-square distribution with $n-1$ degrees of freedom and where $1-\alpha$ is the confidence coefficient.

Using Excel to Construct a Confidence Interval

Excel can be used to construct a 95% confidence interval of the population variance for the example involving filling containers with a liquid detergent product. Refer to Figure 11.3 as we describe the tasks involved. The formula worksheet is in the background; the value worksheet is in the foreground.

CD file

Detergent

Enter Data: Column A shows the number of ounces of detergent for each of the 20 containers.

Enter Functions and Formulas: The descriptive statistics needed are provided in cells D3:D4. Excel's COUNT and VAR functions are used to compute the sample size and the sample variance, respectively.

FIGURE 11.3   EXCEL WORKSHEET FOR THE LIQUID DETERGENT FILLING PROCESS

	A	B	C	D	E
1	Ounces		Interval Estimate of a Population Variance		
2	15.92				
3	16.02		Sample Size	=COUNT(A2:A21)	
4	15.99		Variance	=VAR(A2:A21)	
5	16.02				
6	15.91		Confidence Coefficient	0.95	
7	15.98		Level of Significance	=1-D6	
8	16.06		Chi-Square Value (lower tail)	=CHIINV(1-D7/2,D3-1)	
9	15.97		Chi-Square Value (upper tail)	=CHIINV(D7/2,D3-1)	
10	15.97				
11	16.07		Point Estimate	=D4	
12	15.94		Lower Limit	=((D3-1)*D4)/D9	
13	15.96		Upper Limit	=((D3-1)*D4)/D8	
14	16.04				
15	16.01				
16	16.07				
17	16.01				
18	15.9				
19	15.96				
20	16				
21	15.99				
22					

	A	B	C	D	E
1	Ounces		Interval Estimate of a Population Variance		
2	15.92				
3	16.02		Sample Size	20	
4	15.99		Variance	0.0025	
5	16.02				
6	15.91		Confidence Coefficient	0.95	
7	15.98		Level of Significance	0.05	
8	16.06		Chi-Square Value (lower tail)	8.9065	
9	15.97		Chi-Square Value (upper tail)	32.8523	
10	15.97				
11	16.07		Point Estimate	0.0025	
12	15.94		Lower Limit	0.0014	
13	15.96		Upper Limit	0.0053	
14	16.04				
15	16.01				
16	16.07				
17	16.01				
18	15.90				
19	15.96				
20	16.00				
21	15.99				
22					

Cells D6:D9 are used to compute the appropriate chi-square values. The confidence coefficient was entered into cell D6 and the level of significance (α) was computed in cell D7 by entering the formula =1-D6. Excel's CHIINV function was used to compute the lower- and upper-tail chi-square values. The form of the CHIINV function is CHIINV(upper-tail probability, degrees of freedom). The formula =CHIINV(1-D7/2,D3-1) was entered into cell D8 to compute the chi-square value in the lower tail. The value worksheet shows that the chi-square value for 19 degrees of freedom is $\chi^2_{.975} = 8.9065$. Then, to compute the chi-square value corresponding to an upper-tail probability of .025, the function =CHIINV(D7/2,D3-1) was entered into cell D9. The value worksheet shows that the chi-square value obtained is $\chi^2_{.025} = 32.8523$.

Cells D11:D13 provide the point estimate and the lower and upper limits for the confidence interval. Because the point estimate is just the sample variance, we entered the formula =D4 into cell D11. Inequality (11.7) shows that the lower limit of the 95% confidence interval is

$$\frac{(n-1)s^2}{\chi^2_{\alpha/2}} = \frac{(n-1)s^2}{\chi^2_{.025}}$$

Thus, to compute the lower limit of the 95% confidence interval, the formula =((D3-1)*D4)/D9 was entered into cell D12. Inequality (11.7) also shows that the upper limit of the confidence interval is

$$\frac{(n-1)s^2}{\chi^2_{(1-\alpha/2)}} = \frac{(n-1)s^2}{\chi^2_{.975}}$$

Thus, to compute the upper limit of the 95% confidence interval, the formula =((D3-1)*D4)/D8 was entered into cell D13. The value worksheet shows a lower limit of .0014 and an upper limit of .0053. In other words, the 95% confidence interval estimate of the population variance is from .0014 to .0053.

Hypothesis Testing

When we use σ_0^2 to denote the hypothesized value for the population variance, the three forms for a hypothesis test about a population variance are as follows:

$$H_0: \sigma^2 \geq \sigma_0^2 \qquad H_0: \sigma^2 \leq \sigma_0^2 \qquad H_0: \sigma^2 = \sigma_0^2$$
$$H_a: \sigma^2 < \sigma_0^2 \qquad H_a: \sigma^2 > \sigma_0^2 \qquad H_a: \sigma^2 \neq \sigma_0^2$$

These three forms are similar to the three forms that we used to conduct one-tailed and two-tailed hypothesis tests about population means and proportions in Chapters 9 and 10.

The procedure for conducting a hypothesis test about a population variance uses the hypothesized value for the population variance σ_0^2 and the sample variance s^2 to compute the value of a χ^2 test statistic. Assuming that the population has a normal distribution, the test statistic is as follows:

TEST STATISTIC FOR HYPOTHESIS TESTS ABOUT A POPULATION VARIANCE

$$\chi^2 = \frac{(n-1)s^2}{\sigma_0^2} \tag{11.8}$$

where χ^2 has a chi-square distribution with $n-1$ degrees of freedom.

After computing the value of the χ^2 test statistic, either the *p*-value approach or the critical value approach may be used to determine whether the null hypothesis can be rejected.

An arrival time variance of 4 or less means that the standard deviation of arrival times must be 2 minutes or less.

Let us consider the following example. The St. Louis Metro Bus Company wants to promote an image of reliability by encouraging its drivers to maintain consistent schedules. As a standard policy the company would like arrival times at bus stops to have low variability. In terms of the variance of arrival times, the company standard specifies an arrival time variance of 4 or less when arrival times are measured in minutes. The following hypothesis test is formulated to help the company determine whether the arrival time population variance is excessive.

$$H_0: \sigma^2 \leq 4$$
$$H_a: \sigma^2 > 4$$

In tentatively assuming H_0 is true, we are assuming that the population variance of arrival times is within the company guideline. We reject H_0 if the sample evidence indicates that the population variance exceeds the guideline. In this case, follow-up steps should be taken to reduce the population variance. We will conduct the hypothesis test using a level of significance of $\alpha = .05$.

ArrivalTimes

Suppose that a particular bus stop at a downtown intersection has a scheduled arrival time of 12:15 P.M. and that a random sample of 24 arrival times for this stop has been selected in order to test whether the company standard of an arrival time variance of 4 or less is being met. The 24 arrival times were recorded as the number of minutes past 12:00 noon; for instance, an arrival time of 14 corresponds to a bus arriving at 12:14 P.M. (one minute early). The sample mean for the 24 arrival times is $\bar{x} = 14.76$ minutes and the sample variance is $s^2 = 4.9$. Although the sample mean is close to the scheduled time, the sample variance of 4.9 suggests that the company standard of an arrival time variance of 4 or less is not being met. If the population distribution of arrival times is approximately normal, the value of the test statistic is as follows:

$$\chi^2 = \frac{(n-1)s^2}{\sigma_0^2} = \frac{(24-1)(4.9)}{4} = 28.18$$

The chi-square distribution with $n - 1 = 24 - 1 = 23$ degrees of freedom is shown in Figure 11.4. Because this is an upper tail test, the area under the curve to the right of the test statistic $\chi^2 = 28.18$ is the *p*-value for the test.

Like the *t* distribution table, the chi-square distribution table does not contain sufficient detail to enable us to determine the *p*-value exactly. However, we can use the chi-square distribution table to obtain a range for the *p*-value. For example, using Table 11.1, we find the following information for a chi-square distribution with 23 degrees of freedom.

Area in Upper Tail	.10	.05	.025	.01
χ^2 Value (23 df)	32.007	35.172	38.076	41.638

$$\chi^2 = 28.18$$

Using Excel, p-value = CHIDIST (28.18,23) = .2091.

Because $\chi^2 = 28.18$ is less than 32.007, the area in the upper tail (the *p*-value) is greater than .10. Excel can be used to show that $\chi^2 = 28.18$ provides a *p*-value = .2091. With the *p*-value $> \alpha = .05$, we cannot reject the null hypothesis. The sample does not support the conclusion that the population variance of the arrival times is excessive.

As with other hypothesis testing procedures, the critical value approach can also be used to draw the hypothesis testing conclusion. With $\alpha = .05$, $\chi_{.05}^2$ provides the critical value for

FIGURE 11.4   CHI-SQUARE DISTRIBUTION FOR THE ST. LOUIS METRO BUS EXAMPLE

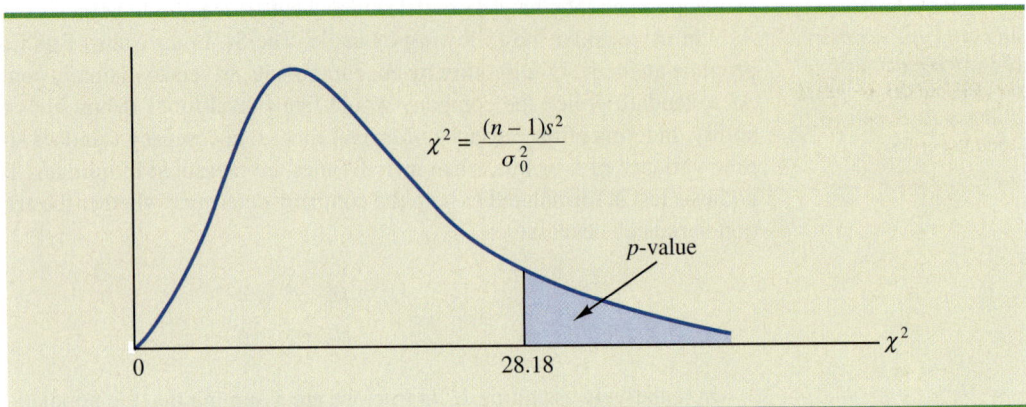

the upper tail hypothesis test. Using Table 11.1 and 23 degrees of freedom, $\chi^2_{.05} = 35.172$. Thus, the rejection rule for the bus arrival time example is as follows:

$$\text{Reject } H_0 \text{ if } \chi^2 \geq 35.172$$

Because the value of the test statistic is $\chi^2 = 28.18$, we cannot reject the null hypothesis.

In practice, upper tail tests as presented here are the most frequently encountered tests about a population variance. In situations involving arrival times, production times, filling weights, part dimensions, and so on, low variances are desirable, whereas large variances are unacceptable. With a statement about the maximum allowable population variance, we can test the null hypothesis that the population variance is less than or equal to the maximum allowable value against the alternative hypothesis that the population variance is greater than the maximum allowable value. With this test structure, corrective action will be taken whenever rejection of the null hypothesis indicates the presence of an excessive population variance.

As we saw with population means and proportions, other forms of hypothesis tests can be developed. Let us demonstrate a two-tailed test about a population variance by considering a situation faced by a bureau of motor vehicles. Historically, the variance in test scores for individuals applying for driver's licenses has been $\sigma^2 = 100$. A new examination with new test questions has been developed. Administrators of the bureau of motor vehicles would like the variance in the test scores for the new examination to remain at the historical level. To evaluate the variance in the new examination test scores, the following two-tailed hypothesis test has been proposed.

$$H_0: \sigma^2 = 100$$
$$H_a: \sigma^2 \neq 100$$

Rejection of H_0 will indicate that a change in the variance has occurred and suggest that some questions in the new examination may need revision to make the variance of the new test scores similar to the variance of the old test scores. A sample of 30 applicants for driver's licenses will be given the new version of the examination. We will use a level of significance $\alpha = .05$ to conduct the hypothesis test.

The sample of 30 examination scores provided a sample variance $s^2 = 162$. The value of the chi-square test statistic is as follows:

$$\chi^2 = \frac{(n-1)s^2}{\sigma^2_0} = \frac{(30-1)(162)}{100} = 46.98$$

Now, let us compute the p-value. Using Table 11.1 and $n - 1 = 30 - 1 = 29$ degrees of freedom, we find the following.

Area in Upper Tail	.10	.05	.025	.01
χ^2 **Value (29 df)**	39.087	42.557	45.722	49.588

$$\chi^2 = 46.98$$

*Using Excel, p-value =
2*CHIDIST(46.98,29) =
.0374.*

Thus, the value of the test statistic $\chi^2 = 46.98$ provides an area between .025 and .01 in the upper tail of the chi-square distribution. Doubling these values shows that the two-tailed p-value is between .05 and .02. Excel can be used to show that $\chi^2 = 46.98$ provides a p-value = .0374. With p-value $\leq \alpha = .05$, we reject H_0 and conclude that the new examination test scores have a population variance different from the historical variance of $\sigma^2 = 100$. A summary of the hypothesis testing procedures for a population variance is shown in Table 11.2.

Using Excel to Conduct a Hypothesis Test

In Chapters 9 and 10 we used Excel to conduct a variety of hypothesis tests. The procedure was general in that, once the test statistic was computed, three p-values were obtained: a p-value (Lower Tail), a p-value (Upper Tail), and a p-value (Two Tail). Then, depending on the form of the hypothesis test, the appropriate p-value was used to make the rejection decision. We will now adapt that approach and use Excel to conduct a hypothesis test about a population variance. The St. Louis Metro Bus example will serve as an illustration. Refer to Figure 11.5 as we describe the tasks involved. The formula worksheet is in the background; the value worksheet is in the foreground.

ArrivalTimes

Enter Data: The 24 arrival times in number of minutes past 12:00 noon have been entered into column A.

Enter Functions and Formulas: The descriptive statistics we need are provided in cells D3:D5. Excel's COUNT function has been used to compute the sample size and Excel's AVERAGE and VAR functions have been used to compute the sample mean and sample variance. The value worksheet shows $n = 24$, $\bar{x} = 14.76$, and $s^2 = 4.9$.

TABLE 11.2   SUMMARY OF HYPOTHESIS TESTS ABOUT A POPULATION VARIANCE

	Lower Tail Test	Upper Tail Test	Two-Tailed Test
Hypotheses	$H_0: \sigma^2 \geq \sigma_0^2$ $H_a: \sigma^2 < \sigma_0^2$	$H_0: \sigma^2 \leq \sigma_0^2$ $H_a: \sigma^2 > \sigma_0^2$	$H_0: \sigma^2 = \sigma_0^2$ $H_a: \sigma^2 \neq \sigma_0^2$
Test Statistic	$\chi^2 = \dfrac{(n-1)s^2}{\sigma_0^2}$	$\chi^2 = \dfrac{(n-1)s^2}{\sigma_0^2}$	$\chi^2 = \dfrac{(n-1)s^2}{\sigma_0^2}$
Rejection Rule: **p-value Approach**	Reject H_0 if p-value $\leq \alpha$	Reject H_0 if p-value $\leq \alpha$	Reject H_0 if p-value $\leq \alpha$
Rejection Rule: **Critical Value** **Approach**	Reject H_0 if $\chi^2 \leq \chi_{(1-\alpha)}^2$	Reject H_0 if $\chi^2 \geq \chi_\alpha^2$	Reject H_0 if $\chi^2 \leq \chi_{(1-\alpha/2)}^2$ or if $\chi^2 \geq \chi_{\alpha/2}^2$

FIGURE 11.5 HYPOTHESIS TEST FOR VARIANCE IN BUS ARRIVAL TIMES

	A	B	C	D	E
1	Times		Hypothesis Test About a Population Variance		
2	15.7				
3	16.9		Sample Size	=COUNT(A2:A25)	
4	12.8		Sample Mean	=AVERAGE(A2:A25)	
5	15.6		Sample Variance	=VAR(A2:A25)	
6	14				
7	16.2		Hypothesized Value	4	
8	14.8				
9	19.8		Test Statistic	=(D3-1)*D5/D7	
10	13.2		Degrees of Freedom	=D3-1	
11	15.3				
12	14.7		*p*-value (Lower Tail)	=1-CHIDIST(D9,D10)	
13	10.2		*p*-value (Upper Tail)	=CHIDIST(D9,D10)	
14	16.7		*p*-value (Two Tail)	=2*MIN(D12,D13)	
15	13.6				
25	12.7				
26					

Note: Rows 16–24 are hidden.

	A	B	C	D	E
1	Times		Hypothesis Test About a Population Variance		
2	15.7				
3	16.9		Sample Size	24	
4	12.8		Sample Mean	14.76	
5	15.6		Sample Variance	4.9	
6	14.0				
7	16.2		Hypothesized Value	4	
8	14.8				
9	19.8		Test Statistic	28.18	
10	13.2		Degrees of Freedom	23	
11	15.3				
12	14.7		*p*-value (Lower Tail)	0.7909	
13	10.2		*p*-value (Upper Tail)	0.2091	
14	16.7		*p*-value (Two Tail)	0.4181	
15	13.6				
25	12.7				
26					

The hypothesized value of the population variance, $\sigma_0^2 = 4$, was entered into cell D7. The formula =(D3-1)*D5/D7 was entered into cell D9 to compute the χ^2 test statistic (28.18), and the formula =D3-1 was entered into cell D10 to compute the degrees of freedom associated with the test statistic. Finally, the CHIDIST function was used to compute the *p*-values in cells D12:D14. The form of the CHIDIST function is CHIDIST(test statistic, degrees of freedom); the value returned by the CHIDIST function is the upper tail probability associated with the test statistic. To compute the *p*-value for a one-tailed test in which the rejection region is in the lower tail, we entered the function =1-CHIDIST(D9,D10) into cell D12. Similarly, to compute the *p*-value for a one-tailed test in which the rejection region is in the upper tail, we entered the function =CHIDIST(D9,D10) into cell D13. Finally, to compute the *p*-value for a two-tailed test, we entered the function =2*MIN(D12,D13) into cell D14. The value worksheet shows that *p*-value (Lower Tail) = .7909, *p*-value (Upper Tail) = .2091, and *p*-value (Two Tail) = .4181. The rejection region for the St. Louis Metro Bus example is in the upper tail; thus, the appropriate *p*-value is .2091. At a .05 level of significance, we cannot reject H_0 because .2091 > .05. Hence, the sample variance of $s^2 = 4.9$ is insufficient evidence to conclude that the arrival time variance is not meeting the company standard.

To avoid having to revise the cell ranges for functions in cells D3:D5, the A:A method of specifying cell ranges can be used.

This worksheet can be used as a template for other hypothesis tests about a population variance. Enter the data in column A, revise the ranges for the functions in cells D3 and D4 as appropriate for the data, and type the hypothesized value σ_0^2 in cell D6. The *p*-value appropriate for the test can then be selected from cells D11:D13. The worksheet can also be used for exercises in which the sample size, sample variance, and hypothesized value are given. For instance, in the previous subsection we conducted a two-tailed hypothesis test about the variance in scores on a new examination given by the bureau of motor vehicles. The sample size was 30, the sample variance was $s^2 = 162$, and the hypothesized value for the population variance was $\sigma_0^2 = 100$. Using the worksheet in Figure 11.5, we can type 30 into cell D3, 162 into cell D5, and 100 into cell D7. The correct two-tailed *p*-value will then be given in cell D14. Try it. You should get a *p*-value of .0374.

Exercises

Methods

1. Find the following chi-square distribution values from Table 11.1 or Table 3 of Appendix B.
    a. $\chi^2_{.05}$ with df = 5
    b. $\chi^2_{.025}$ with df = 15
    c. $\chi^2_{.975}$ with df = 20
    d. $\chi^2_{.01}$ with df = 10
    e. $\chi^2_{.95}$ with df = 18

2. A sample of 20 items provides a sample standard deviation of 5.
    a.   Compute the 90% confidence interval estimate of the population variance.
    b.   Compute the 95% confidence interval estimate of the population variance.
    c.   Compute the 95% confidence interval estimate of the population standard deviation.

3. A sample of 16 items provides a sample standard deviation of 9.5. Test the following hypotheses using $\alpha = .05$. What is your conclusion? Use both the p-value approach and the critical value approach.

$$H_0: \sigma^2 \le 50$$
$$H_a: \sigma^2 > 50$$

Applications

4. The variance in drug weights is critical in the pharmaceutical industry. For a specific drug, with weights measured in grams, a sample of 18 units provided a sample variance of $s^2 = .36$.
    a.   Construct a 90% confidence interval estimate of the population variance for the weight of this drug.
    b.   Construct a 90% confidence interval estimate of the population standard deviation.

5. The daily car rental rates for a sample of eight cities follow.

City	Daily Car Rental Rate ($)	City	Daily Car Rental Rate ($)
Atlanta	47	Phoenix	40
Chicago	50	Pittsburgh	43
Dallas	53	San Francisco	39
New Orleans	45	Seattle	37

   a.   Compute the variance and the standard deviation for these data.
   b.   What is the 95% confidence interval estimate of the variance of car rental rates for the population?
   c.   What is the 95% confidence interval estimate of the standard deviation for the population?

6. The Oppenheimer Capital Appreciation mutual fund provided a 17.6% average annual return over a five-year period (*Fortune,* August 18, 1997). Assume that the following data show the annual returns for each of the five years: 10.8, 34.2, 4.2, 9.4, and 29.4. The standard deviation of the annual returns can be used as a measure of risk, with a larger standard deviation indicating more variation and therefore more uncertainty in the annual returns.
    a.   Use the data as a sample of five annual returns to determine the sample standard deviation measure of risk for the Oppenheimer Capital Appreciation mutual fund.
    b.   What is the 95% confidence interval for the population standard deviation of annual returns for the Oppenheimer Capital Appreciation mutual fund?

7. A sample of eight earnings per share estimates for 1998 is shown here (*Barron's*, December 8, 1997).

Company	Estimated Earnings per Share
AT&T	2.92
Caterpillar	4.65
Eastman Kodak	4.27
Exxon	3.09
Hewlett-Packard	3.57
IBM	7.04
McDonald's	2.64
Wal-Mart	1.74

  a. Compute the sample variance and sample standard deviation for these data.
  b. What is the 95% confidence interval for the population variance?
  c. What is the 95% confidence interval for the population standard deviation?

8. A group of 12 security analysts provided estimates of the year 2001 earnings per share for Qualcomm, Inc. (Zacks.com, June 13, 2000). The data are as follows:

  1.40   1.40   1.45   1.49   1.37   1.27   1.40   1.55   1.40   1.42   1.48   1.63

  a. Compute the sample variance for the earnings per share estimate.
  b. Compute the sample standard deviation for the earnings per share estimate.
  c. Provide 95% confidence interval estimates of the population variance and the population standard deviation.

9. An automotive part must be machined to close tolerances to be acceptable to customers. Production specifications call for a maximum variance in the lengths of the parts of .0004. Suppose the sample variance for 30 parts turns out to be $s^2 = .0005$. Using $\alpha = .05$, test to see whether the population variance specification is being violated.

10. Suppose the average useful life of a DVD player is 6 years with a standard deviation of .75 year. A sample of the useful life of 30 television sets provided a sample standard deviation of .95 year. Construct a hypothesis test that can be used to determine whether the standard deviation of the useful life of television sets is significantly greater than the standard deviation of the useful life of DVD players. With a .05 level of significance, what is your conclusion?

11. Home mortgage interest rates for 30-year fixed-rate loans vary throughout the country. During the summer of 2000, data available from various parts of the country suggested that the standard deviation of the interest rates was .096 (*The Wall Street Journal*, September 8, 2000). The corresponding variance in interest rates would be $(.096)^2 = .009216$. Consider a follow-up study in the summer of 2005. The interest rates for 30-year fixed rate loans at a sample of 20 lending institutions had a sample standard deviation of .114. Conduct a hypothesis test using $H_0: \sigma^2 = .009216$ to see whether the sample data indicate that the variability in interest rates changed. Use $\alpha = .05$. What is your conclusion?

12. A *Fortune* study found that the variance in the number of vehicles owned or leased by subscribers to *Fortune* magazine is .94. Assume a sample of 12 subscribers to another magazine provided the following data on the number of vehicles owned or leased: 2, 1, 2, 0, 3, 2, 2, 1, 2, 1, 0, and 1.
  a. Compute the sample variance in the number of vehicles owned or leased by the 12 subscribers.
  b. Test the hypothesis $H_0: \sigma^2 = .94$ to determine whether the variance in the number of vehicles owned or leased by subscribers of the other magazine differs from $\sigma^2 = .94$ for *Fortune*. At a .05 level of significance, what is your conclusion?

11.2 Inferences About Two Population Variances

In some statistical applications we may want to compare the variances in product quality resulting from two different production processes, the variances in assembly times for two assembly methods, or the variances in temperatures for two heating devices. In making comparisons about the two population variances, we will be using data collected from two independent random samples, one from population 1 and another from population 2. The two sample variances s_1^2 and s_2^2 will be the basis for making inferences about the two population variances σ_1^2 and σ_2^2. Whenever the variances of two normal populations are equal ($\sigma_1^2 = \sigma_2^2$), the sampling distribution of the ratio of the two sample variances s_1^2/s_2^2 is as follows.

SAMPLING DISTRIBUTION OF s_1^2/s_2^2 WHEN $\sigma_1^2 = \sigma_2^2$

Whenever independent simple random samples of sizes n_1 and n_2 are selected from two normal populations with equal variances, the sampling distribution of

$$\frac{s_1^2}{s_2^2} \qquad\qquad (11.9)$$

The F distribution is based on sampling from two normal populations.

has an F distribution with $n_1 - 1$ degrees of freedom for the numerator and $n_2 - 1$ degrees of freedom for the denominator; s_1^2 is the sample variance for the random sample of n_1 items from population 1, and s_2^2 is the sample variance for the random sample of n_2 items from population 2.

Figure 11.6 is a graph of the F distribution with 20 degrees of freedom for both the numerator and denominator. As can be seen from this graph, the F distribution is not symmetric, and the F values can never be negative. The shape of any particular F distribution depends on its numerator and denominator degrees of freedom.

FIGURE 11.6 *F* DISTRIBUTION WITH 20 DEGREES OF FREEDOM FOR THE NUMERATOR AND 20 DEGREES OF FREEDOM FOR THE DENOMINATOR

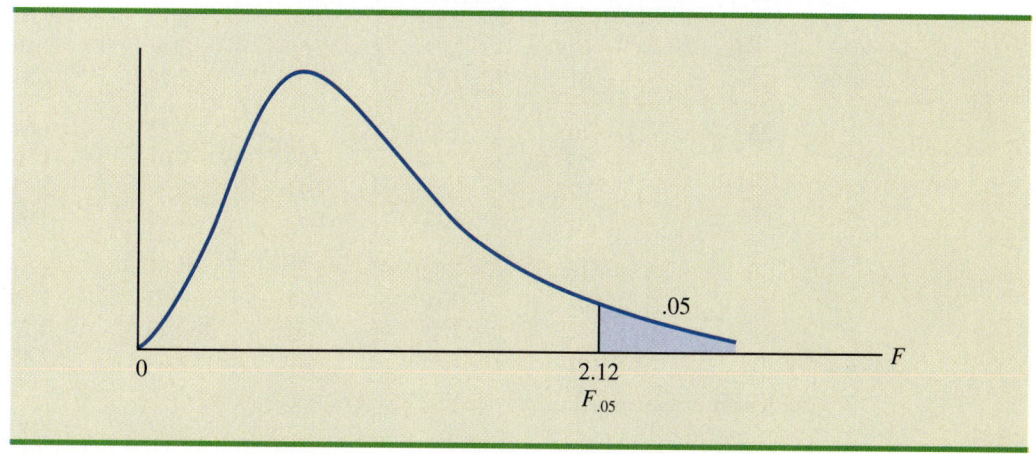

We will use F_α to denote the value of F that provides an area or probability of α in the upper tail of the distribution. For example, as noted in Figure 11.6, $F_{.05}$ denotes the upper tail area of .05 for an F distribution with 20 degrees of freedom for the numerator and 20 degrees of freedom for the denominator. The specific value of $F_{.05}$ can be found by referring to the F distribution table, a portion of which is shown in Table 11.3. Using 20 degrees of freedom for the numerator, 20 degrees of freedom for the denominator, and the row corresponding to an area of .05 in the upper tail, we find $F_{.05} = 2.12$. Note that the table can be used to find F values for upper tail areas of .10, .05, .025, and .01. See Table 4 of Appendix B for a more extensive table for the F distribution.

TABLE 11.3 SELECTED VALUES FROM THE F DISTRIBUTION TABLE

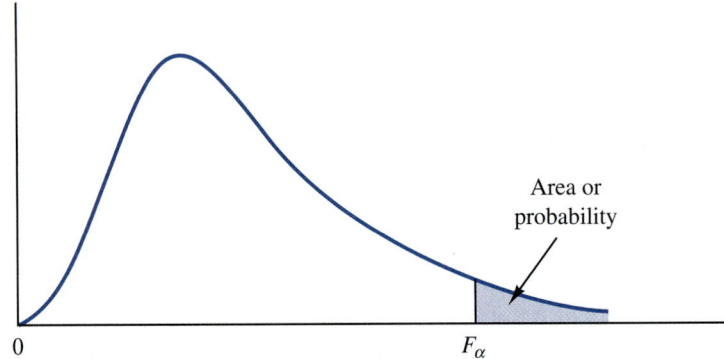

Denominator Degrees of Freedom	Area in Upper Tail	Numerator Degrees of Freedom				
		10	15	20	25	30
10	.10	2.32	2.24	2.20	2.17	2.16
	.05	2.98	2.85	2.77	2.73	2.70
	.025	3.72	3.52	3.42	3.35	3.31
	.01	4.85	4.56	4.41	4.31	4.25
15	.10	2.06	1.97	1.92	1.89	1.87
	.05	2.54	2.40	2.33	2.28	2.25
	.025	3.06	2.86	2.76	2.69	2.64
	.01	3.80	3.52	3.37	3.28	3.21
20	.10	1.94	1.84	1.79	1.76	1.74
	.05	2.35	2.20	2.12	2.07	2.04
	.025	2.77	2.57	2.46	2.40	2.35
	.01	3.37	3.09	2.94	2.84	2.78
25	.10	1.87	1.77	1.72	1.68	1.66
	.05	2.24	2.09	2.01	1.96	1.92
	.025	2.61	2.41	2.30	2.23	2.18
	.01	3.13	2.85	2.70	2.60	2.54
30	.10	1.82	1.72	1.67	1.63	1.61
	.05	2.16	2.01	1.93	1.88	1.84
	.025	2.51	2.31	2.20	2.12	2.07
	.01	2.98	2.70	2.55	2.45	2.39

Note: A more extensive table is provided as Table 4 of Appendix B.

Let us show how the F distribution can be used to conduct a hypothesis test about the variances of two populations. We begin with a test of the equality of two population variances. The hypotheses are stated as follows.

$$H_0: \sigma_1^2 = \sigma_2^2$$
$$H_a: \sigma_1^2 \neq \sigma_2^2$$

We make the tentative assumption that the population variances are equal. If H_0 is rejected, we will draw the conclusion that the population variances are not equal.

The procedure used to conduct the hypothesis test requires two independent random samples, one from each population. The two sample variances are then computed. We refer to the population providing the *larger* sample variance as population 1. Thus, a sample size of n_1 and a sample variance of s_1^2 correspond to the population with the larger sample variance, and a sample size of n_2 and a sample variance of s_2^2 correspond to the population with the smaller sample variance. Based on the assumption that both populations have a normal distribution, the ratio of sample variances provides the following F test statistic.

TEST STATISTIC FOR HYPOTHESIS TESTS ABOUT POPULATION VARIANCES WITH $\sigma_1^2 = \sigma_2^2$

$$F = \frac{s_1^2}{s_2^2} \tag{11.10}$$

Denoting the population with the larger sample variance as population 1, the test statistic has an F distribution with $n_1 - 1$ degrees of freedom for the numerator and $n_2 - 1$ degrees of freedom for the denominator.

Because the F test statistic is constructed with the larger sample variance s_1^2 in the numerator, the value of the test statistic will be in the upper tail of the F distribution. Therefore, the F distribution table as shown in Table 11.3 and in Table 4 of Appendix B need only provide upper tail areas or probabilities. If we did not construct the test statistic in this manner, lower tail areas or probabilities would be needed. In this case, additional calculations or more extensive F distribution tables would be required. Let us now consider an example of a hypothesis test about the equality of two population variances.

Dullus County Schools is renewing its school bus service contract for the coming year and must select one of two bus companies, the Milbank Company or the Gulf Park Company. We will use the variance of the arrival or pickup/delivery times as a primary measure of the quality of the bus service. Low variance values indicate the more consistent and higher-quality service. If the variances of arrival times associated with the two services are equal, Dullus School administrators will select the company offering the better financial terms. However, if the sample data on bus arrival times for the two companies indicate a significant difference between the variances, the administrators may want to give special consideration to the company with the better or lower variance service. The appropriate hypotheses follow.

$$H_0: \sigma_1^2 = \sigma_2^2$$
$$H_a: \sigma_1^2 \neq \sigma_2^2$$

If H_0 can be rejected, the conclusion of unequal service quality is appropriate. We will use a level of significance of $\alpha = .10$ to conduct the hypothesis test.

SchoolBus

A sample of 26 arrival times for the Milbank service provides a sample variance of 48, and a sample of 16 arrival times for the Gulf Park service provides a sample variance of 20. Because the Milbank sample provided the larger sample variance, we will denote Milbank as population 1. Using equation (11.10), the value of the test statistic is

$$F = \frac{s_1^2}{s_2^2} = \frac{48}{20} = 2.40$$

The corresponding F distribution has $n_1 - 1 = 26 - 1 = 25$ numerator degrees of freedom and $n_2 - 1 = 16 - 1 = 15$ denominator degrees of freedom.

As with other hypothesis testing procedures, we can use the p-value approach or the critical value approach to obtain the hypothesis testing conclusion. Table 11.3 shows the following areas in the upper tail and corresponding F values for an F distribution with 25 numerator degrees of freedom and 15 denominator degrees of freedom.

Area in Upper Tail	.10	.05	.025	.01
F Value (df$_1$ = 25, df$_2$ = 15)	1.89	2.28	2.69	3.28

$F = 2.40$

Because $F = 2.40$ is between 2.28 and 2.69, the area in the upper tail of the distribution is between .05 and .025. Since this is a two-tailed test, we double the upper tail area, which results in a p-value between .10 and .05. For this test, we selected $\alpha = .10$ as the level of significance. Because the p-value is less than $\alpha = .10$, the null hypothesis is rejected. This finding leads to the conclusion that the two bus services differ in terms of pickup/delivery time variances. The recommendation is that the Dullus County School administrators give special consideration to the better or lower variance service offered by the Gulf Park Company.

Using Excel, p-value = 2*FDIST(2.4,25,15) = .081.

We can use Excel to show that the test statistic $F = 2.40$ provides a two-tailed p-value $= .081$. With $.081 < \alpha = .10$, the null hypothesis of equal population variances is rejected.

To use the critical value approach to conduct the two-tailed hypothesis test at the $\alpha = .10$ level of significance, we would select critical values with an area of $\alpha/2 = .10/2 = .05$ in each tail of the distribution. Because the value of the test statistic computed using equation (11.10) will always be in the upper tail, we only need to determine the upper tail critical value. From Table 11.3, we see that $F_{.05} = 2.28$. Thus, even though we use a two-tailed test, the rejection rule is stated as follows.

$$\text{Reject } H_0 \text{ if } F \geq 2.28$$

Because the test statistic $F = 2.40$ is greater than 2.28, we reject H_0 and conclude that the two bus services differ in terms of pickup/delivery time variances.

One-tailed tests involving two population variances are also possible. In this case, we use the F distribution to determine whether one population variance is significantly greater than the other. A one-tailed hypothesis test about two population variances will always be formulated as an *upper tail* test:

A one-tailed hypothesis test about two population variances can always be formulated as an upper tail test. This approach eliminates the need for lower tail F values.

$$H_0: \sigma_1^2 \leq \sigma_2^2$$
$$H_a: \sigma_1^2 > \sigma_2^2$$

This form of the hypothesis test always places the p-value and the critical value in the upper tail of the F distribution. As a result, only upper tail F values will be needed, simplifying both the computations and the table for the F distribution.

Let us demonstrate the use of the F distribution to conduct a one-tailed test about the variances of two populations by considering a public opinion survey. Samples of 31 men and 41 women will be used to study attitudes about current political issues. The researcher conducting the study wants to test to see whether the sample data indicate that women show a greater variation in attitude on political issues than men. In the form of the one-tailed hypothesis test given previously, women will be denoted as population 1 and men will be denoted as population 2. The hypothesis test will be stated as follows.

$$H_0: \sigma^2_{\text{women}} \leq \sigma^2_{\text{men}}$$
$$H_a: \sigma^2_{\text{women}} > \sigma^2_{\text{men}}$$

A rejection of H_0 gives the researcher the statistical support necessary to conclude that women show a greater variation in attitude on political issues.

With the sample variance for women in the numerator and the sample variance for men in the denominator, the F distribution will have $n_1 - 1 = 41 - 1 = 40$ numerator degrees of freedom and $n_2 - 1 = 31 - 1 = 30$ denominator degrees of freedom. We will use a level of significance $\alpha = .05$ to conduct the hypothesis test. The survey results provide a sample variance of $s^2_1 = 120$ for women and a sample variance of $s^2_2 = 80$ for men. The test statistic is as follows.

$$F = \frac{s^2_1}{s^2_2} = \frac{120}{80} = 1.50$$

Using Excel, p-value = 2*FDIST(1.5,40,30) = .1256.

Referring to Table 4 in Appendix B, we find that an F distribution with 40 numerator degrees of freedom and 30 denominator degrees of freedom has $F_{.10} = 1.57$. Because the test statistic $F = 1.50$ is less than 1.57, the area in the upper tail must be greater than .10. Thus, we can conclude that the p-value is greater than .10. Excel can be used to show that $F = 1.50$ provides a p-value = .1256. Because the p-value $> \alpha = .05$, H_0 cannot be rejected. Hence, the sample results do not support the conclusion that women show greater variation in attitude on political issues than men. Table 11.4 provides a summary of hypothesis tests about two population variances.

TABLE 11.4   SUMMARY OF HYPOTHESIS TESTS ABOUT TWO POPULATION VARIANCES

	Upper Tail Test	**Two-Tailed Test**
Hypotheses	$H_0: \sigma^2_1 \leq \sigma^2_2$ $H_a: \sigma^2_1 > \sigma^2_2$	$H_0: \sigma^2_1 = \sigma^2_2$ $H_a: \sigma^2_1 \neq \sigma^2_2$
		Note: Population 1 has the larger sample variance
Test Statistic	$F = \dfrac{s^2_1}{s^2_2}$	$F = \dfrac{s^2_1}{s^2_2}$
Rejection Rule: ***p*-value Approach**	Reject H_0 if p-value $\leq \alpha$	Reject H_0 if p-value $\leq \alpha$
Rejection Rule: **Critical Value** **Approach**	Reject H_0 if $F \geq F_\alpha$	Reject H_0 if $F \geq F_{\alpha/2}$

Using Excel to Conduct a Hypothesis Test

Excel's F-Test Two-Sample for Variances tool can be used to conduct a hypothesis test comparing the variances of two populations. We illustrate by using Excel to conduct the two-tailed hypothesis test for the Dullus County School Bus study. Refer to Figure 11.7 and the dialog box in Figure 11.8 as we describe the tasks involved.

Enter Data: Column A contains the sample of 26 arrival times for the Milbank Company and column B contains the sample of 16 arrival times for the Gulf Park Company.

Apply Tools: The following steps describe how to use Excel's F-Test Two-Sample for Variances tool.

Step 1. Select the **Tools** menu
Step 2. Choose **Data Analysis**
Step 3. When the Data Analysis dialog box appears:
　　Choose **F-Test Two-Sample for Variances** from the list of Analysis Tools
　　Click **OK**
Step 4. When the F-Test Two-Sample for Variances dialog box appears (Figure 11.8):
　　Enter A1:A27 in the **Variable 1 Range** box
　　Enter B1:B17 in the **Variable 2 Range** box
　　Select **Labels**
　　Enter .05 in the **Alpha** box
　　　　(*Note:* This Excel procedure uses alpha as the area in the upper tail.)
　　Select **Output Range** and enter D1 in the box
　　Click **OK**

The output, P(F<=f) one-tail = .0405, is the one-tail area associated with the test statistic $F = 2.401$. Thus, the two-tailed p-value is 2(.0405) = .081; we reject the null hypothesis at the .10 level of significance. If the hypothesis test had been a one-tail test (with $\alpha = .05$), the one-tail area in cell E9 would provide the p-value directly. We would not need to double it.

FIGURE 11.7   HYPOTHESIS TEST COMPARING VARIANCE IN PICKUP TIMES FOR TWO SCHOOL BUS SERVICES

	A	B	C	D	E	F	G
1	**Milbank**	**Gulf Park**		F-Test Two-Sample for Variances			
2	35.9	21.6					
3	29.9	20.5			*Milbank*	*Gulf Park*	
4	31.2	23.3		Mean	20.2308	20.2438	
5	16.2	18.8		Variance	48.0206	20.0000	
6	19.0	17.2		Observations	26	16	
7	15.9	7.7		df	25	15	
8	18.8	18.6		F	2.4010		
9	22.2	18.7		P(F<=f) one-tail	0.0405		
10	19.9	20.4		F Critical one-tail	2.2797		
11	16.4	22.4					
16	18.0	27.9					
17	28.1	20.8					
18	12.1						
26	15.2						
27	28.2						
28							

Note: Rows 12–15 and 19–25 are hidden.

FIGURE 11.8   DIALOG BOX FOR F-TEST TWO-SAMPLE FOR VARIANCES

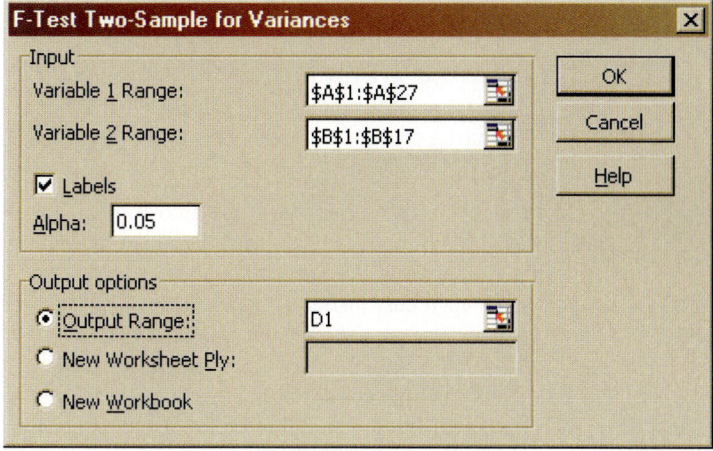

NOTES AND COMMENTS

Research confirms the fact that the F distribution is sensitive to the assumption of normal populations. The F distribution should not be used unless it is reasonable to assume that both populations are at least approximately normally distributed.

Exercises

Methods

13. Find the following F distribution values from Table 4 of Appendix B.
     a. $F_{.05}$ with degrees of freedom 5 and 10
     b. $F_{.025}$ with degrees of freedom 20 and 15
     c. $F_{.01}$ with degrees of freedom 8 and 12
     d. $F_{.10}$ with degrees of freedom 10 and 20

14. A sample of 16 items from population 1 has a sample variance $s_1^2 = 5.8$ and a sample of 21 items from population 2 has a sample variance $s_2^2 = 2.4$. Test the following hypotheses at the .05 level of significance.

$$H_0: \sigma_1^2 \leq \sigma_2^2$$
$$H_a: \sigma_1^2 > \sigma_2^2$$

     a.   What is your conclusion using the p-value approach?
     b.   Repeat the test using the critical value approach.

15. Consider the following hypothesis test.

$$H_0: \sigma_1^2 = \sigma_2^2$$
$$H_a: \sigma_1^2 \neq \sigma_2^2$$

     a.   What is your conclusion if $n_1 = 21$, $s_1^2 = 8.2$, $n_2 = 26$, and $s_2^2 = 4.0$? Use $\alpha = .05$ and the p-value approach.
     b.   Repeat the test using the critical value approach.

Applications

16. Media Metrix and Jupiter Communications gathered data on the time adults and the time teens spend online during a month (*USA Today,* September 14, 2000). The study concluded that on average, adults spend more time online than teens. Assume that a follow-up study sampled 26 adults and 30 teens. The standard deviations of the time online during a month were 94 minutes and 58 minutes, respectively. Do the sample results support the conclusion that adults have a greater variance in online time than teens? Use $\alpha = .01$. What is the *p*-value?

17. Most individuals are aware of the fact that the average annual repair cost for an automobile depends on the age of the automobile. A researcher is interested in finding out whether the variance of the annual repair costs also increases with the age of the automobile. A sample of 26 automobiles 4 years old showed a sample standard deviation for annual repair costs of $170 and a sample of 25 automobiles 2 years old showed a sample standard deviation for annual repair costs of $100.
    a. State the null and alternative versions of the research hypothesis that the variance in annual repair costs is larger for the older automobiles.
    b. At a .01 level of significance, what is your conclusion? What is the *p*-value? Discuss the reasonableness of your findings.

18. The standard deviation in the 12-month earnings per share for 10 companies in the airline industry was 4.27 and the standard deviation in the 12-month earnings per share for 7 companies in the automotive industry was 2.27 (*BusinessWeek,* August 14, 2000). Conduct a test for equal variances at $\alpha = .05$. What is your conclusion about the variability in earnings per share for the airline industry and the automotive industry?

19. The variance in a production process is an important measure of the quality of the process. A large variance often signals an opportunity for improvement in the process by finding ways to reduce the process variance. Conduct a statistical test to determine whether there is a significant difference between the variances in the bag weights for the two machines. Use a .05 level of significance. What is your conclusion? Which machine, if either, provides the greater opportunity for quality improvements?

Machine 1	2.95	3.45	3.50	3.75	3.48	3.26	3.33	3.20
	3.16	3.20	3.22	3.38	3.90	3.36	3.25	3.28
	3.20	3.22	2.98	3.45	3.70	3.34	3.18	3.35
	3.12							
Machine 2	3.22	3.30	3.34	3.28	3.29	3.25	3.30	3.27
	3.38	3.34	3.35	3.19	3.35	3.05	3.36	3.28
	3.30	3.28	3.30	3.20	3.16	3.33		

20. On the basis of data provided by a Romac salary survey, the variance in annual salaries for seniors in public accounting firms is approximately 2.1 and the variance in annual salaries for managers in public accounting firms is approximately 11.1. The salary data were provided in thousands of dollars. Assuming that the salary data were based on samples of 25 seniors and 26 managers, test the hypothesis that the population variances in the salaries are equal. At a .05 level of significance, what is your conclusion?

21. The Dow Jones Industrial Average varies as investors buy and sell shares of the 30 stocks that make up the average. Samples of the Dow Jones Industrial Average taken at different times during the first five days of November 1997 and the first five days of December 1997 are as follows (*Barron's,* December 8, 1997).

November	December
7493	8066
7525	8209
7760	7842
7499	7943
7555	7846
7690	8071
7668	8055
7600	8159
7516	7828
7711	8109

DowJones

a. Compute the variances of the Dow Jones Industrial Average for the two time periods.
b. Use a .05 level of significance and test to determine whether the population variances for the two time periods are equal. What is the *p*-value? What is your conclusion?

22. A research hypothesis is that the variance of stopping distances of automobiles on wet pavement is substantially greater than the variance of stopping distances of automobiles on dry pavement. In the research study, 16 automobiles traveling at the same speeds are tested for stopping distances on wet pavement and then tested for stopping distances on dry pavement. On wet pavement, the standard deviation of stopping distances is 32 feet. On dry pavement, the standard deviation is 16 feet.
   a. At a .05 level of significance, do the sample data justify the conclusion that the variance in stopping distances on wet pavement is greater than the variance in stopping distances on dry pavement? What is the *p*-value?
   b. What are the implications of your statistical conclusions in terms of driving safety recommendations?

Summary

In this chapter we presented statistical procedures that can be used to make inferences about population variances. In the process we introduced two new probability distributions: the chi-square distribution and the F distribution. The chi-square distribution can be used as the basis for interval estimation and hypothesis tests about the variance of a normal population, and the F distribution can be used to conduct hypothesis tests about the variances of two normal populations. In particular, we showed that with independent simple random samples of sizes n_1 and n_2 selected from two normal populations with equal variances $\sigma_1^2 = \sigma_2^2$, the sampling distribution of the ratio of the two sample variances s_1^2/s_2^2 has an F distribution with $n_1 - 1$ degrees of freedom for the numerator and $n_2 - 1$ degrees of freedom for the denominator.

Key Formulas

Interval Estimate of a Population Variance

$$\frac{(n-1)s^2}{\chi_{\alpha/2}^2} \leq \sigma^2 \leq \frac{(n-1)s^2}{\chi_{(1-\alpha/2)}^2} \qquad (11.7)$$

Test Statistic for Hypothesis Tests About a Population Variance

$$\chi^2 = \frac{(n-1)s^2}{\sigma_0^2} \qquad \text{(11.8)}$$

Test Statistic for Hypothesis Tests About Population Variances with $\sigma_1^2 = \sigma_2^2$

$$F = \frac{s_1^2}{s_2^2} \qquad \text{(11.10)}$$

Supplementary Exercises

23. Because of staffing decisions, managers of the Gibson-Marimont Hotel are interested in the variability in the number of rooms occupied per day during a particular season of the year. A sample of 20 days of operation shows a sample mean of 290 rooms occupied per day and a sample standard deviation of 30 rooms.
    a. What is the point estimate of the population variance?
    b. Provide a 90% confidence interval estimate of the population variance.
    c. Provide a 90% confidence interval estimate of the population standard deviation.

24. Initial public offerings (IPOs) of stocks are on average underpriced. The standard deviation measures the dispersion, or variation, in the underpricing-overpricing indicator. A sample of 13 Canadian IPOs that were subsequently traded on the Toronto Stock Exchange had a standard deviation of 14.95. Develop a 95% confidence interval estimate of the population standard deviation for the underpricing-overpricing indicator.

25. The estimated daily living costs for an executive traveling to various major cities follow. The estimates include a single room at a four-star hotel, beverages, breakfast, taxi fares, and incidental costs.

CD file

Travel

City	Daily Living Cost ($)	City	Daily Living Cost ($)
Bangkok	242.87	Madrid	283.56
Bogota	260.93	Mexico City	212.00
Bombay	139.16	Milan	284.08
Cairo	194.19	Paris	436.72
Dublin	260.76	Rio de Janeiro	240.87
Frankfurt	355.36	Seoul	310.41
Hong Kong	346.32	Tel Aviv	223.73
Johannesburg	165.37	Toronto	181.25
Lima	250.08	Warsaw	238.20
London	326.76	Washington, D.C.	250.61

   a. Compute the sample mean.
   b. Compute the sample standard deviation.
   c. Compute a 95% confidence interval for the population standard deviation.

26. Part variability is critical in the manufacturing of ball bearings. Large variances in the size of the ball bearings cause bearing failure and rapid wearout. Production standards call for a maximum variance of .0001 when the bearing diameters are measured in inches. A sample of 15 bearings shows a sample standard deviation of .014 inches.
    a. Use $\alpha = .10$ to determine whether the sample indicates that the maximum acceptable variance is being exceeded.
    b. Compute the 90% confidence interval estimate of the variance of the ball bearings in the population.

27. The filling weight for boxes of cereal is designed to have a variance .02 ounces or less. A sample of 41 boxes of cereal shows a sample standard deviation of .16 ounces. Use $\alpha = .05$ to determine whether the variance in the cereal box filling weight is exceeding the design specification.

28. City Trucking, Inc., claims consistent delivery times for its routine customer deliveries. A sample of 22 truck deliveries shows a sample variance of 1.5 minutes. Test to determine whether $H_0: \sigma^2 \leq 1$ can be rejected. Use $\alpha = .10$.

29. Using a sample of 9 days over the past 6 months, a dentist treated the following numbers of patients: 22, 25, 20, 18, 15, 22, 24, 19, and 26. If the number of patients seen per day is normally distributed, would an analysis of these sample data reject the hypothesis that the variance in the number of patients seen per day is equal to 10? Use a .10 level of significance. What is your conclusion?

30. A sample standard deviation for the number of passengers taking a particular airline flight is 8. A 95% confidence interval estimate of the population standard deviation is 5.86 passengers to 12.62 passengers.
    a. Was a sample size of 10 or 15 used in the statistical analysis?
    b. Suppose the sample standard deviation of $s = 8$ was based on a sample of 25 flights. What change would you expect in the confidence interval for the population standard deviation? Compute a 95% confidence interval estimate of σ with a sample size of 25.

31. Each day the major stock markets have a group of leading gainers in price (stocks that go up the most). On one day the standard deviation in the percentage change for a sample of 10 NASDAQ leading gainers was 15.8. On the same day, the standard deviation in the percentage change for a sample of 10 NYSE leading gainers was 7.9 (*USA Today,* September 14, 2000). Conduct a test for equal population variances to see whether it can be concluded that there is a difference in the volatility of the leading gainers on the two exchanges. Use $\alpha = .10$. What is your conclusion?

32. The grade point averages of 352 students who completed a college course in financial accounting have a standard deviation of .940. The grade point averages of 73 students who dropped out of the same course have a standard deviation of .797. Do the data indicate a difference between the variances of grade point averages for students who completed a financial accounting course and students who dropped out? Use a .05 level of significance. *Note:* $F_{.025}$ with 351 and 72 degrees of freedom is 1.466.

33. The accounting department analyzes the variance of the weekly unit costs reported by two production departments. A sample of 16 cost reports for each of the two departments shows cost variances of 2.3 and 5.4, respectively. Is this sample sufficient to conclude that the two production departments differ in terms of unit cost variance? Use $\alpha = .10$.

34. Two new assembly methods are tested and the variances in assembly times are reported. Use $\alpha = .10$ and test for equality of the two population variances.

	Method A	Method B
Sample Size	$n_1 = 31$	$n_2 = 25$
Sample Variation	$s_1^2 = 25$	$s_2^2 = 12$

Case Problem Air Force Training Program

An Air Force introductory course in electronics uses a personalized system of instruction whereby each student views a videotaped lecture and then is given a programmed instruction text. The students work independently with the text until they have completed the training and passed a test. Of concern is the varying pace at which the students complete this portion of their training program. Some students are able to cover the programmed instruction text relatively quickly, whereas other students work much longer with the text and require additional time to complete the course. The fast students wait until the slow students complete the introductory course before the entire group proceeds together with other aspects of their training.

A proposed alternative system involves use of computer-assisted instruction. In this method, all students view the same videotaped lecture and then each is assigned to a computer terminal for further instruction. The computer guides the student, working independently, through the self-training portion of the course.

To compare the proposed and current methods of instruction, an entering class of 122 students was assigned randomly to one of the two methods. One group of 61 students used the current programmed-text method and the other group of 61 students used the proposed computer-assisted method. The time in hours was recorded for each student in the study. The following data are provided on the CD that accompanies the text in the data set named Training.

Course Completion Times (hours) for Current Training Method

76	76	77	74	76	74	74	77	72	78	73
78	75	80	79	72	69	79	72	70	70	81
76	78	72	82	72	73	71	70	77	78	73
79	82	65	77	79	73	76	81	69	75	75
77	79	76	78	76	76	73	77	84	74	74
69	79	66	70	74	72					

Training

Course Completion Times (hours) for Proposed Computer-Assisted Method

74	75	77	78	74	80	73	73	78	76	76
74	77	69	76	75	72	75	72	76	72	77
73	77	69	77	75	76	74	77	75	78	72
77	78	78	76	75	76	76	75	76	80	77
76	75	73	77	77	77	79	75	75	72	82
76	76	74	72	78	71					

Managerial Report

1. Use appropriate descriptive statistics to summarize the training time data for each method. What similarities or differences do you observe from the sample data?
2. Use the methods of Chapter 10 to comment on any difference between the population means for the two methods. Discuss your findings.
3. Compute the standard deviation and variance for each training method. Conduct a hypothesis test about the equality of population variances for the two training methods. Discuss your findings.
4. What conclusion can you reach about any differences between the two methods? What is your recommendation? Explain.
5. Can you suggest other data or testing that might be desirable before making a final decision on the training program to be used in the future?

CHAPTER 12

Tests of Goodness of Fit and Independence

CONTENTS

STATISTICS IN PRACTICE:
UNITED WAY

12.1 GOODNESS OF FIT TEST: A
MULTINOMIAL POPULATION
Using Excel to Conduct a
Goodness of Fit Test

12.2 TEST OF INDEPENDENCE
Using Excel to Conduct a Test of
Independence

12.3 GOODNESS OF FIT TEST:
POISSON AND NORMAL
DISTRIBUTIONS
Poisson Distribution
Using Excel to Conduct a
Goodness of Fit Test
Normal Distribution
Using Excel to Conduct a
Goodness of Fit Test

STATISTICS *in* PRACTICE

UNITED WAY*
ROCHESTER, NEW YORK

United Way of Greater Rochester is a nonprofit organization dedicated to improving the quality of life for all people in the seven counties it serves by meeting the community's most important human care needs.

The annual United Way/Red Cross fund-raising campaign, conducted each spring, funds hundreds of programs offered by more than 200 service providers. These providers meet a wide variety of human needs—physical, mental, and social—and serve people of all ages, backgrounds, and economic means.

Because of enormous volunteer involvement, United Way of Greater Rochester is able to hold its operating costs at just eight cents of every dollar raised.

The United Way of Greater Rochester decided to conduct a survey to learn more about community perceptions of charities. Focus-group interviews were held with professional, service, and general worker groups to get preliminary information on perceptions. The information obtained was then used to help develop the questionnaire for the survey. The questionnaire was pretested, modified, and distributed to 440 individuals; 323 completed questionnaires were obtained.

A variety of descriptive statistics, including frequency distributions and crosstabulations, were provided from the data collected. An important part of the analysis involved the use of contingency tables and chi-square tests of independence. One use of such statistical tests was to determine whether perceptions of administrative expenses were independent of occupation.

The hypotheses for the test of independence were:

H_0: Perception of United Way administrative expenses is independent of the occupation of the respondent.

H_a: Perception of United Way administrative expenses is not independent of the occupation of the respondent.

Statistical surveys help United Way adjust its program to better meet the needs of the people it serves. © Tony Freeman/PhotoEdit.

Two questions in the survey provided the data for the statistical test. One question obtained data on perceptions of the percentage of funds going to administrative expenses (up to 10%, 11–20%, and 21% or more). The other question asked for the occupation of the respondent.

The chi-square test at a .05 level of significance led to rejection of the null hypothesis of independence and to the conclusion that perceptions of United Way's administrative expenses did vary by occupation. Actual administrative expenses were less than 9%, but 35% of the respondents perceived that administrative expenses were 21% or more. Hence, many had inaccurate perceptions of administrative costs. In this group, production-line, clerical, sales, and professional-technical employees had more inaccurate perceptions than other groups.

The community perceptions study helped United Way of Greater Rochester to develop adjustments to its program and fund-raising activities. In this chapter, you will learn how a statistical test of independence, such as that described here, is conducted.

---

*The authors are indebted to Dr. Philip R. Tyler, Marketing Consultant to the United Way, for providing this Statistics in Practice.

In Chapter 11 we showed how the chi-square distribution could be used in estimation and in hypothesis tests about a population variance. In Chapter 12, we introduce two additional hypothesis testing procedures, both based on the use of the chi-square distribution. Like other hypothesis testing procedures, these tests compare sample results with those that are expected when the null hypothesis is true. The conclusion of the hypothesis test is based on how "close" the sample results are to the expected results.

In the following section we introduce a goodness of fit test for a multinomial population. Later we discuss the test for independence using contingency tables and then show goodness of fit tests for the Poisson and normal distributions.

12.1 Goodness of Fit Test: A Multinomial Population

In this section we consider the case in which each element of a population is assigned to one and only one of several classes or categories. Such a population is a **multinomial population**. The multinomial distribution can be thought of as an extension of the binomial distribution to the case of three or more categories of outcomes. On each trial of a multinomial experiment, one and only one of the outcomes occurs. Each trial of the experiment is assumed to be independent, and the probabilities of the outcomes remain the same for each trial.

The assumptions for the multinomial experiment parallel those for the binomial experiment with the exception that the multinomial has three or more outcomes per trial.

As an example, consider the market share study being conducted by Scott Marketing Research. Over the past year market shares stabilized at 30% for company A, 50% for company B, and 20% for company C. Recently company C developed a "new and improved" product to replace its current entry in the market. Company C retained Scott Marketing Research to determine whether the new product will alter market shares.

In this case, the population of interest is a multinomial population; each customer is classified as buying from company A, company B, or company C. Thus, we have a multinomial population with three outcomes. Let us use the following notation for the proportions.

$$p_A = \text{market share for company A}$$
$$p_B = \text{market share for company B}$$
$$p_C = \text{market share for company C}$$

Scott Marketing Research will conduct a sample survey and compute the proportion preferring each company's product. A hypothesis test will then be conducted to see whether the new product caused a change in market shares. For the null hypothesis, we assume that company C's new product will not alter the market shares. The null and alternative hypotheses are stated as follows.

$$H_0: p_A = .30, p_B = .50, \text{ and } p_C = .20$$
$$H_a: \text{The population proportions are not}$$
$$p_A = .30, p_B = .50, \text{ and } p_C = .20$$

If the sample results lead to the rejection of H_0, Scott Marketing Research will have evidence that the introduction of the new product affects market shares.

Let us assume that the market research firm has used a consumer panel of 200 customers for the study. Each individual was asked to specify a purchase preference among the three alternatives: company A's product, company B's product, and company C's new product. The 200 responses are summarized here.

The consumer panel of 200 customers in which each individual is asked to select one of three alternatives is equivalent to a multinomial experiment consisting of 200 trials.

Observed Frequency		
Company A's Product	**Company B's Product**	**Company C's New Product**
48	98	54

We now can perform a **goodness of fit test** that will determine whether the sample of 200 customer purchase preferences is consistent with the null hypothesis. The goodness of fit test is based on a comparison of the sample of *observed* results with the *expected* results under the assumption that the null hypothesis is true. Hence, the next step is to compute expected purchase preferences for the 200 customers under the assumption that $p_A = .30$, $p_B = .50$, and $p_C = .20$. Doing so provides the expected results.

	Expected Frequency	
Company A's Product	Company B's Product	Company C's New Product
200(.30) = 60	200(.50) = 100	200(.20) = 40

Thus, we see that the expected frequency for each category is found by multiplying the sample size of 200 by the hypothesized proportion for the category.

The goodness of fit test now focuses on the differences between the observed frequencies and the expected frequencies. Large differences between observed and expected frequencies cast doubt on the assumption that the hypothesized proportions or market shares are correct. Whether the differences between the observed and expected frequencies are "large" or "small" is a question answered with the aid of the following test statistic.

TEST STATISTIC FOR GOODNESS OF FIT

$$\chi^2 = \sum_{i=1}^{k} \frac{(f_i - e_i)^2}{e_i} \qquad (12.1)$$

where

f_i = observed frequency for category i
e_i = expected frequency for category i
k = the number of categories

Note: The test statistic has a chi-square distribution with $k - 1$ degrees of freedom provided that the expected frequencies are 5 *or more* for all categories.

Let us continue with the Scott Marketing Research example and use the sample data to test the hypothesis that the multinomial population retains the proportions $p_A = .30$, $p_B = .50$, and $p_C = .20$. We will use an $\alpha = .05$ level of significance. Let us proceed by using the observed and expected frequencies to compute the value of the test statistic. With the expected frequencies all 5 or more, the computation of the chi-square test statistic is shown in Table 12.1. At the bottom of the last column, we see that $\chi^2 = 7.34$.

The test for goodness of fit is always a one-tailed test with the rejection occurring in the upper tail of the chi-square distribution.

We will reject the null hypothesis if the differences between the observed and expected frequencies are *large*. Large differences between the observed and expected frequencies will result in a large value for the test statistic. Thus the test of goodness of fit will always be an upper tail test. We can use the upper tail area for the test statistic and the *p*-value approach to determine whether the null hypothesis can be rejected. With $k - 1 = 3 - 1 = 2$ degrees of freedom, the chi-square table (Table 3 of Appendix B) provides the following:

An introduction to the chi-square distribution and the use of the chi-square table were presented in Section 11.1.

Area in Upper Tail	.10	.05	.025	.01
χ^2 **Value (2 df)**	4.605	5.991	7.378	9.210

$$\chi^2 = 7.34$$

TABLE 12.1   COMPUTATION OF THE CHI-SQUARE TEST STATISTIC FOR THE SCOTT MARKETING RESEARCH MARKET SHARE STUDY

Category	Hypothesized Proportion	Observed Frequency (f_i)	Expected Frequency (e_i)	Difference $(f_i - e_i)$	Squared Difference $(f_i - e_i)^2$	Squared Difference Divided by Expected Frequency $(f_i - e_i)^2/e_i$
Company A	.30	48	60	-12	144	2.40
Company B	.50	98	100	-2	4	0.04
Company C	.20	54	40	14	196	4.90
Total		200				$\chi^2 = 7.34$

Using Excel, CHIDIST (7.34,2) = .0255.

The test statistic $\chi^2 = 7.34$ is between 5.991 and 7.378. Thus, the corresponding upper tail area or p-value must be between .05 and .025. Excel can be used to show that $\chi^2 = 7.34$ provides a p-value $= .0255$. With the p-value $\leq \alpha = .05$, we reject H_0 and conclude that the introduction of the new product by company C will alter the current market share structure.

Instead of using the p-value, we could use the critical value approach to draw the same conclusion. With $\alpha = .05$ and 2 degrees of freedom, the critical value for the test statistic is $\chi^2_{.05} = 5.991$. The upper tail rejection rule becomes

$$\text{Reject } H_0 \text{ if } \chi^2 \geq 5.991$$

With $7.34 > 5.991$, we reject H_0. The p-value approach and critical value approach provide the same hypothesis testing conclusion.

Although no further conclusions can be made as a result of the test, we can compare the observed and expected frequencies informally to obtain an idea of how the market share structure may change. Considering company C, we find that the observed frequency of 54 is larger than the expected frequency of 40. Because the expected frequency was based on current market shares, the larger observed frequency suggests that the new product will have a positive effect on company C's market share. Comparisons of the observed and expected frequencies for the other two companies indicate that company C's gain in market share will hurt company A more than company B.

Let us summarize the general steps that can be used to conduct a goodness of fit test for a hypothesized multinomial population distribution.

MULTINOMIAL DISTRIBUTION GOODNESS OF FIT TEST: A SUMMARY

1. State the null and alternative hypotheses.

   H_0: The population follows a multinomial distribution with specified probabilities for each of the k categories

   H_a: The population does not follow a multinomial distribution with the specified probabilities for each of the k categories

2. Select a random sample and record the observed frequencies f_i for each category.
3. Assume the null hypothesis is true and determine the expected frequency e_i in each category by multiplying the category probability by the sample size.

4. Compute the value of the test statistic.

$$\chi^2 = \sum_{i=1}^{k} \frac{(f_i - e_i)^2}{e_i}$$

5. Rejection rule:

p-value approach: Reject H_0 if p-value $\leq \alpha$
Critical value approach: Reject H_0 if $\chi^2 \geq \chi_\alpha^2$

where α is the level of significance for the test and there are $k - 1$ degrees of freedom.

Using Excel to Conduct a Goodness of Fit Test

Excel can be used to conduct a goodness of fit test for the Scott Marketing Research Study. Refer to Figure 12.1 as we describe the tasks involved. The formula worksheet is in the background; the value worksheet is in the foreground.

CD file
Research

Enter Data: Column A is used to identify each of the 200 customers who made up the consumer panel in the study. Column B shows the purchase preference (A, B, or C) for each customer. The hypothesized proportions, 0.3, 0.5, and 0.2, were entered into cells E4:E6.

FIGURE 12.1   EXCEL WORKSHEET FOR GOODNESS OF FIT TEST CONCERNING MARKET SHARE CHANGE

	A	B	C	D	E	F	G	H	I	J	K
1	Customer	Product								Squared Diff.	
2	1	B			Hyp.	Obs.	Exp.		Squared	Divided by	
3	2	A		Category	Proportion	Freq.	Freq.	Diff.	Diff.	Exp. Freq.	
4	3	C		Company A	0.3	=COUNTIF(B2:B201,"A")	=E4*F7	=F4-G4	=H4^2	=I4/G4	
5	4	C		Company B	0.5	=COUNTIF(B2:B201,"B")	=E5*F7	=F5-G5	=H5^2	=I5/G5	
6	5	C		Company C	0.2	=COUNTIF(B2:B201,"C")	=E6*F7	=F6-G6	=H6^2	=I6/G6	
7	6	A		Total	=SUM(F4:F6)					=SUM(J4:J6)	
8	7	A									
9	8	A		Number of Categories	3						
10	9	C									
11	10	A		Test Statistic	=J7						
12	11	C		Degrees of Freedom	=F9-1						
13	12	B									
14	13	C		p-value	=CHIDIST(F11,F12)						
15	14	A									
200	199	C									
201	200	C									
202											

Note: Rows 16–199 are hidden.

	A	B	C	D	E	F	G	H	I	J	K
1	Customer	Product								Squared Diff.	
2	1	B			Hyp.	Obs.	Exp.		Squared	Divided by	
3	2	A		Category	Proportion	Freq.	Freq.	Diff.	Diff.	Exp. Freq.	
4	3	C		Company A	0.3	48	60	-12	144	2.4	
5	4	C		Company B	0.5	98	100	-2	4	0.04	
6	5	C		Company C	0.2	54	40	14	196	4.9	
7	6	A		Total	200					7.34	
8	7	A									
9	8	A		Number of Categories	3						
10	9	C									
11	10	A		Test Statistic	7.34						
12	11	C		Degrees of Freedom	2						
13	12	B									
14	13	C		p-value	0.0255						
15	14	A									
200	199	C									
201	200	C									
202											

Enter Functions and Formulas: The Excel formulas in cells F4:J7 are used to compute the chi-square test statistic in a fashion parallel to that shown in Table 12.1. The result is the chi-square test statistic shown in cell J7 (7.34). The number of categories, 3, was entered into cell F9 and the two inputs used by Excel's CHIDIST function (test statistic and degrees of freedom) are in cells F11 and F12. The value computed in cell F14 using Excel's CHIDIST function is the area in the upper tail of the chi-square distribution to the right of the test statistic. So, this value is the appropriate p-value for our upper tail hypothesis test.

The value worksheet shows that the resulting p-value is 0.0255. Thus, with $\alpha = .05$, we reject H_0 and conclude that the introduction of the new product by company C will alter the current market share structure.

Exercises

Methods

1. Test the following hypotheses by using the χ^2 goodness of fit test.

$$H_0: p_A = .40, p_B = .40, \text{ and } p_C = .20$$
$$H_a: \text{The population proportions are not}$$
$$p_A = .40, p_B = .40, \text{ and } p_C = .20$$

   A sample of size 200 yielded 60 in category A, 120 in category B, and 20 in category C. Use $\alpha = .01$ and test to see whether the proportions are as stated in H_0.
   a. Use the p-value approach.
   b. Repeat the test using the critical value approach.

2. Suppose we have a multinomial population with four categories: A, B, C, and D. The null hypothesis is that the proportion of items is the same in every category. The null hypothesis is

$$H_0: p_A = p_B = p_C = p_D = .25$$

   A sample of size 300 yielded the following results.

$$A: 85 \quad B: 95 \quad C: 50 \quad D: 70$$

   Use $\alpha = .05$ to determine whether H_0 should be rejected. What is the p-value?

Applications

3. During the first 13 weeks of the television season, the Saturday evening 8:00 P.M. to 9:00 P.M. audience proportions were recorded as ABC 29%, CBS 28%, NBC 25%, and independents 18%. A sample of 300 homes two weeks after a Saturday night schedule revision yielded the following viewing audience data: ABC 95 homes, CBS 70 homes, NBC 89 homes, and independents 46 homes. Test with $\alpha = .05$ to determine whether the viewing audience proportions changed.

4. M&M/MARS, makers of M&M® Chocolate Candies, conducted a national poll in which consumers indicated their preference for colors. In the brochure "Colors," made available by M&M/MARS Consumer Affairs, the traditional distribution of colors for the plain candies is as follows:

Brown	Yellow	Red	Orange	Green	Blue
30%	20%	20%	10%	10%	10%

In a follow-up study, 1-pound bags were used to determine whether the reported percentages were valid. The following results were obtained for a sample of 506 plain candies.

Brown	Yellow	Red	Orange	Green	Blue
177	135	79	41	36	38

Use $\alpha = .05$ to determine whether these data support the percentages reported by the company.

5. Where do women most often buy casual clothing? Data from the U.S. Shopper Database provided the following percentages for women shopping at each of the various outlets (*The Wall Street Journal,* January 28, 2004).

Outlet	Percentage	Outlet	Percentage
Wal-Mart	24	Kohl's	8
Traditional department stores	11	Mail order	12
J.C. Penney	8	Other	37

The other category included outlets such as Target, Kmart, and Sears as well as numerous smaller specialty outlets. No individual outlet in this group accounted for more than 5% of the women shoppers. A recent survey using a sample of 140 women shoppers in Atlanta, Georgia, found 42 Wal-Mart, 20 traditional department store, 8 J.C. Penney, 10 Kohl's, 21 mail order, and 39 other outlet shoppers. Does this sample suggest that women shoppers in Atlanta differ from the shopping preferences expressed in the U.S. Shopper Database? What is the *p*-value? Use $\alpha = .05$. What is your conclusion?

6. The American Bankers Association collects data on the use of credit cards, debit cards, personal checks, and cash when consumers pay for in-store purchases (*The Wall Street Journal,* December 16, 2003). In 1999, the following usages were reported.

In-Store Purchase	Percentage
Credit card	22
Debit card	21
Personal check	18
Cash	39

A sample taken in 2003 found that for 220 in-stores purchases, 46 used a credit card, 67 used a debit card, 33 used a personal check, and 74 used cash.

a. At $\alpha = .01$, can we conclude that a change occurred in how customers paid for in-store purchases over the four-year period from 1999 to 2003? What is the *p*-value?

b. Compute the percentage of use for each method of payment using the 2003 sample data. What appears to have been the major change or changes over the four-year period?

c. In 2003, what percentage of payments was made using plastic (credit card or debit card)?

7. *The Wall Street Journal*'s Shareholder Scoreboard tracks the performance of 1000 major U.S. companies (*The Wall Street Journal,* March 10, 2003). The performance of each company is rated based on the annual total return, including stock price changes and the reinvestment of dividends. Ratings are assigned by dividing all 1000 companies into five groups from A (top

20%), B (next 20%), to E (bottom 20%). Shown here are the one-year ratings for a sample of 60 of the largest companies. Do the largest companies differ in performance from the performance of the 1000 companies in the Shareholder Scoreboard? Use $\alpha = .05$.

A	B	C	D	E
5	8	15	20	12

8. How well do airline companies serve their customers? A study showed the following customer ratings: 3% excellent, 28% good, 45% fair, and 24% poor (*Business Week,* September 11, 2000). In a follow-up study of service by telephone companies, assume that a sample of 400 adults found the following customer ratings: 24 excellent, 124 good, 172 fair, and 80 poor. Is the distribution of the customer ratings for telephone companies different from the distribution of customer ratings for airline companies? Test with $\alpha = .01$. What is your conclusion?

12.2 Test of Independence

Another important application of the chi-square distribution involves using sample data to test for the independence of two variables. Let us illustrate the test of independence by considering the study conducted by the Alber's Brewery of Tucson, Arizona. Alber's manufactures and distributes three types of beer: light, regular, and dark. In an analysis of the market segments for the three beers, the firm's market research group raised the question of whether preferences for the three beers differ among male and female beer drinkers. If beer preference is independent of the gender of the beer drinker, one advertising campaign will be initiated for all of Alber's beers. However, if beer preference depends on the gender of the beer drinker, the firm will tailor its promotions to different target markets.

A test of independence addresses the question of whether the beer preference (light, regular, or dark) is independent of the gender of the beer drinker (male, female). The hypotheses for this test of independence are

H_0: Beer preference is independent of the gender of the beer drinker

H_a: Beer preference is not independent of the gender of the beer drinker

To test whether two variables are independent, one sample is selected and crosstabulation is used to summarize the data for the two variables simultaneously.

Table 12.2 can be used to describe the situation being studied. After identification of the population as all male and female beer drinkers, a sample can be selected and each individual asked to state his or her preference for the three Alber's beers. Every individual in the sample will be classified in one of the six cells in the table. For example, an individual may be a male preferring regular beer (cell (1,2)), a female preferring light beer (cell (2,1)), a

TABLE 12.2 CONTINGENCY TABLE FOR BEER PREFERENCE AND GENDER OF BEER DRINKER

		Beer Preference		
		Light	**Regular**	**Dark**
Gender	**Male**	cell(1,1)	cell(1,2)	cell(1,3)
	Female	cell(2,1)	cell(2,2)	cell(2,3)

TABLE 12.3   SAMPLE RESULTS FOR BEER PREFERENCES OF MALE AND FEMALE BEER DRINKERS (OBSERVED FREQUENCIES)

		Beer Preference			
		Light	**Regular**	**Dark**	**Total**
Gender	**Male**	20	40	20	80
	Female	30	30	10	70
	Total	50	70	30	150

female preferring dark beer (cell (2,3)), and so on. Because we have listed all possible combinations of beer preference and gender or, in other words, listed all possible contingencies, Table 12.2 is called a **contingency table**. The test of independence uses the contingency table format and for that reason is sometimes referred to as a *contingency table test*.

Suppose a simple random sample of 150 beer drinkers is selected. After tasting each beer, the individuals in the sample are asked to state their preference or first choice. The crosstabulation in Table 12.3 summarizes the responses for the study. As we see, the data for the test of independence are collected in terms of counts or frequencies for each cell or category. Of the 150 individuals in the sample, 20 were men who favored light beer, 40 were men who favored regular beer, 20 were men who favored dark beer, and so on.

The data in Table 12.3 are the observed frequencies for the six classes or categories. If we can determine the expected frequencies under the assumption of independence between beer preference and gender of the beer drinker, we can use the chi-square distribution to determine whether there is a significant difference between observed and expected frequencies.

Expected frequencies for the cells of the contingency table are based on the following rationale. First we assume that the null hypothesis of independence between beer preference and gender of the beer drinker is true. Then we note that in the entire sample of 150 beer drinkers, a total of 50 prefer light beer, 70 prefer regular beer, and 30 prefer dark beer. In terms of fractions we conclude that $^{50}/_{150} = \frac{1}{3}$ of the beer drinkers prefer light beer, $^{70}/_{150} = \frac{7}{15}$ prefer regular beer, and $^{30}/_{150} = \frac{1}{5}$ prefer dark beer. If the *independence* assumption is valid, we argue that these fractions must be applicable to both male and female beer drinkers. Thus, under the assumption of independence, we would expect the sample of 80 male beer drinkers to show that $(\frac{1}{3})80 = 26.67$ prefer light beer, $(\frac{7}{15})80 = 37.33$ prefer regular beer, and $(\frac{1}{5})80 = 16$ prefer dark beer. Application of the same fractions to the 70 female beer drinkers provides the expected frequencies shown in Table 12.4.

Let e_{ij} denote the expected frequency for the contingency table category in row i and column j. With this notation, let us reconsider the expected frequency calculation for males

TABLE 12.4   EXPECTED FREQUENCIES IF BEER PREFERENCE IS INDEPENDENT OF THE GENDER OF THE BEER DRINKER

		Beer Preference			
		Light	**Regular**	**Dark**	**Total**
Gender	**Male**	26.67	37.33	16.00	80
	Female	23.33	32.67	14.00	70
	Total	50.00	70.00	30.00	150

(row $i = 1$) who prefer regular beer (column $j = 2$); that is, expected frequency e_{12}. Following the preceding argument for the computation of expected frequencies, we can show that

$$e_{12} = (\tfrac{7}{15})80 = 37.33$$

This expression can be written slightly differently as

$$e_{12} = (\tfrac{7}{15})80 = (\tfrac{70}{150})80 = \frac{(80)(70)}{150} = 37.33$$

Note that 80 in the expression is the total number of males (row 1 total), 70 is the total number of individuals preferring regular beer (column 2 total), and 150 is the total sample size. Hence, we see that

$$e_{12} = \frac{(\text{Row 1 Total})(\text{Column 2 Total})}{\text{Sample Size}}$$

Generalization of the expression shows that the following formula provides the expected frequencies for a contingency table in the test of independence.

EXPECTED FREQUENCIES FOR CONTINGENCY TABLES UNDER THE ASSUMPTION OF INDEPENDENCE

$$e_{ij} = \frac{(\text{Row } i \text{ Total})(\text{Column } j \text{ Total})}{\text{Sample Size}} \qquad \textbf{(12.2)}$$

Using equation (12.2) for male beer drinkers who prefer dark beer, we find an expected frequency of $e_{13} = (80)(30)/150 = 16.00$, as shown in Table 12.4. Use equation (12.2) to verify the other expected frequencies shown in Table 12.4.

The test procedure for comparing the observed frequencies of Table 12.3 with the expected frequencies of Table 12.4 is similar to the goodness of fit calculations made in Section 12.1. Specifically, the χ^2 value based on the observed and expected frequencies is computed as follows.

TEST STATISTIC FOR INDEPENDENCE

$$\chi^2 = \sum_i \sum_j \frac{(f_{ij} - e_{ij})^2}{e_{ij}} \qquad \textbf{(12.3)}$$

where

f_{ij} = observed frequency for contingency table category in row i and column j

e_{ij} = expected frequency for contingency table category in row i and column j based on the assumption of independence

Note: With n rows and m columns in the contingency table, the test statistic has a chi-square distribution with $(n - 1)(m - 1)$ degrees of freedom provided that the expected frequencies are 5 or more for all categories.

TABLE 12.5   COMPUTATION OF THE CHI-SQUARE TEST STATISTIC FOR DETERMINING WHETHER BEER PREFERENCE IS INDEPENDENT OF THE GENDER OF THE BEER DRINKER

Gender	Beer Preference	Observed Frequency (f_{ij})	Expected Frequency (e_{ij})	Difference $(f_{ij} - e_{ij})$	Squared Difference $(f_{ij} - e_{ij})^2$	Squared Difference Divided by Expected Frequency $(f_{ij} - e_{ij})^2/e_{ij}$
Male	Light	20	26.67	−6.67	44.44	1.67
Male	Regular	40	37.33	2.67	7.11	0.19
Male	Dark	20	16.00	4.00	16.00	1.00
Female	Light	30	23.33	6.67	44.44	1.90
Female	Regular	30	32.67	−2.67	7.11	0.22
Female	Dark	10	14.00	−4.00	16.00	1.14
Total		150				$\chi^2 = 6.12$

The double summation in equation (12.3) is used to indicate that the calculation must be made for all the cells in the contingency table.

By reviewing the expected frequencies in Table 12.4, we see that the expected frequencies are 5 or more for each category. We therefore proceed with the computation of the chi-square test statistic. The calculations necessary to compute the chi-square test statistic for determining whether beer preference is independent of the gender of the beer drinker are shown in Table 12.5. We see that the value of the test statistic is $\chi^2 = 6.12$.

The number of degrees of freedom for the appropriate chi-square distribution is computed by multiplying the number of rows minus 1 by the number of columns minus 1. With two rows and three columns, we have $(2 - 1)(3 - 1) = 2$ degrees of freedom. Just like the test for goodness of fit, the test for independence rejects H_0 if the differences between observed and expected frequencies provide a large value for the test statistic. Thus the test for independence is also an upper tail test. Using the chi-square table (Table 3 of Appendix B), we conclude that the upper tail area or p-value at $\chi^2 = 6.12$ is between .025 and .05. Excel can be used to show that $\chi^2 = 6.12$ provides a p-value $= .0468$. At the .05 level of significance, p-value $\leq \alpha = .05$. We reject the null hypothesis of independence and conclude that beer preference is not independent of the gender of the beer drinker.

The test for independence is always a one-tailed test with the rejection region in the upper tail of the chi-square distribution.

Although no further conclusions can be made as a result of the test, we can compare the observed and expected frequencies informally to obtain an idea about the dependence between beer preference and gender. Refer to Tables 12.3 and 12.4. We see that male beer drinkers have higher observed than expected frequencies for both regular and dark beers, whereas female beer drinkers have a higher observed than expected frequency only for light beer. These observations give us insight about the beer preference differences between male and female beer drinkers.

Let us summarize the steps in a contingency table test of independence.

TEST OF INDEPENDENCE: A SUMMARY

1. State the null and alternative hypotheses.

   H_0: The column variable is independent of the row variable
   H_a: The column variable is not independent of the row variable

2. Select a random sample and record the observed frequencies for each cell of the contingency table.

3. Use equation (12.2) to compute the expected frequency for each cell.
4. Use equation (12.3) to compute the value of the test statistic.
5. Rejection rule:

$$p\text{-value approach:} \qquad \text{Reject } H_0 \text{ if } p\text{-value} \leq \alpha$$
$$\text{Critical value approach:} \qquad \text{Reject } H_0 \text{ if } \chi^2 \geq \chi_\alpha^2$$

where α is the level of significance, with n rows and m columns providing $(n-1)(m-1)$ degrees of freedom.

Using Excel to Conduct a Test of Independence

Excel can be used to conduct a test of independence for the Alber's Brewery example. Refer to Figure 12.2 as we describe the tasks involved. The formula worksheet is in the background; the value worksheet is in the foreground.

Alber's

Enter Data: Column A is used to identify each of the 150 individuals in the study. Column B shows the gender and column C shows the beer preference (Light, Regular, or Dark) for each individual.

Apply Tools: Using Excel's PivotTable tool (see Section 2.4 for details regarding how to use this tool), we developed the crosstabulation shown in cells E3:I7. The values in cells F5:H6 are the observed frequencies for the Alber's Brewery study.

FIGURE 12.2 EXCEL WORKSHEET FOR THE ALBER'S BREWERY TEST OF INDEPENDENCE

	A	B	C	D	E	F	G	H	I	J
1	Individual	Gender	Preference							
2	1	Female	Light							
3	2	Female	Regular		Count of Individual	Preference				
4	3	Male	Regular		Gender	Light	Regular	Dark	Grand Total	
5	4	Female	Light		Male	20	40	20	80	
6	5	Female	Light		Female	30	30	10	70	
7	6	Female	Regular		Grand Total	50	70	30	150	
8	7	Male	Regular							
9	8	Female	Dark		Expected Frequencies					
10	9	Female	Regular			Light	Regular	Dark		
11	10	Male	Dark		Male	=F7*I5/I7	=G7*I5/I7	=H7*I5/I7		
12	11	Male	Regular		Female	=F7*I6/I7	=G7*I6/I7	=H7*I6/I7		
13	12	Male	Regular							
14	13	Female	Regular				p-value	=CHITEST(F5:H6,F11:H12)		
15	14	Female	Regular							
16	15	Male	Light							
149	148	Male	Regular							
150	149	Female	Light							
151	150	Female	Regular							
152										

Note: Rows 17–148 are hidden.

	A	B	C	D	E	F	G	H	I	J
1	Individual	Gender	Preference							
2	1	Female	Light							
3	2	Female	Regular		Count of Individual	Preference				
4	3	Male	Regular		Gender	Light	Regular	Dark	Grand Total	
5	4	Female	Light		Male	20	40	20	80	
6	5	Female	Light		Female	30	30	10	70	
7	6	Female	Regular		Grand Total	50	70	30	150	
8	7	Male	Regular							
9	8	Female	Dark		Expected Frequencies					
10	9	Female	Regular			Light	Regular	Dark		
11	10	Male	Dark		Male	26.6667	37.3333	16		
12	11	Male	Regular		Female	23.3333	32.6667	14		
13	12	Male	Regular							
14	13	Female	Regular				p-value	0.0468		
15	14	Female	Regular							
16	15	Male	Light							
149	148	Male	Regular							
150	149	Female	Light							
151	150	Female	Regular							
152										

Enter Functions and Formulas: To compute the expected frequencies for the Alber's Brewery contingency table under the assumption of independence, we use equation (12.2). The formulas in cells F11:H12 are used to compute these expected frequencies. Once the observed and expected frequencies have been computed, Excel's CHITEST function can be used to compute the *p*-value for a test of independence. The inputs to the CHITEST function are the range of values for the observed and expected frequencies. To compute the *p*-value for this test of independence, we entered the following function into cell H14:

$$=\text{CHITEST(F5:H6,F11:H12)}$$

The value worksheet shows that the resulting *p*-value is .0468. Thus, with $\alpha = .05$ we reject H_0 and conclude that beer preference is not independent of the gender of the beer drinker.

NOTES AND COMMENTS

The test statistic for the chi-square tests in this chapter requires an expected frequency of five for each category. When a category has fewer than five, it is often appropriate to combine two adjacent categories to obtain an expected frequency of five or more in each category.

Exercises

Methods

9. The following 2×3 contingency table contains observed frequencies for a sample of 200. Test for independence of the row and column variables using the χ^2 test with $\alpha = .05$.

	Column Variable		
Row Variable	A	B	C
P	20	44	50
Q	30	26	30

10. The following 3×3 contingency table contains observed frequencies for a sample of 240. Test for independence of the row and column variables using the χ^2 test with $\alpha = .05$.

	Column Variable		
Row Variable	A	B	C
P	20	30	20
Q	30	60	25
R	10	15	30

Applications

11. One of the questions on the *BusinessWeek* Subscriber Study was, "In the past 12 months, when traveling for business, what type of airline ticket did you purchase most often?" The data obtained are shown in the following contingency table.

Type of Ticket	Type of Flight	
	Domestic Flights	International Flights
First class	29	22
Business/executive class	95	121
Full fare economy/coach class	518	135

Use $\alpha = .05$ and test for the independence of type of flight and type of ticket. What is your conclusion?

12. In a study of brand loyalty in the automotive industry, new-car customers were asked whether the make of their new car was the same as the make of their previous car (*Business Week,* May 8, 2000). The breakdown of 600 responses shows the brand loyalty for domestic, European, and Asian cars.

Purchased	Manufacturer		
	Domestic	European	Asian
Same Make	125	55	68
Different Make	140	105	107

a. Conduct a hypothesis test to determine whether brand loyalty is independent of the manufacturer. Use $\alpha = .05$. What is your conclusion?
b. If a significant difference is found, which manufacturer appears to have the greatest brand loyalty?

13. With double-digit annual percentage increases in the cost of health insurance, more and more workers are likely to lack health insurance coverage (*USA Today,* January 23, 2004). The following sample data provide a comparison of workers with and without health insurance coverage for small, medium, and large companies. For the purposes of this study, small companies are companies that have fewer than 100 employees. Medium companies have 100 to 999 employees, and large companies have 1000 or more employees. Sample data are reported for 50 employees of small companies, 75 employees of medium companies, and 100 employees of large companies.

Size of Company	Health Insurance		Total
	Yes	No	
Small	36	14	50
Medium	65	10	75
Large	88	12	100

a. Conduct a test of independence to determine whether employee health insurance coverage is independent of the size of the company. Use $\alpha = .05$. What is the p-value, and what is your conclusion?
b. The *USA Today* article indicated employees of small companies are more likely to lack health insurance coverage. Use percentages based on the preceding data to support this conclusion.

14. A State of Washington's Public Interest Research Group (PIRG) study showed that 46% of full-time college students work 25 or more hours per week. The PIRG study provided data on the effects of working on grades (*USA Today,* April 17, 2002). A sample of 200 students included 90 who worked 1–15 hours per week, 60 who worked 16–24 hours per week, and 50 who worked 25–34 hours per week. The sample number of students indicating their work had a positive effect, no effect, or a negative effect on grades is as follows.

	Effect on Grades			
Hours Worked per Week	**Positive**	**None**	**Negative**	**Total**
1–15 hours	26	50	14	90
16–24 hours	16	27	17	60
25–34 hours	11	19	20	50

a. Conduct a test of independence to determine whether the effect on grades is independent of the hours worked per week. Use $\alpha = .05$. What is the *p*-value, and what is your conclusion?

b. Use row percentages to learn more about how working affects grades. What is your conclusion?

15. Negative appeal is recognized as an effective method of persuasion in advertising. A study in *The Journal of Advertising* reported the results of a content analysis of guilt and fear advertisements in 24 magazines. The number of ads with guilt and fear appeals that appeared in selected magazine types follows.

	Type of Appeal	
Magazine Type	**Number of Ads with Guilt Appeals**	**Number of Ads with Fear Appeals**
News and opinion	20	10
General editorial	15	11
Family-oriented	30	19
Business/financial	22	17
Female-oriented	16	14
African-American	12	15

Use the chi-square test of independence with a .01 level of significance to analyze the data. What is your conclusion?

16. Businesses are increasingly placing orders online. The Performance Measurement Group collected data on the rates of correctly filled electronic orders by industry (*Investor's Business Daily,* May 8, 2000). Assume a sample of 700 electronic orders provided the following results.

	Industry			
Order	**Pharmaceutical**	**Consumer**	**Computers**	**Telecommunications**
Correct	207	136	151	178
Incorrect	3	4	9	12

a. Conduct a hypothesis test to determine whether correctness of order fulfillment is independent of industry. Use $\alpha = .05$. What is your conclusion?

b. Which industry has the highest percentage of correctly filled orders?

17. The National Sleep Foundation used a survey to determine whether hours of sleeping per night are independent of age (*Newsweek,* January 19, 2004). The following show the hours of sleep on weeknights for a sample of individuals age 49 and younger and for a sample of individuals age 50 and older.

	Hours of Sleep				
Age	Fewer than 6	6 to 6.9	7 to 7.9	8 or more	Total
49 or younger	38	60	77	65	240
50 or older	36	57	75	92	260

a. Conduct a test of independence to determine whether the hours of sleep on weeknights are independent of age. Use $\alpha = .05$. What is the *p*-value, and what is your conclusion?

b. What is your estimate of the percentage of people who sleep fewer than 6 hours, 6 to 6.9 hours, 7 to 7.9 hours, and 8 or more hours on weeknights?

Goodness of Fit Test: Poisson and Normal Distributions

In Section 12.1 we introduced the goodness of fit test for a multinomial population. In general, the goodness of fit test can be used with any hypothesized probability distribution. In this section we illustrate the goodness of fit test procedure for cases in which the population is hypothesized to have a Poisson or a normal distribution. As we shall see, the goodness of fit test and the use of the chi-square distribution for the test follow the same general procedure used for the goodness of fit test in Section 12.1.

Poisson Distribution

Let us illustrate the goodness of fit test for the case in which the hypothesized population distribution is a Poisson distribution. As an example, consider the arrival of customers at Dubek's Food Market in Tallahassee, Florida. Because of some recent staffing problems, Dubek's managers asked a local consulting firm to assist with the scheduling of clerks for the checkout lanes. After reviewing the checkout lane operation, the consulting firm will make a recommendation for a clerk-scheduling procedure. The procedure, based on a mathematical analysis of waiting lines, is applicable only if the number of customers arriving during a specified time period follows the Poisson distribution. Therefore, before the scheduling process is implemented, data on customer arrivals must be collected and a statistical test conducted to see whether an assumption of a Poisson distribution for arrivals is reasonable.

We define the arrivals at the store in terms of the *number of customers* entering the store during 5-minute intervals. Hence, the following null and alternative hypotheses are appropriate for the Dubek's Food Market study.

H_0: The number of customers entering the store during 5-minute intervals has a Poisson probability distribution

H_a: The number of customers entering the store during 5-minute intervals does not have a Poisson distribution

If a sample of customer arrivals indicates H_0 cannot be rejected, Dubek's will proceed with the implementation of the consulting firm's scheduling procedure. However, if the sample

TABLE 12.6

OBSERVED
FREQUENCY
OF DUBEK'S
CUSTOMER
ARRIVALS FOR
A SAMPLE OF
128 5-MINUTE
TIME PERIODS

Number of Customers Arriving	Observed Frequency
0	2
1	8
2	10
3	12
4	18
5	22
6	22
7	16
8	12
9	6
Total	128

Excel's POISSON function (see Section 5.5) was used to compute the probabilities in Table 12.7.

When the expected number in some category is less than five, the assumptions for the χ^2 test are not satisfied. When this happens, adjacent categories can be combined to increase the expected number to five.

leads to the rejection of H_0, the assumption of the Poisson distribution for the arrivals cannot be made, and other scheduling procedures will be considered.

To test the assumption of a Poisson distribution for the number of arrivals during weekday morning hours, a store employee randomly selects a sample of 128 5-minute intervals during weekday mornings over a 3-week period. For each 5-minute interval in the sample, the store employee records the number of customer arrivals. In summarizing the data, the employee determines the number of 5-minute intervals having no arrivals, the number of 5-minute intervals having one arrival, the number of 5-minute intervals having two arrivals, and so on. These data are summarized in Table 12.6.

Table 12.6 gives the observed frequencies for the 10 categories. We now want to use a goodness of fit test to determine whether the sample of 128 time periods supports the hypothesized Poisson distribution. To conduct the goodness of fit test, we need to consider the expected frequency for each of the 10 categories under the assumption that the Poisson distribution of arrivals is true. That is, we need to compute the expected number of time periods in which no customers, one customer, two customers, and so on would arrive if, in fact, the customer arrivals follow a Poisson distribution.

The Poisson probability function, which was first introduced in Chapter 5, is

$$f(x) = \frac{\mu^x e^{-\mu}}{x!} \tag{12.4}$$

In this function, μ represents the mean or expected number of customers arriving per 5-minute period, x is the random variable indicating the number of customers arriving during a 5-minute period, and $f(x)$ is the probability that x customers will arrive in a 5-minute interval.

Before we use equation (12.4) to compute Poisson probabilities, we must obtain an estimate of μ, the mean number of customer arrivals during a 5-minute time period. The sample mean for the data in Table 12.6 provides this estimate. With no customers arriving in two 5-minute time periods, one customer arriving in eight 5-minute time periods, and so on, the total number of customers who arrived during the sample of 128 5-minute time periods is given by $0(2) + 1(8) + 2(10) + \cdots + 9(6) = 640$. The 640 customer arrivals over the sample of 128 periods provide a mean arrival rate of $\mu = 640/128 = 5$ customers per 5-minute period. With this value for the mean of the Poisson distribution, an estimate of the Poisson probability function for Dubek's Food Market is

$$f(x) = \frac{5^x e^{-5}}{x!} \tag{12.5}$$

This probability function can be evaluated for different values of x to determine the probability associated with each category of arrivals. These probabilities are given in Table 12.7. For example, the probability of zero customers arriving during a 5-minute interval is $f(0) = .0067$, the probability of one customer arriving during a 5-minute interval is $f(1) = .0337$, and so on. As we saw in Section 12.1, the expected frequencies for the categories are found by multiplying the category probabilities by the sample size. For example, the expected number of periods with zero arrivals is given by $(.0067)(128) = .86$, the expected number of periods with one arrival is given by $(.0337)(128) = 4.31$, and so on.

Before we make the usual chi-square calculations to compare the observed and expected frequencies, note that in Table 12.7, four of the categories have an expected frequency less than five. This condition violates the requirements for use of the chi-square distribution. However, expected category frequencies less than five cause no difficulty, because adjacent categories can be combined to satisfy the "at least five" expected frequency requirement. In particular, we will combine 0 and 1 into a single category and then combine 9 with "10 or more" into another single category. Thus, the rule of a minimum expected

TABLE 12.7   EXPECTED FREQUENCY OF DUBEK'S CUSTOMER ARRIVALS, ASSUMING A POISSON DISTRIBUTION WITH $\mu = 5$

Number of Customers Arriving (x)	Poisson Probability $f(x)$	Expected Number of 5-Minute Time Periods with x Arrivals, $128 f(x)$
0	.0067	0.86
1	.0337	4.31
2	.0842	10.78
3	.1404	17.97
4	.1755	22.46
5	.1755	22.46
6	.1462	18.72
7	.1044	13.37
8	.0653	8.36
9	.0363	4.65
10 or more	.0318	4.07
	Total	128.00

frequency of five in each category is satisfied. Table 12.8 shows the observed and expected frequencies after combining categories.

As in Section 12.1, the goodness of fit test focuses on the differences between observed and expected frequencies, $f_i - e_i$. Thus, we will use the observed and expected frequencies shown in Table 12.8 to compute the chi-square test statistic.

$$\chi^2 = \sum_{i=1}^{k} \frac{(f_i - e_i)^2}{e_i}$$

The calculations necessary to compute the chi-square test statistic are shown in Table 12.9. The value of the test statistic is $\chi^2 = 10.96$.

TABLE 12.8   OBSERVED AND EXPECTED FREQUENCIES FOR DUBEK'S CUSTOMER ARRIVALS AFTER COMBINING CATEGORIES

Number of Customers Arriving	Observed Frequency (f_i)	Expected Frequency (e_i)
0 or 1	10	5.17
2	10	10.78
3	12	17.97
4	18	22.46
5	22	22.46
6	22	18.72
7	16	13.37
8	12	8.36
9 or more	6	8.72
Total	128	128.00

TABLE 12.9   COMPUTATION OF THE CHI-SQUARE TEST STATISTIC FOR THE DUBEK'S FOOD MARKET STUDY

Number of Customers Arriving (x)	Observed Frequency (f_i)	Expected Frequency (e_i)	Difference ($f_i - e_i$)	Squared Difference ($f_i - e_i)^2$	Squared Difference Divided by Expected Frequency ($f_i - e_i)^2/e_i$
0 or 1	10	5.17	4.83	23.28	4.50
2	10	10.78	−0.78	0.61	0.06
3	12	17.97	−5.97	35.62	1.98
4	18	22.46	−4.46	19.89	0.89
5	22	22.46	−0.46	0.21	0.01
6	22	18.72	3.28	10.78	0.58
7	16	13.37	2.63	6.92	0.52
8	12	8.36	3.64	13.28	1.59
9 or more	6	8.72	−2.72	7.38	0.85
Total	128	128.00			$\chi^2 = 10.96$

In general, the chi-square distribution for a goodness of fit test has $k - p - 1$ degrees of freedom, where k is the number of categories and p is the number of population parameters estimated from the sample data. For the Poisson distribution goodness of fit test, Table 12.9 shows $k = 9$ categories. Because the sample data were used to estimate the mean of the Poisson distribution, $p = 1$. Thus, there are $k - p - 1 = k - 2$ degrees of freedom. With $k = 9$, we have $9 - 2 = 7$ degrees of freedom.

Suppose we test the null hypothesis that the probability distribution for the customer arrivals is a Poisson distribution with a .05 level of significance. To test this hypothesis, we need to determine the p-value for the test statistic $\chi^2 = 10.96$ by finding the area in the upper tail of a chi-square distribution with 7 degrees of freedom. Using Table 3 of Appendix B, we find that $\chi^2 = 10.96$ provides an area in the upper tail greater than .10. Thus, we know that the p-value is greater than .10. Excel shows the p-value $= .1403$. With p-value $> \alpha = .05$, we cannot reject H_0. Hence, the assumption of a Poisson probability distribution for weekday morning customer arrivals cannot be rejected. As a result, Dubek's management may proceed with the consulting firm's scheduling procedure for weekday mornings.

POISSON DISTRIBUTION GOODNESS OF FIT TEST: A SUMMARY

1. State the null and alternative hypotheses.

H_0: The population has a Poisson distribution
H_a: The population does not have a Poisson distribution

2. Select a random sample and
   a. Record the observed frequency f_i for each value of the Poisson random variable.
   b. Compute the mean number of occurrences μ.

> **3.** Compute the expected frequency of occurrences e_i for each value of the Poisson random variable. Multiply the sample size by the Poisson probability of occurrence for each value of the Poisson random variable. If there are fewer than five expected occurrences for some values, combine adjacent values and reduce the number of categories as necessary.
> **4.** Compute the value of the test statistic.
>
> $$\chi^2 = \sum_{i=1}^{k} \frac{(f_i - e_i)^2}{e_i}$$
>
> **5.** Rejection rule:
>
> p-value approach: Reject H_0 if p-value $\leq \alpha$
> Critical value approach: Reject H_0 if $\chi^2 \geq \chi^2_\alpha$
>
> where α is the level of significance and there are $k - 2$ degrees of freedom.

Using Excel to Conduct a Goodness of Fit Test

In Section 12.1 we showed how Excel could be used to conduct a multinomial goodness of fit test. A similar approach can be used to conduct a Poisson distribution goodness of fit test. Refer to Figure 12.1 as we discuss the approach. The nine categories corresponding to the number of arrivals in Table 12.9 would replace the three companies listed in column D of the worksheet, and the probability associated with each category of arrivals would be computed in column E using Excel's POISSON function. The only data are the observed frequencies, which would be typed directly into column F. The expected frequencies would be computed in column G by multiplying the probabilities in column E by the sample size. The formulas in columns H, I, and J used to compute the χ^2 test statistic using equation (12.1) are the same as in the worksheet in Figure 12.1. The chi-square value obtained is 10.9628. The only other change necessary is that the cell formula for the degrees of freedom must be changed from $k - 1$ for the multinomial goodness of fit test to $k - 2$ for the Poisson distribution goodness of fit test. With these changes, the p-value for the test is computed using Excel's CHIDIST function as we described in Section 12.1. For the Dubek's Food Market goodness of fit test, CHIDIST(10.9628,7) provides a p-value of .1403. With .1403 $> \alpha = .05$, we cannot reject the null hypothesis that the number of customers entering the store during 5-minute intervals has a Poisson distribution.

Normal Distribution

The goodness of fit test for a normal distribution is also based on the use of the chi-square distribution. It is similar to the procedure we discussed for the Poisson distribution. In particular, observed frequencies for several categories of sample data are compared to expected frequencies under the assumption that the population has a normal distribution. Because the normal distribution is continuous, we must modify the way the categories are defined and how the expected frequencies are computed. Let us demonstrate the goodness of fit test for a normal distribution by considering the job applicant test data for Chemline, Inc., listed in Table 12.10.

Chemline hires approximately 400 new employees annually for its four plants located throughout the United States. The personnel director asks whether a normal distribution

TABLE 12.10

CHEMLINE
EMPLOYEE
APTITUDE TEST
SCORES FOR
50 RANDOMLY
CHOSEN JOB
APPLICANTS

71	66	61	65	54	93
60	86	70	70	73	73
55	63	56	62	76	54
82	79	76	68	53	58
85	80	56	61	61	64
65	62	90	69	76	79
77	54	64	74	65	65
61	56	63	80	56	71
79	84				

applies for the population of test scores. If such a distribution can be used, the distribution would be helpful in evaluating specific test scores; that is, scores in the upper 20%, lower 40%, and so on, could be identified quickly. Hence, we want to test the null hypothesis that the population of test scores has a normal distribution.

Let us first use the data in Table 12.10 to develop estimates of the mean and standard deviation of the normal distribution that will be considered in the null hypothesis. We use the sample mean $\bar{x}$ and the sample standard deviation s as point estimators of the mean and standard deviation of the normal distribution. The calculations follow.

$$\bar{x} = \frac{\Sigma x_i}{n} = \frac{3421}{50} = 68.42$$

$$s = \sqrt{\frac{\Sigma(x_i - \bar{x})^2}{n - 1}} = \sqrt{\frac{5310.0369}{49}} = 10.41$$

CD file

Chemline

Using these values, we state the following hypotheses about the distribution of the job applicant test scores.

H_0: The population of test scores has a normal distribution with mean 68.42 and standard deviation 10.41

H_a: The population of test scores does not have a normal distribution with mean 68.42 and standard deviation 10.41

The hypothesized normal distribution is shown in Figure 12.3.

Now let us consider a way of defining the categories for a goodness of fit test involving a normal distribution. For the discrete probability distribution in the Poisson distribution test, the categories were readily defined in terms of the number of customers arriving, such as 0, 1, 2, and so on. However, with the continuous normal probability distribution, we must use a different procedure for defining the categories. We need to define the categories in terms of *intervals* of test scores.

Recall the rule of thumb for an expected frequency of at least five in each interval or category. We define the categories of test scores such that the expected frequencies will be at least five for each category. With a sample size of 50, one way of establishing categories

FIGURE 12.3   HYPOTHESIZED NORMAL DISTRIBUTION OF TEST SCORES FOR THE CHEMLINE JOB APPLICANTS

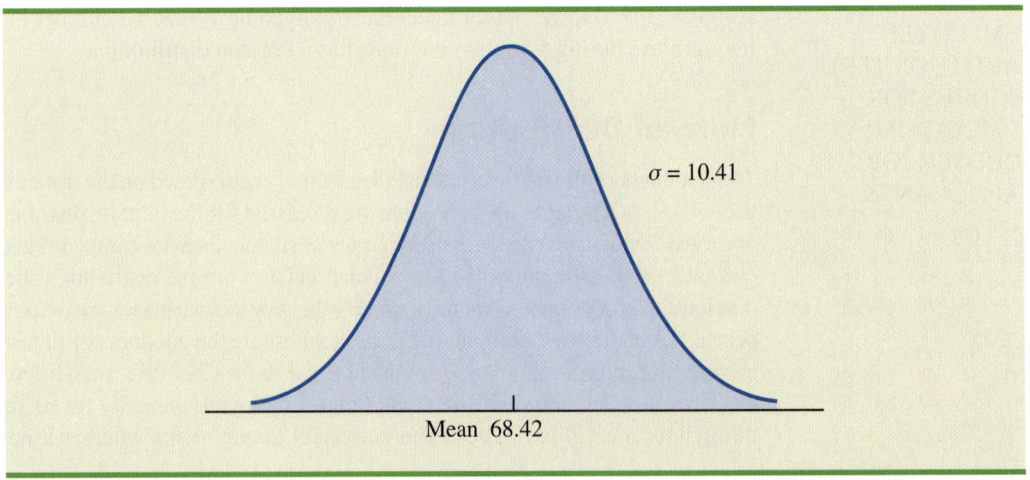

FIGURE 12.4   NORMAL DISTRIBUTION FOR THE CHEMLINE EXAMPLE
WITH 10 EQUAL-PROBABILITY INTERVALS

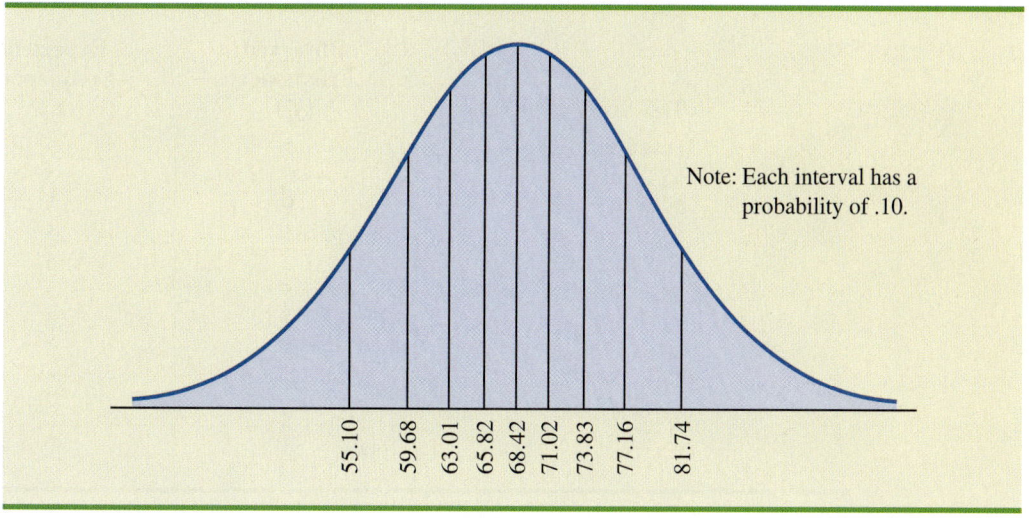

Note: Each interval has a
probability of .10.

55.10 59.68 63.01 65.82 68.42 71.02 73.83 77.16 81.74

With a continuous probability distribution, establish intervals such that each interval has an expected frequency of five or more.

is to divide the normal distribution into 10 equal-probability intervals (see Figure 12.4). With a sample size of 50, we would expect five outcomes in each interval or category, and the rule of thumb for expected frequencies would be satisfied.

Let us look more closely at the procedure for calculating the category boundaries. When the normal probability distribution is assumed, the standard normal distribution table can be used to determine these boundaries. First consider the test score cutting off the lowest 10% of the test scores. From the standard normal probability table we find that the z value for this test score is -1.28. Therefore, the test score of $x = 68.42 - 1.28(10.41) = 55.10$ provides this cutoff value for the lowest 10% of the scores. For the lowest 20%, we find $z = -.84$, and thus $x = 68.42 - .84(10.41) = 59.68$. Working through the normal distribution in this way provides the following test score values.

Lower 10%:	$68.42 - 1.28(10.41) = 55.10$
Lower 20%:	$68.42 - .84(10.41) = 59.68$
Lower 30%:	$68.42 - .52(10.41) = 63.01$
Lower 40%:	$68.42 - .25(10.41) = 65.82$
Mid-score:	$68.42 + 0(10.41) = 68.42$
Upper 40%:	$68.42 + .25(10.41) = 71.02$
Upper 30%:	$68.42 + .52(10.41) = 73.83$
Upper 20%:	$68.42 + .84(10.41) = 77.16$
Upper 10%:	$68.42 + 1.28(10.41) = 81.74$

These cutoff or interval boundary points are identified on the graph in Figure 12.4.

With the categories or intervals of test scores now defined and with the known expected frequency of five per category, we can return to the sample data of Table 12.10 and determine the observed frequencies for the categories. Doing so provides the results in Table 12.11.

With the results in Table 12.11, the goodness of fit calculations proceed exactly as before. Namely, we compare the observed and expected results by computing a χ^2 value. The computations necessary to compute the chi-square test statistic are shown in Table 12.12. We see that the value of the test statistic is $\chi^2 = 7.2$.

TABLE 12.11   OBSERVED AND EXPECTED FREQUENCIES FOR CHEMLINE JOB APPLICANT TEST SCORES

Test Score Interval	Observed Frequency (f_i)	Expected Frequency (e_i)
Less than 55.10	5	5
55.10 to 59.68	5	5
59.68 to 63.01	9	5
63.01 to 65.82	6	5
65.82 to 68.42	2	5
68.42 to 71.02	5	5
71.02 to 73.83	2	5
73.83 to 77.16	5	5
77.16 to 81.74	5	5
81.74 and Over	6	5
Total	50	50

Estimating μ and σ, the two parameters of the normal distribution, will cause a loss of two degrees of freedom in the χ^2 test.

To determine whether the computed χ^2 value of 7.2 is large enough to reject H_0, we need to refer to the appropriate chi-square distribution tables. Using the rule for computing the number of degrees of freedom for the goodness of fit test, we have $k - p - 1 = 10 - 2 - 1 = 7$ degrees of freedom based on $k = 10$ categories and $p = 2$ parameters (mean and standard deviation) estimated from the sample data.

Suppose that we test the null hypothesis that the distribution for the test scores is a normal distribution with a .10 level of significance. To test this hypothesis, we need to determine the p-value for the test statistic $\chi^2 = 7.2$ by finding the area in the upper tail of a chi-square distribution with 7 degrees of freedom. Using Table 3 of Appendix B, we find that $\chi^2 = 7.2$ provides an area in the upper tail greater than .10. Thus, we know that the

TABLE 12.12   COMPUTATION OF THE CHI-SQUARE TEST STATISTIC FOR THE CHEMLINE JOB APPLICANT EXAMPLE

Test Score Interval	Observed Frequency (f_i)	Expected Frequency (e_i)	Difference $(f_i - e_i)$	Squared Difference $(f_i - e_i)^2$	Squared Difference Divided by Expected Frequency $(f_i - e_i)^2/e_i$
Less than 55.10	5	5	0	0	0.0
55.10 to 59.68	5	5	0	0	0.0
59.68 to 63.01	9	5	4	16	3.2
63.01 to 65.82	6	5	1	1	0.2
65.82 to 68.42	2	5	-3	9	1.8
68.42 to 71.02	5	5	0	0	0.0
71.02 to 73.83	2	5	-3	9	1.8
73.83 to 77.16	5	5	0	0	0.0
77.16 to 81.74	5	5	0	0	0.0
81.74 and Over	6	5	1	1	0.2
Total	50	50			$\chi^2 = 7.2$

p-value is greater than .10. Using Excel the exact *p*-value = .4084. With the *p*-value > α = .10, the hypothesis that the probability distribution for the Chemline job applicant test scores is a normal distribution cannot be rejected. The normal distribution may be applied to assist in the interpretation of test scores. A summary of the goodness fit test for a normal distribution follows.

NORMAL DISTRIBUTION GOODNESS OF FIT TEST: A SUMMARY

1. State the null and alternative hypotheses.

H_0: The population has a normal distribution

H_a: The population does not have a normal distribution

2. Select a random sample and
   a. Compute the sample mean and sample standard deviation.
   b. Define intervals of values so that the expected frequency is at least five for each interval. Using equal probability intervals is a good approach.
   c. Record the observed frequency of data values f_i in each interval defined.
3. Compute the expected number of occurrences e_i for each interval of values defined in step 2(b). Multiply the sample size by the probability of a normal random variable being in the interval.
4. Compute the value of the test statistic.

$$\chi^2 = \sum_{i=1}^{k} \frac{(f_i - e_i)^2}{e_i}$$

5. Rejection rule:

   p-value approach: Reject H_0 if *p*-value $\leq \alpha$
   Critical value approach: Reject H_0 if $\chi^2 \geq \chi_\alpha^2$

   where α is the level of significance and there are $k - 3$ degrees of freedom.

Using Excel to Conduct a Goodness of Fit Test

In Section 12.1 we showed how Excel could be used to conduct a multinomial goodness of fit test. A similar approach can be used to conduct a normal distribution goodness of fit test. Refer to Figure 12.1 as we discuss the approach. The 10 categories corresponding to the test score intervals would replace the three companies listed in column D of the worksheet. The only data would be the observed and expected frequencies; they would be typed directly into columns F and G. The formulas in columns H, I, and J used to compute the χ^2 test statistic using equation (12.1) are the same as in the worksheet in Figure 12.1. The only other change necessary is that the cell formula for the degrees of freedom must be changed from $k - 1$ for the multinomial goodness of fit test to $k - 3$ for the normal distribution goodness of fit test. With these changes, the *p*-value for the test is computed using Excel's CHIDIST function as we described in Section 12.1. For the Chemline goodness of fit test CHIDIST(7.2,7) provides a *p*-value of .4084. With .4084 > α = .10, we cannot reject the null hypothesis that the Chemline applicant test scores follow a normal distribution.

Exercises

Methods

18. Data on the number of occurrences per time period and observed frequencies follow. Use $\alpha = .05$ and the goodness of fit test to see whether the data fit a Poisson distribution.

Number of Occurrences	Observed Frequency
0	39
1	30
2	30
3	18
4	3

19. The following data are believed to have come from a normal distribution. Use the goodness of fit test and $\alpha = .05$ to test this claim.

17	23	22	24	19	23	18	22	20	13	11	21	18	20	21
21	18	15	24	23	23	43	29	27	26	30	28	33	23	29

Applications

20. The number of automobile accidents per day in a particular city is believed to have a Poisson distribution. A sample of 80 days during the past year gives the following data. Do these data support the belief that the number of accidents per day has a Poisson distribution? Use $\alpha = .05$.

Number of Accidents	Observed Frequency (days)
0	34
1	25
2	11
3	7
4	3

21. The number of incoming phone calls at a company switchboard during 1-minute intervals is believed to have a Poisson distribution. Use $\alpha = .10$ and the following data to test the assumption that the incoming phone calls follow a Poisson distribution.

Number of Incoming Phone Calls During a 1-Minute Interval	Observed Frequency
0	15
1	31
2	20
3	15
4	13
5	4
6	2
Total	100

22. The weekly demand for a product is believed to be normally distributed. Use a goodness of fit test and the following data to test this assumption. Use $\alpha = .10$. The sample mean is 24.5 and the sample standard deviation is 3.

18	20	22	27	22
25	22	27	25	24
26	23	20	24	26
27	25	19	21	25
26	25	31	29	25
25	28	26	28	24

23. Use $\alpha = .01$ and conduct a goodness of fit test to see whether the following sample appears to have been selected from a normal distribution.

55	86	94	58	55	95	55	52	69	95	90	65	87	50	56
55	57	98	58	79	92	62	59	88	65					

After you complete the goodness of fit calculations, construct a histogram of the data. Does the histogram representation support the conclusion reached with the goodness of fit test? (*Note:* $\bar{x} = 71$ and $s = 17$.)

Summary

In this chapter we introduced the goodness of fit test and the test of independence, both of which are based on the use of the chi-square distribution. The purpose of the goodness of fit test is to determine whether a hypothesized probability distribution can be used as a model for a particular population of interest. The computations for conducting the goodness of fit test involve comparing observed frequencies from a sample with expected frequencies when the hypothesized probability distribution is assumed true. A chi-square distribution is used to determine whether the differences between observed and expected frequencies are large enough to reject the hypothesized probability distribution. We illustrated the goodness of fit test for multinomial, Poisson, and normal distributions.

A test of independence for two variables is an extension of the methodology employed in the goodness of fit test for a multinomial population. A contingency table is used to determine the observed and expected frequencies. Then a chi-square value is computed. Large chi-square values, caused by large differences between observed and expected frequencies, lead to the rejection of the null hypothesis of independence.

Glossary

Multinomial population A population in which each element is assigned to one and only one of several categories. The multinomial distribution extends the binomial distribution from two to three or more outcomes.

Goodness of fit test A statistical test conducted to determine whether to reject a hypothesized probability distribution for a population.

Contingency table A table used to summarize observed and expected frequencies for a test of independence.

Key Formulas

Test Statistic for Goodness of Fit

$$\chi^2 = \sum_{i=1}^{k} \frac{(f_i - e_i)^2}{e_i}$$ (12.1)

Expected Frequencies for Contingency Tables Under the Assumption of Independence

$$e_{ij} = \frac{(\text{Row } i \text{ Total})(\text{Column } j \text{ Total})}{\text{Sample Size}}$$ (12.2)

Test Statistic for Independence

$$\chi^2 = \sum_i \sum_j \frac{(f_{ij} - e_{ij})^2}{e_{ij}}$$ (12.3)

Supplementary Exercises

24. In setting sales quotas, the marketing manager makes the assumption that order potentials are the same for each of four sales territories. A sample of 200 sales follows. Should the manager's assumption be rejected? Use $\alpha = .05$.

Sales Territories			
I	**II**	**III**	**IV**
60	45	59	36

25. Seven percent of mutual fund investors rate corporate stocks "very safe," 58% rate them "somewhat safe," 24% rate them "not very safe," 4% rate them "not at all safe," and 7% are "not sure." A *BusinessWeek*/Harris poll asked 529 mutual fund investors how they would rate corporate bonds on safety. The responses are as follows.

Safety Rating	Frequency
Very safe	48
Somewhat safe	323
Not very safe	79
Not at all safe	16
Not sure	63
Total	529

Do mutual fund investors' attitudes toward corporate bonds differ from their attitudes toward corporate stocks? Support your conclusion with a statistical test. Use $\alpha = .01$.

26. Since 2000, the Toyota Camry, Honda Accord, and Ford Taurus have been the three best-selling passenger cars in the United States. Based on the 2003 sales data, the market shares among the top three are as follows: Toyota Camry 37%, Honda Accord 34%, and Ford Taurus 29% (*The World Almanac,* 2004). Assume a sample of 1200 sales of passenger cars during the first quarter of 2004 shows the following.

Passenger Car	Units Sold
Toyota Camry	480
Honda Accord	390
Ford Taurus	330

Can these data be used to conclude that the market shares among the top three passenger cars have changed during the first quarter of 2004? What is the p-value? Use a .05 level of significance. What is your conclusion?

27. A regional transit authority is concerned about the number of riders on one of its bus routes. In setting up the route, the assumption is that the number of riders is the same on every day from Monday through Friday. Using the following data, test with $\alpha = .05$ to determine whether the transit authority's assumption is correct.

Day	Number of Riders
Monday	13
Tuesday	16
Wednesday	28
Thursday	17
Friday	16

28. The results of *Computerworld*'s Annual Job Satisfaction Survey showed that 28% of Information Systems (IS) managers are very satisfied with their job, 46% are somewhat satisfied, 12% are neither satisfied nor dissatisfied, 10% are somewhat dissatisfied, and 4% are very dissatisfied. Suppose that a sample of 500 computer programmers yielded the following results.

Category	Number of Respondents
Very satisfied	105
Somewhat satisfied	235
Neither	55
Somewhat dissatisfied	90
Very dissatisfied	15

Use $\alpha = .05$ and test to determine whether the job satisfaction for computer programmers is different from the job satisfaction for IS managers.

29. A sample of parts provided the following contingency table data on part quality by production shift.

Shift	Number Good	Number Defective
First	368	32
Second	285	15
Third	176	24

Use $\alpha = .05$ and test the hypothesis that part quality is independent of the production shift. What is your conclusion?

30. *The Wall Street Journal* Subscriber Study showed data on the employment status of subscribers. Sample results corresponding to subscribers of the eastern and western editions are shown here.

	Region	
Employment Status	**Eastern Edition**	**Western Edition**
Full-time	1105	574
Part-time	31	15
Self-employed/consultant	229	186
Not employed	485	344

Use $\alpha = .05$ and test the hypothesis that employment status is independent of the region. What is your conclusion?

31. A lending institution supplied the following data on loan approvals by four loan officers. Use $\alpha = .05$ and test to determine whether the loan approval decision is independent of the loan officer reviewing the loan application.

	Loan Approval Decision	
Loan Officer	**Approved**	**Rejected**
Miller	24	16
McMahon	17	13
Games	35	15
Runk	11	9

32. Data on the marital status of men and women ages 20 to 29 were obtained as part of a national survey. The results from a sample of 350 men and 400 women follow.

	Marital Status		
Gender	**Never Married**	**Married**	**Divorced**
Men	234	106	10
Women	216	168	16

a. Use $\alpha = .01$ and test for independence between marital status and gender. What is your conclusion?

b. Summarize the percentage in each marital status category for men and for women.

33. Barna Research Group collected data showing church attendance by age group (*USA Today*, November 20, 2003). Use the sample data to determine whether attending church is independent of age. Use a .05 level of significance. What is your conclusion? What conclusion can you draw about church attendance as individuals grow older?

	Church Attendance		
Age	**Yes**	**No**	**Total**
20 to 29	31	69	100
30 to 39	63	87	150
40 to 49	94	106	200
50 to 59	72	78	150

34. The following data were collected on the number of emergency ambulance calls for an urban county and a rural county in Virginia.

		Day of Week							
		Sun	**Mon**	**Tue**	**Wed**	**Thur**	**Fri**	**Sat**	**Total**
County	**Urban**	61	48	50	55	63	73	43	393
	Rural	7	9	16	13	9	14	10	78
	Total	68	57	66	68	72	87	53	471

Conduct a test for independence using $\alpha = .05$. What is your conclusion?

35. A random sample of final examination grades for a college course follows.

55	85	72	99	48	71	88	70	59	98	80	74	93	85	74
82	90	71	83	60	95	77	84	73	63	72	95	79	51	85
76	81	78	65	75	87	86	70	80	64					

Use $\alpha = .05$ and test to determine whether a normal distribution should be rejected as being representative of the population's distribution of grades.

36. The office occupancy rates were reported for four California metropolitan areas. Do the following data suggest that the office vacancies were independent of metropolitan area? Use a .05 level of significance. What is your conclusion?

Occupancy Status	Los Angeles	San Diego	San Francisco	San Jose
Occupied	160	116	192	174
Vacant	40	34	33	26

37. A salesperson makes four calls per day. A sample of 100 days gives the following frequencies of sales volumes.

Number of Sales	Observed Frequency (days)
0	30
1	32
2	25
3	10
4	3
Total	100

Records show sales are made to 30% of all sales calls. Assuming independent sales calls, the number of sales per day should follow a binomial distribution. The binomial probability function presented in Chapter 5 is

$$f(x) = \frac{n!}{x!(n-x)!} p^x (1-p)^{n-x}$$

For this exercise, assume that the population has a binomial distribution with $n = 4$, $p = .30$, and $x = 0, 1, 2, 3$, and 4.

a. Compute the expected frequencies for $x = 0, 1, 2, 3$, and 4 by using the binomial probability function. Combine categories if necessary to satisfy the requirement that the expected frequency is five or more for all categories.

b. Use the goodness of fit test to determine whether the assumption of a binomial distribution should be rejected. Use $\alpha = .05$. Because no parameters of the binomial distribution were estimated from the sample data, the degrees of freedom are $k - 1$ when k is the number of categories.

Case Problem   A Bipartisan Agenda for Change

In a study conducted by Zogby International for the *Democrat and Chronicle,* more than 700 New Yorkers were polled to determine whether the New York state government works. Respondents surveyed were asked questions involving pay cuts for state legislators, restrictions on lobbyists, term limits for legislators, and whether state citizens should be able to put matters directly on the state ballot for a vote (*Democrat and Chronicle,* December 7, 1997). The results regarding several proposed reforms had broad support, crossing all demographic and political lines.

Suppose that a follow-up survey of 100 individuals who live in the western region of New York was conducted. The party affiliation (Democrat, Independent, Republican) of each individual surveyed was recorded, as well as their responses to the following three questions.

1. Should legislative pay be cut for every day the state budget is late?
    Yes ____   No ____
2. Should there be more restrictions on lobbyists?
    Yes ____   No ____
3. Should there be term limits requiring that legislators serve a fixed number of years?
    Yes ____   No ____

NYReform

The responses were coded using 1 for a *yes* response and 2 for a *no* response. The complete data set is available on the data disk in the data set named NYReform.

Managerial Report

1. Use descriptive statistics to summarize the data from this study. What are your preliminary conclusions about the independence of the response (Yes or No) and party affiliation for each of the three questions in the survey?
2. With regard to question 1, test for the independence of the response (Yes and No) and party affiliation. Use $\alpha = .05$.
3. With regard to question 2, test for the independence of the response (Yes and No) and party affiliation. Use $\alpha = .05$.
4. With regard to question 3, test for the independence of the response (Yes and No) and party affiliation. Use $\alpha = .05$.
5. Does it appear that there is broad support for change across all political lines? Explain.

CHAPTER 13

Analysis of Variance and Experimental Design

CONTENTS

STATISTICS IN PRACTICE: BURKE
MARKETING SERVICES, INC.

13.1 INTRODUCTION TO
ANALYSIS OF VARIANCE
Assumptions for Analysis of
Variance
A Conceptual Overview

13.2 ANALYSIS OF VARIANCE:
TESTING FOR THE
EQUALITY OF k
POPULATION MEANS
Between-Treatments Estimate of
Population Variance
Within-Treatments Estimate of
Population Variance
Comparing the Variance
Estimates: The F Test
ANOVA Table
Using Excel

13.3 MULTIPLE COMPARISON
PROCEDURES
Fisher's LSD
Type I Error Rates

13.4 INTRODUCTION TO
EXPERIMENTAL DESIGN
Data Collection

13.5 COMPLETELY RANDOMIZED
DESIGN
Between-Treatments Estimate of
Population Variance
Within-Treatments Estimate of
Population Variance
Comparing the Variance
Estimates: The F Test
ANOVA Table
Using Excel
Pairwise Comparisons

13.6 RANDOMIZED BLOCK
DESIGN
Air Traffic Controller Stress Test
ANOVA Procedure
Computations and Conclusions
Using Excel

13.7 FACTORIAL EXPERIMENT
ANOVA Procedure
Computations and Conclusions
Using Excel

STATISTICS *in* PRACTICE

BURKE MARKETING SERVICES, INC.*
CINCINNATI, OHIO

Burke Marketing Services, Inc., is one of the most experienced market research firms in the industry. Burke writes more proposals, on more projects, every day than any other market research company in the world. Supported by state-of-the-art technology, Burke offers a wide variety of research capabilities, providing answers to nearly any marketing question.

In one study, a firm retained Burke to evaluate potential new versions of a children's dry cereal. To maintain confidentiality, we refer to the cereal manufacturer as the Anon Company. The four key factors that Anon's product developers thought would enhance the taste of the cereal were the following:

1. Ratio of wheat to corn in the cereal flake
2. Type of sweetener: sugar, honey, or artificial
3. Presence or absence of flavor bits with a fruit taste
4. Short or long cooking time

Burke designed an experiment to determine what effects these four factors had on cereal taste. For example, one test cereal was made with a specified ratio of wheat to corn, sugar as the sweetener, flavor bits, and a short cooking time; another test cereal was made with a different ratio of wheat to corn and the other three factors the same, and so on. Groups of children then taste-tested the cereals and stated what they thought about the taste of each.

Analysis of variance was the statistical method used to study the data obtained from the taste tests. The results of the analysis showed the following:

Burke's research provides valuable statistical information on what customers want from a product. © Mary Kate Denny/PhotoEdit.

- The flake composition and sweetener type were highly influential in taste evaluation.
- The flavor bits actually detracted from the taste of the cereal.
- The cooking time had no effect on the taste.

This information helped Anon identify the factors that would lead to the best-tasting cereal.

The experimental design employed by Burke and the subsequent analysis of variance were helpful in making a product design recommendation. In this chapter, we will see how such procedures are carried out.

*The authors are indebted to Dr. Ronald Tatham of Burke Marketing Services for providing this Statistics in Practice.

Sir Ronald Alymer Fisher (1890–1962) invented the branch of statistics known as experimental design. In addition to being accomplished in statistics, he was a noted scientist in the field of genetics.

In this chapter we introduce a statistical procedure called *analysis of variance* (ANOVA). First, we show how ANOVA can be used to test for the equality of three or more population means using data obtained from an observational study. Then, we discuss the use of ANOVA for analyzing data obtained from three types of experimental studies: a completely randomized design, a randomized block design, and a factorial experiment. In the following chapters we will see that ANOVA plays a key role in analyzing the results of regression analysis involving both experimental and observational data.

13.1   Introduction to Analysis of Variance

National Computer Products, Inc. (NCP), manufactures printers and fax machines at plants located in Atlanta, Dallas, and Seattle. To measure how much employees at these plants know about the concept of total quality, a random sample of six employees was selected from each plant and given a quality awareness examination. The examination scores obtained for these 18 employees are listed in Table 13.1. The sample means, sample variances, and sample standard deviations for each group are also provided. Managers want to use these data to test the hypothesis that the mean examination score is the same for all three plants.

We will define population 1 as all employees at the Atlanta plant, population 2 as all employees at the Dallas plant, and population 3 as all employees at the Seattle plant. Let

$$\mu_1 = \text{mean examination score for population 1}$$
$$\mu_2 = \text{mean examination score for population 2}$$
$$\mu_3 = \text{mean examination score for population 3}$$

Although we will never know the actual values of μ_1, μ_2, and μ_3, we want to use the sample results to test the following hypotheses.

$$H_0: \mu_1 = \mu_2 = \mu_3$$
$$H_a: \text{Not all population means are equal}$$

If H_0 is rejected, we cannot conclude that all population means are different. Rejecting H_0 means that at least two population means have different values.

As we will demonstrate shortly, analysis of variance is a statistical procedure that can be used to determine whether the observed differences in the three sample means are large enough to reject H_0.

In the introduction to this chapter we stated that analysis of variance can be used to analyze data obtained from both an observational study and an experimental study. In order to provide a common set of terminology for discussing the use of analysis of variance in both types of studies, we need to introduce the concepts of a response variable, a factor, and a treatment.

The two variables in the NCP example are plant location and score on the quality awareness examination. Because the objective is to determine whether the mean examination score is the same for plants located in Atlanta, Dallas, and Seattle, examination score is referred to as the dependent or *response variable* and plant location as the independent variable or *factor*. In general, the values of a factor selected for investigation are referred to as levels of the factor or *treatments*. Thus, in the NCP example the three treatments are Atlanta, Dallas, and Seattle. These three treatments define the populations of interest in the NCP example. For each treatment or population, the response variable is the examination score.

TABLE 13.1 EXAMINATION SCORES FOR 18 EMPLOYEES

Observation	Plant 1 Atlanta	Plant 2 Dallas	Plant 3 Seattle
1	85	71	59
2	75	75	64
3	82	73	62
4	76	74	69
5	71	69	75
6	85	82	67
Sample mean	79	74	66
Sample variance	34	20	32
Sample standard deviation	5.83	4.47	5.66

Assumptions for Analysis of Variance

Three assumptions are required to use analysis of variance.

If the sample sizes are equal, analysis of variance is not sensitive to departures from the assumption of normally distributed populations.

1. **For each population, the response variable is normally distributed.** Implication: In the NCP example, the examination scores (response variable) must be normally distributed at each plant.
2. **The variance of the response variable, denoted σ^2, is the same for all of the populations.** Implication: In the NCP example, the variance of examination scores must be the same for all three plants.
3. **The observations must be independent.** Implication: In the NCP example, the examination score for each employee must be independent of the examination score for any other employee.

A Conceptual Overview

If the means for the three populations are equal, we would expect the three sample means to be close together. In fact, the closer the three sample means are to one another, the more evidence we have for the conclusion that the population means are equal. Alternatively, the more the sample means differ, the more evidence we have for the conclusion that the population means are not equal. In other words, if the variability among the sample means is "small," it supports H_0; if the variability among the sample means is "large," it supports H_a.

If the null hypothesis, $H_0: \mu_1 = \mu_2 = \mu_3$, is true, we can use the variability among the sample means to develop an estimate of σ^2. First, note that if the assumptions for analysis of variance are satisfied, each sample will have come from the same normal distribution with mean μ and variance σ^2. Recall from Chapter 7 that the sampling distribution of the sample mean $\bar{x}$ for a simple random sample of size n from a normal population will be normally distributed with mean μ and variance σ^2/n. Figure 13.1 illustrates such a sampling distribution.

Thus, if the null hypothesis is true, we can think of each of the three sample means, $\bar{x}_1 = 79$, $\bar{x}_2 = 74$, and $\bar{x}_3 = 66$, from Table 13.1 as values drawn at random from the sampling distribution shown in Figure 13.1. In this case, the mean and variance of the three $\bar{x}$ values can be used to estimate the mean and variance of the sampling distribution. When the sample sizes are equal, as in the NCP example, the best estimate of the mean of the

FIGURE 13.1   SAMPLING DISTRIBUTION OF $\bar{x}$ GIVEN H_0 IS TRUE

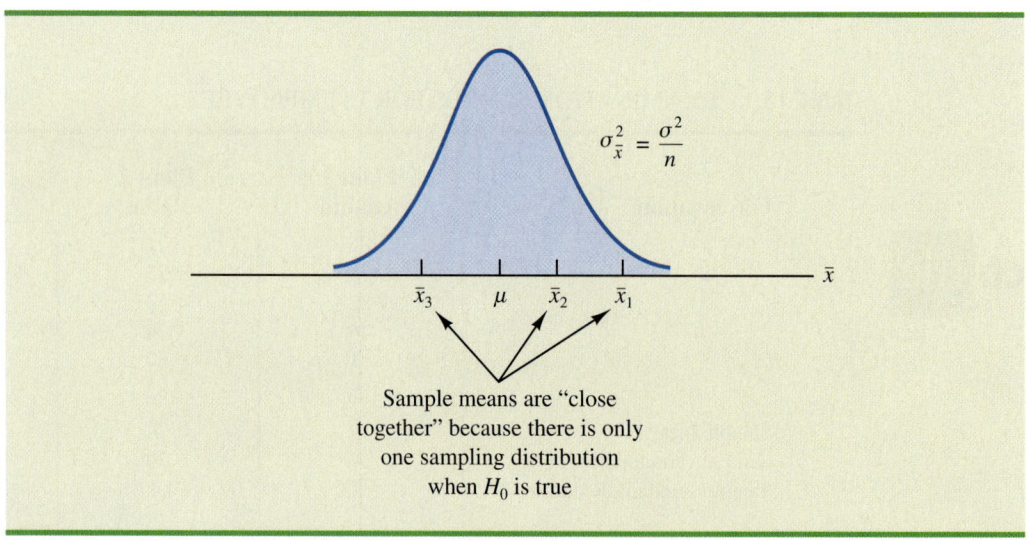

sampling distribution of $\bar{x}$ is the mean or average of the sample means. Thus, in the NCP example, an estimate of the mean of the sampling distribution of $\bar{x}$ is $(79 + 74 + 66)/3 = 73$. We refer to this estimate as the *overall sample mean*. An estimate of the variance of the sampling distribution of $\bar{x}$, $\sigma_{\bar{x}}^2$, is provided by the variance of the three sample means.

$$s_{\bar{x}}^2 = \frac{(79 - 73)^2 + (74 - 73)^2 + (66 - 73)^2}{3 - 1} = \frac{86}{2} = 43$$

Because $\sigma_{\bar{x}}^2 = \sigma^2/n$, solving for σ^2 gives

$$\sigma^2 = n\sigma_{\bar{x}}^2$$

Hence,

$$\text{Estimate of } \sigma^2 = n(\text{Estimate of } \sigma_{\bar{x}}^2) = ns_{\bar{x}}^2 = 6(43) = 258$$

The result, $ns_{\bar{x}}^2 = 258$, is referred to as the *between-treatments* estimate of σ^2.

The between-treatments estimate of σ^2 is based on the assumption that the null hypothesis is true. In this case, each sample comes from the same population, and there is only one sampling distribution of $\bar{x}$. To illustrate what happens when H_0 is false, suppose the population means all differ. Note that because the three samples are from normal populations with different means, they will result in three different sampling distributions. Figure 13.2 shows that in this case, the sample means are not as close together as they were when H_0 was true. Thus, $\sigma_{\bar{x}}^2$ will be larger, causing the between-treatments estimate of σ^2 to be larger. In general, when the population means are not equal, the between-treatments estimate will overestimate the population variance σ^2.

The variation within each of the samples also has an effect on the conclusion we reach in analysis of variance. When a simple random sample is selected from each population, each of the sample variances provides an unbiased estimate of σ^2. Hence, we can combine or pool the individual estimates of σ^2 into one overall estimate. The estimate of σ^2 obtained in this way is called the *pooled* or *within-treatments* estimate of σ^2. Because each sample variance provides an estimate of σ^2 based only on the variation within each sample, the within-treatments estimate of σ^2 is not affected by whether the population means are equal.

FIGURE 13.2   SAMPLING DISTRIBUTIONS OF $\bar{x}$ GIVEN H_0 IS FALSE

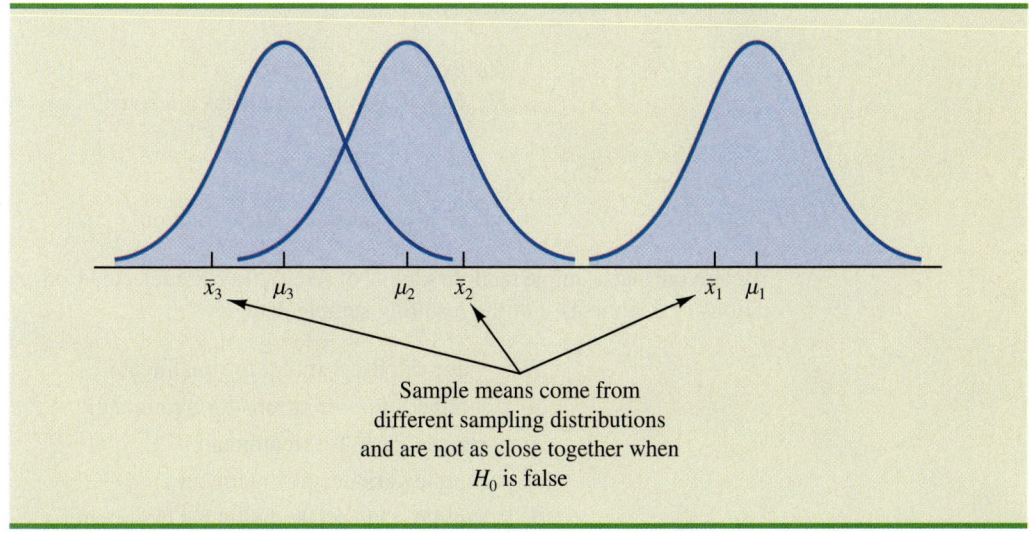

Sample means come from
different sampling distributions
and are not as close together when
H_0 is false

When the sample sizes are equal, the within-treatments estimate of σ^2 can be obtained by computing the average of the individual sample variances. For the NCP example we obtain

$$\text{Within-treatments estimate of } \sigma^2 = \frac{34 + 20 + 32}{3} = \frac{86}{3} = 28.67$$

In the NCP example, the between-treatments estimate of σ^2 (258) is much larger than the within-treatments estimate of σ^2 (28.67). In fact, the ratio of these two estimates is $258/28.67 = 9.00$. Recall, however, that the between-treatments approach provides a good estimate of σ^2 only if the null hypothesis is true; if the null hypothesis is false, the between-treatments approach overestimates σ^2. The within-treatments approach provides a good estimate of σ^2 in either case. Thus, if the null hypothesis is true, the two estimates will be similar and their ratio will be close to 1. If the null hypothesis is false, the between-treatments estimate will be larger than the within-treatments estimate, and their ratio will be large. In the next section we will show how large this ratio must be to reject H_0.

In summary, the logic behind ANOVA is based on the development of two independent estimates of the common population variance σ^2. One estimate of σ^2 is based on the variability among the sample means themselves, and the other estimate of σ^2 is based on the variability of the data within each sample. By comparing these two estimates of σ^2, we will be able to determine whether the population means are equal.

NOTES AND COMMENTS

In Sections 10.1 and 10.2 we presented statistical methods for testing the hypothesis that the means of two populations are equal. ANOVA can also be used to test the hypothesis that the means of two populations are equal. In practice, however, analysis of variance is usually not used except when dealing with three or more population means.

13.2 Analysis of Variance: Testing for the Equality of k Population Means

Analysis of variance can be used to test for the equality of k population means. The general form of the hypotheses tested is

$$H_0: \mu_1 = \mu_2 = \cdots = \mu_k$$
$$H_a: \text{Not all population means are equal}$$

where

$$\mu_j = \text{mean of the } j\text{th population}$$

We assume that a simple random sample of size n_j has been selected from each of the k populations or treatments. For the resulting sample data, let

$$x_{ij} = \text{value of observation } i \text{ for treatment } j$$
$$n_j = \text{number of observations for treatment } j$$
$$\bar{x}_j = \text{sample mean for treatment } j$$
$$s_j^2 = \text{sample variance for treatment } j$$
$$s_j = \text{sample standard deviation for treatment } j$$

The formulas for the sample mean and sample variance for treatment *j* are as follows.

$$\bar{x}_j = \frac{\sum\limits_{i=1}^{n_j} x_{ij}}{n_j} \tag{13.1}$$

$$s_j^2 = \frac{\sum\limits_{i=1}^{n_j} (x_{ij} - \bar{x}_j)^2}{n_j - 1} \tag{13.2}$$

The overall sample mean, denoted $\bar{\bar{x}}$, is the sum of all the observations divided by the total number of observations. That is,

$$\bar{\bar{x}} = \frac{\sum\limits_{j=1}^{k} \sum\limits_{i=1}^{n_j} x_{ij}}{n_T} \tag{13.3}$$

where

$$n_T = n_1 + n_2 + \cdots + n_k \tag{13.4}$$

If the size of each sample is *n*, $n_T = kn$; in this case equation (13.3) reduces to

$$\bar{\bar{x}} = \frac{\sum\limits_{j=1}^{k} \sum\limits_{i=1}^{n_j} x_{ij}}{kn} = \frac{\sum\limits_{j=1}^{k} \sum\limits_{i=1}^{n_j} x_{ij}/n}{k} = \frac{\sum\limits_{j=1}^{k} \bar{x}_j}{k} \tag{13.5}$$

In other words, whenever the sample sizes are the same, the overall sample mean is just the average of the *k* treatment means.

Because each sample in the NCP example consists of $n = 6$ observations, the overall sample mean can be computed by using equation (13.5). For the data in Table 13.1 we obtained the following result.

$$\bar{\bar{x}} = \frac{79 + 74 + 66}{3} = 73$$

If the null hypothesis is true ($\mu_1 = \mu_2 = \mu_3 = \mu$), the overall sample mean of 73 is the best estimate of the population mean μ.

Between-Treatments Estimate of Population Variance

In the preceding section, we introduced the concept of a between-treatments estimate of σ^2 and showed how to compute it when the sample sizes were equal. This estimate of σ^2 is called the *mean square due to treatments* and is denoted MSTR. The general formula for computing MSTR is

$$\text{MSTR} = \frac{\sum\limits_{j=1}^{k} n_j (\bar{x}_j - \bar{\bar{x}})^2}{k - 1} \tag{13.6}$$

The numerator in equation (13.6) is called the *sum of squares due to treatments* and is denoted SSTR. The denominator, $k - 1$, represents the degrees of freedom associated with SSTR. Hence, the mean square due to treatments can be computed by the following formula.

MEAN SQUARE DUE TO TREATMENTS

$$\text{MSTR} = \frac{\text{SSTR}}{k - 1} \tag{13.7}$$

where

$$\text{SSTR} = \sum_{j=1}^{k} n_j (\bar{x}_j - \bar{\bar{x}})^2 \tag{13.8}$$

If H_0 is true, MSTR provides an unbiased estimate of σ^2. However, if the means of the k populations are not equal, MSTR is not an unbiased estimate of σ^2; in fact, in that case, MSTR should overestimate σ^2.

For the NCP data in Table 13.1, we obtain the following results.

$$\text{SSTR} = \sum_{j=1}^{k} n_j (\bar{x}_j - \bar{\bar{x}})^2 = 6(79 - 73)^2 + 6(74 - 73)^2 + 6(66 - 73)^2 = 516$$

$$\text{MSTR} = \frac{\text{SSTR}}{k - 1} = \frac{516}{2} = 258$$

Within-Treatments Estimate of Population Variance

Earlier, we introduced the concept of a within-treatments estimate of σ^2 and showed how to compute it when the sample sizes were equal. This estimate of σ^2 is called the *mean square due to error* and is denoted MSE. The general formula for computing MSE is

$$\text{MSE} = \frac{\sum_{j=1}^{k} (n_j - 1) s_j^2}{n_T - k} \tag{13.9}$$

The numerator in equation (13.9) is called the *sum of squares due to error* and is denoted SSE. The denominator of MSE is referred to as the degrees of freedom associated with SSE. Hence, the formula for MSE can also be stated as follows.

MEAN SQUARE DUE TO ERROR

$$\text{MSE} = \frac{\text{SSE}}{n_T - k} \tag{13.10}$$

where

$$\text{SSE} = \sum_{j=1}^{k} (n_j - 1) s_j^2 \tag{13.11}$$

Note that MSE is based on the variation within each of the treatments; it is not influenced by whether the null hypothesis is true. Thus, MSE always provides an unbiased estimate of σ^2.

For the NCP data in Table 13.1 we obtain the following results.

$$SSE = \sum_{j=1}^{k}(n_j - 1)s_j^2 = (6 - 1)34 + (6 - 1)20 + (6 - 1)32 = 430$$

$$MSE = \frac{SSE}{n_T - k} = \frac{430}{18 - 3} = \frac{430}{15} = 28.67$$

Comparing the Variance Estimates: The F Test

An introduction to the F distribution and the use of the F distribution table were presented in Section 11.2.

If the null hypothesis is true, MSTR and MSE provide two independent, unbiased estimates of σ^2. Based on the material covered in Chapter 11 we know that for normal populations, the sampling distribution of the ratio of two independent estimates of σ^2 follows an F distribution. Hence, if the null hypothesis is true and the ANOVA assumptions are valid, the sampling distribution of MSTR/MSE is an F distribution with numerator degrees of freedom equal to $k - 1$ and denominator degrees of freedom equal to $n_T - k$. In other words, if the null hypothesis is true, the value of MSTR/MSE should appear to have been selected from this F distribution.

However, if the null hypothesis is false, the value of MSTR/MSE will be inflated because MSTR overestimates σ^2. Hence, we will reject H_0 if the resulting value of MSTR/MSE appears to be too large to have been selected from an F distribution with $k - 1$ numerator degrees of freedom and $n_T - k$ denominator degrees of freedom. Because the decision to reject H_0 is based on the value of MSTR/MSE, the test statistic used to test for the equality of k population means is as follows.

TEST STATISTIC FOR THE EQUALITY OF k POPULATION MEANS

$$F = \frac{MSTR}{MSE} \tag{13.12}$$

The test statistic follows an F distribution with $k - 1$ degrees of freedom in the numerator and $n_T - k$ degrees of freedom in the denominator.

Let us return to the National Computer Products example and use a level of significance $\alpha = .05$ to conduct the hypothesis test. The value of the test statistic is

$$F = \frac{MSTR}{MSE} = \frac{258}{28.67} = 9$$

The numerator degrees of freedom is $k - 1 = 3 - 1 = 2$ and the denominator degrees of freedom is $n_T - k = 18 - 3 = 15$. Because we will only reject the null hypothesis for large values of the test statistic, the p-value is the upper tail area of the F distribution to the right of the test statistic $F = 9$. Figure 13.3 shows the sampling distribution of $F =$ MSTR/MSE, the value of the test statistic, and the upper tail area that is the p-value for the hypothesis test.

From Table 4 of Appendix B we find the following areas in the upper tail of an F distribution with 2 numerator degrees of freedom and 15 denominator degrees of freedom.

Area in Upper Tail	.10	.05	.025	.01
F Value (df$_1$ = 2, df$_2$ = 15)	2.70	3.68	4.77	6.36

$F = 9$

FIGURE 13.3 COMPUTATION OF p-VALUE USING THE SAMPLING DISTRIBUTION OF MSTR/MSE

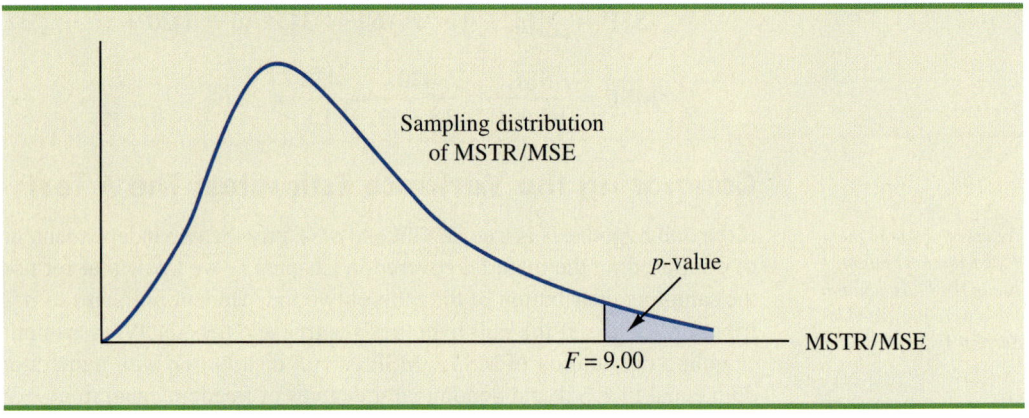

Because $F = 9$ is greater than 6.36, the area in the upper tail at $F = 9$ is less than .01. Thus, the p-value is less than .01. Because the p-value $\leq \alpha = .05$, H_0 is rejected. The test provides sufficient evidence to conclude that the means of the three populations are not equal. In other words, analysis of variance supports the conclusion that the population mean examination scores at the three NCP plants are not equal.

*Using Excel, p-value =
FDIST(9,2,15) = .0027.*

Because the F table only provides values for upper tail areas of .10, .05, .025, and .01, we cannot determine the exact p-value directly from the table. Excel provides the p-value as part of the standard ANOVA output. In the subsection "Using Excel" we show that for the NCP example, the exact p-value corresponding to the test statistic $F = 9$ is .0027.

As with other hypothesis testing procedures, the critical value approach may also be used. With $\alpha = .05$, the critical F value occurs with an area of .05 in the upper tail of an F distribution with 2 and 15 degrees of freedom. From the F distribution table, we find $F_{.05} = 3.68$. Hence, the appropriate upper tail rejection rule for the NCP example is

$$\text{Reject } H_0 \text{ if } F \geq 3.68$$

With $F = 9$, we reject H_0 and conclude that the means of the three populations are not equal. A summary of the overall procedure for testing for the equality of k population means follows.

TEST FOR THE EQUALITY OF k POPULATION MEANS

$$H_0: \mu_1 = \mu_2 = \cdots = \mu_k$$
$$H_a: \text{Not all population means are equal}$$

TEST STATISTIC

$$F = \frac{\text{MSTR}}{\text{MSE}}$$

REJECTION RULE

p-value approach: Reject H_0 if p-value $\leq \alpha$
Critical value approach: Reject H_0 if $F \geq F_\alpha$

where the value of F_α is based on an F distribution with $k - 1$ numerator degrees of freedom and $n_T - k$ denominator degrees of freedom.

ANOVA Table

The results of the preceding calculations can be displayed conveniently in a table referred to as the analysis of variance or **ANOVA table**. Table 13.2 is the analysis of variance table for the National Computer Products example. The sum of squares associated with the source of variation referred to as "Total" is called the total sum of squares (SST). Note that the results for the NCP example suggest that SST = SSTR + SSE, and that the degrees of freedom associated with this total sum of squares is the sum of the degrees of freedom associated with the between-treatments estimate of σ^2 and the within-treatments estimate of σ^2.

We point out that SST divided by its degrees of freedom $n_T - 1$ is nothing more than the overall sample variance that would be obtained if we treated the entire set of 18 observations as one data set. With the entire data set as one sample, the formula for computing the total sum of squares, SST, is

$$\text{SST} = \sum_{j=1}^{k} \sum_{i=1}^{n_j} (x_{ij} - \bar{\bar{x}})^2 \qquad \textbf{(13.13)}$$

It can be shown that the results we observed for the analysis of variance table for the NCP example also apply to other problems. That is,

$$\text{SST} = \text{SSTR} + \text{SSE} \qquad \textbf{(13.14)}$$

Analysis of variance can be thought of as a statistical procedure for partitioning the total sum of squares into separate components.

In other words, SST can be partitioned into two sums of squares: the sum of squares due to treatments and the sum of squares due to error. Note also that the degrees of freedom corresponding to SST, $n_T - 1$, can be partitioned into the degrees of freedom corresponding to SSTR, $k - 1$, and the degrees of freedom corresponding to SSE, $n_T - k$. The analysis of variance can be viewed as the process of **partitioning** the total sum of squares and the degrees of freedom into their corresponding sources: treatments and error. Dividing the sum of squares by the appropriate degrees of freedom provides the variance estimates and the *F* value used to test the hypothesis of equal population means.

Using Excel

Excel's Anova: Single Factor tool can be used to conduct a hypothesis test about the difference between the population means for the National Computer Products example. Refer to the Excel worksheet shown in Figure 13.4 as we describe the tasks involved.

Enter Data: Column A is used to identify the observations at each of the plants. Columns B, C, and D contain the examination scores for the three plants.

Apply Tools: The following steps describe how to use Excel's Anova: Single Factor tool to test the hypothesis that the mean examination score is the same for all three plants.

    Step 1. Select the **Tools** menu
    Step 2. Choose the **Data Analysis** option

TABLE 13.2   ANALYSIS OF VARIANCE TABLE FOR THE NCP EXAMPLE

Source of Variation	Sum of Squares	Degrees of Freedom	Mean Square	*F*
Treatments	516	2	258.00	9.00
Error	430	15	28.67	
Total	946	17		

FIGURE 13.4   EXCEL'S ANOVA: SINGLE FACTOR TOOL OUTPUT FOR THE NCP EXAMPLE

	A	B	C	D	E	F	G	H
1	Observation	Atlanta	Dallas	Seattle				
2	1	85	71	59				
3	2	75	75	64				
4	3	82	73	62				
5	4	76	74	69				
6	5	71	69	75				
7	6	85	82	67				
8								
9	Anova: Single Factor							
10								
11	SUMMARY							
12	*Groups*	*Count*	*Sum*	*Average*	*Variance*			
13	Atlanta	6	474	79	34			
14	Dallas	6	444	74	20			
15	Seattle	6	396	66	32			
16								
17								
18	ANOVA							
19	*Source of Variation*	*SS*	*df*	*MS*	*F*	*P-value*	*F crit*	
20	Between Groups	516	2	258	9	0.0027	3.6823	
21	Within Groups	430	15	28.6667				
22								
23	Total	946	17					
24								

Step 3. Choose **Anova: Single Factor** from the list of Analysis Tools

Step 4. When the Anova: Single Factor dialog box appears (see Figure 13.5):

Enter B1:D7 in the **Input Range** box

Select **Grouped By: Columns**

Select **Labels in First Row**

Enter .05 in the **Alpha** box

Select **Output Range**

Enter A9 in the **Output Range** box (to identify the upper left corner of the section of the worksheet where the output will appear)

Click **OK**

The output, titled *Anova: Single Factor,* appears in cells A9:G23 of the worksheet. Cells A11:E15 provide a summary of the data. Note that the sample mean and sample variance for each plant is the same as shown in Table 13.1. The ANOVA table, shown in cells A18:G23, is basically the same as the ANOVA table shown in Table 13.2. Excel identifies the treatments source of variation using the label *Between Groups* and the error source of variation using the label *Within Groups*. In addition, the Excel output provides the *p*-value associated with the test as well as the critical *F* value.

We can use the *p*-value shown in cell F20, 0.0027, to make the hypothesis testing decision. Thus, at the $\alpha = .05$ level of significance, we reject H_0 because the *p*-value $= 0.0027 < \alpha = .05$. Hence, using the *p*-value approach we still conclude that the mean examination scores differ among the three plants.

FIGURE 13.5 DIALOG BOX FOR ANOVA: SINGLE FACTOR

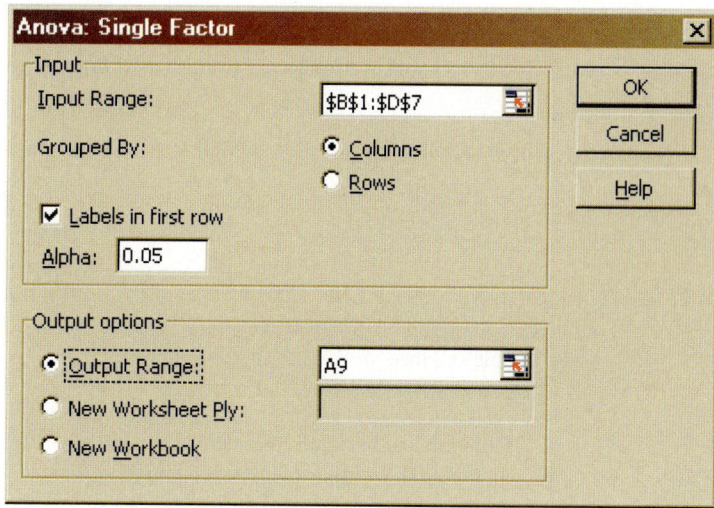

NOTES AND COMMENTS

1. The overall sample mean can also be computed as a weighted average of the *k* sample means.

$$\bar{\bar{x}} = \frac{n_1\bar{x}_1 + n_2\bar{x}_2 + \cdots + n_k\bar{x}_k}{n_T}$$

In problems where the sample means are provided, this formula is simpler than equation (13.3) for computing the overall mean.

2. If each sample consists of *n* observations, equation (13.6) can be written as

$$MSTR = \frac{n\sum_{j=1}^{k}(\bar{x}_j - \bar{\bar{x}})^2}{k - 1} = n\left[\frac{\sum_{j=1}^{k}(\bar{x}_j - \bar{\bar{x}})^2}{k - 1}\right]$$
$$= ns_{\bar{x}}^2$$

Note that this result is the same as presented in Section 13.1 when we introduced the concept of the between-treatments estimate of σ^2. Equation (13.6) is simply a generalization of this result to the unequal sample–size case.

3. If each sample has *n* observations, $n_T = kn$; thus, $n_T - k = k(n - 1)$, and equation (13.9) can be rewritten as

$$MSE = \frac{\sum_{j=1}^{k}(n - 1)s_j^2}{k(n - 1)} = \frac{(n - 1)\sum_{j=1}^{k}s_j^2}{k(n - 1)} = \frac{\sum_{j=1}^{k}s_j^2}{k}$$

In other words, if the sample sizes are the same, MSE is just the average of the *k* sample variances. Note that it is the same result we used in Section 13.1 when we introduced the concept of the within-treatments estimate of σ^2.

4. Confidence interval estimates for each of the *k* population means can be developed using

$$\bar{x} \pm t_{\alpha/2}\frac{\sqrt{MSE}}{\sqrt{n}}$$

The degrees of freedom for the *t* value are the degrees of freedom associated with the within-treatments estimate of σ^2.

Exercises

Methods

1. Five observations were selected from each of three populations. The data obtained follow.

Observation	Sample 1	Sample 2	Sample 3
1	32	44	33
2	30	43	36
3	30	44	35
4	26	46	36
5	32	48	40
Sample mean	30	45	36
Sample variance	6.00	4.00	6.50

   a. Compute the between-treatments estimate of σ^2.
   b. Compute the within-treatments estimate of σ^2.
   c. At the $\alpha = .05$ level of significance, can we reject the null hypothesis that the means of the three populations are equal?
   d. Set up the ANOVA table for this problem.

2. Four observations were selected from each of three populations. The data obtained follow.

Observation	Sample 1	Sample 2	Sample 3
1	165	174	169
2	149	164	154
3	156	180	161
4	142	158	148
Sample mean	153	169	158
Sample variance	96.67	97.33	82.00

   a. Compute the between-treatments estimate of σ^2.
   b. Compute the within-treatments estimate of σ^2.
   c. At the $\alpha = .05$ level of significance, can we reject the null hypothesis that the three population means are equal? Explain.
   d. Set up the ANOVA table for this problem.

3. Samples were selected from three populations. The data obtained follow.

	Sample 1	Sample 2	Sample 3
	93	77	88
	98	87	75
	107	84	73
	102	95	84
		85	75
		82	
$\bar{x}_j$	100	85	79
s_j^2	35.33	35.60	43.50

   a. Compute the between-treatments estimate of σ^2.
   b. Compute the within-treatments estimate of σ^2.

    c. At the $\alpha = .05$ level of significance, can we reject the null hypothesis that the three population means are equal? Explain.

    d. Set up the ANOVA table for this problem.

4. A random sample of 16 observations was selected from each of four populations. A portion of the ANOVA table follows.

Source of Variation	Sum of Squares	Degrees of Freedom	Mean Square	F
Treatments			400	
Error				
Total	1500			

    a. Provide the missing entries for the ANOVA table.

    b. At the $\alpha = .05$ level of significance, can we reject the null hypothesis that the means of the four populations are equal?

5. Random samples of 25 observations were selected from each of three populations. For these data, SSTR = 120 and SSE = 216.

    a. Set up the ANOVA table for this problem.

    b. At the $\alpha = .05$ level of significance, can we reject the null hypothesis that the three population means are equal?

Applications

6. To test whether the mean time needed to mix a batch of material is the same for machines produced by three manufacturers, the Jacobs Chemical Company obtained the following data on the time (in minutes) needed to mix the material. Use these data to test whether the population mean times for mixing a batch of material differ for the three manufacturers. Use $\alpha = .05$.

	Manufacturer	
1	**2**	**3**
20	28	20
26	26	19
24	31	23
22	27	22

7. The Texas Transportation Institute at Texas A&M University conducted a survey to determine the number of hours per year drivers waste sitting in traffic. Of 75 urban areas studied, the most jammed urban area was Los Angeles where drivers wasted an average of 90 hours per year (*U.S. News & World Report,* October 13, 2003). Other jammed urban areas included Denver, Miami, and San Francisco. Assume sample data for six drivers in each of these cities show the following number of hours wasted per year sitting in traffic.

Traffic

Denver	Miami	San Francisco
70	66	65
62	70	62
71	55	74
58	65	69
57	56	63
66	66	75

a. Compute the sample mean hours wasted per year for each of these urban areas.

b. Using $\alpha = .05$, test for significant differences among the population mean wasted time for these three urban areas. What is the p-value? What is your conclusion?

8. New York City, Boston, and the Silicon Valley of California are among the areas with the highest technology salaries in the United States (*USA Today,* February 28, 2002). The following sample data show individual annual salaries reported in thousands of dollars.

Technology

New York City	Boston	Silicon Valley
82	85	82
79	80	91
72	74	94
89	78	88
79	75	85
85	80	
	86	
	74	

Use $\alpha = .05$ and test for a significant difference among the population mean annual technology salaries for these three locations. What is the p-value? What is your conclusion? If a difference exists, which location appears to have the highest mean technology salary?

9. A study reported in the *Journal of Small Business Management* concluded that self-employed individuals experience higher job stress than individuals who are not self-employed. In this study job stress was assessed with a 15-item scale designed to measure various aspects of ambiguity and role conflict. Ratings for each of the 15 items were made using a scale with 1–5 response options ranging from strong agreement to strong disagreement. The sum of the ratings for the 15 items for each individual surveyed is between 15 and 75, with higher values indicating a higher degree of job stress. Suppose that a similar approach, using a 20-item scale with 1–5 response options, was used to measure the job stress of individuals for 15 randomly selected real estate agents, 15 architects, and 15 stockbrokers. The results obtained follow.

Stress

Real Estate Agent	Architect	Stockbroker
81	43	65
48	63	48
68	60	57
69	52	91
54	54	70
62	77	67
76	68	83
56	57	75
61	61	53
65	80	71
64	50	54
69	37	72
83	73	65
85	84	58
75	58	58

Use $\alpha = .05$ to test for any significant difference in job stress among the three professions.

10. *Condé Nast Traveler* conducts an annual survey in which readers rate their favorite cruise ships. Ratings are provided for small ships (carrying up to 500 passengers), medium ships (carrying 500 to 1500 passengers), and large ships (carrying a minimum of 1500 passengers). The following data show the service ratings for eight randomly selected small ships, eight randomly selected medium ships, and eight randomly selected large ships. All ships are rated on a 100-point scale, with higher values indicating better service (*Condé Nast Traveler,* February 2003).

Ships

Small Ships		Medium Ships		Large Ships	
Name	**Rating**	**Name**	**Rating**	**Name**	**Rating**
Hanseactic	90.5	*Amsterdam*	91.1	*Century*	89.2
Mississippi Queen	78.2	*Crystal Symphony*	98.9	*Disney Wonder*	90.2
Philae	92.3	*Maasdam*	94.2	*Enchantment of the Seas*	85.9
Royal Clipper	95.7	*Noordam*	84.3	*Grand Princess*	84.2
Seabourn Pride	94.1	*Royal Princess*	84.8	*Infinity*	90.2
Seabourn Spirit	100	*Ryndam*	89.2	*Legend of the Seas*	80.6
Silver Cloud	91.8	*Statendam*	86.4	*Paradise*	75.8
Silver Wind	95	*Veendam*	88.3	*Sun Princess*	82.3

Use $\alpha = .05$ to test for any significant difference in the mean service ratings among the three sizes of cruise ships.

13.3 Multiple Comparison Procedures

When we use analysis of variance to test whether the means of k populations are equal, rejection of the null hypothesis allows us to conclude only that the population means are *not all equal.* In some cases we will want to go a step further and determine where the differences among means occur. The purpose of this section is to introduce two **multiple comparison procedures** that can be used to conduct statistical comparisons between pairs of population means.

Fisher's LSD

Suppose that analysis of variance provides statistical evidence to reject the null hypothesis of equal population means. In this case, Fisher's least significant difference (LSD) procedure can be used to determine where the differences occur. To illustrate the use of Fisher's LSD procedure in making pairwise comparisons of population means, recall the NCP example introduced in Section 13.1. Using analysis of variance, we concluded that the population mean examination scores are not the same at the three plants. In this case, the follow-up question is: We believe the plants differ, but where do the differences occur? That is, do the means of populations 1 and 2 differ? Or those of populations 1 and 3? Or those of populations 2 and 3?

In Chapter 10 we presented a statistical procedure for testing the hypothesis that the means of two populations are equal. With a slight modification in how we estimate the population variance, Fisher's LSD procedure is based on the t test statistic presented for the two-population case. The following table summarizes Fisher's LSD procedure.

FISHER'S LSD PROCEDURE

$$H_0: \mu_i = \mu_j$$
$$H_a: \mu_i \neq \mu_j$$

TEST STATISTIC

$$t = \frac{\bar{x}_i - \bar{x}_j}{\sqrt{\text{MSE}\left(\dfrac{1}{n_i} + \dfrac{1}{n_j}\right)}} \qquad (13.16)$$

REJECTION RULE

p-value approach: Reject H_0 if p-value $\leq \alpha$

Critical value approach: Reject H_0 if $t \leq -t_{\alpha/2}$ or $t \geq t_{\alpha/2}$

where the value of $t_{\alpha/2}$ is based on a t distribution with $n_T - k$ degrees of freedom.

Let us now apply this procedure to determine whether there is a significant difference between the means of population 1 (Atlanta) and population 2 (Dallas) at the $\alpha = .05$ level of significance. Table 13.1 shows that the sample mean is 79 for the Atlanta plant and 74 for the Dallas plant. Table 13.2 shows that the value of MSE is 28.67; it is the estimate of σ^2 and is based on 15 degrees of freedom. For the NCP data the value of the test statistic is

$$t = \frac{79 - 74}{\sqrt{28.67\left(\dfrac{1}{6} + \dfrac{1}{6}\right)}} = 1.62$$

Using Excel, p-value = TDIST(1.62,15,2) = .1261.

The t distribution table (Table 2 in Appendix B) shows that with 15 degrees of freedom $t = 1.341$ for an area of .10 in the upper tail and $t = 1.753$ for an area of .05 in the upper tail. Because the test statistic $t = 1.62$ is between 1.341 and 1.753, we know that the area in the upper tail must be between .05 and .10. Because this test is a two-tailed test, we double these values to conclude that the p-value is between .10 and .20. Excel can be used to show that the p-value corresponding to $t = 1.62$ is .1261. Because the p-value is greater than $\alpha = .05$, we cannot reject the null hypothesis. Hence, we cannot conclude that the population mean score at the Atlanta plant is different from the population mean score at the Dallas plant.

Many practitioners find it easier to determine how large the difference between the sample means must be to reject H_0. In this case the test statistic is $\bar{x}_i - \bar{x}_j$, and the test is conducted by the following procedure.

FISHER'S LSD PROCEDURE BASED ON THE TEST STATISTIC $\bar{x}_i - \bar{x}_j$

$$H_0: \mu_i = \mu_j$$
$$H_a: \mu_i \neq \mu_j$$

TEST STATISTIC

$$\bar{x}_i - \bar{x}_j$$

REJECTION RULE AT A LEVEL OF SIGNIFICANCE α

Reject H_0 if $|\bar{x}_i - \bar{x}_j| > \text{LSD}$

where

$$LSD = t_{\alpha/2}\sqrt{MSE\left(\frac{1}{n_i} + \frac{1}{n_j}\right)}$$ (13.17)

and $t_{\alpha/2}$ is based on a t distribution with $n_T - k$ degrees of freedom.

For the NCP example, $t_{.025} = 2.131$ and the value of LSD is

The value of t used here is based on $\alpha = .05$ and 15 degrees of freedom.

$$LSD = 2.131\sqrt{28.67\left(\frac{1}{6} + \frac{1}{6}\right)} = 6.59$$

Note that when the sample sizes are equal, only one value for LSD is computed. In such cases we can simply compare the magnitude of the difference between any two sample means with the value of LSD. For example, the difference between the sample means for population 1 (Atlanta) and population 3 (Seattle) is $79 - 66 = 13$. This difference is greater than 6.59, which means we can reject the null hypothesis that the population mean examination score for the Atlanta plant is equal to the population mean score for the Seattle plant. Similarly, with the difference between the sample means for populations 2 and 3 of $74 - 66 = 8 > 6.59$, we can also reject the hypothesis that the population mean examination score for the Dallas plant is equal to the population mean examination score for the Seattle plant. In effect, our conclusion is that the Atlanta and Dallas plants both differ from the Seattle plant.

Fisher's LSD can also be used to develop a confidence interval estimate of the difference between the means of two populations. The general procedure follows.

CONFIDENCE INTERVAL ESTIMATE OF THE DIFFERENCE BETWEEN TWO POPULATION MEANS USING FISHER'S LSD PROCEDURE

$$\bar{x}_i - \bar{x}_j \pm LSD$$ (13.18)

where

$$LSD = t_{\alpha/2}\sqrt{MSE\left(\frac{1}{n_i} + \frac{1}{n_j}\right)}$$ (13.19)

and $t_{\alpha/2}$ is based on a t distribution with $n_T - k$ degrees of freedom.

If the confidence interval in expression (13.18) includes the value zero, we cannot reject the hypothesis that the two population means are equal. However, if the confidence interval does not include the value zero, we conclude that there is a difference between the population means. For the NCP example, recall that $LSD = 6.59$ (corresponding to $t_{.025} = 2.131$). Thus, a 95% confidence interval estimate of the difference between the means of populations 1 and 2 is $79 - 74 \pm 6.59 = 5 \pm 6.59 = -1.59$ to 11.59; because this interval includes zero, we cannot reject the hypothesis that the two population means are equal.

Type I Error Rates

We began the discussion of Fisher's LSD procedure with the premise that analysis of variance gave us statistical evidence to reject the null hypothesis of equal population means. We showed how Fisher's LSD procedure can be used in such cases to determine where the differences occur. Technically, it is referred to as a *protected* or *restricted* LSD test because it is employed only if we first find a significant F value by using analysis of variance. To see why this distinction is important in multiple comparison tests, we need to explain the difference between a *comparisonwise* Type I error rate and an *experimentwise* Type I error rate.

In the NCP example we used Fisher's LSD procedure to make three pairwise comparisons.

Test 1	**Test 2**	**Test 3**
$H_0: \mu_1 = \mu_2$	$H_0: \mu_1 = \mu_3$	$H_0: \mu_2 = \mu_3$
$H_a: \mu_1 \neq \mu_2$	$H_a: \mu_1 \neq \mu_3$	$H_a: \mu_2 \neq \mu_3$

In each case, we used a level of significance of $\alpha = .05$. Therefore, for each test, if the null hypothesis is true, the probability that we will make a Type I error is $\alpha = .05$; hence, the probability that we will not make a Type I error on each test is $1 - .05 = .95$. In discussing multiple comparison procedures we refer to this probability of a Type I error ($\alpha = .05$) as the **comparisonwise Type I error rate**; comparisonwise Type I error rates indicate the level of significance associated with a single pairwise comparison.

Let us now consider a slightly different question. What is the probability that in making three pairwise comparisons, we will commit a Type I error on at least one of the three tests? To answer this question, note that the probability that we will not make a Type I error on any of the three tests is $(.95)(.95)(.95) = .8574$.* Therefore, the probability of making at least one Type I error is $1 - .8574 = .1426$. Thus, when we use Fisher's LSD procedure to make all three pairwise comparisons, the Type I error rate associated with this approach is not .05, but actually .1426; we refer to this error rate as the *overall* or **experimentwise Type I error rate**. To avoid confusion, we denote the experimentwise Type I error rate as α_{EW}.

The experimentwise Type I error rate gets larger for problems with more populations. For example, a problem with five populations has 10 possible pairwise comparisons. If we tested all possible pairwise comparisons by using Fisher's LSD with a comparisonwise error rate of $\alpha = .05$, the experimentwise Type I error rate would be $1 - (1 - .05)^{10} = .40$. In such cases, practitioners look to alternatives that provide better control over the experimentwise error rate.

One alternative for controlling the overall experimentwise error rate, referred to as the Bonferroni adjustment, involves using a smaller comparisonwise error rate for each test. For example, if we want to test C pairwise comparisons and want the maximum probability of making a Type I error for the overall experiment to be α_{EW}, we simply use a comparisonwise error rate equal to α_{EW}/C. In the NCP example, if we want to use Fisher's LSD procedure to test all three pairwise comparisons with a maximum experimentwise error rate of $\alpha_{EW} = .05$, we set the comparisonwise error rate to be $\alpha = .05/3 = .017$. For a problem with five populations and 10 possible pairwise comparisons, the Bonferroni adjustment would suggest a comparisonwise error rate of $.05/10 = .005$.

For a fixed sample size, any decrease in the probability of making a Type I error will result in an increase in the probability of making a Type II error, which corresponds to accepting the hypothesis that the two population means are equal when in fact they are not equal. As a result, many practitioners are reluctant to perform individual tests with a low comparisonwise Type I error rate because of the increased risk of making a Type II error. Several other procedures, such as Tukey's procedure and Duncan's multiple range test, have

---

*The assumption is that the three tests are independent, and hence the joint probability of the three events can be obtained by simply multiplying the individual probabilities. In fact, the three tests are not independent because MSE is used in each test; therefore, the error involved is even greater than that shown.

been developed to help in such situations. However, there is considerable controversy in the statistical community as to which procedure is "best." The truth is that no one procedure is best for all types of problems.

Exercises

Methods

11. In exercise 1, five observations were selected from each of three populations. For these data, $\bar{x}_1 = 30$, $\bar{x}_2 = 45$, $\bar{x}_3 = 36$, and MSE = 5.5. At the $\alpha = .05$ level of significance, the null hypothesis of equal population means was rejected. In the following calculations, use $\alpha = .05$.
    a. Use Fisher's LSD procedure to test whether there is a significant difference between the means of populations 1 and 2, populations 1 and 3, and populations 2 and 3.
    b. Use Fisher's LSD procedure to develop a 95% confidence interval estimate of the difference between the means of populations 1 and 2.

12. Four observations were selected from each of three populations. The data obtained are shown. In the following calculations, use $\alpha = .05$.

	Sample 1	Sample 2	Sample 3
	63	82	69
	47	72	54
	54	88	61
	40	66	48
$\bar{x}_j$	51	77	58
s_j^2	96.67	97.34	81.99

    a. Use analysis of variance to test for a significant difference among the means of the three populations.
    b. Use Fisher's LSD procedure to see which means are different.

Applications

13. Refer to exercise 6. At the $\alpha = .05$ level of significance, use Fisher's LSD procedure to test for the equality of the population means for manufacturers 1 and 3. What conclusion can you draw after carrying out this test?

14. Refer to exercise 13. Use Fisher's LSD procedure to develop a 95% confidence interval estimate of the difference between the population means for manufacturers 1 and 2.

15. To study the ethical values among individuals specializing in marketing, a sample of six marketing managers, six individuals working in marketing research, and six individuals working in advertising was selected. For each individual sampled, a measure of ethical value was obtained; higher scores indicate higher ethical values. The data obtained are shown here:

Marketing Managers	Marketing Researchers	Advertising Employees
6	5	6
5	5	7
4	4	6
5	4	5
6	5	6
4	4	6

a. At the .05 level of significance, what is the difference, if any, in the population mean ethical values among the three groups?

b. Use the procedures in this section to determine where the differences occur. Use $\alpha = .05$.

16. To test for any significant difference in the number of hours between breakdowns for four machines, the following data were obtained.

Machine 1	Machine 2	Machine 3	Machine 4
6.4	8.7	11.1	9.9
7.8	7.4	10.3	12.8
5.3	9.4	9.7	12.1
7.4	10.1	10.3	10.8
8.4	9.2	9.2	11.3
7.3	9.8	8.8	11.5

a. At the $\alpha = .05$ level of significance, what is the difference, if any, in the population mean times among the four machines?

b. Use Fisher's LSD procedure to test for the equality of the means for machines 2 and 4. Use a .05 level of significance.

17. Refer to exercise 16. Use the Bonferroni adjustment to test for a significant difference between all pairs of means. Assume that a maximum overall experimentwise error rate of .05 is desired.

18. Refer to exercise 10. At the .05 level of significance, we can conclude that the mean service ratings of small ships, medium ships, and large ships differ. Use the procedures in this section to determine where the differences occur. Use $\alpha = .05$.

Introduction to Experimental Design

Cause-and-effect relationships can be difficult to establish in observational studies; such relationships are easier to establish in experimental studies.

Statistical studies can be classified as being either experimental or observational. In an experimental study, variables of interest are identified. Then, one or more factors in the study are controlled so that data can be obtained about how the factors influence the variables. In *observational* or *nonexperimental* studies, no attempt is made to control the factors. A survey is perhaps the most common type of observational study.

The NCP example that we used to introduce analysis of variance is an illustration of an observational statistical study. To measure how much NCP employees knew about quality management, a random sample of six employees was selected from each of NCP's three plants and given a quality-awareness examination. The examination scores for these employees were then analyzed by analysis of variance to test the hypothesis that the population mean examination scores were equal for the three plants.

As an example of an experimental statistical study, let us consider the problem facing Chemitech, Inc. Chemitech developed a new filtration system for municipal water supplies. The components for the new filtration system will be purchased from several suppliers, and Chemitech will assemble the components at its plant in Columbia, South Carolina. The industrial engineering group is responsible for determining the best assembly method for the new filtration system. After considering a variety of possible approaches, the group narrows the alternatives to three: method A, method B, and method C. These methods differ in the sequence of steps used to assemble the product. Managers at Chemitech want to determine which assembly method can produce the greatest number of filtration systems per week.

In the Chemitech experiment, assembly method is the independent variable or **factor**. Because three assembly methods correspond to this factor, we say that three treatments are associated with this experiment; each **treatment** corresponds to each of the three assembly methods. The Chemitech problem is an example of a **single-factor experiment** involving a qualitative factor (method of assembly). Other experiments may consist of multiple factors; some factors may be qualitative and some may be quantitative.

The three assembly methods or treatments define the three populations of interest for the Chemitech experiment. One population is all Chemitech employees who use assembly method A, another is those who use method B, and the third is those who use method C. Note that for each population the dependent or response variable is the number of filtration systems assembled per week, and the primary statistical objective of the experiment is to determine whether the mean number of units produced per week is the same for all three populations.

Randomization is the process of assigning the treatments to the experimental units at random. Prior to the work of Sir R. A. Fisher, treatments were assigned on a systematic or subjective basis.

Suppose a random sample of three employees is selected from all assembly workers at the Chemitech production facility. In experimental design terminology, the three randomly selected workers are the **experimental units**. The experimental design that we will use for the Chemitech problem is called a **completely randomized design**. This type of design requires that each of the three assembly methods or treatments be assigned randomly to one of the experimental units or workers. For example, method A might be randomly assigned to the second worker, method B to the first worker, and method C to the third worker. The concept of *randomization*, as illustrated in this example, is an important principle of all experimental designs.

Note that this experiment would result in only one measurement or number of units assembled for each treatment. To obtain additional data for each assembly method, we must repeat or replicate the basic experimental process. Suppose, for example, that instead of selecting just three workers at random we selected 15 workers and then randomly assigned each of the three treatments to five of the workers. Because each method of assembly is assigned to five workers, we say that five replicates have been obtained. The process of *replication* is another important principle of experimental design. Figure 13.6 shows the completely randomized design for the Chemitech experiment.

FIGURE 13.6   COMPLETELY RANDOMIZED DESIGN FOR EVALUATING THE CHEMITECH ASSEMBLY METHOD EXPERIMENT

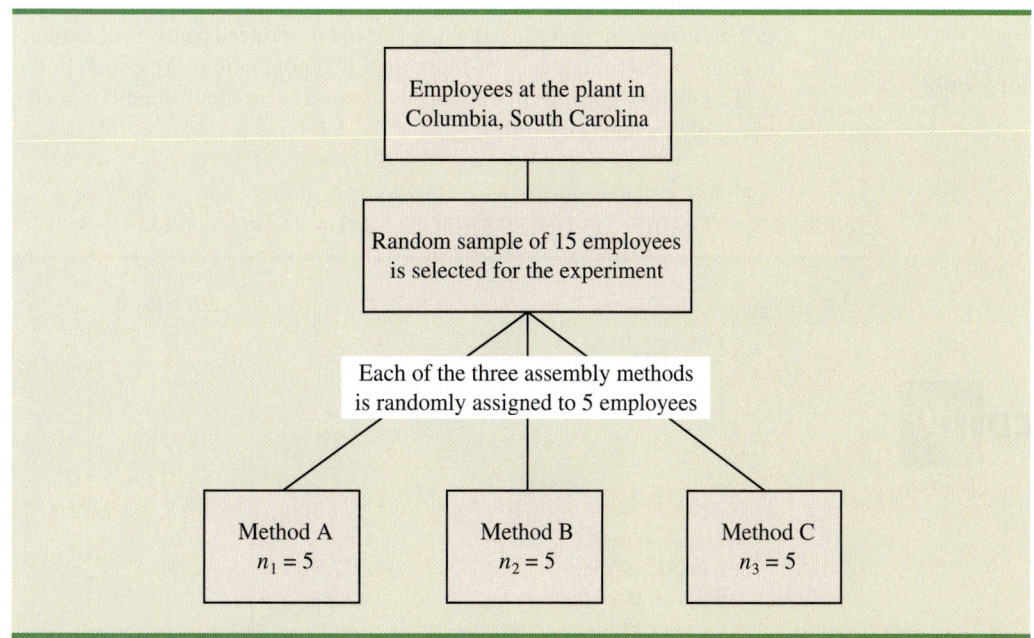

Data Collection

Once we are satisfied with the experimental design, we proceed by collecting and analyzing the data. In the Chemitech case, the employees would be instructed in how to perform the assembly method assigned to them and then would begin assembling the new filtration systems using that method. After this assignment and training, the number of units assembled by each employee during one week is as shown in Table 13.3. The sample mean number of units produced with each of the three assembly methods is reported in the following table.

Assembly Method	Mean Number Produced
A	62
B	66
C	52

From these data, method B appears to result in higher production rates than either of the other methods.

The real issue is whether the three sample means observed are different enough for us to conclude that the means of the populations corresponding to the three methods of assembly are different. To write this question in statistical terms, we introduce the following notation.

μ_1 = mean number of units produced per week for method A
μ_2 = mean number of units produced per week for method B
μ_3 = mean number of units produced per week for method C

Although we will never know the actual values of μ_1, μ_2, and μ_3, we want to use the sample means to test the following hypotheses.

$$H_0: \mu_1 = \mu_2 = \mu_3$$
$$H_a: \text{Not all population means are equal}$$

Excel's Data Analysis tool, Anova: Single Factor, can be used for this completely randomized design.

The problem we face in analyzing data from a completely randomized experimental design is the same problem we faced when we first introduced analysis of variance as a method for testing whether the means of more than two populations are equal. In the next section we will show how analysis of variance is applied in problem situations such as the Chemitech assembly method experiment.

TABLE 13.3 NUMBER OF UNITS PRODUCED BY 15 WORKERS

CD file

ChemTech

		Method		
Observation		A	B	C
1		58	58	48
2		64	69	57
3		55	71	59
4		66	64	47
5		67	68	49
Sample mean		62	66	52
Sample variance		27.5	26.5	31.0
Sample standard deviation		5.24	5.15	5.57

1. Randomization in experimental design is the analog of probability sampling in an observational study.
2. In many medical experiments, potential bias is eliminated by using a double-blind study. In such studies neither the physician applying the treatment nor the subject knows which treatment is being applied. Many other types of experiments could benefit from this type of study.

 # Completely Randomized Design

The hypotheses we want to test when analyzing the data from a completely randomized design are exactly the same as the general form of the hypotheses we presented in Section 13.2.

$$H_0: \mu_1 = \mu_2 = \cdots = \mu_k$$
$$H_a: \text{Not all population means are equal}$$

Hence, to test for the equality of means in situations where the data are collected in a completely randomized experimental design, we can use analysis of variance as introduced in Sections 13.1 and 13.2. Recall that analysis of variance requires the calculation of two independent estimates of the population variance σ^2.

Between-Treatments Estimate of Population Variance

The between-treatments estimate of σ^2 is referred to as the *mean square due to treatments* and is denoted MSTR. The formula for computing MSTR follows:

$$\text{MSTR} = \frac{\sum_{j=1}^{k} n_j (\bar{x}_j - \bar{\bar{x}})^2}{k - 1} \tag{13.20}$$

The numerator in equation (13.20) is called the *sum of squares between* or *sum of squares due to treatments* and is denoted SSTR. The denominator $k - 1$ represents the degrees of freedom associated with SSTR.

For the Chemitech data in Table 13.3, we obtain the following results (note: $\bar{\bar{x}} = 60$).

$$\text{SSTR} = \sum_{j=1}^{k} n_j (\bar{x}_j - \bar{\bar{x}})^2 = 5(62 - 60)^2 + 5(66 - 60)^2 + 5(52 - 60)^2 = 520$$

$$\text{MSTR} = \frac{\text{SSTR}}{k - 1} = \frac{520}{3 - 1} = 260$$

Within-Treatments Estimate of Population Variance

The within-treatments estimate of σ^2 is referred to as the *mean square due to error* and is denoted MSE. The formula for computing MSE follows.

$$\text{MSE} = \frac{\sum_{j=1}^{k} (n_j - 1)s_j^2}{n_T - k} \tag{13.21}$$

The numerator in equation (13.21) is called the *sum of squares within* or *sum of squares due to error* and is denoted SSE. The denominator of MSE is referred to as the degrees of freedom associated with SSE.

For the Chemitech data in Table 13.3, we obtain the following results.

$$SSE = \sum_{j=1}^{k}(n_j - 1)s_j^2 = 4(27.5) + 4(26.5) + 4(31) = 340$$

$$MSE = \frac{SSE}{n_T - k} = \frac{340}{15 - 3} = 28.33$$

Comparing the Variance Estimates: The F Test

If the null hypothesis is true and the ANOVA assumptions are valid, the sampling distribution of MSTR/MSE is an F distribution with numerator degrees of freedom equal to $k - 1$ and denominator degrees of freedom equal to $n_T - k$. Recall also that if the means of the k populations are not equal, the value of MSTR/MSE will be inflated because MSTR overestimates σ^2. Hence we will reject H_0 if the resulting value of MSTR/MSE appears to be too large to have been selected at random from an F distribution with degrees of freedom $k - 1$ in the numerator and $n_T - k$ in the denominator. Thus, the test statistic for a completely randomized design is

$$F = \frac{MSTR}{MSE} \tag{13.22}$$

Let us return to the Chemitech problem and use a level of significance $\alpha = .05$ to conduct the hypothesis test. The value of the test statistic is

$$F = \frac{MSTR}{MSE} = \frac{260}{28.33} = 9.18$$

The numerator degrees of freedom is $k - 1 = 3 - 1 = 2$ and the denominator degrees of freedom is $n_T - k = 15 - 3 = 12$. Because we will only reject the null hypothesis for large values of the test statistic, the p-value is the area under the F distribution to the right of $F = 9.18$. From Table 4 of Appendix B we find that the F value with an area of .01 in the upper tail is 6.93. Because the area in the upper tail for an F value of 9.18 must be less than .01, the p-value for the Chemitech hypothesis test is less than .01. Alternatively, we can use Excel to show that the exact p-value corresponding to $F = 9.18$ is .0038. Because the p-value $\leq \alpha = .05$, H_0 is rejected. The test gives us sufficient evidence to conclude that not all the population means are equal.

Using Excel, p-value = FDIST(9.18,2,12) = .0038.

ANOVA Table

We can now write the result that shows how the total sum of squares, SST, is partitioned.

$$SST = SSTR + SSE \tag{13.23}$$

This result also holds true for the degrees of freedom associated with each of these sums of squares; that is, the total degrees of freedom is the sum of the degrees of freedom associated with SSTR and SSE. The general form of the ANOVA table for a completely randomized design is shown in Table 13.4; Table 13.5 is the corresponding ANOVA table for the Chemitech problem.

Using Excel

In Section 13.2 we showed how Excel's Anova: Single Factor tool could be used to test for the equality of k population means in an observational study. Because the hypotheses we want to test when analyzing the data from a completely randomized experimental design

TABLE 13.4   ANOVA TABLE FOR A COMPLETELY RANDOMIZED DESIGN

Source of Variation	Sum of Squares	Degrees of Freedom	Mean Square	F
Treatments	SSTR	$k - 1$	$\text{MSTR} = \dfrac{\text{SSTR}}{k - 1}$	$\dfrac{\text{MSTR}}{\text{MSE}}$
Error	SSE	$n_T - k$	$\text{MSE} = \dfrac{\text{SSE}}{n_T - k}$	
Total	SST	$n_T - 1$		

are exactly the same as the general form of the hypotheses we presented in Section 13.2, Excel's Anova: Single Factor tool can also be used to test for the equality of means in situations where the data have been collected in a completely randomized design.

The data for the Chemitech problem and the corresponding Anova: Singe Factor tool output are shown in Figure 13.7. We can use the p-value shown in cell F19, 0.0038, to make the hypothesis testing decision. Thus, at the $\alpha = .05$ level of significance, we reject H_0 because the p-value $= 0.0038 < \alpha = .05$.

Pairwise Comparisons

We can use Fisher's LSD procedure to test all possible pairwise comparisons for the Chemitech problem. At the 5% level of significance, the t distribution table shows that with $n_T - k = 15 - 3 = 12$ degrees of freedom, $t_{.025} = 2.179$. Using MSE $= 28.33$ in equation (13.17), we obtain Fisher's least significant difference.

$$\text{LSD} = t_{\alpha/2}\sqrt{\text{MSE}\left(\frac{1}{n_i} + \frac{1}{n_j}\right)} = 2.179\sqrt{28.33\left(\frac{1}{5} + \frac{1}{5}\right)} = 7.34$$

If the magnitude of the difference between any two sample means exceeds 7.34, we can reject the hypothesis that the corresponding population means are equal. For the Chemitech data in Table 13.3, we obtain the following results.

Sample Differences	Significant?
Method A − Method B = 62 − 66 = −4	No
Method A − Method C = 62 − 52 = 10	Yes
Method B − Method C = 66 − 52 = 14	Yes

Thus, the difference in the population means is attributable to the difference between the means for method A and method C and the difference between the means for method B and

TABLE 13.5   ANOVA TABLE FOR THE CHEMITECH PROBLEM

Source of Variation	Sum of Squares	Degrees of Freedom	Mean Square	F
Treatments	520	2	260.00	9.18
Error	340	12	28.33	
Total	860	14		

FIGURE 13.7   EXCEL'S ANOVA: SINGLE FACTOR TOOL OUTPUT FOR THE CHEMITECH PROBLEM

	A	B	C	D	E	F	G	H
1	Observation	Method A	Method B	Method C				
2	1	58	58	48				
3	2	64	69	57				
4	3	55	71	59				
5	4	66	64	47				
6	5	67	68	49				
7								
8	Anova: Single Factor							
9								
10	SUMMARY							
11	*Groups*	*Count*	*Sum*	*Average*	*Variance*			
12	Method A	5	310	62	27.5			
13	Method B	5	330	66	26.5			
14	Method C	5	260	52	31			
15								
16								
17	ANOVA							
18	*Source of Variation*	*SS*	*df*	*MS*	*F*	*P-value*	*F crit*	
19	Between Groups	520	2	260	9.1765	0.0038	3.8853	
20	Within Groups	340	12	28.3333				
21								
22	Total	860	14					
23								

method C. Methods A and B therefore are preferred to method C. However, more testing should be done to compare method A with method B. The current study does not provide sufficient evidence to conclude that these two methods differ.

Exercises

Methods

19. The following data are from a completely randomized design.

		Treatment	
	A	B	C
	162	142	126
	142	156	122
	165	124	138
	145	142	140
	148	136	150
	174	152	128
Sample mean	156	142	134
Sample variance	164.4	131.2	110.4

    a.   Compute the sum of squares between treatments.

    b.   Compute the mean square between treatments.

    c.   Compute the sum of squares due to error.

    d.   Compute the mean square due to error.

    e.   At the $\alpha = .05$ level of significance, test whether the means for the three treatments are equal.

20. Refer to exercise 19.

    a.   Set up the ANOVA table.

    b.   At the $\alpha = .05$ level of significance, use Fisher's least significant difference procedure to test all possible pairwise comparisons. What conclusion can you draw after carrying out this procedure?

21. In a completely randomized experimental design, seven experimental units were used for each of the five levels of the factor. Complete the following ANOVA table.

Source of Variation	Sum of Squares	Degrees of Freedom	Mean Square	F
Treatments	300			
Error				
Total	460			

22. Refer to exercise 21.

    a.   What hypotheses are implied in this problem?

    b.   At the $\alpha = .05$ level of significance, can we reject the null hypothesis in part (a)? Explain.

23. In an experiment designed to test the output levels of three different treatments, the following results were obtained: SST $= 400$, SSTR $= 150$, $n_T = 19$. Set up the ANOVA table and test for any significant difference between the mean output levels of the three treatments. Use $\alpha = .05$.

24. In a completely randomized experimental design, 12 experimental units were used for the first treatment, 15 for the second treatment, and 20 for the third treatment. Complete the following analysis of variance. At a .05 level of significance, is there a significant difference between the treatment means?

Source of Variation	Sum of Squares	Degrees of Freedom	Mean Square	F
Treatments	1200			
Error				
Total	1800			

25. Develop the analysis of variance computations for the following experimental design. At $\alpha = .05$, is there a significant difference between the treatment means?

CD file

Exer25

	Treatment		
	A	**B**	**C**
	136	107	92
	120	114	82
	113	125	85
	107	104	101
	131	107	89

(continued)

	Treatment		
	A	**B**	**C**
	114	109	117
	129	97	110
	102	114	120
		104	98
		89	106
Sample mean	119	107	100
Sample variance	146.86	96.44	173.78

Applications

26. Three different methods for assembling a product were proposed by an industrial engineer. To investigate the number of units assembled correctly with each method, 30 employees were randomly selected and randomly assigned to the three proposed methods in such a way that each method was used by 10 workers. The number of units assembled correctly was recorded, and the analysis of variance procedure was applied to the resulting data set. The following results were obtained: SST = 10,800; SSTR = 4560.
    a. Set up the ANOVA table for this problem.
    b. Use $\alpha = .05$ to test for any significant difference in the means for the three assembly methods.

27. In an experiment designed to test the breaking strength of four types of cables, the following results were obtained: SST = 85.05, SSTR = 61.64, $n_T = 24$. Set up the ANOVA table and test for any significant difference in the mean breaking strength of the four cables. Use $\alpha = .05$.

28. To study the effect of temperature on yield in a chemical process, five batches were produced at each of three temperature levels. The results follow. Construct an analysis of variance table. Use a .05 level of significance to test whether the temperature level has an effect on the mean yield of the process.

Temperature		
50°C	**60°C**	**70°C**
34	30	23
24	31	28
36	34	28
39	23	30
32	27	31

29. Auditors must make judgments about various aspects of an audit on the basis of their own direct experience, indirect experience, or a combination of the two. In a study, auditors were asked to make judgments about the frequency of errors to be found in an audit. The judgments by the auditors were then compared to the actual results. Suppose the following data were obtained from a similar study; lower scores indicate better judgments.

AudJudg

Direct	**Indirect**	**Combination**
17.0	16.6	25.2
18.5	22.2	24.0
15.8	20.5	21.5

Direct	Indirect	Combination
18.2	18.3	26.8
20.2	24.2	27.5
16.0	19.8	25.8
13.3	21.2	24.2

Use $\alpha = .05$ to test to see whether the basis for the judgment affects the quality of the judgment. What is your conclusion?

30. Four different paints are advertised as having the same drying time. To check the manufacturer's claims, five samples were tested for each of the paints. The time in minutes until the paint was dry enough for a second coat to be applied was recorded. The following data were obtained.

Paint

Paint 1	Paint 2	Paint 3	Paint 4
128	144	133	150
137	133	143	142
135	142	137	135
124	146	136	140
141	130	131	153

At the $\alpha = .05$ level of significance, test to see whether the mean drying time is the same for each type of paint.

31. A well-known automotive magazine took three top-of-the-line midsize automobiles manufactured in the United States, test-drove them, and compared them on a variety of criteria. In the area of gasoline mileage performance, five automobiles of each brand were each test-driven 500 miles; the miles per gallon data obtained follow. Use the analysis of variance procedure with $\alpha = .05$ to determine whether there is a significant difference in the mean number of miles per gallon for the three types of automobiles.

Automobile		
A	B	C
19	19	24
21	20	26
20	22	23
19	21	25
21	23	27

32. Refer to exercise 29. Use Fisher's least significant difference procedure to test all possible pairwise comparisons. What conclusion can you draw after carrying out this procedure? Use $\alpha = .05$.

33. Refer to exercise 31. Use Fisher's least significant difference procedure to test all possible pairwise comparisons. What conclusion can you draw after carrying out this procedure? Use $\alpha = .05$.

13.6 Randomized Block Design

Thus far we considered the completely randomized experimental design. Recall that to test for a difference among treatment means, we computed an F value using the ratio

$$F = \frac{\text{MSTR}}{\text{MSE}}$$

*A completely randomized design is useful when the experimental units are homogeneous. If the experimental units are heterogeneous, **blocking** is often used to form homogeneous groups.*

A problem can arise whenever differences due to extraneous factors (ones not considered in the experiment) cause the MSE term in this ratio to become large. In such cases, the F value in equation (13.23) can become small, signaling no difference among treatment means when in fact such a difference exists.

In this section we present an experimental design known as a **randomized block design**. Its purpose is to control some of the extraneous sources of variation by removing such variation from the MSE term. This design tends to provide a better estimate of the true error variance and leads to a more powerful hypothesis test in terms of the ability to detect differences among treatment means. To illustrate, let us consider a stress study for air traffic controllers.

Air Traffic Controller Stress Test

A study measuring the fatigue and stress of air traffic controllers resulted in proposals for modification and redesign of the controller's work station. After consideration of several designs for the work station, three specific alternatives are selected as having the best potential for reducing controller stress. The key question is: To what extent do the three alternatives differ in terms of their effect on controller stress? To answer this question, we need to design an experiment that will provide measurements of air traffic controller stress under each alternative.

Experimental studies in business often involve experimental units that are highly heterogeneous; as a result, randomized block designs are often employed.

In a completely randomized design, a random sample of controllers would be assigned to each work station alternative. However, controllers are believed to differ substantially in their ability to handle stressful situations. What is high stress to one controller might be only moderate or even low stress to another. Hence, when considering the within-group source of variation (MSE), we must realize that this variation includes both random error and error due to individual controller differences. In fact, managers expected controller variability to be a major contributor to the MSE term.

Blocking in experimental design is similar to stratification in sampling.

One way to separate the effect of the individual differences is to use a randomized block design. Such a design will identify the variability stemming from individual controller differences and remove it from the MSE term. The randomized block design calls for a single sample of controllers. Each controller in the sample is tested with each of the three work station alternatives. In experimental design terminology, the work station is the *factor of interest* and the controllers are the *blocks*. The three treatments or populations associated with the work station factor correspond to the three work station alternatives. For simplicity, we refer to the work station alternatives as system A, system B, and system C.

The *randomized* aspect of the randomized block design is the random order in which the treatments (systems) are assigned to the controllers. If every controller were to test the three systems in the same order, any observed difference in systems might be due to the order of the test rather than to true differences in the systems.

To provide the necessary data, the three work station alternatives were installed at the Cleveland Control Center in Oberlin, Ohio. Six controllers were selected at random and assigned to operate each of the systems. A follow-up interview and a medical examination of each controller participating in the study provided a measure of the stress for each controller on each system. The data are reported in Table 13.6.

TABLE 13.6   A RANDOMIZED BLOCK DESIGN FOR THE AIR TRAFFIC CONTROLLER STRESS TEST

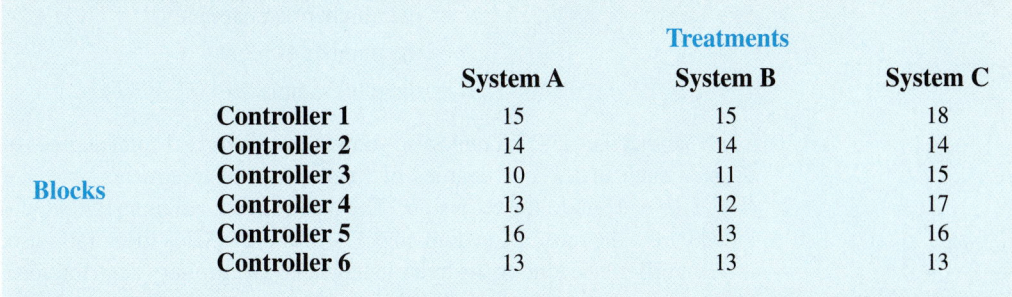

		Treatments		
		System A	System B	System C
	Controller 1	15	15	18
	Controller 2	14	14	14
Blocks	Controller 3	10	11	15
	Controller 4	13	12	17
	Controller 5	16	13	16
	Controller 6	13	13	13

Table 13.7 is a summary of the stress data collected. In this table we include column totals (treatments) and row totals (blocks) as well as some sample means that will be helpful in making the sum of squares computations for the ANOVA procedure. Because lower stress values are viewed as better, the sample data seem to favor system B with its mean stress rating of 13. However, the usual question remains: Do the sample results justify the conclusion that the population mean stress levels for the three systems differ? That is, are the differences statistically significant? An analysis of variance computation similar to the one performed for the completely randomized design can be used to answer this statistical question.

ANOVA Procedure

The ANOVA procedure for the randomized block design requires us to partition the sum of squares total (SST) into three groups: sum of squares due to treatments (SSTR), sum of squares due to blocks (SSBL), and sum of squares due to error (SSE). The formula for this partitioning follows.

$$SST = SSTR + SSBL + SSE \qquad \textbf{(13.24)}$$

TABLE 13.7   SUMMARY OF STRESS DATA FOR THE AIR TRAFFIC CONTROLLER STRESS TEST

		Treatments			Row or Block Totals	Block Means
		System A	System B	System C		
	Controller 1	15	15	18	48	$\bar{x}_{1.} = 48/3 = 16.0$
	Controller 2	14	14	14	42	$\bar{x}_{2.} = 42/3 = 14.0$
Blocks	Controller 3	10	11	15	36	$\bar{x}_{3.} = 36/3 = 12.0$
	Controller 4	13	12	17	42	$\bar{x}_{4.} = 42/3 = 14.0$
	Controller 5	16	13	16	45	$\bar{x}_{5.} = 45/3 = 15.0$
	Controller 6	13	13	13	39	$\bar{x}_{6.} = 39/3 = 13.0$
Column or Treatment Totals		81	78	93	252	$\bar{\bar{x}} = \dfrac{252}{18} = 14.0$
Treatment Means		$\bar{x}_{.1} = \dfrac{81}{6}$ $= 13.5$	$\bar{x}_{.2} = \dfrac{78}{6}$ $= 13.0$	$\bar{x}_{.3} = \dfrac{93}{6}$ $= 15.5$		

This sum of squares partition is summarized in the ANOVA table for the randomized block design as shown in Table 13.8. The notation used in the table is

$$k = \text{the number of treatments}$$
$$b = \text{the number of blocks}$$
$$n_T = \text{the total sample size } (n_T = kb)$$

Note that the ANOVA table also shows how the $n_T - 1$ total degrees of freedom are partitioned such that $k - 1$ degrees of freedom go to treatments, $b - 1$ go to blocks, and $(k - 1)(b - 1)$ go to the error term. The mean square column shows the sum of squares divided by the degrees of freedom, and $F = \text{MSTR/MSE}$ is the F ratio used to test for a significant difference among the treatment means. The primary contribution of the randomized block design is that, by including blocks, we remove the individual controller differences from the MSE term and obtain a more powerful test to determine it the population mean stress levels for the three systems differ.

Computations and Conclusions

To compute the F statistic needed to test for a difference among treatment means with a randomized block design, we need to compute MSTR and MSE. To calculate these two mean squares, we must first compute SSTR and SSE; in doing so, we will also compute SSBL and SST. To simplify the presentation, we perform the calculations in four steps. In addition to k, b, and n_T as previously defined, the following notation is used.

$$x_{ij} = \text{value of the observation corresponding to treatment } j \text{ in block } i$$
$$\bar{x}_{.j} = \text{sample mean of the } j\text{th treatment}$$
$$\bar{x}_{i.} = \text{sample mean for the } i\text{th block}$$
$$\bar{\bar{x}} = \text{overall sample mean}$$

Step 1. Compute the total sum of squares (SST).

$$\text{SST} = \sum_{i=1}^{b}\sum_{j=1}^{k}(x_{ij} - \bar{\bar{x}})^2 \tag{13.25}$$

Step 2. Compute the sum of squares due to treatments (SSTR).

$$\text{SSTR} = b\sum_{j=1}^{k}(\bar{x}_{.j} - \bar{\bar{x}})^2 \tag{13.26}$$

TABLE 13.8   ANOVA TABLE FOR THE RANDOMIZED BLOCK DESIGN
WITH k TREATMENTS AND b BLOCKS

Source of Variation	Sum of Squares	Degrees of Freedom	Mean Square	F
Treatments	SSTR	$k - 1$	$\text{MSTR} = \dfrac{\text{SSTR}}{k-1}$	$\dfrac{\text{MSTR}}{\text{MSE}}$
Blocks	SSBL	$b - 1$	$\text{MSBL} = \dfrac{\text{SSBL}}{b-1}$	
Error	SSE	$(k - 1)(b - 1)$	$\text{MSE} = \dfrac{\text{SSE}}{(k-1)(b-1)}$	
Total	SST	$n_T - 1$		

Step 3. Compute the sum of squares due to blocks (SSBL).

$$\text{SSBL} = k \sum_{i=1}^{b} (\bar{x}_{i\cdot} - \bar{\bar{x}})^2 \qquad \textbf{(13.27)}$$

Step 4. Compute the sum of squares due to error (SSE).

$$\text{SSE} = \text{SST} - \text{SSTR} - \text{SSBL} \qquad \textbf{(13.28)}$$

For the air traffic controller data in Table 13.7, these steps lead to the following sums of squares.

Step 1. $\text{SST} = (15 - 14)^2 + (15 - 14)^2 + (18 - 14)^2 + \cdots + (13 - 14)^2 = 70$

Step 2. $\text{SSTR} = 6[(13.5 - 14)^2 + (13.0 - 14)^2 + (15.5 - 14)^2] = 21$

Step 3. $\text{SSBL} = 3[(16 - 14)^2 + (14 - 14)^2 + (12 - 14)^2 + (14 - 14)^2 +$
$(15 - 14)^2 + (13 - 14)^2] = 30$

Step 4. $\text{SSE} = 70 - 21 - 30 = 19$

These sums of squares divided by their degrees of freedom provide the corresponding mean square values shown in Table 13.9.

Let us use a level of significance $\alpha = .05$ to conduct the hypothesis test. The value of the test statistic is

$$F = \frac{\text{MSTR}}{\text{MSE}} = \frac{10.5}{1.9} = 5.53$$

The numerator degrees of freedom is $k - 1 = 3 - 1 = 2$ and the denominator degrees of freedom is $(k - 1)(b - 1) = (3 - 1)(6 - 1) = 10$. Because we will only reject the null hypothesis for large values of the test statistic, the p-value is the area under the F distribution to the right of $F = 5.53$. From Table 4 of Appendix B we find that with the degrees of freedom 2 and 10, $F = 5.53$ is between $F_{.025} = 5.46$ and $F_{.01} = 7.56$. As a result, the area in the upper tail, or the p-value, is between .01 and .025. Alternatively, we can use Excel to show that the exact p-value for $F = 5.53$ is .0241. Because the p-value $\leq \alpha = .05$, we reject the null hypothesis $H_0: \mu_1 = \mu_2 = \mu_3$ and conclude that the population mean stress levels differ for the three work station alternatives.

Using Excel, p-value = FDIST(5.53,2,10) = .0241.

Some general comments can be made about the randomized block design. The experimental design described in this section is a *complete* block design; the word "complete" indicates that each block is subjected to all k treatments. That is, all controllers (blocks) were tested with all three systems (treatments). Experimental designs in which some but not all treatments are applied to each block are referred to as *incomplete* block designs. A discussion of incomplete block designs is beyond the scope of this text.

TABLE 13.9   ANOVA TABLE FOR THE AIR TRAFFIC CONTROLLER STRESS TEST

Source of Variation	Sum of Squares	Degrees of Freedom	Mean Square	F
Treatments	21	2	10.5	10.5/1.9 = 5.53
Blocks	30	5	6.0	
Error	19	10	1.9	
Total	70	17		

Because each controller in the air traffic controller stress test was required to use all three systems, this approach guarantees a complete block design. In some cases, however, blocking is carried out with "similar" experimental units in each block. For example, assume that in a pretest of air traffic controllers, the population of controllers was divided into groups ranging from extremely high-stress individuals to extremely low-stress individuals. The blocking could still be accomplished by having three controllers from each of the stress classifications participate in the study. Each block would then consist of three controllers in the same stress group. The randomized aspect of the block design would be the random assignment of the three controllers in each block to the three systems.

Finally, note that the ANOVA table shown in Table 13.8 provides an F value to test for treatment effects but *not* for blocks. The reason is that the experiment was designed to test a single factor—work station design. The blocking based on individual stress differences was conducted to remove such variation from the MSE term. However, the study was not designed to test specifically for individual differences in stress.

Some analysts compute $F = $ MSB/MSE and use that statistic to test for significance of the blocks. Then they use the result as a guide to whether the same type of blocking would be desired in future experiments. However, if individual stress difference is to be a factor in the study, a different experimental design should be used. A test of significance on blocks should not be performed as a basis for a conclusion about a second factor.

Using Excel

Excel's Anova: Two-Factor Without Replication tool can be used to test whether the mean stress levels for air traffic controllers are the same for the three work stations. Refer to the Excel worksheet shown in Figure 13.8 as we describe the tasks involved.

Enter Data: Column A is used to identify each of the air traffic controllers in the study. Columns B, C, and D contain the stress level scores for the three systems.

Apply Tools: The following steps describe how to use Excel's Anova: Two-Factor Without Replication tool to test the hypothesis that the mean stress level score is the same for all three systems.

Step 1. Select the **Tools** menu
Step 2. Choose the **Data Analysis** option
Step 3. Choose **Anova: Two-Factor Without Replication** from the list of Analysis Tools
Step 4. When the Anova: Two-Factor Without Replication dialog box appears:
   Enter A1:D7 in the **Input Range** box
   Select **Labels**
   Enter .05 in the **Alpha** box
   Select **Output Range**
   Enter A9 in the **Output Range** box (to identify the upper left corner of the section of the worksheet where the output will appear)
   Click **OK**

The output, titled Anova: Two-Factor Without Replication, appears in cells A9:G30 of the worksheet. Cells A11:E21 provide a summary of the data. The ANOVA table shown in cells A24:G30 is basically the same as the ANOVA table shown in Table 13.9. The label Rows corresponds to the blocks in the problem, and the label Columns corresponds to the treatments. The Excel output provides the p-value associated with the test as well as the critical F value.

FIGURE 13.8   EXCEL'S ANOVA: TWO-FACTOR WITHOUT REPLICATION TOOL OUTPUT
FOR THE AIR TRAFFIC CONTROLLER STRESS TEST

	A	B	C	D	E	F	G	H
1	Controller	System A	System B	System C				
2	1	15	15	18				
3	2	14	14	14				
4	3	10	11	15				
5	4	13	12	17				
6	5	16	13	16				
7	6	13	13	13				
8								
9	Anova: Two-Factor Without Replication							
10								
11	SUMMARY	Count	Sum	Average	Variance			
12	1	3	48	16	3			
13	2	3	42	14	0			
14	3	3	36	12	7			
15	4	3	42	14	7			
16	5	3	45	15	3			
17	6	3	39	13	0			
18								
19	System A	6	81	13.5	4.3			
20	System B	6	78	13	2			
21	System C	6	93	15.5	3.5			
22								
23								
24	ANOVA							
25	Source of Variation	SS	df	MS	F	P-value	F crit	
26	Rows	30	5	6	3.1579	0.0574	3.3258	
27	Columns	21	2	10.5	5.5263	0.0242	4.1028	
28	Error	19	10	1.9				
29								
30	Total	70	17					
31								

We can use the p-value shown in cell F27, 0.0242, to make the hypothesis testing decision. Thus, at the $\alpha = .05$ level of significance, we reject H_0 because the p-value $= .0242 < \alpha = .05$. Hence, we conclude that the mean stress scores differ among the three systems.

NOTES AND COMMENTS

The error degrees of freedom are less for a randomized block design than for a completely randomized design because $b - 1$ degrees of freedom are lost for the b blocks. If n is small, the potential effects due to blocks can be masked because of the loss of error degrees of freedom; for large n, the effects are minimized.

Exercises

Methods

34. Consider the experimental results for the following randomized block design. Make the calculations necessary to set up the analysis of variance table.

		Treatments		
		A	**B**	**C**
	1	10	9	8
	2	12	6	5
Blocks	**3**	18	15	14
	4	20	18	18
	5	8	7	8

Use $\alpha = .05$ to test for any significant differences.

35. The following data were obtained for a randomized block design involving five treatments and three blocks: SST = 430, SSTR = 310, SSBL = 85. Set up the ANOVA table and test for any significant differences. Use $\alpha = .05$.

36. An experiment has been conducted for four treatments with eight blocks. Complete the following analysis of variance table.

Source of Variation	Sum of Squares	Degrees of Freedom	Mean Square	F
Treatments	900			
Blocks	400			
Error				
Total	1800			

Use $\alpha = .05$ to test for any significant differences.

Applications

37. An automobile dealer conducted a test to determine if the time in minutes needed to complete a minor engine tune-up depends on whether a computerized engine analyzer or an electronic analyzer is used. Because tune-up time varies among compact, intermediate, and full-sized cars, the three types of cars were used as blocks in the experiment. The data obtained follow.

		Analyzer	
		Computerized	**Electronic**
	Compact	50	42
Car	**Intermediate**	55	44
	Full-sized	63	46

Use $\alpha = .05$ to test for any significant differences.

38. Five different auditing procedures were compared in terms of total audit time. To control for possible variation due to the person conducting the audit, four accountants were selected randomly and treated as blocks in the experiment. The following values were obtained by the ANOVA procedure: SST = 100, SSTR = 45, SSBL = 36. Use $\alpha = .05$ to test for any significant difference in the mean total audit time for the five auditing procedures.

39. An important consideration in selecting software for word-processing and database management systems is the time required to learn how to use the system. To evaluate three file management systems, a firm designed a test involving five word-processing operators. Because operator variability was believed to be a significant factor, each of the five operators was trained on each of the three file management systems. The data obtained follow.

			System	
		A	**B**	**C**
	1	16	16	24
	2	19	17	22
Operator	**3**	14	13	19
	4	13	12	18
	5	18	17	22

Use $\alpha = .05$ to test for any difference in the mean training time (in hours) for the three systems.

40. A study reported in the *Journal of the American Medical Association* investigated the cardiac demands of heavy snow shoveling. Ten healthy men underwent exercise testing with a treadmill and a cycle ergometer modified for arm cranking. The men then cleared two tracts of heavy, wet snow by using a lightweight plastic snow shovel and an electric snow thrower. Each subject's heart rate, blood pressure, oxygen uptake, and perceived exertion during snow removal were compared with the values obtained during treadmill and arm-crank ergometer testing. Suppose the following table gives the heart rates in beats per minute for each of the 10 subjects.

Snow

Subject	Treadmill	Arm-Crank Ergometer	Snow Shovel	Snow Thrower
1	177	205	180	98
2	151	177	164	120
3	184	166	167	111
4	161	152	173	122
5	192	142	179	151
6	193	172	205	158
7	164	191	156	117
8	207	170	160	123
9	177	181	175	127
10	174	154	191	109

At the .05 level of significance, test for any significant differences.

13.7 Factorial Experiment

The experimental designs we considered thus far enable us to draw statistical conclusions about one factor. However, in some experiments we want to draw conclusions about more than one variable or factor. A **factorial experiment** and its corresponding ANOVA computations is a valuable design when simultaneous conclusions about two or more factors are required. The term *factorial* is used because the experimental conditions include all possible combinations of the factors. For example, for *a* levels of factor A and *b* levels of factor B, the experiment will involve collecting data on *ab* treatment combinations. In this section we will show the analysis for a two-factor factorial experiment. The basic approach can be extended to experiments involving more than two factors.

As an illustration of a two-factor factorial experiment, we will consider a study involving the Graduate Management Admissions Test (GMAT), a standardized test used by graduate schools of business to evaluate an applicant's ability to pursue a graduate program in that field. Scores on the GMAT range from 200 to 800, with higher scores implying higher aptitude.

In an attempt to improve students' performance on the GMAT exam, a major Texas university is considering offering the following three GMAT preparation programs.

1. A three-hour review session covering the types of questions generally asked on the GMAT.
2. A one-day program covering relevant exam material, along with the taking and grading of a sample exam.
3. An intensive 10-week course involving the identification of each student's weaknesses and the setting up of individualized programs for improvement.

Hence, one factor in this study is the GMAT preparation program, which has three treatments: three-hour review, one-day program, and 10-week course. Before selecting the preparation program to adopt, further study will be conducted to determine how the proposed programs affect GMAT scores.

The GMAT is usually taken by students from three colleges: the College of Business, the College of Engineering, and the College of Arts and Sciences. Therefore, a second factor of interest in the experiment is whether a student's undergraduate college affects the GMAT score. This second factor, undergraduate college, also has three treatments: business, engineering, and arts and sciences. The factorial design for this experiment with three treatments corresponding to factor A, the preparation program, and three treatments corresponding to factor B, the undergraduate college, will have a total of $3 \times 3 = 9$ treatment combinations. These treatment combinations or experimental conditions are summarized in Table 13.10.

Assume that a sample of two students will be selected corresponding to each of the nine treatment combinations shown in Table 13.10: two business students will take the three-hour review, two will take the one-day program, and two will take the 10-week course. In addition, two engineering students and two arts and sciences students will take each of the three preparation programs. In experimental design terminology, the sample size of two for each treatment combination indicates that we have two **replications**. Additional replications and a larger sample size could easily be used, but we elect to minimize the computational aspects for this illustration.

TABLE 13.10   NINE TREATMENT COMBINATIONS FOR THE TWO-FACTOR GMAT EXPERIMENT

		Factor B: College		
		Business	Engineering	Arts and Sciences
Factor A:	Three-hour review	1	2	3
Preparation	One-day program	4	5	6
Program	10-week course	7	8	9

This experimental design requires that six students who plan to attend graduate school be randomly selected from *each* of the three undergraduate colleges. Then two students from each college should be assigned randomly to each preparation program, resulting in a total of 18 students being used in the study.

Let us assume that the randomly selected students participated in the preparation programs and then took the GMAT. The scores obtained are reported in Table 13.11.

The analysis of variance computations with the data in Table 13.11 will provide answers to the following questions.

- **Main effect (factor A):** Do the preparation programs differ in terms of effect on GMAT scores?
- **Main effect (factor B):** Do the undergraduate colleges differ in terms of effect on GMAT scores?
- **Interaction effect (factors A and B):** Do students in some colleges do better in one type of preparation program whereas others do better in a different type of preparation program?

The term **interaction** refers to a new effect that we can now study because we used a factorial experiment. If the interaction effect has a significant impact on the GMAT scores, we can conclude that the effect of the type of preparation program depends on the undergraduate college.

ANOVA Procedure

The ANOVA procedure for the two-factor factorial experiment is similar to the completely randomized experiment and the randomized block experiment in that we again partition the sum of squares and the degrees of freedom into their respective sources. The formula for partitioning the sum of squares for the two-factor factorial experiments follows.

$$SST = SSA + SSB + SSAB + SSE \tag{13.29}$$

The partitioning of the sum of squares and degrees of freedom is summarized in Table 13.12. The following notation is used.

$$a = \text{number of levels of factor A}$$
$$b = \text{number of levels of factor B}$$
$$r = \text{number of replications}$$
$$n_T = \text{total number of observations taken in the experiment; } n_T = abr$$

TABLE 13.11   GMAT SCORES FOR THE TWO-FACTOR EXPERIMENT

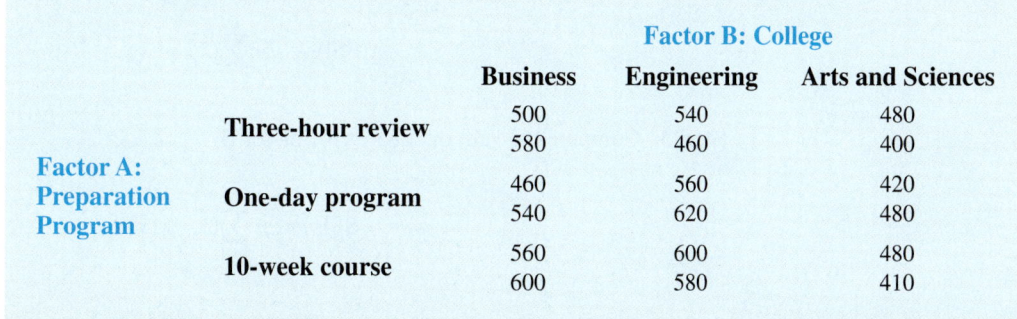

		Factor B: College		
		Business	**Engineering**	**Arts and Sciences**
Factor A: Preparation Program	**Three-hour review**	500 / 580	540 / 460	480 / 400
	One-day program	460 / 540	560 / 620	420 / 480
	10-week course	560 / 600	600 / 580	480 / 410

TABLE 13.12   ANOVA TABLE FOR THE TWO-FACTOR FACTORIAL EXPERIMENT WITH r REPLICATIONS

Source of Variation	Sum of Squares	Degrees of Freedom	Mean Square	F
Factor A	SSA	$a - 1$	$\text{MSA} = \dfrac{\text{SSA}}{a - 1}$	$\dfrac{\text{MSA}}{\text{MSE}}$
Factor B	SSB	$b - 1$	$\text{MSB} = \dfrac{\text{SSB}}{b - 1}$	$\dfrac{\text{MSB}}{\text{MSE}}$
Interaction	SSAB	$(a - 1)(b - 1)$	$\text{MSAB} = \dfrac{\text{SSAB}}{(a - 1)(b - 1)}$	$\dfrac{\text{MSAB}}{\text{MSE}}$
Error	SSE	$ab(r - 1)$	$\text{MSE} = \dfrac{\text{SSE}}{ab(r - 1)}$	
Total	SST	$n_T - 1$		

Computations and Conclusions

To compute the F statistics needed to test for the significance of factor A, factor B, and interaction, we need to compute MSA, MSB, MSAB, and MSE. To calculate these four mean squares, we must first compute SSA, SSB, SSAB, and SSE; in doing so we will also compute SST. To simplify the presentation, we perform the calculations in five steps. In addition to a, b, r, and n_T as previously defined, the following notation is used.

> x_{ijk} = observation corresponding to the kth replicate taken from treatment i of factor A and treatment j of factor B
>
> $\bar{x}_{i\cdot}$ = sample mean for the observations in treatment i (factor A)
>
> $\bar{x}_{\cdot j}$ = sample mean for the observations in treatment j (factor B)
>
> $\bar{x}_{ij}$ = sample mean for the observations corresponding to the combination of treatment i (factor A) and treatment j (factor B)
>
> $\bar{\bar{x}}$ = overall sample mean of all n_T observations

Step 1.   Compute the total sum of squares.

$$\text{SST} = \sum_{i=1}^{a}\sum_{j=1}^{b}\sum_{k=1}^{r}(x_{ijk} - \bar{\bar{x}})^2 \tag{13.30}$$

Step 2.   Compute the sum of squares for factor A.

$$\text{SSA} = br\sum_{i=1}^{a}(\bar{x}_{i\cdot} - \bar{\bar{x}})^2 \tag{13.31}$$

Step 3.   Compute the sum of squares for factor B.

$$\text{SSB} = ar\sum_{j=1}^{b}(\bar{x}_{\cdot j} - \bar{\bar{x}})^2 \tag{13.32}$$

Step 4. Compute the sum of squares for interaction.

$$\text{SSAB} = r \sum_{i=1}^{a} \sum_{j=1}^{b} (\bar{x}_{ij} - \bar{x}_{i\cdot} - \bar{x}_{\cdot j} + \bar{\bar{x}})^2 \qquad \textbf{(13.33)}$$

Step 5. Compute the sum of squares due to error.

$$\text{SSE} = \text{SST} - \text{SSA} - \text{SSB} - \text{SSAB} \qquad \textbf{(13.34)}$$

Table 13.13 reports the data collected in the experiment and the various sums that will help us with the sum of squares computations. Using equations (13.30) through (13.34), we calculate the following sums of squares for the GMAT two-factor factorial experiment.

Step 1. $\text{SST} = (500 - 515)^2 + (580 - 515)^2 + (540 - 515)^2 + \cdots + (410 - 515)^2 = 82{,}450$

Step 2. $\text{SSA} = (3)(2)[(493.33 - 515)^2 + (513.33 - 515)^2 + (538.33 - 515)^2] = 6100$

Step 3. $\text{SSB} = (3)(2)[(540 - 515)^2 + (560 - 515)^2 + (445 - 515)^2] = 45{,}300$

Step 4. $\text{SSAB} = 2[(540 - 493.33 - 540 + 515)^2 + (500 - 493.33 - 560 + 515)^2 + \cdots + (445 - 538.33 - 445 + 515)^2] = 11{,}200$

Step 5. $\text{SSE} = 82{,}450 - 6100 - 45{,}300 - 11{,}200 = 19{,}850$

These sums of squares divided by their corresponding degrees of freedom, as shown in Table 13.14, provide the appropriate mean square values for testing the two main effects (preparation program and undergraduate college) and the interaction effect. The F ratio used to test for differences among preparation programs is 1.38. We can use Excel to show that the p-value corresponding to $F = 1.38$ is .2994. Because the p-value $= .2994 > \alpha = .05$, we cannot reject the null hypothesis and must conclude that there is no significant difference among the three preparation programs. However, for the undergraduate college effect, the p-value corresponding to $F = 10.27$ is .0048. Hence, the analysis of variance results enable us to conclude that the GMAT test scores do differ among the three undergraduate colleges; that is, the three undergraduate colleges do not provide the same preparation for performance on the GMAT. Finally, the interaction F value of $F = 1.27$ and its corresponding p-value of .3503 mean that we cannot identify a significant interaction effect. Therefore, we have no reason to believe that the three preparation programs differ in their ability to prepare students from the different colleges for the GMAT.

Excel's FDIST function makes it easy to compute the p-value for each F value.

Undergraduate college was found to be a significant factor. Checking the calculations in Table 13.13, we see that the sample means are: business students $\bar{x}_{\cdot 1} = 540$, engineering students $\bar{x}_{\cdot 2} = 560$, and arts and sciences students $\bar{x}_{\cdot 3} = 445$. Tests on individual treatment means can be conducted; yet after reviewing the three sample means, we would anticipate no difference in preparation for business and engineering graduates. However, the arts and sciences students appear to be significantly less prepared for the GMAT than students in the other colleges. Perhaps this observation will lead the university to consider other options for assisting these students in preparing for graduate management admission tests.

Using Excel

Excel's Anova: Two-Factor With Replication tool can be used to analyze the data for the two-factor GMAT experiment. Refer to the Excel worksheet shown in Figure 13.9 as we describe the tasks involved.

TABLE 13.13 GMAT SUMMARY DATA FOR THE TWO-FACTOR EXPERIMENT

Factor A: Preparation Program	Factor B: College			Row Totals	Factor A Means
(Treatment combination totals)	**Business**	**Engineering**	**Arts and Sciences**		
Three-hour review	500 580 1080 $\bar{x}_{11} = \dfrac{1080}{2} = 540$	540 460 1000 $\bar{x}_{12} = \dfrac{1000}{2} = 500$	480 400 880 $\bar{x}_{13} = \dfrac{880}{2} = 440$	2960	$\bar{x}_{1\cdot} = \dfrac{2960}{6} = 493.33$
One-day program	460 540 1000 $\bar{x}_{21} = \dfrac{1000}{2} = 500$	560 620 1180 $\bar{x}_{22} = \dfrac{1180}{2} = 590$	420 480 900 $\bar{x}_{23} = \dfrac{900}{2} = 450$	3080	$\bar{x}_{2\cdot} = \dfrac{3080}{6} = 513.33$
10-week course	560 600 1160 $\bar{x}_{31} = \dfrac{1160}{2} = 580$	600 580 1180 $\bar{x}_{32} = \dfrac{1180}{2} = 590$	480 410 890 $\bar{x}_{33} = \dfrac{890}{2} = 445$	3230	$\bar{x}_{3\cdot} = \dfrac{3230}{6} = 538.33$
Column Totals	3240	3360	2670	9270	Overall total
Factor B Means	$\bar{x}_{\cdot 1} = \dfrac{3240}{6} = 540$	$\bar{x}_{\cdot 2} = \dfrac{3360}{6} = 560$	$\bar{x}_{\cdot 3} = \dfrac{2670}{6} = 445$		$\bar{\bar{x}} = \dfrac{9270}{18} = 515$

TABLE 13.14 ANOVA TABLE FOR THE TWO-FACTOR GMAT STUDY

Source of Variation	Sum of Squares	Degrees of Freedom	Mean Square	F
Factor A	6,100	2	3,050	3,050/2206 = 1.38
Factor B	45,300	2	22,650	22,650/2206 = 10.27
Interaction	11,200	4	2,800	2,800/2206 = 1.27
Error	19,850	9	2,206	
Total	82,450	17		

FIGURE 13.9 EXCEL'S ANOVA: TWO-FACTOR WITH REPLICATION TOOL OUTPUT FOR THE GMAT EXPERIMENT

	A	B	C	D	E	F	G	H
1		Business	Engineering	Arts and Sciences				
2	3-hour review	500	540	480				
3		580	460	400				
4	1-day program	460	560	420				
5		540	620	480				
6	10-week course	560	600	480				
7		600	580	410				
8								
9	Anova: Two-Factor With Replication							
10								
11	SUMMARY	Business	Engineering	Arts and Sciences	Total			
12	*3-hour review*							
13	Count	2	2	2	6			
14	Sum	1080	1000	880	2960			
15	Average	540	500	440	493.3333			
16	Variance	3200	3200	3200	3946.667			
17								
18	*1-day program*							
19	Count	2	2	2	6			
20	Sum	1000	1180	900	3080			
21	Average	500	590	450	513.3333			
22	Variance	3200	1800	1800	5386.667			
23								
24	*10-week course*							
25	Count	2	2	2	6			
26	Sum	1160	1180	890	3230			
27	Average	580	590	445	538.3333			
28	Variance	800	200	2450	5936.667			
29								
30	*Total*							
31	Count	6	6	6				
32	Sum	3240	3360	2670				
33	Average	540	560	445				
34	Variance	2720	3200	1510				
35								
36								
37	ANOVA							
38	*Source of Variation*	*SS*	*df*	*MS*	*F*	*P-value*	*F crit*	
39	Sample	6100	2	3050	1.3829	0.2994	4.2565	
40	Columns	45300	2	22650	10.2695	0.0048	4.2565	
41	Interaction	11200	4	2800	1.2695	0.3503	3.6331	
42	Within	19850	9	2205.5556				
43								
44	Total	82450	17					
45								

Enter Data: Column A is used to identify each of the preparation programs (factor A) in the study. Column B contains the GMAT scores for the Business students, column C contains the GMAT scores for the Engineering students, and column D contains the GMAT scores for the Arts and Sciences students.

Apply Tools: The following steps describe how Excel's Anova: Two-Factor With Replication tool can be used to analyze the data for the two-factor GMAT experiment.

> **Step 1.** Select the **Tools** menu
> **Step 2.** Choose the **Data Analysis** option
> **Step 3.** Choose **Anova: Two-Factor With Replication** from the list of Analysis Tools
> **Step 4.** When the Anova: Two-Factor With Replication dialog box appears (see Figure 13.10):
>> Enter A1:D7 in the **Input Range** box
>> Enter 2 in the **Rows per sample** box
>> Enter .05 in the **Alpha** box
>> Select **Output Range**
>> Enter A9 in the Output Range box (to identify the upper left corner of the section of the worksheet where the output will appear)
>> Click **OK**

The output, titled Anova: Two-Factor With Replication, appears in cells A9:G44 of the worksheet. Cells A11:E34 provide a summary of the data. The ANOVA table, shown in cells A37:G44, is basically the same as the ANOVA table shown in Table 13.14. The label Sample corresponds to factor A, the label Columns corresponds to factor B, and the label Within corresponds to error. The Excel output provides the p-value associated with each F test as well as the critical F values.

We can use the p-value of .2994 in cell F39 to make the hypothesis testing decision for factor A (Preparation Program). At the $\alpha = .05$ level of significance, we cannot reject H_0 because the p-value $= 0.2994 > \alpha = .05$. We can make the hypothesis testing decision for factor B (College) by using the p-value of 0.0048 shown in cell F40. At the $\alpha = .05$ level of significance, we reject H_0 because the p-value $= 0.0048 < \alpha = .05$. Finally, the

FIGURE 13.10   EXCEL'S ANOVA: TWO-FACTOR WITH REPLICATION DIALOG BOX

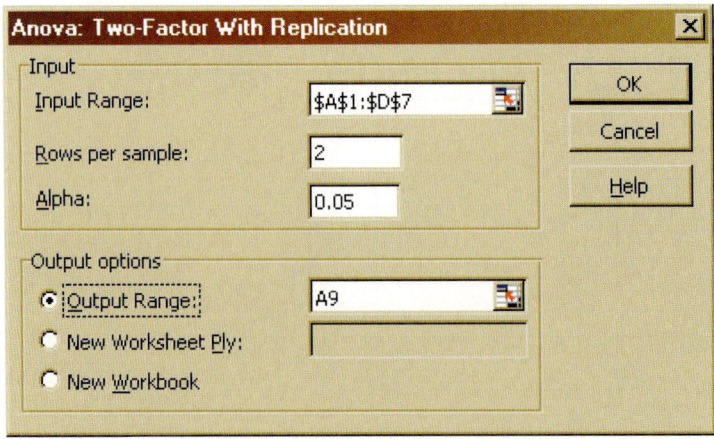

interaction *p*-value of 0.3503 in cell F41 means that we cannot identify a significant interaction effect.

Exercises

Methods

41.   A factorial experiment involving two levels of factor A and three levels of factor B resulted in the following data.

			Factor B	
		Level 1	Level 2	Level 3
	Level 1	135 165	90 66	75 93
Factor A				
	Level 2	125 95	127 105	120 136

Test for any significant main effects and any interaction. Use $\alpha = .05$.

42.   The calculations for a factorial experiment involving four levels of factor A, three levels of factor B, and three replications resulted in the following data: SST = 280, SSA = 26, SSB = 23, SSAB = 175. Set up the ANOVA table and test for any significant main effects and any interaction effect. Use $\alpha = .05$.

Applications

43.   A mail-order catalog firm designed a factorial experiment to test the effect of the size of a magazine advertisement and the advertisement design on the number of catalog requests received (data in 1000s). Three advertising designs and two different-sized advertisements were considered. The data obtained follow. Use the ANOVA procedure for factorial designs to test for any significant effects due to type of design, size of advertisement, or interaction. Use $\alpha = .05$.

		Size of Advertisement	
		Small	Large
	A	8 12	12 8
Design	B	22 14	26 30
	C	10 18	18 14

44.   An amusement park studied methods for decreasing the waiting time (minutes) for rides by loading and unloading riders more efficiently. Two alternative loading/unloading methods have been proposed. To account for potential differences due to the type of ride and the possible interaction between the method of loading and unloading and the type of ride, a

factorial experiment was designed. Use the following data to test for any significant effect due to the loading and unloading method, the type of ride, and interaction. Use $\alpha = .05$.

		Type of Ride	
	Roller Coaster	Screaming Demon	Log Flume
Method 1	41 43	52 44	50 46
Method 2	49 51	50 46	48 44

45. The U.S. Bureau of Labor Statistics collects information on the earnings of men and women for different occupations. Suppose that a reporter for *The Tampa Tribune* wanted to investigate whether there were any differences between the weekly salaries of men and women employed as financial managers, computer programmers, and pharmacists. A sample of five men and women was selected from each of the three occupations, and the weekly salary for each individual in the sample was recorded. The data obtained follow.

CD file

Salaries

Weekly Salary ($)	Occupation	Gender
872	Financial Manager	Male
859	Financial Manager	Male
1028	Financial Manager	Male
1117	Financial Manager	Male
1019	Financial Manager	Male
519	Financial Manager	Female
702	Financial Manager	Female
805	Financial Manager	Female
558	Financial Manager	Female
591	Financial Manager	Female
747	Computer Programmer	Male
766	Computer Programmer	Male
901	Computer Programmer	Male
690	Computer Programmer	Male
881	Computer Programmer	Male
884	Computer Programmer	Female
765	Computer Programmer	Female
685	Computer Programmer	Female
700	Computer Programmer	Female
671	Computer Programmer	Female
1105	Pharmacist	Male
1144	Pharmacist	Male
1085	Pharmacist	Male
903	Pharmacist	Male
998	Pharmacist	Male
813	Pharmacist	Female
985	Pharmacist	Female
1006	Pharmacist	Female
1034	Pharmacist	Female
817	Pharmacist	Female

At the $\alpha = .05$ level of significance, test for any significant effect due to occupation, gender, and interaction.

46. A study reported in *The Accounting Review* examined the separate and joint effects of two levels of time pressure (low and moderate) and three levels of knowledge (naive, declarative, and procedural) on keyword selection behavior in tax research. Subjects were given

a tax case containing a set of facts, a tax issue, and a keyword index consisting of 1336 keywords. They were asked to select the keywords they believed would refer them to a tax authority relevant to resolving the tax case. Prior to the experiment, a group of tax experts determined that the text contained 19 relevant keywords. Subjects in the naive group had little or no declarative or procedural knowledge, subjects in the declarative group had significant declarative knowledge but little or no procedural knowledge, and subjects in the procedural group had significant declarative knowledge and procedural knowledge. Declarative knowledge consists of knowledge of both the applicable tax rules and the technical terms used to describe such rules. Procedural knowledge is knowledge of the rules that guide the tax researcher's search for relevant keywords. Subjects in the low time pressure situation were told they had 25 minutes to complete the problem, an amount of time which should be "more than adequate" to complete the case; subjects in the moderate time pressure situation were told they would have "only" 11 minutes to complete the case. Suppose 25 subjects were selected for each of the six treatment combinations and the sample means for each treatment combination are as follows (standard deviations are in parentheses).

		Knowledge		
		Naive	Declarative	Procedural
Time Pressure	Low	1.13 (1.12)	1.56 (1.33)	2.00 (1.54)
	Moderate	0.48 (0.80)	1.68 (1.36)	2.86 (1.80)

Use the ANOVA procedure to test for any significant differences due to time pressure, knowledge, and interaction. Use a .05 level of significance. Assume that the total sum of squares for this experiment is 327.50.

Summary

In this chapter we showed how analysis of variance can be used to test for differences among means of several populations or treatments. We introduced the completely randomized design, the randomized block design, and the two-factor factorial experiment. The completely randomized design and the randomized block design are used to draw conclusions about differences in the means of a single factor. The primary purpose of blocking in the randomized block design is to remove extraneous sources of variation from the error term. Such blocking provides a better estimate of the true error variance and a better test to determine whether the population or treatment means of the factor differ significantly.

We showed that the basis for the statistical tests used in analysis of variance and experimental design is the development of two independent estimates of the population variance σ^2. In the single-factor case, one estimator is based on the variation between the treatments; this estimator provides an unbiased estimate of σ^2 only if the means $\mu_1, \mu_2, \ldots, \mu_k$ are all equal. A second estimator of σ^2 is based on the variation of the observations within each sample; this estimator will always provide an unbiased estimate of σ^2. By computing the ratio of these two estimators (the F statistic) we developed a rejection rule for determining whether to reject the null hypothesis that the population or treatment means are equal. In all the experimental designs considered, the partitioning of the sum of squares and degrees of freedom into their various sources enabled us to compute the appropriate values for the analysis of variance calculations and tests. We also showed how Fisher's LSD procedure and the Bonferroni adjustment can be used to perform pairwise comparisons to determine which means are different.

Glossary

ANOVA table A table used to summarize the analysis of variance computations and results. It contains columns showing the source of variation, the sum of squares, the degrees of freedom, the mean square, and the F value(s).

Partitioning The process of allocating the total sum of squares and degrees of freedom to the various components.

Multiple comparison procedures Statistical procedures that can be used to conduct comparisons between pairs of population means.

Comparisonwise Type I error rate The probability of a Type I error associated with a single pairwise comparison.

Experimentwise Type I error rate The probability of making a Type I error on at least one of several pairwise comparisons.

Factor Another word for the independent variable of interest.

Treatments Different levels of a factor.

Single-factor experiment An experiment involving only one factor with k populations or treatments.

Experimental units The objects of interest in the experiment.

Completely randomized design An experimental design in which the treatments are randomly assigned to the experimental units.

Blocking The process of using the same or similar experimental units for all treatments. The purpose of blocking is to remove a source of variation from the error term and hence provide a more powerful test for a difference in population or treatment means.

Randomized block design An experimental design employing blocking.

Factorial experiment An experimental design that allows statistical conclusions about two or more factors.

Replications The number of times each experimental condition is repeated in an experiment.

Interaction The effect produced when the levels of one factor interact with the levels of another factor in influencing the response variable.

Key Formulas

Testing for the Equality of k Population Means

Sample Mean for Treatment j

$$\bar{x}_j = \frac{\sum_{i=1}^{n_j} x_{ij}}{n_j} \tag{13.1}$$

Sample Variance for Treatment j

$$s_j^2 = \frac{\sum_{i=1}^{n_j} (x_{ij} - \bar{x}_j)^2}{n_j - 1} \tag{13.2}$$

Overall Sample Mean

$$\bar{\bar{x}} = \frac{\sum_{j=1}^{k} \sum_{i=1}^{n_j} x_{ij}}{n_T} \tag{13.3}$$

$$n_T = n_1 + n_2 + \cdots + n_k \tag{13.4}$$

Mean Square Due to Treatments

$$\text{MSTR} = \frac{\text{SSTR}}{k - 1} \tag{13.7}$$

Sum of Squares Due to Treatments

$$\text{SSTR} = \sum_{j=1}^{k} n_j (\bar{x}_j - \bar{\bar{x}})^2 \tag{13.8}$$

Mean Square Due to Error

$$\text{MSE} = \frac{\text{SSE}}{n_T - k} \tag{13.10}$$

Sum of Squares Due to Error

$$\text{SSE} = \sum_{j=1}^{k} (n_j - 1)s_j^2 \tag{13.11}$$

Test Statistic for the Equality of k Population Means

$$F = \frac{\text{MSTR}}{\text{MSE}} \tag{13.12}$$

Total Sum of Squares

$$\text{SST} = \sum_{j=1}^{k} \sum_{i=1}^{n_j} (x_{ij} - \bar{\bar{x}})^2 \tag{13.13}$$

Partitioning of the Total Sum of Squares

$$\text{SST} = \text{SSTR} + \text{SSE} \tag{13.14}$$

Multiple Comparison Procedures

Test Statistic for Fisher's LSD Procedure

$$t = \frac{\bar{x}_i - \bar{x}_j}{\sqrt{\text{MSE}\left(\dfrac{1}{n_i} + \dfrac{1}{n_j}\right)}} \tag{13.16}$$

Fisher's LSD

$$\text{LSD} = t_{\alpha/2}\sqrt{\text{MSE}\left(\frac{1}{n_i} + \frac{1}{n_j}\right)} \tag{13.17}$$

Completely Randomized Design

Mean Square Due to Treatments

$$\text{MSTR} = \frac{\displaystyle\sum_{j=1}^{k} n_j (\bar{x}_j - \bar{\bar{x}})^2}{k - 1} \tag{13.20}$$

Mean Square Due to Error

$$MSE = \frac{\sum_{j=1}^{k}(n_j - 1)s_j^2}{n_T - k} \tag{13.21}$$

_F_ Test Statistic

$$F = \frac{MSTR}{MSE} \tag{13.22}$$

Randomized Block Design

Total Sum of Squares

$$SST = \sum_{i=1}^{b}\sum_{j=1}^{k}(x_{ij} - \bar{\bar{x}})^2 \tag{13.25}$$

Sum of Squares Due to Treatments

$$SSTR = b\sum_{j=1}^{k}(\bar{x}_{\cdot j} - \bar{\bar{x}})^2 \tag{13.26}$$

Sum of Squares Due to Blocks

$$SSBL = k\sum_{i=1}^{b}(\bar{x}_{i\cdot} - \bar{\bar{x}})^2 \tag{13.27}$$

Sum of Squares Due to Error

$$SSE = SST - SSTR - SSBL \tag{13.28}$$

Factorial Experiment

Total Sum of Squares

$$SST = \sum_{i=1}^{a}\sum_{j=1}^{b}\sum_{k=1}^{r}(x_{ijk} - \bar{\bar{x}})^2 \tag{13.30}$$

Sum of Squares for Factor A

$$SSA = br\sum_{i=1}^{a}(\bar{x}_{i\cdot} - \bar{\bar{x}})^2 \tag{13.31}$$

Sum of Squares for Factor B

$$SSB = ar\sum_{j=1}^{b}(\bar{x}_{\cdot j} - \bar{\bar{x}})^2 \tag{13.32}$$

Sum of Squares for Interaction

$$SSAB = r\sum_{i=1}^{a}\sum_{j=1}^{b}(\bar{x}_{ij} - \bar{x}_{i\cdot} - \bar{x}_{\cdot j} + \bar{\bar{x}})^2 \tag{13.33}$$

Sum of Squares Due to Error

$$SSE = SST - SSA - SSB - SSAB \tag{13.34}$$

Supplementary Exercises

47. A simple random sample of the asking prices (in thousands of dollars) of four houses currently for sale in each of two residential areas resulted in the following data.

Area 1	Area 2
92	90
89	102
98	96
105	88

a. Use the ANOVA procedure to test whether the mean asking price is the same. Use $\alpha = .05$.

b. Suppose that data were collected for another residential area. The asking prices for the simple random sample from the third area were $81,000, $86,000, $75,000, and $90,000. Is the mean asking price the same for all three areas? Use $\alpha = .05$.

48. Buyers of sport utility vehicles (SUVs) and pickup trucks find a wide choice in today's marketplace. One of the factors that is important to many buyers is the resale value of the vehicle. The following table shows the resale value (%) after two years for 10 SUVs, 10 small pickup trucks, and 10 large pickup trucks (*Kiplinger's New Cars & Trucks 2000 Buyer's Guide*).

Trucks

Sport Utility	Resale Value (%)	Small Pickup	Resale Value (%)
Chevrolet Blazer LS	55	Chevrolet S-10 Extended Cab	46
Ford Explorer Sport	57	Dodge Dakota Club Cab Sport	53
GMC Yukon XL 1500	67	Ford Ranger XLT Regular Cab	48
Honda CR-V	65	Ford Ranger XLT Supercab	55
Isuzu VehiCross	62	GMC Sonoma Regular Cab	44
Jeep Cherokee Limited	57	Isuzu Hombre Spacecab	41
Mercury Mountaineer	59	Mazda B4000 SE Cab Plus	51
Nissan Pathfinder XE	54	Nissan Frontier XE Regular Cab	51
Toyota 4Runner	55	Toyota Tacoma Xtracab	49
Toyota RAV4	55	Toyota Tacoma Xtracab V6	50

Full-Size Pickup	Resale Value (%)
Chevrolet K2500	60
Chevrolet Silverado 2500 Ext	64
Dodge Ram 1500	54
Dodge Ram Quad Cab 2500	63
Dodge Ram Regular Cab 2500	59
Ford F150 XL	58
Ford F350 Super Duty Crew Cab XL	64
GMC New Sierra 1500 Ext Cab	68
Toyota Tundra Access Cab Limited	53
Toyota Tundra Regular Cab	58

At the $\alpha = .05$ level of significance, test for any significant difference in the mean resale value for the three types of vehicles.

49. *Money* magazine reports percentage returns and expense ratios for stock and bond funds. The following data are the expense ratios for 10 midcap stock funds, 10 small-cap stock funds, 10 hybrid stock funds, and 10 specialty stock funds (*Money,* March 2003).

CD file

Funds

Midcap	Small-Cap	Hybrid	Specialty
1.2	2.0	2.0	1.6
1.1	1.2	2.7	2.7
1.0	1.7	1.8	2.6
1.2	1.8	1.5	2.5
1.3	1.5	2.5	1.9
1.8	2.3	1.0	1.5
1.4	1.9	0.9	1.6
1.4	1.3	1.9	2.7
1.0	1.2	1.4	2.2
1.4	1.3	0.3	0.7

Use $\alpha = .05$ to test for any significant difference in the mean expense ratio among the four types of stock funds.

50. A study reported in the *Journal of Small Business Management* concluded that self-employed individuals do not experience higher job satisfaction than individuals who are not self-employed. In this study, job satisfaction is measured using 18 items, each of which is rated using a Likert-type scale with 1–5 response options ranging from strong agreement to strong disagreement. A higher score on this scale indicates a higher degree of job satisfaction. The sum of the ratings for the 18 items, ranging from 18–90, is used as the measure of job satisfaction. Suppose that this approach was used to measure the job satisfaction for lawyers, physical therapists, cabinetmakers, and systems analysts. The results obtained for a sample of 10 individuals from each profession follow.

CD file

SatisJob

Lawyer	Physical Therapist	Cabinetmaker	Systems Analyst
44	55	54	44
42	78	65	73
74	80	79	71
42	86	69	60
53	60	79	64
50	59	64	66
45	62	59	41
48	52	78	55
64	55	84	76
38	50	60	62

At the $\alpha = .05$ level of significance, test for any difference in the job satisfaction among the four professions.

51. Crown Plaza Hotels and Resorts offered special weekend rates at hotels at resorts nationwide. A sample of 30 properties from three regions of the country provided the following room rates (*USA Today,* April 14, 2000).

CD file

Resorts

West	Rate ($)	South	Rate ($)	Northeast	Rate ($)
Albuquerque	89	Atlanta	105	Albany	89
Irvine	79	Dallas	80	Boston	139
Las Vegas	119	Greenville	79	Hartford	85
Los Angeles	99	Houston	79	New York	159

West	Rate ($)	South	Rate ($)	Northeast	Rate ($)
Palo Alto	109	Jackson	69	Philadelphia	99
Phoenix	149	Macon	69	Pittsfield	99
Portland	79	Miami	89	Providence	149
San Francisco	139	Orlando	119	Washington, D.C.	159
San Jose	99	Richmond	109	White Plains	109
Seattle	119	Tampa	119	Worcester	124

At the $\alpha = .05$ level of significance, test whether the mean rates are the same for the three regions.

52. To investigate whether there is any difference in the annual compensation for art directors at advertising agencies, suppose that a sample of 10 art directors was selected from each of four regions: West, South, North Central, and Northeast. The base salary (in thousands of dollars) for each of the individuals sampled follows.

CD file

ArtDir

West	South	North Central	Northeast
60.9	50.8	49.5	65.9
45.9	39.6	42.3	58.6
62.1	44.2	35.5	49.3
66.6	40.0	49.1	52.9
68.0	53.9	56.7	48.5
65.0	45.4	41.4	52.9
49.4	61.1	51.3	52.4
62.3	42.3	49.4	48.1
62.6	38.4	42.1	46.5
57.2	38.3	55.7	45.9

At the $\alpha = .05$ level of significance, test whether the mean base salary for art directors is the same for each of the four regions.

53. The National Football League rates prospects by position on a scale that ranges from 5 to 9. The ratings are interpreted as follows: 8–9 should start the first year; 7.0–7.9 should start; 6.0–6.9 will make the team as backup; and 5.0–5.9 can make the club and contribute. The following table shows the ratings for three positions for 40 NFL prospects (*USA Today*, April 14, 2000). Does there appear to be any significant effect on the rating due to the player's position?

CD file

NFL

Wide Receiver		Guard		Offensive Tackle	
Name	Rating	Name	Rating	Name	Rating
Peter Warrick	9.0	Cosey Coleman	7.4	Chris Samuels	8.5
Plaxico Burress	8.8	Travis Claridge	7.0	Stockar McDougle	8.0
Sylvester Morris	8.3	Kaulana Noa	6.8	Chris McIngosh	7.8
Travis Taylor	8.1	Leander Jordan	6.7	Adrian Klemm	7.6
Laveranues Coles	8.0	Chad Clifton	6.3	Todd Wade	7.3
Dez White	7.9	Manula Savea	6.1	Marvel Smith	7.1
Jerry Porter	7.4	Ryan Johanningmeir	6.0	Michael Thompson	6.8
Ron Dugans	7.1	Mark Tauscher	6.0	Bobby Williams	6.8
Todd Pinkston	7.0	Blaine Saipaia	6.0	Darnell Alford	6.4
Dennis Northcutt	7.0	Richard Mercier	5.8	Terrance Beadles	6.3
Anthony Lucas	6.9	Damion McIntosh	5.3	Tutan Reyes	6.1
Darrell Jackson	6.6	Jeno James	5.5	Greg Robinson-Ran	6.0
Danny Farmer	6.5	Al Jackson	5.5		
Sherrod Gideon	6.4				
Trevor Gaylor	6.2				

54. In a completely randomized experimental design, three brands of paper towels were tested for their ability to absorb water. Equal-sized towels were used, with four sections of towels tested per brand. The absorbency rating data follow. At a .05 level of significance, does there appear to be a difference in the ability of the brands to absorb water?

	Brand	
x	*y*	*z*
91	99	83
100	96	88
88	94	89
89	99	76

55. *Business 2.0*'s first annual employment survey provided data showing the typical annual salary for 97 different jobs. The following data show the annual salary for 30 different jobs in three fields: computer software and hardware, construction, and engineering (*Business 2.0*, March 2003).

JobSalary

Computers		Construction		Engineering	
Job	**Salary**	**Job**	**Salary**	**Job**	**Salary**
Data Mgr.	94	Administrator	55	Aeronautical	75
Mfg. Mgr.	90	Architect	53	Agricultural	70
Programmer	63	Architect Mgr.	77	Chemical	88
Project Mgr.	84	Const. Mgr.	60	Civil	77
Software Dev.	73	Foreperson	41	Electrical	89
Sr. Design	75	Interior Design	54	Mechanical	85
Staff Systems	94	Landscape Architect	51	Mining	96
Systems Analyst	77	Sr. Estimator	64	Nuclear	105

Use $\alpha = .05$ to test for any significant difference in the mean annual salary among the three job fields.

56. Three different assembly methods have been proposed for a new product. A completely randomized experimental design was chosen to determine which assembly method results in the greatest number of parts produced per hour, and 30 workers were randomly selected and assigned to use one of the proposed methods. The number of units produced by each worker follows.

Assembly

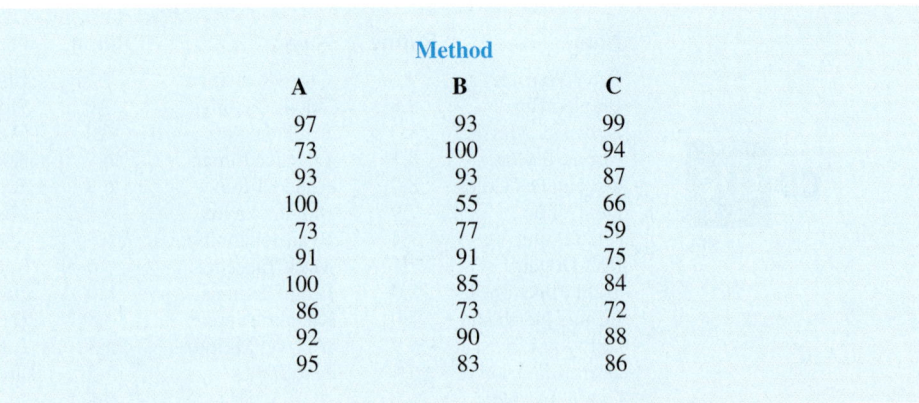

	Method	
A	**B**	**C**
97	93	99
73	100	94
93	93	87
100	55	66
73	77	59
91	91	75
100	85	84
86	73	72
92	90	88
95	83	86

Use these data and test to see whether the mean number of parts produced is the same with each method. Use $\alpha = .05$.

57. Hargreaves Automotive Parts, Inc., wanted to compare the mileage for four different types of brake linings. Thirty linings of each type were produced and placed on a fleet of rental cars. The number of miles that each brake lining lasted until it no longer met the required federal safety standard was recorded, and an average value was computed for each type of lining. The following data were obtained.

Type	Sample Size	Sample Mean	Standard Deviation
A	30	32000	1450
B	30	27500	1525
C	30	34200	1650
D	30	30300	1400

Test to see whether the corresponding population means are equal. Use $\alpha = .05$.

58. A manufacturer of batteries for electronic toys and calculators is considering three new battery designs. Data were collected to determine whether the mean lifetime in hours is the same for each of the three designs.

Design A	Design B	Design C
78	112	115
98	99	101
88	101	100
96	116	120

Test to see whether the population means are equal. Use $\alpha = .05$.

59. In a study conducted to investigate browsing activity by shoppers, each shopper was initially classified as a nonbrowser, light browser, or heavy browser. For each shopper, the study obtained a measure to determine how comfortable the shopper was in a store. Higher scores indicated greater comfort. Suppose the following data were collected.

Nonbrowser	Light Browser	Heavy Browser
4	5	5
5	6	7
6	5	5
3	4	7
3	7	4
4	4	6
5	6	5
4	5	7

a. Use $\alpha = .05$ to test for differences among comfort levels for the three types of browsers.
b. Use Fisher's LSD procedure to compare the comfort levels of nonbrowsers and light browsers. Use $\alpha = .05$. What is your conclusion?

60. A research firm tests the miles-per-gallon characteristics of three brands of gasoline. Because of different gasoline performance characteristics in different brands of automobiles, five brands of automobiles are selected and treated as blocks in the experiment; that is, each brand of automobile is tested with each type of gasoline. The results of the experiment (in miles per gallon) follow.

| | | Gasoline Brand | | |
		I	II	III
	A	18	21	20
	B	24	26	27
Automobile	C	30	29	34
	D	22	25	24
	E	20	23	24

a. At $\alpha = .05$, is there a significant difference in the mean miles-per-gallon characteristics of the three brands of gasoline?

b. Analyze the experimental data using the ANOVA procedure for completely randomized designs. Compare your findings with those obtained in part (a). What is the advantage of attempting to remove the block effect?

61. Wegman's Food Markets and Tops Friendly Markets are the major grocery chains in the Rochester, New York, area. When Wal-Mart opened a Supercenter in one of the Rochester suburbs, experts predicted that Wal-Mart would undersell both local stores. The *Democrat and Chronicle* obtained the price data ($) in the following table for a 15-item market basket (*Democrat and Chronicle,* March 17, 2002).

Grocery

Item	Tops	Wal-Mart	Wegmans
Bananas (1 lb.)	0.49	0.48	0.49
Campbell's soup (10.75 oz.)	0.60	0.54	0.77
Chicken breasts (3 lbs.)	10.47	8.61	8.07
Colgate toothpaste (6.2 oz.)	1.99	2.40	1.97
Large eggs (1 dozen)	1.59	0.88	0.79
Heinz ketchup (36 oz.)	2.59	1.78	2.59
Jell-O (cherry, 3 oz.)	0.67	0.42	0.65
Jif peanut butter (18 oz.)	2.29	1.78	2.09
Milk (fat free, 1/2 gal.)	1.34	1.24	1.34
Oscar Meyer hotdogs (1 lb.)	3.29	1.50	3.39
Ragu pasta sauce (1 lb., 10 oz.)	2.09	1.50	1.25
Ritz crackers (1 lb.)	3.29	2.00	3.39
Tide detergent (liquid, 100 oz.)	6.79	5.24	5.99
Tropicana orange juice (1/2 gal.)	2.50	2.50	2.50
Twizzlers (strawberry, 1 lb.)	1.19	1.27	1.69

At the .05 level of significance, test for any significant difference in the mean price for the 15-item shopping basket for the three stores.

62. Each month *Internet Magazine* accesses more than 100 Internet service providers (ISPs) in order to check the availability of the ISP and test the speed of the connection by measuring the time (seconds) it takes to download a number of popular Web pages. The fol-

lowing data show the download time for 22 free ISPs for Web sites located in the United Kingdom, United States, and Europe (*Internet Magazine,* January 2000).

ISP

ISP Name	U.K.	U.S.	Europe
Abel Gratis	10.62	14.64	17.08
Breathe	11.67	14.14	19.86
btclick.com	12.12	16.43	21.30
Bun	11.13	14.09	15.83
Cable & Wireless Life	9.99	13.07	18.43
conX	12.63	15.97	22.12
Freebeeb	11.71	15.52	19.57
Free-Online	13.77	13.98	23.35
Freeserve	10.65	13.62	25.56
FreeUK	12.20	14.96	18.95
Icom-Web	9.62	11.66	15.91
IPNet	13.82	16.70	22.86
I-way Soho	14.86	12.86	19.32
LineOne	12.01	17.82	21.88
Madasafish	13.38	15.59	19.61
NetDirect Online	11.71	15.52	19.57
Netscape Online	10.84	12.66	16.52
Screaming.net (BT Line)	13.23	15.91	23.08
Telinco Internet Services	12.83	15.34	18.76
UK Online	10.39	13.28	21.04
UKPeople	13.79	19.82	19.76
Virgin Net	12.17	15.47	21.94

At $\alpha = .05$, is there a significant difference in the mean download time for Web sites located in the United Kingdom, United States, and Europe?

63. A factorial experiment was designed to test for any significant differences in the time needed to perform English to foreign language translations with two computerized language translators. Because the type of language translated was also considered a significant factor, translations were made with both systems for three different languages: Spanish, French, and German. Use the following data for translation time in hours.

	Language		
	Spanish	**French**	**German**
System 1	8	10	12
	12	14	16
System 2	6	14	16
	10	16	22

Test for any significant differences due to language translator, type of language, and interaction. Use $\alpha = .05$.

64. A manufacturing company designed a factorial experiment to determine whether the number of defective parts produced by two machines differed and if the number of defective parts produced also depended on whether the raw material needed by each machine was loaded manually or by an automatic feed system. The following data give the numbers of defective parts produced. Use $\alpha = .05$ to test for any significant effect due to machine, loading system, and interaction.

	Loading System	
	Manual	**Automatic**
Machine 1	30 34	30 26
Machine 2	20 22	24 28

Case Problem 1   Wentworth Medical Center

As part of a long-term study of individuals 65 years of age or older, sociologists and physicians at the Wentworth Medical Center in upstate New York investigated the relationship between geographic location and depression. A sample of 60 individuals, all in reasonably good health, was selected; 20 individuals were residents of Florida, 20 were residents of New York, and 20 were residents of North Carolina. Each of the individuals sampled was given a standardized test to measure depression. The data collected follow; higher test scores indicate higher levels of depression. These data are available on the data disk in the file Medical1.

A second part of the study considered the relationship between geographic location and depression for individuals 65 years of age or older who had a chronic health condition such as arthritis, hypertension, and/or heart ailment. A sample of 60 individuals with such conditions was identified. Again, 20 were residents of Florida, 20 were residents of New York, and 20 were residents of North Carolina. The levels of depression recorded for this study follow. These data are available on the CD accompanying the text in the file named Medical2.

Medical1

Medical2

Data from Medical1			Data from Medical2		
Florida	**New York**	**North Carolina**	**Florida**	**New York**	**North Carolina**
3	8	10	13	14	10
7	11	7	12	9	12
7	9	3	17	15	15
3	7	5	17	12	18
8	8	11	20	16	12
8	7	8	21	24	14
8	8	4	16	18	17
5	4	3	14	14	8
5	13	7	13	15	14
2	10	8	17	17	16
6	6	8	12	20	18
2	8	7	9	11	17
6	12	3	12	23	19
6	8	9	15	19	15
9	6	8	16	17	13
7	8	12	15	14	14
5	5	6	13	9	11
4	7	3	10	14	12
7	7	8	11	13	13
3	8	11	17	11	11

Managerial Report

1. Use descriptive statistics to summarize the data from the two studies. What are your preliminary observations about the depression scores?
2. Use analysis of variance on both data sets. State the hypotheses being tested in each case. What are your conclusions?
3. Use inferences about individual treatment means where appropriate. What are your conclusions?
4. Discuss extensions of this study or other analyses that you feel might be helpful.

Case Problem 2   Compensation for ID Professionals

For the preceding 10 years *Industrial Distribution* tracked compensation of industrial distribution (ID) professionals. Results for the 358 respondents in the 1997 Annual Salary Survey showed that 27% of the respondents work for companies with sales over $40 million, with the typical ID professional working for a $12 million firm. Those who work for small to mid-sized companies (between $6 million and $20 million) report higher earnings than those in larger firms. The lowest paid employees work for firms with sales of less than $1 million. The typical outside salesperson made $50,000 in 1996, and the typical inside salesperson earned just $30,000 (*Industrial Distribution*, November 1997). Suppose that a local chapter of ID professionals in the greater San Francisco area conducted a survey of its membership to study the relationship, if any, between the years of experience and salary for individuals employed in outside and inside sales positions. On the survey, respondents were asked to specify one of three levels of years of experience: low (1–10 years), medium (11–20 years), and high (21 or more years). A portion of the data obtained follows. The complete data set, consisting of 120 observations, is available on the CD accompanying the text in the file named IDSalary.

IDSalary

Observation	Salary ($)	Position	Experience
1	28938	Inside	Medium
2	27694	Inside	Medium
3	45515	Outside	Low
4	27031	Inside	Medium
5	37283	Outside	Low
6	32718	Inside	Low
7	54081	Outside	High
8	23621	Inside	Low
9	47835	Outside	High
10	29768	Inside	Medium
.	.	.	.
.	.	.	.
.	.	.	.
115	33080	Inside	High
116	53702	Outside	Medium
117	58131	Outside	Medium
118	32788	Inside	High
119	28070	Inside	Medium
120	35259	Outside	Low

Managerial Report

1. Use descriptive statistics to summarize the data.
2. Develop a 95% confidence interval estimate of the mean annual salary for all salespersons, regardless of years of experience and type of position.
3. Develop a 95% confidence interval estimate of the mean salary for outside salespersons. Compare your results with the national value reported by *Industrial Distribution.*
4. Develop a 95% confidence interval estimate of the mean salary for inside salespersons. Compare your results with the national value reported by *Industrial Distribution.*
5. Ignoring the years of experience, develop a 95% confidence interval estimate of the mean difference between the annual salary for outside salespersons and the mean annual salary for inside salespersons. What is your conclusion?
6. Use analysis of variance to test for any significant differences due to position. Use a .05 level of significance, and for now, ignore the effect of years of experience.
7. Use analysis of variance to test for any significant differences due to years of experience. Use a .05 level of significance, and for now, ignore the effect of position.
8. At the .05 level of significance test for any significant differences due to position, years of experience, and interaction. Use inferences about individual treatment means where appropriate.

CHAPTER 14

Simple Linear Regression

CONTENTS

STATISTICS IN PRACTICE:
ALLIANCE DATA SYSTEMS

14.1 SIMPLE LINEAR
REGRESSION MODEL
Regression Model and
Regression Equation
Estimated Regression Equation

14.2 LEAST SQUARES METHOD
Using Excel to Develop a Scatter
Diagram and Compute the
Estimated Regression Equation

14.3 COEFFICIENT OF
DETERMINATION
Using Excel to Compute the
Coefficient of Determination
Correlation Coefficient

14.4 MODEL ASSUMPTIONS

14.5 TESTING FOR SIGNIFICANCE
Estimate of σ^2
t Test
Confidence Interval for β_1
F Test
Some Cautions About
the Interpretation of
Significance Tests

14.6 EXCEL'S REGRESSION TOOL
Using Excel's Regression Tool
for the Armand's Pizza Parlors
Problem
Interpretation of Estimated
Regression Equation Output

Interpretation of ANOVA Output
Interpretation of Regression
Statistics Output

14.7 USING THE ESTIMATED
REGRESSION EQUATION
FOR ESTIMATION AND
PREDICTION
Point Estimation
Interval Estimation
Confidence Interval Estimate of
the Mean Value of y
Prediction Interval Estimate of an
Individual Value of y
Using Excel to Develop
Confidence and Prediction
Interval Estimates

14.8 RESIDUAL ANALYSIS:
VALIDATING MODEL
ASSUMPTIONS
Residual Plot Against x
Residual Plot Against $\hat{y}$
Using Excel's Regression Tool to
Construct a Residual Plot
Standardized Residuals
Using Excel to Construct a
Standardized Residual Plot
Normal Probability Plot

14.9 OUTLIERS AND
INFLUENTIAL
OBSERVATIONS
Detecting Outliers
Detecting Influential
Observations

STATISTICS *in* PRACTICE

ALLIANCE DATA SYSTEMS*
DALLAS, TEXAS

Alliance Data Systems (ADS) provides transaction processing, credit services, and marketing services for clients in the rapidly growing customer relationship management (CRM) industry. ADS clients are concentrated in four industries: retail, petroleum/convenience stores, utilities, and transportation. In 1983, Alliance began offering end-to-end credit processing services to the retail, petroleum, and casual dining industries; today they employ more than 6500 employees who provide services to clients around the world. Operating more than 140,000 point-of-sale terminals in the United States alone, ADS processes in excess of 2.5 billion transactions annually. The company ranks second in the United States in private label credit services by representing 49 private label programs with nearly 72 million cardholders. In 2001, ADS made an initial public offering and is now listed on the New York Stock Exchange.

As one of its marketing services, ADS designs direct mail campaigns and promotions. With its database containing information on the spending habits of more than 100 million consumers, ADS can target those consumers most likely to benefit from a direct mail promotion. The Analytical Development Group uses regression analysis to build models that measure and predict the responsiveness of consumers to direct market campaigns. Some regression models predict the probability of purchase for individuals receiving a promotion, and others predict the amount spent by those consumers making a purchase.

For one particular campaign, a retail store chain wanted to attract new customers. To predict the effect of the campaign, ADS analysts selected a sample from the consumer database, sent the sampled individuals promotional materials, and then collected transaction data on the consumers' response. Sample data were collected on the amount of purchase made by the consumers responding to the campaign, as well as a variety of consumer-specific variables thought to be useful in predicting sales. The consumer-specific variable that contributed most to predicting the amount purchased was the total amount of credit purchases at related stores over the past 39 months. ADS analysts

*The authors are indebted to Philip Clemance, Director of Analytical Development at Alliance Data Systems, for providing this Statistics in Practice.

Alliance Data analysts discuss use of a regression model to predict sales for a direct marketing campaign. © Courtesy of Alliance Data Systems.

developed an estimated regression equation relating the amount of purchase to the amount spent at related stores:

$$\hat{y} = 26.7 + 0.00205x$$

where

$$\hat{y} = \text{amount of purchase}$$
$$x = \text{amount spent at related stores}$$

Using this equation, we could predict that someone spending $10,000 over the past 39 months at related stores would spend $47.20 when responding to the direct mail promotion. In this chapter, you will learn how to develop this type of estimated regression equation.

The final model developed by ADS analysts also included several other variables that increased the predictive power of the preceding equation. Some of these variables included the absence/presence of a bank credit card, estimated income, and the average amount spent per trip at a selected store. In the following chapter, we will learn how such additional variables can be incorporated into a multiple regression model.

Managerial decisions often are based on the relationship between two or more variables. For example, after considering the relationship between advertising expenditures and sales, a marketing manager might attempt to predict sales for a given level of advertising expenditures. In another case, a public utility might use the relationship between the daily high temperature and the demand for electricity to predict electricity usage on the basis of next month's anticipated daily high temperatures. Sometimes a manager will rely on intuition to judge how two variables are related. However, if data can be obtained, a statistical procedure called *regression analysis* can be used to develop an equation showing how the variables are related.

The statistical methods used in studying the relationship between two variables were first employed by Sir Francis Galton (1822–1911). Galton was interested in studying the relationship between a father's height and the son's height. Galton's disciple, Karl Pearson (1857–1936), analyzed the relationship between the father's height and the son's height for 1078 pairs of subjects.

In regression terminology, the variable being predicted is called the **dependent variable**. The variable or variables being used to predict the value of the dependent variable are called the **independent variables**. For example, in analyzing the effect of advertising expenditures on sales, a marketing manager's desire to predict sales would suggest making sales the dependent variable. Advertising expenditure would be the independent variable used to help predict sales. In statistical notation, y denotes the dependent variable and x denotes the independent variable.

In this chapter we consider the simplest type of regression analysis involving one independent variable and one dependent variable in which the relationship between the variables is approximated by a straight line. It is called **simple linear regression**. Regression analysis involving two or more independent variables is called multiple regression analysis; multiple regression and cases involving curvilinear relationships are covered in Chapters 15 and 16.

(14.1) Simple Linear Regression Model

Armand's Pizza Parlors is a chain of Italian-food restaurants located in a five-state area. Armand's most successful locations are near college campuses. The managers believe that quarterly sales for these restaurants (denoted by y) are related positively to the size of the student population (denoted by x); that is, restaurants near campuses with a large student population tend to generate more sales than those located near campuses with a small student population. Using regression analysis, we can develop an equation showing how the dependent variable y is related to the independent variable x.

Regression Model and Regression Equation

In the Armand's example, the population consists of all the Armand's restaurants. For every restaurant in the population, a value of x (student population) corresponds to a value of y (quarterly sales). The equation that describes how y is related to x and an error term is called the **regression model**. The regression model used in simple linear regression follows.

> SIMPLE LINEAR REGRESSION MODEL
>
> $$y = \beta_0 + \beta_1 x + \epsilon \qquad (14.1)$$

β_0 and β_1 are referred to as the parameters of the model, and ϵ (the Greek letter epsilon) is a random variable referred to as the error term. The error term accounts for the variability in y that cannot be explained by the linear relationship between x and y.

The population of all Armand's restaurants can also be viewed as a collection of sub-populations, one for each distinct value of x. For example, one subpopulation consists of all Armand's restaurants located near college campuses with 8000 students; another subpopulation consists of all Armand's restaurants located near college campuses with 9000 students; and so on. Each subpopulation has a corresponding distribution of y values. Thus, a distribution of y values is associated with restaurants located near campuses with 8000 students; a distribution of y values is associated with restaurants located near campuses with 9000 students; and so on. Each distribution of y values has its own mean or expected value. The equation that describes how the expected value of y, denoted $E(y)$, is related to x is called the **regression equation**. The regression equation for simple linear regression follows.

SIMPLE LINEAR REGRESSION EQUATION

$$E(y) = \beta_0 + \beta_1 x \qquad \textbf{(14.2)}$$

The graph of the simple linear regression equation is a straight line; β_0 is the y-intercept of the regression line, β_1 is the slope, and $E(y)$ is the mean or expected value of y for a given value of x.

Examples of possible regression lines are shown in Figure 14.1. The regression line in Panel A shows that the mean value of y is related positively to x, with larger values of $E(y)$ associated with larger values of x. The regression line in Panel B shows the mean value of y is related negatively to x, with smaller values of $E(y)$ associated with larger values of x. The regression line in Panel C shows the case in which the mean value of y is not related to x; that is, the mean value of y is the same for every value of x.

Estimated Regression Equation

If the values of the population parameters β_0 and β_1 were known, we could use equation (14.2) to compute the mean value of y for a given value of x. In practice, the parameter values are not known and must be estimated using sample data. Sample statistics (denoted b_0 and b_1) are computed as estimates of the population parameters β_0 and β_1. Substituting the values of the sample statistics b_0 and b_1 for β_0 and β_1 in the regression equation, we obtain

FIGURE 14.1   POSSIBLE REGRESSION LINES IN SIMPLE LINEAR REGRESSION

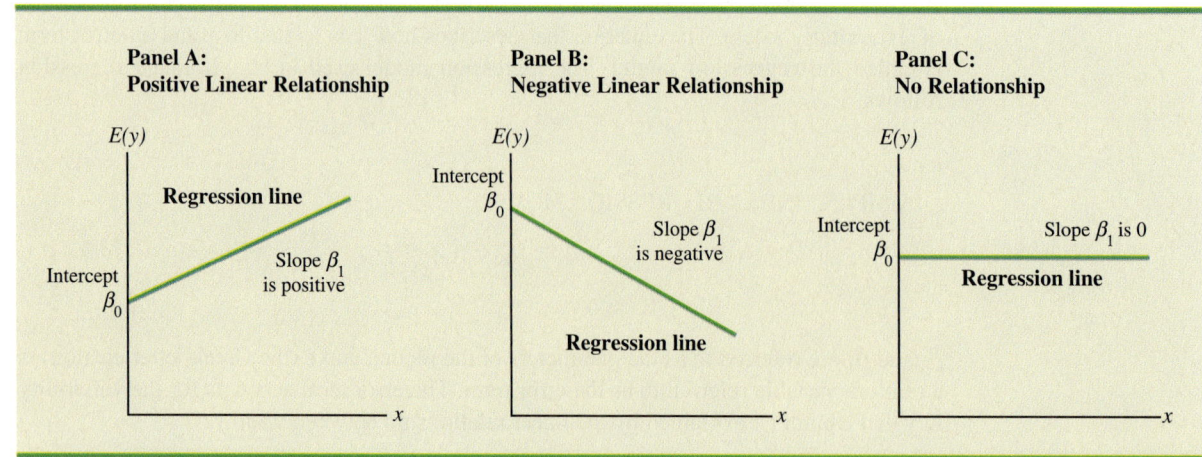

the **estimated regression equation**. The estimated regression equation for simple linear regression follows.

ESTIMATED SIMPLE LINEAR REGRESSION EQUATION

$$\hat{y} = b_0 + b_1 x \qquad (14.3)$$

The graph of the estimated simple linear regression equation is called the *estimated regression line*; b_0 is the y-intercept and b_1 is the slope. In the next section, we show how the least squares method can be used to compute the values of b_0 and b_1 in the estimated regression equation.

In general, $\hat{y}$ is the point estimator of $E(y)$, the mean value of y for a given value of x. Thus, to estimate the mean or expected value of quarterly sales for all restaurants located near campuses with 10,000 students, Armand's would substitute the value of 10,000 for x in equation (14.3). In some cases, however, Armand's may be more interested in predicting sales for one particular restaurant. For example, suppose Armand's would like to predict quarterly sales for the restaurant located near Talbot College, a school with 10,000 students. As it turns out, the best estimate of y for a given value of x is also provided by $\hat{y}$. Thus, to predict quarterly sales for the restaurant located near Talbot College, Armand's would also substitute the value of 10,000 for x in equation (14.3).

Because the value of $\hat{y}$ provides both a point estimate of $E(y)$ for a given value of x and a point estimate of an individual value of y for a given value of x, we will refer to $\hat{y}$ simply as the *estimated value of y*. Figure 14.2 provides a summary of the estimation process for simple linear regression.

FIGURE 14.2   THE ESTIMATION PROCESS IN SIMPLE LINEAR REGRESSION

The estimation of β_0 and β_1 is a statistical process much like the estimation of μ discussed in Chapter 7. β_0 and β_1 are the unknown parameters of interest, and b_0 and b_1 are the sample statistics used to estimate the parameters.

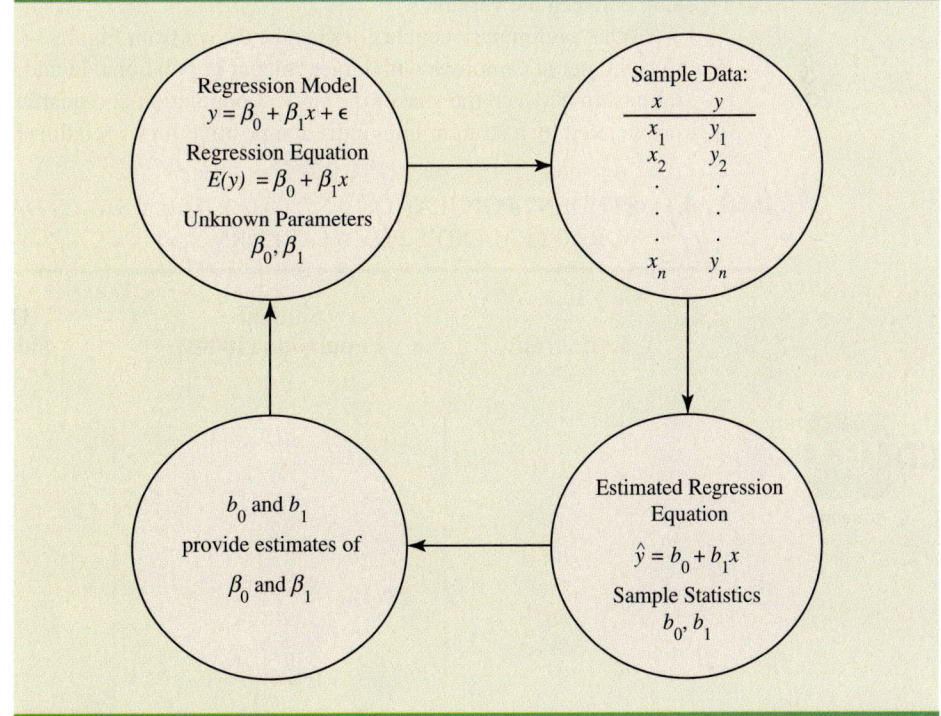

NOTES AND COMMENTS

1. Regression analysis cannot be interpreted as a procedure for establishing a cause-and-effect relationship between variables. It can only indicate how or to what extent variables are associated with each other. Any conclusions about cause and effect must be based upon the judgment of those individuals most knowledgeable about the application.

2. The regression equation in simple linear regression is $E(y) = \beta_0 + \beta_1 x$. More advanced texts in regression analysis often write the regression equation as $E(y|x) = \beta_0 + \beta_1 x$ to emphasize that the regression equation provides the mean value of y for a given value of x.

14.2   Least Squares Method

In simple linear regression, each observation consists of two values: one for the independent variable and one for the dependent variable.

The **least squares method** is a procedure for using sample data to find the estimated regression equation. To illustrate the least squares method, suppose data were collected from a sample of 10 Armand's restaurants located near college campuses. For the ith observation or restaurant in the sample, x_i is the size of the student population (in thousands) and y_i is the quarterly sales (in thousands of dollars). The values of x_i and y_i for the 10 restaurants in the sample are summarized in Table 14.1. We see that restaurant 1, with $x_1 = 2$ and $y_1 = 58$, is near a campus with 2000 students and has quarterly sales of $58,000. Restaurant 2, with $x_2 = 6$ and $y_2 = 105$, is near a campus with 6000 students and has quarterly sales of $105,000. The largest sales value is for restaurant 10, which is near a campus with 26,000 students and has quarterly sales of $202,000.

Figure 14.3 is a scatter diagram of the data in Table 14.1. Student population is shown on the horizontal axis and quarterly sales is shown on the vertical axis. **Scatter diagrams** for regression analysis are constructed with the independent variable x on the horizontal axis and the dependent variable y on the vertical axis. The scatter diagram enables us to observe the data graphically and to draw preliminary conclusions about the possible relationship between the variables.

What preliminary conclusions can be drawn from Figure 14.3? Quarterly sales appear to be higher at campuses with larger student populations. In addition, for these data the relationship between the size of the student population and quarterly sales appears to be approximated by a straight line; indeed, a positive linear relationship is indicated between x

TABLE 14.1   STUDENT POPULATION AND QUARTERLY SALES DATA FOR 10 ARMAND'S PIZZA PARLORS

CD file
Armand's

Restaurant i	Student Population (1000s) x_i	Quarterly Sales ($1000s) y_i
1	2	58
2	6	105
3	8	88
4	8	118
5	12	117
6	16	137
7	20	157
8	20	169
9	22	149
10	26	202

FIGURE 14.3 SCATTER DIAGRAM OF STUDENT POPULATION AND QUARTERLY SALES FOR ARMAND'S PIZZA PARLORS

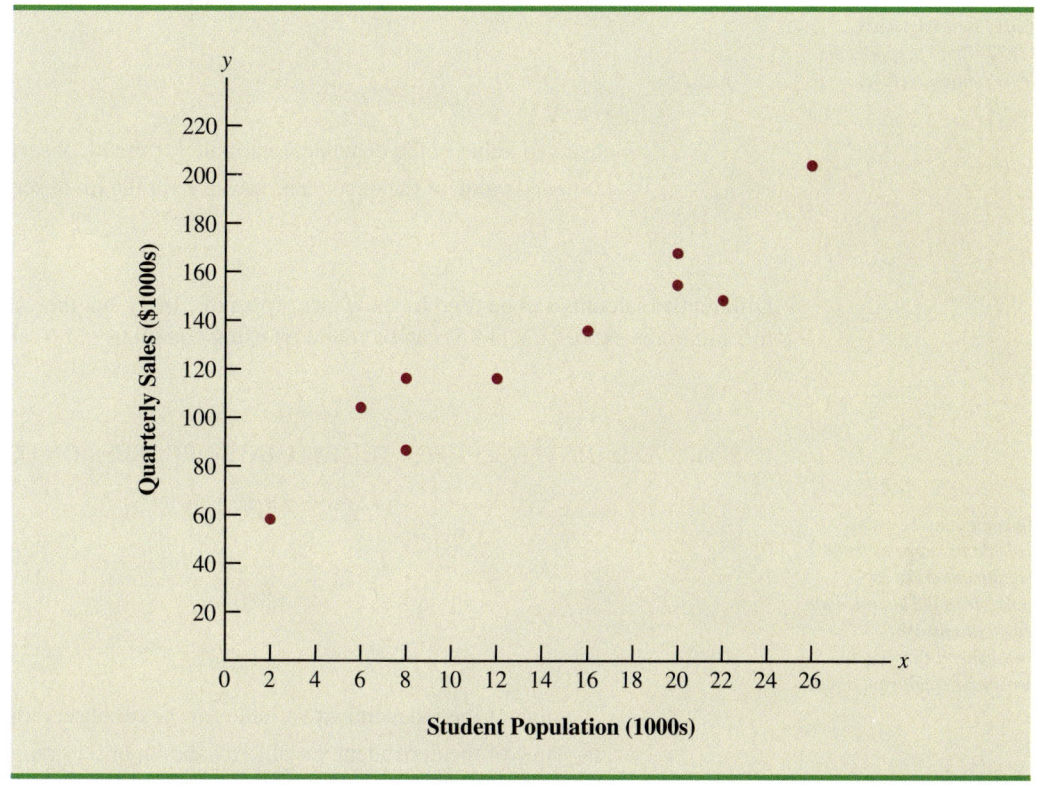

and y. We therefore choose the simple linear regression model to represent the relationship between quarterly sales and student population. Given that choice, our next task is to use the sample data in Table 14.1 to determine the values of b_0 and b_1 in the estimated simple linear regression equation. For the ith restaurant, the estimated regression equation provides

$$\hat{y}_i = b_0 + b_1 x_i \tag{14.4}$$

where

$\hat{y}_i$ = estimated value of quarterly sales ($1000s) for the ith restaurant

b_0 = the y-intercept of the estimated regression line

b_1 = the slope of the estimated regression line

x_i = size of the student population (1000s) for the ith restaurant

With y_i denoting the observed (actual) sales for restaurant i and $\hat{y}_i$ in equation (14.4) representing the estimated value of sales for restaurant i, every restaurant in the sample will have an observed value of sales y_i and an estimated value of sales $\hat{y}_i$. For the estimated regression line to provide a good fit to the data, we want the differences between the observed sales values and the estimated sales values to be small.

The least squares method uses the sample data to provide the values of b_0 and b_1 that minimize the *sum of the squares of the deviations* between the observed values of the dependent variable y_i and the estimated values of the dependent variable. The criterion for the least squares method is given by expression (14.5).

*Carl Friedrich Gauss
(1777–1855) proposed the
least squares method.*

LEAST SQUARES CRITERION

$$\min \Sigma(y_i - \hat{y}_i)^2 \qquad \text{(14.5)}$$

where

y_i = observed value of the dependent variable for the ith observation

$\hat{y}_i$ = estimated value of the dependent variable for the ith observation

Differential calculus can be used to show (see Appendix 14.1) that the values of b_0 and b_1 that minimize expression (14.5) can be found by using equations (14.6) and (14.7).

SLOPE AND y-INTERCEPT FOR THE ESTIMATED REGRESSION EQUATION*

$$b_1 = \frac{\Sigma(x_i - \bar{x})(y_i - \bar{y})}{\Sigma(x_i - \bar{x})^2} \qquad \text{(14.6)}$$

$$b_0 = \bar{y} - b_1\bar{x} \qquad \text{(14.7)}$$

*In computing b_1 with a
calculator, carry as many
significant digits as
possible in the intermediate
calculations. We
recommend carrying at
least four significant digits.*

where

x_i = value of the independent variable for the ith observation

y_i = value of the dependent variable for the ith observation

$\bar{x}$ = mean value for the independent variable

$\bar{y}$ = mean value for the dependent variable

n = total number of observations

Some of the calculations necessary to develop the least squares estimated regression equation for Armand's restaurants are shown in Table 14.2. With the sample of 10 restaurants, we have $n = 10$ observations. Because equations (14.6) and (14.7) require $\bar{x}$ and $\bar{y}$ we begin the calculations by computing $\bar{x}$ and $\bar{y}$.

$$\bar{x} = \frac{\Sigma x_i}{n} = \frac{140}{10} = 14$$

$$\bar{y} = \frac{\Sigma y_i}{n} = \frac{1300}{10} = 130$$

Using equations (14.6) and (14.7) and the information in Table 14.2, we can compute the slope and intercept of the estimated regression equation for Armand's restaurants. The calculation of the slope (b_1) proceeds as follows.

---

*An alternate formula for b_1 is

$$b_1 = \frac{\Sigma x_i y_i - (\Sigma x_i \Sigma y_i)/n}{\Sigma x_i^2 - (\Sigma x_i)^2/n}$$

This form of equation (14.6) is often recommended when using a calculator to compute b_1.

TABLE 14.2   CALCULATIONS FOR THE LEAST SQUARES ESTIMATED REGRESSION EQUATION FOR ARMAND'S PIZZA PARLORS

Restaurant i	x_i	y_i	$x_i - \bar{x}$	$y_i - \bar{y}$	$(x_i - \bar{x})(y_i - \bar{y})$	$(x_i - \bar{x})^2$
1	2	58	−12	−72	864	144
2	6	105	−8	−25	200	64
3	8	88	−6	−42	252	36
4	8	118	−6	−12	72	36
5	12	117	−2	−13	26	4
6	16	137	2	7	14	4
7	20	157	6	27	162	36
8	20	169	6	39	234	36
9	22	149	8	19	152	64
10	26	202	12	72	864	144
Totals	140	1300			2840	568
	Σx_i	Σy_i			$\Sigma(x_i - \bar{x})(y_i - \bar{y})$	$\Sigma(x_i - \bar{x})^2$

$$b_1 = \frac{\Sigma(x_i - \bar{x})(y_i - \bar{y})}{\Sigma(x_i - \bar{x})^2}$$
$$= \frac{2840}{568}$$
$$= 5$$

The calculation of the y-intercept (b_0) follows.

$$b_0 = \bar{y} - b_1\bar{x}$$
$$= 130 - 5(14)$$
$$= 60$$

Thus, the estimated regression equation is

$$\hat{y} = 60 + 5x$$

Figure 14.4 shows the graph of this equation on the scatter diagram.

The slope of the estimated regression equation ($b_1 = 5$) is positive, implying that as student population increases, sales increase. In fact, we can conclude (based on sales measured in $1000s and student population in 1000s) that an increase in the student population of 1000 is associated with an increase of $5000 in expected sales; that is, quarterly sales are expected to increase by $5 per student.

Using the estimated regression equation to make predictions outside the range of the values of the independent variable should be done with caution because outside that range we cannot be sure that the same relationship is valid.

If we believe the least squares estimated regression equation adequately describes the relationship between x and y, it would seem reasonable to use the estimated regression equation to predict the value of y for a given value of x. For example, if we wanted to predict quarterly sales for a restaurant to be located near a campus with 16,000 students, we would compute

$$\hat{y} = 60 + 5(16) = 140$$

Hence, we would predict quarterly sales of $140,000 for this restaurant. In the following sections we will discuss methods for assessing the appropriateness of using the estimated regression equation for estimation and prediction.

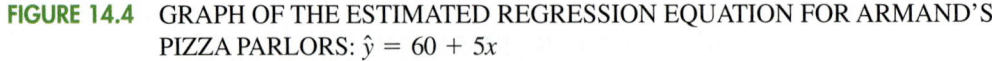

FIGURE 14.4   GRAPH OF THE ESTIMATED REGRESSION EQUATION FOR ARMAND'S
PIZZA PARLORS: $\hat{y} = 60 + 5x$

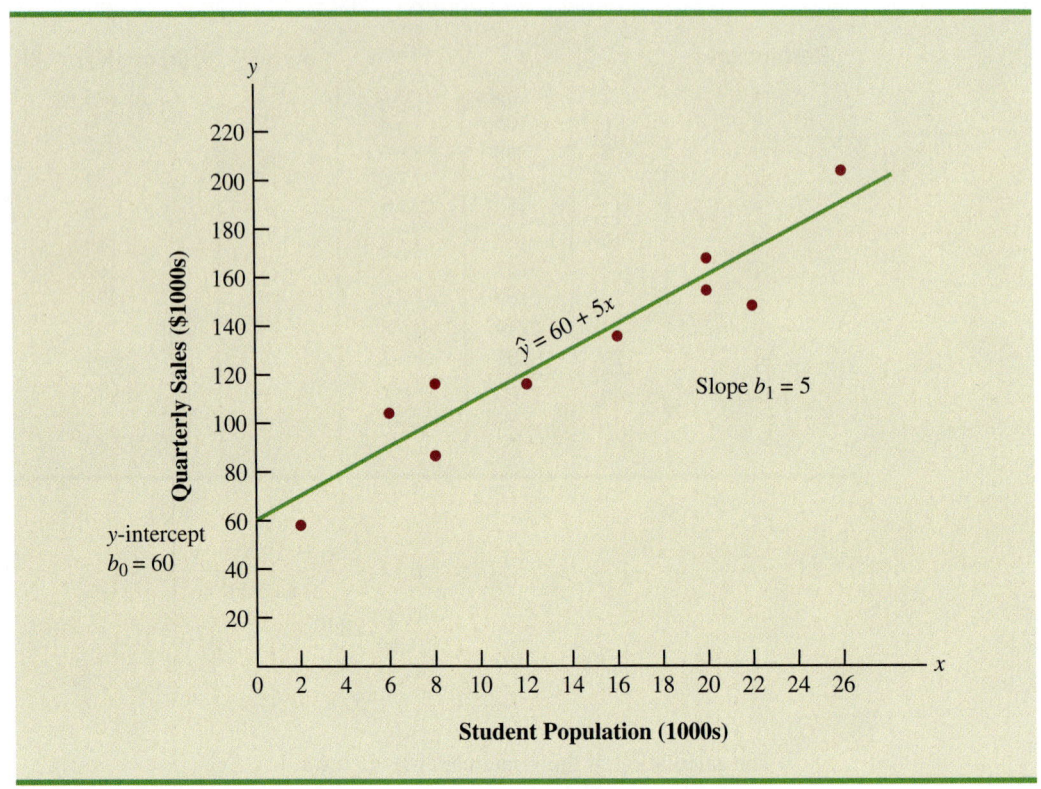

Using Excel to Develop a Scatter Diagram and Compute the Estimated Regression Equation

In Section 2.4 we showed how Excel's Chart Wizard could be used to construct a scatter diagram. Once a scatter diagram has been developed, Excel's Chart menu provides options for computing the estimated regression equation and displaying the graph of the estimated regression equation. We will demonstrate these capabilities using the Armand's Pizza Parlors data appearing in Table 14.1. Refer to Figure 14.5 as we describe the tasks involved.

Enter Data: The labels Restaurant, Population, and Sales are entered into cells A1:C1 of the worksheet. To identify each of the 10 observations, we entered the numbers 1 through 10 into cells A2:A11. The sample data have been entered into cells B2:C11.

Apply Tools: We will first use Excel's Chart Wizard to produce a scatter diagram. We will then show how options available on the Chart menu can be used to compute the estimated regression equation and to display the estimated regression line.

   Step 1. Select cells B1:C11
   Step 2. Click the **Chart Wizard** button on the standard toolbar (or select the **Insert** menu and choose the **Chart** option)
   Step 3. When the **Chart Wizard - Step 1 of 4 - Chart Type** dialog box appears:
         Choose **XY (Scatter)** in the **Chart type** list
         Choose **Scatter** from the **Chart sub-type** display
         Select **Next >**

FIGURE 14.5   SCATTER DIAGRAM, ESTIMATED REGRESSION EQUATION, AND THE ESTIMATED REGRESSION LINE FOR ARMAND'S PIZZA PARLORS

	A	B	C	D	E	F	G	H	I
1	Restaurant	Population	Sales						
2	1	2	58						
3	2	6	105						
4	3	8	88						
5	4	8	118						
6	5	12	117						
7	6	16	137						
8	7	20	157						
9	8	20	169						
10	9	22	149						
11	10	26	202						
12									
13									
14									
15									
16									
17									
18									
19									
20									
21									
22									
23									
24									
25									
26									
27									
28									
29									
30									

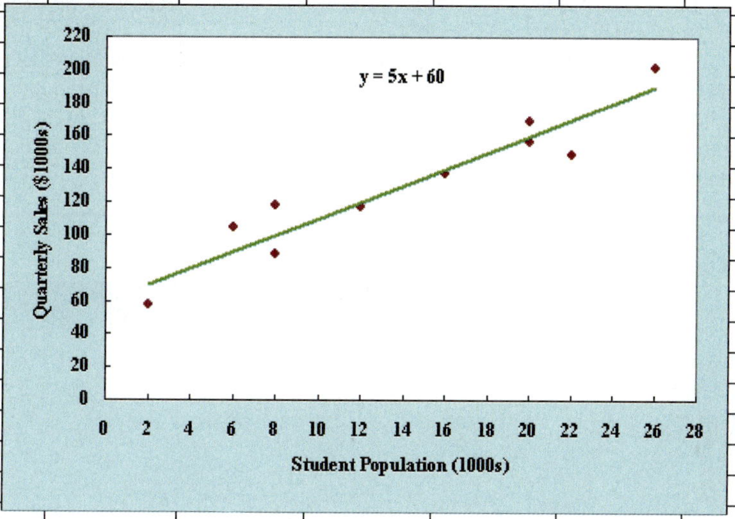

Step 4. When the **Chart Wizard - Step 2 of 4 - Chart Source Data** dialog box appears:
Select **Next >**

Step 5. When the **Chart Wizard - Step 3 of 4 - Chart Options** dialog box appears:
Select the **Titles** tab and then
Delete **Sales** in the Chart title box
Enter **Student Population (1000s)** in the **Value (X) axis** box
Enter **Quarterly Sales ($1000s)** in the **Value (Y) axis** box
Select the **Legend** tab and then
Remove the check in the **Show Legend** box
Select **Next >**

Step 6. When the **Chart Wizard - Step 4 of 4 - Chart Location** dialog box appears:
Specify a location for the new chart (we used the default setting of the current worksheet)
Select **Finish** to display the scatter diagram

Step 7. Position the mouse pointer over any data point and right-click to display the **Chart** menu

Step 8. Select the **Add Trendline** option

Step 9. When the Add Trendline dialog box appears:

On the **Type** tab select **Linear**

On the **Options** tab select the **Display equation on chart** box

Click **OK**

Figure 14.5 shows the scatter diagram, the estimated regression equation, and the graph of the estimated regression equation obtained.

NOTES AND COMMENTS

1. The least squares method provides an estimated regression equation that minimizes the sum of squared deviations between the observed values of the dependent variable y_i and the estimated values of the dependent variable $\hat{y}_i$. The least squares criterion chooses the equation that provides the best fit. If some other criterion were used, such as minimizing the sum of the absolute deviations between y_i and $\hat{y}_i$, a different equation would be obtained. In practice, the least squares method is the most widely used.

2. Excel's INTERCEPT and SLOPE functions can also be used to compute the y-intercept and slope of the estimated regression equation. For instance, for the Armand's data shown in columns B and C of Figure 14.5, the formula =INTERCEPT (C2:C11,B2:B11) can be entered into any empty cell of the worksheet to compute the y-intercept of the estimated regression line, and the formula =SLOPE(C2:C11,B2:B11) can be entered into any empty cell to compute the slope of the estimated regression line.

Exercises

Methods

1. Given are five observations for two variables, x and y.

x_i	1	2	3	4	5
y_i	3	7	5	11	14

   a. Develop a scatter diagram for these data.
   b. What does the scatter diagram developed in part (a) indicate about the relationship between the two variables?
   c. Try to approximate the relationship between x and y by drawing a straight line through the data.
   d. Develop the estimated regression equation by computing the values of b_0 and b_1 using equations (14.6) and (14.7).
   e. Use the estimated regression equation to predict the value of y when $x = 4$.

2. Given are five observations for two variables, x and y.

x_i	2	3	5	1	8
y_i	25	25	20	30	16

   a. Develop a scatter diagram for these data.
   b. What does the scatter diagram developed in part (a) indicate about the relationship between the two variables?
   c. Try to approximate the relationship between x and y by drawing a straight line through the data.
   d. Develop the estimated regression equation by computing the values of b_0 and b_1 using equations (14.6) and (14.7).
   e. Use the estimated regression equation to predict the value of y when $x = 6$.

3. Given are five observations collected in a regression study on two variables.

x_i	2	4	5	7	8
y_i	2	3	2	6	4

   a.   Develop a scatter diagram for these data.
   b.   Develop the estimated regression equation for these data.
   c.   Use the estimated regression equation to predict the value of y when $x = 4$.

Applications

4. The following data were collected on the height (inches) and weight (pounds) of women swimmers.

Height	68	64	62	65	66
Weight	132	108	102	115	128

   a.   Develop a scatter diagram for these data with height as the independent variable.
   b.   What does the scatter diagram developed in part (a) indicate about the relationship between the two variables?
   c.   Try to approximate the relationship between height and weight by drawing a straight line through the data.
   d.   Develop the estimated regression equation by computing the values of b_0 and b_1.
   e.   If a swimmer's height is 63 inches, what would you estimate her weight to be?

5. Technological advances helped make inflatable paddlecraft suitable for backcountry use. These blow-up rubber boats, which can be rolled into a bundle not much bigger than a golf bag, are large enough to accommodate one or two paddlers and their camping gear. *Canoe & Kayak* magazine tested boats from nine manufacturers to determine how they would perform on a three-day wilderness paddling trip. One of the criteria in their evaluation was the baggage capacity of the boat, evaluated using a 4-point rating scale from 1 (lowest rating) to 4 (highest rating). The following data show the baggage capacity rating and the price of the boat (*Canoe & Kayak*, March 2003).

Boat	Baggage Capacity	Price ($)
S14	4	1595
Orinoco	4	1399
Outside Pro	4	1890
Explorer 380X	3	795
River XK2	2.5	600
Sea Tiger	4	1995
Maverik II	3	1205
Starlite 100	2	583
Fat Pack Cat	3	1048

   a.   Develop a scatter diagram for these data with baggage capacity rating as the independent variable.
   b.   What does the scatter diagram developed in part (a) indicate about the relationship between baggage capacity and price?
   c.   Draw a straight line through the data to approximate a linear relationship between baggage capacity and price.
   d.   Use the least squares method to develop the estimated regression equation.
   e.   Provide an interpretation for the slope of the estimated regression equation.
   f.   Predict the price for a boat with a baggage capacity rating of 3.

6. Wageweb conducts surveys of salary data and presents summaries on its Web site. Based on salary data as of October 1, 2002, Wageweb reported that the average annual salary for sales vice presidents was $142,111, with an average annual bonus of $15,432 (Wageweb.com, March 13, 2003). Assume the following data are a sample of the annual salary and bonus for 10 sales vice presidents. Data are in thousands of dollars.

Vice President	Salary ($1000s)	Bonus ($1000s)
1	135	12
2	115	14
3	146	16
4	167	19
5	165	22
6	176	24
7	98	7
8	136	17
9	163	18
10	119	11

a. Develop a scatter diagram for these data with salary as the independent variable.
b. What does the scatter diagram developed in part (a) indicate about the relationship between salary and bonus?
c. Use the least squares method to develop the estimated regression equation.
d. Provide an interpretation for the slope of the estimated regression equation.
e. Predict the bonus for a vice president with an annual salary of $120,000.

7. Would you expect more reliable cars to cost more? *Consumer Reports* rated 15 upscale sedans. Reliability was rated on a 5-point scale: poor (1), fair (2), good (3), very good (4), and excellent (5). The price and reliability rating for each of the 15 cars are shown (*Consumer Reports,* February 2004).

Cars

Make and Model	Reliability	Price ($)
Acura TL	4	33,150
BMW 330i	3	40,570
Lexus IS300	5	35,105
Lexus ES330	5	35,174
Mercedes-Benz C320	1	42,230
Lincoln LS Premium (V6)	3	38,225
Audi A4 3.0 Quattro	2	37,605
Cadillac CTS	1	37,695
Nissan Maxima 3.5 SE	4	34,390
Infiniti I35	5	33,845
Saab 9-3 Aero	3	36,910
Infiniti G35	4	34,695
Jaguar X-Type 3.0	1	37,995
Saab 9-5 Arc	3	36,955
Volvo S60 2.5T	3	33,890

a. Develop a scatter diagram for these data with the reliability rating as the independent variable.
b. Develop the least squares estimated regression equation.
c. Based upon your analysis, do you think more reliable cars cost more? Explain.
d. Estimate the price for an upscale sedan that has an average reliability rating.

8. Mountain bikes that cost less than $1000 now contain many of the high-quality components that until recently were only available on high-priced models. Today, even sub-$1000 models often offer supple suspensions, clipless pedals, and highly engineered frames. An interesting question is whether higher price still buys a higher level of handling, as measured by the bike's sidetrack capability. To measure sidetrack capability, *Outside Magazine* used a rating scale from 1 to 5, with 1 representing an average rating and 5 representing an excellent rating. The sidetrack capability and the price for 10 mountain bikes tested by *Outside Magazine* follow (*Outside Magazine Buyer's Guide*, 2001).

MtnBikes

Manufacturer and Model	Sidetrack Capability	Price ($)
Raleigh M80	1	600
Marin Bear Valley Feminina	1	649
GT Avalanche 2.0	2	799
Kona Jake the Snake	1	899
Schwinn Moab 2	3	950
Giant XTC NRS 3	4	1100
Fisher Paragon Genesisters	4	1149
Jamis Dakota XC	3	1300
Trek Fuel 90	5	1550
Specialized Stumpjumper M4	4	1625

a. Develop a scatter diagram for these data with sidetrack capability as the independent variable.
b. Does it appear that higher-priced models have a higher level of handling? Explain.
c. Develop the least squares estimated regression equation.
d. What is the estimated price for a mountain bike if it has a sidetrack capability rating of 4?

9. A sales manager collected the following data on annual sales and years of experience.

Salesperson	Years of Experience	Annual Sales ($1000s)
1	1	80
2	3	97
3	4	92
4	4	102
5	6	103
6	8	111
7	10	119
8	10	123
9	11	117
10	13	136

a. Develop a scatter diagram for these data with years of experience as the independent variable.
b. Develop an estimated regression equation that can be used to predict annual sales given the years of experience.
c. Use the estimated regression equation to predict annual sales for a salesperson with nine years of experience.

10. *PC World* provided ratings for the top 15 notebook PCs (*PC World*, February 2000). The performance score is a measure of how fast a PC can run a mix of common business applications as compared to how fast a baseline machine can run them. For example, a PC with a performance score of 200 is twice as fast as the baseline machine. A 100-point scale

was used to provide an overall rating for each notebook tested in the study. A score in the 90s is exceptional, while one in the 70s is above average. The performance scores and the overall ratings for the 15 notebooks follow.

PCs

Make and Model	Performance Score	Overall Rating
AMS Tech Roadster 15CTA380	115	67
Compaq Armada M700	191	78
Compaq Prosignia Notebook 150	153	79
Dell Inspiron 3700 C466GT	194	80
Dell Inspiron 7500 R500VT	236	84
Dell Latitude Cpi A366XT	184	76
Enpower ENP-313 Pro	184	77
Gateway Solo 9300LS	216	92
HP Pavilion Notebook PC	185	83
IBM ThinkPad I Series 1480	183	78
Micro Express NP7400	189	77
Micron TransPort NX PII-400	202	78
NEC Versa SX	192	78
Sceptre Soundx 5200	141	73
Sony VAIO PCG-F340	187	77

a. Develop a scatter diagram for these data with performance score as the independent variable.
b. Develop the least squares estimated regression equation.
c. Estimate the overall rating for a new PC that has a performance score of 225.

11. Although delays at major airports are now less frequent, it helps to know which airports are likely to throw off your schedule. In addition, if your plane is late arriving at a particular airport where you must make a connection, how likely is it that the departure will be late and thus increase your chances of making the connection? The following data show the percentage of late arrivals and departures during August for 13 airports (*Business 2.0*, February 2002).

Airport

Airport	Late Arrivals (%)	Late Departures (%)
Atlanta	24	22
Charlotte	20	20
Chicago	30	29
Cincinnati	20	19
Dallas	20	22
Denver	23	23
Detroit	18	19
Houston	20	16
Minneapolis	18	18
Phoenix	21	22
Pittsburgh	25	22
Salt Lake City	18	17
St. Louis	16	16

a. Develop a scatter diagram for these data with the percentage of late arrivals as the independent variable.
b. What does the scatter diagram developed in part (a) indicate about the relationship between late arrivals and late departures?
c. Use the least squares method to develop the estimated regression equation.

d. Provide an interpretation for the slope of the estimated regression equation.
e. Suppose the percentage of late arrivals at the Philadelphia airport for August was 22%. What is an estimate of the percentage of late departures?

12. The following table gives the number of employees and the revenue (in millions of dollars) for 20 companies (*Fortune,* April 17, 2000).

EmpRev

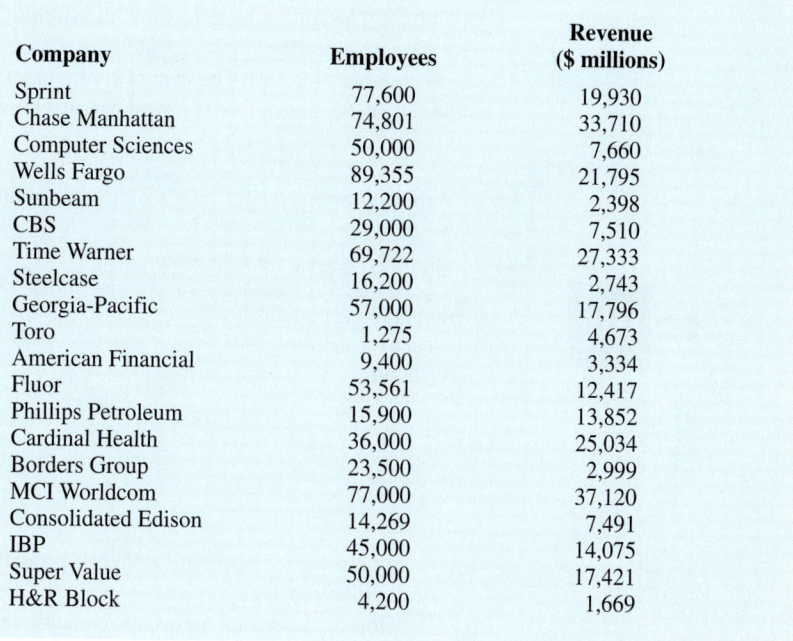

Company	Employees	Revenue ($ millions)
Sprint	77,600	19,930
Chase Manhattan	74,801	33,710
Computer Sciences	50,000	7,660
Wells Fargo	89,355	21,795
Sunbeam	12,200	2,398
CBS	29,000	7,510
Time Warner	69,722	27,333
Steelcase	16,200	2,743
Georgia-Pacific	57,000	17,796
Toro	1,275	4,673
American Financial	9,400	3,334
Fluor	53,561	12,417
Phillips Petroleum	15,900	13,852
Cardinal Health	36,000	25,034
Borders Group	23,500	2,999
MCI Worldcom	77,000	37,120
Consolidated Edison	14,269	7,491
IBP	45,000	14,075
Super Value	50,000	17,421
H&R Block	4,200	1,669

a. Develop a scatter diagram for these data with number of employees as the independent variable.
b. What does the scatter diagram developed in part (a) indicate about the relationship between number of employees and revenue?
c. Develop the estimated regression equation for these data.
d. Use the estimated regression equation to predict the revenue for a firm with 75,000 employees.

13. To the Internal Revenue Service, the reasonableness of total itemized deductions depends on the taxpayer's adjusted gross income. Large deductions, which include charity and medical deductions, are more reasonable for taxpayers with large adjusted gross incomes. If a taxpayer claims larger than average itemized deductions for a given level of income, the chances of an IRS audit are increased. Data (in thousands of dollars) on adjusted gross income and the average or reasonable amount of itemized deductions follow.

Adjusted Gross Income ($1000s)	Reasonable Amount of Itemized Deductions ($1000s)
22	9.6
27	9.6
32	10.1
48	11.1
65	13.5
85	17.7
120	25.5

    a. Develop a scatter diagram for these data with adjusted gross income as the independent variable.

    b. Use the least squares method to develop the estimated regression equation.

    c. Estimate a reasonable level of total itemized deductions for a taxpayer with an adjusted gross income of $52,500. If this taxpayer claimed itemized deductions of $20,400, would the IRS agent's request for an audit appear justified? Explain.

14. Starting salaries for accountants and auditors in Rochester, New York, trail those of many U.S. cities. The following data show the starting salary (in thousands of dollars) and the cost of living index for Rochester and nine other metropolitan areas (*Democrat and Chronicle*, September 1, 2002). The cost of living index, based on a city's food, housing, taxes, and other costs, ranges from 0 (most expensive) to 100 (least expensive).

Metropolitan Area	Index	Salary ($1000s)
Oklahoma City	82.44	23.9
Tampa/St. Petersburg/Clearwater	79.89	24.5
Indianapolis	55.53	27.4
Buffalo/Niagara Falls	41.36	27.7
Atlanta	39.38	27.1
Rochester	28.05	25.6
Sacramento	25.50	28.7
Raleigh/Durham/Chapel Hill	13.32	26.7
San Diego	3.12	27.8
Honolulu	0.57	28.3

Salaries

    a. Develop a scatter diagram for these data with the cost of living index as the independent variable.

    b. Develop the estimated regression equation relating the cost of living index to the starting salary.

    c. Estimate the starting salary for a metropolitan area with a cost of living index of 50.

14.3   Coefficient of Determination

For the Armand's Pizza Parlors example, we developed the estimated regression equation $\hat{y} = 60 + 5x$ to approximate the linear relationship between the size of the student population x and quarterly sales y. A question now is: How well does the estimated regression equation fit the data? In this section, we show that the **coefficient of determination** provides a measure of the goodness of fit for the estimated regression equation.

    For the ith observation, the difference between the observed value of the dependent variable, y_i, and the estimated value of the dependent variable, $\hat{y}_i$, is called the *ith residual*. The ith residual represents the error in using $\hat{y}_i$ to estimate y_i. Thus, for the ith observation, the residual is $y_i - \hat{y}_i$. The sum of squares of these residuals or errors is the quantity that is minimized by the least squares method. This quantity, also known as the *sum of squares due to error*, is denoted by SSE.

SUM OF SQUARES DUE TO ERROR

$$SSE = \Sigma(y_i - \hat{y}_i)^2 \tag{14.8}$$

The value of SSE is a measure of the error in using the estimated regression equation to estimate the values of the dependent variable in the sample.

TABLE 14.3   CALCULATION OF SSE FOR ARMAND'S PIZZA PARLORS

Restaurant i	x_i = Student Population (1000s)	y_i = Quarterly Sales ($1000s)	Predicted Sales $\hat{y}_i = 60 + 5x_i$	Error $y_i - \hat{y}_i$	Squared Error $(y_i - \hat{y}_i)^2$
1	2	58	70	−12	144
2	6	105	90	15	225
3	8	88	100	−12	144
4	8	118	100	18	324
5	12	117	120	−3	9
6	16	137	140	−3	9
7	20	157	160	−3	9
8	20	169	160	9	81
9	22	149	170	−21	441
10	26	202	190	12	144
					SSE = 1530

In Table 14.3 we show the calculations required to compute the sum of squares due to error for the Armand's Pizza Parlors example. For instance, for restaurant 1 the values of the independent and dependent variables are $x_1 = 2$ and $y_1 = 58$. Using the estimated regression equation, we find that the estimated value of quarterly sales for restaurant 1 is $\hat{y}_1 = 60 + 5(2) = 70$. Thus, the error in using $\hat{y}_1$ to estimate y_1 for restaurant 1 is $y_1 - \hat{y}_1 = 58 - 70 = -12$. The squared error, $(-12)^2 = 144$, is shown in the last column of Table 14.3. After computing and squaring the residuals for each restaurant in the sample, we sum them to obtain SSE = 1530. Thus, SSE = 1530 measures the error in using the estimated regression equation $\hat{y} = 60 + 5x$ to predict sales.

Now suppose we are asked to develop an estimate of quarterly sales without knowledge of the size of the student population. Without knowledge of any related variables, we would use the sample mean as an estimate of quarterly sales at any given restaurant. Table 14.2 shows that for the sales data, $\Sigma y_i = 1300$. Hence, the mean value of quarterly sales for the sample of 10 Armand's restaurants is $\bar{y} = \Sigma y_i / n = 1300/10 = 130$. In Table 14.4 we show the sum of squared deviations obtained by using the sample mean $\bar{y} = 130$ to estimate the value of quarterly sales for each restaurant in the sample. For the ith restaurant in the sample, the difference $y_i - \bar{y}$ provides a measure of the error involved in using $\bar{y}$ to estimate sales. The corresponding sum of squares, called the *total sum of squares*, is denoted SST.

TOTAL SUM OF SQUARES

$$SST = \Sigma(y_i - \bar{y})^2 \tag{14.9}$$

The sum at the bottom of the last column in Table 14.4 is the total sum of squares for Armand's Pizza Parlors; it is SST = 15,730.

With SST = 15,370 and SSE = 1530, the estimated regression line provides a much better fit to the data than the line y = ȳ.

In Figure 14.6 we show the estimated regression line $\hat{y} = 60 + 5x$ and the line corresponding to $\bar{y} = 130$. Note that the points cluster more closely around the estimated regression line than they do about the line $\bar{y} = 130$. For example, for the 10th restaurant in the sample we see that the error is much larger when $\bar{y} = 130$ is used as an estimate of y_{10} than when $\hat{y}_{10} = 60 + 5(26) = 190$ is used. We can think of SST as a measure of how well the observations cluster about the $\bar{y}$ line and SSE as a measure of how well the observations cluster about the $\hat{y}$ line.

TABLE 14.4   COMPUTATION OF THE TOTAL SUM OF SQUARES FOR ARMAND'S PIZZA PARLORS

Restaurant i	x_i = Student Population (1000s)	y_i = Quarterly Sales ($1000s)	Deviation $y_i - \bar{y}$	Squared Deviation $(y_i - \bar{y})^2$
1	2	58	−72	5,184
2	6	105	−25	625
3	8	88	−42	1,764
4	8	118	−12	144
5	12	117	−13	169
6	16	137	7	49
7	20	157	27	729
8	20	169	39	1,521
9	22	149	19	361
10	26	202	72	5,184
				SST = 15,730

FIGURE 14.6   DEVIATIONS ABOUT THE ESTIMATED REGRESSION LINE AND THE LINE $y = \bar{y}$ FOR ARMAND'S PIZZA PARLORS

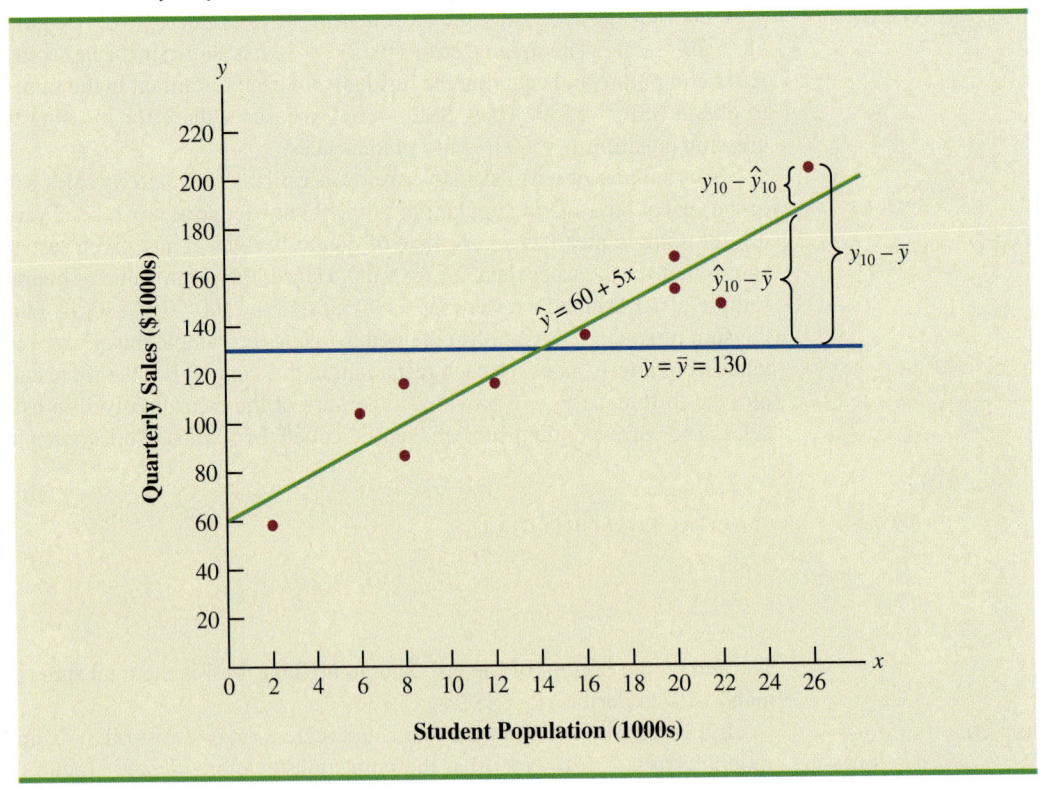

To measure how much the $\hat{y}$ values on the estimated regression line deviate from $\bar{y}$, another sum of squares is computed. This sum of squares, called the *sum of squares due to regression*, is denoted SSR.

SUM OF SQUARES DUE TO REGRESSION

$$SSR = \Sigma(\hat{y}_i - \bar{y})^2 \qquad \textbf{(14.10)}$$

From the preceding discussion, we should expect that SST, SSR, and SSE are related. Indeed, the relationship among these three sums of squares provides one of the most important results in statistics.

RELATIONSHIP AMONG SST, SSR, AND SSE

SSR can be thought of as the explained portion of SST, and SSE can be thought of as the unexplained portion of SST.

$$SST = SSR + SSE \qquad \textbf{(14.11)}$$

where

> SST = total sum of squares
> SSR = sum of squares due to regression
> SSE = sum of squares due to error

Equation (14.11) shows that the total sum of squares can be partitioned into two components, the regression sum of squares and the sum of squares due to error. Hence, if the values of any two of these sums of squares are known, the third sum of squares can be computed easily. For instance, in the Armand's Pizza Parlors example, we already know that SSE = 1530 and SST = 15,730; therefore, solving for SSR in equation (14.11), we find that the sum of squares due to regression is

$$SSR = SST - SSE = 15,730 - 1530 = 14,200$$

Now let us see how the three sums of squares, SST, SSR, and SSE, can be used to provide a measure of the goodness of fit for the estimated regression equation. The estimated regression equation would provide a perfect fit if every value of the dependent variable y_i happened to lie on the estimated regression line. In this case, $y_i - \hat{y}_i$ would be zero for each observation, resulting in SSE = 0. Because SST = SSR + SSE, we see that for a perfect fit SSR must equal SST, and the ratio (SSR/SST) must equal one. Poorer fits will result in larger values for SSE. Solving for SSE in equation (14.11), we see that SSE = SST − SSR. Hence, the largest value for SSE (and hence the poorest fit) occurs when SSR = 0 and SSE = SST.

The ratio SSR/SST, which will take values between zero and one, is used to evaluate the goodness of fit for the estimated regression equation. This ratio is called the *coefficient of determination* and is denoted by r^2.

COEFFICIENT OF DETERMINATION

$$r^2 = \frac{SSR}{SST} \qquad \textbf{(14.12)}$$

For the Armand's Pizza Parlors example, the value of the coefficient of determination is

$$r^2 = \frac{\text{SSR}}{\text{SST}} = \frac{14{,}200}{15{,}730} = .9027$$

The least squares method finds the estimated regression equation that maximizes r^2.

When we express the coefficient of determination as a percentage, r^2 can be interpreted as the percentage of the total sum of squares that can be explained by using the estimated regression equation. For Armand's restaurants, we can conclude that 90.27% of the total sum of squares can be explained by using the estimated regression equation $\hat{y} = 60 + 5x$ to predict quarterly sales. In other words, 90.27% of the variability in sales can be explained by the linear relationship between the size of the student population and sales. We should be pleased to find such a good fit for the estimated regression equation.

Using Excel to Compute the Coefficient of Determination

In Section 14.2 we used Excel's Chart Wizard to construct a scatter diagram for the Armand's Pizza Parlors data. We then showed how options available could be used to compute the estimated regression equation and display its graph. We will now describe how to compute the coefficient of determination.

> **Step 1.** Position the mouse pointer over any data point in the scatter diagram and right-click to display the **Chart** menu
> **Step 2.** Select the **Add Trendline** option
> **Step 3.** When the Add Trendline dialog box appears:
> On the **Options** tab select the **Display R-squared value on chart** box
> Click **OK**

Figure 14.7 displays the scatter diagram, the estimated regression equation, the graph of the estimated regression equation, and the coefficient of determination for the Armand's Pizza Parlors data. We see that $r^2 = .9027$.

Correlation Coefficient

In Chapter 3 we introduced the **correlation coefficient** as a descriptive measure of the strength of linear association between two variables, x and y. Values of the correlation coefficient are always between -1 and $+1$. A value of $+1$ indicates that the two variables x and y are perfectly related in a positive linear sense. That is, all data points are on a straight line that has a positive slope. A value of -1 indicates that x and y are perfectly related in a negative linear sense, with all data points on a straight line that has a negative slope. Values of the correlation coefficient close to zero indicate that x and y are not linearly related.

In Section 3.5 we presented the equation for computing the sample correlation coefficient. If a regression analysis has already been performed and the coefficient of determination r^2 computed, the sample correlation coefficient can be computed as follows.

SAMPLE CORRELATION COEFFICIENT

$$r_{xy} = (\text{sign of } b_1)\sqrt{\text{Coefficient of determination}}$$
$$= (\text{sign of } b_1)\sqrt{r^2}$$

(14.13)

where

$$b_1 = \text{the slope of the estimated regression equation } \hat{y} = b_0 + b_1 x$$

FIGURE 14.7   USING EXCEL TO COMPUTE THE COEFFICIENT OF DETERMINATION

	A	B	C	D	E	F	G	H	I
1	Restaurant	Population	Sales						
2	1	2	58						
3	2	6	105						
4	3	8	88						
5	4	8	118						
6	5	12	117						
7	6	16	137						
8	7	20	157						
9	8	20	169						
10	9	22	149						
11	10	26	202						
12									
13									
14									
15									
16									
17									
18									
19									
20									
21									
22									
23									
24									
25									
26									
27									
28									
29									
30									

The chart within the spreadsheet shows Quarterly Sales ($1000s) versus Student Population (1000s), with the fitted line $y = 5x + 60$ and $R^2 = 0.9027$.

The sign for the sample correlation coefficient is positive if the estimated regression equation has a positive slope ($b_1 > 0$) and negative if the estimated regression equation has a negative slope ($b_1 < 0$).

For the Armand's Pizza Parlors example, the value of the coefficient of determination corresponding to the estimated regression equation $\hat{y} = 60 + 5x$ is .9027. Because the slope of the estimated regression equation is positive, equation (14.13) shows that the sample correlation coefficient is $+\sqrt{.9027} = +.9501$. With a sample correlation coefficient of $r_{xy} = +.9501$, we would conclude that a strong positive linear association exists between x and y.

In the case of a linear relationship between two variables, both the coefficient of determination and the sample correlation coefficient provide measures of the strength of the relationship. The coefficient of determination provides a measure between 0 and 1, whereas the sample correlation coefficient provides a measure between -1 and $+1$. Although the sample correlation coefficient is restricted to a linear relationship between two variables, the coefficient of determination can be used for nonlinear relationships and for relationships that have two or more independent variables. Thus, the coefficient of determination provides a wider range of applicability.

NOTES AND COMMENTS

1. In developing the least squares estimated regression equation and computing the coefficient of determination, we made no probabilistic assumptions about the error term ϵ and no statistical tests for significance of the relationship between x and y were conducted. Larger values of r^2 imply that the least squares line provides a better fit to the data; that is, the observations are more closely grouped about the least squares line. But, using only r^2, we can draw no conclusion about whether the relationship between x and y is statistically significant. Such a conclu-

sion must be based on considerations that involve the sample size and the properties of the appropriate sampling distributions of the least squares estimators.

2. As a practical matter, for typical data found in the social sciences, values of r^2 as low as .25 are often considered useful. For data in the physical and life sciences, r^2 values of .60 or greater are often found; in fact, in some cases, r^2 values greater than .90 can be found. In business applications, r^2 values vary greatly, depending on the unique characteristics of each application.

Exercises

Methods

15. The data from exercise 1 follow.

x_i	1	2	3	4	5
y_i	3	7	5	11	14

The estimated regression equation for these data is $\hat{y} = .20 + 2.60x$.
   a. Compute SSE, SST, and SSR using equations (14.8), (14.9), and (14.10).
   b. Compute the coefficient of determination r^2. Comment on the goodness of fit.
   c. Compute the sample correlation coefficient.

16. The data from exercise 2 follow.

x_i	2	3	5	1	8
y_i	25	25	20	30	16

The estimated regression equation for these data is $\hat{y} = 30.33 - 1.88x$.
   a. Compute SSE, SST, and SSR.
   b. Compute the coefficient of determination r^2. Comment on the goodness of fit.
   c. Compute the sample correlation coefficient.

17. The data from exercise 3 follow.

x_i	2	4	5	7	8
y_i	2	3	2	6	4

The estimated regression equation for these data is $\hat{y} = .75 + .51x$. What percentage of the total sum of squares can be accounted for by the estimated regression equation? What is the value of the sample correlation coefficient?

Applications

18. The following data are the monthly salaries y and the grade point averages x for students who obtained a bachelor's degree in business administration with a major in information systems.

GPA	Monthly Salary ($)
2.6	3300
3.4	3600
3.6	4000
3.2	3500
3.5	3900
2.9	3600

The estimated regression equation for these data is $\hat{y} = 1790.5 + 581.1x$.
   a. Compute SST, SSR, and SSE.
   b. Compute the coefficient of determination r^2. Comment on the goodness of fit.
   c. What is the value of the sample correlation coefficient?

19. The data from exercise 7 follow:

CD file

Cars

Make and Model	x = Reliability	y = Price ($)
Acura TL	4	33,150
BMW 330i	3	40,570
Lexus IS300	5	35,105
Lexus ES330	5	35,174
Mercedes-Benz C320	1	42,230
Lincoln LS Premium (V6)	3	38,225
Audi A4 3.0 Quattro	2	37,605
Cadillac CTS	1	37,695
Nissan Maxima 3.5 SE	4	34,390
Infiniti I35	5	33,845
Saab 9-3 Aero	3	36,910
Infiniti G35	4	34,695
Jaguar X-Type 3.0	1	37,995
Saab 9-5 Arc	3	36,955
Volvo S60 2.5T	3	33,890

The estimated regression equation for these data is $\hat{y} = 40,639 - 1301x$. What percentage of the total sum of squares can be accounted for by the estimated regression equation? Comment on the goodness of fit. What is the sample correlation coefficient?

20. The typical household income and typical home price for a sample of 18 cities follow (*Places Rated Almanac,* 2000). Data are in thousands of dollars.

CD file

Cities

City	Income ($1000s)	Home Price ($1000s)
Akron, OH	74.1	114.9
Atlanta, GA	82.4	126.9
Birmingham, AL	71.2	130.9
Bismarck, ND	62.8	92.8
Cleveland, OH	79.2	135.8
Columbia, SC	66.8	116.7
Denver, CO	82.6	161.9
Detroit, MI	85.3	145.0
Fort Lauderdale, FL	75.8	145.3
Hartford, CT	89.1	162.1
Lancaster, PA	75.2	125.9
Madison, WI	78.8	145.2
Naples, FL	100.0	173.6

(*continued*)

City	Income ($1000s)	Home Price ($1000s)
Nashville, TN	77.3	125.9
Philadelphia, PA	87.0	151.5
Savannah, GA	67.8	108.1
Toledo, OH	71.2	101.1
Washington, DC	97.4	191.9

a. Use these data to develop an estimated regression equation that could be used to esti-mate the typical home price for a city given the typical household income.

b. Compute r^2. Would you feel comfortable using this estimated regression equation to estimate the typical home price for a city?

c. Estimate the typical home price for a city with a typical household income of $95,000.

21. An important application of regression analysis in accounting is in the estimation of cost. By collecting data on production volume (units) and cost and using the least squares method to develop an estimated regression equation relating production volume and cost, an ac-countant can estimate the cost associated with a particular production volume. Consider the following sample of production volume and total cost data for a manufacturing operation.

Production Volume (units)	Total Cost ($)
400	4000
450	5000
550	5400
600	5900
700	6400
750	7000

a. Use these data to develop an estimated regression equation that could be used to pre-dict the total cost for a given production volume.

b. What is the variable cost per unit produced?

c. Compute the coefficient of determination. What percentage of the variation in total cost can be explained by production volume?

d. The company's production schedule shows 500 units must be produced next month. What is the estimated total cost for this operation?

22. *PC World* provided ratings for the top five small-office laser printers and five corporate laser printers (*PC World,* February 2003). The highest rated small-office laser printer was the Minolta-QMS PagePro 1250W, with an overall rating of 91. The highest rated corporate laser printer, the Xerox Phaser 4400/N, had an overall rating of 83. The following data show the speed for plain text printing in pages per minute (ppm) and the price for each printer.

Printers

Name	Type	Speed (ppm)	Price ($)
Minolta-QMS PagePro 1250W	Small Office	12	199
Brother HL-1850	Small Office	10	499
Lexmark E320	Small Office	12.2	299
Minolta-QMS PagePro 1250E	Small Office	10.3	299
HP Laserjet 1200	Small Office	11.7	399
Xerox Phaser 4400/N	Corporate	17.8	1850
Brother HL-2460N	Corporate	16.1	1000
IBM Infoprint 1120n	Corporate	11.8	1387
Lexmark W812	Corporate	19.8	2089
Oki Data B8300n	Corporate	28.2	2200

a.   Develop the estimated regression equation with speed as the independent variable.
b.   Compute r^2. What percentage of the variation in cost can be explained by the printing speed?
c.   What is the sample correlation coefficient between speed and price? Does it reflect a strong or weak relationship between printing speed and cost?

 # 14.4 Model Assumptions

In conducting a regression analysis, we begin by making an assumption about the appropriate model for the relationship between the dependent and independent variable(s). For the case of simple linear regression, the assumed regression model is

$$y = \beta_0 + \beta_1 x + \epsilon$$

Then, the least squares method is used to develop values for b_0 and b_1, the estimates of the model parameters β_0 and β_1, respectively. The resulting estimated regression equation is

$$\hat{y} = b_0 + b_1 x$$

We saw that the value of the coefficient of determination (r^2) is a measure of the goodness of fit of the estimated regression equation. However, even with a large value of r^2, the estimated regression equation should not be used until further analysis of the appropriateness of the assumed model has been conducted. An important step in determining whether the assumed model is appropriate involves testing for the significance of the relationship. The tests of significance in regression analysis are based on the following assumptions about the error term ϵ.

ASSUMPTIONS ABOUT THE ERROR TERM ϵ IN THE REGRESSION MODEL

$$y = \beta_0 + \beta_1 x + \epsilon$$

1. The error term ϵ is a random variable with a mean or expected value of zero; that is, $E(\epsilon) = 0$.
    Implication: Because β_0 and β_1 are constants, $E(\beta_0) = \beta_0$ and $E(\beta_1) = \beta_1$; thus, for a given value of x, the expected value of y is

$$E(y) = \beta_0 + \beta_1 x \qquad\qquad \textbf{(14.14)}$$

    As we indicated previously, equation (14.14) is referred to as the regression equation.
2. The variance of ϵ, denoted by σ^2, is the same for all values of x.
    Implication: The variance of y about the regression line equals σ^2 and is the same for all values of x.
3. The values of ϵ are independent.
    Implication: The value of ϵ for a particular value of x is not related to the value of ϵ for any other value of x; thus, the value of y for a particular value of x is not related to the value of y for any other value of x.
4. The error term ϵ is a normally distributed random variable.
    Implication: Because y is a linear function of ϵ, y is also a normally distributed random variable.

Figure 14.8 illustrates the model assumptions and their implications; note that in this graphical interpretation, the value of $E(y)$ changes according to the specific value of x considered. However, regardless of the x value, the probability distribution of ϵ and hence the probability distributions of y are normally distributed, each with the same variance. The specific value of the error ϵ at any particular point depends on whether the actual value of y is greater than or less than $E(y)$.

At this point, we must keep in mind that we are also making an assumption or hypothesis about the form of the relationship between x and y. That is, we assume that a straight line represented by $\beta_0 + \beta_1 x$ is the basis for the relationship between the variables. We must not lose sight of the fact that some other model, for instance, $y = \beta_0 + \beta_1 x^2 + \epsilon$, may turn out to be a better model for the underlying relationship.

14.5   Testing for Significance

In a simple linear regression equation, the mean or expected value of y is a linear function of x: $E(y) = \beta_0 + \beta_1 x$. If the value of β_1 is zero, $E(y) = \beta_0 + (0)x = \beta_0$. In this case, the mean value of y does not depend on the value of x and hence we would conclude that x and y are not linearly related. Alternatively, if the value of β_1 is not equal to zero, we would conclude that the two variables are related. Thus, to test for a significant regression relationship, we must conduct a hypothesis test to determine whether the value of β_1 is zero. Two tests are commonly used. Both require an estimate of σ^2, the variance of ϵ in the regression model.

FIGURE 14.8   ASSUMPTIONS FOR THE REGRESSION MODEL

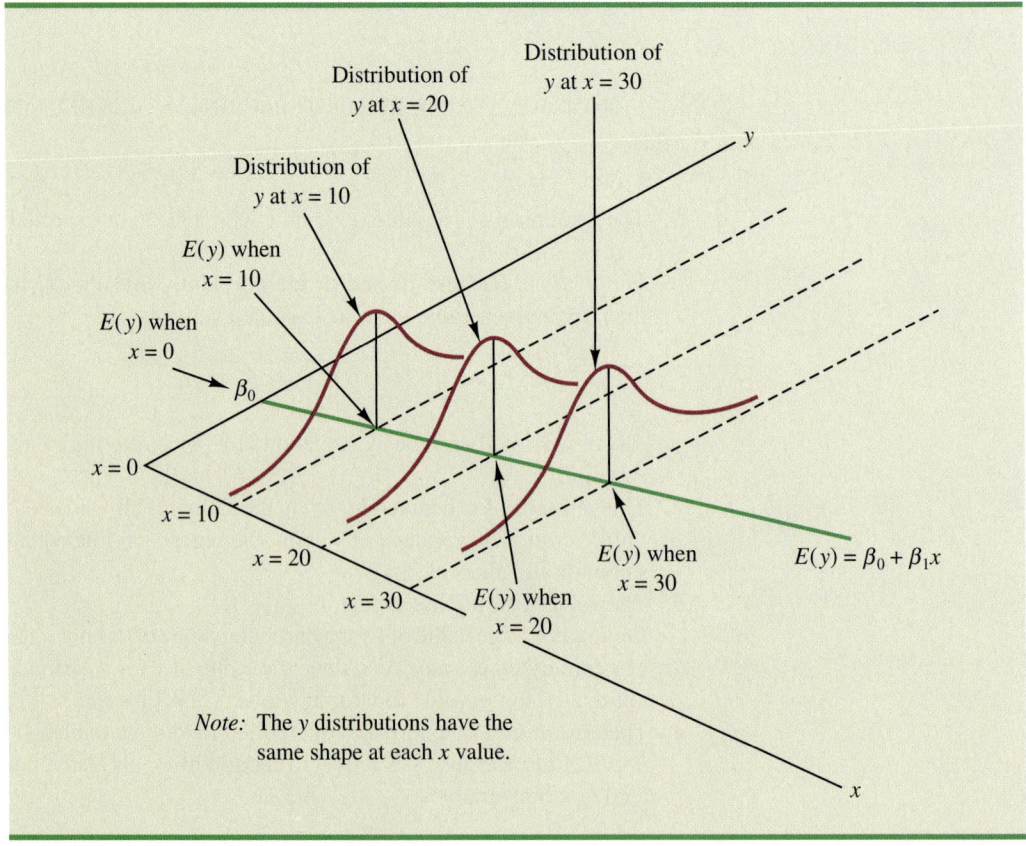

Note: The y distributions have the same shape at each x value.

Estimate of σ^2

From the regression model and its assumptions we can conclude that σ^2, the variance of ϵ, also represents the variance of the y values about the regression line. Recall that the deviations of the y values about the estimated regression line are called residuals. Thus, SSE, the sum of squared residuals, is a measure of the variability of the actual observations about the estimated regression line. The **mean square error** (MSE) provides the estimate of σ^2; it is SSE divided by its degrees of freedom.

With $\hat{y}_i = b_0 + b_1 x_i$, SSE can be written as

$$\text{SSE} = \Sigma(y_i - \hat{y}_i)^2 = \Sigma(y_i - b_0 - b_1 x_i)^2$$

Every sum of squares is associated with a number called its degrees of freedom. Statisticians have shown that SSE has $n - 2$ degrees of freedom because two parameters (β_0 and β_1) must be estimated to compute SSE. Thus, the mean square is computed by dividing SSE by $n - 2$. MSE provides an unbiased estimator of σ^2. Because the value of MSE provides an estimate of σ^2, the notation s^2 is also used.

MEAN SQUARE ERROR (ESTIMATE OF σ^2)

$$s^2 = \text{MSE} = \frac{\text{SSE}}{n - 2} \qquad \textbf{(14.15)}$$

In Section 14.3 we showed that for the Armand's Pizza Parlors example, SSE = 1530; hence,

$$s^2 = \text{MSE} = \frac{1530}{8} = 191.25$$

provides an unbiased estimate of σ^2.

To estimate σ we take the square root of s^2. The resulting value, s, is referred to as the **standard error of the estimate**.

STANDARD ERROR OF THE ESTIMATE

$$s = \sqrt{\text{MSE}} = \sqrt{\frac{\text{SSE}}{n - 2}} \qquad \textbf{(14.16)}$$

For the Armand's Pizza Parlors example, $s = \sqrt{\text{MSE}} = \sqrt{191.25} = 13.829$. In the following discussion, we use the standard error of the estimate in the tests for a significant relationship between x and y.

t Test

The simple linear regression model is $y = \beta_0 + \beta_1 x + \epsilon$. If x and y are linearly related, we must have $\beta_1 \neq 0$. The purpose of the t test is to see whether we can conclude that $\beta_1 \neq 0$. We will use the sample data to test the following hypotheses about the parameter β_1.

$$H_0: \beta_1 = 0$$
$$H_a: \beta_1 \neq 0$$

If H_0 is rejected, we will conclude that $\beta_1 \neq 0$ and that a statistically significant relationship exists between the two variables. However, if H_0 cannot be rejected, we will have insufficient evidence to conclude that a significant relationship exists. The properties of the sampling distribution of b_1, the least squares estimator of β_1, provide the basis for the hypothesis test.

First, let us consider what would happen if we used a different random sample for the same regression study. For example, suppose that Armand's Pizza Parlors used the sales records of a different sample of 10 restaurants. A regression analysis of this new sample might result in an estimated regression equation similar to our previous estimated regression equation $\hat{y} = 60 + 5x$. However, it is doubtful that we would obtain exactly the same equation (with an intercept of exactly 60 and a slope of exactly 5). Indeed, b_0 and b_1, the least squares estimators, are sample statistics with their own sampling distributions. The properties of the sampling distribution of b_1 follow.

SAMPLING DISTRIBUTION OF b_1

Expected Value

$$E(b_1) = \beta_1$$

Standard Deviation

$$\sigma_{b_1} = \frac{\sigma}{\sqrt{\Sigma(x_i - \bar{x})^2}} \qquad \textbf{(14.17)}$$

Distribution Form

Normal

Note that the expected value of b_1 is equal to β_1, so b_1 is an unbiased estimator of β_1.

Because we do not know the value of σ, we develop an estimate of σ_{b_1}, denoted s_{b_1}, by estimating σ with s in equation (14.17). Thus, we obtain the following estimate of σ_{b_1}.

The standard deviation of b_1 is also referred to as the standard error of b_1. Thus, s_{b_1} provides an estimate of the standard error of b_1.

ESTIMATED STANDARD DEVIATION OF b_1

$$s_{b_1} = \frac{s}{\sqrt{\Sigma(x_i - \bar{x})^2}} \qquad \textbf{(14.18)}$$

For Armand's Pizza Parlors, $s = 13.829$. Hence, using $\Sigma(x_i - \bar{x})^2 = 568$ as shown in Table 14.2, we have

$$s_{b_1} = \frac{13.829}{\sqrt{568}} = .5803$$

as the estimated standard deviation of b_1.

The t test for a significant relationship is based on the fact that the test statistic

$$\frac{b_1 - \beta_1}{s_{b_1}}$$

follows a t distribution with $n - 2$ degrees of freedom. If the null hypothesis is true, then $\beta_1 = 0$ and $t = b_1/s_{b_1}$.

Let us conduct this test of significance for Armand's Pizza Parlors at the $\alpha = .01$ level of significance. The test statistic is

$$t = \frac{b_1}{s_{b_1}} = \frac{5}{.5803} = 8.62$$

Using Excel, p-value =
TDIST(8.62,8,2) = .0000.

The t distribution table shows that with $n - 2 = 10 - 2 = 8$ degrees of freedom, $t = 3.355$ provides an area of .005 in the upper tail. Thus, the area in the upper tail of the t distribution corresponding to the test statistic $t = 8.62$ must be less than .005. Because this test is a two-tailed test, we double this value to conclude that the p-value associated with $t = 8.62$ must be less than $2(.005) = .01$. Excel can be used to show that $t = 8.62$ provides a p-value = .0000. Because the p-value $\leq \alpha = .01$, we reject H_0 and conclude that β_1 is not equal to zero. This evidence is sufficient to conclude that a significant relationship exists between student population and quarterly sales. A summary of the t test for significance in simple linear regression follows.

---

t TEST FOR SIGNIFICANCE IN SIMPLE LINEAR REGRESSION

$$H_0: \beta_1 = 0$$
$$H_a: \beta_1 \neq 0$$

TEST STATISTIC

$$t = \frac{b_1}{s_{b_1}} \qquad \textbf{(14.19)}$$

REJECTION RULE

p-value approach:	Reject H_0 if p-value $\leq \alpha$
Critical value approach:	Reject H_0 if $t \leq -t_{\alpha/2}$ or if $t \geq t_{\alpha/2}$

where $t_{\alpha/2}$ is based on a t distribution with $n - 2$ degrees of freedom.

Confidence Interval for β_1

The form of a confidence interval for β_1 is as follows:

$$b_1 \pm t_{\alpha/2} s_{b_1}$$

The point estimator is b_1 and the margin of error is $t_{\alpha/2} s_{b_1}$. The confidence coefficient associated with this interval is $1 - \alpha$, and $t_{\alpha/2}$ is the t value providing an area of $\alpha/2$ in the upper tail of a t distribution with $n - 2$ degrees of freedom. For example, suppose that we wanted to develop a 99% confidence interval estimate of β_1 for Armand's Pizza Parlors. From Table 2 of Appendix B we find that the t value corresponding to $\alpha = .01$ and $n - 2 = 10 - 2 = 8$ degrees of freedom is $t_{.005} = 3.355$. Thus, the 99% confidence interval estimate of β_1 is

$$b_1 \pm t_{\alpha/2} s_{b_1} = 5 \pm 3.355(.5803) = 5 \pm 1.95$$

or 3.05 to 6.95.

In using the t test for significance, the hypotheses tested were

$$H_0: \beta_1 = 0$$
$$H_a: \beta_1 \neq 0$$

At the $\alpha = .01$ level of significance, we can use the 99% confidence interval as an alternative for drawing the hypothesis testing conclusion for the Armand's data. Because 0, the hypothesized value of β_1, is not included in the confidence interval (3.05 to 6.95), we can reject H_0 and conclude that a significant statistical relationship exists between the size of the student population and quarterly sales. In general, a confidence interval can be used to test any two-sided hypothesis about β_1. If the hypothesized value of β_1 is contained in the confidence interval, do not reject H_0. Otherwise, reject H_0.

F Test

An F test, based on the F probability distribution, can also be used to test for significance in regression. With only one independent variable, the F test will provide the same conclusion as the t test; that is, if the t test indicates $\beta_1 \neq 0$ and hence a significant relationship, the F test will also indicate a significant relationship. But with more than one independent variable, only the F test can be used to test for an overall significant relationship.

The logic behind the use of the F test for determining whether the regression relationship is statistically significant is based on the development of two independent estimates of σ^2. We explained how MSE provides an estimate of σ^2. If the null hypothesis $H_0: \beta_1 = 0$ is true, the sum of squares due to regression, SSR, divided by its degrees of freedom provides another independent estimate of σ^2. This estimate is called the *mean square due to regression,* or simply the *mean square regression,* and is denoted MSR. In general,

$$MSR = \frac{SSR}{\text{Regression degrees of freedom}}$$

For the models we consider in this text, the regression degrees of freedom is always equal to the number of independent variables in the model:

$$MSR = \frac{SSR}{\text{Number of independent variables}} \tag{14.20}$$

Because we consider only regression models with one independent variable in this chapter, we have MSR = SSR/1 = SSR. Hence, for Armand's Pizza Parlors, MSR = SSR = 14,200.

If the null hypothesis ($H_0: \beta_1 = 0$) is true, MSR and MSE are two independent estimates of σ^2 and the sampling distribution of MSR/MSE follows an F distribution with numerator degrees of freedom equal to 1 and denominator degrees of freedom equal to $n - 2$. Therefore, when $\beta_1 = 0$, the value of MSR/MSE should be close to one. However, if the null hypothesis is false ($\beta_1 \neq 0$), MSR will overestimate σ^2 and the value of MSR/MSE will be inflated; thus, large values of MSR/MSE lead to the rejection of H_0 and the conclusion that the relationship between x and y is statistically significant.

Let us conduct the F test for the Armand's Pizza Parlors example. The test statistic is

$$F = \frac{MSR}{MSE} = \frac{14,200}{191.25} = 74.25$$

The F test and the t test provide identical results for simple linear regression.

The F distribution table (Table 4 of Appendix B) shows that with 1 degree of freedom in the numerator and $n - 2 = 10 - 2 = 8$ degrees of freedom in the denominator, $F = 11.26$ provides an area of .01 in the upper tail. Thus, the area in the upper tail of the F distribution corresponding to the test statistic $F = 74.25$ must be less than .01. Thus, we conclude that the p-value must be less than .01. Excel can be used to show that $F = 74.25$ provides a p-value = .0000. Because the p-value $\leq \alpha = .01$, we reject H_0 and conclude that a significant relationship exists between the size of the student population and quarterly sales. A summary of the F test for significance in simple linear regression follows.

Using Excel, p-value = FDIST(74.25,1,8) = .0000.

F TEST FOR SIGNIFICANCE IN SIMPLE LINEAR REGRESSION

$$H_0: \beta_1 = 0$$
$$H_a: \beta_1 \neq 0$$

If H_0 is false, MSE still provides an unbiased estimate of σ^2 and MSR overestimates σ^2. If H_0 is true, both MSE and MSR provide unbiased estimates of σ^2; in this case the value of MSR/MSE should be close to 1.

TEST STATISTIC

$$F = \frac{MSR}{MSE} \qquad (14.21)$$

REJECTION RULE

p-value approach:	Reject H_0 if p-value $\leq \alpha$
Critical value approach:	Reject H_0 if $F \geq F_\alpha$

where F_α is based on an F distribution with 1 degree of freedom in the numerator and $n - 2$ degrees of freedom in the denominator.

In Chapter 13 we covered analysis of variance (ANOVA) and showed how an **ANOVA table** could be used to provide a convenient summary of the computational aspects of analysis of variance. A similar ANOVA table can be used to summarize the results of the F test for significance in regression. Table 14.5 is the general form of the ANOVA table for simple linear regression. Table 14.6 is the ANOVA table with the F test computations performed for Armand's Pizza Parlors. Regression, Error, and Total are the labels for the three sources of variation, with SSR, SSE, and SST appearing as the corresponding sum of squares in column 2. The degrees of freedom, 1 for SSR, $n - 2$ for SSE, and $n - 1$ for SST, are shown in

TABLE 14.5 GENERAL FORM OF THE ANOVA TABLE FOR SIMPLE LINEAR REGRESSION

In every analysis of variance table the total sum of squares is the sum of the regression sum of squares and the error sum of squares; in addition, the total degrees of freedom is the sum of the regression degrees of freedom and the error degrees of freedom.

Source of Variation	Sum of Squares	Degrees of Freedom	Mean Square	F
Regression	SSR	1	$MSR = \dfrac{SSR}{1}$	$F = \dfrac{MSR}{MSE}$
Error	SSE	$n - 2$	$MSE = \dfrac{SSE}{n - 2}$	
Total	SST	$n - 1$		

TABLE 14.6 ANOVA TABLE FOR THE ARMAND'S PIZZA PARLORS EXAMPLE

Source of Variation	Sum of Squares	Degrees of Freedom	Mean Square	F
Regression	14,200	1	$\frac{14,200}{1} = 14,200$	$\frac{14,200}{191.25} = 74.25$
Error	1,530	8	$\frac{1530}{8} = 191.25$	
Total	15,730	9		

column 3. Column 4 contains the values of MSR and MSE and column 5 contains the value of $F = \text{MSR}/\text{MSE}$. Almost all computer printouts of regression analysis include an ANOVA table summary of the F test for significance.

Some Cautions About the Interpretation of Significance Tests

Regression analysis, which can be used to identify how variables are associated with one another, cannot be used as evidence of a cause-and-effect relationship.

Rejecting the null hypothesis $H_0: \beta_1 = 0$ and concluding that the relationship between x and y is significant does not enable us to conclude that a cause-and-effect relationship is present between x and y. Concluding a cause-and-effect relationship is warranted only if the analyst can provide some type of theoretical justification that the relationship is in fact causal. In the Armand's Pizza Parlors example, we can conclude that there is a significant relationship between the size of the student population x and quarterly sales y; moreover, the estimated regression equation $\hat{y} = 60 + 5x$ provides the least squares estimate of the relationship. We cannot, however, conclude that changes in student population x *cause* changes in quarterly sales y just because we identified a statistically significant relationship. The appropriateness of such a cause-and-effect conclusion is left to supporting theoretical justification and to good judgment on the part of the analyst. Armand's managers felt that increases in the student population were a likely cause of increased quarterly sales. Thus, the result of the significance test enabled them to conclude that a cause-and-effect relationship was present.

In addition, just because we are able to reject $H_0: \beta_1 = 0$ and demonstrate statistical significance does not enable us to conclude that the relationship between x and y is linear. We can state only that x and y are related and that a linear relationship explains a significant portion of the variability in y over the range of values for x observed in the sample. Figure 14.9 illustrates this situation. The test for significance calls for the rejection of the null hypothesis $H_0: \beta_1 = 0$ and leads to the conclusion that x and y are significantly related, but the figure shows that the actual relationship between x and y is not linear. Although the linear approximation provided by $\hat{y} = b_0 + b_1 x$ is good over the range of x values observed in the sample, it becomes poor for x values outside that range.

Given a significant relationship, we should feel confident in using the estimated regression equation for predictions corresponding to x values within the range of the x values observed in the sample. For Armand's Pizza Parlors, this range corresponds to values of x between 2 and 26. Unless other reasons indicate that the model is valid beyond this range, predictions outside the range of the independent variable should be made with caution. For Armand's Pizza Parlors, because the regression relationship has been found significant at the .01 level, we should feel confident using it to predict sales for restaurants where the associated student population is between 2000 and 26,000.

FIGURE 14.9   EXAMPLE OF A LINEAR APPROXIMATION OF A NONLINEAR
RELATIONSHIP

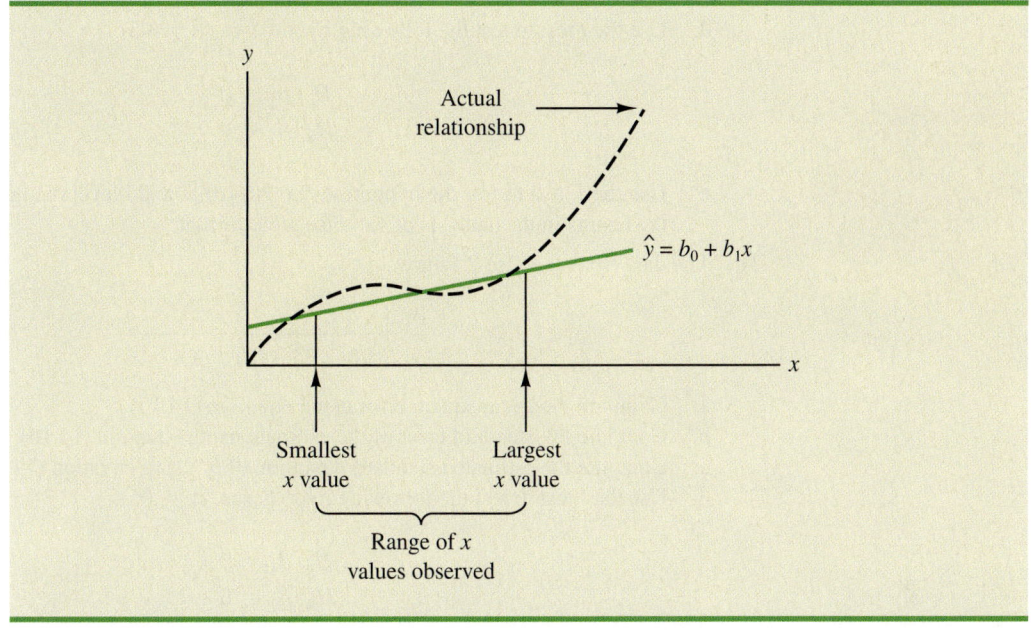

NOTES AND COMMENTS

1. The assumptions made about the error term
(Section 14.4) are what allow the tests of statistical significance in this section. The properties of the sampling distribution of b_1 and the subsequent t and F tests follow directly from these assumptions.

2. Do not confuse statistical significance with practical significance. With very large sample sizes, statistically significant results can be obtained for small values of b_1; in such cases, one must exercise care in concluding that the relationship has practical significance.

3. A test of significance for a linear relationship between x and y can also be performed by using the sample correlation coefficient r_{xy}. With ρ_{xy} denoting the population correlation coefficient, the hypotheses are as follows.

$$H_0: \rho_{xy} = 0$$
$$H_a: \rho_{xy} \neq 0$$

A significant relationship can be concluded if H_0 is rejected. The details of this test are provided in Appendix 14.2. However, the t and F tests presented previously in this section give the same result as the test for significance using the correlation coefficient. Conducting a test for significance using the correlation coefficient therefore is not necessary if a t or F test has already been conducted.

Exercises

Methods

23.   The data from exercise 1 follow.

x_i	1	2	3	4	5
y_i	3	7	5	11	14

a. Compute the mean square error using equation (14.15).
b. Compute the standard error of the estimate using equation (14.16).
c. Compute the estimated standard deviation of b_1 using equation (14.18).
d. Use the t test to test the following hypotheses ($\alpha = .05$):

$$H_0: \beta_1 = 0$$
$$H_a: \beta_1 \neq 0$$

e. Use the F test to test the hypotheses in part (d) at a .05 level of significance. Present the results in the analysis of variance table format.

24. The data from exercise 2 follow.

x_i	2	3	5	1	8
y_i	25	25	20	30	16

a. Compute the mean square error using equation (14.15).
b. Compute the standard error of the estimate using equation (14.16).
c. Compute the estimated standard deviation of b_1 using equation (14.18).
d. Use the t test to test the following hypotheses ($\alpha = .05$):

$$H_0: \beta_1 = 0$$
$$H_a: \beta_1 \neq 0$$

e. Use the F test to test the hypotheses in part (d) at a .05 level of significance. Present the results in the analysis of variance table format.

25. The data from exercise 3 follow.

x_i	2	4	5	7	8
y_i	2	3	2	6	4

a. What is the value of the standard error of the estimate?
b. Test for a significant relationship by using the t test. Use $\alpha = .05$.
c. Use the F test to test for a significant relationship. Use $\alpha = .05$. What is your conclusion?

Applications

26. In exercise 18 the data on grade point average and monthly salary were as follows.

GPA	Monthly Salary ($)	GPA	Monthly Salary ($)
2.6	3300	3.2	3500
3.4	3600	3.5	3900
3.6	4000	2.9	3600

a. Does the t test indicate a significant relationship between grade point average and monthly salary? What is your conclusion? Use $\alpha = .05$.
b. Test for a significant relationship using the F test. What is your conclusion? Use $\alpha = .05$.
c. Show the ANOVA table.

27. *Outside Magazine* tested 10 different models of day hikers and backpacking boots. The following data show the upper support and price for each model tested. Upper support was measured using a rating from 1 to 5, with a rating of 1 denoting average upper support and a rating of 5 denoting excellent upper support (*Outside Magazine Buyer's Guide,* 2001).

Manufacturer and Model	Upper Support	Price ($)
Salomon Super Raid	2	120
Merrell Chameleon Prime	3	125
Teva Challenger	3	130
Vasque Fusion GTX	3	135
Boreal Maigmo	3	150
L.L. Bean GTX Super Guide	5	189
Lowa Kibo	5	190
Asolo AFX 520 GTX	4	195
Raichle Mt. Trail GTX	4	200
Scarpa Delta SL M3	5	220

Boots

a. Use these data to develop an estimated regression equation to estimate the price of a day hiker and backpacking boot given the upper support rating.
b. At the .05 level of significance, determine whether upper support and price are related.
c. Would you feel comfortable using the estimated regression equation developed in part (a) to estimate the price for a day hiker or backpacking boot given the upper support rating?
d. Estimate the price for a day hiker with an upper support rating of 4.

PCs

28. Refer to exercise 10, where an estimated regression equation relating the performance score and the overall rating for notebook PCs was developed. At the .05 level of significance, test whether performance score and overall rating are related. Show the ANOVA table. What is your conclusion?

29. Refer to exercise 21, where data on production volume and cost were used to develop an estimated regression equation relating production volume and cost for a particular manufacturing operation. Use $\alpha = .05$ to test whether the production volume is significantly related to the total cost. Show the ANOVA table. What is your conclusion?

30. Refer to exercise 22 where the following data were used to determine whether the price of a printer is related to the speed for plain text printing (*PC World*, February 2003).

Printers

Name	Type	Speed (ppm)	Price ($)
Minolta-QMS PagePro 1250W	Small Office	12	199
Brother HL-1850	Small Office	10	499
Lexmark E320	Small Office	12.2	299
Minolta-QMS PagePro 1250E	Small Office	10.3	299
HP Laserjet 1200	Small Office	11.7	399
Xerox Phaser 4400/N	Corporate	17.8	1850
Brother HL-2460N	Corporate	16.1	1000
IBM Infoprint 1120n	Corporate	11.8	1387
Lexmark W812	Corporate	19.8	2089
Oki Data B8300n	Corporate	28.2	2200

Does the evidence indicate a significant relationship between printing speed and price? Conduct the appropriate statistical test and state your conclusion. Use $\alpha = .05$.

31. Refer to exercise 20, where an estimated regression equation was developed relating typical household income and typical home price. Test whether the typical household income for a city and the typical home price are related at the .01 level of significance.

14.6 Excel's Regression Tool

In previous sections of this chapter we have shown how Excel can be used for various tasks in a regression analysis. Excel also has a more comprehensive Regression tool. In this section we will illustrate how Excel's Regression tool can be used to perform a complete regression analysis, including statistical tests of significance for the Armand's Pizza Parlors data in Table 14.1.

Using Excel's Regression Tool for the Armand's Pizza Parlors Example

Refer to Figures 14.10 and 14.11 as we describe the tasks involved to use Excel's Regression tool to perform the regression analysis computations for the Armand's data.

Enter Data: The labels Restaurant, Population, and Sales are entered into cells A1:C1 of the worksheet. To identify each of the 10 observations, we entered the numbers 1 through 10 into cells A2:A11. The sample data are entered into cells B2:C11.

Apply Tools: The following steps describe how to use Excel to perform the regression analysis computations performed in Sections 14.2–14.5.

Step 1. Select the **Tools** menu
Step 2. Choose the **Data Analysis** option

FIGURE 14.10   REGRESSION TOOL OUTPUT FOR ARMAND'S PIZZA PARLORS

	A	B	C	D	E	F	G	H	I	J
1	Restaurant	Population	Sales							
2	1	2	58							
3	2	6	105							
4	3	8	88							
5	4	8	118							
6	5	12	117							
7	6	16	137							
8	7	20	157							
9	8	20	169							
10	9	22	149							
11	10	26	202							
12										
13	SUMMARY OUTPUT									
14										
15	*Regression Statistics*									
16	Multiple R	0.9501								
17	R Square	0.9027								
18	Adjusted R Square	0.8906								
19	Standard Error	13.8293								
20	Observations	10								
21										
22	ANOVA									
23		*df*	*SS*	*MS*	*F*	*Significance F*				
24	Regression	1	14200	14200	74.2484	2.55E-05				
25	Residual	8	1530	191.25						
26	Total	9	15730							
27										
28		*Coefficients*	*Standard Error*	*t Stat*	*P-value*	*Lower 95%*	*Upper 95%*	*Lower 99.0%*	*Upper 99.0%*	
29	Intercept	60	9.2260	6.5033	0.0002	38.7247	81.2753	29.0431	90.9569	
30	Population	5	0.5803	8.6167	2.55E-05	3.6619	6.3381	3.0530	6.9470	
31										

FIGURE 14.11   REGRESSION TOOL DIALOG BOX FOR THE ARMAND'S PIZZA
PARLORS EXAMPLE

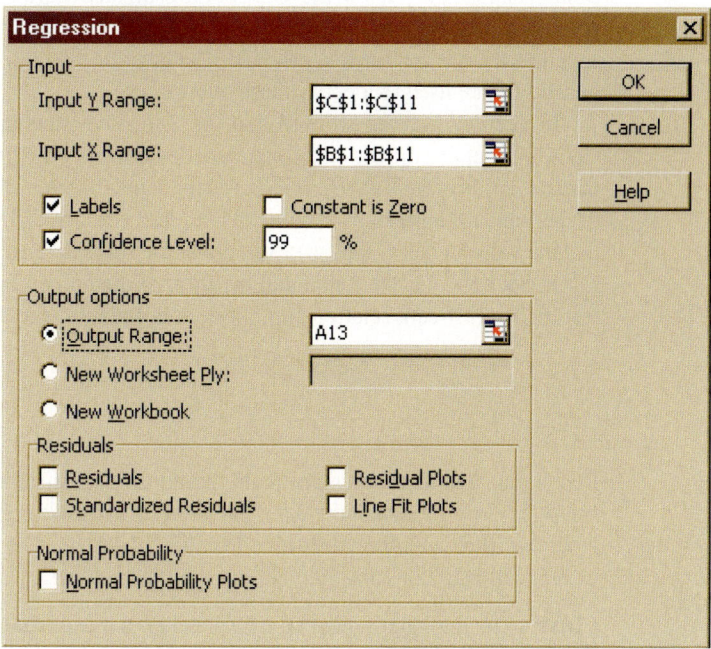

Step 3. Choose **Regression** from the list of Analysis Tools
Step 4. When the Regression dialog box appears (see Figure 14.11):
Enter C1:C11 in the **Input Y Range** box
Enter B1:B11 in the **Input X Range** box
Select **Labels**
Select **Confidence Level**
Enter 99 in the **Confidence Level** box
Select **Output Range**
Enter A13 in the **Output Range** box (to identify the upper left corner of
the section of the worksheet where the output will appear)
Click **OK**

The Excel output can be reformatted to improve readability.

The regression output, titled SUMMARY OUTPUT, begins with row 13 in Figure 14.10. Because Excel initially displays the output using standard column widths, many of the row and column labels are unreadable. In several places we have reformatted to improve readability. We have also reformatted cells displaying numerical values to a maximum of four decimal places. Numbers displayed using scientific notation have not been modified. Regression output in future figures will be similarly reformatted to improve readability.

The first section of the summary output, titled *Regression Statistics,* contains summary statistics such as the coefficient of determination (R Square). The second section of the output, titled ANOVA, contains the analysis of variance table. The last section of the output, which is not titled, contains the estimated regression coefficients and related information. Let us begin our interpretation of the regression output with the information contained in cells A28:I30.

Interpretation of Estimated Regression Equation Output

Row 29 contains information about the y-intercept of the estimated regression line. Row 30 contains information about the slope of the estimated regression line. The y-intercept of the estimated regression line, $b_0 = 60$, is shown in cell B29, and the slope of the estimated regression line, $b_1 = 5$, is shown in cell B30. The label Intercept in cell A29 and the label Population in cell A30 are used to identify these two values.

In Section 14.5 we showed that the estimated standard deviation of b_1 is $s_{b_1} = .5803$. Cell C30 contains the estimated standard deviation of b_1. As we indicated previously, the standard deviation of b_1 is also referred to as the standard error of b_1. Thus, s_{b_1} provides an estimate of the standard error of b_1. The label Standard Error in cell C28 is Excel's way of indicating that the value in cell C30 is the estimate of the standard error, or standard deviation, of b_1.

In Section 14.5 we stated that the form of the null and alternative hypotheses needed to test for a significant relationship between population and sales are as follows:

$$H_0: \beta_1 = 0$$
$$H_a: \beta_1 \neq 0$$

Recall that the t test for a significant relationship required the computation of the t statistic, $t = b_1/s_{b_1}$. For the Armand's data, the value of t that we computed was $t = 5/.5803 = 8.62$. Note that after rounding, the value in cell D30 is 8.62. The label in cell D28, t *Stat,* reminds us that cell D30 contains the value of the t test statistic.

t Test   The information in cell E30 provides a means for conducting a test of significance. The value in cell E30 is the p-value associated with the t test for significance. Excel has displayed the p-value using scientific notation. To obtain the decimal equivalent, we move the decimal point 5 places to the left; we obtain a p-value of .0000255. Thus, the p-value associated with the t test for significance is .0000255. Given the level of significance α, the decision of whether to reject H_0 can be made as follows:

$$\text{Reject } H_0 \text{ if } p\text{-value} \leq \alpha$$

Because the p-value $= .0000255 < \alpha = .01$, we can reject H_0 and conclude that we have a significant relationship between student population and sales. Because p-values are provided as part of the computer output for regression analysis, the p-value approach is most often used for hypothesis tests in regression analysis.

The information in cells F28:I30 can be used to develop confidence interval estimates of the y-intercept and slope of the estimated regression equation. Excel always provides the lower and upper limits for a 95% confidence interval. Recall that in the Regression dialog box (see Figure 14.11) we selected Confidence Level and entered 99 in the Confidence Level box. As a result, Excel's Regression tool also provides the lower and upper limits for a 99% confidence interval. For instance, the value in cell H30 is the lower limit for the 99% confidence interval estimate of β_1 and the value in cell I30 is the upper limit. Thus, after rounding, the 99% confidence interval estimate of β_1 is 3.05 to 6.95. The values in cells F30 and G30 provide the lower and upper limits for the 95% confidence interval. Thus, the 95% confidence interval is 3.66 to 6.34.

Interpretation of ANOVA Output

Excel refers to the error sum of squares as the residual sum of squares.

The information in cells A22:F26 summarizes the analysis of variance computations for the Armand's data. The three sources of variation are labeled Regression, Residual, and Total. The label *df* in cell B23 stands for degrees of freedom, the label *SS* in cell C23 stands for sum of squares, and the label *MS* in cell D23 stands for mean square. Looking at cells C24:C26, we see that the regression sum of squares is 14200, the residual or error sum of squares is 1530, and the total sum of squares is 15730. The values in cells B24:B26 are the degrees of freedom corresponding to each sum of squares. Thus, the regression sum of squares has 1 degree of freedom, the residual or error sum of squares has 8 degrees of freedom, and the total sum of squares has 9 degrees of freedom. As we discussed previously, the regression degrees of freedom plus the residual degrees of freedom are equal to the total degrees of freedom, and the regression sum of squares plus the residual sum of squares are equal to the total sum of squares.

In Section 14.5 we stated that the mean square error, obtained by dividing the error or residual sum of squares by its degrees of freedom, provides an estimate of σ^2. The value in cell D25, 191.25, is the mean square error for the Armand's regression output. We also stated that the mean square regression is the sum of squares due to regression divided by the regression degrees of freedom. The value in cell D24, 14200, is the mean square regression.

F Test   In Section 14.5 we showed that an F test, based upon the F probability distribution, could also be used to test for significance in regression. The value in cell F24, .0000255, is the p-value associated with the F test for significance. Because the p-value $= .0000255 <$ $\alpha = .01$, we can reject H_0 and conclude that we have a significant relationship between student population and sales. Note that it is the same conclusion that we obtained using the p-value approach for the t test for significance. In fact, because the t test for significance is equivalent to the F test for significance in simple linear regression, the p-values provided by both approaches are identical. The label Excel uses to identify the p-value for the F test for significance, shown in cell F23, is *Significance F*. In Chapter 9 we also stated that the p-value is often referred to as the observed level of significance. Thus, the label *Significance F* may be more meaningful if you think of the value in cell F24 as the observed level of significance for the F test.

Interpretation of Regression Statistics Output

The output in cells A15:B20 summarizes the regression statistics. The number of observations in the data set, 10, is shown in cell B20. The coefficient of determination, .9027, appears in cell B17; the corresponding label, R Square, is shown in cell A17. The square root of the coefficient of determination provides the sample correlation coefficient of 0.9501 shown in cell B16. Note that Excel uses the label Multiple R (cell A16) to identify this value. In cell A19, the label Standard Error is used to identify the value of s, the estimate of σ. Cell B19 shows that the value of s is 13.8293. We caution the reader to keep in mind that in the Excel output, the label Standard Error appears in two different places. In the Regression Statistics section of the output the label Standard Error refers to s, the estimate of σ. In the Estimated Regression Equation section of the output, the label Standard Error refers to s_{b_1}, the estimated standard deviation of the sampling distribution of b_1.

NOTES AND COMMENTS

1. The PredInt.xls macro, developed by Professor John O. McClain, Johnson Graduate School of Management, Cornell University, includes a wide variety of regression capabilities in an easy-to-use format. A copy of the PredInt.xls macro is included on the data disk. Instructions for using the macro are provided as part of the macro.

2. In Appendix 14.3 we show how to use SWStat+ to perform the regression analysis computations for the Armand's Pizza Parlors data. The regression analysis capabilities of SWStat+ are more comprehensive than those available using Excel's Regression tool.

EXERCISES

Applications

32. Following is a portion of the Excel output for a regression analysis relating maintenance expense (dollars per month) to usage (hours per week) for a particular brand of computer terminal.

ANOVA

	df	SS
Regression	1	1575.76
Residual	8	349.14
Total	9	1924.90

	Coefficients	Standard Error	t Stat
Intercept	6.1092	.9361	
Usage	0.8951	.149	

a. Write the estimated regression equation.
b. Use a t test to determine whether monthly maintenance expense is related to usage at the .05 level of significance.
c. Did the estimated regression equation provide a good fit? Explain.

33. The commercial division of a real estate firm conducted a study to determine the extent of the relationship between annual gross rents ($1000s) and the selling price ($1000s) for apartment buildings. Data were collected on several properties sold, and Excel's Regression tool was used to develop an estimated regression equation. A portion of the Excel output follows.

ANOVA

	df	SS	MS	F
Regression	1	41587.3		
Residual	7			
Total	8	51984.1		

	Coefficients	Standard Error	t Stat
Intercept	20.000	3.2213	6.21
Annual Gross Rents	7.210	1.3626	5.29

a. How many apartment buildings were in the sample?
b. Write the estimated regression equation.
c. Use the t test to determine whether the selling price is related to annual gross rents. Use $\alpha = .05$.
d. Use the F test to determine whether the selling price is related to annual gross rents. Use $\alpha = .05$.
e. Estimate the selling price of an apartment building with gross annual rents of $50,000.

34. A regression model relating the number of salespersons at a branch office to annual sales at the office (in thousands of dollars) provided the following Excel output.

ANOVA

	df	SS	MS	F
Regression		6828.6		
Residual				
Total		9127.4		

	Coefficients	Standard Error	t Stat	P-value
Intercept	80.0	11.333		
Number of Salespersons	50.0	5.482		

    a.   Write the estimated regression equation.

    b.   Compute the F statistic and test the significance of the relationship at the .05 level of significance.

    c.   Compute the t statistic and test the significance of the relationship at the .05 level of significance.

    d.   Compute the p-value associated with the t test for significance.

35.   Health experts recommend that runners drink 4 ounces of water every 15 minutes they run. Although handheld bottles work well for many types of runs, all-day cross-country runs require hip-mounted or over-the-shoulder hydration systems. In addition to carrying more water, hip-mounted or over-the-shoulder hydration systems offer more storage space for food and extra clothing. As the capacity increases, however, the weight and cost of these larger-capacity systems also increase. The following data show the weight (ounces) and the price for 26 hip-mounted or over-the-shoulder hydration systems (*Trail Runner Gear Guide*, 2003).

Hydration1

Model	Weight (oz.)	Price ($)	Model	Weight (oz.)	Price ($)
Fastdraw	3	10	Elite	14	60
Fastdraw Plus	4	12	Extender	16	65
Fitness	5	12	Stinger	16	65
Access	7	20	GelFlask Belt	3	20
Access Plus	8	25	GelDraw	1	7
Solo	9	25	GelFlask Clip-on Holster	2	10
Serenade	9	35	GelFlask Holster SS	1	10
Solitaire	11	35	Strider (W)	8	30
Gemini	21	45	Walkabout (W)	14	40
Shadow	15	40	Solitude I.C.E.	9	35
SipStream	18	60	Getaway I.C.E.	19	55
Express	9	30	Profile I.C.E.	14	50
Lightning	12	40	Traverse I.C.E.	13	60

    a.   Use these data to develop an estimated regression equation that could be used to predict the price of a hydration system given its weight.

    b.   Test the significance of the relationship at the .05 level of significance.

    c.   Did the estimated regression equation provide a good fit? Explain.

36.   Cushman & Wakefield, Inc., collects data showing the office building vacancy rates and rental rates for markets in the United States. The following data show the overall vacancy rates (%) and the average rental rates (per square foot) for the central business district for 18 selected markets (*The Wall Street Journal Almanac 1998*).

OffRates

Market	Vacancy Rate (%)	Average Rate ($)	Market	Vacancy Rate (%)	Average Rate ($)
Atlanta	21.9	18.54	San Francisco	6.6	31.42
Boston	6.0	33.70	Phoenix	15.9	18.74
Hartford	22.8	19.67	San Jose	9.2	26.76
Baltimore	18.1	21.01	West Palm Beach	19.7	27.72
Washington	12.7	35.09	Detroit	20.0	18.20
Philadelphia	14.5	19.41	Brooklyn	8.3	25.00
Miami	20.0	25.28	Downtown, NY	17.1	29.78
Tampa	19.2	17.02	Midtown, NY	10.8	37.03
Chicago	16.0	24.04	Midtown South, NY	11.1	28.64

a.   Develop a scatter diagram for these data; plot the vacancy rate on the horizontal axis.
b.   Does there appear to be any relationship between these two variables?
c.   Develop the estimated regression equation that could be used to predict the average rental rate given the overall vacancy rate.
d.   Test the significance of the relationship at the .05 level of significance.
e.   Did the estimated regression equation provide a good fit? Explain.

14.7   Using the Estimated Regression Equation for Estimation and Prediction

When using the simple linear regression model we are making an assumption about the relationship between x and y. We then use the least squares method to obtain the estimated simple linear regression equation. If a significant relationship exists between x and y, and the coefficient of determination shows that the fit is good, the estimated regression equation should be useful for estimation and prediction.

Point Estimation

In the Armand's Pizza Parlors example, the estimated regression equation $\hat{y} = 60 + 5x$ provides an estimate of the relationship between the size of the student population x and quarterly sales y. We can use the estimated regression equation to develop a point estimate of the mean value of y for a particular value of x or to predict an individual value of y corresponding to a given value of x. For instance, suppose Armand's managers want a point estimate of the mean quarterly sales for all restaurants located near college campuses with 10,000 students. Using the estimated regression equation $\hat{y} = 60 + 5x$, we see that for $x = 10$ (or 10,000 students), $\hat{y} = 60 + 5(10) = 110$. Thus, a point estimate of the mean quarterly sales for all restaurants located near campuses with 10,000 students is $110,000.

Now suppose Armand's managers want to predict sales for an individual restaurant located near Talbot College, a school with 10,000 students. In this case we are not interested in the mean value for all restaurants located near campuses with 10,000 students; we are just interested in predicting quarterly sales for one individual restaurant. As it turns out, the point estimate for an individual value of y is the same as the point estimate for the mean value of y. Hence, we would predict quarterly sales of $\hat{y} = 60 + 5(10) = 110$ or $110,000 for this one restaurant.

Interval Estimation

Confidence intervals and prediction intervals show the precision of the regression results. Narrower intervals provide a higher degree of precision.

Point estimates do not provide any information about the precision associated with an estimate. For that we must develop interval estimates much like those in Chapters 8, 10, and 11. The first type of interval estimate, a **confidence interval**, is an interval estimate of the *mean value of y* for a given value of x. The second type of interval estimate, a **prediction interval**, is used whenever we want an interval estimate of an *individual value of y* for a given value of x. The point estimate of the mean value of y is the same as the point estimate of an individual value of y. But, the interval estimates we obtain for the two cases are different. The margin of error is larger for a prediction interval.

Confidence Interval Estimate of the Mean Value of y

The estimated regression equation provides a point estimate of the mean value of y for a given value of x. In developing the confidence interval, we will use the following notation.

x_p = the particular or given value of the independent variable x
y_p = the value of the dependent variable y corresponding to the given x_p

$E(y_p)$ = the mean or expected value of the dependent variable y
corresponding to the given x_p

$\hat{y}_p = b_0 + b_1 x_p$ = the point estimate of $E(y_p)$ when $x = x_p$

Using this notation to estimate the mean sales for all Armand's restaurants located near a campus with 10,000 students, we have $x_p = 10$, and $E(y_p)$ denotes the unknown mean value of sales for all restaurants where $x_p = 10$. The point estimate of $E(y_p)$ is provided by $\hat{y}_p = 60 + 5(10) = 110$.

In general, we cannot expect $\hat{y}_p$ to equal $E(y_p)$ exactly. If we want to make an inference about how close $\hat{y}_p$ is to the true mean value $E(y_p)$, we will have to estimate the variance of $\hat{y}_p$. The formula for estimating the variance of $\hat{y}_p$ given x_p, denoted by $s_{\hat{y}_p}^2$, is

$$s_{\hat{y}_p}^2 = s^2 \left[\frac{1}{n} + \frac{(x_p - \bar{x})^2}{\Sigma(x_i - \bar{x})^2} \right] \tag{14.22}$$

The estimate of the standard deviation of $\hat{y}_p$ is given by the square root of equation (14.22).

$$s_{\hat{y}_p} = s \sqrt{\frac{1}{n} + \frac{(x_p - \bar{x})^2}{\Sigma(x_i - \bar{x})^2}} \tag{14.23}$$

The computational results for Armand's Pizza Parlors in Section 14.5 provided $s = 13.829$. With $x_p = 10$, $\bar{x} = 14$, and $\Sigma(x_i - \bar{x})^2 = 568$, we can use equation (14.23) to obtain

$$s_{\hat{y}_p} = 13.829 \sqrt{\frac{1}{10} + \frac{(10 - 14)^2}{568}}$$

$$= 13.829 \sqrt{.1282} = 4.95$$

The general expression for a confidence interval follows.

CONFIDENCE INTERVAL FOR $E(y_p)$

The margin of error associated with this internal estimate is $t_{\alpha/2} s_{\hat{y}_p}$.

$$\hat{y}_p \pm t_{\alpha/2} s_{\hat{y}_p} \tag{14.24}$$

where the confidence coefficient is $1 - \alpha$ and $t_{\alpha/2}$ is based on a t distribution with $n - 2$ degrees of freedom.

Using expression (14.24) to develop a 95% confidence interval of the mean quarterly sales for all Armand's restaurants located near campuses with 10,000 students, we need the value of t for $\alpha/2 = .025$ and $n - 2 = 10 - 2 = 8$ degrees of freedom. Using Table 2 of Appendix B, we have $t_{.025} = 2.306$. Thus, with $\hat{y}_p = 110$ and a margin of error of $t_{\alpha/2} s_{\hat{y}_p} = 2.306(4.95) = 11.415$, the 95% confidence interval estimate is

$$110 \pm 11.415$$

In dollars, the 95% confidence interval for the mean quarterly sales of all restaurants near campuses with 10,000 students is \$110,000 $\pm$ \$11,415. Therefore, the 95% confidence interval for the mean quarterly sales when the student population is 10,000 is \$98,585 to \$121,415.

Note that the estimated standard deviation of $\hat{y}_p$ given by equation (14.23) is smallest when $x_p = \bar{x}$ and the quantity $x_p - \bar{x} = 0$. In this case, the estimated standard deviation of $\hat{y}_p$ becomes

$$s_{\hat{y}_p} = s\sqrt{\frac{1}{n} + \frac{(\bar{x} - \bar{x})^2}{\Sigma(x_i - \bar{x})^2}} = s\sqrt{\frac{1}{n}}$$

This result implies that we can make the best or most precise estimate of the mean value of y whenever $x_p = \bar{x}$. In fact, the farther x_p is from $\bar{x}$, the larger $x_p - \bar{x}$ becomes. As a result, confidence intervals for the mean value of y will become wider as x_p deviates more from $\bar{x}$. This pattern is shown graphically in Figure 14.12.

Prediction Interval Estimate of an Individual Value of y

Suppose that instead of estimating the mean value of sales for all Armand's restaurants located near campuses with 10,000 students, we want to estimate the sales for an individual restaurant located near Talbot College, a school with 10,000 students. As noted previously, the point estimate of y_p, the value of y corresponding to the given x_p, is provided by the estimated regression equation $\hat{y}_p = b_0 + b_1 x_p$. For the restaurant at Talbot College, we have $x_p = 10$ and a corresponding predicted quarterly sales of $\hat{y}_p = 60 + 5(10) = 110$, or $110,000. Note that this value is the same as the point estimate of the mean sales for all restaurants located near campuses with 10,000 students.

FIGURE 14.12   CONFIDENCE INTERVALS FOR THE MEAN SALES y AT GIVEN VALUES OF STUDENT POPULATION x

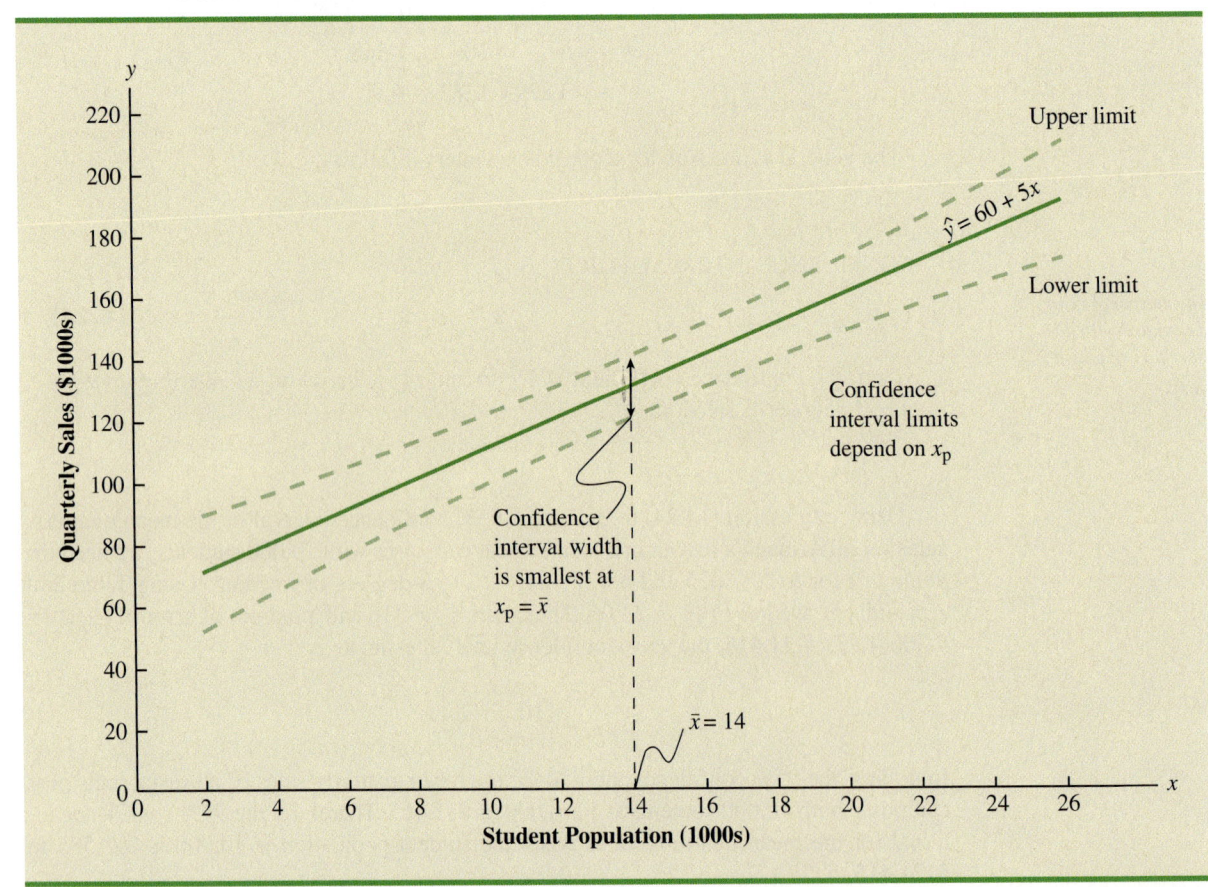

To develop a prediction interval, we must first determine the variance associated with using $\hat{y}_p$ as an estimate of an individual value of y when $x = x_p$. This variance is made up of the sum of the following two components.

1. The variance of individual y values about the mean $E(y_p)$, an estimate of which is given by s^2
2. The variance associated with using $\hat{y}_p$ to estimate $E(y_p)$, an estimate of which is given by $s^2_{\hat{y}_p}$

The formula for estimating the variance of an individual value of y_p, denoted by s^2_{ind}, is

$$
\begin{aligned}
s^2_{ind} &= s^2 + s^2_{\hat{y}_p} \\
&= s^2 + s^2\left[\frac{1}{n} + \frac{(x_p - \bar{x})^2}{\Sigma(x_i - \bar{x})^2}\right] \\
&= s^2\left[1 + \frac{1}{n} + \frac{(x_p - \bar{x})^2}{\Sigma(x_i - \bar{x})^2}\right]
\end{aligned}
\tag{14.25}
$$

Hence, an estimate of the standard deviation of an individual value of y_p is given by

$$
s_{ind} = s\sqrt{1 + \frac{1}{n} + \frac{(x_p - \bar{x})^2}{\Sigma(x_i - \bar{x})^2}}
\tag{14.26}
$$

For Armand's Pizza Parlors, the estimated standard deviation corresponding to the prediction of sales for one specific restaurant located near a campus with 10,000 students is computed as follows.

$$
\begin{aligned}
s_{ind} &= 13.829\sqrt{1 + \frac{1}{10} + \frac{(10 - 14)^2}{568}} \\
&= 13.829\sqrt{1.1282} \\
&= 14.69
\end{aligned}
$$

The general expression for a prediction interval follows.

The margin of error associated with this interval estimate is $t_{\alpha/2}s_{ind}$.

PREDICTION INTERVAL FOR y_p

$$
\hat{y}_p \pm t_{\alpha/2}s_{ind}
\tag{14.27}
$$

where the confidence coefficient is $1 - \alpha$ and $t_{\alpha/2}$ is based on a t distribution with $n - 2$ degrees of freedom.

The 95% prediction interval for quarterly sales at Armand's restaurant located near Talbot College can be found by using $t_{.025} = 2.306$ and $s_{ind} = 14.69$. Thus, with $\hat{y}_p = 110$ and a margin of error of $t_{\alpha/2}s_{ind} = 2.306(14.69) = 33.875$, the 95% prediction interval is

$$
110 \pm 33.875
$$

In dollars, this prediction interval is $110,000 \pm \$33,875$ or $76,125 to \$143,875$. Note that the prediction interval for an individual restaurant located near a campus with 10,000 students is wider than the confidence interval for the mean sales of all restaurants located near campuses with 10,000 students. The difference reflects the fact that we are able to estimate the mean value of y more precisely than we can an individual value of y.

Both confidence interval estimates and prediction interval estimates are most precise when the value of the independent variable is $x_p = \bar{x}$. The general shapes of confidence intervals and the wider prediction intervals are shown together in Figure 14.13.

Using Excel to Develop Confidence and Prediction Interval Estimates

Excel's Regression tool does not have an option for computing confidence and prediction intervals. But, for simple linear regression, formulas can be designed to compute these intervals using equations (14.24) and (14.27) along with the output provided by the Regression tool. The general expression for a confidence or prediction interval is point estimate $\pm$ margin of error. Thus, we must develop formulas for computing a point estimate and the margin of error.

We begin by showing how to develop a 95% confidence interval estimate of the mean quarterly sales for all Armand's restaurants located near a campus with 10,000 students. In Section 14.6, we showed how Excel's Regression tool could be applied to the Armand's problem. The output provided by the Regression tool is shown again in cells A13:I30 of Figure 14.14. Now refer to cells E1:F13 of that figure as we describe the tasks involved in developing a confidence interval. The formula worksheet is in the background; the value worksheet appears in the foreground.

Enter Data: The data (cells B2:C11) and regression output (cells A13:I30) that were initially developed in Figure 14.10 are used as a starting point here.

FIGURE 14.13   CONFIDENCE AND PREDICTION INTERVALS FOR SALES y AT GIVEN VALUES OF STUDENT POPULATION x

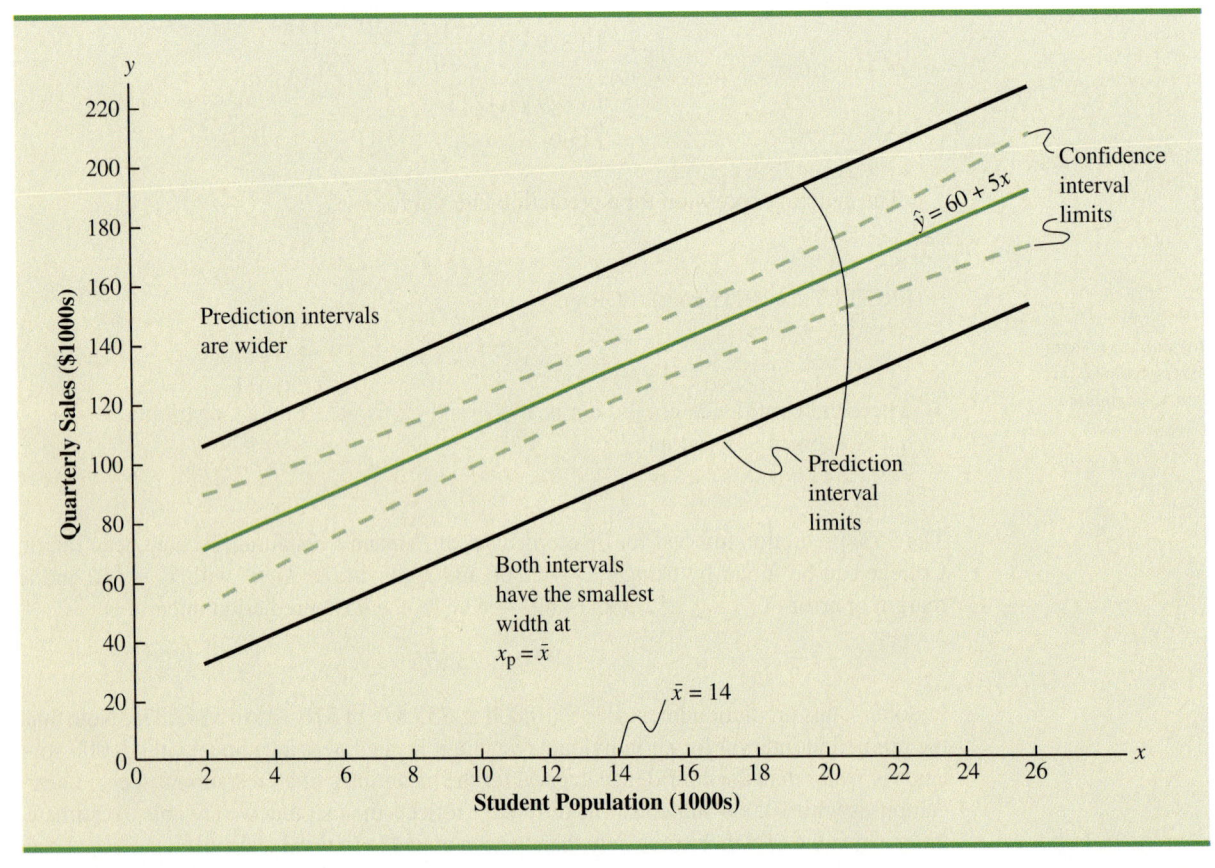

FIGURE 14.14   USING EXCEL TO COMPUTE CONFIDENCE AND PREDICTION INTERVALS

	A	B	C	D	E	F	G	H	I	J
1	Restaurant	Population	Sales		Confidence Interval					
2	1	2	58		Given value of x	10				
3	2	6	105		xbar	=AVERAGE(B2:B11)				
4	3	8	88		x-xbar	=F2-F3				
5	4	8	118		(x-xbar)sq	=F4^2				
6	5	12	117		Sum of (x-xbar)sq	=DEVSQ(B2:B11)				
7	6	16	137		Var of yhat	=D25*(1/B20+F5/F6)				
8	7	20	157		Stdev of yhat	=SQRT(F7)				
9	8	20	169		t value	=TINV(0.05,8)				
10	9	22	149		Margin of Error	=F9*F8				
11	10	26	202		Point Estimate	=B29+B30*F2				
12					Lower Limit	=F11-F10				
13	SUMMARY OUTPUT				Upper Limit	=F11+F10				
14										
15	*Regression Statistics*				Prediction Interval					
16	Multiple R	0.95012295520			Var of yind	=D25+F7				
17	R Square	0.90273363000			Stdev of yind	=SQRT(F16)				
18	Adjusted R Square	0.89057533375			Margin of Error	=F9*F17				
19	Standard Error	13.8293166859			Lower Limit	=F11-F18				
20	Observations	10			Upper Limit	=F11+F18				
21										
22	ANOVA									
23		*df*								
24	Regression	1								
25	Residual	8								
26	Total	9								
27										
28		*Coefficients*								
29	Intercept	60								
30	Population	5								
31										

	A	B	C	D	E	F	G	H	I	J
1	Restaurant	Population	Sales		Confidence Interval					
2	1	2	58		Given value of x	10				
3	2	6	105		xbar	14				
4	3	8	88		x-xbar	-4				
5	4	8	118		(x-xbar)sq	16				
6	5	12	117		Sum of (x-xbar)sq	568				
7	6	16	137		Var of yhat	24.5123				
8	7	20	157		Stdev of yhat	4.9510				
9	8	20	169		t value	2.3060				
10	9	22	149		Margin of Error	11.4170				
11	10	26	202		Point Estimate	110				
12					Lower Limit	98.5830				
13	SUMMARY OUTPUT				Upper Limit	121.4170				
14										
15	*Regression Statistics*				Prediction Interval					
16	Multiple R	0.9501			Var of yind	215.7623				
17	R Square	0.9027			Stdev of yind	14.6889				
18	Adjusted R Square	0.8906			Margin of Error	33.8725				
19	Standard Error	13.8293			Lower Limit	76.1275				
20	Observations	10			Upper Limit	143.8725				
21										
22	ANOVA									
23		*df*	*SS*	*MS*	*F*	*Significance F*				
24	Regression	1	14200	14200	74.2484	2.55E-05				
25	Residual	8	1530	191.25						
26	Total	9	15730							
27										
28		*Coefficients*	*Standard Error*	*t Stat*	*P-value*	*Lower 95%*	*Upper 95%*	*Lower 99.0%*	*Upper 99.0%*	
29	Intercept	60	9.2260	6.5033	0.0002	38.7247	81.2753	29.0431	90.9569	
30	Population	5	0.5803	8.6167	2.55E-05	3.6619	6.3381	3.0530	6.9470	
31										

Enter Functions and Formulas: Because we want to develop a 95% confidence interval estimate of the mean quarterly sales for restaurants near campuses with 10,000 students, $x_p = 10$ and we enter a value of 10 into cell F2. Excel's AVERAGE function is used to compute $\bar{x}$ in cell F3, the formula =F2-F3 is entered into cell F4 to compute the value of $x_p - \bar{x}$, and the formula =F4^2 is entered into cell F5 to compute the value of $(x_p - \bar{x})^2$. Excel's DEVSQ function can be used to compute $\Sigma(x_i - \bar{x})^2$ by entering the following formula into cell F6:

$$=DEVSQ(B2:B11)$$

To identify this sum of squares we entered the label "Sum of (x-xbar)sq" into cell E6.

We can now compute $s_{\hat{y}_p}^2$ using equation (14.22) by entering the formula =D25* (1/B20+F5/F6) into cell F7. We then enter the formula =SQRT(F7) into cell F8 to compute $s_{\hat{y}_p}$, the estimate of the standard deviation of $\hat{y}_p$. To compute the t value required by equation (14.24), we entered the formula =TINV(0.05,8) into cell F9. Finally, the margin of error $t_{\alpha/2}s_{\hat{y}_p}$ is computed by entering the formula =F9*F8 into cell F10. To compute $\hat{y}_p$, the point estimate of $E(y_p)$, we entered the formula =B29+B30*F2 into cell F11. The lower and upper limits of the 95% confidence interval are then computed by entering the formulas =F11-F10 and =F11+F10 into cells F12 and F13, respectively.

The value worksheet shows that the 95% confidence interval estimate is 98.583 to 121.417. In dollars, the 95% confidence interval for the mean quarterly sales of restaurants located near campuses with 10,000 students is $98,583 to $121,417. To develop confidence intervals for other values of x_p we simply use this worksheet as a template and enter another value for student population in cell F2. The new confidence interval will appear in cells F12 and F13. If a confidence interval for another value of α is desired, we can just insert the new value of α for the first argument of the TINV function in cell F9.

The confidence interval formulas developed here cannot be applied directly as a template for other regression problems because the number of observations will likely be different and the location of the regression output will not be in the same worksheet cells. The same cells (E1:F13) can be used to develop the confidence interval but the cell references used in cells F3, F6, F7, and F11 will need to be modified to reflect the location of the data and the regression output. The level of significance and the degrees of freedom used for TINV in cell F9 may also need to be changed.

The design of formulas to compute a prediction interval utilizes some of the same information used to develop a confidence interval. However, equation (14.27) shows that s_{ind}, instead of $s_{\hat{y}_p}$, is used in computing the margin of error. Refer to cells E15:F20 of the worksheet in Figure 14.14 as we describe the tasks involved in computing a 95% prediction interval.

Enter Functions and Formulas: To compute $s_{ind}^2 = s^2 + s_{\hat{y}_p}^2$ we entered the formula =D25+F7 into cell F16. Then, in cell F17 we entered the formula =SQRT(F16) to compute s_{ind}. The labels "Var of yind" and "Stdev of yind" were entered into cells E16 and E17 to identify these values. To compute the margin of error the formula =F9*F17 was entered into cell F18. The formulas =F11-F18 and =F11+F18 were entered into cells F19 and F20, respectively, to compute the lower and upper limits.

The 95% prediction interval is 76.127 to 143.873. In dollars, the 95% prediction interval is $76,127 to $143,873. To develop prediction intervals for other values of x_p we simply enter another value for student population in cell F2 and the new prediction interval will appear in cells F19 and F20. If a prediction interval for another value of α is desired, we can just insert the new value of α for the first argument of the TINV function in cell F9.

NOTES AND COMMENTS

1. The PredInt.xls macro, developed by Professor John O. McClain, Johnson Graduate School of Management, Cornell University, can be used to develop confidence and prediction intervals. A copy of the PredInt.xls macro is included on the data disk. Instructions for using the macro are provided as part of the macro.

2. In Appendix 14.3 we show how to use SWStat+ to develop confidence and prediction interval estimates for the Armand's Pizza Parlors data.

EXERCISES

Methods

37.   The data from exercise 1 follow.

x_i	1	2	3	4	5
y_i	3	7	5	11	14

a.   Use equation (14.23) to estimate the standard deviation of $\hat{y}_p$ when $x = 4$.
b.   Use equation (14.24) to develop a 95% confidence interval estimate of the expected value of y when $x = 4$.
c.   Use equation (14.26) to estimate the standard deviation of an individual value of y when $x = 4$.
d.   Use equation (14.27) to develop a 95% prediction interval for y when $x = 4$.

38.   The data from exercise 2 follow.

x_i	2	3	5	1	8
y_i	25	25	20	30	16

a.   Estimate the standard deviation of $\hat{y}_p$ when $x = 3$.
b.   Develop a 95% confidence interval estimate of the expected value of y when $x = 3$.
c.   Estimate the standard deviation of an individual value of y when $x = 3$.
d.   Develop a 95% prediction interval for y when $x = 3$.

39.   The data from exercise 3 follow.

x_i	2	4	5	7	8
y_i	2	3	2	6	4

Develop the 95% confidence and prediction intervals when $x = 3$. Explain why these two intervals are different.

Applications

40.   In exercise 18, the data on grade point average x and monthly salary y provided the estimated regression equation $\hat{y} = 1790.5 + 581.1x$.
a.   Develop a 95% confidence interval estimate of the mean starting salary for all students with a 3.0 GPA.
b.   Develop a 95% prediction interval estimate of the starting salary for Joe Heller, a student with a GPA of 3.0.

PCs

41.   In exercise 10, data on the performance score (x) and the overall rating (y) for notebook PCs provided the estimated regression equation $\hat{y} = 51.82 + .1452x$ (*PC World*, February 2000).
a.   Develop a point estimate of the overall rating for a PC that has a performance score of 200.
b.   Develop a 95% confidence interval estimate of the mean overall score for all PCs that have a performance score of 200.
c.   Suppose that a new PC developed by Dell has a performance score of 200. Develop a 95% prediction interval estimate of the overall score for this new PC.
d.   Discuss the differences in your answers to parts (b) and (c).

42.   In exercise 13, data were given on the adjusted gross income x and the amount of itemized deductions taken by taxpayers. Data were reported in thousands of dollars. With the estimated regression equation $\hat{y} = 4.68 + .16x$, the point estimate of a reasonable level of total itemized deductions for a taxpayer with an adjusted gross income of $52,500 is $13,080.
a.   Develop a 95% confidence interval estimate of the mean amount of total itemized deductions for all taxpayers with an adjusted gross income of $52,500.
b.   Develop a 95% prediction interval estimate for the amount of total itemized deductions for a particular taxpayer with an adjusted gross income of $52,500.
c.   If the particular taxpayer referred to in part (b) has claimed total itemized deductions of $20,400, would the IRS agent's request for an audit appear to be justified?
d.   Using your answer to part (b), give the IRS agent a guideline as to the amount of total itemized deductions a taxpayer with an adjusted gross income of $52,500 should have before an audit is recommended.

43. Refer to Exercise 21, where data on the production volume x and total cost y for a particular manufacturing operation were used to develop the estimated regression equation $\hat{y} = 1246.67 + 7.6x$.
    a. The company's production schedule shows that 500 units must be produced next month. What is the point estimate of the total cost for the next month?
    b. Develop a 99% prediction interval estimate of the total cost for next month.
    c. If an accounting cost report at the end of next month shows that the actual production cost during the month was $6000, should managers be concerned about incurring such a high total cost for the month? Discuss.

44. Almost all U.S. light-rail systems use electric cars that run on tracks built at street level. The Federal Transit Administration claims light-rail is one of the safest modes of travel, with an accident rate of .99 accidents per million passenger miles as compared to 2.29 for buses. The following data show the miles of track and the weekday ridership in thousands of passengers for six light-rail systems (*USA Today*, January 7, 2003).

City	Miles of Track	Ridership (1000s)
Cleveland	15	15
Denver	17	35
Portland	38	81
Sacramento	21	31
San Diego	47	75
San Jose	31	30
St. Louis	34	42

    a. Use these data to develop an estimated regression equation that could be used to predict the ridership given the miles of track.
    b. Did the estimated regression equation provide a good fit? Explain.
    c. Develop a 95% confidence interval for the mean weekday ridership for all light-rail systems with 30 miles of track.
    d. Suppose that Charlotte is considering construction of a light-rail system with 30 miles of track. Develop a 95% prediction interval for the weekday ridership for the Charlotte system. Do you think that the prediction interval you developed would be of value to Charlotte planners in anticipating the number of weekday riders for their new light-rail system? Explain.

14.8 Residual Analysis: Validating Model Assumptions

Residual analysis is the primary tool for determining whether the assumed regression model is appropriate.

As we noted previously, the *residual* for observation i is the difference between the observed value of the dependent variable (y_i) and the estimated value of the dependent variable ($\hat{y}_i$).

RESIDUAL FOR OBSERVATION i

$$y_i - \hat{y}_i \tag{14.28}$$

where

y_i is the observed value of the dependent variable
$\hat{y}_i$ is the estimated value of the dependent variable

In other words, the ith residual is the error resulting from using the estimated regression equation to predict the value of the dependent variable. The residuals for the Armand's Pizza Parlors example are computed in Table 14.7. The observed values of the dependent variable are in the second column and the estimated values of the dependent variable, obtained using the estimated regression equation $\hat{y} = 60 + 5x$, are in the third column. An analysis of the corresponding residuals in the fourth column will help determine whether the assumptions made about the regression model are appropriate.

Let us now review the regression assumptions for the Armand's Pizza Parlors example. A simple linear regression model was assumed.

$$y = \beta_0 + \beta_1 x + \epsilon \qquad (14.29)$$

This model indicates that we assumed quarterly sales (y) to be a linear function of the size of the student population (x) plus an error term ϵ. In Section 14.4 we made the following assumptions about the error term ϵ.

1. $E(\epsilon) = 0$.
2. The variance of ϵ, denoted by σ^2, is the same for all values of x.
3. The values of ϵ are independent.
4. The error term ϵ has a normal distribution.

These assumptions provide the theoretical basis for the t test and the F test used to determine whether the relationship between x and y is significant, and for the confidence and prediction interval estimates presented in Section 14.6. If the assumptions about the error term ϵ appear questionable, the hypothesis tests about the significance of the regression relationship and the interval estimation results may not be valid.

The residuals provide the best information about ϵ; hence, an analysis of the residuals is an important step in determining whether the assumptions for ϵ are appropriate. Much of residual analysis is based on an examination of graphical plots. In this section, we discuss the following **residual plots**.

1. A plot of the residuals against values of the independent variable x
2. A plot of residuals against the predicted values of the dependent variable $\hat{y}$
3. A standardized residual plot
4. A normal probability plot

TABLE 14.7   RESIDUALS FOR ARMAND'S PIZZA PARLORS

Student Population x_i	Sales y_i	Estimated Sales $\hat{y}_i = 60 + 5x_i$	Residuals $y_i - \hat{y}_i$
2	58	70	−12
6	105	90	15
8	88	100	−12
8	118	100	18
12	117	120	−3
16	137	140	−3
20	157	160	−3
20	169	160	9
22	149	170	−21
26	202	190	12

Residual Plot Against x

A residual plot against the independent variable x is a graph in which the values of the independent variable are represented by the horizontal axis and the corresponding residual values are represented by the vertical axis. A point is plotted for each residual. The first coordinate for each point is given by the value of x_i and the second coordinate is given by the corresponding value of the residual $y_i - \hat{y}_i$. For a residual plot against x with the Armand's Pizza Parlors data from Table 14.7, the coordinates of the first point are $(2, -12)$, corresponding to $x_1 = 2$ and $y_1 - \hat{y}_1 = -12$; the coordinates of the second point are $(6, 15)$, corresponding to $x_2 = 6$ and $y_2 - \hat{y}_2 = 15$, and so on. Figure 14.15 shows the resulting residual plot.

Before interpreting the results for this residual plot, let us consider some general patterns that might be observed in any residual plot. Three examples appear in Figure 14.16. If the assumption that the variance of ϵ is the same for all values of x and the assumed regression model is an adequate representation of the relationship between the variables, the residual plot should give an overall impression of a horizontal band of points such as the one in Panel A of Figure 14.16. However, if the variance of ϵ is not the same for all values of x—for example, if variability about the regression line is greater for larger values of x—a pattern such as the one in Panel B of Figure 14.16 could be observed. In this case, the assumption of a constant variance of ϵ is violated. Another possible residual plot is shown in Panel C. In this case, we would conclude that the assumed regression model is not an adequate representation of the relationship between the variables. A curvilinear regression model or multiple regression model should be considered.

Now let us return to the residual plot for Armand's Pizza Parlors shown in Figure 14.15. The residuals appear to approximate the horizontal pattern in Panel A of Figure 14.16. Hence, we conclude that the residual plot does not provide evidence that the assumptions made for Armand's regression model should be challenged. At this point, we are confident in the conclusion that Armand's simple linear regression model is valid.

FIGURE 14.15   PLOT OF THE RESIDUALS AGAINST THE INDEPENDENT VARIABLE x FOR ARMAND'S PIZZA PARLORS

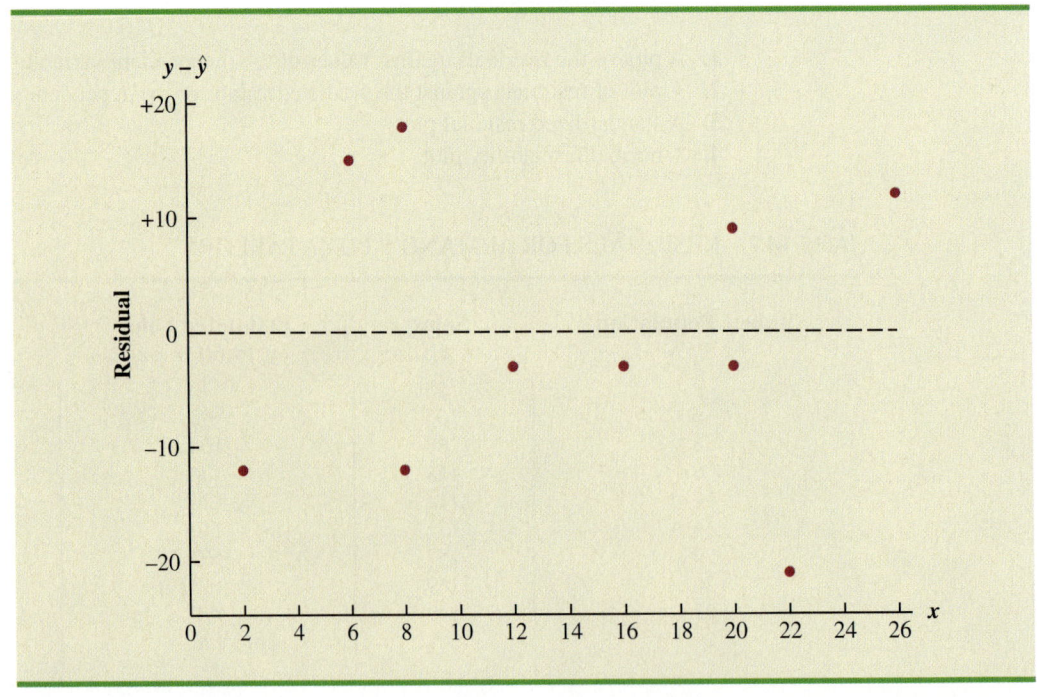

FIGURE 14.16   RESIDUAL PLOTS FROM THREE REGRESSION STUDIES

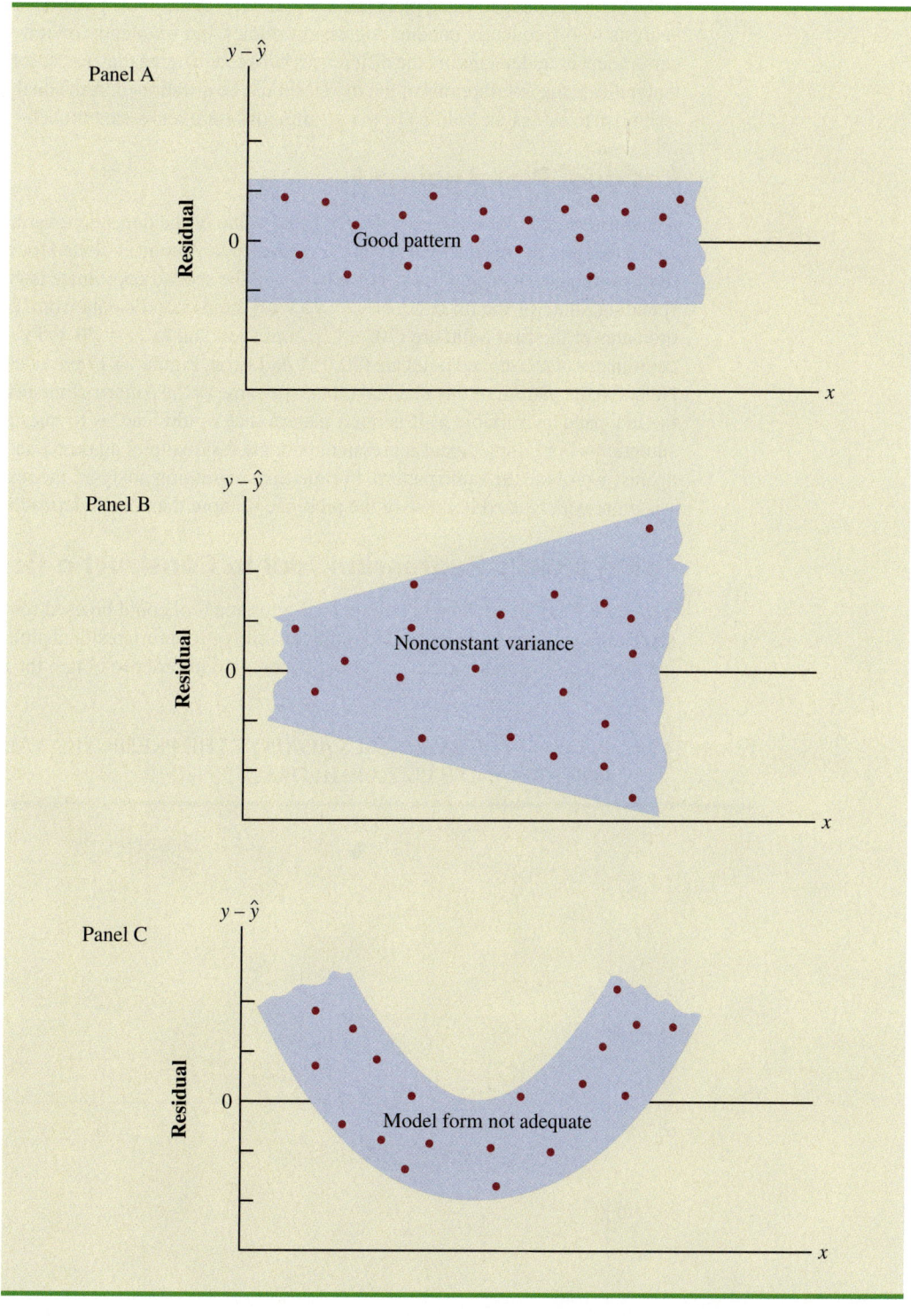

Experience and good judgment are always factors in the effective interpretation of residual plots. Seldom does a residual plot conform precisely to one of the patterns in Figure 14.16. Yet analysts who frequently conduct regression studies and frequently review residual plots become adept at understanding the differences between patterns that are reasonable and patterns that indicate the assumptions of the model should be questioned. A residual plot provides one technique to assess the validity of the assumptions for a regression model.

Residual Plot Against $\hat{y}$

Another residual plot represents the predicted value of the dependent variable $\hat{y}$ on the horizontal axis and the residual values on the vertical axis. A point is plotted for each residual. The first coordinate for each point is given by $\hat{y}_i$ and the second coordinate is given by the corresponding value of the ith residual $y_i - \hat{y}_i$. With the Armand's data from Table 14.7, the coordinates of the first point are $(70, -12)$, corresponding to $\hat{y}_1 = 70$ and $y_1 - \hat{y}_1 = -12$; the coordinates of the second point are $(90, 15)$, and so on. Figure 14.17 provides the residual plot. Note that the pattern of this residual plot is the same as the pattern of the residual plot against the independent variable x. It is not a pattern that would lead us to question the model assumptions. For simple linear regression, both the residual plot against x and the residual plot against $\hat{y}$ provide the same pattern. For multiple regression analysis, the residual plot against $\hat{y}$ is more widely used because of the presence of more than one independent variable.

Using Excel's Regression Tool to Construct a Residual Plot

In Section 14.6 we showed how Excel's Regression tool could be used for regression analysis. The Regression tool also provides the capability to obtain a residual plot. To obtain a residual plot, the steps that we described in Section 14.6 in order to obtain the regression output

FIGURE 14.17   PLOT OF THE RESIDUALS AGAINST THE PREDICTED VALUES $\hat{y}$
FOR ARMAND'S PIZZA PARLORS

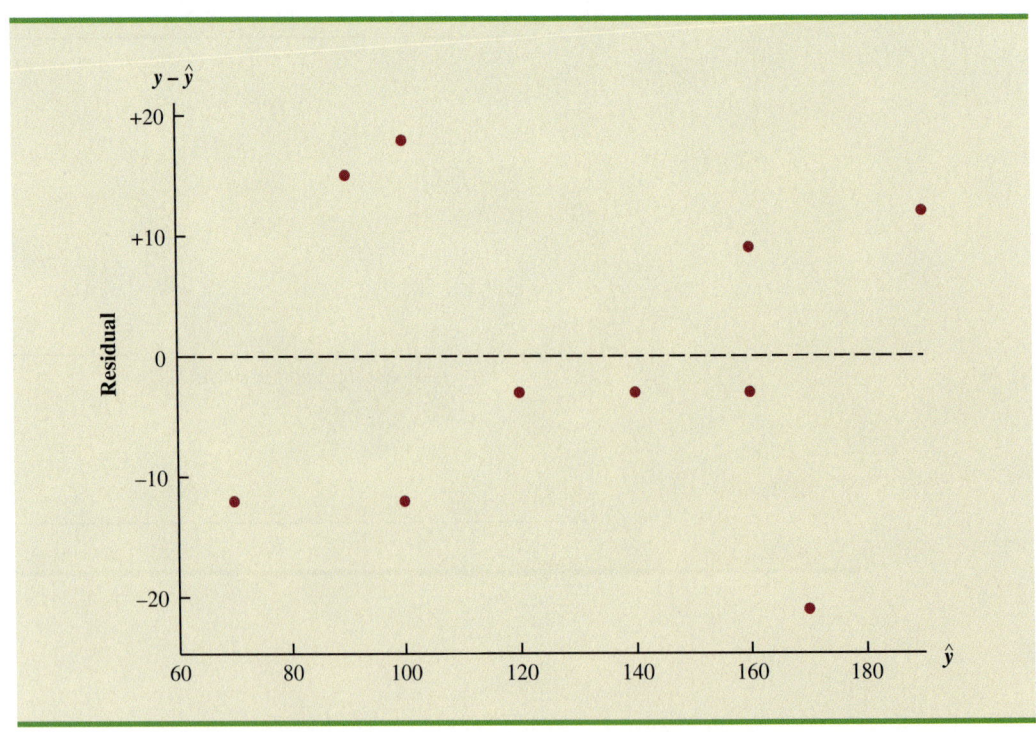

are performed with one change. When the Regression dialog box appears (see Figure 14.11) we must also select the Residual Plots option. The regression output will appear as described previously, and the worksheet will also contain a chart showing a plot of the residuals against the independent variable Population. In addition, a list of predicted values of y and the corresponding residual values is provided below the regression output. Figure 14.18 shows the residual output for the Armand's Pizza Parlors problem. We see that the shape of this plot is the same as shown previously in Figure 14.15.

Standardized Residuals

Many of the residual plots provided by computer software packages use a standardized version of the residuals. As we have seen in preceding chapters, a random variable is standardized by subtracting its mean and dividing the result by its standard deviation. With the least squares method, the mean of the residuals is zero. Thus, simply dividing each residual by its standard deviation provides the **standardized residual.**

It can be shown that the standard deviation of residual i depends on the standard error of the estimate s and the corresponding value of the independent variable x_i.

> **STANDARD DEVIATION OF THE ith RESIDUAL**
>
> $$s_{y_i - \hat{y}_i} = s\sqrt{1 - h_i} \tag{14.30}$$
>
> where
>
> $$s_{y_i - \hat{y}_i} = \text{the standard deviation of residual } i$$
> $$s = \text{the standard error of the estimate}$$
> $$h_i = \frac{1}{n} + \frac{(x_i - \bar{x})^2}{\Sigma(x_i - \bar{x})^2} \tag{14.31}$$
>
> *Note:* This equation actually provides an estimate of the standard deviation of the ith residual, because s is used instead of σ. The value of σ is never known when working with real data and is always estimated by s.

Equation (14.30) shows that the standard deviation of the ith residual depends on x_i because of the presence of h_i in the formula.* Once the standard deviation of each residual has been calculated, we can compute the standardized residual by dividing each residual by its corresponding standard deviation.

> **STANDARDIZED RESIDUAL FOR OBSERVATION i**
>
> $$\frac{y_i - \hat{y}_i}{s_{y_i - \hat{y}_i}} \tag{14.32}$$

Table 14.8 shows the calculation of the standardized residuals for Armand's Pizza Parlors. Recall that previous calculations showed $s = 13.829$. Figure 14.19 is the plot of the standardized residuals against the independent variable x.

---

*h_i is referred to as the leverage of observation i. Leverage will be discussed further when we consider influential observations in Section 14.9.

FIGURE 14.18   EXCEL RESIDUAL OUTPUT FOR THE ARMAND'S PIZZA PARLORS PROBLEM

	A	B	C	D	E	F	G	H	I	J
1	Restaurant	Population	Sales							
2	1	2	58							
3	2	6	105							
4	3	8	88							
5	4	8	118							
6	5	12	117							
7	6	16	137							
8	7	20	157							
9	8	20	169							
10	9	22	149							
11	10	26	202							
33										
34	RESIDUAL OUTPUT									
35										
36	*Observation*	*Predicted Sales*	*Residuals*							
37	1	70	-12							
38	2	90	15							
39	3	100	-12							
40	4	100	18							
41	5	120	-3							
42	6	140	-3							
43	7	160	-3							
44	8	160	9							
45	9	170	-21							
46	10	190	12							
47										

Population Residual Plot

Note: Rows 12–32 are hidden.

TABLE 14.8   COMPUTATION OF STANDARDIZED RESIDUALS FOR ARMAND'S PIZZA PARLORS

Restaurant i	x_i	$x_i - \bar{x}$	$(x_i - \bar{x})^2$	$\dfrac{(x_i - \bar{x})^2}{\Sigma(x_i - \bar{x})^2}$	h_i	$s_{y_i - \hat{y}_i}$	$y_i - \hat{y}_i$	Standardized Residual
1	2	−12	144	.2535	.3535	11.1193	−12	−1.0792
2	6	−8	64	.1127	.2127	12.2709	15	1.2224
3	8	−6	36	.0634	.1634	12.6493	−12	−.9487
4	8	−6	36	.0634	.1634	12.6493	18	1.4230
5	12	−2	4	.0070	.1070	13.0682	−3	−.2296
6	16	2	4	.0070	.1070	13.0682	−3	−.2296
7	20	6	36	.0634	.1634	12.6493	−3	−.2372
8	20	6	36	.0634	.1634	12.6493	9	.7115
9	22	8	64	.1127	.2127	12.2709	−21	−1.7114
10	26	12	144	.2535	.3535	11.1193	12	1.0792
		Total	568					

Note: The values of the residuals were computed in Table 14.7.

FIGURE 14.19   PLOT OF THE STANDARDIZED RESIDUALS AGAINST THE INDEPENDENT VARIABLE x FOR ARMAND'S PIZZA PARLORS

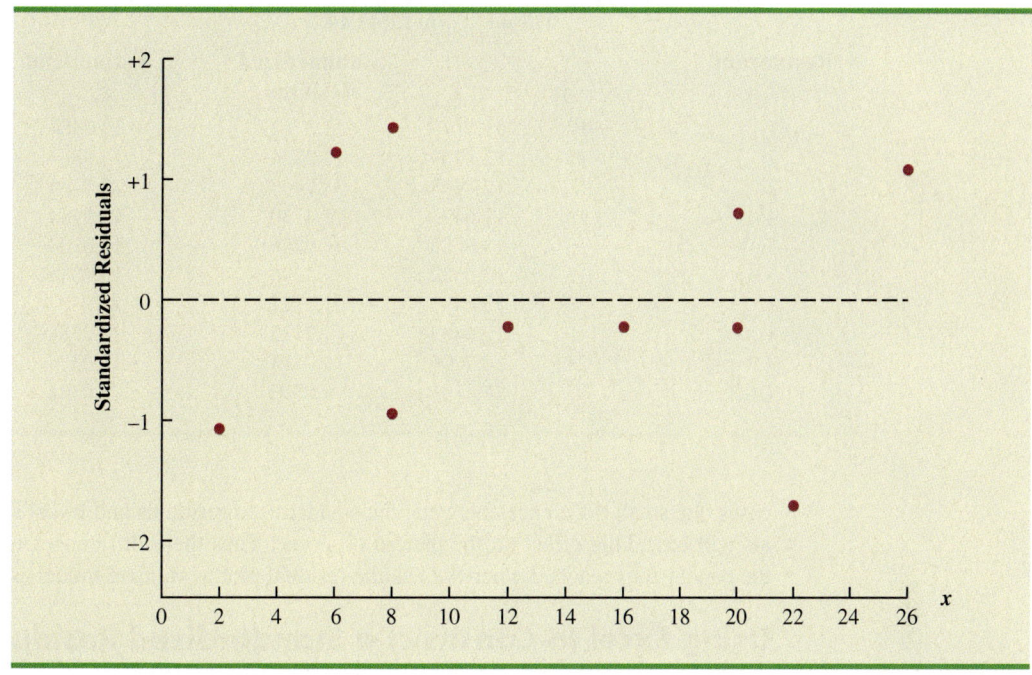

Small departures from normality do not have a great effect on the statistical tests used in regression analysis.

The standardized residual plot can provide insight about the assumption that the error term ϵ has a normal distribution. If this assumption is satisfied, the distribution of the standardized residuals should appear to come from a standard normal probability distribution.* Thus, when looking at a standardized residual plot, we should expect to see approximately 95% of the standardized residuals between -2 and $+2$. We see in Figure 14.19 that for the Armand's example all standardized residuals are between -2 and $+2$. Therefore, on the basis of the standardized residuals, we have no reason to question the assumption that ϵ has a normal distribution.

In the following subsection we will show how Excel can be used to construct what it calls a standardized residual plot. Excel's standardized residual plot is really an approximation of the true standardized residual plot. In Excel, the standard deviation of the ith residual is not computed using equation (14.30). Instead, Excel estimates $s_{y_i - \hat{y}_i}$ using the standard deviation of the n residual values. Then, dividing each residual by this estimate, Excel obtains what it refers to as a standard residual. The plot of these standard residuals is what you get when you request a plot of the standardized residuals using Excel's Regression tool.

We will illustrate how to construct a standardized residual plot using Excel for the Armand's Pizza Parlors problem. The residuals for the Armand's Pizza Parlors problem are -12, 15, -12, 18, -3, -3, -3, 9, -21, and 12. Using Excel's STDEV function, we computed a standard deviation of 13.0384 for these 10 data values. To compute the standard residuals, Excel divides each residual by 13.0384; the results are shown in Table 14.9. Both the standardized residuals, computed in Table 14.8, and Excel's standard residuals are shown. There is not a great deal of difference between Excel's standard residuals and the true standardized residuals. In general, the differences get smaller as the sample size increases. Often we are only interested in identifying the general pattern of the points in a standardized residual plot; in such

---

*Because s is used instead of σ in (14.30), the probability distribution of the standardized residuals is not technically normal. However, in most regression studies, the sample size is large enough that a normal approximation is very good.

TABLE 14.9 COMPUTATION OF EXCEL'S STANDARD RESIDUALS

Restaurant i	Values from Table 14.8			Values Using Excel	
	$y_i - \hat{y}_i$	$s_{y_i - \hat{y}_i}$	Standardized Residual	Estimate of $s_{y_i - \hat{y}_i}$	Standard Residual
1	−12	11.1193	−1.0792	13.0384	−0.9204
2	15	12.2709	1.2224	13.0384	1.1504
3	−12	12.6493	−.9487	13.0384	−0.9204
4	18	12.6493	1.4230	13.0384	1.3805
5	−3	13.0682	−.2296	13.0384	−0.2301
6	−3	13.0682	−.2296	13.0384	−0.2301
7	−3	12.6493	−.2372	13.0384	−0.2301
8	9	12.6493	.7115	13.0384	0.6903
9	−21	12.2709	−1.7114	13.0384	−1.6106
10	12	11.1193	1.0792	13.0384	0.9204

cases, the small differences between the standardized residuals and Excel's standard residuals will have little effect on the pattern observed. Thus these differences will not influence the conclusions reached when we use the residual plot to validate model assumptions.

Using Excel to Construct a Standardized Residual Plot

The Regression tool and the Chart Wizard can be used to obtain Excel's standardized residual plot. First, the steps that we described in Section 14.6 in order to conduct a regression analysis are performed with one change. When the Regression dialog box appears (see Figure 14.11), we must select the Standardized Residuals option. In addition to the regression output described previously, the output will contain a list of predicted values of y, residuals, and standard residuals, as shown in cells A34:D46 in Figure 14.20.

The Standardized Residuals option does not automatically produce a standardized residual plot. But we can use Excel's Chart Wizard to develop a scatter diagram in which the values of the independent variable are placed on the horizontal axis and the values of the standard residuals are placed on the vertical axis. The procedure that describes how to use Excel's Chart Wizard to develop a scatter diagram in regression analysis was described in Section 14.2. Because the Chart Wizard requires that the two variables being plotted be located in adjacent columns of the worksheet, we copied the data and heading for the independent variable Population into cells F36:F46 and the data and heading for the standard residuals into cells G36:G46.

Using the data in cells F36:G46 and the Chart Wizard we obtained the scatter diagram shown in Figure 14.20; this scatter diagram is Excel's version of the standardized residual plot for the Armand's Pizza Parlors example. Comparing Excel's version of the standardized residual plot to the standardized residual plot in Figure 14.19, we see the same pattern evident. All of the standardized residuals in both figures are between −2 and +2, indicating no reason to question the assumption that ϵ has a normal distribution.

Normal Probability Plot

Another approach for determining the validity of the assumption that the error term has a normal distribution is the **normal probability plot**. To show how a normal probability plot is developed, we introduce the concept of *normal scores*.

Suppose 10 values are selected randomly from a standard normal probability distribution with a mean of zero and a standard deviation of one, and that the sampling process is

FIGURE 14.20   EXCEL'S STANDARDIZED RESIDUAL PLOT AGAINST THE INDEPENDENT VARIABLE POPULATION FOR THE ARMAND'S PIZZA PARLORS EXAMPLE

	A	B	C	D	E	F	G	H
34	RESIDUAL OUTPUT							
35								
36	*Observation*	*Predicted Sales*	*Residuals*	*Standard Residuals*		**Population**	**Standard Residuals**	
37	1	70	-12	-0.9204		2	-0.9204	
38	2	90	15	1.1504		6	1.1504	
39	3	100	-12	-0.9204		8	-0.9204	
40	4	100	18	1.3805		8	1.3805	
41	5	120	-3	-0.2301		12	-0.2301	
42	6	140	-3	-0.2301		16	-0.2301	
43	7	160	-3	-0.2301		20	-0.2301	
44	8	160	9	0.6903		20	0.6903	
45	9	170	-21	-1.6106		22	-1.6106	
46	10	190	12	0.9204		26	0.9204	
47								
48								
49								
50								
51								
52								
53								
54								
55								
56								
57								
58								
59								
60								
61								

Note: Rows 1–33 are hidden.

TABLE 14.10

NORMAL SCORES FOR $n = 10$

Order Statistic	Normal Score
1	−1.55
2	−1.00
3	−.65
4	−.37
5	−.12
6	.12
7	.37
8	.65
9	1.00
10	1.55

repeated over and over with the values in each sample of 10 ordered from smallest to largest. For now, let us consider only the smallest value in each sample. The random variable representing the smallest value obtained in repeated sampling is called the first-order statistic.

Statisticians have shown that for samples of size 10 from a standard normal probability distribution, the expected value of the first-order statistic is −1.55. This expected value is called a normal score. For the case with a sample of size $n = 10$, there are 10 order statistics and 10 normal scores (see Table 14.10). In general, if we have a data set consisting of n observations, there are n order statistics and hence n normal scores.

Let us now show how the 10 normal scores can be used to determine whether the standardized residuals for Armand's Pizza Parlors appear to come from a standard normal probability distribution. We begin by ordering the 10 standardized residuals from Table 14.8. The 10 normal scores and the ordered standardized residuals are shown together in Table 14.11. If the normality assumption is satisfied, the smallest standardized residual should be close to the smallest normal score, the next smallest standardized residual should be close to the next smallest normal score, and so on. If we were to develop a plot with the normal scores on the horizontal axis and the corresponding standardized residuals on the vertical axis, the plotted points should cluster closely around a 45-degree line passing through the origin if the

FIGURE 14.21   NORMAL PROBABILITY PLOT FOR ARMAND'S PIZZA PARLORS

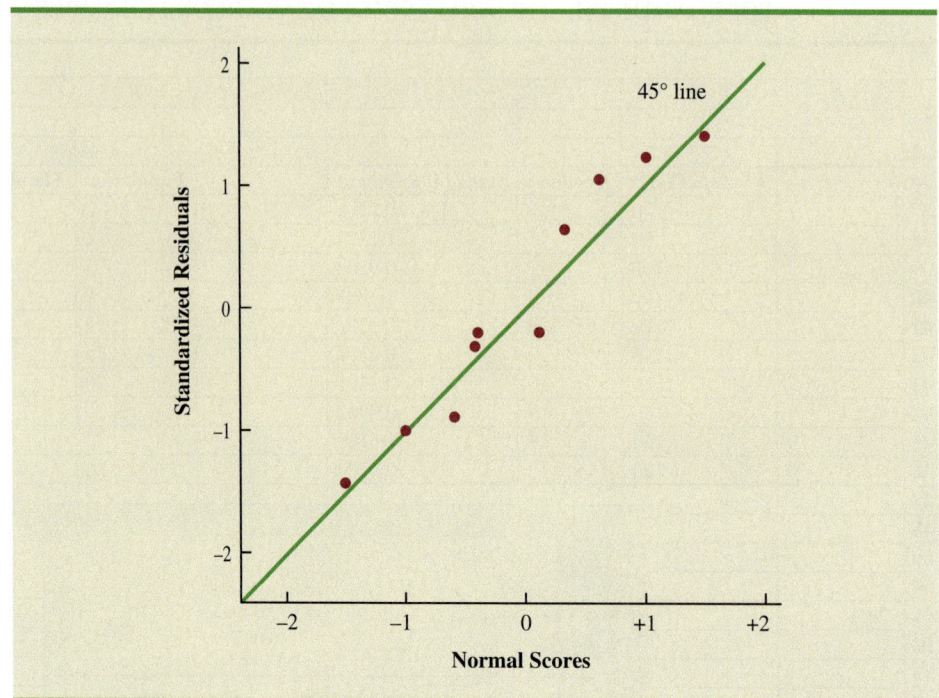

TABLE 14.11

NORMAL SCORES
AND ORDERED
STANDARDIZED
RESIDUALS FOR
ARMAND'S PIZZA
PARLORS

Normal Scores	Ordered Standardized Residuals
−1.55	−1.7114
−1.00	−1.0792
−.65	−.9487
−.37	−.2372
−.12	−.2296
.12	−.2296
.37	.7115
.65	1.0792
1.00	1.2224
1.55	1.4230

standardized residuals are approximately normally distributed. Such a plot is referred to as a *normal probability plot.*

Figure 14.21 is the normal probability plot for the Armand's Pizza Parlors example. Judgment is used to determine whether the pattern observed deviates from the line enough to conclude that the standardized residuals are not from a standard normal probability distribution. In Figure 14.21, we see that the points are grouped closely about the line. We therefore conclude that the assumption of the error term having a normal probability distribution is reasonable. In general, the more closely the points are clustered about the 45-degree line, the stronger the evidence supporting the normality assumption. Any substantial curvature in the normal probability plot is evidence that the residuals have not come from a normal distribution.

NOTES AND COMMENTS

1. The analysis of residuals is the primary method statisticians use to verify that the assumptions associated with a regression model are valid. Even if no violations are found, it does not necessarily follow that the model will yield good predictions. However, if in addition the statistical tests support the conclusion of significance and the coefficient of determination is large, we should be able to develop good estimates using the estimated regression equation.

2. When model assumptions are found to be violated, the appropriate corrective action must be based on good judgment; recommendations from an experienced statistician can be valuable. If one or more assumptions are questionable, but not necessarily invalid, the user should be cautious in using and interpreting the regression results.

3. SWStat+ can be used to develop many different types of residual plots. In Appendix 14.3 we show how to use SWStat+ to develop a standardized residual plot against the predicted values of sales for the Armand's Pizza Parlors data.

EXERCISES

Methods

45.   Given are data for two variables, x and y.

x_i	6	11	15	18	20
y_i	6	8	12	20	30

a.   Develop an estimated regression equation for these data.
b.   Compute the residuals.
c.   Develop a plot of the residuals against the independent variable x. Do the assumptions about the error terms seem to be satisfied?
d.   Compute the standardized residuals.
e.   Develop a plot of the standardized residuals against x. What conclusions can you draw from this plot?

46.   The following data were used in a regression study.

Observation	x_i	y_i	Observation	x_i	y_i
1	2	4	6	7	6
2	3	5	7	7	9
3	4	4	8	8	5
4	5	6	9	9	11
5	7	4			

a.   Develop an estimated regression equation for these data.
b.   Construct a plot of the residuals. Do the assumptions about the error term seem to be satisfied?

Applications

47.   Data on advertising expenditures ($1000s) and revenue ($1000s) for the Four Seasons Restaurant follow.

Advertising Expenditures	Revenue
1	19
2	32
4	44
6	40
10	52
14	53
20	54

a.   Let x equal advertising expenditures ($1000s) and y equal revenue ($1000s). Use the method of least squares to develop a straight-line approximation of the relationship between the two variables.
b.   Test whether revenue and advertising expenditures are related at a .05 level of significance.
c.   Develop a plot of the residuals against the independent variable.
d.   What conclusions can you draw from residual analysis? Should this model be used, or should we look for a better one?

48. Refer to exercise 9, where an estimated regression equation relating years of experience and annual sales was developed.
    a. Compute the residuals and construct a residual plot for this problem.
    b. Do the assumptions about the error terms seem reasonable in light of the residual plot?

49. American Depository Receipts (ADRs) are certificates traded on the NYSE representing shares of a foreign company held on deposit in a bank in its home country. The following table shows the price/earnings (P/E) ratio and the percentage return on investment (ROE) for 10 Indian companies that are likely new ADRs (*Bloomberg Personal Finance,* April 2000).

ADRs

	ROE	P/E
Bharti Televentures	6.43	36.88
Gujarat Ambuja Cements	13.49	27.03
Hindalco Industries	14.04	10.83
ICICI	20.67	5.15
Mahanagar Telephone Nigam	22.74	13.35
NIIT	46.23	95.59
Pentamedia Graphics	28.90	54.85
Satyam Computer Services	54.01	189.21
Silverline Technologies	28.02	75.86
Videsh Sanchar Nigam	27.04	13.17

a. Use Excel to develop an estimated regression equation relating $y =$ P/E and $x =$ ROE.
b. Construct a residual plot of the standardized residuals against the independent variable.
c. Do the assumptions about the error terms and model form seem reasonable in light of the residual plot?

(14.9) Outliers and Influential Observations

In this section we discuss how to identify observations that can be classified as outliers or as being especially influential in determining the estimated regression equation. Some steps that should be taken when such observations are identified are provided.

Detecting Outliers

An **outlier** is a data point (observation) that does not fit the trend shown by the remaining data. Outliers represent observations that are suspect and warrant careful examination. They may represent erroneous data; if so, they should be corrected. They may signal a violation of model assumptions; if so, another model should be considered. Finally, they may simply be unusual values that have occurred by chance. In this case, they should be retained.

To illustrate the process of detecting outliers, consider the data set in Table 14.12; Figure 14.22 shows the scatter diagram for these data and a portion of the Regression tool output, including the tabular residual output obtained using the Standardized Residuals option. The estimated regression equation is $\hat{y} = 64.958 - 7.3305x$ and R Square is .4968; thus, only 49.68% of the variability in the values of y is explained by the estimated regression equation. However, except for observation 4 ($x_4 = 3$, $y_4 = 75$), a pattern suggesting a strong negative linear relationship is apparent. Indeed, given the pattern of the rest of the data, we would have expected y_4 to be much smaller and hence would consider observation 4 to be an outlier. For the case of simple linear regression, one can often detect outliers by simply examining the scatter diagram.

TABLE 14.12

DATA SET ILLUSTRATING THE EFFECT OF AN OUTLIER

x_i	y_i
1	45
1	55
2	50
3	75
3	40
3	45
4	30
4	35
5	25
6	15

FIGURE 14.22   EXCEL OUTPUT FOR THE OUTLIER DATA SET

	A	B	C	D	E	F	G	H	I
1	*x*	*y*							
2	1	45							
3	1	55							
4	2	50							
5	3	75							
6	3	40							
7	3	45							
8	4	30							
9	4	35							
10	5	25							
11	6	15							
12									
13	SUMMARY OUTPUT								
14									
15	*Regression Statistics*								
16	Multiple R	0.7049							
17	R Square	0.4968							
18	Adjusted R Square	0.4339							
19	Standard Error	12.6704							
20	Observations	10							
21									
34	RESIDUAL OUTPUT								
35									
36	*Observation*	*Predicted y*	*Residuals*	*Standard Residuals*					
37	1	57.6271	-12.6271	-1.0570					
38	2	57.6271	-2.6271	-0.2199					
39	3	50.2966	-0.2966	-0.0248					
40	4	42.9661	32.0339	2.6816					
41	5	42.9661	-2.9661	-0.2483					
42	6	42.9661	2.0339	0.1703					
43	7	35.6356	-5.6356	-0.4718					
44	8	35.6356	-0.6356	-0.0532					
45	9	28.3051	-3.3051	-0.2767					
46	10	20.9746	-5.9746	-0.5001					
47									

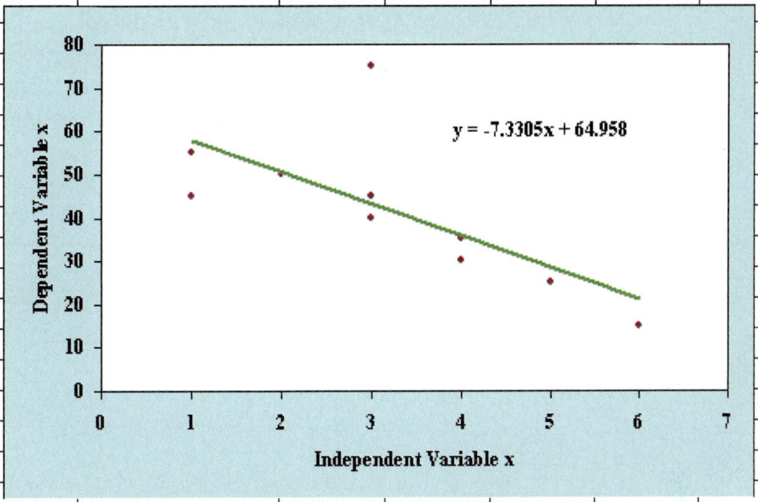

Chart (within cells C3–H20): scatterplot with trend line. Y-axis labeled "Dependent Variable x" from 0 to 80. X-axis labeled "Independent Variable x" from 0 to 7. Equation shown: $y = -7.3305x + 64.958$

Callout: The standard residual for observation 4 is greater than +2; hence, we consider observation 4 to be an outlier.

Note: Rows 22–33 are hidden.

The standardized residuals can also be used to identify outliers. If an observation deviates greatly from the pattern of the rest of the data, the corresponding standardized residual will be large in absolute value. We recommend considering any observation with a standardized residual of less than −2 or greater than +2 as an outlier. With normally distributed errors, standardized residuals should be outside these limits approximately 5% of the time. In the residual output section of Figure 14.22 we see that the standard residual value for observation 4 is 2.68; this value suggests we treat observation 4 as an outlier.

In deciding how to handle an outlier, we should first check to see whether it is a valid observation. Perhaps an error has been made in initially recording the data or in entering

Outlier

the data into the worksheet. For example, suppose that in checking the data in Table 14.12, we find that an error has been made and that the correct value for observation 4 is $x_4 = 3$, $y_4 = 30$. Figure 14.23 shows a portion of the Regression tool output after correction of the value of y_4. The estimated regression equation is $\hat{y} = 59.237 - 6.9492x$ and R Square is .8380. Note also that no standard residuals are less than -2 or greater than $+2$; hence, the revised data contain no outliers. We see that using the incorrect data value had a substantial effect on the goodness of fit. With the correct data, the value of R Square has increased from .4968 to .8380 and the value of b_0 has decreased from 64.958 to 59.237. The slope of the line has changed from -7.3305 to -6.9492. The identification of the outlier enables us to correct the data error and improve the regression results.

FIGURE 14.23   EXCEL OUTPUT FOR THE REVISED OUTLIER DATA SET

	A	B	C	D	E	F	G	H	I
1	x	y							
2	1	45							
3	1	55							
4	2	50							
5	3	30							
6	3	40							
7	3	45							
8	4	30							
9	4	35							
10	5	25							
11	6	15							
12									
13	SUMMARY OUTPUT								
14									
15	*Regression Statistics*								
16	Multiple R	0.9154							
17	R Square	0.8380							
18	Adjusted R Square	0.8177							
19	Standard Error	5.2481							
20	Observations	10							
21									
34	RESIDUAL OUTPUT								
35									
36	*Observation*	*Predicted y*	*Residuals*	*Standard Residuals*					
37	1	52.2881	-7.2881	-1.4730					
38	2	52.2881	2.7119	0.5481					
39	3	45.3390	4.6610	0.9420					
40	4	38.3898	-8.3898	-1.6956					
41	5	38.3898	1.6102	0.3254					
42	6	38.3898	6.6102	1.3359					
43	7	31.4407	-1.4407	-0.2912					
44	8	31.4407	3.5593	0.7194					
45	9	24.4915	0.5085	0.1028					
46	10	17.5424	-2.5424	-0.5138					
47									

The chart embedded in the worksheet shows a scatter plot of Dependent Variable x against Independent Variable x with the fitted line $y = -6.9492x + 59.237$.

Note: Rows 22–33 are hidden.

Detecting Influential Observations

An **influential observation** is an observation that has a strong influence on the regression results. An influential observation may be an outlier (an observation with a y value that deviates substantially from the trend of the remaining data), it may correspond to an x value far from its mean (extreme x value), or it may be caused by a combination of a somewhat off-trend y value and a somewhat extreme x value. Because influential observations may have such a dramatic effect on the estimated regression equation, they must be examined carefully. First, we should check to make sure no error has been made in collecting or recording the data. If such an error has occurred, it can be corrected and a new estimated regression equation developed. If the observation is valid, we might consider ourselves fortunate to have it. Such a point, if valid, can contribute to a better understanding of the appropriate model and can lead to a better estimated regression equation.

To illustrate the process of detecting influential observations, consider the data set in Table 14.13. The top part of Figure 14.24 shows the scatter diagram for these data and the graph of the corresponding estimated regression equation $\hat{y} = 127.47 - .04251x$. The bottom part of Figure 14.24 shows the scatter diagram for the data in Table 14.13 with observation 7 ($x_7 = 70$, $y_7 = 100$) deleted; for these data the estimated regression equation is $\hat{y} = 138.18 - 1.0909x$. With observation 7 deleted, the value of b_0 has increased from 127.47 to 138.18. The slope of the line has changed from -0.4251 to -1.0909. The effect of

TABLE 14.13

DATA SET
ILLUSTRATING
THE EFFECT OF
AN INFLUENTIAL
OBSERVATION

x_i	y_i
10	125
10	130
15	120
20	115
20	120
25	110
70	100

FIGURE 14.24   SCATTER DIAGRAMS FOR THE DATA SET WITH AN INFLUENTIAL OBSERVATION

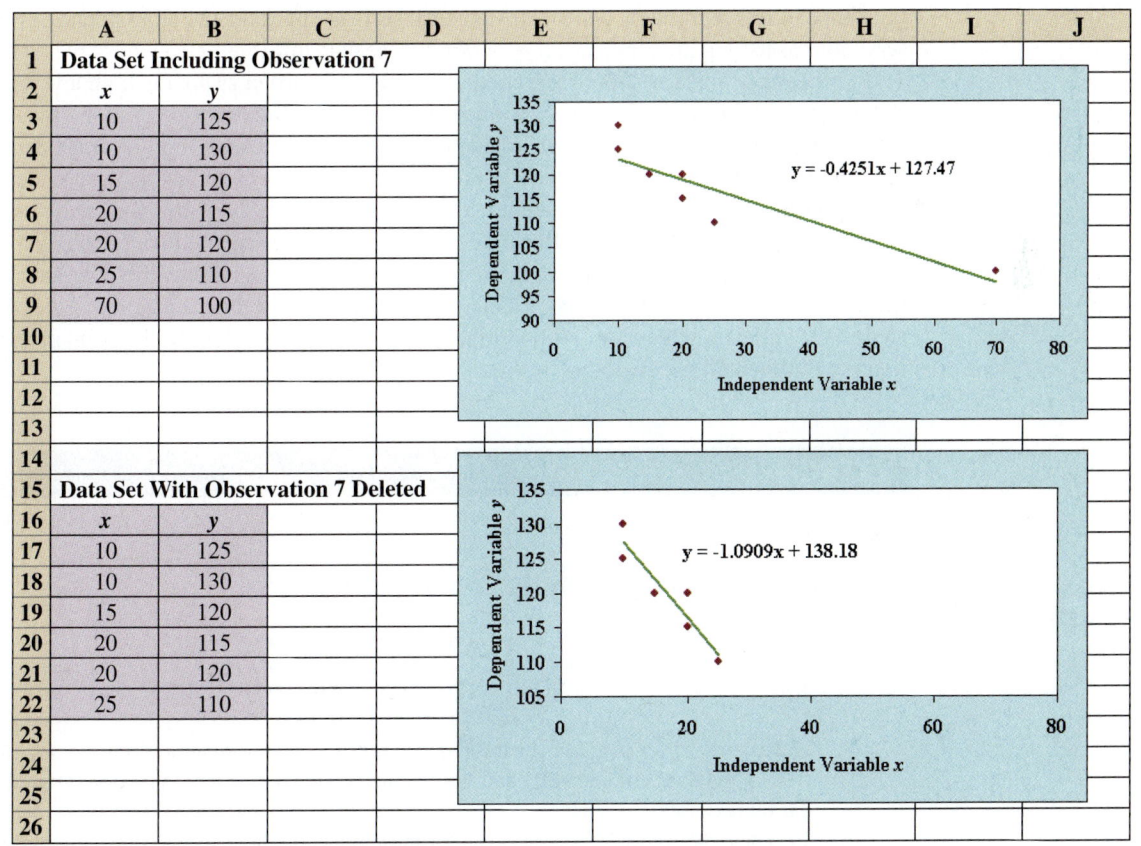

observation 7 on the regression results is dramatic and is confirmed by looking at the graphs of the two estimated regression equations. Clearly observation 7 is influential.

Observations with extreme values for the independent variables are called **high leverage points**. Observation 7 in the data set shown in Table 14.13 (which we have identified as being influential) is a point with high leverage. The leverage of an observation is determined by how far the value of the independent variable is from its mean value. For the single-independent-variable case, the leverage of the ith observation, denoted h_i, can be computed using equation (14.33).

LEVERAGE OF OBSERVATION i

$$h_i = \frac{1}{n} + \frac{(x_i - \bar{x})^2}{\Sigma(x_i - \bar{x})^2} \tag{14.33}$$

From the formula, it is clear that the farther x_i is from its mean $\bar{x}$, the higher the leverage of observation i. For the data in Table 14.13, the leverage of observation 7 is computed using equation (14.33) as follows:

Influential

$$h_i = \frac{1}{n} + \frac{(x_i - \bar{x})^2}{\Sigma(x_i - \bar{x})^2} = \frac{1}{7} + \frac{(70 - 24.286)^2}{2621.43} = .94$$

For simple linear regression, one major statistical software package (Minitab) identifies observations as having high leverage if $h_i > 6/n$; for the data in Table 14.13, $6/n = 6/7 = .86$. Thus, because $h_i = .94 > .86$, observation 7 would be identified as having high leverage. Data points having high leverage are often influential. Influential observations that are caused by an interaction of somewhat large residuals and somewhat high leverage can be difficult to detect. Diagnostic procedures are available that take both into account in determining when an observation is influential. More advanced books on regression analysis discuss the use of such procedures. Excel does not have built-in capabilities for identifying outliers and high leverage points. Thus, we recommend reviewing the scatter diagram after fitting the regression line. For any points significantly off the line, rerun the regression analysis after deleting the observation. If the results change dramatically, the point in question is an influential observation.

EXERCISES

Methods

50. Consider the following data for two variables, x and y.

x_i	135	110	130	145	175	160	120
y_i	145	100	120	120	130	130	110

a. Develop a scatter diagram for these data. Does the scatter diagram indicate any outliers in the data? In general, what implications does this finding have for simple linear regression?

b. Compute the standardized residuals for these data. Do there appear to be any outliers in the data? Explain.

51. Consider the following data for two variables, x and y.

x_i	4	5	7	8	10	12	12	22
y_i	12	14	16	15	18	20	24	19

a. Develop a scatter diagram for these data. Does the scatter diagram indicate any influential observations? Explain.
b. Compute the standardized residuals for these data. Do there appear to be any outliers in the data? Explain.
c. Compute the leverage values for these data. Do there appear to be any influential observations in these data? Explain.

Applications

52. The following data show the media expenditures ($ millions) and the shipments in bbls (millions) for 10 major brands of beer.

Beer

Brand	Media Expenditures ($ millions)	Shipments (bbls millions)
Budweiser	120.0	36.3
Bud Light	68.7	20.7
Miller Lite	100.1	15.9
Coors Light	76.6	13.2
Busch	8.7	8.1
Natural Light	0.1	7.1
Miller Genuine Draft	21.5	5.6
Miller High Life	1.4	4.4
Busch Light	5.3	4.3
Milwaukee's Best	1.7	4.3

a. Develop the estimated regression equation for these data.
b. Use residual analysis to determine whether any outliers and/or influential observations are present. Briefly summarize your findings and conclusions.

53. Health experts recommend that runners drink 4 ounces of water every 15 minutes they run. Runners who run three to eight hours need a larger-capacity hip-mounted or over-the-shoulder hydration system. The following data show the liquid volume (fl oz) and the price for 26 Ultimate Direction hip-mounted or over-the-shoulder hydration systems (*Trail Runner Gear Guide*, 2003).

Hydration2

Model	Volume (fl oz)	Price ($)
Fastdraw	20	10
Fastdraw Plus	20	12
Fitness	20	12
Access	20	20
Access Plus	24	25
Solo	20	25
Serenade	20	35
Solitaire	20	35
Gemini	40	45
Shadow	64	40

(continued)

Model	Volume (fl oz)	Price ($)
SipStream	96	60
Express	20	30
Lightning	28	40
Elite	40	60
Extender	40	65
Stinger	32	65
GelFlask Belt	4	20
GelDraw	4	7
GelFlask Clip-on Holster	4	10
GelFlask Holster SS	4	10
Strider (W)	20	30
Walkabout (W)	230	40
Solitude I.C.E.	20	35
Getaway I.C.E.	40	55
Profile I.C.E.	64	50
Traverse I.C.E.	64	60

a. Develop the estimated regression equation that can be used to predict the price of a hydration system given its liquid volume.

b. Use residual analysis to determine whether any outliers or influential observations are present. Briefly summarize your findings and conclusions.

54. The market capitalization and the salary of the chief executive officer (CEO) for 20 companies are shown in the following table (*The Wall Street Journal,* February 24, 2000, and April 6, 2000).

CEO

	Market Cap. ($ millions)	CEO Salary ($1000s)
Anheuser-Busch	32,977.4	1,130
AT&T	162,365.1	1,400
Charles Schwab	31,363.8	800
Chevron	56,849.0	1,350
DuPont	68,848.0	1,000
General Elec.	507,216.8	3,325
Gillette	44,180.1	978
IBM	194,455.9	2,000
Johnson & Johnson	143,131.0	1,365
Kimberly-Clark	35,377.5	950
Merrill Lynch	31,062.1	700
Motorola	92,923.7	1,275
Philip Morris	54,421.2	1,625
Procter & Gamble	144,152.9	1,318.3
Qualcomm	116,840.8	773
Schering-Plough	62,259.4	1,200
Sun Microsystems	120,966.5	116
Texaco	30,040.7	950
USWest	36,450.8	897
Walt Disney	61,288.1	750

a. Develop the estimated regression equation that can be used to predict the CEO salary given the market capitalization.

b. Use residual analysis to determine whether any outliers and/or influential observations are present. Briefly summarize your findings and conclusions.

Summary

In this chapter we first showed how regression analysis can be used to determine how a dependent variable y is related to an independent variable x. In simple linear regression, the regression model is $y = \beta_0 + \beta_1 x + \epsilon$. The simple linear regression equation $E(y) = \beta_0 + \beta_1 x$ describes how the mean or expected value of y is related to x. We used sample data and the least squares method to develop the estimated regression equation $\hat{y} = b_0 + b_1 x$. In effect, b_0 and b_1 are the sample statistics used to estimate the unknown model parameters β_0 and β_1.

The coefficient of determination was presented as a measure of the goodness of fit for the estimated regression equation; it can be interpreted as the proportion of the variation in the dependent variable y that can be explained by the estimated regression equation. We reviewed correlation as a descriptive measure of the strength of a linear relationship between two variables.

The assumptions about the regression model and its associated error term ϵ were discussed, and t and F tests, based on those assumptions, were presented as a means for determining whether the relationship between two variables is statistically significant. We showed how to use the estimated regression equation to develop confidence interval estimates of the mean value of y and prediction interval estimates of individual values of y.

We used Excel extensively in simple linear regression. We showed how the Chart Wizard could be used to develop a scatter diagram and to fit a trend line to data, and in Section 14.6, we introduced the use of Excel's Regression tool for performing a comprehensive analysis of a regression problem. In Section 14.8 we showed how the Regression tool could also be used to develop a residual plot and how we could use the residuals to validate the regression model assumptions. The chapter concluded with a section on how to identify outliers and influential observations.

Glossary

Dependent variable The variable that is being predicted or explained. It is denoted by y.

Independent variable The variable that is doing the predicting or explaining. It is denoted by x.

Simple linear regression Regression analysis involving one independent variable and one dependent variable in which the relationship between the variables is approximated by a straight line.

Regression model The equation describing how y is related to x and an error term; in simple linear regression, the regression model is $y = \beta_0 + \beta_1 x + \epsilon$.

Regression equation The equation that describes how the mean or expected value of the dependent variable is related to the independent variable; in simple linear regression, $E(y) = \beta_0 + \beta_1 x$.

Estimated regression equation The estimate of the regression equation developed from sample data by using the least squares method. For simple linear regression, the estimated regression equation is $\hat{y} = b_0 + b_1 x$.

Least squares method A procedure used to develop the estimated regression equation. The objective is to minimize $\Sigma(y_i - \hat{y}_i)^2$.

Scatter diagram A graph of bivariate data in which the independent variable is on the horizontal axis and the dependent variable is on the vertical axis.

Coefficient of determination A measure of the goodness of fit of the estimated regression equation. It can be interpreted as the proportion of the variability in the dependent variable y that is explained by the estimated regression equation.

*i*th residual The difference between the observed value of the dependent variable and the value predicted using the estimated regression equation; for the *i*th observation the *i*th residual is $y_i - \hat{y}_i$.

Correlation coefficient A measure of the strength of the linear relationship between two variables (previously discussed in Chapter 3).

Mean square error The unbiased estimate of the variance of the error term σ^2. It is denoted by MSE or s^2.

Standard error of the estimate The square root of the mean square error, denoted by s. It is the estimate of σ, the standard deviation of the error term ϵ.

ANOVA table The analysis of variance table used to summarize the computations associated with the F test for significance.

Confidence interval The interval estimate of the mean value of y for a given value of x.

Prediction interval The interval estimate of an individual value of y for a given value of x.

Residual analysis The analysis of the residuals used to determine whether the assumptions made about the regression model appear to be valid. Residual analysis is also used to identify outliers and influential observations.

Residual plot Graphical representation of the residuals that can be used to determine whether the assumptions made about the regression model appear to be valid.

Standardized residual The value obtained by dividing a residual by its standard deviation.

Normal probability plot A graph of the standardized residuals plotted against values of the normal scores. This plot helps determine whether the assumption that the error term has a normal probability distribution appears to be valid.

Outlier A data point or observation that does not fit the trend shown by the remaining data.

Influential observation An observation that has a strong influence or effect on the regression results.

High leverage points Observations with extreme values for the independent variables.

Key Formulas

Simple Linear Regression Model
$$y = \beta_0 + \beta_1 x + \epsilon \tag{14.1}$$

Simple Linear Regression Equation
$$E(y) = \beta_0 + \beta_1 x \tag{14.2}$$

Estimated Simple Linear Regression Equation
$$\hat{y} = b_0 + b_1 x \tag{14.3}$$

Least Squares Criterion
$$\min \Sigma(y_i - \hat{y}_i)^2 \tag{14.5}$$

Slope and *y*-Intercept for the Estimated Regression Equation
$$b_1 = \frac{\Sigma(x_i - \bar{x})(y_i - \bar{y})}{\Sigma(x_i - \bar{x})^2} \tag{14.6}$$
$$b_0 = \bar{y} - b_1\bar{x} \tag{14.7}$$

Sum of Squares Due to Error
$$SSE = \Sigma(y_i - \hat{y}_i)^2 \tag{14.8}$$

Total Sum of Squares

$$\text{SST} = \Sigma(y_i - \bar{y})^2 \qquad \textbf{(14.9)}$$

Sum of Squares Due to Regression

$$\text{SSR} = \Sigma(\hat{y}_i - \bar{y})^2 \qquad \textbf{(14.10)}$$

Relationship Among SST, SSR, and SSE

$$\text{SST} = \text{SSR} + \text{SSE} \qquad \textbf{(14.11)}$$

Coefficient of Determination

$$r^2 = \frac{\text{SSR}}{\text{SST}} \qquad \textbf{(14.12)}$$

Sample Correlation Coefficient

$$r_{xy} = (\text{sign of } b_1)\sqrt{\text{Coefficient of determination}}$$
$$= (\text{sign of } b_1)\sqrt{r^2} \qquad \textbf{(14.13)}$$

Mean Square Error (Estimate of σ^2)

$$s^2 = \text{MSE} = \frac{\text{SSE}}{n - 2} \qquad \textbf{(14.15)}$$

Standard Error of the Estimate

$$s = \sqrt{\text{MSE}} = \sqrt{\frac{\text{SSE}}{n - 2}} \qquad \textbf{(14.16)}$$

Standard Deviation of b_1

$$\sigma_{b_1} = \frac{\sigma}{\sqrt{\Sigma(x_i - \bar{x})^2}} \qquad \textbf{(14.17)}$$

Estimated Standard Deviation of b_1

$$s_{b_1} = \frac{s}{\sqrt{\Sigma(x_i - \bar{x})^2}} \qquad \textbf{(14.18)}$$

***t* Test Statistic**

$$t = \frac{b_1}{s_{b_1}} \qquad \textbf{(14.19)}$$

Mean Square Regression

$$\text{MSR} = \frac{\text{SSR}}{\text{Number of independent variables}} \qquad \textbf{(14.20)}$$

***F* Test Statistic**

$$F = \frac{\text{MSR}}{\text{MSE}} \qquad \textbf{(14.21)}$$

Estimated Standard Deviation of $\hat{y}_p$

$$s_{\hat{y}_p} = s\sqrt{\frac{1}{n} + \frac{(x_p - \bar{x})^2}{\Sigma(x_i - \bar{x})^2}} \qquad \text{(14.23)}$$

Confidence Interval for $E(y_p)$

$$\hat{y}_p \pm t_{\alpha/2}s_{\hat{y}_p} \qquad \text{(14.24)}$$

Estimated Standard Deviation of an Individual Value

$$s_{\text{ind}} = s\sqrt{1 + \frac{1}{n} + \frac{(x_p - \bar{x})^2}{\Sigma(x_i - \bar{x})^2}} \qquad \text{(14.26)}$$

Prediction Interval for y_p

$$\hat{y}_p \pm t_{\alpha/2}s_{\text{ind}} \qquad \text{(14.27)}$$

Residual for Observation i

$$y_i - \hat{y}_i \qquad \text{(14.28)}$$

Standard Deviation of the ith Residual

$$s_{y_i - \hat{y}_i} = s\sqrt{1 - h_i} \qquad \text{(14.30)}$$

Standardized Residual for Observation i

$$\frac{y_i - \hat{y}_i}{s_{y_i - \hat{y}_i}} \qquad \text{(14.32)}$$

Leverage of Observation i

$$h_i = \frac{1}{n} + \frac{(x_i - \bar{x})^2}{\Sigma(x_i - \bar{x})^2} \qquad \text{(14.33)}$$

Supplementary Exercises

55. Does a high value of r^2 imply that two variables are causally related? Explain.

56. What is the purpose of testing whether $\beta_1 = 0$? If we reject $\beta_1 = 0$, does it imply a good fit?

57. The data in the following table show the number of shares selling (millions) and the expected price (average of projected low price and projected high price) for 10 selected initial public stock offerings.

IPO

Company	Shares Selling	Expected Price ($)
American Physician	5.0	15
Apex Silver Mines	9.0	14
Dan River	6.7	15
Franchise Mortgage	8.75	17
Gene Logic	3.0	11
International Home Foods	13.6	19
PRT Group	4.6	13
Rayovac	6.7	14
RealNetworks	3.0	10
Software AG Systems	7.7	13

a. Develop an estimated regression equation with the number of shares selling as the independent variable and the expected price as the dependent variable.
b. At the .05 level of significance, is there a significant relationship between the two variables?
c. Did the estimated regression equation provide a good fit? Explain.
d. Use the estimated regression equation to estimate the expected price for a firm considering an initial public offering of 6 million shares.

58. Corporate share repurchase programs are often touted as a benefit for shareholders. But Robert Gabele, director of insider research for First Call/Thomson Financial, noted that many of these programs are undertaken solely to acquire stock for a company's incentive options for top managers. Across all companies, existing stock options in 1998 represented 6.2 percent of all common shares outstanding. The following data show the number of shares covered by option grants and the number of shares outstanding for 13 companies (*Bloomberg Personal Finance,* January/February 2000).

CD file

Options

Company	Shares of Option Grants Outstanding (millions)	Common Shares Outstanding (millions)
Adobe Systems	20.3	61.8
Apple Computer	52.7	160.9
Applied Materials	109.1	375.4
Autodesk	15.7	58.9
Best Buy	44.2	203.8
Fruit of the Loom	14.2	66.9
ITT Industries	18.0	87.9
Merrill Lynch	89.9	365.5
Novell	120.2	335.0
Parametric Technology	78.3	269.3
Reebok International	12.8	56.1
Silicon Graphics	52.6	188.8
Toys R Us	54.8	247.6

a. Develop the estimated regression equation that could be used to estimate the number of shares of option grants outstanding given the number of common shares outstanding.
b. Use the estimated regression equation to estimate the number of shares of option grants outstanding for a company that has 150 million shares of common stock outstanding.
c. Do you believe the estimated regression equation would provide a good prediction of the number of shares of option grants outstanding? Use r^2 to support your answer.

59. *Bloomberg Personal Finance* (July/August 2001) reported the market beta for Texas Instruments was 1.46. Market betas for individual stocks are determined by simple linear regression. For each stock, the dependent variable is its quarterly percentage return (capital appreciation plus dividends) minus the percentage return that could be obtained from a risk-free investment (the Treasury Bill rate is used as the risk-free rate). The independent variable is the quarterly percentage return (capital appreciation plus dividends) for the stock market (S&P 500) minus the percentage return from a risk-free investment. An estimated regression equation is developed with quarterly data; the market beta for the stock is the slope of the estimated regression equation (b_1). The value of the market beta is often interpreted as a measure of the risk associated with the stock. Market betas greater than 1 indicate that the stock is more volatile than the market average; market betas less than 1 indicate that the stock is less volatile than the market average. Suppose that the

following figures are the differences between the percentage return and the risk-free return for 10 quarters for the S&P 500 and Horizon Technology.

S&P 500	Horizon
1.2	−0.7
−2.5	−2.0
−3.0	−5.5
2.0	4.7
5.0	1.8
1.2	4.1
3.0	2.6
−1.0	2.0
.5	−1.3
2.5	5.5

a. Develop an estimated regression equation that can be used to determine the market beta for Horizon Technology. What is Horizon Technology's market beta?
b. Test for a significant relationship at the .05 level of significance.
c. Did the estimated regression equation provide a good fit? Explain.
d. Use the market betas of Texas Instruments and Horizon Technology to compare the risk associated with the two stocks.

60. The Australian Public Service Commission's State of the Service Report 2002–2003 reported job satisfaction ratings for employees. One of the survey questions asked employees to choose the five most important workplace factors (from a list of factors) that most affected how satisfied they were with their job. Respondents were then asked to indicate their level of satisfaction with their top five factors. The following data show the percentage of employees who nominated the factor in their top five, and a corresponding satisfaction rating measured using the percentage of employees who nominated the factor in the top five and who were "very satisfied" or "satisfied" with the factor in their current workplace (http://www.apsc.gov.au/stateoftheservice).

CD file

JobSat

Workplace Factor	Top Five (%)	Satisfaction Rating (%)
Appropriate workload	30	49
Chance to be creative/innovative	38	64
Chance to make a useful contribution to society	40	67
Duties/expectations made clear	40	69
Flexible working arrangements	55	86
Good working relationships	60	85
Interesting work provided	48	74
Opportunities for career development	33	43
Opportunities to develop my skills	46	66
Opportunities to utilize my skills	50	70
Regular feedback/recognition for effort	42	53
Salary	47	62
Seeing tangible results from my work	42	69

a. Develop a scatter diagram with Top Five (%) on the horizontal axis and Satisfaction Rating (%) on the vertical axis.
b. What does the scatter diagram developed in part (a) indicate about the relationship between the two variables?

c. Develop the estimated regression equation that could be used to predict the Satisfaction Rating (%) given the Top Five (%).
d. Test for a significant relationship at the .05 level of significance.
e. Did the estimated regression equation provide a good fit? Explain.
f. What is the value of the sample correlation coefficient?

61. Jensen Tire & Auto is in the process of deciding whether to purchase a maintenance contract for its new computer wheel alignment and balancing machine. Managers feel that maintenance expense should be related to usage, and they collected the following information on weekly usage (hours) and annual maintenance expense (in hundreds of dollars).

Weekly Usage (hours)	Annual Maintenance Expense ($ hundreds)
13	17.0
10	22.0
20	30.0
28	37.0
32	47.0
17	30.5
24	32.5
31	39.0
40	51.5
38	40.0

a. Develop the estimated regression equation that relates annual maintenance expense to weekly usage.
b. Test the significance of the relationship in part (a) at a .05 level of significance.
c. Jensen expects to use the new machine 30 hours per week. Develop a 95% prediction interval for the company's annual maintenance expense.
d. If the maintenance contract costs $3000 per year, would you recommend purchasing it? Why or why not?

62. In a manufacturing process the assembly line speed (feet per minute) was thought to affect the number of defective parts found during the inspection process. To test this theory, managers devised a situation in which the same batch of parts was inspected visually at a variety of line speeds. They collected the following data.

Line Speed	Number of Defective Parts Found
20	21
20	19
40	15
30	16
60	14
40	17

a. Develop the estimated regression equation that relates line speed to the number of defective parts found.
b. At a .05 level of significance, determine whether line speed and number of defective parts found are related.

c. Did the estimated regression equation provide a good fit to the data?

d. Develop a 95% confidence interval to predict the mean number of defective parts for a line speed of 50 feet per minute.

63. A sociologist was hired by a large city hospital to investigate the relationship between the number of unauthorized days that employees are absent per year and the distance (miles) between home and work for the employees. A sample of 10 employees was chosen, and the following data were collected.

Distance to Work	Number of Days Absent
1	8
3	5
4	8
6	7
8	6
10	3
12	5
14	2
14	4
18	2

a. Develop a scatter diagram for these data. Does a linear relationship appear reasonable? Explain.

b. Develop the least squares estimated regression equation.

c. Is there a significant relationship between the two variables? Use $\alpha = .05$.

d. Did the estimated regression equation provide a good fit? Explain.

e. Use the estimated regression equation developed in part (b) to develop a 95% confidence interval for the expected number of days absent for employees living 5 miles from the company.

64. The regional transit authority for a major metropolitan area wants to determine whether there is any relationship between the age of a bus and the annual maintenance cost. A sample of 10 buses resulted in the following data.

Age of Bus (years)	Maintenance Cost ($)
1	350
2	370
2	480
2	520
2	590
3	550
4	750
4	800
5	790
5	950

a. Develop the least squares estimated regression equation.

b. Test to see whether the two variables are significantly related with $\alpha = .05$.

c. Did the least squares line provide a good fit to the observed data? Explain.

d. Develop a 95% prediction interval for the maintenance cost for a specific bus that is 4 years old.

65. A marketing professor at Givens College is interested in the relationship between hours spent studying and total points earned in a course. Data collected on 10 students who took the course last quarter follow.

Hours Spent Studying	Total Points Earned
45	40
30	35
90	75
60	65
105	90
65	50
90	90
80	80
55	45
75	65

a. Develop an estimated regression equation showing how total points earned is related to hours spent studying.
b. Test the significance of the model with $\alpha = .05$.
c. Predict the total points earned by Mark Sweeney. He spent 95 hours studying.
d. Develop a 95% prediction interval for the total points earned by Mark Sweeney.

66. The Transactional Records Access Clearinghouse at Syracuse University reported data showing the odds of an Internal Revenue Service audit. The following table shows the average adjusted gross income reported and the percentage of the returns that were audited for 20 selected IRS districts.

CD file

IRSAudit

District	Adjusted Gross Income ($)	Percentage Audited
Los Angeles	36,664	1.3
Sacramento	38,845	1.1
Atlanta	34,886	1.1
Boise	32,512	1.1
Dallas	34,531	1.0
Providence	35,995	1.0
San Jose	37,799	0.9
Cheyenne	33,876	0.9
Fargo	30,513	0.9
New Orleans	30,174	0.9
Oklahoma City	30,060	0.8
Houston	37,153	0.8
Portland	34,918	0.7
Phoenix	33,291	0.7
Augusta	31,504	0.7
Albuquerque	29,199	0.6
Greensboro	33,072	0.6
Columbia	30,859	0.5
Nashville	32,566	0.5
Buffalo	34,296	0.5

a. Develop the estimated regression equation that could be used to predict the percentage audited given the average adjusted gross income reported.
b. At the .05 level of significance, determine whether the adjusted gross income and the percentage audited are related.
c. Did the estimated regression equation provide a good fit? Explain.
d. Use the estimated regression equation developed in part (a) to calculate a 95% confidence interval for the expected percentage audited for districts with an average adjusted gross income of $35,000.

Case Problem 1   # Spending and Student Achievement

Is the educational achievement level of students related to how much the state in which they reside spends on education? In many communities taxpayers are asking this important question as school districts request tax revenue increases for education. In this case, you will be asked to analyze data on spending and achievement scores in order to determine whether there is any relationship between spending and student achievement in the public schools.

The federal government's National Assessment of Educational Progress (NAEP) program is frequently used to measure the educational achievement of students. Table 14.14 shows the total current spending per pupil per year, and the composite NAEP test score for

TABLE 14.14   SPENDING PER PUPIL AND COMPOSITE TEST SCORES FOR STATES THAT PARTICIPATED IN THE NAEP PROGRAM

CD file

NAEP

State	Spending per Pupil ($)	Composite Test Score
Louisiana	4049	581
Mississippi	3423	582
California	4917	580
Hawaii	5532	580
South Carolina	4304	603
Alabama	3777	604
Georgia	4663	611
Florida	4934	611
New Mexico	4097	614
Arkansas	4060	615
Delaware	6208	615
Tennessee	3800	618
Arizona	4041	618
West Virginia	5247	625
Maryland	6100	625
Kentucky	5020	626
Texas	4520	627
New York	8162	628
North Carolina	4521	629
Rhode Island	6554	638
Washington	5338	639
Missouri	4483	641
Colorado	4772	644
Indiana	5128	649
Utah	3280	650
Wyoming	5515	657
Connecticut	7629	657
Massachusetts	6413	658
Nebraska	5410	660
Minnesota	5477	661
Iowa	5060	665
Montana	4985	667
Wisconsin	6055	667
North Dakota	4374	671
Maine	5561	675

TABLE 14.15   SPENDING PER PUPIL FOR STATES THAT DID NOT PARTICIPATE
IN THE NAEP PROGRAM

State	Spending per Pupil ($)
Idaho	3602
South Dakota	4067
Oklahoma	4265
Nevada	4658
Kansas	5164
Illinois	5297
New Hampshire	5387
Ohio	5438
Oregon	5588
Vermont	6269
Michigan	6391
Pennsylvania	6579
Alaska	7890

35 states that participated in the NAEP program. These data are available on the CD accompanying the text in the file named NAEP. The composite test score is the sum of the math, science, and reading scores on the 1996 (1994 for reading) NAEP test. Pupils tested are in grade 8, except for reading, which is given to fourth-graders only. The maximum possible score is 1300. Table 14.15 shows the spending per pupil for 13 states that did not participate in relevant NAEP surveys. These data were reported in an article on spending and achievement level appearing in *Forbes* (November 3, 1997).

Managerial Report

1. Develop numerical and graphical summaries of the data.
2. Use regression analysis to investigate the relationship between the amount spent per pupil and the composite score on the NAEP test. Discuss your findings.
3. Do you think that the estimated regression equation developed for these data could be used to estimate the composite test scores for the states that did not participate in the NAEP program?
4. Suppose that you only considered states that spend at least $4000 per pupil but not more than $6000 per pupil. For these states, does the relationship between the two variables appear to be any different than for the complete data set? Discuss the results of your findings and whether you think deleting states with spending less than $4000 per year and more than $6000 per pupil is appropriate.
5. Develop estimates of the composite test scores for the states that did not participate in the NAEP program.
6. Based upon your analyses, do you think that the educational achievement level of students is related to how much the state spends on education?

Case Problem 2   U.S. Department of Transportation

As part of a study on transportation safety, the U.S. Department of Transportation collected data on the number of fatal accidents per 1000 licenses and the percentage of licensed drivers under the age of 21 in a sample of 42 cities. Data collected over a one-year period follow. These data are available on the CD accompanying the text in the file named Safety.

Safety

Percentage Under 21	Fatal Accidents per 1000 Licenses	Percentage Under 21	Fatal Accidents per 1000 Licenses
13	2.962	17	4.100
12	0.708	8	2.190
8	0.885	16	3.623
12	1.652	15	2.623
11	2.091	9	0.835
17	2.627	8	0.820
18	3.830	14	2.890
8	0.368	8	1.267
13	1.142	15	3.224
8	0.645	10	1.014
9	1.028	10	0.493
16	2.801	14	1.443
12	1.405	18	3.614
9	1.433	10	1.926
10	0.039	14	1.643
9	0.338	16	2.943
11	1.849	12	1.913
12	2.246	15	2.814
14	2.855	13	2.634
14	2.352	9	0.926
11	1.294	17	3.256

Managerial Report

1. Develop numerical and graphical summaries of the data.
2. Use regression analysis to investigate the relationship between the number of fatal accidents and the percentage of drivers under the age of 21. Discuss your findings.
3. What conclusion and recommendations can you derive from your analysis?

Case Problem 3 Alumni Giving

Alumni donations are an important source of revenue for colleges and universities. If administrators could determine the factors that influence increases in the percentage of alumni who make a donation, they might be able to implement policies that could lead to increased revenues. Research shows that students who are more satisfied with their contact with teachers are more likely to graduate. As a result, one might suspect that smaller class sizes and lower student–faculty ratios might lead to a higher percentage of satisfied graduates, which in turn might lead to increases in the percentage of alumni who make a donation. Table 14.16 shows data for 48 national universities (*America's Best Colleges,* Year 2000 Edition). The column labeled % of Classes Under 20 shows the percentage of classes offered with fewer than 20 students. The column labeled Student/Faculty Ratio is the number of students enrolled divided by the total number of faculty. Finally, the column labeled Alumni Giving Rate is the percentage of alumni that made a donation to the university.

TABLE 14.16   DATA FOR 48 NATIONAL UNIVERSITIES

CD file

Alumni

	% of Classes Under 20	Student/Faculty Ratio	Alumni Giving Rate
Boston College	39	13	25
Brandeis University	68	8	33
Brown University	60	8	40
California Institute of Technology	65	3	46
Carnegie Mellon University	67	10	28
Case Western Reserve Univ.	52	8	31
College of William and Mary	45	12	27
Columbia University	69	7	31
Cornell University	72	13	35
Dartmouth College	61	10	53
Duke University	68	8	45
Emory University	65	7	37
Georgetown University	54	10	29
Harvard University	73	8	46
Johns Hopkins University	64	9	27
Lehigh University	55	11	40
Massachusetts Inst. of Technology	65	6	44
New York University	63	13	13
Northwestern University	66	8	30
Pennsylvania State Univ.	32	19	21
Princeton University	68	5	67
Rice University	62	8	40
Stanford University	69	7	34
Tufts University	67	9	29
Tulane University	56	12	17
U. of California–Berkeley	58	17	18
U. of California–Davis	32	19	7
U. of California–Irvine	42	20	9
U. of California–Los Angeles	41	18	13
U. of California–San Diego	48	19	8
U. of California–Santa Barbara	45	20	12
U. of Chicago	65	4	36
U. of Florida	31	23	19
U. of Illinois–Urbana Champaign	29	15	23
U. of Michigan–Ann Arbor	51	15	13
U. of North Carolina–Chapel Hill	40	16	26
U. of Notre Dame	53	13	49
U. of Pennsylvania	65	7	41
U. of Rochester	63	10	23
U. of Southern California	53	13	22
U. of Texas–Austin	39	21	13
U. of Virginia	44	13	28
U. of Washington	37	12	12
U. of Wisconsin–Madison	37	13	13
Vanderbilt University	68	9	31
Wake Forest University	59	11	38
Washington University–St. Louis	73	7	33
Yale University	77	7	50

Managerial Report

1. Develop numerical and graphical summaries of the data.
2. Use regression analysis to develop an estimated regression equation that could be used to predict the alumni giving rate given the percentage of classes with fewer than 20 students.
3. Use regression analysis to develop an estimated regression equation that could be used to predict the alumni giving rate given the student–faculty ratio.
4. Which of the two estimated regression equations provides the best fit? For this estimated regression equation, perform an analysis of the residuals and discuss your findings and conclusions.
5. What conclusions and recommendations can you derive from your analysis?

Case Problem 4 Major League Baseball Team Values

A group led by John Henry paid $700 million to purchase the Boston Red Sox in 2002, even though the Red Sox had not won the World Series since 1918 and posted an operating loss of $11.4 million for 2001. Moreover, *Forbes* magazine estimates that the current value of the team is actually $426 million. *Forbes* attributes the difference between the current value for a team and the price investors are willing to pay to the fact that the purchase of a team often includes the acquisition of a grossly undervalued cable network. For instance, in purchasing the Boston Red Sox, the new owners also got an 80% interest in the New England Sports Network. Table 14.17 shows data for the 30 major league teams (*Forbes,* April 15, 2002). The column labeled Value contains the values of the teams based on current stadium deals, without deduction for debt. The column labeled Income indicates the earnings before interest, taxes, and depreciation.

Managerial Report

1. Develop numerical and graphical summaries of the data.
2. Use regression analysis to investigate the relationship between value and income. Discuss your findings.
3. Use regression analysis to investigate the relationship between value and revenue. Discuss your findings.
4. What conclusions and recommendations can you derive from your analysis?

Appendix 14.1 Calculus-Based Derivation of Least Squares Formulas

As mentioned in the chapter, the least squares method is a procedure for determining the values of b_0 and b_1 that minimize the sum of squared residuals. The sum of squared residuals is given by

$$\Sigma(y_i - \hat{y}_i)^2$$

Substituting $\hat{y}_i = b_0 + b_1 x_i$, we get

$$\Sigma(y_i - b_0 - b_1 x_i)^2 \qquad \textbf{(14.34)}$$

as the expression that must be minimized.

TABLE 14.17   DATA FOR MAJOR LEAGUE BASEBALL TEAMS

Team	Value	Revenue	Income
New York Yankees	730	215	18.7
New York Mets	482	169	14.3
Los Angeles Dodgers	435	143	−29.6
Boston Red Sox	426	152	−11.4
Atlanta Braves	424	160	9.5
Seattle Mariners	373	166	14.1
Cleveland Indians	360	150	−3.6
Texas Rangers	356	134	−6.5
San Francisco Giants	355	142	16.8
Colorado Rockies	347	129	6.7
Houston Astros	337	125	4.1
Baltimore Orioles	319	133	3.2
Chicago Cubs	287	131	7.9
Arizona Diamondbacks	280	127	−3.9
St. Louis Cardinals	271	123	−5.1
Detroit Tigers	262	114	12.3
Pittsburgh Pirates	242	108	9.5
Milwaukee Brewers	238	108	18.8
Philadelphia Phillies	231	94	2.6
Chicago White Sox	223	101	−3.8
San Diego Padres	207	92	5.7
Cincinnati Reds	204	87	4.3
Anaheim Angels	195	103	5.7
Toronto Blue Jays	182	91	−20.6
Oakland Athletics	157	90	6.8
Kansas City Royals	152	85	2.2
Tampa Bay Devil Rays	142	92	−6.1
Florida Marlins	137	81	1.4
Minnesota Twins	127	75	3.6
Montreal Expos	108	63	−3.4

To minimize expression (14.34), we must take the partial derivatives with respect to b_0 and b_1, set them equal to zero, and solve. Doing so, we get

$$\frac{\partial \Sigma(y_i - b_0 - b_1 x_i)^2}{\partial b_0} = -2\Sigma(y_i - b_0 - b_1 x_i) = 0 \qquad \textbf{(14.35)}$$

$$\frac{\partial \Sigma(y_i - b_0 - b_1 x_i)^2}{\partial b_1} = -2\Sigma x_i(y_i - b_0 - b_1 x_i) = 0 \qquad \textbf{(14.36)}$$

Dividing equation (14.35) by two and summing each term individually yields

$$-\Sigma y_i + \Sigma b_0 + \Sigma b_1 x_i = 0$$

Bringing Σy_i to the other side of the equal sign and noting that $\Sigma b_0 = nb_0$, we obtain

$$nb_0 + (\Sigma x_i)b_1 = \Sigma y_i \qquad \textbf{(14.37)}$$

Similar algebraic simplification applied to equation (14.36) yields

$$(\Sigma x_i)b_0 + (\Sigma x_i^2)b_1 = \Sigma x_i y_i \tag{14.38}$$

Equations (14.37) and (14.38) are known as the *normal equations*. Solving equation (14.37) for b_0 yields

$$b_0 = \frac{\Sigma y_i}{n} - b_1 \frac{\Sigma x_i}{n} \tag{14.39}$$

Using equation (14.39) to substitute for b_0 in equation (14.38) provides

$$\frac{\Sigma x_i \Sigma y_i}{n} - \frac{(\Sigma x_i)^2}{n} b_1 + (\Sigma x_i^2)b_1 = \Sigma x_i y_i \tag{14.40}$$

By rearranging the terms in equation (14.40), we obtain

$$b_1 = \frac{\Sigma x_i y_i - (\Sigma x_i \Sigma y_i)/n}{\Sigma x_i^2 - (\Sigma x_i)^2/n} = \frac{\Sigma(x_i - \bar{x})(y_i - \bar{y})}{\Sigma(x_i - \bar{x})^2} \tag{14.41}$$

Because $\bar{y} = \Sigma y_i/n$ and $\bar{x} = \Sigma x_i/n$, we can rewrite equation (14.39) as

$$b_0 = \bar{y} - b_1 \bar{x} \tag{14.42}$$

Equations (14.41) and (14.42) are the formulas (14.6) and (14.7) we used in the chapter to compute the coefficients in the estimated regression equation.

Appendix 14.2   Test for Significance Using Correlation

Using the sample correlation coefficient r_{xy}, we can determine whether the linear relationship between x and y is significant by testing the following hypotheses about the population correlation coefficient ρ_{xy}.

$$H_0: \rho_{xy} = 0$$
$$H_a: \rho_{xy} \neq 0$$

If H_0 is rejected, we can conclude that the population correlation coefficient is not equal to zero and that the linear relationship between the two variables is significant. This test for significance follows.

A TEST FOR SIGNIFICANCE USING CORRELATION

$$H_0: \rho_{xy} = 0$$
$$H_a: \rho_{xy} \neq 0$$

TEST STATISTIC

$$t = r_{xy} \sqrt{\frac{n-2}{1-r_{xy}^2}} \tag{14.43}$$

In Section 14.4, we found that the sample with $n = 10$ provided the sample correlation coefficient for student population and quarterly sales of $r_{xy} = .9501$. The test statistic is

$$t = r_{xy} \sqrt{\frac{n - 2}{1 - r_{xy}^2}} = .9501 \sqrt{\frac{10 - 2}{1 - (.9501)^2}} = 8.61$$

Using Excel, p-value = TDIST(8.61,8,2) = .0000.

The t distribution table shows that with $n - 2 = 10 - 2 = 8$ degrees of freedom, $t = 3.355$ provides an area of .005 in the upper tail. Thus, the area in the upper tail of the t distribution corresponding to the test statistic $t = 8.61$ must be less than .005. Because this test is a two-tailed test, we double this value to conclude that the p-value associated with $t = 8.62$ must be less than $2(.005) = .01$. Excel shows the p-value $= .0000$. Because the p-value is less than $\alpha = .01$, we reject H_0 and conclude that ρ_{xy} is not equal to zero. This evidence is sufficient to conclude that a significant linear relationship exists between student population and quarterly sales.

Note that the test statistic t and the conclusion of a significant relationship are identical to the results obtained in Section 14.5 for the t test conducted using Armand's estimated regression equation $\hat{y} = 60 + 5x$. Performing regression analysis provides the conclusion of a significant relationship between x and y and in addition provides the equation showing how the variables are related. Most analysts therefore use modern computer packages to perform regression analysis and find that using correlation as a separate test of significance is unnecessary.

Appendix 14.3   Regression Analysis with SWStat+

In Section 14.6 we showed how Excel's Regression tool can be used to perform a complete regression analysis for the Armand's Pizza Parlors data in Table 14.1. In this appendix we describe the steps required to perform regression analysis for Armand's Pizza Parlors using SWStat+. First we must create the data area for the Armand's Pizza Parlors data.

Creating the Data Area

Step 1. Select any cell in the Armand's data set
Step 2. Select the **SWStat+** menu
Step 3. Choose **Data Area**
Step 4. Choose **Set New Data Area** from the Data Area options
Step 5. When the SWStat+ Data Area dialog box appears:
Select the **Set New** tab
Select **With column headers**
Select **With row headers**
Click **Set data area**

After creating the data area, the row and column labels will be highlighted in yellow and the entire data set (including labels) will have a blue border. In addition, a Results worksheet is added to the workbook. The Results worksheet will contain all the output generated using SWStat+. We are now ready to use SWStat+ to perform a complete regression analysis for the Armand's Pizza Parlors data.

Simple Linear Regression

The steps necessary to generate the regression analysis output in the Results worksheet shown in Figure 14.25 are as follows:

Step 1. Select the **SWStat+** menu
Step 2. Choose **Statistics**
Step 3. Choose **Regression and Correlation**
Step 4. When the SWStat+: Regression and Correlation dialog box appears:
     Select the **Regression** tab
     Choose **Sales** in the **Dependent (Y)** box
     Choose **Population** in the **Independent (X)** box
     Click **Calculate**

The regression analysis output shown in Figure 14.25 is similar to the standard regression analysis output using Excel's Regression tool. The primary difference is in the order in which the results are presented.

FIGURE 14.25   SWStat+ RESULTS WORKSHEET SHOWING REGRESSION OUTPUT

	A	B	C	D	E	F	G	H	I	J
1	SWStat+ Results Sheet									
2										
3	SWStat+: Regression									
4		Analysis of Variance, ANOVA								
5			Degrees Freedom, df	Sum of Squares, SS	Mean Square, MS	F-Ratio	p-Value			
6		Regression	1	14200.000	14200.000	74.248	0.00003			
7		Error	8	1530.000	191.250					
8		Total	9	15730.000						
9										
10		Regression Equation Results								
11		Dependent Variable, Y: Sales								
12		Sales = 60.000 + 5.000 Population								
13										
14		Indep. X Variables	Coefficient	Standard Error	t Statistic	p-Value	95% Conf. Lower	95% Conf. Upper	VIF	
15		Intercept	60.0	9.226	6.5033	0.00019	38.725	81.275		
16		Population	5.0	0.58	8.6167	0.00003	3.662	6.338	-1.0	
17										
18		R-squared	90.27%							
19		Multiple R	0.9501							
20		Adj. R-squared	89.06%							
21		Standard Error of Estimate	13.829							
22		Durbin-Watson	3.224							
23		Number of Observations	10							
24										

Confidence and Prediction Intervals

To develop a 95% confidence interval and a 95% prediction interval when the student population is 10,000, we would perform the following steps after obtaining the regression results shown in Figure 14.25.

Step 1. Select the **SWStat+** menu
Step 2. Choose **Statistics**
Step 3. Choose **Regression and Correlation**
Step 4. When the SWStat+: Regression and Correlation dialog box appears:
Select the **Predictions** tab
Enter a value of **10** in the predictor value box
Click **Predict Y**

Standardized Residual Plot

To develop a standardized residual plot against the predicted values of sales, we would perform the following steps after obtaining the regression results shown in Figure 14.25.

Step 1. Select the **SWStat+** menu
Step 2. Choose **Statistics**
Step 3. Choose **Regression and Correlation**
Step 4. When the SWStat+: Regression and Correlation dialog box appears:
Select the **Regression Plots** tab
Choose **Standardized Residuals**
Choose **Fitted Value** in the **Style** box
Click **Show Plot**

CHAPTER 15

Multiple Regression

CONTENTS

STATISTICS IN PRACTICE:
INTERNATIONAL PAPER

15.1 MULTIPLE REGRESSION MODEL
Regression Model and
Regression Equation
Estimated Multiple Regression
Equation

15.2 LEAST SQUARES METHOD
An Example: Butler Trucking
Company
Using Excel's Regression Tool to
Develop the Estimated
Multiple Regression Equation
Note on Interpretation of
Coefficients

15.3 MULTIPLE COEFFICIENT OF DETERMINATION

15.4 MODEL ASSUMPTIONS

15.5 TESTING FOR SIGNIFICANCE
F Test
t Test
Multicollinearity

15.6 USING THE ESTIMATED REGRESSION EQUATION FOR ESTIMATION AND PREDICTION

15.7 QUALITATIVE INDEPENDENT VARIABLES
An Example: Johnson
Filtration, Inc.
Interpreting the Parameters
More Complex Qualitative
Variables

15.8 RESIDUAL ANALYSIS
Residual Plot Against $\hat{y}$
Standardized Residual Plot
Against $\hat{y}$

INTERNATIONAL PAPER*
PURCHASE, NEW YORK

International Paper is the world's largest paper and forest products company. The company employs more than 117,000 people in its operations in nearly 50 countries and exports its products to more than 130 nations. International Paper produces building materials such as lumber and plywood; consumer packaging materials such as disposable cups and containers; industrial packaging materials such as corrugated boxes and shipping containers; and a variety of papers for use in photocopiers, printers, books, and advertising materials.

To make paper products, pulp mills process wood chips and chemicals to produce wood pulp. The wood pulp is then used at a paper mill to produce paper products. In the production of white paper products, the pulp must be bleached to remove any discoloration. A key bleaching agent used in the process is chlorine dioxide, which, because of its combustible nature, is usually produced at a pulp mill facility and then piped in solution form into the bleaching tower of the pulp mill. To improve one of the processes used to produce chlorine dioxide, researchers studied the process's control and efficiency. One aspect of the study looked at the chemical-feed rate for chlorine dioxide production.

To produce the chlorine dioxide, four chemicals flow at metered rates into the chlorine dioxide generator. The chlorine dioxide produced in the generator flows to an absorber where chilled water absorbs the chlorine dioxide gas to form a chlorine dioxide solution. The solution is then piped into the paper mill. A key part of controlling the process involves the chemical-feed rates. Historically, experienced operators set the chemical-feed rates, but this approach led to overcontrol by the operators. Consequently, chemical engineers at the mill requested that a set of control equations, one for each chemical feed, be developed to aid the operators in setting the rates.

Multiple regression analysis assisted in the development of a better bleaching process for making white paper products. © Lester Lefkowitz/Corbis.

Using multiple regression analysis, statistical analysts developed an estimated multiple regression equation for each of the four chemicals used in the process. Each equation related the production of chlorine dioxide to the amount of chemical used and the concentration level of the chlorine dioxide solution. The resulting set of four equations was programmed into a microcomputer at each mill. In the new system, operators enter the concentration of the chlorine dioxide solution and the desired production rate; the computer software then calculates the chemical feed needed to achieve the desired production rate. After the operators began using the control equations, the chlorine dioxide generator efficiency increased, and the number of times the concentrations fell within acceptable ranges increased significantly.

This example shows how multiple regression analysis can be used to develop a better bleaching process for producing white paper products. In this chapter we will discuss how computer software packages are used for such purposes. Most of the concepts introduced in Chapter 14 for simple linear regression can be directly extended to the multiple regression case.

*The authors are indebted to Marian Williams and Bill Griggs for providing this Statistics in Practice. This application was originally developed at Champion International Corporation, which became part of International Paper in 2000.

In Chapter 14 we presented simple linear regression and demonstrated its use in developing an estimated regression equation that describes the relationship between two variables. Recall that the variable being predicted or explained is called the dependent variable and the variable being used to predict or explain the dependent variable is called the independent variable. In this chapter we continue our study of regression analysis by considering situations involving two or more independent variables. This subject area, called **multiple regression analysis**, enables us to consider more factors and thus often obtain better estimates than are possible with simple linear regression.

15.1 Multiple Regression Model

Multiple regression analysis is the study of how a dependent variable y is related to two or more independent variables. In the general case, we will use p to denote the number of independent variables.

Regression Model and Regression Equation

The concepts of a regression model and a regression equation introduced in the preceding chapter are applicable in the multiple regression case. The equation that describes how the dependent variable y is related to the independent variables $x_1, x_2, \ldots x_p$ and an error term is called the **multiple regression model**. We begin with the assumption that the multiple regression model takes the following form.

> **MULTIPLE REGRESSION MODEL**
>
> $$y = \beta_0 + \beta_1 x_1 + \beta_2 x_2 + \cdots + \beta_p x_p + \epsilon \qquad (15.1)$$

In the multiple regression model, $\beta_0, \beta_1, \beta_2, \ldots, \beta_p$ are the parameters and ϵ (the Greek letter epsilon) is a random variable. A close examination of this model reveals that y is a linear function of $x_1, x_2, \ldots, x_p$ (the $\beta_0 + \beta_1 x_1 + \beta_2 x_2 + \cdots + \beta_p x_p$ part) plus an error term ϵ. The error term accounts for the variability in y that cannot be explained by the linear effect of the p independent variables.

In Section 15.4 we will discuss the assumptions for the multiple regression model and ϵ. One of the assumptions is that the mean or expected value of ϵ is zero. A consequence of this assumption is that the mean or expected value of y, denoted $E(y)$, is equal to $\beta_0 + \beta_1 x_1 + \beta_2 x_2 + \cdots + \beta_p x_p$. The equation that describes how the mean value of y is related to $x_1, x_2, \ldots, x_p$ is called the **multiple regression equation**.

> **MULTIPLE REGRESSION EQUATION**
>
> $$E(y) = \beta_0 + \beta_1 x_1 + \beta_2 x_2 + \cdots + \beta_p x_p \qquad (15.2)$$

Estimated Multiple Regression Equation

If the values of $\beta_0, \beta_1, \beta_2, \ldots, \beta_p$ were known, equation (15.2) could be used to compute the mean value of y at given values of $x_1, x_2, \ldots, x_p$. Unfortunately, these parameter values will not, in general, be known and must be estimated from sample data. A simple random sample is used to compute sample statistics $b_0, b_1, b_2, \ldots, b_p$ that are used as the point

FIGURE 15.1 THE ESTIMATION PROCESS FOR MULTIPLE REGRESSION

In simple linear regression, b_0 and b_1 were the sample statistics used to estimate the parameters β_0 and β_1. Multiple regression parallels this statistical inference process, with b_0, $b_1, b_2, \ldots, b_p$ denoting the sample statistics used to estimate the parameters $\beta_0, \beta_1, \beta_2, \ldots, \beta_p$.

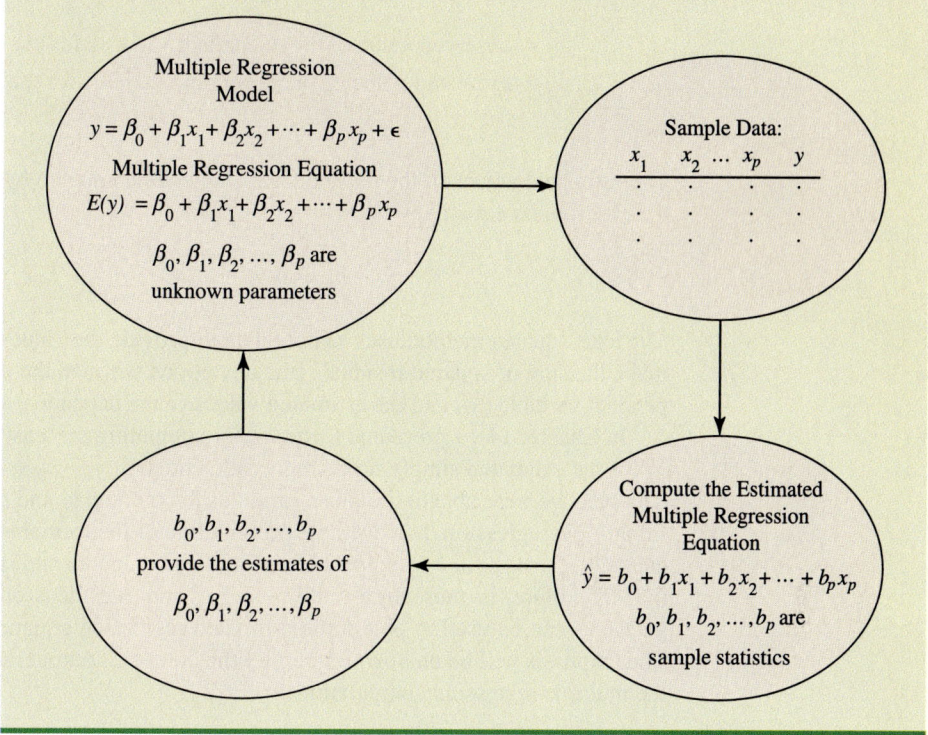

Multiple Regression Model

$$y = \beta_0 + \beta_1 x_1 + \beta_2 x_2 + \cdots + \beta_p x_p + \epsilon$$

Multiple Regression Equation

$$E(y) = \beta_0 + \beta_1 x_1 + \beta_2 x_2 + \cdots + \beta_p x_p$$

$\beta_0, \beta_1, \beta_2, \ldots, \beta_p$ are unknown parameters

Sample Data:

x_1	x_2	$\cdots$	x_p	y
.	.		.	.
.	.		.	.
.	.		.	.

Compute the Estimated Multiple Regression Equation

$$\hat{y} = b_0 + b_1 x_1 + b_2 x_2 + \cdots + b_p x_p$$

$b_0, b_1, b_2, \ldots, b_p$ are sample statistics

$b_0, b_1, b_2, \ldots, b_p$ provide the estimates of $\beta_0, \beta_1, \beta_2, \ldots, \beta_p$

estimators of the parameters $\beta_0, \beta_1, \beta_2, \ldots, \beta_p$. These sample statistics provide the following **estimated multiple regression equation**.

ESTIMATED MULTIPLE REGRESSION EQUATION

$$\hat{y} = b_0 + b_1 x_1 + b_2 x_2 + \cdots + b_p x_p \qquad \textbf{(15.3)}$$

where

$b_0, b_1, b_2, \ldots, b_p$ are the estimates of $\beta_0, \beta_1, \beta_2, \ldots, \beta_p$
$\hat{y}$ = estimated value of the dependent variable

The estimation process for multiple regression is shown in Figure 15.1.

15.2 Least Squares Method

In Chapter 14, we used the **least squares method** to develop the estimated regression equation that best approximated the straight-line relationship between the dependent and independent variables. This same approach is used to develop the estimated multiple regression equation. The least squares criterion is restated as follows.

LEAST SQUARES CRITERION

$$\min \Sigma(y_i - \hat{y}_i)^2 \qquad \textbf{(15.4)}$$

where

y_i = observed value of the dependent variable for the ith observation

$\hat{y}_i$ = estimated value of the dependent variable for the ith observation

The estimated values of the dependent variable are computed by using the estimated multiple regression equation,

$$\hat{y} = b_0 + b_1 x_1 + b_2 x_2 + \cdots + b_p x_p$$

The least squares method uses sample data to provide the values of $b_0, b_1, b_2, \ldots, b_p$ that make the sum of squared residuals [the deviations between the observed values of the dependent variable (y_i) and the estimated values of the dependent variable ($\hat{y}_i$)] a minimum.

In Chapter 14 we presented formulas for computing the least squares estimators b_0 and b_1 for the estimated simple linear regression equation $\hat{y} = b_0 + b_1 x$. With relatively small data sets, we were able to use those formulas to compute b_0 and b_1 by manual calculations. In multiple regression, however, the presentation of the formulas for the regression coefficients $b_0, b_1, b_2, \ldots, b_p$ involves the use of matrix algebra and is beyond the scope of this text. Therefore, in presenting multiple regression, we focus on how computer software packages can be used to obtain the estimated regression equation and other information. The emphasis will be on how to interpret the computer output rather than on how to make the multiple regression computations.

An Example: Butler Trucking Company

As an illustration of multiple regression analysis, we will consider a problem faced by the Butler Trucking Company, an independent trucking company in southern California. A major portion of Butler's business involves deliveries throughout its local area. To develop better work schedules, the managers want to estimate the total daily travel time for their drivers.

Initially the managers believed that the total daily travel time would be closely related to the number of miles traveled in making the daily deliveries. A simple random sample of 10 driving assignments provided the data shown in Table 15.1 and the scatter diagram shown in Figure 15.2. After reviewing this scatter diagram, the managers hypothesized that

TABLE 15.1 PRELIMINARY DATA FOR BUTLER TRUCKING

Butler

Driving Assignment	x_1 = Miles Traveled	y = Travel Time (hours)
1	100	9.3
2	50	4.8
3	100	8.9
4	100	6.5
5	50	4.2
6	80	6.2
7	75	7.4
8	65	6.0
9	90	7.6
10	90	6.1

FIGURE 15.2   SCATTER DIAGRAM OF PRELIMINARY DATA FOR BUTLER TRUCKING

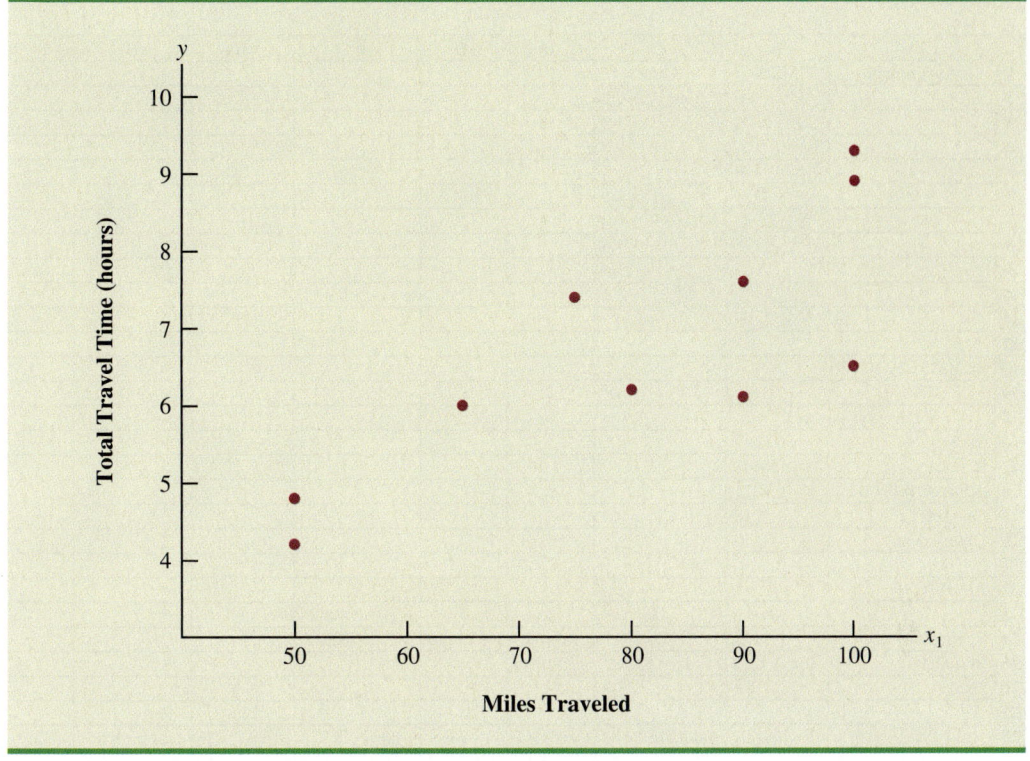

the simple linear regression model $y = \beta_0 + \beta_1 x_1 + \epsilon$ could be used to describe the relationship between the total travel time (y) and the number of miles traveled (x_1). To estimate the parameters β_0 and β_1, the least squares method was used to develop the estimated regression equation.

$$\hat{y} = b_0 + b_1 x_1 \tag{15.5}$$

In Figure 15.3, we show the Excel output* from applying simple linear regression to the data in Table 15.1. The estimated regression equation is

$$\hat{y} = 1.2739 + .0678 x_1$$

At the .05 level of significance, the F value of 15.8146 and its corresponding p-value of .0041 indicate that the relationship is significant; that is, we can reject H_0: $\beta_1 = 0$ because the p-value is less than $\alpha = .05$. Note that the same conclusion is obtained from the t value of 3.9768 and its associated p-value of .0041. Thus, we can conclude that the relationship between the total travel time and the number of miles traveled is significant; longer travel times are associated with more miles traveled. With a coefficient of determination of R Square = .6641, we see that 66.41% of the variability in travel time can be explained by the linear effect of the number of miles traveled. This finding is fairly good, but the managers might want to consider adding a second independent variable to explain some of the remaining variability in the dependent variable.

---

*Excel's Regression tool was used to obtain the output. Section 14.6 describes how to use Excel's Regression tool for simple linear regression.

FIGURE 15.3   REGRESSION TOOL OUTPUT FOR BUTLER TRUCKING WITH ONE INDEPENDENT VARIABLE

	A	B	C	D	E	F	G	H	I	J
1	Assignment	Miles	Time							
2	1	100	9.3							
3	2	50	4.8							
4	3	100	8.9							
5	4	100	6.5							
6	5	50	4.2							
7	6	80	6.2							
8	7	75	7.4							
9	8	65	6							
10	9	90	7.6							
11	10	90	6.1							
12										
13	SUMMARY OUTPUT									
14										
15	*Regression Statistics*									
16	Multiple R	0.8149								
17	R Square	0.6641								
18	Adjusted R Square	0.6221								
19	Standard Error	1.0018								
20	Observations	10								
21										
22	ANOVA									
23		*df*	*SS*	*MS*	*F*	*Significance F*				
24	Regression	1	15.8713	15.8713	15.8146	0.0041				
25	Residual	8	8.0287	1.0036						
26	Total	9	23.9							
27										
28		*Coefficients*	*Standard Error*	*t Stat*	*P-value*	*Lower 95%*	*Upper 95%*	*Lower 99.0%*	*Upper 99.0%*	
29	Intercept	1.2739	1.4007	0.9095	0.3897	-1.9562	4.5040	-3.4261	5.9739	
30	Miles	0.0678	0.0171	3.9768	0.0041	0.0285	0.1072	0.0106	0.1251	
31										

In attempting to identify another independent variable, the managers felt that the number of deliveries could also contribute to the total travel time. The Butler Trucking data, with the number of deliveries added, are shown in Table 15.2. To develop the estimated multiple regression equation with both miles traveled (x_1) and number of deliveries (x_2) as independent variables, we will use Excel's Regression tool.

TABLE 15.2   DATA FOR BUTLER TRUCKING WITH MILES TRAVELED (x_1) AND NUMBER OF DELIVERIES (x_2) AS THE INDEPENDENT VARIABLES

Butler

Driving Assignment	x_1 = Miles Traveled	x_2 = Number of Deliveries	y = Travel Time (hours)
1	100	4	9.3
2	50	3	4.8
3	100	4	8.9
4	100	2	6.5
5	50	2	4.2
6	80	2	6.2
7	75	3	7.4
8	65	4	6.0
9	90	3	7.6
10	90	2	6.1

Using Excel's Regression Tool to Develop the Estimated Multiple Regression Equation

In Section 14.6 we showed how Excel's Regression tool could be used to determine the estimated regression equation for Armand's Pizza Parlors. We can use the same procedure with minor modifications to develop the estimated multiple regression equation for Butler Trucking. Refer to Figures 15.4 and 15.5 as we describe the tasks involved.

Enter Data: The labels Assignment, Miles, Deliveries, and Time are entered into cells A1:D1 of the worksheet, and the sample data are entered into cells B2:D11. The numbers 1–10 are entered into cells A2:A11 to identify each observation.

Apply Tools: The following steps describe how to use the Regression tool for the multiple regression analysis.

Step 1. Select the **Tools** menu
Step 2. Choose the **Data Analysis** option
Step 3. Choose **Regression** from the list of Analysis Tools
Step 4. When the Regression dialog box appears (see Figure 15.5):
Enter D1:D11 in the **Input Y Range** box
Enter B1:C11 in the **Input X Range** box
Select **Labels**

FIGURE 15.4   REGRESSION TOOL OUTPUT FOR BUTLER TRUCKING WITH TWO INDEPENDENT VARIABLES

	A	B	C	D	E	F	G	H	I	J
1	Assignment	Miles	Deliveries	Time						
2	1	100	4	9.3						
3	2	50	3	4.8						
4	3	100	4	8.9						
5	4	100	2	6.5						
6	5	50	2	4.2						
7	6	80	2	6.2						
8	7	75	3	7.4						
9	8	65	4	6						
10	9	90	3	7.6						
11	10	90	2	6.1						
12										
13	SUMMARY OUTPUT									
14										
15	*Regression Statistics*									
16	Multiple R	0.9507								
17	R Square	0.9038								
18	Adjusted R Square	0.8763								
19	Standard Error	0.5731								
20	Observations	10								
21										
22	ANOVA									
23		*df*	*SS*	*MS*	*F*	*Significance F*				
24	Regression	2	21.6006	10.8003	32.8784	0.0003				
25	Residual	7	2.2994	0.3285						
26	Total	9	23.9							
27										
28		*Coefficients*	*Standard Error*	*t Stat*	*P-value*	*Lower 95%*	*Upper 95%*	*Lower 99.0%*	*Upper 99.0%*	
29	Intercept	-0.8687	0.9515	-0.9129	0.3916	-3.1188	1.3813	-4.1986	2.4612	
30	Miles	0.0611	0.0099	6.1824	0.0005	0.0378	0.0845	0.0265	0.0957	
31	Deliveries	0.9234	0.2211	4.1763	0.0042	0.4006	1.4463	0.1496	1.6972	
32										

FIGURE 15.5 REGRESSION DIALOG BOX FOR THE BUTLER TRUCKING EXAMPLE

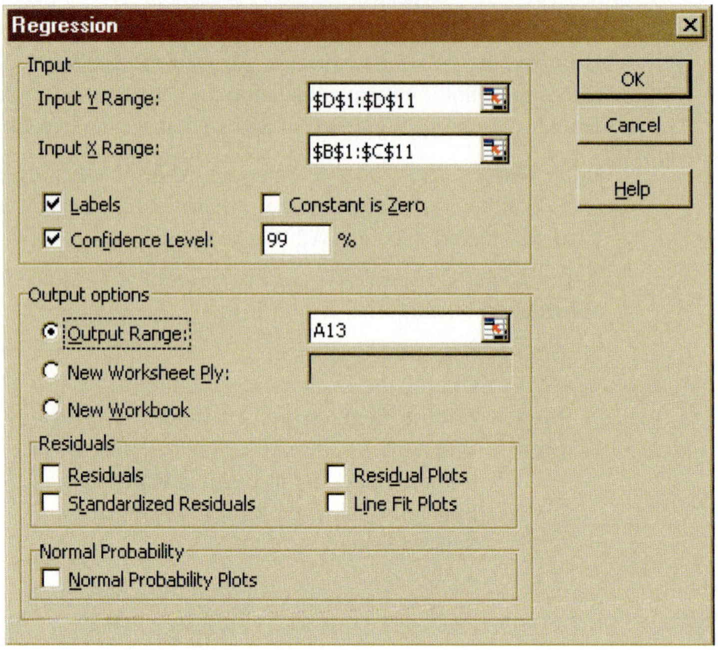

Select **Confidence Level**
Enter 99 in the **Confidence Level** box
Select **Output Range**
Enter A13 in the **Output Range** box (to identify the upper left corner of the
   section of the worksheet where the output will appear)
Click **OK**

In the Excel output shown in Figure 15.4 the label for the independent variable x_1 is Miles (see cell A30), and the label for the independent variable x_2 is Deliveries (see cell A31). The estimated regression equation is

$$\hat{y} = -.8687 + .0611x_1 + .9234x_2 \tag{15.6}$$

Note that using Excel's Regression tool for multiple regression is almost the same as using it for simple linear regression. The major difference is that in the multiple regression case a larger range of cells has to be provided in order to identify the independent variables.

Note on Interpretation of Coefficients

Compare the relationship between the estimated regression equation with only the miles traveled as an independent variable and the estimated regression equation that includes the number of deliveries as a second independent variable. Note that the value of b_1 is not the same in both cases. In simple linear regression, we interpret b_1 as an estimate of the change in y for a 1-unit change in the independent variable. For example, in the Butler Trucking Company example involving only one independent variable, number of miles traveled, $b_1 = .0678$. Thus, .0678 is an estimate of the expected increase in travel time corresponding to an increase of 1 mile in the distance traveled. In multiple regression analysis, this interpretation must be modified somewhat. That is, in multiple regression analysis, we interpret each regression coefficient as follows: b_i represents an estimate of the change in y corresponding to a 1-unit change in x_i when all other independent variables are held constant. In the Butler Trucking example involving two independent variables, $b_1 = .0611$. Thus, .0611 hours is an estimate of the expected increase in travel time corresponding to an increase of 1 mile in the distance traveled when the number of deliveries is held constant. Similarly, because $b_2 = .9234$, an estimate of the expected increase in travel time corresponding to an increase of one delivery when the number of miles traveled is held constant is .9234 hours.

NOTES AND COMMENTS

In Appendix 15.1 we show how to use SWStat+ to perform multiple regression analysis for the Butler Trucking data. The regression analysis capabilities of SWStat+ are more comprehensive than those available using Excel's Regression tool.

Exercises

Note to student: The exercises involving data in this and subsequent sections were designed to be solved using Excel.

Methods

1. The estimated regression equation for a model involving two independent variables and 10 observations follows.

$$\hat{y} = 29.1270 + .5906x_1 + .4980x_2$$

   a. Interpret b_1 and b_2 in this estimated regression equation.
   b. Estimate y when $x_1 = 180$ and $x_2 = 310$.

2. Consider the following data for a dependent variable y and two independent variables, x_1 and x_2.

Exer2

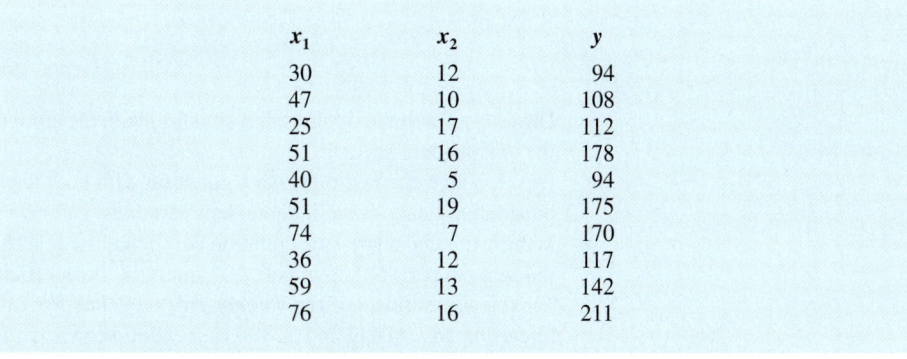

x_1	x_2	y
30	12	94
47	10	108
25	17	112
51	16	178
40	5	94
51	19	175
74	7	170
36	12	117
59	13	142
76	16	211

   a. Develop an estimated regression equation relating y to x_1. Estimate y if $x_1 = 45$.
   b. Develop an estimated regression equation relating y to x_2. Estimate y if $x_2 = 15$.
   c. Develop an estimated regression equation relating y to x_1 and x_2. Estimate y if $x_1 = 45$ and $x_2 = 15$.

3. In a regression analysis involving 30 observations, the following estimated regression equation was obtained.

$$\hat{y} = 17.6 + 3.8x_1 - 2.3x_2 + 7.6x_3 + 2.7x_4$$

   a. Interpret b_1, b_2, b_3, and b_4 in this estimated regression equation.
   b. Estimate y when $x_1 = 10$, $x_2 = 5$, $x_3 = 1$, and $x_4 = 2$.

Applications

4. A shoe store developed the following estimated regression equation relating sales to inventory investment and advertising expenditures.

$$\hat{y} = 25 + 10x_1 + 8x_2$$

   where

$$x_1 = \text{inventory investment (\$1000s)}$$
$$x_2 = \text{advertising expenditures (\$1000s)}$$
$$y = \text{sales (\$1000s)}$$

   a. Estimate sales resulting from a $15,000 investment in inventory and an advertising budget of $10,000.
   b. Interpret b_1 and b_2 in this estimated regression equation.

5. The owner of Showtime Movie Theaters, Inc., would like to estimate weekly gross revenue as a function of advertising expenditures. Historical data for a sample of eight weeks follow.

Showtime

Weekly Gross Revenue ($1000s)	Television Advertising ($1000s)	Newspaper Advertising ($1000s)
96	5.0	1.5
90	2.0	2.0
95	4.0	1.5
92	2.5	2.5
95	3.0	3.3
94	3.5	2.3
94	2.5	4.2
94	3.0	2.5

   a. Develop an estimated regression equation with the amount of television advertising as the independent variable.
   b. Develop an estimated regression equation with both television advertising and newspaper advertising as the independent variables.
   c. Is the estimated regression equation coefficient for television advertising expenditures the same in part (a) and in part (b)? Interpret the coefficient in each case.
   d. What is the estimate of the weekly gross revenue for a week when $3500 is spent on television advertising and $1800 is spent on newspaper advertising?

6. In baseball, a team's success is often thought to be a function of the team's hitting and pitching performance. One measure of hitting performance is the number of home runs the team hits, and one measure of pitching performance is the earned run average for the team's pitching staff. It is generally believed that teams that hit more home runs and have a lower earned run average will win a higher percentage of the games played. The following data show the

proportion of games won, the number of team home runs (HR), and the earned run average (ERA) for the 16 teams in the National League for the 2003 Major League Baseball season (http://www.usatoday.com, January 7, 2004).

MLB

Team	Proportion Won	HR	ERA	Team	Proportion Won	HR	ERA
Arizona	0.519	152	3.857	Milwaukee	0.420	196	5.058
Atlanta	0.623	235	4.106	Montreal	0.512	144	4.027
Chicago	0.543	172	3.842	New York	0.410	124	4.517
Cincinnati	0.426	182	5.127	Philadelphia	0.531	166	4.072
Colorado	0.457	198	5.269	Pittsburgh	0.463	163	4.664
Florida	0.562	157	4.059	San Diego	0.395	128	4.904
Houston	0.537	191	3.880	San Francisco	0.621	180	3.734
Los Angeles	0.525	124	3.162	St. Louis	0.525	196	4.642

a. Determine the estimated regression equation that could be used to predict the proportion of games won given the number of team home runs.

b. Determine the estimated regression equation that could be used to predict the proportion of games won given the earned run average for the team's pitching staff.

c. Determine the estimated regression equation that could be used to predict the proportion of games won given the number of team home runs and the earned run average for the team's pitching staff.

d. For the 2003 season San Diego won only 39.5% of the games they played, the lowest in the National League. To improve next year's record, the team is trying to acquire new players who will increase the number of team home runs to 180 and decrease the earned run average for the team's pitching staff to 4.0. Use the estimated regression equation developed in part (c) to estimate the percentage of games San Diego will win if they have 180 team home runs and have an earned run average of 4.0.

7. Designers of backpacks use exotic material such as supernylon Delrin, high-density polyethylene, aircraft aluminum, and thermomolded foam to make packs that fit comfortably and distribute weight to eliminate pressure points. The following data show the capacity (cubic inches), comfort rating, and price for 10 backpacks tested by *Outside Magazine.* Comfort was measured using a rating from 1 to 5, with a rating of 1 denoting average comfort and a rating of 5 denoting excellent comfort (*Outside Buyer's Guide,* 2001).

Backpack

Manufacturer and Model	Capacity	Comfort	Price ($)
Camp Trails Paragon II	4330	2	190
EMS 5500	5500	3	219
Lowe Alpomayo 90+20	5500	4	249
Marmot Muir	4700	3	249
Kelly Bigfoot 5200	5200	4	250
Gregory Whitney	5500	4	340
Osprey 75	4700	4	389
Arc'Teryx Bora 95	5500	5	395
Dana Design Terraplane LTW	5800	5	439
The Works @ Mystery Ranch Jazz	5000	5	525

a. Determine the estimated regression equation that can be used to predict the price of a backpack given the capacity and the comfort rating.

b. Interpret b_1 and b_2.

c. Predict the price for a backpack with a capacity of 4500 cubic inches and a comfort rating of 4.

8. The following table gives the annual return, the safety rating (0 = riskiest, 10 = safest), and the annual expense ratio for 20 foreign funds (*Mutual Funds,* March 2000).

ForFunds

Fund	Safety Rating	Annual Expense Ratio (%)	Annual Return (%)
Accessor Int'l Equity "Adv"	7.1	1.59	49
Aetna "I" International	7.2	1.35	52
Amer Century Int'l Discovery "Inv"	6.8	1.68	89
Columbia International Stock	7.1	1.56	58
Concert Inv "A" Int'l Equity	6.2	2.16	131
Dreyfus Founders Int'l Equity "F"	7.4	1.80	59
Driehaus International Growth	6.5	1.88	99
Excelsior "Inst" Int'l Equity	7.0	0.90	53
Julius Baer International Equity	6.9	1.79	77
Marshall International Stock "Y"	7.2	1.49	54
MassMutual Int'l Equity "S"	7.1	1.05	57
Morgan Grenfell Int'l Sm Cap "Inst"	7.7	1.25	61
New England "A" Int'l Equity	7.0	1.83	88
Pilgrim Int'l Small Cap "A"	7.0	1.94	122
Republic International Equity	7.2	1.09	71
Sit International Growth	6.9	1.50	51
Smith Barney "A" Int'l Equity	7.0	1.28	60
State St Research "S" Int'l Equity	7.1	1.65	50
Strong International Stock	6.5	1.61	93
Vontobel International Equity	7.0	1.50	47

a. Develop an estimated regression equation relating the annual return to the safety rating and the annual expense ratio.
b. Estimate the annual return for a firm that has a safety rating of 7.5 and annual expense ratio of 2.

9. Two experts provided subjective lists of school districts that they think are among the best in the country. For each school district the average class size, the combined SAT score, and the percentage of students who attended a four-year college were provided.

Schools

District	Average Class Size	Combined SAT Score	% Attend Four-Year College
Blue Springs, MO	25	1083	74
Garden City, NY	18	997	77
Indianapolis, IN	30	716	40
Newport Beach, CA	26	977	51
Novi, MI	20	980	53
Piedmont, CA	28	1042	75
Pittsburgh, PA	21	983	66
Scarsdale, NY	20	1110	87
Wayne, PA	22	1040	85
Weston, MA	21	1031	89
Farmingdale, NY	22	947	81
Mamaroneck, NY	20	1000	69
Mayfield, OH	24	1003	48
Morristown, NJ	22	972	64
New Rochelle, NY	23	1039	55
Newtown Square, PA	17	963	79
Omaha, NE	23	1059	81
Shaker Heights, OH	23	940	82

a.   Using these data, develop an estimated regression equation relating the percentage of students who attend a four-year college to the average class size and the combined SAT score.
b.   Estimate the percentage of students who attend a four-year college if the average class size is 20 and the combined SAT score is 1000.

10.   The National Basketball Association (NBA) records a variety of statistics for each team. Four of these statistics are the proportion of games won (PCT), the proportion of field goals made by the team (FG%), the proportion of three-point shots made by the team's opponent (Opp 3 Pt%), and the number of turnovers committed by the team's opponent (Opp TO). The following data show the values of these statistics for the 29 teams in the NBA for a portion of the 2004 season (www.nba.com, January 3, 2004).

NBA

Team	PCT	FG%	Opp 3 Pt%	Opp TO	Team	PCT	FG%	Opp 3 Pt%	Opp TO
Atlanta	0.265	0.435	0.346	13.206	Minnesota	0.677	0.473	0.348	13.839
Boston	0.471	0.449	0.369	16.176	New Jersey	0.563	0.435	0.338	17.063
Chicago	0.313	0.417	0.372	15.031	New Orleans	0.636	0.421	0.330	16.909
Cleveland	0.303	0.438	0.345	12.515	New York	0.412	0.442	0.330	13.588
Dallas	0.581	0.439	0.332	15.000	Orlando	0.242	0.417	0.360	14.242
Denver	0.606	0.431	0.366	17.818	Philadelphia	0.438	0.428	0.364	16.938
Detroit	0.606	0.423	0.262	15.788	Phoenix	0.364	0.438	0.326	16.515
Golden State	0.452	0.445	0.384	14.290	Portland	0.484	0.447	0.367	12.548
Houston	0.548	0.426	0.324	13.161	Sacramento	0.724	0.466	0.327	15.207
Indiana	0.706	0.428	0.317	15.647	San Antonio	0.688	0.429	0.293	15.344
L.A. Clippers	0.464	0.424	0.326	14.357	Seattle	0.533	0.436	0.350	16.767
L.A. Lakers	0.724	0.465	0.323	16.000	Toronto	0.516	0.424	0.314	14.129
Memphis	0.485	0.432	0.358	17.848	Utah	0.531	0.456	0.368	15.469
Miami	0.424	0.410	0.369	14.970	Washington	0.300	0.411	0.341	16.133
Milwaukee	0.500	0.438	0.349	14.750					

a.   Determine the estimated regression equation that can be used to predict the proportion of games won given the proportion of field goals made by the team.
b.   Provide an interpretation for the slope of the estimated regression equation developed in part (a).
c.   Determine the estimated regression equation that can be used to predict the proportion of games won given the proportion of field goals made by the team, the proportion of three-point shots made by the team's opponent, and the number of turnovers committed by the team's opponent.
d.   Discuss the practical implications of the estimated regression equation developed in part (c).
e.   Estimate the proportion of games won for a team with the following values for the three independent variables: FG% = .45, Opp 3 Pt% = .34, and Opp TO = 17.

15.3 Multiple Coefficient of Determination

In simple linear regression we showed that the total sum of squares can be partitioned into two components: the sum of squares due to regression and the sum of squares due to error. The same relationship applies to the sum of squares in multiple regression.

> RELATIONSHIP AMONG SST, SSR, AND SSE
>
> $$SST = SSR + SSE \qquad \textbf{(15.7)}$$

where

$$SST = \text{total sum of squares} = \Sigma(y_i - \bar{y})^2$$
$$SSR = \text{sum of squares due to regression} = \Sigma(\hat{y}_i - \bar{y})^2$$
$$SSE = \text{sum of squares due to error} = \Sigma(y_i - \hat{y}_i)^2$$

Because of the computational difficulty in computing the three sums of squares, we rely on computer packages to determine those values. The analysis of variance part of the Excel output in Figure 15.4 shows the three values for the Butler Trucking example with two independent variables: SST = 23.9, SSR = 21.6006, and SSE = 2.2994. With only one independent variable (number of miles traveled), the Excel output in Figure 15.3 shows that SST = 23.9, SSR = 15.8713, and SSE = 8.0287. The value of SST is the same in both cases because it does not depend on $\hat{y}$, but SSR increases and SSE decreases when a second independent variable (number of deliveries) is added. The implication is that the estimated multiple regression equation provides a better fit for the observed data.

In Chapter 14, we used the coefficient of determination, $r^2 = SSR/SST$, to measure the goodness of fit for the estimated regression equation. The same concept applies to multiple regression. The term **multiple coefficient of determination** indicates that we are measuring the goodness of fit for the estimated multiple regression equation. The multiple coefficient of determination, denoted R^2, is computed as follows.

In the Excel Regression tool output the label R square is used to identify the value of R^2.

MULTIPLE COEFFICIENT OF DETERMINATION

$$R^2 = \frac{SSR}{SST} \tag{15.8}$$

The multiple coefficient of determination can be interpreted as the proportion of the variability in the dependent variable that can be explained by the estimated multiple regression equation. Hence, when multiplied by 100, it can be interpreted as the percentage of the variability in y that can be explained by the estimated regression equation.

In the two-independent-variable Butler Trucking example, with SSR = 21.6006 and SST = 23.9, we have

$$R^2 = \frac{21.6006}{23.9} = .9038$$

Therefore, 90.38% of the variability in travel time y is explained by the estimated multiple regression equation with miles traveled and number of deliveries as the independent variables. In Figure 15.4, we see that the multiple coefficient of determination is also provided by the Excel output; it is denoted by R square = .9038 (see cell B17).

Adding independent variables causes the prediction errors to become smaller, thus reducing the sum of squares due to error, SSE. Because SSR = SST − SSE, when SSE becomes smaller, SSR becomes larger, causing $R^2 = SSR/SST$ to increase.

Figure 15.3 shows that the R square value for the estimated regression equation with only one independent variable, number of miles traveled (x_1), is .6641. Thus, the percentage of the variability in travel times that is explained by the estimated regression equation increases from 66.41% to 90.38% when number of deliveries is added as a second independent variable. In general, R^2 always increases as independent variables are added to the model.

Many analysts prefer adjusting R^2 for the number of independent variables to avoid overestimating the impact of adding an independent variable on the amount of variability explained by the estimated regression equation. With n denoting the number of observations and p denoting the number of independent variables, the **adjusted multiple coefficient of determination** is computed as follows.

If a variable is added to the model, R^2 becomes larger even if the variable added is not statistically significant. The adjusted multiple coefficient of determination compensates for the number of independent variables in the model.

ADJUSTED MULTIPLE COEFFICIENT OF DETERMINATION

$$R_a^2 = 1 - (1 - R^2)\frac{n - 1}{n - p - 1}$$

(15.9)

For the Butler Trucking example with $n = 10$ and $p = 2$, we have

$$R_a^2 = 1 - (1 - .9038)\frac{10 - 1}{10 - 2 - 1} = .8763$$

Thus, after adjusting for the two independent variables, we have an adjusted multiple coefficient of determination of .8763. This value is provided by the Excel output in Figure 15.4 as Adjusted R Square = .8763 (see cell B18).

Exercises

Methods

11. In exercise 1, the following estimated regression equation based on 10 observations was presented.

$$\hat{y} = 29.1270 + .5906x_1 + .4980x_2$$

The values of SST and SSR are 6724.125 and 6216.375, respectively.
  a. Find SSE.
  b. Compute R^2.
  c. Compute R_a^2.
  d. Comment on the goodness of fit.

12. In exercise 2, 10 observations were provided for a dependent variable y and two independent variables x_1 and x_2; for these data SST = 15,182.9, and SSR = 14,052.2.
  a. Compute R^2.
  b. Compute R_a^2.
  c. Does the estimated regression equation explain a large amount of the variability in the data? Explain.

13. In exercise 3, the following estimated regression equation based on 30 observations was presented.

$$\hat{y} = 17.6 + 3.8x_1 - 2.3x_2 + 7.6x_3 + 2.7x_4$$

The values of SST and SSR are 1805 and 1760, respectively.
  a. Compute R^2.
  b. Compute R_a^2.
  c. Comment on the goodness of fit.

Applications

14. In exercise 4, the following estimated regression equation relating sales to inventory investment and advertising expenditures was given.

$$\hat{y} = 25 + 10x_1 + 8x_2$$

The data used to develop the model came from a survey of 10 stores; for those data, SST = 16,000 and SSR = 12,000.

a. For the estimated regression equation given, compute R^2.
b. Compute R_a^2.
c. Does the model appear to explain a large amount of variability in the data? Explain.

15. In exercise 5, the owner of Showtime Movie Theaters, Inc., used multiple regression analysis to predict gross revenue (y) as a function of television advertising (x_1) and newspaper advertising (x_2). The estimated regression equation was

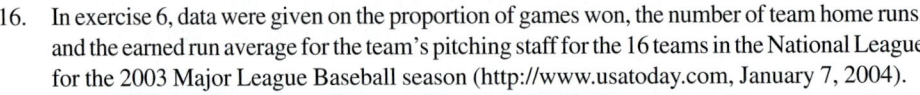

$$\hat{y} = 83.2 + 2.29x_1 + 1.30x_2$$

The computer solution provided SST = 25.5 and SSR = 23.435.
a. Compute and interpret R^2 and R_a^2.
b. When television advertising was the only independent variable, $R^2 = .653$ and $R_a^2 = .595$. Do you prefer the multiple regression results? Explain.

16. In exercise 6, data were given on the proportion of games won, the number of team home runs, and the earned run average for the team's pitching staff for the 16 teams in the National League for the 2003 Major League Baseball season (http://www.usatoday.com, January 7, 2004).
a. Did the estimated regression equation that uses only the number of home runs as the independent variable to predict the proportion of games won provide a good fit? Explain.
b. Discuss the benefits of using both the number of home runs and the earned run average to predict the proportion of games won.

17. In exercise 9, an estimated regression equation was developed relating the proportion of students who attend a four-year college to the average class size and the combined SAT score.
a. Compute and interpret R^2 and R_a^2.
b. Does the estimated regression equation provide a good fit to the data? Explain.

18. Refer to exercise 10, where data were reported on a variety of statistics for the 29 teams in the National Basketball Association for a portion of the 2004 season (http://www.nba.com, January 3, 2004).
a. In part (c) of exercise 10, an estimated regression equation was developed relating the proportion of games won given the percentage of field goals made by the team, the proportion of three-point shots made by the team's opponent, and the number of turnovers committed by the team's opponent. What are the values of R^2 and R_a^2?
b. Does the estimated regression equation provide a good fit to the data? Explain.

SELF test

CD file

Showtime

CD file

MLB

CD file

Schools

CD file

NBA

15.4 ## Model Assumptions

In Section 15.1 we introduced the following multiple regression model.

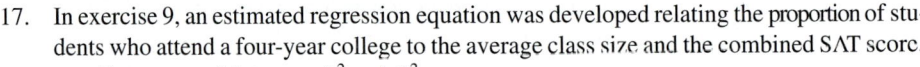

MULTIPLE REGRESSION MODEL

$$y = \beta_0 + \beta_1 x_1 + \beta_2 x_2 + \cdots + \beta_p x_p + \epsilon \qquad \textbf{(15.10)}$$

The assumptions about the error term ϵ in the multiple regression model parallel those for the simple linear regression model.

ASSUMPTIONS ABOUT THE ERROR TERM ϵ IN THE MULTIPLE REGRESSION MODEL $y = \beta_0 + \beta_1 x_1 + \cdots + \beta_p x_p + \epsilon$

1. The error ϵ is a random variable with mean or expected value of zero; that is, $E(\epsilon) = 0$.

Implication: For given values of $x_1, x_2, \ldots, x_p$, the expected, or average, value of y is given by

$$E(y) = \beta_0 + \beta_1 x_1 + \beta_2 x_2 + \cdots + \beta_p x_p \qquad \textbf{(15.11)}$$

Equation (15.11) is the multiple regression equation we introduced in Section 15.1. In this equation, $E(y)$ represents the average of all possible values of y that might occur for the given values of $x_1, x_2, \ldots, x_p$.

2. The variance of ϵ is denoted by σ^2 and is the same for all values of the independent variables $x_1, x_2, \ldots, x_p$.
   Implication: The variance of y about the regression line equals σ^2 and is the same for all values of $x_1, x_2, \ldots, x_p$.

3. The values of ϵ are independent.
   Implication: The size of the error for a particular set of values for the independent variables is not related to the size of the error for any other set of values.

4. The error ϵ is a normally distributed random variable reflecting the deviation between the y value and the expected value of y given by $\beta_0 + \beta_1 x_1 + \beta_2 x_2 + \cdots + \beta_p x_p$.
   Implication: Because $\beta_0, \beta_1, \ldots, \beta_p$ are constants, for the given values of $x_1, x_2, \ldots, x_p$, the dependent variable y is also a normally distributed random variable.

To obtain more insight about the form of the relationship given by equation (15.11), consider the following two-independent-variable multiple regression equation.

$$E(y) = \beta_0 + \beta_1 x_1 + \beta_2 x_2$$

The graph of this equation is a plane in three-dimensional space. Figure 15.6 provides an example of such a graph. Note that the value of ϵ shown is the difference between the actual y value and the expected value of y, $E(y)$, when $x_1 = x_1^*$ and $x_2 = x_2^*$.

FIGURE 15.6   GRAPH OF THE REGRESSION EQUATION FOR MULTIPLE REGRESSION ANALYSIS WITH TWO INDEPENDENT VARIABLES

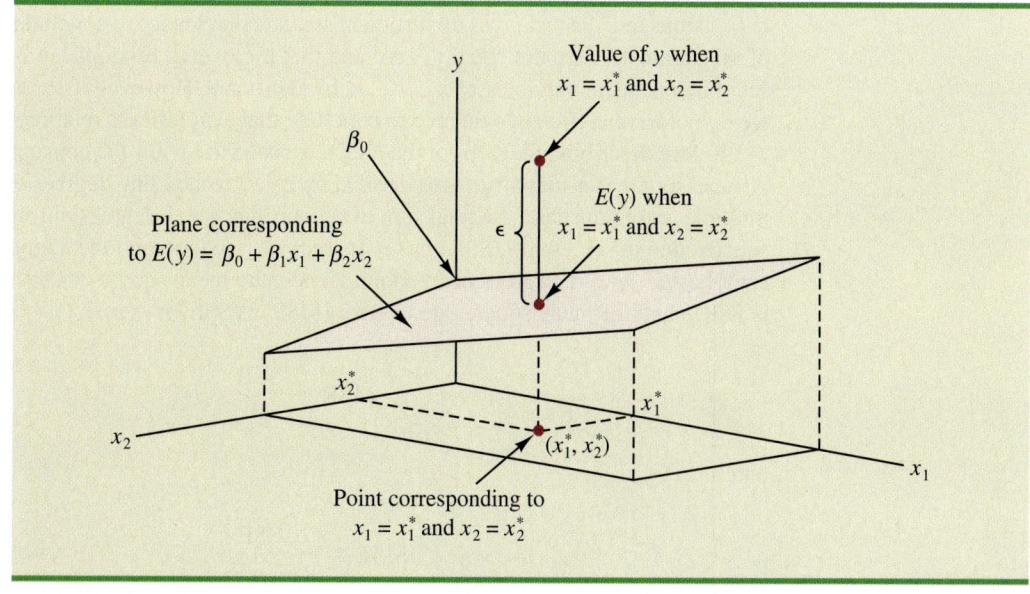

In regression analysis, the term *response variable* is often used in place of the term *dependent variable*. Furthermore, since the multiple regression equation generates a plane or surface, its graph is called a *response surface*.

 15.5   # Testing for Significance

In this section we show how to conduct significance tests for a multiple regression relationship. The significance tests we used in simple linear regression were a *t* test and an *F* test. In simple linear regression, both tests provide the same conclusion; that is, if the null hypothesis is rejected, we conclude that $\beta_1 \neq 0$. In multiple regression, the *t* test and the *F* test have different purposes.

1. The *F* test is used to determine whether a significant relationship exists between the dependent variable and the set of all the independent variables; we will refer to the *F* test as the test for *overall significance*.
2. If the *F* test shows an overall significance, the *t* test is used to determine whether each of the individual independent variables is significant. A separate *t* test is conducted for each of the independent variables in the model; we refer to each of these *t* tests as a test for *individual significance*.

In the material that follows, we will explain the *F* test and the *t* test and apply each to the Butler Trucking Company example.

F **Test**

The multiple regression model as defined in Section 15.1 is

$$y = \beta_0 + \beta_1 x_1 + \beta_2 x_2 + \cdots + \beta_p x_p + \epsilon$$

The hypotheses for the *F* test involve the parameters of the multiple regression model.

$$H_0: \beta_1 = \beta_2 = \cdots = \beta_p = 0$$
$$H_a: \text{One or more of the parameters are not equal to zero}$$

If H_0 is rejected, the test gives us sufficient statistical evidence to conclude that one or more of the parameters are not equal to zero and that the overall relationship between y and the set of independent variables $x_1, x_2, \ldots, x_p$ is significant. However, if H_0 cannot be rejected, we do not have sufficient evidence to conclude that a significant relationship is present.

Before describing the steps of the *F* test, we need to review the concept of *mean square*. A mean square is a sum of squares divided by its corresponding degrees of freedom. In the multiple regression case, the total sum of squares has $n - 1$ degrees of freedom, the sum of squares due to regression (SSR) has p degrees of freedom, and the sum of squares due to error has $n - p - 1$ degrees of freedom. Hence, the mean square due to regression (MSR) is SSR/p and the mean square due to error (MSE) is SSE/$(n - p - 1)$.

$$\text{MSR} = \frac{\text{SSR}}{p} \tag{15.12}$$

and

$$\text{MSE} = \frac{\text{SSE}}{n - p - 1} \tag{15.13}$$

As discussed in Chapter 14, MSE provides an unbiased estimate of σ^2, the variance of the error term ϵ. If $H_0: \beta_1 = \beta_2 = \cdots = \beta_p = 0$ is true, MSR also provides an unbiased estimate of σ^2, and the value of MSR/MSE should be close to 1. However, if H_0 is false, MSR overestimates σ^2 and the value of MSR/MSE becomes larger. To determine how large the value of MSR/MSE must be to reject H_0, we make use of the fact that if H_0 is true and the assumptions about the multiple regression model are valid, the sampling distribution of MSR/MSE is an F distribution with p degrees of freedom in the numerator and $n - p - 1$ degrees of freedom in the denominator. A summary of the F test for significance in multiple regression follows.

F TEST FOR OVERALL SIGNIFICANCE

$$H_0: \beta_1 = \beta_2 = \cdots = \beta_p = 0$$
$$H_a: \text{One or more of the parameters are not equal to zero}$$

TEST STATISTIC

$$F = \frac{\text{MSR}}{\text{MSE}} \tag{15.14}$$

REJECTION RULE

p-value approach:	Reject H_0 if p-value $\leq \alpha$
Critical value approach:	Reject H_0 if $F \geq F_\alpha$

where F_α is based on an F distribution with p degrees of freedom in the numerator and $n - p - 1$ degrees of freedom in the denominator.

Let us apply the F test to the Butler Trucking Company multiple regression example. With two independent variables, the hypotheses are written as follows.

$$H_0: \beta_1 = \beta_2 = 0$$
$$H_a: \beta_1 \text{ and/or } \beta_2 \text{ is not equal to zero}$$

Figure 15.7 shows a portion of the Excel output shown previously in Figure 15.4, with miles traveled (x_1) and number of deliveries (x_2) as the two independent variables. In the analysis of variance part of the output, we see that MSR = 10.8003 and MSE = .3285. Using equation (15.14), we obtain the test statistic.

$$F = \frac{10.8003}{.3285} = 32.9$$

Note that the F value in the Excel output is $F = 32.8784$; the value we calculated differs because we used rounded values for MSR and MSE in the calculation. Using $\alpha = .01$, the p-value (labeled *Significance F*) = 0.0003 in the last column of the analysis of variance table (Figure 15.7) indicates that we can reject $H_0: \beta_1 = \beta_2 = 0$ because the p-value is less than $\alpha = .01$. Alternatively, Table 4 of Appendix B shows that with two degrees of freedom in the numerator and seven degrees of freedom in the denominator, $F_{.01} = 9.55$. Because $F = 32.9 > 9.55$, we reject $H_0: \beta_1 = \beta_2 = 0$ and conclude that a significant relationship is present between travel time y and the two independent variables, miles traveled and number of deliveries.

As noted previously, the mean square error provides an unbiased estimate of σ^2, the variance of the error term ϵ. Referring to Figure 15.7, we see that the estimate of σ^2 is

FIGURE 15.7 PARTIAL EXCEL OUTPUT FOR THE BUTLER TRUCKING EXAMPLE WITH TWO INDEPENDENT VARIABLES

	A	B	C	D	E	F	G	H	I
13	SUMMARY OUTPUT								
14									
15	*Regression Statistics*								
16	Multiple R	0.9507							
17	R Square	0.9038							
18	Adjusted R Square	0.8763							
19	Standard Error	0.5731							
20	Observations	10							
21									
22	ANOVA								
23		*df*	*SS*	*MS*	*F*	*Significance F*			
24	Regression	2	21.6006	10.8003	32.8784	0.0003			
25	Residual	7	2.2994	0.3285					
26	Total	9	23.9						
27									
28		*Coefficients*	*Standard Error*	*t Stat*	*P-value*				
29	Intercept	-0.8687	0.9515	-0.9129	0.3916				
30	Miles	0.0611	0.0099	6.1824	0.0005				
31	Deliveries	0.9234	0.2211	4.1763	0.0042				
32									
33									
34									
35									
36									

> The *Significance F* value in cell F24 is the *p*-value used to test for overall significance.

> The *p*-value in cell E30 is used to test for the individual significance of Miles.

> The *p*-value in cell E31 is used to test for the individual significance of Deliveries.

Note: Rows 1–12 are hidden.

MSE $= .3285$. The square root of MSE is the estimate of the standard deviation of the error term. As defined in Section 14.5, this standard deviation is called the standard error of the estimate and is denoted s. Hence, we have $s = \sqrt{\text{MSE}} = \sqrt{.3285} = .5731$. Note that the value of the standard error of the estimate appears in cell B19 of Figure 15.7.

Table 15.3 is the general analysis of variance (ANOVA) table that provides the F test results for a multiple regression model. The value of the F test statistic appears in the last

TABLE 15.3 ANOVA TABLE FOR A MULTIPLE REGRESSION MODEL WITH p INDEPENDENT VARIABLES

Source	Sum of Squares	Degrees of Freedom	Mean Square	F
Regression	SSR	p	$MSR = \dfrac{SSR}{p}$	$F = \dfrac{MSR}{MSE}$
Error	SSE	$n - p - 1$	$MSE = \dfrac{SSE}{n - p - 1}$	
Total	SST	$n - 1$		

column and can be compared to F_α with p degrees of freedom in the numerator and $n - p - 1$ degrees of freedom in the denominator to make the hypothesis test conclusion. By reviewing the Excel output for Butler Trucking Company in Figure 15.7, we see that Excel's analysis of variance table contains this information. In addition, Excel also provides the p-value corresponding to the F test statistic.

t **Test**

If the F test shows that the multiple regression relationship is significant, a t test can be conducted to determine the significance of each of the individual parameters. The t test for individual significance follows.

---

t TEST FOR INDIVIDUAL SIGNIFICANCE

For any parameter β_i

$$H_0: \beta_i = 0$$
$$H_a: \beta_i \neq 0$$

TEST STATISTIC

$$t = \frac{b_i}{s_{b_i}} \tag{15.15}$$

REJECTION RULE

p-value approach: Reject H_0 if p-value $\leq \alpha$

Critical value approach: Reject H_0 if $t \leq t_{\alpha/2}$ or if $t \geq t_{\alpha/2}$

where $t_{\alpha/2}$ is based on a t distribution with $n - p - 1$ degrees of freedom.

In the test statistic, s_{b_i} is the estimate of the standard deviation of b_i. The value of s_{b_i} will be provided by the computer software package.

Let us conduct the t test for the Butler Trucking regression problem. Refer to cells B30:E31 in the Excel output shown in Figure 15.7. Values of b_1, b_2, s_{b_1}, and s_{b_2} are as follows.

$$b_1 = .0611 \quad s_{b_1} = .0099$$
$$b_2 = .9234 \quad s_{b_2} = .2211$$

Using equation (15.15), we obtain the test statistic for the hypotheses involving the individual parameters β_1 and β_2.

$$t = .0611/.0099 = 6.1717$$
$$t = .9234/.2211 = 4.1764$$

The t values in the Excel output are 6.1824 and 4.1763. The difference is due to rounding.

Note that both of these t-ratio values and the corresponding p-values are provided by the Excel output in Figure 15.7. Using $\alpha = .01$, the p-values of .0005 and .0042 on the Excel output indicate that we can reject $H_0: \beta_1 = 0$ and $H_0: \beta_2 = 0$. Hence, both parameters are statistically significant. Alternatively, Table 2 of Appendix B shows that with $n - p - 1 = 10 - 2 - 1 = 7$ degrees of freedom, $t_{.005} = 3.499$. Because $t = 6.1717 > 3.499$, we reject $H_0: \beta_1 = 0$. Similarly, with $4.1764 > 3.499$, we reject $H_0: \beta_2 = 0$.

Multicollinearity

We used the term *independent variable* in regression analysis to refer to any variable being used to predict or explain the value of the dependent variable. The term does not mean, however, that the independent variables themselves are independent in any statistical sense. On the contrary, most independent variables in a multiple regression problem are correlated to some degree with one another. For example, in the Butler Trucking example involving the two independent variables x_1 (miles traveled) and x_2 (number of deliveries), we could treat the miles traveled as the dependent variable and the number of deliveries as the independent variable to determine whether those two variables are themselves related. We could then compute the sample correlation coefficient $r_{x_1 x_2}$ to determine the extent to which the variables are related. Doing so yields $r_{x_1 x_2} = .16$. Thus, we find some degree of linear association between the two independent variables. In multiple regression analysis, **multicollinearity** refers to the correlation among the independent variables.

To provide a better perspective of the potential problems of multicollinearity, let us consider a modification of the Butler Trucking example. Instead of x_2 being the number of deliveries, let x_2 denote the number of gallons of gasoline consumed. Clearly, x_1 (the miles traveled) and x_2 are related; that is, we know that the number of gallons of gasoline used depends on the number of miles traveled. Hence, we would conclude logically that x_1 and x_2 are highly correlated independent variables.

Assume that we obtain the equation $\hat{y} = b_0 + b_1 x_1 + b_2 x_2$ and find that the F test shows the relationship to be significant. Then suppose we conduct a t test on β_1 to determine whether $\beta_1 \neq 0$, and we cannot reject $H_0: \beta_1 = 0$. Does this result mean that travel time is not related to miles traveled? Not necessarily. What it probably means is that with x_2 already in the model, x_1 does not make a significant additional contribution to determining the value of y. This interpretation makes sense in our example; if we know the amount of gasoline consumed, we do not gain much additional information useful in predicting y by knowing the miles traveled. Similarly, a t test might lead us to conclude $\beta_2 = 0$ on the grounds that, with x_1 in the model, knowledge of the amount of gasoline consumed does not add much.

When the independent variables are highly correlated, it is not possible to determine the separate effect of any particular independent variable on the dependent variable.

In t tests for the significance of individual parameters, the difficulty caused by multicollinearity is that it is possible to conclude that none of the individual parameters are significantly different from zero when an F test on the overall multiple regression equation indicates a significant relationship. This problem is avoided when there is little correlation among the independent variables.

Statisticians have developed several tests for determining whether multicollinearity is high enough to cause problems. According to the rule of thumb test, multicollinearity is a potential problem if the absolute value of the sample correlation coefficient exceeds .7 for any two of the independent variables. The other types of tests are more advanced and beyond the scope of this text.

If possible, every attempt should be made to avoid including independent variables that are highly correlated. In practice, however, strict adherence to this policy is rarely possible. When decision makers have reason to believe substantial multicollinearity is present, they must realize that separating the effects of the individual independent variables on the dependent variable is difficult.

NOTES AND COMMENTS

Ordinarily, multicollinearity does not affect the way in which we perform our regression analysis or interpret the output from a study. However, when multicollinearity is severe—that is, when two or more of the independent variables are highly correlated with one another—we can have difficulty interpreting the results of t tests on the individual parameters. In addition to the type of problem illustrated in this section, severe cases of multicollinearity have been shown to result in least squares estimates that have the wrong sign. That is, in simulated studies where researchers created the underlying regression model and then applied the least squares technique to develop estimates of β_0, β_1, β_2, and so on, it has been shown that under conditions of high multicollinearity the least squares estimates can have a sign opposite that of the parameter being estimated. For example, β_2 might actually be $+10$ and b_2, its estimate, might turn out to be -2. Thus, little faith can be placed in the individual coefficients if multicollinearity is present to a high degree.

Exercises

Methods

19. In exercise 1, the following estimated regression equation based on 10 observations was presented.

$$\hat{y} = 29.1270 + .5906x_1 + .4980x_2$$

Here SST $= 6724.125$, SSR $= 6216.375$, $s_{b_1} = .0813$, and $s_{b_2} = .0567$.
   a. Compute MSR and MSE.
   b. Compute F and perform the appropriate F test. Use $\alpha = .05$.
   c. Perform a t test for the significance of β_1. Use $\alpha = .05$.
   d. Perform a t test for the significance of β_2. Use $\alpha = .05$.

20. Refer to the data presented in exercise 2. The estimated regression equation for these data is

$$\hat{y} = -18.4 + 2.01x_1 + 4.74x_2$$

Here SST $= 15,182.9$, SSR $= 14,052.2$, $s_{b_1} = .2471$, and $s_{b_2} = .9484$.
   a. Test for a significant relationship among x_1, x_2, and y. Use $\alpha = .05$.
   b. Is β_1 significant? Use $\alpha = .05$.
   c. Is β_2 significant? Use $\alpha = .05$.

21. The following estimated regression equation was developed for a model involving two independent variables.

$$\hat{y} = 40.7 + 8.63x_1 + 2.71x_2$$

After x_2 was dropped from the model, the least squares method was used to obtain an estimated regression equation involving only x_1 as an independent variable.

$$\hat{y} = 42.0 + 9.01x_1$$

   a. Give an interpretation of the coefficient of x_1 in both models.
   b. Could multicollinearity explain why the coefficient of x_1 differs in the two models? If so, how?

Applications

22. In exercise 4 the following estimated regression equation relating sales to inventory investment and advertising expenditures was given.

$$\hat{y} = 25 + 10x_1 + 8x_2$$

The data used to develop the model came from a survey of 10 stores; for these data SST $= 16,000$ and SSR $= 12,000$.

a. Compute SSE, MSE, and MSR.
b. Use an *F* test and a .05 level of significance to determine whether there is a relationship among the variables.

23. Refer to Exercise 5.

a. Use $\alpha = .01$ to test the hypotheses

$$H_0: \beta_1 = \beta_2 = 0$$
$$H_a: \beta_1 \text{ and/or } \beta_2 \text{ is not equal to zero}$$

Showtime

for the model $y = \beta_0 + \beta_1 x_1 + \beta_2 x_2 + \epsilon$, where

$$x_1 = \text{television advertising (\$1000s)}$$
$$x_2 = \text{newspaper advertising (\$1000s)}$$

b. Use $\alpha = .05$ to test the significance of β_1. Should x_1 be dropped from the model?
c. Use $\alpha = .05$ to test the significance of β_2. Should x_2 be dropped from the model?

24. Refer to the data in exercise 6. Use the number of team home runs and the earned run average for the team's pitching staff to predict the proportion of games won.

MLB

a. Use the *F* test to determine the overall significance of the relationship. What is your conclusion at the .05 level of significance?
b. Use the *t* test to determine the significance of each independent variable. What is your conclusion at the .05 level of significance?

25. *Barron's* conducts an annual review of online brokers, including both brokers that can be accessed via a Web browser, as well as direct-access brokers that connect customers directly with the broker's network server. Each broker's offerings and performance are evaluated in six areas, using a point value of 0–5 in each category. The results are weighted to obtain an overall score, and a final star rating, ranging from zero to five, is assigned to each broker. Trade execution, ease of use, and range of offerings are three of the areas evaluated. A point value of 5 in the trade execution area means the order entry and execution process flowed easily from one step to the next. A value of 5 in the ease of use area means that the site was easy to use and can be tailored to show what the user wants to see. A value of 5 in the range of offerings area means that all of the investment transactions can be executed online. The following data show the point values for trade execution, ease of use, range of offerings, and the star rating for a sample of 10 of the online brokers that *Barron's* evaluated (*Barron's,* March 10, 2003).

Brokers

Broker	Trade Execution	Ease of Use	Range of Offerings	Rating
Wall St. Access	3.7	4.5	4.8	4.0
E*TRADE (Power)	3.4	3.0	4.2	3.5
E*TRADE (Standard)	2.5	4.0	4.0	3.5
Preferred Trade	4.8	3.7	3.4	3.5
my Track	4.0	3.5	3.2	3.5
TD Waterhouse	3.0	3.0	4.6	3.5
Brown & Co.	2.7	2.5	3.3	3.0
Brokerage America	1.7	3.5	3.1	3.0
Merrill Lynch Direct	2.2	2.7	3.0	2.5
Strong Funds	1.4	3.6	2.5	2.0

a. Determine the estimated regression equation that can be used to predict the star rating given the point values for execution, ease of use, and range of offerings.
b. Use the *F* test to determine the overall significance of the relationship. What is the conclusion at the .05 level of significance?

c. Use the t test to determine the significance of each independent variable. What is your conclusion at the .05 level of significance?

d. Remove any independent variable that is not significant from the estimated regression equation. What is your recommended estimated regression equation? Compare the R^2 with the value of R^2 from part (a). Discuss the differences.

NBA

26. In exercise 10 an estimated regression equation was developed relating the proportion of games won given the proportion of field goals made by the team, the proportion of three-point shots made by the team's opponent, and the number of turnovers committed by the team's opponent.

a. Use the F test to determine the overall significance of the relationship. What is your conclusion at the .05 level of significance?

b. Use the t test to determine the significance of each independent variable. What is your conclusion at the .05 level of significance?

15.6 Using the Estimated Regression Equation for Estimation and Prediction

The procedures for estimating the mean value of y and predicting an individual value of y in multiple regression are similar to those in regression analysis involving one independent variable. First, recall that in Chapter 14 we showed that the point estimate of the expected value of y for a given value of x was the same as the point estimate of an individual value of y. In both cases, we used $\hat{y} = b_0 + b_1 x$ as the point estimate.

In multiple regression we use the same procedure. That is, we substitute the given values of $x_1, x_2, \ldots, x_p$ into the estimated regression equation and use the corresponding value of $\hat{y}$ as the point estimate. Suppose that for the Butler Trucking example we want to use the estimated regression equation involving x_1 (miles traveled) and x_2 (number of deliveries) to develop two interval estimates:

1. A *confidence interval* of the mean travel time for all trucks that travel 100 miles and make two deliveries
2. A *prediction interval* of the travel time for *one specific* truck that travels 100 miles and makes two deliveries

Using the estimated regression equation $\hat{y} = -.869 + .0611 x_1 + .923 x_2$ with $x_1 = 100$ and $x_2 = 2$, we obtain the following value of $\hat{y}$.

$$\hat{y} = -.8687 + .0611(100) + .9234(2) = 7.09$$

Hence, the point estimate of travel time in both cases is approximately seven hours.

To develop interval estimates for the mean value of y and for an individual value of y, we use a procedure similar to that for regression analysis involving one independent variable. The formulas required are beyond the scope of the text, but computer packages for multiple regression analysis will often provide confidence intervals once the values of x_1, $x_2, \ldots, x_p$ are specified by the user. Unfortunately, Excel's Regression tool does not have this capability. However, by running the PredInt.xls macro included on the data disk, you will be able to develop confidence and prediction interval estimates. In Table 15.4 we show 95% confidence and prediction interval estimates for the Butler Trucking example for selected values of x_1 and x_2; these values were obtained by using the PredInt macro. Note that the interval estimate for an individual value of y is wider than the interval estimate for the expected value of y. This difference simply reflects the fact that for given values of x_1 and x_2 we can estimate the mean travel time for all trucks with more precision than we can predict the travel time for one specific truck.

The PredInt.xls macro included on the data disk can be used to develop confidence and prediction intervals.

TABLE 15.4   THE 95% CONFIDENCE AND PREDICTION INTERVAL ESTIMATES
FOR BUTLER TRUCKING

Value of x_1	Value of x_2	Value of $\hat{y}$	Confidence Interval		Prediction Interval	
			Lower Limit	Upper Limit	Lower Limit	Upper Limit
50	2	4.035	3.146	4.924	2.414	5.656
50	3	4.958	4.127	5.789	3.369	6.548
50	4	5.882	4.815	6.948	4.157	7.606
100	2	7.092	6.258	7.925	5.500	8.683
100	3	8.015	7.385	8.645	6.520	9.510
100	4	8.938	8.135	9.742	7.363	10.514

NOTES AND COMMENTS

In Appendix 15.1 we show how to use SWStat+ to develop confidence and prediction interval estimates for the Butler Trucking data.

Exercises

Methods

27. In exercise 1, the following estimated regression equation based on 10 observations was presented.

$$\hat{y} = 29.1270 + .5906x_1 + .4980x_2$$

a. Develop a point estimate of the mean value of y when $x_1 = 180$ and $x_2 = 310$.
b. Develop a point estimate for an individual value of y when $x_1 = 180$ and $x_2 = 310$.

28. Refer to the data in exercise 2. The estimated regression equation for those data is

$$\hat{y} = -18.4 + 2.01x_1 + 4.74x_2$$

a. Develop a 95% confidence interval for the mean value of y when $x_1 = 45$ and $x_2 = 15$.
b. Develop a 95% prediction interval for y when $x_1 = 45$ and $x_2 = 15$.

Applications

Showtime

29. In exercise 5, the owner of Showtime Movie Theaters, Inc., used multiple regression analysis to predict gross revenue (y) as a function of television advertising (x_1) and newspaper advertising (x_2). The estimated regression equation was

$$\hat{y} = 83.2 + 2.29x_1 + 1.30x_2$$

a. What is the gross revenue expected for a week when $3500 is spent on television advertising ($x_1 = 3.5$) and $1800 is spent on newspaper advertising ($x_2 = 1.8$)?
b. Provide a 95% confidence interval for the mean revenue of all weeks with the expenditures listed in part (a).
c. Provide a 95% prediction interval for next week's revenue, assuming that the advertising expenditures will be allocated as in part (a).

Schools

30. In exercise 9, an estimated regression equation was developed relating the percentage of students who attend a four-year college to the average class size and the combined SAT score.
    a. Develop a 95% confidence interval for the mean percentage of students who attend a four-year college for a school district that has an average class size of 25 and whose students have a combined SAT score of 1000.
    b. Suppose that a school district in Conway, South Carolina, has an average class size of 25 and a combined SAT score of 950. Develop a 95% prediction interval for the percentage of students who attend a four-year college.

31. The Buyer's Guide section of the Web site for *Car and Driver* magazine provides reviews and road tests for cars, trucks, SUVs, and vans. The average ratings of overall quality, vehicle styling, braking, handling, fuel economy, interior comfort, acceleration, dependability, fit and finish, transmission, and ride are summarized for each vehicle using a scale ranging from 1 (worst) to 10 (best). A portion of the data for 14 Sports/GT cars is shown here (http://www.caranddriver.com, January 7, 2004).

SportsCar

Sports/GT	Overall	Handling	Dependability	Fit and Finish
Acura 3.2CL	7.80	7.83	8.17	7.67
Acura RSX	9.02	9.46	9.35	8.97
Audi TT	9.00	9.58	8.74	9.38
BMW 3-Series/M3	8.39	9.52	8.39	8.55
Chevrolet Corvette	8.82	9.64	8.54	7.87
Ford Mustang	8.34	8.85	8.70	7.34
Honda Civic Si	8.92	9.31	9.50	7.93
Infiniti G35	8.70	9.34	8.96	8.07
Mazda RX-8	8.58	9.79	8.96	8.12
Mini Cooper	8.76	10.00	8.69	8.33
Mitsubishi Eclipse	8.17	8.95	8.25	7.36
Nissan 350Z	8.07	9.35	7.56	8.21
Porsche 911	9.55	9.91	8.86	9.55
Toyota Celica	8.77	9.29	9.04	7.97

   a. Develop an estimated regression equation using handling, dependability, and fit and finish to predict overall quality.
   b. Another Sports/GT car rated by *Car and Driver* is the Honda Accord. The ratings for handling, dependability, and fit and finish for the Honda Accord were 8.28, 9.06, and 8.07, respectively. Estimate the overall rating for this car.
   c. Provide a 95% confidence interval for overall quality for all sports and GT cars with the characteristics listed in part (a).
   d. Provide a 95% prediction interval for overall quality for the Honda Accord described in part (b).
   e. The overall rating reported by *Car and Driver* for the Honda Accord was 8.65. How does this rating compare to the estimates you developed in parts (b) and (d)?

Qualitative Independent Variables

Independent variables may be qualitative or quantitative.

Thus far, the examples we have considered have involved quantitative independent variables such as student population, distance traveled, and number of deliveries. In many situations, however, we must work with **qualitative independent variables** such as gender (male, female), method of payment (cash, credit card, check), and so on. The purpose of this section is to show how qualitative variables are handled in regression analysis. To illustrate the use and interpretation of a qualitative independent variable, we will consider a problem facing the managers of Johnson Filtration, Inc.

An Example: Johnson Filtration, Inc.

Johnson Filtration, Inc., provides maintenance service for water-filtration systems throughout southern Florida. Customers contact Johnson with requests for maintenance service on their water-filtration systems. To estimate the service time and the service cost, Johnson's managers want to predict the repair time necessary for each maintenance request. Hence, repair time in hours is the dependent variable. Repair time is believed to be related to two factors, the number of months since the last maintenance service and the type of repair problem (mechanical or electrical). Data for a sample of 10 service calls are reported in Table 15.5.

Let y denote the repair time in hours and x_1 denote the number of months since the last maintenance service. The regression model that uses only x_1 to predict y is

$$y = \beta_0 + \beta_1 x_1 + \epsilon$$

Using Excel's Regression tool to develop the estimated regression equation, we obtained the partial Excel output shown in Figure 15.8. The estimated regression equation is

$$\hat{y} = 2.1473 + .3041 x_1 \qquad (15.16)$$

At the .05 level of significance, the p-value of .0163 for the t (or F) test indicates that the number of months since the last service is significantly related to repair time. R Square = .5342 indicates that x_1 alone explains 53.42% of the variability in repair time.

To incorporate the type of failure into the regression model, we define the following variable.

$$x_2 = \begin{cases} 0 \text{ if the type of repair is mechanical} \\ 1 \text{ if the type of repair is electrical} \end{cases}$$

In regression analysis x_2 is called an *indicator* or **dummy variable.** Using this dummy variable, we can write the multiple regression model as

$$y = \beta_0 + \beta_1 x_1 + \beta_2 x_2 + \epsilon$$

Table 15.6 is the revised data set that includes the values of the dummy variable. Using Excel and the data in Table 15.6, we can develop estimates of the model parameters. The Excel output in Figure 15.9 shows that the estimated multiple regression equation is

$$\hat{y} = .9305 + .3876 x_1 + 1.2627 x_2 \qquad (15.17)$$

TABLE 15.5 DATA FOR THE JOHNSON FILTRATION EXAMPLE

Service Call	Months Since Last Service	Type of Repair	Repair Time in Hours
1	2	Electrical	2.9
2	6	Mechanical	3.0
3	8	Electrical	4.8
4	3	Mechanical	1.8
5	2	Electrical	2.9
6	7	Electrical	4.9
7	9	Mechanical	4.2
8	8	Mechanical	4.8
9	4	Electrical	4.4
10	6	Electrical	4.5

FIGURE 15.8   PARTIAL EXCEL OUTPUT FOR THE JOHNSON FILTRATION EXAMPLE WITH MONTHS SINCE LAST SERVICE CALL AS THE INDEPENDENT VARIABLE

The Excel regression output appears in a new worksheet because we selected New Worksheet Ply as the Output option in the Regression dialog box.

	A	B	C	D	E	F	G
1	SUMMARY OUTPUT						
2							
3	*Regression Statistics*						
4	Multiple R	0.7309					
5	R Square	0.5342					
6	Adjusted R Square	0.4759					
7	Standard Error	0.7810					
8	Observations	10					
9							
10	ANOVA						
11		*df*	*SS*	*MS*	*F*	*Significance F*	
12	Regression	1	5.5960	5.5960	9.1739	0.0163	
13	Residual	8	4.8800	0.6100			
14	Total	9	10.476				
15							
16		*Coefficients*	*Standard Error*	*t Stat*	*P-value*		
17	Intercept	2.1473	0.6050	3.5493	0.0075		
18	Months	0.3041	0.1004	3.0288	0.0163		
19							

At the .05 level of significance, the Significance F or p-value of .0010 associated with the F test ($F = 21.3570$) indicates that the regression relationship is significant. The t test part of the output in Figure 15.9 shows that both months since last service (p-value = .0004) and type of repair (p-value = .0051) are statistically significant. In addition, R Square = .8592 and Adjusted R Square = .8190 indicate that the estimated regression equation does a good job of explaining the variability in repair times. Thus, equation (15.17) should prove helpful in estimating the repair time necessary for the various service calls.

TABLE 15.6   DATA FOR THE JOHNSON FILTRATION EXAMPLE WITH TYPE OF REPAIR INDICATED BY A DUMMY VARIABLE ($x_2 = 0$ FOR MECHANICAL; $x_2 = 1$ FOR ELECTRICAL)

CD file

Johnson

Customer	Months Since Last Service (x_1)	Type of Repair (x_2)	Repair Time in Hours (y)
1	2	1	2.9
2	6	0	3.0
3	8	1	4.8
4	3	0	1.8
5	2	1	2.9
6	7	1	4.9
7	9	0	4.2
8	8	0	4.8
9	4	1	4.4
10	6	1	4.5

FIGURE 15.9 PARTIAL EXCEL OUTPUT FOR THE JOHNSON FILTRATION EXAMPLE WITH MONTHS SINCE LAST SERVICE CALL AND TYPE OF REPAIR AS THE INDEPENDENT VARIABLES

	A	B	C	D	E	F	G
1	SUMMARY OUTPUT						
2							
3	*Regression Statistics*						
4	Multiple R	0.9269					
5	R Square	0.8592					
6	Adjusted R Square	0.8190					
7	Standard Error	0.4590					
8	Observations	10					
9							
10	ANOVA						
11		*df*	*SS*	*MS*	*F*	*Significance F*	
12	Regression	2	9.0009	4.5005	21.3570	0.0010	
13	Residual	7	1.4751	0.2107			
14	Total	9	10.476				
15							
16		*Coefficients*	*Standard Error*	*t Stat*	*P-value*		
17	Intercept	0.9305	0.4670	1.9926	0.0866		
18	Months	0.3876	0.0626	6.1954	0.0004		
19	Type	1.2627	0.3141	4.0197	0.0051		
20							

Interpreting the Parameters

The multiple regression equation for the Johnson Filtration example is

$$E(y) = \beta_0 + \beta_1 x_1 + \beta_2 x_2 \tag{15.18}$$

To understand how to interpret the parameters β_0, β_1, and β_2 when a qualitative variable is present, consider the case when $x_2 = 0$ (mechanical repair). Using $E(y \mid \text{mechanical})$ to denote the mean repair time *given* a mechanical repair, we have

$$E(y \mid \text{mechanical}) = \beta_0 + \beta_1 x_1 + \beta_2(0) = \beta_0 + \beta_1 x_1 \tag{15.19}$$

Similarly, for an electrical repair ($x_2 = 1$), we have

$$E(y \mid \text{electrical}) = \beta_0 + \beta_1 x_1 + \beta_2(1) = \beta_0 + \beta_1 x_1 + \beta_2 \tag{15.20}$$
$$= (\beta_0 + \beta_2) + \beta_1 x_1$$

Comparing equations (15.19) and (15.20), we see that the expected repair time is a linear function of x_1 for both mechanical and electrical repairs. The slope of both equations is β_1, but the y-intercept differs. The y-intercept is β_0 in equation (15.19) for mechanical repairs and $(\beta_0 + \beta_2)$ in equation (15.20) for electrical repairs. The interpretation of β_2 is that it indicates the difference between the expected repair time for an electrical repair and the expected repair time for a mechanical repair.

If β_2 is positive, the expected repair time for an electrical repair will be greater than that for a mechanical repair; if β_2 is negative, the expected repair time for an electrical repair will be less than that for a mechanical repair. Finally, if $\beta_2 = 0$, there is no difference in repair time between electrical and mechanical repairs and the type of repair is not related to the repair time.

Using the estimated multiple regression equation $\hat{y} = .9305 + .3876x_1 + 1.2627x_2$, we see that .9305 is the estimate of β_0 and 1.2627 is the estimate of β_2. Thus, when $x_2 = 0$ (mechanical repair)

$$\hat{y} = .9305 + .3876x_1 \qquad \textbf{(15.21)}$$

and when $x_2 = 1$ (electrical repair)

$$\begin{aligned} \hat{y} &= .9305 + .3876x_1 + 1.2627(1) \\ &= 2.1932 + .3876x_1 \end{aligned} \qquad \textbf{(15.22)}$$

In effect, the use of a dummy variable for type of repair has provided two equations that can be used to predict the repair time, one corresponding to mechanical repairs and one corresponding to electrical repairs. In addition, with $b_2 = 1.2627$, we have learned that, on average, electrical repairs require 1.2627 hours longer than mechanical repairs.

Figure 15.10 is the plot of the Johnson data from Table 15.6. Repair time in hours (y) is represented by the vertical axis and months since last service (x_1) is represented by the horizontal axis. A data point for a mechanical repair is indicated by an M and a data point for an electrical repair is indicated by an E. Equations (15.21) and (15.22) are plotted on the graph to show graphically the two equations that can be used to predict the repair time, one corresponding to mechanical repairs and one corresponding to electrical repairs.

FIGURE 15.10   SCATTER DIAGRAM FOR THE JOHNSON FILTRATION REPAIR DATA FROM TABLE 15.6

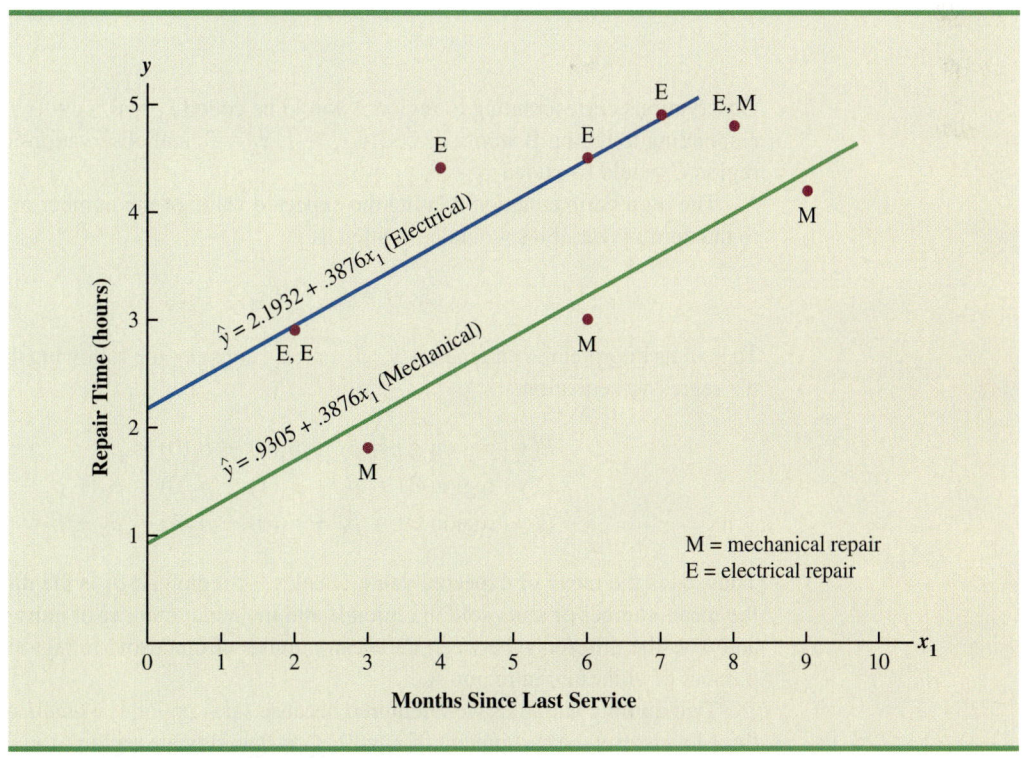

More Complex Qualitative Variables

A qualitative variable with k levels must be modeled using k − 1 dummy variables. Care must be taken in defining and interpreting the dummy variables.

Because the qualitative variable for the Johnson Filtration example had two levels (mechanical and electrical), defining a dummy variable with zero indicating a mechanical repair and one indicating an electrical repair was easy. However, when a qualitative variable has more than two levels, care must be taken in both defining and interpreting the dummy variables. As we will show, if a qualitative variable has k levels, $k − 1$ dummy variables are required, with each dummy variable being coded as 0 or 1.

For example, suppose a manufacturer of copy machines organized the sales territories for a particular state into three regions: A, B, and C. The managers want to use regression analysis to help predict the number of copiers sold per week. With the number of units sold as the dependent variable, they are considering several independent variables (the number of sales personnel, advertising expenditures, and so on). Suppose the managers believe sales region is also an important factor in predicting the number of copiers sold. Because sales region is a qualitative variable with three levels, A, B and C, we will need $3 − 1 = 2$ dummy variables to represent the sales region. Each variable can be coded 0 or 1 as follows.

$$x_1 = \begin{cases} 1 \text{ if sales region B} \\ 0 \text{ otherwise} \end{cases}$$

$$x_2 = \begin{cases} 1 \text{ if sales region C} \\ 0 \text{ otherwise} \end{cases}$$

With this definition, we have the following values of x_1 and x_2.

Region	x_1	x_2
A	0	0
B	1	0
C	0	1

Observations corresponding to region A would be coded $x_1 = 0$, $x_2 = 0$; observations corresponding to region B would be coded $x_1 = 1$, $x_2 = 0$; and observations corresponding to region C would be coded $x_1 = 0$, $x_2 = 1$.

The regression equation relating the expected value of the number of units sold, $E(y)$, to the dummy variables would be written as

$$E(y) = \beta_0 + \beta_1 x_1 + \beta_2 x_2$$

To help us interpret the parameters β_0, β_1, and β_2, consider the following three variations of the regression equation.

$$E(y \mid \text{region A}) = \beta_0 + \beta_1(0) + \beta_2(0) = \beta_0$$
$$E(y \mid \text{region B}) = \beta_0 + \beta_1(1) + \beta_2(0) = \beta_0 + \beta_1$$
$$E(y \mid \text{region C}) = \beta_0 + \beta_1(0) + \beta_2(1) = \beta_0 + \beta_2$$

Thus, β_0 is the mean or expected value of sales for region A; β_1 is the difference between the mean number of units sold in region B and the mean number of units sold in region A; and β_2 is the difference between the mean number of units sold in region C and the mean number of units sold in region A.

Two dummy variables were required because sales region is a qualitative variable with three levels. But the assignment of $x_1 = 0$, $x_2 = 0$ to indicate region A, $x_1 = 1$, $x_2 = 0$ to indicate region B, and $x_1 = 0, x_2 = 1$ to indicate region C was arbitrary. For example, we could have chosen $x_1 = 1$, $x_2 = 0$ to indicate region A, $x_1 = 0$, $x_2 = 0$ to indicate region B, and $x_1 = 0, x_2 = 1$ to indicate region C. In that case, β_1 would have been interpreted as the mean difference between regions A and B and β_2 as the mean difference between regions C and B.

The important point to remember is that when a qualitative variable has k levels, $k - 1$ dummy variables are required in the multiple regression analysis. Thus, if the sales region example had a fourth region, labeled D, three dummy variables would be necessary. For example, the three dummy variables can be coded as follows.

$$x_1 = \begin{cases} 1 \text{ if sales region B} \\ 0 \text{ otherwise} \end{cases} \qquad x_2 = \begin{cases} 1 \text{ if sales region C} \\ 0 \text{ otherwise} \end{cases} \qquad x_3 = \begin{cases} 1 \text{ if sales region D} \\ 0 \text{ otherwise} \end{cases}$$

Exercises

Methods

32. Consider a regression study involving a dependent variable y, a quantitative independent variable x_1, and a qualitative variable with two levels (level 1 and level 2).
    a. Write a multiple regression equation relating x_1 and the qualitative variable to y.
    b. What is the expected value of y corresponding to level 1 of the qualitative variable?
    c. What is the expected value of y corresponding to level 2 of the qualitative variable?
    d. Interpret the parameters in your regression equation.

33. Consider a regression study involving a dependent variable y, a quantitative independent variable x_1, and a qualitative independent variable with three possible levels (level 1, level 2, and level 3).
    a. How many dummy variables are required to represent the qualitative variable?
    b. Write a multiple regression equation relating x_1 and the qualitative variable to y.
    c. Interpret the parameters in your regression equation.

Applications

34. Management proposed the following regression model to predict sales at a fast-food outlet.

$$y = \beta_0 + \beta_1 x_1 + \beta_2 x_2 + \beta_3 x_3 + \epsilon$$

where

$$x_1 = \text{number of competitors within one mile}$$
$$x_2 = \text{population within one mile (1000s)}$$
$$x_3 = \begin{cases} 1 \text{ if drive-up window present} \\ 0 \text{ otherwise} \end{cases}$$
$$y = \text{sales (\$1000s)}$$

The following estimated regression equation was developed after 20 outlets were surveyed.

$$\hat{y} = 10.1 - 4.2x_1 + 6.8x_2 + 15.3x_3$$

a. What is the expected amount of sales attributable to the drive-up window?
b. Predict sales for a store with two competitors, a population of 8000 within one mile, and no drive-up window.
c. Predict sales for a store with one competitor, a population of 3000 within one mile, and a drive-up window.

35. Refer to the Johnson Filtration example introduced in this section. Suppose that in addition to information on the number of months since the machine was serviced and whether a mechanical or an electrical failure had occurred, the managers obtained a list showing which repairperson performed the service. The revised data follow.

Repair

Repair Time in Hours	Months Since Last Service	Type of Repair	Repairperson
2.9	2	Electrical	Dave Newton
3.0	6	Mechanical	Dave Newton
4.8	8	Electrical	Bob Jones
1.8	3	Mechanical	Dave Newton
2.9	2	Electrical	Dave Newton
4.9	7	Electrical	Bob Jones
4.2	9	Mechanical	Bob Jones
4.8	8	Mechanical	Bob Jones
4.4	4	Electrical	Bob Jones
4.5	6	Electrical	Dave Newton

a. Ignore for now the months since the last maintenance service (x_1) and the repairperson who performed the service. Develop the estimated simple linear regression equation to predict the repair time (y) given the type of repair (x_2). Recall that $x_2 = 0$ if the type of repair is mechanical and 1 if the type of repair is electrical.

b. Does the equation that you developed in part (a) provide a good fit for the observed data? Explain.

c. Ignore for now the months since the last maintenance service and the type of repair associated with the machine. Develop the estimated simple linear regression equation to predict the repair time given the repairperson who performed the service. Let $x_3 = 0$ if Bob Jones performed the service and $x_3 = 1$ if Dave Newton performed the service.

d. Does the equation that you developed in part (c) provide a good fit for the observed data? Explain.

36. This problem is an extension of the situation described in exercise 35.

a. Develop the estimated regression equation to predict the repair time given the number of months since the last maintenance service, the type of repair, and the repairperson who performed the service.

b. At the .05 level of significance, test whether the estimated regression equation developed in part (a) represents a significant relationship between the independent variables and the dependent variable.

c. Is the addition of the independent variable x_3, the repairperson who performed the service, statistically significant? Use $\alpha = .05$. What explanation can you give for the results observed?

37. The National Football League rates prospects by position on a scale that ranges from 5 to 9. The ratings are interpreted as follows: 8–9 should start the first year; 7.0–7.9 should start; 6.0–6.9 will make the team as backup; and 5.0–5.9 can make the club and contribute. The following table shows the position, weight, speed (for 40 yards), and ratings for 25 NFL prospects (*USA Today*, April 14, 2000).

Football

Player	Position	Weight (pounds)	Speed (seconds)	Rating
Cosey Coleman	Guard	322	5.38	7.4
Travis Claridge	Guard	303	5.18	7.0
Kaulana Noa	Guard	317	5.34	6.8
Leander Jordan	Guard	330	5.46	6.7
Chad Clifton	Guard	334	5.18	6.3

Player	Position	Weight (pounds)	Speed (seconds)	Rating
Manula Savea	Guard	308	5.32	6.1
Ryan Johanningmeir	Guard	310	5.28	6.0
Mark Tauscher	Guard	318	5.37	6.0
Blaine Saipaia	Guard	321	5.25	6.0
Richard Mercier	Guard	295	5.34	5.8
Damion McIntosh	Guard	328	5.31	5.3
Jeno James	Guard	320	5.64	5.0
Al Jackson	Guard	304	5.20	5.0
Chris Samuels	Offensive tackle	325	4.95	8.5
Stockar McDougle	Offensive tackle	361	5.50	8.0
Chris McIngosh	Offensive tackle	315	5.39	7.8
Adrian Klemm	Offensive tackle	307	4.98	7.6
Todd Wade	Offensive tackle	326	5.20	7.3
Marvel Smith	Offensive tackle	320	5.36	7.1
Michael Thompson	Offensive tackle	287	5.05	6.8
Bobby Williams	Offensive tackle	332	5.26	6.8
Darnell Alford	Offensive tackle	334	5.55	6.4
Terrance Beadles	Offensive tackle	312	5.15	6.3
Tutan Reyes	Offensive tackle	299	5.35	6.1
Greg Robinson-Ran	Offensive tackle	333	5.59	6.0

a. Develop a dummy variable that will account for the player's position.
b. Develop an estimated regression equation to show how rating is related to position, weight, and speed.
c. At the .05 level of significance, test whether the estimated regression equation developed in part (b) indicates a significant relationship between the independent variables and the dependent variable.
d. Does the estimated regression equation provide a good fit for the observed data? Explain.
e. Is position a significant factor in the player's rating? Use $\alpha = .05$. Explain.
f. Suppose a new offensive tackle prospect who weighs 300 pounds ran the 40 yards in 5.1 seconds. Use the estimated regression equation developed in part (b) to estimate the rating for this player.

38. A 10-year study conducted by the American Heart Association provided data on how age, blood pressure, and smoking relate to the risk of strokes. Assume that the following data are from a portion of this study. Risk is interpreted as the probability (times 100) that the patient will have a stroke over the next 10-year period. For the smoking variable, define a dummy variable with 1 indicating a smoker and 0 indicating a nonsmoker.

Risk	Age	Pressure	Smoker
12	57	152	No
24	67	163	No
13	58	155	No
56	86	177	Yes
28	59	196	No
51	76	189	Yes
18	56	155	Yes
31	78	120	No
37	80	135	Yes
15	78	98	No
22	71	152	No
36	70	173	Yes
15	67	135	Yes
48	77	209	Yes

CD file

Stroke

(continued)

Risk	Age	Pressure	Smoker
15	60	199	No
36	82	119	Yes
8	66	166	No
34	80	125	Yes
3	62	117	No
37	59	207	Yes

a.   Develop an estimated regression equation that relates risk of a stroke to the person's age, blood pressure, and whether the person is a smoker.

b.   Is smoking a significant factor in the risk of a stroke? Explain. Use $\alpha = .05$.

c.   What is the probability of a stroke over the next 10 years for Art Speen, a 68-year-old smoker who has blood pressure of 175? What action might the physician recommend for this patient?

 15.8 # Residual Analysis

In Chapter 14 we showed how a residual plot against the independent variable x can be used to validate the assumptions for a simple linear regression model. Because multiple regression analysis deals with two or more independent variables, we would have to examine a residual plot against each of the independent variables to use this approach. The more common approach in multiple regression analysis is to develop a residual plot against the predicted values $\hat{y}$.

Residual Plot Against $\hat{y}$

A residual plot against the predicted values $\hat{y}$ represents the predicted value of the dependent variable $\hat{y}$ on the horizontal axis and the residual values on the vertical axis. A point is plotted for each residual. The first coordinate for each point is given by $\hat{y}_i$ and the second coordinate is given by the corresponding value of the ith residual $y_i - \hat{y}_i$. For the Butler Trucking multiple regression example, the estimated regression equation that we developed using Excel (see Figure 15.4) was

$$\hat{y}_i = -.8687 + .0611x_1 + .9234x_2$$

where x_1 = miles traveled and x_2 = number of deliveries. Table 15.7 shows the predicted values and residuals based on this equation. The residual plot against $\hat{y}$ for Butler Trucking is shown in Figure 15.11. The residual plot does not indicate any abnormalities.

A residual plot against $\hat{y}$ can also be used when performing residual analysis in simple linear regression. In fact, the pattern for a residual plot against $\hat{y}$ in simple linear regression is the same as the pattern of the residual plot against x. Thus, for simple linear regression the residual plot against $\hat{y}$ and the residual plot against x provide the same information. In multiple regression analysis, however, it is preferable to use the residual plot against $\hat{y}$ to determine whether the model's assumptions are satisfied.

Standardized Residual Plot Against $\hat{y}$

In Chapter 14 we pointed out that standardized residuals were frequently used in residual plots. We showed how to construct a standardized residual plot against x and discussed how the standardized residual plot could be used to identify outliers and provide insight about the assumption that the error term ϵ has a normal distribution. Recall that we recommended considering any observation with a standardized residual of less than -2 or greater than $+2$ as an outlier. With normally distributed errors, standardized residuals should be outside these limits approximately 5% of the time.

TABLE 15.7 PREDICTED VALUES AND RESIDUALS FOR BUTLER TRUCKING

Miles Traveled (x_1)	Deliveries (x_2)	Travel Time (y)	Predicted Time ($\hat{y}$)	Residual ($y - \hat{y}$)
100	4	9.3	8.9385	0.3615
50	3	4.8	4.9583	−0.1583
100	4	8.9	8.9385	−0.0385
100	2	6.5	7.0916	−0.5916
50	2	4.2	4.0349	0.1651
80	2	6.2	5.8689	0.3311
75	3	7.4	6.4867	0.9133
65	4	6.0	6.7987	−0.7987
90	3	7.6	7.4037	0.1963
90	2	6.1	6.4803	−0.3803

In multiple regression analysis, the computation of the standardized residuals is too complex to be done by hand. As we showed in Section 14.8, Excel's Regression tool can be used to compute the standard residuals. In multiple regression analysis we use the same procedure to compute the standard residuals. Instead of developing a standardized residual plot against each of the independent variables, we will construct one standardized residual plot against the predicted values $\hat{y}$.

Figure 15.12 shows the standard residuals and the corresponding standardized residual plot against $\hat{y}$ (Predicted Time) for Butler Trucking developed using Excel's Regression tool and the Chart Wizard. The standardized residual plot does not indicate any abnormalities, and no standard residual is less than −2 or greater than +2. Note that the pattern of the standardized

FIGURE 15.11 RESIDUAL PLOT AGAINST THE PREDICTED TIME $\hat{y}$
FOR BUTLER TRUCKING

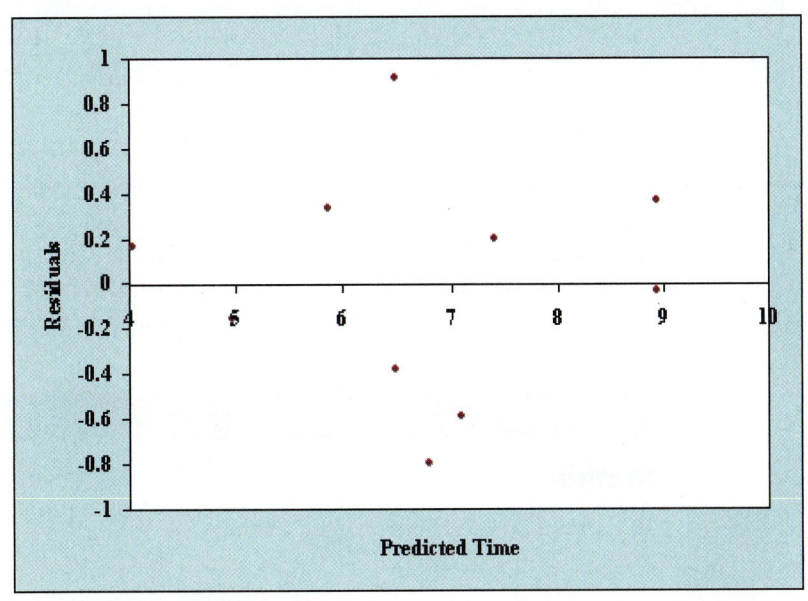

FIGURE 15.12 STANDARDIZED RESIDUAL PLOT AGAINST THE PREDICTED VALUES $\hat{y}$ FOR BUTLER TRUCKING

	A	B	C	D	E	F	G	H
35	RESIDUAL OUTPUT							
36								
37	*Observation*	*Predicted Time*	*Residuals*	*Standard Residuals*		*Predicted Time*	*Standard Residuals*	
38	1	8.9385	0.3615	0.7153		8.9385	0.7153	
39	2	4.9583	-0.1583	-0.3132		4.9583	-0.3132	
40	3	8.9385	-0.0385	-0.0761		8.9385	-0.0761	
41	4	7.0916	-0.5916	-1.1704		7.0916	-1.1704	
42	5	4.0349	0.1651	0.3267		4.0349	0.3267	
43	6	5.8689	0.3311	0.6550		5.8689	0.6550	
44	7	6.4867	0.9133	1.8069		6.4867	1.8069	
45	8	6.7987	-0.7987	-1.5802		6.7987	-1.5802	
46	9	7.4037	0.1963	0.3884		7.4037	0.3884	
47	10	6.4803	-0.3803	-0.7523		6.4803	-0.7523	
48								
49								
50								
51								
52								
53								
54								
55								
56								
57								
58								
59								
60								
61								
62								
63								
64								
65								
66								

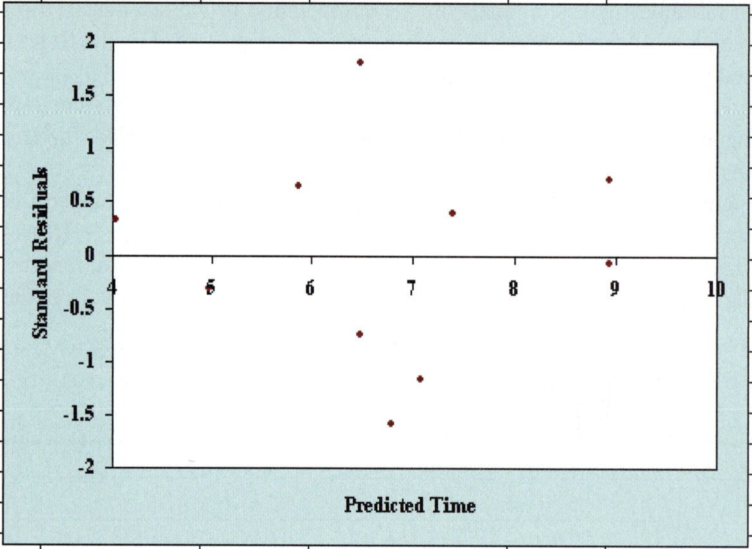

Note: Rows 1–34 are hidden.

residual plot against $\hat{y}$ is the same as the pattern of the residual plot against $\hat{y}$ shown in Figure 15.11. But the standardized residual plot is preferred because it enables us to check for outliers and determine whether the assumption of normality for the regression model is reasonable.

EXERCISES

Methods

SELF test

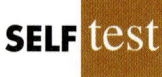

39. Data for two variables, x and y, follow.

x_i	1	2	3	4	5
y_i	3	7	5	11	14

    a.   Develop the estimated regression equation for these data.

    b.   Plot the residuals against $\hat{y}$. Does the residual plot support the assumptions about ϵ? Explain.

    c.   Plot the standardized residuals against $\hat{y}$. Do any outliers appear in these data? Explain.

40.   Data for two variables, x and y, follow.

x_i	22	24	26	28	40
y_i	12	21	31	35	70

    a.   Develop the estimated regression equation for these data.

    b.   Compute the standardized residuals for these data. Can any of these observations be classified as an outlier? Explain.

    c.   Develop a standardized residual plot against $\hat{y}$. Does the residual plot support the assumptions about ϵ? Explain.

Applications

41.   Exercise 5 gave the following data on weekly gross revenue ($1000s), television advertising expenditures ($1000s), and newspaper advertising expenditures ($1000s) for Showtime Movie Theaters.

Showtime

Weekly Gross Revenue ($1000s)	Television Advertising ($1000s)	Newspaper Advertising ($1000s)
96	5.0	1.5
90	2.0	2.0
95	4.0	1.5
92	2.5	2.5
95	3.0	3.3
94	3.5	2.3
94	2.5	4.2
94	3.0	2.5

    a.   Find an estimated regression equation relating weekly gross revenue to television advertising expenditures and newspaper advertising expenditures.

    b.   Plot the standardized residuals against $\hat{y}$. Does the residual plot support the assumptions about ϵ? Explain.

    c.   Check for any outliers in these data. What are your conclusions?

42.   The following table reports the price, horsepower, and ¼-mile speed for 16 popular sports and GT cars.

Auto1

Sports & GT Car	Price ($1000s)	Curb Weight (lb.)	Horsepower	Speed at ¼ mile (mph)
Accura Integra Type R	25.035	2577	195	90.7
Accura NSX-T	93.758	3066	290	108.0
BMW Z3 2.8	40.900	2844	189	93.2
Chevrolet Camaro Z28	24.865	3439	305	103.2
Chevrolet Corvette Convertible	50.144	3246	345	102.1
Dodge Viper RT/10	69.742	3319	450	116.2
Ford Mustang GT	23.200	3227	225	91.7

(continued)

Sports & GT Car	Price ($1000s)	Curb Weight (lb.)	Horsepower	Speed at ¼ mile (mph)
Honda Prelude Type SH	26.382	3042	195	89.7
Mercedes-Benz CLK320	44.988	3240	215	93.0
Mercedes-Benz SLK230	42.762	3025	185	92.3
Mitsubishi 3000GT VR-4	47.518	3737	320	99.0
Nissan 240SX SE	25.066	2862	155	84.6
Pontiac Firebird Trans Am	27.770	3455	305	103.2
Porsche Boxster	45.560	2822	201	93.2
Toyota Supra Turbo	40.989	3505	320	105.0
Volvo C70	41.120	3285	236	97.0

a. Find the estimated regression equation, which uses price and horsepower to predict ¼-mile speed.

b. Plot the standardized residuals against $\hat{y}$. Does the residual plot support the assumption about ϵ? Explain.

c. Check for any outliers. What are your conclusions?

43. In exercise 9, data were provided showing the percentage of students who attend a four-year college, the average class size, and the combined SAT score.

a. Develop an estimated regression equation that can be used to predict the percentage of students who attend a four-year college given the combined SAT score.

b. Based on the estimated regression equation developed in part (a), do these data contain any outliers? Explain.

c. Develop an estimated regression equation that can be used to predict the percentage of students who attend a four-year college given the average class size and the combined SAT score.

d. Based upon the estimated regression equation developed in part (c), do these data contain any outliers? Explain.

Summary

In this chapter, we introduced multiple regression analysis as an extension of simple linear regression analysis presented in Chapter 14. Multiple regression analysis enables us to understand how a dependent variable is related to two or more independent variables. The regression equation $E(y) = \beta_0 + \beta_1 x_1 + \beta_2 x_2 + \cdots + \beta_p x_p$ shows that the expected value or mean value of the dependent variable y is related to the values of the independent variables $x_1, x_2, \ldots, x_p$. Sample data and the least squares method are used to develop the estimated regression equation $\hat{y} = b_0 + b_1 x_1 + b_2 x_2 + \ldots + b_p x_p$. In effect $b_0, b_1, b_2, \ldots, b_p$ are sample statistics used to estimate the unknown model parameters $\beta_0, \beta_1, \beta_2, \ldots, \beta_p$. Excel's Regression tool was used throughout the chapter to emphasize the fact that statistical software packages are the only realistic means of performing the numerous computations required in multiple regression analysis.

The multiple coefficient of determination was presented as a measure of the goodness of fit of the estimated regression equation. It determines the proportion of the variation of y that can be explained by the estimated regression equation. The adjusted multiple coefficient of determination is a similar measure of goodness of fit that adjusts for the number of independent variables and thus avoids overestimating the impact of adding more independent variables.

An F test and a t test were presented as ways to determine statistically whether the relationship among the variables is significant. The F test is used to determine whether there is a significant overall relationship between the dependent variable and the set of all independent variables. The t test is used to determine whether there is a significant relationship between the dependent variable and an individual independent variable given the other independent variables in the regression model. Correlation among the independent variables, known as multicollinearity, was discussed.

The section on qualitative independent variables showed how dummy variables can be used to incorporate qualitative data into multiple regression analysis. The section on residual analysis showed how residual analysis can be used to validate the model assumptions and detect outliers.

Glossary

Multiple regression analysis Regression analysis involving two or more independent variables.

Multiple regression model The mathematical equation that describes how the dependent variable y is related to the independent variables $x_1, x_2, \ldots, x_p$ and an error term ϵ.

Multiple regression equation The mathematical equation relating the expected value or mean value of the dependent variable to the values of the independent variables; that is, $E(y) = \beta_0 + \beta_1 x_1 + \beta_2 x_2 + \ldots + \beta_p x_p$.

Estimated multiple regression equation The estimate of the multiple regression equation based on sample data and the least squares method; it is $\hat{y} = b_0 + b_1 x_1 + b_2 x_2 + \ldots + b_p x_p$.

Least squares method The method used to develop the estimated regression equation. It minimizes the sum of squared residuals (the deviations between the observed values of the dependent variable, y_i, and the estimated values of the dependent variable, $\hat{y}_i$).

Multiple coefficient of determination A measure of the goodness of fit of the estimated multiple regression equation. It can be interpreted as the proportion of the variability in the dependent variable that is explained by the estimated regression equation.

Adjusted multiple coefficient of determination A measure of the goodness of fit of the estimated multiple regression equation that adjusts for the number of independent variables in the model and thus avoids overestimating the impact of adding more independent variables.

Multicollinearity The term used to describe the correlation among the independent variables.

Qualitative independent variable An independent variable with qualitative data.

Dummy variable A variable, coded as 0 or 1, used to model the effect of qualitative independent variables.

Key Formulas

Multiple Regression Model

$$y = \beta_0 + \beta_1 x_1 + \beta_2 x_2 + \cdots + \beta_p x_p + \epsilon \qquad \textbf{(15.1)}$$

Multiple Regression Equation

$$E(y) = \beta_0 + \beta_1 x_1 + \beta_2 x_2 + \cdots + \beta_p x_p \qquad \textbf{(15.2)}$$

Estimated Multiple Regression Equation

$$\hat{y} = b_0 + b_1 x_1 + b_2 x_2 + \cdots + b_p x_p \qquad \textbf{(15.3)}$$

Least Squares Criterion

$$\min \Sigma (y_i - \hat{y}_i)^2 \qquad \textbf{(15.4)}$$

Relationship Among SST, SSR, and SSE

$$\text{SST} = \text{SSR} + \text{SSE} \tag{15.7}$$

Multiple Coefficient of Determination

$$R^2 = \frac{\text{SSR}}{\text{SST}} \tag{15.8}$$

Adjusted Multiple Coefficient of Determination

$$R_a^2 = 1 - (1 - R^2)\frac{n - 1}{n - p - 1} \tag{15.9}$$

Mean Square Regression

$$\text{MSR} = \frac{\text{SSR}}{p} \tag{15.12}$$

Mean Square Error

$$\text{MSE} = \frac{\text{SSE}}{n - p - 1} \tag{15.13}$$

_F_ Test Statistic

$$F = \frac{\text{MSR}}{\text{MSE}} \tag{15.14}$$

_t_ Test Statistic

$$t = \frac{b_i}{s_{b_i}} \tag{15.15}$$

Supplementary Exercises

44. The admissions officer for Clearwater College developed the following estimated regression equation relating the final college GPA to the student's SAT mathematics score and high-school GPA.

$$\hat{y} = -1.41 + .0235x_1 + .00486x_2$$

where

$$x_1 = \text{high-school grade point average}$$
$$x_2 = \text{SAT mathematics score}$$
$$y = \text{final college grade point average}$$

a. Interpret the coefficients in this estimated regression equation.
b. Estimate the final college GPA for a student who has a high-school average of 84 and a score of 540 on the SAT mathematics test.

45. The personnel director for Electronics Associates developed the following estimated regression equation relating an employee's score on a job satisfaction test to his or her length of service and wage rate.

$$\hat{y} = 14.4 - 8.69x_1 + 13.5x_2$$

where

$x_1 =$ length of service (years)
$x_2 =$ wage rate (dollars)
$y =$ job satisfaction test score (higher scores indicate greater job satisfaction)

a. Interpret the coefficients in this estimated regression equation.
b. Develop an estimate of the job satisfaction test score for an employee who has four years of service and makes $6.50 per hour.

46. A partial computer output from a regression analysis using Excel's Regression tool follows.

	A	B	C	D	E	F	G
1	SUMMARY OUTPUT						
2							
3	*Regression Statistics*						
4	Multiple R						
5	R Square	0.923					
6	Adjusted R Square						
7	Standard Error	3.35					
8	Observations						
9							
10	ANOVA						
11		*df*	*SS*	*MS*	*F*	*Significance F*	
12	Regression		1612				
13	Residual	12					
14	Total						
15							
16		*Coefficients*	*Standard Error*	*t Stat*	*P-value*		
17	Intercept	8.103	2.667				
18	X1	7.602	2.105				
19	X2	3.111	0.613				
20							

a. Compute the missing entries in this output.
b. Using $\alpha = .05$, test for overall significance.
c. Use the t test and $\alpha = .05$ to test $H_0: \beta_1 = 0$ and $H_0: \beta_2 = 0$.

47. Recall that in exercise 44, the admissions officer for Clearwater College developed the following estimated regression equation relating final college GPA to the student's SAT mathematics score and high-school GPA.

$$\hat{y} = -1.41 + .0235x_1 + .00486x_2$$

where

$$x_1 = \text{high-school grade point average}$$
$$x_2 = \text{SAT mathematics score}$$
$$y = \text{final college grade point average}$$

A portion of the Excel Regression tool output follows.

	A	B	C	D	E	F	G
1	SUMMARY OUTPUT						
2							
3	*Regression Statistics*						
4	Multiple R						
5	R Square						
6	Adjusted R Square						
7	Standard Error						
8	Observations						
9							
10	ANOVA						
11		*df*	*SS*	*MS*	*F*	*Significance F*	
12	Regression		1.76209				
13	Residual						
14	Total	9	1.88				
15							
16		*Coefficients*	*Standard Error*	*t Stat*	*P-value*		
17	Intercept	-1.4053	0.4848				
18	X1	0.023467	0.0086666				
19	X2	0.00486	0.001077				
20							

a. Complete the missing entries in this output.
b. Using $\alpha = .05$, test for overall significance.
c. Did the estimated regression equation provide a good fit to the data? Explain.
d. Use the t test and $\alpha = .05$ to test $H_0: \beta_1 = 0$ and $H_0: \beta_2 = 0$.

48. Recall that in exercise 45 the personnel director for Electronics Associates developed the following estimated regression equation relating an employee's score on a job satisfaction test to length of service and wage rate.

$$\hat{y} = 14.4 - 8.69x_1 + 13.5x_2$$

where

$$x_1 = \text{length of service (years)}$$
$$x_2 = \text{wage rate (dollars)}$$
$$y = \text{job satisfaction test score (higher scores}$$
$$\text{indicate greater job satisfaction)}$$

A portion of Excel's Regression tool output follows.

	A	B	C	D	E	F	G
1	SUMMARY OUTPUT						
2							
3	*Regression Statistics*						
4	Multiple R						
5	R Square						
6	Adjusted R Square						
7	Standard Error	3.773					
8	Observations						
9							
10	ANOVA						
11		*df*	*SS*	*MS*	*F*	*Significance F*	
12	Regression						
13	Residual		71.17				
14	Total		720				
15							
16		*Coefficients*	*Standard Error*	*t Stat*	*P-value*		
17	Intercept	14.4	8.191				
18	X1	-8.69	1.555				
19	X2	13.517	2.085				
20							

a. Complete the missing entries in this output.

b. Using $\alpha = .05$, test for overall significance.

c. Did the estimated regression equation provide a good fit to the data? Explain.

d. Use the *t* test and $\alpha = .05$ to test $H_0: \beta_1 = 0$ and $H_0: \beta_2 = 0$.

49. *SmartMoney* magazine evaluated 65 metropolitan areas to determine where home values are headed. An ideal city would get a score of 100 if all factors measured were as favorable as possible. Areas with a score of 60 or greater are considered to be primed for price appreciation, and areas with a score of below 50 may see housing values erode. Two of the factors evaluated were the recession resistance of the area and its affordability. Both of these factors were rated using a scale ranging from 0 (low score) to 10 (high score). The data obtained for a sample of 20 cities evaluated by *SmartMoney* follow (*SmartMoney,* February 2002).

HomeValue

Metro Area	Recession Resistance	Affordability	Score
Tucson	10	7	70.7
Fort Worth	10	7	68.5
San Antonio	6	8	65.5
Richmond	8	6	63.6
Indianapolis	4	8	62.5
Philadelphia	0	10	61.9
Atlanta	2	6	60.7

(continued)

Metro Area	Recession Resistance	Affordability	Score
Phoenix	4	5	60.3
Cincinnati	2	7	57.0
Miami	6	5	56.5
Hartford	0	7	56.2
Birmingham	0	8	55.7
San Diego	8	2	54.6
Raleigh	2	7	50.9
Oklahoma City	1	6	49.6
Orange County	4	2	49.1
Denver	4	4	48.6
Los Angeles	0	7	45.7
Detroit	0	5	44.3
New Orleans	0	5	41.2

a. Develop an estimated regression equation that can be used to predict the score given the recession resistance rating. At the .05 level of significance, test for a significant relationship.

b. Did the estimated regression equation developed in part (a) provide a good fit to the data? Explain.

c. Develop an estimated regression equation that can be used to predict the score given the recession resistance rating and the affordability rating. At the .05 level of significance, test for overall significance.

50. Following are data on price, curb weight, horsepower, time to go from 0 to 60 miles per hour, and the speed at ¼ mile for 16 sports and GT cars.

CD file

Auto2

Car	Price ($1000s)	Curb Weight (lb.)	Horse-power	0 to 60 (seconds)	Speed at ¼ mile (mph)
Acura Integra Type R	25.035	2577	195	7.0	90.7
Acura NSX-T	93.758	3066	290	5.0	108.0
BMW Z3 2.8	40.900	2844	189	6.6	93.2
Chevrolet Camaro Z28	24.865	3439	305	5.4	103.2
Chevrolet Corvette Convertible	50.144	3246	345	5.2	102.1
Dodge Viper RT/10	69.742	3319	450	4.4	116.2
Ford Mustang GT	23.200	3227	225	6.8	91.7
Honda Prelude Type SH	26.382	3042	195	7.7	89.7
Mercedes-Benz CLK320	44.988	3240	215	7.2	93.0
Mercedes-Benz SLK230	42.762	3025	185	6.6	92.3
Mitsubishi 3000GT VR-4	47.518	3737	320	5.7	99.0
Nissan 240SX SE	25.066	2862	155	9.1	84.6
Pontiac Firebird Trans Am	27.770	3455	305	5.4	103.2
Porsche Boxster	45.560	2822	201	6.1	93.2
Toyota Supra Turbo	40.989	3505	320	5.3	105.0
Volvo C70	41.120	3285	236	6.3	97.0

a. Develop an estimated regression equation with price, curb weight, horsepower, and time to go from 0 to 60 mph as four independent variables to predict the speed at ¼ mile.

b. Use the F test to determine the significance of the regression results. At a .05 level of significance, what is your conclusion?

c. Use the *t* test to determine the significance of each independent variable. At a .05 level of significance, what is your conclusion?

d. Delete any independent variable that is not significant and provide your recommended estimated regression equation.

e. Develop a standardized residual plot. Does the pattern of the residual plot appear to be reasonable?

f. Do the data contain any outliers?

51. The U.S. Department of Energy's *Fuel Economy Guide* provides fuel efficiency data for cars and trucks. A portion of the data for 35 standard pickup trucks produced by Chevrolet and General Motors follows (http://www.fueleconomy.gov, March 21, 2003). The column labeled Drive identifies whether the vehicle has two-wheel drive (2WD) or four-wheel drive (4WD). The column labeled Displacement shows the engine's displacement in liters, the column labeled Cylinders specifies the number of cylinders the engine has, and the column labeled Transmission shows whether the truck has an automatic transmission or a manual transmission. The column labeled City MPG shows the fuel efficiency rating for the truck for city driving in terms of miles per gallon (mpg).

FuelEcon

Truck	Name	Drive	Displacement	Cylinders	Transmission	City MPG
1	C1500 Silverado	2WD	4.3	6	Auto	15
2	C1500 Silverado	2WD	4.3	6	Manual	15
3	C1500 Silverado	2WD	4.8	8	Auto	15
4	C1500 Silverado	2WD	4.8	8	Manual	16
5	C1500 Silverado	2WD	5.3	8	Auto	11
.	.	.	.	.	.	.
.	.	.	.	.	.	.
.	.	.	.	.	.	.
33	K1500 Sierra	4WD	5.3	8	Auto	15
34	Sonoma	4WD	4.3	6	Auto	17
35	Sonoma	4WD	4.3	6	Manual	15

a. Develop an estimated regression equation that can be used to predict the fuel efficiency for city driving given the engine's displacement. Test for significance using $\alpha = .05$.

b. Consider the addition of the dummy variable Drive4, where the value of Drive4 is 0 if the truck has two-wheel drive and 1 if the truck has four-wheel drive. Develop the estimated regression equation that can be used to predict the fuel efficiency for city driving given the engine's displacement and the dummy variable Drive4.

c. Use $\alpha = .05$ to determine whether the dummy variable added in part (b) is significant.

d. Consider the addition of the dummy variable EightCyl, where the value of EightCyl is 0 if the truck's engine has six cylinders and 1 if the truck's engine has eight cylinders. Develop the estimated regression equation that can be used to predict the fuel efficiency for city driving given the engine's displacement and the dummy variables Drive4 and EightCyl.

e. For the estimated regression equation developed in part (d), test for overall significance and individual significance using $\alpha = .05$.

52. Today's marketplace offers a wide choice to buyers of sport utility vehicles (SUVs) and pickup trucks. An important factor to many buyers is the resale value of the vehicle. The following table shows the resale value (%) after two years and the suggested retail price for 10 SUVs, 10 small pickup trucks, and 10 large pickup trucks (*Kiplinger's New Cars & Trucks 2000 Buyer's Guide*).

Trucks

	Type of Vehicle	Suggested Retail Price ($)	Resale Value (%)
Chevrolet Blazer LS	Sport utility	19,495	55
Ford Explorer Sport	Sport utility	20,495	57
GMC Yukon XL 1500	Sport utility	26,789	67
Honda CR-V	Sport utility	18,965	65
Isuzu VehiCross	Sport utility	30,186	62
Jeep Cherokee Limited	Sport utility	25,745	57
Mercury Mountaineer Monterrey	Sport utility	29,895	59
Nissan Pathfinder XE	Sport utility	26,919	54
Toyota 4Runner	Sport utility	22,418	55
Toyota RAV4	Sport utility	17,148	55
Chevrolet S-10 Extended Cab	Small pickup	18,847	46
Dodge Dakota Club Cab Sport	Small pickup	16,870	53
Ford Ranger XLT Regular Cab	Small pickup	18,510	48
Ford Ranger XLT Supercab	Small pickup	20,225	55
GMC Sonoma Regular Cab	Small pickup	16,938	44
Isuzu Hombre Spacecab	Small pickup	18,820	41
Mazda B4000 SE Cab Plus	Small pickup	23,050	51
Nissan Frontier XE Regular Cab	Small pickup	12,110	51
Toyota Tacoma Xtracab	Small pickup	18,228	49
Toyota Tacoma Xtracab V6	Small pickup	19,318	50
Chevrolet K2500	Full-size pickup	24,417	60
Chevrolet Silverado 2500 Ext	Full-size pickup	24,140	64
Dodge Ram 1500	Full-size pickup	17,460	54
Dodge Ram Quad Cab 2500	Full-size pickup	32,770	63
Dodge Ram Regular Cab 2500	Full-size pickup	23,140	59
Ford F150 XL	Full-size pickup	22,875	58
Ford F-350 Super Duty Crew Cab XL	Full-size pickup	34,295	64
GMC New Sierra 1500 Ext Cab	Full-size pickup	27,089	68
Toyota Tundra Access Cab Limited	Full-size pickup	25,605	53
Toyota Tundra Regular Cab	Full-size pickup	15,835	58

a. Develop an estimated regression equation that can be used to predict the resale value given the suggested retail price. At the .05 level of significance, test for a significant relationship.

b. Did the estimated regression equation developed in part (a) provide a good fit to the data? Explain.

c. Develop an estimated regression equation that can be used to predict the resale value given the suggested retail price and the type of vehicle.

d. Use the F test to determine the significance of the regression results. At a .05 level of significance, what is your conclusion?

Case Problem 1   Consumer Research, Inc.

Consumer Research, Inc., is an independent agency that conducts research on consumer attitudes and behaviors for a variety of firms. In one study, a client asked for an investigation of consumer characteristics that can be used to predict the amount charged by credit card users. Data were collected on annual income, household size, and annual credit card charges for a sample of 50 consumers. The following data are on the CD accompanying the text in the data set named Consumer.

CD file

Consumer

Income ($1000s)	Household Size	Amount Charged ($)	Income ($1000s)	Household Size	Amount Charged ($)
54	3	4016	54	6	5573
30	2	3159	30	1	2583
32	4	5100	48	2	3866
50	5	4742	34	5	3586
31	2	1864	67	4	5037
55	2	4070	50	2	3605
37	1	2731	67	5	5345
40	2	3348	55	6	5370
66	4	4764	52	2	3890
51	3	4110	62	3	4705
25	3	4208	64	2	4157
48	4	4219	22	3	3579
27	1	2477	29	4	3890
33	2	2514	39	2	2972
65	3	4214	35	1	3121
63	4	4965	39	4	4183
42	6	4412	54	3	3730
21	2	2448	23	6	4127
44	1	2995	27	2	2921
37	5	4171	26	7	4603
62	6	5678	61	2	4273
21	3	3623	30	2	3067
55	7	5301	22	4	3074
42	2	3020	46	5	4820
41	7	4828	66	4	5149

Managerial Report

1. Use methods of descriptive statistics to summarize the data. Comment on the findings.
2. Develop estimated regression equations, first using annual income as the independent variable and then using household size as the independent variable. Which variable is the better predictor of annual credit card charges? Discuss your findings.
3. Develop an estimated regression equation with annual income and household size as the independent variables. Discuss your findings.
4. What is the predicted annual credit card charge for a three-person household with an annual income of $40,000?
5. Discuss the need for other independent variables that could be added to the model. What additional variables might be helpful?

Case Problem 2   Predicting Student Proficiency Test Scores

In order to predict how a school district would have scored when accounting for poverty and other income measures, *The Cincinnati Enquirer* gathered data from the Ohio Department of Education's Education Management Services and the Ohio Department of Taxation (*The Cincinnati Enquirer,* November 30, 1997). First, the newspaper obtained passage-rate data on the math, reading, science, writing, and citizenship proficiency exams given to 4th-, 6th-, 9th-, and 12th-graders in early 1996. By combining these data, they computed an overall percentage of students that passed the tests for each district.

The percentage of a school district's students on Aid for Dependent Children (ADC), the percentage who qualify for free or reduced-price lunches, and the district's median family income were also recorded. A portion of the data collected for the 608 school districts follows. The complete data set is available on the CD accompanying the text in the data set named Enquirer.

Enquirer

Rank	School District	County	% Passed	% on ADC	% Free Lunch	Median Income ($)
1	Ottawa Hills Local	Lucas	93.85	0.11	0.00	48231
2	Wyoming City	Hamilton	93.08	2.95	4.59	42672
3	Oakwood City	Montgomery	92.92	0.20	0.38	42403
4	Madeira City	Hamilton	92.37	1.50	4.83	32889
5	Indian Hill Ex Vill	Hamilton	91.77	1.23	2.70	44135
6	Solon City	Cuyahoga	90.77	0.68	2.24	34993
7	Chagrin Falls Ex Vill	Cuyahoga	89.89	0.47	0.44	38921
8	Mariemont City	Hamilton	89.80	3.00	2.97	31823
9	Upper Arlington City	Franklin	89.77	0.24	0.92	38358
10	Granville Ex Vill	Licking	89.22	1.14	0.00	36235
⋮	⋮	⋮	⋮	⋮	⋮	⋮

The data have been ranked based on the values in the column labeled % Passed; these data are the overall percentage of students passing the tests. Data in the column labeled % on ADC are the percentage of each school district's students on ADC, and the data in the column labeled % Free Lunch are the percentage of students who qualify for free or reduced-price lunches. The column labeled Median Income shows each district's median family income. Also shown for each school district is the county in which the school district is located. Note that in some cases the value in the % Free Lunch column is 0, indicating that the district did not participate in the free lunch program.

Managerial Report

Use the methods presented in this and previous chapters to analyze this data set. Present a summary of your analysis, including key statistical results, conclusions, and recommendations, in a managerial report. Include any technical material you feel is appropriate in an appendix.

Case Problem 3 ## Alumni Giving

Alumni donations are an important source of revenue for colleges and universities. If administrators could determine the factors that could lead to increases in the percentage of alumni who make a donation, they might be able to implement policies that could lead to increased revenues. Research shows that students who are more satisfied with their contact with teachers are more likely to graduate. As a result, one might suspect that smaller class sizes and lower student–faculty ratios might lead to a higher percentage of satisfied graduates, which in turn might lead to increases in the percentage of alumni who make a donation. Table 15.18 shows data for 48 national universities (*America's Best Colleges,* Year 2000 Edition). The column labeled Graduation Rate is the percentage of students who initially enrolled at the university and graduated. The column labeled % of Classes Under 20 shows the percentage of classes offered with fewer than 20 students. The column labeled Student-Faculty Ratio is the number of students enrolled divided by the total number of faculty. Finally, the column labeled Alumni Giving Rate is the percentage of alumni who made a donation to the university.

TABLE 15.8   DATA FOR 48 NATIONAL UNIVERSITIES

Alumni

	State	Graduation Rate (%)	% of Classes Under 20	Student-Faculty Ratio	Alumni Giving Rate (%)
Boston College	MA	85	39	13	25
Brandeis University	MA	79	68	8	33
Brown University	RI	93	60	8	40
California Institute of Technology	CA	85	65	3	46
Carnegie Mellon University	PA	75	67	10	28
Case Western Reserve Univ.	OH	72	52	8	31
College of William and Mary	VA	89	45	12	27
Columbia University	NY	90	69	7	31
Cornell University	NY	91	72	13	35
Dartmouth College	NH	94	61	10	53
Duke University	NC	92	68	8	45
Emory University	GA	84	65	7	37
Georgetown University	DC	91	54	10	29
Harvard University	MA	97	73	8	46
Johns Hopkins University	MD	89	64	9	27
Lehigh University	PA	81	55	11	40
Massachusetts Inst. of Technology	MA	92	65	6	44
New York University	NY	72	63	13	13
Northwestern University	IL	90	66	8	30
Pennsylvania State Univ.	PA	80	32	19	21
Princeton University	NJ	95	68	5	67
Rice University	TX	92	62	8	40
Stanford University	CA	92	69	7	34
Tufts University	MA	87	67	9	29
Tulane University	LA	72	56	12	17
U. of California–Berkeley	CA	83	58	17	18
U. of California–Davis	CA	74	32	19	7
U. of California–Irvine	CA	74	42	20	9
U. of California–Los Angeles	CA	78	41	18	13
U. of California–San Diego	CA	80	48	19	8
U. of California–Santa Barbara	CA	70	45	20	12
U. of Chicago	IL	84	65	4	36
U. of Florida	FL	67	31	23	19
U. of Illinois–Urbana Champaign	IL	77	29	15	23
U. of Michigan–Ann Arbor	MI	83	51	15	13
U. of North Carolina–Chapel Hill	NC	82	40	16	26
U. of Notre Dame	IN	94	53	13	49
U. of Pennsylvania	PA	90	65	7	41
U. of Rochester	NY	76	63	10	23
U. of Southern California	CA	70	53	13	22
U. of Texas–Austin	TX	66	39	21	13
U. of Virginia	VA	92	44	13	28
U. of Washington	WA	70	37	12	12
U. of Wisconsin–Madison	WI	73	37	13	13
Vanderbilt University	TN	82	68	9	31
Wake Forest University	NC	82	59	11	38
Washington University–St. Louis	MO	86	73	7	33
Yale University	CT	94	77	7	50

Managerial Report

1. Use methods of descriptive statistics to summarize the data.
2. Develop an estimated regression equation that can be used to predict the alumni giving rate given the percentage of students who graduate. Discuss your findings.
3. Develop an estimated regression equation that could be used to predict the alumni giving rate using the data provided.
4. What conclusions and recommendations can you derive from your analysis?

Appendix 15.1   Multiple Regression Analysis with SWStat+

In Appendix 14.3 we showed how SWStat+ can be used for simple linear regression. In this appendix we describe the steps required to use SWStat+ to perform multiple regression analysis for the Butler Trucking Company example. First we must create the data area for the Butler Trucking data.

Creating the Data Area

Step 1. Select any cell in the data set
Step 2. Select the **SWStat+** menu
Step 3. Choose **Data Area**
Step 4. Choose **Set New Data Area** from the list of Data Area options
Step 5. When the SWStat+ Data Area dialog box appears:
  Select the **Set New** tab
  Select **With column headers**
  Select **With row headers**
  Click **Set data area**

The Results worksheet which was created will contain all the output generated using SWStat+. We are now ready to use SWStat+ to perform multiple regression analysis for the Butler Trucking data.

Multiple Regression

The steps necessary to generate the regression analysis output in the Results worksheet shown in Figure 15.13 are as follows:

Step 1. Select the **SWStat+** menu
Step 2. Choose **Statistics**
Step 3. Choose **Regression and Correlation**
Step 4. When the SWStat+: Regression and Correlation dialog box appears:
  Select the **Regression** tab
  Choose **Time** in the **Dependent (Y)** box
  Choose **Miles** in the **Independent (X)** box
  Choose **Deliveries** in the **Independent (X)** box
  Click **Calculate**

The regression analysis output shown in Figure 15.13 is similar to the multiple regression analysis output using Excel's Regression tool. The primary difference is the order in which the results are presented.

FIGURE 15.13   SWStat+ RESULTS WORKSHEET SHOWING MULTIPLE REGRESSION OUTPUT

	A	B	C	D	E	F	G	H	I	J
1	SWStat+ Results Sheet									
2										
3	SWStat+: Regression									
4		Analysis of Variance, ANOVA								
5			Degrees Freedom, df	Sum of Squares, SS	Mean Square, MS	F-Ratio	p-Value			
6		Regression	2	21.601	10.800	32.878	0.00028			
7		Error	7	2.299	0.328					
8		Total	9	23.900						
9										
10		Regression Equation Results								
11		Dependent Variable, Y: Time								
12		Time = -0.869 + 0.061 Miles + 0.923 Deliveries								
13										
14		Indep. X Variables	Coefficient	Standard Error	t Statistic	p-Value	95% Conf. Lower	95% Conf. Upper	VIF	
15		Intercept	-0.869	0.952	-0.9129	0.39163	-3.119	1.381		
16		Miles	0.061	0.01	6.1824	0.00045	0.038	0.085	1.027	
17		Deliveries	0.923	0.221	4.1763	0.00416	0.401	1.446	1.027	
18										
19		R-squared	90.38%							
20		Multiple R	0.9507							
21		Adj. R-squared	87.63%							
22		Standard Error of Estimate	0.573							
23		Durbin-Watson	2.515							
24		Number of Observations	10							
25										

Confidence and Prediction Intervals

To develop a 95% confidence interval and a 95% prediction interval corresponding to 100 miles traveled and two deliveries, we would perform the following steps after obtaining the regression results shown in Figure 15.13.

Step 1.   Select the **SWStat+** menu
Step 2.   Choose **Statistics**
Step 3.   Choose **Regression and Correlation**
Step 4.   When the SWStat+: Regression and Correlation dialog box appears:
 Select the **Predictions** tab
 Select **Miles**
 Enter 100 in the predictor value box
 Press Enter
 Select **Deliveries**
 Enter 2 in the predictor value box
 Press Enter
 Click **Predict Y**

CHAPTER 16

Regression Analysis: Model Building

CONTENTS

STATISTICS IN PRACTICE:
MONSANTO COMPANY

16.1 GENERAL LINEAR MODEL
Modeling Curvilinear
    Relationships
Interaction
Transformations Involving the
    Dependent Variable
Nonlinear Models That Are
    Intrinsically Linear

16.2 DETERMINING WHEN TO
ADD OR DELETE VARIABLES
General Case

16.3 ANALYSIS OF A LARGER
PROBLEM

16.4 VARIABLE SELECTION
PROCEDURES
Stepwise Regression
Forward Selection
Backward Elimination
Using Excel to Perform the
    Backward Elimination
    Procedure
Best-Subsets Regression

16.5 RESIDUAL ANALYSIS
Autocorrelation and the Durbin-
    Watson Test

16.6 MULTIPLE REGRESSION
APPROACH TO ANALYSIS OF
VARIANCE AND
EXPERIMENTAL DESIGN

STATISTICS *in* PRACTICE

MONSANTO COMPANY*
St. Louis, Missouri

Monsanto Company traces its roots to one entrepreneur's investment of $500 and a dusty warehouse on the Mississippi riverfront, where in 1901 John F. Queeney began manufacturing saccharin. Today, Monsanto is one of the nation's largest chemical companies, producing more than a thousand products ranging from industrial chemicals to synthetic playing surfaces used in modern sports stadiums. Monsanto is a worldwide corporation with manufacturing facilities, laboratories, technical centers, and marketing operations in 65 countries.

Monsanto's Nutrition Chemical Division manufactures and markets a methionine supplement used in poultry, swine, and cattle feed products. Because poultry growers work with high volumes and low profit margins, cost-effective poultry feed products with the best possible nutritional value are needed. Optimal feed composition will result in rapid growth and high final body weight for a given level of feed intake. The chemical industry has worked closely with poultry growers to optimize poultry feed products. Ultimately, success depends on keeping the cost of poultry low in comparison with the cost of beef and other meat products.

Monsanto used regression analysis to model the relationship between body weight y and the amount of methionine x added to the poultry feed. Initially, the following simple linear estimated regression equation was developed.

$$\hat{y} = .21 + .42x$$

This estimated regression equation proved statistically significant; however, the analysis of the residuals indicated that a curvilinear relationship would be a better model of the relationship between body weight and methionine.

Monsanto researchers used regression analysis to develop an optimal feed composition for poultry growers. Photo © PhotoDisc/Getty Images

Further research conducted by Monsanto showed that although small amounts of methionine tended to increase body weight, at some point body weight leveled off and additional amounts of the methionine were of little or no benefit. In fact, when the amount of methionine increased beyond nutritional requirements, body weight tended to decline. The following estimated multiple regression equation was used to model the curvilinear relationship between body weight and methionine.

$$\hat{y} = -1.89 + 1.32x - .506x^2$$

Use of the regression results enabled Monsanto to determine the optimal level of methionine to be used in poultry feed products.

In this chapter we will extend the discussion of regression analysis by showing how curvilinear models such as the one used by Monsanto can be developed. In addition, we will describe a variety of tools that help determine which independent variables lead to the best estimated regression equation.

*The authors are indebted to James R. Ryland and Robert M. Schisla, Senior Research Specialists, Monsanto Nutrition Chemical Division, for providing this Statistics in Practice.

Model building is the process of developing an estimated regression equation that describes the relationship between a dependent variable and one or more independent variables. The major issues in model building are finding the proper functional form of the relationship and selecting the independent variables to be included in the model. In Section 16.1 we establish the framework for model building by introducing the concept of a general linear model. Section 16.2, which provides the foundation for the more sophisticated computer-based procedures, introduces a general approach for determining when to add or delete independent variables. In Section 16.3 we consider a larger regression problem involving eight independent variables. In Section 16.4 we discuss the use of variable selection procedures, including stepwise regression, the forward selection procedure, the backward elimination procedure, and best-subsets regression. We also show how to implement the backward elimination procedure using Excel. In Section 16.5 we show how the Durbin-Watson test can be used to detect serial or autocorrelation, and in Section 16.6 we show how regression analysis can be used for analysis of variance and experimental design problems.

16.1 General Linear Model

Suppose we have collected data for one dependent variable y and k independent variables $x_1, x_2, \ldots, x_k$. Our objective is to use these data to develop an estimated regression equation that provides the best relationship between the dependent and the independent variables. As a general framework for developing more complex relationships among the independent variables, we introduce the concept of a **general linear model** involving p independent variables.

If you can write a regression model in the form of equation (16.1), the standard multiple regression procedures described in Chapter 15 are applicable.

GENERAL LINEAR MODEL

$$y = \beta_0 + \beta_1 z_1 + \beta_2 z_2 + \cdots + \beta_p z_p + \epsilon \qquad (16.1)$$

In equation (16.1), each of the independent variables z_j (where $j = 1, 2, \ldots, p$) is a function of $x_1, x_2, \ldots, x_k$ (the variables for which data have been collected). In some cases, each z_j may be a function of only one x variable. The simplest case is when we have collected data for just one variable (x_1) and want to estimate y by using a straight-line relationship. In this case $z_1 = x_1$, and equation (16.1) becomes

$$y = \beta_0 + \beta_1 x_1 + \epsilon \qquad (16.2)$$

Note that equation (16.2) is the simple linear regression model introduced in Chapter 14 with the exception that the independent variable is labeled x_1 instead of x. In the statistical modeling literature, this model is called a *simple first-order model with one predictor variable*.

Modeling Curvilinear Relationships

More complex types of relationships can be modeled with equation (16.1). To illustrate, let us consider the problem facing Reynolds, Inc., a manufacturer of industrial scales and laboratory equipment. Managers at Reynolds want to investigate the relationship between length of employment of their salespeople and the number of electronic laboratory scales sold. Table 16.1 gives the number of months each salesperson has been employed by the firm and the number of scales sold by 15 randomly selected salespeople for the most recent sales period. Figure 16.1 is the scatter diagram for these data. The scatter diagram indicates a possible curvilinear relationship between the length of time employed and the number of units sold. Before considering how to develop a curvilinear relationship for Reynolds, let us consider the Excel output in Figure 16.2 corresponding to a simple first-order model; the estimated regression equation is

$$\text{Sales} = 111.2279 + 2.3768 \text{ Months}$$

FIGURE 16.1 SCATTER DIAGRAM FOR THE REYNOLDS EXAMPLE

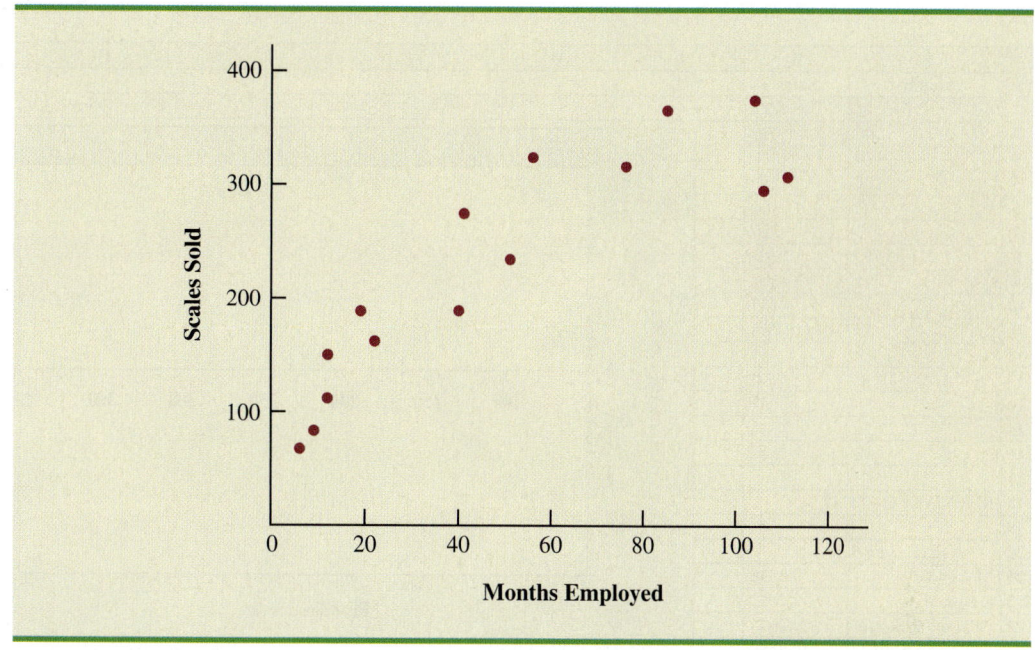

TABLE 16.1

DATA FOR THE
REYNOLDS
EXAMPLE

Months Employed	Scales Sold
41	275
106	296
76	317
104	376
22	162
12	150
85	367
111	308
40	189
51	235
9	83
12	112
6	67
56	325
19	189

where

Sales = number of electronic laboratory scales sold

Months = the number of months the salesperson has been employed

A standardized residual plot against $\hat{y}$ (predicted Sales) is also displayed. Although the computer output shows that a linear relationship explains a high percentage of the variability in sales (R Square = .7812), the standardized residual plot suggests that a curvilinear relationship is present.

To account for the curvilinear relationship, we set $z_1 = x_1$ and $z_2 = x_1^2$ in equation (16.1) to obtain the model

$$y = \beta_0 + \beta_1 x_1 + \beta_2 x_1^2 + \epsilon \tag{16.3}$$

This model is called a *second-order model with one predictor variable*. To develop an estimated regression equation corresponding to this second-order model, Excel's Regression tool needs the original data in Table 16.1, as well as those data corresponding to adding a second independent variable that is the square of the number of months the employee has been with the firm. In Figure 16.3 we show the Excel output corresponding to the second-order model (the months squared data are in column B); the estimated regression equation is

Sales = 45.3476 + 6.3448 Months − .0345 MonthsSq

where

MonthsSq = the square of the number of months the
salesperson has been employed

The corresponding standardized residual plot is also shown. It shows that the previous curvilinear pattern has been removed. At the .05 level of significance, the computer output shows that the overall model is significant (*p*-value for the *F* test is 8.75E-07); note also that the *p*-value

FIGURE 16.2   EXCEL OUTPUT FOR THE REYNOLDS EXAMPLE: FIRST-ORDER MODEL

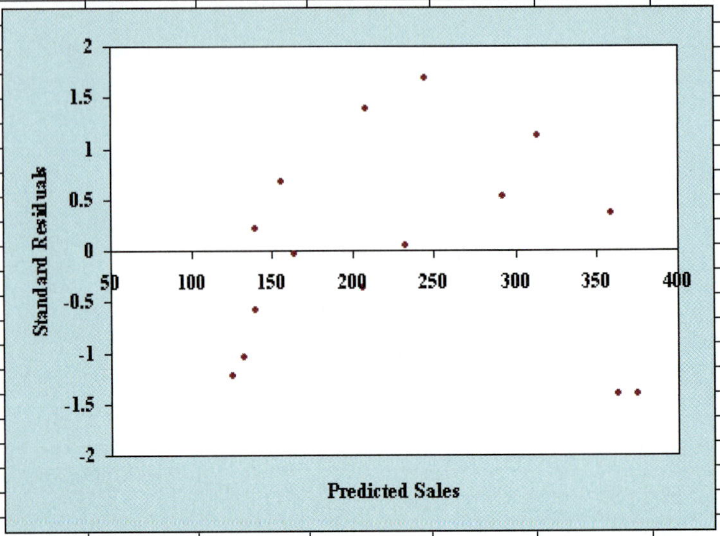

corresponding to the *t* Stat value for MonthsSq is less than .05, and hence we can conclude that adding MonthsSq to the model involving Months is significant. With an Adjusted R Square value of .8859, we should be pleased with the fit provided by this estimated regression equation. Thus, we see how easy it is to handle curvilinear relationships in regression analysis.

Many types of relationships can be modeled by using equation (16.1). The regression techniques with which we have been working are definitely not limited to linear, or straight-line, relationships. In multiple regression analysis the word *linear* in the term "general linear model" refers only to the fact that $\beta_0, \beta_1, \ldots, \beta_p$ all have exponents of one; it does not imply that the relationship between *y* and the underlying x_i variables is linear. Indeed, in this section we have seen one example of equation (16.1) being used to model a curvilinear relationship.

Interaction

If the original data set consists of observations for *y* and two independent variables x_1 and x_2, we can develop a second-order model with two predictor variables by substituting $z_1 = x_1, z_2 = x_2, z_3 = x_1^2, z_4 = x_2^2$, and $z_5 = x_1 x_2$ into the general linear model of equation (16.1). The model obtained is

$$y = \beta_0 + \beta_1 x_1 + \beta_2 x_2 + \beta_3 x_1^2 + \beta_4 x_2^2 + \beta_5 x_1 x_2 + \epsilon \qquad (16.4)$$

FIGURE 16.3   EXCEL OUTPUT FOR THE REYNOLDS EXAMPLE: SECOND-ORDER MODEL

	A	B	C	D	E	F	G	H	I	J
1	Months	MonthsSq	Sales							
2	41	1681	275							
3	106	11236	296							
4	76	5776	317							
5	104	10816	376							
6	22	484	162							
7	12	144	150							
8	85	7225	367							
9	111	12321	308							
10	40	1600	189							
11	51	2601	235							
12	9	81	83							
13	12	144	112							
14	6	36	67							
15	56	3136	325							
16	19	361	189							
17										
18	SUMMARY OUTPUT									
19										
20	*Regression Statistics*									
21	Multiple R	0.9498								
22	R Square	0.9022								
23	Adjusted R Square	0.8859								
24	Standard Error	34.4528								
25	Observations	15								
26										
27	ANOVA									
28		*df*	*SS*	*MS*	*F*	*Significance F*				
29	Regression	2	131413.0156	65706.51	55.3554	8.75E-07				
30	Residual	12	14243.9177	1186.993						
31	Total	14	145656.9333							
32										
33		*Coefficients*	*Standard Error*	*t Stat*	*P-value*	*Lower 95%*	*Upper 95%*	*Lower 99.0%*	*Upper 99.0%*	
34	Intercept	45.3476	22.7747	1.9911	0.0697	-4.2741	94.9693	-24.2185	114.9137	
35	Months	6.3448	1.0579	5.9978	6.24E-05	4.0399	8.6497	3.1136	9.5761	
36	MonthsSq	-0.0345	0.0089	-3.8539	0.0023	-0.0540	-0.0150	-0.0618	-0.0072	
37										

In this second-order model, the variable $z_5 = x_1 x_2$ is added to account for the potential effects of the two variables acting together. This type of effect is called **interaction.**

To provide an illustration of interaction and what it means, let us review the regression study conducted by Tyler Personal Care for one of its new shampoo products. Two factors believed to have the most influence on sales are unit selling price and advertising expenditure. To investigate the effects of these two variables on sales, prices of $2.00, $2.50, and $3.00 were paired with advertising expenditures of $50,000 and $100,000 in 24 test markets. The unit sales that were observed (in 1000s) are reported in Table 16.2.

Table 16.3 is a summary of these data. Note that the mean sales corresponding to a price of $2.00 and an advertising expenditure of $50,000 is 461,000, and the mean sales corresponding to a price of $2.00 and an advertising expenditure of $100,000 is 808,000. Hence, with price held constant at $2.00, the difference in mean sales between advertising expenditures of $50,000 and $100,000 is 808,000 − 461,000 = 347,000 units. When the price of the product is $2.50, the difference in mean sales is 646,000 − 364,000 = 282,000 units. Finally, when the price is $3.00, the difference in mean sales is 375,000 − 332,000 = 43,000 units. Clearly, the difference in mean sales between advertising expenditures of $50,000 and $100,000 depends on the price of the product. In other words, at higher selling

TABLE 16.2   DATA FOR THE TYLER PERSONAL CARE EXAMPLE

Tyler

Price	Advertising Expenditure ($1000s)	Sales (1000s)	Price	Advertising Expenditure ($1000s)	Sales (1000s)
$2.00	50	478	$2.00	100	810
$2.50	50	373	$2.50	100	653
$3.00	50	335	$3.00	100	345
$2.00	50	473	$2.00	100	832
$2.50	50	358	$2.50	100	641
$3.00	50	329	$3.00	100	372
$2.00	50	456	$2.00	100	800
$2.50	50	360	$2.50	100	620
$3.00	50	322	$3.00	100	390
$2.00	50	437	$2.00	100	790
$2.50	50	365	$2.50	100	670
$3.00	50	342	$3.00	100	393

prices, the effect of increased advertising expenditure diminishes. These observations provide evidence of interaction between the price and advertising expenditure variables.

To provide another perspective of interaction, Figure 16.4 shows a graph of the mean sales for the six price-advertising expenditure combinations. This graph also shows that the effect of advertising expenditure on mean sales depends on the price of the product; we again see the effect of interaction. When interaction between two variables is present, we cannot study the effect of one variable on the response y independently of the other variable. In other words, meaningful conclusions can be developed only if we consider the joint effect that both variables have on the response.

To account for the effect of interaction, we will use the following regression model.

$$y = \beta_0 + \beta_1 x_1 + \beta_2 x_2 + \beta_3 x_1 x_2 + \epsilon \tag{16.5}$$

where

$$y = \text{unit sales (1000s)}$$
$$x_1 = \text{price (\$)}$$
$$x_2 = \text{advertising expenditure (\$1000s)}$$

TABLE 16.3   MEAN SALES (1000S) FOR THE TYLER PERSONAL CARE EXAMPLE

		Price		
		$2.00	**$2.50**	**$3.00**
Advertising	$50,000	461	364	332
Expenditure	$100,000	808	646	375

Mean sales of 808,000 units when price = $2.00 and advertising expenditure = $100,000

FIGURE 16.4 MEAN SALES AS A FUNCTION OF SELLING AND ADVERTISING EXPENDITURE

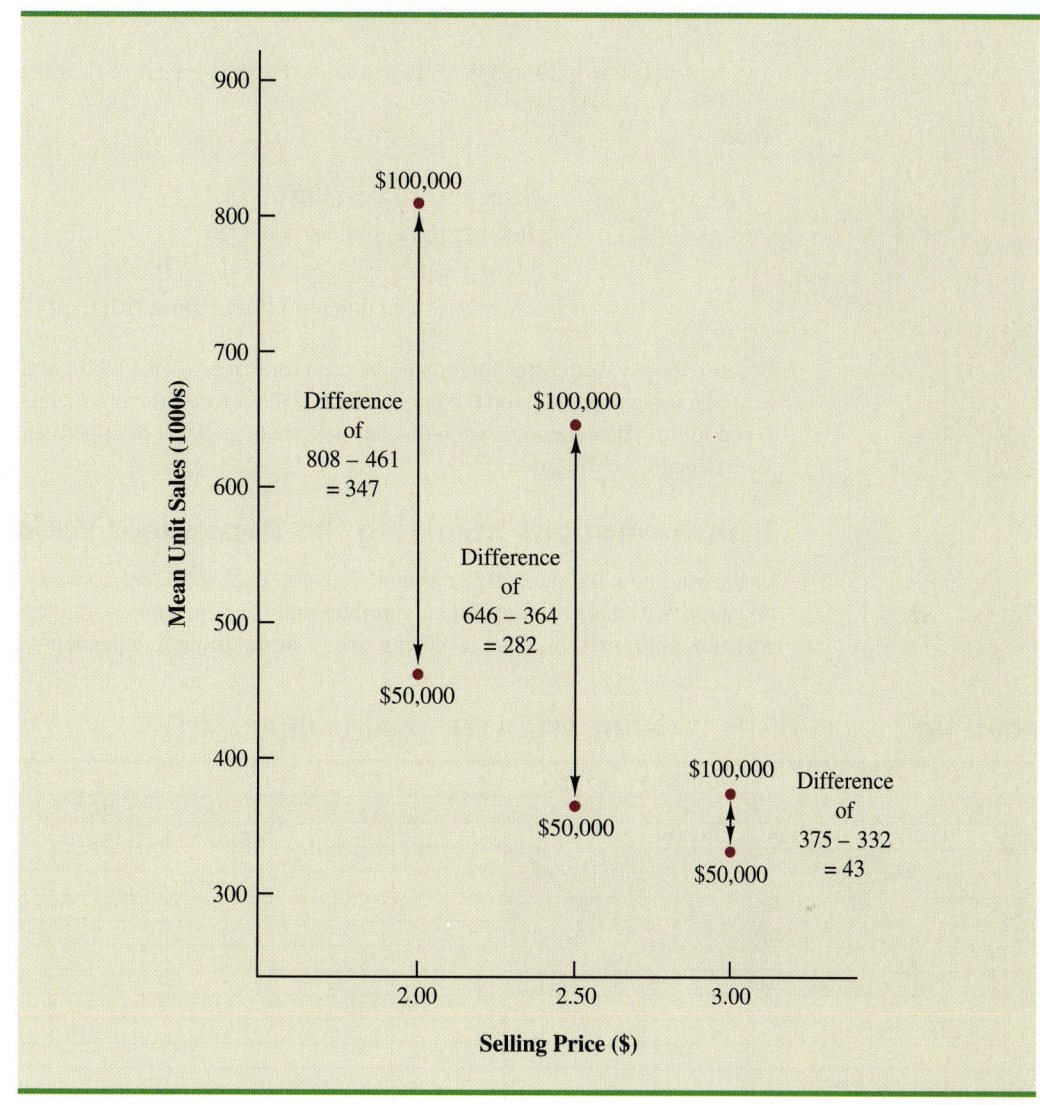

Note that equation (16.5) reflects Tyler's belief that the number of units sold depends linearly on selling price and advertising expenditure (accounted for by the $\beta_1 x_1$ and $\beta_2 x_2$ terms), and that there is interaction between the two variables (accounted for by the $\beta_3 x_1 x_2$ term).

To develop an estimated regression equation, a general linear model involving three independent variables (z_1, z_2, and z_3) was used.

$$y = \beta_0 + \beta_1 z_1 + \beta_2 z_2 + \beta_3 z_3 + \epsilon \qquad (16.6)$$

where

$$z_1 = x_1$$
$$z_2 = x_2$$
$$z_3 = x_1 x_2$$

Figure 16.5 is the Excel output corresponding to the interaction model for the Tyler Personal Care example. The resulting estimated regression equation is

$$\text{Sales} = -275.8333 + 175 \text{ Price} + 19.68 \text{ AdvExp} - 6.08 \text{ PriceAdv}$$

where

$$
\begin{aligned}
\text{Sales} &= \text{unit sales (1000s)} \\
\text{Price} &= \text{price of the product (\$)} \\
\text{AdvExp} &= \text{advertising expenditure (\$1000s)} \\
\text{PriceAdv} &= \text{interaction term (Price times AdvExp)}
\end{aligned}
$$

Because the p-value corresponding to the t test for PriceAdv is 0.0000, we conclude that interaction is significant given the linear effect of the price of the product and the advertising expenditure. Thus, the regression results show that the effect of advertising expenditure on sales depends on the price.

Transformations Involving the Dependent Variable

In showing how the general linear model can be used to model a variety of possible relationships between the independent variables and the dependent variable, we have focused attention on transformations involving one or more of the independent variables. Often it

FIGURE 16.5 EXCEL OUTPUT FOR THE TYLER PERSONAL CARE EXAMPLE

	A	B	C	D	E	F	G	H	I	J
1	Price	AdvExp	PriceAdv	Sales						
2	2	50	100	478						
3	2.5	50	125	373						
4	3	50	150	335						
23	2	100	200	790						
24	2.5	100	250	670						
25	3	100	300	393						
26										
27	SUMMARY OUTPUT									
28										
29	*Regression Statistics*									
30	Multiple R	0.9890								
31	R Square	0.9781								
32	Adjusted R Square	0.9748								
33	Standard Error	28.1739								
34	Observations	24								
35										
36	ANOVA									
37		*df*	*SS*	*MS*	*F*	*Significance F*				
38	Regression	3	709316	236438.7	297.8692	9.26E-17				
39	Residual	20	15875.3333	793.7667						
40	Total	23	725191.3333							
41										
42		*Coefficients*	*Standard Error*	*t Stat*	*P-value*	*Lower 95%*	*Upper 95%*	*Lower 99.0%*	*Upper 99.0%*	
43	Intercept	-275.8333	112.8421	-2.4444	0.0239	-511.2178	-40.4488	-596.9075	45.2408	
44	Price	175	44.5468	3.9285	0.0008	82.0770	267.9230	48.2492	301.7508	
45	AdvExp	19.68	1.4274	13.7878	1.13E-11	16.7026	22.6574	15.6187	23.7413	
46	PriceAdv	-6.08	0.5635	-10.7901	8.68E-10	-7.2554	-4.9046	-7.6833	-4.4767	
47										

Note: Rows 5–22 are hidden.

MPG

TABLE 16.4

WEIGHT AND
MILES-PER-
GALLON
RATING FOR
12 AUTOMOBILES

Weight	Miles per Gallon
2289	28.7
2113	29.2
2180	34.2
2448	27.9
2026	33.3
2702	26.4
2657	23.9
2106	30.5
3226	18.1
3213	19.5
3607	14.3
2888	20.9

is worthwhile to consider transformations involving the dependent variable y. As an illustration of when we might want to transform the dependent variable, consider the data in Table 16.4, the weight and miles-per-gallon rating for 12 automobiles. The scatter diagram in Figure 16.6 shows a negative linear relationship between these two variables. Therefore, we use a simple first-order model to relate the two variables. The Excel output is in Figure 16.7; the resulting estimated regression equation is

$$MPG = 56.0957 - 0.0116 \text{ Weight}$$

where

$$MPG = \text{miles-per-gallon rating}$$
$$Weight = \text{weight of the car in pounds}$$

The model is significant (Significance F or p-value for the F test is 0.000) and the fit is very good (R Square = .9354).

A standardized residual plot is also displayed. The pattern we observe does not look like the horizontal band we should expect to find if the assumptions about the error term are valid. Instead, the variability in the residuals appears to increase as the value of $\hat{y}$ (weight) increases. In other words, we have the wedge-shaped pattern referred to in Chapter 14 as being indicative of a nonconstant variance. We are not justified in reaching any conclusions about the statistical significance of the resulting estimated regression equation when the underlying assumptions for the tests of significance do not appear to be satisfied.

Often the problem of nonconstant variance can be corrected by transforming the dependent variable to a different scale. For instance, if we work with the logarithm of the dependent variable instead of the original dependent variable, the effect will be to compress the values of the dependent variable and thus diminish the effects of nonconstant variance. Excel provides the ability to apply logarithmic transformations using either the base 10

FIGURE 16.6   SCATTER DIAGRAM FOR THE MILES-PER-GALLON EXAMPLE

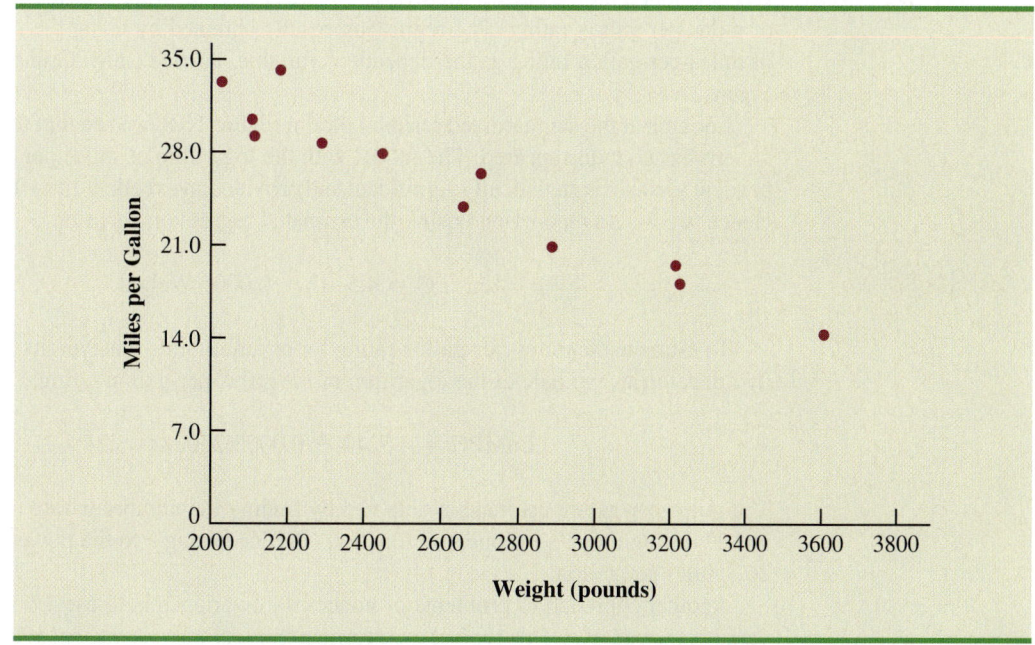

FIGURE 16.7   EXCEL OUTPUT FOR THE MILES-PER-GALLON EXAMPLE

	A	B	C	D	E	F	G	H	I	J
1	Weight	MPG								
2	2289	28.7								
3	2113	29.2								
4	2180	34.2								
11	3213	19.5								
12	3607	14.3								
13	2888	20.9								
14										
15	SUMMARY OUTPUT									
16										
17	*Regression Statistics*									
18	Multiple R	0.9672								
19	R Square	0.9354								
20	Adjusted R Square	0.9289								
21	Standard Error	1.6705								
22	Observations	12								
23										
24	ANOVA									
25		*df*	*SS*	*MS*	*F*	*Significance F*				
26	Regression	1	403.9759	403.9759	144.7601	2.85E-07				
27	Residual	10	27.9066	2.7907						
28	Total	11	431.8825							
29										
30		*Coefficients*	*Standard Error*	*t Stat*	*P-value*	*Lower 95%*	*Upper 95%*	*Lower 99.0%*	*Upper 99.0%*	
31	Intercept	56.0957	2.5821	21.7245	9.55E-10	50.3423	61.8490	47.9122	64.2792	
32	Weight	-0.0116	0.0010	-12.0316	2.85E-07	-0.0138	-0.0095	-0.0147	-0.0086	
33										

Note: Rows 5–10 are hidden.

(common logarithm) or the base $e = 2.71828 \ldots$ (natural logarithm). We applied a natural logarithmic transformation to the miles-per-gallon data (see note on cell C2 in Figure 16.8) and developed the estimated regression equation relating weight to the natural logarithm of miles-per-gallon rating. The regression results obtained by using the natural logarithm of miles-per-gallon rating as the dependent variable, labeled LnMPG in the output, are in Figure 16.8.

Looking at the standardized residual plot in Figure 16.8, we see that the wedge-shaped pattern has now disappeared. The model with the logarithm of miles per gallon as the dependent variable is statistically significant and provides an excellent fit to the observed data. Hence, we would recommend using the estimated regression equation

$$\text{LnMPG} = 4.5242 - 0.0005 \text{ Weight}$$

To estimate the miles-per-gallon rating for an automobile that weighs 2500 pounds, we first develop an estimate of the logarithm of the miles-per-gallon rating.

$$\text{LnMPG} = 4.5242 - 0.0005(2500) = 3.27$$

The miles-per-gallon estimate is obtained by finding the number whose natural logarithm is 3.27. Using Excel's exponential function EXP, or raising e to the power 3.27, we obtain 26.3 miles per gallon.

Another approach to problems of nonconstant variance is to use $1/y$ as the dependent variable instead of y. This type of transformation is called a *reciprocal transformation*. For

FIGURE 16.8   EXCEL OUTPUT FOR THE MILES-PER-GALLON EXAMPLE:
LOGARITHMIC TRANSFORMATION

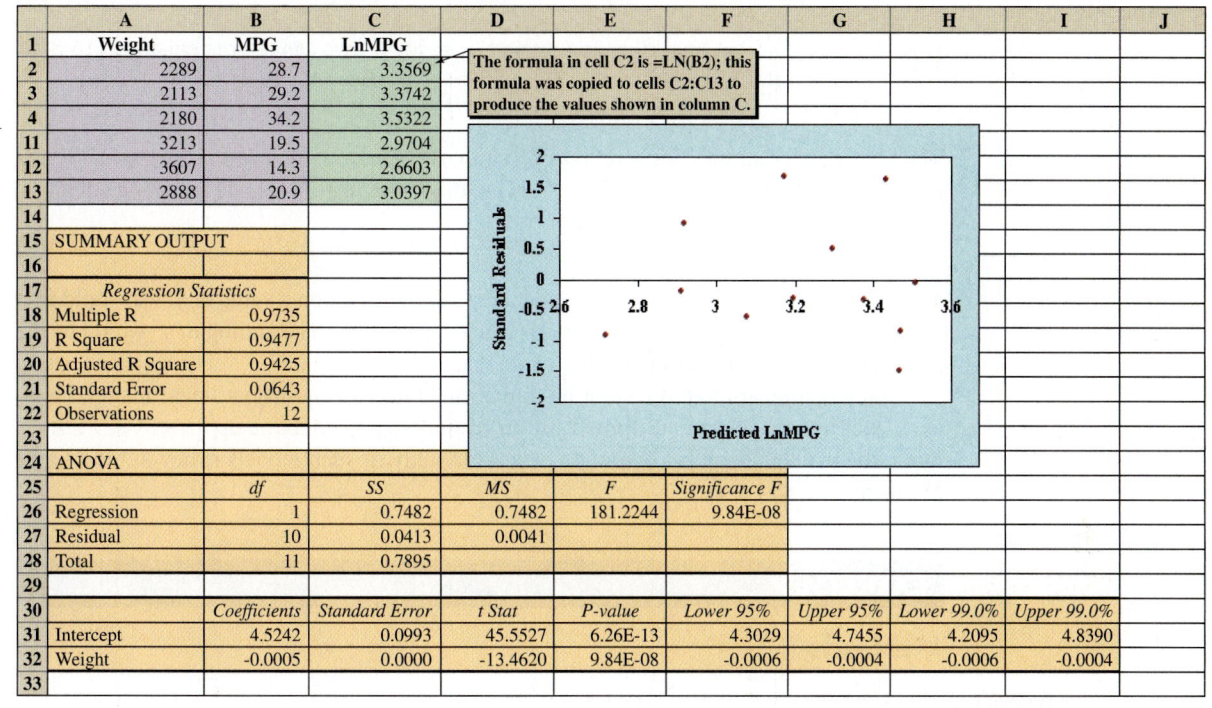

	A	B	C	D	E	F	G	H	I	J
1	Weight	MPG	LnMPG							
2	2289	28.7	3.3569							
3	2113	29.2	3.3742							
4	2180	34.2	3.5322							
11	3213	19.5	2.9704							
12	3607	14.3	2.6603							
13	2888	20.9	3.0397							
14										
15	SUMMARY OUTPUT									
16										
17	*Regression Statistics*									
18	Multiple R	0.9735								
19	R Square	0.9477								
20	Adjusted R Square	0.9425								
21	Standard Error	0.0643								
22	Observations	12								
23										
24	ANOVA									
25		*df*	*SS*	*MS*	*F*	*Significance F*				
26	Regression	1	0.7482	0.7482	181.2244	9.84E-08				
27	Residual	10	0.0413	0.0041						
28	Total	11	0.7895							
29										
30		*Coefficients*	*Standard Error*	*t Stat*	*P-value*	*Lower 95%*	*Upper 95%*	*Lower 99.0%*	*Upper 99.0%*	
31	Intercept	4.5242	0.0993	45.5527	6.26E-13	4.3029	4.7455	4.2095	4.8390	
32	Weight	-0.0005	0.0000	-13.4620	9.84E-08	-0.0006	-0.0004	-0.0006	-0.0004	
33										

The formula in cell C2 is =LN(B2); this formula was copied to cells C2:C13 to produce the values shown in column C.

Note: Rows 5–10 are hidden.

instance, if the dependent variable is measured in miles per gallon, the reciprocal transformation would result in a new dependent variable whose units would be 1/(miles per gallon) or gallons per mile. In general, there is no way to determine whether a logarithmic transformation or a reciprocal transformation will perform best without actually trying each of them.

Nonlinear Models That Are Intrinsically Linear

Models in which the parameters $(\beta_0, \beta_1, \ldots, \beta_p)$ have exponents other than one are called nonlinear models. However, for the case of the exponential model, we can perform a transformation of variables that will enable us to perform regression analysis with equation (16.1), the general linear model. The exponential model involves the following regression equation.

$$E(y) = \beta_0 \beta_1^x \qquad \textbf{(16.7)}$$

This model is appropriate when the dependent variable y increases or decreases by a constant percentage, instead of by a fixed amount, as x increases.

As an example, suppose sales for a product y are related to advertising expenditure x (in $1000s) according to the following regression equation.

$$E(y) = 500(1.2)^x$$

Thus, for $x = 1$, $E(y) = 500(1.2)^1 = 600$; for $x = 2$, $E(y) = 500(1.2)^2 = 720$; and for $x = 3$, $E(y) = 500(1.2)^3 = 864$. Note that $E(y)$ is not increasing by a constant amount in this case, but by a constant percentage; the percentage increase is 20%.

We can transform this nonlinear model to a linear model by taking the logarithm of both sides of equation (16.7).

$$\log E(y) = \log \beta_0 + x \log \beta_1 \qquad \textbf{(16.8)}$$

Now if we let $y' = \log E(y)$ $\beta_0' = \log \beta_0$, and $\beta_1' = \log \beta_1$, we can rewrite equation (16.8) as

$$y' = \beta_0' + \beta_1' x$$

The formulas for simple linear regression can now be used to develop estimates of β_0' and β_1'. Denoting the estimates as b_0' and b_1' leads to the following estimated regression equation.

$$\hat{y}' = b_0' + b_1' x \qquad \textbf{(16.9)}$$

To obtain predictions of the original dependent variable y given a value of x, we would first substitute the value of x into equation (16.9) and compute $\hat{y}'$. The antilog of $\hat{y}'$ would be the prediction of y, or the expected value of y.

Many nonlinear models cannot be transformed into an equivalent linear model. However, such models have had limited use in business and economic applications. Furthermore, the mathematical background needed for study of such models is beyond the scope of this text.

EXERCISES

Methods

1. Consider the following data for two variables, x and y.

x	22	24	26	30	35	40
y	12	21	33	35	40	36

    a. Develop an estimated regression equation for the data of the form $\hat{y} = b_0 + b_1 x$.
    b. Using the results from part (a), test for a significant relationship between x and y; use $\alpha = .05$.
    c. Develop a scatter diagram for the data. Does the scatter diagram suggest an estimated regression equation of the form $\hat{y} = b_0 + b_1 x + b_2 x^2$? Explain.
    d. Develop an estimated regression equation for the data of the form $\hat{y} = b_0 + b_1 x + b_2 x^2$.
    e. Refer to part (d). Is the relationship between x, x^2, and y significant? Use $\alpha = .05$.
    f. Predict the value of y when $x = 25$.

2. Consider the following data for two variables, x and y.

x	9	32	18	15	26
y	10	20	21	16	22

    a. Develop an estimated regression equation for the data of the form $\hat{y} = b_0 + b_1 x$. Comment on the adequacy of this equation for predicting y.
    b. Develop an estimated regression equation for the data of the form $\hat{y} = b_0 + b_1 x + b_2 x^2$. Comment on the adequacy of this equation for predicting y.
    c. Predict the value of y when $x = 20$.

3. Consider the following data for two variables, x and y.

x	2	3	4	5	7	7	7	8	9
y	4	5	4	6	4	6	9	5	11

    a. Does there appear to be a linear relationship between x and y? Explain.
    b. Develop the estimated regression equation relating x and y.

c.   Plot the standardized residuals versus $\hat{y}$ for the estimated regression equation developed in part (b). Do the model assumptions appear to be satisfied? Explain.

d.   Perform a logarithmic transformation on the dependent variable y. Develop an estimated regression equation using the transformed dependent variable. Do the model assumptions appear to be satisfied by using the transformed dependent variable? Does a reciprocal transformation work better in this case? Explain.

Applications

4.   A highway department is studying the relationship between traffic flow and speed. The following model has been hypothesized.

$$y = \beta_0 + \beta_1 x + \epsilon$$

where

$$y = \text{traffic flow in vehicles per hour}$$
$$x = \text{vehicle speed in miles per hour}$$

The following data were collected during rush hour for six highways leading out of the city.

Traffic Flow (y)	Vehicle Speed (x)
1256	35
1329	40
1226	30
1335	45
1349	50
1124	25

a.   Develop an estimated regression equation for the data.

b.   Using $\alpha = .01$, test for a significant relationship.

5.   In working further with the problem of exercise 4, statisticians suggested the use of the following curvilinear estimated regression equation.

$$\hat{y} = b_0 + b_1 x + b_2 x^2$$

a.   Use the data of exercise 4 to compute the coefficients of this estimated regression equation.

b.   Using $\alpha = .01$, test for a significant relationship.

c.   Estimate the traffic flow in vehicles per hour at a speed of 38 miles per hour.

6.   A study of emergency service facilities investigated the relationship between the number of facilities and the average distance traveled to provide the emergency service. The following table gives the data collected.

Number of Facilities	Average Distance (miles)
9	1.66
11	1.12
16	.83
21	.62
27	.51
30	.47

a. Develop a scatter diagram for these data, treating average distance traveled as the dependent variable.

b. Does a simple linear model appear to be appropriate? Explain.

c. Develop an estimated regression equation for the data that you believe will best explain the relationship between these two variables.

7. An important factor in purchasing a suitable computer monitor is the field of view. If a monitor has a wide field of view slight head turns can still provide an acceptable image and someone standing next to the monitor can still clearly see the image on the screen. In a review of 19-inch LCD monitors, *PCWORLD* found that although all the monitors they tested claimed a 170-degree arc—both horizontally and vertically—the actual angles for the monitors ranged from 108 to 167 degrees. The following data show the horizontal viewing angle for eight 19-inch monitors and *PCWORLD*'s overall rating based upon image quality, price, features, and support policies (*PCWORLD,* February 2003).

CD file

Monitors

Monitor	Angle	Rating
Samsung SyncMaster 191T	167	86
ViewSonic VX900	159	82
Sceptre Technologies X9S-Naga	126	81
Planar PL191M	108	81
Dell UltraSharp 1900FP	153	81
AOC LM914	123	81
KDS USA Radius Rad-9	118	80
NEC MultiSync LCD 1920NX	123	80
Iiyama Pro Lite 4821DT-BK	119	80

a. Develop a scatter diagram for these data with horizontal viewing angles as the independent variable.

b. Does a simple linear regression model appear to be appropriate?

c. Develop an estimated regression equation for the data you believe will best explain the relationship between these two variables.

8. In Europe the number of Internet users varies widely from country to country. In 1999, 44.3% of all Swedes used the Internet, while in France the audience was less than 10%. The disparities are expected to persist even though the usage is expected to grow dramatically over the next several years. The following table shows the number of Internet users in 1999 and the projected number of users in 2005 for European countries.

CD file

Internet

Country	1999 Internet Users (%)	2005 Projected Users (%)
Austria	12.6	53.4
Belgium	24.2	60.2
Denmark	40.4	71.2
Finland	40.9	71.4
France	9.7	53.1
Germany	15.0	59.6
Greece	3.4	15.8
Ireland	12.1	46.7
Italy	8.4	34.4
Netherlands	18.6	61.4
Norway	38.0	71.7
Portugal	4.63	36.6
Spain	7.4	39.9
Sweden	44.3	71.9
Switzerland	28.1	66.7
United Kingdom	23.6	66.8

a.   Develop a scatter diagram of the data using the 1999 Internet user percentage as the independent variable. Does a simple linear regression model appear to be appropriate? Discuss.

b.   Develop an estimated multiple regression equation with x = the percentage of 1999 Internet users and x^2 as the two independent variables.

c.   Consider the nonlinear relationship shown by equation (16.7). Use logarithms to develop an estimated regression equation for this model.

d.   Do you prefer the estimated regression equation developed in part (b) or part (c)? Explain.

9.   Almost all U.S. light-rail systems use electric cars that run on tracks built at street level. According to the Federal Transit Administration, light-rail is one of the safest modes of travel, with an accident rate of .99 accidents per million passenger miles as compared to 2.29 for buses. The following data show the miles of track and the weekday ridership in thousands of passengers for selected light-rail systems (*USA Today,* January 7, 2003).

LightRail

City	Miles	Riders
Los Angeles	22	70
San Diego	47	75
Portland	38	81
Sacramento	21	31
San Jose	31	30
San Francisco	73	164
Philadelphia	69	84
Boston	51	231
Denver	17	35
Salt Lake City	18	28
Dallas	44	39
New Orleans	16	14
St. Louis	34	42
Pittsburgh	18	25
Buffalo	6	23
Cleveland	15	15
Newark	9	8

a.   Develop a scatter diagram for these data, treating the number of miles of track as the independent variable. Does a simple linear regression model appear to be appropriate?

b.   Use a simple linear regression model to develop an estimated regression equation to predict the weekday ridership given the miles of track. Construct a standardized residual plot. Based upon the standardized residual plot, does a simple linear regression model appear to be appropriate?

c.   Perform a logarithmic transformation on the dependent variable. Develop an estimated regression equation using the transformed dependent variable. Do the model assumptions appear to be satisfied by using the transformed dependent variable?

d.   Perform a reciprocal transformation on the dependent variable. Develop an estimated regression equation using the transformed dependent variable.

e.   What estimated regression equation would you recommend? Explain.

16.2   Determining When to Add or Delete Variables

In this section we will show how an F test can be used to determine whether it is advantageous to add one or more independent variables to a multiple regression model. This test is based on a determination of the amount of reduction in the error sum of squares resulting from adding one or more independent variables to the model. We will first illustrate how the test can be used in the context of the Butler Trucking example.

In Chapter 15, the Butler Trucking example was introduced to illustrate the use of multiple regression analysis. Recall that the managers wanted to develop an estimated regression equation to predict total daily travel time for trucks using two independent variables: miles traveled and number of deliveries. With miles traveled x_1 as the only independent variable, the least squares procedure provided the following estimated regression equation.

$$\hat{y} = 1.2739 + .0678x_1$$

In Chapter 15 we showed that the error sum of squares for this model was SSE = 8.0287. When x_2, the number of deliveries, was added as a second independent variable, we obtained the following estimated regression equation.

$$\hat{y} = -.8687 + .0611x_1 + .9234x_2$$

The error sum of squares for this model was SSE = 2.2994. Clearly, adding x_2 resulted in a reduction of SSE. The question we want to answer is: Does adding the variable x_2 lead to a *significant* reduction in SSE?

We use the notation $SSE(x_1)$ to denote the error sum of squares when x_1 is the only independent variable in the model, $SSE(x_1, x_2)$ to denote the error sum of squares when x_1 and x_2 are both in the model, and so on. Hence, the reduction in SSE resulting from adding x_2 to the Butler Trucking model involving just x_1 is

$$SSE(x_1) - SSE(x_1, x_2) = 8.0287 - 2.2994 = 5.7293$$

An F test is conducted to determine whether this reduction is significant.

The numerator of the F statistic is the reduction in SSE divided by the number of independent variables added to the original model. Here only one variable, x_2, has been added; thus, the numerator of the F statistic is

$$\frac{SSE(x_1) - SSE(x_1, x_2)}{1} = 5.7293$$

The numerator is a measure of the reduction in SSE per independent variable added to the model. The denominator of the F statistic is the mean square error for the model that includes all of the independent variables. For Butler Trucking this corresponds to the model containing both x_1 and x_2; thus, $p = 2$ and

$$MSE = \frac{SSE(x_1, x_2)}{n - p - 1} = \frac{2.2994}{7} = .3285$$

The following F statistic provides the basis for testing whether the addition of x_2 is statistically significant.

$$F = \frac{\dfrac{SSE(x_1) - SSE(x_1, x_2)}{1}}{\dfrac{SSE(x_1, x_2)}{n - p - 1}} \tag{16.10}$$

The numerator degrees of freedom for this F test is equal to the number of variables added to the model, and the denominator degrees of freedom is equal to $n - p - 1$.

For the Butler Trucking example, we obtain

$$F = \frac{\dfrac{5.7293}{1}}{\dfrac{2.2994}{7}} = \frac{5.7293}{.3285} = 17.44$$

Using Excel, p-value = FDIST(17.44,1,7) = .0042.
Excel can be used to show that $F = 17.44$ provides a p-value $= .0042$. For a level of significance of $\alpha = .05$, we can reject the null hypothesis that x_2 is not statistically significant because the p-value $= .0042 < \alpha = .05$; in other words, adding x_2 to the model involving only x_1 results in a significant reduction in the error sum of squares.

When we want to test for the significance of adding only one independent variable to a model, the result found using the F test just described could also be obtained by using the t test for the significance of an individual parameter (described in Section 15.5). Indeed, the F statistic we just computed is the square of the t statistic used to test the significance of an individual parameter.

Because the t test is equivalent to the F test when only one independent variable is being added to the model, we can now further clarify the proper use of the t test for testing the significance of an individual parameter. If the t test shows that only one parameter is not significant, the corresponding variable can be dropped from the model. However, if the t test shows that two or more parameters are not significant, no more than one independent variable can ever be dropped from a model on the basis of a t test; if one variable is dropped, another variable that was not significant initially might become significant.

We now turn to a consideration of whether the addition of more than one independent variable—as a set—results in a significant reduction in the error sum of squares.

General Case

Consider the following multiple regression model involving q independent variables, where $q < p$.

$$y = \beta_0 + \beta_1 x_1 + \beta_2 x_2 + \cdots + \beta_q x_q + \epsilon \tag{16.11}$$

If we add variables $x_{q+1}, x_{q+2}, \ldots, x_p$ to this model, we obtain a model involving p independent variables.

$$\begin{aligned} y = \beta_0 + \beta_1 x_1 + \beta_2 x_2 + \cdots + \beta_q x_q \\ + \beta_{q+1} x_{q+1} + \beta_{q+2} x_{q+2} + \cdots + \beta_p x_p + \epsilon \end{aligned} \tag{16.12}$$

To test whether the addition of $x_{q+1}, x_{q+2}, \ldots, x_p$ is statistically significant, the null and alternative hypotheses can be stated as follows.

$$H_0: \beta_{q+1} = \beta_{q+2} = \cdots = \beta_p = 0$$
$$H_a: \text{One or more of the parameters are not equal to zero}$$

The following F statistic provides the basis for testing whether the additional independent variables are statistically significant.

$$F = \frac{\dfrac{\text{SSE}(x_1, x_2, \ldots, x_q) - \text{SSE}(x_1, x_2, \ldots, x_q, x_{q+1}, \ldots, x_p)}{p - q}}{\dfrac{\text{SSE}(x_1, x_2, \ldots, x_q, x_{q+1}, \ldots, x_p)}{n - p - 1}} \tag{16.13}$$

This F statistic has $p - q$ numerator degrees of freedom and $n - p - 1$ denominator degrees of freedom. If the corresponding p-value $\leq \alpha$ or $F > F_\alpha$, we reject H_0 and conclude that the set of additional independent variables is statistically significant. Note that for the special case where $q = 1$ and $p = 2$, equation (16.13) reduces to equation (16.10).

Many students find equation (16.13) somewhat complex. To provide a simpler description of this F statistic, we can refer to the model with the smaller number of independent variables as the reduced model and the model with the larger number of independent variables as the full model. If we let SSE(reduced) denote the error sum of squares for the reduced model and SSE(full) denote the error sum of squares for the full model, we can write the numerator of equation (16.13) as

$$\frac{\text{SSE(reduced)} - \text{SSE(full)}}{\text{Number of extra terms}} \tag{16.14}$$

Note that Number of extra terms denotes the difference between the number of independent variables in the full model and the number of independent variables in the reduced model. The denominator of equation (16.13) is the error sum of squares for the full model divided by the corresponding degrees of freedom; in other words, the denominator is the mean square error for the full model. Denoting the mean square error for the full model as MSE(full) enables us to write the F statistic as

$$F = \frac{\dfrac{\text{SSE(reduced)} - \text{SSE(full)}}{\text{Number of extra terms}}}{\text{MSE(full)}} \tag{16.15}$$

To illustrate the use of this F statistic, suppose we have a regression problem involving 30 observations. One model with the independent variables x_1, x_2, and x_3 has an error sum of squares of 150 and a second model with the independent variables x_1, x_2, x_3, x_4, and x_5 has an error sum of squares of 100. Did the addition of the two independent variables x_4 and x_5 result in a significant reduction in the error sum of squares?

First, note that the degrees of freedom for SST is $30 - 1 = 29$ and that the degrees of freedom for the regression sum of squares for the full model is 5 (the number of independent variables in the full model). Thus, the degrees of freedom for the error sum of squares for the full model is $n - p - 1 = 30 - 5 - 1 = 24$, and hence MSE(full) $= 100/24 = 4.17$. Therefore, the F statistic is

$$F = \frac{\dfrac{150 - 100}{2}}{4.17} = 6.00$$

Using Excel, p-value =
FDIST(6,2,24) = .0077.

This computed F value is compared with the table F value with 2 numerator and 24 denominator degrees of freedom. Excel can be used to show that $F = 6.00$ provides a p-value $= .0077$ at the .05 level of significance. Because p-value $= .0077 < \alpha = .05$, we conclude that the addition of variables x_4 and x_5 is statistically significant.

NOTES AND COMMENTS

Computation of the F statistic can also be based on the difference in the regression sums of squares. To show this form of the F statistic, we first note that

$$\text{SSE(reduced)} = \text{SST} - \text{SSR(reduced)}$$
$$\text{SSE(full)} = \text{SST} - \text{SSR(full)}$$

Hence

$$\text{SSE(reduced)} - \text{SSE(full)} = [\text{SST} - \text{SSR(reduced)}] - [\text{SST} - \text{SSR(full)}]$$
$$= \text{SSR (full)} - \text{SSR(reduced)}$$

Thus,

$$F = \frac{\dfrac{\text{SSR(full)} - \text{SSR(reduced)}}{\text{Number of extra terms}}}{\text{MSE(full)}}$$

EXERCISES

Methods

10. In a regression analysis involving 27 observations, the following estimated regression equation was developed.

$$\hat{y} = 25.2 + 5.5x_1$$

For this estimated regression equation SST = 1550 and SSE = 520.
a.   At $\alpha = .05$, test whether x_1 is significant.

Suppose that variables x_2 and x_3 are added to the model and the following regression equation is obtained.

$$\hat{y} = 16.3 + 2.3x_1 + 12.1x_2 - 5.8x_3$$

For this estimated regression equation SST = 1550 and SSE = 100.
b.   Use an F test and a .05 level of significance to determine whether x_2 and x_3 together contribute significantly to the model.

11. In a regression analysis involving 30 observations, the following estimated regression equation was obtained.

$$\hat{y} = 17.6 + 3.8x_1 - 2.3x_2 + 7.6x_3 + 2.7x_4$$

For this estimated regression equation SST = 1805 and SSR = 1760.
a.   At $\alpha = .05$, test the significance of the relationship among the variables.

Suppose variables x_1 and x_4 are dropped from the model and the following estimated regression equation is obtained.

$$\hat{y} = 11.1 - 3.6x_2 + 8.1x_3$$

For this model SST = 1805 and SSR = 1705.
b.   Compute SSE(x_1, x_2, x_3, x_4).
c.   Compute SSE(x_2, x_3).
d.   Use an F test and a .05 level of significance to determine whether x_1 and x_4 contribute significantly to the model.

Applications

12. The following table gives some of the data available for 14 teams in the National Football League after 15 games.

Football

Team	Won–Lost	Total Points	Rushing Yards	Passing Yards	Interceptions Made by Team	Interceptions Made by Opponent
Atlanta	5–10	305	1907	2473	19	23
Chicago	12–3	187	2134	2718	14	24
Dallas	3–12	358	1858	3386	24	10
Detroit	4–11	292	1184	1971	15	12
Green Bay	3–12	298	1274	3046	22	20
St. Louis	9–6	277	1882	3604	17	22
Minnesota	10–5	206	1744	3633	16	35
New Orleans	9–6	274	1843	2963	15	17
N.Y. Giants	10–5	277	1492	3096	14	15
Philadelphia	9–6	312	1812	3247	17	29
Phoenix	7–8	372	1909	3633	19	14
San Francisco	10–5	256	2453	3131	14	21
Tampa Bay	4–11	340	1650	3169	33	18
Washington	7–8	367	1377	3930	24	14

a. Develop an estimated regression equation that can be used to predict the total points scored given the number of interceptions made by the team.
b. Develop an estimated regression equation that can be used to predict the total points scored given the number of interceptions made by the team, the number of rushing yards, and the number of interceptions made by the opponents.
c. At a .05 level of significance, test to see whether the addition of the number of rushing yards and the number of interceptions made by the opponents contributes significantly to the estimated regression equation developed in part (a). Explain.

13. Refer to exercise 12.
a. Develop an estimated regression equation that relates the total points scored to the number of passing yards, the number of interceptions made by the team, and the number of interceptions made by the opponents.
b. Develop an estimated regression equation using the independent variables in part (a) and the number of rushing yards.
c. At a .05 level of significance, did the number of rushing yards contribute significantly to the estimated regression equation developed in part (a)? Explain.

14. A 10-year study conducted by the American Heart Association provided data on how age, systolic blood pressure, and smoking relate to the risk of strokes. Data from a portion of this study follow. Risk is interpreted as the probability (times 100) that a person will have a stroke over the next 10-year period. For the smoker variable, 1 indicates a smoker and 0 indicates a nonsmoker.

Stroke

Risk	Age	Blood Pressure	Smoker
12	57	152	0
24	67	163	0
13	58	155	0
56	86	177	1
28	59	196	0

Risk	Age	Blood Pressure	Smoker
51	76	189	1
18	56	155	1
31	78	120	0
37	80	135	1
15	78	98	0
22	71	152	0
36	70	173	1
15	67	135	1
48	77	209	1
15	60	199	0
36	82	119	1
8	66	166	0
34	80	125	1
3	62	117	0
37	59	207	1

a.   Develop an estimated regression equation that can be used to predict the risk of stroke given the age and blood-pressure level.

b.   Consider adding two independent variables to the model developed in part (a), one for the interaction between age and blood-pressure level and the other for whether the person is a smoker. Develop an estimated regression equation using these four independent variables.

c.   At a .05 level of significance, test to see whether the addition of the interaction term and the smoker variable contribute significantly to the estimated regression equation developed in part (a).

15.   The National Football League rates prospects position by position on a scale that ranges from 5 to 9. The ratings are interpreted as follows: 8–9 should start the first year; 7.0–7.9 should start; 6.0–6.9 will make the team as backup; and 5.0–5.9 can make the club and contribute. The following table shows the position, weight, speed (for 40 yards), and ratings for 40 NFL prospects (*USA Today,* April 14, 2000).

CD file

NFL

Observation	Name	Position	Weight	Speed	Rating
1	Peter Warrick	Wide receiver	194	4.53	9.0
2	Plaxico Burress	Wide receiver	231	4.52	8.8
3	Sylvester Morris	Wide receiver	216	4.59	8.3
4	Travis Taylor	Wide receiver	199	4.36	8.1
5	Laveranues Coles	Wide receiver	192	4.29	8.0
6	Dez White	Wide receiver	218	4.49	7.9
7	Jerry Porter	Wide receiver	221	4.55	7.4
8	Ron Dugans	Wide receiver	206	4.47	7.1
9	Todd Pinkston	Wide receiver	169	4.37	7.0
10	Dennis Northcutt	Wide receiver	175	4.43	7.0
11	Anthony Lucas	Wide receiver	194	4.51	6.9
12	Darrell Jackson	Wide receiver	197	4.56	6.6
13	Danny Farmer	Wide receiver	217	4.60	6.5
14	Sherrod Gideon	Wide receiver	173	4.57	6.4
15	Trevor Gaylor	Wide receiver	199	4.57	6.2
16	Cosey Coleman	Guard	322	5.38	7.4
17	Travis Claridge	Guard	303	5.18	7.0
18	Kaulana Noa	Guard	317	5.34	6.8
19	Leander Jordan	Guard	330	5.46	6.7

(continued)

Observation	Name	Position	Weight	Speed	Rating
20	Chad Clifton	Guard	334	5.18	6.3
21	Manula Savea	Guard	308	5.32	6.1
22	Ryan Johanningmeir	Guard	310	5.28	6.0
23	Mark Tauscher	Guard	318	5.37	6.0
24	Blaine Saipaia	Guard	321	5.25	6.0
25	Richard Mercier	Guard	295	5.34	5.8
26	Damion McIntosh	Guard	328	5.31	5.3
27	Jeno James	Guard	320	5.64	5.0
28	Al Jackson	Guard	304	5.20	5.0
29	Chris Samuels	Offensive tackle	325	4.95	8.5
30	Stockar McDougle	Offensive tackle	361	5.50	8.0
31	Chris McIngosh	Offensive tackle	315	5.39	7.8
32	Adrian Klemm	Offensive tackle	307	4.98	7.6
33	Todd Wade	Offensive tackle	326	5.20	7.3
34	Marvel Smith	Offensive tackle	320	5.36	7.1
35	Michael Thompson	Offensive tackle	287	5.05	6.8
36	Bobby Williams	Offensive tackle	332	5.26	6.8
37	Darnell Alford	Offensive tackle	334	5.55	6.4
38	Terrance Beadles	Offensive tackle	312	5.15	6.3
39	Tutan Reyes	Offensive tackle	299	5.35	6.1
40	Greg Robinson-Ran	Offensive tackle	333	5.59	6.0

a. Develop dummy variables that will account for the player's position.
b. Develop an estimated regression equation to show how rating is related to position, weight, and speed.
c. At the .05 level of significance, test whether the estimated regression equation developed in part (b) represents a significant relationship between the independent variables and the dependent variable.
d. Is position a significant factor in the player's rating? Use $\alpha = .05$. Explain.

16.3   Analysis of a Larger Problem

In introducing multiple regression analysis, we used the Butler Trucking example extensively. The small size of this problem was an advantage in exploring introductory concepts, but would make it difficult to illustrate some of the variable selection issues involved in model building. To provide an illustration of the variable selection procedures discussed in the next section, we introduce a data set consisting of 25 observations on eight independent variables. Permission to use these data was provided by Dr. David W. Cravens of the Department of Marketing at Texas Christian University. Consequently, we refer to the data set as the Cravens data.*

The Cravens data are for a company that sells products in several sales territories, each of which is assigned to a single sales representative. A regression analysis was conducted to determine whether a variety of predictor (independent) variables could explain sales in each territory. A random sample of 25 sales territories resulted in the data in Table 16.5; the variable definitions are given in Table 16.6.

As a preliminary step, let us consider the sample correlation coefficients between each pair of variables. Figure 16.9 is the correlation matrix obtained by using Excel's Correlation

*For details see David W. Cravens, Robert B. Woodruff, and Joe C. Stamper, "An Analytical Approach for Evaluating Sales Territory Performance," *Journal of Marketing*, 36 (January 1972): 31–37. Copyright © 1972 American Marketing Association.

TABLE 16.5   THE CRAVENS DATA

Cravens

Sales	Time	Poten	AdvExp	Share	Change	Accounts	Work	Rating
3,669.88	43.10	74,065.1	4,582.9	2.51	0.34	74.86	15.05	4.9
3,473.95	108.13	58,117.3	5,539.8	5.51	0.15	107.32	19.97	5.1
2,295.10	13.82	21,118.5	2,950.4	10.91	−0.72	96.75	17.34	2.9
4,675.56	186.18	68,521.3	2,243.1	8.27	0.17	195.12	13.40	3.4
6,125.96	161.79	57,805.1	7,747.1	9.15	0.50	180.44	17.64	4.6
2,134.94	8.94	37,806.9	402.4	5.51	0.15	104.88	16.22	4.5
5,031.66	365.04	50,935.3	3,140.6	8.54	0.55	256.10	18.80	4.6
3,367.45	220.32	35,602.1	2,086.2	7.07	−0.49	126.83	19.86	2.3
6,519.45	127.64	46,176.8	8,846.2	12.54	1.24	203.25	17.42	4.9
4,876.37	105.69	42,053.2	5,673.1	8.85	0.31	119.51	21.41	2.8
2,468.27	57.72	36,829.7	2,761.8	5.38	0.37	116.26	16.32	3.1
2,533.31	23.58	33,612.7	1,991.8	5.43	−0.65	142.28	14.51	4.2
2,408.11	13.82	21,412.8	1,971.5	8.48	0.64	89.43	19.35	4.3
2,337.38	13.82	20,416.9	1,737.4	7.80	1.01	84.55	20.02	4.2
4,586.95	86.99	36,272.0	10,694.2	10.34	0.11	119.51	15.26	5.5
2,729.24	165.85	23,093.3	8,618.6	5.15	0.04	80.49	15.87	3.6
3,289.40	116.26	26,878.6	7,747.9	6.64	0.68	136.58	7.81	3.4
2,800.78	42.28	39,572.0	4,565.8	5.45	0.66	78.86	16.00	4.2
3,264.20	52.84	51,866.1	6,022.7	6.31	−0.10	136.58	17.44	3.6
3,453.62	165.04	58,749.8	3,721.1	6.35	−0.03	138.21	17.98	3.1
1,741.45	10.57	23,990.8	861.0	7.37	−1.63	75.61	20.99	1.6
2,035.75	13.82	25,694.9	3,571.5	8.39	−0.43	102.44	21.66	3.4
1,578.00	8.13	23,736.3	2,845.5	5.15	0.04	76.42	21.46	2.7
4,167.44	58.44	34,314.3	5,060.1	12.88	0.22	136.58	24.78	2.8
2,799.97	21.14	22,809.5	3,552.0	9.14	−0.74	88.62	24.96	3.9

tool. Note that the sample correlation coefficient between Sales and Time is .623, between Sales and Poten is .598, and so on.

Looking at the sample correlation coefficients between the independent variables, we see that the correlation between Time and Accounts is .758; hence, if Accounts were used as an independent variable, Time would not add much more explanatory power to the model. Recall the rule-of-thumb test from the discussion of multicollinearity in Section 15.5:

TABLE 16.6   VARIABLE DEFINITIONS FOR THE CRAVENS DATA

Variable	Definition
Sales	Total sales credited to the sales representative
Time	Length of time employed in months
Poten	Market potential; total industry sales in units for the sales territory*
AdvExp	Advertising expenditure in the sales territory
Share	Market share; weighted average for the past 4 years
Change	Change in the market share over the previous 4 years
Accounts	Number of accounts assigned to the sales representative*
Work	Workload; a weighted index based on annual purchases and concentrations of accounts
Rating	Sales representative overall rating on eight performance dimensions; an aggregate rating on a 1–7 scale

*These data were coded to preserve confidentiality.

FIGURE 16.9 SAMPLE CORRELATION COEFFICIENTS FOR THE CRAVENS DATA

	Sales	Time	Poten	AdvExp	Share	Change	Accounts	Work
Time	0.623							
Poten	0.598	0.454						
AdvExp	0.596	0.249	0.174					
Share	0.484	0.106	-0.211	0.264				
Change	0.489	0.251	0.268	0.377	0.085			
Accounts	0.754	0.758	0.479	0.200	0.403	0.327		
Work	-0.117	-0.179	-0.259	-0.272	0.349	-0.288	-0.199	
Rating	0.402	0.101	0.359	0.411	-0.024	0.549	0.229	-0.277

multicollinearity can cause problems if the absolute value of the sample correlation coefficient exceeds .7 for any two of the independent variables. If possible, then, we should avoid including both Time and Accounts in the same regression model. The sample correlation coefficient of .549 between Change and Rating is also high and may warrant further consideration.

Looking at the sample correlation coefficients between Sales and each of the independent variables can give us a quick indication of which independent variables are, by themselves, good predictors. We see that the single best predictor of Sales is Accounts, because it has the highest sample correlation coefficient (.754). Recall that for the case of one independent variable, the square of the sample correlation coefficient is the coefficient of determination. Thus, Accounts can explain $(.754)^2(100)$, or 56.85%, of the variability in Sales. The next most important independent variables are Time, Poten, and AdvExp, each with a sample correlation coefficient of approximately .6.

Although the potential for multicollinearity problems is present, let us consider developing an estimated regression equation using all eight independent variables. Excel's Regression tool provided the results in Figure 16.10. The eight-variable multiple regression model has an adjusted coefficient of determination of .8331. Note, however, that the *P-value* column (the *p*-values for the *t* tests of individual parameters) shows that only Poten, AdvExp, and Share are significant at the $\alpha = .05$ level, given the effect of all the other variables. Hence, we might be inclined to investigate the results that would be obtained if we used just those three variables. Figure 16.11 shows the Excel results obtained for the estimated regression equation with those three variables. We see that the estimated regression equation has an adjusted coefficient of determination of .8274, which is almost as high as that for the eight-independent-variable estimated regression equation.

How can we find an estimated regression equation that will do the best job given the data available? One approach is to compute all possible regressions. That is, we could develop 8 one-variable estimated regression equations (each of which corresponds to one of the independent variables), 28 two-variable estimated regression equations (the number of combinations of eight variables taken two at a time), and so on. In all, for the Cravens data, 255 different estimated regression equations involving one or more independent variables would have to be fitted to the data.

With the excellent computer packages available today, it is possible to compute all possible regressions. But doing so involves a great amount of computation and requires the model builder to review a large volume of computer output, much of which is associated with obviously poor models. Statisticians prefer a more systematic approach to selecting the subset of independent variables that provide the best estimated regression equation. In the next section, we introduce some of the more popular approaches.

FIGURE 16.10 EXCEL OUTPUT USING ALL EIGHT INDEPENDENT VARIABLES

	A	B	C	D	E	F	G	H	I	J
1	SUMMARY OUTPUT									
2										
3	*Regression Statistics*									
4	Multiple R	0.9602								
5	R Square	0.9220								
6	Adjusted R Square	0.8331								
7	Standard Error	449.0154								
8	Observations	25								
9										
10	ANOVA									
11		*df*	*SS*	*MS*	*F*	*Significance F*				
12	Regression	8	38153712.11	4769214	23.6551	1.81E-07				
13	Residual	16	3225836.813	201614.8						
14	Total	24	41379548.93							
15										
16		*Coefficients*	*Standard Error*	*t Stat*	*P-value*	*Lower 95%*	*Upper 95%*	*Lower 95.0%*	*Upper 95.0%*	
17	Intercept	-1507.8358	778.6084	-1.9366	0.0707	-3158.4119	142.7403	-3158.4119	142.7403	
18	Time	2.0101	1.9305	1.0412	0.3132	-2.0824	6.1026	-2.0824	6.1026	
19	Poten	0.0372	0.0082	4.5361	0.0003	0.0198	0.0546	0.0198	0.0546	
20	AdvExp	0.1510	0.0471	3.2051	0.0055	0.0511	0.2508	0.0511	0.2508	
21	Share	199.0402	67.0291	2.9695	0.0090	56.9447	341.1356	56.9447	341.1356	
22	Change	290.8666	186.7769	1.5573	0.1390	-105.0827	686.8159	-105.0827	686.8159	
23	Accounts	5.5497	4.7754	1.1621	0.2622	-4.5737	15.6732	-4.5737	15.6732	
24	Work	19.7939	33.6752	0.5878	0.5649	-51.5943	91.1821	-51.5943	91.1821	
25	Rating	8.1890	128.4985	0.0637	0.9500	-264.2155	280.5936	-264.2155	280.5936	
26										

FIGURE 16.11 EXCEL OUTPUT USING THREE INDEPENDENT VARIABLES: Poten, AdvExp, AND Share

	A	B	C	D	E	F	G	H	I	J
1	SUMMARY OUTPUT									
2										
3	*Regression Statistics*									
4	Multiple R	0.9214								
5	R Square	0.8490								
6	Adjusted R Square	0.8274								
7	Standard Error	545.5151								
8	Observations	25								
9										
10	ANOVA									
11		*df*	*SS*	*MS*	*F*	*Significance F*				
12	Regression	3	35130228.29	11710076	39.3501	8.43E-09				
13	Residual	21	6249320.641	297586.7						
14	Total	24	41379548.93							
15										
16		*Coefficients*	*Standard Error*	*t Stat*	*P-value*	*Lower 95%*	*Upper 95%*	*Lower 99.0%*	*Upper 99.0%*	
17	Intercept	-1603.5821	505.5509	-3.1719	0.0046	-2654.9328	-552.2315	-3034.9786	-172.1857	
18	Poten	0.0543	0.0075	7.2632	3.74E-07	0.0387	0.0698	0.0331	0.0754	
19	AdvExp	0.1675	0.0443	3.7829	0.0011	0.0754	0.2596	0.0421	0.2928	
20	Share	282.7469	48.7556	5.7993	9.33E-06	181.3541	384.1398	144.7023	420.7916	
21										

16.4 Variable Selection Procedures

Variable selection procedures are particularly useful in the early stages of building a model, but they cannot substitute for experience and judgment on the part of the analyst.

In this section we discuss four **variable selection procedures**: stepwise regression, forward selection, backward elimination, and best-subsets regression. Given a data set with several possible independent variables, these variable selection procedures provide a systematic approach to selecting a subset of the independent variables that provide the best model. The first three procedures are iterative; at each step of the procedure a single independent variable is added or deleted and the new model is evaluated. The process continues until a stopping criterion indicates that the procedure cannot find a better model. The best-subsets procedure is not a one-variable-at-a-time procedure; it evaluates regression models involving different subsets of the independent variables.

In the stepwise regression, forward selection, and backward elimination procedures, the criterion for selecting an independent variable to add or delete from the model at each step is based on the F statistic introduced in Section 16.2. Suppose, for instance, that we are considering adding x_2 to a model involving x_1 or deleting x_2 from a model involving x_1 and x_2. To test whether the addition or deletion of x_2 is statistically significant, the null and alternative hypotheses can be stated as follows:

$$H_0: \beta_2 = 0$$
$$H_a: \beta_2 \neq 0$$

In equation (16.10) in Section 16.2 we showed that

$$F = \frac{\dfrac{\text{SSE}(x_1) - \text{SSE}(x_1, x_2)}{1}}{\dfrac{\text{SSE}(x_1, x_2)}{n - p - 1}}$$

can be used as a criterion for determining whether the presence of x_2 in the model causes a significant reduction in the error sum of squares. The p-value corresponding to this F statistic is the criterion used to determine whether an independent variable should be added or deleted from the regression model. The usual rejection rule applies: Reject H_0 if p-value $< \alpha$.

Stepwise Regression

The stepwise regression procedure begins each step by determining whether any of the variables already in the model should be removed. It does so by first computing an F statistic (as shown previously) and corresponding p-value for each independent variable in the model. The level of significance α for determining whether an independent variable should be removed from the model is referred to as *Alpha to remove*. If the p-value for any independent variable is greater than *Alpha to remove,* the independent variable with the largest p-value is removed from the model and the stepwise regression procedure begins a new step.

If no independent variable can be removed from the model, the procedure attempts to enter another independent variable into the model. It does so by first computing an F statistic and corresponding p-value for each independent variable that is not in the model. The level of significance α for determining whether an independent variable should be entered into the model is referred to as *Alpha to enter*. The independent variable with the smallest p-value is entered into the model provided its p-value is less than *Alpha to enter.* The procedure continues in this manner until no independent variables can be deleted from or added to the model.

Forward Selection

The forward selection procedure starts with no independent variables. It adds variables one at a time using the same procedure as stepwise regression for determining whether an independent variable should be entered into the model. However, the forward selection procedure does not permit a variable to be removed from the model once it has been entered. The procedure stops if the p-value for each of the independent variables not in the model is greater than *Alpha to enter*.

Backward Elimination

The backward elimination procedure begins with a model that includes all the independent variables. It then deletes one independent variable at a time using the same procedure as stepwise regression. However, the backward elimination procedure does not permit an independent variable to be reentered once it has been removed. The procedure stops when none of the independent variables in the model have a p-value greater than *Alpha to remove*.

Using Excel to Perform the Backward Elimination Procedure

Excel does not have built-in capabilities for performing the stepwise regression, forward selection, or backward elimination procedures. However, Excel's Regression tool can be used to perform the backward elimination procedure by running a series of regression problems starting with a model that involves all of the independent variables. We will illustrate the procedure using the Cravens data and a value of .05 for *Alpha to remove*.

Figure 16.10 (shown earlier) shows the Excel output for the Cravens problem using all eight independent variables. At step 1 of the backward elimination procedure, we first check to see whether the p-value for any independent variable is greater than *Alpha to remove* = .05. The Cravens data contain five independent variables with a p-value greater than .05: Time (.3132), Change (.1390), Accounts (.2622), Work (.5649), and Rating (.9500). Because Rating has the largest p-value, we will remove Rating from the current model and develop a new estimated regression equation involving the remaining seven independent variables; Figure 16.12 shows the Excel output for the new estimated regression equation.

Figure 16.12 shows that four of the seven independent variables have a p-value greater than .05: Time (.2867), Change (.0896), Accounts (.2340), and Work (.5501). Because Work has the largest p-value greater than .05, it is selected as the next independent variable to be removed from the model. Thus, we must now develop a new estimated regression equation corresponding to six independent variables: Time, Poten, AdvExp, Share, Change, and Accounts. Instead of showing the complete regression output for this and subsequent steps of the procedure, we will summarize the key results in Table 16.7.

The column labeled All Variables in Table 16.7 shows the p-values for each of the eight independent variables at the start of the backward elimination procedure. Recall that we used these p-values to determine that Rating should be the first independent variable to remove from the model. The results after deleting Rating and developing a new estimated regression equation are shown in the column labeled Step 1. At each step, the label Deleted indicates the independent variable to be removed from the model. Thus the p-values shown in the Step 1 column correspond to the estimated regression equation obtained after deleting Rating; in other words, they are the p-values shown in the regression output in Figure 16.12. Similarly, the column labeled Step 2 in Table 16.7 shows that at step 2 Work was selected as the next independent variable to be removed. The p-values in the Step 2

FIGURE 16.12   EXCEL OUTPUT FOR THE CRAVENS DATA AFTER DELETING RATING

	A	B	C	D	E	F	G	H	I	J
1	SUMMARY OUTPUT									
2										
3	*Regression Statistics*									
4	Multiple R	0.9602								
5	R Square	0.9220								
6	Adjusted R Square	0.8899								
7	Standard Error	435.6642								
8	Observations	25								
9										
10	ANOVA									
11		*df*	*SS*	*MS*	*F*	*Significance F*				
12	Regression	7	38152893.29	5450413	28.7161	3.21E-08				
13	Residual	17	3226655.64	189803.3						
14	Total	24	41379548.93							
15										
16		*Coefficients*	*Standard Error*	*t Stat*	*P-value*	*Lower 95%*	*Upper 95%*	*Lower 99.0%*	*Upper 99.0%*	
17	Intercept	-1485.9001	677.6281	-2.1928	0.0425	-2915.5705	-56.2297	-3449.8227	478.0224	
18	Time	1.9751	1.7957	1.0999	0.2867	-1.8134	5.7637	-3.2292	7.1794	
19	Poten	0.0373	0.0079	4.7499	0.0002	0.0207	0.0539	0.0145	0.0600	
20	AdvExp	0.1520	0.0432	3.5139	0.0027	0.0607	0.2432	0.0266	0.2773	
21	Share	198.3252	64.1187	3.0931	0.0066	63.0466	333.6038	12.4945	384.1560	
22	Change	295.8774	164.3831	1.7999	0.0896	-50.9407	642.6954	-180.5427	772.2975	
23	Accounts	5.6089	4.5449	1.2341	0.2340	-3.9800	15.1979	-7.5633	18.7812	
24	Work	19.8989	32.6347	0.6097	0.5501	-48.9543	88.7521	-74.6840	114.4818	
25										

column correspond to a new estimated regression equation involving only six independent variables Time, Poten, AdvExp, Share, Change, and Accounts. Note that the independent variable with the largest p-value is now Accounts (p-value = .2882); thus, in step 3 Accounts is removed from the model and a new estimated regression equation is developed. In step 4, because Change is the only independent variable remaining with a p-value greater than .05, it is removed from the model. Because no independent variables remain with a p-value greater than *Alpha to remove* = .05, the procedure now stops.

Figure 16.13 shows the Excel output corresponding to the four independent variables selected in the final step of the backward elimination procedure: Time, Poten, AdvExp,

TABLE 16.7   SUMMARY OF THE BACKWARD ELIMINATION PROCEDURE FOR THE CRAVENS DATA

	All Variables p-value	Step 1 p-value	Step 2 p-value	Step 3 p-value	Step 4 p-value
Intercept	0.0707	0.0425	0.01255	0.0125	0.0074
Time	0.3132	0.2867	0.1982	0.1982	0.0070
Poten	0.0003	0.0002	7.94E-05	7.94E-05	4.65E-06
AdvExp	0.0055	0.0027	0.0018	0.0018	0.0007
Share	0.0090	0.0066	0.0004	0.0004	5.2E-06
Change	0.1390	0.0896	0.0927	0.0927	**Deleted**
Accounts	0.2622	0.2340	0.2882	**Deleted**	
Work	0.5649	0.5501	**Deleted**		
Rating	0.9500	**Deleted**			

FIGURE 16.13   EXCEL RESULTS AFTER STEP 4 OF THE BACKWARD ELIMINATION PROCEDURE

	A	B	C	D	E	F	G	H	I	J
1	SUMMARY OUTPUT									
2										
3	*Regression Statistics*									
4	Multiple R	0.9466								
5	R Square	0.8960								
6	Adjusted R Square	0.8752								
7	Standard Error	463.9334								
8	Observations	25								
9										
10	ANOVA									
11		*df*	*SS*	*MS*	*F*	*Significance F*				
12	Regression	4	37074865.43	9268716	43.0634	1.48E-09				
13	Residual	20	4304683.495	215234.2						
14	Total	24	41379548.93							
15										
16		*Coefficients*	*Standard Error*	*t Stat*	*P-value*	*Lower 95%*	*Upper 95%*	*Lower 99.0%*	*Upper 99.0%*	
17	Intercept	-1312.3817	440.7254	-2.9778	0.0074	-2231.7188	-393.0445	-2566.3953	-58.3680	
18	Time	3.8166	1.2697	3.0058	0.0070	1.1680	6.4652	0.2038	7.4294	
19	Poten	0.0444	0.0072	6.2027	4.65E-06	0.0295	0.0593	0.0240	0.0648	
20	AdvExp	0.1525	0.0380	4.0144	0.0007	0.0732	0.2317	0.0444	0.2605	
21	Share	259.4843	42.1803	6.1518	5.2E-06	171.4978	347.4708	139.4671	379.5015	
22										

and Share. The estimated regression equation obtained using the backward elimination procedure is

$$\hat{y} = -1312.3817 + 3.8166\text{Time} + .0444\text{Poten} + .1525\text{AdvExp} + 259.4843\text{Share}$$

With an Adjusted R Square of .8752 we see that the estimated regression equation provides a good fit.

Forward selection and backward elimination are different approaches that may lead to different models.

Forward selection and backward elimination are the two extremes of model building; the forward selection procedure starts with no independent variables in the model and adds independent variables one at a time, whereas the backward elimination procedure starts with all independent variables in the model and deletes variables one at a time. The two procedures may lead to the same estimated regression equation. But it is possible for them to lead to two different estimated regression equations. Which estimated regression equation to use remains a topic for discussion. Ultimately, the analyst's judgment must be applied. The best-subsets model-building procedure we discuss next provides additional information to be considered before a final decision is made.

Best-Subsets Regression

Stepwise regression, forward selection, and backward elimination are approaches to choosing the regression model by adding or deleting independent variables one at a time. Hence, they offer no guarantee that the best model for a given number of variables will be found. These one-variable-at-a-time procedures are properly viewed as heuristics for selecting a good regression model.

Some statistical software packages have a procedure called best-subsets regression that enables the user to find, given a specified number of independent variables, the best regression equation. Typical output from such packages will enable the user to identify the two best one-variable estimated regression equations, the two best two-variable regression equations, the two best three-variable regression equations, and so on. The criterion used in determining which estimated regression equations are best for any number of predictors is usually the value of the coefficient of determination.

NOTES AND COMMENTS

1. Functions of the independent variables can be used to create new independent variables for use with any of the procedures in this section. For instance, if we wanted x_1x_2 in the model to account for interaction, we would use the data for x_1 and x_2 to create the data for $z = x_1x_2$.

2. None of the procedures that add or delete variables one at a time can be guaranteed to identify the best regression model. But they are excellent approaches to finding good models—especially when little multicollinearity is present.

3. The Excel add-in SWStat+ has the capability to perform stepwise regression, forward selection, backward elimination, and best-subsets regression. Users of SWStat+ will find these features fairly easy to implement.

EXERCISES

Applications

16. Two experts provided subjective lists of school districts that they think are among the best in the country. For each school district, the following data were obtained: average class size, instructional spending per student, average teacher salary, combined SAT score, percentage of students taking the SAT, and percentage of graduates attending a four-year college.

Schools

City	Average Class Size	Average Instructional Spending per Student ($)	Average Teacher Salary ($)	Combined SAT Score/ % Taking Test	Attend Four-Year College (%)
Blue Springs, MO	25	3,060	29,359	1083/(8)	74
Garden City, NY	18	9,700	51,000	997/(99)	77
Indianapolis, IN	30	3,222	30,482	716/(42)	40
Newport Beach, CA (Newport–Mesa)	26	4,028	37,043	977/(46)	51
Novi, MI	20	3,067	39,797	980/(15)	53
Piedmont, CA (Piedmont City)	28	4,208	37,274	1,042/(91)	75
Pittsburgh, PA (Fox Chapel area)	21	4,884	37,156	983/(80)	66
Scarsdale, NY (Edgemont)	20	9,853	31,555	1,110/(98)	87
Wayne, PA (Radnor Township)	22	5,022	40,406	1,040/(95)	85
Weston, MA	21	4,680	39,800	1,031/(99)	89
Farmingdale, NY	22	6,729	45,846	947/(75)	81
Mamaroneck, NY	20	10,405	49,625	1,000/(90)	69
Mayfield, OH	24	5,881	36,228	1,003/(25)	48
Morristown, NJ	22	6,300	37,000	972/(80)	64
New Rochelle, NY	23	8,875	41,650	1,039/(80)	55
Newtown Square, PA (Marple–Newtown)	17	5,313	38,000	963/(75)	79
Omaha, NE (Westside)	23	4,815	32,500	1,059/(31)	81
Shaker Heights, OH	23	4,370	38,639	940/(56)	82

Let the dependent variable be the percentage of graduates attending a four-year college.
a. Develop the best one-variable estimated regression equation.
b. Develop an estimated regression equation using all five independent variables.
c. Use the backward elimination procedure to develop the best estimated regression equation.

17. Refer to the data in exercise 12. Let the dependent variable be the number of wins.
a. Develop the best one-variable estimated regression equation.
b. Develop an estimated regression equation using all of the independent variables.
c. Use the backward elimination procedure to develop the best estimated regression equation.

18. The Ladies Professional Golfers Association (LPGA) maintains statistics on performance and earnings for members of the LPGA Tour. Year-end LPGA Tour statistics for 1997 follow (*Golfweek,* December 6, 1997). Scoring Avg. is the average score per 18 holes of golf; Driving Distance is the average number of yards per drive; Fairways is the percentage of drives ending in the fairway; Greens is the percentage of times a player was able to hit the green in regulation; Putts is the average number of putts per round; Sand Saves is the percentage of times a player was able to get "up and down" from a greenside sand bunker. A green is considered hit in regulation if any part of the ball is touching the putting surface and the number of strokes taken to hit the green is not more than the value of par minus two.

CD file

LPGATour

Player	Scoring Avg.	Driving Distance	Fairways	Greens	Putts	Sand Saves
Annika Sorenstam	70.04	249.00	75.4	73.2	29.67	47.3
Karrie Webb	70.00	254.60	72.1	75.1	30.20	38.0
Kelly Robbins	70.35	256.00	69.3	78.6	29.96	44.9
Chris Johnson	70.84	249.40	66.9	70.4	30.17	39.6
Tammie Green	71.24	239.40	70.4	68.6	29.64	47.2
Juli Inkster	70.64	251.60	69.0	69.8	29.35	46.0
Liselotte Neumann	71.28	243.50	66.6	65.9	29.36	48.4
Laura Davies	70.86	258.40	56.4	68.8	29.90	40.0
Nancy Lopez	70.70	245.50	73.4	73.0	30.23	43.1
Betsy King	71.52	245.70	65.9	66.9	29.63	37.6
Lorie Kane	71.47	243.30	74.9	69.4	30.22	47.8
Michelle McGann	71.52	256.20	57.8	69.6	30.05	51.0
Donna Andrews	71.01	230.60	79.1	71.7	29.94	42.3
Colleen Walker	72.31	230.00	73.6	63.3	29.58	40.9
Rosie Jones	71.77	227.20	77.0	66.0	29.86	41.0
Lisa Hackney	71.34	246.00	69.8	65.1	29.91	36.4
Jane Geddes	71.34	261.20	64.5	70.0	30.15	44.2
Alison Nicholas	72.31	241.70	71.8	66.4	30.43	39.4
Pat Hurst	72.14	251.50	62.4	69.1	30.58	29.9
Cindy Figg-Currier	71.90	237.20	70.1	68.0	30.40	39.3

a. If the average score per 18 holes of golf is the dependent variable, what is the best one-variable estimated regression equation? What does the estimated regression equation suggest for players on the LPGA Tour?
b. Use the methods in this section to develop the best estimated multiple regression equation for estimating a player's average score.
c. Does the estimated regression equation developed in part (b) appear reasonable in terms of interpretation?
d. Michele Redman has the following data: Driving Distance 231.6 yards, Fairways 75.7%, Greens 65.2%, Putts 30.69, and Sand Saves 50.5%. Estimate the average score for this professional golfer.

19. A sample of 16 companies taken from the *Stock Investor Pro* database was used to obtain the following data on the price/earnings (P/E) ratio, the gross profit margin, and the sales growth for each company (*Stock Investor Pro,* American Association of Individual Investors, August 21, 1997). The data in the Industry column are codes used to define the industry for each company: 1 = energy-international oil; 2 = health-drugs; and 3 = other.

StkData

Firm	P/E Ratio	Gross Profit Margin (%)	Sales Growth (%)	Industry
Abbott Laboratories	22.3	23.7	10.0	2
American Home Products	22.6	21.1	5.3	2
Amoco	16.7	11.0	16.5	1
Bristol Meyers Squibb Co.	25.9	26.6	9.4	2
Chevron	18.3	11.6	18.4	1
Exxon	18.7	9.8	8.3	1
General Electric Company	13.1	13.4	13.1	3
Hewlett-Packard	23.3	9.7	21.9	3
IBM	17.3	11.5	5.6	3
Merck & Co. Inc.	26.2	25.6	18.9	2
Mobil	18.7	8.2	8.1	1
Pfizer	34.6	25.1	12.8	2
Pharmacia & Upjohn, Inc.	22.3	15.0	2.7	2
Procter & Gamble Co.	5.4	14.9	5.4	3
Texaco	12.3	7.3	23.7	1
Travelers Group Inc.	28.7	17.8	28.7	3

Develop an estimated regression equation that can be used to predict price/earnings ratio. Briefly discuss the process you used to develop a recommended estimated regression equation for these data.

20. Refer to exercise 14. Using age, blood pressure, whether a person is a smoker, and any interaction involving those variables, develop an estimated regression equation that can be used to predict the risk of a stroke. Briefly describe the process you used to develop an estimated regression equation for these data.

16.5   Residual Analysis

In Chapters 14 and 15 we showed how residual plots can be used to detect violations of assumptions about the regression model. We looked for violations of assumptions about the error term ϵ and the assumed functional form of the model. Some of the actions that can be taken when such violations are detected have been discussed in this chapter. When a different functional form is needed, curvilinear and interaction terms can be included through the use of the general linear model. When several independent variables are considered, the variable selection procedures of the preceding section may be appropriate.

We also discussed how residual analysis can be used to identify observations that can be classified as outliers or as being influential in determining the estimated regression equation. Some steps that should be taken when such observations are found were noted. In many regression studies involving data collected over time, a special type of correlation among the error terms can cause problems; it is called **serial correlation** or **autocorrelation**. In this section we show how the **Durbin-Watson test** can be used to detect significant autocorrelation.

Autocorrelation and the Durbin-Watson Test

Often, the data used for regression studies in business and economics are collected over time. It is not uncommon for the value of y at time t, denoted by y_t, to be related to the value of y at previous time periods. In such cases, we say autocorrelation (also called serial correlation) is present in the data. If the value of y in time period t is related to its value in time period $t - 1$, first-order autocorrelation is present. If the value of y in time period t is related to the value of y in time period $t - 2$, second-order autocorrelation is present, and so on.

When autocorrelation is present, one of the assumptions of the regression model is violated: the error terms are not independent. In the case of first-order autocorrelation, the error at time t, denoted ϵ_t, will be related to the error at time period $t - 1$, denoted ϵ_{t-1}. Two cases of first-order autocorrelation are illustrated in Figure 16.14. Panel A is the case of positive autocorrelation; Panel B is the case of negative autocorrelation. With positive autocorrelation we expect a positive residual in one period to be followed by a positive residual in the next period, a negative residual in one period to be followed by a negative residual in the next period, and so on. With negative autocorrelation, we expect a positive residual in one period to be followed by a negative residual in the next period, then a positive residual, and so on.

When autocorrelation is present, serious errors can be made in performing tests of statistical significance based upon the assumed regression model. It is therefore important to be able to detect autocorrelation and take corrective action. We will show how the Durbin-Watson statistic can be used to detect first-order autocorrelation.

Suppose the values of ϵ are not independent but are related in the following manner:

$$\epsilon_t = \rho \epsilon_{t-1} + z_t \tag{16.16}$$

where ρ is a parameter with an absolute value less than one and z_t is a normally and independently distributed random variable with a mean of zero and a variance of σ^2. From equation (16.16) we see that if $\rho = 0$, the error terms are not related, and each has a mean of zero and a variance of σ^2. In this case, there is no autocorrelation and the regression assumptions are satisfied. If $\rho > 0$, we have positive autocorrelation; if $\rho < 0$, we have

FIGURE 16.14   RESIDUAL PLOTS FOR TWO DATA SETS WITH FIRST-ORDER AUTOCORRELATION

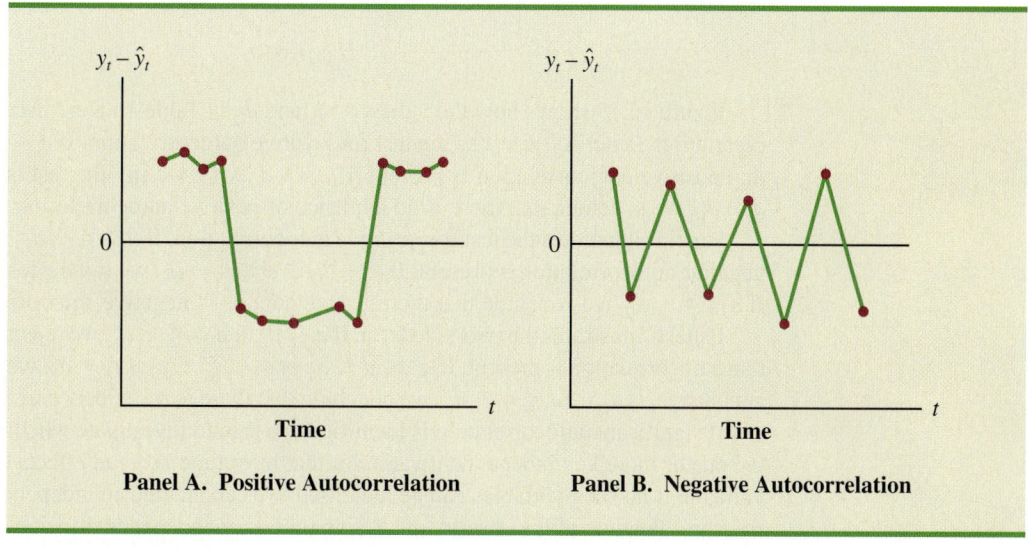

Panel A. Positive Autocorrelation   Panel B. Negative Autocorrelation

negative autocorrelation. In either of these cases, the regression assumptions about the error term are violated.

The Durbin-Watson test for autocorrelation uses the residuals to determine whether $\rho = 0$. To simplify the notation for the Durbin-Watson statistic, we denote the ith residual by $e_i = y_i - \hat{y}_i$. The Durbin-Watson test statistic is computed as follows.

DURBIN-WATSON TEST STATISTIC

$$d = \frac{\sum_{t=2}^{n}(e_t - e_{t-1})^2}{\sum_{t=1}^{n}e_t^2} \tag{16.17}$$

If successive values of the residuals are close together (positive autocorrelation), the value of the Durbin-Watson test statistic will be small. If successive values of the residuals are far apart (negative autocorrelation), the value of the Durbin-Watson test statistic will be large.

The Durbin-Watson test statistic ranges in value from zero to four, with a value of two indicating no autocorrelation is present. Durbin and Watson have developed tables that can be used to determine when their test statistic indicates the presence of autocorrelation. Table 16.8 shows lower and upper bounds (d_L and d_U) for hypothesis tests using $\alpha = .05$, $\alpha = .025$, and $\alpha = .01$; n denotes the number of observations. The null hypothesis to be tested is always that there is no autocorrelation.

$$H_0: \rho = 0$$

The alternative hypothesis to test for positive autocorrelation is

$$H_a: \rho > 0$$

The alternative hypothesis to test for negative autocorrelation is

$$H_a: \rho < 0$$

A two-sided test is also possible. In this case the alternative hypothesis is

$$H_a: \rho \neq 0$$

Figure 16.15 shows how the values of d_L and d_U in Table 16.8 are used to test for autocorrelation. Panel A illustrates the test for positive autocorrelation. If $d < d_L$, we conclude that positive autocorrelation is present. If $d_L \leq d \leq d_U$, we say the test is inconclusive. If $d > d_U$, we conclude that there is no evidence of positive autocorrelation.

Panel B illustrates the test for negative autocorrelation. If $d > 4 - d_L$, we conclude that negative autocorrelation is present. If $4 - d_U \leq d \leq 4 - d_L$, we say the test is inconclusive. If $d < 4 - d_U$, we conclude that there is no evidence of negative autocorrelation.

Panel C illustrates the two-sided test. If $d < d_L$ or $d > 4 - d_L$, we reject H_0 and conclude that autocorrelation is present. If $d_L \leq d \leq d_U$ or $4 - d_U \leq d \leq 4 - d_L$, we say the test is inconclusive. If $d_U < d < 4 - d_U$, we conclude that there is no evidence of autocorrelation.

If significant autocorrelation is identified, we should investigate whether we have omitted one or more key independent variables that have time-ordered effects on the dependent variable. If no such variables can be identified, we can include an independent variable that measures the time of the observation. Using time as an independent variable will sometimes

TABLE 16.8 CRITICAL VALUES FOR THE DURBIN-WATSON TEST FOR AUTOCORRELATION

Note: Entries in the table are the critical values for a one-tailed Durbin-Watson test for autocorrelation. For a two-tailed test, the level of significance is doubled.

Significance Points of d_L and d_U: $\alpha = .05$
Number of Independent Variables

	1		2		3		4		5	
n	d_L	d_U	d_L	d_U	d_L	d_U	d_L	d_U	d_L	d_U
15	1.08	1.36	0.95	1.54	0.82	1.75	0.69	1.97	0.56	2.21
16	1.10	1.37	0.98	1.54	0.86	1.73	0.74	1.93	0.62	2.15
17	1.13	1.38	1.02	1.54	0.90	1.71	0.78	1.90	0.67	2.10
18	1.16	1.39	1.05	1.53	0.93	1.69	0.82	1.87	0.71	2.06
19	1.18	1.40	1.08	1.53	0.97	1.68	0.86	1.85	0.75	2.02
20	1.20	1.41	1.10	1.54	1.00	1.68	0.90	1.83	0.79	1.99
21	1.22	1.42	1.13	1.54	1.03	1.67	0.93	1.81	0.83	1.96
22	1.24	1.43	1.15	1.54	1.05	1.66	0.96	1.80	0.86	1.94
23	1.26	1.44	1.17	1.54	1.08	1.66	0.99	1.79	0.90	1.92
24	1.27	1.45	1.19	1.55	1.10	1.66	1.01	1.78	0.93	1.90
25	1.29	1.45	1.21	1.55	1.12	1.66	1.04	1.77	0.95	1.89
26	1.30	1.46	1.22	1.55	1.14	1.65	1.06	1.76	0.98	1.88
27	1.32	1.47	1.24	1.56	1.16	1.65	1.08	1.76	1.01	1.86
28	1.33	1.48	1.26	1.56	1.18	1.65	1.10	1.75	1.03	1.85
29	1.34	1.48	1.27	1.56	1.20	1.65	1.12	1.74	1.05	1.84
30	1.35	1.49	1.28	1.57	1.21	1.65	1.14	1.74	1.07	1.83
31	1.36	1.50	1.30	1.57	1.23	1.65	1.16	1.74	1.09	1.83
32	1.37	1.50	1.31	1.57	1.24	1.65	1.18	1.73	1.11	1.82
33	1.38	1.51	1.32	1.58	1.26	1.65	1.19	1.73	1.13	1.81
34	1.39	1.51	1.33	1.58	1.27	1.65	1.21	1.73	1.15	1.81
35	1.40	1.52	1.34	1.58	1.28	1.65	1.22	1.73	1.16	1.80
36	1.41	1.52	1.35	1.59	1.29	1.65	1.24	1.73	1.18	1.80
37	1.42	1.53	1.36	1.59	1.31	1.66	1.25	1.72	1.19	1.80
38	1.43	1.54	1.37	1.59	1.32	1.66	1.26	1.72	1.21	1.79
39	1.43	1.54	1.38	1.60	1.33	1.66	1.27	1.72	1.22	1.79
40	1.44	1.54	1.39	1.60	1.34	1.66	1.29	1.72	1.23	1.79
45	1.48	1.57	1.43	1.62	1.38	1.67	1.34	1.72	1.29	1.78
50	1.50	1.59	1.46	1.63	1.42	1.67	1.38	1.72	1.34	1.77
55	1.53	1.60	1.49	1.64	1.45	1.68	1.41	1.72	1.38	1.77
60	1.55	1.62	1.51	1.65	1.48	1.69	1.44	1.73	1.41	1.77
65	1.57	1.63	1.54	1.66	1.50	1.70	1.47	1.73	1.44	1.77
70	1.58	1.64	1.55	1.67	1.52	1.70	1.49	1.74	1.46	1.77
75	1.60	1.65	1.57	1.68	1.54	1.71	1.51	1.74	1.49	1.77
80	1.61	1.66	1.59	1.69	1.56	1.72	1.53	1.74	1.51	1.77
85	1.62	1.67	1.60	1.70	1.57	1.72	1.55	1.75	1.52	1.77
90	1.63	1.68	1.61	1.70	1.59	1.73	1.57	1.75	1.54	1.78
95	1.64	1.69	1.62	1.71	1.60	1.73	1.58	1.75	1.56	1.78
100	1.65	1.69	1.63	1.72	1.61	1.74	1.59	1.76	1.57	1.78

(continued)

TABLE 16.8   (*continued*)

Significance Points of d_L and d_U: $\alpha = .025$
Number of Independent Variables

	1		2		3		4		5	
n	d_L	d_U	d_L	d_U	d_L	d_U	d_L	d_U	d_L	d_U
15	0.95	1.23	0.83	1.40	0.71	1.61	0.59	1.84	0.48	2.09
16	0.98	1.24	0.86	1.40	0.75	1.59	0.64	1.80	0.53	2.03
17	1.01	1.25	0.90	1.40	0.79	1.58	0.68	1.77	0.57	1.98
18	1.03	1.26	0.93	1.40	0.82	1.56	0.72	1.74	0.62	1.93
19	1.06	1.28	0.96	1.41	0.86	1.55	0.76	1.72	0.66	1.90
20	1.08	1.28	0.99	1.41	0.89	1.55	0.79	1.70	0.70	1.87
21	1.10	1.30	1.01	1.41	0.92	1.54	0.83	1.69	0.73	1.84
22	1.12	1.31	1.04	1.42	0.95	1.54	0.86	1.68	0.77	1.82
23	1.14	1.32	1.06	1.42	0.97	1.54	0.89	1.67	0.80	1.80
24	1.16	1.33	1.08	1.43	1.00	1.54	0.91	1.66	0.83	1.79
25	1.18	1.34	1.10	1.43	1.02	1.54	0.94	1.65	0.86	1.77
26	1.19	1.35	1.12	1.44	1.04	1.54	0.96	1.65	0.88	1.76
27	1.21	1.36	1.13	1.44	1.06	1.54	0.99	1.64	0.91	1.75
28	1.22	1.37	1.15	1.45	1.08	1.54	1.01	1.64	0.93	1.74
29	1.24	1.38	1.17	1.45	1.10	1.54	1.03	1.63	0.96	1.73
30	1.25	1.38	1.18	1.46	1.12	1.54	1.05	1.63	0.98	1.73
31	1.26	1.39	1.20	1.47	1.13	1.55	1.07	1.63	1.00	1.72
32	1.27	1.40	1.21	1.47	1.15	1.55	1.08	1.63	1.02	1.71
33	1.28	1.41	1.22	1.48	1.16	1.55	1.10	1.63	1.04	1.71
34	1.29	1.41	1.24	1.48	1.17	1.55	1.12	1.63	1.06	1.70
35	1.30	1.42	1.25	1.48	1.19	1.55	1.13	1.63	1.07	1.70
36	1.31	1.43	1.26	1.49	1.20	1.56	1.15	1.63	1.09	1.70
37	1.32	1.43	1.27	1.49	1.21	1.56	1.16	1.62	1.10	1.70
38	1.33	1.44	1.28	1.50	1.23	1.56	1.17	1.62	1.12	1.70
39	1.34	1.44	1.29	1.50	1.24	1.56	1.19	1.63	1.13	1.69
40	1.35	1.45	1.30	1.51	1.25	1.57	1.20	1.63	1.15	1.69
45	1.39	1.48	1.34	1.53	1.30	1.58	1.25	1.63	1.21	1.69
50	1.42	1.50	1.38	1.54	1.34	1.59	1.30	1.64	1.26	1.69
55	1.45	1.52	1.41	1.56	1.37	1.60	1.33	1.64	1.30	1.69
60	1.47	1.54	1.44	1.57	1.40	1.61	1.37	1.65	1.33	1.69
65	1.49	1.55	1.46	1.59	1.43	1.62	1.40	1.66	1.36	1.69
70	1.51	1.57	1.48	1.60	1.45	1.63	1.42	1.66	1.39	1.70
75	1.53	1.58	1.50	1.61	1.47	1.64	1.45	1.67	1.42	1.70
80	1.54	1.59	1.52	1.62	1.49	1.65	1.47	1.67	1.44	1.70
85	1.56	1.60	1.53	1.63	1.51	1.65	1.49	1.68	1.46	1.71
90	1.57	1.61	1.55	1.64	1.53	1.66	1.50	1.69	1.48	1.71
95	1.58	1.62	1.56	1.65	1.54	1.67	1.52	1.69	1.50	1.71
100	1.59	1.63	1.57	1.65	1.55	1.67	1.53	1.70	1.51	1.72

TABLE 16.8 *(continued)*

Significance Points of d_L and d_U: $\alpha = .01$

Number of Independent Variables

	1		2		3		4		5	
n	d_L	d_U	d_L	d_U	d_L	d_U	d_L	d_U	d_L	d_U
15	0.81	1.07	0.70	1.25	0.59	1.46	0.49	1.70	0.39	1.96
16	0.84	1.09	0.74	1.25	0.63	1.44	0.53	1.66	0.44	1.90
17	0.87	1.10	0.77	1.25	0.67	1.43	0.57	1.63	0.48	1.85
18	0.90	1.12	0.80	1.26	0.71	1.42	0.61	1.60	0.52	1.80
19	0.93	1.13	0.83	1.26	0.74	1.41	0.65	1.58	0.56	1.77
20	0.95	1.15	0.86	1.27	0.77	1.41	0.68	1.57	0.60	1.74
21	0.97	1.16	0.89	1.27	0.80	1.41	0.72	1.55	0.63	1.71
22	1.00	1.17	0.91	1.28	0.83	1.40	0.75	1.54	0.66	1.69
23	1.02	1.19	0.94	1.29	0.86	1.40	0.77	1.53	0.70	1.67
24	1.04	1.20	0.96	1.30	0.88	1.41	0.80	1.53	0.72	1.66
25	1.05	1.21	0.98	1.30	0.90	1.41	0.83	1.52	0.75	1.65
26	1.07	1.22	1.00	1.31	0.93	1.41	0.85	1.52	0.78	1.64
27	1.09	1.23	1.02	1.32	0.95	1.41	0.88	1.51	0.81	1.63
28	1.10	1.24	1.04	1.32	0.97	1.41	0.90	1.51	0.83	1.62
29	1.12	1.25	1.05	1.33	0.99	1.42	0.92	1.51	0.85	1.61
30	1.13	1.26	1.07	1.34	1.01	1.42	0.94	1.51	0.88	1.61
31	1.15	1.27	1.08	1.34	1.02	1.42	0.96	1.51	0.90	1.60
32	1.16	1.28	1.10	1.35	1.04	1.43	0.98	1.51	0.92	1.60
33	1.17	1.29	1.11	1.36	1.05	1.43	1.00	1.51	0.94	1.59
34	1.18	1.30	1.13	1.36	1.07	1.43	1.01	1.51	0.95	1.59
35	1.19	1.31	1.14	1.37	1.08	1.44	1.03	1.51	0.97	1.59
36	1.21	1.32	1.15	1.38	1.10	1.44	1.04	1.51	0.99	1.59
37	1.22	1.32	1.16	1.38	1.11	1.45	1.06	1.51	1.00	1.59
38	1.23	1.33	1.18	1.39	1.12	1.45	1.07	1.52	1.02	1.58
39	1.24	1.34	1.19	1.39	1.14	1.45	1.09	1.52	1.03	1.58
40	1.25	1.34	1.20	1.40	1.15	1.46	1.10	1.52	1.05	1.58
45	1.29	1.38	1.24	1.42	1.20	1.48	1.16	1.53	1.11	1.58
50	1.32	1.40	1.28	1.45	1.24	1.49	1.20	1.54	1.16	1.59
55	1.36	1.43	1.32	1.47	1.28	1.51	1.25	1.55	1.21	1.59
60	1.38	1.45	1.35	1.48	1.32	1.52	1.28	1.56	1.25	1.60
65	1.41	1.47	1.38	1.50	1.35	1.53	1.31	1.57	1.28	1.61
70	1.43	1.49	1.40	1.52	1.37	1.55	1.34	1.58	1.31	1.61
75	1.45	1.50	1.42	1.53	1.39	1.56	1.37	1.59	1.34	1.62
80	1.47	1.52	1.44	1.54	1.42	1.57	1.39	1.60	1.36	1.62
85	1.48	1.53	1.46	1.55	1.43	1.58	1.41	1.60	1.39	1.63
90	1.50	1.54	1.47	1.56	1.45	1.59	1.43	1.61	1.41	1.64
95	1.51	1.55	1.49	1.57	1.47	1.60	1.45	1.62	1.42	1.64
100	1.52	1.56	1.50	1.58	1.48	1.60	1.46	1.63	1.44	1.65

Source: J. Durbin and G. S. Watson, "Testing for Serial Correlation in Least Squares Regression II," *Biometrika*, 38 (1951): 159–178.

FIGURE 16.15   HYPOTHESIS TEST FOR AUTOCORRELATION USING
THE DURBIN-WATSON TEST

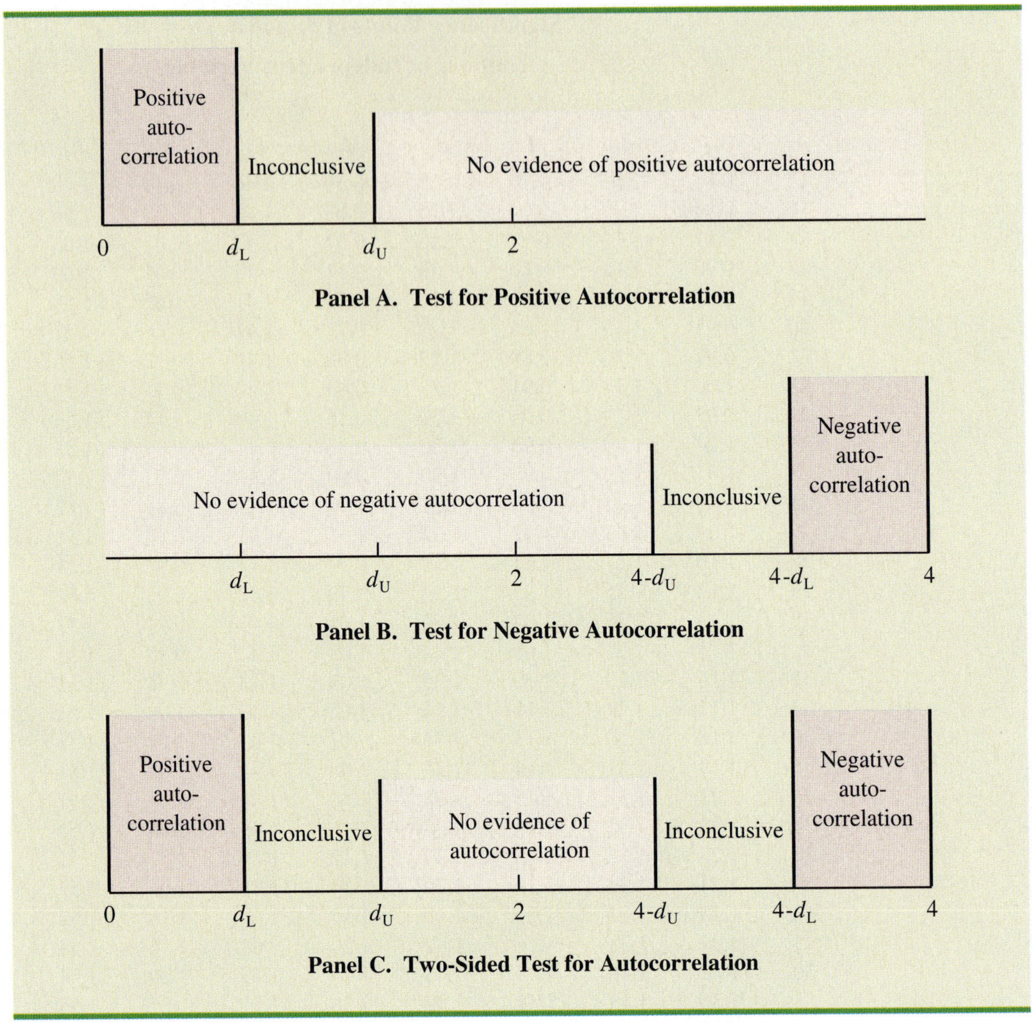

Positive
auto-
correlation | Inconclusive | No evidence of positive autocorrelation

0   d_L d_U 2

Panel A. Test for Positive Autocorrelation

No evidence of negative autocorrelation | Inconclusive | Negative
auto-
correlation

d_L d_U 2 $4-d_U$ $4-d_L$ 4

Panel B. Test for Negative Autocorrelation

Positive
auto-
correlation | Inconclusive | No evidence of
autocorrelation | Inconclusive | Negative
auto-
correlation

0   d_L d_U 2 $4-d_U$ $4-d_L$ 4

Panel C. Two-Sided Test for Autocorrelation

eliminate or reduce the autocorrelation. When these attempts to reduce or remove auto-correlation do not work, transformations on the dependent or independent variables can prove helpful; a discussion of such transformations can be found in more advanced texts on regression analysis.

Note that the Durbin-Watson tables list the smallest sample size as 15. The reason is that the test is generally inconclusive for smaller sample sizes; in fact, many statisticians believe the sample size should be at least 50 for the test to produce worthwhile results.

EXERCISES

Applications

21. Consider the data set in exercise 19.
     a. Develop the estimated regression equation that can be used to predict the price/earnings ratio given the gross profit margin.
     b. At the .05 level of significance, test for any positive autocorrelation in the data.

22.   Refer to the Cravens data set in Table 16.5. In Section 16.3 we showed that the estimated regression equation involving Poten, AdvExp, and Share had an adjusted coefficient of determination of .8274. Use the .05 level of significance and apply the Durbin-Watson test to determine whether positive autocorrelation is present.

16.6   Multiple Regression Approach to Analysis of Variance and Experimental Design

In Section 15.7 we discussed the use of dummy variables in multiple regression analysis. In this section we show how the use of dummy variables in a multiple regression equation can provide another approach to solving analysis of variance and experimental design problems. We will demonstrate the multiple regression approach to analysis of variance by applying it to the National Computer Products, Inc. (NCP) problem introduced in Chapter 13.

Recall that NCP manufactures printers and fax machines at plants in Atlanta, Dallas, and Seattle. To measure how much the employees know about quality management, a random sample of six employees was selected from each plant and given a quality-awareness exam. The examination scores for these 18 employees are listed in Table 16.9. Managers want to use the exam scores of the 18 employees to determine whether the mean examination scores are the same at each plant.

We begin the regression approach to this problem by defining two dummy variables that will be used to indicate the plant from which each sample observation was selected. Because the NCP problem has three plants or populations, we need two dummy variables. In general, if the factor being investigated involves k distinct levels or populations, we need to define $k - 1$ dummy variables. For the NCP problem we define D and S as shown in Table 16.10.

We can use the dummy variables D and S to relate the score on the quality awareness examination to the plant at which the employee works.

E(Score) = Expected value of the score on the quality awareness examination

$$= \beta_0 + \beta_1 D + \beta_2 S$$

Thus, if we are interested in the expected value of the examination score for an employee who works at the Atlanta plant, our procedure for assigning numerical values to the dummy variables D and S would result in setting $D = S = 0$. The multiple regression equation then reduces to

$$E(\text{Score}) = \beta_0 + \beta_1(0) + \beta_2(0) = \beta_0$$

TABLE 16.10

NCP PROBLEM WITH DUMMY VARIABLES

D	S	
0	0	Observation is associated with the Atlanta plant
1	0	Observation is associated with the Dallas plant
0	1	Observation is associated with the Seattle plant

TABLE 16.9   EXAMINATION SCORES FOR 18 EMPLOYEES

Plant 1 Atlanta	Plant 2 Dallas	Plant 3 Seattle
85	71	59
75	75	64
82	73	62
76	74	69
71	69	75
85	82	67

We can interpret β_0 as the expected value of the examination score for employees who work at the Atlanta plant.

Next let us consider the forms of the multiple regression equation for each of the other plants. For the Dallas plant, $D = 1$ and $S = 0$, and

$$E(\text{Score}) = \beta_0 + \beta_1(1) + \beta_2(0) = \beta_0 + \beta_1$$

For the Seattle plant, $D = 0$ and $S = 1$, and

$$E(\text{Score}) = \beta_0 + \beta_1(0) + \beta_2(1) = \beta_0 + \beta_2$$

We see that $\beta_0 + \beta_1$ represents the expected value of the examination score for employees at the Dallas plant, and $\beta_0 + \beta_2$ represents the expected value of the examination score for employees at the Seattle plant.

We now want to estimate the coefficients β_0, β_1, and β_2 and hence develop an estimate of the expected value of the examination score for each plant. The sample data consisting of 18 observations of D, S, and Score were entered into Excel. The actual input data and the output from Excel's Regression tool are in Table 16.11 and Figure 16.16, respectively.

In Figure 16.16, we see that the estimates of β_0, β_1, and β_2 are $b_0 = 79$, $b_1 = -5$, and $b_2 = -13$. Thus, the best estimate of the expected value of the examination score for each plant is as follows.

Plant	Estimate of $E(\text{Score})$
Atlanta	$b_0 = 79$
Dallas	$b_0 + b_1 = 79 - 5 = 74$
Seattle	$b_0 + b_2 = 79 - 13 = 66$

TABLE 16.11   REGRESSION INPUT DATA FOR THE NCP PROBLEM

CD file

NCP

Observation	D	S	Score
1	0	0	85
2	0	0	75
3	0	0	82
4	0	0	76
5	0	0	71
6	0	0	85
7	1	0	71
8	1	0	75
9	1	0	73
10	1	0	74
11	1	0	69
12	1	0	82
13	0	1	59
14	0	1	64
15	0	1	62
16	0	1	69
17	0	1	75
18	0	1	67

FIGURE 16.16   EXCEL REGRESSION TOOL OUTPUT FOR THE NCP PROBLEM

	A	B	C	D	E	F	G	H	I	J
1	Observation	D	S	Score						
2	1	0	0	85						
3	2	0	0	75						
4	3	0	0	82						
5	4	0	0	76						
6	5	0	0	71						
7	6	0	0	85						
8	7	1	0	71						
9	8	1	0	75						
10	9	1	0	73						
11	10	1	0	74						
12	11	1	0	69						
13	12	1	0	82						
14	13	0	1	59						
15	14	0	1	64						
16	15	0	1	62						
17	16	0	1	69						
18	17	0	1	75						
19	18	0	1	67						
20										
21	SUMMARY OUTPUT									
22										
23	*Regression Statistics*									
24	Multiple R	0.7385								
25	R Square	0.5455								
26	Adjusted R Square	0.4848								
27	Standard Error	5.3541								
28	Observations	18								
29										
30	ANOVA									
31		*df*	*SS*	*MS*	*F*	*Significance F*				
32	Regression	2	516	258	9	0.0027				
33	Residual	15	430	28.6667						
34	Total	17	946							
35										
36		*Coefficients*	*Standard Error*	*t Stat*	*P-value*	*Lower 95%*	*Upper 95%*	*Lower 99.0%*	*Upper 99.0%*	
37	Intercept	79	2.1858	36.1422	5.27E-16	74.3411	83.6589	72.5590	85.4410	
38	D	-5	3.0912	-1.6175	0.1266	-11.5887	1.5887	-14.1089	4.1089	
39	S	-13	3.0912	-4.2055	0.0008	-19.5887	-6.4113	-22.1089	-3.8911	
40										

Note that the best estimate of the expected value of the examination score for each plant obtained from the regression analysis is the same as the sample mean found previously by applying the ANOVA procedure. That is, 79 for Atlanta, 74 for Dallas, and 66 for Seattle.

Now let us see how we can use the output from the multiple regression package to perform the ANOVA test on the difference in the means for the three plants. First, we observe that if there is no difference in the means,

$$E(\text{Score}) \text{ for the Dallas plant} - E(\text{Score}) \text{ for the Atlanta plant} = 0$$

$$E(\text{Score}) \text{ for the Seattle plant} - E(\text{Score}) \text{ for the Atlanta plant} = 0$$

Because β_0 equals $E(\text{Score})$ for the Atlanta plant and $\beta_0 + \beta_1$ equals $E(\text{Score})$ for the Dallas plant, the first difference is equal to $(\beta_0 + \beta_1) - \beta_0 = \beta_1$. Moreover, because $\beta_0 + \beta_2$ equals $E(\text{Score})$ for the Seattle plant, the second difference is equal to $(\beta_0 + \beta_2) - \beta_0 = \beta_2$.

We would conclude that there is no difference in the three means if $\beta_1 = 0$ and $\beta_2 = 0$. Hence, the null hypothesis for a test for difference of means can be stated as

$$H_0: \beta_1 = \beta_2 = 0$$

Figure 16.16 shows that the p-value associated with the F test for overall significance is .0027. Thus, at a .05 level of significance the p-value $= .0027 < \alpha = .05$. Hence, we can reject H_0 and conclude that the means for the three plants are different.

EXERCISES

Methods

23. Consider a completely randomized design involving four treatments: A, B, C, and D. Write a multiple regression equation that can be used to analyze these data. Define all variables.

24. Write a multiple regression equation that can be used to analyze the data for a randomized block design involving three treatments and two blocks. Define all variables.

25. Write a multiple regression equation that can be used to analyze the data for a two-factorial design with two levels for factor A and three levels for factor B. Define all variables.

Applications

26. The Jacobs Chemical Company wants to estimate the mean time (minutes) required to mix a batch of material on machines produced by three different manufacturers. To limit the cost of testing, four batches of material were mixed on machines produced by each of the three manufacturers. The times needed to mix the material follow.

Manufacturer 1	Manufacturer 2	Manufacturer 3
20	28	20
26	26	19
24	31	23
22	27	22

   a. Write a multiple regression equation that can be used to analyze the data.
   b. What are the best estimates of the coefficients in your regression equation?
   c. In terms of the regression equation coefficients, what hypotheses must we test to see whether the mean time to mix a batch of material is the same for all three manufacturers?
   d. Using $\alpha = .05$, what conclusion should be drawn?

27. Four different paints are advertised as having the same drying time. To check the manufacturers' claims, five samples were tested for each of the paints. The time in minutes until the paint was dry enough for a second coat to be applied was recorded for each sample. The data obtained follow.

Paint 1	Paint 2	Paint 3	Paint 4
128	144	133	150
137	133	143	142
135	142	137	135
124	146	136	140
141	130	131	153

a. Using $\alpha = .05$, test for any significant differences in mean drying time among the paints.

b. What is your estimate of mean drying time for paint 2? How is it obtained from the computer output?

28. An automobile dealer conducted a test to determine if the time needed to complete a minor engine tune-up depends on whether a computerized engine analyzer or an electronic analyzer is used. Because tune-up time varies among compact, intermediate, and full-sized cars, the three types of cars were used as blocks in the experiment. The data (time in minutes) obtained follow.

		Car		
		Compact	Intermediate	Full-Sized
Analyzer	Computerized	50	55	63
	Electronic	42	44	46

Using $\alpha = .05$, test for any significant differences.

29. A mail-order catalog firm designed a factorial experiment to test the effect of the size of a magazine advertisement and the advertisement design on the number of catalog requests received (1000s). Three advertising designs and two sizes of advertisements were considered. The following data were obtained. Test for any significant effects due to type of design, size of advertisement, or interaction. Use $\alpha = .05$.

		Size of Advertisement	
		Small	Large
Design	A	8 12	12 8
	B	22 14	26 30
	C	10 18	18 14

Summary

In this chapter we discussed several concepts used by model builders in identifying the best estimated regression equation. First, we introduced the concept of a general linear model to show how the methods discussed in Chapters 14 and 15 could be extended to handle curvilinear relationships and interaction effects. Then we discussed how transformations involving the dependent variable could be used to account for problems such as nonconstant variance in the error term.

In many applications of regression analysis, a large number of independent variables are considered. We presented a general approach based on an F statistic for adding or deleting variables from a regression model. We then introduced a larger problem involving eight independent variables. We saw that one issue encountered in solving larger problems is finding the best subset of the independent variables. To help in that task, we discussed several variable selection procedures: stepwise regression, forward selection, backward elimination, and best-subsets regression.

In Section 16.5, we extended the applications of residual analysis to show the Durbin-Watson test for autocorrelation. The chapter concluded with a discussion of how multiple regression models could be developed to provide another approach for solving analysis of variance and experimental design problems.

Glossary

General linear model A model of the form $y = \beta_0 + \beta_1 z_1 + \beta_2 z_2 + \cdots + \beta_p z_p + \epsilon$, where each of the independent variables $z_j, j = 1, 2, \ldots, p$, is a function of $x_1, x_2, \ldots, x_k$, the variables for which data have been collected.

Interaction The effect of two independent variables acting together.

Variable selection procedures Methods for selecting a subset of the independent variables for a regression model.

Autocorrelation Correlation in the errors that arises when the error terms at successive points in time are related.

Serial correlation Same as autocorrelation.

Durbin-Watson test A test to determine whether first-order autocorrelation is present.

Key Formulas

General Linear Model

$$y = \beta_0 + \beta_1 z_1 + \beta_2 z_2 + \cdots + \beta_p z_p + \epsilon \tag{16.1}$$

General F Test for Adding or Deleting $p - q$ Independent Variables

$$F = \dfrac{\dfrac{\text{SSE}(x_1, x_2, \ldots, x_q) - \text{SSE}(x_1, x_2, \ldots, x_q, x_{q+1}, \ldots, x_p)}{p - q}}{\dfrac{\text{SSE}(x_1, x_2, \ldots, x_q, x_{q+1}, \ldots, x_p)}{n - p - 1}} \tag{16.13}$$

First-Order Autocorrelation ($\rho \neq 0$)

$$\epsilon_t = \rho \epsilon_{t-1} + z_t \tag{16.16}$$

Durbin-Watson Test Statistic

$$d = \frac{\sum\limits_{t=2}^{n}(e_t - e_{t-1})^2}{\sum\limits_{t=1}^{n} e_t^2} \tag{16.17}$$

Supplementary Exercises

30. Many international funds offer more reasonable equity valuations than those found in the United States. Because international markets often move in directions different from the U.S. market, investments in foreign markets can also reduce an investor's overall risk. The following table shows the one-year performance through December 10, 1999, fund type (load or no-load), expense ratio (%), and safety rating (0 = riskiest, 10 = safest) for 20 international funds (*Mutual Funds,* February 2000).

MutFunds

Fund	Fund Type	Expense Ratio (%)	Safety Rating	Performance (%)
ABN AMRO Int'l Equity "Com"	No-load	1.38	6.9	36
Accessor Int'l Equity "Adv"	No-load	1.59	7.1	42
Artisan International	No-load	1.45	6.8	72
Columbia Int'l Stock	No-load	1.56	7.1	54
Concert Inv. "A" Int'l Equity	Load	2.16	6.3	116
Diversified Invstr Int'l Eqty	No-load	1.40	7.3	54
Driehaus Int'l Growth	No-load	1.88	6.5	92
Founders Passport	No-load	1.52	7.0	86
Guardian Baillie Fifford Int'l "A"	Load	1.62	7.1	37
Jamestown Int'l Equity	No-load	1.56	7.1	35
Julius Baer Int'l Equity	No-load	1.79	6.9	71
Aetna "I" Int'l	No-load	1.35	7.3	46
Pilgrim Int'l Value "A"	Load	1.80	7.1	42
Fidelity Diversified Int'l	No-load	1.48	7.5	42
Putnam "A" Int'l Growth	Load	1.59	6.9	55
Sit Int'l Growth	No-load	1.50	6.9	49
Touchstone Int'l Equity "A"	Load	1.60	7.5	35
United Int'l Growth "A"	Load	1.28	7.1	47
Vontobel Int'l Equity	No-load	1.50	7.0	43
Waddell & Reed Int'l Growth "B"	Load	2.46	7.0	75

   a. Use the methods in this chapter to develop an estimated regression equation that can be used to estimate the performance of a fund on the basis of the data provided.

   b. Did the estimated regression equation developed in part (a) provide a good fit? Explain.

   c. Acorn International is a no-load fund that has an annual expense ratio of 1.12% and a safety rating of 7.6. Use the estimated regression equation developed in part (a) to estimate the one-year performance for Acorn International.

31. A study investigated the relationship between audit delay (Delay), the length of time from a company's fiscal year-end to the date of the auditor's report, and variables that describe the client and the auditor. Some of the independent variables that were included in this study follow.

   Industry   A dummy variable coded 1 if the firm was an industrial company or 0 if the firm was a bank, savings and loan, or insurance company.

   Public   A dummy variable coded 1 if the company was traded on an organized exchange or over the counter; otherwise coded 0.

   Quality   A measure of overall quality of internal controls, as judged by the auditor, on a five-point scale ranging from "virtually none" (1) to "excellent" (5).

   Finished   A measure ranging from 1 to 4, as judged by the auditor, where 1 indicates "all work performed subsequent to year-end" and 4 indicates "most work performed prior to year-end."

Suppose that a sample of 40 companies provided the following data.

Audit

Delay	Industry	Public	Quality	Finished
62	0	0	3	1
45	0	1	3	3
54	0	0	2	2
71	0	1	1	2
91	0	0	1	1

(continued)

Delay	Industry	Public	Quality	Finished
62	0	0	4	4
61	0	0	3	2
69	0	1	5	2
80	0	0	1	1
52	0	0	5	3
47	0	0	3	2
65	0	1	2	3
60	0	0	1	3
81	1	0	1	2
73	1	0	2	2
89	1	0	2	1
71	1	0	5	4
76	1	0	2	2
68	1	0	1	2
68	1	0	5	2
86	1	0	2	2
76	1	1	3	1
67	1	0	2	3
57	1	0	4	2
55	1	1	3	2
54	1	0	5	2
69	1	0	3	3
82	1	0	5	1
94	1	0	1	1
74	1	1	5	2
75	1	1	4	3
69	1	0	2	2
71	1	0	4	4
79	1	0	5	2
80	1	0	1	4
91	1	0	4	1
92	1	0	1	4
46	1	1	4	3
72	1	0	5	2
85	1	0	5	1

    a.   Develop the estimated regression equation using all of the independent variables.

    b.   Did the estimated regression equation developed in part (a) provide a good fit? Explain.

    c.   Develop a scatter diagram showing Delay as a function of Finished. What does this scatter diagram indicate about the relationship between Delay and Finished?

    d.   On the basis of your observations about the relationship between Delay and Finished, develop an alternative estimated regression equation to the one developed in part (a) to explain as much of the variability in Delay as possible.

32.   Refer to the data in exercise 31. Consider a model in which only Industry is used to predict Delay. At a .01 level of significance, test for any positive autocorrelation in the data.

33.   Refer to the data in exercise 31.

    a.   Develop an estimated regression equation that can be used to predict Delay by using Industry and Quality.

    b.   At the .05 level of significance, test for any positive autocorrelation in the data.

34.   A study was conducted to investigate browsing activity by shoppers. Shoppers were classified as nonbrowsers, light browsers, and heavy browsers. For each shopper in the study, a measure was obtained to determine how comfortable the shopper was in the store. Higher scores indi-

cated greater comfort. Assume that the following data are from this study. Use a .05 level of significance to test for differences in comfort levels among the three types of browsers.

Browsing

Nonbrowser	Light Browser	Heavy Browser
4	5	5
5	6	7
6	5	5
3	4	7
3	7	4
4	4	6
5	6	5
4	5	7

35. The following data show the percentage changes in the Dow Jones Industrial Average (DJIA) in each of the four years of eight presidential terms (*1998 Stock Trader's Almanac*). Use regression analysis to determine what effect party and year of term in office have on the change in the Dow Jones Industrial Average.

Election

President	Party	Year Elected	Year of Term	Year's Change in DJIA
Johnson	Democrat	1964	First	10.9
Johnson	Democrat		Second	−18.9
Johnson	Democrat		Third	15.2
Johnson	Democrat		Fourth	4.3
Nixon	Republican	1968	First	−15.2
Nixon	Republican		Second	4.8
Nixon	Republican		Third	6.1
Nixon	Republican		Fourth	14.6
Nixon	Republican	1972	First	−16.6
Nixon	Republican		Second	−27.6
Nixon*	Republican		Third	38.3
Nixon*	Republican		Fourth	17.9
Carter	Democrat	1976	First	−17.3
Carter	Democrat		Second	−3.1
Carter	Democrat		Third	4.2
Carter	Democrat		Fourth	14.9
Reagan	Republican	1980	First	−9.2
Reagan	Republican		Second	19.6
Reagan	Republican		Third	20.3
Reagan	Republican		Fourth	−3.7
Reagan	Republican	1984	First	−27.7
Reagan	Republican		Second	22.6
Reagan	Republican		Third	2.3
Reagan	Republican		Fourth	11.8
Bush	Republican	1988	First	27.0
Bush	Republican		Second	−4.3
Bush	Republican		Third	20.3
Bush	Republican		Fourth	4.2
Clinton	Democrat	1992	First	13.7
Clinton	Democrat		Second	2.1
Clinton	Democrat		Third	33.5
Clinton	Democrat		Fourth	26.0

*Because President Nixon resigned from office in August 1974, Gerald Ford became president and completed the remainder of Nixon's term in office.

36. *Money* magazine reported price and related data for 418 of the most popular vehicles of the 2003 model year. One of the variables reported was the vehicle's resale value, expressed as a percentage of the manufacturer's suggested resale price. The data were classified according to size and type of vehicle. The following table shows the resale value for 10 randomly selected small cars, 10 randomly selected mid-size cars, 10 randomly selected luxury cars, and 10 randomly selected sports cars (*Money,* March 2003).

Resale

Small	Mid-size	Luxury	Sports
26	26	36	41
31	29	38	39
41	41	38	30
32	27	39	34
27	26	35	40
34	33	26	43
31	27	40	42
38	29	47	39
27	35	41	44
42	39	32	50

Use $\alpha = .05$ and test for any significant difference in the mean resale value among the four types of vehicles.

Case Problem 1   Unemployment Study

A study provided data on variables that may be related to the number of weeks a manufacturing worker has been jobless. The dependent variable in the study (Weeks) was defined as the number of weeks a worker has been jobless due to a layoff. The following independent variables were used in the study.

Age   The age of the worker

Educ   The number of years of education

Married   A dummy variable: 1 if married, 0 otherwise

Head   A dummy variable: 1 if the head of household, 0 otherwise

Tenure   The number of years on the old job

Manager   A dummy variable: 1 if management occupation, 0 otherwise

Sales   A dummy variable: 1 if sales occupation, 0 otherwise

Assume the data on the following page were collected for 50 displaced workers. These data are available on the CD accompanying the text in the data set named Layoffs.

Managerial Report

Use the methods presented in this and previous chapters to analyze this data set. Present a summary of your analysis, including key statistical results, conclusions, and recommendations in a managerial report. Include any appropriate technical material (computer output, residual plots, etc.) in an appendix.

Layoffs

Weeks	Age	Educ	Married	Head	Tenure	Manager	Sales
37	30	14	1	1	1	0	0
62	27	14	1	0	6	0	0
49	32	10	0	1	11	0	0
73	44	11	1	0	2	0	0
8	21	14	1	1	2	0	0
15	26	13	1	0	7	1	0
52	26	15	1	0	6	0	0
72	33	13	0	1	6	0	0
11	27	12	1	1	8	0	0
13	33	12	0	1	2	0	0
39	20	11	1	0	1	0	0
59	35	7	1	1	6	0	0
39	36	17	0	1	9	1	0
44	26	12	1	1	8	0	0
56	36	15	0	1	8	0	0
31	38	16	1	1	11	0	1
62	34	13	0	1	13	0	0
25	27	19	1	0	8	0	0
72	44	13	1	0	22	0	0
65	45	15	1	1	6	0	0
44	28	17	0	1	3	0	1
49	25	10	1	1	1	0	0
80	31	15	1	0	12	0	0
7	23	15	1	0	2	0	0
14	24	13	1	1	7	0	0
94	62	13	0	1	8	0	0
48	31	16	1	0	11	0	0
82	48	18	0	1	30	0	0
50	35	18	1	1	5	0	0
37	33	14	0	1	6	0	1
62	46	15	0	1	6	0	0
37	35	8	0	1	6	0	0
40	32	9	1	1	13	0	0
16	40	17	1	0	8	1	0
34	23	12	1	1	1	0	0
4	36	16	0	1	8	0	1
55	33	12	1	0	10	0	1
39	32	16	0	1	11	0	0
80	62	15	1	0	16	0	1
19	29	14	1	1	12	0	0
98	45	12	1	0	17	0	0
30	38	15	0	1	6	0	1
22	40	8	1	1	16	0	1
57	42	13	1	0	2	1	0
64	45	16	1	1	22	0	0
22	39	11	1	1	4	0	0
27	27	15	1	0	10	0	1
20	42	14	1	1	6	1	0
30	31	10	1	1	8	0	0
23	33	13	1	1	8	0	0

Case Problem 2   Fuel Economy for Cars

Posted on every new car sold in the United States is a fuel economy rating that shows the miles per gallon the car is expected to achieve in actual city and highway use. Data showing these ratings for all cars and trucks are available in the U.S. Department of Energy's *Fuel Economy Guide*. A portion of the data for 230 cars is available on the CD accompanying the text in the file named Cars (http://www.fueleconomy.gov, March 21, 2003). Descriptions for the data follow.

Cars

Class	The class of the car (Compact, Midsize, Large)
Manufacturer	The manufacturer of the car
carline name	The name of the car
displ	The displacement of the engine in liters
cyl	The number of cylinders in the engine (4, 6, 8)
trans	The type of transmission (Automatic, Manual)
cty	The fuel economy rating for city driving in miles per gallon
hwy	The fuel economy rating for highway driving in miles per gallon

Managerial Report

Use the methods presented in this and previous chapters to analyze this data set. The objective of your study is to develop an estimated regression equation that can be used to estimate the fuel economy rating for city driving and an estimated regression equation that can be used to estimate the fuel economy rating for highway driving. Present a summary of your analysis, including key statistical results, conclusions, and recommendations in a managerial report. Include any appropriate technical material (computer output, residual plots, etc.) in an appendix.

Case Problem 3   Predicting Graduation Rates for Colleges and Universities

The percentage of students who enroll at a college or university and actually graduate is an important statistic for university administrators. Some of the factors related to the graduation rate include the percentage of classes with fewer than 20 students, the percentage of classes with more than 50 students, the student–faculty ratio, the percentage of students who apply to the university and are admitted, the percentage of first-year students in the top 10% of their high school class, and the academic reputation of the university. To study the effect of these factors on the graduation rate, data for 48 national universities was collected (*America's Best Colleges,* Year 2000 Edition). These data are available on the CD accompanying the text in the file named GradRate. Descriptions for the data follow.

GradRate

State	The state in which the university is located
Region	The region of the country in which the university is located (North, South, Midwest, West)
Graduation Rate	The percentage of students who enroll at the university and graduate
% of Classes Under 20	The percentage of classes with fewer than 20 students
% of Classes of 50 or More	The percentage of classes with more than 50 students

Student-Faculty Ratio	The ratio of the number of students enrolled divided by the total number of faculty
Acceptance Rate	The percentage of students who apply and are accepted
1st-Year Students in Top 10% of HS Class	The percentage of students admitted who were in the top 10% of their high school class
Academic Reputation Score	A measure of the school's reputation determined by surveying administrators at other universities: measured on a scale from 1 (marginal) to 5 (distinguished)

Managerial Report

Use the methods presented in this and previous chapters to analyze this data set. Present a summary of your analysis, including key statistical results, conclusions, and recommendations in a managerial report. Include any appropriate technical material (computer output, residual plots, etc.) in an appendix.

CHAPTER 17

Nonparametric Methods

CONTENTS

STATISTICS IN PRACTICE:
WEST SHELL REALTORS

17.1 SIGN TEST
Small-Sample Case
Using Excel
Large-Sample Case
Using Excel
Hypothesis Test About a Median
Using Excel

17.2 WILCOXON SIGNED RANK
TEST
Using Excel

17.3 MANN-WHITNEY-
WILCOXON RANK SUM TEST
Small-Sample Case
Large-Sample Case
Using Excel

17.4 KRUSKAL-WALLIS TEST
Using Excel

17.5 RANK CORRELATION
Test for Significant Rank
Correlation
Using Excel

WEST SHELL REALTORS*
CINCINNATI, OHIO

West Shell Realtors was founded in 1958 with one office and a sales staff of three people. In 1964, the company began a long-term expansion program, with new offices added almost yearly. Over the years, West Shell grew to become one of the largest realtors in Greater Cincinnati, with offices in southwest Ohio, southeast Indiana, and northern Kentucky.

Statistical analysis helps real estate firms such as West Shell monitor sales performance. Monthly reports are generated for each of West Shell's offices as well as for the total company. Statistical summaries of total sales dollars, number of units sold, and median selling price per unit are essential in keeping both office managers and the company's top managers informed of progress and trouble spots in the organization.

In addition to monthly summaries of ongoing operations, the company uses statistical considerations to guide corporate plans and strategies. West Shell has implemented a strategy of planned expansion. Each time an expansion plan calls for the establishment of a new sales office, the company must address the question of office location. Selling prices of homes, turnover rates, and forecast sales volumes are the types of data used in evaluating and comparing alternative locations.

In one instance, West Shell identified two suburbs, Clifton and Roselawn, as prime candidates for a new office. A variety of factors were considered in comparing the two areas, including selling prices of homes. West Shell employed nonparametric

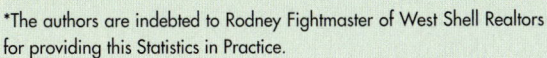

---

*The authors are indebted to Rodney Fightmaster of West Shell Realtors for providing this Statistics in Practice.

Realtors use statistical analysis of home sales to remain competitive. © PhotoDisc Red/Getty Images

statistical methods to help identify any differences in sales patterns for the two areas.

Samples of 25 sales in the Clifton area and 18 sales in the Roselawn area were taken, and the Mann-Whitney-Wilcoxon rank sum test was chosen as an appropriate statistical test of the difference in the pattern of selling prices. At the .05 level of significance, the Mann-Whitney-Wilcoxon rank sum test did not allow rejection of the null hypothesis that the two populations of selling prices were identical. Thus, West Shell was able to focus on criteria other than selling prices of homes in the site selection process.

In this chapter we will show how nonparametric statistical tests such as the Mann-Whitney-Wilcoxon rank sum test are applied. We will also discuss the proper interpretation of such tests.

The statistical methods presented thus far in the text are generally known as *parametric methods*. In this chapter we introduce several **nonparametric methods**. Such methods are often applicable in situations where the parametric methods of the preceding chapters are not. Nonparametric methods typically require less restrictive assumptions about the level of data measurement and fewer assumptions about the form of the probability distributions generating the sample data.

One consideration in determining whether a parametric or a nonparametric method is appropriate is the scale of measurement used to generate the data. All data are generated by one of four scales of measurement: nominal, ordinal, interval, and ratio. Hence, all statistical analyses are conducted with either nominal, ordinal, interval, or ratio data.

Let us define and provide examples of the four scales of measurement.

1. *Nominal scale.* The scale of measurement is nominal if the data are labels or categories used to define an attribute of an element. Nominal data may be numeric or nonnumeric.

    Examples. The exchange where a stock is listed (NYSE, NASDAQ, or AMEX) is nonnumeric nominal data. An individual's social security number is numeric nominal data.

In Chapter 1 we pointed out that nominal and ordinal scales provide qualitative data. Interval and ratio scales provide quantitative data.

2. *Ordinal scale.* The scale of measurement is ordinal if the data can be used to rank, or order, the observations. Ordinal data may be numeric or nonnumeric.

> **Examples.** The measures small, medium, and large for the size of an item are nonnumeric ordinal data. The class ranks of individuals measured as 1, 2, 3, . . . are numeric ordinal data.

3. *Interval scale.* The scale of measurement is interval if the data have the properties of ordinal data and the interval between observations is expressed in terms of a fixed unit of measure. Interval data must be numeric.

> **Examples.** Measures of temperature are interval data. Suppose it is 70 degrees in one location and 40 degrees in another. We can rank the locations with respect to warmth: the first location is warmer than the second. The fixed unit of measure, a degree, enables us to say how much warmer it is at the first location: 30 degrees.

4. *Ratio scale.* The scale of measurement is ratio if the data have the properties of interval data and the ratio of measures is meaningful. Ratio data must be numeric.

> **Examples.** Variables such as distance, height, weight, and time are measured on a ratio scale. Temperature measures are interval, but not ratio, data because there is no inherently defined zero point. For instance, the freezing point of water is 32 degrees on a Fahrenheit scale and 0 degrees on a Celsius scale. Ratios are not meaningful with temperature data. For instance, it makes no sense to say that 80 degrees is twice as warm as 40 degrees.

If the level of data measurement is nominal or ordinal, computations of means, variances, and standard deviations are not meaningful. Thus, with these kinds of data, many of the statistical procedures discussed previously cannot be employed.

Most of the statistical methods referred to as parametric require the use of interval- or ratio-scaled data. With these types of data, arithmetic operations are meaningful, and means, variances, standard deviations, and so on can be computed, interpreted, and used in the analysis. However, for nominal or ordinal data, it is inappropriate to compute means, variances, and standard deviations; hence, parametric methods normally cannot be used. Nonparametric methods are often the only way to analyze such data and draw statistical conclusions.

In general, for a statistical method to be classified as nonparametric, it must satisfy at least one of the following conditions.*

1. The method can be used with nominal data.
2. The method can be used with ordinal data.
3. The method can be used with interval or ratio data when no assumption can be made about the population probability distribution.

If the scale of measurement is interval or ratio and if the necessary probability distribution assumptions for the population are appropriate, parametric methods provide more powerful or more discriminating statistical procedures. In many cases where a nonparametric method as well as a parametric method can be applied, the nonparametric method is almost as good or almost as powerful as the parametric method. In cases where the data are nominal or ordinal or in cases where the assumptions required by parametric methods are inappropriate, only nonparametric methods are available. Because of the less restrictive data measurement requirements and the fewer assumptions needed about the population distribution, nonparametric methods are regarded as more generally applicable than parametric methods. The sign test, the Wilcoxon signed rank test, the Mann-Whitney-Wilcoxon rank sum test, the Kruskal-Wallis test, and Spearman rank correlation are the nonparametric methods presented in this chapter.

---

*See W. J. Conover, *Practical Nonparametric Statistics*, 3rd ed. (New York: John Wiley & Sons, 1998).

17.1 Sign Test

A common market-research application of the **sign test** involves using a sample of n potential customers to identify a preference for one of two brands of a product such as coffee, soft drinks, or detergents. The n expressions of preference are nominal data because the consumer simply names, or labels, a preference. Given these data, our objective is to determine whether a difference in preference exists between the two items being compared. The sign test is a nonparametric statistical procedure for answering this question.

Small-Sample Case

The small-sample case for the sign test should be used whenever $n \le 20$. Let us illustrate the use of the sign test for the small-sample case by considering a study conducted for Sun Coast Farms. Sun Coast produces a brand of orange juice marketed under the name Citrus Valley. A competitor of Sun Coast Farms produces a brand of orange juice known as Tropical Orange. In a study of consumer preferences for the two brands, 12 individuals were given unmarked samples of each product. The brand each individual tasted first was selected randomly. After tasting the two products, the individuals were asked to state a preference for one of the two brands. The purpose of the study is to determine whether consumers prefer one product over the other. Letting p indicate the proportion of the population of consumers favoring Citrus Valley, we want to test the following hypotheses.

$$H_0: p = .50$$
$$H_a: p \ne .50$$

If H_0 cannot be rejected, we will have no evidence indicating a difference in preference for the two brands of orange juice. However, if H_0 can be rejected, we can conclude that the consumer preferences are different for the two brands. In that case, the brand selected by the greater number of consumers can be considered the more preferred brand.

In the following discussion we will show how the small-sample version of the sign test can be used to test the hypothesis and draw a conclusion about consumer preference. To record the preference data for the 12 individuals participating in the study, we use a plus sign if the individual expresses a preference for Citrus Valley and a minus sign if the individual expresses a preference for Tropical Orange. Because the data are recorded in terms of plus or minus signs, this nonparametric test is called the sign test.

The number of plus signs is the test statistic. Under the assumption that H_0 is true ($p = .50$), its sampling distribution is a binomial distribution with $p = .50$. With a sample size of $n = 12$, Excel's BINOMDIST function (see Chapter 5) was used to compute the probabilities displayed in Table 17.1. Figure 17.1 is a graphical representation of this binomial sampling distribution. It shows the probability of the number of plus signs under the assumption that H_0 is true. Let us proceed with the test to determine whether there is a difference in consumer preference for the two brands of orange juice. We will use a .05 level of significance.

The preference data obtained are shown in Table 17.2. The two plus signs indicate two consumers preferred Citrus Valley. We can now use the binomial probabilities to determine the p-value for the test. With a two-tailed test, the p-value is found by doubling the probability in the tail of the binomial sampling distribution. For Sun Coast Farms, the number of plus signs (2) is in the lower tail of the distribution. So the probability in the tail is the probability of 2, 1, and 0 plus signs. Adding these probabilities, we obtain $.0161 + .0029 + .0002 = .0192$. Doubling this value, we obtain the p-value $= 2(.0192) = .0384$. With the p-value $\le \alpha = .05$, we reject H_0. The taste test provides evidence that consumer preference differs significantly for the two brands of orange juice. We would advise Sun Coast Farms that consumers prefer Tropical Orange.

TABLE 17.1

BINOMIAL PROBABILITIES WITH $n = 12$, $p = .50$

Number of Plus Signs	Probability
0	.0002
1	.0029
2	.0161
3	.0537
4	.1208
5	.1934
6	.2256
7	.1934
8	.1208
9	.0537
10	.0161
11	.0029
12	.0002

FIGURE 17.1   BINOMIAL SAMPLING DISTRIBUTION FOR THE NUMBER OF PLUS SIGNS
WHEN $n = 12$ AND $p = .50$

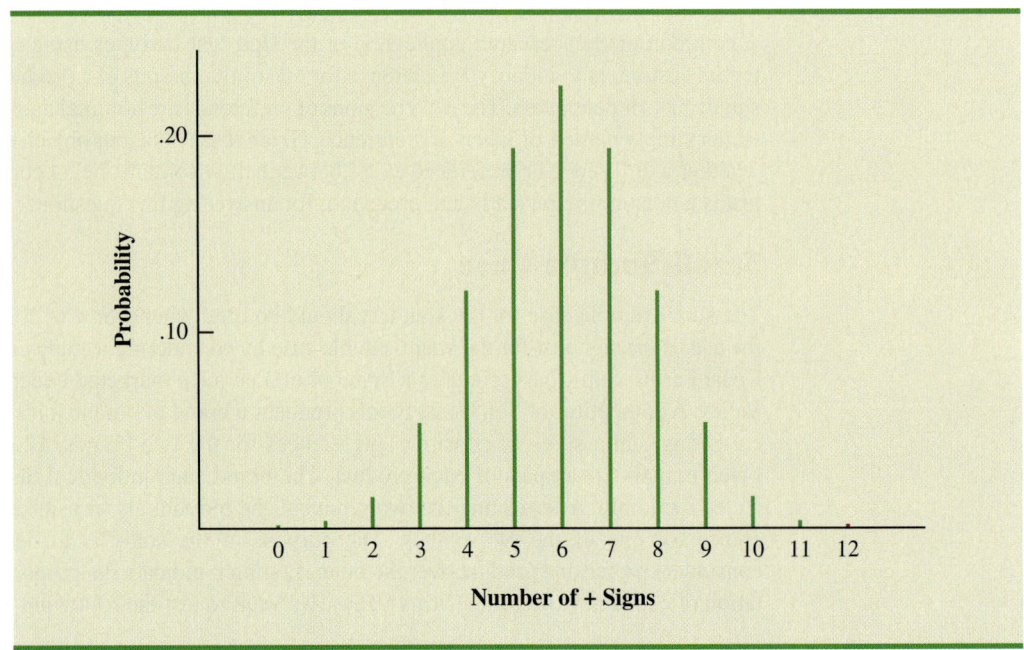

The Sun Coast Farms hypothesis test is a two-tailed test. As a result, the p-value is found by doubling the probability in the tail of the binomial sampling distribution. One-tailed sign tests are also possible. If the test is a lower tail test, the p-value is the probability that the number of plus signs is less than or equal to the observed number. If the test is an upper tail test, the p-value is the probability that the number of plus signs is greater than or equal to the observed number.

In the Sun Coast Farms taste test, all 12 individuals were able to state a preference for one of the two brands of orange juice. In other applications of the sign test, one or more individuals in the sample may not be able to state a preference. If a preference cannot be

TABLE 17.2   PREFERENCE DATA FOR THE SUN COAST FARMS TASTE TEST

SunCoast

Individual	Brand Preference	Recorded Data
1	Tropical Orange	−
2	Tropical Orange	−
3	Citrus Valley	+
4	Tropical Orange	−
5	Tropical Orange	−
6	Tropical Orange	−
7	Tropical Orange	−
8	Tropical Orange	−
9	Citrus Valley	+
10	Tropical Orange	−
11	Tropical Orange	−
12	Tropical Orange	−

indicated, the response is discarded from the sample and the sign test is based on a smaller sample size.

Using Excel

Excel's BINOMDIST function can be used to conduct a sign test. Here we show how to develop an Excel worksheet for the Sun Coast Farms sign test. Refer to Figure 17.2 as we describe the tasks involved. The formula worksheet is in the background; the value worksheet is in the foreground. When using Excel, it is not necessary to record the brand preference data using $+$ and $-$ signs. Instead we can work directly with the actual brand names: Citrus Valley and Tropical Orange.

Enter Data: The brand preference data are entered in column A.

Enter Functions and Formulas: The descriptive statistics needed are computed in cells D3 and D5. The COUNTA function is used in cell D3 to count the number of persons in the sample. Citrus Valley is entered in cell D4 to identify the response of interest (the one considered a $+$) and the COUNTIF function is used in cell D5 to count the number of persons stating a preference for the response of interest. All that remains is to compute the p-value.

The p-value (Lower Tail) is computed in cell D7 using Excel's BINOMDIST function. Recall that the form of the BINOMDIST function is BINOMDIST(x, n, p, cumulative), where x is the number of successes in a sample of size n with a probability of success given by p. We enter TRUE for cumulative if a cumulative probability (lower-tail area) is desired and FALSE for cumulative if an individual probability is desired. So we entered the formula

FIGURE 17.2 EXCEL WORKSHEET FOR SUN COAST FARMS SIGN TEST

	A	B	C	D	E	F
1	**Brand Preference**		**Sign Test Using Binomial Distribution**			
2	Tropical Orange					
3	Tropical Orange		**Sample Size**	=COUNTA(A2:A13)		
4	Citrus Valley		**Response of Interest**	Citrus Valley		
5	Tropical Orange		**Count of Response**	=COUNTIF(A2:A13,D4)		
6	Tropical Orange					
7	Tropical Orange		**p-value (Lower tail)**	=BINOMDIST(D5,D3,0.5,TRUE)		
8	Tropical Orange		**p-value (Upper tail)**	=1-BINOMDIST(D5-1,D3,0.5,TRUE)		
9	Tropical Orange		**p-value (Two tail)**	=2*MIN(D7,D8)		
10	Citrus Valley					
11	Tropical Orange					
12	Tropical Orange					
13	Tropical Orange					
14						

	A	B	C	D	E	F
1	**Brand Preference**		**Sign Test Using Binomial Distribution**			
2	Tropical Orange					
3	Tropical Orange		**Sample Size**	12		
4	Citrus Valley		**Response of Interest**	Citrus Valley		
5	Tropical Orange		**Count of Response**	2		
6	Tropical Orange					
7	Tropical Orange		**p-value (Lower tail)**	0.0193		
8	Tropical Orange		**p-value (Upper tail)**	0.9968		
9	Tropical Orange		**p-value (Two tail)**	0.0386		
10	Citrus Valley					
11	Tropical Orange					
12	Tropical Orange					
13	Tropical Orange					
14						

=BINOMDIST (D5,D3,0.5,TRUE) into cell D7 to compute the cumulative probability of the number of successes shown in cell D5. The value worksheet shows a cumulative probability of 0.0193. For a discrete probability distribution, the p-value (Upper Tail) is not just 1 minus the p-value (Lower Tail). For instance, in the Sun Coast Farms case, the p-value (Upper Tail) is the probability of two or more successes in 12 trials. But we must compute it as 1 minus the probability of 1 or fewer successes. Therefore, to compute p-value (Upper Tail) we enter the formula =1-BINOMDIST (D5-1,D3,0.5,TRUE) into cell D8. The value worksheet shows a p-value (Upper Tail) of 0.9968. The p-value (Two Tail) is computed in the usual way (see cell D9) as twice the minimum of the two one-tailed p-values. The value worksheet shows a p-value (Two Tail) value of 0.0386. Because the p-value (Two Tail) = .0386 < α = .05, we reject H_0 and conclude that consumer preference differs for the two brands of orange juice. Note that the p-value computed using Excel (.0386) differs slightly from the p-value we computed by hand (.0384); this difference is due simply to the fact that the binomial probabilities shown in Table 17.1 were rounded to four decimal places.

This worksheet can be used as a template for a different problem by entering the new data in column A, modifying the ranges in cells D3 and D5 to fit the new data, and entering the appropriate response in cell D4. The hypothesis test can then be conducted by choosing the appropriate p-value in cells D7:D9. To use this worksheet for exercises in which only the sample size and number of plus signs are given, one can ignore the data in column A, type in the sample size in cell D3, and type in the number of plus signs in cell D5. The appropriate p-values will then appear in cells D7:D9. We illustrate this use of the template later in the section.

Large-Sample Case

The large-sample sign test is equivalent to the test of a population proportion with p = .50 as presented in Chapter 9.

Using the null hypothesis H_0: p = .50 and a sample size of $n > 20$, the sampling distribution for the number of plus signs can be approximated by a normal distribution.

NORMAL APPROXIMATION OF THE SAMPLING DISTRIBUTION OF THE
NUMBER OF PLUS SIGNS WHEN H_0: p = .50

$$\text{Mean: } \mu = .50n \qquad \textbf{(17.1)}$$
$$\text{Standard Deviation: } \sigma = \sqrt{.25n} \qquad \textbf{(17.2)}$$

Distribution form: Approximately normal provided $n > 20$.

Let us consider an application of the sign test to political polling. A poll taken during a recent presidential election campaign asked 200 registered voters to rate the Democratic and Republican candidates in terms of best overall foreign policy. Results of the poll showed 72 rated the Democratic candidate higher, 103 rated the Republican candidate higher, and 25 indicated no difference between the candidates. Does the poll indicate a significant difference between the two candidates in terms of public opinion about their foreign policies?

Ties are handled by dropping the items from the analysis.

Using the sign test, we see that n = 200 − 25 = 175 individuals were able to indicate the candidate they believed had the best overall foreign policy. Using equations (17.1) and (17.2), we find that the sampling distribution of the number of plus signs has the following properties.

$$\mu = .50n = .50(175) = 87.5$$
$$\sigma = \sqrt{.25n} = \sqrt{.25(175)} = 6.6$$

In addition, with n = 175 we can assume that the sampling distribution is approximately normal. This distribution is shown in Figure 17.3.

Let us proceed with the sign test and use a .05 level of significance to draw a conclusion. Based on the number of times the Democratic candidate received the higher foreign

FIGURE 17.3   SAMPLING DISTRIBUTION FOR THE NUMBER OF PLUS SIGNS
IN A SIGN TEST WITH $n = 175$

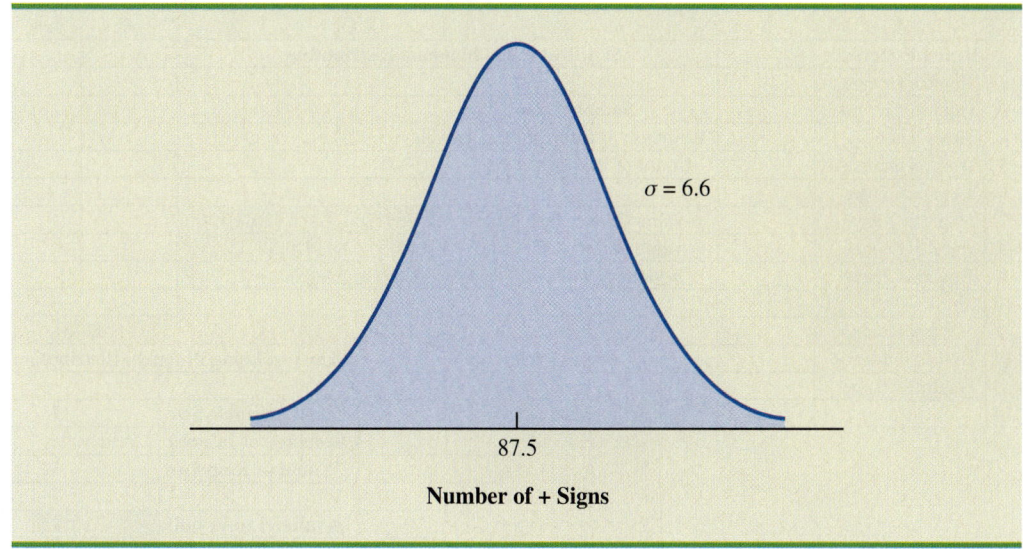

Number of + Signs

policy rating as the number of plus signs ($x = 72$), we can calculate the following value for
the test statistic.

$$z = \frac{x - \mu}{\sigma} = \frac{72 - 87.5}{6.6} = -2.35$$

*If the analysis used the
number of times the
Republican candidate was
rated higher, $z = 2.35$
would lead us to the same
conclusion.*

The standard normal probability table shows that the area in the tail to the left of $z = -2.35$
is .0094. With a two-tailed test, the p-value $= 2(.0094) = .0188$. Because the p-value $\leq$
$\alpha = .05$, we reject H_0. The study indicates that the candidates are perceived to differ in
terms of public opinion about their foreign policy.

Using Excel

For the large sample case, the sampling distribution can be approximated by a normal distribution. This is fine for hand calculations. But, when using Excel, it is unnecessary to use
the normal approximation for the large sample case. We will use the worksheet in Figure 17.2
as a template and modify it to conduct the hypothesis test involving the political candidates.
The sample size is 175 and 72 people rated the Democratic candidate higher. Therefore, we
enter 175 into cell D3 and 72 into cell D5 of the worksheet in Figure 17.2. The results obtained are shown in Figure 17.4. Note that p-value (Two Tail) $= 0.0231$ leads us to reject
H_0 with $\alpha = .05$. This p-value is actually slightly larger than the one found using the normal approximation. In general, we recommend using the binomial probabilities (as this
worksheet does) whenever possible, even in the large-sample case. However, the difference
caused by using the normal approximation is not that great, and both approaches lead to rejection of the null hypothesis and the conclusion of no difference in the foreign policy rating of the two candidates.

A final note about using the worksheet in Figure 17.2 as a template is in order. Although the Sun Coast Farms data are still in column A, they are not used in the computation of the p-values. Only the sample size in cell D3 and the number of pluses in cell D5
are used, and these are the values we just typed in for the current hypothesis test. If desired,
the data in column A and the label in cell D4 can be deleted in order to clean up the worksheet when it is used to solve exercises in which the sample data are not provided.

FIGURE 17.4   EXCEL WORKSHEET FOR THE PRESIDENTIAL ELECTION POLL EXAMPLE

	A	B	C	D	E	F
1	**Brand Preference**		**Sign Test Using Binomial Distribution**			
2	Tropical Orange					
3	Tropical Orange		Sample Size	175		
4	Citrus Valley		Response of Interest	Citrus Valley		
5	Tropical Orange		Count of Response	72		
6	Tropical Orange					
7	Tropical Orange		*p*-value (Lower tail)	=BINOMDIST(D5,D3,0.5,TRUE)		
8	Tropical Orange		*p*-value (Upper tail)	=1-BINOMDIST(D5-1,D3,0.5,TRUE)		
9	Tropical Orange		*p*-value (Two tail)	=2*MIN(D7,D8)		
10	Citrus Valley					
11	Tropical Orange					
12	Tropical Orange					
13	Tropical Orange					
14						

	A	B	C	D	E	F
1	**Brand Preference**		**Sign Test Using Binomial Distribution**			
2	Tropical Orange					
3	Tropical Orange		Sample Size	175		
4	Citrus Valley		Response of Interest	Citrus Valley		
5	Tropical Orange		Count of Response	72		
6	Tropical Orange					
7	Tropical Orange		*p*-value (Lower tail)	0.0115		
8	Tropical Orange		*p*-value (Upper tail)	0.9923		
9	Tropical Orange		*p*-value (Two tail)	0.0231		
10	Citrus Valley					
11	Tropical Orange					
12	Tropical Orange					
13	Tropical Orange					
14						

Hypothesis Test About a Median

In Chapter 9 we described how hypothesis tests can be used to make an inference about a population mean. We now show how the sign test can be used to conduct hypothesis tests about a population median. Recall that the median splits a population in such a way that 50% of the values are at the median or above and 50% are at the median or below. We can apply the sign test by using a plus sign whenever the data in the sample are above the hypothesized value of the median and a minus sign whenever the data in the sample are below the hypothesized value of the median. Any data exactly equal to the hypothesized value of the median should be discarded. The computations for the sign test are done in exactly the same way as before.

For example, the following hypothesis test is being conducted about the median price of new homes in St. Louis, Missouri.

$$H_0: \text{Median} = \$130{,}000$$
$$H_a: \text{Median} \neq \$130{,}000$$

In a sample of 62 new homes, 34 have prices above $130,000, 26 have prices below $130,000, and two have prices of exactly $130,000.

With $n = 60$, the large sample case applies. Using equations (17.1) and (17.2) for the $n = 60$ homes with prices different from $130,000, we obtain

$$\mu = .50n = .50(60) = 30$$
$$\sigma = \sqrt{.25n} = \sqrt{.25(60)} = 3.87$$

With $x = 34$ as the number of plus signs, the test statistic becomes

$$z = \frac{x - \mu}{\sigma} = \frac{34 - 30}{3.87} = 1.03$$

Using the standard normal distribution table and $z = 1.03$, we find the two-tailed p-value = $2(1.0000 - .8485) = .303$. With p-value $> .05$, we cannot reject H_0. Based on the sample data, we are unable to reject the null hypothesis that the median selling price of a new home in St. Louis is $130,000.

Using Excel

Again, instead of using the large sample normal approximation, we can use the worksheet in Figure 17.2 as a template and modify it to conduct the hypothesis test involving the median selling price of new homes in St. Louis. The sample size is 60 and 34 of the selling prices were above $130,000. Therefore, we enter 60 into cell D3 and 34 into cell D5 of the worksheet in Figure 17.2. The results obtained are shown in Figure 17.5. Note that p-value (Two Tail) = 0.3663. For any reasonable level of significance, the p-value would not be less than α and hence we would not reject H_0. Thus, we would not challenge the claim that the median selling price is $130,000. Note again that the worksheet we used here is just a modification of the worksheet in Figure 17.2. Although the Sun Coast Farms data still appear in column A, the formulas in cells D3 and D5 have been replaced by the values that we typed in for the sample size and number of plus signs. Thus, if desired, the data in column A and the label in cell D4 can be deleted in order to clean up the worksheet when it is used to solve exercises in which the sample data are not provided.

FIGURE 17.5   EXCEL WORKSHEET FOR SIGN TEST INVOLVING MEDIAN SELLING PRICE OF HOMES

	A	B	C	D	E	F
1	**Brand Preference**		**Sign Test Using Binomial Distribution**			
2	Tropical Orange					
3	Tropical Orange		**Sample Size**	60		
4	Citrus Valley		**Response of Interest**	Citrus Valley		
5	Tropical Orange		**Count of Response**	34		
6	Tropical Orange					
7	Tropical Orange		**p-value (Lower tail)**	=BINOMDIST(D5,D3,0.5,TRUE)		
8	Tropical Orange		**p-value (Upper tail)**	=1-BINOMDIST(D5-1,D3,0.5,TRUE)		
9	Tropical Orange		**p-value (Two tail)**	=2*MIN(D7,D8)		
10	Citrus Valley					
11	Tropical Orange					
12	Tropical Orange					
13	Tropical Orange					
14						

	A	B	C	D	E	F
1	**Brand Preference**		**Sign Test Using Binomial Distribution**			
2	Tropical Orange					
3	Tropical Orange		**Sample Size**	60		
4	Citrus Valley		**Response of Interest**	Citrus Valley		
5	Tropical Orange		**Count of Response**	34		
6	Tropical Orange					
7	Tropical Orange		**p-value (Lower tail)**	0.8775		
8	Tropical Orange		**p-value (Upper tail)**	0.1831		
9	Tropical Orange		**p-value (Two tail)**	0.3663		
10	Citrus Valley					
11	Tropical Orange					
12	Tropical Orange					
13	Tropical Orange					
14						

Exercises

Methods

1. The following table lists the preferences indicated by 10 individuals in taste tests involving two brands of a product.

Individual	Brand A Versus Brand B	Individual	Brand A Versus Brand B
1	+	6	+
2	+	7	−
3	+	8	+
4	−	9	−
5	+	10	+

With $\alpha = .05$, test for a significant difference in the preferences for the two brands. A plus indicates a preference for brand A over brand B.

2. The following hypothesis test is to be conducted.

$$H_0: \text{Median} \leq 150$$
$$H_a: \text{Median} > 150$$

A sample of size 30 yields 22 cases in which a value greater than 150 is obtained, 3 cases in which a value of exactly 150 is obtained, and 5 cases in which a value less than 150 is obtained. Use $\alpha = .01$ and conduct the hypothesis test.

Applications

3. Are stock splits beneficial to stockholders? SNL Securities studied stock splits in the banking industry over an 18-month period and found that stock splits tended to increase the value of an individual's stock holding. Assume that of a sample of 20 recent stock splits, 14 led to an increase in value, 4 led to a decrease in value, and 2 resulted in no change. Suppose a sign test is to be used to determine whether stock splits continue to be beneficial for holders of bank stocks.
    a. What are the null and alternative hypotheses?
    b. With $\alpha = .05$, what is your conclusion?

4. A poll asked 1253 adults a series of questions about the state of the economy and their children's future. One question was, "Do you expect your children to have a better life than you have had, a worse life, or a life about as good as yours?" The responses were 34% better, 29% worse, 33% about the same, and 4% not sure. Use the sign test and a .05 level of significance to determine whether more adults feel their children will have a better future than feel their children will have a worse future. What is your conclusion?

5. Nielsen Media Research identified *ER* and *Seinfeld* as the top-rated network television shows for 1996–1997. Assume that in a local television preference poll, 410 individuals were asked to indicate their favorite network television show: 185 selected *ER*, 165 selected *Seinfeld*, and 60 selected another television show. Use a .05 level of significance to test the hypothesis that *ER* and *Seinfeld* have the same level of preference. What is your conclusion?

6. Competition in the personal computer market is intense. A sample of 500 purchases showed 202 Brand A computers, 158 Brand B computers, and 140 other computers. Use a .05 level of significance to test the hypothesis that Brand A and Brand B have the same share of the personal computer market. What is your conclusion?

7. The median annual income of subscribers to *Barron's* magazine is $131,000 (http://www. barronsmag.com, July 28, 2000). Assume a sample of 300 subscribers to *The Wall Street Journal* found 165 subscribers with an income over $131,000 and 135 subscribers with an income under $131,000. Can you conclude that there is any difference between the median incomes of the two subscriber groups? At $\alpha = .05$, what is your conclusion?

8. In a sample of 150 college basketball games, the home team won 98 games. Test to see whether the data support the claim of a home-team advantage in college basketball. Use a .05 level of significance. What is your conclusion?

9. The median number of part-time employees at fast-food restaurants in a particular city was known to be 15 last year. City officials think the use of part-time employees may be increasing. A sample of nine fast-food restaurants showed that more than 15 part-time employees worked at seven of the restaurants, one restaurant had exactly 15 part-time employees, and one had fewer than 15 part-time employees. Test at $\alpha = .05$ to see whether the median number of part-time employees increased.

10. According to a national survey, the median annual income adults say would make their dreams come true is $152,000. Suppose that of a sample of 225 individuals in Ohio, 122 individuals report that the amount of income needed to make their dreams come true is less than $152,000, and 103 report that the amount needed is more than $152,000. Test the null hypothesis that the median amount of annual income needed to make dreams come true in Ohio is $152,000. Use $\alpha = .05$. What is your conclusion?

11. A sample of women working as executive assistants in the Chicago area provided the following weekly wage data ($). Use the sample data to test H_0: median ≤ 585, H_a: median > 585 for the population of female executive assistants in Chicago. Use a .05 level of significance. What is your conclusion?

Chicago

622	516	631	498	715
571	494	525	664	721
657	692	551	580	649
706	597	518	725	635
548	604	671	607	487
583	702	622	714	693
600	721	662	633	681
624	551	632	544	485
655	721	669	677	609
656	562	721	489	582

17.2 Wilcoxon Signed Rank Test

The **Wilcoxon signed rank test** is the nonparametric alternative to the parametric matched-sample test presented in Chapter 10. In the matched-sample situation, each experimental unit generates two paired or matched observations, one from population 1 and one from population 2. The differences between the matched observations provide insight about the differences between the two populations.

A manufacturing firm is attempting to determine whether two production methods differ in task completion time. A sample of 11 workers was selected, and each worker completed a production task using each of the production methods. The production method that each worker used first was selected randomly. Thus, each worker in the sample provided a pair of observations, as shown in Table 17.3. A positive difference in task completion times indicates that method 1 required more time, and a negative difference in times indicates that method 2 required more time. Do the data indicate that the methods are significantly different in terms of task completion times?

TABLE 17.3 PRODUCTION TASK COMPLETION TIMES (MINUTES)

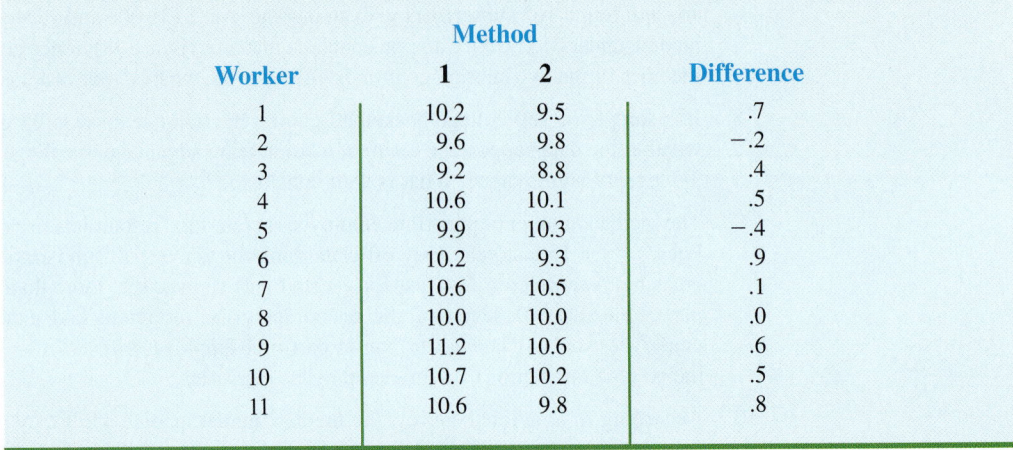

	Method		
Worker	**1**	**2**	**Difference**
1	10.2	9.5	.7
2	9.6	9.8	−.2
3	9.2	8.8	.4
4	10.6	10.1	.5
5	9.9	10.3	−.4
6	10.2	9.3	.9
7	10.6	10.5	.1
8	10.0	10.0	.0
9	11.2	10.6	.6
10	10.7	10.2	.5
11	10.6	9.8	.8

In effect, we have two populations of task completion times, one population associated with each method. The following hypotheses will be tested.

H_0: The populations are identical

H_a: The populations are not identical

If H_0 cannot be rejected, we will not have evidence to conclude that the task completion times differ for the two methods. However, if H_0 can be rejected, we will conclude that the two methods differ in task completion time.

The first step of the Wilcoxon signed rank test requires a ranking of the *absolute value* of the differences between the two methods. We discard any differences of zero and then rank the remaining absolute differences from lowest to highest. Tied differences are assigned the average ranking of their positions in the combined data set. The ranking of the absolute values of differences is shown in the fourth column of Table 17.4. Note that the

TABLE 17.4 RANKING OF ABSOLUTE DIFFERENCES FOR THE PRODUCTION TASK COMPLETION TIME EXAMPLE

Worker	Difference	Absolute Value of Difference	Rank	Signed Rank
1	.7	.7	8	+ 8
2	−.2	.2	2	− 2
3	.4	.4	3.5	+ 3.5
4	.5	.5	5.5	+ 5.5
5	−.4	.4	3.5	− 3.5
6	.9	.9	10	+10
7	.1	.1	1	+ 1
8	.0	.0	—	—
9	.6	.6	7	+ 7
10	.5	.5	5.5	+ 5.5
11	.8	.8	9	+ 9
			Sum of Signed Ranks	+44.0

difference of zero for worker 8 is discarded from the rankings; then the smallest absolute difference of .1 is assigned the rank of 1. This ranking of absolute differences continues with the largest absolute difference of .9 assigned the rank of 10. The tied absolute differences for workers 3 and 5 are assigned the average rank of 3.5 and the tied absolute differences for workers 4 and 10 are assigned the average rank of 5.5.

Once the ranks of the absolute differences have been determined, the ranks are given the sign of the original difference in the data. For example, the .1 difference for worker 7, which was assigned the rank of 1, is given the value of $+1$ because the observed difference between the two methods was positive. The .2 difference, which was assigned the rank of 2, is given the value of -2 because the observed difference between the two methods was negative for worker 2. The complete list of signed ranks, as well as their sum, is shown in the last column of Table 17.4.

Let us return to the original hypothesis of identical population task completion times for the two methods. If the populations representing task completion times for each of the two methods are identical, we would expect the positive ranks and the negative ranks to cancel each other, so that the sum of the signed rank values would be approximately zero. Thus, the test for significance under the Wilcoxon signed rank test involves determining whether the computed sum of signed ranks ($+44$ in our example) is significantly different from zero.

Let T denote the sum of the signed rank values in a Wilcoxon signed rank test. It can be shown that if the two populations are identical and the number of matched pairs of data is 10 or more, the sampling distribution of T can be approximated by a normal distribution as follows.

SAMPLING DISTRIBUTION OF T FOR IDENTICAL POPULATIONS

$$\text{Mean: } \mu_T = 0 \tag{17.3}$$

$$\text{Standard Deviation: } \sigma_T = \sqrt{\frac{n(n+1)(2n+1)}{6}} \tag{17.4}$$

Distribution form: Approximately normal provided $n \geq 10$.

For the example, we have $n = 10$ after discarding the observation with the difference of zero (worker 8). Thus, using equation (17.4), we have

$$\sigma_T = \sqrt{\frac{10(11)(21)}{6}} = 19.62$$

Figure 17.6 is the sampling distribution of T under the assumption of identical populations.

Let us proceed with the Wilcoxon signed rank test and use a .05 level of significance to draw a conclusion. With the sum of the signed rank values $T = 44$, we calculate the following value for the test statistic.

$$z = \frac{T - \mu_T}{\sigma_T} = \frac{44 - 0}{19.62} = 2.24$$

Using the standard normal distribution table and $z = 2.24$, we find the two-tailed p-value $= 2(1.0000 - .9875) = .025$. With p-value $\leq \alpha = .05$, we reject H_0 and conclude that the two populations are not identical and that the methods differ in task completion time.

FIGURE 17.6   SAMPLING DISTRIBUTION OF *T* FOR THE PRODUCTION TASK
COMPLETION TIME EXAMPLE

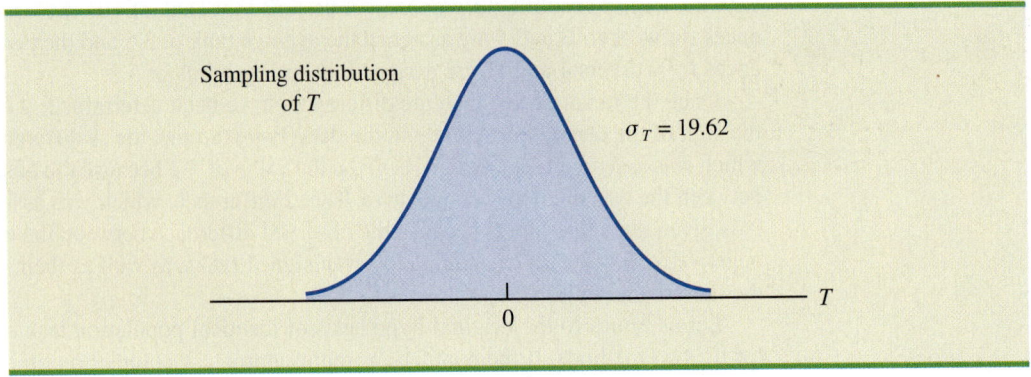

Method 2's shorter completion times for 8 of the workers lead us to conclude that method 2 is the preferred production method.

Using Excel

Excel does not provide any tools specifically designed for the Wilcoxon signed rank test. But using Excel's ABS, RANK, and SIGN functions allows us to develop a worksheet to assist in conducting the test. We now describe the development of such a worksheet. Refer to Figure 17.7 as we describe the tasks involved. The formula worksheet is in the background; the value worksheet is in the foreground.

Enter Data: The task completion time data are entered in columns B and C. Note that the data for worker 8 (the case of no difference) have been deleted.

Enter Functions and Formulas: The formulas in cells D2:D11 compute the differences in task completion times, and Excel's ABS function is used in cells E2:E11 to compute the absolute value of the differences. Excel's RANK function has been used in column F to rank the absolute differences in ascending order (smallest to largest). The first input for the RANK function is the data value to be ranked, the second input is the range of values for it to be ranked among, and the third input is a one. If the third argument is a nonzero number, an ascending order ranking is performed. Our difficulty in using the results provided by the RANK function is that the RANK function does not assign an average rank to tied values. Therefore, we must modify the results provided by the function by typing in the average values for ties (see cells F4:F6 and F10 in the formula worksheet). With the differences ranked, we used Excel's SIGN function in column G to assign each of the ranked differences their original sign from column D. The sum of the signed ranks is then computed using Excel's SUM function in cell G12.

Now we are ready to compute the test statistic and the *p*-value. The effective sample size (the sample size after discarding any differences of zero) is computed using Excel's COUNT function in cell C14. The standard deviation is computed in cell C15 using equation (17.4) and Excel's SQRT function. The test statistic is computed in cell C16 as the sum of the signed ranks divided by the standard deviation. With this test statistic, *p*-value (Lower Tail) and *p*-value (Upper Tail) are computed using the NORMSDIST function in cells G14 and G15, respectively. Then, *p*-value (Two Tail) is computed in cell G16 as twice the minimum of the two one-tailed *p*-values. Because the task completion time example is a two-tailed test, we use *p*-value (Two Tail) = .0249 to conduct the hypothesis test. Because $.0249 < \alpha = .05$, we reject the null hypothesis of no difference between the two production methods.

FIGURE 17.7   EXCEL WORKSHEET FOR SIGNED RANK TEST OF DIFFERENCES IN PRODUCTION METHODS

	A	B	C	D	E	F	G	H
1	Worker	Method 1	Method 2	Difference	Absolute Value	Rank	Signed Rank	
2	1	10.2	9.5	=B2-C2	=ABS(D2)	=RANK(E2,$E$2:$E$11,1)	=SIGN(D2)*F2	
3	2	9.6	9.8	=B3-C3	=ABS(D3)	=RANK(E3,$E$2:$E$11,1)	=SIGN(D3)*F3	
4	3	9.2	8.8	=B4-C4	=ABS(D4)	3.5	=SIGN(D4)*F4	
5	4	10.6	10.1	=B5-C5	=ABS(D5)	5.5	=SIGN(D5)*F5	
6	5	9.9	10.3	=B6-C6	=ABS(D6)	3.5	=SIGN(D6)*F6	
7	6	10.2	9.3	=B7-C7	=ABS(D7)	=RANK(E7,$E$2:$E$11,1)	=SIGN(D7)*F7	
8	7	10.6	10.5	=B8-C8	=ABS(D8)	=RANK(E8,$E$2:$E$11,1)	=SIGN(D8)*F8	
9	9	11.2	10.6	=B9-C9	=ABS(D9)	=RANK(E9,$E$2:$E$11,1)	=SIGN(D9)*F9	
10	10	10.7	10.2	=B10-C10	=ABS(D10)	5.5	=SIGN(D10)*F10	
11	11	10.6	9.8	=B11-C11	=ABS(D11)	=RANK(E11,$E$2:$E$11,1)	=SIGN(D11)*F11	
12							=SUM(G2:G11)	
13								
14	Effective Sample Size	=COUNT(A2:A11)				*p*-value (Lower Tail)	=NORMSDIST(C16)	
15	Standard Deviation	=SQRT(C14*(C14+1)*(2*C14+1)/6)				*p*-value (Upper Tail)	=1-NORMSDIST(C16)	
16	Test Statistic	=G12/C15				*p*-value (Two Tail)	=2*MIN(G14,G15)	
17								

	A	B	C	D	E	F	G	H
1	Worker	Method 1	Method 2	Difference	Absolute Value	Rank	Signed Rank	
2	1	10.2	9.5	0.7	0.7	8	8	
3	2	9.6	9.8	-0.2	0.2	2	-2	
4	3	9.2	8.8	0.4	0.4	3.5	3.5	
5	4	10.6	10.1	0.5	0.5	5.5	5.5	
6	5	9.9	10.3	-0.4	0.4	3.5	-3.5	
7	6	10.2	9.3	0.9	0.9	10	10	
8	7	10.6	10.5	0.1	0.1	1	1	
9	9	11.2	10.6	0.6	0.6	7	7	
10	10	10.7	10.2	0.5	0.5	5.5	5.5	
11	11	10.6	9.8	0.8	0.8	9	9	
12							44	
13								
14	Effective Sample Size	10				*p*-value (Lower Tail)	0.9875	
15	Standard Deviation	19.62				*p*-value (Upper Tail)	0.0125	
16	Test Statistic	2.24				*p*-value (Two Tail)	0.0249	
17								

Exercises

Applications

12. Two fuel additives are tested to determine their effect on miles per gallon for passenger cars. Test results for 12 cars follow; each car was tested with both fuel additives. Use $\alpha = .05$ and the Wilcoxon signed rank test to see whether there is a significant difference in the additives.

MPG

	Additive			Additive	
Car	1	2	Car	1	2
1	20.12	18.05	7	16.16	17.20
2	23.56	21.77	8	18.55	14.98
3	22.03	22.57	9	21.87	20.03
4	19.15	17.06	10	24.23	21.15
5	21.23	21.22	11	23.21	22.78
6	24.77	23.80	12	25.02	23.70

13. A sample of 10 men was used in a study to test the effects of a relaxant on the time required to fall asleep for male adults. Data for 10 subjects showing the number of minutes required to fall asleep with and without the relaxant follow. Use a .05 level of significance to determine whether the relaxant reduces the time required to fall asleep. What is your conclusion?

Subject	Without Relaxant	With Relaxant	Subject	Without Relaxant	With Relaxant
1	15	10	6	7	5
2	12	10	7	8	10
3	22	12	8	10	7
4	8	11	9	14	11
5	10	9	10	9	6

14. Rental car gasoline prices per gallon were sampled at 10 major airports. Data for Avis and Budget car rental companies follow (*USA Today*, April 4, 2000).

Airport	Avis	Budget
Boston Logan	1.58	1.39
Chicago O'Hare	1.60	1.55
Chicago Midway	1.53	1.55
Denver	1.55	1.51
Fort Lauderdale	1.57	1.58
Los Angeles	1.80	1.74
Miami	1.62	1.60
New York (JFK)	1.69	1.60
Orange County, CA	1.75	1.59
Washington (Dulles)	1.55	1.54

Use $\alpha = .05$ to test the hypothesis that there is no difference between the two populations. What is your conclusion?

15. A test was conducted of two overnight mail delivery services. Two samples of identical deliveries were set up so that both delivery services were notified of the need for a delivery at the same time. The hours required to make each delivery follow. Do the data shown suggest a difference in the delivery times for the two services? Use a .05 level of significance for the test.

Delivery	Service 1	Service 2
1	24.5	28.0
2	26.0	25.5
3	28.0	32.0
4	21.0	20.0
5	18.0	19.5
6	36.0	28.0
7	25.0	29.0
8	21.0	22.0
9	24.0	23.5
10	26.0	29.5
11	31.0	30.0

16. The 1997 price/earnings ratios for a sample of 12 stocks are shown in the following list (*Barron's,* December 8, 1997). Assume that a financial analyst provided the estimated price/earnings ratio for 1998. Using a .05 level of significance, what is your conclusion about the differences between the price/earnings ratios for 1997 and 1998?

PERatio

Stock	1997 P/E Ratio	1998 P/E Ratio (Est.)
Coca-Cola	40	32
Du Pont	24	22
Eastman Kodak	21	23
General Electric	30	23
General Mills	25	19
IBM	19	19
McDonald's	20	17
Merck	29	19
Motorola	35	20
Philip Morris	17	18
Walt Disney	33	27
Xerox	20	16

17. Ten test-market cities were selected as part of a market research study designed to evaluate the effectiveness of a particular advertising campaign. The sales dollars for each city were recorded for the week prior to the promotional program. Then the campaign was conducted for two weeks and new sales data were collected for the week immediately after the campaign. The two sets of sales data (in thousands of dollars) follow.

Advertising

City	Precampaign Sales ($1000s)	Postcampaign Sales ($1000s)
Kansas City	130	160
Dayton	100	105
Cincinnati	120	140
Columbus	95	90
Cleveland	140	130
Indianapolis	80	82
Louisville	65	55
St. Louis	90	105
Pittsburgh	140	152
Peoria	125	140

Use $\alpha = .05$. What conclusion would you draw about the value of the advertising program?

17.3 Mann-Whitney-Wilcoxon Rank Sum Test

In this section we present another nonparametric method that can be used to determine whether a difference exists between two populations. This test, unlike the signed rank test, is not based on a matched sample. Two independent samples, one from each population, are used. The test was developed jointly by Mann, Whitney, and Wilcoxon. It is sometimes called the *Mann-Whitney test* and sometimes the *Wilcoxon rank sum test.* Both the Mann-Whitney and Wilcoxon versions of this test are equivalent; we refer to it as the **Mann-Whitney-Wilcoxon (MWW) rank sum test**, or simply the MWW test.

The nonparametric MWW test does not require interval data or the assumption that the populations are normally distributed. The only requirement of the MWW test is that the measurement scale for the data is at least ordinal. Then, instead of testing for the difference between the means of the two populations, the MWW test determines whether the two populations are identical. The hypotheses for the MWW test are as follows.

H_0: The two populations are identical

H_a: The two populations are not identical

We demonstrate how the MWW test can be applied by first showing an application for the small-sample case.

Small-Sample Case

The small-sample case for the MWW test should be used whenever the sample sizes for both populations are less than or equal to 10. We illustrate the use of the MWW test for the small-sample case by considering the academic potential of students attending Johnston High School. The majority of students attending Johnston High School previously attended either Garfield Junior High School or Mulberry Junior High School. The question raised by school administrators was whether the population of students who had attended Garfield was identical to the population of students who had attended Mulberry in terms of academic potential. The following hypotheses were considered.

H_0: The two populations are identical in terms of academic potential

H_a: The two populations are not identical in terms of academic potential

Using high school records, Johnston High School administrators selected a random sample of four high school students who attended Garfield Junior High and another random sample of five students who attended Mulberry Junior High. The current high school class standing was recorded for each of the nine students used in the study. The ordinal class standings for the nine students are listed in Table 17.5.

The first step in the MWW test is to rank the *combined* data from the two samples from low to high. The lowest value (class standing 8) receives a rank of 1 and the highest value (class standing 202) receives a rank of 9. The ranking of the nine students is given in Table 17.6.

The next step is to sum the ranks for each sample separately. This calculation is shown in Table 17.7. The MWW test can use the sum of the ranks for either sample. In the following discussion, we use the sum of the ranks for the sample of four students from Garfield. We denote this sum by the symbol T. Thus, for our example, $T = 11$.

Let us consider the properties of the sum of the ranks for the Garfield sample. With four students in the sample, Garfield could have the top four students in the study. If this were the case, $T = 1 + 2 + 3 + 4 = 10$ would be the smallest value possible for the rank sum T.

TABLE 17.5   HIGH SCHOOL CLASS STANDING DATA

Garfield Students		Mulberry Students	
Student	**Class Standing**	**Student**	**Class Standing**
Fields	8	Hart	70
Clark	52	Phipps	202
Jones	112	Kirkwood	144
Tibbs	21	Abbott	175
		Guest	146

TABLE 17.6   RANKING OF HIGH SCHOOL STUDENTS

Student	Class Standing	Combined Sample Rank	Student	Class Standing	Combined Sample Rank
Fields	8	1	Kirkwood	144	6
Tibbs	21	2	Guest	146	7
Clark	52	3	Abbott	175	8
Hart	70	4	Phipps	202	9
Jones	112	5			

Conversely, Garfield could have the bottom four students, in which case $T = 6 + 7 + 8 + 9 = 30$ would be the largest value possible for T. Hence, T for the Garfield sample must take a value between 10 and 30.

Note that values of T near 10 imply that Garfield has the significantly better, or higher ranking, students, whereas values of T near 30 imply that Garfield has the significantly weaker, or lower ranking, students. Thus, if the two populations of students were identical in terms of academic potential, we would expect the value of T to be near the average of the two values, or $(10 + 30)/2 = 20$.

Critical values of the MWW T statistic are provided in Table 17.8 for cases in which both sample sizes are less than or equal to 10. In that table, n_1 refers to the sample size corresponding to the sample whose rank sum is being used in the test. T_L is the lower tail critical value, its value is read directly from the table. T_U is the upper tail critical value; its value is computed from equation (17.5).

$$T_U = n_1(n_1 + n_2 + 1) - T_L \qquad (17.5)$$

Neither the value of T_L nor the value of T_U is in the rejection region. The null hypothesis of identical populations should be rejected only if T is strictly less than T_L or strictly greater than T_U.

For example, using Table 17.8 with a .05 level of significance, we see that the lower tail critical value for the MWW statistic with $n_1 = 4$ (Garfield) and $n_2 = 5$ (Mulberry) is $T_L = 12$. The upper tail critical value for the MWW statistic computed by using equation (17.5) is

$$T_U = 4(4 + 5 + 1) - 12 = 28$$

TABLE 17.7   RANK SUMS FOR HIGH SCHOOL STUDENTS FROM EACH JUNIOR HIGH SCHOOL

	Garfield Students			Mulberry Students	
Student	Class Standing	Sample Rank	Student	Class Standing	Sample Rank
Fields	8	1	Hart	70	4
Clark	52	3	Phipps	202	9
Jones	112	5	Kirkwood	144	6
Tibbs	21	2	Abbott	175	8
			Guest	146	7
	Sum of Ranks	11		Sum of Ranks	34

TABLE 17.8   CRITICAL VALUES (T_L AND T_U) FOR THE MANN-WHITNEY-WILCOXON RANK SUM TEST

Reject the hypothesis of identical populations if the sum of the ranks for the n_1 items is *less* than the value T_L shown in the following table or if the sum of the ranks for the n_1 items is *greater* than the value T_U where

$$T_U = n_1(n_1 + n_2 + 1) - T_L$$

$\alpha = .05$		n_2								
		2	3	4	5	6	7	8	9	10
	2	3	3	3	3	3	3	4	4	4
	3	6	6	6	7	8	8	9	9	10
	4	10	10	11	12	13	14	15	15	16
	5	15	16	17	18	19	21	22	23	24
n_1	6	21	23	24	25	27	28	30	32	33
	7	28	30	32	34	35	37	39	41	43
	8	37	39	41	43	45	47	50	52	54
	9	46	48	50	53	56	58	61	63	66
	10	56	59	61	64	67	70	73	76	79

$\alpha = .10$		n_2								
		2	3	4	5	6	7	8	9	10
	2	3	3	3	4	4	4	5	5	5
	3	6	7	7	8	9	9	10	11	11
	4	10	11	12	13	14	15	16	17	18
	5	16	17	18	20	21	22	24	25	27
n_1	6	22	24	25	27	29	30	32	34	36
	7	29	31	33	35	37	40	42	44	46
	8	38	40	42	45	47	50	52	55	57
	9	47	50	52	55	58	61	64	67	70
	10	57	60	63	67	70	73	76	80	83

Thus, the MWW decision rule indicates that the null hypothesis of identical populations can be rejected if the sum of the ranks for the first sample (Garfield) is less than 12 or greater than 28. The rejection rule can be written as

$$\text{Reject } H_0 \text{ if } T < 12 \text{ or if } T > 28$$

If we conducted the test with the rank sum of the Mulberry students, we would have $n_1 = 5$, $n_2 = 4$, $T_L = 17$, $T_U = 33$, and $T = 34$. With $T > T_U$, we would reach the same conclusion to reject H_0.

Referring to Table 17.7, we see that $T = 11$. Hence, the null hypothesis H_0 is rejected, and we can conclude that the population of students at Garfield differs from the population of students at Mulberry in terms of academic potential. The higher class ranking obtained by the sample of Garfield students suggests that Garfield students are better prepared for high school than the Mulberry students.

Large-Sample Case

When both sample sizes are greater than or equal to 10, a normal approximation of the sampling distribution of T can be used to conduct the analysis for the MWW test. We illustrate the large-sample case by considering a situation at Third National Bank.

Third National Bank has two branch offices. Data collected from two independent simple random samples, one from each branch, are given in Table 17.9. Do the data indicate whether the populations of checking account balances at the two branch banks are identical?

The first step in the MWW test is to rank the *combined* data from the lowest to the highest values. Using the combined set of 22 observations in Table 17.9, we find the lowest data value of $750 (sixth item of sample 2) and assign to it a rank of 1. Continuing the ranking gives us the following list.

Balance ($)	Item	Assigned Rank
750	6th of sample 2	1
800	5th of sample 2	2
805	7th of sample 1	3
850	2nd of sample 2	4
.	.	.
.	.	.
.	.	.
1195	4th of sample 1	21
1200	3rd of sample 1	22

In ranking the combined data, we may find that two or more data values are the same. In that case, the tied values are given the *average* ranking of their positions in the combined data set. For example, the balance of $945 (eighth item of sample 1) will be assigned the rank of 11. However, the next two values in the data set are tied with values of $950 (see the sixth item of sample 1 and the fourth item of sample 2). Because these two values will be considered for assigned ranks of 12 and 13, they are both assigned the rank of 12.5. At

TABLE 17.9   ACCOUNT BALANCES FOR TWO BRANCHES OF THIRD NATIONAL BANK

	Branch 1		Branch 2
Account	Balance ($)	Account	Balance ($)
1	1095	1	885
2	955	2	850
3	1200	3	915
4	1195	4	950
5	925	5	800
6	950	6	750
7	805	7	865
8	945	8	1000
9	875	9	1050
10	1055	10	935
11	1025		
12	975		

TABLE 17.10   COMBINED RANKING OF THE DATA IN THE TWO SAMPLES FROM THIRD NATIONAL BANK

Branch 1			Branch 2		
Account	Balance ($)	Rank	Account	Balance ($)	Rank
1	1095	20	1	885	7
2	955	14	2	850	4
3	1200	22	3	915	8
4	1195	21	4	950	12.5
5	925	9	5	800	2
6	950	12.5	6	750	1
7	805	3	7	865	5
8	945	11	8	1000	16
9	875	6	9	1050	18
10	1055	19	10	935	10
11	1025	17		Sum of Ranks	83.5
12	975	15			
	Sum of Ranks	169.5			

the next highest data value of $955, we continue the ranking process by assigning $955 the rank of 14. Table 17.10 is the entire data set with the assigned rank of each observation.

The next step in the MWW test is to sum the ranks for each sample. The sums are given in Table 17.10. The test procedure can be based on the sum of the ranks for either sample. We use the sum of the ranks for the sample from branch 1. Thus, for this example, $T = 169.5$.

Given that the sample sizes are $n_1 = 12$ and $n_2 = 10$, we can use the normal approximation to the sampling distribution of the rank sum T. The appropriate sampling distribution is given by the following expressions.

SAMPLING DISTRIBUTION OF T FOR IDENTICAL POPULATIONS

$$\text{Mean: } \mu_T = \tfrac{1}{2} n_1(n_1 + n_2 + 1) \qquad (17.6)$$

$$\text{Standard Deviation: } \sigma_T = \sqrt{\tfrac{1}{12} n_1 n_2(n_1 + n_2 + 1)} \qquad (17.7)$$

Distribution form: Approximately normal provided $n_1 \geq 10$ and $n_2 \geq 10$.

For branch 1, we have

$$\mu_T = \tfrac{1}{2} 12(12 + 10 + 1) = 138$$
$$\sigma_T = \sqrt{\tfrac{1}{12} 12(10)(12 + 10 + 1)} = 15.17$$

Figure 17.8 is the sampling distribution of T. Let us proceed with the MWW test and use a .05 level of significance to draw a conclusion. With the sum of the ranks for branch 1 $T = 169.5$, we calculate the following value for the test statistic.

$$z = \frac{T - \mu_T}{\sigma_T} = \frac{169.5 - 138}{15.17} = 2.08$$

FIGURE 17.8   SAMPLING DISTRIBUTION OF *T* FOR THE THIRD NATIONAL BANK EXAMPLE

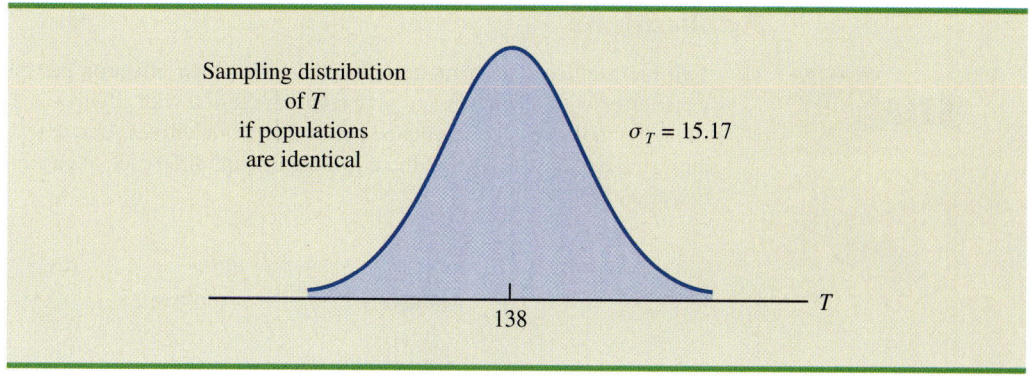

Using the standard normal distribution table and $z = 2.08$, we find the two-tailed *p*-value = $2(1.0000 - .9812) = .0376$. With the *p*-value $\leq \alpha = .05$, we reject H_0 and conclude the two populations are not identical; that is, the populations of account balances at the branch banks are not the same.

In summary, the Mann-Whitney-Wilcoxon rank sum test consists of the following steps to determine whether two independent random samples are selected from identical populations.

1. Rank the combined sample observations from lowest to highest, with tied values being assigned the average of the tied rankings.
2. Compute *T*, the sum of the ranks for the first sample.
3. In the large-sample case, make the test for significant differences between the two populations by using the observed value of *T* and comparing it to the sampling distribution of *T* for identical populations using equations (17.6) and (17.7). The value of the standardized test statistic *z* and the *p*-value provide the basis for deciding whether to reject H_0. In the small-sample case, use Table 17.8 to find the critical values for the test.

Using Excel

Excel does not have any special tools for the Mann-Whitney-Wilcoxon rank sum test. However, an Excel worksheet can be used to advantage in ranking the data, summing the ranks, computing the test statistic, and computing the *p*-value in the large-sample case. The usage is similar to the use of Excel in the previous section except for assigning signs to the ranks so we will not develop a separate worksheet here.

NOTES AND COMMENTS

The nonparametric test discussed in this section is used to determine whether two populations are identical. The parametric statistical tests described in Chapter 10 test the equality of two population means. When we reject the hypothesis that the means are equal, we conclude that the populations differ in their means. When we reject the hypothesis that the populations are identical using the MWW rank sum test, we cannot state how they differ. The populations could have different means, different medians, different variances, or different forms. Nonetheless, if we believe that the populations are the same in every aspect but the means, a rejection of H_0 by the nonparametric method implies that the means differ.

Exercises

Applications

18. Two fuel additives are being tested to determine their effect on gas mileage. Seven cars were tested with additive 1 and nine cars were tested with additive 2. The following data show the miles per gallon obtained with the two additives. Use $\alpha = .05$ and the MWW rank sum test to see whether there is a significant difference in gasoline mileage for the two additives.

Additive 1	Additive 2
17.3	18.7
18.4	17.8
19.1	21.3
16.7	21.0
18.2	22.1
18.6	18.7
17.5	19.8
	20.7
	20.2

19. Samples of starting annual salaries for individuals entering the public accounting and financial planning professions follow. Annual salaries are shown in thousands of dollars.

Salaries

Public Accountant	Financial Planner	Public Accountant	Financial Planner
35.2	34.0	40.0	38.6
43.8	34.2	35.9	34.7
41.3	38.1	44.5	38.9
43.2	40.9	41.7	36.8
39.2	36.9	36.9	33.9

a. Use a .05 level of significance and test the hypothesis that there is no difference between the starting annual salaries of public accountants and financial planners. What is your conclusion?

b. What are the sample mean annual salaries for the two professions?

20. The gap between the earnings of men and women with equal education is narrowing but has not closed (*USA Today*, September 15, 2000). Sample data for seven men and seven women with bachelor's degrees are as follows. Data are shown in thousands of dollars.

Men	30.6	75.5	45.2	62.2	38.2	49.9	55.3
Women	44.5	35.4	27.9	40.5	25.8	47.5	24.8

a. What is the median salary for men? For women?

b. Use $\alpha = .05$ and conduct the hypothesis test for equal populations. What is your conclusion?

21. Mileage performance tests were conducted for two models of automobiles. Twelve automobiles of each model were selected randomly and a miles-per-gallon rating for each model was developed on the basis of 1000 miles of highway driving. The data follow.

Model 1		Model 2	
Automobile	**Miles per Gallon**	**Automobile**	**Miles per Gallon**
1	20.6	1	21.3
2	19.9	2	17.6
3	18.6	3	17.4
4	18.9	4	18.5
5	18.8	5	19.7
6	20.2	6	21.1
7	21.0	7	17.3
8	20.5	8	18.8
9	19.8	9	17.8
10	19.8	10	16.9
11	19.2	11	18.0
12	20.5	12	20.1

Automobile

Use $\alpha = .10$ and test for a significant difference in the populations of miles-per-gallon ratings for the two models.

22. *BusinessWeek* annually publishes statistics on the world's 1000 largest companies. A company's price/earnings (P/E) ratio is the company's current stock price divided by the latest 12 months' earnings per share. Listed in Table 17.11 are the P/E ratios for a sample of 10 Japanese and 12 U.S. companies. Is the difference in P/E ratios between the two countries significant? Use the MWW test and $\alpha = .01$ to support your conclusion.

TABLE 17.11   P/E RATIOS FOR JAPANESE AND U.S. COMPANIES

Japan		United States	
Company	**P/E Ratio**	**Company**	**P/E Ratio**
Sumitomo Corp.	153	Gannet	19
Kinden	21	Motorola	24
Heiwa	18	Schlumberger	24
NCR Japan	125	Oracle Systems	43
Suzuki Motor	31	Gap	22
Fuji Bank	213	Winn-Dixie	14
Sumitomo Chemical	64	Ingersoll-Rand	21
Seibu Railway	666	American Electric Power	14
Shiseido	33	Hercules	21
Toho Gas	68	Times Mirror	38
		WellPoint Health	15
		Northern States Power	14

23. Police records show the following numbers of daily crime reports for a sample of days during the winter months and a sample of days during the summer months. Use a .05 level of significance to determine whether there is a significant difference between the winter and summer months in terms of the number of crime reports.

Winter	Summer	Winter	Summer
18	28	20	29
20	18	12	23
15	24	16	38
16	32	19	28
21	18	20	18

24. A certain brand of microwave oven was priced at 10 stores in Dallas and 13 stores in San Antonio. The data follow. Use a .05 level of significance and test whether prices for the microwave oven are the same in the two cities.

Dallas	San Antonio
445	460
489	451
405	435
485	479
439	475
449	445
436	429
420	434
430	410
405	422
	425
	459
	430

25. The National Association of Home Builders provided data on the cost of the most popular home remodeling projects. Use the Mann-Whitney-Wilcoxon rank sum test to see whether it can be concluded that the cost of kitchen remodeling differs from the cost of master bedroom remodeling. Use a .05 level of significance.

Kitchen	Master Bedroom
25,200	18,000
17,400	22,900
22,800	26,400
21,900	24,800
19,700	26,900
23,000	17,800
19,700	24,600
16,900	21,000
21,800	
23,600	

17.4 Kruskal–Wallis Test

The MWW rank sum test in Section 17.3 can be used to test whether two populations are identical. Kruskal and Wallis extended the test to the case of three or more populations. The hypotheses for the **Kruskal-Wallis test** with $k \geq 3$ populations can be written as follows.

$$H_0: \text{All populations are identical}$$
$$H_a: \text{Not all populations are identical}$$

The Kruskal-Wallis test is based on the analysis of independent random samples from each of the k populations.

This test is an alternative to ANOVA in Chapter 13, which focused on the equality of the means of k populations.

In Chapter 13 we showed that analysis of variance (ANOVA) can be used to test for the equality of means among three or more populations. The ANOVA procedure requires interval or ratio data and the assumption that the k populations are normally distributed.

TABLE 17.12

PERFORMANCE
EVALUATION
RATINGS FOR
20 WILLIAMS
EMPLOYEES

College A	College B	College C
25	60	50
70	20	70
60	30	60
85	15	80
95	40	90
90	35	70
80		75

The nonparametric Kruskal-Wallis test can be used with ordinal data as well as with interval or ratio data. In addition, the Kruskal-Wallis test does not require the assumption of normally distributed populations. Hence, whenever the data from $k \geq 3$ populations are ordinal, or whenever the assumption of normally distributed populations is questionable, the Kruskal-Wallis test provides an alternate statistical procedure for testing whether the populations are identical. We demonstrate the Kruskal-Wallis test by using it in an employee selection application.

Williams Manufacturing hires employees for its management staff from three local colleges. Recently, the company's personnel department began collecting and reviewing annual performance ratings in an attempt to determine whether there are differences in performance among the managers hired from these colleges. Performance rating data are available from independent samples of seven employees from college A, six employees from college B, and seven employees from college C. These data are summarized in Table 17.12; the overall performance rating of each manager is given on a 0–100 scale, with 100 being the highest possible performance rating.

Suppose we want to test whether the three populations are identical in terms of performance evaluations. We will use a .05 level of significance. The Kruskal-Wallis test statistic, which is based on the sum of ranks for each of the samples, can be computed as follows.

KRUSKAL-WALLIS TEST STATISTIC

$$W = \left[\frac{12}{n_T(n_T + 1)} \sum_{i=1}^{k} \frac{R_i^2}{n_i} \right] - 3(n_T + 1) \qquad \textbf{(17.8)}$$

where

$$k = \text{the number of populations}$$
$$n_i = \text{the number of items in sample } i$$
$$n_T = \Sigma n_i = \text{total number of items in all samples}$$
$$R_i = \text{sum of the ranks for sample } i$$

Kruskal and Wallis were able to show that, under the null hypothesis in which the populations are identical, the sampling distribution of W can be approximated by a chi-square distribution with $k - 1$ degrees of freedom. This approximation is generally acceptable if each of the sample sizes is greater than or equal to 5. The null hypothesis of identical populations will be rejected if the test statistic is large. As a result, the procedure uses an upper tail test.

The Kruskal-Wallis test uses only the ordinal rank of the data.

To compute the W statistic for our example, we must first rank all 20 data items. The lowest data value of 15 from the college B sample receives a rank of 1, whereas the highest data value of 95 from the college A sample receives a rank of 20. The data values, their associated ranks, and the sum of the ranks for the three samples are given in Table 17.13. Note that we assign the average rank to tied items;* for example, the data values of 60, 70, 80, and 90 had ties.

The sample sizes are

$$n_1 = 7 \qquad n_2 = 6 \qquad n_3 = 7$$

---

*If numerous tied ranks are observed, equation (17.8) must be modified; the modified formula is given in *Practical Non-parametric Statistics*, 3rd ed. (New York: John Wiley & Sons, 1998) by W. J. Conover.

TABLE 17.13   COMBINED RANKINGS FOR THE 20 WILLIAMS MANUFACTURING
EMPLOYEES

Willams

College A	Rank	College B	Rank	College C	Rank
25	3	60	9	50	7
70	12	20	2	70	12
60	9	30	4	60	9
85	17	15	1	80	15.5
95	20	40	6	90	18.5
90	18.5	35	5	70	12
80	15.5			75	14
Sum of Ranks	95		27		88

and

$$n_T = \Sigma n_i = 7 + 6 + 7 = 20$$

We compute the W statistic by using equation (17.8).

$$W = \frac{12}{20(21)}\left[\frac{(95)^2}{7} + \frac{(27)^2}{6} + \frac{(88)^2}{7}\right] - 3(20 + 1) = 8.92$$

We can now use the chi-square distribution table (Table 3 of Appendix B) to determine the p-value for the test. Using $k - 1 = 3 - 1 = 2$ degrees of freedom, we find $\chi^2 = 7.378$ has an area of .025 in the upper tail of the distribution and $\chi^2 = 9.21$ has an area of .01 in the upper tail distribution. With $W = 8.92$ between 7.378 and 9.21, we can conclude that the area in the upper tail of the distribution is between .025 and .01. Because it is an upper tail test, we can conclude that the p-value is between .025 and .01. Excel will show p-value = .0116. Because the p-value $\leq \alpha = .05$, we reject H_0 and conclude that the three populations are not identical. Manager performance differs significantly depending on the college attended. Furthermore, because the performance ratings are lowest for college B, it would be reasonable for the company to either cut back recruiting from college B or at least evaluate its graduates more thoroughly.

Using Excel

Excel does not have a special tool for the Kruskal-Wallis test. However, an Excel worksheet can be used to simplify ranking the data and summing the ranks, as well as computing the test statistic and corresponding p-value. Excel's CHIDIST function is used to compute the p-value. We show the development of a worksheet for the Williams Manufacturing example. Refer to Figure 17.9 as we describe the tasks involved. The formula worksheet is in the background; the value worksheet is in the foreground.

Enter Data: The data are in columns A and B. The college attended is in column A and the performance rating is in column B. Note that rows 2 through 8 contain the sample of college A employees, rows 9 through 14 contain the sample of college B employees, and rows 15 through 21 contain the sample of college C employees.

Enter Functions and Formulas: We have used Excel's RANK function in column C to determine the rank order for the 20 employees. As in Section 17.2 we had to modify the results provided by the RANK function by typing in the average ranks for ties. In reviewing the formula worksheet, we see several places where providing the average rank for ties was

FIGURE 17.9 EXCEL WORKSHEET FOR THE KRUSKAL-WALLIS TEST ON THE WILLIAMS MANUFACTURING EXAMPLE

	A	B	C	D	E	F
1	College	Performance Rating	Rank			
2	A	25	=RANK(B2,$B$2:$B$21,1)			
3	A	70	12			
4	A	60	9			
5	A	85	=RANK(B5,$B$2:$B$21,1)			
6	A	95	=RANK(B6,$B$2:$B$21,1)			
7	A	90	18.5	n_1	=COUNT(B2:B8)	
8	A	80	15.5	Sum A	=SUM(C2:C8)	
9	B	60	9			
10	B	20	=RANK(B10,$B$2:$B$21,1)			
11	B	30	=RANK(B11,$B$2:$B$21,1)			
12	B	15	=RANK(B12,$B$2:$B$21,1)			
13	B	40	=RANK(B13,$B$2:$B$21,1)	n_2	=COUNT(B9:B14)	
14	B	35	=RANK(B14,$B$2:$B$21,1)	Sum B	=SUM(C9:C14)	
15	C	50	=RANK(B15,$B$2:$B$21,1)			
16	C	70	12			
17	C	60	9			
18	C	80	15.5			
19	C	90	18.5			
20	C	70	12	n_3	=COUNT(B15:B21)	
21	C	75	=RANK(B21,$B$2:$B$21,1)	Sum C	=SUM(C15:C21)	
22				n_T	=COUNT(B2:B21)	
23		Test Statistic	=(12/(E22*(E22+1)))*(E8^2/E7+E14^2/E13+E21^2/E20)-3*(E22+1)			
24		Degrees of Freedom	2			
25						
26		p-value (Lower Tail)	=1-CHIDIST(C23,C24)			
27		p-value (Upper Tail)	=CHIDIST(C23,C24)			
28		p-value (Two Tail)	=2*MIN(C26,C27)			
29						

	A	B	C	D	E	F
1	College	Performance Rating	Rank			
2	A	25	3			
3	A	70	12			
4	A	60	9			
5	A	85	17			
6	A	95	20			
7	A	90	18.5	n_1	7	
8	A	80	15.5	Sum A	95	
9	B	60	9			
10	B	20	2			
11	B	30	4			
12	B	15	1			
13	B	40	6	n_2	6	
14	B	35	5	Sum B	27	
15	C	50	7			
16	C	70	12			
17	C	60	9			
18	C	80	15.5			
19	C	90	18.5			
20	C	70	12	n_3	7	
21	C	75	14	Sum C	88	
22				n_T	20	
23		Test Statistic	8.92			
24		Degrees of Freedom	2			
25						
26		p-value (Lower Tail)	0.9884			
27		p-value (Upper Tail)	0.0116			
28		p-value (Two Tail)	0.0232			
29						

necessary. Excel's COUNT function was used in cells E7, E13, and E20 to compute the sample size for each college, and the SUM function was used in cells E8, E14, and E21 to compute the sum of ranks for each college.

The test statistic is computed in cell C23 using an Excel formula to implement equation (17.8). A value of $k - 1 = 2$ has been entered into cell C24 for the degrees of freedom. Excel's CHIDIST function is then used to compute the p-values associated with the test statistic in cells C26:C28. Recall that the form of the CHIDIST function is CHIDIST (test statistic, degrees of freedom), and that the value provided by the function is the area in the upper tail of the chi-square distribution. Thus, to obtain the p-value (Lower Tail) we enter the formula =1-CHIDIST(C23,C24) into cell C26. The p-value (Upper Tail) is obtained by entering the formula =CHIDIST(C23, C24) into cell C27, and the p-value (Two Tail) is obtained in cell C28 as two times the minimum of the 2 one-tailed p-values. Because the Williams Manufacturing example is an upper tail hypothesis test, we compare the p-value (Upper Tail) = .0116 to $\alpha = .05$. With $.0116 < \alpha = .05$, we reject H_0 and conclude that the three populations are not identical.

NOTES AND COMMENTS

The Kruskal-Wallis procedure illustrated in the example began with the collection of interval-scaled data showing employee performance evaluation ratings. The procedure also would work if the data were the ordinal rankings of the 20 employees. In that case, the Kruskal-Wallis test could be applied directly to the original data; the step of constructing the rank orderings from the performance evaluation ratings would be omitted.

Exercises

Methods

26. Three products received the following performance ratings by a panel of 15 consumers.

Product		
A	**B**	**C**
50	80	60
62	95	45
75	98	30
48	87	58
65	90	57

Use the Kruskal-Wallis test and $\alpha = .05$ to determine whether there is a significant difference in the performance ratings for the products.

27. Three admission test preparation programs are being evaluated. The scores obtained by a sample of 20 people who used the test preparation programs provided the following data. Use the Kruskal-Wallis test to determine whether there is a significant difference among the three test preparation programs. Use $\alpha = .01$.

Program		
A	**B**	**C**
540	450	600
400	540	630
490	400	580
530	410	490
490	480	590
610	370	620
	550	570

Applications

28. Forty-minute workouts of one of the following activities three days a week will lead to a loss of weight. The following sample data show the number of calories burned during 40-minute workouts for three different activities. Do these data indicate differences in the amount of calories burned for the three activities? Use a .05 level of significance. What is your conclusion?

Swimming	**Tennis**	**Cycling**
408	415	385
380	485	250
425	450	295
400	420	402
427	530	268

29.   The miles-per-gallon data obtained from tests on three different automobiles are reported as follows. Use the Kruskal-Wallis test with $\alpha = .05$ to determine whether there is a significant difference in the gasoline mileage for the three automobiles.

Automobile		
A	**B**	**C**
19	19	24
21	20	26
20	22	23
19	21	25
21	23	27

30.   A large corporation sends many of its first-level managers to an off-site supervisory skills course. Four different management development centers offer this course, and the corporation wants to determine whether they differ in the quality of training provided. A sample of 20 employees who attended these programs is chosen and the employees were ranked in terms of supervisory skills. The results follow.

Course	Supervisory Skills Rank				
1	3	14	10	12	13
2	2	7	1	5	11
3	19	16	9	18	17
4	20	4	15	6	8

Note that the top-ranked supervisor attended course 2 and the lowest-ranked supervisor attended course 4. Use $\alpha = .05$ and test to see whether there is a significant difference in the training provided by the four programs.

31.   The better-selling candies are high in calories. Assume that the following data show the calorie content from samples of M&Ms, Kit Kat, and Milky Way II. Test for significant differences in the calorie content of these three candies. At a .05 level of significance, what is your conclusion?

M&Ms	Kit Kat	Milky Way II
230	225	200
210	205	208
240	245	202
250	235	190
230	220	180

Rank Correlation

The correlation coefficient is a measure of the linear association between two variables for which interval or ratio data are available. In this section, we consider measures of association between two variables when only ordinal data are available. The **Spearman rank correlation coefficient** r_s has been developed for this purpose.

SPEARMAN RANK CORRELATION COEFFICIENT

$$r_s = 1 - \frac{6\Sigma d_i^2}{n(n^2 - 1)}$$ (17.9)

where

n = the number of items or individuals being ranked
x_i = the rank of item i with respect to one variable
y_i = the rank of item i with respect to a second variable
$d_i = x_i - y_i$

Let us illustrate the use of the Spearman rank correlation coefficient with an example. A company wants to determine whether individuals who were expected at the time of employment to be better salespersons actually turn out to have better sales records. To investigate this question, the vice president in charge of personnel carefully reviewed the original job interview summaries, academic records, and letters of recommendation for 10 current members of the firm's salesforce. After the review, the vice president ranked the 10 individuals in terms of their potential for success, basing the assessment solely on the information available at the time of employment. Then a list was obtained of the number of units sold by each salesperson over the first two years. On the basis of actual sales performance, a second ranking of the 10 salespersons was carried out. Table 17.14 gives the relevant data and the two rankings. The statistical question is whether there is agreement between the ranking of potential at the time of employment and the ranking based on the actual sales performance over the first two years.

Let us compute the Spearman rank correlation coefficient for the data in Table 17.14. The computations are summarized in Table 17.15. We see that the rank correlation coefficient is a positive .73. The Spearman rank correlation coefficient ranges from −1.0 to +1.0 and its interpretation is similar to that of the sample correlation coefficient in that positive values near 1.0 indicate a strong association between the rankings; as one rank increases, the other rank increases. Rank correlations near −1.0 indicate a strong negative association

TABLE 17.14   SALES POTENTIAL AND ACTUAL TWO-YEAR SALES DATA FOR 10 SALESPEOPLE

Salesperson	Ranking of Potential	Two-Year Sales (units)	Ranking According to Two-Year Sales
A	2	400	1
B	4	360	3
C	7	300	5
D	1	295	6
E	6	280	7
F	3	350	4
G	10	200	10
H	9	260	8
I	8	220	9
J	5	385	2

TABLE 17.15   COMPUTATION OF THE SPEARMAN RANK CORRELATION COEFFICIENT FOR SALES POTENTIAL AND SALES PERFORMANCE

Salesperson	x_i = Ranking of Potential	y_i = Ranking of Sales Performance	$d_i = x_i - y_i$	d_i^2
A	2	1	1	1
B	4	3	1	1
C	7	5	2	4
D	1	6	−5	25
E	6	7	−1	1
F	3	4	−1	1
G	10	10	0	0
H	9	8	1	1
I	8	9	−1	1
J	5	2	3	9
				$\Sigma d_i^2 = 44$

$$r_s = 1 - \frac{6\Sigma d_i^2}{n(n^2 - 1)} = 1 - \frac{6(44)}{10(100 - 1)} = .73$$

between the rankings; as one rank increases, the other rank decreases. The value $r_s = .73$ indicates a positive correlation between potential and actual performance. Individuals ranked high on potential tend to rank high on performance.

Test for Significant Rank Correlation

At this point, we have seen how sample results can be used to compute the sample rank correlation coefficient. As with many other statistical procedures, we may want to use the sample results to make an inference about the population rank correlation ρ_s. To make an inference about the population rank correlation, we must test the following hypotheses.

$$H_0: \rho_s = 0$$
$$H_a: \rho_s \neq 0$$

Under the null hypothesis of no rank correlation ($\rho_s = 0$), the rankings are independent, and the sampling distribution of r_s is as follows.

SAMPLING DISTRIBUTION OF r_s

$$\text{Mean: } \mu_{r_s} = 0 \qquad \textbf{(17.10)}$$

$$\text{Standard Deviation: } \sigma_{r_s} = \sqrt{\frac{1}{n - 1}} \qquad \textbf{(17.11)}$$

Distribution form: Approximately normal provided $n \geq 10$.

The sample rank correlation coefficient for sales potential and sales performance is $r_s = .73$. With this value, we can test for a significant rank correlation. From equation (17.10) we have $\mu_{r_s} = 0$ and from (17.11) we have $\sigma_{r_s} = \sqrt{1/(10 - 1)} = .33$. Using the standard normal random variable z as the test statistic, we have

$$z = \frac{r_s - \mu_{r_s}}{\sigma_{r_s}} = \frac{.73 - 0}{.33} = 2.20$$

Using the standard normal distribution table and $z = 2.20$, we find the p-value = $2(1.0000 - .9861) = .0278$. With a .05 level of significance, the p-value $\leq \alpha = .05$ leads to the rejection of the hypothesis that the rank correlation is zero. Thus, we can conclude that there is a significant rank correlation between sales potential and sales performance.

Using Excel

The Spearman rank correlation coefficient is equal to the Pearson correlation coefficient applied to ordinal or rank data.

In Chapter 3, we showed how to use Excel's CORREL function for computing the Pearson product moment correlation coefficient. The Spearman rank correlation coefficient is the same as the Pearson correlation coefficient applied to the ranked data. We develop a worksheet for making the necessary calculations. Refer to Figure 17.10 as we describe the tasks involved. The formula worksheet is in the background; the value worksheet appears in the foreground.

Enter Data: The data for the salespersons are entered in cells B2:C11. The data in column B are the ranks of the potential of the salespersons, and the data in column C are sales over the first two years.

Enter Functions and Formulas: We have used Excel's RANK function in column D to rank the salespersons with respect to sales over the first two years. We now want to apply Excel's CORREL function to compute the correlation between the ranks in columns B and D. Excel's CORREL function is used in cell C13 to make this calculation. In the value worksheet we see that the result is .73 and that the Pearson correlation coefficient applied to the ranked data does indeed provide the same value as the Spearman rank correlation coefficient.

FIGURE 17.10 EXCEL WORKSHEET FOR COMPUTING THE SPEARMAN RANK CORRELATION COEFFICIENT

	A	B	C	D	E
1	Salesperson	Ranking of Potential	Two-Year Sales (units)	Sales Ranking	
2	A	2	400	=RANK(C2,$C$2:$C$11)	
3	B	4	360	=RANK(C3,$C$2:$C$11)	
4	C	7	300	=RANK(C4,$C$2:$C$11)	
5	D	1	295	=RANK(C5,$C$2:$C$11)	
6	E	6	280	=RANK(C6,$C$2:$C$11)	
7	F	3	350	=RANK(C7,$C$2:$C$11)	
8	G	10	200	=RANK(C8,$C$2:$C$11)	
9	H	9	260	=RANK(C9,$C$2:$C$11)	
10	I	8	220	=RANK(C10,$C$2:$C$11)	
11	J	5	385	=RANK(C11,$C$2:$C$11)	
12					
13	Spearman Correlation		=CORREL($B$2:$B$11,$D$2:$D$11)		
14					

	A	B	C	D	E
1	Salesperson	Ranking of Potential	Two-Year Sales (units)	Sales Ranking	
2	A	2	400	1	
3	B	4	360	3	
4	C	7	300	5	
5	D	1	295	6	
6	E	6	280	7	
7	F	3	350	4	
8	G	10	200	10	
9	H	9	260	8	
10	I	8	220	9	
11	J	5	385	2	
12					
13	Spearman Correlation		0.73		
14					

Exercises

Methods

32. Consider the following set of rankings for a sample of 10 elements.

Element	x_i	y_i	Element	x_i	y_i
1	10	8	6	2	7
2	6	4	7	8	6
3	7	10	8	5	3
4	3	2	9	1	1
5	4	5	10	9	9

    a. Compute the Spearman rank correlation coefficient for the data.
    b. Use $\alpha = .05$ and test for significant rank correlation. What is your conclusion?

33. Consider the following two sets of rankings for six items.

	Case One			Case Two	
Item	**First Ranking**	**Second Ranking**	**Item**	**First Ranking**	**Second Ranking**
A	1	1	A	1	6
B	2	2	B	2	5
C	3	3	C	3	4
D	4	4	D	4	3
E	5	5	E	5	2
F	6	6	F	6	1

Note that in the first case the rankings are identical, whereas in the second case the rankings are exactly opposite. What value should you expect for the Spearman rank correlation coefficient for each of these cases? Explain. Calculate the rank correlation coefficient for each case.

Applications

34. For a sample of 11 states, the following table gives the ranks on pupil–teacher ratio (1 = lowest, 11 = highest) and expenditure per pupil (1 = highest, 11 = lowest).

	Rank			Rank	
State	**Pupil–Teacher Ratio**	**Expenditure per Pupil**	**State**	**Pupil–Teacher Ratio**	**Expenditure per Pupil**
Arizona	10	9	Massachusetts	1	1
Colorado	8	5	Nebraska	2	7
Florida	6	4	North Dakota	7	8
Idaho	11	2	South Dakota	5	10
Iowa	4	6	Washington	9	3
Louisiana	3	11			

At the $\alpha = .05$ level, does there appear to be a relationship between expenditure per pupil and pupil–teacher ratio?

35. A national study by Harris Interactive, Inc., evaluated the top Internet companies and their reputations (*The Wall Street Journal,* November 18, 1999). The following two lists show how 10 Internet companies ranked in terms of reputation and percentage of respondents

who said they would purchase the company's stock. A positive rank correlation is anticipated because it seems reasonable to expect that a company with a higher reputation would be a more desirable purchase.

	Reputation	Probable Purchase
Microsoft	1	3
Intel	2	4
Dell	3	1
Lucent	4	2
Texas Instruments	5	9
Cisco Systems	6	5
Hewlett-Packard	7	10
IBM	8	6
Motorola	9	7
Yahoo!	10	8

a. Compute the rank correlation between reputation and probable purchase.
b. Test for a significant positive rank correlation. What is the p-value?
c. At $\alpha = .05$, what is your conclusion?

36. The 1996 rankings of a sample of professional golfers in both driving distance and putting follows (*Golf Digest*, January 1997). What is the rank correlation between driving distance and putting? Use a .10 level of significance.

Professional Golfer	Driving Distance	Putting
Fred Couples	1	5
David Duval	5	6
Ernie Els	4	10
Nick Faldo	9	2
Tom Lehman	6	7
Justin Leonard	10	3
Davis Love III	2	8
Phil Mickelson	3	9
Greg Norman	7	4
Mark O'Meara	8	1

37. A student organization surveyed both recent graduates and current students to obtain information on the quality of teaching at a particular university. An analysis of the responses provided the following teaching-ability rankings. Do the rankings given by the current students agree with the rankings given by the recent graduates? Use $\alpha = .10$ and test for a significant rank correlation.

	Ranking by	
Professor	Current Students	Recent Graduates
1	4	6
2	6	8
3	8	5
4	3	1
5	1	2
6	2	3
7	5	7
8	10	9
9	7	4
10	9	10

Summary

In this chapter we presented several statistical procedures that are classified as nonparametric methods. Because nonparametric methods can be applied to nominal and ordinal data as well as interval and ratio data and do not require population distribution assumptions, they expand the class of problems that can be subjected to statistical analysis.

The sign test is a nonparametric procedure for identifying differences between two populations when the only data available are nominal data. In the small-sample case, the binominal probability distribution can be used to determine the critical values for the sign test; in the large-sample case, a normal approximation can be used. The Wilcoxon signed rank test is a procedure for analyzing matched-sample data whenever interval- or ratio-scaled data are available for each matched pair. No assumptions are made about the population distribution. The Wilcoxon procedure tests the hypothesis that the two populations being considered are identical.

The Mann-Whitney-Wilcoxon rank sum test is a nonparametric method for testing for a difference between two populations based on two independent random samples. Tables were presented for the small-sample case, and a normal approximation was provided for the large-sample case. The Kruskal-Wallis test extends the Mann-Whitney-Wilcoxon rank sum test to the case of three or more populations. The Kruskal-Wallis test is the nonparametric analog of the parametric ANOVA test for differences among population means.

In the last section of this chapter we introduced the Spearman rank correlation coefficient as a measure of association for two ordinal or rank-ordered sets of items.

Glossary

Nonparametric methods Statistical methods that require few, if any, assumptions about the population probability distributions and the level of measurement. These methods can be applied when nominal or ordinal data are available.

Sign test A nonparametric statistical test for identifying differences between two populations based on the analysis of nominal data.

Wilcoxon signed rank test A nonparametric statistical test for identifying differences between two populations based on the analysis of two matched or paired samples.

Mann-Whitney-Wilcoxon (MWW) rank sum test A nonparametric statistical test for identifying differences between two populations based on the analysis of two independent samples.

Kruskal-Wallis test A nonparametric test for identifying differences among three or more populations.

Spearman rank correlation coefficient A correlation measure based on rank-ordered data for two variables.

Key Formulas

Sign Test (Large-Sample Case)—Normal Approximation of Sampling Distribution

$$\text{Mean: } \mu = .50n \tag{17.1}$$
$$\text{Standard Deviation: } \sigma = \sqrt{.25n} \tag{17.2}$$

Wilcoxon Signed Rank Test—Normal Approximation of Sampling Distribution

$$\text{Mean: } \mu_T = 0 \tag{17.3}$$
$$\text{Standard Deviation: } \sigma_T = \sqrt{\frac{n(n+1)(2n+1)}{6}} \tag{17.4}$$

Mann-Whitney-Wilcoxon Rank Sum Test (Large-Sample)—Normal Approximation of Sampling Distribution

$$\text{Mean: } \mu_T = \tfrac{1}{2} n_1(n_1 + n_2 + 1) \tag{17.6}$$

$$\text{Standard Deviation: } \sigma_T = \sqrt{\tfrac{1}{12} n_1 n_2 (n_1 + n_2 + 1)} \tag{17.7}$$

Kruskal-Wallis Test Statistic

$$W = \left[\frac{12}{n_T(n_T + 1)} \sum_{i=1}^{k} \frac{R_i^2}{n_i} \right] - 3(n_T + 1) \tag{17.8}$$

Spearman Rank Correlation Coefficient

$$r_s = 1 - \frac{6 \Sigma d_i^2}{n(n^2 - 1)} \tag{17.9}$$

Supplementary Exercises

38. A survey asked the following question: Do you favor or oppose providing tax-funded vouchers or tax deductions to parents who send their children to private schools? Of the 2010 individuals surveyed, 905 favored the support, 1045 opposed the support, and 60 offered no opinion. Do the data indicate a significant difference in the preferences for the support for parents who send their children to private schools? Use a .05 level of significance.

39. The national median sales price of existing one-family homes is $118,000 (*The Wall Street Journal Almanac*, 1998). Assume that the following data were obtained for sales of existing one-family homes in Houston and Boston.

	Greater than $118,000	Equal to $118,000	Less than $118,000
Houston	11	2	32
Boston	27	1	13

    a. Is the median resale price in Houston lower than the national median of $118,000? Use a statistical test with $\alpha = .05$ to support your conclusion.
    b. Is the median resale price in Boston higher than the national median of $118,000? Use a statistical test with $\alpha = .05$ to support your conclusion.

40. Twelve homemakers were asked to estimate the retail selling price of two models of refrigerators. Their estimates of selling price are shown in the following table. Use these data and test at the .05 level of significance to determine whether there is a difference between the two models in terms of homemakers' perceptions of selling price.

CD file

Refrigerator

Homemaker	Model 1 ($)	Model 2 ($)	Homemaker	Model 1 ($)	Model 2 ($)
1	650	900	7	700	890
2	760	720	8	690	920
3	740	690	9	900	1000
4	700	850	10	500	690
5	590	920	11	610	700
6	620	800	12	720	700

41. A study was designed to evaluate the weight-gain potential of a new poultry feed. A sample of 12 chickens was used in a six-week study. The weight of each chicken was recorded before and after the six-week test period. The differences between the before and after

weights of the 12 chickens are 1.5, 1.2, −.2, .0, .5, .7, .8, 1.0, .0, .6, .2, −.01. A negative value indicates a weight loss during the test period, whereas .0 indicates no weight change over the period. Use a .05 level of significance to determine whether the new feed appears to provide a weight gain for the chickens.

42. The following data are product weights for items produced on two production lines. Test for a difference between the product weights for the two lines. Use $\alpha = .10$.

Production Line 1	Production Line 2
13.6	13.7
13.8	14.1
14.0	14.2
13.9	14.0
13.4	14.6
13.2	13.5
13.3	14.4
13.6	14.8
12.9	14.5
14.4	14.3
	15.0
	14.9

43. A client wants to determine whether there is a significant difference in the time required to complete a program evaluation with the three different methods that are in common use. The times (in hours) required for each of 18 evaluators to conduct a program evaluation follow.

Method 1	Method 2	Method 3
68	62	58
74	73	67
65	75	69
76	68	57
77	72	59
72	70	62

Use $\alpha = .05$ and test to see whether there is a significant difference in the time required by the three methods.

44. A sample of 20 engineers employed with a company for three years has been rank-ordered with respect to managerial potential. Some of the engineers attended the company's management-development course, others attended an off-site management-development program at a local university, and the remainder did not attend any program. Use the following rankings and $\alpha = .025$ to test for a significant difference in the managerial potential of the three groups.

No Program	Company Program	Off-Site Program
16	12	7
9	20	1
10	17	4
15	19	2
11	6	3
13	18	8
	14	5

45. Course-evaluation ratings for four instructors follow. Use $\alpha = .05$ and the Kruskal-Wallis test to test for a significant difference in teaching abilities.

Instructor	Course-Evaluation Rating							
Black	88	80	79	68	96	69		
Jennings	87	78	82	85	99	99	85	94
Swanson	88	76	68	82	85	82	84	83	81
Wilson	80	85	56	71	89	87		

46. A sample of 15 students received the following rankings on midterm and final examinations in a statistics course.

Rank		Rank		Rank	
Midterm	**Final**	**Midterm**	**Final**	**Midterm**	**Final**
1	4	6	2	11	14
2	7	7	5	12	15
3	1	8	12	13	11
4	3	9	6	14	10
5	8	10	9	15	13

Compute the Spearman rank correlation coefficient for the data and test for a significant correlation. Use $\alpha = .10$.

CHAPTER 18

Statistical Methods for Quality Control

CONTENTS

STATISTICS IN PRACTICE:
DOW CHEMICAL

18.1 PHILOSOPHIES AND
FRAMEWORKS
Malcolm Baldrige National
Quality Award
ISO 9000
Six Sigma

18.2 STATISTICAL PROCESS
CONTROL
Control Charts
$\bar{x}$ Chart: Process Mean and
Standard Deviation Known
$\bar{x}$ Chart: Process Mean and
Standard Deviation Unknown

R Chart
Using Excel to Construct an
R Chart and an $\bar{x}$ Chart
p Chart
np Chart
Interpretation of Control Charts

18.3 ACCEPTANCE SAMPLING
KALI, Inc.: An Example of
Acceptance Sampling
Computing the Probability of
Accepting a Lot
Selecting an Acceptance
Sampling Plan
Multiple Sampling Plans

STATISTICS *in* PRACTICE

DOW CHEMICAL*
FREEPORT, TEXAS

Dow Chemical, Texas Operations, began in 1940 when The Dow Chemical Company purchased 800 acres of Texas land on the Gulf Coast to build a magnesium production facility. That original site, expanded to cover more than 5000 acres, holds one of the largest petrochemical complexes in the world. Among the products from Texas Operations are magnesium, styrene, plastics, adhesives, solvent, glycol, and chlorine. Some products are made solely for use in other processes, but many end up as essential ingredients in products such as pharmaceuticals, toothpastes, dog food, water hoses, ice chests, milk cartons, garbage bags, shampoos, and furniture.

Dow's Texas Operations produce more than 30% of the world's magnesium, an extremely lightweight metal used in products ranging from tennis rackets to suitcases to "mag" wheels. The Magnesium Department was the first group in Texas Operations to train its technical people and managers in the use of statistical quality control. Some of the earliest successful applications of statistical quality control were in chemical processing.

In one application involving the operation of a dryer, samples of the output were taken at periodic intervals; the average value for each sample was computed and recorded on a chart called an $\bar{x}$ chart. Such a chart enabled Dow analysts to monitor trends in the output that might indicate the process was not operating correctly. In one instance, analysts began to observe values for the sample mean that were not indicative of a process operating within its design limits. On further examination of the

Statistical quality control has enabled Dow Chemical to improve its processing methods and output.
© PhotoDisc, Inc.

control chart and the operation itself, the analysts found that the variation could be traced to problems involving one operator. The $\bar{x}$ chart recorded after retraining of the operator showed a significant improvement in the process quality.

Dow Chemical achieves quality improvements everywhere statistical quality control is applied. Documented savings of several hundred thousand dollars per year are realized, and new applications are continually being discovered.

In this chapter we will show how an $\bar{x}$ chart such as the one used by Dow Chemical can be developed. Such charts are a part of statistical quality control known as statistical process control. We will also discuss methods of quality control for situations in which a decision to accept or reject a group of items is based on a sample.

*The authors are indebted to Clifford B. Wilson, Magnesium Technical Manager, The Dow Chemical Company, for providing this Statistics in Practice.

The American Society for Quality (ASQ) defines quality as "the totality of features and characteristics of a product or service that bears on its ability to satisfy given needs." In other words, quality measures how well a product or service meets customer needs. Organizations recognize that to be competitive in today's global economy, they must strive for a high level of quality. As a result, they place increased emphasis on methods for monitoring and maintaining quality.

Today, the customer-driven focus that is fundamental to high-performing organizations has changed the scope that quality issues encompass, from simply eliminating defects on a production line to developing broad-based corporate quality strategies. Broadening the scope of quality naturally leads to the concept of **total quality (TQ)**.

Total Quality (TQ) is a people-focused management system that aims at continual increase in customer satisfaction at continually lower real cost. TQ is a total system approach (not a separate area or work program) and an integral part of high-level strategy; it works horizontally across function and departments, involves all employees, top to bottom, and extends backward and forward to include the supply chain and the customer chain. TQ stresses learning and adaptation to continual change as keys to organization success.*

Regardless of how it is implemented in different organizations, total quality is based on three fundamental principles: a focus on customers and stakeholders; participation and teamwork throughout the organization; and a focus on continuous improvement and learning. In the first section of the chapter we provide a brief introduction to the three quality management frameworks: the Malcolm Baldrige Quality Award, ISO 9000 standards, and the Six Sigma philosophy. In the last two sections we introduce two statistical tools that can be used to monitor quality: statistical process control and acceptance sampling.

 # Philosophies and Frameworks

Two individuals who have had great influence on quality are Dr. W. Edwards Deming and Joseph Juran. These men helped educate the Japanese in quality management shortly after World War II. Although quality is everybody's job, Deming stressed that the focus on quality must be led by managers. He developed a list of 14 points that he believed represent the key responsibilities of managers. For instance, Deming stated that managers must cease dependence on mass inspection; must end the practice of awarding business solely on the basis of price; must seek continual improvement in all production processes and service; must foster a team-oriented environment; and must eliminate goals, slogans, and work standards that prescribe numerical quotas. Perhaps most important, managers must create a work environment in which a commitment to quality and productivity is maintained at all times.

Juran proposed a simple definition of quality: *fitness for use*. Juran's approach to quality focused on three quality processes: quality planning, quality control, and quality improvement. In contrast to Deming's philosophy, which required a major cultural change in the organization, Juran's programs were designed to improve quality by working within the current organizational system. Nonetheless, the two philosophies are similar in that they both focus on the need for top management to be involved and stress the need for continuous improvement, the importance of training, and the use of quality control techniques.

Many other individuals played significant roles in the quality movement, including Philip B. Crosby, A. V. Feigenbaum, Karou Ishikawa, and Genichi Taguchi. More specialized texts dealing exclusively with quality provide details of the contributions of each of these individuals. The contributions of all individuals involved in the quality movement helped define a set of best practices and led to numerous awards and certification programs. The two most significant programs are the U.S. Malcolm Baldrige National Quality Award and the International ISO 9000 certification process. In recent years, use of Six Sigma—a methodology for improving organizational performance based on rigorous data collection and statistical analysis—has also increased.

Malcolm Baldrige National Quality Award

The Malcolm Baldrige National Quality Award is given by the president of the United States to organizations that apply and are judged to be outstanding in seven areas: leadership; strategic planning; customer and market focus; measurement, analysis, and knowledge management; human resource focus; process management; and business results. Congress established the award program in 1987 to recognize U.S. organizations for their

---

*J. R. Evans and W. M. Lindsay, *The Management and Control of Quality*, 6th ed. (Cincinnati, OH: South-Western, 2005), pp. 18–19.

The U.S. Commerce Department's National Institute of Standards and Technology (NIST) manages the Baldrige National Quality Program. More information can be obtained at www.quality.nist.gov.

achievements in quality and performance and to raise awareness about the importance of quality as a competitive edge. The award is named for Malcolm Baldrige who served as Secretary of Commerce from 1981 until his death in 1987.

Since the presentation of the first awards in 1988, the Baldrige National Quality Program has grown in stature and impact. Approximately 2 million copies of the criteria have been distributed since 1988, and wide-scale reproduction by organizations and electronic access add to that number significantly. For the eighth year in a row, a hypothetical stock index, made up of publicly traded U.S. companies that have received the Baldrige Award, outperformed the Standard & Poor's 500. In 2003, the "Baldrige Index" outperformed the S&P 500 by 4.4 to 1. At the 2003 Baldrige Award Ceremony, Bob Barnett, executive vice president of Motorola, Inc., said, "We applied for the Award, not with the idea of winning, but with the goal of receiving the evaluation of the Baldrige Examiners. That evaluation was comprehensive, professional, and insightful . . . making it perhaps the most cost-effective, value-added business consultation available anywhere in the world today."

ISO 9000

ISO 9000 is a series of five international standards published in 1987 by the International Organization for Standardization (ISO), Geneva, Switzerland. Companies can use the standards to help determine what is needed to maintain an efficient quality conformance system. For example, the standards describe the need for an effective quality system, for ensuring that measuring and testing equipment is calibrated regularly, and for maintaining an adequate record-keeping system. ISO 9000 registration determines whether a company complies with its own quality system. Overall, ISO 9000 registration covers less than 10% of the Baldrige Award criteria.

Six Sigma

In the late 1980s Motorola recognized the need to improve the quality of its products and services; their goal was to achieve a level of quality so good that, for every million opportunities, no more than 3.4 defects will occur. This level of quality is referred to as the six sigma level of quality, and the methodology created to reach this quality goal is referred to as **Six Sigma**.

An organization may undertake two kinds of Six Sigma projects:

- DMAIC (Define, Measure, Analyze, Improve, and Control) to help redesign existing processes
- DFSS (Design for Six Sigma) to design new products, processes, or services

In helping to redesign existing processes and design new processes, Six Sigma places a heavy emphasis on statistical analysis and careful measurement. Today, Six Sigma is a major tool in helping organizations achieve Baldrige levels of business performance and process quality. Many Baldrige examiners view Six Sigma as the ideal approach for implementing Baldrige improvement programs.

Six Sigma Limits and Defects per Million Opportunities   In Six Sigma terminology, a *defect* is any mistake or error that is passed on to the customer. The Six Sigma process defines quality performance as defects per million opportunities (dpmo). As we indicated previously, Six Sigma represents a quality level of at most 3.4 dpmo. To illustrate how this quality level is measured, let us consider the situation at KJW Packaging.

KJW operates a production line where boxes of cereal are filled. The filling process has a mean of $\mu = 16.05$ ounces and a standard deviation of $\sigma = .10$ ounces. In addition, assume the filling weights are normally distributed. The distribution of filling weights is shown in Figure 18.1. Suppose management considers 15.45 to 16.65 ounces to be acceptable quality

FIGURE 18.1   NORMAL DISTRIBUTION OF CEREAL BOX FILLING WEIGHTS
WITH A PROCESS MEAN $\mu = 16.05$

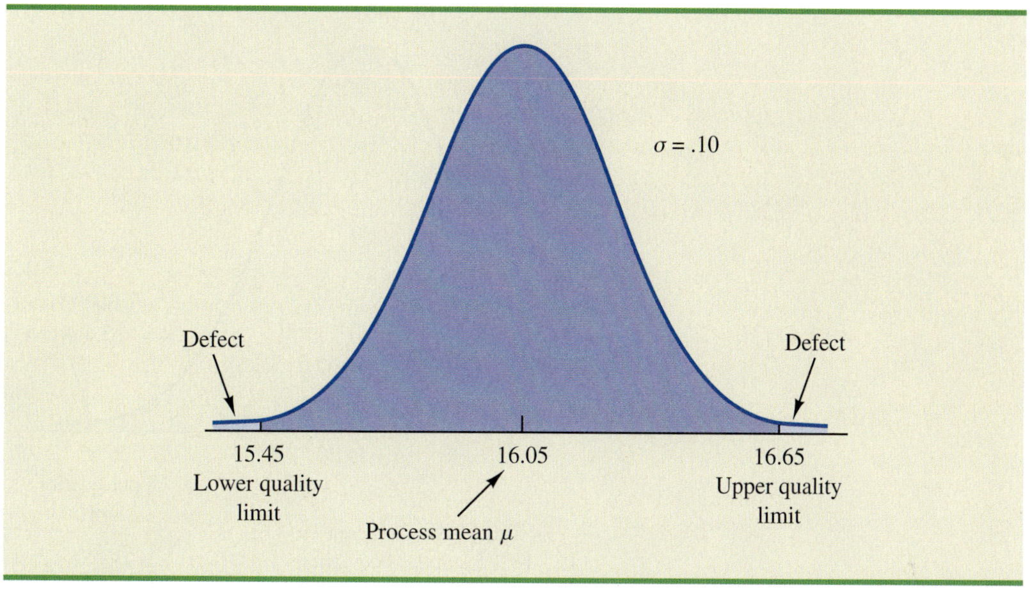

$\sigma = .10$

Defect   Defect

15.45	16.05	16.65
Lower quality limit		Upper quality limit

Process mean μ

*Using Excel,
NORMSDIST(6) −
NORMSDIST(−6) =
0.999999998.*

limits for the filling process. Thus, any box of cereal that contains less than 15.45 or more than 16.65 ounces is considered to be a defect. Using Excel's NORMSDIST function it can be shown that 99.9999998% of the boxes filled will have between $16.05 - 6(.10) = 15.45$ ounces and $16.05 + 6(.10) = 16.65$ ounces. In other words, only .0000002% of the boxes filled will contain less than 15.45 ounces or more than 16.65 ounces. Thus, the likelihood of obtaining a defective box of cereal from the filling process appears to be extremely unlikely, because on average only two boxes in 10 million will be defective.

Motorola's early work on Six Sigma convinced them that a process mean can shift on average by as much as 1.5 standard deviations. For instance, suppose that the process mean for KJW increases by 1.5 standard deviations or $1.5(.10) = .15$ ounces. With such a shift, the normal distribution of filling weights would now be centered at $\mu = 16.05 + .15 = 16.20$ ounces. With a process mean of $\mu = 16.05$ ounces, the probability of obtaining a box of cereal with more than 16.65 ounces is extremely small. But how does this probability change if the mean of the process shifts up to $\mu = 16.20$ ounces? Figure 18.2 shows that for this case, the upper quality limit of 16.65 is 4.5 standard deviations to the right of the new

*Using Excel, 1 −
NORMSDIST(4.5) =
0.0000034.*

mean $\mu = 16.20$ ounces. Using this mean and Excel's NORMSDIST function we find that the probability of obtaining a box with more than 16.65 ounces is .0000034. Thus, if the process mean shifts up by 1.5 standard deviations, approximately $1,000,000(.0000034) = 3.4$ boxes of cereal will exceed the upper limit of 16.65 ounces. Using Six Sigma terminology, the quality level of the process is said to be 3.4 defects per million opportunities. If management of KJW considers 15.45 to 16.65 ounces to be acceptable quality limits for the filling process, the KJW filling process would be considered a Six Sigma process. Thus, if the process mean stays within 1.5 standard deviations of its target value $\mu = 16.05$ ounces, a maximum of only 3.4 defects per million boxes filled can be expected.

Organizations that want to achieve and maintain a Six Sigma level of quality must emphasize methods for monitoring and maintaining quality. *Quality assurance* refers to the entire system of policies, procedures, and guidelines established by an organization to achieve and maintain quality. Quality assurance consists of two principal functions: quality engineering and quality control. The object of *quality engineering* is to include quality in the

FIGURE 18.2   NORMAL DISTRIBUTION OF CEREAL BOX FILLING WEIGHTS
WITH A PROCESS MEAN $\mu = 16.20$

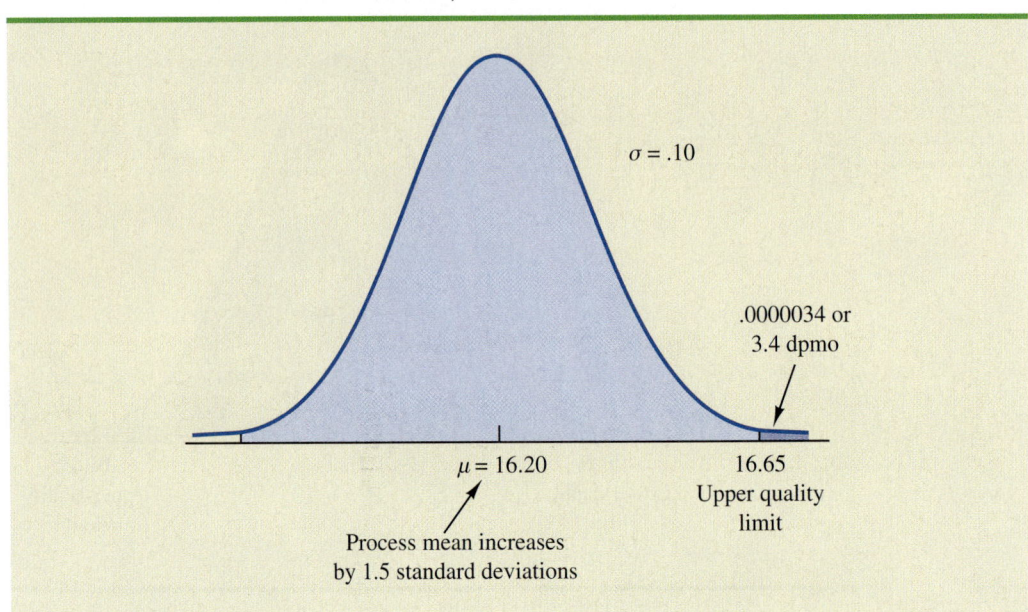

design of products and processes and to identify quality problems prior to production.
Quality control consists of a series of inspections and measurements used to determine
whether quality standards are being met. If quality standards are not being met, corrective
or preventive action can be taken to achieve and maintain conformance. In the next two sections we present two statistical methods used in quality control. The first method, *statistical process control,* uses graphical displays known as control charts to monitor a process;
the goal is to determine whether the process can be continued or whether corrective action
should be taken to achieve a desired quality level. The second method, *acceptance sampling,* is used in situations where a decision to accept or reject a group of items must be
based on the quality found in a sample.

 ## Statistical Process Control

In this section we consider quality control procedures for a production process whereby
goods are manufactured continuously. On the basis of sampling and inspection of production output, a decision will be made to either continue the production process or adjust it to
bring the items or goods being produced up to acceptable quality standards.

Despite high standards of quality in manufacturing and production operations, machine
tools invariably wear out, vibrations throw machine settings out of adjustment, purchased
materials contain defects, and human operators make mistakes. Any or all of these factors
can result in poor quality output. Fortunately, procedures available to monitor production
output help detect poor quality early, which allows for the adjustment and correction of the
production process.

If the variation in the quality of the production output is due to **assignable causes** such
as tools wearing out, incorrect machine settings, poor quality raw materials, or operator
error, the process should be adjusted or corrected as soon as possible. Alternatively, if the
variation results from **common causes**—that is, randomly occurring variations in materials, temperature, humidity, and so on, which the manufacturer cannot possibly control—

the process does not need to be adjusted. The main objective of statistical process control is to determine whether variations in output are due to assignable causes or common causes.

Whenever assignable causes are detected, we conclude that the process is *out of control.* In that case, corrective action should be taken to bring the process back to an acceptable level of quality. However, if the variation in the output of a production process is due only to common causes, we conclude that the process is in *statistical control,* or simply *in control;* in such cases, no changes or adjustments are necessary.

Process control procedures are closely related to hypothesis testing procedures discussed earlier in this text. Control charts provide an ongoing test of the hypothesis that the process is in control.

The statistical procedures for process control are based on the hypothesis testing methodology presented in Chapter 9. The null hypothesis H_0 is formulated in terms of the production process being in control. The alternative hypothesis H_a is formulated in terms of the production process being out of control. Table 18.1 shows that correct decisions correspond to continuing an in-control process and adjusting an out-of-control process. However, as with other hypothesis testing procedures, both a Type I error (adjusting an in-control process) and a Type II error (allowing an out-of-control process to continue) are possible.

Control Charts

A **control chart** provides a basis for deciding whether the variation in the output is due to common causes (in control) or assignable causes (out of control). Whenever an out-of-control situation is detected, adjustments or other corrective action will be taken to bring the process back into control.

Control charts based on data that can be measured on a continuous scale are called variables control charts. The $\bar{x}$ chart is a variables control chart.

Control charts can be classified by the type of data they contain. An $\bar{x}$ **chart** is used if the quality of the output is measured in terms of a variable such as length, weight, temperature, and so on. In that case, the decision to continue or to adjust the production process will be based on the mean value found in a sample of the output. To introduce some of the concepts common to all control charts, let us consider some specific features of an $\bar{x}$ chart.

Figure 18.3 shows the general structure of an $\bar{x}$ chart. The center line of the chart corresponds to the mean of the process when the process is in control. The vertical axis measures $\bar{x}$ for the variable of interest. Each time a sample is taken from the production process, a value of the sample mean $\bar{x}$ is computed and a data point showing the value of $\bar{x}$ is plotted on the control chart.

The two lines labeled UCL and LCL are important in determining whether the process is in control or out of control. The lines are called the *upper control limit* and the *lower control limit,* respectively. They are chosen so that when the process is in control, there will be a high probability that the value of $\bar{x}$ will be between the two control limits. Values outside the control limits provide strong statistical evidence that the process is out of control and corrective action should be taken.

TABLE 18.1   DECISIONS AND STATES OF THE PROCESS

		State of Production Process	
		H_0 True Process in Control	H_0 False Process Out of Control
Decision	**Continue Process**	Correct decision	Type II error (allowing an out-of-control process to continue)
	Adjust Process	Type I error (adjusting an in-control process)	Correct decision

FIGURE 18.3   GENERAL STRUCTURE OF AN $\bar{x}$ CHART

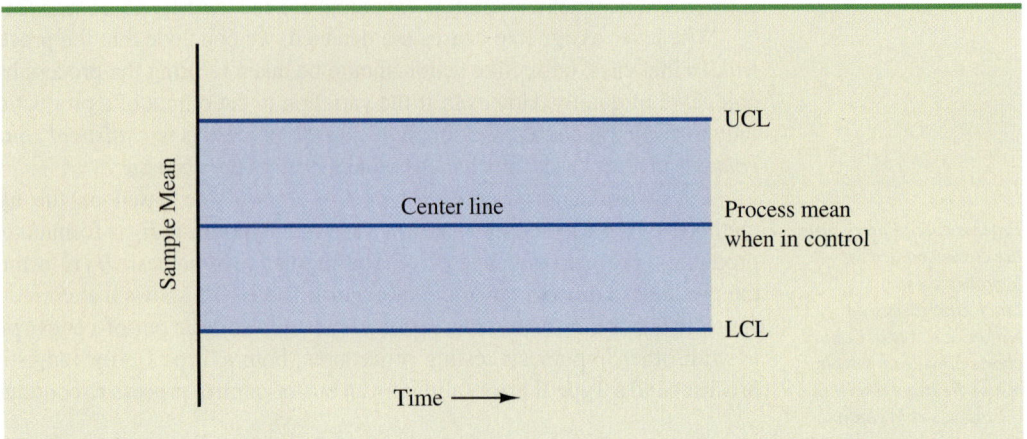

Over time, more and more data points ($\bar{x}$ values) will be added to the control chart. The order of the data points will be from left to right as the process is sampled. In essence, every time a point is plotted on the control chart, we are carrying out a hypothesis test to determine whether the process is in control.

In addition to the $\bar{x}$ chart, other control charts can be used to monitor the range of the measurements in the sample (R chart), the proportion of defective items in the sample (p chart), and the number of defective items in the sample (np chart). In each case, the control chart contains a LCL line, a center line, and a UCL line similar to the $\bar{x}$ chart in Figure 18.3. The major difference among the charts is what the vertical axis measures; for instance, in a p chart the vertical axis denotes the proportion of defective items in the sample instead of the sample mean. In the following discussion, we will illustrate the construction and use of the $\bar{x}$ chart, R chart, p chart, and np chart.

$\bar{x}$ Chart: Process Mean and Standard Deviation Known

We will use the KJW Packaging example introduced in Section 18.1 to illustrate the construction of an $\bar{x}$ chart. Recall that KJW operates a production line that fills cereal boxes. They designed the process so that when it is operating correctly—and hence the system is in control—the mean filling weight is $\mu = 16.05$ ounces and the process standard deviation is $\sigma = .10$ ounces. In addition, assume the filling weights (x) are normally distributed. The normal probability distribution of filling weights is shown in Figure 18.4.

The sampling distribution of $\bar{x}$, as presented in Chapter 7, can be used to determine the expected variation in $\bar{x}$ values for a process that is in control. Let us first briefly review the properties of the sampling distribution of $\bar{x}$. First, recall that $E(\bar{x})$, the expected value or mean of $\bar{x}$, is equal to μ, the mean filling weight when the production process is in control. For samples of size n, the formula for the standard deviation of $\bar{x}$, called the *standard error of the mean,* is

$$\sigma_{\bar{x}} = \frac{\sigma}{\sqrt{n}}$$

(18.1)

In addition, because the filling weights (x) are normally distributed, the sampling distribution of $\bar{x}$ is normal for any sample size. Thus, the sampling distribution of $\bar{x}$ is a normal probability distribution with mean μ and standard deviation $\sigma_{\bar{x}}$. This probability distribu-

FIGURE 18.4 NORMAL PROBABILITY DISTRIBUTION OF CEREAL BOX FILLING WEIGHTS WHEN THE PROCESS IS IN CONTROL

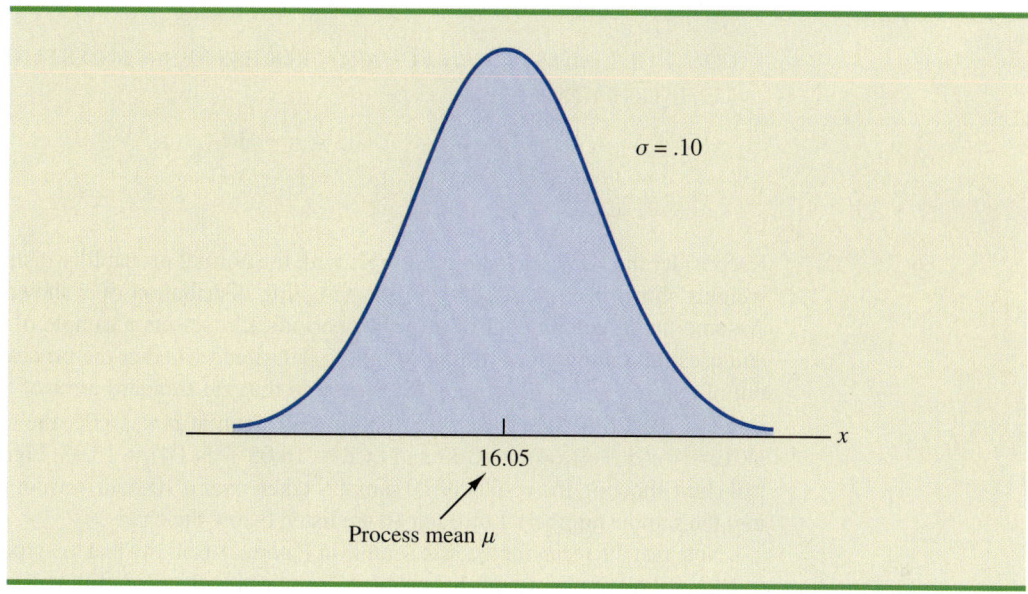

tion is shown in Figure 18.5. Note that the sampling distribution of $\bar{x}$ has the same mean (16.05) as the probability distribution of individual filling weights.

The sampling distribution of $\bar{x}$ is used to determine what values of $\bar{x}$ are reasonable if the process is in control. The general practice in quality control is to define as reasonable any value of $\bar{x}$ that is within 3 standard deviations above or below the mean value μ. Recall from the study of the normal probability distribution that approximately 99.7% of the values of a normally distributed random variable are within ± 3 standard deviations of its mean value. Thus, if a value of $\bar{x}$ is within the interval $\mu - 3\sigma_{\bar{x}}$ to $\mu + 3\sigma_{\bar{x}}$, we will

FIGURE 18.5   SAMPLING DISTRIBUTION OF $\bar{x}$ FOR A SAMPLE OF n FILLING WEIGHTS

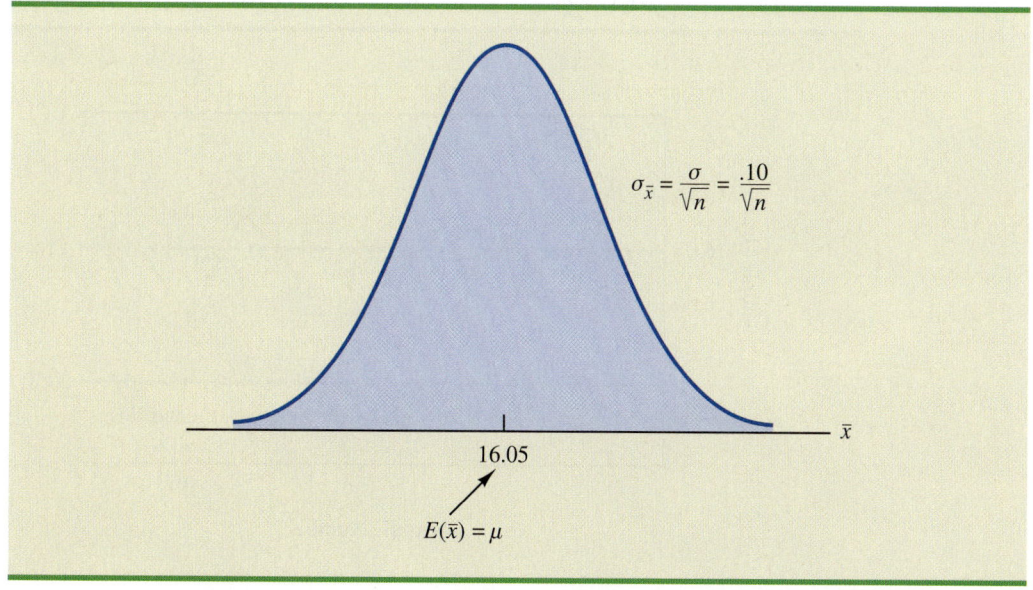

assume that the process is in control. In summary, then, the control limits for an $\bar{x}$ chart are as follows.

CONTROL LIMITS FOR AN $\bar{x}$ CHART: PROCESS MEAN AND STANDARD DEVIATION KNOWN

$$UCL = \mu + 3\sigma_{\bar{x}} \qquad \textbf{(18.2)}$$
$$LCL = \mu - 3\sigma_{\bar{x}} \qquad \textbf{(18.3)}$$

Reconsider the KJW Packaging example with the normal probability distribution of filling weights shown in Figure 18.4 and the sampling distribution of $\bar{x}$ shown in Figure 18.5. Assume that a quality control inspector periodically selects a sample of six cereal boxes and uses the sample mean filling weight to determine whether the process is in control or out of control. Using equation (18.1), we find that the standard error of the mean is $\sigma_{\bar{x}} = \sigma/\sqrt{n} = .10/\sqrt{6} = .04$. Thus, with the process mean at $\mu = 16.05$, the control limits are UCL = $16.05 + 3(.04) = 16.17$ and LCL = $16.05 - 3(.04) = 15.93$. Figure 18.6 is a control chart showing the results of 10 samples taken over a 10-hour period. For ease of reading, the sample numbers 1 through 10 are listed below the chart.

Note that the mean for the fifth sample in Figure 18.6 shows that the process is out of control. The fifth sample mean is below the LCL indicating that underfilling is occurring and that assignable causes of output variation are present. As a result, corrective action was taken at this point to bring the process back into control. The fact that the remaining points on the $\bar{x}$ chart are within the upper and lower control limits indicates that the corrective action was successful.

$\bar{x}$ Chart: Process Mean and Standard Deviation Unknown

In the KJW Packaging example, we showed how an $\bar{x}$ chart can be developed when the mean and standard deviation of the process are known before sampling. In many situations, the process mean and standard deviation must be estimated by using samples that are selected from the process when it is assumed to be operating in control. For instance, KJW might select a random sample of five boxes each morning and five boxes each afternoon for 10 days of operation. For

FIGURE 18.6 $\bar{x}$ CHART FOR THE CEREAL BOX FILLING PROCESS

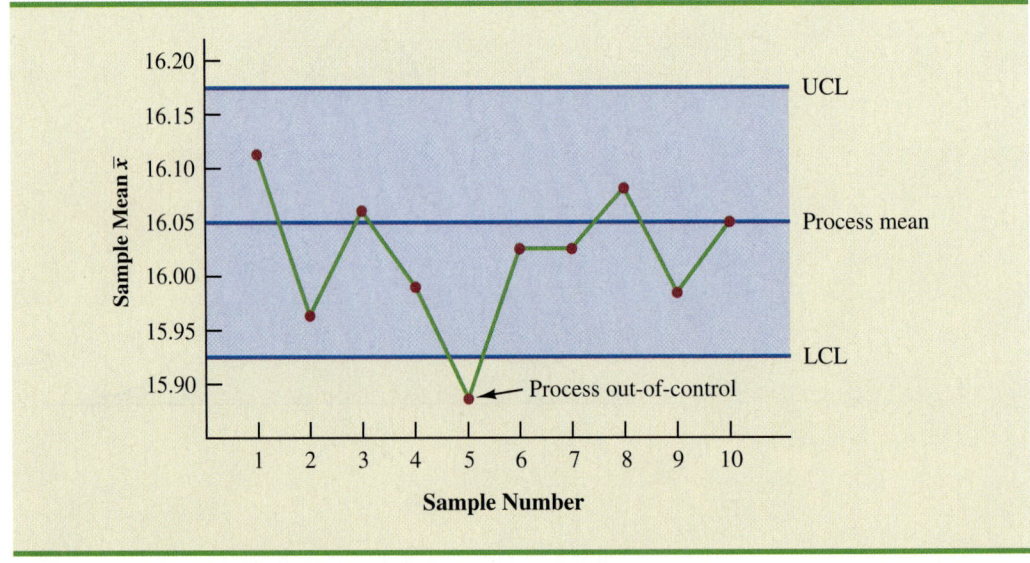

each subgroup, or sample, the mean and standard deviation of the sample are computed. The overall averages of both the sample means and the sample standard deviations can then be used to construct control charts for both the process mean and the process standard deviation.

In practice, it is common to monitor the variability of a production process by using the range instead of the standard deviation because the range is easier to compute. The range can then be used to provide good estimates of the process standard deviation; thus it can be used to construct upper and lower control limits for the $\bar{x}$ chart with little computational effort. To illustrate, let us consider the problem facing Jensen Computer Supplies, Inc.

Jensen Computer Supplies (JCS) manufactures 3.5-inch-diameter computer disks; they have just finished adjusting their production process so that it is operating in control. Suppose random samples of five disks are taken during the first hour of operation, during the second hour of operation, and so on, until 20 samples have been selected. Table 18.2 provides the diameter of each disk sampled as well as the mean $\bar{x}_j$ and range R_j for each of the samples.

The estimate of the process mean μ developed using k samples of size n is given by the overall sample mean.

OVERALL SAMPLE MEAN

$$\bar{\bar{x}} = \frac{\bar{x}_1 + \bar{x}_2 + \cdots + \bar{x}_k}{k} \tag{18.4}$$

where

$$\bar{x}_j = \text{mean of the } j\text{th sample } j = 1, 2, \ldots, k$$
$$k = \text{number of samples}$$

TABLE 18.2   DATA FOR JENSEN COMPUTER SUPPLIES

Sample Number	Observations					Sample Mean $\bar{x}_j$	Sample Range R_j
1	3.5056	3.5086	3.5144	3.5009	3.5030	3.5065	.0135
2	3.4882	3.5085	3.4884	3.5250	3.5031	3.5026	.0368
3	3.4897	3.4898	3.4995	3.5130	3.4969	3.4978	.0233
4	3.5153	3.5120	3.4989	3.4900	3.4837	3.5000	.0316
5	3.5059	3.5113	3.5011	3.4773	3.4801	3.4951	.0340
6	3.4977	3.4961	3.5050	3.5014	3.5060	3.5012	.0099
7	3.4910	3.4913	3.4976	3.4831	3.5044	3.4935	.0213
8	3.4991	3.4853	3.4830	3.5083	3.5094	3.4970	.0264
9	3.5099	3.5162	3.5228	3.4958	3.5004	3.5090	.0270
10	3.4880	3.5015	3.5094	3.5102	3.5146	3.5047	.0266
11	3.4881	3.4887	3.5141	3.5175	3.4863	3.4989	.0312
12	3.5043	3.4867	3.4946	3.5018	3.4784	3.4932	.0259
13	3.5043	3.4769	3.4944	3.5014	3.4904	3.4935	.0274
14	3.5004	3.5030	3.5082	3.5045	3.5234	3.5079	.0230
15	3.4846	3.4938	3.5065	3.5089	3.5011	3.4990	.0243
16	3.5145	3.4832	3.5188	3.4935	3.4989	3.5018	.0356
17	3.5004	3.5042	3.4954	3.5020	3.4889	3.4982	.0153
18	3.4959	3.4823	3.4964	3.5082	3.4871	3.4940	.0259
19	3.4878	3.4864	3.4960	3.5070	3.4984	3.4951	.0206
20	3.4969	3.5144	3.5053	3.4985	3.4885	3.5007	.0259

For the JCS data in Table 18.2, $k = 20$ and the overall sample mean is $\bar{\bar{x}} = 3.4995$. This value will be the center line for the $\bar{x}$ chart. The range of each sample, denoted R_j, is simply the difference between the largest and smallest values in each sample. The average range for k samples is computed as follows.

AVERAGE RANGE

$$\bar{R} = \frac{R_1 + R_2 + \cdots + R_k}{k} \tag{18.5}$$

where

$$R_j = \text{range of the } j\text{th sample}, j = 1, 2, \ldots, k$$
$$k = \text{number of samples}$$

For the JCS data in Table 18.2, the average range is $\bar{R} = .0253$.

In the preceding section we showed that the upper and lower control limits for the $\bar{x}$ chart are

$$\mu \pm 3 \frac{\sigma}{\sqrt{n}} \tag{18.6}$$

The overall sample mean $\bar{\bar{x}}$ is used to estimate μ and the sample ranges are used to develop an estimate of σ.
Hence, to construct the control limits for the $\bar{x}$ chart, we need to estimate μ and σ, the mean and standard deviation of the process. An estimate of μ is given by $\bar{\bar{x}}$. An estimate of σ can be developed by using the range data.

It can be shown that an estimator of the process standard deviation σ is the average range divided by d_2, a constant that depends on the sample size n. That is,

$$\text{Estimator of } \sigma = \frac{\bar{R}}{d_2} \tag{18.7}$$

The *American Society for Testing and Materials Manual on Presentation of Data and Control Chart Analysis* provides values for d_2 as shown in Table 18.3. For instance, when $n = 5$, $d_2 = 2.326$, and the estimate of σ is the average range divided by 2.326. If we substitute $\bar{\bar{x}}$ for μ and $\bar{R}/d_2$ for σ in equation (18.6), we can write the control limits for the $\bar{x}$ chart as

$$\bar{\bar{x}} \pm 3 \frac{\bar{R}/d_2}{\sqrt{n}} = \bar{\bar{x}} \pm \frac{3}{d_2\sqrt{n}} \bar{R} = \bar{\bar{x}} \pm A_2\bar{R} \tag{18.8}$$

Note that $A_2 = 3/(d_2\sqrt{n})$ is a constant that depends only on the sample size. Values for A_2 are also provided in Table 18.3. For $n = 5$, $A_2 = .577$; thus, the control limits for Jensen's $\bar{x}$ chart are

$$3.4995 \pm (.577)(.0253) = 3.4995 \pm .0146$$

Hence, UCL $= 3.514$ and LCL $= 3.485$.

Figure 18.7 shows the $\bar{x}$ chart for Jensen Computer Supplies. One can use the data in Table 18.2 and Excel's Chart Wizard to construct the chart. The center line is shown at the

TABLE 18.3   FACTORS FOR $\bar{x}$ AND R CONTROL CHARTS

Observations in Sample, n	d_2	A_2	d_3	D_3	D_4
2	1.128	1.880	0.853	0	3.267
3	1.693	1.023	0.888	0	2.574
4	2.059	0.729	0.880	0	2.282
5	2.326	0.577	0.864	0	2.114
6	2.534	0.483	0.848	0	2.004
7	2.704	0.419	0.833	0.076	1.924
8	2.847	0.373	0.820	0.136	1.864
9	2.970	0.337	0.808	0.184	1.816
10	3.078	0.308	0.797	0.223	1.777
11	3.173	0.285	0.787	0.256	1.744
12	3.258	0.266	0.778	0.283	1.717
13	3.336	0.249	0.770	0.307	1.693
14	3.407	0.235	0.763	0.328	1.672
15	3.472	0.223	0.756	0.347	1.653
16	3.532	0.212	0.750	0.363	1.637
17	3.588	0.203	0.744	0.378	1.622
18	3.640	0.194	0.739	0.391	1.608
19	3.689	0.187	0.734	0.403	1.597
20	3.735	0.180	0.729	0.415	1.585
21	3.778	0.173	0.724	0.425	1.575
22	3.819	0.167	0.720	0.434	1.566
23	3.858	0.162	0.716	0.443	1.557
24	3.895	0.157	0.712	0.451	1.548
25	3.931	0.153	0.708	0.459	1.541

Source: Adapted from Table 27 of ASTM STP 15D, *ASTM Manual on Presentation of Data and Control Chart Analysis.* Copyright © 1976 American Society of Testing and Materials, Philadelphia, PA. Reprinted with permission.

overall sample mean $\bar{\bar{x}} = 3.499$. The upper control limit (UCL) is 3.514, which is 3 "sigma limits" above $\bar{\bar{x}}$. The lower control limit (LCL) is 3.485, which is 3 "sigma limits" below $\bar{\bar{x}}$. The $\bar{x}$ chart shows the 20 sample means plotted over time. Because all 20 sample means fall within the control limits, our assumption is confirmed that the data were collected during a period the process was in control. This chart can now be used to monitor the process mean on an ongoing basis.

R Chart

Let us now consider a range chart or **R chart** that can be used to control the variability of a process. To develop the R chart, we need to think of the range of a sample as a random variable with its own mean and standard deviation. The average range $\bar{R}$ provides an estimate of the mean of this random variable. Moreover, it can be shown that an estimate of the standard deviation of the range, denoted $\hat{\sigma}_R$, is

$$\hat{\sigma}_R = d_3 \frac{\bar{R}}{d_2}$$

(18.9)

FIGURE 18.7 $\bar{x}$ CHART FOR JENSEN COMPUTER SUPPLIES

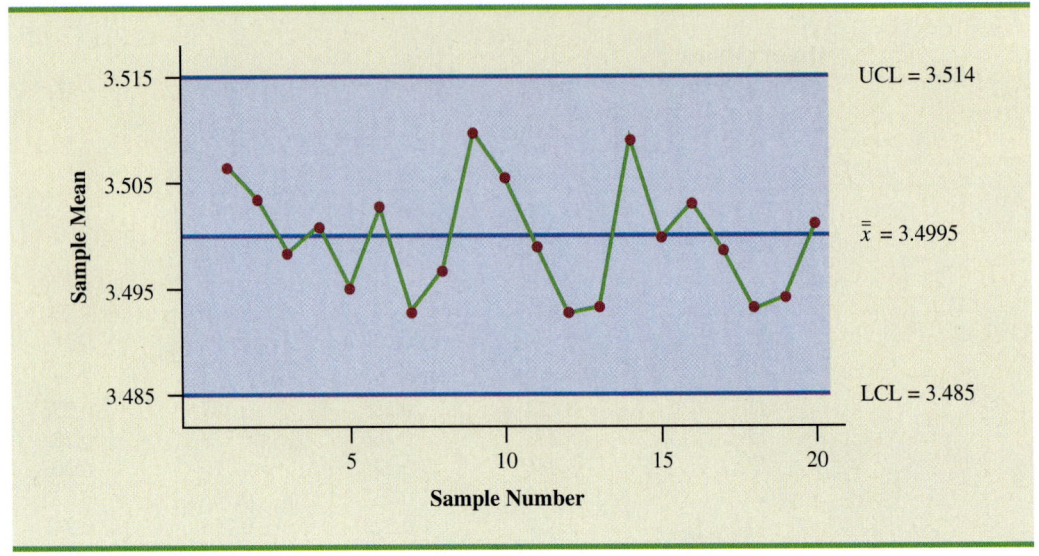

where d_2 and d_3 are constants that depend on the sample size; values of d_2 and d_3 are provided in Table 18.3. Thus, the UCL for the R chart is given by

$$\bar{R} + 3\hat{\sigma}_R = \bar{R} + 3d_3 \frac{\bar{R}}{d_2} = \bar{R}\left(1 + 3\frac{d_3}{d_2}\right) \tag{18.10}$$

and the LCL is

$$\bar{R} - 3\hat{\sigma}_R = \bar{R} - 3d_3 \frac{\bar{R}}{d_2} = \bar{R}\left(1 - 3\frac{d_3}{d_2}\right) \tag{18.11}$$

If we let

$$D_4 = 1 + 3\frac{d_3}{d_2} \tag{18.12}$$

$$D_3 = 1 - 3\frac{d_3}{d_2} \tag{18.13}$$

we can write the control limits for the R chart as

$$UCL = \bar{R}D_4 \tag{18.14}$$
$$LCL = \bar{R}D_3 \tag{18.15}$$

Values for D_3 and D_4 are also provided in Table 18.3. Note that for $n = 5$, $D_3 = 0$ and $D_4 = 2.114$. Thus, with $\bar{R} = .0253$, the control limits are

$$UCL = .0253(2.114) = .0535$$
$$LCL = .0253(0) = 0$$

If the R chart indicates that the process is out of control, the $\bar{x}$ chart should not be interpreted until the R chart indicates the process variability is in control.

Figure 18.8 shows the R chart for Jensen Computer Supplies. One can use the data in Table 18.2 and Excel's Chart Wizard to construct the chart. The center line is shown at the overall mean of the 20 sample ranges, $\bar{R} = .0253$. The UCL is .0535 or 3 sigma limits above $\bar{R}$. The LCL is 0.0 or 3 sigma limits below $\bar{R}$. The R chart shows the 20 sample ranges plotted over time. Because all 20 sample ranges are within the control limits, we confirm that the process was in control during the sampling period.

Using Excel to Construct an R Chart and an $\bar{x}$ Chart

The $\bar{x}$ chart in Figure 18.7 and the R chart in Figure 18.8 can be constructed using Excel. Here we show how the data in Table 18.2 can be used to construct an R chart and an $\bar{x}$ chart using Excel. Figure 18.9 is an Excel worksheet containing the Jensen Computer Supplies data. The average value for the range is needed to compute the lower and upper control limits for the $\bar{x}$ chart. So we will construct the R chart first. Our approach will be to first develop a worksheet with the needed data. Then the Chart Wizard will be used to develop the R chart. A similar procedure is followed to construct the $\bar{x}$ chart. Figure 18.10 contains the data developed for the R chart. The formula worksheet is in the background; the value worksheet appears in the foreground.

Enter Data: The data for the diameter measurements for the 20 samples selected by Jensen Computer Supplies are contained in the worksheet in Figure 18.9. We will use the data in this worksheet to construct the worksheets shown in Figures 18.10 and 18.11. For future reference, the worksheet in Figure 18.9 is named Data. The only values entered directly into the worksheets in Figures 18.10 and 18.11 are the sample numbers 1–20 in column A, the heading in cells A1:E1, and cells C23 and C24.

Enter Functions and Formulas: The worksheet in Figure 18.10 contains the formulas needed to construct an R chart using the Chart Wizard. Here we describe how this worksheet was constructed. Column A contains the sample numbers 1–20 as noted. Column B contains the Excel formulas needed to compute the range for each sample from the data in

FIGURE 18.8 R CHART FOR JENSEN COMPUTER SUPPLIES

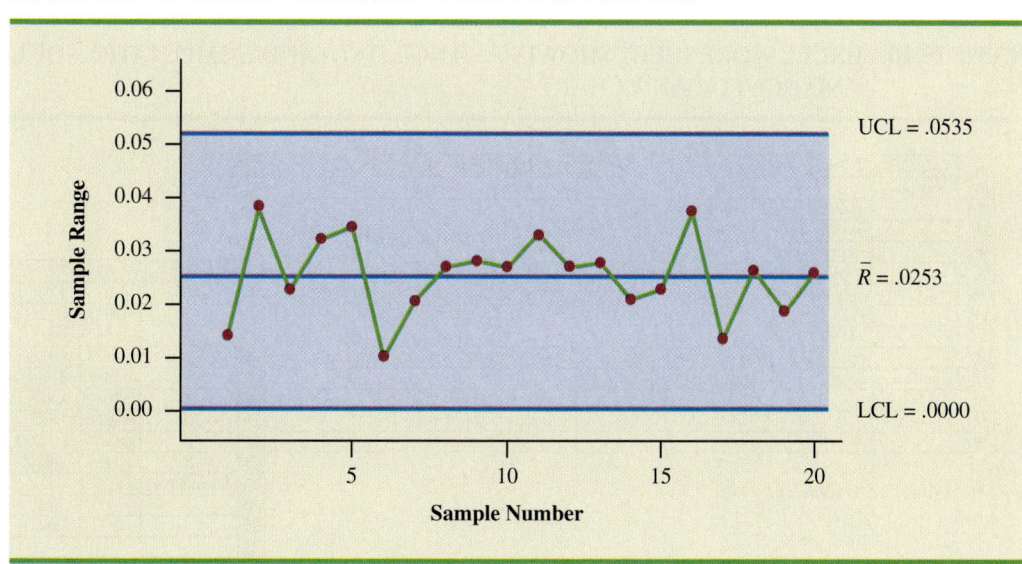

FIGURE 18.9 EXCEL DATA WORKSHEET FOR JENSEN COMPUTER SUPPLIES

	A	B	C	D	E	F	G
1	Sample	Observation 1	Observation 2	Observation 3	Observation 4	Observation 5	
2	1	3.5056	3.5086	3.5144	3.5009	3.5030	
3	2	3.4882	3.5085	3.4884	3.5250	3.5031	
4	3	3.4897	3.4898	3.4995	3.5130	3.4969	
5	4	3.5153	3.5120	3.4989	3.4900	3.4837	
6	5	3.5059	3.5113	3.5011	3.4773	3.4801	
7	6	3.4977	3.4961	3.5050	3.5014	3.5060	
8	7	3.4910	3.4913	3.4976	3.4831	3.5044	
9	8	3.4991	3.4853	3.4830	3.5083	3.5094	
10	9	3.5099	3.5162	3.5228	3.4958	3.5004	
11	10	3.4880	3.5015	3.5094	3.5102	3.5146	
12	11	3.4881	3.4887	3.5141	3.5175	3.4863	
13	12	3.5043	3.4867	3.4946	3.5018	3.4784	
14	13	3.5043	3.4769	3.4944	3.5014	3.4904	
15	14	3.5004	3.5030	3.5082	3.5045	3.5234	
16	15	3.4846	3.4938	3.5065	3.5089	3.5011	
17	16	3.5145	3.4832	3.5188	3.4935	3.4989	
18	17	3.5004	3.5042	3.4954	3.5020	3.4889	
19	18	3.4959	3.4823	3.4964	3.5082	3.4871	
20	19	3.4878	3.4864	3.4960	3.5070	3.4984	
21	20	3.4969	3.5144	3.5053	3.4985	3.4885	
22							

cells B2:F21 of the Data worksheet shown in Figure 18.9. Excel's MAX and MIN functions are used. The cell references in the formulas are to cells in the Data worksheet; note that the worksheet name followed by an exclamation point must precede a cell reference when the cells referenced are in another worksheet of the same workbook. The value worksheet shows that the ranges computed are the same as in Table 18.2. The AVERAGE function used in cell B22 computes the average of the ranges for the 20 samples.

FIGURE 18.10 EXCEL WORKSHEET SHOWING RANGE DATA AND COMPUTATION OF LCL, MEAN, AND UCL FOR AN R CHART

	A	B	C	D	E	F
1	Sample	R	LCL	Mean	UCL	
2	1	=MAX(Data!B2:F2)-MIN(Data!B2:F2)	=$D$23*$B$22	=$B$22	=$D$24*$B$22	
3	2	=MAX(Data!B3:F3)-MIN(Data!B3:F3)	=$D$23*$B$22	=$B$22	=$D$24*$B$22	
4	3	=MAX(Data!B4:F4)-MIN(Data!B4:F4)	=$D$23*$B$22	=$B$22	=$D$24*$B$22	
5	4	=MAX(Data!B5:F5)-MIN(Data!B5:F5)	=$D$23*$B$22	=$B$22	=$D$24*$B$22	
6	5	=MAX(Data!B6:F6)-MIN(Data!B6:F6)	=$D$23*$B$22	=$B$22	=$D$24*$B$22	
19	18	=MAX(Data!B19:F19)-MIN(Data!B19:F19)	=$D$23*$B$22	=$B$22	=$D$24*$B$22	
20	19	=MAX(Data!B20:F20)-MIN(Data!B20:F20)	=$D$23*$B$22	=$B$22	=$D$24*$B$22	
21	20	=MAX(Data!B21:F21)-MIN(Data!B21:F21)	=$D$23*$B$22	=$B$22	=$D$24*$B$22	
22	Mean(Rbar)	=AVERAGE($B$2:$B$21)				
23			D3	0		
24			D4	2.114		
25						

	A	B	C	D	E	F
1	Sample	R	LCL	Mean	UCL	
2	1	0.0135	0.0000	0.0253	0.0534	
3	2	0.0368	0.0000	0.0253	0.0534	
4	3	0.0233	0.0000	0.0253	0.0534	
5	4	0.0316	0.0000	0.0253	0.0534	
6	5	0.0340	0.0000	0.0253	0.0534	
19	18	0.0259	0.0000	0.0253	0.0534	
20	19	0.0206	0.0000	0.0253	0.0534	
21	20	0.0259	0.0000	0.0253	0.0534	
22	Mean(Rbar)	0.0253				
23			D3	0.0000		
24			D4	2.1140		
25						

Note: Rows 7–18 (samples 6–17) are hidden.

FIGURE 18.11   EXCEL WORKSHEET SHOWING $\bar{x}$ DATA AND COMPUTATION OF LCL, MEAN, AND UCL

	A	B	C	D	E	F
1	Sample	xbar	LCL	Mean	UCL	
2	1	=AVERAGE(Data!B2:F2)	=$B$22-$D$23*$D$24	=$B$22	=$B$22+$D$23*$D$24	
3	2	=AVERAGE(Data!B3:F3)	=$B$22-$D$23*$D$24	=$B$22	=$B$22+$D$23*$D$24	
4	3	=AVERAGE(Data!B4:F4)	=$B$22-$D$23*$D$24	=$B$22	=$B$22+$D$23*$D$24	
5	4	=AVERAGE(Data!B5:F5)	=$B$22-$D$23*$D$24	=$B$22	=$B$22+$D$23*$D$24	
6	5	=AVERAGE(Data!B6:F6)	=$B$22-$D$23*$D$24	=$B$22	=$B$22+$D$23*$D$24	
19	18	=AVERAGE(Data!B19:F19)	=$B$22-$D$23*$D$24	=$B$22	=$B$22+$D$23*$D$24	
20	19	=AVERAGE(Data!B20:F20)	=$B$22-$D$23*$D$24	=$B$22	=$B$22+$D$23*$D$24	
21	20	=AVERAGE(Data!B21:F21)	=$B$22-$D$23*$D$24	=$B$22	=$B$22+$D$23*$D$24	
22	Mean	=AVERAGE(B2:B21)				
23			A2	0.577		
24			Rbar	0.025275		
25						

	A	B	C	D	E	F
1	Sample	xbar	LCL	Mean	UCL	
2	1	3.5065	3.4849	3.4995	3.5141	
3	2	3.5026	3.4849	3.4995	3.5141	
4	3	3.4978	3.4849	3.4995	3.5141	
5	4	3.5000	3.4849	3.4995	3.5141	
6	5	3.4951	3.4849	3.4995	3.5141	
19	18	3.4940	3.4849	3.4995	3.5141	
20	19	3.4951	3.4849	3.4995	3.5141	
21	20	3.5007	3.4849	3.4995	3.5141	
22	Mean	3.4995				
23			A2	0.577		
24			Rbar	0.0253		
25						

Note: Rows 7–18 (samples 6–17) are hidden.

In order to compute the LCL and UCL we must know D_3 and D_4. These values are obtained from Table 18.3 and placed into cells D23 and D24, respectively. The formulas in cells C2:C21 are identical; they compute the LCL by multiplying D_3 (cell D23) times the average range (cell B22). The formulas in cells D2:D21 are also identical; they provide the average range. Finally, the formulas in cells E2:E21 (also identical) compute the UCL by multiplying D_4 (cell D24) times the average range (cell B22).

Apply Tools: The following steps describe how to use Excel's Chart Wizard to construct the *R* chart from the data in cells A2:E21 of Figure 18.10.

Step 1. Select cells A2:E21
Step 2. Click the **Chart Wizard** button on the Standard toolbar (or select the **Insert** menu and choose the **Chart** option)
Step 3. When the **Chart Wizard - Step 1 of 4 - Chart Type** dialog box appears:
Choose **XY (Scatter)** in the **Chart type** list
Choose **Scatter with data points connected by Lines** from the **Chart sub-type** display
Click **Next>**
Step 4. When the **Chart Wizard - Step 2 of 4 - Chart Source Data** dialog box appears:
Click **Next>**
Step 5. When the **Chart Wizard - Step 3 of 4 - Chart Options** dialog box appears:
Select the **Titles** tab and then
Type **R Chart for Jensen Computer Supplies** in the **Chart title** box
Type **Sample Number** in the **Value (X) axis** box
Type **Sample Range R** in the **Value (Y) axis** box
Select the **Legend** tab and remove the check in the **Show Legend** box
Select the **Gridlines** tab and remove the check in the **Major gridlines** box
Click **Next>**
Step 6. When the **Chart Wizard - Step 4 of 4 - Chart Location** dialog box appears:
Specify a location for the chart (we chose the **As new sheet** option)
Click **Finish**

The resulting *R* chart will appear in a new sheet entitled "Chart 1" in your workbook.

You will need to do some editing of your chart to make it look like Figure 18.8. To make the UCL line a solid line like it is in Figure 18.8 follow these steps:

Step 1. Right-click on the UCL line at one of the data points and select **Format Data Series**

Step 2. When the Format Data Series dialog box appears, select the **Patterns** tab:

> In the **Line** section:
>> Choose black for **Color**
>> Choose the second line from the bottom for **Weight**
> In the **Marker** section:
>> Choose the "long dash" for **Style**
>> Choose black for **Foreground**
>> Click **OK**

Control charts based on data indicating the presence of a defect or the number of defects are called attributes control charts. A p chart is an attributes control chart.

The UCL line will now appear as a solid black line. You should then follow the same steps for the average and LCL lines to make them look as they do in Figure 18.8. As a final step you will need to right-click on the vertical axis to format the axis labels as shown in Figure 18.8. You will probably also want to resize the chart to satisfy your own preference. Just select the chart and move the drag handles until the chart looks the way you want it.

The procedure for constructing an $\bar{x}$ chart is similar. Figure 18.11 shows the worksheet developed to provide the data needed to construct an $\bar{x}$ chart. It is analogous to the worksheet developed for the R chart in Figure 18.10. One can use the Chart Wizard with this worksheet to construct the $\bar{x}$ chart shown in Figure 18.7. The steps followed are almost identical to those we just described for the R chart, so we will not repeat them here.

p Chart

Let us consider the case in which the output quality is measured in terms of the items being either nondefective or defective. The decision to continue or to adjust the production process will be based on $\bar{p}$, the proportion of defective items found in a sample of the output. The control chart used to monitor the proportion of defective items is called a **p chart.**

To illustrate the construction of a p chart, consider the use of automated mail-sorting machines in a post office. These automated machines scan the zip codes on letters and divert each letter to its proper carrier route. Even when a machine is operating properly, some letters are diverted to incorrect routes. Suppose that when a machine is operating correctly, or in a state of control, 3% of the letters are incorrectly diverted. Thus p, the proportion of letters incorrectly diverted when the process is in control, is .03.

The sampling distribution of $\bar{p}$, as presented in Chapter 7, can be used to determine the variation that can be expected in $\bar{p}$ values for a process that is in control. Recall that the expected value or mean of $\bar{p}$ is p, the proportion defective when the process is in control. With samples of size n, the formula for the standard deviation of $\bar{p}$, called the standard error of the proportion, is

$$\sigma_{\bar{p}} = \sqrt{\frac{p(1-p)}{n}} \tag{18.16}$$

We also learned in Chapter 7 that the sampling distribution of $\bar{p}$ can be approximated by a normal probability distribution whenever the following two conditions are satisfied.

$$np \geq 5$$
$$n(1-p) \geq 5$$

Thus, if these two conditions are satisfied, the sampling distribution of $\bar{p}$ can be approximated by a normal probability distribution with mean p and standard deviation $\sigma_{\bar{p}}$. This distribution is shown in Figure 18.12.

FIGURE 18.12   SAMPLING DISTRIBUTION OF $\bar{p}$

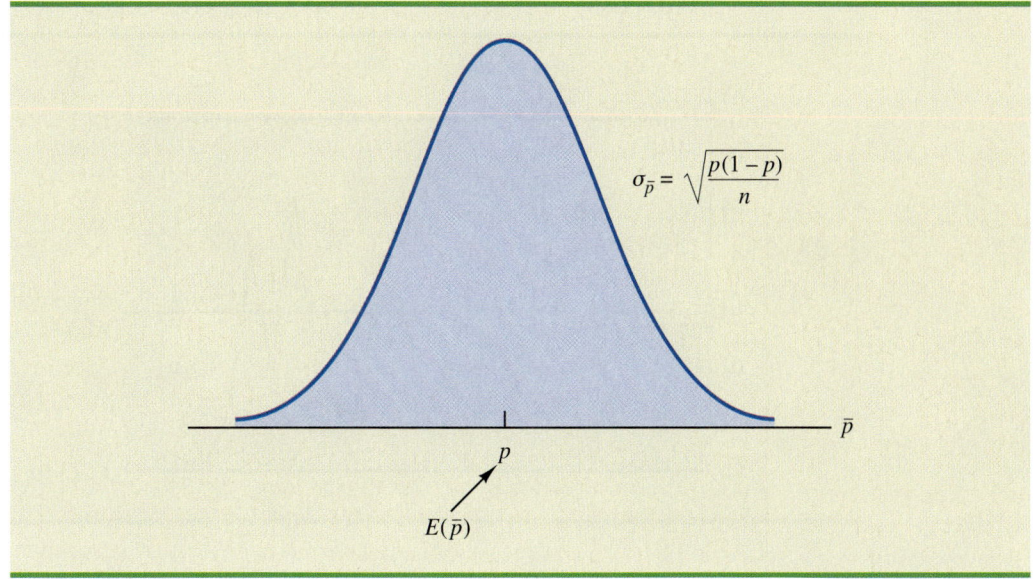

$$\sigma_{\bar{p}} = \sqrt{\frac{p(1-p)}{n}}$$

$E(\bar{p})$

To establish control limits for a p chart, we follow the same procedure we used to establish control limits for an $\bar{x}$ chart. That is, the limits for the control chart are set at 3 standard errors above and below the proportion defective when the process is in control. Thus, we have the following control limits.

CONTROL LIMITS FOR A p CHART

$$UCL = p + 3\sigma_{\bar{p}} \qquad\qquad \textbf{(18.17)}$$
$$LCL = p - 3\sigma_{\bar{p}} \qquad\qquad \textbf{(18.18)}$$

With $p = .03$ and samples of size $n = 200$, equation (18.16) shows that the standard error is

$$\sigma_{\bar{p}} = \sqrt{\frac{.03(1 - .03)}{200}} = .0121$$

Hence, the control limits are UCL $= .03 + 3(.0121) = .0663$, and LCL $= .03 - 3(.0121) = -.0063$. Whenever equation (18.18) provides a negative value for LCL, LCL is reset to zero in the control chart.

Figure 18.13 is the control chart for the mail-sorting process. The points plotted show the sample proportion defective found in samples of letters taken from the process. All points are within the control limits, and the sorting process shows no evidence of being out of control. In fact, the p chart indicates that the process should continue to operate.

If the proportion of defective items for a process that is in control is not known, that value is first estimated by using sample data. Suppose, for example, that k different samples, each of size n, are selected from a process that is in control. The fraction or proportion of defective items in each sample is then determined. Treating all the data collected as one large sample, we can determine the average number of defective items for all the data; that value can then be used to provide an estimate of p, the proportion of defective items observed when the process is in control. Note that this estimate of p also enables us to estimate the standard error of the proportion; upper and lower control limits can then be established.

FIGURE 18.13 *p* CHART FOR THE PROPORTION DEFECTIVE IN A MAIL-SORTING PROCESS

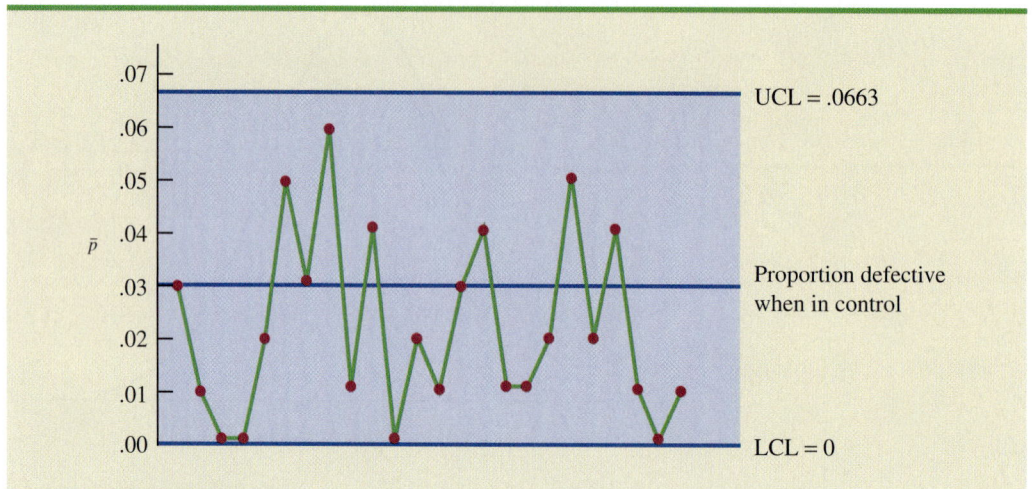

np **Chart**

An ***np* chart** is a control chart developed for the number of defective items observed in a sample. In this case, n is the sample size and p is the probability of observing a defective item when the process is in control. Whenever $np \geq 5$ and $n(1 - p) \geq 5$, the distribution of the number of defective items observed in a sample size n can be approximated by a normal probability distribution with mean np and standard deviation $\sqrt{np(1 - p)}$. Thus, for the mail-sorting example, with $n = 200$ and $p = .03$, the number of defective items observed in a sample of 200 letters can be approximated by a normal probability distribution with a mean of $200(.03) = 6$ and a standard deviation of $\sqrt{200(.03)(.97)} = 2.4125$.

The control limits for an *np* chart are set at 3 standard deviations above and below the expected number of defective items observed when the process is in control. Thus, we have the following control limits.

CONTROL LIMITS FOR AN *np* CHART

$$\text{UCL} = np + 3\sqrt{np(1 - p)} \tag{18.19}$$
$$\text{LCL} = np - 3\sqrt{np(1 - p)} \tag{18.20}$$

For the mail-sorting process example, with $p = .03$ and $n = 200$, the control limits are UCL $= 6 + 3(2.4125) = 13.2375$, and LCL $= 6 - 3(2.4125) = -1.2375$. Because equation (18.20) provides a negative value for LCL, it is reset to zero in the control chart. Hence, if the number of letters diverted to incorrect routes is 14 or more, the process is concluded to be out of control.

The information provided by an *np* chart is equivalent to the information provided by the *p* chart; the only difference is that the *np* chart is a plot of the number of defective items observed, whereas the *p* chart is a plot of the proportion of defective items observed. Thus, if we were to conclude that a particular process is out of control on the basis of a *p* chart, the process would also be concluded to be out of control on the basis of an *np* chart.

Interpretation of Control Charts

Control charts are designed to identify when assignable causes of variation are present. Managers must then authorize action to eliminate the assignable cause and return the process to an in-control state.

The location and pattern of points in a control chart enable us to determine, with a small probability of error, whether a process is in statistical control. A primary indication that a process may be out of control is a data point outside the control limits, such as point 5 in Figure 18.6. Such a point is statistical evidence that the process is out of control; in such cases, corrective action should be taken as soon as possible.

In addition to points outside the control limits, certain patterns of the points within the control limits can be warning signals of quality control problems. For example, assume that all the data points are within the control limits but that a large number of points are on one side of the center line. This pattern may indicate that an equipment problem, a change in materials, or some other assignable cause has led to a shift in quality. Careful investigation of the production process should be undertaken to determine whether quality has changed.

Even if all points are within the upper and lower control limits, a process may not be in control. Trends in the sample data points or unusually long runs above or below the center line may also indicate out-of-control conditions.

Another pattern to watch for in control charts is a gradual shift, or trend, over time. For example, as tools wear out, the dimensions of machined parts will gradually deviate from their designed levels. Gradual changes in temperature or humidity, general equipment deterioration, dirt buildup, or operator fatigue may also result in a trend pattern in control charts. Six or seven points in a row that indicate either an increasing or decreasing trend should be cause for concern, even if the data points are all within the control limits. When such a pattern occurs, the process should be reviewed for possible changes or shifts in quality. Corrective action to bring the process back into control may be necessary.

NOTES AND COMMENTS

1. Because the control limits for the $\bar{x}$ chart depend on the value of the average range, these limits will not have much meaning unless the process variability is in control. In practice, the R chart is usually constructed before the $\bar{x}$ chart; if the R chart indicates that the process variability is in control, then the $\bar{x}$ chart is constructed.

2. The p and np control charts can also be constructed using Excel's Chart Wizard. For instance, to develop a p chart, start by organizing the data for $\bar{p}$, LCL, mean, and UCL in a worksheet similar to Figures 18.10 or 18.11. Then use the Chart Wizard in the same way we did earlier to construct an R chart.

Exercises

Methods

1. A process that is in control has a mean of $\mu = 12.5$ and a standard deviation of $\sigma = .8$.
    a. Construct an $\bar{x}$ chart if samples of size 4 are to be used.
    b. Repeat part (a) for samples of size 8 and 16.
    c. What happens to the limits of the control chart as the sample size is increased? Discuss why this change is reasonable.

2. Twenty-five samples, each of size 5, were selected from a process that was in control. The sum of all the data collected was 677.5 pounds.
    a. What is an estimate of the process mean (in terms of pounds per unit) when the process is in control?
    b. Develop the control chart for this process if samples of size 5 will be used. Assume that the process standard deviation is .5 when the process is in control and that the mean of the process is the estimate developed in part (a).

3. Twenty-five samples of 100 items each were inspected when a process was considered to be operating satisfactorily. In the 25 samples, 135 items were found to be defective.
   a. What is an estimate of the proportion defective when the process is in control?
   b. What is the standard error of the proportion if samples of size 100 will be used for statistical process control?
   c. Compute the upper and lower control limits for the control chart.

4. An in-control process sampled 20 times with a sample of size 8 resulted in $\bar{\bar{x}} = 28.5$ and $\bar{R} = 1.6$. Compute the upper and lower control limits for the $\bar{x}$ and R charts for this process.

SELF test

Applications

5. Temperature is used to measure the output of a production process. When the process is in control, the mean of the process is $\mu = 128.5$ and the standard deviation is $\sigma = .4$.
   a. Construct an $\bar{x}$ chart if samples of size 6 are to be used.
   b. Is the process in control for a sample providing the following data?

   | 128.8 | 128.2 | 129.1 | 128.7 | 128.4 | 129.2 |

   c. Is the process in control for a sample providing the following data?

   | 129.3 | 128.7 | 128.6 | 129.2 | 129.5 | 129.0 |

6. A quality control process monitors the weight per carton of laundry detergent. Control limits are set at UCL = 20.12 ounces and LCL = 19.90 ounces. Samples of size 5 are used for the sampling and inspection process. What are the process mean and process standard deviation for the manufacturing operation?

7. The Goodman Tire and Rubber Company periodically tests its tires for tread wear under simulated road conditions. To study and control the manufacturing process, 20 samples, each containing three radial tires, were chosen from different shifts over several days of operation; the data collected are shown below. Assuming that these data were collected when the manufacturing process was believed to be operating in control, develop the R and $\bar{x}$ charts.

Tires

Sample	Tread Wear*		
1	31	42	28
2	26	18	35
3	25	30	34
4	17	25	21
5	38	29	35
6	41	42	36
7	21	17	29
8	32	26	28
9	41	34	33
10	29	17	30
11	26	31	40
12	23	19	25
13	17	24	32
14	43	35	17
15	18	25	29
16	30	42	31
17	28	36	32
18	40	29	31
19	18	29	28
20	22	34	26

*Hundredths of an inch

8. Over several weeks of normal, or in-control, operation, 20 samples of 150 packages each of synthetic-gut tennis strings were tested for breaking strength. A total of 141 packages of the 3000 tested failed to conform to the manufacturer's specifications.

    a. What is an estimate of the process proportion defective when the system is in control?
    b. Compute the upper and lower control limits for a p chart.
    c. With the results of part (b), what conclusion should be drawn about the process if tests on a new sample of 150 packages find 12 defective? Do there appear to be assignable causes in this situation?
    d. Compute the upper and lower control limits for an np chart.
    e. Answer part (c) using the results of part (d).
    f. Which control chart would be preferred in this situation? Explain.

9. An automotive industry supplier produces pistons for several models of automobiles. Twenty samples, each consisting of 200 pistons, were selected when the process was known to be operating in control. The numbers of defective pistons found in the samples follow.

8	10	6	4	5	7	8	12	8	15
14	10	10	7	5	8	6	10	4	8

    a. What is an estimate of the proportion defective for the piston manufacturing process when it is in control?
    b. Construct a p chart for the manufacturing process, assuming each sample has 200 pistons.
    c. With the results of part (b), what conclusion should be drawn if a sample of 200 has 20 defective pistons?
    d. Compute the upper and lower control limits for an np chart.
    e. Answer part (c) using the results of part (d).

18.3   Acceptance Sampling

In acceptance sampling, the items of interest can be incoming shipments of raw materials or purchased parts as well as finished goods from final assembly. Suppose we want to decide whether to accept or reject a group of items on the basis of specified quality characteristics. In quality control terminology, the group of items is a **lot**, and **acceptance sampling** is a statistical method that enables us to make an accept-reject decision based on the sample of items from the lot.

The general steps of acceptance sampling are shown in Figure 18.14. After a lot is received, a sample is selected for inspection. The results of the inspection are compared to specified quality characteristics. If the quality is satisfactory, the lot is accepted and sent to production or shipped to customers. If the quality is not satisfactory, the lot is rejected. Managers must then decide on the disposition of the lot. In some cases, the decision may be to keep the lot and remove the unacceptable or nonconforming items. In other cases, the lot may be returned to the supplier at the supplier's expense; the extra work and cost placed on the supplier can motivate the supplier to provide high-quality lots. Finally, if the rejected lot consists of finished goods, the goods must be scrapped or reworked to meet acceptable quality standards.

The statistical procedure of acceptance sampling is based on the hypothesis testing methodology presented in Chapter 9. The null and alternative hypotheses are stated as follows.

Acceptance sampling has the following advantages over 100% inspection:
1. *Usually less expensive*
2. *Less product damage due to less handling and testing*
3. *Fewer inspectors required*
4. *Provides only approach possible if destructive testing must be used*

$$H_0: \text{Good-quality lot}$$
$$H_a: \text{Poor-quality lot}$$

Table 18.4 shows the outcomes of the hypothesis testing procedure. Note that correct decisions correspond to accepting a good-quality lot and rejecting a poor-quality lot. However, as with

FIGURE 18.14   ACCEPTANCE SAMPLING PROCEDURE

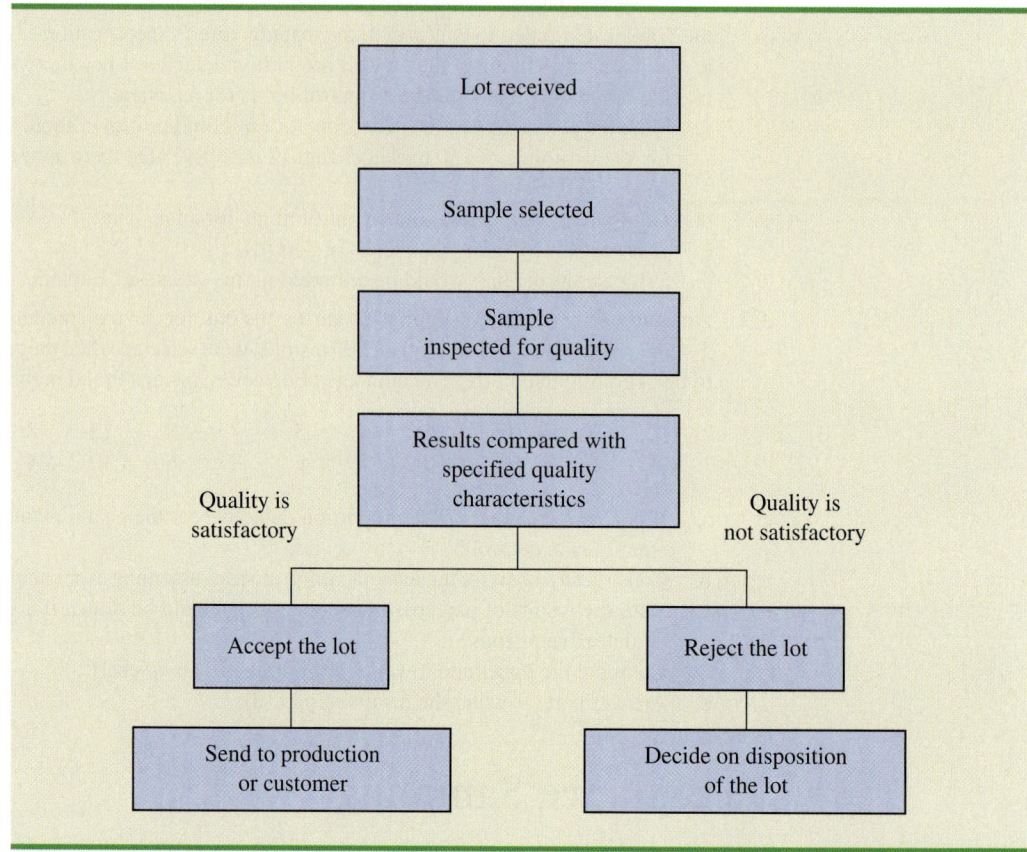

other hypothesis testing procedures, we need to be aware of the possibilities of making a Type I error (rejecting a good-quality lot) or a Type II error (accepting a poor-quality lot).

Because the probability of a Type I error creates a risk for the producer of the lot, it is known as the **producer's risk.** For example, a producer's risk of .05 indicates a 5% chance that a good-quality lot will be erroneously rejected. Because the probability of a Type II error creates a risk for the consumer of the lot, it is known as the **consumer's risk.** For example, a consumer's risk of .10 means that there is a 10% chance that a poor-quality lot will be erroneously accepted and thus used in production or shipped to the customer. Spe-

TABLE 18.4   OUTCOMES OF ACCEPTANCE SAMPLING

		State of the Lot	
		H_0 **True** **Good-Quality Lot**	H_0 **False** **Poor-Quality Lot**
Decision	**Accept the Lot**	Correct decision	Type II error (accepting a poor-quality lot)
	Reject the Lot	Type I error (rejecting a good-quality lot)	Correct decision

cific values for the producer's risk and the consumer's risk can be controlled by the person designing the acceptance sampling procedure. To illustrate how to assign risk values, let us consider the problem faced by KALI, Inc.

KALI, Inc.: An Example of Acceptance Sampling

KALI, Inc., manufactures home appliances that are marketed under a variety of trade names. However, KALI does not manufacture every component used in its products. Several components are purchased directly from suppliers. For example, one of the components that KALI purchases for use in home air conditioners is an overload protector, a device that turns off the compressor if it overheats. The compressor can be seriously damaged if the overload protector does not function properly; therefore, KALI is concerned about the quality of the overload protectors. One way to ensure quality would be to test every component received; this approach is known as 100% inspection. However, to determine proper functioning of an overload protector, the device must be subjected to time-consuming and expensive tests, and KALI cannot justify testing every overload protector it receives.

Instead, KALI uses an acceptance sampling plan to monitor the quality of the overload protectors. The acceptance sampling plan requires that KALI's quality control inspectors select and test a sample of overload protectors from each shipment. If very few defective units are found in the sample, the lot is probably of good quality and should be accepted. However, if a large number of defective units are found in the sample, the lot is probably of poor quality and should be rejected.

An *acceptance sampling plan* consists of a sample size n and an acceptance criterion c. The **acceptance criterion** is the maximum number of defective items that can be found in the sample and still indicate an acceptable lot. For example, for the KALI example let us suppose that a sample of 15 items will be selected from each incoming shipment or lot. Furthermore, suppose that the manager of quality control states that the lot can be accepted only if no defective items are found. In this case, the acceptance sampling plan established by the quality control manager is $n = 15$ and $c = 0$.

This acceptance sampling plan is easy for the quality control inspector to implement. The inspector simply selects a sample of 15 items, performs the tests, and reaches a conclusion based on the following decision rule.

- *Accept the lot* if zero defects are found.
- *Reject the lot* if one or more defects are found.

Before implementing this acceptance sampling plan, the quality control manager wants to evaluate the risks or errors possible under the plan. The plan will be implemented only if both the producer's risk (Type I error) and the consumer's risk (Type II error) are controlled at reasonable levels.

Computing the Probability of Accepting a Lot

The key to analyzing both the producer's risk and the consumer's risk is a what-if type of analysis; that is, we assume that a lot has some known percentage of defective items and compute the probability of accepting the lot for a given sampling plan. By varying the assumed percentage of defective items, we can examine the effect of the sampling plan on both types of risks.

Let us begin by assuming that in a large shipment of overload protectors 5% of the overload protectors are defective. For a shipment or lot with 5% of the items defective, what is the probability that the $n = 15$, $c = 0$ sampling plan will lead us to accept the lot? Because each overload protector tested will be either defective or nondefective and because the lot size is large, the number of defective items in a sample of 15 has a *binomial probability distribution.* The binomial probability function, which was presented in Chapter 5, follows.

BINOMIAL PROBABILITY FUNCTION FOR ACCEPTANCE SAMPLING

$$f(x) = \frac{n!}{x!(n-x)!} p^x (1-p)^{(n-x)} \qquad \textbf{(18.21)}$$

where

$$n = \text{sample size}$$
$$p = \text{proportion of defective items in the lot}$$
$$x = \text{number of defective items in the sample}$$
$$f(x) = \text{probability of } x \text{ defective items in the sample}$$

For the KALI acceptance sampling plan, $n = 15$; thus, for a lot with 5% defective ($p = .05$), we have

$$f(x) = \frac{15!}{x!(15-x)!} (.05)^x (1 - .05)^{(15-x)} \qquad \textbf{(18.22)}$$

Using equation (18.22), $f(0)$ will provide the probability that zero overload protectors will be defective and the lot will be accepted. In using equation (18.22), recall that $0! = 1$. Thus, the probability computation for $f(0)$ is

$$f(0) = \frac{15!}{0!(15-0)!} (.05)^0 (1 - .05)^{(15-0)}$$

$$= \frac{15!}{0!(15)!} (.05)^0 (.95)^{15} = (.95)^{15} = .4633$$

We now know that the $n = 15$, $c = 0$ sampling plan has a .4633 probability of accepting a lot with 5% defective items. Hence, a corresponding probability of rejecting a lot with 5% defective items is $1 - .4633 = .5367$.

Excel's BINOMDIST function can also be used to compute these probabilities. See Chapter 5.

In Table 18.5 we show the probability that the $n = 15$, $c = 0$ sampling plan will lead to the acceptance of lots with 1%, 2%, 3%, . . . defective items. The probabilities in the table were computed by using $p = .01, p = .02, p = .03, \ldots$ in the binomial probability function (18.21).

TABLE 18.5   PROBABILITY OF ACCEPTING THE LOT FOR THE KALI EXAMPLE WITH $n = 15$ AND $c = 0$

Percent Defective in the Lot	Probability of Accepting the Lot
1	.8601
2	.7386
3	.6333
4	.5421
5	.4633
10	.2059
15	.0874
20	.0352
25	.0134

FIGURE 18.15   OPERATING CHARACTERISTIC CURVE FOR THE $n = 15, c = 0$ ACCEPTANCE SAMPLING PLAN

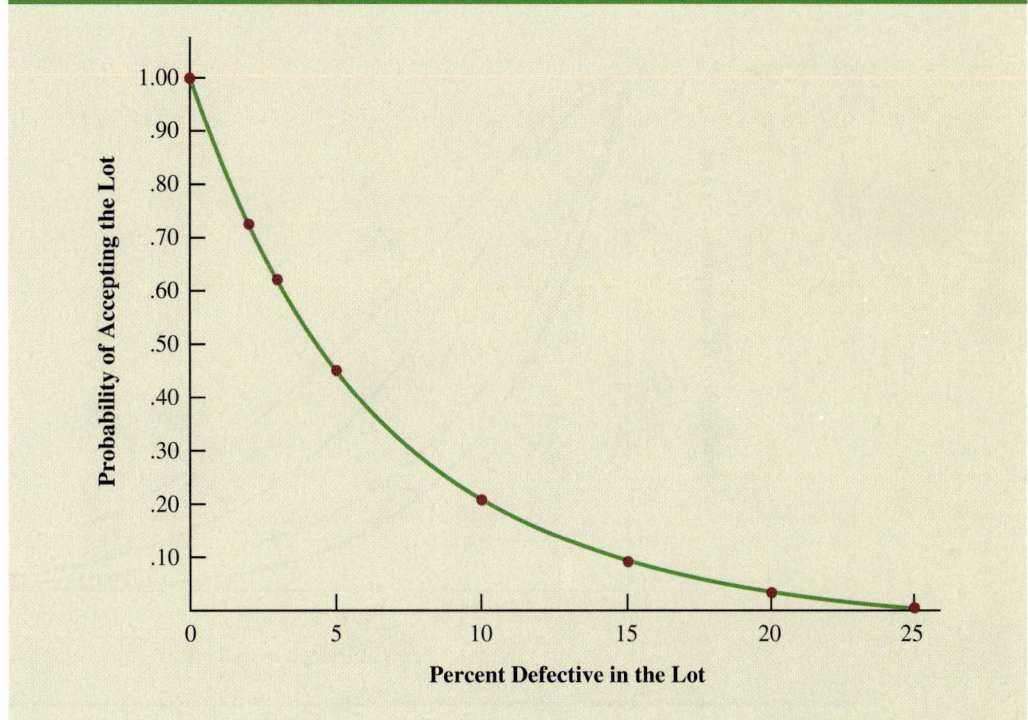

With the data in Table 18.5, a graph of the probability of accepting the lot versus the percent defective in the lot can be drawn as shown in Figure 18.15. This graph, or curve, is called the **operating characteristic (OC) curve** for the $n = 15, c = 0$ acceptance sampling plan.

Perhaps we should consider other sampling plans, ones with different sample sizes n and/or different acceptance criteria c. First consider the case in which the sample size remains $n = 15$ but the acceptance criterion increases from $c = 0$ to $c = 1$; that is, we will now accept the lot if zero or one defective item is found in the sample. For a lot with 5% defective items ($p = .05$), the binomial probability function in equation (18.21) can be used to compute $f(0)$ and $f(1)$. Summing these two probabilities provides the probability that the $n = 15, c = 1$ sampling plan will accept the lot. We find that with $n = 15$ and $p = .05$, $f(0) = .4633$ and $f(1) = .3658$. Thus, we find a $.4633 + .3658 = .8291$ probability that the $n = 15, c = 1$ plan will lead to the acceptance of a lot with 5% defective items.

Figure 18.16 shows the operating characteristic curves for four alternative acceptance sampling plans for the KALI example. Samples of size 15 and 20 are considered. Note that regardless of the proportion defective in the lot, the $n = 15, c = 1$ sampling plan provides the highest probabilities of accepting the lot. The $n = 20, c = 0$ sampling plan provides the lowest probabilities of accepting the lot; however, that plan also provides the highest probabilities of rejecting the lot.

Selecting an Acceptance Sampling Plan

Now that we know how to use the binomial probability distribution to compute the probability of accepting a lot with a given proportion defective, we are ready to select the values of n and c that determine the desired acceptance sampling plan for the application being studied. In formulating an acceptance plan, managers must specify two values for the proportion

FIGURE 18.16 OPERATING CHARACTERISTIC CURVES FOR FOUR ACCEPTANCE SAMPLING PLANS

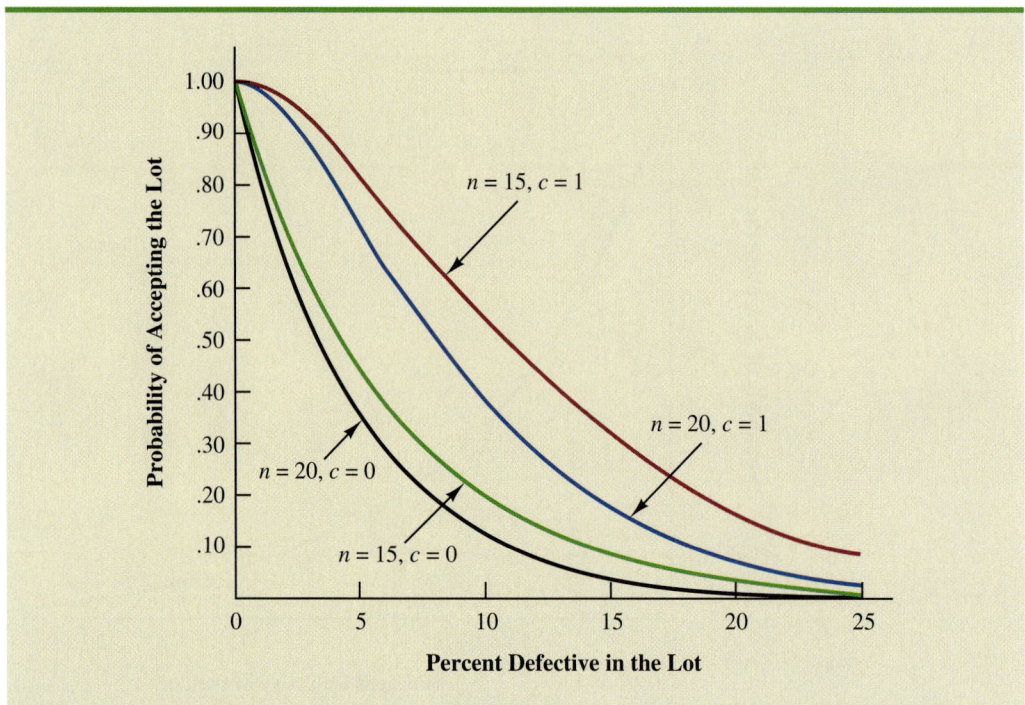

defective in the lot. One value, denoted p_0, will be used to control for the producer's risk, and the other value, denoted p_1, will be used to control for the consumer's risk.

In showing how this formulation can be done, we will use the following notation.

α = the producer's risk; the probability that a lot with p_0 defective will be rejected

β = the consumer's risk; the probability that a lot with p_1 defective will be accepted

Suppose that for the KALI example, the managers specify that $p_0 = .03$ and $p_1 = .15$. From the OC curve for $n = 15$, $c = 0$ in Figure 18.17, we see that $p_0 = .03$ provides a producer's risk of approximately $1 - .63 = .37$, and $p_1 = .15$ provides a consumer's risk of approximately .09. Thus, if the managers are willing to tolerate both a .37 probability of rejecting a lot with 3% defective items (producer's risk) and a .09 probability of accepting a lot with 15% defective items (consumer's risk), the $n = 15$, $c = 0$ acceptance sampling plan would be acceptable.

Suppose, however, that the managers request a producer's risk of $\alpha = .10$ and a consumer's risk of $\beta = .20$. We see that now the $n = 15$, $c = 0$ sampling plan offers a better-than-desired consumer's risk but an unacceptably large producer's risk. The fact that $\alpha = .37$ indicates that 37% of the lots will be erroneously rejected when only 3% of the items in them are defective. The producer's risk is too high, and a different acceptance sampling plan should be considered.

Using $p_0 = .03$, $\alpha = .10$, $p_1 = .15$, and $\beta = .20$ in Figure 18.16 shows that the acceptance sampling plan with $n = 20$ and $c = 1$ comes closest to meeting both the producer's and the consumer's risk requirements. Exercise 13 at the end of this section will ask you to compute the producer's risk and the consumer's risk for the $n = 20$, $c = 1$ sampling plan.

As shown in this section, several computations and several operating characteristic curves may need to be considered to determine the sampling plan with the desired pro-

FIGURE 18.17 OPERATING CHARACTERISTIC CURVE FOR $n = 15$, $c = 0$ WITH $p_0 = .03$ AND $p_1 = .15$

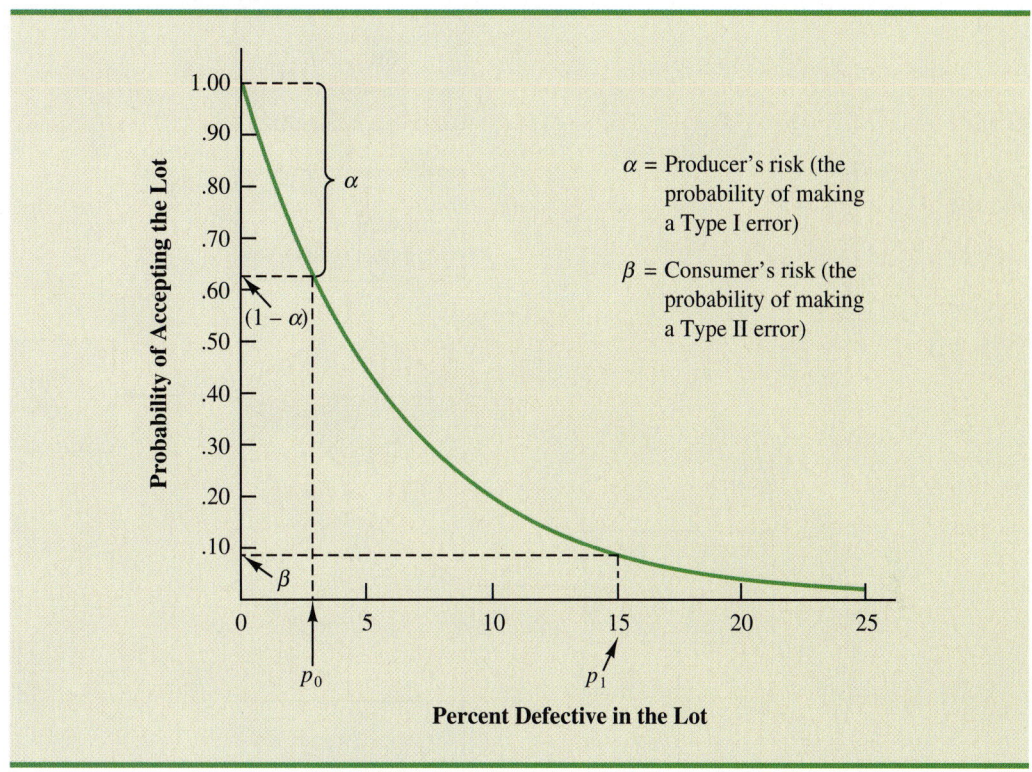

α = Producer's risk (the probability of making a Type I error)

β = Consumer's risk (the probability of making a Type II error)

ducer's and consumer's risks. Fortunately, tables of sampling plans are published. For example, the American Military Standard Table, MIL-STD-105D, provides information helpful in designing acceptance sampling plans. More advanced texts on quality control, such as those listed in the bibliography, describe the use of such tables. The advanced texts also discuss the role of sampling costs in determining the optimal sampling plan.

Multiple Sampling Plans

The acceptance sampling procedure presented for the KALI example is called a *single-sample plan,* because only one sample or sampling stage is used. After the number of defective components in the sample is determined, a decision must be made to accept or reject the lot. An alternative to the single-sample plan is a **multiple sampling plan,** in which two or more stages of sampling are used. At each stage a decision is made among three possibilities: stop sampling and accept the lot, stop sampling and reject the lot, or continue sampling. Although more complex, multiple sampling plans often result in a smaller total sample size than single-sample plans with the same α and β probabilities.

The logic of a two-stage, or double-sample, plan is shown in Figure 18.18. Initially a sample of n_1 items is selected. If the number of defective components x_1 is less than or equal to c_1, accept the lot. If x_1 is greater than or equal to c_2, reject the lot. If x_1 is between c_1 and c_2 ($c_1 < x_1 < c_2$), select a second sample of n_2 items. Determine the total number of defects from the first sample (x_1) and the second sample (x_2). If $x_1 + x_2 \leq c_3$, accept the lot; otherwise reject the lot. The development of the double-sample plan is more difficult because the sample sizes n_1 and n_2 and the acceptance numbers c_1, c_2, and c_3 must meet acceptable levels of both the producer's and consumer's risks.

FIGURE 18.18   A TWO-STAGE ACCEPTANCE SAMPLING PLAN

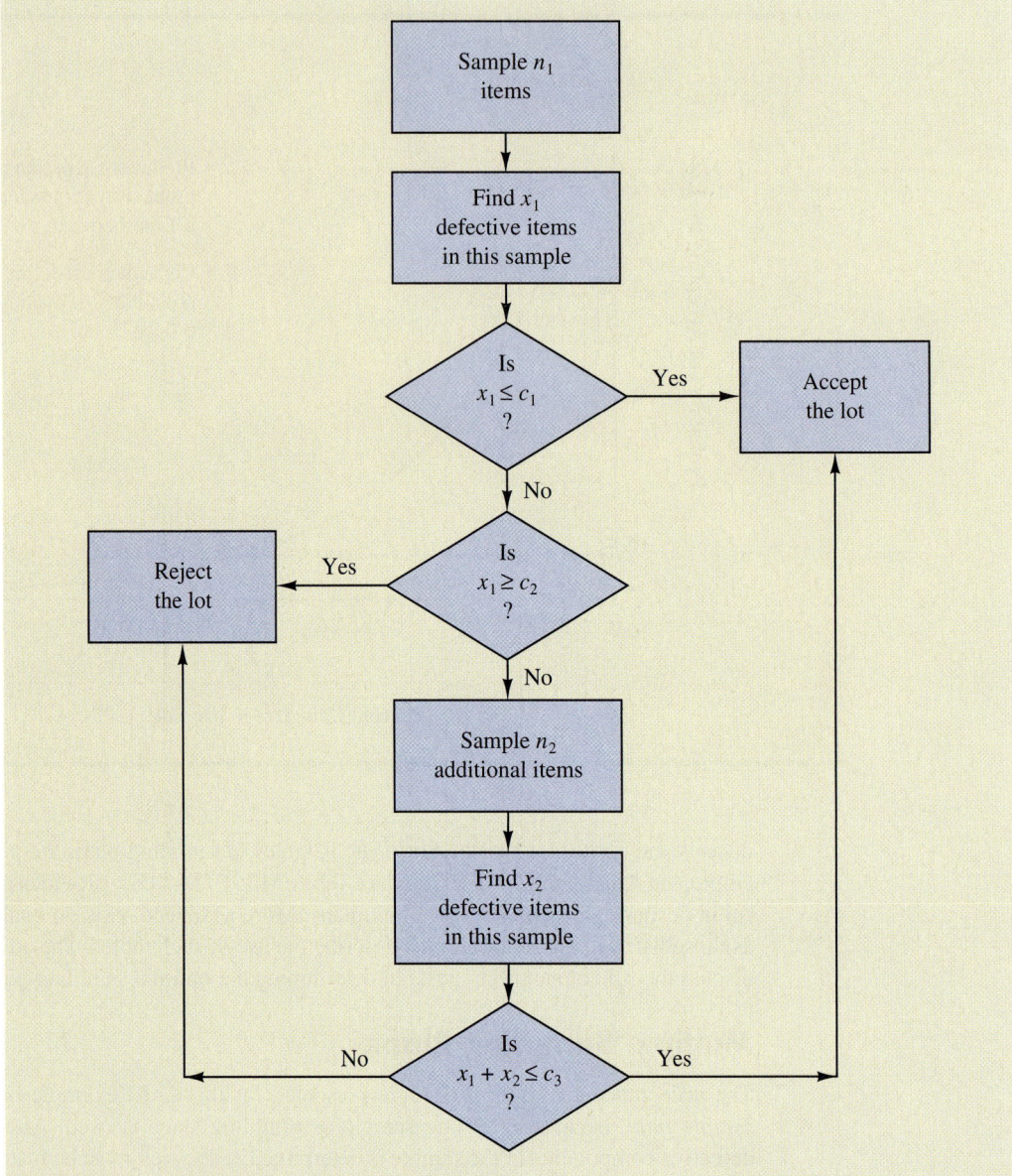

1. The use of the binomial probability distribution for acceptance sampling is based on the assumption of large lots. If the lot size is small, the hypergeometric probability distribution is the appropriate distribution.

2. In the MIL-STD-105D sampling tables, p_0 is called the acceptable quality level (AQL). In some sampling tables, p_1 is called the lot tolerance percent defective (LTPD) or the rejectable

quality level (RQL). Many of the published sampling plans also use quality indexes such as the indifference quality level (IQL) and the average outgoing quality limit (AOQL). The more advanced texts listed in the bibliography provide a complete discussion of these other indexes.

3. In this section we provided an introduction to *attributes sampling plans*. In these plans each item sampled is classified as nondefective or de-

fective. In *variables sampling plans,* a sample is taken and a measurement of the quality characteristic is taken. For example, for gold jewelry a measurement of quality may be the amount of gold it contains. A simple statistic such as the average amount of gold in the sample jewelry is computed and compared with an allowable value to determine whether to accept or reject the lot.

Exercises

Methods

10. For an acceptance sampling plan with $n = 25$ and $c = 0$, find the probability of accepting a lot when the defect rate is 2%. What is the probability of accepting the lot if the defect rate is 6%?

11. Consider an acceptance sampling plan with $n = 20$ and $c = 0$. Compute the producer's risk for each of the following cases.
    a. The lot has a defect rate of 2%.
    b. The lot has a defect rate of 6%.

12. Repeat exercise 11 for the acceptance sampling plan with $n = 20$ and $c = 1$. What happens to the producer's risk as the acceptance number c is increased? Explain.

Applications

13. Refer to the KALI example presented in this section. The quality control manager requested a producer's risk of .10 or less when p_0 was .03 and a consumer's risk of .20 or less when p_1 was .15. Consider the acceptance sampling plan based on a sample size of 20 and an acceptance criterion of $c = 1$. Answer the following questions.
    a. What is the producer's risk for the $n = 20$, $c = 1$ sampling plan?
    b. What is the consumer's risk for the $n = 20$, $c = 1$ sampling plan?
    c. Does the $n = 20$, $c = 1$ sampling plan satisfy the risk limits as requested by the quality control manager? Discuss.

14. To inspect incoming shipments of raw materials, a manufacturer is considering samples of sizes 10, 15, and 20. Use binomial probabilities to select a sampling plan that provides a producer's risk of $\alpha = .03$ when p_0 is .05 and a consumer's risk of $\beta = .12$ when p_1 is .30.

15. A domestic manufacturer of watches purchases quartz crystals from a Swiss firm. The crystals are shipped in lots of 1000. The acceptance sampling procedure uses 20 randomly selected crystals.
    a. Construct operating characteristic curves for acceptance criteria of 0, 1, and 2.
    b. If p_0 is .01 and $p_1 = .08$, what are the producer's and consumer's risks for each sampling plan in part (a)?

Summary

In this chapter we discussed how statistical methods can be used to assist in the control of quality. First, we presented a brief introduction to three quality management frameworks: the Malcolm Baldrige Quality Award, ISO 9000 standards, and the Six Sigma philosophy. In Six Sigma terminology a defect is any mistake or error passed on to the customer, and Six Sigma represents a quality level of at most 3.4 defects per million opportunities.

Quality control consists of a series of inspections and measurements used to determine whether quality standards are being met. Two of the statistical methods used in quality control are statistical process control and acceptance sampling. We first presented the $\bar{x}$, R, p, and np control charts as graphical aids in monitoring process quality. Control limits are established for each chart; samples are selected periodically and the data plotted on the control chart. Data outside the control limits indicate that the process is out of control and that corrective action should be taken. Patterns of data within the control limits can also indicate potential quality control problems and suggest that corrective action may be warranted.

With the technique known as acceptance sampling, a sample is selected and inspected. The number of defective items in the sample provides the basis for accepting or rejecting the lot. The sample size and the acceptance criterion can be adjusted to control both the producer's risk (Type I error) and the consumer's risk (Type II error).

Glossary

Total quality (TQ) A people-focused management system that aims at continual increase in customer satisfaction at continually lower real cost.

Six Sigma A methodology used to provide a level of quality so good that for every 1 million opportunities, no more than 3.4 defects will occur. This level of quality is referred to as the Six Sigma level of quality.

Quality control A series of inspections and measurements used to determine whether quality standards are being met.

Assignable causes Variations in process outputs that are due to factors such as machine tools wearing out, incorrect machine settings, poor-quality raw materials, operator error, and so on. Corrective action should be taken whenever assignable causes are detected.

Common causes Normal or natural variations in process outputs that are due purely to chance. No corrective action is necessary when output variations are due to common causes.

Control chart A graphical tool used to help determine whether a process is in control or out of control.

$\bar{x}$ chart A control chart used to monitor the mean value of a variable such as a length, weight, temperature, and so on.

R chart A control chart used to control the variability of a process.

p chart A control chart used to monitor the proportion of defective items generated by a process.

np chart A control chart used to monitor the number of defective items generated by a process.

Lot A group of items such as an incoming shipment of raw materials, a shipment of purchased parts, or a batch of finished goods from final assembly.

Acceptance sampling A statistical procedure in which the number of defective items found in a sample is used to determine whether a lot should be accepted or rejected.

Producer's risk The risk of rejecting a good-quality lot; a Type I error.

Consumer's risk The risk of accepting a poor-quality lot; a Type II error.

Acceptance criterion The maximum number of defective items that can be found in the sample and still indicate an acceptable lot.

Operating characteristic (OC) curve A graph showing the probability of accepting the lot as a function of the percent defective in the lot. This curve can be used to determine whether a particular acceptance sampling plan meets both the producer's and the consumer's risk requirements.

Multiple sampling plan A form of acceptance sampling in which more than one sample or stage is used. On the basis of the number of defective items found in a sample, a decision will be made to accept the lot, reject the lot, or continue sampling.

Key Formulas

Standard Error of the Mean

$$\sigma_{\bar{x}} = \frac{\sigma}{\sqrt{n}} \tag{18.1}$$

Control Limits for an $\bar{x}$ Chart: Process Mean and Standard Deviation Known

$$\text{UCL} = \mu + 3\sigma_{\bar{x}} \tag{18.2}$$
$$\text{LCL} = \mu - 3\sigma_{\bar{x}} \tag{18.3}$$

Overall Sample Mean

$$\bar{\bar{x}} = \frac{\bar{x}_1 + \bar{x}_2 + \cdots + \bar{x}_k}{k} \tag{18.4}$$

Average Range

$$\bar{R} = \frac{R_1 + R_2 + \cdots + R_k}{k} \tag{18.5}$$

Control Limits for an $\bar{x}$ Chart: Process Mean and Standard Deviation Unknown

$$\bar{\bar{x}} \pm A_2\bar{R} \tag{18.8}$$

Control Limits for an R Chart

$$\text{UCL} = \bar{R}D_4 \tag{18.14}$$
$$\text{LCL} = \bar{R}D_3 \tag{18.15}$$

Standard Error of the Proportion

$$\sigma_{\bar{p}} = \sqrt{\frac{p(1 - p)}{n}} \tag{18.16}$$

Control Limits for a p Chart

$$\text{UCL} = p + 3\sigma_{\bar{p}} \tag{18.17}$$
$$\text{LCL} = p - 3\sigma_{\bar{p}} \tag{18.18}$$

Control Limits for an np Chart

$$\text{UCL} = np + 3\sqrt{np(1 - p)} \tag{18.19}$$
$$\text{LCL} = np - 3\sqrt{np(1 - p)} \tag{18.20}$$

Binomial Probability Function for Acceptance Sampling

$$f(x) = \frac{n!}{x!(n - x)!} p^x(1 - p)^{(n-x)} \tag{18.21}$$

Supplementary Exercises

16. Samples of size 5 provided the following 20 sample means for a production process that is believed to be in control.

95.72	95.24	95.18
95.44	95.46	95.32
95.40	95.44	95.08
95.50	95.80	95.22
95.56	95.22	95.04
95.72	94.82	95.46
95.60	95.78	

a. Based on these data, what is an estimate of the mean when the process is in control?
b. Assuming that the process standard deviation is $\sigma = .50$, develop an $\bar{x}$ control chart for this production process. Assume that the mean of the process is the estimate developed in part (a).
c. Are any of the 20 sample means outside the control limits?

17. Product filling weights are normally distributed with a mean of 350 grams and a standard deviation of 15 grams.
a. Develop the control limits for samples of size 10, 20, and 30.
b. What happens to the control limits as the sample size is increased?
c. What happens when a Type I error is made?
d. What happens when a Type II error is made?
e. What is the probability of a Type I error for samples of size 10, 20, and 30?
f. What is the advantage of increasing the sample size for control chart purposes? What error probability is reduced as the sample size is increased?

18. Twenty-five samples of size 5 resulted in $\bar{\bar{x}} = 5.42$ and $\bar{R} = 2.0$. Compute control limits for the $\bar{x}$ and R charts, and estimate the standard deviation of the process.

19. The following quality control data for a manufacturing process at Kensport Chemical Company show the temperature in degrees centigrade at five points in time during a manufacturing cycle. The company is interested in using control charts to monitor the temperature of its manufacturing process. Construct the $\bar{x}$ and R charts. What conclusions can be drawn about the quality of the process?

Sample	$\bar{x}$	R	Sample	$\bar{x}$	R
1	95.72	1.0	11	95.80	.6
2	95.24	.9	12	95.22	.2
3	95.18	.8	13	95.56	1.3
4	95.44	.4	14	95.22	.5
5	95.46	.5	15	95.04	.8
6	95.32	1.1	16	95.72	1.1
7	95.40	.9	17	94.82	.6
8	95.44	.3	18	95.46	.5
9	95.08	.2	19	95.60	.4
10	95.50	.6	20	95.74	.6

20. The following data were collected for the Master Blend Coffee production process. The data show the filling weights based on samples of 3-pound cans of coffee. Use these data to construct the $\bar{x}$ and R charts. What conclusions can be drawn about the quality of the production process?

Sample	Observations 1	2	3	4	5
1	3.05	3.08	3.07	3.11	3.11
2	3.13	3.07	3.05	3.10	3.10
3	3.06	3.04	3.12	3.11	3.10
4	3.09	3.08	3.09	3.09	3.07
5	3.10	3.06	3.06	3.07	3.08
6	3.08	3.10	3.13	3.03	3.06
7	3.06	3.06	3.08	3.10	3.08
8	3.11	3.08	3.07	3.07	3.07
9	3.09	3.09	3.08	3.07	3.09
10	3.06	3.11	3.07	3.09	3.07

CD file

Coffee

21. Consider the following situations and comment on whether the sample results might cause concern about the quality of the process.
    a. A p chart has LCL = 0 and UCL = .068. When the process is in control, the proportion defective is .033. Plot the following seven sample results: .035, .062, .055, .049, .058, .066, and .055. Discuss.
    b. An $\bar{x}$ chart has LCL = 22.2 and UCL = 24.5. The mean is μ = 23.35 when the process is in control. Plot the following seven sample results: 22.4, 22.6, 22.65, 23.2, 23.4, 23.85, and 24.1. Discuss.

22. Managers of 1200 different retail outlets make twice-a-month restocking orders from a central warehouse. Past experience shows 4% of the orders contain one or more errors such as wrong item shipped, wrong quantity shipped, and item requested but not shipped. Random samples of 200 orders are selected monthly and checked for accuracy.
    a. Construct a control chart for this situation.
    b. Six months of data show the following numbers of orders with one or more errors: 10, 15, 6, 13, 8, and 17. Plot the data on the control chart. What does your plot indicate about the order process?

23. An n = 10, c = 2 acceptance sampling plan is being considered; assume that p_0 = .05 and p_1 = .20.
    a. Compute both the producer's and the consumer's risks for this acceptance sampling plan.
    b. Would the producer, the consumer, or both be unhappy with the proposed sampling plan?
    c. What change in the sampling plan, if any, would you recommend?

24. An acceptance sampling plan with n = 15 and c = 1 was designed with a producer's risk of .075.
    a. Was the value of p_0 equal to .01, .02, .03, .04, or .05? What does this value mean?
    b. What is the consumer's risk associated with this plan if p_1 is .25?

25. A manufacturer produces lots of a canned food product. Let p denote the proportion of the lots that do not meet the product quality specifications. An n = 25, c = 0 acceptance sampling plan will be used.
    a. Compute points on the operating characteristic curve when p = .01, .03, .10, and .20.
    b. Plot the operating characteristic curve.
    c. What is the probability that the acceptance sampling plan will reject a lot that has .01 defective?

CHAPTER 19

Decision Analysis

CONTENTS

STATISTICS IN PRACTICE:
OHIO EDISON COMPANY

19.1 PROBLEM FORMULATION
Payoff Tables
Decision Trees

19.2 DECISION MAKING WITH
PROBABILITIES
Expected Value Approach
Expected Value of Perfect
Information

19.3 DECISION ANALYSIS WITH
SAMPLE INFORMATION
Decision Tree
Decision Strategy
Expected Value of Sample
Information

19.4 COMPUTING BRANCH
PROBABILITIES USING
BAYES' THEOREM

STATISTICS *in* PRACTICE

OHIO EDISON COMPANY*
AKRON, OHIO

Ohio Edison Company is an operating company of FirstEnergy Corporation. Ohio Edison and its subsidiary, Pennsylvania Power Company, provide electrical service to more than 1 million customers in central and northeastern Ohio and western Pennsylvania. Most of the electricity is generated by coal-fired power plants. Because of evolving pollution-control requirements, Ohio Edison embarked on a program to replace the existing pollution-control equipment at most of its generating plants.

To meet new emission limits for sulfur dioxide at one of its largest power plants, Ohio Edison decided to burn low-sulfur coal in four of the smaller units at the plant and to install fabric filters on those units to control particulate emissions. Fabric filters use thousands of fabric bags to filter out particles and function in much the same way as a household vacuum cleaner.

It was considered likely, although not certain, that the three larger units at the plant would burn medium- to high-sulfur coal. Preliminary studies narrowed the particulate equipment choice for these larger units to fabric filters and electrostatic precipitators (which remove particles suspended in the flue gas by passing it through a strong electrical field). Among the uncertainties that would affect the final choice were the way some air quality laws and regulations might be interpreted, potential future changes in air quality laws and regulations, and fluctuations in construction costs.

Because of the complexity of the problem, the high degree of uncertainty associated with factors affecting the decision, and the cost impact on Ohio Edison, decision analysis was used in the selection process. A graphical description of the problem, referred to as a decision tree, was developed. The measure used to evaluate the outcomes depicted on the decision tree was the annual revenue requirements for the three large units over their remaining lifetime. Revenue requirements were the monies that would have to be collected from the utility customers to recover costs resulting from the installation of the new pollution-control

Ohio Edison Company used decision analysis in the selection process for replacement pollution control equipment.

equipment. An analysis of the decision tree led to the following conclusions.

- The expected value of annual revenue requirements for the electrostatic precipitators was approximately $1 million less than that for the fabric filters.
- The fabric filters had a higher probability of high revenue requirements than the electrostatic precipitators.
- The electrostatic precipitators had nearly a .8 probability of having lower annual revenue requirements.

These results led Ohio Edison to select the electrostatic precipitators for the generating units in question. Had the decision analysis not been performed, the particulate-control decision might have been based chiefly on capital cost, a decision measure that favored the fabric filter equipment. It was felt that the use of decision analysis identified the option with both lower expected revenue requirements and lower risk.

In this chapter we will introduce the methodology of decision analysis that Ohio Edison used. The focus will be on showing how decision analysis can identify the best decision alternative given an uncertain or risk-filled pattern of future events.

---

*The authors are indebted to Thomas J. Madden and M. S. Hyrnick of Ohio Edison Company for providing this Statistics in Practice.

Decision analysis can be used to develop an optimal decision strategy when a decision maker is faced with several decision alternatives and an uncertain or risk-filled pattern of future events. We begin the study of decision analysis by considering decision problems that involve reasonably few decision alternatives and reasonably few future events. Payoff tables are introduced to provide a structure for decision problems. We then introduce decision trees to show the sequential nature of the problems. Decision trees are used to analyze more complex problems and to identify an optimal sequence of decisions, referred to as an optimal decision strategy. In the last section, we show how Bayes' theorem, presented in Chapter 4, can be used to compute branch probabilities for decision trees. TreePlan is an Excel add-in that can be used to develop decision trees. The software and instructions for using TreePlan are provided on the CD accompanying the text.

An example using the decision analysis software TreePlan is provided in Appendix 19.1.

 ## 19.1 Problem Formulation

The first step in the decision analysis process is problem formulation. We begin with a verbal statement of the problem. We then identify the decision alternatives, the uncertain future events, referred to as **chance events**, and the **consequences** associated with each decision alternative and chance event outcome. Let us begin by considering a construction project of the Pittsburgh Development Corporation.

Pittsburgh Development Corporation (PDC) purchased land that will be the site of a new luxury condominium complex. The location provides a spectacular view of downtown Pittsburgh and the Golden Triangle where the Allegheny and Monongahela rivers meet to form the Ohio River. PDC plans to price the individual condominium units between $300,000 and $1,400,000.

PDC commissioned preliminary architectural drawings for three different-sized projects: one with 30 condominiums, one with 60 condominiums, and one with 90 condominiums. The financial success of the project depends upon the size of the condominium complex (the decision alternative) and the demand for the condominiums (the chance event). The statement of the PDC decision problem is to select the size of the new luxury condominium project that will lead to the largest profit given the uncertainty concerning the demand for the condominiums.

Given the statement of the problem, it is clear that PDC's objective is to select the best size for the condominium complex. The three decision alternatives are

d_1 = a small complex with 30 condominiums
d_2 = a medium complex with 60 condominiums
d_3 = a large complex with 90 condominiums

A factor in selecting the best decision alternative is the uncertainty associated with the chance event concerning the demand for the condominiums. When asked about the possible demand for the condominiums, PDC's president acknowledged a wide range of possibilities, but decided that it would be adequate to consider two possible outcomes for the chance event: a strong demand and a weak demand.

In decision analysis, the possible outcomes for a chance event are referred to as the **states of nature**. The states of nature are defined so that one and only one of the possible states of nature will occur. For the PDC problem, the chance event concerning the demand for the condominiums has two states of nature:

s_1 = strong demand for the condominiums
s_2 = weak demand for the condominiums

Management must first select a decision alternative (complex size), then a state of nature follows (demand for the condominiums), and finally a consequence will occur. In this case, the consequence is PDC's profit.

Payoff Tables

Given the three decision alternatives and the two states of nature, which complex size should PDC choose? To answer this question, PDC will need to know the consequence associated with each decision alternative and each state of nature. In decision analysis, we refer to the consequence resulting from a specific combination of a decision alternative and a state of nature as a **payoff**. A table showing payoffs for all combinations of decision alternatives and states of nature is a **payoff table**.

Payoffs can be expressed in terms of profit, cost, time, distance, or any other measure appropriate for the decision problem being analyzed.

Because PDC wants to select the complex size that provides the largest profit, profit is used as the consequence. The payoff table with profits expressed in millions of dollars is shown in Table 19.1. Note, for example, that if a medium complex is built and demand turns out to be strong, a profit of \$14 million will be realized. We will use the notation V_{ij} to denote the payoff associated with decision alternative i and state of nature j. Using Table 19.1, $V_{31} = 20$ indicates a payoff of \$20 million occurs if the decision is to build a large complex (d_3) and the strong demand state of nature (s_1) occurs. Similarly, $V_{32} = -9$ indicates a loss of \$9 million if the decision is to build a large complex (d_3) and the weak demand state of nature (s_2) occurs.

Decision Trees

A **decision tree** graphically shows the sequential nature of the decision-making process. Figure 19.1 presents a decision tree for the PDC project, demonstrating the natural or logical progression that will occur over time. First, PDC must make a decision regarding the size of the condominium complex (d_1, d_2, or d_3). Then, after the decision is implemented, either state of nature s_1 or s_2 will occur. The number at each end point of the tree indicates the payoff associated with a particular sequence. For example the topmost payoff of 8 indicates that an \$8 million profit is anticipated if PDC constructs a small condominium complex (d_1) and demand turns out to be strong (s_1). The next payoff of 7 indicates an anticipated profit of \$7 million if PDC constructs a small condominium complex (d_1) and demand turns out to be weak (s_2). Thus, the decision tree shows graphically the sequences of decision alternatives and states of nature that provide the six possible payoffs.

The decision tree in Figure 19.1 has four **nodes**, numbered 1–4, that represent the decisions and chance events. Squares are used to represent **decision nodes** and circles are used to represent **chance nodes**. Thus, node 1 is a decision node, and nodes 2, 3, and 4 are chance nodes. The **branches** leaving the decision node correspond to the decision alternatives. The branches leaving each chance node correspond to the states of nature. The payoffs are shown at the end of the state-of-nature branches. We now turn to the

TABLE 19.1   PAYOFF TABLE FOR THE PDC CONDOMINIUM PROJECT
(PAYOFFS IN \$ MILLIONS)

Decision Alternative	State of Nature	
	Strong Demand s_1	Weak Demand s_2
Small complex, d_1	8	7
Medium complex, d_2	14	5
Large complex, d_3	20	−9

FIGURE 19.1   DECISION TREE FOR THE PDC CONDOMINIUM PROJECT
(PAYOFFS IN $ MILLIONS)

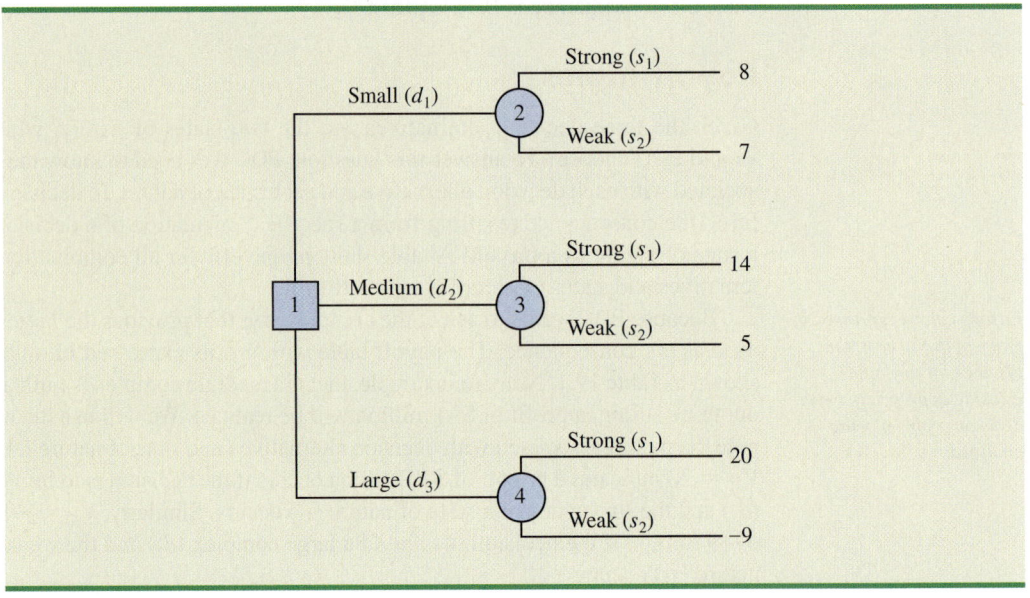

question: How can the decision maker use the information in the payoff table or the decision tree to select the best decision alternative?

NOTES AND COMMENTS

1. Experts in problem solving agree that the first step in solving a complex problem is to decompose it into a series of smaller subproblems. Decision trees provide a useful way to show how a problem can be decomposed and the sequential nature of the decision process.

2. People often view the same problem from different perspectives. Thus, the discussion regarding the development of a decision tree may provide additional insight about the problem.

 # Decision Making with Probabilities

Once we define the decision alternatives and the states of nature for the chance events, we can focus on determining probabilities for the states of nature. The classical method, the relative frequency method, or the subjective method of assigning probabilities discussed in Chapter 4 may be used to identify these probabilities. After determining the appropriate probabilities, we show how to use the **expected value approach** to identify the best, or recommended, decision alternative for the problem.

Expected Value Approach

We begin by defining the expected value of a decision alternative. Let

$$N = \text{the number of states of nature}$$
$$P(s_j) = \text{the probability of state of nature } s_j$$

Because one and only one of the N states of nature can occur, the probabilities must satisfy two conditions:

The probabilities for the states of nature must satisfy the basic requirements for assigning probabilities introduced in Chapter 4.

$$P(s_j) \geq 0 \qquad \text{for all states of nature} \tag{19.1}$$

$$\sum_{j=1}^{N} P(s_j) = P(s_1) + P(s_2) + \cdots + P(s_N) = 1 \tag{19.2}$$

The **expected value (EV)** of decision alternative d_i is as follows.

> EXPECTED VALUE
>
> $$EV(d_i) = \sum_{j=1}^{N} P(s_j)V_{ij} \tag{19.3}$$
>
> where
>
> $V_{ij} =$ the value of the payoff for decision alternative d_i and state of nature s_j

In words, the expected value of a decision alternative is the sum of weighted payoffs for the decision alternative. The weight for a payoff is the probability of the associated state of nature and therefore the probability that the payoff will occur. Let us return to the PDC project to see how the expected value approach can be applied.

PDC is optimistic about the potential for the luxury high-rise condominium complex. Suppose that this optimism leads to an initial subjective probability assessment of .8 that demand will be strong (s_1) and a corresponding probability of .2 that demand will be weak (s_2). Thus, $P(s_1) = .8$ and $P(s_2) = .2$. Using the payoff values in Table 19.1 and equation (19.3), we compute the expected value for each of the three decision alternatives as follows:

$$EV(d_1) = .8(8) \; + .2(7) \quad = \; 7.8$$
$$EV(d_2) = .8(14) + .2(5) \quad = 12.2$$
$$EV(d_3) = .8(20) + .2(-9) = 14.2$$

Thus, using the expected value approach, we find that the large condominium complex, with an expected value of \$14.2 million, is the recommended decision.

The calculations required to identify the decision alternative with the best expected value can be conveniently carried out on a decision tree. Figure 19.2 shows the decision tree for the PDC project with state-of-nature branch probabilities. Working backward through the decision tree, we first compute the expected value at each chance node; that is, at each chance node, we weight each possible payoff by its probability of occurrence. By doing so, we obtain the expected values for nodes 2, 3, and 4, as shown in Figure 19.3.

Because the decision maker controls the branch leaving decision node 1 and because we are trying to maximize the expected profit, the best decision alternative at node 1 is d_3. Thus, the decision tree analysis leads to a recommendation of d_3 with an expected value of \$14.2 million. Note that this recommendation is also obtained with the expected value approach using the payoff table.

In Appendix 19.1, we show how the Excel add-in TreePlan can build this decision tree.

Other decision problems may be substantially more complex than the PDC project, but if a reasonable number of decision alternatives and states of nature are present, you can use the decision tree approach outlined here. First, draw a decision tree consisting of decision nodes, chance nodes, and branches that describe the sequential nature of the problem. If you use the expected value approach, the next step is to determine the probabilities for each of

FIGURE 19.2   PDC DECISION TREE WITH STATE-OF-NATURE BRANCH PROBABILITIES

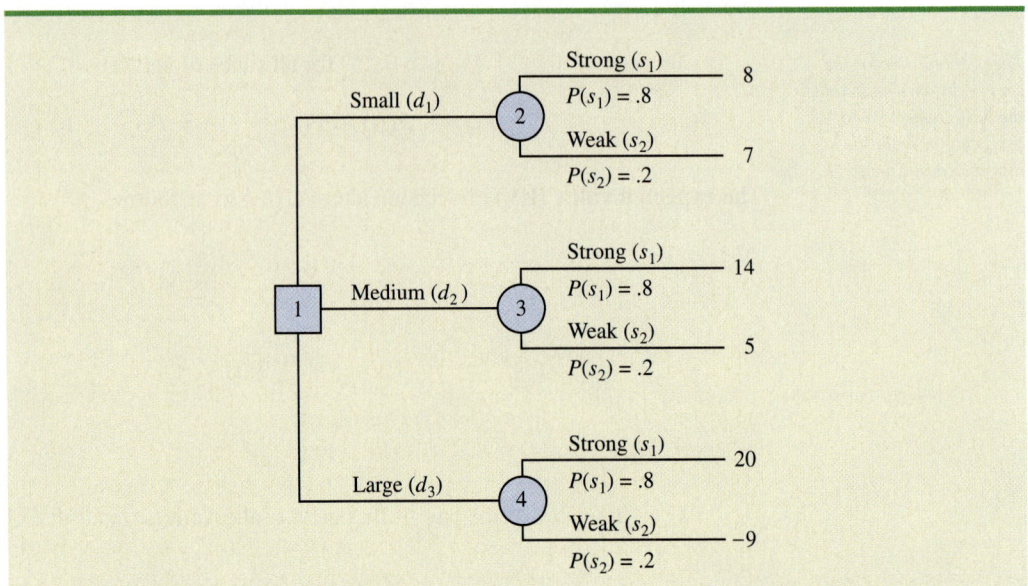

the states of nature and compute the expected value at each chance node. Then select the decision branch leading to the chance node with the best expected value. The decision alternative associated with this branch is the recommended decision.

Expected Value of Perfect Information

Suppose that PDC has the opportunity to conduct a market research study that would help evaluate buyer interest in the condominium project and provide information that management could use to improve the probability assessments for the states of nature. To determine the potential value of this information, we begin by supposing that the study could provide *perfect information* regarding the states of nature; that is, we assume for the moment that

FIGURE 19.3   APPLYING THE EXPECTED VALUE APPROACH USING DECISION TREES

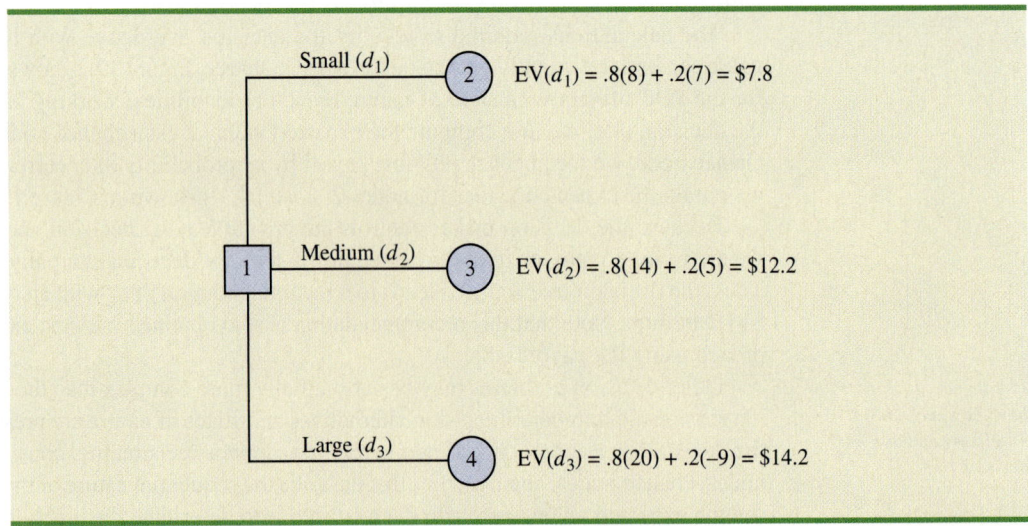

PDC could determine with certainty, prior to making a decision, which state of nature is going to occur. To make use of this perfect information, we will develop a decision strategy that PDC should follow once it knows which state of nature will occur. A decision strategy is simply a decision rule that specifies the decision alternative to be selected after new information becomes available.

To help determine the decision strategy for PDC, we reproduce PDC's payoff table in Table 19.2. Note that, if PDC knew for sure that state of nature s_1 would occur, the best decision alternative would be d_3, with a payoff of $20 million. Similarly, if PDC knew for sure that state of nature s_2 would occur, the best decision alternative would be d_1, with a payoff of $7 million. Thus, we can state PDC's optimal decision strategy if the perfect information becomes available as follows:

If s_1, select d_3 and receive a payoff of $20 million.

If s_2, select d_1 and receive a payoff of $7 million.

What is the expected value for this decision strategy? To compute the expected value with perfect information, we return to the original probabilities for the states of nature: $P(s_1) = .8$, and $P(s_2) = .2$. Thus, there is a .8 probability that the perfect information will indicate state of nature s_1 and the resulting decision alternative d_3 will provide a $20 million profit. Similarly, with a .2 probability for state of nature s_2, the optimal decision alternative d_1 will provide a $7 million profit. Thus, using equation (19.3), the expected value of the decision strategy based on perfect information is

$$.8(20) + .2(7) = 17.4$$

We refer to the expected value of $17.4 million as the *expected value with perfect information* (EVwPI).

Earlier in this section we showed that the recommended decision using the expected value approach is decision alternative d_3, with an expected value of $14.2 million. Because this decision recommendation and expected value computation were made without the benefit of perfect information, $14.2 million is referred to as the *expected value without perfect information* (EVwoPI).

It would be worth $3.2 million for PDC to learn the level of market acceptance before selecting a decision alternative.

The expected value with perfect information is $17.4 million, and the expected value without perfect information is $14.2; therefore, the expected value of the perfect information (EVPI) is $17.4 − $14.2 = $3.2 million. In other words, $3.2 million represents the additional expected value that can be obtained if perfect information were available about the states of nature. Generally speaking, a market research study will not provide "perfect" information; however, if the market research study is a good one, the information gathered might be worth a sizable portion of the $3.2 million. Given the EVPI of $3.2 million, PDC might seriously consider a market survey as a way to obtain more information about the states of nature.

TABLE 19.2   PAYOFF TABLE FOR THE PDC CONDOMINIUM PROJECT ($ MILLIONS)

	State of Nature	
Decision Alternative	**Strong Demand s_1**	**Weak Demand s_2**
Small complex, d_1	8	7
Medium complex, d_2	14	5
Large complex, d_3	20	−9

In general, the **expected value of perfect information (EVPI)** is computed as follows:

EXPECTED VALUE OF PERFECT INFORMATION

$$\text{EVPI} = \left| \text{EVwPI} - \text{EVwoPI} \right| \qquad (19.4)$$

where

$\text{EVPI} =$ expected value of perfect information
$\text{EVwPI} =$ expected value *with* perfect information about the states of nature
$\text{EVwoPI} =$ expected value *without* perfect information about the states of nature

Note the role of the absolute value in equation (19.4). For minimization problems, information helps reduce or lower cost, thus the expected value with perfect information is less than or equal to the expected value without perfect information. In this case, EVPI is the magnitude of the difference between EVwPI and EVwoPI, or the absolute value of the difference as shown in equation (19.4).

Exercises

Methods

1. The following payoff table shows profit for a decision analysis problem with two decision alternatives and three states of nature.

	State of Nature		
Decision Alternative	s_1	s_2	s_3
d_1	250	100	25
d_2	100	100	75

a. Construct a decision tree for this problem.
b. Suppose that the decision maker obtains the probabilities $P(s_1) = .65$, $P(s_2) = .15$, and $P(s_3) = .20$. Use the expected value approach to determine the optimal decision.

2. A decision maker faced with four decision alternatives and four states of nature develops the following profit payoff table.

	State of Nature			
Decision Alternative	s_1	s_2	s_3	s_4
d_1	14	9	10	5
d_2	11	10	8	7
d_3	9	10	10	11
d_4	8	10	11	13

The decision maker obtains information that enables the following probabilities assessments: $P(s_1) = .5$, $P(s_2) = .2$, $P(s_3) = .2$, and $P(s_1) = .1$.
a. Use the expected value approach to determine the optimal decision.
b. Now assume that the entries in the payoff table are costs. Use the expected value approach to determine the optimal decision.

Applications

3. Hudson Corporation is considering three options for managing its data processing opera-tion: continue with its own staff, hire an outside vendor to do the managing (referred to as *outsourcing*), or use a combination of its own staff and an outside vendor. The cost of the operation depends on future demand. The annual cost of each option (in thousands of dol-lars) depends on demand as follows.

		Demand	
Staffing Option	**High**	**Medium**	**Low**
Own staff	650	650	600
Outside vendor	900	600	300
Combination	800	650	500

   a. If the demand probabilities are .2, .5, and .3, which decision alternative will minimize the expected cost of the data processing operation? What is the expected annual cost associated with your recommendation?
   b. What is the expected value of perfect information?

4. Myrtle Air Express decided to offer direct service from Cleveland to Myrtle Beach. Man-agement must decide between a full price service using the company's new fleet of jet air-craft and a discount service using smaller capacity commuter planes. It is clear that the best choice depends on the market reaction to the service Myrtle Air offers. Management de-veloped estimates of the contribution to profit for each type of service based upon two pos-sible levels of demand for service to Myrtle Beach: strong and weak. The following table shows the estimated quarterly profits (in thousands of dollars).

	Demand for Service	
Service	**Strong**	**Weak**
Full Price	$960	−$490
Discount	$670	$320

   a. What is the decision to be made, what is the chance event, and what is the consequence for this problem? How many decision alternatives are there? How many outcomes are there for the chance event?
   b. Suppose that management of Myrtle Air Express believes that the probability of strong demand is .7 and the probability of weak demand is .3. Use the expected value ap-proach to determine an optimal decision.
   c. Suppose that the probability of strong demand is .8 and the probability of weak de-mand is .2. What is the optimal decision using the expected value approach?

5. The distance from Potsdam to larger markets and limited air service have hindered the town in attracting new industry. Air Express, a major overnight delivery service, is con-sidering establishing a regional distribution center in Potsdam. But Air Express will not es-tablish the center unless the length of the runway at the local airport is increased. Another candidate for new development is Diagnostic Research, Inc. (DRI), a leading producer of medical testing equipment. DRI is considering building a new manufacturing plant. In-creasing the length of the runway is not a requirement for DRI, but the planning commis-sion feels that doing so will help convince DRI to locate their new plant in Potsdam.

Assuming that the town lengthens the runway, the Potsdam planning commission believes that the probabilities shown in the following table are applicable.

	DRI Plant	**No DRI Plant**
Air Express Center	.30	.10
No Air Express Center	.40	.20

For instance, the probability that Air Express will establish a distribution center and DRI will build a plant is .30.

The estimated annual revenue to the town, after deducting the cost of lengthening the runway, is as follows:

	DRI Plant	**No DRI Plant**
Air Express Center	$600,000	$150,000
No Air Express Center	$250,000	−$200,000

If the runway expansion project is not conducted, the planning commission assesses the probability DRI will locate their new plant in Potsdam at .6; in this case, the estimated annual revenue to the town will be $450,000. If the runway expansion project is not conducted and DRI does not locate in Potsdam, the annual revenue will be $0 since no cost will have been incurred and no revenues will be forthcoming.

a. What is the decision to be made, what is the chance event, and what is the consequence?
b. Compute the expected annual revenue associated with the decision alternative to lengthen the runway.
c. Compute the expected annual revenue associated with the decision alternative to not lengthen the runway.
d. Should the town elect to lengthen the runway? Explain.
e. Suppose that the probabilities associated with lengthening the runway were as follows:

	DRI Plant	**No DRI Plant**
Air Express Center	.40	.10
No Air Express Center	.30	.20

What effect, if any, would this change in the probabilities have on the recommended decision?

6. Seneca Hill Winery recently purchased land for the purpose of establishing a new vineyard. Management is considering two varieties of white grapes for the new vineyard: Chardonnay and Riesling. The Chardonnay grapes would be used to produce a dry Chardonnay wine, and the Riesling grapes would be used to produce a semi-dry Riesling wine. It takes approximately four years from the time of planting before new grapes can be harvested. This length of time creates a great deal of uncertainty concerning future demand and makes the decision concerning the type of grapes to plant difficult. Three possibilities are being considered: Chardonnay grapes only; Riesling grapes only; and both Chardonnay and Riesling grapes. Seneca management decided that for planning purposes it would be adequate to consider only two demand possibilities for each type of

wine: strong or weak. With two possibilities for each type of wine it was necessary to assess four probabilities. With the help of some forecasts in industry publications management made the following probability assessments.

	Riesling Demand	
Chardonnay Demand	**Weak**	**Strong**
Weak	.05	.50
Strong	.25	.20

Revenue projections show an annual contribution to profit of $20,000 if Seneca Hill only plants Chardonnay grapes and demand is weak for Chardonnay wine, and $70,000 if they only plant Chardonnay grapes and demand is strong for Chardonnay wine. If they only plant Riesling grapes, the annual profit projection is $25,000 if demand is weak for Riesling grapes and $45,000 if demand is strong for Riesling grapes. If Seneca plants both types of grapes, the annual profit projections are shown in the following table.

	Riesling Demand	
Chardonnay Demand	**Weak**	**Strong**
Weak	$22,000	$40,000
Strong	$26,000	$60,000

a. What is the decision to be made, what is the chance event, and what is the consequence? Identify the alternatives for the decisions and the possible outcomes for the chance events.
b. Develop a decision tree.
c. Use the expected value approach to recommend which alternative Seneca Hill Winery should follow in order to maximize expected annual profit.
d. Suppose management is concerned about the probability assessments when demand for Chardonnay wine is strong. Some believe it is likely for Riesling demand to also be strong in this case. Suppose the probability of strong demand for Chardonnay and weak demand for Riesling is .05 and that the probability of strong demand for Chardonnay and strong demand for Riesling is .40. How does this change the recommended decision? Assume that the probabilities when Chardonnay demand is weak are still .05 and .50.
e. Other members of the management team expect the Chardonnay market to become saturated at some point in the future causing a fall in prices. Suppose that the annual profit projections fall to $50,000 when demand for Chardonnay is strong and Chardonnay grapes only are planted. Using the original probability assessments, determine how this change would affect the optimal decision.

7. The Lake Placid Town Council has decided to build a new community center to be used for conventions, concerts, and other public events, but considerable controversy surrounds the appropriate size. Many influential citizens want a large center that would be a showcase for the area, but the mayor feels that if demand does not support such a center, the community will lose a large amount of money. To provide structure for the decision process, the council narrowed the building alternatives to three sizes: small, medium, and large. Everybody agreed that the critical factor in choosing the best size is the number of people who will want to use the new facility. A regional planning consultant provided demand estimates under three scenarios: worst case, base case, and best case. The worst-case scenario corresponds to a situation in which tourism drops significantly; the base-case scenario corresponds to a situation in which Lake Placid continues to attract visitors at cur-

rent levels; and the best-case scenario corresponds to a significant increase in tourism. The consultant has provided probability assessments of .10, .60, and .30 for the worst-case, base-case, and best-case scenarios, respectively.

The town council suggested using net cash flow over a five-year planning horizon as the criterion for deciding on the best size. A consultant developed the following projections of net cash flow (in thousands of dollars) for a five-year planning horizon. All costs, including the consultant's fee, are included.

	Demand Scenario		
Center Size	Worst Case	Base Case	Best Case
Small	400	500	660
Medium	−250	650	800
Large	−400	580	990

a. What decision should Lake Placid make using the expected value approach?
b. Compute the expected value of perfect information. Do you think it would be worth trying to obtain additional information concerning which scenario is likely to occur?
c. Suppose the probability of the worst-case scenario increases to .2, the probability of the base-case scenario decreases to .5, and the probability of the best-case scenario remains at .3. What effect, if any, would these changes have on the decision recommendation?
d. The consultant suggested that an expenditure of $150,000 on a promotional campaign over the planning horizon will effectively reduce the probability of the worst-case scenario to zero. If the campaign can be expected to also increase the probability of the best-case scenario to .4, is it a good investment?

19.3 Decision Analysis with Sample Information

In applying the expected value approach, we showed how probability information about the states of nature affects the expected value calculations and thus the decision recommendation. Frequently, decision makers have preliminary or **prior probability** assessments for the states of nature that are the best probability values available at that time. However, to make the best possible decision, the decision maker may want to seek additional information about the states of nature. This new information can be used to revise or update the prior probabilities so that the final decision is based on more accurate probabilities for the states of nature. Most often, additional information is obtained through experiments designed to provide **sample information** about the states of nature. Raw material sampling, product testing, and market research studies are examples of experiments (or studies) that may enable management to revise or update the state-of-nature probabilities. These revised probabilities are called **posterior probabilities**.

Let us return to the PDC project and assume that management is considering a six-month market research study designed to learn more about potential market acceptance of the PDC condominium project. Management anticipates that the market research study will provide one of the following two results:

1. Favorable report: A significant number of the individuals contacted express interest in purchasing a PDC condominium.
2. Unfavorable report: Very few of the individuals contacted express interest in purchasing a PDC condominium.

Decision Tree

The decision tree for the PDC project with sample information shows the logical sequence for the decisions and the chance events in Figure 19.4. First, PDC's management must decide whether the market research should be conducted. If it is conducted, PDC's management must be prepared to make a decision about the size of the condominium project if the market research report is favorable and, possibly, a different decision about the size of the condominium project if the market research report is unfavorable.

FIGURE 19.4 THE PDC DECISION TREE INCLUDING THE MARKET RESEARCH STUDY

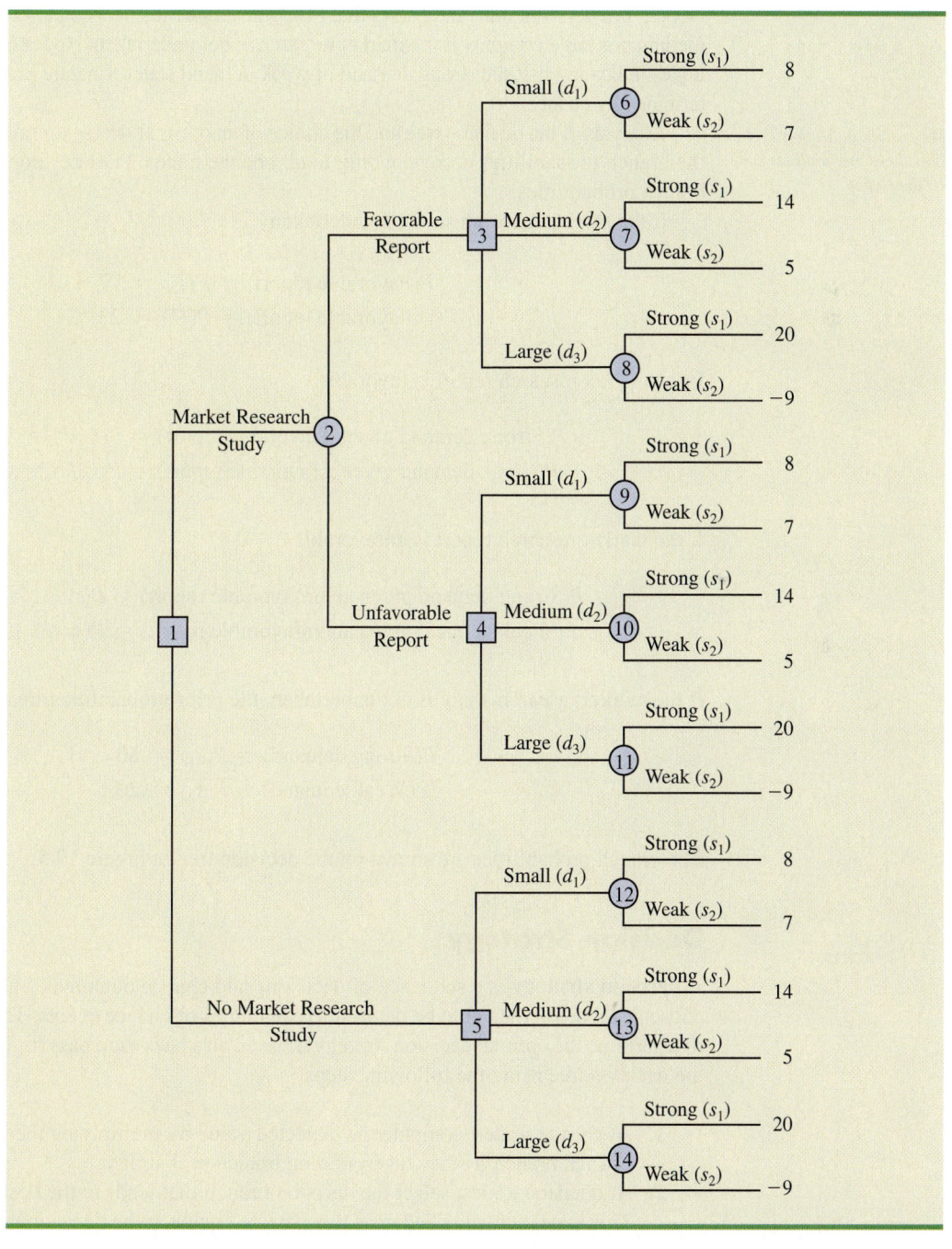

In Figure 19.4, the squares are decision nodes and the circles are chance nodes. At each decision node, the branch of the tree that is taken is based on the decision made. At each chance node, the branch of the tree that is taken is based on probability or chance. For example, decision node 1 shows that PDC must first make the decision whether to conduct the market research study. If the market research study is undertaken, chance node 2 indicates that both the favorable report branch and the unfavorable report branch are not under PDC's control and will be determined by chance. Node 3 is a decision node, indicating that PDC must make the decision to construct the small, medium, or large complex if the market research report is favorable. Node 4 is a decision node showing that PDC must make the decision to construct the small, medium, or large complex if the market research report is unfavorable. Node 5 is a decision node indicating that PDC must make the decision to construct the small, medium, or large complex if the market research is not undertaken. Nodes 6 to 14 are chance nodes indicating that the strong demand or weak demand state-of-nature branches will be determined by chance.

We explain in Section 19.4 how these probabilities can be developed.

Analysis of the decision tree and the choice of an optimal strategy requires that we know the branch probabilities corresponding to all chance nodes. PDC developed the following branch probabilities.

If the market research study is undertaken

$$P(\text{Favorable report}) = P(F) = .77$$
$$P(\text{Unfavorable report}) = P(U) = .23$$

If the market research report is favorable

$$P(\text{Strong demand given a favorable report}) = P(s_1|F) = .94$$
$$P(\text{Weak demand given a favorable report}) = P(s_2|F) = .06$$

If the market research report is unfavorable

$$P(\text{Strong demand given an unfavorable report}) = P(s_1|U) = .35$$
$$P(\text{Weak demand given an unfavorable report}) = P(s_2|U) = .65$$

If the market research study is not undertaken, the prior probabilities are applicable.

$$P(\text{Strong demand}) = P(s_1) = .80$$
$$P(\text{Weak demand}) = P(s_2) = .20$$

The branch probabilities are shown on the decision tree in Figure 19.5.

Decision Strategy

A **decision strategy** is a sequence of decisions and chance outcomes where the decisions chosen depend on the yet to be determined outcomes of chance events. The approach used to determine the optimal decision strategy is based on a backward pass (right to left) through the decision tree using the following steps:

1. At chance nodes, compute the expected value by multiplying the payoff at the end of each branch by the corresponding branch probability.
2. At decision nodes, select the decision branch that leads to the best expected value. This expected value becomes the expected value at the decision node.

FIGURE 19.5   THE PDC DECISION TREE WITH BRANCH PROBABILITIES

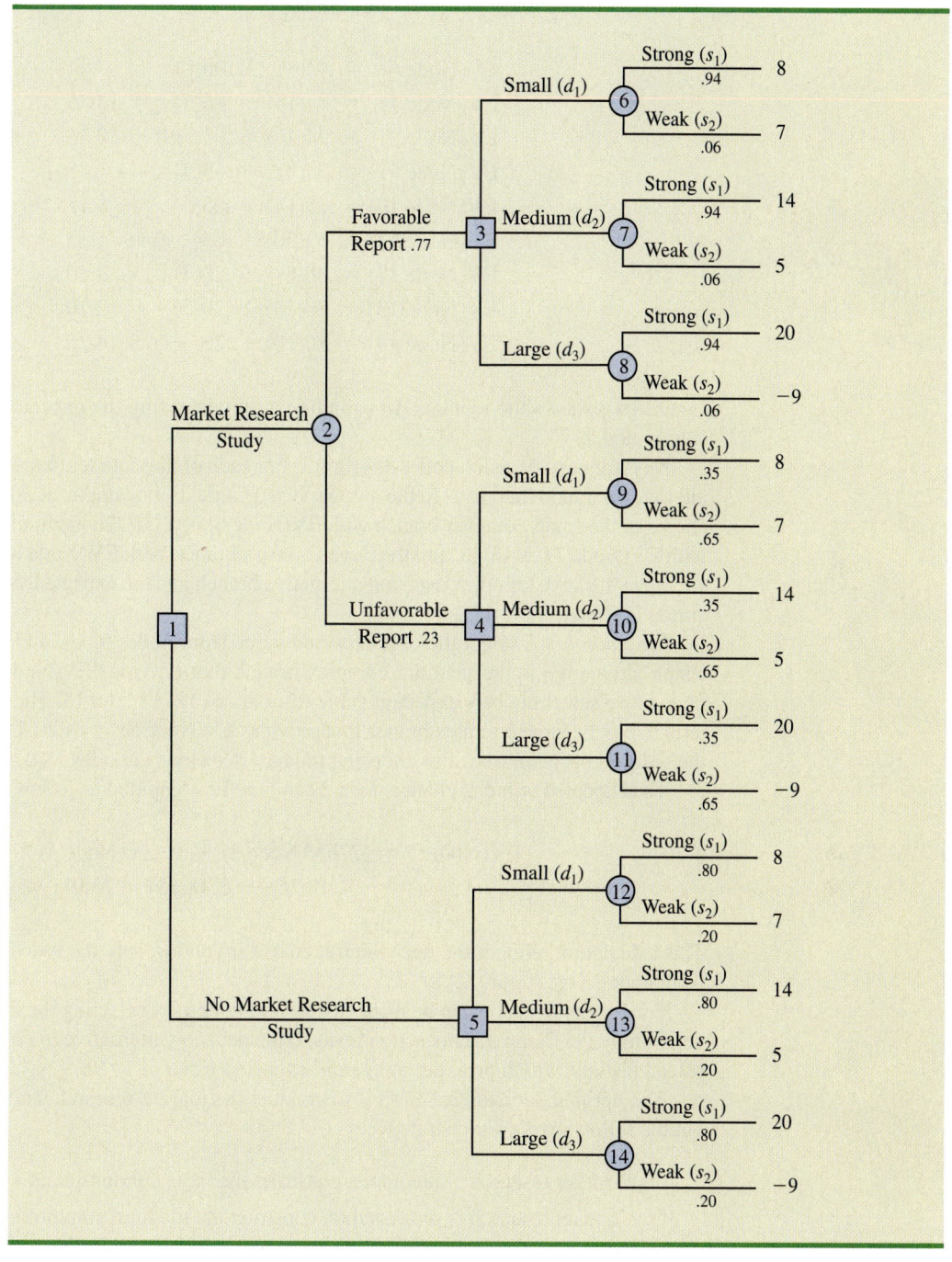

Starting the backward pass calculations by computing the expected values at chance nodes 6 to 14 provides the following results.

$$
\begin{aligned}
\text{EV(Node 6)} &= .94(8) \;+ .06(7) \;= \;7.94 \\
\text{EV(Node 7)} &= .94(14) + .06(5) \;= 13.46 \\
\text{EV(Node 8)} &= .94(20) + .06(-9) = 18.26 \\
\text{EV(Node 9)} &= .35(8) \;+ .65(7) \;= \;7.35 \\
\text{EV(Node 10)} &= .35(14) + .65(5) \;= \;8.15 \\
\text{EV(Node 11)} &= .35(20) + .65(-9) = \;1.15 \\
\text{EV(Node 12)} &= .80(8) \;+ .20(7) \;= \;7.80 \\
\text{EV(Node 13)} &= .80(14) + .20(5) \;= 12.20 \\
\text{EV(Node 14)} &= .80(20) + .20(-9) = 14.20
\end{aligned}
$$

Figure 19.6 shows the reduced decision tree after computing the expected values at these chance nodes.

Next move to decision nodes 3, 4, and 5. For each of these nodes, we select the decision alternative branch that leads to the best expected value. For example, at node 3 we have the choice of the small complex branch with EV(Node 6) = 7.94, the medium complex branch with EV(Node 7) = 13.46, and the large complex branch with EV(Node 8) = 18.26. Thus, we select the large complex decision alternative branch and the expected value at node 3 becomes EV(Node 3) = 18.26.

For node 4, we select the best expected value from nodes 9, 10, and 11. The best decision alternative is the medium complex branch that provides EV(Node 4) = 8.15. For node 5, we select the best expected value from nodes 12, 13, and 14. The best decision alternative is the large complex branch that provides EV(Node 5) = 14.20. Figure 19.7 shows the reduced decision tree after choosing the best decisions at nodes 3, 4, and 5.

The expected value at chance node 2 can now be computed as follows:

$$
\begin{aligned}
\text{EV(Node 2)} &= .77\text{EV(Node 3)} + .23\text{EV(Node 4)} \\
&= .77(18.26) + .23(8.15) = 15.93
\end{aligned}
$$

This calculation reduces the decision tree to one involving only the two decision branches from node 1 (see Figure 19.8).

Finally, the decision can be made at decision node 1 by selecting the best expected values from nodes 2 and 5. This action leads to the decision alternative to conduct the market research study, which provides an overall expected value of 15.93.

The optimal decision for PDC is to conduct the market research study and then carry out the following decision strategy:

If the market research is favorable, construct the large condominium complex.

If the market research is unfavorable, construct the medium condominium complex.

The analysis of the PDC decision tree illustrates the methods that can be used to analyze more complex sequential decision problems. First, draw a decision tree consisting of decision and chance nodes and branches that describe the sequential nature of the problem. Determine the probabilities for all chance outcomes. Then, by working backward through the tree, compute expected values at all chance nodes and select the best decision branch at all decision nodes. The sequence of optimal decision branches determines the optimal decision strategy for the problem.

FIGURE 19.6 PDC DECISION TREE AFTER COMPUTING EXPECTED VALUES AT CHANCE NODES 6 TO 14

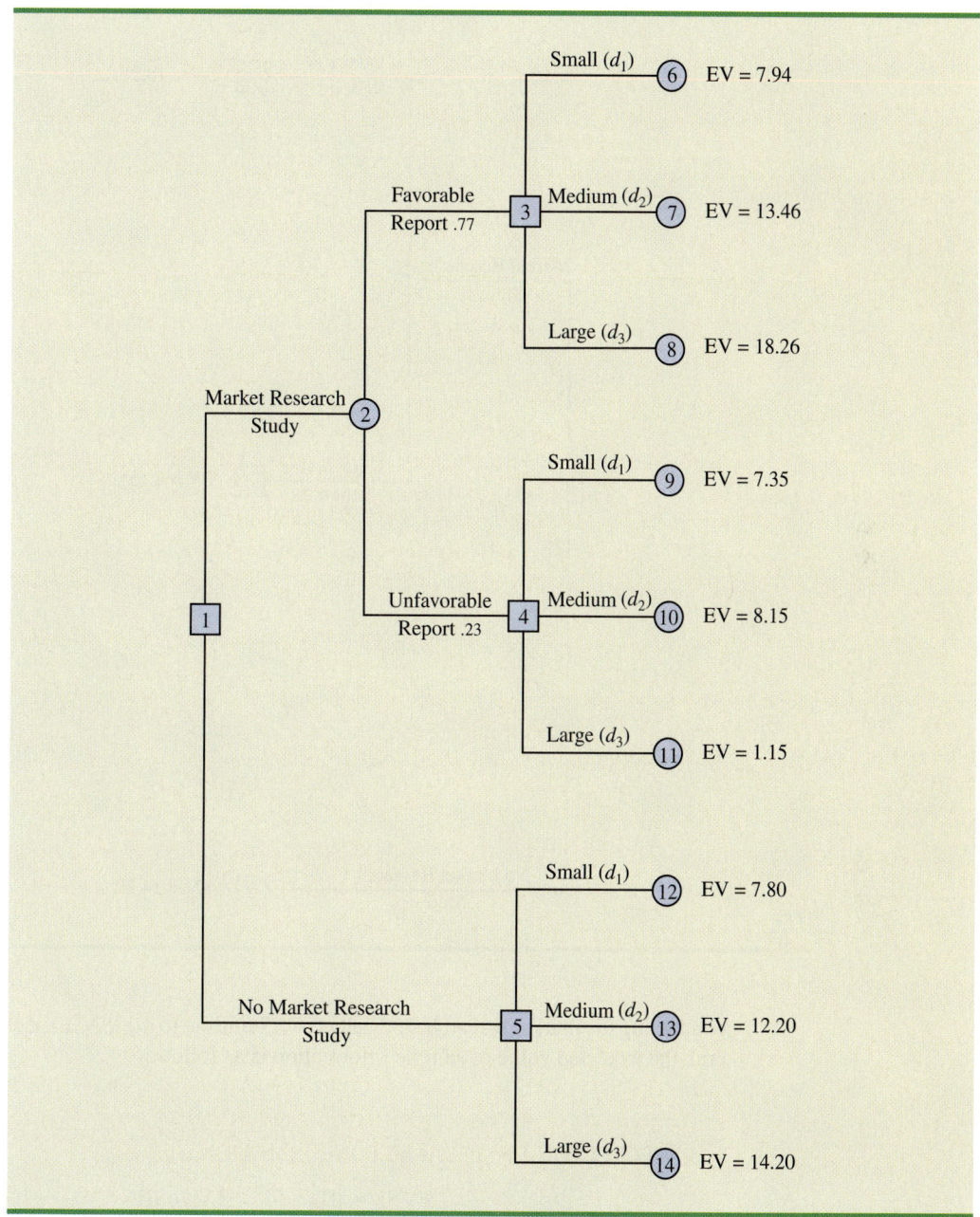

Expected Value of Sample Information

The EVSI = $1.73 million suggests PDC should be willing to pay up to $1.73 million to conduct the market research study.

In the PDC project, the market research study is the sample information used to determine the optimal decision strategy. The expected value associated with the market research study is $15.93. In Section 19.2 we showed that the best expected value if the market research study is *not* undertaken is $14.20. Thus, we can conclude that the difference, $15.93 − $14.20 = $1.73, is the **expected value of sample information (EVSI)**. In other words,

FIGURE 19.7 PDC DECISION TREE AFTER CHOOSING BEST DECISIONS AT NODES 3, 4, AND 5

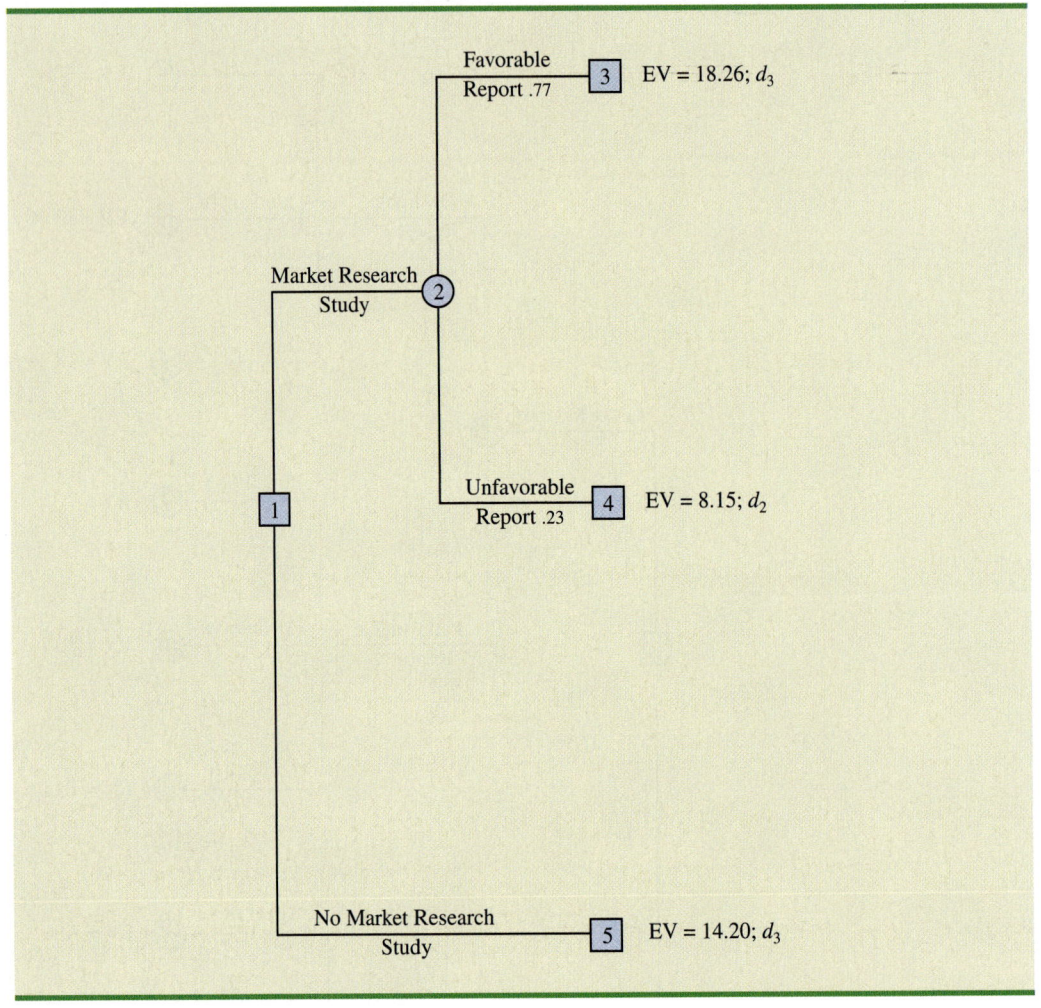

conducting the market research study adds $1.73 million to the PDC expected value. In general, the expected value of sample information is as follows:

EXPECTED VALUE OF SAMPLE INFORMATION

$$EVSI = |EVwSI - EVwoSI| \qquad (19.5)$$

where

$EVSI$ = expected value of sample information
$EVwSI$ = expected value *with* sample information about the states of nature
$EVwoSI$ = expected value *without* sample information about the states of nature

---

Note the role of the absolute value in equation (19.5). For minimization problems the expected value with sample information is always less than or equal to the expected value without

FIGURE 19.8   PDC DECISION TREE REDUCED TO TWO DECISION BRANCHES

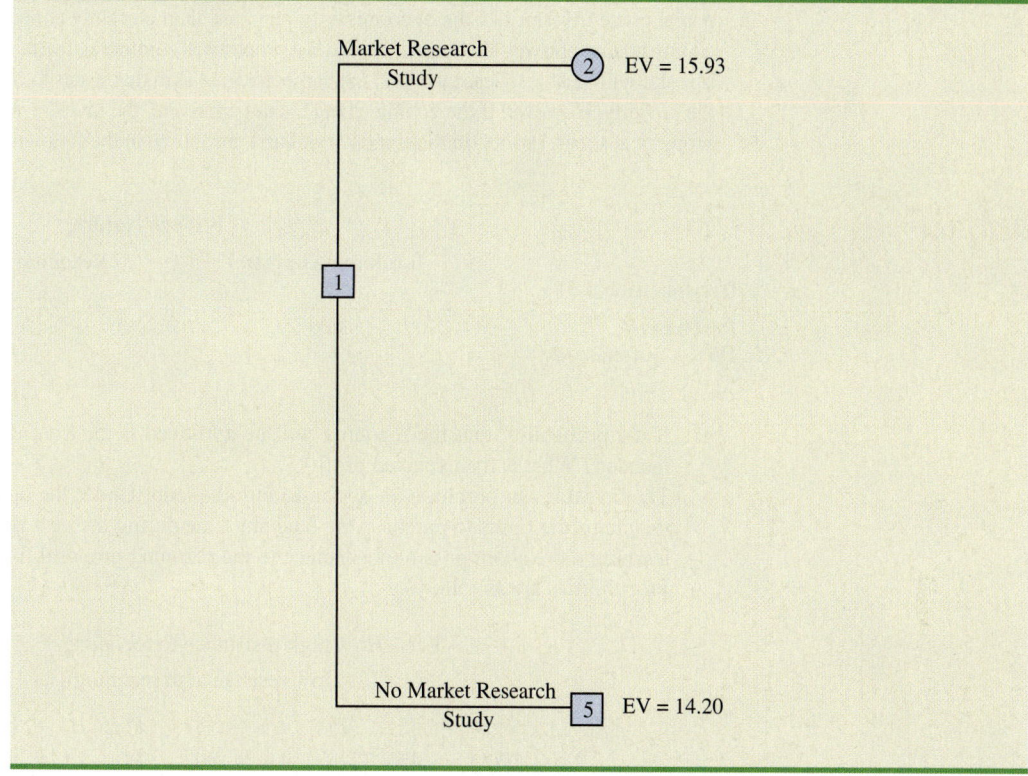

sample information. In this case, EVSI is the magnitude of the difference between EVwSI and EVwoSI; thus, by taking the absolute value of the difference as shown in equation (19.5), we can handle both the maximization and minimization cases with one equation.

Exercises

Methods

8.   Consider a variation of the PDC decision tree shown in Figure 19.5. As before, the company must first decide whether to undertake the market research study. If the market research study is conducted, the outcome will either be favorable (F) or unfavorable (U). However, for this exercise, assume there are only two decision alternatives d_1 and d_2 and two states of nature s_1 and s_2. The payoff table showing profit is as follows:

	State of Nature	
Decision Alternative	s_1	s_2
d_1	100	300
d_2	400	200

a.   Show the decision tree.
b.   Use the following probabilities. What is the optimal decision strategy?

$$P(F) = .56 \quad P(s_1 \mid F) = .57 \quad P(s_1 \mid U) = .18 \quad P(s_1) = .40$$
$$P(U) = .44 \quad P(s_2 \mid F) = .43 \quad P(s_2 \mid U) = .82 \quad P(s_2) = .60$$

Applications

9. A real estate investor has the opportunity to purchase land currently zoned residential. If the county board approves a request to rezone the property as commercial within the next year, the investor will be able to lease the land to a large discount firm that wants to open a new store on the property. However, if the zoning change is not approved, the investor will have to sell the property at a loss. Profits (in thousands of dollars) are shown in the following payoff table.

	State of Nature	
	Rezoning Approved	Rezoning Not Approved
Decision Alternative	s_1	s_2
Purchase, d_1	600	-200
Do not purchase, d_2	0	0

   a. If the probability that the rezoning will be approved is .5, what decision is recommended? What is the expected profit?
   b. The investor can purchase an option to buy the land. Under the option, the investor maintains the rights to purchase the land any time during the next three months while learning more about possible resistance to the rezoning proposal from area residents. Probabilities are as follows.

$$\text{Let} \quad H = \text{high resistance to rezoning}$$
$$L = \text{low resistance to rezoning}$$

$$P(H) = .55 \quad P(s_1 \mid H) = .18 \quad P(s_2 \mid H) = .82$$
$$P(L) = .45 \quad P(s_1 \mid L) = .89 \quad P(s_2 \mid L) = .11$$

   What is the optimal decision strategy if the investor uses the option period to learn more about the resistance from area residents before making the purchase decision?
   c. If the option will cost the investor an additional $10,000, should the investor purchase the option? Why or why not? What is the maximum that the investor should be willing to pay for the option?

10. Dante Development Corporation is considering bidding on a contract for a new office building complex. Figure 19.9 shows the decision tree prepared by one of Dante's analysts. At node 1, the company must decide whether to bid on the contract. The cost of preparing the bid is $200,000. The upper branch from node 2 shows that the company has a .8 probability of winning the contract if it submits a bid. If the company wins the bid, it will have to pay $2,000,000 to become a partner in the project. Node 3 shows that the company will then consider doing a market research study to forecast demand for the office units prior to beginning construction. The cost of this study is $150,000. Node 4 is a chance node showing the possible outcomes of the market research study.

   Nodes 5, 6, and 7 are similar in that they are the decision nodes for Dante to either build the office complex or sell the rights in the project to another developer. The decision to build the complex will result in an income of $5,000,000 if demand is high and $3,000,000 if demand is moderate. If Dante chooses to sell its rights in the project to another developer, income from the sale is estimated to be $3,500,000. The probabilities shown at nodes 4, 8, and 9 are based on the projected outcomes of the market research study.
   a. Verify Dante's profit projections shown at the ending branches of the decision tree by calculating the payoffs of $2,650,000 and $650,000 for first two outcomes.
   b. What is the optimal decision strategy for Dante, and what is the expected profit for this project?
   c. What would the cost of the market research study have to be before Dante would change its decision about conducting the study?

FIGURE 19.9 DECISION TREE FOR THE DANTE DEVELOPMENT CORPORATION

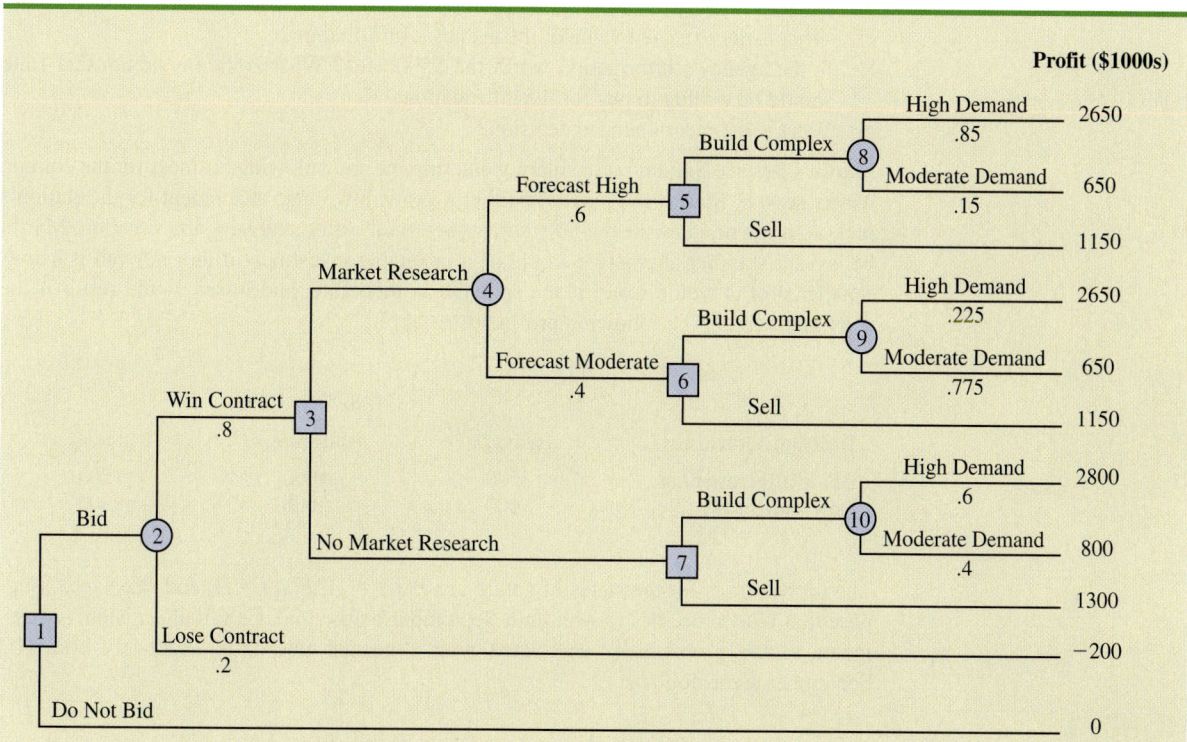

11. Hale's TV Productions is considering producing a pilot for a comedy series in the hope of selling it to a major television network. The network may decide to reject the series, but it may also decide to purchase the rights to the series for either one or two years. At this point in time, Hale may either produce the pilot and wait for the network's decision or transfer the rights for the pilot and series to a competitor for $100,000. Hale's decision alternatives and profits (in thousands of dollars) are as follows:

	State of Nature		
Decision Alternative	**Reject, s_1**	**1 Year, s_2**	**2 Years, s_3**
Produce pilot, d_1	-100	50	150
Sell to competitor, d_2	100	100	100

The probabilities for the states of nature are $P(s_1) = .2$, $P(s_2) = .3$, and $P(s_3) = .5$. For a consulting fee of $5000, an agency will review the plans for the comedy series and indicate the overall chances of a favorable network reaction to the series. Assume that the agency review will result in a favorable (F) or an unfavorable (U) review and that the following probabilities are relevant.

$$P(F) = .69 \qquad P(s_1 \mid F) = .09 \qquad P(s_1 \mid U) = .45$$
$$P(U) = .31 \qquad P(s_2 \mid F) = .26 \qquad P(s_2 \mid U) = .39$$
$$P(s_3 \mid F) = .65 \qquad P(s_3 \mid U) = .16$$

a. Construct a decision tree for this problem.
b. What is the recommended decision if the agency opinion is not used? What is the expected value?

   c. What is the expected value of perfect information?
   d. What is Hale's optimal decision strategy assuming the agency's information is used?
   e. What is the expected value of the agency's information?
   f. Is the agency's information worth the $5000 fee? What is the maximum that Hale should be willing to pay for the information?
   g. What is the recommended decision?

12. Martin's Service Station is considering entering the snowplowing business for the coming winter season. Martin can purchase either a snowplow blade attachment for the station's pick-up truck or a new heavy-duty snowplow truck. After analyzing the situation, Martin believes that either alternative would be a profitable investment if the snowfall is heavy. Smaller profits would result if the snowfall is moderate, and losses would result if the snowfall is light. The following profits/losses apply.

| | State of Nature | | |
Decision Alternative	Heavy, s_1	Moderate, s_2	Light, s_3
Blade attachment, d_1	3500	1000	−1500
New snowplow, d_2	7000	2000	−9000

The probabilities for the states of nature are $P(s_1) = .4$, $P(s_2) = .3$, and $P(s_3) = .3$. Suppose that Martin decides to wait until September before making a final decision. Assessments of the probabilities associated with a normal (N) or unseasonably cold (U) September are as follows:

$$P(N) = .8 \qquad P(s_1 \mid N) = .35 \qquad P(s_1 \mid U) = .62$$
$$P(U) = .2 \qquad P(s_2 \mid N) = .30 \qquad P(s_2 \mid U) = .31$$
$$\qquad\qquad P(s_3 \mid N) = .35 \qquad P(s_3 \mid U) = .07$$

   a. Construct a decision tree for this problem.
   b. What is the recommended decision if Martin does not wait until September? What is the expected value?
   c. What is the expected value of perfect information?
   d. What is Martin's optimal decision strategy if the decision is not made until the September weather is determined? What is the expected value of this decision strategy?

13. Lawson's Department Store faces a buying decision for a seasonal product for which demand can be high, medium, or low. The purchaser for Lawson's can order 1, 2, or 3 lots of the product before the season begins but cannot reorder later. Profit projections (in thousands of dollars) are shown.

| | State of Nature | | |
| | High Demand | Medium Demand | Low Demand |
Decision Alternative	s_1	s_2	s_3
Order 1 lot, d_1	60	60	50
Order 2 lots, d_2	80	80	30
Order 3 lots, d_3	100	70	10

   a. If the prior probabilities for the three states of nature are .3, .3, and .4, respectively, what is the recommended order quantity?
   b. At each preseason sales meeting, the vice president of sales provides a personal opinion regarding potential demand for this product. Because of the vice president's enthusiasm and optimistic nature, the predictions of market conditions have always been

either "excellent" (E) or "very good" (V). Probabilities are as follows. What is the optimal decision strategy?

$$P(E) = .7 \qquad P(s_1 \mid E) = .34 \qquad P(s_1 \mid V) = .20$$
$$P(V) = .3 \qquad P(s_2 \mid E) = .32 \qquad P(s_2 \mid V) = .26$$
$$P(s_3 \mid E) = .34 \qquad P(s_3 \mid V) = .54$$

   c.   Compute EVPI and EVSI. Discuss whether the firm should consider a consulting expert who could provide independent forecasts of market conditions for the product.

19.4   Computing Branch Probabilities Using Bayes' Theorem

In Section 19.3 the branch probabilities for the PDC decision tree chance nodes were specified in the problem description. No computations were required to determine these probabilities. In this section we show how **Bayes' theorem**, a topic covered in Chapter 4, can be used to compute branch probabilities for decision trees.

The PDC decision tree is shown again in Figure 19.10. Let

$$F = \text{favorable market research report}$$
$$U = \text{unfavorable market research report}$$
$$s_1 = \text{strong demand (state of nature 1)}$$
$$s_2 = \text{weak demand (state of nature 2)}$$

At chance node 2, we need to know the branch probabilities $P(F)$ and $P(U)$. At chance nodes 6, 7, and 8, we need to know the branch probabilities $P(s_1 \mid F)$, the probability of state of nature 1 given a favorable market research report, and $P(s_2 \mid F)$, the probability of state of nature 2 given a favorable market research report. $P(s_1 \mid F)$ and $P(s_2 \mid F)$ are referred to as *posterior probabilities* because they are conditional probabilities based on the outcome of the sample information. At chance nodes 9, 10, and 11, we need to know the branch probabilities $P(s_1 \mid U)$ and $P(s_2 \mid U)$; note that these are also posterior probabilities, denoting the probabilities of the two states of nature *given* that the market research report is unfavorable. Finally at chance nodes 12, 13, and 14, we need the probabilities for the states of nature, $P(s_1)$ and $P(s_2)$, if the market research study is not undertaken.

In making the probability computations, we need to know PDC's assessment of the probabilities for the two states of nature, $P(s_1)$ and $P(s_2)$, which are the prior probabilities as discussed earlier. In addition, we must know the **conditional probability** of the market research outcomes (the sample information) *given* each state of nature. For example, we need to know the conditional probability of a favorable market research report given that strong demand exists for the PDC project; note that this conditional probability of F given state of nature s_1 is written $P(F \mid s_1)$. To carry out the probability calculations, we will need conditional probabilities for all sample outcomes given all states of nature, that is, $P(F \mid s_1)$, $P(F \mid s_2)$, $P(U \mid s_1)$, and $P(U \mid s_2)$. In the PDC project, we assume that the following assessments are available for these conditional probabilities.

	Market Research Report	
State of Nature	**Favorable, F**	**Unfavorable, U**
Strong demand, s_1	$P(F \mid s_1) = .90$	$P(U \mid s_1) = .10$
Weak demand, s_2	$P(F \mid s_2) = .25$	$P(U \mid s_2) = .75$

FIGURE 19.10   THE PDC DECISION TREE

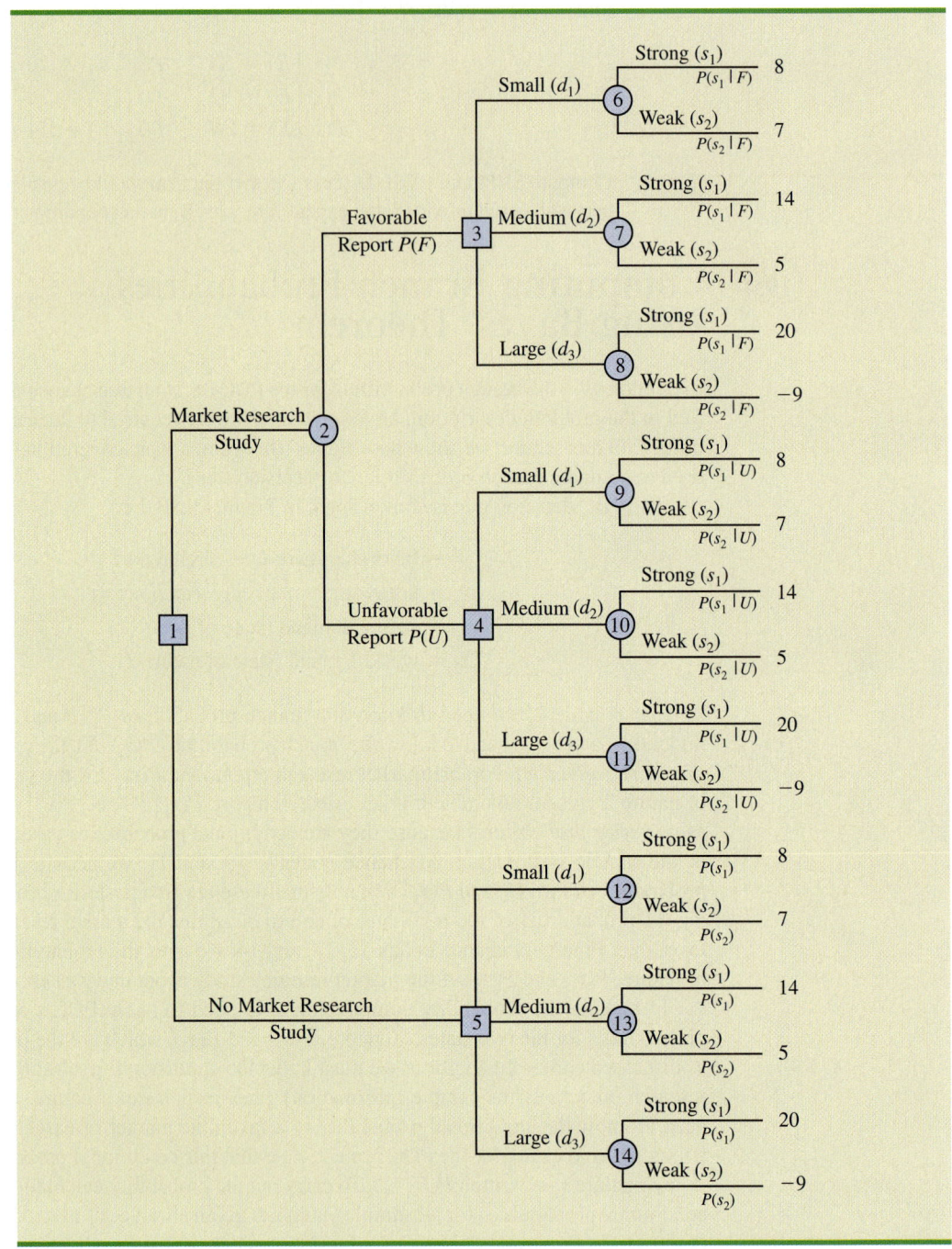

Note that the preceding probability assessments provide a reasonable degree of confidence in the market research study. If the true state of nature is s_1 (strong demand), the probability of a favorable market research report is .90, and the probability of an unfavorable market research report is .10. If the true state of nature is s_2 (weak demand), the probability of a favorable market research report is .25, and the probability of an unfavorable market research report is .75. The reason for a .25 probability of a potentially misleading favorable market research report for state of nature s_2 is that when some potential buyers

TABLE 19.3   BRANCH PROBABILITIES FOR THE PDC CONDOMINIUM PROJECT BASED ON A FAVORABLE MARKET RESEARCH REPORT

State of Nature s_j	Prior Probability $P(s_j)$	Conditional Probability $P(F \mid s_j)$	Joint Probability $P(F \cap s_j)$	Posterior Probability $P(s_j \mid F)$
s_1	.8	.90	.72	.94
s_2	.2	.25	.05	.06
	1.0		$P(F) = .77$	1.00

first hear about the new condominium project, their enthusiasm may lead them to overstate their real interest in it. A potential buyer's initial favorable response can change quickly to a "no thank you" when later faced with the reality of signing a purchase contract and making a down payment.

In the following discussion, we present a tabular approach as a convenient method for carrying out the probability computations. The computations for the PDC project based on a favorable market research report (F) are summarized in Table 19.3. The steps used to develop this table are as follows.

Step 1. In column 1 enter the states of nature. In column 2 enter the *prior probabilities* for the states of nature. In column 3 enter the *conditional probabilities* of a favorable market research report (F) given each state of nature.

Step 2. In column 4 compute the **joint probabilities** by multiplying the prior probability values in column 2 by the corresponding conditional probability values in column 3.

Step 3. Sum the joint probabilities in column 4 to obtain the probability of a favorable market research report, $P(F)$.

Step 4. Divide each joint probability in column 4 by $P(F) = .77$ to obtain the revised or *posterior probabilities,* $P(s_1 \mid F)$ and $P(s_2 \mid F)$.

Table 19.3 shows that the probability of obtaining a favorable market research report is $P(F) = .77$. In addition, $P(s_1 \mid F) = .94$ and $P(s_2 \mid F) = .06$. In particular, note that a favorable market research report will prompt a revised or posterior probability of .94 that the market demand for the condominium project will be strong, s_1.

The tabular probability computation procedure must be repeated for each possible sample information outcome. Thus, Table 19.4 shows the computations of the branch probabilities of the PDC project based on an unfavorable market research report. Note

TABLE 19.4   BRANCH PROBABILITIES FOR THE PDC CONDOMINIUM PROJECT BASED ON AN UNFAVORABLE MARKET RESEARCH REPORT

State of Nature s_j	Prior Probability $P(s_j)$	Conditional Probability $P(U \mid s_j)$	Joint Probability $P(U \cap s_j)$	Posterior Probability $P(s_j \mid U)$
s_1	.8	.10	.08	.35
s_2	.2	.75	.15	.65
	1.0		$P(U) = .23$	1.00

that the probability of obtaining an unfavorable market research report is $P(U) = .23$. If an unfavorable report is obtained, the posterior probability of a strong market demand, s_1, is .35 and of a weak market demand, s_2, is .65. The branch probabilities from Tables 19.3 and 19.4 were shown on the PDC decision tree in Figure 19.5.

Exercise 14 asks you to compute posterior probabilities.

The discussion in this section shows an underlying relationship between the probabilities on the various branches in a decision tree. To assume different prior probabilities, $P(s_1)$ and $P(s_2)$, without determining how these changes would alter $P(F)$ and $P(U)$, as well as the posterior probabilities $P(s_1 \mid F)$, $P(s_2 \mid F)$, $P(s_1 \mid U)$, and $P(s_2 \mid U)$, would be inappropriate.

Exercises

Methods

14. Suppose that a decision analysis problem involves three possible states of nature: s_1, s_2, and s_3. The prior probabilities are $P(s_1) = .2$, $P(s_2) = .5$, and $P(s_3) = .3$. The sample information I, has associated probabilities $P(I \mid s_1) = .1$, $P(I \mid s_2) = .05$, and $P(I \mid s_3) = .2$. Compute the revised or posterior probabilities: $P(s_1 \mid I)$, $P(s_2 \mid I)$, and $P(s_3 \mid I)$.

15. In the following profit payoff table for a decision problem with two states of nature and three decision alternatives, the prior probabilities for s_1 and s_2 are $P(s_1) = .8$ and $P(s_2) = .2$.

	State of Nature	
Decision Alternative	s_1	s_2
d_1	15	10
d_2	10	12
d_3	8	20

a. What is the optimal decision?
b. Find the EVPI.
c. Suppose that sample information I is obtained, with $P(I \mid s_1) = .20$ and $P(I \mid s_2) = .75$. Find the posterior probabilities $P(s_1 \mid I)$ and $P(s_2 \mid I)$. Recommend a decision alternative based on these probabilities.

Applications

16. To save on expenses, Rona and Jerry agreed to form a carpool for traveling to and from work. Rona preferred to use the somewhat longer but more consistent Queen City Avenue. Although Jerry preferred the quicker expressway, he agreed with Rona that they should take Queen City Avenue if the expressway had a traffic jam. The following payoff table provides the one-way time estimate in minutes for traveling to and from work.

	State of Nature	
	Expressway Open	Expressway Jammed
Decision Alternative	s_1	s_2
Queen City Avenue, d_1	30	30
Expressway, d_2	25	45

Based on their experience with traffic problems, Rona and Jerry agreed on a .15 probability that the expressway would be jammed.

In addition, they agreed that weather seemed to affect the traffic conditions on the expressway. Let

$$C = \text{clear}$$
$$O = \text{overcast}$$
$$R = \text{rain}$$

The following conditional probabilities apply.

$$P(C \mid s_1) = .8 \qquad P(O \mid s_1) = .2 \qquad P(R \mid s_1) = .0$$
$$P(C \mid s_2) = .1 \qquad P(O \mid s_2) = .3 \qquad P(R \mid s_2) = .6$$

a. Use Bayes' theorem for probability revision to compute the probability of each weather condition and the conditional probability of the expressway open s_1 or jammed s_2 given each weather condition.
b. Show the decision tree for this problem.
c. What is the optimal decision strategy, and what is the expected travel time?

17. The Gorman Manufacturing Company must decide whether to manufacture a component part at its Milan, Michigan, plant or purchase the component part from a supplier. The resulting profit is dependent upon the demand for the product. The following payoff table shows the projected profit (in thousands of dollars).

	State of Nature		
	Low Demand	**Medium Demand**	**High Demand**
Decision Alternative	s_1	s_2	s_3
Manufacture, d_1	−20	40	100
Purchase, d_2	10	45	70

The state-of-nature probabilities are $P(s_1) = .35$, $P(s_2) = .35$, and $P(s_3) = .30$.
a. Use a decision tree to recommend a decision.
b. Use EVPI to determine whether Gorman should attempt to obtain a better estimate of demand.
c. A test market study of the potential demand for the product is expected to report either a favorable (F) or unfavorable (U) condition. The relevant conditional probabilities are as follows:

$$P(F \mid s_1) = .10 \qquad P(U \mid s_1) = .90$$
$$P(F \mid s_2) = .40 \qquad P(U \mid s_2) = .60$$
$$P(F \mid s_3) = .60 \qquad P(U \mid s_3) = .40$$

What is the probability that the market research report will be favorable?
d. What is Gorman's optimal decision strategy?
e. What is the expected value of the market research information?

Summary

Decision analysis can be used to determine a recommended decision alternative or an optimal decision strategy when a decision maker is faced with an uncertain and risk-filled pattern of future events. The goal of decision analysis is to identify the best decision alternative or the optimal decision strategy given information about the uncertain events and the possible consequences or payoffs. The uncertain future events are called chance events and the outcomes of the chance events are called states of nature.

We showed how payoff tables and decision trees could be used to structure a decision problem and describe the relationships among the decisions, the chance events, and the consequences. With probability assessments provided for the states of nature, the expected value approach was used to identify the recommended decision alternative or decision strategy.

In cases where sample information about the chance events is available, a sequence of decisions can be made. First we decide whether to obtain the sample information. If the answer to this decision is yes, an optimal decision strategy based on the specific sample information must be developed. In this situation, decision trees and the expected value approach can be used to determine the optimal decision strategy.

The Excel add-in TreePlan is available at the ASW Web site (http://asw.swlearning.com).

The Excel add-in TreePlan can be used to set up the decision trees and solve the decision problems presented in this chapter. The TreePlan software and a manual for using TreePlan are on the CD accompanying the text. An example showing how to use TreePlan for the PDC project in Section 19.1 is provided in Appendix 19.1.

Glossary

Chance event An uncertain future event affecting the consequence, or payoff, associated with a decision.

Consequence The result obtained when a decision alternative is chosen and a chance event occurs. A measure of the consequence is often called a payoff.

States of nature The possible outcomes for chance events that affect the payoff associated with a decision alternative.

Payoff A measure of the consequence of a decision such as profit, cost, or time. Each combination of a decision alternative and a state of nature has an associated payoff (consequence).

Payoff table A tabular representation of the payoffs for a decision problem.

Decision tree A graphical representation of the decision problem that shows the sequential nature of the decision-making process.

Node An intersection or junction point of a decision tree.

Decision nodes Nodes indicating points where a decision is made.

Chance nodes Nodes indicating points where a chance event will occur.

Branches Lines showing the alternatives from decision nodes and the outcomes from chance nodes.

Expected value approach An approach to choosing a decision alternative that is based on the expected value of each decision alternative. The recommended decision alternative is the one that provides the best expected value.

Expected value (EV) For a chance node, it is the weighted average of the payoffs. The weights are the state-of-nature probabilities.

Expected value of perfect information (EVPI) The expected value of information that would tell the decision maker exactly which state of nature is going to occur (i.e., perfect information).

Prior probabilities The probabilities of the states of nature prior to obtaining sample information.

Sample information New information obtained through research or experimentation that enables an updating or revision of the state-of-nature probabilities.

Posterior (revised) probabilities The probabilities of the states of nature after revising the prior probabilities based on sample information.

Decision strategy A strategy involving a sequence of decisions and chance outcomes to provide the optimal solution to a decision problem.

Expected value of sample information (EVSI) The difference between the expected value of an optimal strategy based on sample information and the "best" expected value without any sample information.

Bayes' theorem A theorem that uses sample information to revise prior probabilities.

Conditional probability The probability of one event given the known outcome of a (possibly) related event.

Joint probability The probability of both sample information and a particular state of nature occurring simultaneously.

Key Formulas

Expected Value

$$EV(d_i) = \sum_{j=1}^{N} P(s_j)V_{ij} \tag{19.3}$$

Expected Value of Perfect Information

$$EVPI = \left| EVwPI - EVwoPI \right| \tag{19.4}$$

Expected Value of Sample Information

$$EVSI = \left| EVwSI - EVwoSI \right| \tag{19.5}$$

Case Problem   Lawsuit Defense Strategy

John Campbell, an employee of Manhattan Construction Company, claims to have injured his back as a result of a fall while repairing the roof at one of the Eastview apartment buildings. In a lawsuit asking for damages of $1,500,000, filed against Doug Reynolds, the owner of Eastview Apartments, John claims that the roof had rotten sections and that his fall could have been prevented if Mr. Reynolds had told Manhattan Construction about the problem. Mr. Reynolds notified his insurance company, Allied Insurance, of the lawsuit. Allied must defend Mr. Reynolds and decide what action to take regarding the lawsuit.

Following some depositions and a series of discussions between both sides, John Campbell offered to accept a settlement of $750,000. Thus, one option is for Allied to pay John $750,000 to settle the claim. Allied is also considering making John a counteroffer of $400,000 in the hope that he will accept a lesser amount to avoid the time and cost of going to trial. Allied's preliminary investigation shows that John has a strong case; Allied is concerned that John may reject their counteroffer and request a jury trial. Allied's lawyers spent some time exploring John's likely reaction if they make a counteroffer of $400,000.

The lawyers concluded that it is adequate to consider three possible outcomes to represent John's possible reaction to a counteroffer of $400,000: (1) John will accept the counteroffer and the case will be closed; (2) John will reject the counteroffer and elect to have a jury decide the settlement amount; or (3) John will make a counteroffer to Allied of $600,000.

If John does make a counteroffer, Allied has decided that they will not make additional counteroffers. They will either accept John's counteroffer of $600,000 or go to trial.

If the case goes to a jury trial, Allied considers three outcomes possible: (1) the jury rejects John's claim and Allied will not be required to pay any damages; (2) the jury finds in favor of John and awards him $750,000 in damages; or (3) the jury concludes that John has a strong case and awards him the full amount of $1,500,000.

Key considerations as Allied develops its strategy for disposing of the case are the probabilities associated with John's response to an Allied counteroffer of $400,000 and the probabilities associated with the three possible trial outcomes. Allied's lawyers believe the probability that John will accept a counteroffer of $400,000 is .10, the probability that John will reject a counteroffer of $400,000 is .40, and the probability that John will, himself, make a counteroffer to Allied of $600,000 is .50. If the case goes to court, they believe that the probability the jury will award John damages of $1,500,000 is .30, the probability that the jury will award John damages of $750,000 is .50, and the probability that the jury will award John nothing is .20.

Managerial Report

Perform an analysis of the problem facing Allied Insurance and prepare a report that summarizes your findings and recommendations. Be sure to include the following items:

1. A decision tree
2. A recommendation regarding whether Allied should accept John's initial offer to settle the claim for $750,000
3. A decision strategy that Allied should follow if they decide to make John a counteroffer of $400,000
4. Compute the probability for each final outcome using your recommended strategy. That is, develop a risk profile for your recommended strategy

Appendix 19.1 Solving the PDC Problem with TreePlan

TreePlan* is an Excel add-in that can be used to develop decision trees for decision analysis problems. The software package is provided on the CD accompanying the text. A manual containing additional information on starting and using TreePlan is also included. In the following example, we show how to use TreePlan to build a decision tree and solve the PDC problem presented in Section 19.1. The decision tree for the PDC project is shown in Figure 19.11.

Getting Started: An Initial Decision Tree

We begin by assuming that TreePlan has been installed and an Excel workbook is open. To build a TreePlan version of the PDC decision tree proceed as follows:

Step 1. Select cell A1
Step 2. Select the **Tools** menu and choose **Decision Tree**
Step 3. When the TreePlan New dialog box appears:
        Click **New Tree**

---

*TreePlan was developed by Professor Michael R. Middleton at the University of San Francisco and modified for use by Professor James E. Smith at Duke University. The TreePlan Web site is located at http://www.treeplan.com.

FIGURE 19.11   PDC DECISION TREE

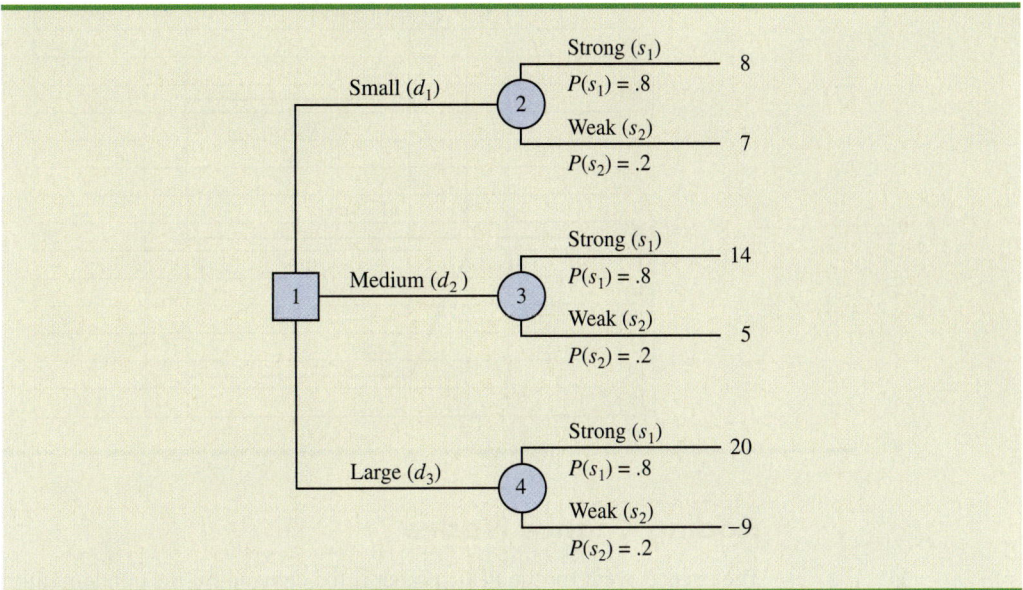

A decision tree with one decision node and two branches appears as follows:

	A	B	C	D	E	F	G
1							
2				Decision 1			
3							0
4				0	0		
5			1				
6		0					
7				Decision 2			
8							0
9				0	0		

Adding a Branch

The PDC problem includes three decision alternatives (small, medium, and large condominium complexes), so we must add another decision branch to the tree.

>**Step 1.** Select cell B5
>**Step 2.** Select the **Tools** menu and choose **Decision Tree**
>**Step 3.** When the TreePlan Decision dialog box appears:
>>Select **Add branch**
>>Click **OK**

A revised tree with three decision branches now appears in the Excel worksheet.

Naming the Decision Alternatives

The decision alternatives can be named by selecting the cells containing the labels Decision 1 (cell D2), Decision 2 (cell D7), and Decision 3 (cell D12), and then entering the corresponding PDC names Small, Medium, and Large. After naming the alternatives, the PDC tree with three decision branches appears as follows:

	A	B	C	D	E	F	G
1							
2				Small			
3							0
4				0	0		
5							
6							
7				Medium			
8			1				0
9		0		0	0		
10							
11							
12				Large			
13							0
14				0	0		

Adding Chance Nodes

The chance event for the PDC project is the demand for the condominiums, which may be either strong or weak. Thus, a chance node with two branches must be added at the end of each decision alternative branch.

Step 1. Select cell F3
Step 2. Select the **Tools** menu and choose **Decision Tree**
Step 3. When the TreePlan Terminal dialog box appears:
Select **Change to event node**
Select **Two** in the **Branches** section
Click **OK**

The tree now appears as follows:

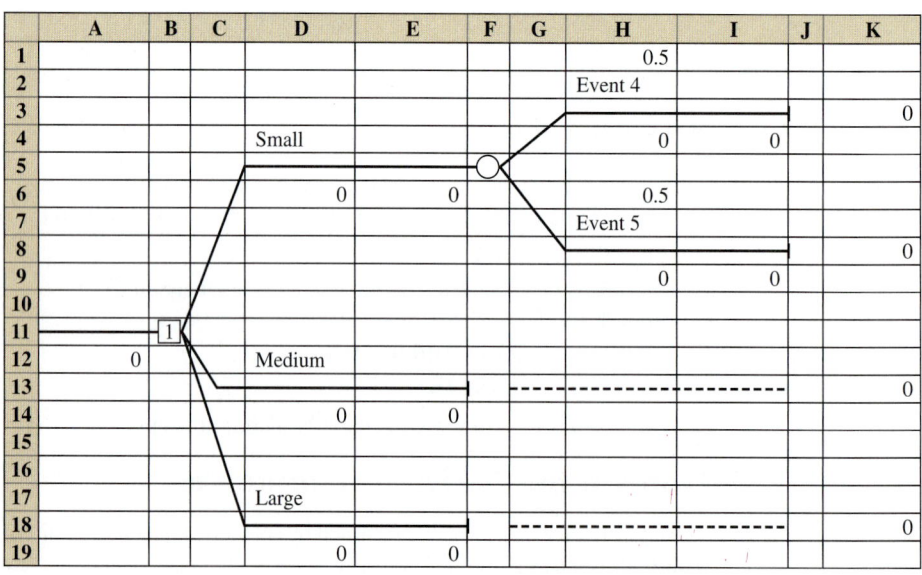

	A	B	C	D	E	F	G	H	I	J	K
1								0.5			
2								Event 4			
3											0
4				Small				0	0		
5											
6					0	0		0.5			
7								Event 5			
8											0
9								0	0		
10											
11			1								
12		0		Medium							
13											0
14					0	0					
15											
16											
17				Large							
18											0
19					0	0					

We next select the cells containing Event 4 (cell H2) and Event 5 (cell H7) and rename them Strong and Weak to provide the proper names for the PDC states of nature. After doing so we can copy the subtree for the chance node in cell F5 to the other two decision branches to complete the structure of the PDC decision tree.

Step 1. Select cell F5
Step 2. Select the **Tools** menu and choose **Decision Tree**
Step 3. When the TreePlan Event dialog box appears:
      Select **Copy subtree**
      Click **OK**
Step 4. Select cell F13
Step 5. Select the **Tools** menu and choose **Decision Tree**
Step 6. When the TreePlan Terminal dialog box appears:
      Select **Paste subtree**
      Click **OK**

This copy/paste procedure places a chance node at the end of the Medium decision branch. Repeating the same copy/paste procedure for the Large decision branch completes the structure of the PDC decision tree as shown in Figure 19.12.

FIGURE 19.12   THE PDC DECISION TREE DEVELOPED BY TREEPLAN

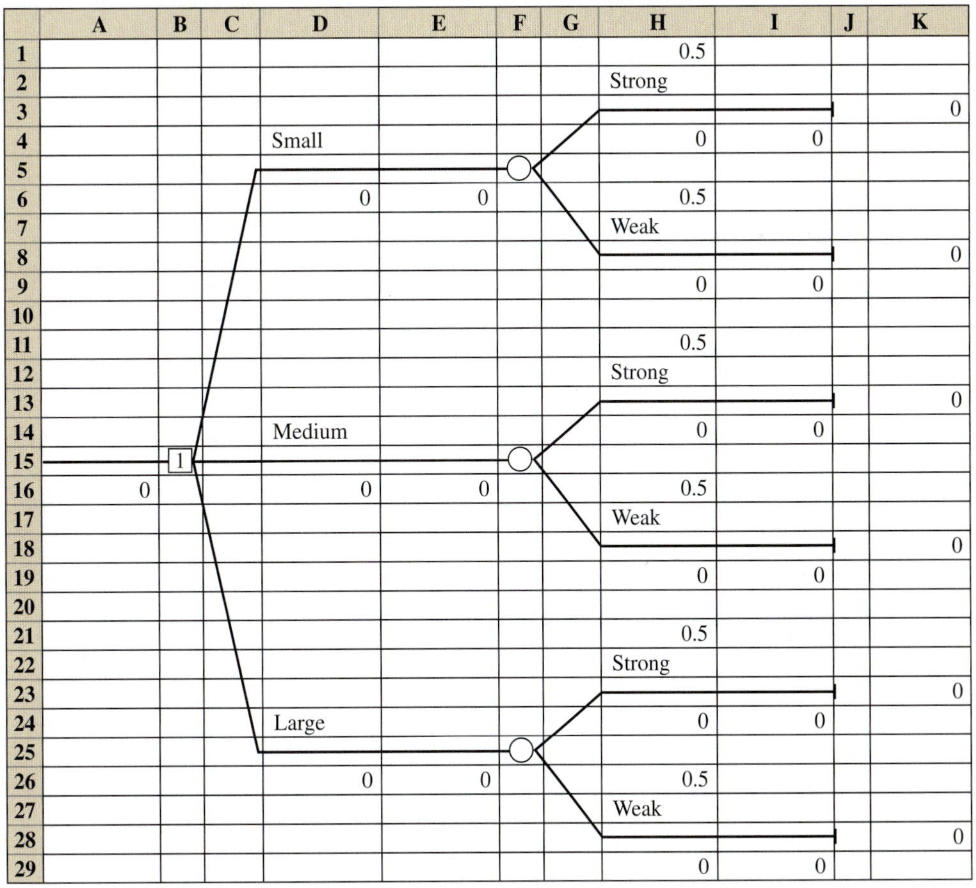

Inserting Probabilities and Payoffs

TreePlan provides the capability of inserting probabilities and payoffs into the decision tree. In Figure 19.12, we see that TreePlan automatically assigned an equal probability .5 to each of the states of nature. For PDC, the probability of strong demand is .8 and the probability of weak demand is .2. We can select cells H1, H6, H11, H16, H21, and H26 and insert the appropriate probabilities. The payoffs for the chance outcomes are inserted in cells H4, H9, H14, H19, H24, and H29. After inserting the PDC probabilities and payoffs, the PDC decision tree appears as shown in Figure 19.13.

Note that the payoffs also appear in the right-hand margin (column K) of the decision tree. These payoffs are computed by a formula that adds the payoffs on all of the branches leading to the associated terminal node. For the PDC project, no payoffs are associated with the decision alternative branches so we leave the default values of zero in cells D6, D16, and D26. The PDC decision tree is now complete.

Interpreting the Result

When probabilities and payoffs are inserted, TreePlan automatically makes the backward pass computations necessary to compute expected values and determine the optimal solution. Optimal decisions are identified by the number in the corresponding decision node. In

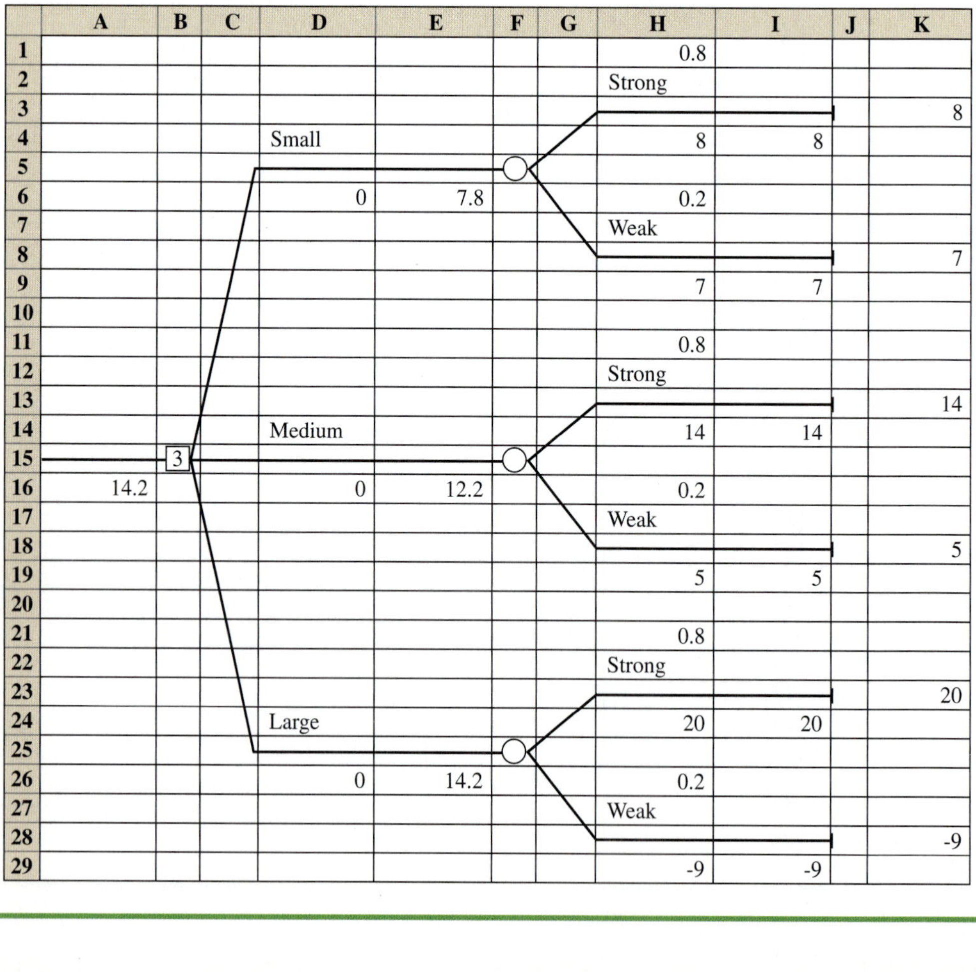

FIGURE 19.13   THE PDC DECISION TREE WITH BRANCH PROBABILITIES AND PAYOFFS

the PDC decision tree in Figure 19.13, cell B15 contains the decision node. Note that a 3 appears in this node, which tells us that decision alternative branch 3 provides the optimal decision. Thus, decision analysis recommends PDC construct the Large condominium complex. The expected value of this decision appears at the beginning of the tree in cell A16. Thus, we see the optimal expected value is $14.2 million. The expected values of the other decision alternatives are displayed at the end of the corresponding decision branch. Thus, referring to cells E6 and E16, we see that the expected value of the Small complex is $7.8 million and the expected value of the Medium complex is $12.2 million.

Other Options

TreePlan defaults to a maximization objective. If you would like a minimization objective, follow these steps:

Step 1. Select the **Tools** menu and choose **Decision Tree**
Step 2. Select **Options**
Step 3. Choose **Minimize (costs)**
Step 4. Click **OK**

In using a TreePlan decision tree, we can modify probabilities and payoffs and quickly observe the impact of the changes on the optimal solution. Using this "what if" type of sensitivity analysis, we can identify changes in probabilities and payoffs that would change the optimal decision. Also, because TreePlan is an Excel add-in, most of Excel's capabilities are available. For instance, we could use boldface to highlight the name of the optimal decision alternative on the final decision tree solution. A variety of other options provided by TreePlan is contained in the TreePlan manual.

APPENDIXES

APPENDIX A
    References and Bibliography

APPENDIX B
    Tables

APPENDIX C
    Summation Notation

APPENDIX D
    Self-Test Solutions and Answers
        to Even-Numbered Exercises

APPENDIX E
    Using Excel Functions

General

Bowerman, B. L., and R. T. O'Connell. *Applied Statistics: Improving Business Processes.* Irwin, 1996.

Freedman, D., R. Pisani, and R. Purves. *Statistics,* 3rd ed. W. W. Norton, 1997.

Hogg, R. V., and A. T. Craig. *Introduction to Mathematical Statistics,* 5th ed. Prentice Hall, 1994.

Hogg, R. V., and E. A. Tanis. *Probability and Statistical Inference,* 6th ed. Prentice Hall, 2001.

Joiner, B. L., and B. F. Ryan. *Minitab Handbook.* Brooks/Cole, 2000.

Miller, I., and M. Miller. *John E. Freund's Mathematical Statistics.* Prentice Hall, 1998.

Moore, D. S., and G. P. McCabe. *Introduction to the Practice of Statistics,* 4th ed. Freeman, 2003.

Roberts, H. *Data Analysis for Managers with Minitab.* Scientific Press, 1991.

Tanur, J. M. *Statistics: A Guide to the Unknown,* 4th ed. Brooks/Cole, 2002.

Tukey, J. W. *Exploratory Data Analysis.* Addison-Wesley, 1977.

Probability

Hogg, R. V., and E. A. Tanis. *Probability and Statistical Inference,* 6th ed. Prentice Hall, 2001.

Ross, S. M. *Introduction to Probability Models,* 7th ed. Academic Press, 2000.

Wackerly, D. D., W. Mendenhall, and R. L. Scheaffer. *Mathematical Statistics with Applications,* 6th ed. Duxbury Press, 2002.

Sampling

Cochran, W. G. *Sampling Techniques,* 3rd ed. Wiley, 1977.

Deming, W. E. *Some Theory of Sampling.* Dover, 1984.

Hansen, M. H., W. N. Hurwitz, W. G. Madow, and M. N. Hanson. *Sample Survey Methods and Theory.* Wiley, 1993.

Kish, L. *Survey Sampling.* Wiley, 1995.

Levy, P. S., and S. Lemeshow. *Sampling of Populations: Methods and Applications,* 3rd ed. Wiley, 1999.

Scheaffer, R. L., W. Mendenhall, and L. Ott. *Elementary Survey Sampling,* 5th ed. Duxbury Press, 1996.

Experimental Design

Cochran, W. G., and G. M. Cox. *Experimental Designs,* 2nd ed. Wiley, 1992.

Hicks, C. R., and K. V. Turner. *Fundamental Concepts in the Design of Experiments,* 5th ed. Oxford University Press, 1999.

Montgomery, D. C. *Design and Analysis of Experiments,* 5th ed. Wiley, 2000.

Winer, B. J., K. M. Michels, and D. R. Brown. *Statistical Principles in Experimental Design,* 3rd ed. McGraw-Hill, 1991.

Wu, C. F. Jeff, and M. Hamada. *Experiments: Planning, Analysis, and Parameter Optimization.* Wiley, 2000.

Regression Analysis

Belsley, D. A. *Conditioning Diagnostics: Collinearity and Weak Data in Regression.* Wiley, 1991.

Chatterjee, S., and B. Price. *Regression Analysis by Example,* 3rd ed. Wiley, 1999.

Draper, N. R., and H. Smith. *Applied Regression Analysis,* 3rd ed. Wiley, 1998.

Graybill, F. A., and H. Iyer. *Regression Analysis: Concepts and Applications.* Duxbury Press, 1994.

Hosmer, D. W., and S. Lemeshow. *Applied Logistic Regression,* 2nd ed. Wiley, 2000.

Kleinbaum, D. G., L. L. Kupper, and K. E. Muller. *Applied Regression Analysis and Other Multivariate Methods,* 3rd ed. Duxbury Press, 1997.

Kutner, M. H., C. J. Nachtschiem, W. Wasserman, and J. Neter. *Applied Linear Statistical Models,* 4th ed. Irwin, 1996.

Mendenhall, M., and T. Sincich. *A Second Course in Statistics: Regression Analysis,* 5th ed. Prentice Hall, 1996.

Myers, R. H. *Classical and Modern Regression with Applications,* 2nd ed. PWS, 1990.

Nonparametric Methods

Conover, W. J. *Practical Nonparametric Statistics,* 3rd ed. Wiley, 1998.

Gibbons, J. D., and S. Chakraborti. *Nonparametric Statistical Inference,* 3rd ed. Marcel Dekker, 1992.

Siegel, S., and N. J. Castellan. *Nonparametric Statistics for the Behavioral Sciences,* 2nd ed. McGraw-Hill, 1990.

Sprent, P. *Applied Non-Parametric Statistical Methods.* CRC, 1993.

Quality Control

Deming, W. E. *Quality, Productivity, and Competitive Position.* MIT, 1982.

Evans, J. R., and W. M. Lindsay. *The Management and Control of Quality,* 6th ed. South-Western, 2005.

Gryna, F. M., and I. M. Juran. *Quality Planning and Analysis: From Product Development Through Use,* 3rd ed. McGraw-Hill, 1993.

Ishikawa, K. *Introduction to Quality Control.* Kluwer Academic, 1991.

Montgomery, D. C. *Introduction to Statistical Quality Control,* 4th ed. Wiley, 2000.

Decision Analysis

Chernoff, H., and L. E. Moses. *Elementary Decision Theory.* Dover, 1987.

Clemen, R. T., and T. Reilly. *Making Hard Decisions with Decision Tools.* Duxbury Press, 2001.

Goodwin, P., and G. Wright. *Decision Analysis for Management Judgment.* 2nd ed. Wiley, 1999.

Pratt, J. W., H. Raiffa, and R. Schlaifer. *Introduction to Statistical Decision Theory.* MIT Press, 1995.

Raiffa, H. *Decision Analysis.* McGraw-Hill, 1997.

Appendix B: Tables

TABLE 1   CUMULATIVE PROBABILITIES FOR THE STANDARD NORMAL
DISTRIBUTION

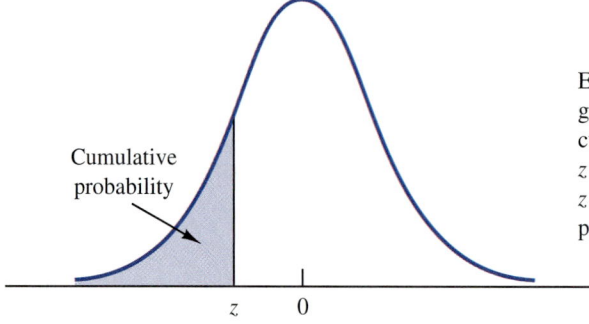

Cumulative
probability

Entries in the table
give the area under the
curve to the left of the
z value. For example, for
$z = -.85$, the cumulative
probability is .1977.

z	.00	.01	.02	.03	.04	.05	.06	.07	.08	.09
−3.0	.0013	.0013	.0013	.0012	.0012	.0011	.0011	.0011	.0010	.0010
−2.9	.0019	.0018	.0018	.0017	.0016	.0016	.0015	.0015	.0014	.0014
−2.8	.0026	.0025	.0024	.0023	.0023	.0022	.0021	.0021	.0020	.0019
−2.7	.0035	.0034	.0033	.0032	.0031	.0030	.0029	.0028	.0027	.0026
−2.6	.0047	.0045	.0044	.0043	.0041	.0040	.0039	.0038	.0037	.0036
−2.5	.0062	.0060	.0059	.0057	.0055	.0054	.0052	.0051	.0049	.0048
−2.4	.0082	.0080	.0078	.0075	.0073	.0071	.0069	.0068	.0066	.0064
−2.3	.0107	.0104	.0102	.0099	.0096	.0094	.0091	.0089	.0087	.0084
−2.2	.0139	.0136	.0132	.0129	.0125	.0122	.0119	.0116	.0113	.0110
−2.1	.0179	.0174	.0170	.0166	.0162	.0158	.0154	.0150	.0146	.0143
−2.0	.0228	.0222	.0217	.0212	.0207	.0202	.0197	.0192	.0188	.0183
−1.9	.0287	.0281	.0274	.0268	.0262	.0256	.0250	.0244	.0239	.0233
−1.8	.0359	.0351	.0344	.0336	.0329	.0322	.0314	.0307	.0301	.0294
−1.7	.0446	.0436	.0427	.0418	.0409	.0401	.0392	.0384	.0375	.0367
−1.6	.0548	.0537	.0526	.0516	.0505	.0495	.0485	.0475	.0465	.0455
−1.5	.0668	.0655	.0643	.0630	.0618	.0606	.0594	.0582	.0571	.0559
−1.4	.0808	.0793	.0778	.0764	.0749	.0735	.0721	.0708	.0694	.0681
−1.3	.0968	.0951	.0934	.0918	.0901	.0885	.0869	.0853	.0838	.0823
−1.2	.1151	.1131	.1112	.1093	.1075	.1056	.1038	.1020	.1003	.0985
−1.1	.1357	.1335	.1314	.1292	.1271	.1251	.1230	.1210	.1190	.1170
−1.0	.1587	.1562	.1539	.1515	.1492	.1469	.1446	.1423	.1401	.1379
−.9	.1841	.1814	.1788	.1762	.1736	.1711	.1685	.1660	.1635	.1611
−.8	.2119	.2090	.2061	.2033	.2005	.1977	.1949	.1922	.1894	.1867
−.7	.2420	.2389	.2358	.2327	.2296	.2266	.2236	.2206	.2177	.2148
−.6	.2743	.2709	.2676	.2643	.2611	.2578	.2546	.2514	.2483	.2451
−.5	.3085	.3050	.3015	.2981	.2946	.2912	.2877	.2843	.2810	.2776
−.4	.3446	.3409	.3372	.3336	.3300	.3264	.3228	.3192	.3156	.3121
−.3	.3821	.3783	.3745	.3707	.3669	.3632	.3594	.3557	.3520	.3483
−.2	.4207	.4168	.4129	.4090	.4052	.4013	.3974	.3936	.3897	.3859
−.1	.4602	.4562	.4522	.4483	.4443	.4404	.4364	.4325	.4286	.4247
−.0	.5000	.4960	.4920	.4880	.4840	.4801	.4761	.4721	.4681	.4641

TABLE 1 CUMULATIVE PROBABILITIES FOR THE STANDARD NORMAL DISTRIBUTION (*Continued*)

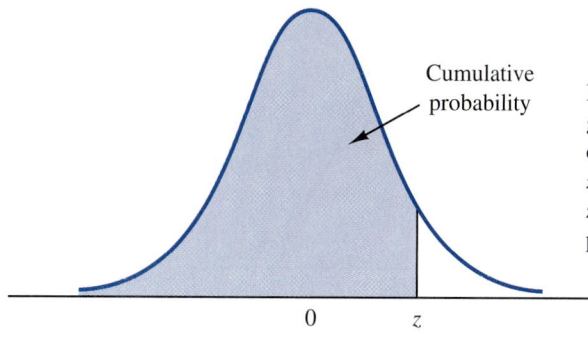

Cumulative probability

Entries in the table give the area under the curve to the left of the *z* value. For example, for *z* = 1.25, the cumulative probability is .8944.

0   z

z	.00	.01	.02	.03	.04	.05	.06	.07	.08	.09
.0	.5000	.5040	.5080	.5120	.5160	.5199	.5239	.5279	.5319	.5359
.1	.5398	.5438	.5478	.5517	.5557	.5596	.5636	.5675	.5714	.5753
.2	.5793	.5832	.5871	.5910	.5948	.5987	.6026	.6064	.6103	.6141
.3	.6179	.6217	.6255	.6293	.6331	.6368	.6406	.6443	.6480	.6517
.4	.6554	.6591	.6628	.6664	.6700	.6736	.6772	.6808	.6844	.6879
.5	.6915	.6950	.6985	.7019	.7054	.7088	.7123	.7157	.7190	.7224
.6	.7257	.7291	.7324	.7357	.7389	.7422	.7454	.7486	.7517	.7549
.7	.7580	.7611	.7642	.7673	.7704	.7734	.7764	.7794	.7823	.7852
.8	.7881	.7910	.7939	.7967	.7995	.8023	.8051	.8078	.8106	.8133
.9	.8159	.8186	.8212	.8238	.8264	.8289	.8315	.8340	.8365	.8389
1.0	.8413	.8438	.8461	.8485	.8508	.8531	.8554	.8577	.8599	.8621
1.1	.8643	.8665	.8686	.8708	.8729	.8749	.8770	.8790	.8810	.8830
1.2	.8849	.8869	.8888	.8907	.8925	.8944	.8962	.8980	.8997	.9015
1.3	.9032	.9049	.9066	.9082	.9099	.9115	.9131	.9147	.9162	.9177
1.4	.9192	.9207	.9222	.9236	.9251	.9265	.9279	.9292	.9306	.9319
1.5	.9332	.9345	.9357	.9370	.9382	.9394	.9406	.9418	.9429	.9441
1.6	.9452	.9463	.9474	.9484	.9495	.9505	.9515	.9525	.9535	.9545
1.7	.9554	.9564	.9573	.9582	.9591	.9599	.9608	.9616	.9625	.9633
1.8	.9641	.9649	.9656	.9664	.9671	.9678	.9686	.9693	.9699	.9706
1.9	.9713	.9719	.9726	.9732	.9738	.9744	.9750	.9756	.9761	.9767
2.0	.9772	.9778	.9783	.9788	.9793	.9798	.9803	.9808	.9812	.9817
2.1	.9821	.9826	.9830	.9834	.9838	.9842	.9846	.9850	.9854	.9857
2.2	.9861	.9864	.9868	.9871	.9875	.9878	.9881	.9884	.9887	.9890
2.3	.9893	.9896	.9898	.9901	.9904	.9906	.9909	.9911	.9913	.9913
2.4	.9918	.9920	.9922	.9925	.9927	.9929	.9931	.9932	.9934	.9936
2.5	.9938	.9940	.9941	.9943	.9945	.9946	.9948	.9949	.9951	.9952
2.6	.9953	.9955	.9956	.9957	.9959	.9960	.9961	.9962	.9963	.9964
2.7	.9965	.9966	.9967	.9968	.9969	.9970	.9971	.9972	.9973	.9974
2.8	.9974	.9975	.9976	.9977	.9977	.9978	.9979	.9979	.9980	.9981
2.9	.9981	.9982	.9982	.9983	.9984	.9984	.9985	.9985	.9986	.9986
3.0	.9986	.9987	.9987	.9988	.9988	.9989	.9989	.9989	.9990	.9990

TABLE 2 t DISTRIBUTION

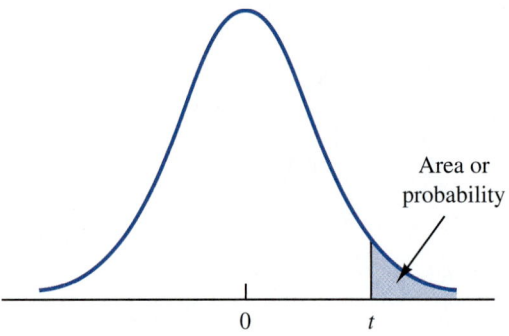

Entries in the table give the t values for an area or probability in the upper tail of the t distribution. For example, with 10 degrees of freedom and a .05 area in the upper tail, $t_{.05} = 1.812$.

Area or probability

0   t

Degrees of Freedom	Area in Upper Tail					
	.20	**.10**	**.05**	**.025**	**.01**	**.005**
1	1.376	3.078	6.314	12.706	31.821	63.656
2	1.061	1.886	2.920	4.303	6.965	9.925
3	.978	1.638	2.353	3.182	4.541	5.841
4	.941	1.533	2.132	2.776	3.747	4.604
5	.920	1.476	2.015	2.571	3.365	4.032
6	.906	1.440	1.943	2.447	3.143	3.707
7	.896	1.415	1.895	2.365	2.998	3.499
8	.889	1.397	1.860	2.306	2.896	3.355
9	.883	1.383	1.833	2.262	2.821	3.250
10	.879	1.372	1.812	2.228	2.764	3.169
11	.876	1.363	1.796	2.201	2.718	3.106
12	.873	1.356	1.782	2.179	2.681	3.055
13	.870	1.350	1.771	2.160	2.650	3.012
14	.868	1.345	1.761	2.145	2.624	2.977
15	.866	1.341	1.753	2.131	2.602	2.947
16	.865	1.337	1.746	2.120	2.583	2.921
17	.863	1.333	1.740	2.110	2.567	2.898
18	.862	1.330	1.734	2.101	2.552	2.878
19	.861	1.328	1.729	2.093	2.539	2.861
20	.860	1.325	1.725	2.086	2.528	2.845
21	.859	1.323	1.721	2.080	2.518	2.831
22	.858	1.321	1.717	2.074	2.508	2.819
23	.858	1.319	1.714	2.069	2.500	2.807
24	.857	1.318	1.711	2.064	2.492	2.797
25	.856	1.316	1.708	2.060	2.485	2.787
26	.856	1.315	1.706	2.056	2.479	2.779
27	.855	1.314	1.703	2.052	2.473	2.771
28	.855	1.313	1.701	2.048	2.467	2.763
29	.854	1.311	1.699	2.045	2.462	2.756
30	.854	1.310	1.697	2.042	2.457	2.750
31	.853	1.309	1.696	2.040	2.453	2.744
32	.853	1.309	1.694	2.037	2.449	2.738
33	.853	1.308	1.692	2.035	2.445	2.733
34	.852	1.307	1.691	2.032	2.441	2.728

TABLE 2   *t* DISTRIBUTION (*Continued*)

Degrees of Freedom	_____ Area in Upper Tail _____					
	.20	**.10**	**.05**	**.025**	**.01**	**.005**
35	.852	1.306	1.690	2.030	2.438	2.724
36	.852	1.306	1.688	2.028	2.434	2.719
37	.851	1.305	1.687	2.026	2.431	2.715
38	.851	1.304	1.686	2.024	2.429	2.712
39	.851	1.304	1.685	2.023	2.426	2.708
40	.851	1.303	1.684	2.021	2.423	2.704
41	.850	1.303	1.683	2.020	2.421	2.701
42	.850	1.302	1.682	2.018	2.418	2.698
43	.850	1.302	1.681	2.017	2.416	2.695
44	.850	1.301	1.680	2.015	2.414	2.692
45	.850	1.301	1.679	2.014	2.412	2.690
46	.850	1.300	1.679	2.013	2.410	2.687
47	.849	1.300	1.678	2.012	2.408	2.685
48	.849	1.299	1.677	2.011	2.407	2.682
49	.849	1.299	1.677	2.010	2.405	2.680
50	.849	1.299	1.676	2.009	2.403	2.678
51	.849	1.298	1.675	2.008	2.402	2.676
52	.849	1.298	1.675	2.007	2.400	2.674
53	.848	1.298	1.674	2.006	2.399	2.672
54	.848	1.297	1.674	2.005	2.397	2.670
55	.848	1.297	1.673	2.004	2.396	2.668
56	.848	1.297	1.673	2.003	2.395	2.667
57	.848	1.297	1.672	2.002	2.394	2.665
58	.848	1.296	1.672	2.002	2.392	2.663
59	.848	1.296	1.671	2.001	2.391	2.662
60	.848	1.296	1.671	2.000	2.390	2.660
61	.848	1.296	1.670	2.000	2.389	2.659
62	.847	1.295	1.670	1.999	2.388	2.657
63	.847	1.295	1.669	1.998	2.387	2.656
64	.847	1.295	1.669	1.998	2.386	2.655
65	.847	1.295	1.669	1.997	2.385	2.654
66	.847	1.295	1.668	1.997	2.384	2.652
67	.847	1.294	1.668	1.996	2.383	2.651
68	.847	1.294	1.668	1.995	2.382	2.650
69	.847	1.294	1.667	1.995	2.382	2.649
70	.847	1.294	1.667	1.994	2.381	2.648
71	.847	1.294	1.667	1.994	2.380	2.647
72	.847	1.293	1.666	1.993	2.379	2.646
73	.847	1.293	1.666	1.993	2.379	2.645
74	.847	1.293	1.666	1.993	2.378	2.644
75	.846	1.293	1.665	1.992	2.377	2.643
76	.846	1.293	1.665	1.992	2.376	2.642
77	.846	1.293	1.665	1.991	2.376	2.641
78	.846	1.292	1.665	1.991	2.375	2.640
79	.846	1.292	1.664	1.990	2.374	2.639

(*Continued*)

TABLE 2   *t* DISTRIBUTION (*Continued*)

Degrees of Freedom	Area in Upper Tail					
	.20	**.10**	**.05**	**.025**	**.01**	**.005**
80	.846	1.292	1.664	1.990	2.374	2.639
81	.846	1.292	1.664	1.990	2.373	2.638
82	.846	1.292	1.664	1.989	2.373	2.637
83	.846	1.292	1.663	1.989	2.372	2.636
84	.846	1.292	1.663	1.989	2.372	2.636
85	.846	1.292	1.663	1.988	2.371	2.635
86	.846	1.291	1.663	1.988	2.370	2.634
87	.846	1.291	1.663	1.988	2.370	2.634
88	.846	1.291	1.662	1.987	2.369	2.633
89	.846	1.291	1.662	1.987	2.369	2.632
90	.846	1.291	1.662	1.987	2.368	2.632
91	.846	1.291	1.662	1.986	2.368	2.631
92	.846	1.291	1.662	1.986	2.368	2.630
93	.846	1.291	1.661	1.986	2.367	2.630
94	.845	1.291	1.661	1.986	2.367	2.629
95	.845	1.291	1.661	1.985	2.366	2.629
96	.845	1.290	1.661	1.985	2.366	2.628
97	.845	1.290	1.661	1.985	2.365	2.627
98	.845	1.290	1.661	1.984	2.365	2.627
99	.845	1.290	1.660	1.984	2.364	2.626
100	.845	1.290	1.660	1.984	2.364	2.626
∞	.842	1.282	1.645	1.960	2.326	2.576

TABLE 3   CHI-SQUARE DISTRIBUTION

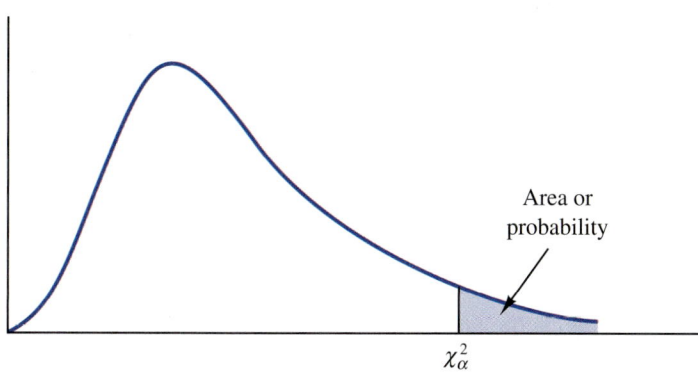

Entries in the table give χ_α^2 values, where α is the area or probability in the upper tail of the chi-square distribution. For example, with 10 degrees of freedom and a .01 area in the upper tail, $\chi_{.01}^2 = 23.209$.

Area or probability

χ_α^2

Degrees of Freedom	Area in Upper Tail									
	.995	.99	.975	.95	.90	.10	.05	.025	.01	.005
1	.000	.000	.001	.004	.016	2.706	3.841	5.024	6.635	7.879
2	.010	.020	.051	.103	.211	4.605	5.991	7.378	9.210	10.597
3	.072	.115	.216	.352	.584	6.251	7.815	9.348	11.345	12.838
4	.207	.297	.484	.711	1.064	7.779	9.488	11.143	13.277	14.860
5	.412	.554	.831	1.145	1.610	9.236	11.070	12.832	15.086	16.750
6	.676	.872	1.237	1.635	2.204	10.645	12.592	14.449	16.812	18.548
7	.989	1.239	1.690	2.167	2.833	12.017	14.067	16.013	18.475	20.278
8	1.344	1.647	2.180	2.733	3.490	13.362	15.507	17.535	20.090	21.955
9	1.735	2.088	2.700	3.325	4.168	14.684	16.919	19.023	21.666	23.589
10	2.156	2.558	3.247	3.940	4.865	15.987	18.307	20.483	23.209	25.188
11	2.603	3.053	3.816	4.575	5.578	17.275	19.675	21.920	24.725	26.757
12	3.074	3.571	4.404	5.226	6.304	18.549	21.026	23.337	26.217	28.300
13	3.565	4.107	5.009	5.892	7.041	19.812	22.362	24.736	27.688	29.819
14	4.075	4.660	5.629	6.571	7.790	21.064	23.685	26.119	29.141	31.319
15	4.601	5.229	6.262	7.261	8.547	22.307	24.996	27.488	30.578	32.801
16	5.142	5.812	6.908	7.962	9.312	23.542	26.296	28.845	32.000	34.267
17	5.697	6.408	7.564	8.672	10.085	24.769	27.587	30.191	33.409	35.718
18	6.265	7.015	8.231	9.390	10.865	25.989	28.869	31.526	34.805	37.156
19	6.844	7.633	8.907	10.117	11.651	27.204	30.144	32.852	36.191	38.582
20	7.434	8.260	9.591	10.851	12.443	28.412	31.410	34.170	37.566	39.997
21	8.034	8.897	10.283	11.591	13.240	29.615	32.671	35.479	38.932	41.401
22	8.643	9.542	10.982	12.338	14.041	30.813	33.924	36.781	40.289	42.796
23	9.260	10.196	11.689	13.091	14.848	32.007	35.172	38.076	41.638	44.181
24	9.886	10.856	12.401	13.848	15.659	33.196	36.415	39.364	42.980	45.558
25	10.520	11.524	13.120	14.611	16.473	34.382	37.652	40.646	44.314	46.928
26	11.160	12.198	13.844	15.379	17.292	35.563	38.885	41.923	45.642	48.290
27	11.808	12.878	14.573	16.151	18.114	36.741	40.113	43.195	46.963	49.645
28	12.461	13.565	15.308	16.928	18.939	37.916	41.337	44.461	48.278	50.994
29	13.121	14.256	16.047	17.708	19.768	39.087	42.557	45.722	49.588	52.335

(Continued)

TABLE 3   CHI-SQUARE DISTRIBUTION (*Continued*)

Degrees of Freedom	Area in Upper Tail									
	.995	.99	.975	.95	.90	.10	.05	.025	.01	.005
30	13.787	14.953	16.791	18.493	20.599	40.256	43.773	46.979	50.892	53.672
35	17.192	18.509	20.569	22.465	24.797	46.059	49.802	53.203	57.342	60.275
40	20.707	22.164	24.433	26.509	29.051	51.805	55.758	59.342	63.691	66.766
45	24.311	25.901	28.366	30.612	33.350	57.505	61.656	65.410	69.957	73.166
50	27.991	29.707	32.357	34.764	37.689	63.167	67.505	71.420	76.154	79.490
55	31.735	33.571	36.398	38.958	42.060	68.796	73.311	77.380	82.292	85.749
60	35.534	37.485	40.482	43.188	46.459	74.397	79.082	83.298	88.379	91.952
65	39.383	41.444	44.603	47.450	50.883	79.973	84.821	89.177	94.422	98.105
70	43.275	45.442	48.758	51.739	55.329	85.527	90.531	95.023	100.425	104.215
75	47.206	49.475	52.942	56.054	59.795	91.061	96.217	100.839	106.393	110.285
80	51.172	53.540	57.153	60.391	64.278	96.578	101.879	106.629	112.329	116.321
85	55.170	57.634	61.389	64.749	68.777	102.079	107.522	112.393	118.236	122.324
90	59.196	61.754	65.647	69.126	73.291	107.565	113.145	118.136	124.116	128.299
95	63.250	65.898	69.925	73.520	77.818	113.038	118.752	123.858	129.973	134.247
100	67.328	70.065	74.222	77.929	82.358	118.498	124.342	129.561	135.807	140.170

TABLE 4   F DISTRIBUTION

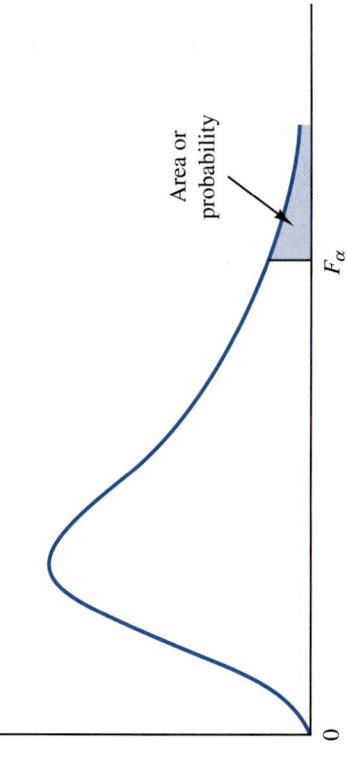

Area or probability

F_α

Entries in the table give F_α values, where α is the area or probability in the upper tail of the F distribution. For example, with 4 numerator degrees of freedom, 8 denominator degrees of freedom, and a .05 area in the upper tail, $F_{.05} = 3.84$.

Denominator Degrees of Freedom	Area in Upper Tail	Numerator Degrees of Freedom																	
		1	2	3	4	5	6	7	8	9	10	15	20	25	30	40	60	100	1000
1	.10	39.86	49.50	53.59	55.83	57.24	58.20	58.91	59.44	59.86	60.19	61.22	61.74	62.05	62.26	62.53	62.79	63.01	63.30
	.05	161.45	199.50	215.71	224.58	230.16	233.99	236.77	238.88	240.54	241.88	245.95	248.01	249.26	250.10	251.14	252.20	253.04	254.19
	.025	647.79	799.48	864.15	899.60	921.83	937.11	948.20	956.64	963.28	968.63	984.87	993.08	998.09	1001.40	1005.60	1009.79	1013.16	1017.76
	.01	4052.18	4999.34	5403.53	5624.26	5763.96	5858.95	5928.33	5980.95	6022.40	6055.93	6156.97	6208.66	6239.86	6260.35	6286.43	6312.97	6333.92	6362.80
2	.10	8.53	9.00	9.16	9.24	9.29	9.33	9.35	9.37	9.38	9.39	9.42	9.44	9.45	9.46	9.47	9.47	9.48	9.49
	.05	18.51	19.00	19.16	19.25	19.30	19.33	19.35	19.37	19.38	19.40	19.43	19.45	19.46	19.46	19.47	19.48	19.49	19.49
	.025	38.51	39.00	39.17	39.25	39.30	39.33	39.36	39.37	39.39	39.40	39.43	39.45	39.46	39.46	39.47	39.48	39.49	39.50
	.01	98.50	99.00	99.16	99.25	99.30	99.33	99.36	99.38	99.39	99.40	99.43	99.45	99.46	99.47	99.48	99.48	99.49	99.50
3	.10	5.54	5.46	5.39	5.34	5.31	5.28	5.27	5.25	5.24	5.23	5.20	5.18	5.17	5.17	5.16	5.15	5.14	5.13
	.05	10.13	9.55	9.28	9.12	9.01	8.94	8.89	8.85	8.81	8.79	8.70	8.66	8.63	8.62	8.59	8.57	8.55	8.53
	.025	17.44	16.04	15.44	15.10	14.88	14.73	14.62	14.54	14.47	14.42	14.25	14.17	14.12	14.08	14.04	13.99	13.96	13.91
	.01	34.12	30.82	29.46	28.71	28.24	27.91	27.67	27.49	27.34	27.23	26.87	26.69	26.58	26.50	26.41	26.32	26.24	26.14
4	.10	4.54	4.32	4.19	4.11	4.05	4.01	3.98	3.95	3.94	3.92	3.87	3.84	3.83	3.82	3.80	3.79	3.78	3.76
	.05	7.71	6.94	6.59	6.39	6.26	6.16	6.09	6.04	6.00	5.96	5.86	5.80	5.77	5.75	5.72	5.69	5.66	5.63
	.025	12.22	10.65	9.98	9.60	9.36	9.20	9.07	8.98	8.90	8.84	8.66	8.56	8.50	8.46	8.41	8.36	8.32	8.26
	.01	21.20	18.00	16.69	15.98	15.52	15.21	14.98	14.80	14.66	14.55	14.20	14.02	13.91	13.84	13.75	13.65	13.58	13.47
5	.10	4.06	3.78	3.62	3.52	3.45	3.40	3.37	3.34	3.32	3.30	3.324	3.21	3.19	3.17	3.16	3.14	3.13	3.11
	.05	6.61	5.79	5.41	5.19	5.05	4.95	4.88	4.82	4.77	4.74	4.62	4.56	4.52	4.50	4.46	4.43	4.41	4.37
	.025	10.01	8.43	7.76	7.39	7.15	6.98	6.85	6.76	6.68	6.62	6.43	6.33	6.27	6.23	6.18	6.12	6.08	6.02
	.01	16.26	13.27	12.06	11.39	10.97	10.67	10.46	10.29	10.16	10.05	9.72	9.55	9.45	9.38	9.29	9.20	9.13	9.03

(Continued)

TABLE 4 *F* DISTRIBUTION (*Continued*)

Denominator Degrees of Freedom	Area in Upper Tail	Numerator Degrees of Freedom																	
		1	2	3	4	5	6	7	8	9	10	15	20	25	30	40	60	100	1000
6	.10	3.78	3.46	3.29	3.18	3.11	3.05	3.01	2.98	2.96	2.94	2.87	2.84	2.81	2.80	2.78	2.76	2.75	2.72
	.05	5.99	5.14	4.76	4.53	4.39	4.28	4.21	4.15	4.10	4.06	3.94	3.87	3.83	3.81	3.77	3.74	3.71	3.67
	.025	8.81	7.26	6.60	6.23	5.99	5.82	5.70	5.60	5.52	5.46	5.27	5.17	5.11	5.07	5.01	4.96	4.92	4.86
	.01	13.75	10.92	9.78	9.15	8.75	8.47	8.26	8.10	7.98	7.87	7.56	7.40	7.30	7.23	7.14	7.06	6.99	6.89
7	.10	3.59	3.26	3.07	2.96	2.88	2.83	2.78	2.75	2.72	2.70	2.63	2.59	2.57	2.56	2.54	2.51	2.50	2.47
	.05	5.59	4.74	4.35	4.12	3.97	3.87	3.79	3.73	3.68	3.64	3.51	3.44	3.40	3.38	3.34	3.30	3.27	3.23
	.025	8.07	6.54	5.89	5.52	5.29	5.12	4.99	4.90	4.82	4.76	4.57	4.47	4.40	4.36	4.31	4.25	4.21	4.15
	.01	12.25	9.55	8.45	7.85	7.46	7.19	6.99	6.84	6.72	6.62	6.31	6.16	6.06	5.99	5.91	5.82	5.75	5.66
8	.10	3.46	3.11	2.92	2.81	2.73	2.67	2.62	2.59	2.56	2.54	2.46	2.42	2.40	2.38	2.36	2.34	2.32	2.30
	.05	5.32	4.46	4.07	3.84	3.69	3.58	3.50	3.44	3.39	3.35	3.22	3.15	3.11	3.08	3.04	3.01	2.97	2.93
	.025	7.57	6.06	5.42	5.05	4.82	4.65	4.53	4.43	4.36	4.30	4.10	4.00	3.94	3.89	3.84	3.78	3.74	3.68
	.01	11.26	8.65	7.59	7.01	6.63	6.37	6.18	6.03	5.91	5.81	5.52	5.36	5.26	5.20	5.12	5.03	4.96	4.87
9	.10	3.36	3.01	2.81	2.69	2.61	2.55	2.51	2.47	2.44	2.42	2.34	2.30	2.27	2.25	2.23	2.21	2.19	2.16
	.05	5.12	4.26	3.86	3.63	3.48	3.37	3.29	3.23	3.18	3.14	3.01	2.94	2.89	2.86	2.83	2.79	2.76	2.71
	.025	7.21	5.71	5.08	4.72	4.48	4.32	4.20	4.10	4.03	3.96	3.77	3.67	3.60	3.56	3.51	3.45	3.40	3.34
	.01	10.56	8.02	6.99	6.42	6.06	5.80	5.61	5.47	5.35	5.26	4.96	4.81	4.71	4.65	4.57	4.48	4.41	4.32
10	.10	3.29	2.92	2.73	2.61	2.52	2.46	2.41	2.38	2.35	2.32	2.24	2.20	2.17	2.16	2.13	2.11	2.09	2.06
	.05	4.96	4.10	3.71	3.48	3.33	3.22	3.14	3.07	3.02	2.98	2.85	2.77	2.73	2.70	2.66	2.62	2.59	2.54
	.025	6.94	5.46	4.83	4.47	4.24	4.07	3.95	3.85	3.78	3.72	3.52	3.42	3.35	3.31	3.26	3.20	3.15	3.09
	.01	10.04	7.56	6.55	5.99	5.64	5.39	5.20	5.06	4.94	4.85	4.56	4.41	4.31	4.25	4.17	4.08	4.01	3.92
11	.10	3.23	2.86	2.66	2.54	2.45	2.39	2.34	2.30	2.27	2.25	2.17	2.12	2.10	2.08	2.05	2.03	2.01	1.98
	.05	4.84	3.98	3.59	3.36	3.20	3.09	3.01	2.95	2.90	2.85	2.72	2.65	2.60	2.57	2.53	2.49	2.46	2.41
	.025	6.72	5.26	4.63	4.28	4.04	3.88	3.76	3.66	3.59	3.53	3.33	3.23	3.16	3.12	3.06	3.00	2.96	2.89
	.01	9.65	7.21	6.22	5.67	5.32	5.07	4.89	4.74	4.63	4.54	4.25	4.10	4.01	3.94	3.86	3.78	3.71	3.61
12	.10	3.18	2.81	2.61	2.48	2.39	2.33	2.28	2.24	2.21	2.19	2.10	2.06	2.03	2.01	1.99	1.96	1.94	1.91
	.05	4.75	3.89	3.49	3.26	3.11	3.00	2.91	2.85	2.80	2.75	2.62	2.54	2.50	2.47	2.43	2.38	2.35	2.30
	.025	6.55	5.10	4.47	4.12	3.89	3.73	3.61	3.51	3.44	3.37	3.18	3.07	3.01	2.96	2.91	2.85	2.80	2.73
	.01	9.33	6.93	5.95	5.41	5.06	4.82	4.64	4.50	4.39	4.30	4.01	3.86	3.76	3.70	3.62	3.54	3.47	3.37
13	.10	3.14	2.76	2.56	2.43	2.35	2.28	2.23	2.20	2.16	2.14	2.05	2.01	1.98	1.96	1.93	1.90	1.88	1.85
	.05	4.67	3.81	3.41	3.18	3.03	2.92	2.83	2.77	2.71	2.67	2.53	2.46	2.41	2.38	2.34	2.30	2.26	2.21
	.025	6.41	4.97	4.35	4.00	3.77	3.60	3.48	3.39	3.31	3.25	3.05	2.95	2.88	2.84	2.78	2.72	2.67	2.60
	.01	9.07	6.70	5.74	5.21	4.86	4.62	4.44	4.30	4.19	4.10	3.82	3.66	3.57	3.51	3.43	3.34	3.27	3.18
14	.10	3.10	2.73	2.52	2.39	2.31	2.24	2.19	2.15	2.12	2.10	2.01	1.96	1.93	1.91	1.89	1.86	1.83	1.80
	.05	4.60	3.74	3.34	3.11	2.96	2.85	2.76	2.70	2.65	2.60	2.46	2.39	2.34	2.31	2.27	2.22	2.19	2.14
	.025	6.30	4.86	4.24	3.89	3.66	3.50	3.38	3.29	3.21	3.15	2.95	2.84	2.78	2.73	2.67	2.61	2.56	2.50
	.01	8.86	6.51	5.56	5.04	4.69	4.46	4.28	4.14	4.03	3.94	3.66	3.51	3.41	3.35	3.27	3.18	3.11	3.02
15	.10	3.07	2.70	2.49	2.36	2.27	2.21	2.16	2.12	2.09	2.06	1.97	1.92	1.89	1.87	1.85	1.82	1.79	1.76
	.05	4.54	3.68	3.29	3.06	2.90	2.79	2.71	2.64	2.59	2.54	2.40	2.33	2.28	2.25	2.20	2.16	2.12	2.07
	.025	6.20	4.77	4.15	3.80	3.58	3.41	3.29	3.20	3.12	3.06	2.86	2.76	2.69	2.64	2.59	2.52	2.47	2.40
	.01	8.68	6.36	5.42	4.89	4.56	4.32	4.14	4.00	3.89	3.80	3.52	3.37	3.28	3.21	3.13	3.05	2.98	2.88

TABLE 4 *F* DISTRIBUTION (*Continued*)

Denominator Degrees of Freedom	Area in Upper Tail	Numerator Degrees of Freedom																	
		1	2	3	4	5	6	7	8	9	10	15	20	25	30	40	60	100	1000
16	.10	3.05	2.67	2.46	2.33	2.24	2.18	2.13	2.09	2.06	2.03	1.94	1.89	1.86	1.84	1.81	1.78	1.76	1.72
	.05	4.49	3.63	3.24	3.01	2.85	2.74	2.66	2.59	2.54	2.49	2.35	2.28	2.23	2.19	2.15	2.11	2.07	2.02
	.025	6.12	4.69	4.08	3.73	3.50	3.34	3.22	3.12	3.05	2.99	2.79	2.68	2.61	2.57	2.51	2.45	2.40	2.32
	.01	8.53	6.23	5.29	4.77	4.44	4.20	4.03	3.89	3.78	3.69	3.41	3.26	3.16	3.10	3.02	2.93	2.86	2.76
17	.10	3.03	2.64	2.44	2.31	2.22	2.15	2.10	2.06	2.03	2.00	1.91	1.86	1.83	1.81	1.78	1.75	1.73	1.69
	.05	4.45	3.59	3.20	2.96	2.81	2.70	2.61	2.55	2.49	2.45	2.31	2.23	2.18	2.15	2.10	2.06	2.02	1.97
	.025	6.04	4.62	4.01	3.66	3.44	3.28	3.16	3.06	2.98	2.92	2.72	2.62	2.55	2.50	2.44	2.38	2.33	2.26
	.01	8.40	6.11	5.19	4.67	4.34	4.10	3.93	3.79	3.68	3.59	3.31	3.16	3.07	3.00	2.92	2.83	2.76	2.66
18	.10	3.01	2.62	2.42	2.29	2.20	2.13	2.08	2.04	2.00	1.98	1.89	1.84	1.80	1.78	1.75	1.72	1.70	1.66
	.05	4.41	3.55	3.16	2.93	2.77	2.66	2.58	2.51	2.46	2.41	2.27	2.19	2.14	2.11	2.06	2.02	1.98	1.92
	.025	5.98	4.56	3.95	3.61	3.38	3.22	3.10	3.01	2.93	2.87	2.67	2.56	2.49	2.44	2.38	2.32	2.27	2.20
	.01	8.29	6.01	5.09	4.58	4.25	4.01	3.84	3.71	3.60	3.51	3.23	3.08	2.98	2.92	2.84	2.75	2.68	2.58
19	.10	2.99	2.61	2.40	2.27	2.18	2.11	2.06	2.02	1.98	1.96	1.86	1.81	1.78	1.76	1.73	1.70	1.67	1.64
	.05	4.38	3.52	3.13	2.90	2.74	2.63	2.54	2.48	2.42	2.38	2.23	2.16	2.11	2.07	2.03	1.98	1.94	1.88
	.025	5.92	4.51	3.90	3.56	3.33	3.17	3.05	2.96	2.88	2.82	2.62	2.51	2.44	2.39	2.33	2.27	2.22	2.14
	.01	8.18	5.93	5.01	4.50	4.17	3.94	3.77	3.63	3.52	3.43	3.15	3.00	2.91	2.84	2.76	2.67	2.60	2.50
20	.10	2.97	2.59	2.38	2.25	2.16	2.09	2.04	2.00	1.96	1.94	1.84	1.79	1.76	1.74	1.71	1.68	1.65	1.61
	.05	4.35	3.49	3.10	2.87	2.71	2.60	2.51	2.45	2.39	2.35	2.20	2.12	2.07	2.04	1.99	1.95	1.91	1.85
	.025	5.87	4.46	3.86	3.51	3.29	3.13	3.01	2.91	2.84	2.77	2.57	2.46	2.40	2.35	2.29	2.22	2.17	2.09
	.01	8.10	5.85	4.94	4.43	4.10	3.87	3.70	3.56	3.46	3.37	3.09	2.94	2.84	2.78	2.69	2.61	2.54	2.43
21	.10	2.96	2.57	2.36	2.23	2.14	2.08	2.02	1.98	1.95	1.92	1.83	1.78	1.74	1.72	1.69	1.66	1.63	1.59
	.05	4.32	3.47	3.07	2.84	2.68	2.57	2.49	2.42	2.37	2.32	2.18	2.10	2.05	2.01	1.96	1.92	1.88	1.82
	.025	5.83	4.42	3.82	3.48	3.25	3.09	2.97	2.87	2.80	2.73	2.53	2.42	2.36	2.31	2.25	2.18	2.13	2.05
	.01	8.02	5.78	4.87	4.37	4.04	3.81	3.64	3.51	3.40	3.31	3.03	2.88	2.79	2.72	2.64	2.55	2.48	2.37
22	.10	2.95	2.56	2.35	2.22	2.13	2.06	2.01	1.97	1.93	1.90	1.81	1.76	1.73	1.70	1.67	1.64	1.61	1.57
	.05	4.30	3.44	3.05	2.82	2.66	2.55	2.46	2.40	2.34	2.30	2.15	2.07	2.02	1.98	1.94	1.89	1.85	1.79
	.025	5.79	4.38	3.78	3.44	3.22	3.05	2.93	2.84	2.76	2.70	2.50	2.39	2.32	2.27	2.21	2.14	2.09	2.01
	.01	7.95	5.72	4.82	4.31	3.99	3.76	3.59	3.45	3.35	3.26	2.98	2.83	2.73	2.67	2.58	2.50	2.42	2.32
23	.10	2.94	2.55	2.34	2.21	2.11	2.05	1.99	1.95	1.92	1.89	1.80	1.74	1.71	1.69	1.66	1.62	1.59	1.55
	.05	4.28	3.42	3.03	2.80	2.64	2.53	2.44	2.37	2.32	2.27	2.13	2.05	2.00	1.96	1.91	1.86	1.82	1.76
	.025	5.75	4.35	3.75	3.41	3.18	3.02	2.90	2.81	2.73	2.67	2.47	2.36	2.29	2.24	2.18	2.11	2.06	1.98
	.01	7.88	5.66	4.76	4.26	3.94	3.71	3.54	3.41	3.30	3.21	2.93	2.78	2.69	2.62	2.54	2.45	2.37	2.27
24	.10	2.93	2.54	2.33	2.19	2.10	2.04	1.98	1.94	1.91	1.88	1.78	1.73	1.70	1.67	1.64	1.61	1.58	1.54
	.05	4.26	3.40	3.01	2.78	2.62	2.51	2.42	2.36	2.30	2.25	2.11	2.03	1.97	1.94	1.89	1.84	1.80	1.74
	.025	5.72	4.32	3.72	3.38	3.15	2.99	2.87	2.78	2.70	2.64	2.44	2.33	2.26	2.21	2.15	2.08	2.02	1.94
	.01	7.82	5.61	4.72	4.22	3.90	3.67	3.50	3.36	3.26	3.17	2.89	2.74	2.64	2.58	2.49	2.40	2.33	2.22

(*Continued*)

TABLE 4 *F* DISTRIBUTION (*Continued*)

| | | | | | | | Numerator Degrees of Freedom | | | | | | | | | | | | |
Denominator Degrees of Freedom	Area in Upper Tail	1	2	3	4	5	6	7	8	9	10	15	20	25	30	40	60	100	1000
25	.10	2.92	2.53	2.32	2.18	2.09	2.02	1.97	1.93	1.89	1.87	1.77	1.72	1.68	1.66	1.63	1.59	1.56	1.52
	.05	4.24	3.39	2.99	2.76	2.60	2.49	2.40	2.34	2.28	2.24	2.09	2.01	1.96	1.92	1.87	1.82	1.78	1.72
	.025	5.69	4.29	3.69	3.35	3.13	2.97	2.85	2.75	2.68	2.61	2.41	2.30	2.23	2.18	2.12	2.05	2.00	1.91
	.01	7.77	5.57	4.68	4.18	3.85	3.63	3.46	3.32	3.22	3.13	2.85	2.70	2.60	2.54	2.45	2.36	2.29	2.18
26	.10	2.91	2.52	2.31	2.17	2.08	2.01	1.96	1.92	1.88	1.86	1.76	1.71	1.67	1.65	1.61	1.58	1.55	1.51
	.05	4.23	3.37	2.98	2.74	2.59	2.47	2.39	2.32	2.27	2.22	2.07	1.99	1.94	1.90	1.85	1.80	1.76	1.70
	.025	5.66	4.27	3.67	3.33	3.10	2.94	2.82	2.73	2.65	2.59	2.39	2.28	2.21	2.16	2.09	2.03	1.97	1.89
	.01	7.72	5.53	4.64	4.14	3.82	3.59	3.42	3.29	3.18	3.09	2.81	2.66	2.57	2.50	2.42	2.33	2.25	2.14
27	.10	2.90	2.51	2.30	2.17	2.07	2.00	1.95	1.91	1.87	1.85	1.75	1.70	1.66	1.64	1.60	1.57	1.54	1.50
	.05	4.21	3.35	2.96	2.73	2.57	2.46	2.37	2.31	2.25	2.20	2.06	1.97	1.92	1.88	1.84	1.79	1.74	1.68
	.025	5.63	4.24	3.65	3.31	3.08	2.92	2.80	2.71	2.63	2.57	2.36	2.25	2.18	2.13	2.07	2.00	1.94	1.86
	.01	7.68	5.49	4.60	4.11	3.78	3.56	3.39	3.26	3.15	3.06	2.78	2.63	2.54	2.47	2.38	2.29	2.22	2.11
28	.10	2.89	2.50	2.29	2.16	2.06	2.00	1.94	1.90	1.87	1.84	1.74	1.69	1.65	1.63	1.59	1.56	1.53	1.48
	.05	4.20	3.34	2.95	2.71	2.56	2.45	2.36	2.29	2.24	2.19	2.04	1.96	1.91	1.87	1.82	1.77	1.73	1.66
	.025	5.61	4.22	3.63	3.29	3.06	2.90	2.78	2.69	2.61	2.55	2.34	2.23	2.16	2.11	2.05	1.98	1.92	1.84
	.01	7.64	5.45	4.57	4.07	3.75	3.53	3.36	3.23	3.12	3.03	2.75	2.60	2.51	2.44	2.35	2.26	2.19	2.08
29	.10	2.89	2.50	2.28	2.15	2.06	1.99	1.93	1.89	1.86	1.83	1.73	1.68	1.64	1.62	1.58	1.55	1.52	1.47
	.05	4.18	3.33	2.93	2.70	2.55	2.43	2.35	2.28	2.22	2.18	2.03	1.94	1.89	1.85	1.81	1.75	1.71	1.65
	.025	5.59	4.20	3.61	3.27	3.04	2.88	2.76	2.67	2.59	2.53	2.32	2.21	2.14	2.09	2.03	1.96	1.90	1.82
	.01	7.60	5.42	4.54	4.04	3.73	3.50	3.33	3.20	3.09	3.00	2.73	2.57	2.48	2.41	2.33	2.23	2.16	2.05
30	.10	2.88	2.49	2.28	2.14	2.05	1.98	1.93	1.88	1.85	1.82	1.72	1.67	1.63	1.61	1.57	1.54	1.51	1.46
	.05	4.17	3.32	2.92	2.69	2.53	2.42	2.33	2.27	2.21	2.16	2.01	1.93	1.88	1.84	1.79	1.74	1.70	1.63
	.025	5.57	4.18	3.59	3.25	3.03	2.87	2.75	2.65	2.57	2.51	2.31	2.20	2.12	2.07	2.01	1.94	1.88	1.80
	.01	7.56	5.39	4.51	4.02	3.70	3.47	3.30	3.17	3.07	2.98	2.70	2.55	2.45	2.39	2.30	2.21	2.13	2.02
40	.10	2.84	2.44	2.23	2.09	2.00	1.93	1.87	1.83	1.79	1.76	1.66	1.61	1.57	1.54	1.51	1.47	1.43	1.38
	.05	4.08	3.23	2.84	2.61	2.45	2.34	2.25	2.18	2.12	2.08	1.92	1.84	1.78	1.74	1.69	1.64	1.59	1.52
	.025	5.42	4.05	3.46	3.13	2.90	2.74	2.62	2.53	2.45	2.39	2.18	2.07	1.99	1.94	1.88	1.80	1.74	1.65
	.01	7.31	5.18	4.31	3.83	3.51	3.29	3.12	2.99	2.89	2.80	2.52	2.37	2.27	2.20	2.11	2.02	1.94	1.82
60	.10	2.79	2.39	2.18	2.04	1.95	1.87	1.82	1.77	1.74	1.71	1.60	1.54	1.50	1.48	1.44	1.40	1.36	1.30
	.05	4.00	3.15	2.76	2.53	2.37	2.25	2.17	2.10	2.04	1.99	1.84	1.75	1.69	1.65	1.59	1.53	1.48	1.40
	.025	5.29	3.93	3.34	3.01	2.79	2.63	2.51	2.41	2.33	2.27	2.06	1.94	1.87	1.82	1.74	1.67	1.60	1.49
	.01	7.08	4.98	4.13	3.65	3.34	3.12	2.95	2.82	2.72	2.63	2.35	2.20	2.10	2.03	1.94	1.84	1.75	1.62
100	.10	2.76	2.36	2.14	2.00	1.91	1.83	1.78	1.73	1.69	1.66	1.56	1.49	1.45	1.42	1.38	1.34	1.29	1.22
	.05	3.94	3.09	2.70	2.46	2.31	2.19	2.10	2.03	1.97	1.93	1.77	1.68	1.62	1.57	1.52	1.45	1.39	1.30
	.025	5.18	3.83	3.25	2.92	2.70	2.54	2.42	2.32	2.24	2.18	1.97	1.85	1.77	1.71	1.64	1.56	1.48	1.36
	.01	6.90	4.82	3.98	3.51	3.21	2.99	2.82	2.69	2.59	2.50	2.22	2.07	1.97	1.89	1.80	1.69	1.60	1.45
1000	.10	2.71	2.31	2.09	1.95	1.85	1.78	1.72	1.68	1.64	1.61	1.49	1.43	1.38	1.35	1.30	1.25	1.20	1.08
	.05	3.85	3.00	2.61	2.38	2.22	2.11	2.02	1.95	1.89	1.84	1.68	1.58	1.52	1.47	1.41	1.33	1.26	1.11
	.025	5.04	3.70	3.13	2.80	2.58	2.42	2.30	2.20	2.13	2.06	1.85	1.72	1.64	1.58	1.50	1.41	1.32	1.13
	.01	6.66	4.63	3.80	3.34	3.04	2.82	2.66	2.53	2.43	2.34	2.06	1.90	1.79	1.72	1.61	1.50	1.38	1.16

Appendix C: Summation Notation

Summation

Definition

$$\sum_{i=1}^{n} x_i = x_1 + x_2 + \cdots + x_n \tag{C.1}$$

Example for $x_1 = 5, x_2 = 8, x_3 = 14$:

$$\sum_{i=1}^{3} x_i = x_1 + x_2 + x_3$$
$$= 5 + 8 + 14$$
$$= 27$$

Result 1

For a constant c:

$$\sum_{i=1}^{n} c = \underbrace{(c + c + \cdots + c)}_{n \text{ times}} = nc \tag{C.2}$$

Example for $c = 5, n = 10$:

$$\sum_{i=1}^{10} 5 = 10(5) = 50$$

Example for $c = \bar{x}$:

$$\sum_{i=1}^{n} \bar{x} = n\bar{x}$$

Result 2

$$\sum_{i=1}^{n} cx_i = cx_1 + cx_2 + \cdots + cx_n$$
$$= c(x_1 + x_2 + \cdots + x_n) = c\sum_{i=1}^{n} x_i \tag{C.3}$$

Example for $x_1 = 5, x_2 = 8, x_3 = 14, c = 2$:

$$\sum_{i=1}^{3} 2x_i = 2\sum_{i=1}^{3} x_i = 2(27) = 54$$

Result 3

$$\sum_{i=1}^{n} (ax_i + by_i) = a\sum_{i=1}^{n} x_i + b\sum_{i=1}^{n} y_i \tag{C.4}$$

Example for $x_1 = 5, x_2 = 8, x_3 = 14, a = 2, y_1 = 7, y_2 = 3, y_3 = 8, b = 4$:

$$\sum_{i=1}^{3} (2x_i + 4y_i) = 2 \sum_{i=1}^{3} x_i + 4 \sum_{i=1}^{3} y_i$$
$$= 2(27) + 4(18)$$
$$= 54 + 72$$
$$= 126$$

Double Summation

Consider the following data involving the variable x_{ij}, where i is the subscript denoting the row position and j is the subscript denoting the column position:

		Column		
		1	**2**	**3**
Row	**1**	$x_{11} = 10$	$x_{12} = 8$	$x_{13} = 6$
	2	$x_{21} = 7$	$x_{22} = 4$	$x_{23} = 12$

Definition

$$\sum_{i=1}^{n} \sum_{j=1}^{m} x_{ij} = (x_{11} + x_{12} + \cdots + x_{1m}) + (x_{21} + x_{22} + \cdots + x_{2m})$$
$$+ (x_{31} + x_{32} + \cdots + x_{3m}) + \cdots + (x_{n1} + x_{n2} + \cdots + x_{nm}) \qquad \text{(C.5)}$$

Example:

$$\sum_{i=1}^{2} \sum_{j=1}^{3} x_{ij} = x_{11} + x_{12} + x_{13} + x_{21} + x_{22} + x_{23}$$
$$= 10 + 8 + 6 + 7 + 4 + 12$$
$$= 47$$

Definition

$$\sum_{i=1}^{n} x_{ij} = x_{1j} + x_{2j} + \cdots + x_{nj} \qquad \text{(C.6)}$$

Example:

$$\sum_{i=1}^{2} x_{i2} = x_{12} + x_{22}$$
$$= 8 + 4$$
$$= 12$$

Shorthand Notation

Sometimes when a summation is for all values of the subscript, we use the following shorthand notations:

$$\sum_{i=1}^{n} x_i = \sum_i x_i \qquad \text{(C.7)}$$

$$\sum_{i=1}^{n} \sum_{j=1}^{m} x_{ij} = \sum \sum x_{ij} \qquad \text{(C.8)}$$

$$\sum_{i=1}^{n} x_{ij} = \sum_i x_{ij} \qquad \text{(C.9)}$$

Chapter 1

2. a. 9
  b. 4
  c. Qualitative: country and room rate
     Quantitative: number of rooms and overall score
  d. Country is nominal; room rate is ordinal; number of rooms is ratio; overall score is interval

3. a. Average number of rooms = 808/9 = 89.78, or approximately 90 rooms
  b. Average overall score = 732.1/9 = 81.3
  c. 2 of 9 are located in England; approximately 22%
  d. 4 of 9 have a room rate of $$; approximately 44%

4. a. 10
  b. All brands of minisystems manufactured
  c. $314
  d. $314

6. Questions a, c, and d provide quantitative data
   Questions b and e provide qualitative data

8. a. 1005
  b. Qualitative
  c. Percentages
  d. Approximately 291

10. a. Quantitative; ratio
  b. Qualitative; nominal
  c. Qualitative; ordinal
  d. Quantitative; ratio
  e. Qualitative; nominal

12. a. All visitors to Hawaii
  b. Yes
  c. First and fourth questions provide quantitative data
     Second and third questions provide qualitative data

13. a. Quantitative
  b. Time series with 6 observations
  c. Earnings for Volkswagen
  d. An increase would be expected in 2003, but it appears that the rate of increase is slowing

14. a. Qualitative

16. a. Product taste tests and test marketing
  b. Specially designed statistical studies

18. a. 36%
  b. 189
  c. Qualitative

20. a. 43% of managers were bullish or very bullish, and 21% of managers expected health care to be the leading industry over the next 12 months

b. The average 12-month return estimate is 11.2% for the population of investment managers
  c. The sample average of 2.5 years is an estimate of how long the population of investment managers think it will take to resume sustainable growth

22. a. All registered voters in California
  b. Registered voters contacted by the Policy Institute
  c. Too time consuming and costly to reach the entire population

24. a. Correct
  b. Incorrect
  c. Correct
  d. Incorrect
  e. Incorrect

Chapter 2

2. a. .20
  b. 40
  c/d.

Class	Frequency	Percent Frequency
A	44	22
B	36	18
C	80	40
D	40	20
Total	200	100

3. a. 360° × 58/120 = 174°
  b. 360° × 42/120 = 126°
  c.

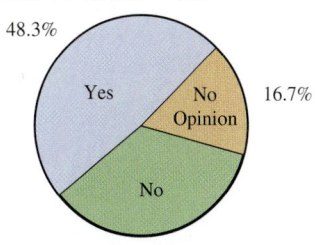

d.

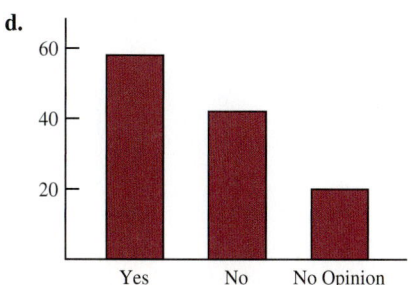

4. a. Qualitative

b.

TV Show	Frequency	Percent Frequency
CSI	18	36
ER	11	22
Friends	15	30
Raymond	6	12
Total	50	100

d. CSI had the largest; Friends was second

6. a.

Book	Frequency	Percent Frequency
7 Habits	10	16.66
Millionaire	16	26.67
Motley	9	15.00
Dad	13	21.67
WSJ Guide	6	10.00
Other	6	10.00
Total	60	100.00

b. First 5: *Millionaire, Dad, 7 Habits, Motley, WSJ Guide*
c. 48.33%

7.

Rating	Frequency	Relative Frequency
Outstanding	19	.38
Very good	13	.26
Good	10	.20
Average	6	.12
Poor	2	.04

Management should be pleased with these results: 64% of the ratings are very good to outstanding, and 84% of the ratings are good or better; comparing these ratings to previous results will show whether the restaurant is making improvements in its customers' ratings of food quality

8. a.

Position	Frequency	Relative Frequency
P	17	.309
H	4	.073
1	5	.091
2	4	.073
3	2	.036
S	5	.091
L	6	.109
C	5	.091
R	7	.127
Total	55	1.000

b. Pitcher
c. 3rd base

d. Right field
e. Infielders 16 to outfielders 18

10. a. The data are ordinal; they simply provide quality classifications

b.

Response	Frequency	Relative Frequency
3	2	.03
4	4	.07
5	12	.20
6	24	.40
7	18	.30
Total	60	1.00

12.

Class	Cumulative Frequency	Cumulative Relative Frequency
≤ 19	10	.20
≤ 29	24	.48
≤ 39	41	.82
≤ 49	48	.96
≤ 59	50	1.00

14. b/c.

Class	Frequency	Percent Frequency
6.0–7.9	4	20
8.0–9.9	2	10
10.0–11.9	8	40
12.0–13.9	3	15
14.0–15.9	3	15
Total	20	100

15. a/b.

Waiting Time	Frequency	Relative Frequency
0–4	4	.20
5–9	8	.40
10–14	5	.25
15–19	2	.10
20–24	1	.05
Total	20	1.00

c/d.

Waiting Time	Cumulative Frequency	Cumulative Relative Frequency
≤ 4	4	.20
≤ 9	12	.60
≤ 14	17	.85
≤ 19	19	.95
≤ 24	20	1.00

e. $12/20 = .60$

16. a. Adjusted Gross Income

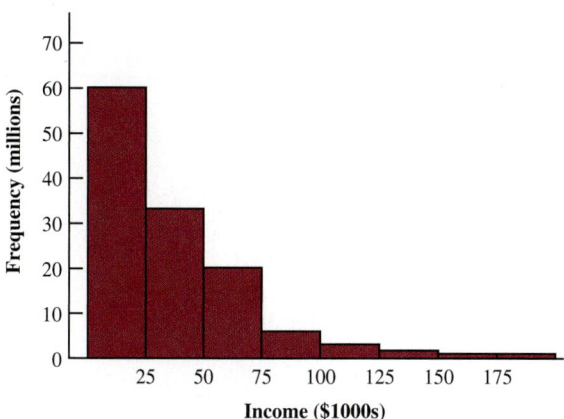

Histogram is skewed to the right

b. Exam Scores

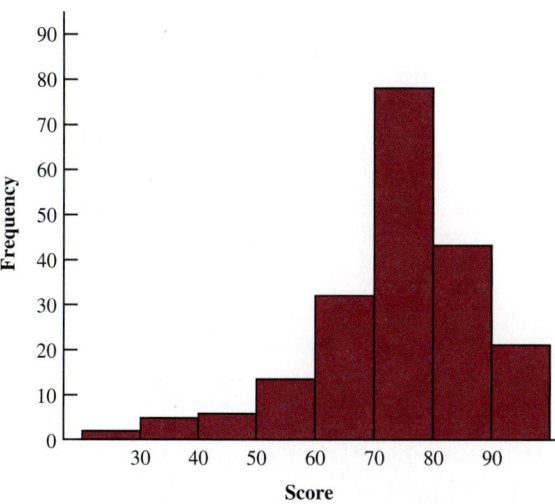

Histogram is skewed to the left

c.

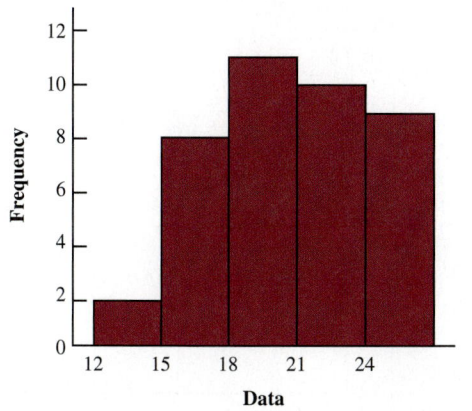

Histogram skewed slightly to the left, but roughly symmetric

18. a. Lowest salary: $93,000
Highest salary: $178,000

b.

Salary ($1000s)	Frequency	Relative Frequency	Percent Frequency
91–105	4	0.08	8
106–120	5	0.10	10
121–135	11	0.22	22
136–150	18	0.36	36
151–165	9	0.18	18
166–180	3	0.06	6
Total	50	1.00	100

c. 20/50

d. 24%

20. a.

Price	Frequency	Percent Frequency
30–39.99	7	35
40–49.99	5	25
50–59.99	2	10
60–69.99	3	15
70–79.99	3	15
Total	20	100

c. Fleetwood Mac, Harper/Johnson

22.

```
5 | 7  8
6 | 4  5  8
7 | 0  2  2  5  5  6  8
8 | 0  2  3  5
```

23. Leaf unit = .1

```
 6 | 3
 7 | 5  5  7
 8 | 1  3  4  8
 9 | 3  6
10 | 0  4  5
11 | 3
```

24. Leaf unit = 10

```
11 | 6
12 | 0  2
13 | 0  6  7
14 | 2  2  7
15 | 5
16 | 0  2  8
17 | 0  2  3
```

25.
```
 9 | 8 9
10 | 2 4 6 6
11 | 4 5 7 8 8 9
12 | 2 4 5 7
13 | 1 2
14 | 4
15 | 1
```

26. a.
```
1 | 0 3 7 7
2 | 4 5 5
3 | 0 0 5 5 9
4 | 0 0 0 5 5 8
5 | 0 0 0 4 5 5
```

b.
```
0 | 5 7
1 | 0 1 1 3 4
1 | 5 5 5 8
2 | 0 0 0 0 0 0
2 | 5 5
3 | 0 0 0
3 | 6
4 |
4 |
5 |
5 |
6 | 3
```

28. a.
```
2 | 1 4
2 | 6 7
3 | 0 1 1 1 2 3
3 | 5 6 7 7
4 | 0 0 3 3 3 3 3 4 4
4 | 6 6 7 9
5 | 0 0 0 2 2
5 | 5 6 7 9
6 | 1 4
6 | 6
7 | 2
```

b. 40–44 with 9

c. 43 with 5

d. 10%; relative small participation in the race

29. a.

		y 1	2	Total
	A	5	0	5
x	B	11	2	13
	C	2	10	12
	Total	18	12	30

b.

		y 1	2	Total
	A	100.0	0.0	100.0
x	B	84.6	15.4	100.0
	C	16.7	83.3	100.0

c.

		y 1	2
	A	27.8	0.0
x	B	61.1	16.7
	C	11.1	83.3
	Total	100.0	100.0

d. A values are always in $y = 1$
B values are most often in $y = 1$
C values are most often in $y = 2$

30. a.

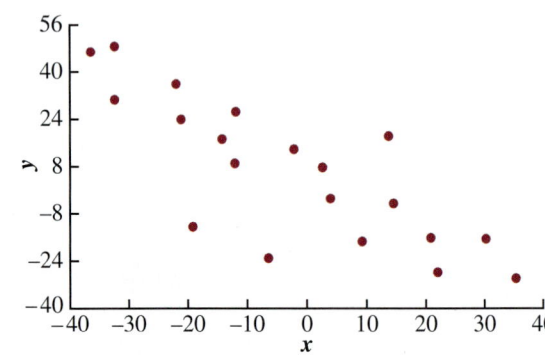

b. A negative relationship between x and y; y decreases as x increases

32. a.

Education Level	Household Income ($1000s) Under 25	25.0–49.9	50.0–74.9	75.0–99.9	100 or more	Total
Not H.S. Graduate	32.70	14.82	8.27	5.02	2.53	15.86
H.S. Graduate	35.74	35.56	31.48	25.39	14.47	30.78
Some College	21.17	29.77	30.25	29.82	22.26	26.37
Bachelor's Degree	7.53	14.43	20.56	25.03	33.88	17.52
Beyond Bach. Deg.	2.86	5.42	9.44	14.74	26.86	9.48
Total	100.00	100.00	100.00	100.00	100.00	100.00

15.86% of the heads of households did not graduate from high school

b. 26.86%, 39.72%

34. a.

Sales/ Margins/ ROE	EPS Rating 0– 19	20– 39	40– 59	60– 79	80– 100	Total
A				1	8	9
B		1	4	5	2	12
C	1		1	2	3	7
D	3	1		1		5
E		2	1			3
Total	4	4	6	9	13	36

b.

Sales/ Margins/ ROE	EPS Rating 0– 19	20– 39	40– 59	60– 79	80– 100	Total
A				11.11	88.89	100
B		8.33	33.33	41.67	16.67	100
C	14.29		14.29	28.57	42.86	100
D	60.00	20.00		20.00		100
E		66.67	33.33			100

Higher EPS ratings seem to be associated with higher ratings on Sales/Margins/ROE

36. b. No apparent relationship

38. a.

Vehicle	Frequency	Percent Frequency
Accord	6	12
Camry	7	14
F-Series	14	28
Ram	10	20
Silverado	13	26

b. Ford F-Series and the Toyota Camry

40. a.

Response	Frequency	Percent Frequency
Accuracy	16	16
Approach shots	3	3
Mental approach	17	17
Power	8	8
Practice	15	15
Putting	10	10
Short game	24	24
Strategic decisions	7	7
Total	100	100

b. Poor short game, poor mental approach, lack of accuracy, and limited practice

42. a/b.

Closing Price	Freq.	Rel. Freq.	Cum. Freq.	Cum. Rel. Freq.
0–9.99	9	.225	9	.225
10–19.99	10	.250	19	.475
20–29.99	5	.125	24	.600
30–39.99	11	.275	35	.875
40–49.99	2	.050	37	.925
50–59.99	2	.050	39	.975
60–69.99	0	.000	39	.975
70–79.99	1	.025	40	1.000
Total	40	1.000		

44.

Income ($)	Frequency	Relative Frequency
18,000–21,999	13	0.255
22,000–25,999	20	0.392
26,000–29,999	12	0.235
30,000–33,999	4	0.078
34,000–37,999	2	0.039
Total	51	1.000

46. a. High Temperature

```
3 |
4 |
5 | 7
6 | 1  4  4  4  4  6  8
7 | 3  5  7  9
8 | 0  1  1  4  6
9 | 0  2  3
```

b. Low Temperature

```
3 | 9
4 | 3  6  8
5 | 0  0  0  2  4  4  5  5  7  9
6 | 1  8
7 | 2  4  5  5
8 |
9 |
```

c. The range of low temperatures is below the range of high temperatures

d. 8 cities

e.

Temperature	Frequency High Temp.	Low Temp.
30–39	0	1
40–49	0	3
50–59	1	10
60–69	7	2
70–79	4	4
80–89	5	0
90–99	3	0
Total	20	20

48. a.

Occupation	Satisfaction Score 30– 39	40– 49	50– 59	60– 69	70– 79	80– 89	Total
Cabinetmaker			2	4	3	1	10
Lawyer	1	5	2	1	1		10
Physical Therapist			5	2	1	2	10
Systems Analyst		2	1	4	3		10
Total	1	7	10	11	8	3	40

b.

| | Satisfaction Score | | | | | | |
| | 30– 39 | 40– 49 | 50– 59 | 60– 69 | 70– 79 | 80– 89 | Total |
Occupation							
Cabinetmaker			20	40	30	10	100
Lawyer	10	50	20	10	10		100
Physical Therapist				50	20	10	20	100
Systems Analyst			20	10	40	30	100

c. Cabinetmakers seem to have the highest job satisfaction scores; lawyers seem to have the lowest

50. a. Row totals: 247; 54; 82; 121
Column totals: 149; 317; 17; 7; 14

b.

Year	Freq.	Fuel	Freq.
1973 or before	247	Elect.	149
1974–79	54	Nat. Gas	317
1980–86	82	Oil	17
1987–91	121	Propane	7
Total	504	Other	14
		Total	504

c. Crosstabulation of column percentages

| Year Constructed | Fuel Type | | | | |
	Elect.	Nat. Gas	Oil	Propane	Other
1973 or before	26.9	57.7	70.5	71.4	50.0
1974–1979	16.1	8.2	11.8	28.6	0.0
1980–1986	24.8	12.0	5.9	0.0	42.9
1987–1991	32.2	22.1	11.8	0.0	7.1
Total	100.0	100.0	100.0	100.0	100.0

d. Crosstabulation of row percentages.

| Year Constructed | Fuel Type | | | | | |
	Elect.	Nat. Gas	Oil	Propane	Other	Total
1973 or before	16.2	74.1	4.9	2.0	2.8	100.0
1974–1979	44.5	48.1	3.7	3.7	0.0	100.0
1980–1986	45.1	46.4	1.2	0.0	7.3	100.0
1987–1991	39.7	57.8	1.7	0.0	0.8	100.0

52. a. Crosstabulation of market value and profit

| Market Value ($1000s) | Profit ($1000s) | | | | |
	0– 300	300– 600	600– 900	900– 1200	Total
0–8000	23	4			27
8000–16,000	4	4	2	2	12
16,000–24,000		2	1	1	4
24,000–32,000		1	2	1	4
32,000–40,000		2	1		3
Total	27	13	6	4	50

b. Crosstabulation of row percentages

| Market Value ($1000s) | Profit ($1000s) | | | | |
	0– 300	300– 600	600– 900	900– 1200	Total
0–8000	85.19	14.81	0.00	0.00	100
8000–16,000	33.33	33.33	16.67	16.67	100
16,000–24,000	0.00	50.00	25.00	25.00	100
24,000–32,000	0.00	25.00	50.00	25.00	100
32,000–40,000	0.00	66.67	33.33	0.00	100

c. A positive relationship is indicated between profit and market value; as profit goes up, market value goes up

54. b. A positive relationship is demonstrated between market value and stockholders' equity

Chapter 3

2. 16, 16.5

3. Arrange data in order: 15, 20, 25, 25, 27, 28, 30, 34

$i = \dfrac{20}{100}(8) = 1.6$; round up to position 2

20th percentile = 20

$i = \dfrac{25}{100}(8) = 2$; use positions 2 and 3

25th percentile $= \dfrac{20 + 25}{2} = 22.5$

$i = \dfrac{65}{100}(8) = 5.2$; round up to position 6

65th percentile = 28

$i = \dfrac{75}{100}(8) = 6$; use positions 6 and 7

75th percentile $= \dfrac{28 + 30}{2} = 29$

4. 59.727, 57, 53

6. a. 422
b. 380
c. 690
d. Not using capacity

8. a. $\bar{x} = \dfrac{\Sigma x_i}{n} = \dfrac{695}{20} = 34.75$

Mode = 25 (appears three times)

b. Data in order: 18, 20, 25, 25, 25, 26, 27, 27, 28, 33, 36, 37, 40, 40, 42, 45, 46, 48, 53, 54

Median (10th and 11th positions)

$\dfrac{33 + 36}{2} = 34.5$

At-home workers are slightly younger

c. $i = \dfrac{25}{100}(20) = 5$; use positions 5 and 6

$Q_1 = \dfrac{25 + 26}{2} = 25.5$

$$i = \frac{75}{100}(20) = 15; \text{ use positions 15 and 16}$$

$$Q_3 = \frac{42 + 45}{2} = 43.5$$

d. $i = \frac{32}{100}(20) = 6.4$; round up to position 7

32nd percentile = 27
At least 32% of the people are 27 or younger

10. a. 76, 76
   b. 39, 37.5
   c. Yes; emergency wait too long

12. a. \$639
   b. 98.8 pictures
   c. 110.2 minutes

14. 16, 4

15. Range = 34 − 15 = 19
Arrange data in order: 15, 20, 25, 25, 27, 28, 30, 34

$$i = \frac{25}{100}(8) = 2; Q_1 = \frac{20 + 25}{2} = 22.5$$

$$i = \frac{75}{100}(8) = 6; Q_3 = \frac{28 + 30}{2} = 29$$

$$IQR = Q_3 - Q_1 = 29 - 22.5 = 6.5$$

$$\bar{x} = \frac{\Sigma x_i}{n} = \frac{204}{8} = 25.5$$

x_i	$(x_i - \bar{x})$	$(x_i - \bar{x})^2$
27	1.5	2.25
25	−.5	.25
20	−5.5	30.25
15	−10.5	110.25
30	4.5	20.25
34	8.5	72.25
28	2.5	6.25
25	−.5	.25
		242.00

$$s^2 = \frac{\Sigma(x_i - \bar{x})^2}{n - 1} = \frac{242}{8 - 1} = 34.57$$

$$s = \sqrt{34.57} = 5.88$$

16. a. Range = 190 − 168 = 22
   b. $\bar{x} = \dfrac{\Sigma x_i}{n} = \dfrac{1068}{6} = 178$

$$s^2 = \frac{\Sigma(x_i - \bar{x})^2}{n - 1}$$

$$= \frac{4^2 + (-10)^2 + 6^2 + 12^2 + (-8)^2 + (-4)^2}{6 - 1}$$

$$= \frac{376}{5} = 75.2$$

   c. $s = \sqrt{75.2} = 8.67$

   d. $\dfrac{s}{\bar{x}}(100) = \dfrac{8.67}{178}(100\%) = 4.87\%$

18. a. 38, 97, 9.85
   b. Eastern shows more variation

20. *Dawson:* range = 2, s = .67
     Clark: range = 8, s = 2.58

22. a. 45.05, 23.98; 57.50, 11.475
   b. 190.67, 13.81; 140.63, 11.86
   c. 38.02%; 57.97%
   d. Greater for broker-assisted trades

24. *Quarter-milers:* s = .0564, Coef. of Var. = 5.8%
     Milers: s = .1295, Coef. of Var. = 2.9%

26. .20, 1.50, 0, −.50, −2.20

27. Chebyshev's theorem: *at least* $(1 - 1/z^2)$

   a. $z = \dfrac{40 - 30}{5} = 2; 1 - \dfrac{1}{(2)^2} = .75$

   b. $z = \dfrac{45 - 30}{5} = 3; 1 - \dfrac{1}{(3)^2} = .89$

   c. $z = \dfrac{38 - 30}{5} = 1.6; 1 - \dfrac{1}{(1.6)^2} = .61$

   d. $z = \dfrac{42 - 30}{5} = 2.4; 1 - \dfrac{1}{(2.4)^2} = .83$

   e. $z = \dfrac{48 - 30}{5} = 3.6; 1 - \dfrac{1}{(3.6)^2} = .92$

28. a. 95%
   b. Almost all
   c. 68%

29. a. $z = 2$ standard deviations

$$1 - \frac{1}{z^2} = 1 - \frac{1}{2^2} = \frac{3}{4}; \text{ at least 75\%}$$

   b. $z = 2.5$ standard deviations

$$1 - \frac{1}{z^2} = 1 - \frac{1}{2.5^2} = .84; \text{ at least 84\%}$$

   c. $z = 2$ standard deviations
      Empirical rule: 95%

30. a. 68%
   b. 81.5%
   c. 2.5%

32. a. −.67
   b. 1.50
   c. Neither an outlier
   d. Yes; z = 8.25

34. a. 76.5, 7
   b. 16%, 2.5%
   c. 12.2, 7.89; no

36. 15, 22.5, 26, 29, 34

38. Arrange data in order: 5, 6, 8, 10, 10, 12, 15, 16, 18

$$i = \frac{25}{100}(9) = 2.25; \text{ round up to position 3}$$

$$Q_1 = 8$$

Median (5th position) = 10

$i = \dfrac{75}{100}(9) = 6.75$; round up to position 7

$Q_3 = 15$

5-number summary: 5, 8, 10, 15, 18

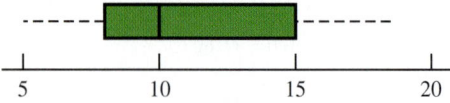

40. a. 619, 725, 1016, 1699, 4450
   b. Limits: 0, 3160
   c. Yes
   d. No

41. a. Arrange data in order low to high

$i = \dfrac{25}{100}(21) = 5.25$; round up to 6th position

$Q_1 = 1872$

Median (11th position) = 4019

$i = \dfrac{75}{100}(21) = 15.75$; round up to 16th position

$Q_3 = 8305$

5-number summary: 608, 1872, 4019, 8305, 14138
   b. IQR $= Q_3 - Q_1 = 8305 - 1872 = 6433$
   Lower limit: $1872 - 1.5(6433) = -7777$
   Upper limit: $8305 + 1.5(6433) = 17,955$
   c. No; data are within limits
   d. $41,138 > 27,604$; 41,138 would be an outlier; data value would be reviewed and corrected
   e.

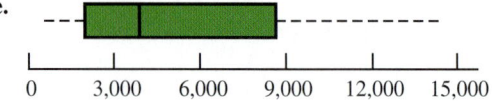

42. a. 61
   b. 34, 45, 61, 90, 126
   c. No; upper limit $= 157.5$

44. a. 18.2, 15.35
   b. 11.7, 23.5
   c. 3.4, 11.7, 15.35, 23.5, 41.3
   d. Yes; Alger Small Cap 41.3

45. b. There appears to be a negative linear relationship between x and y
   c.

x_i	y_i	$x_i - \bar{x}$	$y_i - \bar{y}$	$(x_i - \bar{x})(y_i - \bar{y})$
4	50	−4	4	−16
6	50	−2	4	−8
11	40	3	−6	−18
3	60	−5	14	−70
16	30	8	−16	−128
40	230	0	0	−240

$\bar{x} = 8; \bar{y} = 46$

$s_{xy} = \dfrac{\Sigma(x_i - \bar{x})(y_i - \bar{y})}{n - 1} = \dfrac{-240}{4} = -60$

The sample covariance indicates a negative linear association between x and y

d. $r_{xy} = \dfrac{s_{xy}}{s_x s_y} = \dfrac{-60}{(5.43)(11.40)} = -.969$

The sample correlation coefficient of $-.969$ is indicative of a strong negative linear relationship

46. b. There appears to be a positive linear relationship between x and y
   c. $s_{xy} = 26.5$
   d. $r_{xy} = .693$

48. $-.91$; negative relationship

50. a. .92
   b. Strong positive linear relationship

52. a. 3.69
   b. 3.175

53. a.

f_i	M_i	$f_i M_i$
4	5	20
7	10	70
9	15	135
5	20	100
25		325

$\bar{x} = \dfrac{\Sigma f_i M_i}{n} = \dfrac{325}{25} = 13$

   b.

f_i	M_i	$(M_i - \bar{x})$	$(M_i - \bar{x})^2$	$f_i(M_i - \bar{x})^2$
4	5	−8	64	256
7	10	−3	9	63
9	15	2	4	36
5	20	7	49	245
25				600

$s^2 = \dfrac{\Sigma f_i(M_i - \bar{x})^2}{n - 1} = \dfrac{600}{25 - 1} = 25$

$s = \sqrt{25} = 5$

54. a.

Grade x_i	Weight w_i
4 (A)	9
3 (B)	15
2 (C)	33
1 (D)	3
0 (F)	0
	60 credit hours

$\bar{x} = \dfrac{\Sigma w_i x_i}{\Sigma w_i} = \dfrac{9(4) + 15(3) + 33(2) + 3(1)}{9 + 15 + 33 + 3}$

$= \dfrac{150}{60} = 2.5$

   b. Yes

56. 10.74, 25.63, 5.06; estimate $= 1288.8$

58. a. 1800, 1351
  b. 387, 1710
  c. 7280, 1323
  d. 3,675,303, 1917
  e. 9271.01, 96.29
  f. High positive
  g. Using a box plot: 4135 and 7450

60. a. 2.3, 1.85
  b. 1.90, 1.38
  c. Altria Group 5%
  d. −.51, below mean
  e. 1.02, above mean
  f. No

62. a. $\bar{x} = 83.135$, $s = 16.173$
  b. \$50,789 to \$115,481
  c. Same range as in part (b); higher probability
  d. Danbury, CT, is an outlier

64. a. 502.67; positive linear relationship
  b. .933

66. b. .9856, strong positive relationship

68. a. 817
  b. 833

70. a. 60.68
  b. $s^2 = 31.23$; $s = 5.59$

Chapter 4

2. $\binom{6}{3} = \dfrac{6!}{3!3!} = \dfrac{6 \cdot 5 \cdot 4 \cdot 3 \cdot 2 \cdot 1}{(3 \cdot 2 \cdot 1)(3 \cdot 2 \cdot 1)} = 20$

ABC	ACE	BCD	BEF
ABD	ACF	BCE	CDE
ABE	ADE	BCF	CDF
ABF	ADF	BDE	CEF
ACD	AEF	BDF	DEF

4. b. (H,H,H), (H,H,T), (H,T,H), (H,T,T),
    (T,H,H), (T,H,T), (T,T,H), (T,T,T)
  c. $\frac{1}{8}$

6. $P(E_1) = .40$, $P(E_2) = .26$, $P(E_3) = .34$
    The relative frequency method was used

8. a. 4: Commission Positive—Council Approves
      Commission Positive—Council Disapproves
      Commission Negative—Council Approves
      Commission Negative—Council Disapproves

9. $\binom{50}{4} = \dfrac{50!}{4!46!} = \dfrac{50 \cdot 49 \cdot 48 \cdot 47}{4 \cdot 3 \cdot 2 \cdot 1} = 230,300$

10. a. Use the relative frequency approach
      $P(\text{California}) = 1,434/2,374 = .60$
  b. Number not from four states
          $= 2,374 - 1,434 - 390 - 217 - 112$
          $= 221$
      $P(\text{Not from 4 states}) = 221/2,374 = .09$
  c. $P(\text{Not in early stages}) = 1 - .22 = .78$
  d. Estimate of number of Massachusetts' companies in
      early stage of development $= (.22)390 \approx 86$

e. If we assume the size of the awards did not differ by
    state, we can multiply the probability an award went to
    Colorado by the total venture funds disbursed to get an
    estimate
    Estimate of Colorado funds $= (112/2374)(\$32.4)$
    $= \$1.53$ billion
    Authors' Note: The actual amount going to Colorado
    was \$1.74 billion

12. a. 2,869,685
  b. 1/2,869,685
  c. 1/120,526,770

14. a. $\frac{1}{4}$
  b. $\frac{1}{2}$
  c. $\frac{3}{4}$

15. a. $S = $ (ace of clubs, ace of diamonds, ace of hearts, ace
      of spades)
  b. $S = $ (2 of clubs, 3 of clubs, . . . , 10 of clubs, J of clubs,
      Q of clubs, K of clubs, A of clubs)
  c. There are 12; jack, queen, or king in each of the four suits
  d. For (a): $4/52 = 1/13 = .08$
      For (b): $13/52 = 1/4 = .25$
      For (c): $12/52 = .23$

16. a. 36
  c. $\frac{1}{6}$
  d. $\frac{5}{18}$
  e. No; $P(\text{odd}) = P(\text{even}) = \frac{1}{2}$
  f. Classical

17. a. (4, 6), (4, 7), (4, 8)
  b. $.05 + .10 + .15 = .30$
  c. (2, 8), (3, 8), (4, 8)
  d. $.05 + .05 + .15 = .25$
  e. .15

18. a. $P(0) = .05$
  b. $P(4 \text{ or } 5) = .20$
  c. $P(0, 1, \text{ or } 2) = .55$

20. a. .112
  b. .086
  c. .49

22. a. .40, .40, .60
  b. .80, yes
  c. $A^c = (E_3, E_4, E_5)$; $C^c = (E_1, E_4)$;
      $P(A^c) = .60$; $P(C^c) = .40$
  d. (E_1, E_2, E_5); .60
  e. .80

23. a. $P(A) = P(E_1) + P(E_4) + P(E_6)$
        $= .05 + .25 + .10 = .40$
      $P(B) = P(E_2) + P(E_4) + P(E_7)$
        $= .20 + .25 + .05 = .50$
      $P(C) = P(E_2) + P(E_3) + P(E_5) + P(E_7)$
        $= .20 + .20 + .15 + .05 = .60$
  b. $A \cup B = \{E_1, E_2, E_4, E_6, E_7\}$;
      $P(A \cup B) = P(E_1) + P(E_2) + P(E_4) + P(E_6) + P(E_7)$
          $= .05 + .20 + .25 + .10 + .05$
          $= .65$
  c. $A \cap B = \{E_4\}$; $P(A \cap B) = P(E_4) = .25$

d. Yes, they are mutually exclusive

e. $B^c = \{E_1, E_3, E_5, E_6\}$;
$$P(B^c) = P(E_1) + P(E_3) + P(E_5) + P(E_6)$$
$$= .05 + .20 + .15 + .10$$
$$= .50$$

24. a. .05
   b. .70

26. a. .30, .23
   b. .17
   c. .64

28. Let B = rented a car for business reasons
   P = rented a car for personal reasons
   a. $P(B \cup P) = P(B) + P(P) - P(B \cap P)$
   $$= .540 + .458 - .300$$
   $$= .698$$
   b. $P(\text{Neither}) = 1 - .698 = .302$

30. a. $P(A \mid B) = \dfrac{P(A \cap B)}{P(B)} = \dfrac{.40}{.60} = .6667$

   b. $P(B \mid A) = \dfrac{P(A \cap B)}{P(A)} = \dfrac{.40}{.50} = .80$

   c. No, because $P(A \mid B) \neq P(A)$

32. a.

Age	Yes	No	Total
18 to 34	.375	.085	.46
35 and over	.475	.065	.54
Total	.850	.150	1.00

   b. 46% 18 to 34; 54% 35 and over
   c. .15
   d. .1848
   e. .1204
   f. .5667
   g. Higher probability of No for 18 to 34

33. a.

	Reason for Applying			
		Cost/		
Status	**Quality**	**Convenience**	**Other**	**Total**
Full-time	.218	.204	.039	.461
Part-time	.208	.307	.024	.539
Total	.426	.511	.063	1.000

   b. A student is most likely to cite cost or convenience as the first reason (probability = .511); school quality is the reason cited by the second largest number of students (probability = .426)
   c. $P(\text{quality} \mid \text{full-time}) = .218/.461 = .473$
   d. $P(\text{quality} \mid \text{part-time}) = .208/.539 = .386$
   e. For independence, we must have $P(A)P(B) = P(A \cap B)$; from the table

   $P(A \cap B) = .218$, $P(A) = .461$, $P(B) = .426$
   $P(A)P(B) = (.461)(.426) = .196$

   Because $P(A)P(B) \neq P(A \cap B)$, the events are not independent

34. a. .44
   b. .15
   c. .136
   d. .106
   e. .0225
   f. .0025

36. a. .7921
   b. .9879
   c. .0121
   d. .3364, .8236, .1764
       Don't foul Reggie Miller

38. a. .0209
   b. .0141, .027
   c. No
   d. .0202, .0458
   e. Yes

39. a. Yes, because $P(A_1 \cap A_2) = 0$
   b. $P(A_1 \cap B) = P(A_1)P(B \mid A_1) = .40(.20) = .08$
       $P(A_2 \cap B) = P(A_2)P(B \mid A_2) = .60(.05) = .03$
   c. $P(B) = P(A_1 \cap B) + P(A_2 \cap B) = .08 + .03 = .11$
   d. $P(A_1 \mid B) = \dfrac{.08}{.11} = .7273$

   $P(A_2 \mid B) = \dfrac{.03}{.11} = .2727$

40. a. .10, .20, .09
   b. .51
   c. .26, .51, .23

42. M = missed payment
   D_1 = customer defaults
   D_2 = customer does not default
   $P(D_1) = .05, P(D_2) = .95, P(M \mid D_2) = .2, P(M \mid D_1) = 1$

   a. $P(D_1 \mid M) = \dfrac{P(D_1)P(M \mid D_1)}{P(D_1)P(M \mid D_1) + P(D_2)P(M \mid D_2)}$
   $$= \dfrac{(.05)(1)}{(.05)(1) + (.95)(.2)}$$
   $$= \dfrac{.05}{.24} = .21$$

   b. Yes, the probability of default is greater than .20

44. a. .47, .53, .50, .45
   b. .4963
   c. .4463
   d. 47%, 53%

46. a. .68
   b. 52
   c. 10

48. a. 315
   b. .29
   c. No
   d. Republicans

50. a. .76
   b. .24

52. b. .2022
   c. .4618
   d. .4005

54. a. .49
   b. .44
   c. .54
   d. No
   e. Yes

56. a. .25
   b. .125
   c. .0125
   d. .10
   e. No

58. 3.44%

60. a. .40
   b. .67

Chapter 5

1. a. Head, Head (H, H)
   Head, Tail (H, T)
   Tail, Head (T, H)
   Tail, Tail (T, T)
   b. $x =$ number of heads on two coin tosses
   c.

Outcome	Values of x
(H, H)	2
(H, T)	1
(T, H)	1
(T, T)	0

   d. Discrete; it may assume 3 values: 0, 1, and 2

2. a. $x =$ time in minutes to assemble product
   b. Any positive value: $x > 0$
   c. Continuous

3. Let $Y =$ position is offered
   $N =$ position is not offered
   a. $S = \{(Y, Y, Y), (Y, Y, N), (Y, N, Y), (Y, N, N), (N, Y, Y),$
   $(N, Y, N), (N, N, Y), (N, N, N)\}$
   b. Let $N =$ number of offers made; N is a discrete random variable
   c.

Experimental Outcome	(Y, Y, Y)	(Y, Y, N)	(Y, N, Y)	(Y, N, N)	(N, Y, Y)	(N, Y, N)	(N, N, Y)	(N, N, N)
Value of N	3	2	2	1	2	1	1	0

4. $x = 0, 1, 2, \ldots, 12$

6. a. 0, 1, 2, . . . , 20; discrete
   b. 0, 1, 2, . . . ; discrete
   c. 0, 1, 2, . . . , 50; discrete
   d. $0 \leq x \leq 8$; continuous
   e. $x > 0$; continuous

7. a. $f(x) \geq 0$ for all values of x
   $\Sigma f(x) = 1$; therefore, it is a valid probability distribution
   b. Probability $x = 30$ is $f(30) = .25$
   c. Probability $x \leq 25$ is $f(20) + f(25) = .20 + .15 = .35$
   d. Probability $x > 30$ is $f(35) = .40$

8. a.

x	$f(x)$
1	3/20 = .15
2	5/20 = .25
3	8/20 = .40
4	4/20 = .20
	Total 1.00

   b.

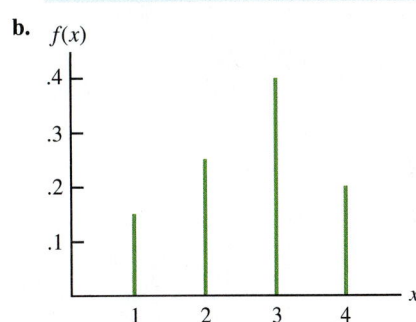

   c. $f(x) \geq 0$ for $x = 1, 2, 3, 4$
   $\Sigma f(x) = 1$

10. a.

x	1	2	3	4	5
$f(x)$	.05	.09	.03	.42	.41

   b.

x	1	2	3	4	5
$f(x)$	.04	.10	.12	.46	.28

   c. .83
   d. .28
   e. Senior executives more satisfied

12. a. Yes
   b. .65

14. a. .05
   b. .70
   c. .40

16. a.

y	$f(y)$	$yf(y)$
2	.20	.40
4	.30	1.20
7	.40	2.80
8	.10	.80
Totals	1.00	5.20

$E(y) = \mu = 5.20$

b.

y	$y - \mu$	$(y - \mu)^2$	$f(y)$	$(y - \mu)^2 f(y)$
2	-3.20	10.24	.20	2.048
4	-1.20	1.44	.30	.432
7	1.80	3.24	.40	1.296
8	2.80	7.84	.10	.784
			Total	4.560

$$\text{Var}(y) = 4.56$$
$$\sigma = \sqrt{4.56} = 2.14$$

18. a/b.

x	$f(x)$	$xf(x)$	$x - \mu$	$(x - \mu)^2$	$(x - \mu)^2 f(x)$
0	0.04	0.00	-1.84	3.39	0.12
1	0.34	0.34	-0.84	0.71	0.24
2	0.41	0.82	0.16	0.02	0.01
3	0.18	0.53	1.16	1.34	0.24
4	0.04	0.15	2.16	4.66	0.17
Total	1.00	1.84			0.79
		↑			↑
		$E(x)$			$\text{Var}(x)$

c/d.

y	$f(y)$	$yf(y)$	$y - \mu$	$(y - \mu)^2$	$y - \mu^2 f(y)$
0	0.00	0.00	-2.93	8.58	0.01
1	0.03	0.03	-1.93	3.72	0.12
2	0.23	0.45	-0.93	0.86	0.20
3	0.52	1.55	0.07	0.01	0.00
4	0.22	0.90	1.07	1.15	0.26
Total	1.00	2.93			0.59
		↑			↑
		$E(y)$			$\text{Var}(y)$

e. The number of bedrooms in owner-occupied houses is greater than in renter-occupied houses; the expected number of bedrooms is $1.09 = 2.93 - 1.84$ greater and the variability in the number of bedrooms is less for the owner-occupied houses

20. a. 166

b. -94; concern is to protect against the expense of a big accident

22. a. 445

b. $1250 loss

24. a. Medium: 145; large: 140

b. Medium: 2725; large: 12,400

25. a.

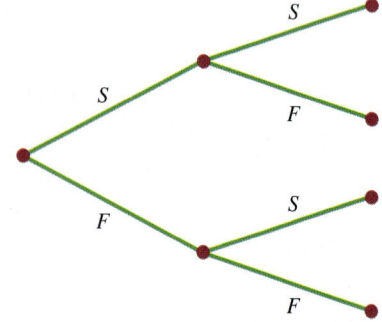

b. $f(1) = \binom{2}{1}(.4)^1(.6)^1 = \dfrac{2!}{1!1!}(.4)(.6) = .48$

Using Excel: BINOMDIST(1,2,.4,FALSE) = .48

c. $f(0) = \binom{2}{0}(.4)^0(.6)^2 = \dfrac{2!}{0!2!}(1)(.36) = .36$

Using Excel: BINOMDIST(0,2,.4,FALSE) = .36

d. $f(2) = \binom{2}{2}(.4)^2(.6)^0 = \dfrac{2!}{2!0!}(.16)(.1) = .16$

Using Excel: BINOMDIST(2,2,.4,FALSE) = .16

e. $P(x \geq 1) = f(1) + f(2) = .48 + .16 = .64$

f. $E(x) = np = 2(.4) = .8$
$\text{Var}(x) = np(1 - p) = 2(.4)(.6) = .48$
$\sigma = \sqrt{.48} = .6928$

26. a. $f(0) = .3487$

b. $f(2) = .1937$

c. .9298

d. .6513

e. 1

f. $\sigma^2 = .9000, \sigma = .9487$

28. a. .2789

b. .4181

c. .0733

30. a. Probability of a defective part being produced must be .03 for each part selected; parts must be selected independently

b. Let D = defective
G = not defective

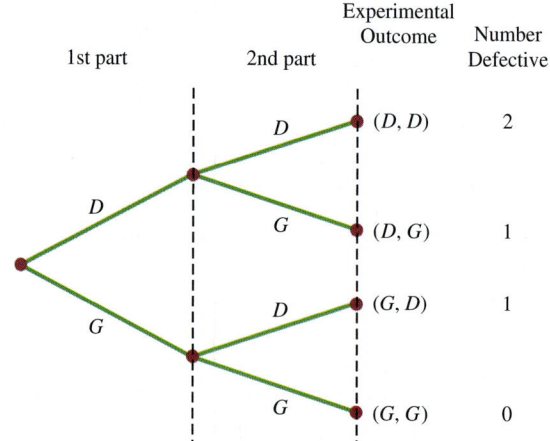

c. Two outcomes result in exactly one defect

d. $P(\text{no defects}) = (.97)(.97) = .9409$
$P(1 \text{ defect}) = 2(.03)(.97) = .0582$
$P(2 \text{ defects}) = (.03)(.03) = .0009$

32. a. .90

b. .99

c. .999

d. Yes

34. a. .0634

b. .0634

c. .9729

38. a. $f(x) = \dfrac{3^x e^{-3}}{x!}$

  b. .224

  c. .149

  d. .801

39. a. $f(x) = \dfrac{2^x e^{-2}}{x!}$

  b. $\mu = 6$ for 3 time periods

  c. $f(x) = \dfrac{6^x e^{-6}}{x!}$

  d. $f(2) = \dfrac{2^2 e^{-2}}{2!} = \dfrac{4(.1353)}{2} = .2706$

   Using Excel: POISSON(2,2,FALSE) = .2707

  e. $f(6) = \dfrac{6^6 e^{-6}}{6!} = .1606$

   Using Excel: POISSON(6,6,FALSE) = .1606

  f. $f(5) = \dfrac{4^5 e^{-4}}{5!} = .1563$

   Using Excel: POISSON(5,4,FALSE) = .1563

40. a. $\mu = 48(5/60) = 4$

   $f(3) = \dfrac{4^3 e^{-4}}{3!} = \dfrac{(64)(.0183)}{6} = .1952$

  b. $\mu = 48(15/60) = 12$

   $f(10) = \dfrac{12^{10} e^{-12}}{10!} = .1048$

  c. $\mu = 48(5/60) = 4$; one can expect four callers to be waiting after 5 minutes

   $f(0) = \dfrac{4^0 e^{-4}}{0!} = .0183$; the probability none will be waiting after 5 minutes is .0183

  d. $\mu = 48(3/60) = 2.4$

   $f(0) = \dfrac{2.4^0 e^{-2.4}}{0!} = .0907$; the probability of no interruptions in 3 minutes is .0907

42. a. $f(0) = \dfrac{7^0 e^{-7}}{0!} = e^{-7} = \text{POISSON}(0,7,\text{FALSE})$

   $= .0009$

  b. Probability $= 1 - [f(0) + f(1)]$

   $= 1 - \text{POISSON}(1,7,\text{TRUE}) = .9927$

  c. $\mu = 3.5$

   $f(0) = \dfrac{3.5^0 e^{-3.5}}{0!} = e^{-3.5} = \text{POISSON}(0,3.5,\text{FALSE})$

   $= .0302$

   Probability $= 1 - f(0) = 1 - .0302 = .9698$

  d.

   Probability $= 1 - [f(0) + f(1) + f(2) + f(3) + f(4)]$

   $= 1 - \text{POISSON}(4,7,\text{TRUE})$

   $= .8270$

44. a. $\mu = 1.25$

  b. .2865

  c. .3581

  d. .3554

46. a. $f(1) = \dfrac{\binom{3}{1}\binom{10-3}{4-1}}{\binom{10}{4}} = \dfrac{\left(\dfrac{3!}{1!2!}\right)\left(\dfrac{7!}{3!4!}\right)}{\dfrac{10!}{4!6!}}$

   $= \dfrac{(3)(35)}{210} = .50$

   Using Excel: HYPGEOMDIST(1,4,3,10) = .5000

  b. $f(2) = \dfrac{\binom{3}{2}\binom{10-3}{2-2}}{\binom{10}{2}} = \dfrac{(3)(1)}{45} = .067$

   Using Excel: HYPGEOMDIST(2,2,3,10) = .0667

  c. $f(0) = \dfrac{\binom{3}{0}\binom{10-3}{2-0}}{\binom{10}{2}} = \dfrac{(1)(21)}{45} = .4667$

   Using Excel: HYPGEOMDIST(0,2,3,10) = .4667

  d. $f(2) = \dfrac{\binom{3}{2}\binom{10-3}{4-2}}{\binom{10}{4}} = \dfrac{(3)(21)}{210} = .30$

   Using Excel: HYPGEOMDIST(2,4,3,10) = .3000

48. a. .5250

  b. .8167

50. $N = 60, n = 10$

  a. $r = 20, x = 0$

   $f(0) = \dfrac{\binom{20}{0}\binom{40}{10}}{\binom{60}{10}} = \dfrac{(1)\left(\dfrac{40!}{10!30!}\right)}{\dfrac{60!}{10!50!}}$

   $= \left(\dfrac{40!}{10!30!}\right)\left(\dfrac{10!50!}{60!}\right)$

   $= \dfrac{40\cdot 39\cdot 38\cdot 37\cdot 36\cdot 35\cdot 34\cdot 33\cdot 32\cdot 31}{60\cdot 59\cdot 58\cdot 57\cdot 56\cdot 55\cdot 54\cdot 53\cdot 52\cdot 51}$

   $\approx .01$

   Using Excel: HYPGEOMDIST(1,10,20,60) = .0112

  b. $r = 20, x = 1$

   $f(1) = \dfrac{\binom{20}{1}\binom{40}{9}}{\binom{60}{10}} = 20\left(\dfrac{40!}{9!31!}\right)\left(\dfrac{10!50!}{60!}\right)$

   $\approx .07$

   Using Excel: HYPGEOMDIST(1,10,20,60) = .0725

  c. $1 - f(0) - f(1) = 1 - .08 = .92$

  d. Same as the probability one will be from Hawaii; in part (b) it was equal to approximately .07

52. a. .5333

  b. .6667

  c. .7778

  d. $n = 7$

54. a.

x	1	2	3	4	5
$f(x)$	.24	.21	.10	.21	.24

b. 3.00, 2.34
c. Bonds: $E(x) = 1.36$, $\text{Var}(x) = .23$
    Stocks: $E(x) = 4$, $\text{Var}(x) = 1$

56. a. .0596
b. .3585
c. 100
d. 95, 9.7468

58. a. .9510
b. .0480
c. .0490

60. a. 240
b. 12.9615
c. 12.9615

62. .1912

64. a. .2240
b. .5767

66. a. .4667
b. .4667
c. .0667

Chapter 6

1. a.

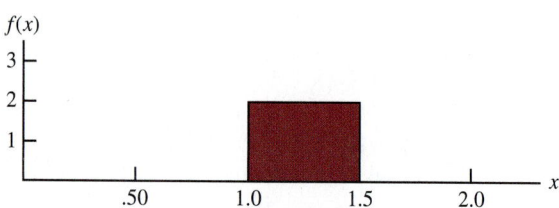

b. $P(x = 1.25) = 0$; the probability of any single point is zero because the area under the curve above any single point is zero
c. $P(1.0 \leq x \leq 1.25) = 2(.25) = .50$
d. $P(1.20 < x < 1.5) = 2(.30) = .60$

2. b. .50
c. .60
d. 15
e. 8.33

4. a.

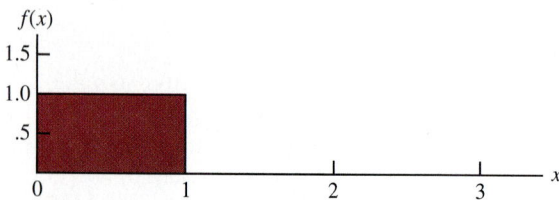

b. $P(.25 < x < .75) = 1(.50) = .50$
c. $P(x \leq .30) = 1(.30) = .30$
d. $P(x > .60) = 1(.40) = .40$

6. a. .40
b. .64
c. .68

10. a. .9332
b. .8413
c. .0919
d. .4938

12. a. .2967
b. .4418
c. .3300
d. .5910
e. .8849
f. .2389

13. a. $.6879 - .0239 = .6640$
b. $.8888 - .6985 = .1903$
c. $.1492 - .0401 = .1091$

14. a. $z = 1.96$
b. $z = 1.96$
c. $z = .61$
d. $z = 1.12$
e. $z = .44$
f. $z = .44$

15. a. The z-value corresponding to a cumulative probability of .2119 is $z = -.80$
b. Compute $.9030/2 = .4515$; the cumulative probability of $.5000 + .4515 = .9515$ corresponds to $z = 1.66$
c. Compute $.2052/2 = .1026$; z corresponds to a cumulative probability of $.5000 + .1026 = .6026$, so $z = .26$
d. The z-value corresponding to a cumulative probability of .9948 is $z = 2.56$
e. The area to the left of z is $1 - .6915 = .3085$, so $z = -.50$

16. a. $z = 2.33$
b. $z = 1.96$
c. $z = 1.645$
d. $z = 1.28$

18. $\mu = 30$ and $\sigma = 8.2$
a. At $x = 40$, $z = \dfrac{40 - 30}{8.2} = 1.22$
    $P(z \leq 1.22) = .8888$
    $P(x \geq 40) = 1.000 - .8888 = .1112$
b. At $x = 20$, $z = \dfrac{20 - 30}{8.2} = -1.22$
    $P(z \leq -1.22) = .1112$
    $P(x \leq 20) = .1112$
c. A z-value of 1.28 cuts off an area of approximately 10% in the upper tail
    $x = 30 + 8.2(1.28)$
    $= 40.50$
    A stock price of $40.50 or higher will put a company in the top 10%

20. a. .0885
b. 12.51%
c. 93.8 hours or more

22. a. .4194; using NORMDIST: .4199
b. $517.44 or more; using NORMINV: $517.59
c. .0166; using NORMDIST: .0165

24. a. 902.75, 114.185

 b. .1841

 c. .1977; using NORMDIST: .1972

 d. 1,091 million

26. a. .5276

 b. .3935

 c. .4724

 d. .1341; using EXPONDIST: .1342

27. a. $P(x \leq x_0) = 1 - e^{-x_0/3}$

 b. $P(x \leq 2) = 1 - e^{-2/3} = 1 - .5134 = .4866$

 c. $P(x \geq 3) = 1 - P(x \leq 3) = 1 - (1 - e^{-3/3})$
 $= e^{-1} = .3679$

 d. $P(x \leq 5) = 1 - e^{-5/3} = 1 - .1889 = .8111$

 e. $P(2 \leq x \leq 5) = P(x \leq 5) - P(x \leq 2)$
 $= .8111 - .4866 = .3245$

28. a. .3935

 b. .2231

 c. .3834

29. a.

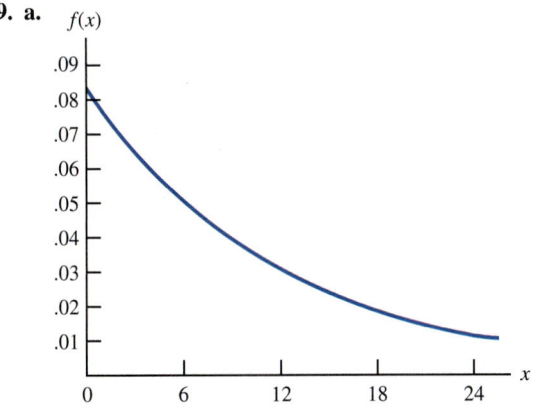

 b. $P(x \leq 12) = 1 - e^{-12/12} = 1 - .3679 = .6321$

 c. $P(x \leq 6) = 1 - e^{-6/12} = 1 - .6065 = .3935$

 d. $P(x \geq 30) = 1 - P(x < 30)$
 $= 1 - (1 - e^{-30/12})$
 $= .0821$

30. a. 50 hours

 b. .3935

 c. .1353

32. a. $f(x) = 30e^{-30x}$

 b. .0821

 c. .7135

34. a. $3780 or less

 b. 19.22%

 c. $8167.50

36. a. 3229

 b. .2244

 c. $12,382 or more

38. a. .0228

 b. $50

40. a. 38.3%

 b. 3.59% better, 96.41% worse

 c. 38.21%

42. $\mu = 19.23$ ounces

44. a. $\frac{1}{7}$ minute

 b. $7e^{-7x}$

 c. .0009

 d. .2466

46. a. 2 minutes

 b. .2212

 c. .3935

 d. .0821

Chapter 7

1. a. AB, AC, AD, AE, BC, BD, BE, CD, CE, DE

 b. With 10 samples, each has a $\frac{1}{10}$ probability

 c. B and D because the two smallest random numbers are .0476 and .0957

2. Elements 2, 3, 5, and 10

3. The simple random sample consists of New York, Detroit, Oakland, Boston, and Kansas City

4. Step 1. Generate a random number for each company
 Step 2. Sort with respect to random numbers and select the first three companies

6. Finite, infinite, infinite, infinite, finite

7. a. $\bar{x} = \dfrac{\Sigma x_i}{n} = \dfrac{54}{6} = 9$

 b. $s = \sqrt{\dfrac{\Sigma(x_i - \bar{x})^2}{n - 1}}$

 $\Sigma(x_i - \bar{x})^2 = (-4)^2 + (-1)^2 + 1^2 + (-2)^2 + 1^2 + 5^2$
 $= 48$

 $s = \sqrt{\dfrac{48}{6 - 1}} = 3.1$

8. a. .50

 b. .3667

9. a. $\bar{x} = \dfrac{\Sigma x_i}{n} = \dfrac{465}{5} = 93$

 b.

x_i	$(x_i - \bar{x})$	$(x_i - \bar{x})^2$
94	+1	1
100	+7	49
85	−8	64
94	+1	1
92	−1	1
Totals 465	0	116

 $s = \sqrt{\dfrac{\Sigma(x_i - \bar{x})^2}{n - 1}} = \sqrt{\dfrac{116}{4}} = 5.39$

10. a. .45

 b. .15

 c. .45

12. a. .10
  b. 20
  c. .72

15. a. The sampling distribution is normal with:

$$E(\bar{x}) = \mu = 200$$

$$\sigma_{\bar{x}} = \frac{\sigma}{\sqrt{n}} = \frac{50}{\sqrt{100}} = 5$$

For $+5$, $(\bar{x} - \mu) = 5$,

$$z = \frac{\bar{x} - \mu}{\sigma_{\bar{x}}} = \frac{5}{5} = 1$$

Area $= .8413 - .1587 = .6826$

  b. For ± 10, $(\bar{x} - \mu) = 10$,

$$z = \frac{\bar{x} - \mu}{\sigma_{\bar{x}}} = \frac{10}{5} = 2$$

Area $= .9772 - .0228 = .9544$

16. 3.54, 2.50, 2.04, 1.77
  $\sigma_{\bar{x}}$ decreases as n increases

18. a. Normal with $E(\bar{x}) = 51{,}800$ and $\sigma_{\bar{x}} = 516.40$
  b. $\sigma_{\bar{x}}$ decreases to 365.15
  c. $\sigma_{\bar{x}}$ decreases as n increases

19. a.

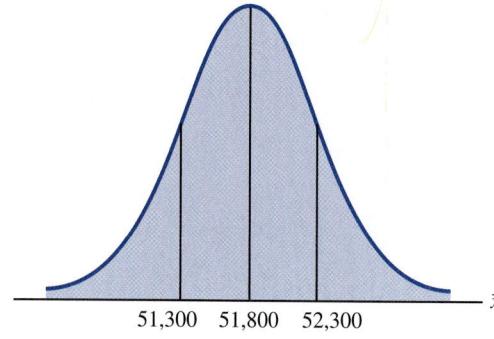

$$\sigma_{\bar{x}} = \frac{\sigma}{\sqrt{n}} = \frac{4000}{\sqrt{60}} = 516.40$$

At $\bar{x} = 52{,}300$, $z = \dfrac{52{,}300 - 51{,}800}{516.40} = .97$

$$P(\bar{x} \le 52{,}300) = P(z \le .97) = .8340$$

At $\bar{x} = 51{,}300$, $z = \dfrac{51{,}300 - 51{,}800}{516.40} = -.97$

$$P(\bar{x} < 51{,}300) = P(z < -.97) = .1660$$

$$P(51{,}300 \le \bar{x} \le 52{,}300) = .8340 - .1660 = .6680$$

Using Excel:
=NORMDIST(52300,51800,516.40,TRUE)-
     NORMDIST(51300,51800,516.40,TRUE) = .6671

  b. $\sigma_{\bar{x}} = \dfrac{\sigma}{\sqrt{n}} = \dfrac{4000}{\sqrt{120}} = 365.15$

At $\bar{x} = 52{,}300$, $z = \dfrac{52{,}300 - 51{,}800}{365.15} = 1.37$

$$P(\bar{x} \le 52{,}300) = P(z \le 1.37) = .9147$$

At $\bar{x} = 51{,}300$, $z = \dfrac{51{,}300 - 51{,}800}{365.15} = -1.37$

$$P(\bar{x} < 51{,}300) = P(z < -1.37) = .0853$$

$$P(51{,}300 \le \bar{x} \le 52{,}300) = .9147 - .0853 = .8294$$

Using Excel:
=NORMDIST(52300,51800,365.15,TRUE)-
     NORMDIST(51300,51800,365.15,TRUE) = .8291

20. a. Normal with $E(\bar{x}) = 4260$ and $\sigma_{\bar{x}} = 127.28$
  b. .95
  c. .5704

22. a. Using table: .5034, .6212, .7888, .9232, .9876
  b. Higher probability within ± 250

24. a. Normal with $E(\bar{x}) = 687$ and $\sigma_{\bar{x}} = 34.29$
  b. Using table: .9964; using NORMDIST: .9965
  c. Using table: .5346; using NORMDIST: .5340
  d. Increase the sample size

26. a. $n/N = .01$; no
  b. 1.29, 1.30; little difference
  c. Using table: .8764

28. a. $E(\bar{p}) = .40$

$$\sigma_{\bar{p}} = \sqrt{\frac{p(1 - p)}{n}} = \sqrt{\frac{(.40)(.60)}{200}} = .0346$$

Within $\pm .03$ means $.37 \le \bar{p} \le .43$

Using table: $z = \dfrac{\bar{p} - p}{\sigma_{\bar{p}}} = \dfrac{.03}{.0346} = .87$

$$P(.37 \le \bar{p} \le .43) = P(-.87 \le z \le .87)$$
$$= .8078 - .1922$$
$$= .6156$$

Using Excel:
=NORMDIST(.43,.40,.0346,TRUE)-
     NORMDIST(.37,.40,.0346,TRUE) = .6141

  b. Using table: $z = \dfrac{\bar{p} - p}{\sigma_{\bar{p}}} = \dfrac{.05}{.0346} = 1.44$

$$P(.35 \le \bar{p} \le .45) = P(-1.44 \le z \le 1.44)$$
$$= .9251 - .0749$$
$$= .8502$$

Using Excel:
=NORMDIST(.45,.40,.0346,TRUE)-
     NORMDIST(.35,.40,.0346,TRUE) = .8516

30. a. Using table: .6156; using NORMDIST: .6175
  b. Using table: .7814; using NORMDIST: .7830
  c. Using table: .9488; using NORMDIST: .9490
  d. Using table: .9942; using NORMDIST: .9942
  e. Higher probability with larger n

31. a.

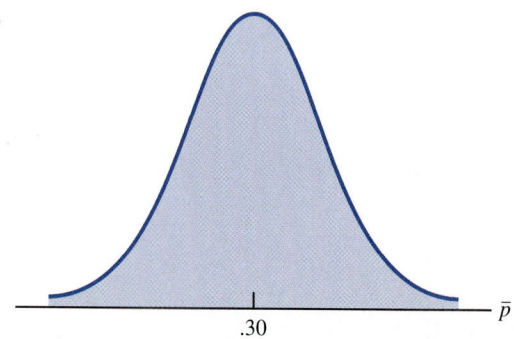

$$\sigma_{\bar{p}} = \sqrt{\frac{p(1 - p)}{n}} = \sqrt{\frac{.30(.70)}{100}} = .0458$$

The normal distribution is appropriate because $np = 100(.30) = 30$ and $n(1 - p) = 100(.70) = 70$ are both greater than 5

b. $P(.20 \leq \bar{p} \leq .40) = ?$

$$z = \frac{.40 - .30}{.0458} = 2.18$$

$$P(.20 \leq \bar{p} \leq .40) = P(-2.18 \leq z \leq 2.18)$$
$$= .9854 - .0146$$
$$= .9708$$

Using Excel:
=NORMDIST(.40,.30,.0458,TRUE)-
    NORMDIST(.20,.30,.0458,TRUE) = .9710

c. $P(.25 \leq \bar{p} \leq .35) = ?$

$$z = \frac{.35 - .30}{.0458} = 1.09$$

$$P(.25 \leq \bar{p} \leq .35) = P(-1.09 \leq z \leq 1.09)$$
$$= .8621 - .1379$$
$$= .7242$$

Using Excel:
=NORMDIST(.35,.30,.0458,TRUE)-
    NORMDIST(.25,.30,.0458,TRUE) = .7250

32. a. Normal with $E(\bar{p}) = .56$ and $\sigma_{\bar{p}} = .0287$
 b. Using table: .7062; using NORMDIST: .7041
 c. Using table: .8612; using NORMDIST: .8605
     Using table: .9438; using NORMDIST: .9440

34. a. Normal with $E(\bar{p}) = .56$ and $\sigma_{\bar{p}} = .0248$
 b. Using table: .5820; using NORMDIST: .5800
 c. Using table: .8926; using NORMDIST: .8932

36. a. Normal with $E(\bar{p}) = .76$ and $\sigma_{\bar{p}} = .0214$
 b. Using table: .8384; using NORMDIST: .8390
 c. Using table: .9452; using NORMDIST: .9455

38. Thoroughbreds, The Marker, Officers Club, SeaBlue, Crickets

40. a. Normal with $E(\bar{x}) = 115.50$ and $\sigma_{\bar{x}} = 5.53$
 b. Using table: .9298; using NORMDIST: .9292
 c. Using table: $z = -2.71$, .0034;
     using NORMDIST: .0025

42. a. 707
 b. .50
 c. Using table: $z = \pm 1.41$, .8414;
     using NORMDIST: .8428
 d. .9544

44. a. 625
 b. .7888

46. a. Normal with $E(\bar{p}) = .305$ and $\sigma_{\bar{p}} = .0326$
 b. Using table: $z = \pm 1.23$, .7814;
     using NORMDIST: .7802
 c. Using table: $z = \pm .61$, .4582;
     using NORMDIST: .4605

48. a. Using table: $z = \pm 2.06$, .9606; using NORMDIST: .9604
 b. Using table: $z = 1.65$, .0495; using NORMDIST: .0499

50. a. 48
 b. Normal, $E(\bar{p}) = .25$, $\sigma_{\bar{p}} = .0625$
 c. .2119

Chapter 8

2. Use $\bar{x} \pm z_{\alpha/2}(\sigma/\sqrt{n})$
 a. $32 \pm 1.645 (6/\sqrt{50})$
     32 ± 1.4; 30.6 to 33.4
 b. $32 \pm 1.96(6/\sqrt{50})$
     32 ± 1.66; 30.34 to 33.66
 c. $32 \pm 2.576(6/\sqrt{50})$
     32 ± 2.19; 29.81 to 34.19

4. 54

5. a. $1.96\sigma/\sqrt{n} = 1.96(5/\sqrt{49}) = 1.40$
 b. 24.80 ± 1.40; 23.40 to 26.20

6. 8.1 to 8.9

8. a. Population is at least approximately normal
 b. 3.1
 c. 4.1

10. a. \$113,638 to \$124,672
 b. \$112,581 to \$125,729
 c. \$110,515 to \$127,795
 d. Width increases as confidence level increases

12. a. 2.179
 b. -1.676
 c. 2.457
 d. -1.708 and 1.708
 e. -2.014 and 2.014

13. a. $\bar{x} = \dfrac{\Sigma x_i}{n} = \dfrac{80}{8} = 10$

 b. $s = \sqrt{\dfrac{\Sigma(x_i - \bar{x})^2}{n - 1}} = \sqrt{\dfrac{84}{7}} = 3.46$

 c. $t_{.025}\left(\dfrac{s}{\sqrt{n}}\right) = 2.365\left(\dfrac{3.46}{\sqrt{8}}\right) = 2.9$

 d. $\bar{x} \pm t_{.025}\left(\dfrac{s}{\sqrt{n}}\right)$
     10 ± 2.9 (7.1 to 12.9)

14. a. 21.5 to 23.5
 b. 21.3 to 23.7
 c. 20.9 to 24.1
 d. A larger margin of error and a wider interval

15. $\bar{x} \pm t_{\alpha/2}(s/\sqrt{n})$
 90% confidence: $df = 64$ and $t_{.05} = 1.669$

 $19.5 \pm 1.669\left(\dfrac{5.2}{\sqrt{65}}\right)$

 19.5 ± 1.08 (18.42 to 20.58)
 95% confidence: $df = 64$ and $t_{.025} = 1.998$

 $19.5 \pm 1.998\left(\dfrac{5.2}{\sqrt{65}}\right)$

 19.5 ± 1.29 (18.21 to 20.79)

16. a. 1.69
  b. 47.31 to 50.69
  c. Fewer hours and higher cost for United

18. a. 3.8
  b. .8429
  c. 2.96 to 4.64
  d. Larger n next time

20. 6.27 to 6.78

22. a. 3.348%
  b. 2.40% to 4.29%

24. a. Planning value of $\sigma = \dfrac{\text{Range}}{4} = \dfrac{36}{4} = 9$

  b. $n = \dfrac{z_{.025}^2 \sigma^2}{E^2} = \dfrac{(1.96)^2 (9)^2}{(3)^2} = 34.57$; use $n = 35$

  c. $n = \dfrac{(1.96)^2 (9)^2}{(2)^2} = 77.79$; use $n = 78$

25. a. Use $n = \dfrac{z_{\alpha/2}^2 \sigma^2}{E^2}$

  $n = \dfrac{(1.96)^2 (6.84)^2}{(1.5)^2} = 79.88$; use $n = 80$

  b. $n = \dfrac{(1.645)^2 (6.84)^2}{(2)^2} = 31.65$; use $n = 32$

26. a. 340
  b. 1358
  c. 8487

28. a. 343
  b. 487
  c. 840
  d. n gets larger; no to 99% confidence

30. 81

31. a. $\bar{p} = \dfrac{100}{400} = .25$

  b. $\sqrt{\dfrac{\bar{p}(1 - \bar{p})}{n}} = \sqrt{\dfrac{.25(.75)}{400}} = .0217$

  c. $\bar{p} \pm z_{.025} \sqrt{\dfrac{\bar{p}(1 - \bar{p})}{n}}$
  $.25 \pm 1.96(.0217)$
  $.25 \pm .0424$; .2076 to .2924

32. a. .6733 to .7267
  b. .6682 to .7318

34. 1068

35. a. $\bar{p} = \dfrac{281}{611} = .4599$ (46%)

  b. $z_{.05} \sqrt{\dfrac{\bar{p}(1 - \bar{p})}{n}} = 1.645 \sqrt{\dfrac{4599(1 - .4599)}{611}} = .0332$

  c. $\bar{p} \pm .0332$
  $.4599 \pm .0332$ (.4267 to .4931)

36. a. .4393
  b. .3870 to .4916

38. a. .0430
  b. .2170 to .3030
  c. 822

39. a. $n = \dfrac{1.96^2 p^*(1 - p^*)}{E^2}$

  $n = \dfrac{1.96^2 (.33)(.67)}{(.03)^2} = 943.75$; use $n = 944$

  b. $n = \dfrac{2.576^2 (.33)(.67)}{(.03)^2} = 1630.19$; use $n = 1631$

40. .0267, .8333 to .8867

42. a. .0442
  b. 601, 1068, 2401, 9604

44. a. 2009
  b. 47,991 to 52,009

46. a. 998
  b. $24,479 to $26,455
  c. $93.5 million
  d. Yes; $21.4 (30%) over *Lost World*

48. a. 14 minutes
  b. 13.38 to 14.62
  c. 32 per day
  d. Staff reduction

50. 37

52. 176

54. a. .5420
  b. .0508
  c. .4912 to .5928

56. a. .68
  b. .6391 to .7209

58. a. 1267
  b. 1509

60. a. .3101
  b. .2898 to .3304
  c. 8219; no, this sample size is unnecessarily large

Chapter 9

2. a. $H_0: \mu \le 14$
  $H_a: \mu > 14$
  b. No evidence that the new plan increases sales
  c. The research hypothesis $\mu > 14$ is supported; the new plan increases sales

4. a. $H_0: \mu \ge 220$
  $H_a: \mu < 220$

5. a. Rejecting $H_0: \mu \le 56.2$ when it is true
  b. Accepting $H_0: \mu \le 56.2$ when it is false

6. a. $H_0: \mu \le 1$
  $H_a: \mu > 1$
  b. Claiming $\mu > 1$ when it is not true
  c. Claiming $\mu \le 1$ when it is not true

8. a. $H_0: \mu \geq 220$
$H_a: \mu < 220$

b. Claiming $\mu < 220$ when it is not true

c. Claiming $\mu \geq 220$ when it is not true

10. a. $z = \dfrac{\bar{x} - \mu_0}{\sigma/\sqrt{n}} = \dfrac{26.4 - 25}{6/\sqrt{40}} = 1.48$

b. Using normal table with $z = 1.48$: p-value = $1.0000 - .9306 = .0694$
Using Excel: p-value = $1 - \text{NORMSDIST}(1.48)$
$= .0694$

c. p-value $> .01$, do not reject H_0

d. Reject H_0 if $z \geq 2.33$
$1.48 < 2.33$, do not reject H_0

11. a. $z = \dfrac{\bar{x} - \mu_0}{\sigma/\sqrt{n}} = \dfrac{14.15 - 15}{3/\sqrt{50}} = -2.00$

b. p-value = $2(.0228) = .0456$

c. p-value $\leq .05$, reject H_0

d. Reject H_0 if $z \leq -1.96$ or $z \geq 1.96$
$-2.00 \leq -1.96$, reject H_0

12. a. .1056; do not reject H_0

b. .0062; reject H_0

c. ≈ 0; reject H_0

d. .7967; do not reject H_0

14. a. .3844; do not reject H_0

b. .0074; reject H_0

c. .0836; do not reject H_0

15. a. $H_0: \mu \geq 1056$
$H_a: \mu < 1056$

b. $z = \dfrac{\bar{x} - \mu_0}{\sigma/\sqrt{n}} = \dfrac{910 - 1056}{1600/\sqrt{400}} = -1.83$
p-value = .0336

c. p-value $\leq .05$, reject H_0; the mean refund of "last-minute" filers is less than $1056

d. Reject H_0 if $z \leq -1.645$
$-1.83 \leq -1.645$; reject H_0

16. a. $H_0: \mu \leq 895$
$H_a: \mu > 895$

b. .1170

c. Do not reject H_0

d. Withhold judgment; collect more data

18. a. $H_0: \mu = 4.1$
$H_a: \mu \neq 4.1$

b. -2.21, .0272

c. Reject H_0

20. a. $H_0: \mu \geq 181,900$
$H_a: \mu < 181,900$

b. -2.93

c. .0017

d. Reject H_0

22. a. $H_0: \mu = 8$
$H_a: \mu \neq 8$

b. .1706

c. Do not reject H_0

d. 7.83 to 8.97; yes

24. a. $t = \dfrac{\bar{x} - \mu_0}{s/\sqrt{n}} = \dfrac{17 - 18}{4.5/\sqrt{48}} = -1.54$

b. Degrees of freedom $= n - 1 = 47$
Area in lower tail is between .05 and .10
p-value (two-tail) is between .10 and .20
Using Excel: p-value = TDIST(1.54,47,2) = .1303

c. p-value $> .05$; do not reject H_0

d. With $df = 47$, $t_{.025} = 2.012$
Reject H_0 if $t \leq -2.012$ or $t \geq 2.012$
$t = -1.54$; do not reject H_0

26. a. Between .02 and .05; using Excel: p-value = TDIST(2.10,64,2) = .0397; reject H_0

b. Between .01 and .02; using Excel: p-value = TDIST(2.57,64,2) = .0125; reject H_0

c. Between .10 and .20; using Excel: p-value = TDIST(1.54,64,2) = .1285; do not reject H_0

27. a. $H_0: \mu \geq 238$
$H_a: \mu < 238$

b. $t = \dfrac{\bar{x} - \mu_0}{s/\sqrt{n}} = \dfrac{231 - 238}{80/\sqrt{100}} = -.88$
Degrees of freedom $= n - 1 = 99$
p-value is between .10 and .20
Using Excel: p-value = TDIST(.88,99,1) = .1905

c. p-value $> .05$; do not reject H_0
Cannot conclude mean weekly benefit in Virginia is less than the national mean

d. $df = 99$, $t_{.05} = -1.66$
Reject H_0 if $t \leq -1.66$
$-.88 > -1.66$; do not reject H_0

28. a. $H_0: \mu \leq 3530$
$H_a: \mu > 3530$

b. Between .005 and .01
Using Excel: p-value = TDIST(2.49,91,1) = .0072

c. Reject H_0

30. a. $H_0: \mu = 600$
$H_a: \mu \neq 600$

b. Between .20 and .40
Using Excel: p-value = TDIST(1.17,39,2) = .2491

c. Do not reject H_0

d. A larger sample size

32. a. $H_0: \mu = 10,192$
$H_a: \mu \neq 10,192$

b. Between .02 and .05
Using Excel: p-value = TDIST(2.23,49,2) = .0304

c. Reject H_0

34. a. $H_0: \mu = 2$
$H_a: \mu \neq 2$

b. 2.2

c. .52

d. Between .20 and .40
Using Excel: p-value = TDIST(1.22,9,2) = .2535

e. Do not reject H_0

36. a. $z = \dfrac{\bar{p} - p_0}{\sqrt{\dfrac{p_0(1 - p_0)}{n}}} = \dfrac{.68 - .75}{\sqrt{\dfrac{.75(1 - .75)}{300}}} = -2.80$

p-value = .0026

p-value $\le$ .05; reject H_0

b. $z = \dfrac{.72 - .75}{\sqrt{\dfrac{.75(1 - .75)}{300}}} = -1.20$

p-value = .1151

p-value $>$ .05; do not reject H_0

c. $z = \dfrac{.70 - .75}{\sqrt{\dfrac{.75(1 - .75)}{300}}} = -2.00$

p-value = .0228

p-value $\le$ .05; reject H_0

d. $z = \dfrac{.77 - .75}{\sqrt{\dfrac{.75(1 - .75)}{300}}} = .80$

p-value = .7881

p-value $>$ .05; do not reject H_0

38. a. H_0: $p = .64$

H_a: $p \ne .64$

b. $\bar{p} = 52/100 = .52$

$z = \dfrac{\bar{p} - p_0}{\sqrt{\dfrac{p_0(1 - p_0)}{n}}} = \dfrac{.52 - .64}{\sqrt{\dfrac{.64(1 - .64)}{100}}} = -2.50$

Area = .4938

p-value = 2(.0062) = .0124

c. p-value $\le$ .05; reject H_0

Proportion differs from the reported .64

d. Yes, because $\bar{p} = .52$ indicates that fewer believe the supermarket brand is as good as the name brand

40. a. .2702

b. H_0: $p \le .22$

H_a: $p > .22$

p-value $\approx$ 0; reject H_0

c. Helps evaluate the effectiveness of commercials

42. H_0: $p \le .24$

H_a: $p > .24$

p-value = .0023; reject H_0

44. a. H_0: $p \le .51$

H_a: $p > .51$

b. $\bar{p} = .58$, p-value = .00263

c. Reject H_0

46. a. H_0: $\mu = 16$

H_a: $\mu \ne 16$

b. .0286; reject H_0

Readjust line

c. .2186; do not reject H_0

Continue operation

d. $z = 2.19$; reject H_0

$z = -1.23$; do not reject H_0

Yes, same conclusion

48. a. H_0: $\mu \le 45{,}250$

H_a: $\mu > 45{,}250$

b. .0034

c. Reject H_0

50. $t = -.93$

p-value between .20 and .40

Using Excel: p-value = TDIST(.93,31,2) = .3596

Do not reject H_0

52. $t = 2.26$

p-value between .01 and .025

Using Excel: p-value = TDIST(2.26,31,1) = .0155

Reject H_0

54. a. H_0: $p \le .50$

H_a: $p > .50$

b. .64

c. .0026; reject H_0

56. a. H_0: $p \le .50$

H_a: $p > .50$

b. .6381

c. .0023; reject H_0

58. H_0: $p \ge .90$

H_a: $p < .90$

p-value = .0808

Do not reject H_0

Chapter 10

1. a. $\bar{x}_1 - \bar{x}_2 = 13.6 - 11.6 = 2$

b. $z_{\alpha/2} = z_{.05} = 1.645$

$\bar{x}_1 - \bar{x}_2 \pm 1.645\sqrt{\dfrac{\sigma_1^2}{n_1} + \dfrac{\sigma_2^2}{n_2}}$

$2 \pm 1.645\sqrt{\dfrac{(2.2)^2}{50} + \dfrac{(3)^2}{35}}$

$2 \pm .98 \quad (1.02 \text{ to } 2.98)$

c. $z_{\alpha/2} = z_{.05} = 1.96$

$2 \pm 1.96\sqrt{\dfrac{(2.2)^2}{50} + \dfrac{(3)^2}{35}}$

$2 \pm 1.17 \quad (.83 \text{ to } 3.17)$

2. a. $z = \dfrac{(\bar{x}_1 - \bar{x}_2) - D_0}{\sqrt{\dfrac{\sigma_1^2}{n_1} + \dfrac{\sigma_2^2}{n_2}}} = \dfrac{(25.2 - 22.8) - 0}{\sqrt{\dfrac{(5.2)^2}{40} + \dfrac{(6)^2}{50}}} = 2.03$

b. p-value = $1.0000 - .9788 = .0212$

c. p-value $\le$ .05; reject H_0

4. a. $\bar{x}_1 - \bar{x}_2 = 2.04 - 1.72 = .32$

b. $z_{.025}\sqrt{\dfrac{\sigma_1^2}{n_1} + \dfrac{\sigma_2^2}{n_2}} = 1.96\sqrt{\dfrac{(.10)^2}{40} + \dfrac{(.08)^2}{35}} = .04$

c. $.32 \pm .04 \quad (.28 \text{ to } .36)$

6. p-value = .015

Reject H_0; an increase

8. a. 1.08

b. .2802

c. Do not reject H_0; cannot conclude a difference exists

9. a. $\bar{x}_1 - \bar{x}_2 = 22.5 - 20.1 = 2.4$

b. $df = \dfrac{\left(\dfrac{s_1^2}{n_1} + \dfrac{s_2^2}{n_2}\right)^2}{\dfrac{1}{n_1 - 1}\left(\dfrac{s_1^2}{n_1}\right)^2 + \dfrac{1}{n_2 - 1}\left(\dfrac{s_2^2}{n_2}\right)^2}$

$= \dfrac{\left(\dfrac{2.5^2}{20} + \dfrac{4.8^2}{30}\right)^2}{\dfrac{1}{19}\left(\dfrac{2.5^2}{20}\right)^2 + \dfrac{1}{29}\left(\dfrac{4.8^2}{30}\right)^2} = 45.8$

c. $df = 45, \; t_{.025} = 2.014$

$t_{.025}\sqrt{\dfrac{s_1^2}{n_1} + \dfrac{s_2^2}{n_2}} = 2.014\sqrt{\dfrac{2.5^2}{20} + \dfrac{4.8^2}{30}} = 2.1$

d. 2.4 ± 2.1 (.3 to 4.5)

10. a. $t = \dfrac{(\bar{x}_1 - \bar{x}_2) - 0}{\sqrt{\dfrac{s_1^2}{n_1} + \dfrac{s_2^2}{n_2}}} = \dfrac{(13.6 - 10.1) - 0}{\sqrt{\dfrac{5.2^2}{35} + \dfrac{8.5^2}{40}}} = 2.18$

b. $df = \dfrac{\left(\dfrac{s_1^2}{n_1} + \dfrac{s_2^2}{n_2}\right)^2}{\dfrac{1}{n_1 - 1}\left(\dfrac{s_1^2}{n_1}\right)^2 + \dfrac{1}{n_2 - 1}\left(\dfrac{s_2^2}{n_2}\right)^2}$

$= \dfrac{\left(\dfrac{5.2^2}{35} + \dfrac{8.5^2}{40}\right)^2}{\dfrac{1}{34}\left(\dfrac{5.2^2}{35}\right)^2 + \dfrac{1}{39}\left(\dfrac{8.5^2}{40}\right)^2} = 65.7$

Use $df = 65$

c. $df = 65$, area in tail is between .01 and .025; two-tailed p-value is between .02 and .05

d. p-value $\leq .05$; reject H_0

12. a. $\bar{x}_1 - \bar{x}_2 = 22.5 - 18.6 = 3.9$ miles

b. $df = \dfrac{\left(\dfrac{s_1^2}{n_1} + \dfrac{s_2^2}{n_2}\right)^2}{\dfrac{1}{n_1 - 1}\left(\dfrac{s_1^2}{n_1}\right)^2 + \dfrac{1}{n_2 - 1}\left(\dfrac{s_2^2}{n_2}\right)^2}$

$= \dfrac{\left(\dfrac{8.4^2}{50} + \dfrac{7.4^2}{40}\right)^2}{\dfrac{1}{49}\left(\dfrac{8.4^2}{50}\right)^2 + \dfrac{1}{39}\left(\dfrac{7.4^2}{40}\right)^2} = 87.1$

Use $df = 87, \; t_{.025} = 1.988$

$3.9 \pm 1.988\sqrt{\dfrac{8.4^2}{50} + \dfrac{7.4^2}{40}}$

3.9 ± 3.3 (.6 to 7.2)

14. a. $H_0: \mu_1 - \mu_2 = 0$
$H_a: \mu_1 - \mu_2 \neq 0$

b. 2.18

c. Between .02 and .05

d. Reject H_0; mean ages differ

16. a. $H_0: \mu_1 - \mu_2 \leq 0$
$H_a: \mu_1 - \mu_2 > 0$

b. 38

c. $t = 1.80, df = 25$
p-value between .025 and .05

d. Reject H_0; conclude higher mean score if college grad

18. a. $H_0: \mu_1 - \mu_2 \geq 120$
$H_a: \mu_1 - \mu_2 < 120$

b. -2.10
Between .01 and .025

c. 32 to 118

d. Larger sample size

19. a. 1, 2, 0, 0, 2

b. $\bar{d} = \Sigma d_i / n = 5/5 = 1$

c. $s_d = \sqrt{\dfrac{\Sigma(d_i - \bar{d})^2}{n - 1}} = \sqrt{\dfrac{4}{5 - 1}} = 1$

d. $t = \dfrac{\bar{d} - \mu}{s_d/\sqrt{n}} = \dfrac{1 - 0}{1/\sqrt{5}} = 2.24$

$df = n - 1 = 4$
p-value is between .025 and .05
p-value $\leq .05$; reject H_0

20. a. 3, -1, 3, 5, 3, 0, 1

b. 2

c. 2.08

d. 2

e. .07 to 3.93

21. $H_0: \mu_d \leq 0$
$H_a: \mu_d > 0$
$\bar{d} = .625$
$s_d = 1.30$
$t = \dfrac{\bar{d} - \mu_d}{s_d/\sqrt{n}} = \dfrac{.625 - 0}{1.30/\sqrt{8}} = 1.36$

$df = n - 1 = 7$
p-value is between .10 and .20
p-value $> .05$; do not reject H_0

22. .16 to .35

24. $t = 1.63$
p-value between .10 and .20
Do not reject H_0

26. a. $t = -.60$
p-value greater than .40
Do not reject H_0

b. $-.103$

c. .39; larger sample size

28. a. $\bar{p} = \dfrac{n_1\bar{p}_1 + n_2\bar{p}_2}{n_1 + n_2} = \dfrac{200(.22) + 300(.16)}{200 + 300} = .1840$

$z = \dfrac{\bar{p}_1 - \bar{p}_2}{\sqrt{\bar{p}(1 - \bar{p})\left(\dfrac{1}{n_1} + \dfrac{1}{n_2}\right)}}$

$= \dfrac{.22 - .16}{\sqrt{.1840(1 - .1840)\left(\dfrac{1}{200} + \dfrac{1}{300}\right)}} = 1.70$

p-value $= 1.0000 - .9554 = .0446$

b. p-value $\leq .05$; reject H_0

29. $\bar{p}_1 = 220/400 = .55$ $\bar{p}_2 = 192/400 = .48$

$$\bar{p}_1 - \bar{p}_2 \pm z_{.025}\sqrt{\frac{\bar{p}_1(1 - \bar{p}_1)}{n_1} + \frac{\bar{p}_2(1 - \bar{p}_2)}{n_2}}$$

$$.55 - .48 \pm 1.96\sqrt{\frac{.55(1 - .55)}{400} + \frac{.48(1 - .48)}{400}}$$

$.07 \pm .0691$ (.0009 to .1391)

7% more executives are predicting an increase in full-time jobs; the confidence interval shows the difference may be from 0% to 14%

30. a. .46, .28
   b. .18
   c. .0777
   d. .1023 to .2577, higher for Republicans

32. a. .803
   b. .849
   c. $H_0: p_1 - p_2 \geq 0$
      $H_a: p_1 - p_2 < 0$
   d. p-value = .0055
      Reject H_0

34. a. $H_0: p_1 - p_2 = 0$
      $H_a: p_1 - p_2 \neq 0$
   b. .13
   c. p-value = .0404

36. p-value = .0322
   Proportion in Washington greater

38. 8934 to 11,066

40. a. $H_0: \mu_1 - \mu_2 \leq 0$
      $H_a: \mu_1 - \mu_2 > 0$
   b. $t = .60$, $df = 57$
      p-value greater than .20
      Do not reject H_0

42. a. 15 (or $15,000)
   b. 9.81 to 20.19
   c. 11.5%

44. a. p-value ≈ 0, reject H_0
   b. .0468 to .1332

46. a. 163, 66
   b. .025 to .275
   c. Yes

Chapter 11

2. $s^2 = 25$
   a. With 19 degrees of freedom, $\chi^2_{.05} = 30.144$ and $\chi^2_{.95} = 10.117$

$$\frac{19(25)}{30.144} \leq \sigma^2 \leq \frac{19(25)}{10.117}$$

$$15.76 \leq \sigma^2 \leq 46.95$$

   b. With 19 degrees of freedom, $\chi^2_{.025} = 32.852$ and $\chi^2_{.975} = 8.907$

$$\frac{19(25)}{32.852} \leq \sigma^2 \leq \frac{19(25)}{8.907}$$

$$14.46 \leq \sigma^2 \leq 53.33$$

   c. $3.8 \leq \sigma \leq 7.3$

4. a. .22 to .71
   b. .47 to .84

6. a. 13.3
   b. 8.0 to 38.2

8. a. .00845
   b. .092
   c. .0042 to .0244
      .065 to .156

9. $H_0: \sigma^2 \leq .0004$
   $H_a: \sigma^2 > .0004$

$$\chi^2 = \frac{(n-1)s^2}{\sigma_0^2} = \frac{(30-1)(.0005)}{.0004} = 36.25$$

From table with 29 degrees of freedom, p-value greater than .10
p-value $> .05$; do not reject H_0
The product specification does not appear to be violated

10. $\chi^2 = 46.53$
   p-value between .01 and .025
   Reject H_0

12. a. .8106
   b. $\chi^2 = 9.49$
      p-value greater than .20
      Do not reject H_0

14. a. $F = 2.4$
      p-value between .025 and .05
      Reject H_0
   b. $F_{.05} = 2.2$; reject H_0

15. a. Larger sample variance is s_1^2

$$F = \frac{s_1^2}{s_2^2} = \frac{8.2}{4} = 2.05$$

Degrees of freedom: 20, 25
From table, area in tail is between .025 and .05
p-value for two-tailed test is between .05 and .10
p-value $> .05$; do not reject H_0
   b. For a two-tailed test:
      $F_{\alpha/2} = F_{.025} = 2.30$
      Reject H_0 if $F \geq 2.30$
      $2.05 < 2.30$; do not reject H_0

16. $F = 2.63$
   p-value less than .01
   Reject H_0

17. a. Population 1 is 4-year-old automobiles
      $H_0: \sigma_1^2 \leq \sigma_2^2$
      $H_a: \sigma_1^2 > \sigma_2^2$

b. $F = \dfrac{s_1^2}{s_2^2} = \dfrac{170^2}{100^2} = 2.89$

Degrees of freedom: 25, 24

From tables, p-value is less than .01

p-value $\le .01$; reject H_0

Conclude that 4-year-old automobiles have a larger variance in annual repair costs compared to 2-year-old automobiles, which is expected because older automobiles are more likely to have more expensive repairs that lead to greater variance in the annual repair costs

18. $F = 3.54$

p-value between .10 and .20

Do not reject H_0

20. $F = 5.29$

p-value ≈ 0

Reject H_0

22. a. $F = 4$

p-value less than .01

Reject H_0

24. 10.72 to 24.68

26. a. $\chi^2 = 27.44$

p-value between .01 and .025

Reject H_0

b. .00012 to .00042

28. $\chi^2 = 31.50$

p-value between .05 and .10

Reject H_0

30. a. $n = 15$

b. 6.25 to 11.13

32. $F = 1.39$

Do not reject H_0

34. $F = 2.08$

p-value between .05 and .10

Reject H_0

Chapter 12

1. a. Expected frequencies: $e_1 = 200(.40) = 80$

$e_2 = 200(.40) = 80$

$e_3 = 200(.20) = 40$

Actual frequencies: $f_1 = 60, f_2 = 120, f_3 = 20$

$\chi^2 = \dfrac{(60-80)^2}{80} + \dfrac{(120-80)^2}{80} + \dfrac{(20-40)^2}{40}$

$= \dfrac{400}{80} + \dfrac{1600}{80} + \dfrac{400}{40}$

$= 5 + 20 + 10 = 35$

Degrees of freedom: $k - 1 = 2$

$\chi^2 = 35$ shows p-value ≈ 0

p-value $\le .01$; reject H_0

b. Reject H_0 if $\chi^2 \ge 9.210$

$\chi^2 = 35$; reject H_0

2. $\chi^2 = 15.33, df = 3$

p-value less than .005

Reject H_0

3. $H_0: p_{ABC} = .29, p_{CBS} = .28, p_{NBC} = .25, p_{IND} = .18$

$H_a:$ The proportions are not

$p_{ABC} = .29, p_{CBS} = .28, p_{NBC} = .25, p_{IND} = .18$

Expected frequencies: $300(.29) = 87, 300(.28) = 84$

$300(.25) = 75, 300(.18) = 54$

$e_1 = 87, e_2 = 84, e_3 = 75, e_4 = 54$

Actual frequencies: $f_1 = 95, f_2 = 70, f_3 = 89, f_4 = 46$

$\chi^2 = \dfrac{(95-87)^2}{87} + \dfrac{(70-84)^2}{84} + \dfrac{(89-75)^2}{75}$

$+ \dfrac{(46-54)^2}{54} = 6.87$

Degrees of freedom: $k - 1 = 3$

$\chi^2 = 6.87, p$-value between .05 and .10

Do not reject H_0

4. $\chi^2 = 29.51, df = 5$

p-value ≈ 0

Reject H_0

6. a. $\chi^2 = 12.21, df = 3$

p-value is between .005 and .01

Conclude difference for 2003

b. 21%, 30%, 15%, 34%

Increased use of debit card

c. 51%

8. $\chi^2 = 16.31, df = 3$

p-value less than .005

Reject H_0

9. $H_0:$ The column variable is independent of the row variable

$H_a:$ The column variable is not independent of the row variable

Expected frequencies:

	A	B	C
P	28.5	39.9	45.6
Q	21.5	30.1	34.4

$\chi^2 = \dfrac{(20-28.5)^2}{28.5} + \dfrac{(44-39.9)^2}{39.9} + \dfrac{(50-45.6)^2}{45.6}$

$+ \dfrac{(30-21.5)^2}{21.5} + \dfrac{(26-30.1)^2}{30.1} + \dfrac{(30-34.4)^2}{34.4}$

$= 7.86$

Degrees of freedom: $(2-1)(3-1) = 2$

$\chi^2 = 7.86, p$-value between .01 and .025

Reject H_0

10. $\chi^2 = 19.77, df = 4$

p-value less than .005

Reject H_0

11. $H_0:$ Type of ticket purchased is independent of the type of flight

$H_a:$ Type of ticket purchased is not independent of the type of flight

Expected frequencies:

$e_{11} = 35.59$ $e_{12} = 15.41$
$e_{21} = 150.73$ $e_{22} = 65.27$
$e_{31} = 455.68$ $e_{32} = 197.32$

Ticket	Flight	Observed Frequency (f_i)	Expected Frequency (e_i)	$(f_i - e_i)^2/e_i$
First	Domestic	29	35.59	1.22
First	International	22	15.41	2.82
Business	Domestic	95	150.73	20.61
Business	International	121	65.27	47.59
Full-fare	Domestic	518	455.68	8.52
Full-fare	International	135	197.32	19.68
Totals		920		$\chi^2 = 100.43$

Degrees of freedom: $(3 - 1)(2 - 1) = 2$
$\chi^2 = 100.43$, p-value ≈ 0
Reject H_0

12. a. $\chi^2 = 7.36$, $df = 2$
   p-value between .025 and .05
   Reject H_0
   b. Domestic 47.2%

14. a. $\chi^2 = 10.60$, $df = 4$
   p-value between .025 and .05
   Reject H_0; not independent
   b. Higher negative effect on grades as hours increase

16. a. $\chi^2 = 7.85$, $df = 3$
   p-value between .025 and .05
   Reject H_0
   b. Pharmaceutical, 98.6%

18. First estimate μ from the sample data (sample size = 120)

$$\mu = \frac{0(39) + 1(30) + 2(30) + 3(18) + 4(3)}{120}$$

$$= \frac{156}{120} = 1.3$$

Therefore, we use Poisson probabilities with $\mu = 1.3$ to compute expected frequencies

x	Observed Frequency	Poisson Probability	Expected Frequency	Difference $(f_i - e_i)$
0	39	.2725	32.70	6.30
1	30	.3543	42.51	−12.51
2	30	.2303	27.63	2.37
3	18	.0998	11.98	6.02
4 or more	3	.0431	5.16	−2.17

$$\chi^2 = \frac{(6.30)^2}{32.70} + \frac{(-12.51)^2}{42.51} + \frac{(2.37)^2}{27.63} + \frac{(6.02)^2}{11.98}$$

$$+ \frac{(-2.17)^2}{5.16} = 9.04$$

Degrees of freedom: $5 - 1 - 1 = 3$
$\chi^2 = 9.04$, p-value between .025 and .05
Reject H_0; not a Poisson distribution

19. With $n = 30$ we will use six classes with .1667 of the probability associated with each class

$$\bar{x} = 22.8, s = 6.27$$

The z values that create 6 intervals, each with probability .1667 are $-.98$, $-.43$, 0, $.43$, $.98$

z	Cutoff Value of x
−.98	$22.8 - .98(6.27) = 16.66$
−.43	$22.8 - .43(6.27) = 20.11$
0	$22.8 + .00(6.27) = 22.80$
.43	$22.8 + .43(6.27) = 25.49$
.98	$22.8 + .98(6.27) = 28.94$

Interval	Observed Frequency	Expected Frequency	Difference
less than 16.66	3	5	−2
16.66–20.11	7	5	2
20.11–22.80	5	5	0
22.80–25.49	7	5	2
25.49–28.94	3	5	−2
28.94 and up	5	5	0

$$\chi^2 = \frac{(-2)^2}{5} + \frac{(2)^2}{5} + \frac{(0)^2}{5} + \frac{(2)^2}{5} + \frac{(-2)^2}{5} + \frac{(0)^2}{5}$$

$$= \frac{16}{5} = 3.20$$

Degrees of freedom: $6 - 2 - 1 = 3$
$\chi^2 = 3.20$, p-value greater than .10
Do not reject H_0
Assumption of a normal distribution is not rejected

20. $\chi^2 = 4.30$, $df = 2$
   p-value greater than .10
   Do not reject H_0

22. $\chi^2 = 2.8$, $df = 3$
   p-value greater than .10
   Do not reject H_0

24. $\chi^2 = 8.04$, $df = 3$
   p-value between .025 and .05
   Reject H_0

26. $\chi^2 = 4.64$, $df = 2$
   p-value between .05 and .10
   Do not reject H_0

28. $\chi^2 = 42.53$, $df = 4$
   p-value ≈ 0
   Reject H_0

30. $\chi^2 = 23.37$, $df = 3$
   p-value ≈ 0
   Reject H_0

32. a. $\chi^2 = 12.86$, $df = 2$

p-value less than .005

Reject H_0

b. 66.9, 30.3, 2.9

54.0, 42.0, 4.0

34. $\chi^2 = 6.17$, $df = 6$

p-value greater than .10

Do not reject H_0

36. $\chi^2 = 7.75$, $df = 3$

p-value between .05 and .10

Do not reject H_0

Chapter 13

1. a. $\bar{\bar{x}} = (30 + 45 + 36)/3 = 37$

$$\text{SSTR} = \sum_{j=1}^{k} n_j(\bar{x}_j - \bar{\bar{x}})^2$$

$$= 5(30 - 37)^2 + 5(45 - 37)^2 + 5(36 - 37)^2$$

$$= 570$$

$$\text{MSTR} = \frac{\text{SSTR}}{k-1} = \frac{570}{2} = 285$$

b. $\text{SSE} = \sum_{j=1}^{k} (n_j - 1)s_j^2$

$$= 4(6) + 4(4) + 4(6.5) = 66$$

$$\text{MSE} = \frac{\text{SSE}}{n_T - k} = \frac{66}{15 - 3} = 5.5$$

c. $F = \dfrac{\text{MSTR}}{\text{MSE}} = \dfrac{285}{5.5} = 51.82$

From the F table (2 degrees of freedom numerator and 12 denominator), p-value is less than .01

Because the p-value $\le \alpha = .05$, we reject the null hypothesis that the means of the three populations are equal

d.

Source of Variation	Sum of Squares	Degrees of Freedom	Mean Square	F
Treatments	570	2	285	51.82
Error	66	12	5.5	
Total	636	14		

2. a. MSTR = 268

b. MSE = 92

c. Cannot reject H_0 because p-value is greater than .10

d.

Source of Variation	Sum of Squares	Degrees of Freedom	Mean Square	F
Treatments	536	2	268	2.91
Error	828	9	92	
Total	1364	11		

4. b. Reject H_0 because p-value is less than .01

6.

	Mfg 1	Mfg 2	Mfg 3
Sample mean	23	28	21
Sample variance	6.67	4.67	3.33

$$\bar{\bar{x}} = (23 + 28 + 21)/3 = 24$$

$$\text{SSTR} = \sum_{j=1}^{k} n_j(\bar{x}_j - \bar{\bar{x}})^2$$

$$= 4(23 - 24)^2 + 4(28 - 24)^2 + 4(21 - 24)^2 = 104$$

$$\text{MSTR} = \frac{\text{SSTR}}{k-1} = \frac{104}{2} = 52$$

$$\text{SSE} = \sum_{j=1}^{k} (n_j - 1)s_j^2$$

$$= 3(6.67) + 3(4.67) + 3(3.33) = 44.01$$

$$\text{MSE} = \frac{\text{SSE}}{n_T - k} = \frac{44.01}{12 - 3} = 4.89$$

$$F = \frac{\text{MSTR}}{\text{MSE}} = \frac{52}{4.89} = 10.63$$

From the F table (2 degrees of freedom numerator and 9 denominator), p-value is less than .01

Actual p-value = .0043

Because the p-value $\le \alpha = .05$, we reject the null hypothesis that the mean time needed to mix a batch of material is the same for each manufacturer

8. Significant; p-value is less than .05

10. Significant; p-value = .0419

11. a. $\text{LSD} = t_{\alpha/2} \sqrt{\text{MSE}\left(\dfrac{1}{n_i} + \dfrac{1}{n_j}\right)}$

$$= t_{.025} \sqrt{5.5\left(\frac{1}{5} + \frac{1}{5}\right)}$$

$$= 2.179\sqrt{2.2} = 3.23$$

$|\bar{x}_1 - \bar{x}_2| = |30 - 45| = 15 > \text{LSD}$; significant

$|\bar{x}_1 - \bar{x}_3| = |30 - 36| = 6 > \text{LSD}$; significant

$|\bar{x}_2 - \bar{x}_3| = |45 - 36| = 9 > \text{LSD}$; significant

b. $\bar{x}_1 - \bar{x}_2 \pm t_{\alpha/2} \sqrt{\text{MSE}\left(\dfrac{1}{n_1} + \dfrac{1}{n_2}\right)}$

$$(30 - 45) \pm 2.179 \sqrt{5.5\left(\frac{1}{5} + \frac{1}{5}\right)}$$

$$-15 \pm 3.23 = -18.23 \text{ to } -11.77$$

12. a. Significant; p-value is between .01 and .025

b. LSD = 15.34

1 and 2; significant

1 and 3; not significant

2 and 3; significant

13. $\text{LSD} = t_{\alpha/2}\sqrt{\text{MSE}\left(\dfrac{1}{n_1} + \dfrac{1}{n_3}\right)}$

$\qquad = t_{.025}\sqrt{4.89\left(\dfrac{1}{4} + \dfrac{1}{4}\right)}$

$\qquad = 2.262\sqrt{2.45} = 3.54$

Because $|\bar{x}_1 - \bar{x}_3| = |23 - 21| = 2 < 3.54$, there does not appear to be any significant difference between the means of populations 1 and 3

14. $\bar{x}_1 - \bar{x}_2 \pm \text{LSD}$
$23 - 28 \pm 3.54$
$\quad -5 \pm 3.54 = -8.54 \text{ to } -1.46$

16. a. Significant; p-value is less than .01
    b. Significant; $2.3 > \text{LSD} = 1.19$

18. $\text{LSD} = 5.74$
Small and medium: not significant
Small and large: significant
Medium and large: not significant

19. a. $\bar{\bar{x}} = (156 + 142 + 134)/3 = 144$

$\text{SSTR} = \displaystyle\sum_{j=1}^{k} n_j(\bar{x}_j - \bar{\bar{x}})^2$

$\qquad = 6(156 - 144)^2 + 6(142 - 144)^2 + 6(134 - 144)^2$

$\qquad = 1488$

b. $\text{MSTR} = \dfrac{\text{SSTR}}{k-1} = \dfrac{1488}{2} = 744$

c. $s_1^2 = 164.4, \quad s_2^2 = 131.2, \quad s_3^2 = 110.4$

$\text{SSE} = \displaystyle\sum_{j=1}^{k} (n_j - 1)s_j^2$

$\qquad = 5(164.4) + 5(131.2) + 5(110.4)$

$\qquad = 2030$

d. $\text{MSE} = \dfrac{\text{SSE}}{n_T - k} = \dfrac{2030}{18 - 3} = 135.3$

e. $F = \dfrac{\text{MSTR}}{\text{MSE}} = \dfrac{744}{135.3} = 5.50$

From the F table (2 degrees of freedom numerator and 15 denominator), p-value is between .01 and .025

Actual p-value = .0162

Because p-value $\leq \alpha = .05$, we reject the hypothesis that the means for the three treatments are equal

20. a.

Source of Variation	Sum of Squares	Degrees of Freedom	Mean Square	F
Treatments	1488	2	744	5.50
Error	2030	15	135.3	
Total	3518	17		

b. Significant difference between A and C

22. a. $H_0: \mu_1 = \mu_2 = \mu_3 = \mu_4 = \mu_5$
      H_a: Not all the population means are equal
   b. Reject H_0; p-value is less than .01

24. Significant; p-value is less than .01

26. b. Significant; p-value is less than .01

28. Not significant; p-value is greater than .10

30. Not significant; p-value is between .05 and .10

32. Means are all different (LSD = 2.53)

34. ***Treatment Means***
    $\bar{x}_{.1} = 13.6, \quad \bar{x}_{.2} = 11.0, \quad \bar{x}_{.3} = 10.6$
    Block Means
    $\bar{x}_{1.} = 9, \ \bar{x}_{2.} = 7.67, \ \bar{x}_{3.} = 15.67, \ \bar{x}_{4.} = 18.67, \ \bar{x}_{5.} = 7.67$
    Overall Mean
    $\bar{\bar{x}} = 176/15 = 11.73$

Step 1

$\text{SST} = \displaystyle\sum_i\sum_j (x_{ij} - \bar{\bar{x}})^2$

$\qquad = (10 - 11.73)^2 + (9 - 11.73)^2 + \cdots + (8 - 11.73)^2$

$\qquad = 354.93$

Step 2

$\text{SSTR} = b\displaystyle\sum_j (\bar{x}_{.j} - \bar{\bar{x}})^2$

$\qquad = 5[(13.6 - 11.73)^2 + (11.0 - 11.73)^2$
$\qquad\qquad + (10.6 - 11.73)^2] = 26.53$

Step 3

$\text{SSBL} = k\displaystyle\sum_j (\bar{x}_{i.} - \bar{\bar{x}})^2$

$\qquad = 3[(9 - 11.73)^2 + (7.67 - 11.73)^2$
$\qquad\qquad + (15.67 - 11.73)^2 + (18.67 - 11.73)^2$
$\qquad\qquad + (7.67 - 11.73)^2] = 312.32$

Step 4
$\text{SSE} = \text{SST} - \text{SSTR} - \text{SSBL}$
$\qquad = 354.93 - 26.53 - 312.32 = 16.08$

Source of Variation	Sum of Squares	Degrees of Freedom	Mean Square	F
Treatments	26.53	2	13.27	6.60
Blocks	312.32	4	78.08	
Error	16.08	8	2.01	
Total	354.93	14		

From the F table (2 numerator degrees of freedom and 8 denominator), p-value is between .01 and .025

Actual p-value = .0203

Because p-value $\leq \alpha = .05$, we reject the null hypothesis that the means of the three treatments are equal

36. Significant; p-value is less than .01

38. Significant; p-value is less than .01

40. Significant; p-value = .0000

TABLE D13.41

		Factor B			Factor A Means
		Level 1	**Level 2**	**Level 3**	
Factor A	**Level 1**	$\bar{x}_{11} = 150$	$\bar{x}_{12} = 78$	$\bar{x}_{13} = 84$	$\bar{x}_{1.} = 104$
	Level 2	$\bar{x}_{21} = 110$	$\bar{x}_{22} = 116$	$\bar{x}_{23} = 128$	$\bar{x}_{2.} = 118$
Factor B Means		$\bar{x}_{.1} = 130$	$\bar{x}_{.2} = 97$	$\bar{x}_{.3} = 106$	$\bar{\bar{x}} = 111$

41. See Table D13.41

Step 1

$$SST = \sum_i \sum_j \sum_k (x_{ijk} - \bar{\bar{x}})^2$$
$$= (135 - 111)^2 + (165 - 111)^2 + \cdots$$
$$+ (136 - 111)^2 = 9028$$

Step 2

$$SSA = br \sum_i (\bar{x}_{i.} - \bar{\bar{x}})^2$$
$$= 3(2)[(104 - 111)^2 + (118 - 111)^2] = 588$$

Step 3

$$SSB = ar \sum_j (\bar{x}_{.j} - \bar{\bar{x}})^2$$
$$= 2(2)[(130 - 111)^2 + (97 - 111)^2 + (106 - 111)^2]$$
$$= 2328$$

Step 4

$$SSAB = r \sum_i \sum_j (\bar{x}_{ij} - \bar{x}_{i.} - \bar{x}_{.j} + \bar{\bar{x}})^2$$
$$= 2[(150 - 104 - 130 + 111)^2$$
$$+ (78 - 104 - 97 + 111)^2 + \cdots$$
$$+ (128 - 118 - 106 + 111)^2] = 4392$$

Step 5

$$SSE = SST - SSA - SSB - SSAB$$
$$= 9028 - 588 - 2328 - 4392 = 1720$$

Source of Variation	Sum of Squares	Degrees of Freedom	Mean Square	F
Factor A	588	1	588	2.05
Factor B	2328	2	1164	4.06
Interaction	4392	2	2196	7.66
Error	1720	6	286.67	
Total	9028	11		

Factor A: $F = 2.05$

From the F table (1 degree of freedom numerator and 6 denominator), p-value is greater than .10

Actual p-value $= .2022$

Because p-value $> \alpha = .05$, factor A is not significant

Factor B: $F = 4.06$

From the F table (2 degrees of freedom numerator and 6 denominator), p-value is between .05 and .10

Actual p-value $= .0767$

Because p-value $> \alpha = .05$, factor B is not significant

Interaction: $F = 7.66$

From the F table (2 degrees of freedom numerator and 6 denominator), p-value is between .01 and .025

Actual p-value $= .0223$

Because p-value $\le \alpha = .05$, interaction is significant

42. Factor A is significant; p-value $= .025$

Factor B is significant; p-value is between .01 and .025

Interaction is significant; p-value is less than .01

44. No significant effect due to the loading and unloading method, the type of ride, or interaction; p-value is greater than .10 for each test

46. Factor A is not significant

Factor B is significant

Interaction is significant

48. Significant; p-value $= .0000$

50. Significant; p-value is less than .01

52. Significant; p-value $= .0002$

54. Significant; p-value is between .01 and .025

56. Not significant; p-value is greater than .10

58. Significant; p-value is between .025 and .05

60. a. Significant; p-value is between .01 and .025

62. Significant; p-value $= .0000$

64. Type of machine is significant; type of loading system and interaction are not significant

Chapter 14

1. a.

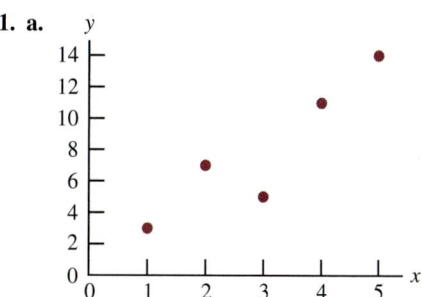

b. There appears to be a linear relationship between x and y

c. Many different straight lines can be drawn to provide a linear approximation of the relationship between x and y; in part (d) we will determine the equation of a straight line that "best" represents the relationship according to the least squares criterion

d. Summations needed to compute the slope and y-intercept:

$$\Sigma x_i = 15, \quad \Sigma y_i = 40, \quad \Sigma(x_i - \bar{x})(y_i - \bar{y}) = 26,$$
$$\Sigma(x_i - \bar{x})^2 = 10$$

$$b_1 = \frac{\Sigma(x_i - \bar{x})(y_i - \bar{y})}{\Sigma(x_i - \bar{x})^2} = \frac{26}{10} = 2.6$$

$$b_0 = \bar{y} - b_1\bar{x} = 8 - (2.6)(3) = 0.2$$

$$\hat{y} = 0.2 - 2.6x$$

e. $\hat{y} = .2 + 2.6x = .2 + 2.6(4) = 10.6$

2. b. There appears to be a linear relationship between x and y

d. $\hat{y} = 30.33 - 1.88x$

e. 19.05

4. a.

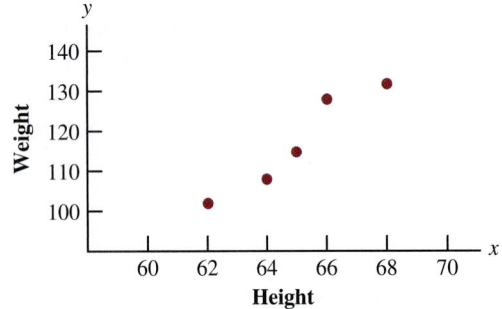

b. It indicates there may be a linear relationship between height and weight

c. Many different straight lines can be drawn to provide a linear approximation of the relationship between height and weight; in part (d) we will determine the equation of a straight line that "best" represents the relationship according to the least squares criterion

d. Summations needed to compute the slope and y-intercept:

$$\Sigma x_i = 325, \quad \Sigma y_i = 585, \quad \Sigma(x_i - \bar{x})(y_i - \bar{y}) = 110,$$
$$\Sigma(x_i - \bar{x})^2 = 20$$

$$b_1 = \frac{\Sigma(x_i - \bar{x})(y_i - \bar{y})}{\Sigma(x_i - \bar{x})^2} = \frac{110}{20} = 5.5$$

$$b_0 = \bar{y} - b_1\bar{x} = 117 - (5.5)(65) = -240.5$$

$$\hat{y} = -240.5 + 5.5x$$

e. $\hat{y} = -240.5 + 5.5(63) = 106$

The estimate of weight is 106 pounds

6. c. $\hat{y} = -10.16 + .18x$

e. 11.95 or approximately \$12,000

8. c. $\hat{y} = 490.21 + 204.24x$

d. \$1307

10. b. $\hat{y} = 51.82 + .145x$

c. 84.4

12. c. $\hat{y} = 1293 + .3165x$

d. 25,031

14. b. $\hat{y} = 28.30 - .0415x$

c. 26.2

15. a. $\hat{y}_i = .2 + 2.6x_i$ and $\bar{y} = 8$

x_i	y_i	$\hat{y}_i$	$y_i - \hat{y}_i$	$(y_i - \hat{y}_i)^2$	$y_i - \bar{y}$	$(y_i - \bar{y})^2$
1	3	2.8	.2	.04	-5	25
2	7	5.4	1.6	2.56	-1	1
3	5	8.0	-3.0	9.00	-3	9
4	11	10.6	.4	.16	3	9
5	14	13.2	.8	.64	6	36
				SSE = 12.40		SST = 80

$$\text{SSR} = \text{SST} - \text{SSE} = 80 - 12.4 = 67.6$$

b. $r^2 = \dfrac{\text{SSR}}{\text{SST}} = \dfrac{67.6}{80} = .845$

The least squares line provided a good fit; 84.5% of the variability in y has been explained by the least squares line

c. $r = \sqrt{.845} = +.9192$

16. a. SSE = 6.3325, SST = 114.80, SSR = 108.47

b. $r^2 = .945$

c. $r = -.9721$

18. a. The estimated regression equation and the mean for the dependent variable:

$$\hat{y} = 1790.5 + 581.1x, \quad \bar{y} = 3650$$

The sum of squares due to error and the total sum of squares:

$$\text{SSE} = \Sigma(y_i - \hat{y}_i)^2 = 85,135.14$$
$$\text{SST} = \Sigma(y_i - \bar{y})^2 = 335,000$$

Thus, SSR = SST − SSE
$$= 335,000 - 85,135.14 = 249,864.86$$

b. $r^2 = \dfrac{\text{SSR}}{\text{SST}} = \dfrac{249,864.86}{335,000} = .746$

The least squares line accounted for 74.6% of the total sum of squares

c. $r = \sqrt{.746} = +.8637$

20. a. $\hat{y} = -48.11 + 2.3325x$

b. $r^2 = .82$

c. \$173,500

22. a. $\hat{y} = -745.80 + 117.917x$

b. $r^2 = .7071$

c. $r = +.84$

23. a. $s^2 = \text{MSE} = \dfrac{\text{SSE}}{n - 2} = \dfrac{12.4}{3} = 4.133$

b. $s = \sqrt{\text{MSE}} = \sqrt{4.133} = 2.033$

c. $\Sigma(x_i - \bar{x})^2 = 10$

$$s_{b_1} = \frac{s}{\sqrt{\Sigma(x_i - \bar{x})^2}} = \frac{2.033}{\sqrt{10}} = .643$$

d. $t = \dfrac{b_1 - \beta_1}{s_{b_1}} = \dfrac{2.6 - 0}{.643} = 4.04$

From the t table (3 degrees of freedom), area in tail is between .01 and .025

p-value is between .02 and .05

Actual p-value $= .0272$

Because the p-value $\leq \alpha$, we reject H_0: $\beta_1 = 0$

e. $\text{MSR} = \dfrac{\text{SSR}}{1} = 67.6$

$F = \dfrac{\text{MSR}}{\text{MSE}} = \dfrac{67.6}{4.133} = 16.36$

From the F table (1 degree of freedom numerator and 3 denominator), p-value is between .025 and .05

Actual p-value $= .0272$

Because the p-value $\leq \alpha$, we reject H_0: $\beta_1 = 0$

Source of Variation	Sum of Squares	Degrees of Freedom	Mean Square	F
Regression	67.6	1	67.6	16.36
Error	12.4	3	4.133	
Total	80	4		

24. a. 2.11

  b. 1.453

  c. .262

  d. Significant; p-value is less than .01

  e. Significant; p-value is less than .01

26. a. $s^2 = \text{MSE} = \dfrac{\text{SSE}}{n-2} = \dfrac{85,135.14}{4} = 21,283.79$

  $s = \sqrt{\text{MSE}} = \sqrt{21,283.79} = 145.89$

  $\Sigma(x_i - \bar{x})^2 = .74$

  $s_{b_1} = \dfrac{s}{\sqrt{\Sigma(x_i - \bar{x})^2}} = \dfrac{145.89}{\sqrt{.74}} = 169.59$

  $t = \dfrac{b_1 - \beta_1}{s_{b_1}} = \dfrac{581.08 - 0}{169.59} = 3.43$

  From the t table (4 degrees of freedom), area in tail is between .01 and .025

  p-value is between .02 and .05

  Actual p-value $= .0266$

  Because the p-value $\leq \alpha$, we reject H_0: $\beta_1 = 0$

  b. $\text{MSR} = \dfrac{\text{SSR}}{1} = \dfrac{249,864.86}{1} = 249,864.86$

  $F = \dfrac{\text{MSR}}{\text{MSE}} = \dfrac{249,864.86}{21,283.79} = 11.74$

  From the F table (1 degree of freedom numerator and 4 denominator), p-value is between .025 and .05

  Actual p-value $= .0266$

  Because the p-value $\leq \alpha$, we reject H_0: $\beta_1 = 0$

c.

Source of Variation	Sum of Squares	Degrees of Freedom	Mean Square	F
Regression	29,864.86	1	29,864.86	11.74
Error	85,135.14	4	21,283.79	
Total	335,000	5		

28. They are related; p-value is less than .01

30. Significant; p-value is less than .01

32. a. $\hat{y} = 6.1092 + .8951x$

  b. Significant relationship

  c. $r^2 = .82$; a good fit

34. a. $\hat{y} = 80.0 + 50.0x$

  b. p-value $\leq \alpha$; reject H_0: $\beta_1 = 0$

  c. p-value $\leq \alpha$; reject H_0: $\beta_1 = 0$

  d. p-value $= .000$

36. b. There appears to be a linear relationship between the two variables

  c. $\hat{y} = 37.0747 - 0.7792x$

  d. Significant relationship

  e. 0.43; not a good fit

37. a. $s = 2.033$

  $\bar{x} = 3,\ \Sigma(x_i - \bar{x})^2 = 10$

  $s_{\hat{y}_p} = s\sqrt{\dfrac{1}{n} + \dfrac{(x_p - \bar{x})^2}{\Sigma(x_i - \bar{x})^2}}$

  $= 2.033\sqrt{\dfrac{1}{5} + \dfrac{(4-3)^2}{10}} = 1.11$

  b. $\hat{y} = .2 + 2.6x = .2 + 2.6(4) = 10.6$

  $\hat{y}_p \pm t_{\alpha/2} s_{\hat{y}_p}$

  $10.6 \pm 3.182(1.11)$

  10.6 ± 3.53, or 7.07 to 14.13

  c. $s_{\text{ind}} = s\sqrt{1 + \dfrac{1}{n} + \dfrac{(x_p - \bar{x})^2}{\Sigma(x_i - \bar{x})^2}}$

  $= 2.033\sqrt{1 + \dfrac{1}{5} + \dfrac{(4-3)^2}{10}} = 2.32$

  d. $\hat{y}_p \pm t_{\alpha/2} s_{\text{ind}}$

  $10.6 \pm 3.182(2.32)$

  10.6 ± 7.38, or 3.22 to 17.98

38. a. 1.453

  b. 22.53 to 26.85

  c. 1.61

  d. 19.57 to 29.81

40. a. $s = 145.89,\ \bar{x} = 3.2,\ \Sigma(x_i - \bar{x})^2 = .74$

  $\hat{y} = 1790.5 + 581.1x = 1790.5 + 581.1(3)$

  $= 3533.8$

  $s_{\hat{y}_p} = s\sqrt{\dfrac{1}{n} + \dfrac{(x_p - \bar{x})^2}{\Sigma(x_i - \bar{x})^2}}$

  $= 145.89\sqrt{\dfrac{1}{6} + \dfrac{(3 - 3.2)^2}{.74}} = 68.54$

  $\hat{y}_p \pm t_{\alpha/2} s_{\hat{y}_p}$

  $3533.8 \pm 2.776(68.54)$

  3533.8 ± 190.27, or \$3343.53 to \$3724.07

b. $\hat{y} = 1790.5 + 581.1x = 1790.5 + 581.1(3)$

$= 3533.8$

$$s_{\text{ind}} = s\sqrt{1 + \frac{1}{n} + \frac{(x_p - \bar{x})^2}{\Sigma(x_i - \bar{x})^2}}$$

$$= 145.89\sqrt{1 + \frac{1}{6} + \frac{(3 - 3.2)^2}{0.74}} = 161.19$$

$\hat{y}_p \pm t_{\alpha/2}s_{\text{ind}}$

$3533.8 \pm 2.776(161.19)$

3533.8 ± 447.46, or \$3086.34 to \$3981.26

42. a. \$11,740 to \$14,420

b. \$9,300 to \$16,860

c. Yes, \$20,400 is much larger than anticipated

d. Any deductions exceeding \$16,800

44. a. $\hat{y} = -6.76 + 1.755x$

b. $r^2 = .713$; a good fit

c. 31.8 to 60

d. 6.3 to 85.5

45. a. Using Excel's Regression tool the estimated regression equation is $\hat{y} = -7.0222 + 1.5873x$ or $\hat{y} = -7.02 + 1.59x$

b.

x_i	y_i	$\hat{y}_i$	$y_i - \hat{y}_i$
6	6	2.52	3.48
11	8	10.47	-2.47
15	12	16.83	-4.83
18	20	21.60	-1.60
20	30	24.78	5.22

c.

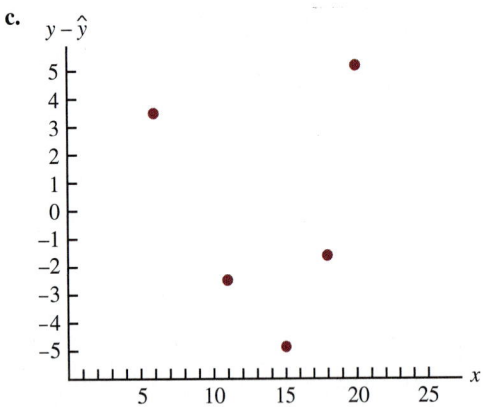

With only five observations, it is difficult to determine whether the assumptions are satisfied; however, the plot does suggest curvature in the residuals, which would indicate that the error term assumptions are not satisfied; the scatter diagram for these data also indicates that the underlying relationship between x and y may be curvilinear

d. $s^2 = 23.78$

$$h_i = \frac{1}{n} + \frac{(x_i - \bar{x})^2}{\Sigma(x_i - \bar{x})^2}$$

$$= \frac{1}{5} + \frac{(x_i - 14)^2}{126}$$

x_i	h_i	$s_{y_i - \hat{y}_i}$	$y_i - \hat{y}_i$	Standardized Residuals
6	.7079	2.6356	3.48	1.32
11	.2714	4.1625	-2.47	-.59
15	.2079	4.3401	-4.83	-1.11
18	.3270	4.0005	-1.60	-.40
20	.4857	3.4972	5.22	1.49

e. The plot of the standardized residuals against x has the same shape as the original residual plot. The conclusions reached in part (c) are also appropriate here.

46. a. $\hat{y} = 2.322 + .6366x$

b. Assumption that variance is the same for all values of x is questionable; the variance appears to increase for larger values of x

47. Using Excel's Regression tool, the estimated regression equation is $\hat{y} = 29.39911 + 1.547458x$ or $\hat{y} = 29.40 + 1.55x$

b. Significant relationship: Significance F (or p-value) $< \alpha = .05$

c.

x_i	y_i	$\hat{y}_i = 29.40 + 1.55x_i$	$y_i - \hat{y}_i$
1	19	30.95	-11.95
2	32	32.50	-.50
4	44	35.60	8.40
6	40	38.70	1.30
10	52	44.90	7.10
14	53	51.10	1.90
20	54	60.40	-6.40

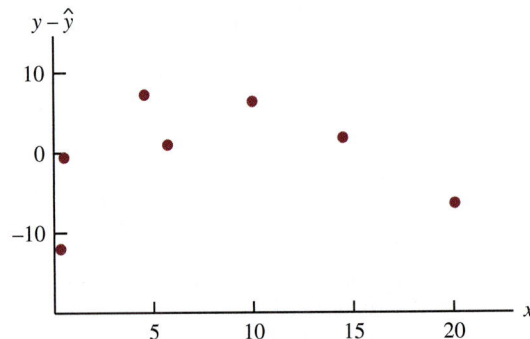

d. The residual plot leads us to question the assumption of a linear relationship between x and y; even though the relationship is significant at the $\alpha = .05$ level, it would be extremely dangerous to extrapolate beyond the range of the data (e.g., $x > 20$)

48. b. The assumptions concerning the error terms appear reasonable

50. a. The scatter diagram indicates that $x = 135$, $y = 145$ may be an outlier

b. The standard residual for $x = 135$, $y = 145$ is 2.13; thus, it is an outlier

52. a. $\hat{y} = 4.0890 + .1995x$
    b. We would treat observation 1 as an outlier

54. a. $\hat{y} = 707.0299 + .0048x$

56. To determine whether there is a significant relationship between x and y; no

58. a. $\hat{y} = -3.8338 + .2957x$
    b. Approximately 40.6 million
    c. Yes; $r^2 = .919$

60. b. There appears to be a positive linear relationship
    c. $\hat{y} = 9.3742 + 1.2875x$
    d. p-value $= .0002$; significant
    e. $r^2 = .7413$; good fit
    f. $r = .8610$

62. a. $\hat{y} = 22.1739 - .1478x$
    b. Significant relationship
    c. $r^2 = .739$; good fit
    d. 12.294 to 17.271

64. a. $\hat{y} = 220 + 131.6667x$
    b. Significant relationship
    c. $r^2 = .873$; good fit
    d. 559.3 to 933.9

66. a. $\hat{y} = -.4710 + .00004x$
    b. Significant relationship; p-value $= .0384$
    c. $r^2 = .217$; not a good fit
    d. .7729 to .9927

Chapter 15

2. a. The estimated regression equation is
$$\hat{y} = 45.0594 + 1.9436x_1$$
An estimate of y when $x_1 = 45$ is
$$\hat{y} = 45.0594 + 1.9436(45) = 132.52$$

    b. The estimated regression equation is
$$\hat{y} = 85.2171 + 4.3215x_2$$
An estimate of y when $x_2 = 15$ is
$$\hat{y} = 85.2171 + 4.3215(15) = 150.04$$
    c. The estimated regression equation is
$$\hat{y} = -18.3683 + 2.0102x_1 + 4.7378x_2$$
An estimate of y when $x_1 = 45$ and $x_2 = 15$ is
$$\hat{y} = -18.3683 + 2.0102(45) + 4.7378(15) = 143.16$$

4. a. \$255,000

5. a. The Excel output is shown in Figure D15.5a
    b. The Excel output is shown in Figure D15.5b
    c. It is 1.6039 in part (a) and 2.2902 in part (b); in part (a) the coefficient is an estimate of the change in revenue due to a one-unit change in television advertising expenditures; in part (b) it represents an estimate of the change in revenue due to a one-unit change in television advertising expenditures when the amount of newspaper advertising is held constant
    d. Revenue $= 83.2301 + 2.2902(3.5) + 1.3010(1.8)$
               $= 93.59$ or \$93,590

6. a. $\hat{y} = .3540 + .0009$ HR
    b. $\hat{y} = .8647 + .0837$ ERA
    c. $\hat{y} = .7092 + .0014$ HR $- .1026$ ERA
    d. .551

8. a. Return $= 247.3579 - 32.8445$ Safety $+$
                  34.5887 ExpRatio
    b. 70.2

10. a. $\hat{y} = -1.2207 + 3.9576$ FG%
    b. .04
    c. $\hat{y} = 1.2346 + 4.8166$ FG% $- 2.5895$ Opp 3 Pt% $+$
        $.0344$ Opp TO
    e. .6372

FIGURE D15.5a

Regression Statistics	
Multiple R	0.8078
R Square	0.6526
Adjusted R Square	0.5946
Standard Error	1.2152
Observations	8

ANOVA

	df	SS	MS	F	Significance F
Regression	1	16.6401	16.6401	11.2688	0.0153
Residual	6	8.8599	1.4767		
Total	7	25.5			

	Coefficients	Standard Error	t Stat	P-value
Intercept	88.6377	1.5824	56.0159	2.174E-09
Television Advertising (\$1000s)	1.6039	0.4778	3.3569	0.0153

FIGURE D15.5b

Regression Statistics	
Multiple R	0.9587
R Square	0.9190
Adjusted R Square	0.8866
Standard Error	0.6426
Observations	8

ANOVA

	df	SS	MS	F	Significance F
Regression	2	23.4354	11.7177	28.3778	0.0019
Residual	5	2.0646	0.4129		
Total	7	25.5			

	Coefficients	Standard Error	t Stat	P-value
Intercept	83.2301	1.5739	52.8825	4.57E-08
Television Advertising ($1000s)	2.2902	0.3041	7.5319	0.0007
Newspaper Advertising ($1000s)	1.3010	0.3207	4.0567	0.0098

12. a. $R^2 = \dfrac{\text{SSR}}{\text{SST}} = \dfrac{14{,}052.2}{15{,}182.9} = .926$

 b. $R_a^2 = 1 - (1 - R^2)\dfrac{n-1}{n-p-1}$

 $= 1 - (1 - .926)\dfrac{10-1}{10-2-1} = .905$

 c. Yes; after adjusting for the number of independent variables in the model, we see that 90.5% of the variability in y has been accounted for

14. a. .75

 b. .68

15. a. $R^2 = \dfrac{\text{SSR}}{\text{SST}} = \dfrac{23.435}{25.5} = .919$

 $R_a^2 = 1 - (1 - R^2)\dfrac{n-1}{n-p-1}$

 $= 1 - (1 - .919)\dfrac{8-1}{8-2-1} = .887$

 b. Multiple regression analysis is preferred because both R^2 and R_a^2 show an increased percentage of the variability of y explained when both independent variables are used

16. a. No, $R^2 = .1532$

 b. Using both independent variables provides a better fit

18. a. $R^2 = .5638$, $R_a^2 = .5114$

 b. The fit is not very good; but it does explain over 50% of the variability in y

19. a. $\text{MSR} = \dfrac{\text{SSR}}{p} = \dfrac{6216.375}{2} = 3108.188$

 $\text{MSE} = \dfrac{\text{SSE}}{n-p-1} = \dfrac{507.75}{10-2-1} = 72.536$

 b. $F = \dfrac{\text{MSR}}{\text{MSE}} = \dfrac{3108.188}{72.536} = 42.85$

 $F_{.05} = 4.74$ (2 degrees of freedom numerator and 7 denominator)

 Because $F = 42.85 > F_{.05} = 4.74$, the overall model is significant

 c. $t = \dfrac{b_1}{s_{b_1}} = \dfrac{.5906}{.0813} = 7.26$

 $t_{.025} = 2.365$ (7 degrees of freedom)

 With $t = 7.26 > t_{.025} = 2.365$, β_1 is significant

 d. $t = \dfrac{b_2}{s_{b_2}} = \dfrac{.4980}{.0567} = 8.78$

 With $t = 8.78 > t_{.025} = 2.365$, β_2 is significant

20. a. Significant; p-value = .0001

 b. Significant; p-value = .0000

 c. Significant; p-value = .0016

22. a. SSE = 4000, MSE = 571.43, MSR = 6000

 b. Significant; $F = 10.50 > F_{.05} = 4.74$

23. a. $F = 28.38$

 $F_{.01} = 13.27$ (2 degrees of freedom numerator and 1 denominator)

 Because $F > F_{.01} = 13.27$, reject H_0

 Alternatively, the p-value of .002 leads to the same conclusion

 b. $t = 7.53$

 $t_{.025} = 2.571$

 Because $t > t_{.025} = 2.571$, β_1 is significant and x_1 should not be dropped from the model

c. $t = 4.06$

$t_{.025} = 2.571$

With $t > t_{.025} = 2.571$, β_2 is significant and x_2 should not be dropped from the model

24. a. Significant relationship
b. Both independent variables are significant

26. a. Significant; p-value $= .0000$
b. All of the independent variables are significant

28. a. Using the PredInt macro, the 95% confidence interval is 132.16 to 154.16
b. Using the PredInt macro, the 95% prediction interval is 111.13 to 175.18

29. a. See Excel output in Figure D15.5b
$\hat{y} = 83.2301 + 2.2902(3.5) + 1.3010(1.8) = 93.588$
or $93,588
b. Using the PredInt macro: 92.840 to 94.335, or $92,840 to $94,335
c. Using the PredInt macro: 91.774 to 95.401, or $91,774 to $95,401

30. a. 101.29
b. 99.490 to 103.089
c. 94.596 to 107.984

32. a. $E(y) = \beta_0 + \beta_1 x_1 + \beta_2 x_2$

where $x_2 = \begin{cases} 0 \text{ if level } 1 \\ 1 \text{ if level } 2 \end{cases}$

b. $E(y) = \beta_0 + \beta_1 x_1 + \beta_2(0) = \beta_0 + \beta_1 x_1$
c. $E(y) = \beta_0 + \beta_1 x_1 + \beta_2(1) = \beta_0 + \beta_1 x_1 + \beta_2$
d. $\beta_2 = E(y \mid \text{level } 2) - E(y \mid \text{level } 1)$
β_1 is the change in $E(y)$ for a 1-unit change in x_1 holding x_2 constant

34. a. $15,300, because $b_3 = 15.3$
b. $\hat{y} = 10.1 - 4.2(2) + 6.8(8) + 15.3(0)$
$= 10.1 - 8.4 + 54.4$
$= 56.1$
Sales prediction: $56,100
c. $\hat{y} = 10.1 - 4.2(1) + 6.8(3) + 15.3(1)$
$= 10.1 - 4.2 + 20.4 + 15.3$
$= 41.6$
Sales prediction: $41,600

36. a. $\hat{y} = 1.8602 + 0.2914 \text{ Months} + 1.1024 \text{ Type} - 0.6091 \text{ Person}$
b. Significant; p-value $= .0021 < \alpha = .05$
c. Person is not significant

38. a. $\hat{y} = -91.7595 + 1.0767 \text{ Age} + .2518 \text{ Pressure} + 8.7399 \text{ Smoker}$
b. Significant; p-value $= .0102 < \alpha = .05$
c. 95% prediction interval is 21.35 to 47.18 or a probability of .2135 to .4718; quit smoking and begin some type of treatment to reduce his blood pressure

39. a. The Excel output is shown in Figure D15.39a
b.

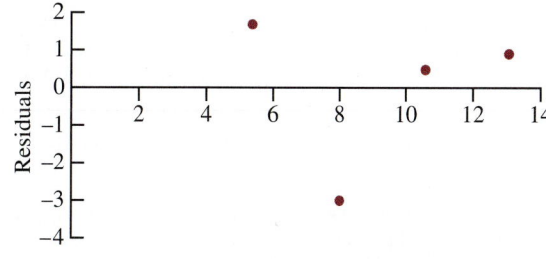

FIGURE D15.39a

Regression Statistics	
Multiple R	0.9192
R Square	0.845
Adjusted R Square	0.7933
Standard Error	2.0331
Observations	5

ANOVA

	df	SS	MS	F	Significance F
Regression	1	67.6	67.6	16.3548	0.0272
Residual	3	12.4	4.1333		
Total	4	80			

	Coefficients	Standard Error	t Stat	P-value
Intercept	0.2	2.1323	0.0938	0.9312
x	2.6	0.6429	4.0441	0.0272

With only 5 observations it is difficult to determine if there are any violations in the assumptions; however, there is nothing unusual in the shape of the plot to question the assumptions

c. The standardized residual plot is shown here:

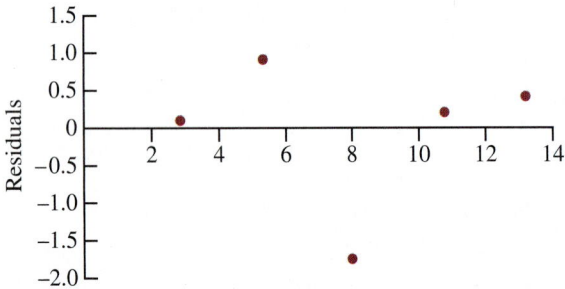

Predicted y

The shape of the standardized residual plot is the same as the shape of the residual plot in part (b); because none of the standard residuals is less than -2 or greater than $+2$, we would conclude that there are no outliers in the data set

40. a. $\hat{y} = -53.28 + 3.11x$
   b. $-1.27, -.15, 1.39, .49, -.45$; no

41. a. The Excel output appears in Figure E15.5b; the estimated regression equation is $\hat{y} = 83.2301 + 2.2902x_1 + 1.3010x_2$ where $x_1 =$ television advertising ($1000s) and $x_2 =$ newspaper advertising ($1000s)
   b. Using Excel, we obtained the following values:

$\hat{y}_i$	Standard Residual	$\hat{y}_i$	Standard Residual
96.63	-1.16	94.39	1.12
90.41	$-.76$	94.24	$-.44$
94.34	1.21	94.42	$-.77$
92.21	$-.38$	93.35	1.19

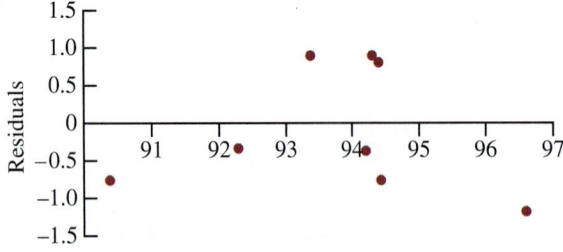

Predicted y

With the relatively few observations, it is difficult to determine if any of the assumptions regarding the error term have been violated (e.g., an argument could be made that there does not appear to be any pattern in the plot; alternatively an argument could be made that there is a curvilinear pattern in the plot)

   c. The values of the standard residuals are greater than -2 and less than $+2$; thus, there are no outliers

42. b. Unusual trend
   c. No outliers

44. b. 3.19

46. b. Significant; p-value $= .000$
   c. Both are significant

48. b. Significant; $F = 22.79 > F_{.05} = 5.79$
   c. $R_a^2 = .861$; good fit
   d. Both are significant

50. a. Speed $= 97.5702 + .0693$ Price $- .0008$ Weight $+ .0590$ Horsepwr $- 2.4836$ Zero60
   b. Significant relationship
   c. Price and Weight are not significant
   d. Speed $= 103.1028 + .0558$ Horsepwr $- 3.1876$ Zero60
   e. Unusual trend
   f. Observation 2 is an outlier

52. a. Resale% $= 38.7718 + .0008$ Price
   b. Not a good fit; R Square $= .3671$
   c. Resale% $= 42.5539 + 9.0903$ Type 1 $+ 7.9172$ Type 2 $+ .0003$ Price
   where Type 1 $= 1$ if a full-size pickup and Type 2 $= 1$ if a sport utility vehicle
   d. Significant relationship; p-value corresponding to $F = 14.7892 = .000 < \alpha = .05$

Chapter 16

1. a. The Excel output is shown in Figure D16.1a
   b. The p-value corresponding to $F = 6.8530$ is $.0589 > \alpha = .05$; therefore, the relationship is not significant
   c.

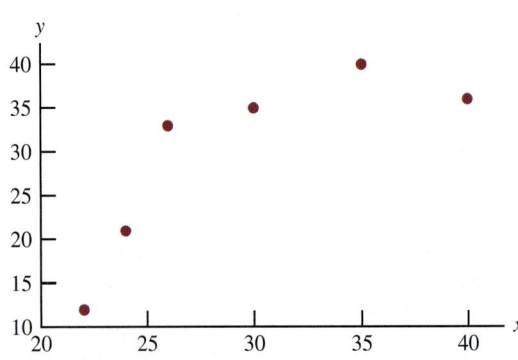

The scatter diagram suggests that a curvilinear relationship may be appropriate
   d. The Excel output is shown in Figure D16.1d
   e. The p-value corresponding to $F = 25.6778$ is $.013 < \alpha = .05$; therefore, the relationship is significant
   f. $\hat{y} = -168.8848 + 12.1870(25) - .1770(25)^2 = 25.165$

2. a. $\hat{y} = 9.3152 + .4242x$; p-value $= .1171$ indicates that the relationship between x and y is not significant
   b. $\hat{y} = -8.1014 + 2.4127x - .0480x^2$
   $R_a^2 = .9324$; good fit
   c. 20.953

FIGURE D16.1a

Regression Statistics	
Multiple R	0.7946
R Square	0.6314
Adjusted R Square	0.5393
Standard Error	7.2693
Observations	6

ANOVA

	df	SS	MS	F	Significance F
Regression	1	362.1304802	362.1305	6.8530	0.0589
Residual	4	211.3695198	52.8424		
Total	5	573.5			

	Coefficients	Standard Error	t Stat	P-value
Intercept	−6.7745	14.1709	−0.4781	0.6576
x	1.2296	0.4697	2.6178	0.0589

4. **a.** $\hat{y} = 943.0476 + 8.7143x$
 b. Significant; p-value $= .0049 < \alpha = .01$

5. **a.** The Excel output is shown in Figure E16.5a
 b. The p-value corresponding to $F = 73.1475$ is $.0028 <$ $\alpha = .01$; therefore, the relationship is significant; we would reject $H_0: \beta_1 = \beta_2 = 0$
 c. The fitted value is 1302.01 with a standard deviation of 9.93. The 95% confidence interval is 1270.41 to 1333.61; the 95% prediction interval is 1242.55 to 1361.47

6. **b.** No, the relationship appears to be curvilinear
 c. Several possible models; e.g.,
 $\hat{y} = 2.90 - .185x + .00351x^2$

8. **a.** It appears that a simple linear regression model is not appropriate
 b. 2005% $= 17.0988 + 3.1462\,1999\% - .0445\,1999\%$Sq
 c. Log 2000% $= 1.1742 + .4489$ Log1999%
 d. Part (b); higher percentage of variability is explained

FIGURE D16.1d

Regression Statistics	
Multiple R	0.9720
R Square	0.9448
Adjusted R Square	0.9080
Standard Error	3.2482
Observations	6

ANOVA

	df	SS	MS	F	Significance F
Regression	2	541.8473	270.9236	25.6778	0.0130
Residual	3	31.6527	10.5509		
Total	5	573.5			

	Coefficients	Standard Error	t Stat	P-value
Intercept	−168.8848	39.7862	−4.2448	0.0239
x	12.1870	2.6632	4.5760	0.0196
xsq	−0.1770	0.0429	−4.1271	0.0258

FIGURE D16.5a

Regression Statistics	
Multiple R	0.9899
R Square	0.9799
Adjusted R Square	0.9665
Standard Error	15.8264
Observations	6

ANOVA

	df	SS	MS	F	Significance F
Regression	2	36643.4048	18321.7024	73.1475	0.0028
Residual	3	751.4286	250.4762		
Total	5	37394.8333			

	Coefficients	Standard Error	t Stat	P-value
Intercept	432.5714	141.1763	3.0641	0.0548
x	37.4286	7.8074	4.7940	0.0173
xsq	−0.3829	0.1036	−3.6952	0.0344

10. a. Significant; p-value = .0000
   b. Significant; p-value = .0000

11. a. SSE = 1805 − 1760 = 45

$$F = \frac{MSR}{MSE} = \left(\frac{1760/4}{45/25}\right) = 244.44$$

p-value (4 degrees of freedom numerator and 25 denominator) = .0000

Because p-value $< \alpha$, we reject H_0; the relationship is significant

b. SSE(x_1, x_2, x_3, x_4) = 45

c. SSE(x_2, x_3) = 1805 − 1705 = 100

d. $F = \dfrac{(100 - 45)/2}{1.8} = 15.28 \qquad F_{.05} = 3.39$

With $F = 15.28 > 3.39$, x_1 and x_2 are significant

12. a. The Excel output is shown in Figure D16.12a
   b. The Excel output is shown in Figure D16.12b

FIGURE D16.12a

Regression Statistics	
Multiple R	0.6456
R Square	0.4167
Adjusted R Square	0.3681
Standard Error	43.9290
Observations	14

ANOVA

	df	SS	MS	F	Significance F
Regression	1	16546.1695	16546.1695	8.5742	0.0126
Residual	12	23157.0447	1929.7537		
Total	13	39703.2143			

	Coefficients	Standard Error	t Stat	P-value
Intercept	170.1274	44.0201	3.8648	0.0022
Team Interceptions	6.6130	2.2584	2.9282	0.0126

FIGURE D16.12b

Regression Statistics	
Multiple R	0.7996
R Square	0.6394
Adjusted R Square	0.5312
Standard Error	37.8376
Observations	14

ANOVA

	df	SS	MS	F	Significance F
Regression	3	25386.3868	8462.1289	5.9106	0.0138
Residual	10	14316.8274	1431.6827		
Total	13	39703.2143			

	Coefficients	Standard Error	t Stat	P-value
Intercept	280.3430	81.4181	3.4433	0.0063
Team Interceptions	5.1762	2.0735	2.4964	0.0316
Rushing Yards	−0.0037	0.0334	−0.1119	0.9131
Opponent Interceptions	−3.9182	1.6509	−2.3733	0.0391

c. $F = \dfrac{[\text{SSE(reduced)} - \text{SSE(full)}]/(\text{\# extra terms})}{\text{MSE(full)}}$

$= \dfrac{(23{,}157 - 14{,}317)/2}{1432} = 3.09$

p-value (2 degrees of freedom numerator and 10 denominator) = .0000

Because the p-value $\le \alpha = .05$, the addition of the two independent variables is not significant

Note: Suppose that we consider adding only the number of interceptions made by the opponents; the corresponding Excel output is shown in Figure D16.12c; in this case,

$F = \dfrac{(23{,}157 - 14{,}335)/1}{1303} = 6.77$

p-value (1 degree of freedom numerator and 11 denominator) = .0246

Because the p-value $\le \alpha = .05$, the addition of the number of interceptions made by the opponents is significant

FIGURE D16.12c

Regression Statistics	
Multiple R	0.7993
R Square	0.6390
Adjusted R Square	0.5733
Standard Error	36.0993
Observations	14

ANOVA

	df	SS	MS	F	Significance F
Regression	2	25368.4476	12684.2238	9.7334	0.0037
Residual	11	14334.7667	1303.1606		
Total	13	39703.2143			

	Coefficients	Standard Error	t Stat	P-value
Intercept	273.7699	53.8077	5.0879	0.0004
Team Interceptions	5.2267	1.9308	2.7070	0.0204
Opponent Interceptions	−3.9650	1.5239	−2.6019	0.0246

FIGURE D16.16a

Regression Statistics	
Multiple R	0.5448
R Square	0.2968
Adjusted R Square	0.2528
Standard Error	12.8264
Observations	18

ANOVA

	df	SS	MS	F	Significance F
Regression	1	1110.8344	1110.8344	6.7521	0.0194
Residual	16	2632.2767	164.5173		
Total	17	3743.1111			

	Coefficients	Standard Error	t Stat	P-value
Intercept	−26.6126	37.2180	−0.7150	0.4849
Combined SAT Score	0.0970	0.0373	2.5985	0.0194

14. a. $\hat{y} = -110.9423 + 1.3150$ Age $+ .2964$ Pressure
  b. $\hat{y} = -123.1650 + 1.5130$ Age $+ .4483$ Pressure $+ 8.8656$ Smoker $- .0028$ AgePress
  c. Significant; *p*-value = .0349

16. a. The Excel output is shown in Figure D16.16a
  b. The Excel output is shown in Figure D16.16b

  c. The backward elimination procedure results in an estimated regression equation with two independent variables (see Figure D16.16c)

18. a. Greens
  b. ScoreAvg = $58.1979 - .0100$ Distance $- .1519$ Greens $+ .8686$ Putts

FIGURE D16.16b

Regression Statistics	
Multiple R	0.7723
R Square	0.5965
Adjusted R Square	0.4283
Standard Error	11.2191
Observations	18

ANOVA

	df	SS	MS	F	Significance F
Regression	5	2232.6895	446.5379	3.5477	0.0336
Residual	12	1510.4217	125.8685		
Total	17	3743.1111			

	Coefficients	Standard Error	t Stat	P-value
Intercept	33.7086	63.2773	0.5327	0.6040
Average Class Size	−1.5577	1.0901	−1.4289	0.1786
Spending Per Student ($)	−0.0024	0.0017	−1.4661	0.1683
Average Teacher Salary ($)	−0.0003	0.0006	−0.4045	0.6930
Combined SAT Score	0.0769	0.0374	2.0573	0.0621
% Taking SAT	0.2852	0.1154	2.4704	0.0295

FIGURE D16.16c

Regression Statistics	
Multiple R	0.6851
R Square	0.4693
Adjusted R Square	0.3986
Standard Error	11.5076
Observations	18

ANOVA

	df	SS	MS	F	Significance F
Regression	2	1756.7232	878.3616	6.6329	0.0086
Residual	15	1986.3879	132.4259		
Total	17	3743.1111			

	Coefficients	Standard Error	t Stat	P-value
Intercept	−26.9312	33.3916	−0.8065	0.4325
Combined SAT Score	0.0838	0.0340	2.4623	0.0264
% Taking SAT	0.2045	0.0926	2.2085	0.0432

    c. Yes

    d. 72.64

20. $\hat{y} = -91.7595 + 1.0767$ Age $+ .2518$ Pressure
      $+ 8.7399$ Smoker

21. a. The Excel output is shown in Figure D16.21a

    b. The Durban-Watson statistic is $d = 1.96$; at $\alpha = .05$,
    $d_L = 1.10$, and $d_U = 1.37$; because $d > d_U$, there is no
    significant positive autocorrelation

22. $d = 1.60$; test is inconclusive

23.

x_1	x_2	x_3	Treatment
0	0	0	A
1	0	0	B
0	1	0	C
0	0	1	D

$$E(y) = \beta_0 + \beta_1 x_1 + \beta_2 x_2 + \beta_3 x_3$$

FIGURE D16.21a

Regression Statistics	
Multiple R	0.6246
R Square	0.3901
Adjusted R Square	0.3465
Standard Error	5.6483
Observations	16

ANOVA

	df	SS	MS	F	Significance F
Regression	1	285.6389	285.6389	8.9534	0.0097
Residual	14	446.6411	31.9029		
Total	15	732.28			

	Coefficients	Standard Error	t Stat	P-value
Intercept	10.0518	3.7355	2.6908	0.0176
Gross Profit Margin (%)	0.6562	0.2193	2.9922	0.0097

FIGURE D16.26b

Regression Statistics	
Multiple R	0.8383
R Square	0.7027
Adjusted R Square	0.6366
Standard Error	2.2111
Observations	12

ANOVA

	df	SS	MS	F	Significance F
Regression	2	104	52	10.6364	0.0043
Residual	9	44	4.8889		
Total	11	148			

	Coefficients	Standard Error	t Stat	P-value
Intercept	23	1.1055	20.8043	0.0000
D1	5	1.5635	3.1980	0.0109
D2	−2	1.5635	−1.2792	0.2328

24.

x_1	x_2	Treatment
0	0	1
1	0	2
0	1	3

$x_3 = 0$ if block 1; $x_3 = 1$ if block 2
$E(y) = \beta_0 + \beta_1 x_1 + \beta_2 x_2 + \beta_3 x_3$

26. a.

D_1	D_2	Manufacturer
0	0	1
1	0	2
0	1	3

$$E(y) = \beta_0 + \beta_1 D_1 + \beta_2 D_2$$

  b. See Figure E16.26b
  c. $H_0: \beta_1 = \beta_2 = 0$
  d. The p-value is $.0043 < \alpha = .05$; therefore, we conclude that the mean time to mix a batch of material is not the same for each manufacturer

28. Significant difference between the two analyzers

30. a. Let ExS denote the interaction between expense ratio and safety rating
  Perform% = 23.3240 + 222.4310 Expense%
    − 28.8689 ExS
  b. Adjusted R Square = .653
  c. 26.7 or approximately 27%

32. a. Delay = 63 + 11.0741 Industry; no significant positive autocorrelation

34. Significant differences between comfort levels for the three types of browsers

Chapter 17

1. Binomial probabilities for $n = 10$, $p = .50$

x	Probability	x	Probability
0	.0010	6	.2051
1	.0098	7	.1172
2	.0439	8	.0439
3	.1172	9	.0098
4	.2051	10	.0010
5	.2461		

Number of plus signs = 7
$$P(x \geq 7) = P(7) + P(8) + P(9) + P(10)$$
$$= .1172 + .0439 + .0098 + .0010$$
$$= .1719$$
p-value = 2(.1719) = .3438
p-value > .05; do not reject H_0
No indication difference exists

2. $n = 27$ cases in which a value different from 150 is obtained
Use normal approximation with $\mu = np = .5(27) = 13.5$ and $\sigma = \sqrt{.25n} = \sqrt{.25(27)} = 2.6$
Use $x = 22$ as the number of plus signs and obtain the following test statistic:
$$z = \frac{x - \mu}{\sigma} = \frac{22 - 13.5}{2.6} = 3.27$$
Largest table value $z = 3.09$
Area in tail = $1.0000 - .9990 = .001$
For $z = 3.27$, p-value less than .001
p-value $\leq .01$; reject H_0 and conclude median > 150

4. We need to determine the number of "better" responses and the number of "worse" responses; the sum of the two is the sample size used for the study

$$n = .34(1253) + .29(1253) = 789.4$$

Use the large-sample test and the normal distribution; the value of $n = 789.4$ need not be integer

Use $\quad \begin{aligned} \mu &= .5n = .5(789.4) = 394.7 \\ \sigma &= \sqrt{.25n} = \sqrt{.25(789.4)} = 14.05 \end{aligned}$

Let p = proportion of adults who feel children will have a better future

$H_0: p \le .50$
$H_a: p > .50$

$$x = .34(1253) = 426.0$$

$$z = \frac{x - \mu}{\sigma} = \frac{426.0 - 394.7}{14.05} = 2.23$$

p-value $= 1.0000 - .9871 = .0129$

Reject H_0 and conclude that more adults feel their children will have a better future

6. $z = 2.32$
p-value $= .0204$
Reject H_0

8. $z = 3.76$
p-value ≈ 0
Reject H_0

10. $z = 1.27$
p-value $= .2040$
Do not reject H_0

12. H_0: The populations are identical
H_a: The populations are not identical

Additive			Absolute		Signed
1	**2**	**Difference**	**Value**	**Rank**	**Rank**
20.12	18.05	2.07	2.07	9	+9
23.56	21.77	1.79	1.79	7	+7
22.03	22.57	−.54	.54	3	−3
19.15	17.06	2.09	2.09	10	+10
21.23	21.22	.01	.01	1	+1
24.77	23.80	.97	.97	4	+4
16.16	17.20	−1.04	1.04	5	−5
18.55	14.98	3.57	3.57	12	+12
21.87	20.03	1.84	1.84	8	+8
24.23	21.15	3.08	3.08	11	+11
23.21	22.78	.43	.43	2	+2
25.02	23.70	1.32	1.32	6	+6
					$T = 62$

$$\mu_T = 0$$

$$\sigma_T = \sqrt{\frac{n(n+1)(2n+1)}{6}} = \sqrt{\frac{12(13)(25)}{6}} = 25.5$$

$$z = \frac{T - \mu_T}{\sigma_T} = \frac{62 - 0}{25.5} = 2.43$$

p-value $= 2(1.0000 - .9925) = .0150$

Reject H_0 and conclude that there is a significant difference between the additives

13.

Without Relaxant	With Relaxant	Difference	Rank of Absolute Difference	Signed Rank
15	10	5	9	+9
12	10	2	3	+3
22	12	10	10	+10
8	11	−3	6.5	−6.5
10	9	1	1	+1
7	5	2	3	+3
8	10	−2	3	−3
10	7	3	6.5	+6.5
14	11	3	6.5	+6.5
9	6	3	6.5	+6.5
				$T = 36$

$$\mu_T = 0$$

$$\sigma_T = \sqrt{\frac{n(n+1)(2n+1)}{6}} = \sqrt{\frac{10(11)(21)}{6}} = 19.62$$

$$z = \frac{T - \mu_T}{\sigma_T} = \frac{36}{19.62} = 1.83$$

p-value $= 1.0000 - .9664 = .0336$

Reject H_0 and conclude there is a significant difference in favor of the relaxant

14. $z = 2.29$
p-value $= .0220$
Reject H_0

16. $z = 2.62$
p-value $= .0088$
Reject H_0

18. Rank the combined samples and find rank sum for each sample; this is a small-sample test because $n_1 = 7$ and $n_2 = 9$

Additive 1		Additive 2	
MPG	**Rank**	**MPG**	**Rank**
17.3	2	18.7	8.5
18.4	6	17.8	4
19.1	10	21.3	15
16.7	1	21.0	14
18.2	5	22.1	16
18.6	7	18.7	8.5
17.5	3	19.8	11
	34	20.7	13
		20.2	12
			102

$T = 34$

With $\alpha = .05$, $n_1 = 7$, and $n_2 = 9$

$$T_L = 41 \text{ and } T_U = 7(7 + 9 + 1) - 41 = 78$$

Because $T = 34 < 41$, reject H_0 and conclude that there is a significant difference in gasoline mileage

19. a.

Public Accountant	Rank	Financial Planner	Rank
35.2	5	34.0	2
43.8	19	34.2	3
41.3	16	38.1	10
43.2	18	40.9	15
39.2	13	36.9	8.5
40.0	14	38.6	11
35.9	6	34.7	4
44.5	20	38.9	12
41.7	17	36.8	7
36.9	8.5	33.9	1
	136.5		73.5

$$\mu_T = \frac{1}{2} n_1(n_1 + n_2 + 1) = \frac{1}{2}(10)(10 + 10 + 1) = 105$$

$$\sigma_T = \sqrt{\frac{1}{12} n_1 n_2(n_1 + n_2 + 1)} = \sqrt{\frac{1}{12}(10)(10)(10 + 10 + 1)}$$
$$= 13.23$$
$$T = 136.5$$

$$z = \frac{136.5 - 105}{13.23} = 2.38$$

p-value $= 2(1.0000 - .9913) = .0174$

Reject H_0 and conclude that salaries differ significantly for the two professions

b. Public Accountant $40,200
Financial Planner $36,700

20. a. Men 49.9, Women 35.4
b. $T = 36$, $T_L = 37$
Reject H_0

22. $z = 2.77$
p-value $= .0056$
Reject H_0

24. $z = -.25$
p-value $= .8026$
Do not reject H_0

26. Rankings:

Product A	Product B	Product C
4	11	7
8	14	2
10	15	1
3	12	6
9	13	5
34	65	21

$$W = \frac{12}{(15)(16)}\left[\frac{34^2}{5} + \frac{65^2}{5} + \frac{21^2}{5}\right] - 3(15 + 1)$$
$$= 58.22 - 48 = 10.22 \quad (df = 2)$$

p-value between .005 and .01
Actual p-value $= .006$
Reject H_0 and conclude the ratings for the products differ

28. Rankings:

Swimming	Tennis	Cycling
8	9	5
4	14	1
11	13	3
6	10	7
12	15	2
41	61	18

$$W = \frac{12}{15(15 + 1)}\left[\frac{41^2}{5} + \frac{61^2}{5} + \frac{18^2}{5}\right] - 3(15 + 1)$$
$$= 9.26 \quad (df = 2)$$

p-value between .005 and .01

Reject H_0 and conclude that activities differ

30. $W = 8.03$; $df = 3$
p-value between .025 and .05
Reject H_0

32. a. $\Sigma d_i^2 = 52$
$$r_s = 1 - \frac{6\Sigma d_i^2}{n(n^2 - 1)} = 1 - \frac{6(52)}{10(99)} = .68$$

b. $\sigma_{r_s} = \sqrt{\frac{1}{n-1}} = \sqrt{\frac{1}{9}} = .33$

$$z = \frac{r_s - 0}{\sigma_{r_s}} = \frac{.68}{.33} = 2.05$$

p-value $= 2(1.000 - .9798) = .0404$

Reject H_0 and conclude that significant rank correlation exists

34. $\Sigma d_i^2 = 250$
$$r_s = 1 - \frac{6\Sigma d_i^2}{n(n^2 - 1)} = 1 - \frac{6(250)}{11(120)} = -.136$$

$$\sigma_{r_s} = \sqrt{\frac{1}{n-1}} = \sqrt{\frac{1}{10}} = .32$$

$$z = \frac{r_s - 0}{\sigma_{r_s}} = \frac{-.136}{.32} = -.43$$

p-value $= 2(.3336) = .6672$

Do not reject H_0; we cannot conclude that there is a significant relationship between the rankings

36. $r_s = -.71$, $z = -2.13$
p-value $= .0332$
Reject H_0

38. $z = -3.17$
p-value less than .002
Reject H_0

40. $z = -2.59$
p-value = .0096
Reject H_0

42. $z = -2.97$
p-value = .003
Reject H_0

44. $W = 12.61$; $df = 2$
p-value between .01 and .025
Reject H_0

46. $r_s = .76$, $z = 2.83$
p-value = .0046
Reject H_0

Chapter 18

2. a. 5.42
b. UCL = 6.09, LCL = 4.75

4. R chart:
UCL = $\bar{R}D_4 = 1.6(1.864) = 2.98$
LCL = $\bar{R}D_3 = 1.6(.136) = .22$
$\bar{x}$ chart:
UCL = $\bar{\bar{x}} + A_2\bar{R} = 28.5 + .373(1.6) = 29.10$
LCL = $\bar{\bar{x}} - A_2\bar{R} = 28.5 - .373(1.6) = 27.90$

6. 20.01, .082

8. a. .0470
b. UCL = .0989, LCL = −.0049 (use LCL = 0)
c. $\bar{p} = .08$; in control
d. UCL = 14.826, LCL = −0.726 (use LCL = 0)
Process is out of control if more than 14 defective
e. In control with 12 defective
f. np chart

10. $f(x) = \dfrac{n!}{x!(n-x)!}p^x(1-p)^{n-x}$

When $p = .02$, the probability of accepting the lot is

$f(0) = \dfrac{25!}{0!(25-0)!}(.02)^0(1-.02)^{25} = .6035$

When $p = .06$, the probability of accepting the lot is

$f(0) = \dfrac{25!}{0!(25-0)!}(.06)^0(1-.06)^{25} = .2129$

12. $p_0 = .02$; producer's risk = .0599
$p_0 = .06$; producer's risk = .3396
Producer's risk decreases as the acceptance criterion c is increased

14. $n = 20$, $c = 3$

16. a. 95.4
b. UCL = 96.07, LCL = 94.73
c. No

18.

	R Chart	$\bar{x}$ Chart
UCL	4.23	6.57
LCL	0	4.27

Estimate of standard deviation = .86

20.

	R Chart	$\bar{x}$ Chart
UCL	.1121	3.112
LCL	0	3.051

22. a. UCL = .0817, LCL = −.0017 (use LCL = 0)

24. a. .03
b. $\beta = .0802$

Chapter 19

1. a.

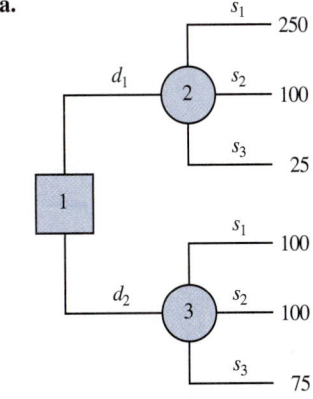

b. $EV(d_1) = .65(250) + .15(100) + .20(25) = 182.5$
$EV(d_2) = .65(100) + .15(100) + .20(75) = 95$
The optimal decision is d_1

2. a. d_1; $EV(d_1) = 11.3$
b. d_4; $EV(d_4) = 9.5$

3. a. EV(own staff) = .2(650) + .5(650) + .3(600)
$= 635$
EV(outside vendor) = .2(900) + .5(600)
$+ .3(300) = 570$
EV(combination) = .2(800) + .5(650) + .3(500)
$= 635$
Optimal decision: Hire an outside vendor with an expected cost of $570,000
b. EVwPI = .2(650) + .5(600) + .3(300)
$= 520$
EVPI = $|520 - 570| = 50$, or $50,000

4. b. Discount; EV = 565
c. Full Price; EV = 670

6. c. Chardonnay only; EV = 42.5
d. Both grapes; EV = 46.4
e. Both grapes; EV = 39.6

8. a.

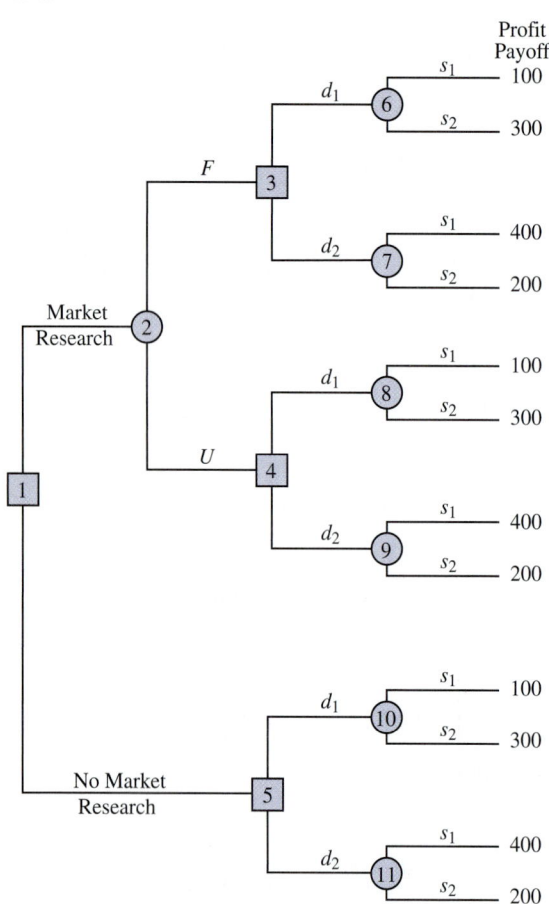

Profit
Payoff

b. EV (node 6) $= .57(100) + .43(300) = 186$
EV (node 7) $= .57(400) + .43(200) = 314$
EV (node 8) $= .18(100) + .82(300) = 264$
EV (node 9) $= .18(400) + .82(200) = 236$
EV (node 10) $= .40(100) + .60(300) = 220$
EV (node 11) $= .40(400) + .60(200) = 280$

EV (node 3) $= \text{Max}(186,314) = 314$ d_2
EV (node 4) $= \text{Max}(264,236) = 264$ d_1
EV (node 5) $= \text{Max}(220,280) = 280$ d_2

EV (node 2) $= .56(314) + .44(264) = 292$
EV (node 1) $= \text{Max}(292,280) = 292$

∴ Market Research
   If Favorable, decision d_2
   If Unfavorable, decision d_1

10. a. $5000 - 200 - 2000 - 150 = 2650$
$3000 - 200 - 2000 - 150 = 650$

b. Expected values at nodes
8: 2350	5: 2350	9: 1100
6: 1150	10: 2000	7: 2000
4: 1870	3: 2000	2: 1560
1: 1560		

c. Cost would have to decrease by at least $130,000

12. b. d_1, 1250
  c. 1700
  d. If N, d_1
     If U, d_2; 1666

14.

State of Nature	$P(s_j)$	$P(I\|s_j)$	$P(I \cap s_j)$	$P(s_j\|I)$
s_1	.2	.10	.020	.1905
s_2	.5	.05	.025	.2381
s_3	.3	.20	.060	.5714
	1.0		$P(I) = .105$	1.0000

16. a. .695, .215, .090
    .98, .02
    .79, .21
    .00, 1.00
  c. If C, Expressway
    If O, Expressway
    If R, Queen City
    26.6 minutes

Excel provides a wealth of functions for data management and statistical analysis. If we know what function is needed, and how to use it, we can simply enter the function into the appropriate worksheet cell. However, if we are not sure what functions are available to accomplish a task or are not sure how to use a particular function, Excel can provide assistance.

Finding the Right Excel Function

*In earlier versions of Excel, the **Paste Function** dialog box serves the same purpose as the **Insert Function** dialog box in Excel 2003.*

To identify the functions available in Excel, select the **Insert** menu and then choose **Function** from the list of options. Alternatively, select the f_x button on the formula bar. Either approach provides the **Insert Function** dialog box shown in Figure 1.

The **Search for a function** box at the top of the Insert Function dialog box enables us to type a brief description of what we want to do. After doing so and clicking **Go**, Excel will search for and display, in the **Select a function** box, the functions that may accomplish our task. In many situations, however, we may want to browse through an entire category of functions to see what is available. For this task, the **Or select a category** box is helpful. It contains a drop-down list of several categories of functions provided by Excel. Figure 1 shows that we selected the **Statistical** category. As a result, Excel's statistical functions ap-

FIGURE 1 INSERT FUNCTION DIALOG BOX

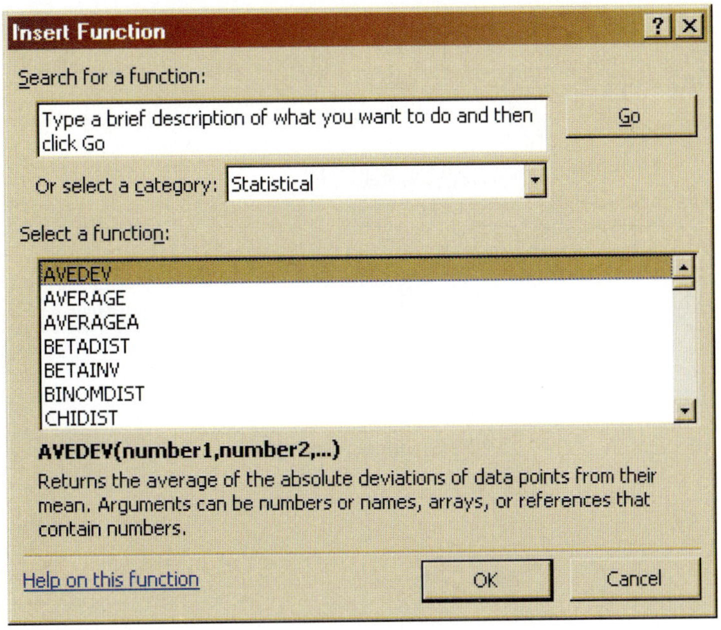

pear in alphabetic order in the Select a function box. We see the AVEDEV function listed first, followed by the AVERAGE function, and so on.

The AVEDEV function is highlighted in Figure 1, indicating it is the function currently selected. The proper syntax for the function and a brief description of the function appear below the Select a function box. We can scroll through the list in the Select a function box to display the syntax and a brief description for each of the statistical functions available. For instance, scrolling down farther, we select the COUNTIF function. See Figure 2. Note that COUNTIF is now highlighted, and that immediately below the Select a function box we see **COUNTIF(range,criteria)**, which indicates that the COUNTIF function contains two arguments, range and criteria. In addition, we see that the description of the COUNTIF function is "Counts the number of cells within a range that meet the given condition."

*In earlier versions of Excel, a similar dialog box will appear. It serves the same purpose as the **Function Arguments** dialog box in Excel 2003.*

If the function selected (highlighted) is the one we want to use, we click **OK**; the **Function Arguments** dialog box then appears. The Function Arguments dialog box for the COUNTIF function is shown in Figure 3. This dialog box assists in creating the appropriate arguments for the function selected. When finished entering the arguments, we click **OK**; Excel then inserts the function into a worksheet cell.

Inserting a Function into a Worksheet Cell

We will now show how to use the Insert Function and Function Arguments dialog boxes to select a function, develop its arguments, and insert the function into a worksheet cell.

In Section 2.1, we used Excel's COUNTIF function to construct a frequency distribution for soft drink purchases. Figure 4 displays an Excel worksheet containing the soft drink

FIGURE 2   DESCRIPTION OF THE COUNTIF FUNCTION IN THE INSERT FUNCTION DIALOG BOX

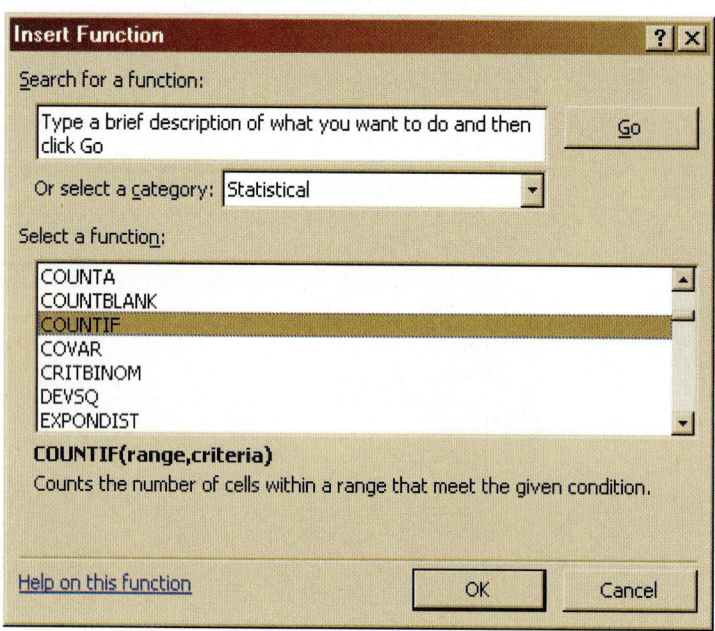

FIGURE 3   FUNCTION ARGUMENTS DIALOG BOX FOR THE COUNTIF FUNCTION

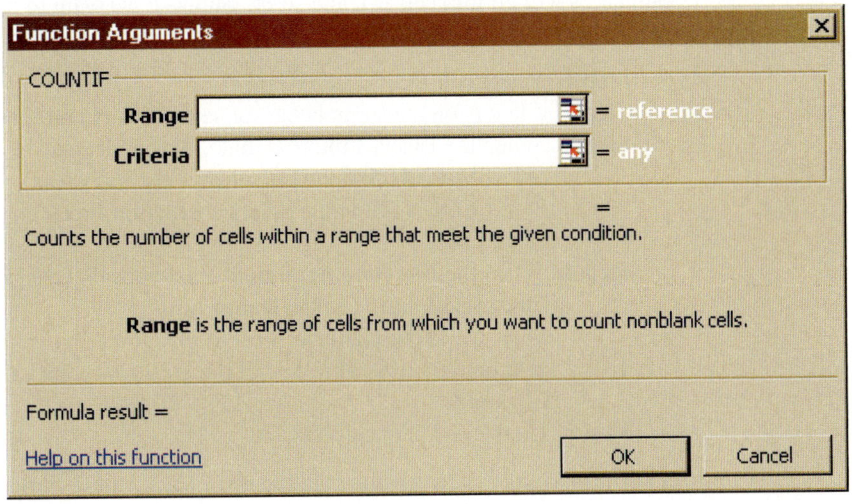

Function Arguments   ×

COUNTIF

Range [   ] 🔢 = reference

Criteria [   ] 🔢 = any

=

Counts the number of cells within a range that meet the given condition.

Range is the range of cells from which you want to count nonblank cells.

Formula result =

Help on this function   OK   Cancel

FIGURE 4   EXCEL WORKSHEET WITH SOFT DRINK DATA AND LABELS FOR THE
FREQUENCY DISTRIBUTION WE WOULD LIKE TO CONSTRUCT

CD file

SoftDrink

*Note: Rows 11–44
are hidden.*

	A	B	C	D	E
1	**Brand Purchased**		**Soft Drink**	**Frequency**	
2	Coke Classic		Coke Classic		
3	Diet Coke		Diet Coke		
4	Pepsi-Cola		Dr. Pepper		
5	Diet Coke		Pepsi-Cola		
6	Coke Classic		Sprite		
7	Coke Classic				
8	Dr. Pepper				
9	Diet Coke				
10	Pepsi-Cola				
45	Pepsi-Cola				
46	Pepsi-Cola				
47	Pepsi-Cola				
48	Coke Classic				
49	Dr. Pepper				
50	Pepsi-Cola				
51	Sprite				
52					

data and labels for the frequency distribution we would like to construct. We see that the frequency of Coke Classic purchases will go into cell D2, the frequency of Diet Coke purchases will go into cell D3, and so on. Suppose we want to use the COUNTIF function to compute the frequencies for these cells and would like some assistance from Excel.

Step 1. Select cell D2

Step 2. Click f_x on the formula bar (or select **Insert** and then choose **Function**)

Step 3. When the **Insert Function** dialog box appears:
Select **Statistical** in the **Or select a category box**
Select **COUNTIF** in the **Select a function box**
Click **OK**

Step 4. When the **Function Arguments** box appears (see Figure 5):
Enter $A$2:$A$51 in the **Range** box
Enter C2 in the **Criteria** box (At this point, the value of the function will appear on the next-to-last line of the dialog box. Its value is 19.)
Click **OK**

Step 5. Copy cell D2 to cells D3:D6

The worksheet then appears as in Figure 6. The formula worksheet is in the background; the value worksheet appears in the foreground. The formula worksheet shows that the COUNTIF function was inserted into cell D2. We copied the contents of cell D2 into cells D3:D6. The value worksheet shows the proper class frequencies as computed.

We illustrated the use of Excel's capability to provide assistance in using the COUNTIF function. The procedure is similar for all Excel functions. This capability is especially helpful if you do not know what function to use or forget the proper name and/or syntax for a function.

FIGURE 5 COMPLETED FUNCTION ARGUMENTS DIALOG BOX
FOR THE COUNTIF FUNCTION

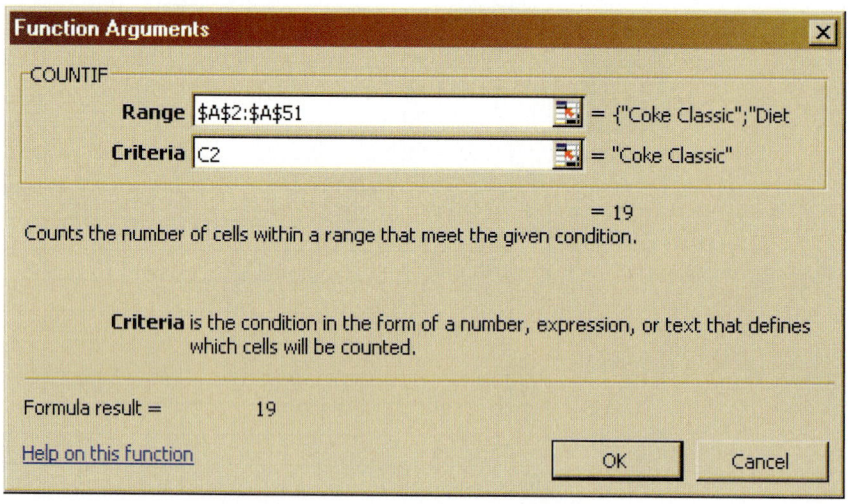

FIGURE 6   EXCEL WORKSHEET SHOWING THE USE OF EXCEL'S COUNTIF FUNCTION
TO CONSTRUCT A FREQUENCY DISTRIBUTION

	A	B	C	D	E
1	**Brand Purchased**		**Soft Drink**	**Frequency**	
2	Coke Classic		Coke Classic	=COUNTIF($A$2:$A$51,C2)	
3	Diet Coke		Diet Coke	=COUNTIF($A$2:$A$51,C3)	
4	Pepsi-Cola		Dr. Pepper	=COUNTIF($A$2:$A$51,C4)	
5	Diet Coke		Pepsi-Cola	=COUNTIF($A$2:$A$51,C5)	
6	Coke Classic		Sprite	=COUNTIF($A$2:$A$51,C6)	
7	Coke Classic				
8	Dr. Pepper				
9	Diet Coke				
10	Pepsi-Cola				
45	Pepsi-Cola				
46	Pepsi-Cola				
47	Pepsi-Cola				
48	Coke Classic				
49	Dr. Pepper				
50	Pepsi-Cola				
51	Sprite				
52					

*Note: Rows 11–44
are hidden.*

	A	B	C	D	E
1	**Brand Purchased**		**Soft Drink**	**Frequency**	
2	Coke Classic		Coke Classic	19	
3	Diet Coke		Diet Coke	8	
4	Pepsi-Cola		Dr. Pepper	5	
5	Diet Coke		Pepsi-Cola	13	
6	Coke Classic		Sprite	5	
7	Coke Classic				
8	Dr. Pepper				
9	Diet Coke				
10	Pepsi-Cola				
45	Pepsi-Cola				
46	Pepsi-Cola				
47	Pepsi-Cola				
48	Coke Classic				
49	Dr. Pepper				
50	Pepsi-Cola				
51	Sprite				
52					

Index

Note: Chapter 20 can be found on the CD-ROM included with this book. Index entries found in this chapter are denoted by chapter number 20, hyphen, and page number.

A

Acceptance criterion, 819
Acceptance sampling, 800, 817–819
  computing probability of accepting a lot, 819–821
  example problem, 819
Acceptance sampling plans, 819
  multiple, 823–824
  selecting, 821–823
Accounting, statistical applications in, 3
Addition law, 170–173
Adjusted multiple coefficient of determination, 662–663
Alliance Data Systems (Statistics in Practice), 560
Alpha to enter, 728
Alpha to remove, 728
Alternative hypothesis, 346–349
Analysis of variance (ANOVA)
  assumptions for, 500
  conceptual overview, 500–502
  interpretation of Excel output, 598–599
  introduction to, 498–499
  multiple comparison procedures, 513
    Fisher's LSD, 513–515
    Type I error rates, 516–517
  multiple regression approach to, 741–744
  testing for equality of *k* population means, 502–503
    ANOVA table, 507
    between-treatments estimate of population variance, 503–504
    comparing variance estimates: *F* test, 505–506
    Excel used for, 507–509
    within-treatments estimate of population variance, 504–505
  See also Completely randomized design; Factorial experiments; Randomized block design
ANOVA
  See Analysis of variance (ANOVA)
ANOVA table, 507
  completely randomized design, 522
  for significance testing in regression, 591–592
Area
  as measure of probability, 241–243
  sampling, 300
Assignable causes, 800

Association between two variables, 123
  correlation coefficient, 127–128
    Excel computation of, 130–131
    interpretation of, 128–129
  covariance, 123–125
    Excel computation of, 130–131
    interpretation of, 125–127
Attributes control charts, 812
Attributes sampling plans, 824–825
Autocorrelation, 734
  Durbin-Watson test and, 735–740
Average
  See Mean

B

Backward elimination, 729
  Excel used for, 729–731
Baldrige, Malcolm, 798
Bar graph, 12–13, 34
  using Excel, 34–36
  using SWStat+, 27
Basic requirements for assigning probabilities, 160
Bayes, Thomas (Reverend), 185
Bayes' theorem, 162, 183–186, 853
  branch probabilities computed using, 853–856
  posterior probabilities computed with Excel, 187–188
  tabular approach, 186–187
Bernoulli, Jakob, 214
Bernoulli process, 214
Best-subsets regression, 731–732
Between-treatments estimate of population variance, 501, 503–504, 521
Bimodal data, 91
Binomial experiment, 214–219
Binomial probability distribution, 213, 214
  acceptance sampling, 819–820, 824
  binomial experiment, 214–219
  Excel computation of, 219–221
  expected value for, 221–222
  variance for, 221–222
Binomial probability function, 215, 218
Blocking, 528
Blocks, 528
Bonferroni adjustment, 516
Bound on the sampling error, 20-7
Box plot, 119–120
  using SWStat+, 149–152

Branches, 833
Branch probabilities computed using Bayes' theorem, 853–856
Burke Marketing Services, Inc. (Statistics in Practice), 498
Business Week (Statistics in Practice), 2
Butler, Marty, 346

C

Categorical data, 7
Census, 14, 20-5
Central limit theorem, 286–288
Chance events, 832
Chance nodes, 833
Chebyshiev's theorem, 114, 115–116
Chi-square distribution, 441–445
Cinergy (Statistics in Practice), 20-2
Citibank (Statistics in Practice), 199
Classes for frequency distribution, 40–41, 53
Classical method of assigning probabilities, 160–161, 167
Class limits, 40–41
Class midpoint, 41
Clemance, Philip, 560
Clusters, 299, 20-26
Cluster sampling, 299–300
  See also Sample surveys
Cochran, William G., 20-12
Coefficient of determination, 576–580
  adjusted multiple, 662–663
  correlation coefficient, 580–582
  Excel computation of, 580
  multiple, 661–663
Coefficient of variation, 106
Coefficients, interpretation of, 656–657
Colgate-Palmolive Company (Statistics in Practice), 29
Collectively exhaustive, 186
Combinations, 159
Common causes, 800–801
Comparisonwise Type I error rate, 516
Complement of an event, 169–170
Complete block design, 531
Completely randomized design, 519, 521
  ANOVA table, 522
  between-treatments estimate of population variance, 521
  comparing variance estimates: *F* test, 522
  Excel used with, 522–523, 524
  pairwise comparisons, 523–524

Completely randomized design (*cont.*)
  within-treatments estimate of population variance, 521–522
Conditional probability, 175–179, 853
  independent events, 179
  multiplication law, 179–180
Confidence coefficient, 311
Confidence interval, 311, 602
  for β_1, 589–590
  Excel used for, 395–397, 606–608
  mean value of *y*, 602–604
  multiple regression, 673–674
  SWStat+ used for, 647, 701
Confidence level, 311
Consequences, 832
Consumer's risk, 818
Contingency table, 474
Continuous probability distributions, 239–240
  exponential probability distribution, 259–260
    computing probabilities for, 260–261
    Excel computation of, 261–262
    Poisson and, 261
  normal probability distribution, 244
    computing probabilities for, 251–252
    example problem, 252–254
    Excel computation of, 254–256
    normal curve, 244–246
    standard, 246–251
  uniform probability distribution, 240–241
    area as measure of probability, 241–243
Continuous quantitative data, 8
Continuous random variables, 201
Control charts, 801–802
  See also Statistical methods for quality control
Convenience sampling, 301, 20-4
Correlation
  serial, 734
  significance testing with, 644–645
Correlation coefficient, 127–128
  Excel computation of, 130–131
  interpretation of, 128–129
  Pearson product moment, 127–128
  simple linear regression, 580–582
Counting rules
  for combinations, 159
  for multiple-step experiments, 156–159
  for permutations, 159–160
Covariance, 123–125
  Excel computation of, 130–131
  interpretation of, 125–127
Cravens, David W. (Dr.), 724
Cravens data, 724–727
Critical value, 354
  one-tailed test, 356–357
  two-tailed test, 360
Crosby, Philip B., 797
Cross-sectional data, 7–8
Crosstabulations, 61–63
  Excel construction of, 64–67
  Simpson's paradox, 67–68

Cumulative distributions, 46–49
Cumulative frequency distributions, 46–49
Cumulative percent frequency distributions, 48, 49
Cumulative relative frequency distributions, 48, 49
Cunningham, Keith, 307
Curvilinear relationships, modeling, 704–706

D

Data acquisition errors, 12
Data and statistics, 2–3
  applications in business and economics, 3–5
  data, 5
    cross-sectional and time series, 7–8
    elements, 5
    observations, 6
    qualitative and quantitative, 7, 30
    variables, 6
  data set, 5
  data sources
    data acquisition errors, 12
    existing, 8–9, 10
    statistical studies, 9, 11–12
  descriptive statistics, 12–14
  scales of measurement, 6–7, 755–756
  statistical analysis using Excel, 16–19
  statistical inference, 14–15
Data collection, 520
Data sources
  See Data and statistics
Decision analysis, 832
  branch probabilities computed using Bayes' theorem, 853–856
  with probabilities, 834
    expected value approach, 834–836
    expected value of perfect information, 836–838
  problem formulation, 832–833
    decision trees, 833–834
    payoff tables, 833
  with sample information, 842
    decision strategy, 844, 846–847
    decision tree, 843–844, 845
    expected value of sample information, 847–849
  TreePlan used for, 860–865
Decision nodes, 833
Decision strategy, 844, 846–847
Decision trees, 833–834, 843–844, 845
de Fermat, Pierre, 154
Degrees of freedom, 316
Deming, W. Edwards (Dr.), 797
de Moivre, Abraham, 244
Dependent events, 179
Dependent variable, 561, 666
Descriptive statistics, 12–14
  Excel's tool for, 106–108
  See also Numerical measures of descriptive statistics; Tabular and graphical methods of descriptive statistics

Deviation about the mean, 103–104, 105
Discrete probability distributions, 199, 202–205
  binomial probability distribution, 213
    binomial experiment, 214–219
    Excel computation of, 219–221
    expected value for, 221–222
    variance for, 221–222
  expected value, 208
    Excel computation of, 209–210
  hypergeometric probability distribution, 229–231
    Excel computation of, 231
  Poisson probability distribution, 224
    Excel computation of, 226–228
    experiment properties, 224
    exponential and, 261
    length or distance interval example, 225–226
    time interval example, 224–225
  random variables, 199–200
    continuous, 201
    discrete, 200
  standard deviation, 209
    Excel computation of, 209–210
  variance, 208–209
    Excel computation of, 209–210
Discrete probability function, required conditions for, 203
Discrete quantitative data, 8
Discrete random variables, 200
Discrete uniform probability distribution, 204
Dispersion
  See Variability measures
Distance intervals, Poisson probability distribution and, 225–226
Distribution shape, 111–112
Double-blind study, 521
Dow Chemical (Statistics in Practice), 796
Dummy variable, 676
Durbin-Watson test, 734
  autocorrelation and, 735–740

E

Economics, statistical applications in, 4–5
Elements, 5
  in sample survey, 20-2, 20-3
Empirical rule, 114–115
Error
  data acquisition, 12
  margin of, 307–312, 317–319
  mean square, 587
  mean square due to, 504, 521
  nonsampling, 20-5
  sampling, 20-5–20-6, 20-7
  standard, 286, 295, 20-6
  sum of squares due to, 504, 522
  Type I, 349–351
  Type II, 349–351

Estimated multiple regression equation, 650–651
  for estimation and prediction, 673–674
  Excel used for, 655–656
Estimated regression equation, 562–564
  for confidence interval estimate of mean value of y, 602–604
  Excel used for, 568–570
  Excel used for confidence and prediction interval estimates, 606–608
  interpretation of Excel output, 598
  for interval estimation, 602
  for point estimation, 602
  for prediction interval estimate of individual value of y, 604–606
Estimated regression line, 563
Estimate of σ^2, 587
Events, 165
  complement of, 169–170
  dependent, 179
  independent, 179, 180
  intersection of, 171
  mutually exclusive, 173, 180
  probabilities of, 165–167
  union of, 170–171
Excel
  ANOVA
    completely randomized design, 522–523, 524
    equality of k population means, 507–509
    factorial experiments, 539, 541–543
    randomized block design, 532–533
  backward elimination, 729–731
  bar graphs, 34–36
  binomial probabilities, 219–221
  cluster sampling, 20-31–20-32
  coefficient of determination, 580
  confidence intervals
    difference between two population means: σ_1 and σ_2 known, 395–397
    difference between two population means: σ_1 and σ_2 unknown, 405–407
    difference between two population proportions, 424–426
    population variance, 445–446
    simple linear regression, 606–608
  correlation coefficient, 130–131
  covariance, 130–131
  crosstabulations, 64–67
  Descriptive Statistics tool, 106–108
  estimated multiple regression equation, 655–656
  estimated regression equation, 568–570
  expected value, 209–210
  exponential probabilities, 261–262
  frequency distributions, 31–32, 41–42, 49–52
    percent, 33
    relative, 33
  goodness of fit test
    multinomial population, 470–471
  normal distribution, 489
  Poisson distribution, 485
histograms, 44–46, 49–52
hypergeometric probabilities, 231
hypothesis testing
  difference between two population means: σ_1 and σ_2 known, 399–400
  difference between two population means: σ_1 and σ_2 unknown, 409–411
  difference between two population means: matched samples, 417–419
  difference between two population proportions, 427–429
  population mean: σ known, 361–362
  population mean: σ unknown, 372–374
  population proportion, 380–382
  population variance, 449–450
  population variances, two, 458–459
interval estimation
  population mean: σ known, 312–314
  population mean: σ unknown, 320–321
  population proportion, 330–332
Kruskal-Wallis test, 782–783
Mann-Whitney-Wilcoxon rank sum test, 777
mean, 92–93
median, 92–93
mode, 92–93
normal probabilities, 254–256
percentiles, 95–97
pie charts, 34–36
Poisson probabilities, 226–228
population mean, 20-16–20-18
population proportion, 20-21
population total, 20-19
posterior probabilities, 187–188
prediction intervals, 606–608
quartiles, 95–97
R chart, 809–812
Regression tool
  example problem, 596–597
  interpretation of ANOVA output, 598–599
  interpretation of estimated regression equation output, 598
  interpretation of regression statistics output, 599
residual analysis, 614–615, 616, 618, 685–686
sample standard deviation, 106, 107
sample variance, 106, 107
scatter diagrams, 70–72, 568–570
sign test
  hypothesis test about a median, 763
  large-sample case, 761–762
  small-sample case, 759–760
simple random sampling, 272–276, 20-9–20-12
Spearman rank correlation coefficient, 788
standard deviation, 209–210
statistical analysis, 16–19
test of independence, 477–478
  trendlines, 70–72
  variance, 209–210
  Wilcoxon signed rank test, 768–769
  $\bar{x}$ chart, 809–812
Expected value (EV), 835
  of binomial probability distribution, 221–222
  as decision making approach, 834–836
  of discrete random variable, 208
  Excel computation of, 209–210
  of $\bar{p}$, 294–295
  of perfect information, 836–838
  with perfect information, 837
  without perfect information, 837
  of sample information, 847–849
  of $\bar{x}$, 284–285
Expected value approach, 834–836
Expected value of perfect information (EVPI), 836–838
Expected value of sample information (EVSI), 847–849
Experiment, 155–160
  binomial, 214–219
  multinomial, 467–471
  Poisson, 224
  random, 163
  single-factor, 519
Experimental design
  data collection, 520
  introduction to, 518–519
  multiple regression approach to, 741–744
  See also Completely randomized design; Factorial experiments; Randomized block design
Experimental statistical studies, 9, 11
Experimental units, 519
Experimentwise Type I error rate, 516
Exploratory data analysis, 56
  box plot, 119–120
    using SWStat+, 149–152
  five-number summary, 118–119
  stem-and-leaf display, 56–59
Exponential probability distribution, 259–260
  computing probabilities for, 260–261
  Excel computation of, 261–262
  Poisson and, 261

F

F distribution, 453–457
F test, 453–457, 505–506, 522
  Excel used for, 458–459
  as significance test, 590–592, 666–669
  interpretation of Excel output, 599
Factor, 499, 519
Factorial, 159, 536
Factorial experiments, 535–537
  ANOVA procedure, 537–538
  computations and conclusions, 538–539, 540
  Excel used for, 539, 541–543
Factor of interest, 528

Feigenbaum, A. V., 797
Fightmaster, Rodney, 755
Finance, statistical applications in, 3–4
Finite population, sampling from, 272–276
Finite population correction factor, 285
Fisher, Ronald Alymer (Sir), 498, 519
Fisher's LSD, 513–515
Fisons Corporation (Statistics in Practice), 392
Five-number summary, 118–119
Food Lion (Statistics in Practice), 307
Foreman, Art, 440
Formula worksheet, 18
Forward selection, 729
Fowle, William R., 29
Frame, 20-3
Frequency distributions, 30
  cumulative, 46–49
  histogram, 43–44
    Excel used for, 44–46, 49–52
  percent, 32
    cumulative, 48, 49
    Excel used for, 33
  qualitative data, 30–31
    Excel used for, 31–32
  quantitative data, 39–41
    Excel used for, 41–42, 49–52
  relative, 32
    cumulative, 48, 49
    Excel used for, 33

G

Galton, Francis (Sir), 561
Gauss, Carl Friedrich, 566
General linear model, 704
  See also Regression analysis: model building
Goodness of fit test, 467
  multinomial population, 467–470
    Excel used for, 470–471
  normal distribution, 485–489
    Excel used for, 489
  Poisson distribution, 481–485
    Excel used for, 485
Gosset, William Sealy, 316
Griggs, Bill, 649
Grouped data, 134–137

H

Harkey, Bobby, 307
Haskell, Michael, 154
High leverage points, 626
Histogram, 12–14, 43–44
  Excel construction of, 44–46, 49–52
Hypergeometric probability distribution, 229–231
  Excel computation of, 231
Hypergeometric probability function, 229–230

Hypothesis tests, 346–347
  interval estimation and, 364–365
  null and alternative hypotheses, 346–347
    summary of forms, 348–349
    testing for decision-making, 348
    testing research hypotheses, 347
    testing validity of claim, 347–348
  population mean: σ known, 352
    Excel used for, 361–362
    one-tailed test, 352–357
    summary and advice, 362–363
    two-tailed test, 358–360
  population mean: σ unknown, 368–369
    Excel used for, 372–374
    one-tailed test, 369–370
    summary and advice, 374–375
    two-tailed test, 370–372
  population median, 762–763
  population proportion, 378–380
    Excel used for, 380–382
  Type I errors, 349–351
  Type II errors, 349–351
  See also Statistical inference
Hyrnick, M. S., 831

I

Incomplete block design, 531
Independence, test of, 473–478
Independent events, 179, 180
Independent samples, 415
Independent simple random samples, 393
Independent variable, 561, 670
  qualitative, 675
Indicator variable, 676
Individual significance, 666
Individual value of y, 602
  prediction interval estimate of, 604–606
Inference
  See Statistical inference
Infinite population, sampling from, 276–277
Influential observations, 625–626
Interaction, 537, 706–710
International Paper (Statistics in Practice), 649
Interquartile range (IQR), 102
Intersection of events, 171
Interval estimation, 307–308
  estimated regression equation for, 602
  hypothesis testing and, 364–365
  of population mean, 308
  of population mean: σ known, 308
    Excel construction of, 312–314
    margin of error, 308–312
    practical advice, 314
  of population mean: σ unknown, 316–317
    Excel construction of, 320–321
    margin of error, 317–319
    practical advice, 321
    small sample size, 321–323
  of population proportion, 308, 329–330
    Excel construction of, 330–332
    sample size determination, 332–334

procedure summary, 323
sample size determination, 326–327
See also Statistical inference
Interval scale, 6–7, 756
Ishikawa, Karou, 797
ISO 9000, 798
ith residual, 576

J

John Morrell & Company (Statistics in Practice), 346
Joint probability, 176, 855
Joint probability table, 176–177
Judgment sampling, 301, 20-4
Juran, Joseph, 797

K

Kahn, Joel, 239
Karter, Stacey, 199
Kruskal-Wallis test, 780–782
  Excel used for, 782–783

L

Leaf unit, 59
Least squares method
  Excel used for, 568–570
  formula derivation, 642–644
  multiple regression, 651–652
  simple linear regression, 564–568
Ledman, Dale, 440
Length intervals, Poisson probability distribution and, 225–226
Level of significance, 311, 350
  observed, 356
Leverage of observation i, 615, 626
Location measures
  mean, 89–90
    Excel computation of, 92–93
  median, 90–91
    Excel computation of, 92–93
  mode, 91–92
    Excel computation of, 92–93
  percentiles, 93–94
    Excel computation of, 95–97
  quartiles, 94–95
    Excel computation of, 95–97
  relative
    Chebyshiev's theorem, 114, 115–116
    empirical rule, 114–115
    z-scores, 113
Lot, 817
  computing probability of accepting, 819–821
Lower control limit, 801

M

Madden, Thomas J., 831
Malcolm Baldrige National Quality Award, 797–798

Mann-Whitney test
See Mann-Whitney-Wilcoxon (MWW) rank sum test
Mann-Whitney-Wilcoxon (MWW) rank sum test, 771–772
Excel used for, 777
large-sample case, 775–777
small-sample case, 772–774
Marginal probabilities, 177
Margin of error, 307–308
interval estimate and, 308–312, 317–319
Marketing, statistical applications in, 4
Matched samples, 415–419
McCarthy, John A., 88
Meadwestvaco Corporation (Statistics in Practice), 270
Mean, 14, 89–90
Excel computation of, 92–93
trimmed, 97
weighted, 133–134
See also Population mean; Sample mean
Mean square, 666
Mean square due to error, 504, 521
Mean square due to regression, 590
Mean square due to treatments, 503–504, 521
Mean square error, 587
Mean value of y, 602
confidence interval estimate of, 602–604
Measurement, scales of, 6–7, 755–756
See also Numerical measures of descriptive statistics
Median, 90–91
Excel computation of, 92–93
hypothesis test about, 762–763
Microsoft Excel
See Excel
Mode, 91–92
Excel computation of, 92–93
Model building
See Regression analysis: model building
Monsanto Company (Statistics in Practice), 703
Morton International (Statistics in Practice), 154
Mulitmodal data, 91
Multicollinearity, 670–671
Multinomial population, 467
goodness of fit test, 467–471
Multiple coefficient of determination, 661–663
adjusted, 662–663
Multiple comparison procedures, 513
Fisher's LSD, 513–515
Type I error rates, 516–517
Multiple regression
analysis, 650
estimated multiple regression equation, 650–651
for estimation and prediction, 673–674
Excel used for, 655–656
least squares method, 651–652
coefficient interpretation, 656–657
example problem, 652–654

model, 650
model assumptions, 664–666
multiple coefficient of determination, 661–663
qualitative independent variables, 675
complex, 680–681
example problem, 676–678
interpreting parameters, 678–679
regression equation, 650
residual analysis, 684
residual plot against $\hat{y}$, 684
standardized residual plot against $\hat{y}$, 684–686
significance testing, 666
F test, 666–669
multicollinearity, 670–671
t test, 666, 669
SWStat+ used for, 700–701
See also Regression analysis: model building
Multiple sampling plans, 823–824
Multiplication law, 179–180
Mutually exclusive events, 173, 180
Myerson, Roger, 244

N

Neyman allocation, 20-22
Nodes, 833
Nominal scale, 6, 755
Nonexperimental statistical studies, 11, 518
Nonlinear models that are intrinsically linear, 713–714
Nonparametric methods, 755–756
Kruskal-Wallis test, 780–782
Excel used for, 782–783
Mann-Whitney-Wilcoxon rank sum test, 771–772
Excel used for, 777
large-sample case, 775–777
small-sample case, 772–774
sign test, 757
Excel used for, 759–763
hypothesis test about a median, 762–763
large-sample case, 760–762
small-sample case, 757–760
Spearman rank correlation coefficient, 785–787
Excel used for, 788
test for significant rank correlation, 787–788
Wilcoxon signed rank test, 765–768
Excel used for, 768–769
Nonprobabilistic sampling, 20-4
Nonprobability sampling, 301
Nonsampling error, 20-5
Normal curve, 244–246
Normal equations, 644
Normal probability distribution, 244
computing probabilities for, 251–252
example problem, 252–254
Excel computation of, 254–256

goodness of fit test, 485–489
Excel used for, 489
normal curve, 244–246
standard, 246–252
Normal probability plot, 618–620
Normal scores, 618–620
np chart, 814
Null hypothesis, 346, 347–349
Numerical measures of descriptive statistics, 14, 88–89
association between two variables, 123
correlation coefficient, 127–129
covariance, 123–127
Excel for computing covariance and correlation coefficient, 130–131
distribution shape, 111–112
Excel's Descriptive Statistics tool, 106–108
exploratory data analysis
box plot, 119–120
box plot using SWStat+, 149–152
five-number summary, 118–119
grouped data, 134–137
location
Excel for computing mean, median, and mode, 92–93
Excel for computing percentiles and quartiles, 95–97
mean, 89–90
median, 90–91
mode, 91–92
percentiles, 93–94
quartiles, 94–95
trimmed mean, 97
outliers, 115
relative location
Chebyshiev's theorem, 114, 115–116
empirical rule, 114–115
z-scores, 113
skewness, 111–112
variability, 101–102
coefficient of variation, 106
Excel for computing variance and standard deviation, 106, 107
interquartile range, 102
range, 102
standard deviation, 104–105, 108
variance, 103–104, 109
weighted mean, 133–134

O

Observational statistical studies, 11
Observational studies, 518
Observations, 6, 8
Observed level of significance, 356
Ogive, 48–49
Ohio Edison Company (Statistics in Practice), 831
One-tailed test, 352
population mean: σ known, 352–357
population mean: σ unknown, 369–370
Open-end class, 53

Operating characteristic (OC) curve, 821
Ordinal scale, 6, 756
Outliers, 115, 119, 622–624
Overall sample mean, 501
Overall significance, 666
Overall Type I error rate, 516

P

$\bar{p}$
  expected value of, 294–295
  sampling distribution of, 294
    form, 295–296
      practical value, 296–297
  standard deviation of, 295
p chart, 812–814
p-value, 354
  one-tailed test, 354–356
  two-tailed test, 359–360
Pairwise comparisons, 523–524
Parameters, 270
  population, 89, 270–271
Parametric methods, 755–756
Pareto, Vilfredo, 34
Pareto diagram, 34
Partitioning, 507
Pascal, Blaise, 154
Payoff, 833
Payoff tables, 833
Pearson, Karl, 561
Pearson product moment correlation
  coefficient
    population data, 128
    sample data, 127
Percent frequency distributions, 32, 43
  cumulative, 48, 49
  Excel construction of, 33
Percentiles, 93–94
Perfect information, 836–837
  expected value of, 836–838
Permutations, 159–160
Pie chart, 34
  using Excel, 34–36
Point estimate, 279
Point estimation, 278–280
  estimated regression equation
    for, 602
Point estimator, 89, 279
Poisson, Siméon, 224
Poisson probability distribution, 224
  Excel computation of, 226–228
  experiment properties, 224
  exponential and, 261
  goodness of fit test, 481–485
    Excel used for, 485
  length or distance interval example,
    225–226
  time interval example, 224–225
Poisson probability function, 224
Pooled estimator of p, 426
Pooled sample variance, 411
Pooled treatments estimate, 501

Population, 14, 270
  finite, sampling from, 272–276
  infinite, sampling from, 276–277
  multinomial, 467
  sampled, 20-3
  in sample survey, 20-2, 20-3
  target, 20-3
Population correlation coefficient, 128
Population covariance, 125
Population mean, 90, 271
  cluster sampling, 20-28–20-29
  simple random sampling, 20-6–20-7
  stratified simple random sampling,
    20-15–20-18
  See also Statistical inference
Population parameters, 89, 270–271
Population proportion, 271
  cluster sampling, 20-30–20-31
  hypothesis testing and, 378–382
  inference about difference between two,
    422–429
  interval estimation and, 308, 329–334
  simple random sampling, 20-9
  stratified simple random sampling,
    20-19–20-21
Population total
  cluster sampling, 20-29–20-30
  simple random sampling, 20-7–20-8
  stratified simple random sampling,
    20-18–20-19
Population variance, 103
  See also Statistical inference
Posterior (revised) probabilities, 183, 842, 853
  Excel computation of, 187–188
Precision, 20-12
Prediction interval, 602
  Excel used for, 606–608
  individual value of y, 604–606
  multiple regression, 673–674
  SWStat+ used for, 647, 701
Prior probability, 183, 842
Probabilistic sampling, 20-4
Probability, 154–155
  addition law, 170–173
  area as measure of, 241–243
  assigning, 160–162, 167
  Bayes' theorem, 162, 183–186, 853
    branch probabilities computed using,
      853–856
    posterior probabilities computed with
      Excel, 187–188
    tabular approach, 186–187
  complement of an event, 169–170
  conditional, 175–179, 853
    independent events, 179, 180
    multiplication law, 179–180
  counting rules
    for combinations, 159
    for multiple-step experiments, 156–159
    for permutations, 159–160
  events and, 165–167
  experiments, 155–160

  joint, 176, 855
  KP&L project example, 162–163
  marginal, 177
  posterior, 183, 187–188, 842, 853
  prior, 183, 842
Probability density function, 240
Probability distributions, 202
  See also Continuous probability distribu-
    tions; Discrete probability distributions;
    Sampling distributions
Probability function, 202
  binomial, 215, 218
  discrete, required conditions for, 203
  hypergeometric, 229–230
  Poisson, 224
Probability sampling, 301
Procter & Gamble (Statistics in
  Practice), 239
Producer's risk, 818
Production, statistical applications in, 4
Proportion
  standard error of, 295
  See also Population proportion
Proportional allocation, 20-24
Protected LSD test, 516

Q

Qualitative data, 7, 30
  See also Tabular and graphical methods of
    descriptive statistics
Qualitative independent variables, 675
  complex, 680–681
  interpreting parameters, 678–679
Qualitative variable, 7
Quality, 796
  ISO 9000, 798
  Malcolm Baldrige National Quality Award,
    797–798
  philosophies and frameworks, 797
  Six Sigma, 798–800
  total, 796–797
  See also Statistical methods for quality
    control
Quality assurance, 799
Quality control, 800
  See also Statistical methods for quality
    control
Quality engineering, 799–800
Quantitative data, 7, 30
  discrete versus continuous, 8
  See also Tabular and graphical methods of
    descriptive statistics
Quantitative variable, 7
Quartiles, 94–95

R

R chart, 807–809
  Excel used for, 809–812
Random experiments, 163
Randomization, 519, 521

Randomized block design, 528
  air traffic controller stress test, 528–529
  ANOVA procedure, 529–530
  computations and conclusions, 530–532
  Excel used for, 532–533
Random sampling
  See Sampling; Simple random sampling
Random variables, 199–200
  continuous, 201
  discrete, 200
Range, 102
  interquartile, 102
Rank correlation
  See Spearman rank correlation coefficient
Ratio scale, 7, 756
Reciprocal transformation, 712–713
Regression analysis, 561, 564
  See also Multiple regression; Regression
    analysis: model building; Simple linear
    regression
Regression analysis: model building,
  703–704
  analysis of larger problem, 724–727
  general linear model, 704
    curvilinear relationships, 704–706
    interaction, 706–710
    nonlinear models that are intrinsically
      linear, 713–714
    transformations involving dependent
      variable, 710–713
  multiple regression approach to analysis of
    variance and experimental design,
    741–744
  residual analysis, 734
    autocorrelation and Durbin-Watson test,
      735–740
  variables, adding or deleting, 717–719
    general case, 719–721
  variable selection procedures, 728
    backward elimination, 729
    backward elimination with Excel,
      729–731
    best-subsets regression, 731–732
    forward selection, 729
    stepwise regression, 728
Regression equation
  multiple, 650
  simple linear, 562
  See also Multiple regression; Simple linear
    regression
Regression model
  multiple, 650
  simple linear, 561
  See also Multiple regression; Simple linear
    regression
Regression statistics, interpretation of Excel
  output, 599
Relative frequency distributions, 32, 43
  cumulative, 48, 49
  Excel construction of, 33
Relative frequency method of assigning
  probabilities, 161

Replications, 519, 536
Residual analysis
  autocorrelation and Durbin-Watson test,
    734–740
  in multiple regression, 684
    residual plot against $\hat{y}$, 684
    standardized residual plot against $\hat{y}$,
      684–686
  in simple linear regression, 610–611
    Excel used for, 614–615, 616, 618
    normal probability plot, 618–620
    residual plot against x, 612–614
    residual plot against $\hat{y}$, 614
    standardized residuals, 615–618
Residual plot, 612
  Excel used for, 614–615, 616, 618
  standardized, against $\hat{y}$, 684–686
  SWStat+ used for, 647
  against x, 612–614
  against $\hat{y}$, 614, 684
Residuals, 587, 610
  standardized, 615–618
Response surface, 666
Response variable, 499, 666
Restricted LSD test, 516
Revised probabilities
  See Posterior probabilities
Riddle, Jim, 20-2
Ryland, James R., 703

S

Sample, 14, 270
  independent, 415
  matched, 415–419
  in sample survey, 20-2, 20-3
Sample correlation coefficient, 127–128
Sample covariance, 123–124
Sampled population, 20-3
Sample information, 842
  decision analysis with, 842–849
Sample mean, 89–90, 271, 280
  overall, 501
Sample point, 155–156
Sample proportion, 271
Sample size
  in cluster sampling, 20-32
  in interval estimation, 326–327
  and sampling distribution of $\bar{x}$, 290–291
  in simple random sampling,
    20-12–20-14
  in stratified simple random sampling,
    20-21–20-24
Sample space, 155–156, 167
Sample statistic, 89, 278
Sample surveys, 14
  cluster sampling, 20-26–20-28
    Excel used for, 20-31–20-32
    population mean, 20-28–20-29
    population proportion, 20-30–20-31
    population total, 20-29–20-30
    sample size determination, 20-32

  errors
    nonsampling, 20-5
    sampling, 20-6
  sampling methods, 20-3–20-4
  simple random sampling, 20-6
    Excel used for, 20-9–20-12
    population mean, 20-6–20-7
    population proportion, 20-9
    population total, 20-7–20-8
    sample size determination, 20-12–20-14
  stratified simple random sampling, 20-15
    population mean, 20-15–20-16
    population mean using Excel,
      20-16–20-18
    population proportion, 20-19–20-21
    population proportion using Excel, 20-21
    population total, 20-18–20-19
    population total using Excel, 20-19
    sample size determination, 20-21–20-24
  systematic sampling, 20-34
  terminology, 20-2–20-3
  types of, 20-3–20-4
Sample variance, 103–104, 109
  pooled, 411
Sampling
  cluster, 299–300
  convenience, 301, 20-4
  example problem, 271–272
  judgment, 301, 20-4
  nonprobabilistic, 20-4
  nonprobability, 301
  point estimation, 278–280
  probabilistic, 20-4
  probability, 301
  stratified random, 299, 300
  systematic, 300–301
  See also Acceptance sampling; Simple ran-
    dom sampling
Sampling distributions, 282
  introduction to, 281–284
  of $\bar{p}$, 294
    expected value of $\bar{p}$, 294–295
    form of, 295–296
    practical value of, 296–297
    standard deviation of $\bar{p}$, 295
  of $\bar{x}$, 284
    for EAI problem, 288
    expected value of $\bar{x}$, 284–285
    form of, 286–288
    practical value of, 288–290
    sample size and, 290–291
    standard deviation of $\bar{x}$, 285–286
Sampling error, 20-6
  bound on the, 20-7
Sampling units, 20-3
Scales of measurement, 6–7, 755–756
Scatter diagrams, 61, 68–70
  Excel construction of, 70–72, 568–570
  regression analysis, 564, 565
Schisla, Robert M., 703
Second-order model with one predictor vari-
  able, 705

Serial correlation, 734
Shape of distribution, 111–112
Significance
    individual, 666
    overall, 666
Significance level, 311, 350
    observed, 356
Significance tests, 351, 586, 666
    confidence interval for β_1, 589–590
    correlation used for, 644–645
    estimate of σ^2, 587
    F test, 590–592, 666–669
    interpretation of, 592–593
    multicollinearity, 670–671
    t test, 587–589, 666, 669
Sign test, 757
    hypothesis test about a median, 762–763
        Excel used for, 763
    large-sample case, 760–761
        Excel used for, 761–762
    small-sample case, 757–759
        Excel used for, 759–760
Simple first-order model with one predictor
    variable, 704
Simple linear regression, 561
    coefficient of determination, 576–580
        correlation coefficient, 580–582
        Excel computation of, 580
    estimated regression equation, 562–564
        for confidence interval estimate of mean
            value of y, 602–604
        Excel used for, 568–570
        Excel used for confidence and prediction
            interval estimates, 606–608
        for interval estimation, 602
        for point estimation, 602
        for prediction interval estimate of indi-
            vidual value of y, 604–606
    Excel's Regression tool
        example problem, 596
        interpretation of ANOVA output,
            598–599
        interpretation of estimated regression
            equation output, 598
        interpretation of regression statistics out-
            put, 599
    influential observations, 625–626
    least squares method, 564–568
        formula derivation, 642–644
    model, 561
    model assumptions, 585–586, 593
    outliers, 622–624
    regression equation, 562
    residual analysis, 610–611
        Excel used for, 614–615, 616, 618
        normal probability plot, 618–620
        residual plot against x, 612–614
        residual plot against ŷ, 614
        standardized residuals, 615–618
    significance testing, 586
        confidence interval for β_1, 589–590
        correlation used for, 644–645

estimate of σ^2, 587
F test, 590–592
    interpretation of, 592–593
    t test, 587–589
    SWStat+ used for, 645–647
Simple random sampling, 272
    from finite population, 272–276
    from infinite population, 276–277
    See also Sample surveys; Sampling
Simpson's paradox, 67–68
Single-factor experiment, 519
Single-stage cluster sampling, 20-26
Six Sigma, 798–800
Skewness, 111–112
Small Fry Design (Statistics in Practice), 88
Spearman rank correlation coefficient,
    785–787
    Excel used for, 788
    test for significant rank correlation,
        787–788
Squared deviation about the mean,
    103–104, 105
Standard deviation, 104–105, 108
    of discrete probability distribution, 209
        Excel computation of, 209–210
    Excel computation of, 106, 107
    of $\bar{p}$, 295
    of $\bar{x}$, 285–286
Standard error, 286, 295, 20-6
Standard error of the estimate, 587
Standard error of the mean, 802
Standard error of the proportion, 295
Standardized residual, 615–618
Standardized residual plot
    Excel used for, 618
    SWStat+ used for, 647
    against ŷ, 684–686
Standardized value, 113
Standard normal probability distribution,
    246–252
States of nature, 832–833
Stationarity assumption, 215
Statistical control, 801
Statistical inference, 14–15, 392–393
    about a population variance, 441
        Excel for confidence intervals, 445–446
        Excel for hypothesis tests, 449–450
        hypothesis testing, 446–449
        interval estimation, 441–445
    about two population variances, 453–457
        Excel for hypothesis tests, 458–459
    difference between two population means:
        σ_1 and σ_2 known, 393
        Excel for confidence intervals, 395–397
        Excel for hypothesis tests, 399–400
        hypothesis tests about $\mu_1 - \mu_2$, 397–399
        interval estimation of $\mu_1 - \mu_2$, 393–395
        practical advice, 401
    difference between two population means:
        σ_1 and σ_2 unknown, 403
        Excel for confidence intervals, 405–407
        Excel for hypothesis tests, 409–411

    hypothesis tests about $\mu_1 - \mu_2$, 407–409
    interval estimation of $\mu_1 - \mu_2$, 404–405
    practical advice, 411
    difference between two population means:
        matched samples, 415–417
        Excel for hypothesis tests, 417–419
    difference between two population propor-
        tions, 422
        Excel for confidence intervals, 424–426
        Excel for hypothesis tests, 427–429
        hypothesis tests about $p_1 - p_2$, 426–427
        interval estimation of $p_1 - p_2$, 422–424
Statistical methods for quality control,
    796–797
    acceptance sampling, 817–819
        computing probability of accepting a lot,
            819–821
        example problem, 819
        multiple sampling plans, 823–824
        selecting a plan, 821–823
    philosophies and frameworks, 797
        ISO 9000, 798
        Malcolm Baldrige National Quality
            Award, 797–798
        Six Sigma, 798–800
    statistical process control, 800–801
        control charts, 801–802
        control charts, interpretation of, 815
        Excel used for R chart and chart $\bar{x}$,
            809–812
        np chart, 814
        p chart, 812–814
        R chart, 807–809
        $\bar{x}$ chart: process mean and standard
            deviation known, 802–804
        $\bar{x}$ chart: process mean and standard
            deviation unknown, 804–807
Statistical process control, 800–801
    See also Statistical methods for quality
        control
Statistical studies, 9, 11–12
Statistics, 3
    sample, 89, 278
    test, 353–354
    See also Data and statistics
Stem-and-leaf display, 56–59
Stepwise regression, 728
Strata, 299
Stratified random sampling, 299, 300
Stratified simple random sampling
    See Sample surveys
Subjective method of assigning probabilities,
    161–162
Sum of squares, total, 507, 576
Sum of squares between treatments
    See Sum of squares due to treatments
Sum of squares due to error, 504, 522, 576
Sum of squares due to regression, 579
Sum of squares due to treatments, 504, 521
Sum of squares of the deviations, 565
Sum of squares within error
    See Sum of squares due to error

Survey, sample
  See Sample surveys
SWStat+, 16
  box plot, 149–152
  installing and running, 26
  multiple regression analysis, 700–701
  regression analysis, 645–647
  using, 26–27
Systematic sampling, 300–301, 20-34

T

t distribution, 316
t test, 587–589, 666, 669
  interpretation of Excel output, 598
Tabular and graphical methods of descriptive
  statistics, 12–14, 29–30
  crosstabulations, 61–63
    Excel construction of, 64–67
    Simpson's paradox, 67–68
  exploratory data analysis, 56–59
  qualitative data, summarizing
    bar graphs, 34
    bar graphs constructed with Excel,
      34–36
    frequency distributions, 30–31
    frequency distributions constructed with
      Excel, 31–32
    percent frequency distributions, 32
    percent frequency distributions con-
      structed with Excel, 33
    pie charts, 34
    pie charts constructed with Excel, 34–36
    relative frequency distributions, 32
    relative frequency distributions con-
      structed with Excel, 33
  quantitative data, summarizing
    cumulative distributions, 46–49
    frequency distributions, 39–41
    frequency distributions constructed with
      Excel, 41–42, 49–52
    histogram, 43–44
    histogram constructed with Excel,
      44–46, 49–52
    percent frequency distributions, 43
    relative frequency distributions, 43
  scatter diagrams, 61, 68–70
    Excel construction of, 70–72
  stem-and-leaf display, 56–59
  trendlines, 68–70
    Excel construction of, 70–72
Taguchi, Genichi, 797
Target population, 20-3
Tatham, Ronald (Dr.), 498
Test of independence, 473–477
  Excel used for, 477–478
Test statistic, 353–354

Time intervals, Poisson probability distribu-
  tion and, 224–225
Time series data, 7–8
Total quality (TQ), 796–797
Total sum of squares, 507, 576
Transformations involving dependent vari-
  able, 710–713
Treatments, 499, 519
  between, 501, 503–504, 521
  mean square due to, 503–504, 521
  pooled (within), 501, 504–505, 521–522
  sum of squares due to, 504, 521
Tree diagram, 157
TreePlan, decision analysis with, 860–865
Trendlines, 68–70
  Excel construction of, 70–72
Trentham, Charlene, 2
Trimmed mean, 97
Two-stage cluster sampling, 20-26–20-27
Two-tailed test, 358
  population mean: σ known, 358–360
  population mean: σ unknown, 370–372
Tyler, Philip R. (Dr.), 466
Type I error, 349–351
Type I error rates, 516–517
Type II error, 349–351

U

Unbiased, 285
Uniform probability distribution, 240–241
  area as measure of probability, 241–243
  discrete, 204
Union of events, 170–171
United Way (Statistics in Practice), 466
Upper control limit, 801
U.S. General Accounting Office (Statistics in
  Practice), 440

V

Validity of data, 116
Value worksheet, 18
Variability measures, 101–102
  coefficient of variation, 106
  range, 102
    interquartile, 102
  standard deviation, 104–105, 108
    Excel computation of, 106, 107
  variance, 103–104, 109
    Excel computation of, 106, 107
Variables, 6
  adding or deleting in multiple regression
    model, 717–721
  dependent, 561, 666
  dummy (indicator), 676

  independent, 561, 670
  qualitative, 7
  qualitative independent, 675
  quantitative, 7
  random, 199–201
  response, 499, 666
    See also Association between two variables
Variables control charts, 801
Variable selection procedures, 728–732
Variables sampling plans, 825
Variance, 103–104, 109
  of binomial probability distribution,
    221–222
  of discrete random variable, 208–209
    Excel computation of, 209–210
  Excel computation of, 106, 107
    See also Analysis of variance (ANOVA)
Venn diagram, 169–170

W

Weighted mean, 133–134
West Shell Realtors (Statistics in
  Practice), 755
Whiskers, 119
Wilcoxon rank sum test
  See Mann-Whitney-Wilcoxon rank
    sum test
Wilcoxon signed rank test, 765–768
  Excel used for, 768–769
Williams, Marian, 649
Wilson, Clifford B., 796
Winkofsky, Edward P. (Dr.), 270
Within-treatments estimate of population
  variance, 501, 504–505, 521–522

X

$\bar{x}$
  expected value of, 284–285
  sampling distribution of, 284
    for EAI problem, 288
    form, 286–288
    practical value, 288–290
    and sample size, 290–291
  standard deviation of, 285–286
$\bar{x}$ chart, 801
  Excel used for, 809–812
  process mean and standard deviation
    known, 802–804
  process mean and standard deviation un-
    known, 804–807

Z

z-scores, 113

Modern Business Statistics with Microsoft Excel, 2e Data Disk

Chapter 1

Music	Exercise 14
Hotel	Table 1.6
Minisystems	Table 1.7
Norris	Table 1.5
Shadow02	Table 1.1

Chapter 2

ApTest	Table 2.9
Audit	Table 2.5
AutoData	Exercise 38
Broker	Exercise 26
BWBooks	Exercise 6
CEOs	Exercise 9
Client	Exercise 10
Computer	Exercise 21
Comstock	Exercise 42
Concerts	Exercise 20
Crosstab	Exercise 29
Dow	Exercise 41
Fortune	Exercise 51
Frequency	Exercise 11
Golf	Exercise 40
HighLow	Exercise 46
IBD	Exercise 34
Income	Exercise 44
Marathon	Exercise 28
Names	Exercise 5
NFL	Exercise 37
OccupSat	Exercise 48
PelicanStores	Case Problem
Restaurant	Table 2.10
RevEmps	Exercise 49
Scatter	Exercise 30
Shadow	Exercise 43
SoftDrink	Table 2.1
Spending	Exercise 17
Stereo	Table 2.13
StockPrices	Exercise 27
TVMedia	Exercise 4
Wageweb	Exercise 18

Chapter 3

Asian	Case Problem 3
Beer	Exercise 65
Broker	Exercises 7 & 22
Cameras	Exercise 12
Cities	Exercise 64
DowS&P	Exercise 50
Health	Case Problem 2
Hotels	Exercise 5
Income	Exercise 62
Mutual	Exercise 44
NCAA	Exercise 34
Notebook	Exercise 23
Payroll	Exercise 42
PCs	Exercise 49
PelicanStores	Case Problem 1
Property	Exercise 40
Retainer	Exercise 59
Salary	Table 3.1
Speakers	Exercise 35
Stereo	Table 3.6
Temperature	Exercise 51
Visa	Exercise 58
WageWeb	Exercise 33
Websites	Exercise 9

Chapter 4

Judge	Case Problem

Chapter 7

American League	Exercise 3
Dining	Exercise 38
EAI	Section 7.1
MutualFund	Exercise 10
National League	Figure 7.1

Chapter 8

ActTemps	Exercise 49
Auto	Case Problem 3
Balance	Table 8.3
Bock	Case Problem 1
FastFood	Exercise 18
Flights	Exercise 48
GPA	Exercise 9
GulfProp	Case Problem 2
JobSatisfaction	Exercise 37
Lloyd's	Section 8.1
Miami	Exercise 17
NYSEStocks	Exercise 47
Nielsen	Exercise 6
OpenEndFunds	Exercise 22
Restaurant	Exercise 5
Scheer	Table 8.4
TeeTimes	Section 8.4
TVtime	Exercise 20

Chapter 9

BLS	Case Problem 2
AirRating	Section 9.4
Coffee	Section 9.3
Diamonds	Exercise 29
Fowle	Exercise 21
GolfTest	Section 9.3
Orders	Section 9.4
Quality	Case Problem 1
RentalRates	Exercise 16
UsedCars	Exercise 32
WomenGolf	Section 9.5

Chapter 10

Cargo	Exercise 13
CheckAcct	Section 10.2
Digital	Exercise 39
Earnings	Exercise 26
ExamScores	Figure 10.3
Florida	Exercise 42
Golf	Case Problem
HomeStyle	Section 10.1
Matched	Table 10.2
Mortgage	Exercise 6
Mutual	Exercise 40
SAT	Exercise 18
SATVerbal	Exercise 16
SoftwareTest	Table 10.1
TaxPrep	Section 10.4
TVRadio	Exercise 25

Chapter 11

ArrivalTimes	Section 11.1
Bags	Exercise 19
Detergent	Figure 11.3
DowJones	Exercise 21
SchoolBus	Section 11.2
Training	Case Problem
Travel	Exercise 25

Chapter 12

Alber's	Figure 12.2
Chemline	Table 12.10
NYReform	Case Problem
Research	Figure 12.1

Chapter 13

AirTraf	Table 13.6
ArtDir	Exercise 52
Assembly	Exercise 56
AudJudg	Exercise 29
Browsing	Exercise 59
ChemTech	Table 13.3
Exer25	Exercise 25
Funds	Exercise 49
GMAT	Table 13.11
Grocery	Exercise 61
IDSalary	Case Problem 2
ISP	Exercise 62
JobSalary	Exercise 55
Medical1	Case Problem 1
Medical2	Case Problem 1
NCP	Table 13.1
NFL	Exercise 53
Paint	Exercise 30
Resorts	Exercise 51
Salaries	Exercise 45
SatisJob	Exercise 50
Ships	Exercise 10
Snow	Exercise 40
Stress	Exercise 9
Technology	Exercise 8
Traffic	Exercise 7
Trucks	Exercise 48

Chapter 14

ADRs	Exercise 49
Airport	Exercise 11
Alumni	Case Problem 3
Armand's	Table 14.1
Beer	Exercise 52
Boots	Exercise 27
Cars	Exercises 7 & 19
CEO	Exercise 54
Cities	Exercise 20
EmpRev	Exercise 12
Hydration1	Exercise 35
Hydration2	Exercise 53
Inflluential	Table 14.13
IPO	Exercise 57
IRSAudit	Exercise 66
JobSat	Exercise 60
MLB	Case Problem 4
MtnBikes	Exercise 8
NAEP	Case Problem 1
OffRates	Exercise 36
Options	Exercise 58
Outlier	Table 14.12
PCs	Exercises 10, 28, & 41
Printers	Exercises 22 & 30
Safety	Case Problem 2
Salaries	Exercise 14

Chapter 15

Alumni	Case Problem 3
Auto1	Exercise 42
Auto2	Exercise 50
Backpack	Exercise 7
Brokers	Exercise 25
Butler	Tables 15.1 & 15.2
Consumer	Case Problem 1
Enquirer	Case Problem 2
Exer2	Exercise 2
Football	Exercise 37
ForFunds	Exercise 8
FuelEcon	Exercise 51
HomeValue	Exercise 49
Johnson	Table 15.6
MLB	Exercises 6, 16, & 24
NBA	Exercises 10, 18, & 26
Repair	Exercises 35 & 36
Schools	Exercises 9, 17, & 30
Showtime	Exercises 5, 15, 23, 29, & 41
SportsCar	Exercise 31
Stroke	Exercise 38
Trucks	Exercise 52

Chapter 16

Audit	Exercise 31
Browsing	Exercise 34
Cars	Case Problem 2
Cravens	Table 16.5
Election	Exercise 35
Football	Exercise 12
GradRate	Case Problem 3
Internet	Exercise 8
Layoffs	Case Problem 1
LightRail	Exercise 9
LPGATour	Exercise 18
Monitors	Exercise 7
NCP	Table 16.11
MPG	Table 16.4
MutFunds	Exercise 30
NFL	Exercise 15
Resale	Exercise 36
Reynolds	Table 16.1
Schools	Exercise 16
StkData	Exercise 19
Stroke	Exercise 14
Tyler	Table 16.2

Chapter 17

Advertising	Exercise 17
Automobile	Exercise 21
CarRental	Exercise 14
Chicago	Exercise 11
Delivery	Exercise 15
Methods	Table 17.3
MPG	Exercise 12
PERatio	Exercise 16
Refrigerator	Exercise 40
Relaxant	Exercise 13
Salaries	Exercise 19
Sales Potential	Table 17.14
SunCoast	Table 17.2
Williams	Figure 17.9

Chapter 18

Coffee	Exercise 20
Jensen	Table 18.2
Tires	Exercise 7

Chapter 20

Lakeland	Section 20.5
NEG	Section 20.4